THE PAPERS OF
Andrew Johnson

Sponsored by
The University of Tennessee
The National Historical Publications and Records Commission
The National Endowment for the Humanities
The Tennessee Historical Commission

Frontispiece: President Andrew Johnson
An engraving in Kenneth Rayner,
Life and Times of Andrew Johnson (1866)

THE PAPERS OF
Andrew Johnson

Volume 10, February-July 1866

PAUL H. BERGERON
EDITOR

PATRICIA J. ANTHONY   LeROY P. GRAF

R. B. ROSENBURG   GLENNA R. SCHROEDER-LEIN

MARION O. SMITH   LISA L. WILLIAMS

THE EDITING STAFF

1992

THE UNIVERSITY OF TENNESSEE PRESS

KNOXVILLE

Library of Congress Cataloging in Publication Data
(Revised for volume 10)

Johnson, Andrew, 1808–1875.
    The papers of Andrew Johnson
    Vols. 8— edited by Paul H. Bergeron.
    Includes bibliographical references and indexes.
    Contents: v.1. 1822–1851.—v.2. 1852–1857.—[etc]—
v. 10. February–July 1866.
        1. United States—Politics and government—1849–
           1877—Sources.
        2. Johnson, Andrew, 1808–1875—Manuscripts.
        3. Presidents—United States—Manuscripts.
I. Graf, LeRoy P., ed.   II. Haskins, Ralph W., ed.
III. Bergeron, Paul H., 1938–   .   IV. Title.
E415.6.J65   1967   973.8′1′0924 [B]   67-25733
ISBN 0-87049-098-2 (v. 2)
[ISBN 0-87049-764-2 (v. 10)]

TO
Sara Dunlap Jackson
(1919–1991)
Extraordinary friend of the
Johnson Project for many years
and in many ways.

Contents

Illustrations

Introduction

On April 2, 1866, President Andrew Johnson formally declared that the war between the United States and the Confederacy (with the exception of Texas) had ended.[1] There was more than a little irony in the timing of this proclamation, for the President was at that moment heavily engaged in war with Congress.

Johnson had fired the first salvo in mid-February when much to the surprise and consternation of many members of Congress he vetoed the recently-passed Freedmen's Bureau bill. Upon learning of this action a former congressman reacted with the exclamation, "The fight is on!" And so it seemed to be. Ten days earlier, Joseph S. Fullerton, at Johnson's request, had sent the President a lengthy list of arguments against the bill.[2] Johnson did not lack for advice from several different quarters, not the least of which was from disgruntled Southerners who had expressed their distrust and dislike of the Freedmen's Bureau.

The President staked out his position in his veto message. As has been summarized by one historian, Johnson emphasized that the bill was unnecessary, unconstitutional and unjust. Instantly letters flowed into the White House from the Midwest, the Northeast, and the South lauding Johnson's stance.[3] It was perhaps the sort of dramatic demonstration of support that he desired. Yet three days later, on the night of the 22nd, an even more exciting episode occurred when a group of well-wishers congregated outside of the President's home. They serenaded him and shouted praises; in reaction he ignored the wishes of his closest advisers who had urged him not to address the crowd.

The infamous speech, if such be the word, delivered that night echoed for weeks and months thereafter. Having been egged on by the intense environment fostered by the crowd, Johnson attacked the Radical Republican leadership, even stooping to calling his principal tormentors by name.[4] In the wake of the President's incredible harangue newspapers

1. See Proclamation *re* End of Insurrection, Apr. 2, 1866. My essay is based upon documents published in this volume and upon several key monographs: Hans L. Trefousse, *Andrew Johnson: A Biography* (New York, 1989); LaWanda Cox and John H. Cox, *Politics, Principle, and Prejudice, 1865–1866* (New York, 1963); Eric L. McKitrick, *Andrew Johnson and Reconstruction* (Chicago, 1960); Albert Castel, *The Presidency of Andrew Johnson* (Lawrence, Kans., 1979); James E. Sefton, *Andrew Johnson and the Uses of Constitutional Power* (Boston, 1980).

2. Cox and Cox, *Politics, Principle, and Prejudice*, 172; Fullerton to Johnson, Feb. 9, 1866.

3. Castel, *Presidency of Johnson*, 67. From February 19 through the remainder of the month, letters supportive of Johnson's veto arrived at the White House; the month of March also saw additional letters backing the President's decision.

4. See Washington's Birthday Address, Feb. 22, 1866.

and private individuals responded. Not surprisingly, many letters arrived at the White House to cheer on Johnson; but elsewhere opinion was hostile or at best mixed.[5] Certainly it was widely believed that he had compounded the possible blunder of the veto with his undignified February 22 speech.

Yet despite the criticisms that abounded on nearly every hand, Johnson still had supporters and defenders, not a few of whom were found among Democrats and even Republicans in Congress. This is to argue that although recognizable warfare had begun, the President's situation was by no means hopeless at this point. In fact in March and beyond there were still opportunities for Congress and Johnson to negotiate a truce and link arms to work harmoniously together.

But the stubborn, conservative-minded President apparently was in no real mood to yield and compromise; after all, he had to defend the Constitution, as he understood it, and to preserve the rightful relationship, as he understood it, between the states and the federal government. Hence, when the next major challenge came, he did not flinch from thwarting the will of Congress. It arrived in the form of the Civil Rights bill that had been working its way through the national legislature since January. Numerous political and personal acquaintances pressed Johnson to approve the measure, but unfortunately he turned a deaf ear to them.[6] Instead, on March 27 he sent a veto message to Congress.

Although the President had indicated in earlier weeks and months an interest in and support of legislation to provide legal protection for blacks, he rejected this professed leaning when the challenge appeared before him in the shape of the Civil Rights bill. He did so largely because he feared that its terms upset the critical balance between the federal and state governments; it was vintage Johnsonian philosophy. This time, unlike on the Freedmen's Bureau bill, Congress mustered the support to override—albeit by a shaky and narrow margin. This action represented the first overturning of a presidential veto on any *major* legislation in the nation's history.[7] Clearly Congress had spoken.

Emboldened by a successful vote and increasingly determined to fashion the Reconstruction agenda, Congress directed its attention to the prospect of a constitutional amendment. Slowly and with some difficulty during the spring, it chiseled out the component parts of the Fourteenth Amendment, the capstone of which would confer citizenship upon blacks and equal protection for all citizens.[8] Unlike the two previous major

5. Among the most prominent who lauded Johnson's speech in its immediate aftermath were William H. Seward and Thurlow Weed, who both sent messages from New York on February 23.

6. Two notable letters are the ones from Henry Ward Beecher, Mar. 17, and Jacob D. Cox, Mar. 22, 1866.

7. See Veto of Civil Rights Bill, Mar. 27, 1866; McKitrick, *Johnson and Reconstruction*, 323.

8. For a very able discussion of the Fourteenth Amendment see McKitrick, *Johnson and Reconstruction*, Chapter 11.

conflicts between the President and Congress, however, the amendment did not require executive approval. Nevertheless, important friends implored Johnson to endorse it.

Yet he could not resist the temptation to raise objections—this time procedural rather than substantive. The President protested that Congress had no right to submit an amendment to the states when eleven of those states remained unrepresented in the national legislature.[9] The amendment nonetheless went forward for ratification or rejection. By this time it was commonly understood by the leadership of Congress that no former Confederate state could be readmitted without having approved the Fourteenth Amendment.

There was ample irony in the fact that Johnson's home state of Tennessee served as a test case. Whereas he resented the additional requirement placed upon the Southern states, the President devoutly wanted the state formally back in the Union. Therefore perhaps after some amount of philosophical torment he officially recognized the ratification of the amendment by Tennessee, although it had taken place under unorthodox and arguably illegal means. Johnson seized the opportunity to offer another objection to the right of Congress "to pass laws preliminary to the admission of duly qualified representatives from any of the States."[10] He may have had additional grounds for complaint, given that his arch-enemy in state politics, Governor William G. Brownlow, had broken overtly with him and had stirred anti-Johnson sentiment in the state. At any rate, Tennessee reentered the Union, the first of the Confederate states to do so; and Johnson's son-in-law, David T. Patterson, took his seat in the U.S. Senate, at long last.

Somewhat lost in the story of the Fourteenth Amendment and its ratification is the fact that Congress returned to the Freedmen's Bureau bill in July and passed a measure very similar to the earlier February one. On July 16, Johnson, not surprisingly, vetoed the new bill, reminding his hearers of the arguments he had offered in his first veto message but adding charges concerning corruption among Bureau officials in the various states. In typical Johnson fashion he concluded with the claim that the bill was repugnant because it represented class legislation.[11] But Congress, virtually unstoppable by now, overrode the veto.

The significant pieces of legislation that Johnson and Congress clashed over fundamentally involved the question of the status and future of the newly-freed blacks in the South. That reality certainly invested the controversies with an important dimension of meaning. The President also had a number of other direct and indirect dealings with racial matters. For example, he had a remarkable interview with a delegation of prominent blacks on February 7. Frederick Douglass and others pleaded in behalf of the voting franchise for blacks and in the process stirred a rather

9. See Message *re* Amending the Constitution, June 22, 1866.
10. See Message *re* Resolution on Restoration of Tennessee, July 24, 1866.
11. Freedmen's Bureau Bill Veto, July 16, 1866.

heated exchange with Johnson. Afterwards they penned a reply to the President which was followed on the next day with an additional response from Johnson. Within days the full report of the interview had been widely distributed throughout the nation. In early March an anonymous writer warned the President that clerks in the Third Auditor's office had invited Douglass to lecture in Washington "against your administration and excite the negroes to rebel."[12]

In the meantime Johnson had already vetoed the Freedmen's Bureau bill and was contemplating similar action against the pending Civil Rights measure. A group of Baltimore blacks sent an impressive argument to him in behalf of the latter bill, but to no avail. The President defended his veto of the Civil Rights legislation in a wide-ranging interview with a London *Times* correspondent in mid-April. Moreover, he explained his relationship with blacks and attacked the actions of the Freedmen's Bureau in certain parts of the South. A few days later a group of Washington blacks, celebrating the anniversary of emancipation in the District, visited Johnson at the White House. He lashed out against the pretended allies of the blacks and predicted that some day he would be recognized as the best friend the blacks had.[13] While the group seemed delighted with his remarks, the President's subsequent reaction to the Fourteenth Amendment and the revised Freedmen's Bureau bill surely must have prompted these citizens to doubt his claims.

Sometimes unnoticed is that to a small degree Johnson was interested in the matter of schooling for Southern blacks. It was an issue of great concern to many persons, North and South, to be sure. In late March, for instance, a North Carolina woman wrote to the President inquiring how the government intended to provide for the education of blacks and how she might secure employment for herself in a school. He routinely referred her letter to General Howard of the Freedmen's Bureau. In a July interview with Dr. Paschal B. Randolph, however, Johnson eagerly agreed to support Randolph's mission to raise money in the Northern states for support of black schools in Louisiana. He also took the occasion to reiterate his friend-of-blacks theme. He demonstrated this in a small way when a few days later an Episcopal clergyman informed the President about a lack of success in the endeavor to raise money in the North for a black school in Charleston. Inasmuch as Johnson had earlier promised the Rev. Porter that he would donate one thousand dollars of his personal funds to the school, the cleric urged the President to forward the gift as soon as possible—which he did.[14]

12. See Interview with Delegation of Blacks, Feb. 7, 1866; Reply of the Black Delegates to the President, Feb. 7, 1866; Further Remarks on Response to Black Delegates, Feb. 8, 1866; Administration Friend to Johnson, Mar 10, 1866.

13. Maryland Blacks to Johnson, Mar. 17, 1866; Interview with *The Times* (London) Correspondent, Apr. 12, 1866; Speech to Washington Blacks, Apr. 19, 1866.

14. Sarah F. Mason to Johnson, Mar. 29, 1866; Interview with Paschal B. Randolph, July 21, 1866; A. Toomer Porter to Johnson, July 28, 1866.

These paternalistic gestures did not, of course, offset the blatant racism so evident in Johnson's speeches, writings, and actions. They merely indicate that he was capable, in somewhat typical Southern fashion, of being civil and polite toward blacks and supportive of conservative nongovernmental methods of dealing with them. Perhaps he is due a modicum of recognition for having hosted a number of group and individual visits by blacks at the White House and for being the first president to receive blacks at the traditional New Year's Day reception.[15]

In addition to racial concerns there were other matters that absorbed the President's attention during the February-July period. For example, the perennial question of patronage simply would not disappear. Numerous documents in this volume deal with requests for appointment, for removal (particularly of "thorough-going Radicals"), etc. Hundreds of collectors, assessors, postmasters, marshals, judges, and others needed to be appointed by Johnson and he received more advice than he could use. The major vacancy unresolved from earlier months was the all-important New York collectorship which in April finally went to Henry A. Smythe as a compromise candidate. In what might be labelled as a nineteenth-century version of "affirmative action," Johnson issued a circular which specified that discharged Union soldiers and sailors, particularly the wounded or ill, should be given preference for appointment to federal positions and should have preference for promotions within the various governmental offices. Veterans responded by petitioning the President for jobs.[16]

The patronage question took on special personal meaning when two of the President's nephews pressured him for federal appointment. The older, Andrew, had just lost his job at the state penitentiary in Nashville; but the younger, Nathan, simply wanted a position, because he needed "money and clothing, and other necessary articles." Besides, argued Nathan, "you have many places of profit at your disposal."[17] Although these are the only extant family letters in this time period, Johnson could not have been overjoyed at receiving them. Indeed evidence indicates that he took no overt steps to place either one in federal offices. So much for family ties.

The most challenging matter concerning appointments revolved around the personnel in Johnson's Cabinet. As early as mid-March a friend urged that Attorney General Speed should be replaced with a stronger man. In the following month correspondents recommended Lewis Campbell for a Cabinet post and Seward and possibly Stanton for removal. Nothing more was heard about shakeups in the Cabinet until July, when

15. Castel, *Presidency of Johnson*, 62.
16. Henry A. Smythe to Johnson, Apr. 13, 1866; Circular *re* Appointments to Office, Apr. 7, 1866. An informative, although brief, discussion of patronage may be found in Cox and Cox, *Politics, Principle, and Prejudice*, Chapter 6.
17. Andrew Johnson, Jr., to Johnson, Mar. 3, 1866; Nathan Johnson to Johnson, May 21, 1866.

three members, under increasing pressure to support Johnson's policies and particularly the call for a Unionist convention in August, submitted their resignations. After Speed, Harlan, and Dennison resigned, they were rapidly replaced by Henry Stanbery, Orville H. Browning, and Alexander W. Randall, respectively.[18] This represented the first overt disturbance within the official family but it would subsequently be overshadowed by even more controversial removals and replacements.

While patronage problems persisted, so did consideration of presidential pardon. But by the spring of 1866 the latter occupied a lesser position, for thousands of repentant Southerners had already been pardoned by Johnson. Nevertheless, a rather steady stream of requests for individual pardon reached the President's desk. Yet perhaps the most extraordinary one was not related to the 1865 Amnesty Proclamation but instead was connected simply to the general pardoning power of the chief executive. Mary Blake had been convicted and fined five hundred dollars for "keeping a bawdy house" in the District of Columbia; but in June, Johnson granted her a pardon.[19]

Closely affiliated with the question of pardons for ex-Rebels was the nagging matter of parole for imprisoned or not-yet pardoned high Confederate officials or alleged Lincoln conspirators. The wives of Jefferson Davis, Clement C. Clay, Jr., and Samuel Mudd, for example, entreated Johnson for special consideration for their incarcerated husbands. In the spring months the President finally permitted Varina Davis and Virginia Clay to visit their husbands at Fortress Monroe but took no steps to release the famous prisoners.[20] Likewise he did nothing about Sarah Mudd's plea for freeing her ailing husband from Dry Tortugas. There is no denying that Johnson remained quite mindful of the situations of the three famous prisoners, thanks to the importunings of their wives. Meanwhile other correspondents sought or acknowledged general or limited paroles for prominent persons such as Robert E. Lee, Alexander H. Stephens, David Yulee, and John H. Reagan.[21]

The two former Confederate states that demanded the President's attention during the February-July period were Texas and Louisiana. The former held its convention in February and March, much later than the other Southern states. Johnson naturally received several reports on the actions of that convention. Then the gubernatorial and legislative

18. Thomas Ewing to Johnson, Mar. 15, 1866; E. C. Parrott to Johnson, Apr. 2, 1866; Montgomery Blair to Johnson, Apr. 11, 1866; William Dennison to Johnson, July 11, 1866; Johnson to Henry Stanbery, July 13, 1866; Anonymous to Johnson, July 14, 1866; James Harlan to Johnson, July 27, 1866.

19. See Pardon of Mary Blake, June 21, 1866.

20. Virginia C. Clay to Johnson, Mar. 12, 16, 1866; Johnson to Lorenzo Thomas, Mar. 19, 1866; Varina Davis to Johnson, May 5, 19, 1866; Sarah F. Mudd to Johnson, June 28, 1866.

21. Alexander H. Stephens to Johnson, Mar. 23, 1866; Ulysses S. Grant to Johnson, Mar. 22, 1866; John H. Reagan to Johnson, June 20, 1866; Ladies of Warren County to Johnson, July 25, 1866.

elections were held in Texas at the end of June, thereby prompting letters to the President concerning the outcome of the elections and the pending inauguration of the new state government.[22]

March was a busy month for Louisiana matters, because among other things elections for New Orleans officials were held then. Controversy immediately erupted over the transfer of power, particularly the mayor's office, in that city; but Johnson seemed eager to accept the legitimacy of the election results and the assumption of office by the newly-elected individuals. Later dispute focused in July upon Governor Wells's desire to reconvene the 1864 convention. The gathering of that conclave touched off the New Orleans riot which occurred at the very end of the month.[23] Johnson was caught in the middle of that tragedy.

Prior to the unfolding of these events the President was ready to consider his political future in terms of the possibility of bringing the Unionists together under a new structure. Accordingly he gave his approval to a plan to call for a convention to meet in Philadelphia in August. There followed a flurry of activity, letter writing, and newspaper editorials in preparation for the forthcoming conclave. Johnson's friends rallied everywhere to assure representation at the meeting. Such stirrings offered a glimmer of hope to the embattled and desperate Johnson crowd.[24]

During the war-like conditions of the congressional session, the President searched for political friends and personal support. His daughters, Martha Patterson and Mary Stover, offered familial encouragement and assistance but his wife seems to have remained largely hidden in the upstairs bedroom. Regrettably, Johnson's son, Robert, continued his alcoholic and carousing ways. So troublesome did this become that the President and Gideon Welles conspired to send Robert on a long cruise. But after all of the arrangements had been made, Robert balked and refused to go.[25] Evidently Johnson experienced a warfare of sorts within his own family as well as with the leaders of Congress.

Doubtless the receipt of an honorary doctoral degree from the University of North Carolina in the summer months afforded a fleeting sense of well being to the President.[26] But the grim reality was that his presidential administration was in great jeopardy. Historian Hans Trefousse has

22. See, for example, Johnson to Andrew J. Hamilton, Feb. 13, 1866; Hamilton to Johnson, Feb. 16, Mar. 1, 7, 28, 1866; John P. White to Johnson, Feb. 19, 1866; Sackfield Maclin to Johnson, Mar. 6, 1866; James H. Bell to Johnson, July 2, 1866; James W. Throckmorton to Johnson, July 24, 1866.

23. There are at least six different March documents published herein that treat the matter of the Louisiana elections. The crucial exchange of communications regarding the calling of a convention in New Orleans is found on July 28, 30, and 31.

24. Examples of such documents are: George W. Morgan to Johnson, July 7, 1866; James Dixon to Johnson, July 8, 1866; William H.C. King to Johnson, July 10, 1866; Lewis D. Campbell to Johnson, July 17, 1866; Robert W. Johnson to Johnson, July 23, 1866.

25. See Trefousse, *Johnson*, 240.

26. Johnson to David L. Swain, June 29, 1866.

declared that the seven months between December 1865 and July 1866 constituted "perhaps the most crucial period in the administration of Andrew Johnson. . . ."[27] The documentary record provided herein corroborates that judgment. Irreparable damage had been done during the first session of the 39th Congress; Johnson's worst features had been in full array. He had demonstrated that he could govern effectively without Congress (April-December 1865) but that he could not do so with the national legislature in session. There would be more battles yet ahead, to be sure, but by the end of the summer of 1866 virtually everyone, save Johnson himself, knew that Congress had already emerged as the victor.

ACKNOWLEDGMENTS

This volume, like all previous volumes, is the result of the labors and support of various individuals and institutions. With a project of the magnitude of this one, it could not be otherwise.

At the University of Tennessee we continue to benefit directly from the constant backing of Dean Lorman A. Ratner and Associate Dean Charles O. Jackson of the College of Liberal Arts. Similarly we have depended heavily upon the assistance of the staffs of the Hodges Library and the Special Collections department, housed in Hoskins Library. The University of Tennessee Press and the University's Development Office have also played a critical role in the production of this volume. Throughout the period of our involvement with Volume 10 we have been aided in a variety of ways by our neighbors at the Andrew Jackson and the James K. Polk projects.

Libraries, archives, and historical societies have continued to provide copies of documents as well as research assistance. We are particularly indebted to the Library of Congress, the National Archives, and the Knox County Public Library (especially its McClung Historical Collection).

Financial support has come from several quarters. Both the National Historical Publications and Records Commission and the National Endowment for the Humanities have continued to provide indispensable monetary backing as well as other forms of assistance and encouragement. At the former we have dealt principally with Mary Giunta, Richard Sheldon, and Timothy Connelly and at the NEH with Gordon B. McKinney. The Tennessee Historical Commission, headed by Herbert L. Harper, has once more provided its much appreciated annual stipend. We again have been aided by the financial assistance donated by our longtime Greeneville benefactors, Margaret Johnson Patterson Bartlett and Ralph M. Phinney. Finally, the Tennessee Presidents Trust has offered

27. Trefousse, *Johnson*, 234.

monetary support garnered from contributions made by Tennesseans across the state.

The staff whose names appear on the title page of this volume deserve even more recognition than that, for they have carried much of the burden and challenge of editing the documents published herein. There are two new names on the list: Glenna Schroeder-Lein and Lisa Williams. Dr. Schroeder-Lein joined the Johnson Project in September 1990 and Ms. Williams in July 1991. Both have made valuable contributions to the preparation and production of this volume.

There are two persons whose names are not included on the list but who have rendered significant service to the Johnson Project; they are Thomas F. Curran and Ruth P. Graf. Mr. Curran served a ten-month stint as a NHPRC Fellow in 1990–91; during that time he undertook regular responsibilities as a staff member. We are indebted to him for his excellent work with us. Mrs. Graf continues as our volunteer-in-residence as she has so ably done for a number of years. We appreciate her willingness to assist with a variety of routine tasks.

Together the persons mentioned here and on the title page have worked to produce a volume that reflects credit upon the field of Reconstruction history and upon us as historical editors. I am immensely grateful to this team of scholars who have made my assignment as Editor both manageable and enjoyable.

I conclude, as is my custom, on a personal note. My wife, Mary Lee, and our three sons, Pierre, Andre, and Louis, have continued, through word and deed, to encourage me in my scholarly endeavors. For this and many other reasons I cherish them beyond measure.

Paul H. Bergeron

Knoxville, Tennessee
January 1992

Editorial Method

Since this volume treats six extremely important months in Andrew Johnson's presidency and in the evolving of the Reconstruction story, we have had to deal with thousands of documents. Therefore, as was the case in the immediately preceding two volumes, we have followed selections guidelines (as discussed in Volume 8) to decide which documents to include and which to exclude. The overwhelming number of published documents herein are from either various record groups in the National Archives or from the Johnson Papers in the Library of Congress. Our search for pertinent Johnson materials has been exhaustive and has been persistent over a long period of time. We admit, with considerable frustration, that we are able to include only a portion of those documents in this volume.

There are only two documents falling within the chronological boundaries of Volume 10 that have previously appeared in our special volume, *Advice After Appomattox: Letters to Andrew Johnson, 1865–1866*. They are: Benjamin C. Truman to Johnson, February 8 and March 24, 1866. For these we refer the reader to *Advice*, pp. 196–98.

Once again, as was the practice in Volume 9, we have published only a very few documents in summarized form. We continue to find an occasional document that warrants inclusion in the volume but because of various factors (length, illegibility, etc.) does not merit publication in full.

In Volume 10 we continue to follow the procedure established in the preceding volume of omitting the inside address and the complimentary closing from the documents which we publish in full. Whenever the complimentary closing is actually a part of the document's concluding sentence, we publish most of the sentence but then provide ellipses marks to indicate the omission of the complimentary closing.

Other than the modifications in editorial methodology described in Volume 8, there are no additional changes in this volume. We continue to strive to provide an identification or explanation for every person or event mentioned in the documents. But from time to time we have had to admit defeat, despite extensive research. Individuals identified in previous volumes are not identified again, unless it seems important to provide a very brief update. The Index for this volume offers information about where a complete identification for a particular person might be found, if there is none in Volume 10.

As in Volume 9, we do not offer a document-by-document listing in the Table of Contents of this volume. Readers wishing to know if a specific individual either wrote to Johnson or else received a letter from him may consult the Index for that information.

In conclusion, we affirm that we have attempted to render the documents as faithfully to the original as possible, given some concessions to modernization (beginning all sentences with capital letters, italicizing underscored words, indenting the first line of all paragraphs, etc.) and given the obvious difficulties of producing a printed document from one that had been a handwritten document.

SYMBOLS AND ABBREVIATIONS

REPOSITORY SYMBOLS

CtHi   Connecticut Historical Society, Hartford
DLC   Library of Congress, Washington, D.C.
DNA   National Archives, Washington, D.C.

RECORD GROUPS USED*

RG15	Records of the Veterans Administration
RG42	Records of the Office of Public Buildings and Grounds
RG46	Records of the United States Senate
RG48	Records of the Office of the Secretary of the Interior
RG56	General Records of the Department of the Treasury
RG58	Records of the Internal Revenue Service
RG59	General Records of the Department of State
RG60	General Records of the Department of Justice
RG75	Records of the Bureau of Indian Affairs
RG84	Records of the Foreign Service Posts of the Department of State
RG92	Records of the Office of the Quartermaster General
RG94	Records of the Adjutant General's Office, 1780s–1917
RG105	Records of the Bureau of Refugees, Freedmen, and Abandoned Lands
RG107	Records of the Office of the Secretary of War
RG108	Records of the Headquarters of the Army
RG109	War Department Collection of Confederate Records
RG153	Records of the Office of the Judge Advocate General (Army)
RG204	Records of the Office of the Pardon Attorney
RG206	Records of the Solicitor of the Treasury

*We have also used a number of microfilm collections from the National Archives, all of which are parts of the various Record Groups listed here.

Ms-Ar	Mississippi Department of Archives and History, Jackson
NcD	Duke University, Durham, North Carolina
NRU	University of Rochester Library, Rochester, New York
OCHP	Cincinnati Historical Society, Cincinnati, Ohio
OFH	Rutherford B. Hayes Library, Fremont, Ohio
OkWeaT	Southwestern State College, Weatherford, Oklahoma
TSLA	Tennessee State Library and Archives, Nashville

MANUSCRIPTS

ALS	Autograph Letter Signed
Copy	Copy, not by writer
Draft	Draft
DS	Document Signed
ES	Endorsement Signed
L	Letter
LBcopy	Letter Book copy
LS	Letter Signed
Mem	Memorial
PD	Printed Document
Pet	Petition
Tel	Telegram

ABBREVIATIONS

ACP	Appointment, Commission, and Personal Branch
Adj.	Adjutant
Appl(s).	Application(s)
Appt(s).	Appointment(s)
Atty. Gen.	Attorney General
Brig.	Brigadier
Btn.	Battalion
Bvt.	Brevet
c/ca.	circa
Cav.	Cavalry
Cld.	Colored
Co.	Company
Commr.	Commissioner
Dist(s).	District(s)
Div.	Division
Enum.	Enumeration
fl	flourishing

Inf.	Infantry
JP	Johnson Papers
Let. Bk.	Letter Book
Lgt.	Light
Mil. Bks.	Military Books
No.	number
n.d.	no date
n.p.	no page; no publisher
Pt.	Part
Recomm.	Recommendation
Res.	Reserve
Rgt.	Regiment
Ser.	Series; Serial
Subdiv.	Subdivision
Tels.	Telegrams
Twp.	Township
USCT	United States Colored Troops
Vet.	Veteran
Vol(s).	Volume(s); volunteer(s)

SHORT TITLES

BOOKS

Advice	Brooks D. Simpson, LeRoy P. Graf, and John Muldowny, eds., *Advice After Appomattox: Letters to Andrew Johnson, 1865–1866* (Knoxville, 1987).
Alexander, *Reconstruction*	Thomas B. Alexander, *Political Reconstruction in Tennessee* (Nashville, 1950).
American Annual Cyclopaedia	*American Annual Cyclopaedia and Register of Important Events* (42 vols. in 3 series, New York, 1862–1903).
Appleton's Cyclopaedia	James G. Wilson and John Fiske, eds., *Appleton's Cyclopaedia of American Biography* (6 vols., New York, 1887–89).
Bailey, *Indian Territory*	M. Thomas Bailey, *Reconstruction in Indian Territory: A Story of Avarice, Discrimination, and Opportunism* (Port Washington, N.Y., 1972).

Basler, *Works of Lincoln*

Roy P. Basler, ed., *The Collected Works of Abraham Lincoln* (9 vols., New Brunswick, 1953–55).

BDAC

Biographical Directory of the American Congress, 1774–1961 (Washington, D.C., 1961).

BDTA

Robert M. McBride et al., comps., *Biographical Directory of the Tennessee General Assembly* (5 vols., Nashville, 1975–).

Beale, *Welles Diary*

Howard K. Beale, ed., *Diary of Gideon Welles* (3 vols., New York, 1960).

Bentley, *Freedmen's Bureau*

George R. Bentley, *A History of the Freedmen's Bureau* (Philadelphia, 1955).

Biographical Cyclopaedia of Ohio

The Biographical Cyclopaedia and Portrait Gallery with an Historical Sketch of the State of Ohio (6 vols., Cincinnati, 1883–95).

Bonadio, *North of Reconstruction*

Felice A. Bonadio, *North of Reconstruction: Ohio Politics, 1865–1870* (New York, 1970).

Bradley, *Militant Republicanism*

Erwin S. Bradley, *The Triumph of Militant Republicanism: A Study of Pennsylvania and Presidential Politics, 1860–1872* (Philadelphia, 1964).

Callahan, *List of Navy and Marine Corps*

Edward W. Callahan, ed., *List of Officers of the Navy of the United States and of the Marine Corps from 1775 to 1900* (New York, 1969 [1901]).

Castel, *Presidency of Johnson*

Albert Castel, *The Presidency of Andrew Johnson* (Lawrence, Kans., 1979).

Conrad, *La. Biography*

Glenn R. Conrad, ed., *A Dictionary of Louisiana Biography* (2 vols., New Orleans, 1988).

Coulter, *Brownlow*

E. Merton Coulter, *William G. Brownlow: Fighting Parson of the Southern Highlands* (Chapel Hill, 1937).

DAB

Allen Johnson and Dumas Malone, eds., *Dictionary of American*

	Biography (20 vols., supps., and index, New York, 1928–).
DNB	Leslie Stephen and Sidney Lee, eds., *The Dictionary of National Biography* (22 vols. and supps., London, 1938– [1885–1901]).
Goodspeed's *Tennessee, East Tennessee, White* [and other counties]	Goodspeed Publishing Company, *History of Tennessee, from the Earliest Time to the Present . . .* (Chicago, 1886–87).
Heitman, *Register*	Francis B. Heitman, *Historical Register and Dictionary of the United States Army, from Its Organization, September 29, 1789 to March 2, 1903* (2 vols., Washington, D.C., 1903).
Hunt and Brown, *Brigadier Generals*	Roger D. Hunt and Jack R. Brown, *Brevet Brigadier Generals in Blue* (Gaithersburg, Md., 1990).
Johnson Papers	LeRoy P. Graf, Ralph W. Haskins, and Paul H. Bergeron, eds., *The Papers of Andrew Johnson* (9 vols., Knoxville, 1967–).
McMullin and Walker, *Territorial Governors*	Thomas A. McMullin and David Walker, *Biographical Directory of American Territorial Governors* (Westport, 1984).
Moulton, *John Ross*	Gary E. Moulton, *John Ross, Cherokee Chief* (Athens, 1978).
NCAB	*National Cyclopaedia of American Biography* . . . (63 vols. and index, New York, 1893–1984 [1–18, Ann Arbor, 1967]).
NUC	Library of Congress, *The National Union Catalog: Pre-1956 Imprints* (754 vols., London, 1968–).
Nuermberger, *Clays*	Ruth K. Nuermberger, *The Clays of Alabama* (Lexington, 1958).
OR	*War of the Rebellion: A Compilation of the Official Records of the Union and Confederate Armies* (70 vols. in 128, Washington, D.C., 1880–1901).
OR-Navy	*Official Records of the Union and Confederate Navies in the War*

	of the Rebellion (30 vols., Washington, D.C., 1894– 1927).
Owen, *History of Ala.*	Thomas M. Owen, *History of Alabama and Dictionary of Alabama Biography* (4 vols., Chicago, 1921).
Parrish, *Radical Rule*	William E. Parrish, *Missouri Under Radical Rule, 1865–1870* (Columbia, Mo., 1965).
Patton, *Unionism and Reconstruction*	James W. Patton, *Unionism and Reconstruction in Tennessee: 1860–1869* (Chapel Hill, 1934).
Pomeroy, *The Territories*	Earl S. Pomeroy, *The Territories and the United States, 1861–1890* (Seattle, 1969 [1947]).
Powell, *Army List*	William H. Powell, *List of Officers of the Army of the United States from 1779 to 1900* (Detroit, 1967 [1900]).
Ramsdell, *Reconstruction in Texas*	Charles W. Ramsdell, *Reconstruction in Texas* (New York, 1910).
Richardson, *Messages*	James D. Richardson, comp., *A Compilation of the Messages and Papers of the Presidents, 1789– 1897* (10 vols., Washington, D.C., 1896–99).
Ritter and Wakelyn, *Legislative Leaders*	Charles F. Ritter and Jon L. Wakelyn, *American Legislative Leaders, 1850–1910* (Westport, 1989).
Simon, *Grant Papers*	John Y. Simon, ed., *The Papers of Ulysses S. Grant* (18 vols., Carbondale, 1967–).
Smith, *Blair Family*	William E. Smith, *The Francis Preston Blair Family in Politics* (2 vols., New York, 1933).
Sobel and Raimo, *Governors*	Robert Sobel and John Raimo, eds., *Biographical Directory of the Governors of the United States, 1789–1978* (4 vols., Westport, 1978).
Taylor, *La. Reconstructed*	Joe Gray Taylor, *Louisiana Reconstructed, 1863–1877* (Baton Rouge, 1974).

Thompson, *Navajo*	Gerald Thompson, *The Army and the Navajo* (Tucson, 1976).
Trefousse, *Johnson*	Hans L. Trefousse, *Andrew Johnson: A Biography* (New York, 1989).
U.S. Off. Reg.	*Register of the Officers and Agents, Civil, Military and Naval in the Service of the United States . . .* (Washington, D.C., 1851–).
Van Deusen, *Seward*	Glyndon G. Van Deusen, *William Henry Seward* (New York, 1967).
Wakelyn, *BDC*	Jon L. Wakelyn, *Biographical Directory of the Confederacy* (Westport, 1977).
Waller, *Hamilton of Texas*	John L. Waller, *Colossal Hamilton of Texas* (El Paso, 1968).
Warner, *Blue*	Ezra J. Warner, *Generals in Blue* (Baton Rouge, 1964).
Warner, *Gray*	Ezra J. Warner, *Generals in Gray* (Baton Rouge, 1959).
Webb et al., *Handbook of Texas*	Walter P. Webb et al., eds., *The Handbook of Texas* (3 vols., Austin, 1952, 1976).
Zuber, *Worth*	Richard L. Zuber, *Jonathan Worth: A Biography of a Southern Unionist* (Chapel Hill, 1965).

JOURNALS

AHR	*American Historical Review*
AR	*The Alabama Review*
Con Vet	*Confederate Veteran*
GHQ	*Georgia Historical Quarterly*
IaJHP	*Iowa Journal of History and Politics*
InMH	*Indiana Magazine of History*
JNH	*Journal of Negro History*
JSH	*Journal of Southern History*
KSHS *Collections*	Kansas State Historical Society *Collections*
La. Hist.	*Louisiana History*
LHQ	*Louisiana Historical Quarterly*
MdHM	*Maryland Historical Magazine*
Minn. Hist.	*Minnesota History*
MoHR	*Missouri Historical Review*
MVHR	*Mississippi Valley Historical Review*
NMHR	*New Mexico Historical Review*

OHQ	*Oregon Historical Quarterly*
PHR	*Pacific Historical Review*
RCHS *Pubs.*	Rutherford County Historical Society *Publications*
Records CHS	*Records of the Columbia Historical Society*
SCHM	*South Carolina Historical Magazine*
SWHQ	*Southwestern Historical Quarterly*
THQ	*Tennessee Historical Quarterly*
VMHB	*Virginia Magazine of History and Biography*
WVaH	*West Virginia History*

Chronology

1808, December 29	Born at Raleigh, North Carolina
1812, January 4	Death of father Jacob Johnson
1826, September	Arrives in Greeneville, Tennessee
1827, May 17	Marries Eliza McCardle
1828, October 25	Birth of daughter Martha
1829–35	Alderman, then mayor
1830, February 19	Birth of son Charles
1832, May 8	Birth of daughter Mary
1834, February 22	Birth of son Robert
1835–37, 1839–41	State representative
1841–43	State senator
1843–53	Congressman, first district
1852, August 5	Birth of son Andrew, Jr.
1853–57	Governor
1857, October 8	Elected to U.S. Senate
1862, March 3	Appointed military governor of Tennessee
1863, April 4	Death of son Charles
1864, June 8	Nominated for Vice President
1864, November 8	Elected Vice President
1865, March 4	Inaugurated as Vice President
1865, April 15	Sworn in as President
1865, May 29	Amnesty Proclamation
	Proclamation Establishing Government for North Carolina
1865, August 22	Circular to Provisional Governors
1865, October 11	Order *re* Release of Prominent Confederate Prisoners
1865, October 24	Death of brother William P.
1865, December 4	First Annual Message to Congress
1866, January 1	New Year's Day White House Reception
1866, February 7	Interview with Delegation of Blacks
1866, February 19	Veto of Freedmen's Bureau Bill
1866, February 22	Washington's Birthday Address
1866, March 27	Veto of Civil Rights Bill
1866, April 2	Proclamation *re* End of Insurrection
1866, April 7	Circular *re* Appointments to Office
1866, April 12	Interview with London *Times* Correspondent

1866, May 15	Veto of Colorado Statehood Bill
1866, June 7	Honorary doctorate conferred by the University of North Carolina
1866, June 22	Message *re* Amending the Constitution
1866, July 16	Veto of Freedmen's Bureau Bill
1866, July 24	Message *re* Resolution on Restoration of Tennessee
1866, August 28-September 15	"Swing around the circle" trip
1868, February 24	Impeachment by House
1868, May 16, 26	Acquittal by Senate
1869, March	Returns to Greeneville
1869, October 22	Defeated for U.S. Senate
1872, November 5	Defeated for congressman-at-large
1875, January 26	Elected to U.S. Senate
1875, March 5–24	Serves in extra Senate session
1875, July 31	Dies at Stover home, Carter County

THE PAPERS OF
Andrew Johnson

February 1866

From Dorothy H. Ball[1]

[Fairfax County, Va., ca. February 1866][2]

The petition of Mrs D. H. Ball, in behalf of the heirs of the "Ball Estate," in Fairfax County, Va, respectfully shows:—

That said estate contains about 1000 Acres, to which there are twelve heirs, & three persons otherwise interested,—in all fifteen,—and that it is largely indebted to men who have never been disloyal to the Government.

That about 700 Acres of the land *was* in timber of the finest quality, *all of which* has been cut down: that all the fencing & three good dwellings, with their out-buildings, have been destroyed entirely, & the land greatly injured by the erection of large fortifications,—& this numerous family have *no home*, & are in entirely destitute circumstances.

That the only dwelling the family occupied (the others being held by tenants) was not "abandoned" during the war, till the head of the family[3] then occupying it was carried off to prison.

That the land was libelled for Confiscation, & the suits have been dismissed, *& all costs & taxes paid*, & all the persons interested, except minor children, have accepted the terms of the "Amnesty Proclamation," & taken the required oaths.

That according to measurement about 1800 cords of wood (the *only* hope of the family & large interest of the creditors) are now lying on the place, which is being rapidly hauled off by Agents of the "Freedman's Bureau" & persons having or pretending to have orders from them:— That the manure deposited by camps is also being taken by a man who claims to have purchased it from one of them—notwithstanding that the land has been released by Gen. Howard's order, dated three days prior to his purchase, & in which the manure is not excepted.

That the "release" of Gen. Howard is of no benefit to the parties interested in the land, as the wood & manure, which are the only available sources of present profit connected with it, are beyond their power to control or possess, & will soon be entirely lost to them, unless they can pay for it the sum of $2700.00 (which the Bureau demands)—an amount utterly beyond their power to raise.

In consideration of which facts which are matters of notoriety in the neighborhood, & can be sustained by affidavits, your petitioner respectfully & earnestly prays for an order from your Excellency restoring to her & to Wm. H. Dulany,[4] the administrators on the several estates, the land, with all its contents, & stopping the hauling of the wood & manure from it.[5]

D. H. Ball

ALS, DNA-RG105, Asst. Commr., D.C., Unregistered Lets. Recd.
1. Ball (1817–1889) was the widow of William Waring Ball (1812–1862) and daughter of a Leesburg physician. Horace E. Hayden, *Virginia Genealogies* (Baltimore, 1959 [1885]), 136, 141.
2. Internal evidence suggests that the letter was written from Fairfax County; the accompanying endorsements of late February and early March 1866 suggest a February 1866 date.
3. Probably William Waring Ball.
4. Dulany (*fl*1870), a lawyer and relative by marriage to the Ball family, had represented Fairfax County as a unionist at the Virginia secession convention. He had briefly fought with the Confederate army and then served in the Virginia senate (1863–65). Afterwards he practiced law with his relative, Mottrom Dulany Ball. Nan Netherton et al., *Fairfax County, Virginia: A History* (Fairfax, 1978), 300, 314, 316; William H. Gaines, Jr., *Biographical Register of Members: Virginia State Convention of 1861, First Session* (Richmond, 1969), 32.
5. The letter was referred to General Howard, who recommended that the wood remaining on the Ball Estate be restored to the family, while the wood previously taken by the army be kept as payment for the cost of cutting the wood. The manure had already been sold and therefore could not be returned. On March 2 Johnson approved of Howard's recommendation. See endorsements attached to Dorothy Ball's letter.

From Columbia County, Pa., Citizens[1]

[February 1866][2]

The Undersigned Citizens of the County of Columbia, in the Thirteenth Revenue District of the State of Pennsylvania, respectfully represent—

That they have heard with regret of the removal of Isaac S. Monroe[3] from the Assessorship of the said District; and of the appointment of Palemon John[4] to that office; and they beg leave to lay before your Excellency some reasons in favor of the reinstatement of Mr. Monroe.

He was originally appointed on the recommendation of Hon. Henry W. Tracy,[5] Member of Congress from the District, and held the office for the period of about Sixteen months. No charges of Corruption or of maladministration were made against him, and no allegation can be made that the duties of the office were not faithfully performed by him. No necessity for a change is believed to have existed, so far as requiring more efficiency in the public service was concerned; and there is this, among other unanswerable arguments in favor of Mr. Monroe—That under his predecessor the Income Tax for 1864 was a little over Forty two thousand dollars; while under Monroe for the year 1865, it was over One hundred and twenty two thousand dollars.

That large additional taxation was so fairly laid and so skilfully adjusted that it was cheerfully acquiesced in, except by those who could be influenced by Palemon John, the present Assessor, and his newspaper, through which he endeavored to make the tax as odious as possible by repeated and reiterated and malicious attacks upon the system.

For four years Palemon John has been holding the lucrative office of Post Master at Bloomsburg in the County of Columbia, and only resigned it to accept the Assessorship; and while that was held in abeyance he declined and refused to print and publish in his newspaper the "Columbia County Republican" a resolution of the Republican County Convention endorsing the President of the United States and his appointments.

Your Memorialists most humbly and respectfully submit, that when an officer has been found who is honest and capable, a change for the mere sake of change is inexpedient, and more especially is this so in an office, the duties of which are so important responsible and complicated as those of Revenue Assessor. To supercede a man just when he has acquired a thorough knowledge of his business is to pay a premium to incompetency; and to make a short tenure of office the rule, is to invite peculation and fraud, because it will not pay to be honest.

We think it would be to the interest of the Government and the satisfaction of the Tax Payers to have the office of Revenue Assessor again in the hands of Isaac S. Monroe.[6]

Pet, DNA-RG56, Appts., Internal Revenue Service, Assessor, Pa., 13th Dist.

1. There were 159 signatures.

2. A docket which accompanies the petition offers this date.

3. A former Democrat who joined the Republican party in 1861, Monroe (c1812–1879) also owned a powder keg factory and later served as a county judge (1870–76). J. H. Battle, ed., *History of Columbia and Montour Counties, Pennsylvania* (Chicago, 1887), 94, 514–15.

4. John (fl1869) had been given a temporary commission as assessor in October 1865. Ibid., 118; David Wilmot to Johnson, Feb. 6, 1866, Appts., Internal Revenue Service, Assessor, Pa., 13th Dist., Palemon John, RG56, NA.

5. Tracy (1807–1886), an Independent Republican while in Congress (1863–65), later served as deputy collector of the port of Philadelphia. *BDAC*; *U.S. Off. Reg.* (1867).

6. Monroe was not reinstated, nor was John's nomination sent to the Senate. Instead, Johnson nominated Robert F. Clark, as recommended by both of Pennsylvania's senators. Edgar Cowan and C. R. Buckalew to Johnson, Jan. 22, 1866, Appts., Internal Revenue Service, Assessor, Pa., 13th Dist., Robert F. Clark, RG56, NA; Ser. 6B, Vol. 4: 82, Johnson Papers, LC.

From Idaho Citizens[1]

[Boise, ca. February 1866][2]

The undersigned citizens of Idaho Territory, would humbly represent to your Excellency that Alex C. Smith,[3] one of the Associate Justices of the Supreme Court of said Territory has proven himself wholly incompetent and unfit to perform the responsible duties of said office, that he does not possess the legal learning and ability necessary to fill the position, with anything like respectibility.[4] In addition to which, and worse than all, he is addicted to habitual intoxication, and even gross drunkenness, to such an extent as to totally disqualify him for the administration of justice.

We send you enclosed, an extract from a letter lately received by the clerk of the Supreme Court at this place,[5] from the Sheriff of Nez Perce County,[6] (Judge Smith's place of residence) and also an affidavit of Judge Cook,[7] an atty of this City. They speak for themselves.[8]

We are sorry to have to say so much of anyone occupying such an honorable position in our midst, but necessity as well as an imperative sense of duty to the Government, and the people of this Territory, as well as to ourselves, absolutely require it. And we can do no less. Not being willing to stand quietly by, and see the best interests of our citizens sacrificed, and our Courts brought disrepute, and justly, made a subject of reproach and contempt in the m[inds] of our enemies, by reason of the unfi[tness] of *one* of our Judges.

We therefore earnestly, but humbly pray that Judge Alec. C. Smith be removed and that some suitable person learned in the law, be appointed in his place.

And in connection with this matter we would beg leave to recommend Wyatt A George Esqr.,[9] an attorney and counseller at law of this City, as a suitable person to fill said office, as Judge Smith's successor. Mr George was born and educated in the State of Indiana and acquired his profession in the Office of Howard & Wright[10] of that State, (la[te] Gov Wright) and came to the bar in 18[?]. He has practiced several years on this coast, and is thoroughly acquainted with the character and wants of our people and with the jurisprudence of this country. He is about forty five years of age, and is residing here with his family. He [is] a firm and consistent Union man, and during the late rebellion rendered most efficient services in his able and zealous support of all those great measures [of] the administration, which so happily brought the war to a close.

The position of Mr George as a citizen, the moral tone and dignity of his character, and his acknowledged legal attainments and ability, render him eminently qualified for the Office, and his appointment would give general satisfaction, and especially would it be appreciated and highly gratifying to our friend and the friends of the Government in this Territory.

We therefore most humbly and sincerely ask the appointment of W. A George and we will ever pray.[11]

Pet, DNA-RG60, Office of Atty. Gen., Lets. Recd., President.

1. Eight individuals, mostly territorial officials, signed the petition.

2. This document cannot be dated later than February 10, 1866, since one of the signatories, Territorial Secretary Horace C. Gilson, departed on that date for San Francisco, absconding with territorial funds. A notation on the manuscript indicates the petition was received at Washington on March 15, 1866, and internal evidence reveals that the document originated in Boise. Merle W. Wells, "Clinton DeWitt Smith, Secretary, Idaho Terri-

tory, 1864–1865," *OHQ*, 52 (1951): 51–52. See also David W. Ballard to Johnson, July 25, 1866.

3. Alleck C. Smith, a native of Kentucky, had been appointed to the Idaho court from the Washington Territory on March 10, 1863. *U.S. Off. Reg.* (1863); John Hailey, *The History of Idaho* (Boise, 1910), 48.

4. Judge Smith had ardently advocated keeping the territorial capitol at Lewiston (in his district) rather than moving it to Boise City as the territorial legislature had decreed. In the supreme court case deciding the location, a Lewiston attorney had to write Smith's minority opinion for him, which "tended to substantiate claims that the judge was illiterate, or at least incompetent." In December 1865 the Democratic legislature, in a move against Radical Republican Judge Milton Kelly, shifted the territorial supreme court justices to different districts, bringing Smith to Boise. This action may have provoked the petition. Wells, "Clinton DeWitt Smith," 46–47; Ronald H. Limbaugh, "The Idaho Spoilsmen: Federal Administrators and Idaho Territorial Politics, 1863–1890," (Ph.D. diss., Univ. of Idaho, 1966), 37–38.

5. A. L. Downer, clerk of the supreme court from June 1864 to March 1866, also signed the petition. Initially Downer, from Wisconsin, had served as U.S. commissioner in Idaho. Hailey, *Idaho*, 168; *History of Idaho Territory* (San Francisco, 1884), 82.

6. James H. Fisk had served as sheriff as early as 1863. Ibid., 226; George Owens, comp., *General Directory and Business Guide of the Principal Towns in the Upper Country* . . . (San Francisco, 1866), 87.

7. A. G. Cook, district attorney of the Third Judicial District, who also signed this petition, had served as postmaster of Boise City during part of 1865. *U.S. Off. Reg.* (1865).

8. Neither document has been found.

9. Not further identified.

10. Tilghman A. Howard and Joseph A. Wright had practiced law together in Parke County, Indiana, in the early 1840s. *A Biographical History of Eminent and Self-Made Men of the State of Indiana* (2 vols., Cincinnati, 1880), 2: 247–48.

11. James M. Ashley of Ohio, chairman of the House Committee on Territories, endorsed the petition: "I *know* that the statement of the petitioners is in the main true." On January 20, 1866, before this petition had been drafted, Johnson nominated George L. Wood, a resident of Oregon, to replace Alleck Smith. Wood's nomination, however, was later withdrawn and on the same date, May 18, 1866, John Cummins, a signer of the petition, was appointed, serving until he himself was removed by July 1867. *Senate Ex. Proceedings*, Vol. 14, pt. 2: 821–22, 835; Ser. 6B, Vol. 4: 398, Johnson Papers, LC.

From James Gordon Bennett

Fort Washington [N.Y.]   1st Feb. 1866

My Dear Sir

General John Cochrane came out to see me to day and had a talk on the present state of public affairs. Stevens and the radicals have now declared war against your administration. It is clear now that something should be done of a practical character. I beleive that with proper skill the Conservative interests of Congress could now be united under the programme of your administration so as to give you a majority for all public purposes. I am perfectly satisfied that the extreme radicals are in a minority in the Congress but they intend to do every thing they can to prevent any divisions in their ranks, so as to be able to carry the next elections for Congress. Now or pretty soon is the time for your friends to act.

General Cochrane will explain to you my general views which would occupy too great a space now to enter upon. I think it is my duty to the country that your administration should be supported to the utmost. I have already said that I take little interest in offices or appointments, but these matters can be used efficiency at the proper time. It will soon arrive but is not yet. I may venture however that as a type or specimen for Collector of New York, you should select a man acquainted with law, with commerce, with the business of the Custom House and with the politics of this state. Such a type is General C. He has been a democrat—went into the war, fought through several campaigns, was then elected by the republicans Attorney general of the state. I do not ask for any appointment, but I only wish to explain the exigences of the time by a living representative. I feel satisfied that the crisis is approaching and that the prospect of triumph is very good.[1]

James G. Bennett

ALS, DLC-JP.
    1. Bennett's letter was enclosed in John Cochrane's of February 12, 1866.

From Berks County, Pa., Committee[1]

Berks County, Penna.   Feb 1st 1866.

Believing that erroneous statements and false representations have been made to the Department concerning a matter in which we feel a deep and lasting interest, we beg to offer the following facts—trusting that our appeal may not be in vain.

When the office of Assessor of Int. Rev. was first created, Mr. A. P. Tutton secured the position through the influence of Mr. Levi B. Smith,[2] (our defeated candidate for Congress in 1861) and other Gentlemen who were not residents of our County, but whose influence at Washington was of a nature to be respected. Mr. Tutton is an honest, unassuming man, but at once obscure, unknown, and without the slightest pretence to influence. Indeed, so far as politics were concerned, at the time of his appointment he scarcely Knew to what political organization he belonged. Mr Tutton has held the position until the present time, and until recently without opposition.

But the termination of the war has brought with it many aspirants for place—Not politicians and wirepulling office seekers, but men, who in the service of their Country have lost their health, or limbs, and in many cases are totally unfitted to follow their former occupations, or to labor with their hands.

Such, in a word, is the case with the Gentleman whom we put forth and urge as the successor of Mr. Tutton, the present incumbent. Col. Geo. W. Alexander was wounded while leading his Regiment the 47th P. V. at Pleasantville La.[3] during the Red River expedition under Maj. Genl. Banks, and though apparently an able bodied man, it is extremely doubtful whether he can ever fully recover from the effects of his wound.

Without wishing to be considered egotistical, we claim to be the representative men of the republican party of Berks County—and we but express the earnest desire of our party when we ask the appointment of Col. Alexander to the Assessorship of Int. Rev. of our district. In the outset we did not suppose there would be any opposition offered on the part of the friends of Mr. Tutton, to the change, basing our opinions upon the late leading principals of our party—That meritorious soldiers, in all cases, and at all times, other things being equal should have the preference of appointment to office; And having also, this principal practically carried out by the appointment of Maj. Briner,[4] a worthy, wounded soldier to the Post Mastership of the city of Reading and by so doing the Department removed Mr. Knabb,[5] a life long politician, and one who, as Editor of the Republican organ of our party has laboured harder and done more real service in the county than any twenty other men, in the District. We preferred above all men, the retention of Mr. Knabb in office, in consideration of services rendered, and we desired that should any civilian be retained in office it might be Mr. Knabb. But our party in Convention assembled soon after, passed a unanimous resolution, thanking the President for so practically carrying out the principles of the Party. Now, if Mr. Knabb is displaced, why, we ask, in the name of Justice is this man who never performed one meritorious act for the party, to be allowed to retain his place?

Every Township within our District (with one single exception that one not being represented) expressed itself publicly in favour of the appointment of Col. Alexander to the Assessorship at our County Convention held last fall. Every Republican councilman as well as the Mayor of the City of Reading,[6] has signed his petition. Every candidate nominated on the Republican County Ticket, for the last County election sign his petition and urge his appointment. At least nine tenths of the Republican members of the County Bar are anxious for Col. Alexander's appointment.

In fact, every representative man within the County, with very few exceptions, ask the same. The City of Reading the home of Col. Alexander, was carried by the Democratic party last fall by nearly two hundred (200) majority—a loss to our party of about three hundred and fifty— (350) over the previous spring election—simply because our appeals were disregarded at Washington.

The retention of Mr. Tutton, if persevered in against our common protest, will demoralize the party here. This may appear strange, but the following will to some extent explain.

There has not been one single soldier appointed to the Asst. Assessorship in this whole district, until quite recently. Lately there were *two* soldiers appointed, and one of those does not act. All the rest in the entire District are civilians. Our County is large, and there is not a sub-district in it that does not contain several worthy soldiers; some of them cripples, able and competent to do the work of an Asst. Assessor. We can instance one old man, gray headed, who served his country faithfully for over three years in the field, as a Lieutenant, and who is now broken down in health, entirely destitute of means to support his family.

This man has made repeated application for the position of Asst. Assessor of his sub-district, which would pay him about six hundred dollars ($600) per year—but his prayers have, so far, been offered in vain. He must find employment elsewhere—while a hearty, robust civilian holds the place. These things are telling fearfully in the rank and file of our party.

Col. Alexander pledges himself if appointed to give all places of profit and benefit within his gift, to the needy and crippled soldier. And as our county placed in the field nearly Four thousand (4000) men to fight the battles of the Country we feel that Justice demands that some attention should be paid to their claims, particularly as the soldiers throughout this County have organized themselves into "Soldiers Leagues," working together, and as a matter of course, *for* and *with* the party which supports them. And by conciliating this element, we feel that we may be able to greatly reduce the heretofore heavy Democratic majorities in the County.[7]

LS, DLC-JP.

1. There were ten signatories, including Jacob Hoffman, committee chairman. Hoffman (1805–1870), an influential lawyer whose specialty was land cases, had been a supporter of Lincoln during the war. Morton L. Montgomery, *History of Berks County in Pennsylvania* (Philadelphia, 1886), 564.

2. Smith (1806–1876) was an attorney, wood stove manufacturer, bank president, and a staunch Republican. Montgomery, *Berks County*, 1155–57.

3. The battle at Pleasant Hill was fought on April 9, 1864.

4. William M. Briner (c1819-c1890) had commanded Co. D, 3rd Pa. Inf. Res., before being mustered out in June 1864. Commissioned postmaster of Reading in July 1866, he later worked as an insurance agent. CSR, Wm. Briner, RG94, NA; Reading directories (1870–95); Ser. 6B, Vol. 4: 83, Johnson Papers, LC.

5. Appointed as postmaster by Lincoln, Jacob Knabb (1817-c1888) edited the *Berks and Schuylkill Journal* at Reading from 1845 until his death. Reading directories (1887–89); Montgomery, *Berks County*, 401–3.

6. Nathan M. Eisenhower (1812–1877), a carpenter who served as mayor of Reading (1865–67), also wrote a letter recommending Alexander. Eisenhower to E. A. Cowan, June 13, 1866, Johnson Papers, LC; Morton L. Montgomery, *Historical and Biographical Annals of Berks County, Pennsylvania* (2 vols., Chicago, 1909), 2: 218.

7. Alexander was nominated by Johnson on May 16, 1866, but the nomination was withdrawn two weeks later. After Tutton had been removed, Alexander was finally commissioned as assessor of the Eighth District in March 1867, only to be removed from office in July 1868. Ser. 6B, Vol. 4: 85, 91, Johnson Papers, LC; *Senate Ex. Proceedings*, Vol. 14, pt. 2: 816, 839.

From James Park et al.[1]

Feby 1, 1866.

Sir:

The undersigned, on behalf of themselves, and the Members and Congregation of the First Presbyterian Church, in Knoxville, Tenn. would respectfully represent: That for more than two years we have been deprived of the use of our House of Worship; that it was taken originally by the U.S. Military authorities and used as a hospital for Federal soldiers; that in the mean time many of the pews were broken and destroyed; that subsequently it was used as a barracks for a period of several weeks; and that for about one year past it has been used, by whose authority we cannot learn, as a school house for freedmen. In the grave yard attached, are the mortal remains of many of the pioneer settlers and earliest citizens of Knoxville, such as the Whites, Williamses, Ramseys, Cowans, Humeses, Blounts &c &c including several ministers and teachers of the past generation. Both the church edifice and the grave-yard have been shamefully abused and mutilated. The house is almost entirely stripped of its pews and other furniture, the walls and painting defaced, and many of the tombstones and monuments are overturned and broken, and the graves are continually trampled under foot and disgustingly defiled. Each day increases the ruin. We have made repeated applications for the restoration of the property, but without avail. Since the middle of Nov. 1865 we have made two appeals to Gen. Fisk, of the Freedmans Bureau, without eliciting any satisfactory reply.[2]

We are now worshipping in a hired house, while our own is going to wreck.

We appeal to your high sense of justice and right, and pray an order for the restoration of the property to its rightful owners; and that it be refitted for use according to its original purpose.[3]

And your petitioners will ever pray for the blessing of Almighty God upon your administration, and that the Grace of the Great Head of the Church be vouchsafed to you forever.[4]

James Park, Minister

ALS, DNA-RG107, Lets. Recd., Executive (M494, Roll 84).

1. Park (1822–1912), a native of Knoxville and graduate of East Tennessee University, became principal of the Tennessee School for the Deaf in Knoxville in 1859. He left the area during the war but returned in January 1866 and became the unofficial and subsequently official pastor of the city's First Presbyterian Church, a post he held until his resignation in 1905. The three church elders who also signed the letter were: David A. Deaderick (1797–1873), who was for many years clerk and master of the chancery court at Knoxville and was also engaged in the mercantile business; William S. Kennedy (c1806–fl1870), a native Tennessean who was fairly prosperous on the eve of the outbreak of the war and is later listed as a miller by trade; and George M. White (1800–1884), a native of Knoxville who served in the prewar years as mayor in the early 1850s, chairman of the county court, and also as recorder, a post White held well into the postwar years. 1860 Census, Tenn., Knox, 1st Dist., Knoxville, 88; (1870), 3rd Ward, Knoxville, 16; Mary U. Rothrock, ed., *The French Broad-Holston Country: A History of Knox County, Tennessee* (Knoxville, 1946), 464–66; *Knoxville Press and Herald*, Aug. 30, 1873; *Knoxville Chronicle*, Dec. 19, 1884.

2. For an account of the church's situation during the war years and in 1866, see James Park, *The First Presbyterian Church in Knoxville, Tennessee* (Knoxville, 1876), 23–24.

3. For information concerning the restoration of the property to the congregation of the First Presbyterian Church in May 1866, see ibid., 24–25. See also the files accompanying Park et al. to Johnson, Lets. Recd., Executive (M494, Roll 84), RG107, NA.

4. Below the signatures of the minister and elders of the church was a statement from non-members of the congregation who supported the petition. This supporting declaration was signed by some sixteen prominent Knoxville and Knox County residents. The petition

was referred to General Howard at the Freedmen's Bureau, who replied to Secretary Stanton on April 26 that "orders for restoration have been issued." Ibid.

From Caroline V. Sayre[1]

Montgomery, Alabama   February 1st 1866.

The petitioner Mrs Caroline V Sayre, a resident of Montgomery Ala. for many years, respectfully sheweth unto your Excellency.

1st That she is the widow of P D Sayre[2] who died in 1850, being at the time of death, a resident of Montgomery, Ala.

2nd. He left your petitioner his widow, and ten children. His estate consisted in real, & personal property.

3rd. When the Federal forces occupied the city of Montgomery on the 9th of May 1865, Maj Genl Smith published an order to the effect that on, and after that date, the Government would pay for all private property which was taken possession of, or used by the army, and that no impressments would be made.

4th. Under this order, a large, & very valuable part of said real estate Known as Estelle, & Concert Halls,[3] which is still in the hands of petitioner as the legal representative thereof, and undivided. (Several of the children being still minors.)

That on or about the 9th day of May 1865, the officers of the division of the United States army under the control and command of Genl A. J. Smith 16th Army Corps, found it necessary to occupy six of the tenements, known as Estelle & Concert Halls for offices connected with the Head quarters of that Division of the Army; and that they took possession of the same, not as your petitioner is advised, as *seized* or *captured* property, for by general order all private property was to be respected—but certainly in a most irregular manner, and notwithstanding the said Genels' order directed that all private property should be respected: and that all property &c. taken for the use of the army should be paid for—they have continued ever since to occupy, and use said property, without the payment of rent. Your petitioner therefore requests an order for the restoration of her property, so soon as it can be given up by said army offices: and that in the meantime she be allowed a fair, and reasonable rent for the use, and occupation of the same and for such other & further relief as justice demands.

Your petitioner was *pardoned* on the 12th Sept 1865. As a lady well advanced in life—your petitioner could not, & did not take part in the rebellion, and she thinks it hard for herself & minor children, who are dependent on the rents, & income of said property to be deprived of their only income, and means of support, because others over whom she had no control, were found in rebellion against the Government of the United States.[4]

Caroline V. Sayre.

LS, DNA-RG107, Lets. Recd., Executive (M494, Roll 84).

1. Sayre (c1806–fl1870), a prewar slaveholder and "Farmer" worth over $200,000, had several sons in the Confederate army. By the end of the decade, she barely managed $7,500 in assets. 1860 Census, Ala., Montgomery, 1st Dist., 47; (1870), 5; Amnesty Papers (M1003, Roll 10), Ala., Caroline V. Sayre, RG94, NA.

2. At the time of his death, Phil D. Sayre (b. c1800) was a Montgomery merchant. Ronald V. Jackson and Gary R. Teeples, eds., *Alabama 1840 Census Index* (Bountiful, Utah, 1977), 108; 1850 Census, Ala., Montgomery, Montgomery, 2nd Ward, 267.

3. During the summer of 1865, "Concert Hall, over Farmers' Bank, Market street," had served as the headquarters of Gen. Eugene A. Carr, commander of the 3rd Div., 16th Army Corps. *Montgomery Advertiser*, July 26, 1865.

4. The petition bore the endorsements of former Generals William B. Woods and Carr and was presented to Johnson on March 12 by Lewis E. Parsons while the ex-provisional Alabama governor was in Washington. Johnson ordered Mrs. Sayre's application to be referred to the quartermaster general, who, because of an earlier decision by the judge advocate general in similar cases, ruled that her "claim could not be entertained" since it had originated in a disloyal state. Stanton to Johnson, Apr. 3, 1866; Montgomery C. Meigs to Stanton, Mar. 21, 1866, Lets. Recd., Executive (M494, Roll 84), RG107, NA.

From John H. Gilmer

[Washington] Feb. 2d [186]6

Sir.

If agreeable to you, I am very anxious to have the privilege of a private interview with you—to day, or to morrow.

I refer you to Hnble Samuel Randall of Phil. the Atty. Genl U.S. and Secretary of state, as *to who and what I am*.

As the chairman of the judiciary committee of the Virginia Senate, I am compelled to be in my seat on Monday, so that I must leave on Sunday.

I wish to know from your *own* lips what—as matters now stand,—you deem the most advantageous policy, *as to yourself*—for Virginia to pursue—*at this time*. As a state—a people—and government—Virginia is with you—though many who *profess* to be your friends—are your wost and most dangerous enemies.[1]

John H. Gilmer

ALS, DLC-JP.

1. During their conversation, which took place the following day, Johnson and Gilmer discussed pending Virginia legislation which would permit the use of "negro evidence" in the state's courts. Two days later Gilmer forwarded to the White House copies of the proposed bills in question, along with a speech he had recently delivered on the subject, and informed the President that a committee would soon pay him a visit. Shortly afterwards the legislature passed a law allowing freedmen to testify only in cases involving other blacks. Gilmer to Johnson, Feb. 5, 1866, Johnson Papers, LC; Hamilton J. Eckenrode, *The Political History of Virginia During the Reconstruction* (Baltimore, 1904), 44. See Response to Virginia Legislative Delegation, Feb. 10, 1866.

From Russell Houston

Louisville   Feby. 2. 1866.

My Dear Friend.

I have delayed writing many things that I have been inclined to write & would have written, but for the fact that I supposed you were annoyed by every body's opinion & worried by every body's advice. But as your friend—than whom you have no better—& as the friend of your country & mine, I must be permitted to express my extreme gratification at the firmness & fidelity with which you have adhered to your plan for the restoration of the Union. The good men of this land are with you. Thus far you have their approbation & warmest sympathies. They rely upon your known courage, & firmness in the right—your stubborn adherence to principle, & therefore they have hopes for the future. Your national character for political integrity leads them to expect you to do your duty. Your positions may be assailed, & your motives, even, be impugned—your measures may be voted down & your plans defeated, but not forever. Be not disheartened. If you are to go down, go down in the right, & you will be sure to rise again. Since the days of Washington, no man has had in his hands, so much of good for his race, & I may say, so much of evil to his generation to avert & defeat; & with no purpose to flatter, I beg to say that, for one, I have no fears as to your course.

The doctrine of the forfeiture of the life of a State for the treason of its citizens[1] will find its proper fate at the proper time. It is a species of forfeiture but recently heard of in this Country. The treason of a State is not mentioned in the Constitution. Treason is defined & forfeitures for treason are limited & guarded—but the forfeiture of the existence of a State of this Union, for any cause, was not thought of, & cannot occur in this Country except by the total destruction of our System of government. The question—what is a state, has been often asked, in recent discussions. It is as easily answered as it [is] asked, if it were of any consequence when asked or answered. There were thirteen States before the formation of our Constitution. They were complete States in the full sense of the term. He who knows what they were then, knows what a State is now. A definition is unnecessary when we have the thing to be defined, plainly before us. These thirteen States & people as States & people, formed our National Government, conferring upon it certain specific powers & all implied powers necessary to carry into effect, the specific powers, & establishing, between the States & this national Government, certain relations which neither can dissolve at pleasure. In the formation of this government, the integrity of the states was maintained & never questioned. They were as much States afterwards as before, & are as much now as ever in the past; & if the South had succeeded in the late struggle, the Southern States would have been States in the Southern

Confederacy. It was not the purpose of either party to the war, to destroy the States; but on the part of the Government, it was, to maintain the integrity of the States & to preserve their relations to the General Government & to each other. The contest was not, by the South to preserve the States, & the Government to destroy them, as is implied in the position assumed by the extreme men of the Country—but on the part of the Government, it was an effort to maintain itself in all of its essential ingredients as created by the Constitution—to hold the Southern States & people up to their duty as States & people of the American Union, & it was successful. The Southern people were defeated & gave up the contest & were pardoned by general Amnesty & pardon & by special pardons in proper cases, & they now propose to return to their loyalty & duty, & as their first & highest *duty*, they elect & send to Congress, Senators & Representatives; I mean what I write. It was not simply a privilege, but an imperious duty. And the first open & traitorous breach of duty by the South was the recall of their Senators & Representatives from Congress. It was their duty to be there & in their seats, & to vote & participate in the legislation of the Country; & had this been done on occasions well remembered by you, perhaps our Country would now be at peace. They now propose to perform their obligations—they have been whipped into their duty & are being kicked out of it. But I grow tedious, I fear, & can suggest little if any thing, that may profit either you or myself.

I see that your first serious trouble is to be the universal suffrage bill for the District of Columbia.[2] I know not your views except from my knowledge of your character. Should the bill of the House be passed by the Senate, I hope you will veto it. I say this not with any special reference to the power to pass it, but with reference to the character of the bill itself. To me, the idea of authorizing such a mass of ignorant negroes as are in & around Washington to exercise the privilege of controling the Municipal Affairs of the Capitol of this Nation, is montrous. It is fraught with untold mischief, & if not checked at once, I fear for the life of the nation. No other people on earth would propose such an act of folly. It argues an ignorance of the character of the negroes of the South that is wholly inexcusable, or a blind & reckless zeal for party interest that forbodes no good to the Country. I have no prejudices against the negro—but would protect him in all of his rights. Let him be free—hold, own & dispose of property— Sue for injuries to person or property & testify in the Courts. These seek not the equality of the races, & provoke not implacable animosities—but universal suffrage would engender & promote both & would finally work the extinction of the colored race. Make the Southern states, *territories*— organize them as such with universal suffrage & admit them as States with enforced negro equality, in less than a quarter of a century, we will have another civil war, not merely to protect the rights of the negro, but his existence also, & no people in the Country would engage more heartily in the extermination of the race than the Northern people who would remove to the South.

But I admit that if the present bill were Stripped of its gross imperfections & made unobjectionable in itself, if it be possible to frame such a bill, the question would be much more difficult to decide in view of the universal opposition of the people of the District. "Congress shall exercise exclusive legislation in all cases whatever &c."—that is, in one view of it—Congress alone shall legislate for the District in exclusion of the States that may cede the District, & all other legislative power—but to legislate exclusively as legislation is understood in a free representative government & as practiced in the States of the Union, according to the will of the majority—that is, it shall exercise this exclusive legislation in a manner, republican—not without limitation of power—not despotic, but limited & constrained by the true genius & Spirit of our government.

On the other hand, it may be claimed that Congress has full power over the question & inasmuch as it is a Subject of legislation & of exclusive legislation with Congress—that the matter involved is a great national question—that its proper solution depends on a fair test of its merits— that the number of negroes in the northern States in comparison with the white race, is so small, that to permit them to vote would not solve the problem—that it cannot be tested in the Southern States because of Constitutional objections, & that therefore the District of Columbia is the only place to make the trial. True men, wishing to promote the interests of the Country & to do their duty might feel & reason in this way, especially being in ignorance of the character & capacity of the African race, & such men deserve to be heard. But as to blind fanaticism or wicked & malicious hatred of the Southern people, I would not swerve an inch. If those in power wish to make an honest experiment & to learn the truth, let them submit to you a bill involving no constitutional objections & in no sense violating the fundamental principles of civil liberty as practiced in this Country from the foundation of the government, & then they may expect co-operation of good people every where. You will, of course, be on your guard. The constitutional provision—the seemingly unlimited power of legislation conferred—the fact, that in a certain sense the District is the property of the nation & not of any particular State, will enable your opponents to place you in a false position, unless all proper points are guarded. Should the bill be made a proper one & you sign it, your opponents will be defeated & sadly disappointed. If you & they are to go before the American people to decide the issues between you, see that these issues are fairly presented & you may be satisfied with the decision. The generally received untruth that the negroes were all loyal in our late struggle, has given to demagogues a good weapon before the ignorant. I think I was pretty well posted as to current events, as the war progressed & I confess that I remember no victory won or battle fought by negroes. The success of our army was the result of the skill & courage of white officers & soldiers. I believe Sherman had not a solitary black soldier with him—Thomas, I think, had only one or two regiments in the battle at Nashville—Sherridan I believe never had any & Grant none to aid him materially. I think nearly every officer in the Southern Armies had his negro servant with him, & of the four millions of slaves in the South, not one tenth sought the Union lines & during the whole war they were more than usually faithful to the wives & children of their masters, most of whom were in the rebel armies.

I know this statement is in conflict with the current assertions of the times & would be considered a monstrous libel upon the character of the "loyal blacks"—but the Statement is nevertheless true. As has been often stated & repeated—"this is a white man's government"—it was won originally by the valor of white men—formed by the wisdom of white men, & *as the Constitution shows on its face*, for white men—has been administered for three quarters of a century by white men, & in our late struggle, it was saved by white men. And I may add *that it will be controled by white men in the future, if controled at all.*

I have been trying to get East to join me in a visit to you, but as his Court is in Session, I fear I will fail. I may come in a few days any way.

Russell Houston

ALS, DLC-JP.

1. A reference to the theory on reconstruction put forward by Rep. Samuel Shellabarger of Ohio on January 8, 1866, that eventually became the majority position in Congress. Shellabarger declared that no state was or could be out of the Union, but that the act of rebellion altered the relationship between the federal government and the former rebellious states, specifically in regard to the states' "body politic." Because the Constitution gave Congress responsibility to guarantee a republican form of government to those states, Congress would determine when such governments were reestablished, thus restoring the rights and powers of government granted to states of the Union. Eric L. McKitrick, *Andrew Johnson and Reconstruction* (Chicago, 1960), 113–15.

2. Houston refers to a bill proposed by William Kelley on December 5, 1865, and passed in the House of Representatives on January 18, 1866, extending the franchise to black males in the District of Columbia. The Senate referred the bill to its Committee on the District of Columbia but never took a vote on it. A black suffrage bill finally passed on December 14, 1866. Johnson vetoed the bill on January 7, 1867; on that same day the Senate repassed the measure over his veto and the House soon followed suit. Ibid., 474n; *Congressional Globe*, 39 Cong., 1 Sess., pp. 10, 311, 313.

From Joseph S. Oliver[1]

Auburn Macon Co Ala   Feby 2nd 1866

Dear Sir—

I wrote you the 3rd of last Novr[2] giving your Excellency an account of my afflicted condition, and of the destitution of my family. About one month after the date of my letter a young man a Federal Soldier came to my house and informed me that a communication had been received at Post head quarters at Tuskegee from Washington directing an officer to be sent to CrossKeys to inquire after J. S. Oliver, and that he had been ordered out on that business and was directed to make inquiry upon the following points. First as to my Standing and, 2d If I was indeed an invalid, and 3d as to the destitution of my family, 4th the number he has in the family, 5th did his house get burnt and how or by whom and did he loose a Horse & mule and by whom. Now I gave the young man all the information I posably could in my great afflictions. I satisfied him that I am indeed an ivalid the evidences of which are plainly visable upon almost every Joint. He also Saw upon my left leg a very bad looking and painfull ulcer. He spoke of it as being a very bad looking sore indeed and that he considered me a confirmed invalid. As to my standing the burning of my house the loose of my horse & mule I wanted him to stay with me and give me time to draw up some cirtisficates and get them sined by my neighbours who have know me variously from 15 to 20 and 25 years but the young man expressed himself as being in a hurry and did not wait for me to inform him upon those points as I desired to do and could have done very easily had he given me reasonable time. I drew up a cirtisficate for a Mr Jones and a Mr Simmons[3] and others who live directly on the young mans Road back to Tuskegee, but I understand he only got Mr Jones' name the others not being at home. I also drew up a cirtificate for a Mr Brumby[4] who I went to School with. This was more in regard to My Standing as Brumby and I have known each other from boy hood. I have not heard whither he got Brumbys name or not. If the young man had given time I could have sent your Excellency satisfactory evidence in regard to all the points in question. From the young mans talk I was led to believe he would make a report decidedly in my favor and which he may have done. I have not heard anything to the contrary. This agent or officer being thus sent to inquire into the situation and condition of my family led me to hope that Something would be done in my behalf, but as yet nothing more than sending the officer has been done, and I have Just received a note from the Q.M. General[5] stating that there is no law to authorize him to pay for stock taken by the U.S. Army. Now the intention of my letter of Novr. 3rd/65 was to call upon your Excellency for assistance not because I had lost a Horse & mule and not because my Negroes had been freed but simply because I am badly afflicted and my family is in a very destitute condition. I mentioned the Horse & mule if I mistake not more as an incidental matter and I think expressed a doubt as to such claims being reimbursed. I would now say to your Excellency that without assistance and that at an early day my family must inevitably suffer. I have five interesting Children[6] all growing up and Suffering daily now for the want of education for the want of propper food and rament. I appeal not to your Excellency on account of anything I have lost by the action of the Government, but I appeal as an afflicted Father who is unable to procure the necessities much less the comforts of life for his suffering and destitute children. Yes in the name and behalf of my children and an aged Mother do I make this appeal to your Excellency, will you lend a helping hand in this the hour of distress and affliction? For the sake of humanity for the sake of suffering Childhood for the sake of old age for the sake of the future prospects of my children who are growing up with out an education and for every consideration I would urge upon and most earnestly appeal to your Excellency to help in this hour of affliction and destitution. If I had the use of my limbs and could labor as in gone by days, your Excellency would never have been troubled with an appeal of this kind from your humble correspondent J. S. Oliver. Many and many a day have I followed the plow, and gladly would I now exchage the tedious seat of affliction for the Joyous and Merry labor of the farm. As stated in my letter of Novr 3d I had 27 negroes not one of them are with me all are gone. Not one have remained to bake the humble corn cake or to make me a fire in the cold bleak mornings of winter. In asking your Excellency to assist me I do not intend to sit down until all is exausted and apply again. If I had a little means Just at this time I could invest in a way that I could turn it to good account in the support of my family. It is true that my State has been in Rebellion against the laws and Constitution of the United States, but I never gave a vote in favor of the Rebellion in any way what ever, and have long since take the oath of alliegence to the United States.

That Your Excellency may more fully understand the extent of my afflictions I would state that I am and have been unable for the last five years to dress and undress myself. I have to be undressed every night and put to bed like a child, and dressed every morning in like manner. It is with the greatest difficulty that I can comb my head. I have not been able to get my hands to my feet in more than five years. I can not use a common chair but have to sit upon a high seat made for the purpose. Altho thus badly afflicted I do not suffer much pane from my Rheumatic afflictions. The Ulcer on my leg causes me a greateal of pane at times. My appetite and general health is good for a man laboring under so great afflictions. Tho not quite 46 years of age my head is nearly white. My cup of sorrow and afflictions have been filled to the brim having been called upon to stand by the death bed of a Father a Wife and Six Children all within a short span of time. I labored hard in early life and denied myself and family many of the comforts and necessaries of life that I might have something to live upon in old age, but now when my head is white with the frost of nearly fifty winters and the hand of affliction pressing heavily upon me, all for which I have labored during youth and manhood is sntched away from me as in a moment and I am left with out the means of procureing the humblest comforts and necessaries of life. Not withstanding all this if I had the ability to labor as in gone by days the authorities of my Country would never be troubled with an appeal for assistance from me. But dire necessity compels me to trouble your Excellency, and as much as I dislike to do to it I must again in conclusion appeal to you ask can you not out of the many thousands yea millions of money that passes through the hands of the Government spair something for an afflicted man with a destitute family whose afflictions and destitution has been brought upon them by circumstances beyond their control. Hoping that your Excellency will lend a helping hang in the hour of affliction detitution and distress I close by assurances of my Kindest and best wishes for the future hapiness and prosperity of yourself and family.

J. S. Oliver

P.S. Please excuse bad writing. My hands partake so largely of my affliction that I write bad. Please answer this at Auburn Macon County Ala as I shall move near that place in a few days.[7]

J. S. O.

ALS, DLC-JP.
1. Oliver (b. *c*1820) was a farmer whose combined estate before the war totaled $30,000. 1860 Census, Ala., Macon, Southern Div., 42.
2. Received on November 17, Oliver's letter had been forwarded to the secretary of war. Ser. 4A, Vol. 3: 263, Johnson Papers, LC.
3. There are too many Macon County Jones and Simmons families to determine the individuals Oliver refers to.
4. Possibly Arnoldus V. Brumby (*c*1812–1887), a West Point graduate who at midcentury was a school teacher in Macon County. Subsequently, he was superintendent of the Georgia Military Institute at Marietta (1851–59), a Confederate colonel, and an Atlanta resident. 1850 Census, Ala., Macon, 21st Dist., 530; *Register of Graduates and Former Cadets of the United States Military Academy: Cullum Memorial Edition* (West Point, 1970), 225; Sarah B.G. Temple, *The First Hundred Years: A Short History of Cobb County, Georgia* (Atlanta, 1935), 183.
5. The note from Montgomery C. Meigs has not been located.
6. Before the war six children were listed in Oliver's household: three boys ranging in age from three to eighteen, and three girls from ten to fourteen. 1860 Census, Ala., Macon, Southern Div., 42.
7. There is no record of a response by Johnson.

From William T. Sherman

Washington, Feb 2, 1866.

Sir.

I have the honor to acknowledge receipt last evening of your letter of Feb 1. and in compliance with your request, enclose herewith a Copy of Field Orders No 15,[1] of 1865 with this brief history of its origin and the reasons for making it.

The Hon E. M Stanton Sec of War came to Savannah[2] soon after its occupation by the Forces under my command, and conferred freely with me as to the best method to provide for the vast number of negros, who had followed the Army from the Interior of Georgia, an also of those who had already congregated on the Island near Hilton Head and were still coming into our Lines. We agreed perfectly that the young and able bodied men should be enlisted as soldiers, or employed by the Quarter Master in the necessary work of unloading ships and for other Army purposes. But this left on our hands the old & feeble, the women and children on our hands who had necessarily to be fed by the United States. Mr

Stanton summoned a large number of the old negros, mostly Preachers with whom he held a long Conference of which he took down notes. After this Conference he was satisfied the negros could with some little aid from us, by means of the abandoned Plantations on the Sea Islands, and along the navigable waters, take care of themselves. He requested me to draw up a plan that would be uniform and practicable. I made the rough draft, and we went over it very carefully, Mr Stanton making many changes, and the present orders No 15, resulted, and were made public.

I knew of course we could not convey title to land, and merely provided "possessory" titles, to be good so long as War, and our military power lasted. I merely aimed to make provision for the negros who were absolutely dependant on us, leaving the value of their possessions to be determined by after events or legislation.

At that time January 1865, it will be remembered that the tone of the people of the South was very defiant and no one could foretell when the period of War would Cease. Therefore I did not contemplate that event, as being so near at hand.

W. T. Sherman   Maj Genl.

ALS, DLC-JP.
1. In response to a visit by a delegation of South Carolina leaders on January 31, Johnson requested from Sherman a "brief and correct statement of the provisions and purposes of" Sherman's Field Orders No. 15, which set aside lands along the South Carolina and Georgia coast for former slaves, because "conflicting opinions [had] been expressed in reference to the intention and effect" of the order. William Henry Trescot to Johnson, Jan. 31, 1866 (two letters), Records of the Commr., Lets. Recd. from Executive Mansion, RG105, NA; Johnson to Sherman, Feb. 1, 1866, Johnson Papers, LC; Paul A. Cimbala, "The Freedmen's Bureau, the Freedmen, and Sherman's Grant in Reconstruction Georgia, 1865–1867," *JSH*, 55 (1989): 597–99; *OR*, Ser. 1, Vol. 47, Pt. 2: 60–62.
2. For an account of Stanton's visit, see Benjamin P. Thomas and Harold M. Hyman, *Stanton: The Life and Times of Lincoln's Secretary of War* (New York, 1962), 344–45.

From Robert J. Walker

Philadelphia   Febr 2, 1866—

Dear Sir

Permit me to call your attention to the case of C. C Clay Jr of Alabama, now languishing with broken health in prison. He heard, when his escape was certain, that he was charged with a horrible crime[1] and he travelled back several hundred miles, to surrender himself for trial. I have known Mr. Clay many years, and unhesitatingly pronounce him incapable of such a crime. There has arisen great public sympathy for him, and a general desire that, if not pardoned, he may be paroled. As his surrender *for trial* was voluntary, and accepted by the Government, is it just to confine him so long without a trial? Under the circumstances of his voluntary surrender for a trial, can there be any apprehension that he would break his parole to avoid a trial? Permit me to say, that, among the hundreds of loyal men, who have conversed with me on this subject, I have *never met one* who believed Mr. Clay guilty of any complicity in the murder of Mr. Lincoln.[2]

R. J. Walker

ALS, DLC-JP.
1. See Proclamation of Rewards for Arrest of Sundry Confederates, May 2, 1865, *Johnson Papers*, 8: 15–16.
2. Concerning parole for Clay, see, for example, Virginia C. Clay to Johnson, Jan. 14, 1866, ibid., 9: 600; Virginia C. Clay to Johnson, Mar. 12, 16, 1866.

From Benjamin Rush

Private.

Mt. Airy, Penna.   3d. Feby 1866.

Mr. President,

In the spirit of cordial approval of your policy, which first induced me to address you on the 5h. of June last,[1] may I, again as one of your constituents, take the liberty to add this to my letter of the 20h. of last month.[2]

Immediately on the passage by The House of the District of Columbia Suffrage Bill, since well described by you as "a mere entering wedge to the agitation of the question throughout the States," and as such, "ill timed, uncalled for, calculated to do great harm,"[3] I sought concert among my political friends, the War Democrats, in reference to a prompt expression of popular opinion.

One of them, a leader in the days of Jackson, clothed with his confidence in high office and an unwavering supporter of the War, and all War measures all through the Rebellion, thus writes to me:—

The acts of the Radicals in Congress are monstrous indeed, and no one abhors them more than I do. No one would go further to stop them, if that were possible, at this time.

But the conservative element in the Republican ranks must be permitted to do this. Then, as our Country is every thing, we can unite with them in the overthrow of the New England fanatics, (he might have added, "*and some most odious ones from this State*," the ringleader[4] of whom I have scorned for 30 years) the enemies of The Union and Constitution.

I think there must be a decided break between The President and the Radical Members before long. When this occurs, it will be the duty of every man, loving his country better than party, to uphold the principles and policy of The President, and sustain him in his efforts to restore the South and preserve The Union.

That the sentiments of my correspondent are sound to the core, and will be heartily responded to by every War Democrat, and every friend to his Country, I am of nothing more confident.

Equally so am I that the broad and statesmanlikeness of the Executive, recently made known in connection with a Senator,[5] will be enthusiastically sustained, when the time comes for The People to speak authoritatively at the Polls.

Perhaps, Mr. President, I ought to apologize for thus venturing to address you.

But the very long connection of my Father[6] with public affairs, at home and abroad, commencing in the days of Mr. Madison and Mr. Monroe, of both of whose Cabinets he was a member; my consequent familiarity with public subjects, through his daily conversations, from boyhood up; and my own subsequent connection with public life, and other public men, will, to some extent, I venture to hope, be accepted as an excuse by one whose lion-hearted devotion to the obligations of his great office, and to the prosperity and glory of his whole Country, I am very sure my Father, had he lived, would have been among the first to appreciate and applaud.

The annexed extract[7] from one of the newspapers of 1861, which recently came under my eye, recalls nothing which can be new to you Sir, but may be a little curious certainly just now to others, with which view I take the liberty to enclose it.

Benjamin Rush.

ALS, DLC-JP.
    1. His letter is found in Johnson Papers, LC.
    2. See *Johnson Papers*, 9: 626.
    3. See Interview with James Dixon, Jan. 28, 1866, ibid., 647–49.
    4. Probably a reference to Thaddeus Stevens.
    5. Undoubtedly another reference to Johnson's interview with James Dixon.
    6. Richard Rush (1780–1859) had served as Madison's attorney general, Monroe's secretary of state *ad interim* and minister to Great Britain, and John Quincy Adams's secretary of the treasury, before assuming diplomatic assignments during the Jackson and Polk administrations. *DAB*.
    7. Not found.

From Green Clay Smith

Executive Mansion.
Washington D.C.   Feb. 3d 1866

Mr. President—

A day or two ago I requested the nominations for Collectors & assessors in Ky. be suspended a few days.[1] My purpose was to ask the Collector in my District be changed. John S. Nixon[2] is the present incumbent. I desire his name to be stricken off, and James Hudnall[3] be appointed in his place. I make this application not only on my own account, but by the request of a large number of my constituents.[4] Mr. Nixon has never been in the service, and is well to do in the way of means while Mr. Hudnall is poor, and served four years in the army and was in fifty seven engagements, besides he is as well qualified as Mr. Nixon. I have conversed with the sety. of the Treasury, and he assured me he would offer no objection to this change.

I trust you will make this change and let the nominations go to the senate—as the Commissioner of Int. Rev.[5] is anxious to have these men at work.

Mine is the 6th Congressional Dst. and is by the proposed order[6] the 6" Rev. Dst.

James Hudnall should be appointed Collector for the 6th Dst. and I earnestly recommend it.[7]

G. Clay Smith

ALS, DNA-RG56, Appts., Internal Revenue Service, Collector, Ky., 6th Dist., James Hudnall.

1. See Smith to Johnson, Jan. 30, 1866, Appts., Internal Revenue Service, Collector, Ky., 6th Dist., James Hudnall, RG56, NA.

2. Nixon (c1824–1875), an Ohio-born lawyer, had been appointed as collector in 1863. 1870 Census, Ky., Kenton, Covington, 2nd Ward, 26; *Cincinnati Enquirer*, Mar. 29, 1875; *U.S. Off. Reg.* (1863–73).

3. Hudnall (c1822–fl1868) had formerly served as a county judge, before enlisting in the 4th Ky. Inf., USA, from which he was mustered out as a captain in October 1864. 1860 Census, Ky., Pendleton, Falmouth, 1; *Off. Army Reg.: Vols.*, 4: 1248; J. W. Campbell et al. to Johnson, [Mar. 1866], Appts., Internal Revenue Service, Collector, Ky., 6th Dist., James Hudnall, RG56, NA.

4. There are at least seven other petitions in favor of Hudnall's appointment within his file. See ibid.

5. Edward A. Rollins.

6. For a copy of the order as signed by Johnson on January 25, 1866, increasing the number of internal revenue districts in Kentucky from four to nine, see Executive Orders (1862–85), RG58, NA.

7. Hudnall was nominated by Johnson on February 6 and confirmed by the Senate less than two weeks later. He was, however, later removed for malfeasance and replaced in April 1868 by Dr. William M. Murphy, who served through the end of Johnson's term. Ser. 6B, Vol. 4: 241–42, Johnson Papers, LC; Murphy to Johnson, Mar. 1868, Appts., Internal Revenue Service, Collector, Ky., 6th Dist., William M. Murphy, RG56, NA; *U.S. Off. Reg.* (1867).

From William H. Tenney[1]

Washington, D.C., Feb. 3, 1866

Sir

You may remember me as calling on you in Jany. 1861 with a friend and getting from you a kind promise to address a Union meeting in Georgetown and also on a subsequent occasion a similar promise both of which for very cogent reasons you were unable to comply with.[2] I had a further interview with you as one of a Committee last Spring in reference to returned District Rebels, after having made a speech[3] at a public meeting in Washington against them which interview possibly you may also remember. I also wrote you[4] requesting a pardon for a Union Soldier in Fort Delaware and had the pleasure of receiving the thanks of that Soldier for his release, and the greater pleasure of knowing that our President amidst his great cares and responsibilities will attend to the petition of the humblest citizen. I refer to these matters to show my uniform loyalty as I see in the Intelligencer this morning a rumor that Chas. S. English[5] has been appointed a Commissioner of Police for Georgetown in place of myself whose Commission has expired. As it has been usual to renew the Commission of a Public Officer except for cause, I presume my actions must have been misrepresented to your Excellency. If it is necessary I could send you the *unaminous* testimony of the *unconditional* union citizens of Georgetown endorsing my loyalty, and the endorsement of the whole Board of Police of my course as Commissioner with perhaps the exception of Mayor Wallach.[6] I noticed an editorial in the Star[7] charging the Board's proceedings with being secret whereas any one present is at liberty to name and publish every thing that takes place, as has been the uniform custom of the Board from its organization in 1861.

Another charge is dictation by the "Bowen clique"[8] a slur against gentlemen who think and act each for himself, in a bill prepared for Congress and recommended by the Secretary of the Interior increasing the force 73 men, and proposing to increase the pay of the Commissioners from $250 to $400 per year by the United States. As the bill greatly increases their labors this increase of pay was put in the bill for Congress to determine. The only dictation in the bill (if a Police regulation is dictation) is a provision that all licenses to sell liquor by the Glass shall be approved by the Board of Police, the object of which is to restrain little low drinking places where no eatables are sold.[9] The bill met the unaminous approval of the Board excepting Mayors Wallach and Addison voting against the supervision of licenses. Mayor Wallach & Dr Nicholls[10] wishing the salaries of the Commissioners left for Congress to fill, and Mayor Wallach voting against retaining $2000 as contingent fund out of liquor fines annually.

I would esteem it a great favor to have a personal interview with you before any further action is taken, and if I cannot satisfy you that I have done my duty as Commissioner & Treasurer which office I hold. The laws requiring one of the Commissioners to be Treasurer, and that my views of public policy correspond with your own I will be satisfied to retire.

Do me the favor to read my brief speech enclosed endorsing your policy made last September and oblige.[11]

W. H. Tenney

LS, DNA-RG48, Appts. Div., Misc. Lets. Recd.
    1. Tenney (1815–1888), a grocer, had served as one of five original D.C. police commissioners appointed under an act that Congress passed in 1861. He later operated a grist mill with his sons. *NUC*; Washington, D.C., directories (1866–88); *U.S. Off. Reg.* (1861–65).
    2. See Tenney to Johnson, Feb. 15, 19, 1862, Johnson Papers, LC.
    3. Tenney had called for the disfranchisement and banishment of all District citizens who had participated in the rebellion. *Washington Morning Chronicle*, May 10, 1865.
    4. Not found.
    5. English (c1826–c1900), a hardware merchant, was later collector of customs at Georgetown under Presidents Grant and Hayes. Johnson had nominated him on January 29, in place of Tenney. English was confirmed by the Senate and received his commission in

March. 1860 Census, D.C., Georgetown, 3rd Ward, 109; Washington, D.C., directories (1866–1901); *U.S. Off. Reg.* (1871–78); Ser. 6B, Vol. 4: 114, Johnson Papers, LC; *National Intelligencer*, Feb. 3, Mar. 29, 1866.

    6. Richard Wallach (1816–1881), an Alexandria, Virginia, native and a former Whig, served as mayor of Washington from 1861 until 1866, when he returned to his law practice. Allen C. Clark, "Richard Wallach and the Times of His Mayoralty," *Records CHS*, 21 (1918): 195–244 passim.

    7. See *Washington Evening Star*, Jan. 31, 1866.

    8. Associates of Sayles J. Bowen.

    9. For the final version of the Metropolitan Police bill, which retained the liquor by the glass regulation but did not raise commissioners' salaries when passed by Congress and approved by Johnson in July 1866, see *U.S. Statutes at Large*, 14: 212–14.

    10. Charles H. Nichols (1820–1889), who had also served with Tenney on the board of police commissioners, was reappointed to a second term by Johnson in March 1866. Formerly affiliated with two mental institutions in New York, Nichols currently superintended the Government Hospital for the Insane (later St. Elizabeth's Hospital). *DAB; U.S. Off. Reg.* (1865).

    11. Tenney enclosed a clipping from the *Washington Morning Chronicle*, September 24, 1865, which reported a speech he had made to a group of New York army band members who had paid a visit to his home. There is no record of a response by Johnson.

From John Cochrane

Washington, February 4, 1866

My Dear Mr President

    I came here with the purpose of repeating to you, the views entertained by Mr Bennett, and which by his written request I was desired to confide to your ear. This charge was the more cheerfully assumed, under the increasing personal conviction, that the multifarious perplexities with which your nominal friends were conspiring to embarrass you, required corresponding efforts by real friends to assist you with advice; and the tender not only of personal sympathy, but of political cooperation. A spectator, however, of the throng of anxious friends, counsellors, and office expectants which densely beleagured your doors yesterday, I began to question the significance of my store of Knowledge, and the propriety of my encumbering your patience with the length of my communication. I accordingly refrained from my quest of an interview, and now with the permission of your friend Edward Cooper,[1] hope to discharge loyally my allegiance to your fortune by submitting, through his corteous and kind intervention a few considerations, in a form least offensive to your time and thought.

    I need not repeat what is so obviously, the direction which current events are giving to those of the masses who are affected to your policy, and who are to be found indiscriminately within the limits of the nominally adverse parties. They are restlessly expectant of the period when an overt act by you, in resistance of systematic congressional encroachment, shall enable them to muster into your service, for the defence of sound constitutional doctrines. It may not be disguised that the large majority of these men are members at present of the titular democratic party. I refer to the rank & file; exclusively of their former leaders, whose personal taint of Copperheadism, infects them with oblivion in the future. Unquestionably, large numbers of those who have guided their action within the bounds of the Union party, stand in similar suspense of expectation. These, very generally, however, are those who advanced to their position, from former democratic antecedents. Combined the two would form a body which to-day, organized, under discipline, into party efficiency, would disclose a popular voting preponderance of fifty thousand in the State of New York, and I think, proportionably a numerical total, in the central & north western States. The strength, success and *recurrence* of your Administration, Mr President, I am sure, is to depend upon this body of men. Their adversaries will be—they are now—your political opponents. The logical sequence of the combination which organizes these disjointed forces is, by necessity, the reproduction of your power in 1868. The political salvation of their opponents, consists alone with the termination of your carreer, at the period presented by the accident which promoted you.

And now, upon this assumption rendered impregnable, I think, by events already passed into record, let me, Mr President, advert to the critical posture your interests have received from the implacable pressure upon you, of the mercenary and insidious hordes of office seekers, from New York, and their howling retinue of *claquers* menials and lackeys. It must be apparent that to embark upon appointments before a political issue with your *nominal* friends, shall have enabled you to divulge them to the country, as your *real* enemies, would be, to permit to appointments the office restricted to principles alone—viz—the formation of party. The suggestion is demonstrative of folly. The government, whose measures, consist in its appointments, is wedded to defeat. But if it be planted upon its avowed championship of Constitutional right, the antagonism of its opponents, will shiver, as the conflict which political enmity, directs against government, under the pretext of injudicious or the proper nominations. Their appointments are as they should be secondary, and subordinate, not primary, & paramount.

Should you, however, Mr President, from whatever reason thought by you sufficient, decide to nominate a Collector for New York, previously to the segregation of your friends, under the effect of an issue declared, from the nebulous condition of present politics, into a compacted party, please to observe the very unequal game of chance with your enemies, which the decision will have imposed upon you. Should the appointee, disappoint you hereafter, with sympathies secret or avowed, with those in the mean time passed, under the order of events, into the denomination of your political enemies, your suffering will be the estimate of their gain. But, should a fortunate felicity, in this respect, approve the wisdom of your choice, still, you will be unable to retrieve, the loss of political strength, by the infusion, through the appointment of a supposed political enemy, of a suspicion, (in politics always armed with the efficacy of a certainty) into the myriads of democrats struggling to support you, that you are carless, if not indifferent to their freindship. No, Mr President I regard this convention of influence which the daily rails wheel to your doors, as "a convocation of politic worms" assembled, as at the body of the dead Polonius, where they are not eaten—*but to eat.* You are to be pressed for a nomination in a game where, evidently, they have all to gain, and you every thing to lose. Their famine is to be filled, and you are to furnish the pasture.

If, however, a political necessity conducts to this catastrophe, clearly, submission becomes a duty. Is there such a necessity?

It is vehemently urged that the government, by your delay, is deprived of the security which a Collectors official bond provides. Now, the sureties of the bond are responsible for the default, only, of the Collector, Defalcation from account stated, and their instruments peculation & fraud, alone, are retrieved by the legal assurance of the bond. In other phrase, a collector's bond assures the honesty of a collector's account—no more. These accounts are habitually, and by legal direction returned & settled at exceedingly short intervals of time. These intervals may be, under official direction, further abbreviated, and all responsibility be reduced to zero, by the material impossibility of perpetrating peculation within twenty four hours time. Daily accounting is a permanent security. In every other particular, even the universal tongue of the dissonant clamours of New York City, asserts that the Custom House in New York is more securely conducted now, by Mr Clinch,[2] than it can be by any possible appointee. I, who am intimate with Custom House routine, and the solid understanding, and imperturbable integrity of Mr Clinch know, and aver the fact. Still, if, Mr President, you perceive that the sanctions of public duty impose the nomination upon you *now*, I would be very far from opposing your conscientious conclusions. As duty is of first magnitude, and of unimpeachable solemnity, he would not truly advise, who could recommend a departure from it, at any point, even of triviality.

But, do not, neither, Mr President mistake the impetuous vociferations of New York delegations, for the deliberate expression of public opinion. A wonderfully capricious, superficial and fluctuating population is that of the Metropolis. Never satisfied, unless the country is sunk to Pluto, or raised ineffably, once every Sun, they uniformly send it to hell at the breakfast table, if their muffins are heavy, and place it in heaven, if the Play is good. And as strange are the vagaries into which its various classes gambol. The lawyer, who has exhausted his energies with hopeless gropings among black letter volumes, suddenly, on occasion, is galvanised with the spirit of public affairs and rushes to Washington, to inform the President of a patent country-saving-machine. The Divine, who for years has been intent upon the Spirit of his people and their souls often takes the rail for the capital where to take in hand the Spirit of the constitution & the soul of the Country, and the Merchant, whose whole intellect gravitates to the balance on his Ledger, always loses his balance, when he seeks the Presidential prasence to enlighten the Chief Executive; evoke his views upon the State of the Country.

The truth is, Mr President New York City has no public opinion. She is a very great Goose that, clothed with her annual coat of feathers, is periodically ravished from her autumnal feeding, and subjected to the furious plucking of the *ring politicians*. A terrible kicking and gabbling occur during the process. Reformers look solemn, and citizens associations cackle. But, soon, the goose is stripped, the pockets of the politicians are filled—the animal is released, and she walks away quietly to her feeding ground, to grow another anual crop of feathers, again to be plucked, again to gabble, but again to be discharged, through every revolving year.

These graceless pluckers are the politicians of New York City. Their visual horizon is limited by the Bells of Mortality, and their object of life is the filling of their pockets. Municipal plunder attracts them, not national politics. Once glutted, and they are torpid, they exhibit gymnastic feats at the City elections in *December*; but, when, in *November* the ballot box speaks with a national tongue, and articulates the political opinions of New York State, these men are quiescent. Then prevail the national politicians, and the work is done which secures to New York her influence in the politics of the nation, & establishes the character of her political power. Consult Mr President the *November* men of New York, and disregard the *December* men, and you will not be misled. These men of *November*, represent public opinion—the *December* men represent feathers. Such are the men, these honest, earnest, sincere men, who, in their study of the interests of their Country see her noblest future in the success of your policy. They desire to support its representative, and to perpetuate his administration. I think that you will not err if you propitiate their freindship, and secure their support. Without these, I see nothing for you, but subordination to the wishes of men, who bode you no good, & restraint within the limits of their policy, only to be ultimately discarded by them for the leader, whose nod they, even now, recognize, whose voice they obey, and whose burden they are stooping to bear.

And now, Mr President, permit one word as to myself. Do not believe me a candidate trained to solicitation for office. You should appoint no candidate simply for the length of his subscription scroll, or the grave character of those whose axes seek their sharpest edge, upon your grind stone. Appoint the fittest and most capable person, who is *your friend*. Grind your *own axe* upon *your own* grind stone. Make that Mr President a part of your policy. Your friends will approve it, and even your enemies cannot condemn it. Appoint no one because he is a candidate. I hold the written recommendations of men of great consideration. But, I refrain from presenting them—for, in my honest judgment, he is no friend of yours who, at this complicated juncture, could embarrass your action by personal application. Your *own* well informed judgment, is your truest guide.

John Cochrane

ALS, DLC-JP.
1. Probably Edmund Cooper, who soon functioned officially as acting private secretary to Johnson.
2. Charles P. Clinch, assistant collector.

From Joshua Hill

Confidential.

Madison, Ga.   Feby' 5, 1866.

Sir.

I may err in supposing that it is my duty to inform you of the condition of affairs in Georgia. Provl. Govr. Johnson, requested me to write you, as he himself designed doing. He and I might be presumed to be in a bad frame of mind, for imparting impartial information on political affairs at home. I *think*, I can speak for him—I know, I can for myself—and declare of a truth that in our defeat for the Senate[1]—we were not disappointed in the result. While affairs remained in a situation for the officials of government, and such as were supposed to have the confidence of the government, to be used for private advantage—he and I were sought after—and seemingly respected for our influence, and the liberality with which it was employed for the benefit of others. But as soon as the Provl. Govr.' functions terminated, his power and influence perished—and there were "none so poor as to do him reverence."[2] The inauguration of Govr. Jenkins—and the regular & usual operations of the State Legislature—were at work—men began to forget past kindnesses, and to revive old prejudices.

I never knew a man in any station more kind than James Johnson was in his—and less disposed to discriminate against former adversaries. His uniform courtesy & kindness failed to excite a sentiment of gratitude—despite, his conceded abilities—which all admit to be of a high order—and alike regardless, of his acknowledged personal worth and private virtues.

Of myself, I can say nothing—other than that I was recognized by all, as the friend of the government—"loving it not wisely, but too well"[3]—and as such much appealed to without fee, to aid the unfortunate of all classes. The opportunity offered, for a manifestation of thanks & regard, or of contempt—and the last, or an indifference approximating to it is promptly shown. After the Senatorial election, members came to me to explain—saying they were compelled there to vote in diference to the will of their constituents. *I believe them.* The war feeling is so strong—especially since the interference of the Freedmans Bureau, with cheap contracts with negroes—that few men dare disregard it—and especially, to the extent of voting for a man opposed to it—and who boasts of having refused to vote during the rebellion—for any of its officers—or to attend a meeting for any purpose, during the struggle. The disgust of the friends of the government—upon my report, drove some of them from the Chamber—others refused to vote at all afterwards—which made Provl. Govr. Johnsons vote even less than mine.

You may rely upon it, the true and full strength of the serious Union men, was polled for me, and a little more besides.

It is well known that Jenkins Stephens & H. V. Johnson, all defend the *right* of secession—and *repudiate* repudiation of the State war debts. I know that I do not mistake.

I am without political ambition—but am free to say—I should be glad to prove to this people, that I am regarded by those in authority at Washington—with respect and favor. It does not become me to indicate in what manner this "should be done.["] The war has greatly reduced me in fortune—and there are few offices that yield money. I must make some, and will if I live.[4]

Provl. Govr. Johnson, is a true man and more needy than I am. I wish your Excellency would bear him in mind—and aid him if opportunity offers.[5] He and I design visiting Washington in a month or so—not in search of office, but to confer with your Excellency on the actual state of the Country.[6] We both feel that we are in the condition of the prophet— "who hath honor, save in his own Country." We may not hope ever again to be regarded cordially by the people of Georgia. *It cannot be.* We have much to say, much that might interest your Excellency—*provided*, we are assured of a wish on your part, to hear it.

In all I have written, I beg to assure you, that I am not influenced by the wish to occupy official station in Georgia—either by election or appointment. Nor have I the slightest desire to interpose an objection to any plan your Excellency may have conceived for the restoration of the State—in all respects. After all I have done and said to their representatives at Milledgeville—no matter how caustic or defiant it may appear I would assist this embittered and unhappy people, to escape from their troubles and annoyances, by any proper and safe means, except accepting office from them, or their Governor.

Your Excellency will pardon the freedom of this communication—and if you should desire any further information—signify it by acknowledging the receipt of this.

Joshua Hill.

P.S. I do not mean to be understood, that I am anxious, because others may wish it—to dispence with the prudential action of government, for the safety of the people, and the preservation of public order. To be very candid, I think Georgia is much as Tennessee, & that Genl. Thomas is right as to Tennessee.

ALS, DLC-JP.

1. On January 30, 1866, the Georgia legislature had elected Alexander H. Stephens and Herschel V. Johnson to the U.S. Senate, over Hill, Lucius J. Gartrell, Cincinnatus Peeples, and James Johnson. Isaac W. Avery, *The History of the State of Georgia From 1850 to 1881* (New York, 1881), 356. See also Stephens to Johnson, Jan. 31, 1866, *Johnson Papers*, 9: 656.

2. From Shakespeare's *Julius Caesar*, act 3, sc. 2, line 124.

3. Adapted from Shakespeare's *Othello*, act 5, sc. 2, line 338.

4. On April 4 Johnson nominated Hill to replace Wylly Woodbridge as collector of customs at Savannah and the Senate confirmed Hill's appointment in June. McCulloch to Woodbridge, Apr. 4, 1866; McCulloch to Johnson, Apr. 4, 1866, Lets. Sent *re* Customs Service Employees (QC Ser.), Vol. 3, RG56, NA; *Senate Ex. Proceedings*, Vol. 14, pt. 2: 713, 849. See also Hill to Johnson, Mar. 19, 1866.

5. Nominated initially in June 1866 as minister to Colombia, James Johnson instead accepted in August the Savannah customs post which Hill apparently had declined. The Senate confirmed Johnson's nomination in place of Hill in February 1867. *Senate Ex. Proceedings*, Vol. 14, pt. 2: 869; Vol. 15, pt. 1: 246; Ser. 6B, Vol. 3: 305, Johnson Papers, LC.

6. Sometime around March 1, James Johnson did visit Washington and had an interview with the President regarding the removal of black troops from Georgia. Hill apparently did not accompany Johnson to the capital at this time. *National Intelligencer*, Mar. 17, 1866. See Charles J. Jenkins to Johnson, Feb. 15, 1866; and Osborne A. Lochrane to Johnson, Mar. 26, 1866.

From James B. Lamb

Nashville, Feby 5, 1866.

My dear Sir:

I had hoped to see you 'ere this but circumstances have prevented.

You know the condition of affairs in our State. I have been here for several days trying to harmonize or conciliate parties. Have had two interviews with Govr Brownlow. He *talks* right. The franchise bill[1]—the great cause of trouble—I propose the modification of to all who have or may receive your pardon, upon the condition that prominent—leading *rebels* (*that were*) honestlly,—bonafide—pledge their support to the administration of *State* & federal Govent. I have hope that an accommodation of this sort can be effected. Can you—will you not help in the work? And let us once more have peace & quiet in our good old State?

I know you have not time to read long letters from *me*; will only add *don't* believe all reports of things in Tennessee or elsewhere made by Freedmen Bureau men or roving officers. The people of the *whole* south are *with* you and *for* you—love & admire you more than ever before. All that men *can* do they will do for you.

Oh, for one hour's *private* talk with you of men & things with us.

J. B. Lamb

ALS, DLC-JP.

1. Lamb, a prominent Fayetteville lawyer, refers here to the very restrictive franchise law enacted by the Brownlow-dominated legislature in the late spring of 1865. Controversial from the outset, it became even more so after the August congressional elections. By January 1866 voices were being raised in behalf of a revision of the franchise law, some, like Lamb, wanting a lessening of restrictions and some, like Brownlow, desiring additional

ones. Patton, *Unionism and Reconstruction*, 108, 111, 114–17. See Samuel P. Walker to
Johnson, Feb. 18, 1866.

From New Mexico Citizens

Metropolitan Hotel   Washington D.C.
February 5th 1866

We the undersigned citizens of New Mexico have learned that Filipe
Delgado[1] the present superintendant of Indian Affairs for New Mexico is
to be removed from office.

We doubt the propriety of such removal.

We have a population in New Mexico of some ninety thousand souls
more than nine tenths of whome are Mexicans and it would seem to be
improper to exclude them entirely from any participation in the federal
appointments for that Territory. It is true that but few of them speak the
English language but this is no fault of theirs. They were forced into
our government by the fortunes of war but they are now citizens of the
United States and during the late rebellion none were more loyal or willing to take up arms in defence of the government and if they are to be
proscribed in this way it will be a poor reccompence for their fidelity and
loyalty. If however it is determined that no Mexican shall fill the office of
superintendant of Indian Affairs we american residents there who know
the Indians and who are in every way qualified to discharge all the duties
of the office in a manner more satisfactory than any stranger who is ignorant of the spanish language through which all the business with the Indians has to be done. They are good men, honest and true to the government and we respectfully submit that if a change is to be made a citizen of
New Mexico should be appointed.

We were willing on account of unfortunate difficulties which exist in
our Territory[2] that the principal officers should be sent from the States;
this has been done in the appointment of a Governor Secretary Chief Justice Marshal and one Indian agent.[3] These officers will all be strangers to
our people and we think you will agree with us that it has gone quite far
enough in that direction and that if any more changes are to be made the
appointees should be taken from our own citizens. It has been universally
the policy of the government heretofore to make appointments, as far as
possible from the residents of the Territories except at the time of the
organization of such Territories. New Mexico was organized in 1850;
Sixteen years ago; during that period many enterprising, and worthy
american citizens have encountered the hardships and perils incident to
emigration to that far off reagon and have taken their all with them and it
is certainly fair and right that they should have, all else being equal, a
share of the public patronage. These men live there, have their families
there and when the Territory was invaded by bands of rebels from Texas
boldly and willingly took up arms in defence of the flag and of their

homes and after many hard fought battles drove the invaders back[4] and it is not just that they should be overlooked in making these appointments.

In conclusion allow us to say that Mr. Delgado is an honest man who will never wrong the Government out of a single dollar and although he does not speak the English language we feel sure his administration of the superintendency will in the end be satisfactory to you.

The citizens of New Mexico now in this city would like to have an interview with you before any further action is taken in the case.[5]

J. L. Collins
John S. Watts
H. B. Denman
W. W. Mills   El Paso Texas[6]

ALS (Watts), DNA-RG75, Gen. Records, Lets. Recd. (M234, Roll 553).

1. Delgado (c1828–fl1882), a Democrat and a Santa Fe merchant, who served variously as a territorial legislator, treasurer, and probate judge, had been superintendent of Indian affairs since early 1865. 1860 Census, N.M., Santa Fe, Santa Fe, 559; Lawrence R. Murphy, *Frontier Crusader—William F.M. Arny* (Tucson, 1972), 130; Thompson, *Navajo* 83–84; Hubert H. Bancroft, *History of Arizona and New Mexico, 1520–1888* (San Francisco, 1889), 636, 704, 706, 708; *U.S. Off. Reg.* (1865); *A Complete Business Directory of New Mexico and Gazeteer of the Territory for 1882* (Santa Fe, 1882), 125; *Senate Ex. Proceedings*, Vol. 14, pt. 1: 191.

2. Probably a reference to the bitter feuds between territorial Republicans and Democrats which had erupted over the Indian policies of Gen. James H. Carleton. Lawrence R. Murphy, "William F.M. Arny: Secretary of the New Mexico Territory, 1862–1867," *Arizona and the West*, 8 (1966): 330; Howard R. Lamar, *The Far Southwest, 1846–1912: A Territorial History* (New Haven, 1966), 125–31. See also Joseph A. LaRue to Johnson, Apr. 9, 1866.

3. There had been a wholesale turnover of New Mexico territorial officials in the past few months, though probably none of the new appointees officially assumed their duties before the summer. Henry Connelly, formerly territorial governor, had been replaced by Gen. Robert B. Mitchell of Kansas. William F.M. Arny, territorial secretary since 1862, was supposed to be replaced by George P. Este of Ohio, who, although nominated and confirmed by January 1866, never took office, thereby leaving Arny in the post until 1867. John P. Slough of the District of Columbia had been appointed as chief justice in place of Kirby Benedict. And Capt. John Pratt, a former aide to General Mitchell, succeeded Abraham Cutler as U.S. marshal. Apparently, there had been no change in the territorial Indian agency as of yet. Ser. 6B, Vol. 4: 370, Johnson Papers, LC; Murphy, "William F.M. Arny," 323, 337; S. J. Crawford to Johnson, May 11, 1865, ACP Branch, File P-932-CB-1865, John Pratt, RG94, NA; *Senate Ex. Proceedings*, Vol. 14, pt. 1: 315. See also David Davis to Johnson, Jan. 10, 1866, *Johnson Papers*, 9: 586–87.

4. For an introduction to these military engagements which occurred from February to April 1862, see Martin H. Hall, *Sibley's New Mexico Campaign* (Austin, 1960). See also Reuben F. Bernard to Johnson, Mar. 20, 1862, *Johnson Papers*, 5: 216–17.

5. A New Mexico delegation is reported to have met with the President sometime on February 7. Whether that group and the signatories for this document are the same is unknown. Nevertheless, on February 6, Johnson nominated A. Baldwin Norton, brother of Sen. Daniel S. Norton of Minnesota, to replace Delgado. The Senate confirmed Norton's appointment on February 15, yet Delgado remained in office for several more months. *Washington Evening Star*, Feb. 7, 1866; *Senate Ex. Proceedings*, Vol. 14, pt. 1: 511; pt. 2: 561; Felipe Delgado to Johnson, May 20, 1866, Gen. Records, Lets. Recd. (M234, Roll 553), RG75, NA.

6. A former superintendent of Indian affairs for New Mexico, James L. Collins (1800–1869) had also published the Democratic *Santa Fe Gazette* intermittently since 1846. In April Johnson nominated him to be receiver of the land office and collector of public monies

for the territory, which position he held until he was murdered by robbers. Watts (1816–1876) was an Indiana lawyer before his appointment as associate justice for the territory (1851–54) and his election as a Republican delegate to Congress (1861–63). In March 1868 Johnson nominated him as chief justice. Hampton B. Denman (c1832–fl1870), a former mayor of Leavenworth, Kansas, was a merchant and a beef cattle contractor for the Indians at the Bosque Redondo reservation at Fort Sumner. He later became Indian superintendent at Omaha, Nebraska, dismissing Radical Republican officeholders in positions under him, and in January 1869 Johnson nominated him as government surveyor for New Mexico Territory. Collector of customs for New Mexico, William W. Mills (1836–1913) was reappointed by Johnson in March 1866. A moderate Republican, he married A. J. Hamilton's daughter in 1869. Omaha directories (1868–70); Aurora Hunt, *Kirby Benedict: Frontier Federal Judge* (Glendale, 1961), 149n; Murphy, "William F.M. Arny," 328–29; *BDAC*; 1860 Census, Kans., Leavenworth, Leavenworth, 4th Ward, 180; Jesse A. Hall and Leroy T. Hand, *History of Leavenworth County, Kansas* (Topeka, 1921), 201; Thompson, *Navajo*, 40, 42, passim; Eugene H. Berwanger, *The West and Reconstruction* (Urbana, 1981), 99; W. W. Mills, *Forty Years at El Paso, 1858–1898*, ed. by Rex W. Strickland (El Paso, 1962), xi–xix; Ser. 6B, Vol. 4: 370–71, Johnson Papers, LC. Johnson ordered the petition referred to Secretary Harlan.

From William L. Sharkey

Washington   February 5th 1866

Sir

Some reflection on the subject of the conversation we had the honor to hold with you yesterday[1] has induced me to venture so far as to submit a few suggestions in regard to the proper time for the appearance of your proclamation. I think you will find a law of 1795 and a supplemental one of 1807 or 8, by which the President is invested with the power to declare when a rebellion commences and when it ends. The laws are not before me and I cannot state their provisions accurately. They may have escaped your notice, and hence I venture to address you. If these provisions are such as I think they are, then the matter would stand thus: It is the province of the President, probably it is his duty, to declare when rebellion exists and when it ends, and this being so, probably the question has been withdrawn from Congress. Then bearing in mind the law of 1862 or 3[2] which declares the purpose for which the war was prosecuted, and it would seem, with great deference, to devolve on you the duty of making the announcement which you have in contemplation in advance of any action of congress. And when Mr Raymonds proposition comes up,[3] Congress may say, "The President has not informed us whether the rebellion has been ended or not." And moreover by taking the initiative you make no issue with any party, but simply discharge a duty required by law. If Congress should not sustain you, it is that body that makes the issue with you, not you with them. Suppose however I should be mistaken in the purport of the laws of 1795 and 1807, still very much the same result will follow from your action on the law of 1862, or resolution as it may be, as remarked to you yesterday. The old laws only make the duty more manifest.

But there are other considerations, I think, that may be looked to. The Country is looking for some distinct declaration of the kind from you, and it will be hailed with general joy.[4] Why let Mr Raymond reap the benefits? I will only add that I fear you may embarrass yourself by allowing Congress to move in advance of you.

I write hastily and but in brief suggestions. I trust that my good intentions may serve as an apology for the liberty I have taken.

W. L. Sharkey

ALS, DLC-JP.
    1. Evidence of a February meeting between Johnson, Sharkey, and others has not been located.
    2. This is perhaps a reference to the July 1862 law, "an act to suppress Insurrection to punish Treason and Rebellion, to seize and confiscate the Property of Rebels, and for other Purposes." *U.S. Statutes at Large*, 12: 589–92.
    3. Sharkey may be referring to New York Rep. Henry J. Raymond's resolution of January 12, 1866, in which the representative requested the President to send to the House all documents pertinent to the former Confederate states and their governmental operations. *Congressional Globe*, 39 Cong., 1 Sess., p. 214.
    4. Approximately two months later, Johnson issued a proclamation which announced the end of the war in all states, except Texas. See Proclamation *re* End of Insurrection, Apr. 2, 1866.

From George W. White

New Orleans La   Feby 5th 1866.

Dear Sir.

I have been in the city for several days. During this time I have had the pleasure of meeting many citizens of Texas. They report every thing quiet, & that the whole people, except a few Radicals, heartily endorse your policy. From what they tell me, I am sure that all will go well in the Texas convention.[1]

On my arrival I learned the gratifying intelligence that Gov. Pease & Judge Bell[2] were both defeated for the convention. The former was beaten by Judge Hancock[3] nearly *three to one*. Hancock is the ablest & one of the most consistent union men in the state—*always loyal* & for two years a refugee at New Orleans. Notwithstanding this, I saw a Washington despatch lately to the Herald calling him an *ex-rebel*. *Never* was he a rebel. He ran for the convention on your platform & endorsed you fully. The result shows the strength of *radicalism* at Austin.

I hope that you are steadily gaining strength in congress, & that in a short time you will be able to administer the Government in such manner as you may deem best for the interest of the people.

I shall return to Winchester in a few days.

Geo. W. White

P. S. Maj. Maclin[4] left here yesterday for Texas.

ALS, DLC-JP.
    1. The constitutional convention lasted from February 7 to April 2. Ramsdell, *Reconstruction in Texas*, 85, 106.

2. Elisha M. Pease and James H. Bell.

3. A moderate during the 1866 convention, John Hancock (1824–1893) was an Austin attorney, planter, and district judge (1851–55) who had lost his legislative seat in 1860 because he refused to take the Confederate oath of allegiance. He was later elected as a Democrat to Congress (1871–77, 1883–85). *BDAC*; Waller, *Hamilton of Texas*, 86.

4. Sackfield Maclin (*c*1812–*fl*1881) served as paymaster in the U.S. Army until his resignation in San Antonio, Texas, with the rank of major, in February 1861. Afterwards, commissioners and troops from the now seceded state of Texas seized $30,000 in U.S. funds that Maclin held. Maclin served as a staff officer in the Confederate Ordnance Bureau and Commissary Department during the war. Gen. Philip H. Sheridan ordered Maclin arrested in November 1865 and confined at Fort Jackson near New Orleans, apparently for alleged collusion with the Rebels. Although Maclin was released on parole after a visit to Washington, no special pardon appears to have been issued. *BDTA*, 1: 490; Powell, *Army List*, 447; *New Orleans Picayune*, Dec. 9, 1865; Amnesty Papers (M1003, Roll 28), La., Sackfield Maclin, RG94, NA; Mrs. A. J. Maclin to Johnson, Aug. 13, 1865; Parole of Sackfield Maclin, Dec. 21, 1865, Johnson Papers, LC. See also Sackfield Maclin to Johnson, Mar. 6, 1866.

From John W. Gorham

Clarksville Tenn   Feby 6th 1866

Dr. Sir

You remember in our last conversation[1] I stated that the People of this Country would sustain your administration with as much earnestness as they did that of Genl. Jackson. I felt when I made the statement that it was correct. Since I returned Home I have travelled over the Country a great deal, and find that I was not mistaken. The People are for Andrew Johnson and his reconstruction placy and I will state further that some of the most earnest supporters you have now has been the most violent Rebbals in the Country. They say publicly that you have shown yourself to be above Party Prejudice and Petty tyrany, and therefore they do desire to sustain you and will do so in every way they can. We had a county meeting to day in this City[2] to appoint delegates to a Convention which is to assemble at Nashville on the 22nd. Inst[3] and thear was but One Sentament among the People and was to Sustain President Johnson and his polacy. Speeches were maid by Col. J. E Bailey *old* Howket Allen, Mr. Hornburger[4] and others. They said in Old Political times that they differed with you and even believed you to be *Demegog* &c. &c. but that they took back every word they had ever uttered against you, and pleasantly remarked Gorham you knew him better than we did &c &c. I mention the facts that you may know that the People are in earnest in Sustaining you. The meeting adjourned untill next Munday, when Resolutions will be addopted &c. &c. which I will send you.[5] Now Sir this is all done in the absence of the Millitary for thank God and President Johnson we have been relieved of Millitary rule. There is no Soldiers of any kind at this place and none needed. The Negro Soldiers are being discharged and returning among us and I am glad to say they are behaving well so far as I know or have hird. I shall *leave* this Place soon and whare I shall stop I cant say for I dont Know. I am broken up, have lost every thing I had. Its all ben Burnt, Stolen, destroyed, and I am left a wanderer without a

Home, but I hope something may turn up for me in the future, but this is a melencolly Subject and I will cloase it. My Kindest regards to your Son Robert and Boys about the White House. I thank you Kindly for the many favours you have done for my friends in Pardning &c. &c.

Jno W Gorham

ALS, DLC-JP.
1. It is unclear when Gorham might have seen Johnson in Washington, but two of his earlier letters refer to having visited the President there. See Gorham to Johnson, Oct. 29, Nov. 18, 1865, *Johnson Papers*, 9: 300–301, 403–4.
2. The Montgomery County meeting was held on February 5; a lengthy list of potential delegates to the proposed Nashville conclave was submitted. Gorham's name was among the recommended delegates. *Clarksville Chronicle*, Feb. 9, 1866.
3. Sponsored by Conservative leaders in Tennessee, the Nashville gathering was principally for the purpose of demonstrating support for Johnson and his policies. Governor Brownlow opposed the meeting. Alexander, *Reconstruction*, 102–3.
4. James Edmund Bailey, Nathaniel H. Allen, and Jacob G. Hornberger, all previously identified, were Clarksville lawyers.
5. On February 12 a second Clarksville meeting was held, as announced. It offered additional names of possible delegates, adopted a resolution in support of the forthcoming Nashville convention, and indicated the travel arrangements that had been made. *Clarksville Chronicle*, Feb. 16, 1866.

From J. Madison Wells

New Orleans, Febr'y 6th 1866

Sir.

Herewith, in response to the telegram of the Secretary of War of 3d inst.,[1] I have the honor to enclose numerous papers[2] which have been placed in my hands by Mayor Kennedy, in relation to military interferences with him in the performance of his civic duties.[3] In matters of still smaller moment, not referred to, Genr'l Canby's officiousness was equally active.

Every one resident or a sojourner here, is surprized at finding the currency indebtedness of this city, now exceeding three millions three hundred thousand dollars, maintained at par with the national paper money; and the fact of itself is the highest compliment that could be paid to the Mayor's financial talent, his administrative capacity and his personal integrity; and may well excite astonishment, because, under similar circumstances, it has no parallel. General Canby, who is so prompt in throwing obstructions in the Mayor's way, does not show any plan of his own, eligible or otherwise, to accomplish the same end; the importance of which your Excellency can weigh when you recollect that of the thirty three hundred thousand dollars of this City currency in circulation, two thirds, at least, are in the hands of classes who would be ruined by its great depreciation or unexchangeability. What would be the condition of the City itself in such a contingency, I am appalled to be obliged to imagine.

There has been a large addition made to what is called the batture property of the City, by the high water of the Mississipi. This is owned conjointly by citizens and the City of New Orleans. The former represented by the Hon: Randall Hunt,[4] now in Washington, deem the present favorable for its sale; and as the City's proportion is expected to be at least half a million of dollars, which can be immediately applied to the extinguishment of a portion of the floating debt, Mayor Kennedy acceded to the proposal to have it sold. If current talk is worthy of consideration, Genr'l Canby intends to prevent this sale also.

This City never was under as good an administration in its history before; and should the secret associations now organizing rapidly, be able to regain the ascendancy which made it a living hell for years preceding the rebellion, I shudder at the consequences. I have the honor to enclose the by-laws of one of these associations.[5]

The Mayor has no wish to retain office, on the contrary, has repeatedly asked to be relieved; and should his health get worse, I really do not know how I am to replace him. Of course his independent, impartial and just conduct has made every bad man his enemy; such men as Jacob Barker, the M.C. whom he was obliged to sue for twenty seven thousand dollars of trust funds he, Barker, had borrowed from the Mayor's immediate predecessor Capt: Hoyt,[6] are active in agitating opposition to him. Such opposition is the only kind known here.

J Madison Wells   Gov Louisiana

LS, DNA-RG107, Lets. Recd., Executive (M494, Roll 84).

1. Stanton, in response to a telegram to Johnson from Wells of February 1 stating that General Canby "assumes the right to control the civil affairs" of New Orleans, informed Wells that the President "directs me to ask you to specify the particular cases in which General Canby makes the assumptions mentioned." Wells to Johnson, Feb. 1, 1866, Tels. Recd., President, Vol. 5 (1866–67), RG107, NA; Stanton to Wells, Feb. 3, 1866, Tels. Sent, Sec. of War (M473, Roll 90), RG107, NA.

2. In a telegram to Johnson the day before he wrote his letter, Wells indicated that he would send papers by mail and in that dispatch he quoted from letters from DeWitt Clinton to Hugh Kennedy of January 30 and 31. Those two documents, as well as letters from Kennedy to Wells, January 31, 1866, Wells to Kennedy, February 1, 1866, and Kennedy to Canby, February 1, 1866, are all found in the Johnson Papers, LC, and are likely the "numerous papers" to which Wells refers here.

3. Evidently also included among the enclosures sent by Wells is a letter from Kennedy in which he complained that General Canby had interfered in his attempts to raise revenue for city expenses, particularly in regard to the city wharves and plans for a street railway. Kennedy to Wells, Feb. 6, 1866, Lets. Recd., Executive (M494, Roll 84), RG107, NA.

4. Lawyer and politician Randell Hunt (1806–1892) was elected to the U.S. Senate by the Louisiana legislature in November 1865 but was not seated by the Congress. Hunt served as president of the University of Louisiana (Tulane) from 1867 to 1884. Conrad, *La. Biography*; Taylor, *La. Reconstructed*, 80–81.

5. Not found.

6. Stephen Hoyt.

From Philip Critz

Washington City   7 Feby 1866

Philip Critz A Citizen of Hawkins County State of Tennessee Pray you will grant him a Special Pardon in an Indicment for treauson against the Goverment of the United States.[1]

P. Critz

ALS, DNA-RG94, Amnesty Papers (M1003, Roll 48), Tenn., Philip Critz.

1. A former member of the Tennessee legislature, Critz was obviously in Washington for the express purpose of securing an individual pardon. Endorsements accompanying his letter include the President's pencilled instruction: "The Atty Genl will issue pardon— This Case. A. J." On February 8 Andrew K. Long wrote the attorney general in behalf of the President requesting that Critz's pardon be sent to Johnson's office immediately "to enable the applicant to leave this city this eve." Critz was in fact pardoned on that date. Amnesty Papers (M1003, Roll 48), Tenn., Philip Critz, RG94, NA.

From James Farrow

Spartanburg S.C.   7 Feby 66

Sir,

Having seen it stated in the Papers that the Members elect from the Southern States were recognized by the various Departments of the Executive Branch of the Govt.—and so far as to accord to Members Elect the franking privilege—; I take the liberty of making direct inquiry in this subject. The "privilege" if recognized would prove of far more value than its mere money price from the fact of it being so extremely difficult in this portion of the country to get stamps. Having no Post Masters regularly installed we are dependent for Postage Stamps upon picking them up now & then and very few at a time.

While writing I will suggest that if there could be some plan adopted for circulating the pamphlet copies of your Messages & such like documents I think much good would be thereby accomplished. In my Cong. Dist—embracing 8 of the Judicial Dists nearest the Mountains which before the war aggregated about twenty Thousand voters—I do not suppose there are in all as many as one hundred City Papers taken. Our Country papers even where we have any are small and had not room to print more than short extracts.

I have addressed my inquiry to you in order the more certainly to have it given the proper direction for an authoritative answer.[1]

Jas. Farrow

ALS, DNA-RG60, Office of Atty. Gen., Lets. Recd., President.

1. According to an endorsement on the letter, the President's staff referred Farrow's letter to the attorney general's office on February 19.

Interview with Delegation of Blacks[1]

[Washington, D.C., February 7, 1866][2]

Mr. George T. Downing then addressed the President as follows:

We present ourselves to your Excellency, to make known with pleasure the respect which we are glad to cherish for you—a respect which is your due, as our Chief Magistrate. It is our desire for you to know that we come feeling that we are friends meeting a friend. We should, however, have manifested our friendship by not coming to further tax your already much burdened and valuable time; but we have another object in calling. We are in a passage to equality before the law. God hath made it by opening a Red Sea. We would have your assistance through the same. We come to you in the name of the colored people of the United States. We are delegated to come by some who have unjustly worn iron manacles on their bodies—by some whose minds have been manacled by class legislation in States called free. The colored people of the States of Illinois, Wisconsin, Alabama, Mississippi, Florida, South Carolina, North Carolina, Virginia, Maryland, Pennsylvania, New York, New England States, and District of Columbia have specially delegated us to come.

Our coming is a marked circumstance, noting determined hope that we are not satisfied with an amendment prohibiting slavery, but that we wish it enforced with appropriate legislation. This is our desire. We ask for it intelligently, with the knowledge and conviction that the fathers of the Revolution intended freedom for every American; that they should be protected in their rights as citizens, and be equal before the law. We are Americans, native born Americans. We are citizens, we are glad to have it known to the world that you bear no doubtful record on this point. On this fact, and with confidence in the triumph of justice we base our hope. We see no recognition of color or race in the organic law of the land. It knows no privileged class, and therefore we cherish the hope that we may be fully enfranchised, not only here in this District, but throughout the land. We respectfully submit that rendering anything less than this will be rendering to us less than our just due; that granting anything less than our full rights will be a disregard of our just rights and of due respect for our feelings. If the powers that be do so it will be used as a license, as it were, or an apology for any community, or for individuals thus disposed, to outrage our rights and feelings. It has been shown in the present war that the Government may justly reach its strong arm into States, and demand for them, from those who owe it allegiance, their assistance and support. May it not reach out a like arm to secure and protect its subjects upon whom it has a claim?

Following upon Mr. Downing, Mr. Fred. Douglass advanced and addressed the President, saying:

Mr. President, we are not here to enlighten you, sir, as to your duties as the Chief Magistrate of this Republic, but to show our respect, and to present in brief the claims of our race to your favorable consideration. In the order of Divine Providence you are placed in a position where you have the power to save or destroy us, to bless or blast us. I mean our whole race. Your noble and humane predecessor placed in our hands the sword to assist in saving the nation, and we do hope that you, his able successor, will favorably regard the placing in our hands the ballot with which to save ourselves.

We shall submit no argument on that point. The fact that we are the subjects of Government, and subject to taxation, subject to volunteer in the service of the country, subject to being drafted, subject to bear the burdens of the State, makes it not improper that we should ask to share in the privileges of this condition.

I have no speech to make on this occasion. I simply submit these observations as a limited expression of the views and feelings of the delegation with which I have come.

RESPONSE OF THE PRESIDENT

In reply to some of your inquiries, not to make a speech about this thing, for it is always best to talk plainly and distinctly about such matters, I will say that if I have not given evidence in my course that I am a friend of humanity, and to that portion of it which constitutes the colored population, I can give no evidence here. Everything that I have had, both as regards life and property, has been perilled in that cause, and I feel and think that I understand—not to be egotistic—what should be the true direction of this question, and what course of policy would result in the melioration and ultimate elevation, not only of the colored, but of the great mass of the people of the United States. I say that if I have not given evidence that I am a friend of humanity, and especially the friend of the colored man, in my past conduct, there is nothing that I can now do that would. I repeat, all that I possessed, life, liberty, and property, have been put up in connection with that question; when I had every inducement held out to take the other course, by adopting which I would have accomplished perhaps all that the most ambitious might have desired. If I know myself, and the feelings of my own heart, they have been for the colored man. I have owned slaves and bought slaves, but I never sold one. I might say, however, that practically, so far as my connection with slaves has gone, I have been their slave instead of their being mine. Some have even followed me here, while others are occupying and enjoying my property with my consent. For the colored race my means, my time, my all has been perilled; and now at this late day, after giving evidence that is tangible, that is practical, I am free to say to you that I do not like to be arraigned by some who can get up handsomely rounded periods and deal in rhetoric, and talk about abstract ideas of liberty, who never perilled life, liberty, or property. This kind of theoretical, hollow, unpractical friendship amounts to but very little. While I say that I am a friend of the colored man, I do not want to adopt a policy that I believe will end in a contest between the races, which if persisted in will result in the extermination of one or the other. God forbid that I should be engaged in such a work!

Now, it is always best to talk about things practically and in a common sense way. Yes, I have said, and I repeat here, that if the colored man in the United States could find no other Moses, or any Moses that would be more able and efficient than myself, I would be his Moses to lead him from bondage to freedom; that I would pass him from a land where he had lived in slavery to a land (if it were in our reach) of freedom. Yes, I would be willing to pass with him through the Red sea to the Land of Promise—to the land of liberty; but I am not willing, under either circumstance, to adopt a policy which I believe will only result in the sacrifice of his life and the shedding of his blood. I think I know what I say. I feel what I say; and I feel well assured that if the policy urged by some be persisted in, it will result in great injury to the white as well as to the colored man. There is a great deal talk about the sword in one hand accomplishing an end, and the ballot accomplishing another at the ballot-box.

These things all do very well, and sometimes have forcible application. We talk about justice; we talk about right; we say that the white man has been in the wrong in keeping the black man in slavery as long as he has. That is all true. Again, we talk about the Declaration of Independence and equality before the law. You understand all that, and know how to appreciate it. But, now, let us look each other in the face; let us go to the great mass of colored men throughout the slave States; let us take the condition in which they are at the present time—and it is bad enough, we all know—and suppose, by some magic touch you could say to every one, "You shall vote to-morrow," how much would that ameliorate their condition at this time?

Now, let us get closer up to this subject, and talk about it. ⟨The President here approached very near to Mr. Douglass.⟩ What relation has the colored man and the white man heretofore occupied in the South? I opposed slavery upon two grounds. First, it was a great monopoly, enabling those who controlled and owned it to constitute an aristocracy, enabling the few to derive great profits and rule the many with an iron rod, as it were. And this is one great objection to it in a government, it being a monopoly. I was opposed to it secondly upon the abstract principle of slavery. Hence, in getting clear of a monopoly, we are getting clear of slavery at the same time. So you see there were two right ends accomplished in the accomplishment of the one.

Mr. Douglass. Mr. President, do you wish—

The President. I am not quite through yet.

Slavery has been abolished, a great national guarantee has been given, one that cannot be revoked. I was getting at the relation that subsisted between the white man and the colored men. A very small proportion of white persons compared with the whole number of such owned the colored people of the South. I might instance the State of Tennessee in illustration. There were there twenty-seven non-slaveholders to one slaveholder, and yet the slave power controlled the State. Let us talk about this matter as it is. Although the colored man was in slavery there, and owned as property in the sense and in the language of that locality and of that community, yet, in comparing his condition, and his position there with the non-slaveholder, he usually estimated his importance just in proportion to the number of slaves that his master owned, with the non-slaveholder.

Have you ever lived upon a plantation?

Mr. Douglass. I have, your Excellency.

The President. When you would look over and see a man who had a large family, struggling hard upon a poor piece of land, you thought a great deal less of him than you did of your own master's negro, did'nt you?

Mr. Douglass. Not I!

The President. Well, I know such was the case with a large number of you in those sections. Where such is the case we know there is an enmity, we know there is a hate. The poor white man, on the other hand, was opposed to the slave and his master; for the colored man and his master, combined, kept him in slavery, by depriving him of a fair participation in the labor and productions of the rich land of the country.

Don't you know that a colored man, in going to hunt a master (as they call it) for the next year, preferred hiring to a man who owned slaves rather than to a man who did not? I know the fact, at all events. They did not consider it quite as respectable to hire to a man who did not own negroes as to one who did.

Mr. Douglass. Because he wouldn't be treated as well.

The President. Then that is another argument in favor of what I am going to say. It shows that the colored man appreciated the slave owner more highly than he did the man who didn't own slaves. Hence the enmity between the colored man and the non-slaveholders. The white man was permitted to vote before—Government was derived from him. He is a part and parcel of the political machinery.

Now by the rebellion or revolution—and when you come back to the objects of this war, you find that the abolition of slavery was not one of the objects; Congress and the President himself declared that it was waged on our part in order to suppress the rebellion—the abolition of slavery has come as an incident to the suppression of a great rebellion—as an incident, and as an incident we should give it the proper direction.

The colored man went into this rebellion a slave; by the operation of the rebellion he came out a freedman—equal to a freeman in any other portion of the country. Then there is a great deal done for him on this point. The non-slaveholder who was forced into the rebellion, who was as loyal as those that lived beyond the limits of the State, but who [was] carried into it, and his property, and in a number of instances, the lives of such were sacrificed, and he who has survived has come out of it with nothing gained but a great deal lost.

Now, upon the principle of justice, should they be placed in a condition different from what they were before? On the one hand, one has gained a great deal; on the other hand, one has lost a great deal, and, in a political point of view, scarcely stands where he did before.

Now, we are talking about where we are going to begin. We have got at the hate that existed between the two races. The query comes up whether these two races, situated as they were before, without preparation, without time for passion and excitement to be appeased, and without time for the slightest improvement, whether the one should be turned loose upon the other, and be thrown together at the ballot-box with this enmity and hate existing between them. The query comes up right there, whether we don't commence a war of races. I think I understand this thing, and especially is this the case when you force it upon a people without their consent.

You have spoken about government. Where is power derived from? We say it is derived from the people. Let us take it so and refer to the District of Columbia by way of illustration. Suppose, for instance, here, in this political community, which, to a certain extent must have government, must have laws, and putting it now upon the broadest basis you can put it—take into consideration the relation which the white has heretofore borne to the colored race—is it proper to force upon this community, without their consent, the elective franchise, without regard to color, making it universal?

Now, where do you begin? Government must have a controlling power; must have a lodgment. For instance, suppose Congress should pass a law authorizing an election to be held at which all over twenty-one years of age, without regard to color, should be allowed to vote, and a majority should decide at such election that the elective franchise should not be universal; what would you do about it? Who would settle it? Do you deny that first great principle of the right of the people to govern themselves? Will you resort to an arbitrary power, and say a majority of the people shall receive a state of things they are opposed to?

Mr. Douglass. That was said before the war.

The President. I am now talking about a principle; not what somebody else said.

Mr. Downing. Apply what you have said, Mr. President, to South Carolina, for instance, where a majority of the inhabitants are colored.

The President. Suppose you go to South Carolina; suppose you go to Ohio. That doesn't change the principle at all. The query to which I have referred still comes up when Government is undergoing a fundamental change. Government commenced upon this principle; it has existed upon it; and you propose now to incorporate into it an element that didn't exist before. I say the query comes up in undertaking this thing, whether we have a right to make a change in regard to the elective franchise in Ohio, for instance, whether we shall not let the people in that State decide the matter for themselves.

Each community is better prepared to determine the depository of its political power than anybody else, and it is for the Legislature, for the people of Ohio to say who shall vote, and not for the Congress of the United States. I might go down here to the ballot-box to-morrow and vote directly for universal suffrage; but if a great majority of the people said no, I should consider it would be tyrannical in me to attempt to force such upon them without their will. It is a fundamental tenet in my creed that the will of the people must be obeyed. Is there anything wrong or unfair in that?

Mr. Douglass (smiling.) A great deal that is wrong, Mr. President, with all respect.

The President. It is the people of the States that must for themselves determine this thing. I do not want to be engaged in a work that will commence a war of races. I want to begin the work of preparation, and the States, or the people in each community, if a man demeans himself well, and shows evidence that this new state of affairs will operate, will protect him in all his rights, and give him every possible advantage when they become reconciled socially and politically to this state of things. Then will this new order of things work harmoniously; but forced upon the people before they are prepared for it, it will be resisted, and work inharmoniously. I feel a conviction that driving this matter upon the people, upon the community, will result in the injury of both races, and the ruin of one or the other. God knows I have no desire but the good of the whole human race. I would it were so that all you advocate could be done in the twinkling of an eye; but it is not in the nature of things, and I do not assume or pretend to be wiser than Providence, or stronger than the laws of nature.

Let us now seek to discover the laws governing this thing. There is a great law controlling it; let us endeavor to find out what that law is, and conform our actions to it. All the details will then properly adjust themselves and work out well in the end.

God knows that anything I can do I will do. In the mighty process by which the great end is to be reached, anything I can do to elevate the races, to soften and ameliorate their condition I will do, and to be able to do so is the sincere desire of my heart.

I am glad to have met you, and thank you for the compliment you have paid me.

Mr. Douglass. I have to return to you our thanks, Mr. President, for so kindly granting us this interview. We did not come here expecting to argue this question with your Excellency, but simply to state what were our views and wishes in the premises. If we were disposed to argue the question, and you would grant us permission, of course we would endeavor to controvert some of the positions you have assumed.

Mr. Downing. Mr. Douglass, I take it that the President, by his kind expressions and his very full treatment of the subject, must have contemplated some reply to the views which he has advanced, and in which we certainly do not concur, and I say this with due respect.

The President. I thought you expected me to indicate to some extent what my views were on the subjects touched upon in your statement.

Mr. Downing. We are very happy, indeed, to have heard them.

Mr. Douglass. If the President will allow me, I would like to say one or two words in reply. You enfranchise your enemies and disfranchise your friends.

The President. All I have done is simply to indicate what my views are, as I supposed you expected me to, from your address.

Mr. Douglass. My own impression is that the very thing that your Excellency would avoid in the Southern States can only be avoided by the very measure that we propose, and I would state to my brother delegates that because I perceive the President has taken strong ground in favor of a given policy, and distrusting my own ability to remove any of those impressions which he has expressed, I thought we had better end the interview with the expression of thanks. (Addressing the President.) But if your Excellency will be pleased to hear, I would like to say a word or two in regard to that one matter of the enfranchisement of the blacks as a means of preventing the very thing which your Excellency seems to apprehend—that is a conflict of races.

The President. I repeat. I merely wanted to indicate my views in reply to your address, and not to enter into any general controversy, as I could not well do so under the circumstances.

Your statement was a very frank one, and I thought it was due to you to meet it in the same spirit.

Mr. Douglass. Thank you, sir.

The President. I think you will find, so far as the South is concerned, that if you will all inculcate there the idea in connection with the one you urge, that the colored people can live and advance in civilization to better advantage elsewhere than crowded right down there in the South, it would be better for them.

Mr. Douglass. But the masters have the making of the laws, and we cannot get away from the plantations.

The President. What prevents you?

Mr. Douglass. We have not the single right of locomotion through the Southern States now.

The President. Why not; the government furnishes you with every facility.

Mr. Douglass. There are six days in the year that the negro is free in the South now, and his master then decides for him where he shall go, where he shall work, how much he shall work—in fact, he is divested of all political power. He is absolutely in the hands of those men.

The President. If the master now controls him or his action, would he not control him in his vote?

Mr. Douglass. Let the negro once understand that he has an organic right to vote, and he will raise up a party in the Southern States among the poor, who will rally with him. There is this conflict that you speak of between the wealthy slaveholder and the poor man.

The President. You touch right upon the point there. There is this conflict, and hence I suggest emigration. If he cannot get employment in the South, he has it in his power to go where he can get it.

In parting, the President said that they were both desirous of accomplishing the same ends, but proposed to do so by following different roads.

Mr. Douglass, on turning to leave, remarked to his fellow delegates: "The President sends us to the people, and we go to the people."

The President. Yes, sir; I have great faith in the people. I believe they will do what is right.[3]

Washington Morning Chronicle, Feb. 8, 1866.

1. The delegation, representing the Equal Rights convention recently held in Washington, included Frederick Douglass (1817–1895), the former slave and leader in the abolition/civil rights movement; and George T. Downing (1819–1903), a northern-born businessman, restauranteur, and civil rights activist. The group met with Johnson at the White House, where he greeted them. Rayford W. Logan and Michael R. Winston, eds., *Dictionary of American Negro Biography* (New York, 1982).

2. The newspaper accounts make clear that the interview took place on February 7, 1866, in Washington.

3. After the delegation left his office, Johnson told one of his secretaries: "Those d----d sons of b-----s thought they had me in a trap! I know that d----d Douglass; he's just like any nigger, and he would sooner cut a white man's throat than not." Quoted in Lawanda and John H. Cox, *Politics, Principle, and Prejudice, 1865–1866: Dilemma of Reconstruction America* (New York, 1963), 163.

From Charles J. Jenkins

Milledgeville Ga.   7, Feby 1866

Sir

Having been informed that the trial of Mr. G. B. Lamar of Savannah had resulted in his conviction,[1] I trust you will not consider it improperly intrusive in me, to invoke in his behalf the interposition of Executive clemency. I will not weary you with many words; but I beg you to consider that Mr Lamar is now an old man, of very large and respectable family connections in our State, and has always sustained a high character for integrity. He has led a very active, and diversified business life, well calculated to test a man's principles, and I know no man, in this state, in whom the people generally place more implicit reliance, in any matter involving trust, and confidence. If he has erred, an acquaintance with him, of more than forty years standing, assures me, it was an error of the head only. I pray you Mr President, deal tenderly with such a man, in his old age.

I have also been requested to ask your clemency in behalf of Dr John H. Gee,[2] who either has been or now is, on trial at Raleigh N.C. Of him, I know nothing personally, but the representations I have of his character, and standing, satisfy me that mercy shown him, would not be misplaced. You will hear from others,[3] better informed, but I think I do no wrong to truth and justice by adding my plea to their's. I trust, Mr President, you are satisfied with the selection our Legislature has made, of Senators. It is true, that they both, after having, in vain, struggled manfully against secession, as long as there was an inch of ground to stand on, took part in the Confederate Government. But it was not for this, nor by reason of their seeking the positions, that they were preferred. They both sought to avoid the result. They were pressed into service, because of their known conservative principles, because of their distinguished ability, and national reputation, and because in every hamlet, within our borders, however retired, they are recognised as Representative men of Georgia. By such men, you know, Sir, the People like to be represented. Aspirants, who were advocates of secession in the beginning, and some whose claims were based on military edict, lately acquired, were rejected.

Charles J. Jenkins

ALS, DLC-JP.

1. At his trial Gazaway B. Lamar, Sr., was convicted of defrauding the United States by stealing sixty-seven bales of cotton from the Treasury Department, formerly belonging to Lamar's Importing and Exporting Company of Georgia, and bribing army officers. Lamar was sentenced to three years' imprisonment and a $25,000 fine. After a very short imprisonment he was released on bail and late in Johnson's administration his sentence was remitted. Thomas R. Hay, "Gazaway Bugg Lamar, Confederate Banker and Businessman," *GHQ*, 37 (1953): 124; Joseph Holt to Edwin M. Stanton, Feb. 12, 1866, Lets. Sent (Record Books), Vol. 18, RG153, NA. See also Jenkins to Johnson, Jan. 1, 1866, *Johnson Papers*, 9: 556–58.

2. Gee (1819–1876), physician, Mexican War veteran, and major, 4th Fla. Btn., CSA, during the latter months of 1864 was the commandant of the Confederate prison at Salisbury, North Carolina. His trial (which began on February 21) for alleged crimes at that prison ended in his acquittal and he was released from confinement in July 1866. Ida B. Williams, "John Henry Gee, Physician and Soldier," *GHQ*, 45 (1961): 238–44; *National Intelligencer*, Apr. 12, 1866; John C. Robinson to E. D. Townsend, July 6, 1866, Lets. Recd. (Main Ser.), File R-260-1866 (M619, Roll 508), RG94, NA.

3. Gov. Jonathan Worth forwarded to Johnson a letter to Worth from Judge Daniel G. Fowle. Invoking Johnson's April 2 proclamation, Fowle questioned the legality of Gee's trial by military commission. But inasmuch as the trial had commenced some six weeks prior to the issuance of the proclamation, the President, through Townsend, ordered that the military trial be brought to "its final termination," although "the execution of any sentence" would be suspended "until the record is reviewed." Worth to Johnson, Apr. 17, 1866; Fowle to Worth, Apr. 14, 1866; Cooper to Worth, Apr. 27, 1866, Johnson Papers, LC; Townsend to Thomas H. Ruger, Apr. 18, 1866, Tels. Sent, Sec. of War (M473, Roll 90), RG107, NA.

From Lewis E. Parsons and George S. Houston[1]

Washington   Feby. 7" 1866—

Sir

Learning that the office of Collector at Mobile is vacant & that Hon. Albert Elmore, at present Secy. of State & Hon. William Garrett, a member of the Senate, are applicants for the place, we respectfully recommend them to your favorable consideration. Each of them is well qualified to discharge the duties of the office & will make an efficient & reliable officer. Each was opposed to secession in principle & policy, and has labored efficiently, from the first, in the work of restoration in alabama, in accordance with your policy and both are firm friends of the constitution and the union. The appointment of either of them would give great satisfaction to the people of that State.[2]

Lewis E. Parsons
Geo. S Houston

ALS (Parsons), DNA-RG56, Appts., Customs Service, Collector, Mobile, Albert Elmore.
    1. Alabama's U.S. senators-elect were in the national capital to present their credentials to Congress.
    2. Both Elmore and Garrett were supported by numerous recommendations from Alabama officials, citizens, or army officers. The current governor of the state, Robert M. Patton, especially backed Garrett. But it was Elmore whom Johnson nominated for the office in March 1866 and whom the Senate confirmed in June. Patton to Johnson, Feb. 5, 1866, Appts., Customs Service, Collector, Mobile, Wm. Garrett, RG56, NA; *U.S. Off. Reg.* (1867); *Senate Ex. Proceedings*, Vol. 14, pt. 2: 679, 849.

Remarks to Citizens of Montana[1]

[February 7, 1866][2]

Gentlemen:

It is no ordinary pleasure for me to meet you here on this occasion and to hear the sentiments you have announced. To receive so large and respectable a body of intelligent gentlemen from that remote region of the country from which you come is extremely gratifying to me. In response, sir, (addressing Mr. Pinney,)[3] to the eloquent manner in which you have expressed the sentiments and feelings of those you represent on this occasion, I might content myself with simply returning my thanks for your kind expressions. But you have made some allusions to which, under the circumstances which surround us, I cannot be indifferent. You have alluded to the great principles of our Government having been enunciated by me in a paper sent a short time since to the Congress of the United States.[4] The declaration by me of those principles was not the result of impulse. It was the result of a thorough and calm consideration of those great truths which lie at the foundations of all free governments. Those who understood those truths, and have laid them down as their guide, cannot fail to understand the doctrine enunciated in the message. It is not necessary to inquire whether they emanate from this man or that man. Those who understand and believe in those principles, no matter from what standpoint they look at them, will find themselves involuntarily, and imperceptibly it may be, but surely coming together in all great struggles that may take place in regard to them: while those who disclaim them, who are willing to repudiate them, and set them at naught, will be found disintegrating and travelling in a divergent direction. For this reason there may be many now coming together without any previous concert or arrangement, but imperceptibly, because they agree on the same great principles. I think, gentlemen, there is no one who can mistake the great cardinal principles that are laid down in that message. They comprehend and embrace the principles upon which the Government rests, and upon which, to be successful, it must be administered. I care not by what name the party administering the Government may be denominated—the Union party, the Republican party, the Democratic party, or whatnot—no party can administer the Government successfully unless it is administered upon the great principles laid down in that paper. You would meet with about the same success in attempting to carry on the Government upon any other principles than those which are found in the Constitution as you would if you should take hold of a piece of machinery that had been constructed and trained to run harmoniously in one direction, and attempt by reverse action to run it in the opposite direction. I say again that I think no one can mistake the doctrines of that message. It is very easy for persons to misrepresent it, and to make assertions that this, that or the other had taken place, or will take place; but I think I may be permitted to say to you on this occasion that, taking all my antecedents, going back to my advent into political life, and continuing down to the present time, the great cardinal principles set forth in that paper have been my constant and unerring guide. After having gone so far, it is impossible for me to turn and take a different direction. They will be my guide from this time onward, and those who understand them may know where I shall always be found when principle is involved.

Here let me say to you, in order to disabuse the public mind as far as it is possible for an individual to do so, that my public career is well-nigh done. The sand of my political glass has well-nigh run out. If I were disposed to refer to myself, I might trace my career back to the log cabin, then an alderman and a mayor in a village, then through both branches of the State Legislature, then for ten consecutive years in the National House of Representatives, then through the gubernatorial chair to the Senate of the United States, then provisional governor, with a slight participation in military affairs, then Vice President, and now in the position

I occupy before you; and now in this position, if I can be instrumental in restoring the Government of the United States, in restoring to their true position in the Union those States whose relations to the National Government have been for a time interrupted by one of the most gigantic rebellions that ever occurred in the world, so that we can proclaim once more that we are a united people, I shall feel that the measure of my ambition has been filled, and filled to overflowing; and at that point, if there be any who are envious and jealous of honor and position, I shall be prepared to make them as polite a bow as I know how, and thank them to take the place I have occupied, for my mission will have been fulfilled.

In saying this, in the performance of my duty, and in response to the encouragement you have given me, I feel that I am in a condition not to be arrogant, not to feel imperious or supercilious. I feel that I can afford to do right, and so feeling, God being willing, I intend to do right, and so far as in me lies I intend to administer this Government upon the principles that lie at the foundation of it.

I can inform all aspirants who are trying to form their combinations for the future, who want to make one organization for one purpose, and another for another, that they are not in my way; I am not a candidate for any position, and hence I repeat I can afford to do right and, being in that condition, I will do right. I make this announcement for the purpose of letting all know that my work is to restore the Government—not to make combinations with any reference to any future candidacy for the Presidency of the United States. I have reached the utmost round; my race is run, so far as that is concerned, my object is to perform my duty, and that I will endeavor to do.

Let us all, then, join in this great work of restoration; and while we are restoring and repairing the breaches that have been made, let us also unite in the work of making new States and populating them with a people who are worthy of the Government that protects them, and let those new State governments be founded on principles in harmony with the great machinery devised by our fathers. So far as regards any aid or assistance that can be given here in the progress and in the consummation of this great work of building up new States, as well as in the restoration of all the former States, you will find me a willing and cordial helper.

Gentlemen, I did not expect this demonstration, but you will please accept my thanks for the compliment you have paid me on this occasion, and the encouragement you have given me in the discharge of my duty.

All I can say in conclusion is to assure you that any assistance you may need from this quarter will be most cheerfully given to advance the interests of the community you represent.[5]

Washington Evening Star, Feb. 8, 1866.

1. The Montana delegation, which visited Commissioner James M. Edmunds of the General Land Office as well as Johnson, numbered twenty-five to thirty members, includ-

ing Walter A. Burleigh, delegate from the Dakota Territory, and Montana Chief Justice Hezekiah L. Hosmer. Hosmer (1814–1893), a native of New York, practiced law and edited a newspaper in Ohio, before becoming secretary to the U.S. House Committee on the Territories in 1861. He served as chief justice of Montana (1864–69), postmaster at Virginia City, Montana (1869–72), and later held several minor positions in San Francisco. *Washington Evening Star*, Feb. 7, 8, 1866; *DAB*.

2. The newspaper account of February 8 notes that on "yesterday morning" citizens from Montana "now in Washington" called upon the President. *Washington Evening Star*, Feb. 8, 1866.

3. George M. Pinney (c1833–fl1869) resided in the Dakota Territory, where he was first speaker of the territorial house, marshal, and then provost marshal, before he became marshal for the Montana Territory in February 1865. In 1867 he served as a special agent of the Treasury Department in Montana, and a year later he became editor of the *Montana Post* in Helena. Ritter and Wakelyn, *Legislative Leaders*; Basler, *Works of Lincoln*, 7: 207, 215; *U.S. Off. Reg.* (1865–67); *History of Montana, 1739–1885* (Chicago, 1885), 321, 322; *New York Times*, Oct. 13, 1868.

4. See Johnson's first annual Message to Congress, Dec. 4, 1865, *Johnson Papers*, 9: 466–85.

5. On February 16 the *Cincinnati Daily Enquirer* reported that the *New Haven Register* had received a letter, supposedly from someone in attendance, attesting that there was another paragraph to the President's Montana speech not published. According to Johnson had remarked that he was aware of the factions, but he was not going to place men in important positions who were opposed to his policies. *Daily Enquirer* (Cincinnati), Feb. 16, 1866.

Reply of the Black Delegates to the President[1]

Washington, February 7, 1866.

Mr. President:

In consideration of a delicate sense of propriety, as well as your own repeated intimations of indisposition to discuss or to listen to a reply to the views and opinions you were pleased to express to us in your elaborate speech to-day, the undersigned would respectfully take this method of replying thereto. Believing as we do that the views and opinions you expressed in that address are entirely unsound and prejudicial to the highest interests of our race as well as our country at large, we cannot do other than expose the same, and, as far as may be in our power, arrest their dangerous influence. It is not necessary at this time to call attention to more than two or three features of your remarkable address:

1. The first point to which we feel especially bound to take exception is your attempt to found a policy opposed to our enfranchisement, upon the alleged ground of an existing hostility on the part of the former slaves toward the poor white people of the South. We admit the existence of this hostility, and hold that it is entirely reciprocal. But you obviously commit an error by drawing an argument from an incident of a state of slavery, and making it a basis for a policy adapted to a state of freedom. The hostility between the whites and blacks of the South is easily explained. It has its root and sap in the relation of slavery, and was incited on both sides by the cunning of the slave masters. Those masters secured their ascen-

dency over both the poor whites and the blacks by putting enmity between them.

They divided both to conquer each. There was no earthly reason why the blacks should not hate and dread the poor whites when in a state of slavery, for it was from this class that their masters received their slave-catchers, slave-drivers, and overseers. They were the men called in upon all occasions by the masters when any fiendish outrage was to be committed upon the slave. Now, sir, you cannot but perceive that, the cause of this hatred removed, the effect must be removed also. Slavery is abolished. The cause of antagonism is removed, and you must see that it is altogether illogical (and "putting new wine into old bottles," "mending new garments with old cloth") to legislate from slaveholding and slave-driving premises for a people whom you have repeatedly declared your purpose to maintain in freedom.

2. Besides, even if it were true, as you allege, that the hostility of the blacks toward the poor whites must necessarily project itself into a state of freedom, and that this enmity between the two races is even more intense in a state of freedom than in a state of slavery, in the name of Heaven, we reverently ask, how can you, in view of your professed desire to promote the welfare of the black man, deprive him of all means of defence, and clothe him whom you regard as his enemy in the panoply of political power? Can it be that you would recommend a policy which would arm the strong and cast down the defenceless? Can you, by any possibility of reasoning, regard this as just, fair, or wise? Experience proves that those are oftenest abused who can be abused with the greatest impunity. Men are whipped oftenest who are whipped easiest. Peace between the races is not to be secured by degrading one race and exalting another, by giving power to one race and withholding it from another, but by maintaining a state of equal justice between all classes. First pure, then peaceable.

3. On the colonization theory you were pleased to broach very much could be said. It is impossible to suppose, in view of the usefulness of the black man in time of peace as a laborer in the South, and in time of war as a soldier at the North, and the growing respect for his rights among the people, and his increasing adaptation to a high state of civilization in this his native land, there can ever come a time when he can be removed from this country without a terrible shock to its prosperity and peace. Besides, the worst enemy of the nation could not cast upon its fair name a greater infamy than to suppose that negroes could be tolerated among them in a state of the most degrading slavery and oppression, and must be cast away, driven into exile, for no other cause than having been freed from their chains.

Washington Morning Chronicle, Feb. 8, 1866.
   1. The published document was signed by Frederick Douglass, George T. Downing, and others. They had met with Johnson earlier in the day.

From Joseph A. Wright

Berlin [Prussia]   February 7th 1866

My Dear President;

As your friend I take the liberty of sending you the enclosed artile,[1] which has been extensively published throughout Europe, the German Papers being most flattering upon your administration. And I thought you might take the time (amid the multiplicity of your cares & duties,) to read what the estimate is that Europe places upon your character.

You have doubtless heard thru Mr. Seward, that I am making some progress towards the settlement of the Military Question,[2] and I hope Mr. S, has shown you the private note of the Prime Minister (Count Bismarck) on this subject, written to me.[3] I doubt not we can and will do better than he proposes. Prussia is now in an excited position; and by no means quiet. She wants our friendship and goodwill, and will at this juncture, yeild almost every thing we ask.

If *you* shall adjust and settle this question satisfactory to those returning to the land of their birth, (which I believe you will accomplish) it will do more to further the cause of Emigration, than any question of the day; and one of the brightest and most important acts of your administration.[4]

This confidential note of the Minister to me is the first instance of any Government yeilding to us, in the slightest degree for what we contend to be our rights. It is not *all* we ask, but it is one step in the right direction. I have read with great interest Senator Doolittles speech,[5] and I will not believe there will be any division in the Union party. A majority of both Houses will stand by your Policy of Reconstruction.

Senator Lane from Indiana writes me there is not the slightest cause for division, and he will doubtless stand by your Administration.

I have been most kindly received, by the Royal family, and treated with the highest respect.

Mrs Wright unites with me in assurances of the kindest regard and wishes for your health and happiness.

Joseph A. Wright

ALS, DLC-JP.

1. Not found.

2. Wright had apprised Johnson of this thorny issue in his letter of September 27, 1865. *Johnson Papers*, 9: 141–42.

3. Not found, but see the "memorandum" enclosed in Wright's communiqué to Seward of December 16, 1865. *Senate Ex. Docs.*, 40 Cong., 1 Sess., No. 4, p. 124 (Ser. 1308).

4. See Wright to Johnson, May 2, 1866.

5. Here Wright probably refers to James R. Doolittle's speech in the Senate on January 17 when he attacked Sumner and the Radicals' reconstruction policy. *Congressional Globe*, 39 Cong., 1 Sess., pp. 266–75; *Philadelphia Evening Bulletin*, Jan. 18, 1866.

From Thomas R. Barry

Gallatin Tennessee   Feb 8th 1866

Dear President

The foregoing contains as I think a very unjustifiable censure of what I done officially.[1] At our last circuit court a negro was brought before me for trial for violating a State Law against Tipling.[2] I did simply what was my sworn duty as a public officer but instead of fining the negroe large sums I simply fined him only one cent in each case.[3] This is the fourth instance of an unjustifiable interference with the civil authority of the Court of the county in the last 10 days. The object of this letter is to inquire of you if you know of and approve of these interferences. No man has more respect for the goverment authorities of the U S than myself. No man in propotion to his means and ability has done more to uphold its power and no man living would now go farther than myself to uphold its rightful Constitutional authority. I have written you two or three letters lately which required no answer but I think the public interest my own feelings and my future course demands a quick answer to this. If Gen Thomas was here I would appeal to him with great confidence for I have always regarded him as a real friend to his country. I will if you require it send you a copy of the orders in the other cases.[4]

T Barry

ALS, DNA-RG108, Lets. Recd. *re* Military Discipline.

1. Barry is referring here to an order from Gen. Richard W. Johnson in which he notified the chancellor (via the clerk) that a case involving a suit over the Union army's impressment of mules and horses during the war should "be discontinued and dismissed forever." Johnson to John R. Barry, Feb. 2, 1866, Lets. Recd. *re* Military Discipline, RG108, NA; and accompanying documents concerning the James Frazier suit found in the same files.

2. On February 7, Bvt. Lt. Col. Jesse E. Jacobs wrote from the Freedmen's Bureau office in Nashville that fines imposed upon a black man, Alfred Lillard, for selling liquor in Sumner County should be negated and restitution made to Lillard. He had sold liquor based upon a permit issued by General Rousseau during the occupation of Sumner County by Federal troops. But Barry refused to recognize the legality of such a permit when Lillard was brought into his court. Jacobs to Thomas C. Trimble, Feb. 7, 1866, ibid.

3. Barry entered a further plea in his own defense concerning the black fined for selling liquor in Sumner County. Barry lashed out at the military authorities who were circumventing the civil laws of Tennessee. He declared that "if these military interferences are not stoped the Constitution and all laws will be obsolete." Barry to Johnson, Feb. 9, 1866, ibid.

4. In March Barry continued his efforts to enlist support for his stance with regard to military authorities and Freedmen's Bureau officials. He entreated Kentucky Rep. Henry Grider to talk directly with the President about the situations. Barry to Grider, Mar. 8, 1866, Johnson Papers, LC.

From Michael Burns

Nashville   Feb 8. 1866

Mr President

I am Impelled to write you as I See a determined effort by a Small clique in this state to get up an impression that your course in Administring the Goverment dont meet the approval of the people. I Say *Emphaticaly* that nine tenths of the people fully indorse your course and are willing to trust you. Let them wait until after the meeting of the 22.[1] It will be a triumph. I wont trespass farther on your time. Your friends are in earnest.

M Burns

ALS, DLC-JP.
1. The Washington Birthday Union convention met at the state capitol in Nashville to hear speeches and adopt resolutions. The tenor of the latter was strongly supportive of President Johnson and his policies, including his "liberal exercise of Executive clemency." For a convenient contemporary report of the deliberations and proceedings, see the *Nashville Union and American*, Feb. 23, 1866. For other references to the Nashville convention, see Gorham to Johnson, Feb. 6, and Nicholson to Johnson, Feb. 27, 1866.

From Benjamin B. French

Washington, Feby. 8. 1866.

My Dear Sir,

I cannot forbear to express to you the great pleasure I felt on reading your remarks to the colored men who visited you yesterday. The principles you enunciated are the same expressed to me in a conversation I had with you last Autumn,[1] and in which I fully agreed with you. You said to me then that every one would, and *must* admit that the white race was superior to the black, and that while we ought to do our best to bring them ⟨the blacks⟩ up to our present level, that, in doing so we should, at the same time raise our own intellectual status so that the relative position of the two races would be the same. I think that was about your idea, and, if success attended the efforts to exalt the black race, which I some doubt, the result would doubtless be that the white race would still hold its natural place above them. Man, with his puny arm, cannot annul the decrees of God!

I am astonished, and more than astonished, at the persistency with which the radical idea of placing negroes on an equality with whites, *in every particular*, is pressed in Congress. And with solemnity I say, that, in my opinion our Union is, at this moment, in greater danger from the fanatical zeal with which this false idea is pressed, than it was from the Rebellion itself! Give the colored race the unlimited right of suffrage, and a fire brand is cast among the people that cannot be extinguished until it is quenched in the blood of hostile factions.

I hope, & trust, and pray that the vision of the sovereign people will be so far carried into the future by the common Father of us all, that they will avert the danger by vetoing, not only the *measures* which tend to so awful a result, but the *men* who initiated and supported them.

I am only one humble citizen, but I love my Country and her Constitution, and I desire, beyond all things, the prosperity, and the honor of that Country. Until the tide of fanaticism, which is now in full flood, shall turn, as it must, unless sanity has departed from the people, we must place our trust in you to keep us safe "from the pestilence that walketh in darkness, and the destruction that wasteth at noon-day."[2]

Permit me to ask if you have read a most forcible article on the races of men, published in the Intelligencer of this morning, from the pen of a Doctor Nott?[3] If you have not read it, I commend it to your perusal.

Pardon me for writing to you at such length. I have known you so long, and so well, and esteemed and respected you so much, that I could not forbear to express my unalloyed pleasure at the noble position you hold as a staesman and a patriot. If my feeble tongue or arm are needed for your defence they are always ready.

B. B. French

ALS, DLC-JP.
1. Perhaps a reference to their interview of August 27, when they sat on the White House lawn and talked for about an hour. Donald B. Cole and John J. McDonough, eds., *Benjamin Brown French, Witness to the Young Republic: A Yankee's Journal, 1828–1870* (Hanover, N.H., 1989), 484–85.
2. A variation of Psalms 91: 6.
3. See Josiah C. Nott's letter to Gen. O. O. Howard, Nov. 25, 1865, *National Intelligencer*, Feb. 8, 1866.

Further Remarks on Response to Black Delegates

[Washington, D.C., February 8, 1866][1]

The Representative[2] said some persons felt, and others would probably, for personal or factious ends, endeavor to show that the President was taking sides against the colored people, or was at least less favorably disposed toward them than he had been.

The President responded that no one could fairly and truthfully do that. He was now what he had always been, the friend of the poor and the lowly. He had never broken faith with anybody, and if his past course and his former language were not a sufficient guarantee that he meant well toward the colored people, and would endeavor to secure to them a fair chance, nothing he could say or do now would give any such guarantee. He thought, however, that it was best to speak plainly, and he did not believe that the effort now making by some who call themselves the negroes' special friends, to force universal suffrage upon the States, was wise or judicious. He thought it tended to embitter feelings, while our effort should be to cultivate calmness and confidence. He believed it would result in great injury to the prospects of the colored people. He did not know whether Mr. DOUGLASS and his friends expected him to talk to them, but he thought it best to take the opportunity to state his views. He would repeat that he was, if he knew his own heart, the colored man's friend. He had great faith in the people, and would endeavor to carry out their will.

The Representative then said that some persons might take, or profess to take, the President's speech as an indication that he was at variance with his party friends, and that some others might endeavor to found upon it the charge that he was preparing to go over.

The President smiled, and answered that if the party which opposed his election indulged in any great expectations on that score, they were likely to be disappointed. He might differ with individuals of what was called the Union party as to the means to be used, but he considered himself in general accord with that party, as a whole, in the ends to be reached. He was not a party man, and he meant to sink the partisan in the patriot. But, so far as he understood the sentiments of the Union party, he was in general accord with it.

The Representative finally, after further conversation, said something about the distribution of offices, about Executive patronage.

The President remarked that he was the servant of the whole people, but he could not entirely forget by what party he had been placed in his present position, and supported in the administration of the duties intrusted to him. He proposed to fight his battles within the lines of the party which elected him to office. He might differ with some of his friends, and he should feel wholly at liberty to so differ, and to state the ground of his contrary belief or opinion; but he considered himself identified with the great Union party, and had no desire or intention of being found outside. He intended to exercise his own judgment, but was ready to yield it when he found it was not sustained by the judgment of the people. He had no sympathies with those who opposed the war for the Union, and while he hoped the whole country would approve the endeavor to restore the Union, he could not forget that some men favored and some opposed the cause of the Union when it was in peril.[3]

New York Times, Feb. 11, 1866.

1. According to the newspaper account, the visit by the delegation of blacks on February 7 was further discussed by the President on the following day in a conversation with "a distinguished Representative" at the White House.

2. Presumably the House member who conferred with the President on the morning of February 8 was Henry J. Raymond of New York. See *Richmond Dispatch*, Feb. 15, 1866.

3. The newspaper correspondent added here an explanatory paragraph in which he stated that the Johnson conversation had lasted about "half an hour." Furthermore, "I have condensed it and left out much that was of a more private character. I have so far as possible given the President's own words." *New York Times*, Feb. 11, 1866.

From William L. Hodge[1]

Washn   8 Feby 1866

Sir

Allow me for one both as a Citizen of the U.S & a resident of the District to proffer my sincere thanks for the sentiments expressed in your speech yesterday to Douglass & his fellows whose impudence is only exceeded by that of his white radical colleagues & to both you gave a just and stinging reproof.

I hope the intimation you gave on the subject will prevent any further attempt to cram the negro wool & all down our throats, against the unanimous sentiment of the people of the District[2] a measure which not one even of the most *ultra of the radicals* would dare attempt against the people of their respective states, without the previous consent of thier constituents.

Wm L Hodge

ALS, DLC-JP.
   1. Hodge (c1789–1868), a former merchant in New Orleans and assistant secretary of the treasury in the early 1850s, was at this time an insurance agent in Washington, D.C. Washington, D.C., directories (1863–67); *Washington Evening Star*, Jan. 24, 1868; Charles Lanman, *Biographical Annals of the Civil Government of the United States* (Detroit, 1976 [1876]), 509.
   2. A reference to both the District suffrage bill and the popular referendum which had defeated a similar proposal. See Henry Addison to Johnson, Jan. 12, 1866, *Johnson Papers*, 9: 593–94; Russell Houston to Johnson, Feb. 2, 1866.

From Joseph S. Ingraham[1]

Bangor, Me.   Feb 8th. 1866.

Dear Sir,

If *hatred* towards the South had not predominated in the hearts of those who came into possession of the Government, Mar 4th 1861, a compromise would have been agreed upon during that memorable session of Congress, in 1860–61—& which would have exercised the noble & christian influence of *preventing* the late calamitous war.

It would afford some consolation, when reflecting upon the terrible scourge with which our poor country has so recently been afflicted, if we could witness, *now*, a disposition on the part of the people of the North to let bye-gones be bye-gones. But, with shame be it said, very little of this Spirit seems to be manifested. Why *should* such a state of things ever have existed, or "have a being" at the present time. What great crime has the South ever committed as against the North. What right that attaches to the latter, by virtue of the Constitution, has the former ever trenched upon, or shown any disposition to thus conduct. Have the people of the South *ever* exhibited other than a National Spirit through their Several legislatures—or their representatives on the floor of Congress? If she was obliged, at last, to show a rebellious spirit, will not posterity, that most impartial of all tribunals, do her the justice to pronounce that she had quite good cause for so doing?

I say, why should those residing north of "Masons & Dixons line" so feel towards the inhabitants living south of it—& in a common country, too. It is clearly not on account of the existence of *Slavery* for that is numbered with the "things that were." And from the conduct of the radicals, today, (& I am afraid they constitute a majority of the people in the North) it would appear that it *never*, really, had anything to do in engendering this spirit of antagonism.

I think it can be explained only on the ground of a *feeling of jealousy, on the part of leading men North*, against a similar class South—for the genius & talents displayed by the latter on the floor of Congress,—& the influence heretofore exercised by her (the South) in the affairs of the Government.

Through legislation, Mess Stevens, Sumner, Wilson & Co hope to curtail the South of the power formerly wielded by her; not, that these *par excellence* Unionists apprehend that if the South is allowed again to occupy the position in the Union, assigned her by the Constitution, she will do anything which would tend to *diminish* the glory & prosperity of the Republic, but rather that she will *add to it*, in too *great a degree*.

And these same individuals are now seeking for some excuse by which they may cause *you* to be removed from the office of President! They will not scruple at anything to carry their point. In Heavens name may they not succeed! I must frankly admit, that often, during the late war, I stated that the South was fighting *the battle of the Revolution over again*—that the same issues were at stake—i.e.—true, republican liberty versus centralization,—and if she was *defeated*, then farewell to all worth preserving of the Republic! Does not every day furnish evidence that it is the *design* of the Republicans (Bl'k) to overthrow our form of Government? I trust you may be able to defeat its consummation.

Excuse me, being a stranger, for thus adressing you.

J. S. Ingraham

ALS, DLC-JP.
    1. Ingraham (b. *c*1830) was a druggist. 1860 Census, Maine, Penobscot, Bangor, 5th Ward, 55; Bangor directories (1848–59).

From James H. Embry

Philadelphia Pa   9— February 1866

Dr Sir

Being a sojourner for a few days in this City, and learning last Evening that one Fred. Douglas, (of Color) intended to discourse at "Concert Hall" on the condition of the Country and that he intended to attack the policy of the Administration, I very quietly walked around and reached there shortly after he commenced speaking.

After scanning the City Papers to-day I find no report of the Speech and a very meagre statement of his utterance.[1] He had a crowded House, about one half white and the other black, so far as I could judge. They seemed to have arranged themselves with reference to the idea of perfect equality among the races.

White & black of both sexes were seated upon the Platform and throughout the Hall "without distinction of color or race." The only *marked distinction* I recognized was that on the Platform the Negro occupied the post of honor *on the right* of the Speaker and the White man was content with the position assigned him on the left.

Frederick's Text, as he announced it, was Abraham Lincoln and his Administration, and as incident thereto his virtues, qualities & characteristicks. Whilst no one could object to what he said in regard to the fallen Patriot and Statesman, yet the purpose of his discourse had a far different object than to review the administration of Mr Lincoln or to offer deserved tribute to his memory and his virtues.

In the manner of the speaker and in the animus and subject-matter and especially the arrangement and drift of the Speech—I read another purpose. I reached the conclusion at once that Fred. Douglas had been sent for by Sumner, Stevens, Kelly[2] & Co to go to Washington to make the demands of you he did make to wield the power of the Administration to force Negro Suffrage upon the South, and in the event of failure to attack you in a public Speech. Several gentlemen with whom I have talked to-day concur with me in this opinion. I am fully convinced that after his interview with you on Wednesday that he was advised by Stevens & Co to make the speech he delivered last night, and that it was planned, arranged and matured by them "in Committee of the whole."

Many of his utterances toward you were grossly insulting and abusive. His clearly defined effort was to attempt to show that the policy of Mr Lincoln's administration was not only to crush out the Rebellion but to elevate the Negro to a civil and political equality with the white man— and then an attempt to show that you had surrendered to the Rebellion and was using the power of the Government to deprive the negro of his rights as a freed man.

His frequent allusion to you, sometimes by name, was cheered loudly of course by his entire audience, as he gave loose rein to Satire, anger and slander. His allusion to John Brown, who deservedly died on the Scaffold, as he held him up to his audience as a *martyr* and a *murdered man*, was of course equally applauded from a different spirit.

He was particularly bitter in commenting upon your advice to the negroes, whenever you addressed them, to go to work and be quiet and orderly and prove by their conduct that they were capable of enjoying freedom, particularly your address to the Negro Soldiers upon one occasion.[3] He thinks you ought to have advised them to strike for the ballot & to assert their equality.

But enough until it is known whether the Speech will be published as delivered. The Speech is *only important* as being the utterance of his friends in Washington, and he merely the *Mask* behind which they strike, fearing to do so upon their own responsibilities as Senators & Representatives, as there are constituencies behind them whose voices they must heed and obey. It is already said here that Kelly cannot be re-elected upon the issues he is now making in Congress and that Sumner's chances are doubtful.[4]

The highest Tribunal in this Nation, in which the rights of person and property are adjudicated, have decided that the Negro is not a Citizen, and yet, in the Second City in the Nation, a man who is not a Citizen of the Country, who, by the almost unanimous voice of the people, is denied the right to vote or hold office, is put forward to discuss the duty of the Nation and the policy it ought to adopt, and to arraign & malign the Chief Magistrate of the Republic.

The Negroes now, aided and seconded by their white allies, are creating the *Second Rebellion*—a Rebellion against the peace and quiet of the people and the unity of the Nation, and they would sever it rather than not accomplish Negro equality. As foreshadowed in his Speech last night, this same Fred. Douglas will be put forward to inculcate through the South the doctrine that the negro ought not to labor for any whites where the Elective Franchise is denied. The issue is being rapidly made between these Destructives and the friends of the Nation, unity & peace.

But pardon, my dear Sir, this long letter. I will only add that so far as I can learn the masses are rapidly uniting to support you.

A very valued friend, a Citizen of Rhode Island, Mr B. H. Cheever,[5] and who has enjoyed a long and an intimate personal acquaintance in N. York City with its leading citizens and business men, and who is and has been an active and zealous supporter of you and your administration, told me to-day that N. York City would speak soon in your behalf with a unanimity and a power unprecedented, and would be the nucleous of popular sentiment around which the masses of the North would rally as a unit.

James H. Embry

ALS, DLC-JP.

1. For the "statement" to which Embry undoubtedly refers, see *Philadelphia Evening Bulletin*, Feb. 9, 1866. The speech, entitled "The Assassination and Its Lessons," was apparently the same one Douglass delivered in New York City and Washington, D.C., during January and February 1866. Philip S. Foner, *Frederick Douglass* (New York, 1964 [1950]), 240–42; *Washington Evening Star*, Feb. 15, 1866.

2. William D. Kelley.

3. See Speech to First Regiment, USCT, Oct. 10, 1865, *Johnson Papers*, 9: 219–23.

4. Embry was woefully inaccurate in his assessment about the political future of both Kelley and Sumner, for Kelley continued to serve in the House until his death in 1890 and Sumner continued in the Senate until his death in 1874. *BDAC*.

5. Having lived in Washington, D.C., and New York City as well as Rhode Island, Ben-

jamin H. Cheever (b. *c*1815) was recommended for the U.S. mission to The Hague but did not receive the appointment. *NCAB*, 22: 357; 1850 Census, D.C., Washington, 2nd Ward, 211; Ser. 6A, Vol. B: 41; Ser. 6B, Vol. 2: 75, Johnson Papers, LC.

From Joseph S. Fullerton[1]

Bureau of Refugees, Freedmen and Abandoned Lands.
Washington, February 9th 1866.

In reply to your verbal request I have the honor to submit the following objections to an Act now before Congress providing for the enlargement of the powers of the Freedmens Bureau.

1st.   It is class legislation, conferring peculiar benefits on certain citizens, excluding or withholding the same from other citizens of the same locality.

2d.   I believe its provisions if carried out will be injurious to the freedman in preventing him from acquiring a position as an independent citizen. This can only be done through his own exertions; by harmonizing his interests with those of the white people of the South; and by exercising such a spirit of forbearance and moderation as will overcome the prejudices that exist against him on the part of the white race of the South.

3d.   There will be great danger of the organization becoming a political machine, thus destroying any usefulness it might otherwise have in the advancement of the interests of the freedman.

4th.   The great expense to the government of conducting the Bureau.

5th.   Objected to, because the contemplated organization is not necessary, as the interests of the freedman can be as well or better cared for by the military arm of the government, at a small expense additional to the necessary expense of supporting the Army.

The Act provides for the relief of "Freedmen and Loyal Refugees," which means that it provides for Freedmen only. There is now no such class as "Loyal Refugees." These are "catch" words which give to the Act the appearance of general legislation—Legislation for both the poor loyal whites and the blacks of the South. Had the intention been to furnish relief to the loyal whites, it would have been easy to insert the words "for relief of Freedmen & Loyal whites." When the Act, approved March 3d. 1865,—originally establishing the bureau, was passed there were a large number of persons in the border States and within the lines of our Armies who on account of their loyalty to the government, had been driven or forced to fly from their homes in the South. These persons, generally being poor and without the necessities of life, were a charge upon the Government, and such were contemplated in the legislation for "Loyal Refugees." The war has ended; the country is at peace, and all of such persons have been provided for elsewhere, or have returned to their *former homes*, So that now there is no class known as "Loyal Refugees."

After the surrender of the rebel armies, and until late in the following fall many refugees were furnished by the Commissioner of this Bureau with transportation to their homes, but none apply for such assistance now. Under the construction of this expression, the Agents of this Bureau have been instructed not to furnish supplies to the poor whites of the South, even to those who had been within the lines of our army and had returned to their homes, for they were not then "refugees." The Act then is to give relief only to "Freedmen." Commissary, Quarter master and Medical supplies are to be furnished to this class of persons; public lands are to be set apart and reserved especially for them; sights for schools and asylums, under certain conditions, are to be purchased, and special courts or tribunals are to be established for them by the Government. For the poor *loyal* whites of the South, even those who have served in our Army, there is nothing.

Aside from the fact of this being class legislation, it is such as will intensify, on the part of the poor whites of the South, the hatred that already exists between them and the blacks. This of course will be more or less disastrous to the latter class. When these poor whites realize that they have no special friends in the Bureau Agents sent south by the Government; that certain lands are not set apart for them; that Schools are not provided; that Government stores are not furnished; and that the freedman even has his special tribunals, backed by military power, where he can obtain very summary process, while they must wait for the slow and uncertain action of Civil Courts, then they will surely think that the Government intends to desert and discriminate against them, instead of raising them up from the political subjection in which they also have been held by the ruling class of the South.

As slavery has been "constitutionally" abolished the old State slave codes are now null and void, and the military force of the Government in the South, if necessary, can prevent their execution. Congress also has power under the Constitutional Amendment abolishing slavery, to enforce said amendment by appropriate legislation. Would it not be better then for Congress to pass an Act declaring all slave codes, or state laws that abridge the personal liberty of the freedmen, inoperative, and give the Agents of the government power to enforce such Act, rather than to set up an immense civil or semi-military government, within a civil government, to be placed in the hands of, in many cases, inexperienced or bad men—strangers to the people—,for the protection of a certain class in the South?

The effect of establishing the Bureau upon the basis contemplated by this Act will be, I believe, to prevent the freedman, in a great measure, from acquiring that independence and self-reliance so necessary for his advancement. The Bureau as at present organized has been in existence for nearly ten months. During this time some damage and much good has been done by its agents. By some the freedman has been told that it is necessary for him, though free, to labor and work out his own salvation; by all he has been told that he is free. He knows now that he is free and with the tuition he has received he is now much better able to take care of himself, if let alone, than is generally supposed by his friends.[2]

The bureau in its operations almost necessarily takes the place of a master. To it many of the freedmen look entirely for support, instruction and assistance. Even in those State where all civil rights have been conferred upon the freedman he does not go to the State Courts for a remedy, but to the bureau, for the process of civil law is too slow and the proceedings are not sufficiently convenient. The agents of the bureau decide for whom he shall work, for how much and when, and approve or disapprove all of his Contracts for labor. They have control in many places of his churches and schools, and some of them are endeavoring to control his finances. Special tribunals are to be organized in certain states for the trial of all cases where freedmen are concerned. Any system of Courts or Laws that look to the protection of a particular class must be objectionable and will be damaging in the end to such persons. It keeps them from endeavoring to gain admission to the state courts where they can obtain justice on the same footing as others. If we can judge from the past these courts will discriminate more against the white man than the State Courts can against the black. Some of these now in existence have been presided over by men inexperienced in law and evidence; men of strong prejudices in favor of the black men, who decide cases without reference to law, but the "right" as the right appears to them. Of course such justice is a farce, that pleases the black and exasperates the white. It is a bad plan by which to compel the people of the south to make just laws for the blacks: wholesome laws cannot be made under force. The longer these Courts remain in existence the harder it will be to give them up, and when given up the freedman, I fear, will be left in a worse condition than if they had not been established. The longer the offices of the bureau extend personal assistance to the freedman the less will he be prepared to take care of himself. Habitual dependence will prevent any class of people from making exertions for themselves.

By the too generous action of some agents of the bureau in furnishing rations & clothing many able bodied freedmen have been lost from the fields. It has been over eight months since the agents of this bureau commenced the "temporary" issue of rations. They are still issued. There appears to be no definite time when "temporary" issues shall cease, & this new act provides that such issues shall continue. There is work for all able bodied men in the South. But many will not engage in it as long as rations and clothing are furnished by the Government. The Asst. Commr. of the Bureau for North Carolina[3] told me a few days ago that there are 3000 able bodied freedmen on Roanoke Island for whom he can get employment, but they will not take it. A short time ago he cut off the temporary issue of rations to these people. They then at once became "destitute & suffering freedmen" and again had to be fed to save them from starving. Some of the philanthropists interested in the freedmen complained of his bad treatment of these people in cutting off the rations. The aged and infirm must be taken care of until the State Governments in the South are able to take care of their own poor—but they will never be able—or show a willingness to do so as long as the general government provides it for them.

An immense number of agents will be required to carry out the provisions of this act. The Army will perhaps be called upon for a small number, the rest must be citizens. There are now on file in this Bureau hundreds of applications for such appointments. The most of these are from men of the North who profess to be philanthropists and wish to work for the good of the freedman, but none of them offer to work without pay, while some are very exorbitant in their demands. The class of men seeking such places are generally those who have strong prejudices in favor of the black and against the white man of the south, and many of them wish to go into the work to carry out some political theory or hobby. Instead of harmonizing capital & labor such men will keep the whites and blacks of the south in a chronic state of hostility. A few will be unprincipled enough to create disturbances in order to prove the existence of the bureau a necessity, so that they may be retained in position with pay. As it is now we have good reason to suppose that a few local agents of the bureau send startling accounts of outrages committed against the freedmen to the press of the country for the same reason or for a political purpose. Again some of the Agents will do as is now done by a few of those at present engaged in this work, i.e take advantage of their positions to improve their finances;—such as renting plantations, and furnishing freedmen laborers to planters for a consideration.

It is true that the appointment of agents of the bureau must be made by your Excellency and the Commissioner. But it will be impossible for you to know much of the many applicants for position. When hundreds are to be appointed many bad men will slip in, and many who will come well recommended will not be able to stand the pecuniary & political temptations to which they will be subjected. It has been admitted to me by some of the warmest friends of the Act that the success of the bureau will depend entirely upon the character of its employees. The increase of its powers and agents is then a dangerous experiment. If the law has not inherent power to prevent evil some new law or remedy should be sought. I believe it to be impossible to have a majority of the agents—selected as they must be—good men. If then the Bureau is not a success it will be much worse for the freedman than if it had never been in existance.

It is almost certain that in certain localities the organization would become a political machine. Already there has been an example of this in the State of Louisiana, notwithstanding the Commissioner had given direct and positive orders against such an abuse of the institution. In such cases the true interest of the freedman would be neglected, to teach him political theories, at present impractical or impolitic, that will insure his enmity towards the white and the whites towards him—thus widening the breach that exists between them.

Another objection to the Act is the great expense that it will Entail upon the Government. Under the Act approved March 3d 1865, organizing the bureau, no appropriation of funds was made. Agents therefore had to be detailed from the Army, and the Hon. Secy. of War furnished all needful QrMaster & Commissary supplies. No person can complain that the freedman has not received sufficient attention and assistance from the bureau up to the present time. Yet it is proposed to increase the institution largely, and the expenses to an enormous amount. The estimate for funds made by the Commissioner for the coming year was not made for the expenses necessary under the Act now under consideration & is therefore not a criterion for the amt. that will be required.[4]

In reference to confirming the posessary titles that the freedmen have to the Estates on the Sea Islands I have only to say that there are legal objections which will present themselves. I am sure that some of the good lawyers who voted in favor of the Act were aware of this fact, or they would have confirmed them forever—as Gen Shermans order provides —instead of for three years.[5] There is no doubt but that the freedmen will remain, under this Act, in posession for three years, for it will take that length of time to bring the matter to a trial and decission in the U.S. Supreme Court. I believe it will be injurious to the freedmen to confirm their posession beyond the time for gathering their present crops, unless confirmed forever.

The freedmen can be better cared for, so far as the government should extend assistance, by the Military Authorities than in any other way: and this at a very small expense additional to the expense of supporting the troops in the south. If the head of the bureau, as at present, is in the War Department and issues orders and instructions from there, and then the officers and subalterns of the army are made ex-officio members of the bureau—or better, if its made part of their military duty to have general supervision of the freedmen, as they have of other persons where civil law is inoperative, the system would be much simplified, a large expense would be saved, and great good could be done. These military agents would be obliged to carry out the orders of the head of the bureau, and they would have the power to do so. They would have no political, selfish, or pecuniary designs to carry out. They would have no desire to promote strife between the whites and blacks, and both of these classes having confidence in them would advance in their interests and become reconciled to the situation. They will have no object to desire the continuance of the bureau longer than its existence is actually demanded in order that they may receive a support, for their offices would still continue.

The objection that some will offer to this proposition will be that the armies are being mustered out & there will not be material enough left for Agents of the bureau. But the Act in providing for a large number of Agents also provides, in Section 2., that the "President of the United States, through the War Department and the Commissioner, shall extend military jurisdiction and protection over all employees, agents and offices of this bureau in the exercise of the duties imposed or authorized by this act, or the act to which this is additional."

If there are enough officers & men in the Military service to extend such protection to the employees &c, surely there are enough to attend, as agents, to the requirements of the Bureau.

J. S. Fullerton   Bv. Brig. Genl. Vols.

ALS, DLC-JP.
   1. Fullerton a few months earlier had been the acting head of the Freedmen's Bureau in Louisiana.
   2. Here Fullerton crossed out a paragraph in which he declared that at the close of the war the freedman was "taken care of and protected by the Government," but that now "he should be allowed to take care of himself" with the government standing by "merely to see that he is protected in his liberty."
   3. Eliphalet Whittlesey (1821–1909), a college professor, served on General Howard's staff before becoming assistant commissioner of the Freedmen's Bureau in North Carolina. By May 1866 he was relieved because of mistreatment of blacks in his district. Hunt and Brown, *Brigadier Generals*; William S. McFeely, *Yankee Stepfather: General O. O. Howard and the Freedmen* (New York, 1968), 78–82; Paul S. Peirce, *The Freedmen's Bureau* (New York, 1971 [1904]), 173.
   4. Three days later, Fullerton, in a detailed financial estimate, stated his belief that the Bureau could not function "for less than twenty millions of dollars per annum." Consequently, Johnson, in his veto of the Bureau, said that double the $11,745,000 appropriation asked for would be needed. Fullerton to Johnson, Feb. 12, 1866, Johnson Papers, LC.
   5. Sherman's Special Field Orders No. 15, January 16, 1865. See Sherman to Johnson, Feb. 2, 1866.

From Ulysses S. Grant[1]

Washington, D.C., Feby. 9th 1866

Sir:

Referring to the Resolutions of the Legislature of Mississippi[2] requesting the withdrawal of Federal troops from that State, &c., referred by yourself to me, I have the honor to remark that the condition of things in the State of Mississippi, does not warrant the belief that the civil authorities of that State "*are amply sufficient*" to execute the laws and good order. When however the civil authorities prove themselves amply sufficient to fairly and justly execute the laws among all her citizens and to perpetuate their loyalty, the troops will not be permitted to interfere in civil matters.

No action is deemed necessary upon the affidavits submitted.

[Ulysses S. Grant]   Lieutenant General

LBcopy, DNA-RG108, Lets. Recd., Let. Bk. C, No. 83 (1865).
   1. The editors of the Grant Papers believe that this letter was probably never sent. Simon, *Grant Papers*, 16: 53.

2. On November 8, 1865, the Mississippi legislature, noting that their state officers had been "elected, and regularly installed," declared that the civil authorities "are amply sufficient to execute the laws, and to perpetuate the loyalty of the citizens." Therefore there was "no further necessity" for federal troops; the legislators requested Johnson to withdraw the soldiers. The resolutions had been referred to General Grant's office in late December. Resolutions from the Mississippi Legislature, Nov. 8, 1865, Johnson Papers, LC.

From Edward Bates

St. Louis Mo.   Feb. 10, 1866

Sir,

Perhaps I do but aggravate my offence, in presuming to write to you, a second time, when my first letter has never been recognized, perhaps never seen by you.[1] But I am constrained by considerations far higher than any personal vanity of my own, or any mere forms of courtesy due to a great magistrate whom I respect & honor.

I am past seventy years old, & in very bad health,[2] & therefore, beyond the reach of all the hopes & fears which commonly, actuate the conduct of men engaged in the strifes of party politics. I belong to no political party, now in existence, & sympahise with no political organization but that which was ordained by the constitution, & which lives & moves & has its being *only* in, under & according to that fundamental law. And I have no respect for either the judgment or the patriotism of any man whose prurient vanity is strong enough to make him believe that he is justified in attempting to do good to his country, in ways forbidden by that fundamental law. I believe, undoubtingly, that if our government be, in any respect, better than the government of any civilized country in Europe, it is only because it is a government of *law*, & not of the *will* of those who happen, for the time being, to be in places of power, whether as Kings, or Presidents or Congressmen.

I believe that the constitution, if reverently preserved, obeyed & acted out in practice, will insure the stability & continuance of the government, & the liberty & prosperity of the people. And I believe, as confidently, that, if the constitution be, habitually, broken & despised, by men in office, the Government will lose all hold upon the affection & respect of the people, & will become weak, irregular & arbitrary, fluctuating, from day to day, with the changing passions of men & factions.

I am aware sir (& the fact grieves me deeply) that since your accession to legal power, you have been constrained, by the novelties & difficulties of your situation, to give your apparent sanction to certain arbitrary measures of government dangerous alike to the liberty of individuals & to the supremacy of the laws of the land. I mean the use of *military commissions*, instead of *Courts* established & regulated by law, to try & punish supposed criminals. I do not allege this as a designed wrong on your part, for I know full well, how you have been misled into that unhappy position. I know that there are men connected with the government who affect to believe (& boldly preach it for doctrine) that *the military* is a separate, independent power in the state—in fact, a government in itself, with authority to constitute courts, & administer penal justice, at its own pleasure, & without any subordination to the written laws of the country! Such men pretend to believe, & teach it openly, that the commander of the army (that is the President) has legitimate power, at his own discretion, & by his mere declaration, to annul the constitution & the statutes, & establish his own will in their stead!

Mr President, I will not trouble you with argument upon this great theme, involving, as it does, the liberty & laws of a nation, on the one side, & upon the other side, the power & passions of a despot; but content myself with remarking that whoever has read the constitution *must know* that "the military" is only one branch or instrument of that "Executive Power" which, by the terms of the constitution, is vested in the President. That *the military* is always & every where, under the command of the President; & that the President himself, is always, every where, & under all possible circumstances, under the command of the constitution. That in fact, if there be, in the nation, any one man who, more than any other man, is the bound servant of the Constitution, that man is the President.

I have spoken freely of what has been done since you came to the Presidency, which in my judgment, is contrary to the constitution & dangerous to liberty & law. I suppose that those wrongs were done, not because you actively approved them, but because, (then fresh in office & surrounded with untried obstacles) you could not at once, perceive that you held in your official hand, the legal means of preventing or curing the evil. And now Sir, I will speak with equal freedom of the altered state of affairs, & of what every law-loving patriot in the nation hopes & expects at your hands. We believe that you are a patriot—an earnest, sincere brave man—determined to fulfill all the legal duties of your station "as you understand them." And that thought gives me great comfort; for I do not doubt that you are armed with all the legal powers which are necessary to maintain the established government, by preserving, protecting & defending the constitution & taking care that the laws be faithfully executed, against all the efforts of a desperate faction, which seems, for the present, to dominate both Houses of Congress, &, in its eagerness to clutch all power into its own hands, has cast off even the outward show of respect for the Constitution. And, having these lawful powers in your own hand, I will not allow myself to doubt that you will use them efficiently, for the public good; for I know you to be too good a constitutional lawyer to suppose that official powers may be treated as *privileges*, & waived at pleasure. The powers of the President do not belong to him, as an individual. They are granted to him *officially* & for the sole purpose of enabling him to perform his duties.

As I write this letter only in the exercise of what I suppose to be my right, as a citizen, & not in the character of a counsellor, whose advice has been asked, I will not obtrude upon you my opinions, in detail, upon the special matters which are now so recklessly thrust upon you & the nation. Nor will I dwell, at any great length, upon the coarse insolence with which you & your benign policy towards the southern states, have been treated in Congress. A leading member of the House has, in effect, denied your official existence, & assumed to consider you an alien & a stranger, by declaring that "The state of Tennessee is not known to this House or to Congress!"[3] A prominent senator has introduced a bill to degrade the states which you have invited to resume their constitutional positions in the Union, by ruling them as so much conquered territory, subject to the arbitrary power of Congress.[4] And both houses have recently passed a bill requiring you, in flat contradiction of your constitutional duty "to extend *military jurisdiction* over all employe's, agents & officers" of the freedman's bureau, & to "extend *military protection &* *jurisdiction* over all cases affecting such persons" as are discriminated against by state laws.[5] And the same bill also provides (without any reference to the intermediate or conflicting authority of the President, the war Department, the chief Freedman of the bureau, or the Courts of law) that "it shall be the duty of the *officers & agents* of this bureau (all & each one of them, of course) *to take jurisdiction*, of, & to *hear and determine all offences* committed against the provisions of this section (8); & also of *all cases* affecting negros, mulattos, freedmen, refugees or *other persons* who are discriminated against, in any of the particulars mentioned in the preceeding section of this act!"

I shall not weary you sir, with comments upon these legislative monstrosities. But I cannot forbear to remark that the faction which now domineers over the two houses of Congress, is itself, not only utterly regardless of the constitution, but is, apparently, determined to force you to be an accomplice in their crime. And that is not all: They will degrade you, if they can, by forcing you to recant & falsify the wisest & best measures which you have yet devised, for the good of your country & your own historic fame.

These are not new opinions of mine. They were formed long ago—before the Radical leaders had dared to declare open war against you & the constitution. And to show this I will close the present writing with an extract from a private letter written by me, as long ago as last September,[6] in answer to an eminent friend in Pennsylvania.

The extract—

You express the opinion that "a split between the Administration & the Radicals is inevitable." I suppose so; & that split may be very formidable if the Radicals be still allowed by the Administration to give tone & direction to all or any of the Departments, whereby the Government is, every day, committed to Radical enormities, & thereby pledged against law & truth. But, if we really have *an administration* (& not seven or eight distinct Departmental Governments, each one scheming for its own ends), if President Johnson will assume what lawfully belongs to him—the headship of the nation the actual control of *an administration* all of whose parts are required to operate harmoniously, for the attainment of *one* great end—the restoration of the Union, with peace & order—& by *one* great means, the strict observance of the constitution—if, I say, the President will only do this, &, with a fixed resolution & a steady hand, perform all his own duties *according to law*, he will have small cause to fear the Radicals. All the honest men among them (& I suppose there may be some) will willingly acquiesce in a course so manifestly just & right; all the timid, the trimmers, the timeservers, (which I take to be the bulk of the Radical faction), will hasten to give in their adhesion, rather than renounce all hope of power & patronage for the next three years. And as for the few truculent leaders who (like the frogs we read of) hoped, by bellowing & blowing, to pass themselves off for bullocks—they have no substance in them, & may be trodden out, like so many sparks on the floor.

It was much easier *then* than *now*, to serve the country by putting down that faction; for then they had not fully organized their conspiracy against the constitution, nor marshalled all their powers for mischief. But the good end can be accomplished, as effectually, now as then, & by the sam simple means—the strict observance of the constitution & the faithful execution of the laws.

Edwd. Bates

ALS, DLC-JP.
   1. Bates probably refers here to his letter to Johnson of April 15, 1865. *Johnson Papers*, 7: 555.
   2. Bates, nearly seventy-three years old, had been seriously ill since the summer of 1865, probably with the lung affliction that eventually caused his death in 1869. Marvin R. Cain, *Lincoln's Attorney General: Edward Bates of Missouri* (Columbia, 1965), 2, 324–26, 329, 333; Howard K. Beale, ed., *The Diary of Edward Bates, 1859–1866* in *Annual Report of the American Historical Association, 1930* (Washington, 1933), 491–570 passim.
   3. See Thaddeus Stevens's speech of December 12, 1865, *Congressional Globe*, 39 Cong., 1 Sess., p. 31.
   4. On January 10, 1866, Sen. Timothy O. Howe introduced the measure referred to by Bates. Ibid., pp. 162–70.
   5. The Freedmen's Bureau bill.
   6. According to an earlier edited version, the Bates letter was written on September 24, 1865. To whom it was sent is not revealed. Duane Mowry, ed., "Letters of Edward Bates and the Blairs from the Private Papers of Senator Doolittle," *MoHR*, 11 (1917): 124–25.

From George Crook

Washington City D.C.   February 10th 1866

I have the honor to make the following statement in behalf of Mr. John T. Peirce,[1] who is desirous of availing himself of the benefits of your Amnesty Proclamation of the 23d of May 1865. It was my fortune to see a good deal of Mr. Peirce when I was a prisoner of war in 1865.[2] From his universal kind treatment of us, the sentiments he expressed & the general character which I have heard responsible persons give him, who know him, I have no hesitancy in saying that I believe he would conscientiously observe any obligations under which he might bind himself.[3]

George Crook   Brevt Brig. Gen. U.S.A.

ALS, DNA-RG94, Amnesty Papers (M1003, Roll 72), W. Va., John T. Peerce.

1. Peerce (c1818–fl1884), a native of Hampshire County, Virginia, and a farmer of substantial means, had applied for executive amnesty seven months earlier. Enlisting in 1861 in the 7th Va. Cav., he spent most of the war on detached duty with a band of partisan rangers which operated in the vicinity of the south branch of the Potomac. 1860 Census, Va., Hampshire, Ridgeville, 171; Peerce, "Capture of a Railroad Train," *Southern Bivouac*, 2 (1884): 352–55; Peerce to Johnson, July 13, 1865, Amnesty Papers (M1003, Roll 72), W. Va., John T. Peerce, RG94, NA.

2. While in command of the Department of West Virginia, Crook and his immediate subordinate, Benjamin F. Kelley, were apprehended in February 1865 at their headquarters in Cumberland, Maryland, by Jesse C. McNeill's partisan rangers. The generals were sent to Richmond, where they remained in Libby Prison until both were paroled on March 14 and officially exchanged the following week. According to a number of eyewitness accounts, Peerce, who did not participate in the actual capture of the generals, had only minimal contact with Crook and Kelley and saw them only while they were being transported to Richmond. Warner, *Blue*; *OR*, Ser. 1, Vol. 46, Pt. 2: 966; Pt. 3: 28, 59; J. B. Fay, "Captors of Gens. Crook and Kelley, U.S.A.," *Con Vet*, 16 (1908): 279.

3. Peerce's amnesty file contains a number of petitions signed by residents from Hampshire and neighboring counties, several of which were in his favor. Among the hundreds of signatories were former members of McNeill's Rangers, including Captain McNeill himself. Gov. Arthur I. Boreman of West Virginia, however, protested against pardoning Peerce, claiming that he "will not be a peaceable or useful citizen" and that during the war he had "conducted himself more like a guerilla than a regular soldier." Nevertheless, Johnson granted Peerce a pardon on April 6, 1866, primarily on the recommendation of Crook. Amnesty Papers (M1003, Roll 72), W. Va., John T. Peerce, RG94, NA.

From William S. Hillyer[1]

New York   Feb 10, 1866

Dear Sir.

In accordance with the suggestion you did me the honor to make during my interview with you at Washington[2] I have given to the public my testimony of the status of the South.

I herewith send you a report cut from one of our dailies.[3]

If in the press of your duties you can find time to glance over it I hope it will meet the approval of your Excellency.

The soldiers of New York have determined to appeal to the people of the city to make such a demonstration of the popular sentiment in approval of your policy as will do justice to both you and them.

Ninetenths of the people of this city heartily endorse your opinions and actions.

As soon as proper arrangements can be made a meeting will be held at Cooper Institute which will represent the intelligence and patriotism of the city regardless of party.[4]

I wish you would add your request to ours that Gens Grant and Sherman will be present.

The meeting will be held under the auspices of the veterans of the War.

Wm. S. Hillyer
52 East 15th St   New York City

ALS, DLC-JP.

1. A former staff officer of General Grant's, Hillyer (1830–1874) was later appointed by Johnson as an internal revenue agent in New York and Brooklyn. Hunt and Brown, *Brigadier Generals; House Reports*, 40 Cong., 1 Sess., No. 7, p. 852 (Ser. 1314).

2. Hillyer had met with Johnson for two hours on or about February 1 in company with General Grant. Ibid., 845.

3. Not found, but the excerpt probably was a condensed version of Hillyer's February 9 speech during which he discussed his recent tour of Alabama, Mississippi, and Tennessee. Supposedly, Johnson had requested Hillyer to make the speech, in part to counter Carl Schurz's unfavorable reports. Ibid., 845, 853–54; *New York Herald*, Feb. 10, 1866.

4. Hillyer may be alluding here to the forthcoming February 22 meeting of New York Democrats and Republicans, which would feature speeches by Johnson cabinet members Seward and Dennison. Or perhaps he refers to a planned "general demonstration" by the United Service Society, comprised of the "soldiers of New York," which soon memorialized the President, thus becoming, according to Hillyer, the "first political party" to endorse the Johnson administration. Ibid., Feb. 10, 23, 1866; Van Deusen, *Seward*, 443; Hillyer to Johnson, June 14, 22, 1866, Appts., Customs Service, Naval Officer, New York, William S. Hillyer, RG56, NA. See William H. Seward to Johnson and Thurlow Weed to Johnson, both Feb. 23, 1866.

Response to Virginia Legislative Delegation[1]

[Washington, February 10, 1866][2]

In reply, gentlemen, to the resolutions you have just presented to me, and the clear and forcible and concise remarks which you have made in explanation of the position of Virginia, I shall not attempt to make a formal speech, but simply enter into a plain conversation in regard to the condition of things in which we stand.

As a premise to what I may say, permit me first to tender you my thanks for this visit, and next to express the gratification I feel in meeting so many intelligent, responsible, and respectable men of Virginia, bearing to me the sentiments which have been expressed in the resolutions of your Legislature, and in the remarks accompanying them.

They are, so far as they refer to the Constitution of the country, the sentiments and the principles embraced in that charter of the Government. The preservation of the Union has been, from my entrance into public life, one of my cardinal tenets. At the very incipiency of this rebellion I set my face against the dissolution of the Union of the States. I do not make this allusion for the purpose of bringing up anything which has transpired which may be regarded as of an unkind or unpleasant character; but I believed then, as I believe now, and as you have most unmistakably indicated, that the security and the protection of the rights of all the people were to be found in the Union; that we were certainly safer in the Union than we were out of it.

Upon this conviction I based my opposition to the efforts which were made to destroy the Union. I have continued those efforts, notwithstanding the perils through which I have passed, and you are not unaware that the trial has been a severe one. When opposition to the Government came from one section of the country, and that the section in which my life had been passed, and with which my interests were identified, I stood, as I stand now, contending for the Union and asseverating that the best and surest way to obtain our rights and to protect our interests was to remain in the Union, under the protection of the Constitution.

The ordeal through which we have passed during the last four or five years demonstrates most conclusively that that opposition was right; and to-day, after the experiment has been made and has failed; after the demonstration has been most conclusively afforded that this Union cannot be dissolved, that it was not designed to be dissolved, it is extremely gratifying to me to meet gentlemen as intelligent and as responsible as yourselves, who are willing and anxious to accept and do accept the terms laid down in the Constitution and obedience to the laws made in pursuance thereof.

We were at one period separated; the separation was to me painful in the extreme; but now, after having gone through a struggle in which the powers of the Government have been tried, when we have swung around to a point at which we meet to agree and are willing to unite our efforts for the preservation of the Government, which I believe is the best in the world, it is exceedingly gratifying to me to meet you to-day, standing upon common ground, rallying around the Constitution and the Union of these States, the preservation of which, as I conscientiously and honestly believe, will result in the promotion and the advancement of this people.

I repeat, I am gratified to meet you to-day, expressing the principles and announcing the sentiments to which you have given utterance, and I trust that the occasion will long be remembered. I have no doubt that your intention is to carry out and comply with every single principle laid down in the resolutions you have submitted. I know that some are distrustful; but I am of those who have confidence in the judgment, in the integrity, in the intelligence, in the virtue of the great mass of the American people; and having such confidence, I am willing to trust them, and I thank God that we have not yet reached that point where we have lost all confidence in each other.

The spirit of the Government can only be preserved, we can only become prosperous and great as a people, by mutual forbearance and confidence. Upon that faith and that confidence alone can the Government be successfully carried on.

On the cardinal principle of representation to which you refer, I will make a single remark. That principle is inherent; it constitutes one of the fundamental elements of this Government. The representatives of the States and of the people should have the qualifications prescribed by the Constitution of the United States, and those qualifications most unquestionably imply loyalty. He who comes as a representative, having the qualifications prescribed by the Constitution to fit him to take a seat in either of the deliberative bodies, which constitute the National Legislature, must necessarily, according to the intendment of the Constitution, be a loyal man, willing to abide by and be devoted to the Union and the Constitution of the States. He cannot be for the Constitution, he cannot be for the Union, he cannot acknowledge obedience to all the laws, unless he is loyal. When the people send such men in good faith, they are entitled to representation through them.

In going into the recent rebellion or insurrection against the Government of the United States we erred, and in returning and resuming our relations with the Federal Government, I am free to say that all the responsible positions and places ought to be confined distinctly and clearly to men who are loyal. If there were only five thousand loyal men in a State, or a less number, but sufficient to take charge of the political machinery of a State, those five thousand men, or the lesser number, are entitled to it, if all the rest should be otherwise inclined. I look upon it as being fundamental that the exercise of political power should be confined to loyal men, and I regard that as implied in the doctrines laid down in these resolutions, and in the eloquent address by which they have been accompanied. I may say, furthermore, that after having passed through the great struggle in which we have been engaged, we should be placed upon much more acceptable ground in resuming all our relations to the General Government if we presented men unmistakably and unquestionably loyal to fill the places of power. This being done, I feel that the day is not distant—I speak confidingly in reference to the great mass of the American people—when they will determine that this Union shall be made whole, and the great right of representation in the councils of the nation be acknowledged.

Gentlemen, that is a fundamental principle. "No taxation without representation" was one of the principles which carried us through the Revolution. This great principle will hold good yet; and if we but perform our duty; if we but comply with the spirit of the resolutions presented to me to-day, the American people will maintain and sustain the great doctrines upon which the Government was inaugurated. It can be done, and it will be done; and I think that if the effort be fairly and fully made, with forbearance and with prudence, and with discretion and wisdom, the end is not very far distant.

It seems to me apparent that from every consideration the best policy which could be adopted at present would be a restoration of these States and of the Government upon correct principles. We have some foreign difficulties, but the moment it can be announced that the Union of the States is again complete, that we have resumed our career of prosperity and greatness, at that very instant, almost, all our foreign difficulties will be settled, for there is no power upon the earth which will care to have a controversy or a rupture with the Government of the United States under such circumstances.

If these States be fully restored, the area for the circulation of the national currency, which is thought by some to be inflated to a very great extent, will be enlarged, the number of persons through whose hands it is to pass will be increased, the quantity of commerce in which it is to be employed as a medium of exchange will be enlarged; and then it will begin to approximate, what we all desire, a specie standard. If all the States were restored—if peace and order reigned throughout the land, and all the industrial pursuits, all the avocations of peace were again resumed— the day would not be far distant when we could put into the commerce of the world $250,000,000 or $300,000,000 worth of cotton and tobacco, and the various products of the Southern States, which would constitute in part a basis of this currency.

Then, instead of the cone being inverted, we should reverse the position, and put the base at the bottom, as it ought to be, and the currency of the country will rest on a sound and enduring basis; and surely that is a result which is calculated to promote the interests not only of one section, but of the whole country from one extremity to the other. Indeed, I look upon the restoration of these States as being indispensable to all our greatness.

Gentlemen, I know nothing further that I could say in the expression of my feelings on this occasion—and they are not affected—more than to add that I shall continue in the same line of policy which I have pursued from the commencement of the rebellion to the present period. My efforts have been to preserve the Union of the States. I never, for a single moment, entertained the opinion that a State could withdraw from the Union of its own will. That attempt was made. It has failed. I continue to pursue the same line of policy which has been my constant guide. I was against dissolution. Dissolution was attempted; it has failed; and now I cannot take the position that a State which attempted to secede is out of the Union, when I contend all the time that it could not go out, and that it never has been out. I cannot be forced into that position. Hence, when the States and their people shall have complied with the requirements of the Government, I shall be in favor of their resuming their former relations to this Government in all respects.

I do not intend to say anything personal, but you know as well as I do that at the beginning, and, indeed, before the beginning of the recent gigantic struggle between the different sections of the country, there were extreme men South, and there were extreme men North. I might make use of a homely figure, (which is sometimes as good as any other, even in the illustrations of great and important questions,) and say that it has been hammer at one end of the line and anvil at the other; and this great Government, the best the world ever saw, was kept upon the anvil and hammered before the rebellion, and it has been hammered since the rebellion; and there seems to be a disposition to continue the hammering until the Government shall be destroyed. I have opposed that system always, and I oppose it now.

The Government, in the assertion of its powers and in the maintenance of the principles of the Constitution, has taken hold of one extreme, and with the strong arm of physical power has put down the rebellion. Now, as we swing around the circle of the Union with a fixed and unalterable determination to stand by it, if we find the counterpart or the duplicate of the same spirit that played to this feeling and these persons in the South, this other extreme which stands in the way must get out of it, and the Government must stand unshaken and unmoved on its basis. The Government must be preserved.

I will only say, in conclusion, that I hope all the people of this country, in good faith and in the fullness of their hearts, will, upon the principles which you have enunciated here to-day, of the maintenance of the Constitution and the preservation of the Union, lay aside every other feeling for the good of our common country, and with uplifted faces to Heaven swear that our gods and our altars and all shall sink in the dust together rather than this glorious Union shall not be preserved. ⟨Great applause.⟩

I am gratified to find the loyal sentiment of the country developing and manifesting itself in these expressions; and now that the attempt to destroy the Government has failed at one end of the line, I trust we shall go on determined to preserve the Union in its original purity against all opposers.

I thank you, gentlemen, for the compliment you have paid me, and respond most cordially to what has been said in your resolutions and address, and I trust in God the time will soon come when we can meet under more favorable auspices than we do now.[3]

Washington Morning Chronicle, Feb. 11, 1866.
1. A delegation of eight members of the current Virginia legislature met with Johnson to present resolutions passed by that body. John B. Baldwin (1820–1873), a lawyer and former member of the Confederate Congress, served as the spokesman for the group. Baldwin read the resolutions to the President and then made a brief speech in which he declared Virginia's acquiescence in the union of the states, in the overthrow of slavery, in devotion to the policies of the federal administration, and in Johnson's position as defender of the Constitution. Washington Morning Chronicle, Feb. 11, 1866; Ezra J. Warner and Wilfred Buck Yearns, Biographical Register of the Confederate Congress (Baton Rouge, 1975).
2. Both the place and date of this meeting are supplied by the newspaper accounts.
3. After Johnson completed his remarks, Baldwin once again briefly addressed the President in order to introduce his colleagues. Upon completion of that, Johnson made some informal comments in which he expressed his pleasure at meeting the Virginia legislators, referred to his longtime political career, and committed himself anew to the restoration of the states (the fulfillment of his ambitions). Washington Morning Chronicle, Feb. 11, 1866.

From Virginia C. Clay

Washington city, D.C.   Feby. 11th 1866.
My dear Sir:

Burdened as you are, with the responsibility of a nation's welfare, and minor cares and perplexations "Thick as leaves in Vallambrosa"[1] pressing upon you, I deeply regret the addition of a feather's weight. But, "Necessity Knows no law"—and you are, in my case, unhappily, the victim of its Lawlessness. But I have been the tortured victim of far more lawlessness than even *"military* necessity" required, in my opinion, *one* item of which, I beg now to present to you for redress.

Since the surrender of Gen Lee, & the "so-called" restoration of Peace, I have been *four* several times thoroughly searched—three times by written authority from the War Department, and once by a band of ruffians, who *said* they were sent by order of Majr. Gen. Wilson,[2] Comdg. at Macon.

In August last, my father's house in Huntsville, (Gov. Clay's) was invaded; & every book-case; desk, drawer, escritoir and trunk rifled of its contents. This plunderer, (Col. or Gen. Baker,[3] so-called) then went to Macon, where he learned I was sojourning, and thoroughly scanned & scoured the contents of five pieces of baggage, containing; all my earthly possessions. These, he left thrown "in most admired disorder," over a room 20 ft. square. He came without Key or lock-smith, *and* was only deterred from breaking the locks by the earnest entreaties of my friends, (for fortunately, or unfortunately, I was absent) who beguiled him into a momentary delay, while one was summoned. He bore off a mail-bag of printed & written matter much of it prior to the revolution;—and not *only that*, but my *private diary* and some books, (one of poems;), & insisted on including the *pictures* of my dead child, and other members of my family. These, I presume he wanted for speculation, but in consideration of the amazement & indignant expostulation of my friends they were finally spared. He exhibited much elation in his rarely privileged task of beholding & manipulating a *lady's* trunks, gloating his Eyes & indulging his tongue in remarks of sublimated coarseness & insolence.

He was deeply moved to find "none of the destitution spoken of in the South in Mrs. Clay's case"—and while admiring the style & finish of sundry articles "not to be mentioned to ears polite,"[4]—deprecated they should still be mine! In short, his whole manner, and *criticism*, during the refreshing operation, (enhanced as it was, by several fragrant Havanas[)] was such as to force the opinion on those present that he had certainly served longer as apprentice to a second-rate mantau-maker or saleswoman than—a *Vidocq*.[5]

It took me a week to repack, when I left for Huntsville, to find, on arrival, that he had insulted my aged parents, (to whom he was presented by our former dining-room man-servant) ransacked their house & departed.

Gen. Croxton[6] to whom I applied for protection in Macon, gave an exemption, co-extensive with his command, & other Generals followed suit—else, I would doubtless have suffered like indignity—at every wood-station & water-tank "en route."

This correspondence, now pleaded for, had been secured at the burning of my house and is the only remaining tangible link now binding me to the Past. All the letters left me from my husband, immediately preceding & succeeding our marriage were taken; all his effusions in Poetry, (to *me*, GEMS) all the communications from those nearest & dearest by blood & affinity—for years past, were remorselessly swept in, & borne off by this official Cormorant to the gaping eyes and heartless scorn of enemies, whose warmest look for me & mine, is cold as the glitter from a serpent's scales. In short, Mr. Johnson, the sanctity of my stricken heart was suddenly & ruthlessly invaded,—every chamber of it desecrated by his insensate touch,—and every idol removed from its hallowed niche, to be exposed to this victor's gaze, *literally*, "bruised monuments" hung up in the Temple of War!

But they are still the precious & sacred ashes from off the altar of my heart,—and tho' "*I* am ashes where once I was fire,"[7] I desire to reclaim them if only to scatter!

As they have been retained quite six months, at the mercy of all who behold them and long Enough to have Served the purpose desired by the Dept. (if possible,) I beg their return. To the Dept. useless, to me, invaluable—grant my request. The Sec: of War, to whom I spoke, relative to them, two months since, promised them, but his promise is unredeemed.

The Judge Av: Gener'l[8] to whom I wrote, a month ago, asking to see his Report in my husband's case, (if any,) and also the return of my correspondence, *diary* etc. (then in his possession) has neither deigned to acknowledge or reply to my communication. It was the third time he had been honored by missives from me—and the last!

Trusting now, Sir to you, for Justice,—and with sincerest wishes for your entire success as the great Peacemaker, the great physician of a nation's ills, allow me Sir, to subscribe myself,

V. C. Clay.

At Mr. Geo: Parkers[9]   Cor. 4½ & C. Streets.

ALS, DLC-JP.
  1. Derived from John Milton, *Paradise Lost*, bk. 1, line 302.
  2. James H. Wilson.
  3. See Order to Lafayette C. Baker, Aug. 7, 1865, *Johnson Papers*, 8: 542.
  4. Adapted from Alexander Pope, *Moral Essays*, epistle 4, line 149.
  5. Probably a reference to Eugène Francois Vidouq (1775–1857), longtime chief of the French detective police in Paris. *NUC*.
  6. John T. Croxton.
  7. From Lord Byron, "To the Countess of Blessington."
  8. Joseph Holt.
  9. George Parker (*c*1804–1876) was a wealthy Pennsylvania Avenue grocer. 1860 Census, D.C., Washington, 4th Ward, 290; Douglass Zevely, "Old Houses on C Street and Those Who Lived There," *Records CHS*, 5 (1902): 163.

From William T. Sherman

Head Quarters Military Division of the Mississippi,
Saint Louis, Mo   Feb 11 1865.[1866][1]

Sir,

I owe you a personal apology for not calling again to pay my respects before leaving the Capitol. I had the honor of a personal interview, and attended two of your General receptions[2] and on all occasions saw enough to satisfy me that it would be doing you a kindness not to intrude unless in case of business, of which I had none.

Without pretending to represent you I endeavored to impress upon all Senators and Representatives, with whom I conversed, that the extreme Radical measures of Sumner & Stevens were calculated to lead to a result that even they ought not to desire viz the everlasting estrangement of all the People of the South, and more over that you as Chief Executive, who have ample means for correct knowledge, should be allowed in your own way to bring about what must obtain, the restoration of our system of Government in all parts of our National Territory. In the end I know you must succeed, for this result is desired heartily by the Great masses of our People, regardless of the noisy innovations of mere theorists and experimental Legislators. I will continue to use what little influence I possess to the same end, and beg to assure your Excellency that I will continue to serve you in any way you choose to command or suggest.

I shall always bear in honorable remembrance your personal expression that you will feel that you have fulfilled your highest ambition, when you complete the entire pacification of our Country by restoring all its parts to the enjoyment of its privileges and protection, and add my absolute faith in your success, because you will be sustained by Natural Laws, that mischievous men may delay but not prevent.

You will pardon me I hope for expressing my earnest wish that you will not only succeed in this, but that by a renewal of the term of office you may perpetuate the Peace that you have done so much already to secure.[3]

W. T. Sherman   Maj Genl.

ALS, DLC-JP.

1. Although clearly dated 1865, internal evidence as well as subsequent correspondence indicate that the correct date for the document is 1866.

2. Sherman and his wife were among the many guests who attended receptions at the Executive Mansion on January 26 and 30, 1866. The date of his interview with the President, however, is unknown. *National Intelligencer*, Jan. 27, 1866; *Washington Morning Chronicle*, Jan. 31, 1866.

3. Months later Johnson requested permission from Sherman to publish this letter and sought Grant's advice in the matter. Speculation by the press regarding the alleged contents of Sherman's letter, coupled with the general's recall to Washington in October 1866, fueled rumors that Johnson would soon appoint Sherman as acting secretary of war in place of Stanton. Grant to Sherman, Oct. 18, 1866, Simon, *Grant Papers*, 16: 337–40; Thomas and Hyman, *Stanton*, 503; Rachel S. Thorndike, ed., *The Sherman Letters: Correspondence*

Between General and Senator Sherman From 1831 to 1891 (New York, 1971 [1894]), 279–80; Johnson to Sherman, Oct. 2, 1866, Tels. Sent, President, Vol. 3 (1865–68), RG107, NA.

From Thomas E. Bramlette

Executive Office   Frankfort Ky
Feby 12th 1866

Mr. President:

I transmit herewith a Resolution adopted in the House of Representatives of the General Assembly on Saturday the 10th Inst[1] with entire unanimity, together with the account taken from the Louisville Journal[2] which accompanied the Resolution. The Account in the Journal you will perceive was taken from the "Mercer Banner" published at Harrodsburg Mercer County—the scene of the outrage upon the civil authorities. I send also a copy of a letter written to me by the Sheriff who had Poor in custody.[3]

I have enquired into the case and am enabled to state that the account taken from the Journal is correct.[4]

This is but a single instance of the constantly recurring outrages committed by the Agents of the "Freedmans Bureau" upon the civil authorities and citizens of Kentucky. When it is considered that the "Freedman's Bureau" has no *legal* existence in Kentucky, and cannot be extended to Kentucky or any State having an organized civil Government in harmony with the Federal Government, the outrages become the more striking. Were it within the Constitutional powers of Congress to extend the "Freedmen's Bureau" to Ky, which I positively deny, its extension will work the ruin of the negro, as well as great injury to the citizen. But for the super-officious intermedling of Military Commandants and now the impertinent interference of the Agents of the "Freedman's Bureau," the utmost harmony would prevail between the citizens and freedmen. The Freedmen have always had protection in life liberty and property in Ky. All now being free—all have that protection by existing laws Coevil with the State. The slave code has no one to operate upon—all being free. The "Freedmans Bureau" has started forth upon a crusade against the citizen and against the civil authorities of the State.

It has already began in some localities to levy *black mail* upon both black & white.

So far as this PANDORA's BOX has been opened in Kentucky, it has been the source of evil and only evil.

It is an insult and an outrage upon our people, assuming to place Northern *Overseers* over the *Governments* and *people* of the heretofore slave states. Though the ravages of war were desolating in Kentucky they were far more tolerable than the "Freedman's Bureau"; for the reason that we bore the ravages of war in order to maintain our Government, which the "Freedman's Bureau" would overthrow with insult, outrage and plunder.

Let this *thing* be taken away from among us and we can get along harmoniously. The interests and rights of the negro will be well guarded and protected, and he will be contented and happy in receiving the reward of his labor.

If fanaticism in its implacable fury will force the "Freedman's Bureau" upon us, painful as may be the necessary course of action, we shall in self defence be compelled to adopt legislation which will compel the negro to leave Kentucky or starve. I shall, should this Pandoras Box be set up as one of the permanent institutions of the Country, convene the General Assemby in extra Session, and recommend and procure the passage of the Acts making it a high misdemeanor for any *citizen of Kentucky or white person* resident therein to *leave* or *rent any lands* or houses to; or employ in any way any negro or mulato or retain them in their service. Such an Act will not trench upon *negro rights* & *Freedman's Bureau*; but will by the prohibition of their employment remove the "Bureau" by emptying its contents upon Ohio and other States north & west.

We are willing and desirous to retain our negro population, to treat them kindly, employ them at fair wages, and secure them amply in life liberty and property; but we are not willing to take with them a "Freedman's Bureau" which places a northern fanatic as overseer over white & black, and over the Government and Civil Authorities of the State. We do not wish to be driven to such extremity, but will not hesitate when the time for self-defensive action shall come.

I have deemed it due to myself and to the people whom I represent as well as to you with whom the *people* of Kentucky are almost unanimously in harmony to make this full and clear statement of our condition and of the course which necessity may compel us to pursue as a disagreeable and painful necessity.

Tho E Bramlette   Gov of Ky

ALS, DLC-JP.

1. Enclosed was a handwritten copy of the resolution adopted by the Kentucky house, the gist of which was that William Goodloe of the Freedmen's Bureau, acting under orders from General Fisk, had taken a prisoner from the civil authorities during a trial. Furthermore, the house asked the governor to launch an inquiry into the circumstances and, in the meanwhile, to call upon the President to have both Fisk and Goodloe removed from command and to have them delivered over to Kentucky authorities to stand trial for violation of state laws.

2. Not found with the letter, the *Louisville Journal* account indicated that on February 3, Captain Goodloe, Freedmen's Bureau superintendent for a tri-county Kentucky area, entered the courthouse at Harrodsburg with a detachment of black troops and ordered that James W. Poor be remanded to the custody of military authorities. The judge consented. Poor (c1838–1905) had served in the Union army (3rd Ky. Inf.) during the war; in early February 1866 he shot a black man for which he was placed on trial. *Louisville Journal*, Feb. 10, 1866; 1860 Census, Ky., Garrad, Lancaster, 117; *Report of the Adjutant General of the State of Kentucky* (2 vols., Utica, 1984 [1866]), 1: 598–99; Pension File, James W. Poor, RG15, NA. See also *Louisville Courier*, Feb. 10, 1866.

3. The sheriff of Mercer County, Henry F. James (b. c1816), a Virginia native and a local farmer, informed Governor Bramlette that after the shooting incident Poor had been immediately taken into custody by the sheriff. James asked the governor "what to do." James to Bramlette, Feb. 3, 1866, Johnson Papers, LC; 1860 Census, Ky., Mercer, 2nd Dist., Eldorado, 96; Michael L. Cook, *Mercer County Kentucky Records* (2 vols., Evansville, 1987–88), 2: 480.

4. Evidently the incident attracted some attention beyond Kentucky's borders, for Fisk reported on the matter to General Howard. He indicated that Poor had shot and killed Peter Branford, a returned black soldier, "without cause or provocation." At about that same time, Bramlette notified the Kentucky legislature that he had received a telegram from Fisk ordering the return of Poor to civil authorities for trial. A preliminary trial was held in May, after which the judge set bail and a date in August for the actual trial of Poor. Fisk to Howard, Feb. 14, 1866, *House Ex. Docs.*, 39 Cong., 1 Sess., No. 70, p. 237 (Ser. 1256); *Louisville Journal*, Feb. 15, May 11, 1866.

From John Cochrane

New York   February 12th 1866

My Dear Sir

I think that every true friend of yours must rejoice in the publicity given by yesterdays (Sunday) Herald, to your Sentiments expressed to the Committee of the Virginia Delegate, and to a member of Congress, as conveyed by the correspondence of the Boston Advocate.[1]

There began to be great danger of your position being misunderstood by the people—and to your detriment. An uninterrupted series of claims persistently iterated by democratic presses, to your political sympathies and antecedents, began to impress the unreflecting, that your nonconcurrence with the Sumner Radicals was the signal both of your withdrawal from the Union ranks, and of your adherence to the democratic party. Such an opinion, generally held, would be as injurious as I have known that it is untrue. A more effectual *Tylerization* cannot be conceived. While resisting that process of political exhaustion, conducted and applied by the Suffrage Bills, and the Kindred measures of Radicalism, it would be strange indeed, were you to invite it in the quite as objectionable shape, of the deadly embrace of a Copperhead democracy. Your original position, is the strong and inelligible one. As the propounder & representative of the only constitutional policy, its adherents, & disciples must and will aggregate about you. These will come from old Republicans—old Whigs—old democrats. The Union party contains a large proportion of men, who will be knit together by this policy; but, from the democratic masses will prodigious accessions acrue. They must come to you. You cannot go to them. All who will "let them come." Thus will you be sustained, not only personally, but, politically you, & your policy will rest at the base of the constitutional party, now approaching consistence, and assuming shape.

I cannot but repeat how rejoiced I am that at these points you are now thoroughly understood by the people. A menacing danger has been removed, and the country sees clearly, again, that you are not the man "to fall into the hand" of men.

I have had the accompanying letter of Mr Bennetts[2] in my possession since its date. When in Washington for the purpose of delivering it, a few days after, I was unwilling farther to involve by additional solicitations the question of the New York Collectorship which just then I thought was injuriously thrust upon you. On my return I informed Mr Bennett of the fact, who assented to my presentation of it at another time. I accordingly transmit it, in evidence of his judgment on the subjects discussed.

I think that the best informed concur in thinking your delay in making the appointment of a Collector, wise.

I wrote you[3] my impression that the want of a Collectors Bond deprived the government, in fact, of no additional security.

On further enquiry I learn that I was quite right. The Collector's account *is* daily sent to Washington, is *settled* here at the Assistant Treasurers office, by balance deposited. At the end of each month, he makes requisition on Washington for an estimated sum to pay the Salaries of Clerks &c. On the day of the receipt of this credit, it is exhausted, and the sum disbursed to the clerks employees &c. You will perceive how little, if any possibility there is of a defalcation by a Collector, and consequently, how little, if any additional security, a Collector's Bond affords the government. Indeed, Bonds are no longer relied on. Vigilance, more than supplies their place, and "*Savast wonting*" is now impossible.

The daily balances in the Assistant Treasurers hands exceed his bonds by hundreds of thousands of dollars.

I will trouble our friend Hon Edward Cooper[4] to hand you this, and the accompanying letter of Mr Bennett.

John Cochrane

ALS, DLC-JP.
1. See Johnson's Further Remarks on Response to Black Delegates, February 8, and his Response to Virginia Legislative Delegation, February 10. The *Herald*'s source for the President's remarks of February 8 was actually a correspondent from the *Boston Advertiser*. *New York Herald*, Feb. 11, 1866.
2. See Bennett to Johnson, Feb. 1, 1866.
3. Cochrane to Johnson, Feb. 4, 1866.
4. Edmund Cooper.

From John B. Purcell[1]

Cincinnati   12 Feb. 1866

Sir

Allow me, I pray you, to intercede for the pardon of the unfortunate and foolish Col. St. Leger Greenfell,[2] now a prisoner at the Dry Tortugas. His four afflicted sisters, in England, acknowledge his guilt and the justice of his punishment. But, with me, they crave that justice may be tempered with mercy, in his regard. He has been severely punished in various manners. And I therefore implore that executive clemency may be extended to him.

J. B. Purcell   Archbp Cin.

ALS, DNA-RG153, Court-Martial Records, NN-3409.
1. Purcell (1800–1883) had been named bishop of Cincinnati in 1832 and then archbishop in 1850. He continued in that influential post until his retirement at the end of the 1870s amidst the scandal surrounding the failure of his trust fund or bank, administered by his brother. Before and during the Civil War, Purcell was an ardent Unionist. *DAB*.
2. George St. Leger Grenfell (1808–1868) was one of the convicted Chicago conspirators whose death sentence was commuted by Johnson in July 1865. Grenfell was sent to the prison at Dry Tortugas, from which he escaped in March 1868 but perished at sea. Archbishop Purcell and others were unsuccessful in their efforts to secure a presidential pardon for Grenfell. Stephen Z. Starr, *Colonel Grenfell's Wars: The Life of a Soldier of Fortune* (Baton Rouge, 1971), 17–325 passim; Joseph Holt to Johnson, July 29, 1865, *Johnson Papers*, 8: 315.

From Trustees of Methodist Episcopal Church, Fernandina, Florida[1]

[February 12, 1866][2]

The petition of the undersigned, residents of Fernandina, Fla, and Trustees of the Methodist Episcopal Church at that place, respectfully Sheweth:

That our church edifice at this place is held by a minister from the State of New Hampshire, and is used exclusively for persons of colour;

That a large congregation of white members are, thus deprived a place of worship, built, and rightfully owned by them;

That the members of this congregation of which your petitioners are Trustees, did project, and at their expense construct, a suitable house of worship for persons of colour, which house is by them kept vacant, notwithstanding its sufficiency for their numbers and purpose;

That there are, besides the present one applied for, *three* church edifices in the possession and use of colored persons here,[3] either of them sufficient to accommodate the fullest assemblage of such persons;

That our Ministers and members are loyal citizens, and firm supporters of your Excellency's reconstruction policy;

We therefore pray respectfully for an order from your Excellency, remanding the Edifice of the Methodist Episcopal Church in this place, to the possession and occupancy of the Trustees and congregation, for their use and benefit.[4]

Pet, DNA-RG107, Lets. Recd., Executive (M494, Roll 84).
1. The three trustees who signed this petition were: George S. Roux (c1830–fl1870), a native of Florida and a sometime commission merchant, who was appointed port collector at Fernandina in the late spring of 1866; Henry Timanus (c1815–fl1870), a Maryland native, who was a merchant in Fernandina; and T. D. Hawkins, not further identified. 1860 Census, Fla., Nassau, Fernandina, 18, 19; (1870), 41, 43; *Charleston Courier*, Aug. 1, 1866; *U.S. Off. Reg.* (1867); Ser. 6B, Vol. 4: 175, Johnson Papers, LC.

2. This date is derived from the attached certification from Fernandina's post commander, Capt. John George Hamel, 34th USCT, testifying that the applicants "are the rightfull owners of the said Church."

3. Evidently the reference here is to the Baptist, Presbyterian, and Episcopal congregations in Fernandina. See Thomas Teddy to S. S. McHenry, Apr. 10, 1866, Lets. Recd., Executive (M494, Roll 84), RG107, NA.

4. The trustees' petition was forwarded from Johnson to the secretary of war, who on March 24 acknowledged the Fernandina petition and informed the President that it had been referred to Gen. John G. Foster, commander in Florida. In early April Foster relayed the matter to Thomas W. Osborn, Freedmen's Bureau commissioner for the state, who then reported on April 16 that the churches in question would "be vacated on the 1st of May & possession granted to the claimants." Endorsements, ibid.

From James E. Wyche[1]

Walla Walla Wash. Territory
Feb 12, 1866

Dear Sir

I was east last summer and fall and called on you but as you are visited by so many I do not know that you will recall me. I visited the south and on my return to this Territory sent a communication to one of our papers which I enclose.[2] I have no business to write about but as some intensely Union men (Who if they had been in your situation at the inauguration of the rebellion would probably have gone into the rebel service) presume to question your loyalty to the Union and to the principles on which you were elected I desire to say that I believe your course a wise and patriotic one and if the whole matter of the readjustment of the Union was in your hands you would bring peace and prosperity to the whole Country at an earlier day than the policy proposed to be pursued by Congress is likely to do.

I cannot speak for public sentiment elsewhere but I believe that a large majority of the people on the Pacific Coast approve of your efforts in the work of restoration and I venture the opinion that Certain persons who seem desirous of breaking your neck are in their warfare on you quite as likely to get their own necks broken.

I do not feel that I ought to apologise for writing this letter and I feel that while you are being assailed as you now are that your friends owe you a word of approval.

With wishes for your prosperity and Success in the arduous labors of your position. . . .

J. E. Wyche
U S Judge of Wash Territory

ALS, DLC-JP.

1. Wyche (1828–1873), who served as an associate justice of the Washington Territory (1861–69), was a native of Mississippi who had moved north and was appointed to office from Michigan. Earle Connette, *Pacific Northwest Quarterly Index* (Hamden, Conn., 1964), 729; *U.S. Off. Reg.* (1861–67); Pomeroy, *The Territories*, 121–22.

2. Not found with the letter, Wyche's communication described conditions in the South as he observed them, and also made a few predictions and suggestions. *Vancouver Register*, Feb. 10, 1866.

From Jeremiah T. Boyle

Louisville City Railway Co.
Louisville, Ky.   Febry 13th 1866

Sir

I have the honor to submit to your Excellency the enclosed letter received yesterday, from one, Will P Thomasson,[1] Supt of Freedman' Beaureau, in this city, that your Excellency may see the spirit and tone and grade of capacity of the head of the Beaureau at this place.

It is evidently the purpose of this official to subject the conductors on the street cars to the humiliation of arrest, and the oppression of fine imprisonment, and costs of proceedings, for use of such silly and harmless words as, *"Let the Beaureau pass,"* ["]*Give way for the Beaureau"* &c. &c. Surely no sensible man, competent and fit, to fill so delicate a trust would for a moment think of taking action, such as is threatened, for the mere use of foolish and harmless words. It would only serve to create discontent, and excite animosities between races, and cause needless and great harm.

That there is reason to apprehend officious interference by this new official, is evident from the last clause of his letter in which he says, *"If after this notice you do not stop this blackguard practice, I will try."*

That this is the exhibition of a tyrannical spirit of a petty officer, expressed in language not very chaste, and not worthy of an official of our great goverment, I am sure your Excellency will agree. And that it exhibits a spirit of injustice and a disposition to wrong, wholly unfitting the man for the position, I believe is equally manifest.

Believing that this letter, in itself, is conclusive of the want of proper qualification and fitness for the official position he occupies, I hopefully and respectfully trust your Excellency will remove him from office and fill the position with a fitter and better man.

I beg leave to assure your Excellency that in addressing you this letter that I am influenced by no personal prejudice to the officer or to the Freedmen. I express a judgment merely on the letter; and for the Freedmen—a number of whom I emancipated in the last fifteen years—I entertain kindly and freindly sympathies and desire to see them fully protected in all their rights of person and property. I desire to see avoided anything which will superinduce animosity and hatred between the races.

It is due to the Conductors of the street cars that I should state that the printed orders of the Railway Company require that they should observe orderly and gentlemanly conduct toward all persons who are passengers on the cars, and the conductors assure me that they have so deported themselves to all persons of all classes and colors. And I believe their statements are true. That persons riding on the cars, boys on the street, &c, &c, may use such expressions as are ascribed to the conductors of the street cars may be true, but it will hardly be esteemed the duty of this officer to correct the use of such frivolous words by arrest and punishment, and fine and imprisonment, of the offenders.

I hopefully trust your Excellency will protect the citizen from the bullying tyranny and oppression of this and all other officials, by removing them from authority, and appointing wiser and more prudent and moderate men to the office.[2]

J. T. Boyle

ALS, DNA-RG105, Records of the Commr., Lets. Recd. from Executive Mansion.

1. William P. Thomasson (1797–1882), a lawyer and veteran of the War of 1812, represented Kentucky in Congress as a Whig and then practiced law in Chicago. During the war he served in the 71st N.Y. Vol. Inf., then returned to Kentucky where, on the recommendation of James Harlan, he received an appointment in the Freedmen's Bureau. Thomasson wrote to Boyle and at least one other local streetcar proprietor complaining of the verbal harassment received by blacks at the hands of conductors. *BDAC*; Thomasson to Harlan, Oct. 5, 1865, Records of the Commr., Lets. Recd. (M752, Roll 24), RG105, NA; Thomasson to Boyle and Thomasson to Isham Henderson, both Feb. 12, 1866, Records of the Commr., Lets. Recd. from Executive Mansion, RG105, NA.

2. Feeling "sure that the conductors are guiltless of the conduct charged against them, frivolous and foolish as it is," Boyle forwarded this and copies of Thomasson's letters to Rep. Lovell H. Rousseau, asking him to present them to the President. Boyle expressed his confidence that Johnson would do what he could to prevent "the harmful influence" of the officers of the Bureau. Boyle also called on the services of Sen. James Guthrie in the matter. In mid-March Thomasson resigned from the Bureau, and was replaced soon after by Gen. John Ely from the Lexington sub-district. Boyle to Rousseau, Feb. 13, 1866; Boyle to Guthrie, Feb. 17, 1866, ibid.; *Louisville Courier*, Mar. 16, 20, 1866.

From Alvan C. Gillem

Head-Quarters   District of East Tennessee,
Chattanooga, Tenn., Feb 13 1866

Dear Sir;

A few days since I saw in one of the Cincinnati papers, an article headed "Conflict between the Civil and Military Authorities in East Tenn." The facts are these. Col Joe Parsons & some of the officers and men of the 9 were charged with killing one John A Thornhill[1] near Morristown in June 65. The parties were tried by Court Martial, and all except Col Parsons and Capt Bell[2] were acquitted it appearing that they were merely obeying orders. Parson's & Bell were sentenced to be *hung* —but were Pardoned by Major Genl Stoneman the Department Commander. So Soon as the 9th Tenn Cav was mustered out all the parties concerned in the killing were indicted for murder and several of them put in jail. They appealed to General Thomas on the ground of having been already tried for the offence charged.

Genl Thomas directed their release, the sheriff[3] of Jefferson County declined obeying the order, an officer and *ten* men failed to execute the order the sheriff having it is reported one hundred men. Genl. Stoneman then directed a larger force to be sent to Dandridge when the men were released.[4] This case and one other where the ownership of a horse was in question are the only instances in which there has been any difference between the civil and military—to my knowledge in East Tenn.

From Bristol to Chattanooga everything is quiet. Courts are held and justice administered. There are instances of personal violence and theft —but this was to be expected. Civil war is always taken advantage of by the evil disposed & this class has been greatly augmented by disbanding two great armies in neither of which was private property much respected. Such are the facts, the assertions in the manifesto of the Vigilace Committee to the contrary notwithstanding. As to the exclusion of loyal men from social society by the rebels I can not speak, never having applied for admission.

I fear the signers of the memorial[5] were not actuated entirely by patriotism. It was the intention originally to introduce a series of resolutions into the Legislature disapproving your course. A copy of these resolutions has been furnished you—but it was found that they could not command a respectable minority—hence the memorial. The most violent of your enemies is E. P. Cone who with Fletcher and Judge Lovering[6] appear to do the talking. There are some others who do not desire to openly break with you yet—but it is useless for me to speak of these men you know them. Hoping to be excused for this intrusion. . . .

Alvan C Gillem

ALS, DLC-JP.

1. Thornhill (b. *c*1841) had been captain of Co. B, 9th Tenn. Cav., USA. CSR, John A. Thornhill, RG94, NA.

2. James W. Bell (*c*1840-*fl*1900) was mustered into service at Nashville as a lieutenant in February 1864 and promoted to captain in June 1865. Subsequent to his military service, he returned to Knoxville and eventually became involved in real estate. 1860 Census, Tenn., Knox, 17th Dist., Mecklenburg, 256; Knoxville directories (1885–1900); CSR, James W. Bell, RG94, NA. For a convenient summary of the proceedings in Bell's case, see *Nashville Union*, Feb. 3, 1866.

3. Nicholas B. Swann (b. *c*1806), a farmer and delegate to the Greeneville Convention, served as sheriff from 1864 to 1866. 1850 Census, Tenn., Jefferson, 13th Dist., 720; (1860), 75; *OR*, Ser. 1, Vol. 52, Pt. 1: 169; Goodspeed's *East Tennessee*, 863.

4. For earlier references to this incident, see Johnson to Thomas, Jan. 3, 1866, *Johnson Papers*, 9: 570; *Nashville Union*, Jan. 3, 1866.

5. Here Gillem undoubtedly refers to a memorial adopted by Tennessee unionists who had convened in Nashville in early January. Among the several memorialists were Andrew J. Fletcher, Edward P. Cone, and Amos Lovering. See Central Committee of the Union Party of Tennessee to Johnson, ca. Jan. 9, 1866, *Johnson Papers*, 9: 582. See also Sam Milligan to Johnson, Jan. 16, 1866, ibid., 602–3.

6. Amos Lovering (*c*1805–*fl*1871), a former Indiana attorney and jurist, resided several years in Nashville before becoming a circuit judge in Mississippi. 1860 Census, Ind., Clark, Monroe Twp., Henryville, 139; Nashville directories (1866–69); *NUC*; Dunbar Rowland, *Courts, Judges, and Lawyers of Mississippi 1798–1935* (Jackson, 1935), 260. Months later, Gillem again warned Johnson about Lovering and others who were not his supporters. See Gillem to Johnson, June 29, 1866.

To Andrew J. Hamilton

Executive Office, Washington, D.C.,
Febuary 13th 1866

I am highly gratified to receive your dispatch,[1] and that your Convention was organized. I hope all will end well. It is of the utmost importance that the proceedings of your convention, be prudent and of the most temperate candour, indicating loyalty, and of the entire willingness to acknowledge the supremacy of the Constitution and of obedience to the laws of the United States. You no doubt understand the posture of affairs here and much will depend upon the future proceedings of your Convention. I am still hopeful that in the end, matters will take a different turn here and that loyal representatives will be admitted to take their seats in the councils of the nation from all the states.

(Sgd) Andrew Johnson   Prest. U S

Tel, DNA-RG107, Tels. Sent, President, Vol. 3 (1865–68).
1. Hamilton had reported that "The radical Union men are in a minority and there are many violent and impracticable men in the body." Hamilton to Johnson, Feb. 11, 1866, Johnson Papers, LC. For a further description of the Texas convention, see Ben C. Truman to Johnson, Feb. 8, 1866, *Advice*, 196.

From John Gill Shorter

Washington, Febry 13th 1866
Sir:

By the earnest request of citizens of Barbour County, Alabama, I have been induced to come to Washington to represent to you as a grievance the arbitrary seizure of cotton at Eufaula, Ala.—the private property of individual citizens,—made by one J. Condit Smith,[1] styling himself a Contract Agent of the U.S. Treasury; over 800 bales of which he has forcibly removed from said town, under protest of the legal owners and claimants thereof, and shipped down the Chattahoochee river to Apalachicola, Florida, consigned to Horatio Page,[2] who is reported to be an Assistant Supervising Special Agent of the Treasury.

The pretended justification of these seizures is the allegation that the original owners of the cotton had subscribed in aid of the so called Produce Loan of the Confederate States, and that if they had done so in any form their right of property was forfeited and they could not claim even the immunity and protection so generously extended to them by your Excellency's warrant of Pardon & Amnesty. I am requested to report to your Excellency that proof was submitted to the said J. Condit Smith, Contract Agent as aforesaid, that some of the parties whose cotton he seized had never subscribed in any form, or in any amount, to the said so called Produce Loan, and that some of the cotton seized by him had been raised since the close of the war & during the year 1865, and some prior to 1865 but since the year 1861, during which year the subscriptions in the locality mentioned were made in aid of the said Produce Loan,—and further that none of the parties had by any form of subscription pledged cotton in kind in aid of the Confederate States, but that those who were thus charged had subscribed the nett proceeds of sale of raw produce merely, and without ever having parted with any right or interest in the same, or having confered any control over the same to the Confederate States or any of its agents, or without any express dedication of the cotton by mark or delivery, or setting aside in aid of the Confederate States, they either sold the same as their own private property, at their own will and pleasure, & paid the proceeds or some part thereof, or the market value thereof, for the bonds of the Confederate States, in full compliance with the express terms of subscription made by them;—but that the said J. Condit Smith, Contract Agent as aforesaid, absolutely refused to allow the said proof & release the cotton thus shown to have been illegally detained by him.

I beg leave further to state to your Excellency that I have been furnished with the necessary proofs by some of the parties whom I represent & am prepared to submit the same with specification of quantity, marks & ownership; and that other proofs in similar cases are probably now on the way from Alabama, and that if the shipment or conversion of the cotton by the said J. Condit Smith & his associates can be promptly arrested & a reasonable opportunity afforded, all the parties who have been oppressed by his unauthorized & unjust exactions will be able to obtain the needful redress.

This statement is respectfully submitted to your Excellency with an assured confidence that whatever remedy in your Excellency's wisdom may be deemed necessary to protect loyal and peaceful citizens in their personal rights will be summarily adopted.[3]

Jno. Gill Shorter

ALS, DNA-RG56, Misc. Div., Claims for Cotton and Captured and Abandoned Property.

1. John Condit Smith (1840–1883), a railroad builder, during the war had been a lieutenant, 42nd Ill. Inf., and a lieutenant colonel, quartermaster, on Gen. W. T. Sherman's staff. His last residence was Buffalo, New York, where he was vice president of a railroad. *New York Times*, Nov. 10, 1883; Heitman, *Register*, 1: 900; *OR*, Ser. 1, Vol. 24, Pt. 2: 281.

2. Not otherwise identified.

3. Shorter also submitted a letter addressed to Johnson by Governor Patton of Alabama, who looked forward to the day when all matters related to the government's confiscation of cotton "shall have passed away." On February 15 the letters were referred to Hugh McCulloch, "who it is hoped will give Mr Shorter an interview." Robert M. Patton to Johnson, Feb. 6, 1866, Misc. Div., Claims for Cotton and Captured and Abandoned Property, RG56, NA.

From John H. Brinton[1]

West Chester Penna   Feb 14, 1866

My dear Sir,

The State Convention of the Democratic Party of Penna: will meet at Harrisburgh on the 5th March next.[2] The Delegates from this County and Senatorial District were chosen two days ago in this place by a Convention.

The endorsement of your policy of Reconstruction will come up before the State Convention. There is a kind feeling towards you personally and politically among Democrats. You have boldly and frankly thrown yourself upon the People for support, to the great distaste of the Abolition wing of the Republican Party. It may refuse to break with you directly for they have a great object in view—which is the carrying the Congressional Elections of next fall throughout the North—and thus have the Congress which will count the Presidential Electoral vote of 1868. Most assuredly if such vantage ground is gained through Federal influence or patronage, the Electoral vote of the South will be counted out—and a minority or sectional man of extreme views like Butler, be smuggled in as your successor. Then the Freedmans policy contemplated in the existing Bill[3] of Congress will be administered with a vengeance—to the degradation of white men every where but specially in the South. It settles hundreds of thousands of Negroes on public lands in sections of five States. Far better that the whole coloured race should be led to Liberia. Emigration is the only sure method of benefitting them and the twenty seven millions of white freemen of our Republic.

Considerations of this kind weigh with our Delegates to the Democratic State Convention of 5th March. As the Senatorial Delegate—after consulting with the three Representative Delegates to that Convention —from this County, I hope you will veto that Freedmans Bill, which may—before the meeting of our State Convention—reach your hands for official action.

John H Brinton

ALS, DLC-JP.

1. Brinton (b. c1812) was an attorney and a native of Pennsylvania. He enclosed this letter in a missive of the same date to ex-Rep. Thomas B. Florence. 1860 Census, Pa., Chester, Westchester, 115; Samuel T. Wiley, *Biographical and Portrait Cyclopedia of Chester County, Pennsylvania* (Philadelphia, 1893), 105; Brinton to Florence, Feb. 14, 1866, Johnson Papers, LC.

2. For the adopted resolutions, including one endorsing the President, see *American Annual Cyclopaedia* (1866), 613.

3. Here Brinton refers to the Southern Homestead bill, as introduced in early January 1866 by Rep. John H. Rice of Maine, which provided for the settlement by anyone, regardless of race or color, of unoccupied lands in the states of Alabama, Arkansas, Florida, Louisiana, and Mississippi. At the time of Brinton's writing, the bill had been passed by the House and referred to the Senate Committee on Public Lands. The bill became law with

Johnson's signature on June 21, 1866. *House Journal*, 39 Cong., 1 Sess., p. 113 (Ser. 1243); *Senate Journal*, 39 Cong., 1 Sess., p. 147 (Ser. 1236); *Congressional Globe*, 39 Cong., 1 Sess., Appendix, p. 329; Michael L. Lanza, *Agrarianism and Reconstruction Politics: The Southern Homestead Act* (Baton Rouge, 1990), 5, 14, 19.

From James M. Chambers[1]

Columbus Ga.   15th Feb. 1866

Sir,

Though I have not the honor of a personal acquaintance or to have been one of your Constituents, yet having obtained your pardon[2] (for which I now thank you) and having taken the oath of allegiance which I am proposing to keep in good faith I do now recognize you as *my* President—and ask to be one of the people of this great nation over which you have been Called to Preside. It is gratifying to see that your elevation has not cut off *your Sympathy with the people*, but that your whole administration has shown that in heart and in practice you have never ceased to feel that you were one of them. That it would be your pleasure to know their wishes and their wants, and that these could not be better known, than from the people themselves. This is the explanation and the apology for the liberty which I now take. Such demonstrations are not only cheering to the subject, but are alike creditable to the head and the heart of a great Ruler. But Mr President from the standpoint which I was occupying when you were chosen to Preside I was not prepared to accord to you even that much. I say this, to show how great has been the change, since "the beam has been removed from my eye,"[3] and Judging you by the acts of your administration, I have to admire that Patriotism which could come up from the din of war when the worst passions of the heart had been stired, and hatred and prejudice had waked up to make their demands. Amid such surroundings, to find you going on & on, and beyond all this, and rising superior to all these conflicting passions, proclaiming pardon to those who in good faith would come back, and planting yourself upon the principles of the Constitution pledging its guarantees and its equities alike to all. This is a Patriotism of which its author and its beneficiaries may be well proud. And yet all this would have been comparatively easy if public sentiment had approved,—if the people with whom you had been identified and associated in the war had condoned the act—and said "Well done." But those endorsements were few and feeble, while the great masses (or rather their Representatives) infuriated and prejudiced demanded terms both degrading and ruinous, and these demands have been made in a spirit which would have undid or revoked (I fear,) all Constitutional barriers, but for *your decision and firmness*. I do not praise you for favors done to the South, but *for doing* RIGHT. I know, and all who have marked your course know, that you will not swerve from your prescribed line of duty, to win new friends at the

South, or to hold old ones at the North. That the Constitution is your bark whether you sail on Northern or Southern waters. This you have told to all men, and very recently repeated emphatically to the delegation from the Montana Territory,—And in your recent interview with Fred Douglas and his co-delegates you were just to the point, no more, nor no less than should have been said by one occupying the high and responsible trust of President of the whole Country. *Our rejoicing thus is, for benefits resulting from right principles.* Mr President it is hardly necessary to say that in the late War we thought we were contending for rights that ought to be ours, and though you differed with us in that conclusion, you were assured that we were in earnest. We did all we could, our sons, our fortunes and our prayers were all contributed. But we were over powered. Our cause was lost,—and we have accepted the result. The negroes have been given up with an astonishing acquiescence, and I should rejoice, if what I infer to be your wish could be carried out, and they could be colonized. Ceasing to be Slaves they ought to be a separate people having their own government—and social relations. But I was proposing to say that having accepted the result—of the war, the people of this part of the Country & I think I may say throughout the South are sincere and without any mental reservations in their desire for reconstruction. Great injustice is done us when isolated cases are paraded or the testimony of mischievious letter writers is taken to prove the unsoundness of the Southern people. *They are in earnest*, but greatly aggrieved at what we think, is an affected want of confidence, affording pretexts for withholding the right of representation, and for keeping up a sort of Military rule. And just here I will ask leave to say, that within the last four weeks, negro troops have been sent here for the first time.[4] They have given much trouble and I fear are to produce serious difficulties. The effect upon the negroes who had entered into contracts & gone to work is said already to be bad. Inducing many of them to quit work or to do it less faithfully. An armed force of negroes begets the expectation that they are to rule, and increases the probabilities of a general insurrection. Those here have been behaving insolently. I have very reliable information that a lady has been rudely pressed from the side walk against the wall, of another who was handed off the side walk and told that was where she belonged—of another who had her purse snatched from her hands and robbed of its money contents. The reply of the Commandant[5] to such complaints is reported to be, "identify the negro." This usually is, an impracticability. A few evenings since a young man walking that street when one of these negroes is said to have thrown him off—cursing him and calling him a damned rebel, drawing his bayonet, where upon the young man shot him with a pistol.[6] Great excitement—spread through the City, the negroes paraded and fired several guns, the citizens turned out, and fortunately, quiet was restored without the loss of life. The same evening as Majr

Warner[7] was walking peacably along the street to his house, on the opposite side to the barracks he was shot at across the street, the ball bursting the knee Joint—and the leg was amputated. We were without troops for a few days before these fellows came and it was generally remarked that the City had not been so quiet—and orderly since the war. I do not seriously object to the presence of troops, but I do hope that these negroes may be removed.[8] But for the arguments which it might have furnished to rabid Politicians against the South it would have been about impossible to have restrained the community upon which such outrages had been committed. My residence is two miles from the City. Personally I have not suffered, but how long I may escape I can not say, nor can I know how soon worse things may happen. There is yet one other subject to which I desire to allude. It is the swarms of Treasury agents real or pretended. Really Mr President I am reminded of Esops fable of the Fox and the fleas. When one set have sucked until they are full and have left us another succeeds. Those who first came to seize cotton subscribed to the Confederate loan, declined to take the cotton when it could be shown that the party subscribing had paid the value in money—another, setting all aside, & often without asking any questions, seizes all he can excuse & gives notice which bears upon that which is to be made to settle for all which has been sold. Thus amid all the varied demands present and prospective the impoverished negroless farmer is paralyzed in his reviving energies, and the more so, as he apprehends that the flow into the treasury is not in exact proportion to that from his purse, but like the streams in the desert—are often lost in the thirsty sand before reaching the ocean.

But—Mr President—there were two things of which I wanted mainly to assure you. The one was that the people of this part of the country were sincere in their professions and in good faith wanted to be back in the Union. The other was that though your administration in the beginning had no supporters here, now all hearts are turned to you and are prepared to sustain you and your administration. All true unprejudiced men every where must and will sustain one who plants himself upon the Constitution. If that fails all must go down.

James M. Chambers

ALS, DLC-JP.
    1. Chambers (c1801–1869), president of an 1861 cotton planters convention, former editor of an agricultural journal, planter, and large slaveholder, during the war had been an avid Confederate who argued for the cultivation of crops other than cotton. Amnesty Papers (M1003, Roll 17), Ga., James M. Chambers, RG94, NA; *Charleston Courier*, Aug. 20, 1861, Mar. 22, 1862; *Rome Courier*, Mar. 18, 1869.
    2. Chambers was pardoned on September 28, 1865. Amnesty Papers (M1003, Roll 17), Ga., James M. Chambers, RG94, NA.
    3. A reference to Matthew 7: 5 and Luke 6: 42.
    4. Two companies of the 103rd USCT, numbering 150 men, had appeared in Columbus on February 6, 1866, with two more companies "expected" to arrive. *Memphis Appeal*, Feb. 11, 1866.

5. Lt. Col. John A. Bogert (1836–1921), a former New York City marble worker, was thought by the *Columbus Sun* staff to have arrived with the two companies of the 103rd USCT. Ibid.; *New York Times*, June 22, 1921; *NUC Manuscript Collections Index* (1963–66), 25.

6. Chambers alludes to a February 12 shooting by Cooper Lindsay (b. c1843), who escaped. 1860 Census, Ga., Muscogee, Wynton, 10; *Augusta Constitutionalist*, Feb. 16, 1866; Nancy Telfair, *A History of Columbus, Georgia, 1828–1928* (Columbus, 1929), 151.

7. James H. Warner (c1830–1866), a former U.S. Navy chief engineer who served the Confederacy in the same capacity at the Columbus Naval Iron Works, died on February 21. 1860 Census, Va., Norfolk, Jackson Ward, 176; Maxine Turner, *Navy Gray: A Story of the Confederate Navy on the Chattahoochee and Apalachicola Rivers* (Tuscaloosa, 1988), 53–54; *Augusta Constitutionalist*, Feb. 27, 1866.

8. By the end of the month, the black troops in Columbus had been ordered out and replaced by "over sixty" white soldiers from the 176th N.Y. Inf. *Memphis Appeal*, Feb. 28, 1866; *Off. Army Reg.: Vols.*, 2: 680; Frederick H. Dyer, *A Compendium of the War of the Rebellion* (Des Moines, 1908), 1469.

From Benjamin Coates[1]

Philadelphia   Feb, 15th 1866

Will you allow one who is no politician yet who takes a deep interest in his country's welfare to occupy a few minutes of your attention. If so I will premise by saying that I am a great admirer of the character of our late President Abraham Lincoln, not only for his honesty & purity, & disinterested patriotism, but also as a man of progress—one who was willing to move forward under the guiding hand of Providence, as the way opened before him. And if it were proper to speak of the living, I should say that when Andrew Johnson in the Senate of the United States, faithful among the faithless, boldly & patriotically denounced both Treason & traitors in uncompromising terms; and when I rembered that this true man was the author of the homestead bill, which perhaps more than any other measure was calculated to carry out the principles of republicanism by giving to every man the opportunity of a right in the soil—it occurred to me as it did to many others that Andrew Johnson of Tennessee was the most proper man to be associated with Abraham Lincoln as the candidates for the two highest offices in the gift of the American people,—and as far as in my power did I feel it my duty to my country, and to mankind to urge, & secure their nomination & election. I had faith in Andrew Johnson then, and I have faith in him now. As Govr. of Tennessee—as the liberator of his slaves,—and in his address to the colored people of Nashville[2] he showed to the World that his principles were superior to his prejudices, and in recognizing the rights of man without regard to the color of his skin,—and that the democracy of christianity is confined to no particular race, he proved himself the man for the times. Great was my satisfaction then when we were all overwhelmed with grief at the loss of our beloved President Lincoln that we had in his successor so worthy & reliable a counterpart as President Johnson.

Your history Mr President and the record of your life are before the country; Your reputation is the property of the American people,— hence it is not without some anxiety that they view the great effort now being made by Semi-loyal men, from the North and the South, through the Press, and by delegations of those who after having failed in their utmost endeavour to break up the best government ever vouchsafed to man & to destroy republican institutions from the face of the earth forever,— now in the most audacious manner, have the effrontery to attempt to sweve you from your position by caresses & flattery at once disgusting, & insulting—knowing that you are not to be driven or coerced by their denunciation their great effort now is to create a bad feeling between you & the great Union party of the country as represented in the U.S. Congress —hoping thereby to divide & conquer. But this cannot be. You have a greater, a nobler destiny before you—disregarding alike the flattery on the one hand & the uncourteous remarks of those from whom, you should have aid & sympathy in the reorganization of the Union, on the principles of the Constitution recognizing the rights of man without distinction of race or color, with the cardinal doctrine of the fathers of the republic that taxation & representation must go together. You have only Mr President to co-operate with the representatives of the loyal masses of the people, in securing the Union of these States on the eternal principles of Right & Justice,—and every true patriot will have cause to thank you, every lover of liberty in the civilized world will cherish your name with those of Washington & Lincoln,—& all will down to posterity together, as benefactors of mankind—on the brightest page of the World's history.

Few men Mr President have ever been placed in so responsible a position as that you now occupy,—with the attention of the whole civilized world directed to your co-operation with the acts of the present Congress, in re-establishing the Union on a firm basis, accepting the situation & its requirements so as to discard forever all *class legislation*, whether for white or black. The oppressed masses of Europe, who are suffering under unequal laws are looking to see the republican principles from Constitution & Declaration of Independence carried out in their true spirit giving to the poor man whoever he may be equal rights under the law with the wealthiest & most aristocratic in the land.

When great principles are being discussed, it may seem out of place to refer to party feelings—or party policy. But may I ask Mr President, is it not certain that every citizen of the Republic will sooner or later possess the right of suffrage; & if so, is it not best that in the reorganization of our union on the republican principles of its Constitution that this right should be recognized *at once* under the protecting care of the *Government*, rather than to leave it to the *favored few* the wealthy & aristocratic ex slaveholders who will give this right to the Colored population in their midst as *a boon from them* to attach the blacks to their interests, (& from whom they do not fear any social equality), so as to retain the governing power in their own hands, and thus establish a barrier against the upward progress of the white democracy who have kept so long in ignorance of their rights & power; reinforced as this latter element will be by emigration from the northern states & from Europe. It is true Sir that our Government is founded on the virtue & intelligence of the people, & *without both virtue & intelligence*, republicanism is a failure. Should not the Government & should not every patriot in the land make increased effort to secure the success of republican institutions—and is there any thing more elevating than the ballot? When every man feels that he is part & parcel of the government & that the great responsibility is thrown upon him of acting wisely & well will it not give a new impulse, a new life, to the whole frame work of society? Already the freedmen of the south are seeking an education with the greatest avidity. Hundreds of thousands are this day being taught where the law a few years ago made it a high crime to teach a human being of a certain class—or who had the smallest admixture of that blood with that of the ruling caste,—now how changed! More than that, following the spirit of the times—all our Freedman's associations in the Northern & Western states have made a union with the "Union Commission for the education of poor white children["]—all being now merged into *one organization* for the education of *all*, irrespective of race or color—that carry out the true democratic principle—leaving the social question to adjust itself. But then while we put ourselves right & establish equal laws for all, the laws of nature—which are the laws of God will gradually cause the black race (the children of the Tropics) to seek a warmer climate taking with them our civilization, our language, the christian religion & republican Institutions, to Mexico, the West Indies, to South America,—& to the land of their forefathers—thus blessing the whole world—and future generations of both whites & blacks in the commercial intercourse with each other will have cause to thank all those who under Divine Providence had the will & power to accomplish this great purpose.

Sincerely hoping that you will feel it your duty to pass approve the late acts of Congress, especially those securing the election franchise of all those paying taxes in the District of Colum & The Freedmen Bureau bill. . . .

                                                    Benjamin Coates.

ALS, DLC-JP.
    1. Probably the Benjamin Coates (1797–1881) who was a physician and longtime member of the Historical Society of Pennsylvania and also the author of at least two antebellum tracts dealing with the emancipation of slaves and the treatment of their diseases. *NUC*.
    2. See Speech to Nashville Freedmen, Nov. 12, 1864, *Johnson Papers*, 7: 281–83.

From Charles J. Jenkins

Executive Department   Milledgeville Georgia
February 15th 1866

Sir:

It has become my duty again to ask your attention to a subject adverted to in a former communication, viz: the keeping in our midst colored troops. After many of them had been withdrawn and the policy of their withdrawal seemed likely soon to be consumated, our people felt great relief, and in many localities where there remained no military force at all, law and order were strictly observed—peace and quiet prevailed—and good business relations, mutually advantageous, were established between white and colored people. Suddenly in certain places, as in the Cities of Macon and Columbus, colored troops were introduced, and settled as if for indefinite occupation. In the latter City, a most unfortunate disturbance of the public peace has already occurred, which from all the information in my possession, I verily believe originated in the grossly improper and insulting conduct of some of those troops. The circumstances are briefly referred to, in the inclosed communication which is the immediate cause of this to you.[1] A majority of the signers, are known to me personally or by reputation, as respectable, intelligent, moral men, such as any City or State might be proud of.

Their statements are altogether reliable. Believe me, Sir, the presence of these troops among us is unfavorable to the public peace and tranquility. When out of the immediate presence of their officers, their conduct is often intolerably insulting, and not unfrequently going to the extent of personal violence. I have myself, when quietly riding in my carriage with my Wife,[2] on the high-way, in the absence of all provocation, by word by gesture or by look, been cursed by them and ordered to get out of the road with that carriage, they wanted the whole road. My old blood, did not boil over quite; but the hot blood of a young man can hardly bear being rudely thrust from the pavement, or seeing a lady wantonly insulted. If it be supposed that these troops are kept in proper subjection by their officers, I respectfully affirm that as a general rule, it is not so.

Mr President, I believe you have full authority in the premises, I know your kindly feelings and purposes towards us and I entreat you, if it do not contravene any policy you deem necessary, to relieve us of this portion of the United States Military.[3]

Charles J. Jenkins   Governor of Geo

LS, DNA-RG108, Lets. Recd. *re* Military Discipline.

1. In a February 13, 1866, petition to Governor Jenkins, thirty-eight citizens of Columbus, Georgia, including Mayor F. G. Wilkins, urged Johnson's "intervention in their behalf," meaning removal of the black troops. Ira Berlin, ed., *Freedom: A Documentary His-*

tory of Emancipation, 1861–1867. Series II, *The Black Military Experience* (Cambridge, 1982), 759.

2. Emily Gertrude Barnes (b. *c*1817) of Philadelphia had married Jenkins in 1854. 1860 Census, Ga., Richmond, 119th Dist., 38; Williard R. Rocker, *Marriages and Obituaries from the Macon Messenger, 1818–1865* (Easley, S.C., 1988), 475.

3. The letter was referred to the secretary of war, who in turn forwarded it to General Grant. See Osborne A. Lochrane to Johnson, Mar. 26, 1866.

From Ralph Phinney[1]

Cambria Mills Mich Feb. [ca. 15] 1866.[2]

Dear Sir

With great anxiety I wated for the reading of you Annual Message to Congress. When I felt in my heart to pray God to protect and keep you Sir from the assan and death Generally and especially from the faction of Blockheads in the present Congress.

I do not think either you or the country have half as much to fear from all Rebeldom as from the thirty or forty Trators in the presnt Congress. But Sir, you doubtless know that three fourths of the people of this country are with you in your wise and true doctrine on the Relation of the States &c and that you wish to *rule by Law* and not *by mob*.

All the good and true people of the nation are with you and pray constantly for you to be guided by power from above. I read with delight your meeting recently with the *negro* delegation. In which I see you was more than a mactch for the great *Fred* Douglass.[3] As many fanatics think their Pet Douglass is far a head of Your Exellency in profound wisdom. But they are of that class of preachs and people that proclaimed at our Late Presidents *funeral*, "that he was so mild *toward the Rebels* that God would not indorse his kindness no longer but removed him by death."[4] I need not say to you that this is blasphemy. But your truth I see closed Mr D's fine argumnts and will open the eyes of many thousands of the blinded in the country. I view your stand to cover all the good there is in all partis in Poletic's. This is the Position I have ocupied for years; and I beliv is the true one.

A man who only serves party is not worthy of the name man; But I am not the only one who prays for God to sustain you in your disinterested work to consolid[ate] the various views of the people and parties to the consolidation of the Union. We have not had a peoples President since Andrew Jackson before you; and I do feel you are indeed the right man in the right place. No matter about the abuse some of the hot heads heap upon you. The people will bless you after you are through with this world and God the great king will crown you in the New Heavn and Earth at the Last day with tresure for your noble deeds in this settlemt if nothing more. Trust in him then daly for he that puteth his trust in me shall not be put to shame or confounded—Jesus.

I Am only a humble man and as nothing of office honors or molument of men but my heart has gone up to God spontanouly for you in prayer and praise for you good deeds that I wanted to let you know that all had not bowed the knees to Mammon and delusion but that the humble and the thinking part of the people could see your good deeds and glorefy our Father which is in heavn.

Ralph Phinney

ALS, DLC-JP.
    1. Not identified.
    2. The approximate date of February 15 is supplied, based upon the fact that Phinney wrote the letter sometime after the Johnson-Douglass interview of February 7 and the assumption that it might have taken a week for Phinney to learn about the interview and to write to Johnson.
    3. See Interview with Delegation of Blacks, Feb. 7, 1866.
    4. The source of this direct quotation remains elusive, despite examination of several funeral sermons. One historian has taken cognizance of the view, expressed by some, that Lincoln had brought the assassination upon himself by being lenient toward the Rebels. See Thomas R. Turner, *Beware the People Weeping: Public Opinion and the Assassination of Abraham Lincoln* (Baton Rouge, 1982), 82.

From William H. Spencer[1]

Lebanon, Ky.   15th Febry 1866.

Sometime since I presented my claims to the Commissioner of Internal Revenue,[2] for the office of Collector for 4th Congressional district Ky. urging that the government had adopted as its policy, to give these appointments to discharged soldiers, and also my fitness for the position by reason of experience in the duties of the office. From the daily papers I see that the appointment has been given to a gentleman residing outside the limits of the district,[3] while we have hundreds of good, true, loyal, competent administration men residing in the district, who, by hard blows against rebels & the rebelion, have earned this, & more, at the hands of their government.

Now Sir I respectfully ask if this is exactly the treatment to be meted out to those of us who have perrilled our lives & property in defence of the dear old flag?

If the appointment had been given to a resident of the district, as I understand the law Clearly to Contemplate, I for one would never have uttered a word of Complaint, but if men, who have sacraficed health, ease, comfort, property, & friends in upholding the Government, are to be rudely thrust aside to make place for those who remained snugly at home, in ease & Comfort when war's rude blast was sounded, and who are at heart opposed to you & your Administration, then I think you will bear with me, when I say we have great grounds for Complaint.

Mr C. C. Smith the appointee to the Collectorship of 4th District Kentucky, and who is now a resident of 7th district, is a gentleman and a Union man, but while he was safely at home, within the bosom of his family, I was at Shiloh, Corinth, Stones River &c. &c. and my wife & children receiving indignities, insult & injury at the hands of the home rebels & rebel soldiery.

The fiat has gone forth, the decision is made, and I submit like all good Citizens should. I do ask however as this precedent has been established, that an appointment either as Assessor, or Collector of Internal Revenue be given me for one of the vacant districts, for my qualifications as a business man, and my experience in the duties of this particular branch, I have only to refer you to the very large & allmost unanimous recommendations & endorsements from 4th Congressional district now in the hands of the Commissioner of Internal Revenue & the Secretary of the Treasury, also to every Revenue officer and a majority of the good people of 4th district. My loyalty Can not be Questioned. I was one of the first men in Kentucky to go to Camp Dick Robinson, and had the pleasure of meeting you while in camp there.[4] As to my political status I can only say that with all my strength & soul I endorse you & your policy and pray god you may triumph.[5]

W. H. Spencer,
late Col 3d Ky Inftry.

ALS, DNA-RG56, Appts., Internal Revenue Service, Assessor, Ky., 4th Dist.

1. Spencer (1828–1898), a former druggist and veteran of the Mexican War, was mustered into the volunteer army at Camp Dick Robinson in October 1861 and served in the 3rd Ky. Inf. until April 1863, when he resigned for health reasons. Afterwards appointed by Lincoln as assessor of the old Second Revenue District of Kentucky, Spencer was renominated by Johnson to the new Fourth District and commissioned on February 15, 1866. 1860 Census, Ky., Adair, Columbia, 1st Div., 3; *U.S. Off. Reg.* (1863–65); CSR, William H. Spencer, RG94, NA; Pension Records, William H. Spencer, RG15, NA; Ser. 6B, Vol. 4: 241, Johnson Papers, LC.

2. Edward A. Rollins. See, for example, George D. Blakey to Rollins, Jan. 20, 1866, in which a petition endorsing Spencer was also enclosed. Appts., Internal Revenue Service, Assessor, Ky., 4th Dist., William M. [H.] Spencer, RG56, NA.

3. Curran C. Smith (1822–*fl*1892), an older brother of Kentucky Rep. Green Clay Smith, was a Lexington physician nominated by Johnson on February 6 upon the recommendation of William H. Randall, Samuel McKee, and Smith's brother. He was commissioned as collector of the Fourth District approximately one week later. Thomas Speed, *Records and Memorials of the Speed Family* (Louisville, 1892), 90; Hugh McCulloch to Johnson, Jan. 27, 1866, Lets. Sent *re* Internal Revenue Service Employees (QD Ser.), Vol. 1, RG56, NA; Ser. 6B, Vol. 4: 241, Johnson Papers, LC.

4. Johnson had made a speech at Camp Dick Robinson in the fall of 1861. Trefousse, *Johnson*, 147.

5. Spencer's letter was referred to the secretary of the treasury. Smith was removed in July 1866 and replaced by John R. Beckley, a resident of the Fourth District, while Spencer continued serving as assessor until the office was abolished. Ser. 6A, Vol. B: 246; Ser. 6B, Vol. 4: 241, Johnson Papers, LC; Green Clay Smith to Johnson, July 2, 1866, Appts., Internal Revenue Service, Collector, Ky., 4th Dist., RG56, NA; *U.S. Off. Reg.* (1867–71). See also Marion C. Taylor to Johnson, June 26, 1866.

From Andrew J. Hamilton

Austin Texas   Feby 16th 1866

President Johnson

Your telegram of the thirteenth recd.[1] There is so far no definite action by the Convention. The Counties are preparing to report and in two or three days there will probably be some decisive action. The Convention is composed of about two thirds original secessionists to one third original Union men. The former are anxious to evade the admission that the ordinance of secession was null and void from the beginning. They say they do not want to nullify themselves. That the majority came very reluctantly up to the work of doing any necessary thing except the re-pudiation of the Rebel state debt but the Union men are earnest and determined and I think will be able to force as favorable action as has been in any Convention in the South. There are four men in the Convention who have petitioned for special pardons. John Ireland[2] first exception, J. W. Whitfield[3] & F. N. Wool[4] Brigadier General in Confederate army and R. N. Runels[5] thirteenth exception. I decided in my proclamation ordering an election that parties in this Convention were not eligable un-til pardoned. It is for you to determine. There petitions have been recom-mended.[6]

A. J. Hamilton

Tel, DLC-JP.

1. See Johnson to Hamilton, Feb. 13, 1866.

2. Ireland (1827–1896) was a lawyer and mayor of Sequin, Texas, before the war. After holding the office of local Confederate states receiver for less than a year, he joined the army, rising to the rank of lieutenant colonel. He was pardoned by Johnson on January 25, 1866. After the war Ireland served in the Texas house of representatives, senate, supreme court, and finally as governor. Webb et al., *Handbook of Texas*, 1: 891–92; Amnesty Papers (M1003, Roll 53), Tex., John Ireland, RG94, NA.

3. John W. Whitfield (1818–1879) was a Mexican War veteran who had served as an Indian agent in Missouri and Arkansas and as a delegate to Congress from the Kansas Ter-ritory. An officer with Texas cavalry regiments in the West, Whitfield became a brigadier general. He was still applying for pardon in August 1866. No individual pardon date has been found. Ibid. (Roll 55), Tex., John W. Whitfield, RG94, NA; Warner, *Gray*.

4. Thomas N. Waul (1813–1903), another brigadier general who served primarily in the Trans-Mississippi West, was a lawyer and planter who had moved to Texas in 1850. There is no evidence that Waul received an individual pardon. Ibid.; Webb et al., *Handbook of Texas*, 2: 871; Amnesty Papers (M1003, Roll 55), Tex., Thomas Neville Waul, RG94, NA.

5. Hardin R. Runnels (1820–1873), former Texas legislator and governor, was a pro-secession member of the state secession convention but otherwise had held no civil or mili-tary office during the war. He applied for pardon in order to avoid persecution in the event his estate was still worth more than $20,000. Johnson pardoned him on March 6, 1866. Webb et al., *Handbook of Texas*, 2: 515; Sobel and Raimo, *Governors*, 4: 518; Runnels to Johnson, Dec. 13, 1865, Amnesty Papers (M1003, Roll 54), Tex., H. R. Runnels, RG94, NA.

6. Ten days later Hamilton sent the President another dispatch, informing him that "No measure has yet been determined by the Convention." But he still expected "satisfac-tory results," and he promised to notify Johnson "as fast as final action is had upon the

important question pending." Hamilton to Johnson, Feb. 26, 1866, Johnson Papers, LC.
See Hamilton to Johnson, Mar. 17, 1866.

From Alexander T. Steele[1]

New Orleans   February 16 1866

Sir

On the 24 Jany 1866, I addressed a letter to the secretary of war en-
quiring whether any board &c had been appointed to carry out the provisions of the act of Congress approved Febry 24 1864 allowing to *loyal*
owners of slaves $100 bounty & not over $300 as compensation for the
property of slaves enlisted or drafted into the army of the United States.

Several of my friends had applied to me to get for them the amount I
have named for each slave &c. A letter from Lt Col A F Rockwell[2] asst adj
Gen of date Febry 7, 1866 informs me that *no Board* had been provided
&c &c.

Please permit me to call this statute to your notice and to ask you to
provide at least for the fifteen parishes which are recognized as loyal—or
for the loyal men in all the parishes of this state *if it be right.*

My own interest in the matter is only some fifteen slaves but the interest of Louisiana is for many more.[3]

Alexr. T Steele   attorney at law
31 Commercial Place   corner St Charles St
See acts of Congress—1844 Chap 13—page 11—Sect 24—requiring
the secretary to appoint a commission &c.

ALS, DNA-RG107, Lets. Recd., Executive (M494, Roll 85).
   1. Two Alexander Steeles practiced law in New Orleans according to the 1860 census.
Probably the author of this letter was the Virginia native (*c*1817–*fl*1886) who also appears
in the 1870 census and continued to practice law until at least 1886. 1860 Census, La.,
Orleans, New Orleans, 3rd Ward, 167, 237; (1870), 2nd Ward, 73; New Orleans directories (1861–87).
   2. Almon F. Rockwell (1835–1903), a native of New York, served in the volunteers
during the war and in the Quartermaster Department of the regular army afterwards. He
retired in February 1897 with the rank of lieutenant colonel, after over thirty years' service.
Powell, *Army List,* 560; *New York Times,* Aug. 1, 1903; *New York Tribune,* Aug. 4, 1903;
Pension File, Henrietta H. Rockwell, RG15, NA.
   3. Congress repealed the act awarding compensation to loyal masters in March 1867.
Boards of commissioners appointed by the secretary of war under the terms of the 1864
measure were also dissolved. *U.S. Statutes at Large,* 15: 29.

From Thomas T. Davis[1]

CONFIDENTIAL

Philadelphia, Feb 17 1866

Mr. President

I called yesterday after noon with the hope of being able to see you a
moment before leaving town for a few days but learned that your engagements would prevent a interview.

There were two points on which I desired to say a word.

First. As to the New York Collectorship.

The paper recommending Mr. DePew[2] was pesented to me for signature and a representation made that the *Entire Delegation* (Union) from New York had signed or had agreed to sign it.[3] I had not bee present at their meetings & acted on this information which I find to be incorrect.

I desire to suggest to you in referce to that office Hon D. C. Littlejohn[4] of Oswego, N.Y who has for several terms been Speaker of our Assembly & who is in every way qualified for the position, by business experience by moral character & by political sentiment.

Governor Morgan knows him well as does Mr. Seward.[5] I think his nomination would be entirely satisfactory to the mercantile interests of New York & that his administration would be in all respects what it ought to be.

Second. As to the Bill extending the powers of the Freedmans Bureau.

Although there were features in this bill which I desired to see modified & which I regarded as highly objectionable, still as all attempts to change them were unavailing, I voted for the measure because all the powers were to be exercised by you & because I think that public sentiment would be better satisfied upon other points, if it appears that the Government is determined to protect the negro in his *freedom*.

I thought on the whole it would strengthen your friends in sustaining the position they have taken in regard to the admission of Representatives from the States lately in Rebellion.

I trust if you should disapprove the Bill, you will be able to suggest something which will if adopted show that the Freedmen shall receive the legal protection which many believe it is so essential to provide by further legislation.

In coming over last night to this City with Kasson,[6] we met Judge Kelly[7] who made the charge against you that *you* had established a Rebel news paper in Memphis Tenn. given a government press & materials for the office, put in charge of a Rebel officer as Editor[8] & taken away the government patronage from Brownlows Paper in Knoxville[9] & in violation of law had given to this secession paper. We called upon him for his proof but he could not give them. He says he has them & will prove it. When will misrepresentation cease?

Thos. T. Davis

ALS, DLC-JP.

1. Congressman representing the Syracuse, New York, district.

2. Chauncey M. DePew (1834–1928), a New York assemblyman and secretary of state, had been appointed in November 1865 as U.S. minister to Japan but declined. Apparently Johnson also favored DePew, a Republican, for the New York collectorship. In fact, as DePew recalled many years later, the appointment papers were made out and the President instructed Secretary McCulloch to have them sent to the Senate for confirmation. Yet DePew's nomination was not submitted, owing to the votes of both senators from New York to override Johnson's veto of the Civil Rights bill. Afterwards DePew became a

railroad magnate and served two full terms in the Senate (1899–1911). *BDAC*; Trefousse, *Johnson*, 247–49; Chauncey M. DePew, *My Memories of Eighty Years* (New York, 1924), 46–48.

3. Davis's own signature appears on the document. See Roswell Hart et al. to Johnson, Jan. 19, 1866, Appts., Customs Service, Collector, N.Y., Chauncey DePew, RG56, NA.

4. DeWitt C. Littlejohn (1818–1892), who commanded an infantry regiment prior to serving in Congress (1863–65), was also Thurlow Weed's and Rep. William Radford's candidate for the collectorship. *BDAC*; Jerome Mushkat, *The Reconstruction of New York Democracy, 1861–1874* (East Brunswick, N.J., 1981), 95; Radford to Johnson, Apr. 6, 1866, Appts., Customs Service, Collector, N.Y., D. C. Littlejohn, RG56, NA. See Henry A. Smythe to Johnson, Apr. 13, 1866.

5. See Thomas Machin to Johnson, Mar. 28, 1866, and Seward to Johnson, Apr. 9, 1866, both in Johnson Papers, LC.

6. Probably John A. Kasson, Iowa congressman.

7. William D. Kelley, Pennsylvania congressman.

8. Perhaps a reference to Matthew C. Gallaway, editor and publisher of the *Memphis Avalanche*. Reportedly, Gallaway visited Johnson in Washington in the fall of 1865. See William Conner to Johnson, Sept. 13, 1865, *Johnson Papers*, 9: 75.

9. Governor Brownlow's *Knoxville Whig and Rebel Ventilator*.

From Charles O. Faxon

Louisville Ky   Feb. 17, 1866

Mr President:—

Will you permit one you once recognized as your friend and who owes much to your clemency,[1] to congratulate you upon the success of your administration thus far, and to express his admiration of the wisdom and Statesmanship which has characterized your policy up to this time? Whether you triumph over those who stand between you and success of the measures for which you have been and are yet so nobly struggling, or not, you will receive the plaudits of your country men and your name will be embalmed in history among those who have labored for the welfare of their kind and the true glory of their country.

I am now, as I have been for several months, the principal writing editor of the Louisville Courier, of which you have doubtless heard; and in connection with this fact my opinions may not be without interest to you. It is fashionable with those who have a more plentiful supply of epithets than arguments to designate the Courier as a rebel sheet, but the charge so implied is not justified by any thing which has appeared in its columns. Whatever the paper may have been in days gone by, and you are familiar with its history it is now the earnest and honest advocate of the restoration of the Union, and I know that those who guide its policy do not intend that it shall occupy any other position. In my first article published in the first issue I announced that we approved warmly of your policy and should give it our support, and upon that issue I have fought the "Democrat" here, from that day to this.

I find much difficulty however in getting along with the continual suspension of the Habeas Corpus, the Freedman's Bureau and the negro troops. They are all irritating and exasperating subjects and I trust you will not consider me impertinent or obtrusive when I express the opinion that peace and good order in this state would be greatly subserved by the removal of each and all of them. I can really see no advantage to grow out of the continuance of either of them in the State but on the contrary evil and only evil.

Of course I shall not attempt to bore you with an argument upon any of these points. I did not sit down for any such purpose. I felt an impulse to express both my admiration of your policy and gratitude to you for conceiving and so boldly and fearlessly urging its adoption. I trust that this candid expression of my approval will be accepted in the friendly spirit in which it is made.[2]

C. O. Faxon

ALS, DLC-JP.

1. In reply to Faxon's initial request for executive clemency in June 1865, Johnson had indicated that no special pardon was needed. But, fearing that his first petition had been overlooked, Faxon wrote again two months later, and Johnson pardoned him on September 5, 1865. Faxon to Johnson, June 6, 1865, *Johnson Papers*, 8: 188–90; Faxon to Johnson, Aug. 10, 1865, Amnesty Papers (M1003, Roll 49), Tenn., Charles O. Faxon, RG94, NA; *House Ex. Docs.*, 39 Cong., 2 Sess., No. 116, p. 39 (Ser. 1293).

2. Three days after Faxon wrote this letter the *Courier* ran an article praising Johnson's veto of the Freedmen's Bureau bill. Faxon personally expressed his approval to Johnson in a letter on February 26, noting that the President's "appeal to the people will not be in vain. Their hearts are with you and you will be sustained." *Louisville Courier*, Feb. 20, 1866; Faxon to Johnson, Feb. 26, 1866, Johnson Papers, LC.

From Ulysses S. Grant

Washington, D.C.   February 17" 1866.

Sir:

I have the honor to submit herewith for your information, reports from the Departments of South Carolina, North Carolina, Mississippi, Georgia and Tennessee, of outrages committed by Whites against Blacks, and by Blacks against Whites, made in pursuance of the accompanying telegraphic instructions.[1]

The following tabulated statement presents a résumé of the papers:

Departments	Assault & Batt'y		Larceny		Murder		Disorderly Conduct		Drunkeness	
	Blacks	Whites	Blacks	Whites	Blacks	Whites	Blacks	Whites	Blacks	Whites
South Carolina	123	60	605	90			45	25	55	135
North Carolina		68		29		13				
Mississippi	2	14		2		22		3		
Georgia & Tennessee	4	65		2		9				
	129	207	605	123		44	45	28	55	135

Assault & Battery, excess committed by Whites 78.
Larceny, excess committed by Blacks 482.
Murders, committed by Whites 44.
Disorderly conduct & Drunkeness, excess by Whites 100.

U. S. Grant   Lieut Gen'l

LS, DLC-JP.
    1. On Christmas Day, 1865, Grant had telegraphed Generals Daniel E. Sickles, Thomas H. Ruger, Alfred H. Terry, and George H. Thomas to report "all known outrages occurring within your commands since the surrender of the rebel armies, committed by white people against the blacks, and the reverse." The information was desired "as soon as possible after the meeting of Congress." Lets. Recd. (Main Ser.), File P-770-1866 (M619, Roll 505), RG94, NA. For a similar report from the Department of Alabama, see Grant to Johnson, Mar. 14, 1866.

To Ulysses S. Grant

Executive Mansion.   Washington, D.C.
Feby. 17th 1866.

General,

H. R. Pollard,[1] Esq, has been again to see me in reference to his case.[2] I would not be considered importunate, but Mr. Pollard seems thoroughly penitent, and to give every reasonable promise for the future course of his paper,[3] and I request that the order in regard to it may be suspended for the present.

If such an order is made, the conditions upon which it is done should be clearly stipulated and expressed.[4]

Andrew Johnson

LS, DNA-RG108, Lets. Recd. re Military Discipline.
    1. Henry Rives Pollard (1833–1868), brother of journalist Edward A. Pollard, edited newspapers in Leavenworth, Kansas, and Baltimore, before serving as news editor of the Richmond Examiner from 1861 to 1867. A year later he was murdered by James Grant (no relation to the general) for a story which appeared in Pollard's Southern Opinion, a Richmond weekly. Leon G. Tyler, ed., Encyclopedia of Virginia Biography (5 vols., New York, 1915), 3: 328; National Intelligencer, Nov. 25, 1868.
    2. On February 13, 1866, Grant, through Col. Theodore S. Bowers, had ordered Gen. Alfred H. Terry to seize the offices of the Examiner owing to the paper's "dangerously inflamatory course." On the morning of the 16th, Pollard had met with Grant and later that day saw Johnson, who referred him again to the commanding general, indicating to Grant that if Pollard "makes satisfactory explanation," and promises to do better hereafter, you will be as moderate with him as possible." In an endorsement written and handed to Pollard on the following day, Grant explained that he could not revoke the suppression of the Examiner, because the paper's tone "has been such as to foster and increase the ill feeling existing towards the Government . . . by the discontented portion of the Southern people." Pollard then sought a second interview with the President, which led to Johnson's February 17 letter to Grant. Bowers to Terry, Feb. 13, 1866; Terry to Bowers, Feb. 14, 1866; Pollard to Grant, Feb. 16, 1866; Grant to [Pollard], Feb. 17, 1866; Johnson to Grant, Feb. 16, 1866, Simon, Grant Papers, 16: 70–72. See also Nashville Union and American, Feb. 20, 1866; Cincinnati Gazette, Feb. 20, 1866.

3. During the course of his interview with the President on the 17th, Pollard pledged in writing that the *Examiner* would "give a cordial support to the Union, the Constitution & the laws of the land" and continue to support Johnson's administration. Simon, *Grant Papers*, 16: 71; *Nashville Press*, Feb. 28, 1866.

4. On February 19 Colonel Bowers notified General Terry that Grant's order of the 13th was "temporarily suspended," and that the *Examiner* would be allowed to resume publication, so long as the paper gave "support, countenance and friendship to acts and expressions of loyalty to the Union and its supporters." Simon, *Grant Papers*, 16: 71–72. See also Benjamin F. Butler to Johnson, Feb. 20, 1866.

From John L. Helm[1]

Frankfort   Febr 17th 1866

The legislature of Kentucky will adjourn on Monday. I once had your acquaintance & presume to address you. I am a member of the Senate. It has pleased many of the publick journals to ascribe to me no small degree of influence in directing its deliberations and action. I think proper to acquaint you with the action of the legislature, & Some what with the publick opinion. Senator Trumbull Sent me his bureau bills. We regard them as violations of the Constitution. An inovation on the rights and powers of the States, and So far as Kentucky is concerned wholly useless and productive of much harm & destructive to the negro. With these opinions I advised that our legislation Conform as near to the provisions of those bills as our manhood would allow. I think I can safely say there are but two points left open for a conflict of law. These are we will not Consent that a negro shall be viewed as a witness between two white men as litigants.[2] We think our laws allow him to be a witness in all other cases. Violence on the person of a white woman by a negro is death, by a white man it is a long confinement in the penitentiary. We would not & will not change that. We desire to leave open one or two points, So if collusion arose we may have an opportunity of getting judicial exposition of the powers Confirmed by the 2 clause of the amendment. We think that necessary to the future harmony of Society.

Touching fedederal relations there was a great variety of opinions as indicated by the resolutions presented[3] & to some extent diverse opinions among the Democratick Conservative party and the Same in regard to what is familiarly known as the radical party. I had presented the most pointed and important which would have passed both houses. I send you a copy & my speech.[4] In view of the Struggle you were making for restoration, and fully appreciating the dificulties by which you were Surrounded tho not agreeing with you in Some things touching the mode I thought publick duty required we should take no step which might possibly give pretext for increasing your dificulties. I led the way and consented that my own proposition should be passed over for action at the adjourned Session next winter, and with it went all others.

The radical party presented in the house two distinct propotins. One asking you to restore the writ of Habeas Corpus. The other to remove the freedmans bureau. These with slight amendment in verbiage in the Senate passed.

I say to you frankly if that is not done, you will not get a cordial endorsement from Kentucky.

The people in this State in overwhelming numbers Sustain you in your position to regard the Seceded States as of the Union. They look with curious interest however to what mode is left you to accomplish your object with your conceded right to Congress to be the exclusive judges of the qualification of their Members. That power has been perverted, there is no doubt of that. But what now the remedy? It seems to me the nation cannot stand the agony of another four years of Suspense. If things are kept as they are till another presidential election, I can See at once all the opposition must rally on you because you have a position to force the right. I imagine a fierce Conflict. You getting all the Southern states & enough from elsewhere to give you a majority of the electoral votes. Your opponent is hard bye, and insists the Southern states shall not be counted. Here is the advent for another revolution. Stevens has boldly proclaimed the purpose of general confiscation to pay the publick debt, and Secure homes for negroes. This is a tempting bate in these degenerate days of pocket patriotism and false philanthropy. Revolutions grow until the occasion is accomplished or they are wasted by exhaustion. You have before you a desperately diseased body politick. You must patiently wait to see if it has vitality enough left in its Constitution to recover if left to a natural process, or there must be applied a desperate remedy. If it is thought best to wait the next congressional election to develope more fully the disease you have the chances for abatement and you run the risk of increased malignity & render the cure more hopeless. You are on the ground and I have much confidence in your political sagacity & prudence. But remember one thing fanaticism & despotism are never conquered by submission. That revolutions are most easily managed in their incipient stages. It is not unfrequently they are crushed by a Single blow made in a bold and dareing thrust at its vitals.

I have thought if you made a proclamation that the rebellion had been quelled, that peace had been restored, that the states were once more united, and general amnesty granted, then pause for a while awaiting theaction of Congress. If they would not yield, I would call all the members elected from the Southern States to Washington. I would Signify to Shearman I desired his presence with a certain number of regulars on a given day. When that day arrived I would at the head of the senatorial delegation, walk into the senate chamber and lift myself at least to the height of old hickory & say it is my duty to see the laws are executed; that I regarded further delay in admitting them revolutionary & direct an officer to swear them in. I would see it was done. If any move was made for expulsion I would ring Sewards bell. If the radicals left I would notify that their seats were vacant. I would go through the same process in the house having duly posted a squad of observation with a request that members remain in their seats. Keep a force there until the process is complete. Rely on it the agony would be over and the Country would manifest their gratitude to you. Kentucky will stand by you by more than 100000 majority. However eratick, & presumptious this may seem to be I hoped your excellency will receive it in the kind spirit which prompts it.[5]

John L. Helm

ALS, DLC-JP.

1. Helm (1802–1867), an Elizabethtown lawyer, was a prewar legislator, lieutenant governor, governor, and president of the Louisville & Nashville Railroad. Elected to the state senate in 1865, Helm chaired the committee on federal relations and worked to repeal laws that placed restrictions upon ex-Confederates. He was elected governor in 1867 but died a few days after taking the oath of office. *DAB*.

2. In February 1866 Governor Bramlette signed a bill which conferred certain civil rights upon blacks, but not the right to testify in the courts. With the exception of the Lexington circuit, all the Kentucky courts eventually denied black testimony against whites, a practice that was not changed until legislation in 1872. Victor B. Howard, "The Black Testimony Controversy in Kentucky, 1866–1872," *JNH*, 58 (1973): 140–42, 146, 164.

3. Helm probably alludes here to the series of resolutions adopted by Union (Republican) members of the legislature who had met in a party caucus on January 17. A copy of the resolutions had earlier been forwarded to the President. See Albert G. Hodges to Johnson, Jan. 20, 1866, *Johnson Papers*, 9: 613–14.

4. Not found. On February 3 Helm, as chair of the senate committee, presented a report protesting against the Thirteenth Amendment. The report incorporated the resolutions passed earlier by the Republican caucus. It condemned the Freedmen's Bureau, requested that the President remove the Bureau, as well as troops, from Kentucky, and it demanded that the writ of habeas corpus be restored. After reading the report, Helm delivered a lengthy speech in favor of the resolutions. Discussion of the committee's report was postponed, however, until after the legislature had reconvened in a later session. See *Louisville Journal*, Feb. 6, 14, 1866.

5. Three days later Helm wrote Johnson to express satisfaction with his veto of the Freedmen's Bureau bill. See Helm to Johnson, Feb. 20, 1866, Johnson Papers, LC.

From David W. Lothrop[1]

West Medford, Ms., Feb. 17/66.

Honored Sir:

I am so well pleased with the wise and firm stand you have taken in regard to the reconstruction of the late rebel states—and especially that relating to negro suffrage—that I am prompted to express to you my congratulations, even though a private and humble individual of Massachusetts.

The people of this State have looked with so much horror upon slavery for the past few years, that now, since the advent of the war and the enlistment of colored men into the Federal army, the freedmen are regarded as beings holding the first place in their hearts, and for whom there can be no check to the gushings of their humanity. Politicians have seized upon this feeling and turned it to their own account. Many national events have favored them, and a party, once small, has been increased into one of great power; the current that at first was a mere ripple has been augmented in volume, increased in power, and accelerated in its flow, so that now many tremble at a reckless torrent which threatens to sweep everything before it, whether good or evil. And although the original impetus may be removed, it will still roll heedlessly along till its momentum is exhausted. A reaction, however, will finally come, and then things will probably be viewed in a more philosophical and calmer temper.

The negro has assisted the Union in its struggle against slavery, and in the overthrow of the latter (as you have intimated) he has his reward. He can go where he pleases—into any State. But few only profess to see this among the Republicans of Massachusetts. The majority demand suffrage as his only recompense, besides claiming it as a right. But Massachusetts has changed her opinion on many important subjects the past ten years, and it is quite likely she will in this.

It would be well now to pause and ask whether in endeavoring to banish all "distinction in color," we are not encouraging the black man to hope for more than can be extended to him, and whether a real *fusion without distinction of color* (if possible) is not in violation of the laws of God and inimical to the welfare of both races. I know, Sir, you think so, and I am happy to agree with one who has had a far better opportunity to judge in the premises than myself. Can we have a harmonious *political* fusion without a *social* fusion? And as every white man, at least, *prefers his own race*, and wishes to see only his own blood and features in his grandchildren, we cannot *encourage* intermarriage, though the laws may permit it. The Irish, Germans, &c. lose, very soon, their *identity* when among us, but the black man never. No humanity can ever bridge over the gulf between the Caucasian and the Negro, though the one may represent as worthy a race as the other. Nevertheless, they are *radically* distinct, to use a popular term. God has made them so, and I would not impeach him, even in the name of humanity.

But, Sir, what is the *real*, *social status* of the colored man in Massachusetts, in Boston, where he has the ballot, and is "equal before the law" in all respects with the white man? Here is the residence of the Hon. Charles Sumner and Gov. John A. Andrew, eloquent, whole-souled men, having a great influence. Although Massachusetts has been intensely antislavery for the past ten or twelve years, the colored people of this State are as much ignored as ever. They hold no office, and can get none; commingle with white men only on business, are debarred the hospitalities of the dominant race at their firesides and in their drawing-rooms, and at the ballot-box can only choose between two men of a different color from their own! The black man complains, as well he may; but Mr. Sumner would naturally reply, "Are you not equal before the law, and do you mean to say that there is now any prejudice against color in old Massachusetts? If so, *I* can't help it."

"Prejudice!" No, Mr. President, it is nature, reason, "higher law." But whatever we term it, it plainly shows that there can be no affiliation worthy of the name between the black and white races on the basis of equality. With anything like equal numbers, the struggle for power begins, each contending for his own race. So the opportune lesson of Jamaica tells us. The truth seems to be self-evident, that while the white man always favors his own race and color, the black man never forgets that he is black. How then can the two races live together on an equality and without unhappy distinctions?

For myself, I prefer my own color, though I can wish well for the black man. When he is by himself, as he ought to be, on a national foundation and independent—when no greater questions underlie the right of suffrage—he can then use the ballot and the sword in his own behalf. But the white American will not yield up to him any power here—in any of the States, not even in Massachusetts—and hence it must be wrong to place him in a position to hope for it. Without this hope or actual power, of what use will his suffrage be at the South? It seems quite plain, in the nature of things, that if the negro covets office and political influence among *us*, he must not only hold *one* rein, but *both*; in other words, he must put us under his feet!

I am glad to see that you speak of "emigration" and "colonization," as did your honored predecessor, Mr Lincoln. They are words as significant now as with our forefathers, when they wisely sought a more congenial home across the pathless ocean. Every people who would be free must endure an allotment of hardships. Many intelligent colored people of the North, who have escaped the seductive influence of the wily politician, have gone to Liberia, firmly believing that this is no place for their proper development; and if they love their race, and wish to preserve it, the body of them will turn their eyes and steps in that direction. Could it take place, it would effectually solve the negro question, and leave a happy void in our national politics, to be occupied with topics more profitable to the nation, and far less exciting.

I should like to say more upon this subject, but fear an apology is necessary for saying what I have. I am a Republican, but have but little time to devote to politics. Still, I think and judge for myself, and take an especial interest in the poblem of the freedmen. Feeling rather diffident about giving my true signature, from the liberty I have taken to address you, I present my *representative*, trusting that that will suffice.[2]

Beechcroft, W. Medford Ms.

L, DLC-JP.

1. Lothrop (c1817–fl1881) was a printer and a Massachusetts native. 1860 Census, Mass., Middlesex, Medford, Somerville, 78; Boston directories (1861–81).

2. Evidently Lothrop placed some sort of mark, perhaps a seal, on the document immediately after the complimentary closing but it is impossible to determine now what it might have been. At any rate, a comparison of this February 1866 letter with a Lothrop letter of April 1867 leaves no doubt that this letter was written by him. Historian William S. McFeely has also reached the same conclusion. See Lothrop to Johnson, Apr. 8, 1867, Johnson Papers, LC; McFeely, *Yankee Stepfather*, 242n.

From Samuel P. Walker

Nashville Tennessee.   Feby. 18th. 1866.

Sir.

Within the last week a "Francise Bill" has been introduced into the House of Representatives (in Lieu of all other Bills on that subject) and hurried to a third Reading by a majority, without printing & with but little discussion & attempted to be forced through, by a call of the "Previous Question."[1] We had no power to amend it, or to offer Amendments to any of its sections or provisions.

Under this Bill the Govorner has the power to appoint Commissioners in every County in the State—all old registrations to be cancelled & the voting population to be restricted to *the few* these Commissioners *may Choose to give Certificates to*, under the severe restrictions of the Law, and the immense *power* given to the Commissioners under the Law.

The minority in the House, (being powerless to prevent its passage, & feeling that it was utterly destructive to Republican-Democratic liberty in Tennessee,) had no alternative, but to be absent from the House & leave them without a quorum.[2]

We do not mean by this to disorganize the State,—but we want time, we want delay, with the hope that reason & reflection may induce the majority to be *just* to the people, & to disfranchise only those, *who are not Loyal to the Govornment*, & if they choose, such as are now disfranchised under the present Law.[3]

If they have the right under a Republican form of Govornment, to pass this Bill—they have the same right & the same *power* to still further restrict it—leaving the people with no voice in the Govornment,—& with no protection, except such as the *limited few* may choose to give them.

If we have done wrong—it has been from an error of judgement & a consciencious desire to preserve, as far as we can, the right of *Loyal Citizens* in the State to exercise the Elective franchise.

I hope you will excuse me for this long letter, in explanation of the Course of the Conservative members of the House.

Saml P. Walker

ALS, DLC-JP.

1. In late January 1866 the house committee on franchise had introduced a revision of the 1865 law. The measure quickly passed the house on first and second readings but was

halted by a filibuster and eventually by lack of a quorum. Beginning on February 13 and continuing for several days no business could be conducted by the house; eventually the speaker issued warrants for the return of eleven absent members. Coulter, *Brownlow*, 283–84; Alexander, *Reconstruction*, 105–6; Patton, *Unionism and Reconstruction*, 115.

2. The strategy escalated from mere absence to actual resignations of some of the conservative legislators. With the legislature thus stalemated, Governor Brownlow denounced the members who had resigned and called for elections to be held on March 31 to replace the resigned lawmakers. Alexander, *Reconstruction*, 106–8; Patton, *Unionism and Reconstruction*, 116; Coulter, *Brownlow*, 284.

3. Eventually parliamentary manipulations enabled the house to establish a quorum in early April, whereupon the new franchise law passed that chamber on April 12. Subsequently it cleared the state senate. Alexander, *Reconstruction*, 108–9; Coulter, *Brownlow*, 285–86; Patton, *Unionism and Reconstruction*, 116, 118.

From Mark W. Delahay

No 362 Mass Avenue   Washington D C
Februay 19th 1866

Sir

It may not be out of place for me, in these exciting times, to offer to you my feeble support. I have perused with some care your *Veto Message* returning the Freedmens' Bureau Bill to the Senate. I had thought it a ponderous measure, involving large expenditures, much of which would be carried into States and Districts when there was neither demand or plausible excuse for its extension. It is not to be supposed, that a law creating patronage that can be lawfully claimed by every member of Congress will be overlooked or refused even where there is not the least necessity for the extension of the Offices created by the Bill. But the following point in your message if we are to foster the true definition of the Constitution Strikes me with paramount force. You correctly Say, "the Constitution imperitively declares in connection with taxation that each *State Shall have* at least *one representative* and fixes the rule for the number to which in future times each State Shall be entitled" and further you Strongly present the following Constitutional obligation, That "no State without its consent Shall be deprived of its equal Suffrage in the Senate."

And again you present a Cardinality to which all men Should Subscribe, when you Say in the language of the Constitution—"The princiqlle is firmly fixed in the minds of the American people that there Should be no taxation without representation." I agree with you fully that your Stand point is quite different from that of a any Single representative. You have to deal with the Union, with *all its parts*. The Union by the *victory* of our *arms* is either maintained in its entirety, else the war closed too Soon. While I think likely *South Carolina* and perhaps Mississippi at present would not likely be able to Send loyal men as representatives, Still Tennessee, perhaps Louisiana and Arkansas Can Send Such as can take the required oath and who are truly loyal. They Should Stand upon their own merits and each other State *lately* in rebellion

Should be judged upon their Seperate merits when they come up for trial and judgement at the bar of Either Branch of Congress.

I congratulate you on the *Significant* firmness of your purpose as shown in that Message to thwart the wild unbridled and ambitious political passion of those who Seek to destroy, rather than reconstruct upon principles of harmony and good will.

I was your early friend in Kansas. I was the first man west of the Mississippi River that ever brought forward the name of the lamented Lincoln for the Presidency.[1] He was my friend for thirty years—he never beleived the States lately in rebellion were out of the Union—and in that view I fully concurred. As I am upon the bench[2] and Seek nothing at your hands, I have thought perhaps a letter from me fully endorsing your general policy might not be regarded out of place.

Mark W Delahay
U.S. District Judge for Kansas—

ALS, DLC-JP.
1. In December 1859 Lincoln visited Kansas and stayed with the Delahays. The judge's daughter recalled helping to serve at a political dinner party at which Delahay predicted that Lincoln would be the next president. After this prediction became true, it was referred to in Kansas as "Delahay's prophecy." Mary E. Delahay, "Judge Mark W. Delahay," KSHS *Collections*, 10 (1907–08): 640.
2. Appointed as a district judge in late 1863, Delahay served until 1873. Frank W. Blackmar, ed., *Kansas: A Cyclopedia of State History . . .* (4 vols., Chicago, 1912), 1: 305.

From Charles Dement[1]

Dixon Ills   Feby 19 1866

Dr Sir

Excuse a plain simple farmer if he ventures to address a line of commendation. In these times of trial it is well for a man to know his friends (I want no office, so you may understand that is not the motive which actuates me). I write to *say stand firm and immovable* in your noble and manly position taken in your reconstruction policy.

The country wants the union of the States, wants it brought about in the least time practicable & with the least cost of money and fraternal good will.

We are groaning under burdensome taxation. If the policy of Stephens & Sumner are carried out, involving additional expenditure of millions if not hundreds of millions in unnecessarily large armies of soldiers and armies of politicians under the Freed mens bureau bill, piling taxes still higher upon the people, it will end in repudiation of the whole government debt. The money can not be raised by the people. And rest assured that if the people come to be convinced that congress has created a fraudulent obligation, one that they are not in justice bound to respect, it will be easy to convince them that they should pay none of it. When men are driven to extremes they will do desperate acts. Do not let such a case arise.

The Man that makes the old Constitution his Chart to sail the Government ship by is sure not to run her on rocks or shoals, but will always find good water, and a *ready crue* to insure her against any *casualties* that may arise. But if the Constitution is to be disregarded by President and Congress, who are sworn to guard it from violation, then the oath administered is a farce, and the constitution in the language of Beecher "a dead sheep skin"[2] in reality.

The policy indicated in your reply to Fred Douglas and other colored men, your response to the Montana Delegation as also your reply to the Virginia Delegation is one of conciliation,[3] a policy that appeals at once to the better impulses of human nature and rest assured will be met in a like friendly spirit by the South, and in a short time commercial intercourse will heal all wounds that can be healed, and the Union of the States will be a fixed fact.

But sir if such men as Wendel Phillipps, Sumner, & Stephens are to have the settling of this question in which every citizen of the whole U.S. is deeply interested I most earnestly believe it will end in the final overthrow of this government and possibly involve us in a worse conflict than that we have just passed through.

Wendell Phillipps I see has just sounded the key note of radicalism, proclaiming bitter war upon your Exellency.[4] *Be not dismayed.* They have sickened the country with their hobby for political position. The people are beginning to think of the old maxim "selfe preservation is the first law of nature,["] after which they are willing to be very charitable to the negroe.

Politically I have always voted the Democratic ticket, never have been a *politician*. I like your Jacksonian independence, and am for the man that will administer the government upon the principles of the *constitution*. Giving traitors whether north or south plainly to understand that they must keep within its provisions.

My father was a native of Galatin Tenn. & his name was David Dement.[5] He left two brothers there, Cater & Charles.[6] I mention their names as you may possibly know them. I have not heard from them since the rebellion. They may have been carried along in the general vortex in which they were. Such most probably is the case.

With every assurance of my high consideration, I subscribe my selfe. . . .

Chas Dement

ALS, DLC-JP.
1. A native of Illinois, Dement (1822–1875) owned and operated Dement House in Fulton, Illinois, before engaging in "land operations" and farming in Dixon. Dement and

his brother were extremely active in locating lands in the Dixon land district. *History of Lee County* (Chicago, 1881), 239–40; James W. Oberly, *Sixty Million Acres: American Veterans and the Public Lands before the Civil War* (Kent, Ohio, 1990), 137.

2. Dement is possibly quoting Edward Beecher (1803–1895), who served as president of Illinois College and later as pastor of the First Congregational Church of Galesburg. Robert Meredith, *The Politics of the Universe: Edward Beecher, Abolition, and Orthodoxy* (Nashville, 1968 [1963]), vii-x, 104.

3. See Interview with Delegation of Blacks and Remarks to Citizens of Montana, both Feb. 7, 1866, and Response to Virginia Legislative Delegation, Feb. 10, 1866.

4. Dement may be reacting here to the editorial, entitled "Our Poor White President," which ran in Phillips's *Standard* on February 17, 1866. Irving H. Bartlett, *Wendell Phillips: Brahmin Radical* (Boston, 1961), 299.

5. Dement was an early Sumner County landowner, juror, and cotton inspector who migrated to the Southern Illinois frontier in 1816. W.P.A., Tenn., *Records of Sumner County, County Court Minutes* (1936), 346, 387, 420, 581, 666; Goodspeed's *History of Gallatin, Saline, Hamilton, Franklin and Williamson Counties, Illinois* (Chicago, 1887), 352.

6. Possibly Cader Dement, whose will was filed in the Rutherford County Court in October 1849, and Charles Dement, also of Rutherford County. Susan G. Daniel, "Index to Some Actual Wills of Rutherford County, TN 1802–1882," RCHS *Pubs.*, 12 (1979), 71; Henry G. Wray, comp., *Rutherford County, Tennessee Deed Abstracts, Vol. 1, 1804–1810* (Smyrna, n.d.), 94.

Freedmen's Bureau Veto Message[1]

Washington, February 19, 1866.

To the Senate of the United States

I have examined with care the bill, which originated in the Senate and has been passed by the two Houses of Congress, to amend an act entitled "An act to establish a bureau for the relief of freedmen and refugees," and for other purposes. Having with much regret come to the conclusion that it would not be consistent with the public welfare to give my approval to the measure, I return the bill to the Senate with my objections to its becoming a law.

I might call to mind in advance of these objections that there is no immediate necessity for the proposed measure. The act to establish a bureau for the relief of freedmen and refugees, which was approved in the month of March last, has not yet expired. It was thought stringent and extensive enough for the purpose in view in time of war. Before it ceases to have effect further experience may assist to guide us to a wise conclusion as to the policy to be adopted in time of peace.

I share with Congress the strongest desire to secure the freedmen the full enjoyment of their freedom and property and their entire independence and equality in making contracts for their labor, but the bill before me contains provisions which in my opinion are not warranted by the Constitution and are not well suited to accomplish the end in view.

The bill proposes to establish by authority of Congress military jurisdiction over all parts of the United States containing refugees and freedmen. It would by its very nature apply with most force to those parts of the United States in which the freedmen most abound, and it expressly extends the existing temporary jurisdiction of the Freedmen's Bureau, with greatly enlarged powers, over those States "in which the ordinary course of judicial proceedings has been interrupted by the rebellion." The source from which this military jurisdiction is to emanate is none other than the President of the United States, acting through the War Department and the Commissioner of the Freedmen's Bureau. The agents to carry out this military jurisdiction are to be selected either from the Army or from civil life; the country is to be divided into districts and subdistricts, and the number of salaried agents to be employed may be equal to the number of counties or parishes in all the United States where freedmen and refugees are to be found.

The subjects over which this military jurisdiction is to extend in every part of the United States include protection to "all employees, agents, and officers of this bureau in the exercise of the duties imposed" upon them by the bill. In eleven States it is further to extend over all cases affecting freedmen and refugees discriminated against "by local law, custom, or prejudice." In those eleven States the bill subjects any white person who may be charged with depriving a freedman of "any civil rights or immunities belonging to white persons" to imprisonment or fine, or both, without, however, defining the "civil rights and immunities" which are thus to be secured to the freedmen by military law. This military jurisdiction also extends to all questions that may arise respecting contracts. The agent who is thus to exercise the office of a military judge may be a stranger, entirely ignorant of the laws of the place, and exposed to the errors of judgment to which all men are liable. The exercise of power over which there is no legal supervision by so vast a number of agents as is contemplated by the bill must, by the very nature of man, be attended by acts of caprice, injustice, and passion.

The trials having their origin under this bill are to take place without the intervention of a jury and without any fixed rules of law or evidence. The rules on which offenses are to be "heard and determined" by the numerous agents are such rules and regulations as the President, through the War Department, shall prescribe. No previous presentment is required nor any indictment charging the commission of a crime against the laws; but the trial must proceed on charges and specifications. The punishment will be, not what the law declares, but such as a court-martial may think proper; and from these arbitrary tribunals there lies no appeal, no writ of error to any of the courts in which the Constitution of the United States vests exclusively the judicial power of the country.

While the territory and the classes of actions and offenses that are made subject to this measure are so extensive, the bill itself, should it become a law, will have no limitation in point of time, but will form a part of the permanent legislation of the country. I can not reconcile a system of military jurisdiction of this kind with the words of the Constitution which declare that "no person shall be held to answer for a capital or otherwise infamous crime unless on a presentment or indictment of a grand jury, except in cases arising in the land or naval forces, or in the militia when in actual service in time of war or public danger," and that "in all criminal prosecutions the accused shall enjoy the right to a speedy and public trial by an impartial jury of the State and district wherein the crime shall have been committed." The safeguards which the experience and wisdom of ages taught our fathers to establish as securities for the protection of the innocent, the punishment of the guilty, and the equal administration of justice are to be set aside, and for the sake of a more vigorous interposition in behalf of justice we are to take the risks of the many acts of injustice that would necessarily follow from an almost countless number of agents established in every parish or county in nearly a third of the States of the Union, over whose decisions there is to be no supervision or control by the Federal courts. The power that would be thus placed in the hands of the President is such as in time of peace certainly ought never to be intrusted to any one man.

If it be asked whether the creation of such a tribunal within a State is warranted as a measure of war, the question immediately presents itself whether we are still engaged in war. Let us not unnecessarily disturb the commerce and credit and industry of the country by declaring to the American people and to the world that the United States are still in a condition of civil war. At present there is no part of our country in which the authority of the United States is disputed. Offenses that may be committed by individuals should not work a forfeiture of the rights of whole communities. The country has returned, or is returning, to a state of peace and industry, and the rebellion is in fact at an end. The measure, therefore, seems to be as inconsistent with the actual condition of the country as it is at variance with the Constitution of the United States.

If, passing from general considerations, we examine the bill in detail, it is open to weighty objections.

In time of war it was eminently proper that we should provide for those who were passing suddenly from a condition of bondage to a state of freedom. But this bill proposes to make the Freedmen's Bureau, established by the act of 1865 as one of many great and extraordinary military measures to suppress a formidable rebellion, a permanent branch of the public administration, with its powers greatly enlarged. I have no reason to suppose, and I do not understand it to be alleged, that the act of March, 1865, has proved deficient for the purpose for which it was passed, although at that time and for a considerable period thereafter the Government of the United States remained unacknowledged in most of the States whose inhabitants had been involved in the rebellion. The institution of slavery, for the military destruction of which the Freedmen's Bureau was called into existence as an auxiliary, has been already effectually and finally abrogated throughout the whole country by an amendment of the Constitution of the United States, and practically its eradication has received the assent and concurrence of most of those States in which it at any time had an existence. I am not, therefore, able to discern in the condition of the country anything to justify an apprehension that the powers and agencies of the Freedmen's Bureau, which were effective for the protection of freedmen and refugees during the actual continuance of hostilities and of African servitude, will now, in a time of peace and after the abolition of slavery, prove inadequate to the same proper ends. If I am correct in these views, there can be no necessity for the enlargement of the powers of the Bureau, for which provision is made in the bill.

The third section of the bill authorizes a general and unlimited grant of support to the destitute and suffering refugees and freedmen, their wives and children. Succeeding sections make provision for the rent or purchase of landed estates for freedmen, and for the erection for their benefit of suitable buildings for asylums and schools, the expenses to be defrayed from the Treasury of the whole people. The Congress of the United States has never heretofore thought itself empowered to establish asylums beyond the limits of the District of Columbia, except for the benefit of our disabled soldiers and sailors. It has never founded schools for any class of our own people, not even for the orphans of those who have fallen in the defense of the Union, but has left the care of education to the much more competent and efficient control of the States, of communities, of private associations, and of individuals. It has never deemed itself authorized to expend the public money for the rent or purchase of homes for the thousands, not to say millions, of the white race who are honestly toiling from day to day for their subsistence. A system for the support of indigent persons in the United States was never contemplated by the authors of the Constitution; nor can any good reason be advanced why, as a permanent establishment, it should be founded for one class or color of our people more than another. Pending the war many refugees and freedmen received support from the Government, but it was never intended that they should thenceforth be fed, clothed, educated, and sheltered by the United States. The idea on which the slaves were assisted to freedom was that on becoming free they would be a self-sustaining population. Any legislation that shall imply that they are not expected to attain a self-sustaining condition must have a tendency injurious alike to their character and their prospects.

The appointment of an agent for every county and parish will create an immense patronage, and the expense of the numerous officers and their clerks, to be appointed by the President, will be great in the beginning, with a tendency steadily to increase. The appropriations asked by the

Freedmen's Bureau as now established, for the year 1866, amount to $11,745,000. It may be safely estimated that the cost to be incurred under the pending bill will require double that amount—more than the entire sum expended in any one year under the Administration of the second Adams. If the presence of agents in every parish and county is to be considered as a war measure, opposition, or even resistance, might be provoked; so that to give effect to their jurisdiction troops would have to be stationed within reach of every one of them, and thus a large standing force be rendered necessary. Large appropriations would therefore be required to sustain and enforce military jurisdiction in every county or parish from the Potomac to the Rio Grande. The condition of our fiscal affairs is encouraging, but in order to sustain the present measure of public confidence it is necessary that we practice not merely customary economy, but, as far as possible, severe retrenchment.

In addition to the objections already stated, the fifth section of the bill proposes to take away land from its former owners without any legal proceedings being first had, contrary to that provision of the Constitution which declares that no person shall "be deprived of life, liberty, or property without due process of law." It does not appear that a part of the lands to which this section refers may not be owned by minors or persons of unsound mind, or by those who have been faithful to all their obligations as citizens of the United States. If any portion of the land is held by such persons, it is not competent for any authority to deprive them of it. If, on the other hand, it be found that the property is liable to confiscation, even then it can not be appropriated to public purposes until by due process of law it shall have been declared forfeited to the Government.

There is still further objection to the bill, on grounds seriously affecting the class of persons to whom it is designed to bring relief. It will tend to keep the mind of the freedman in a state of uncertain expectation and restlessness, while to those among whom he lives it will be a source of constant and vague apprehension.

Undoubtedly the freedman should be protected, but he should be protected by the civil authorities, especially by the exercise of all the constitutional powers of the courts of the United States and of the States. His condition is not so exposed as may at first be imagined. He is in a portion of the country where his labor can not well be spared. Competition for his services from planters, from those who are constructing or repairing railroads, and from capitalists in his vicinage or from other States will enable him to command almost his own terms. He also possesses a perfect right to change his place of abode, and if, therefore, he does not find in one community or State a mode of life suited to his desires or proper remuneration for his labor, he can move to another where that labor is more esteemed and better rewarded. In truth, however, each State, induced by its own wants and interests, will do what is necessary and proper to retain within its borders all the labor that is needed for the development of its resources. The laws that regulate supply and demand will maintain their force, and the wages of the laborer will be regulated thereby. There is no danger that the exceedingly great demand for labor will not operate in favor of the laborer.

Neither is sufficient consideration given to the ability of the freedmen to protect and take care of themselves. It is no more than justice to them to believe that as they have received their freedom with moderation and forbearance, so they will distinguish themselves by their industry and thrift, and soon show the world that in a condition of freedom they are self-sustaining, capable of selecting their own employment and their own places of abode, of insisting for themselves on a proper remuneration, and of establishing and maintaining their own asylums and schools. It is earnestly hoped that instead of wasting away they will by their own efforts establish for themselves a condition of respectability and prosperity. It is certain that they can attain to that condition only through their own merits and exertions.

In this connection the query presents itself whether the system proposed by the bill will not, when put into complete operation, practically transfer the entire care, support, and control of 4,000,000 emancipated slaves to agents, overseers, or taskmasters, who, appointed at Washington, are to be located in every county and parish throughout the United States containing freedmen and refugees. Such a system would inevitably tend to a concentration of power in the Executive which would enable him, if so disposed, to control the action of this numerous class and use them for the attainment of his own political ends.

I can not but add another very grave objection to this bill. The Constitution imperatively declares, in connection with taxation, that each State *shall* have at least one Representative, and fixes the rule for the number to which, in future times, each State shall be entitled. It also provides that the Senate of the United States *shall* be composed of two Senators from each State, and adds with peculiar force "that no State, without its consent, shall be deprived of its equal suffrage in the Senate." The original act was necessarily passed in the absence of the States chiefly to be affected, because their people were then contumaciously engaged in the rebellion. Now the case is changed, and some, at least, of those States are attending Congress by loyal representatives, soliciting the allowance of the constitutional right for representation. At the time, however, of the consideration and the passing of this bill there was no Senator or Representative in Congress from the eleven States which are to be mainly affected by its provisions. The very fact that reports were and are made against the good disposition of the people of that portion of the country is an additional reason why they need and should have representatives of their own in Congress to explain their condition, reply to accusations, and assist by their local knowledge in the perfecting of measures immediately affecting themselves. While the liberty of deliberation would then be free and Congress would have full power to decide according to its judgment, there could be no objection urged that the States most interested had not been permitted to be heard. The principle is firmly fixed in the minds of the American people that there should be no taxation without representation. Great burdens have now to be borne by all the country, and we may best demand that they shall be borne without murmur when they are voted by a majority of the representatives of all the people. I would not interfere with the unquestionable right of Congress to judge, each House for itself, "of the elections, returns, and qualifications of its own members;" but that authority can not be construed as including the right to shut out in time of peace any State from the representation to which it is entitled by the Constitution. At present all the people of eleven States are excluded—those who were most faithful during the war not less than others. The State of Tennessee, for instance, whose authorities engaged in rebellion, was restored to all her constitutional relations to the Union by the patriotism and energy of her injured and betrayed people. Before the war was brought to a termination they had placed themselves in relations with the General Government, had established a State government of their own, and, as they were not included in the emancipation proclamation, they by their own act had amended their constitution so as to abolish slavery within the limits of their State. I know no reason why the State of Tennessee, for example, should not fully enjoy "all her constitutional relations to the United States."

The President of the United States stands toward the country in a somewhat different attitude from that of any member of Congress. Each member of Congress is chosen from a single district or State; the President is chosen by the people of all the States. As eleven States are not at this time represented in either branch of Congress, it would seem to be his duty on all proper occasions to present their just claims to Congress. There always will be differences of opinion in the community, and individuals may be guilty of transgressions of the law, but these do not constitute valid objections against the right of a State to representation. I would in no wise interfere with the discretion of Congress with regard to the qualifications of members; but I hold it my duty to recommend to you, in the interests of peace and the interests of union, the admission of every State to its share in public legislation when, however insubordinate, insurgent, or rebellious its people may have been, it presents itself, not only in an attitude of loyalty and harmony, but in the persons of representatives whose loyalty can not be questioned under any existing constitutional or legal test. It is plain that an indefinite or permanent exclusion of any part of the country from representation must be attended by a spirit of disquiet and complaint. It is unwise and dangerous to pursue a course of measures which will unite a very large section of the country against another section of the country, however much the latter may preponderate. The course of emigration, the development of industry and business, and natural causes will raise up at the South men as devoted to the Union as those of any other part of the land; but if they are all excluded from Congress, if in a permanent statute they are declared not to be in full constitutional relations to the country, they may think they have cause to become a unit in feeling and sentiment against the Government. Under the political education of the American people the idea is inherent and ineradicable that the consent of the majority of the whole people is necessary to secure a willing acquiescence in legislation.

The bill under consideration refers to certain of the States as though they had not "been fully restored in all their constitutional relations to the United States." If they have not, let us at once act together to secure that desirable end at the earliest possible moment. It is hardly necessary for me to inform Congress that in my own judgment most of those States, so far, at least, as depends upon their own action, have already been fully restored, and are to be deemed as entitled to enjoy their constitutional rights as members of the Union. Reasoning from the Constitution itself and from the actual situation of the country, I feel not only entitled but bound to assume that with the Federal courts restored and those of the several States in the full exercise of their functions the rights and interests of all classes of people will, with the aid of the military in cases of resistance to the laws, be essentially protected against unconstitutional infringement or violation. Should this expectation unhappily fail, which I do not anticipate, then the Executive is already fully armed with the powers conferred by the act of March, 1865, establishing the Freedmen's Bureau, and hereafter, as heretofore, he can employ the land and naval forces of the country to suppress insurrection or to overcome obstructions to the laws.

In accordance with the Constitution, I return the bill to the Senate, in the earnest hope that a measure involving questions and interests so important to the country will not become a law, unless upon deliberate consideration by the people it shall receive the sanction of an enlightened public judgment.

ANDREW JOHNSON.

Richardson, *Messages*, 6: 398–405.
1. For a careful analysis of the various drafts of the veto message submitted by several different Johnson advisers, see John H. and LaWanda Cox, "Andrew Johnson and His Ghost Writers: An Analysis of the Freedmen's Bureau and Civil Rights Veto Messages," *MVHR*, 48 (1961–62): 460–79.

From Hugh McCulloch

Treasury Department   February 19. 1866.

Sir:

Concurring in the recommendation of the Solicitor of the Treasury,[1] that the whole subject should be referred to the President for such action

A depiction of Johnson's veto of
the Freedmen's Bureau Bill
Harper's Weekly, April 14, 1866

as he may deem proper in the premises, etc., I have the honor to submit herewith all the papers before this Department in regard to certain gold coin, now held as captured property, which is claimed by some of the banks lately if not now in operation in Richmond, Va.[2]

As it seems to be clearly established that the coin is regarded as captured solely by virtue of your order on the subject, and as it is held as a special deposit in the Treasury by your direction, it is considered that no person other than yourself can properly give any orders or take any action in the case.

The papers are therefore submitted to you, as stated above, for your decision; and I shall take pleasure in receiving and putting into effect, so far as any action of this Department may be concerned such directions as you may see fit to give on the subject.[3]

I will thank you, also, to cause them to be returned with your instructions.

H. McCulloch, Secretary of the Treasury

LBcopy, DNA-RG56, Lets. Sent *re* Restricted Commercial Intercourse (BE Ser.), Vol. 12.

1. Edward Jordan (*fl*1879) served in this capacity under both Lincoln and Johnson. Afterwards he practiced law in the D.C. area. *U.S. Off. Reg.* (1861–69); Washington, D.C., directories (1869–80).

2. In April 1865 Richmond bankers, fearing for the safety of their specie deposits, sent a substantial sum of gold coin and bullion to the town of Washington, Georgia. On August 23, 1865, Johnson ordered that the money be turned over to Treasury Department agents; whereupon it was transported to the nation's capital. A convenient summary of the claims of the Richmond banks is found in *National Intelligencer*, Mar. 6, 1866, and *House Misc. Docs.*, 45 Cong., 2 Sess., No. 5 (Ser. 1815).

3. On March 2 Johnson rendered his decision that the money should be removed from the Treasury Department and returned, under proper procedures, to the Richmond banks. However, a dispute over the ownership of the banks' assets delayed their return for more than thirty years. Ibid.; *U.S. Statutes at Large*, 29: 809; *Washington Evening Star*, Mar. 5, 1866; Decision Concerning Richmond Banks, Mar. 2, 1866, Lets. Recd. from Sec. of the Treasury, RG206, NA.

From John P. White

Nashville Tenn   Feby 19th 1866

Dr Sir

I arrived here from Texas on yesterday where I went on my return from Washington to settle the business of George with Gov Hamilton,[1] but I am sorry to say accomplished nothing after Gov H— had sent the Post Master at Austin[2] all the way to Washington to see and say to George to return and that he should have protection and he would settle the matter with him but on my arrival there he determined the he as Provisional Gov had no power to do it but was willing to accept my proposition which I deemed fair and Just to both the state of Texas and George and the Gov was willing and expressed himself anxious to accept but doubted his power to settle and with this view of the matter he is anxious for George to return and they together will present the matter to the Convention now in sesion & the Legislature soon to Convene. The enclosed Communication[3] he explains itselfe to you and pledges full protection to George if he returns and Gov H— asked me to say to you to give him protection to return and he would see that he was not harshly treated and I now ask as another faver to me on the recpt of this to Telegraph to George W White Austin Texas care of F. W. Chandler[4] giving him your protection to remain there for the purpose of settling his business. He George was at New Orleans on my return and I made him go to Austin on Gov Hamiltons pass so as to be able to meet the Convention before it adjourned and he is there by this time and it would seem from the pledges he made to me and what he says to you in the enclosed paper from him[5] that I ought to have no fears but I must confess that from what I know of the man and the part he has acted in this matter from the beginning I have no confidence in him and I will take it as a kindness to me to Comply with Gov H— request and Telegraph immediately to George or Gov H— giving him your protection to remain there for the purposes mentioned by Gov H.

I found the great mass of the people of Texas sincerely your friends and warm supporters and think you the best *man* on *earth* and say but for you they the people of that state would have been terribly oppressed. Still there has been many wrongs perpetrated but all is now going on very well. The present officers of the state govermt are nearly all known to be unfrindly to you and your reconstruction policy from the Gov. to the lowist officer in the state, but the better class of Union men in Texas are your friends and of course all others.

It has been the custom in other southern states to send your Prov Governors to the senate. This will not be the case from Texas. They will elect Judge's Hancock & Evans[6] two original union men who left the state during the war and are known to be your warm frinds and supporters & men who can take the test oath if required.

My fathers family are very well. I forgot to mention that our friend G W Jones will be here this evening a delegate to the Convention to be held here on Thursday[7] and I hope we will have a speech from him.

John P White

ALS, DLC-JP.
1. This is doubtless a reference to the continuing conflict between George W. White and Texas officials over the matter of bonds. For an earlier reference to this dispute, see George W. Paschal to Johnson, Sept. 20, 1865, *Johnson Papers*, 9: 104–6.
2. Perhaps William Rust (b. c1791), who served as Austin postmaster from the late 1850s through the war years; he had moved to Texas in the early 1850s. Rust sought a presidential pardon in September 1865 and received one in November. Amnesty Papers (M1003, Roll 54), Tex., William Rust, RG94, NA; *U.S. Off. Reg.* (1861–65).
3. Andrew J. Hamilton to Johnson, Jan. 31, 1866, Johnson Papers, LC.

4. Frederick W. Chandler (*c*1814–*fl*1880), an Austin lawyer, was a native of Massachusetts who had moved to Texas in 1847. He sought a presidential pardon from Johnson in August 1865 and received it in November. 1860 Census, Tex., Travis, Austin, 90; (1870), 87; (1880), 5th Ward, 133rd Enum. Dist., 13; Chandler to Johnson, Aug. 19, 1865, Amnesty Papers (M1003, Roll 52), Tex., Frederick W. Chandler, RG94, NA; *House Ex. Docs.*, 39 Cong., 2 Sess., No. 116, p. 57 (Ser. 1293).

5. This is perhaps a reference to the letter from George W. White to Johnson, Feb. 5, 1866, written from New Orleans.

6. John Hancock and Lemuel D. Evans, neither of whom was elected.

7. White refers here to the forthcoming February 22 meeting in Nashville.

From Jeremiah S. Black

Washington   Feb. 20, 1866

Dear Mr. President;

Your message has made millions of good hearts glad and grateful for it has saved the nation. You ought to be—I hope you will be—sustained by every man who loves Peace and Union. The high ground you take will insure you an easy and complete defence against all opposers; and you will realise the great truth that *"Peace hath her victories more renowned than those of War."*[1]

I do not write this because I think that my individual opinion is of any account but because I know that I share what will be the universal sentiment as soon as the passions of the hour shall cool. In the meantime "let the heathen rage;" there is no danger that "the people will imagine a vain thing."[2]

J. S. Black

ALS, DLC-JP.

1. From John Milton's "To the Lord General Cromwell."

2. Variation of Psalms 2:1, "Why do the heathen rage, and the people imagine a vain thing?"

From Benjamin F. Butler

Hoffman House [New York]   Feb 20th. 1866

Dr Sir

I was so struck with a couple of articles from the "New York Sunday Times" in reference to a subject of conversation[1] which I had the honor to suggest to you that I have ventured to cut them out and enclose them.[2]

What concern can the General of the Army have with the *"question of Reconstruction?"* In time of *Peace* what control has he over the liberty of the Press in States of the Union that he should issue "HIS orders?"[3]

Benj. F Butler

ALS, DLC-JP.

1. Butler was in Washington during much of the month of February, and is reported to have had at least one interview with the President, which occurred on the 7th. Jessie A.

Marshall, ed., *Private and Official Correspondence of Gen. Benjamin F. Butler* (5 vols., Norwood, Mass., 1917), 5: 700–701; *Washington Morning Chronicle*, Feb. 13, 1866; *Washington Evening Star*, Feb. 7, 1866.

2. He probably refers to articles entitled, "The Southern Press" and "The Ax to the Root," both concerning General Grant's circular letter of February 17 to department commanders, instructing them to forward copies of Southern papers which "contain sentiments of disloyalty and hostility to the Government." *New York Times*, Feb. 18, 1866; Simon, *Grant Papers*, 16: 72.

3. Butler's hostile feelings toward Grant apparently stemmed from his removal from command of the Army of the James in January 1865 following his aborted attempt to take Fort Fisher. During the summer and fall of 1866 Butler vehemently attacked his former commanding general in public speeches for his leniency toward the defeated Confederate army after Lee's surrender. The two men did not mend their differences until the spring of 1868. William S. McFeely, *Grant: A Biography* (New York, 1981), 197–98; Hans L. Trefousse, *Ben Butler: The South Called Him Beast!* (New York, 1957), 186; Richard S. West, Jr., *Lincoln's Scapegoat General: A Life of Benjamin F. Butler, 1818–1893* (Boston, 1965), 327–28.

From Albert B. Buttles[1]

Columbus Ohio   Feby 20th 1866

Having been from the first announcement of your name, a warm friend of your nomination as Vice President, and having in the opinion of several members of the Ohio Delegation to the Baltimore Con. contributed as much to that result as any member of that body, I take the liberty of saying a few words, as to the political crisis which seems impending. The personal fact above mentioned, would probably never have been brought to your notice, except that it might gain me a hearing, and because it is freshly in my mind from reading the very able Speech of Mr Delano,[2] and observing the striking coincidence between the position of Congress and the Baltimore Convention as to the question discussed by Mr D. Mr Stevens and his friends, in that Convention (mostly members of Congress), were strenuously contending, then as now, against the admission of the Delegation from Tennessee, while Mr Delano, argued precisely as he does now, in their favor. As Secretary of the Ohio Delegation, it fell to me, to take our vote upon the admission of the Tennessee Delegates, and am sorry to say that vote was very close, being only 17 "aye" to 16 "nay"; but by a vote early adopted, the vote of the State was to be cast on all questions, "as a Unit" and the full vote of the State was thus secured in the affirmative. And when in calling the roll of States the Secretary of the Convention came to Ohio, and Mr Delano arose and responded, "Ohio 42 votes *Aye*" there followed such a storm of applause from galleries and convention, that it was sometime before order could be restored & the call proceeded with. Up to that time the vote had been very much divided, but this was felt to be so decisive of the result that many States began to change their votes favorably and the final result was declared "310 Aye, 150 Nay." I may add as a personal reminiscence, which may be of interest that the 42 votes of Ohio were secured for you by a preliminary vote in Caucus of 19 for Johnston, 17 for Dickenson[3] & a few scattering. The facts are sufficiently suggestive, and show at least that your nomination at Baltimore was the result probably, of the very policy you now advocate.

But the sole object in writing you, Mr President, is to implore you to STAND BY the great body of the Union Party who nominated and elected you, and I do assure you, as one who ought to know, in this locality, at least, that they will *stand by you*. In behalf of the Union *people*, I would say that we can stand, do, or give up almost anything, but we cannot and will not affiliate with that party which has been Stabbing in the dark at us, at *you* and at the whole country during the last four years. I believe, earnestly, that whatever position may be taken by the extremists in Congress, that a very large majority of those who voted for Lincoln and Johnson in this District will stand by and sustain you so long as you remain as they believe you are now, in harmony with the Union Party proper, and that very many of the better portion of the Democracy, will *come* over to sustain you & the party—thus purged of its ceaseless agitators and factionists.

The true Copperheads here seem delighted with your veto message, but, as you no doubt well know, not from any thought or care about the freedmen, the Country or yourself but, simply, because they hope it may be the element of discord which is to seperate you from the Party which elected you. God forbid, that so disastrous an event should ever befal the Country. At the suggestion of several of your friends, I have to day, written about the substance of this letter to our member Mr Shellabarger,[4] and *he* knows what authority my opinion is entitled to in this District. I could refer you to Gov Dennison[5] as to any statement I have made.

A B Buttles

ALS, DLC-JP.

1. Buttles (1823-*c*1871) was an attorney, former county clerk, and member of the state Republican central and executive committees. Columbus directories (1856–72); *History of Franklin and Pickaway Counties, Ohio* (Philadelphia, 1880), 83; Buttles to William Dennison, Dec. 1, 1864, Lincoln Papers, LC.

2. In his speech in the House of Representatives on February 10, Columbus Delano, representing the 13th District of Ohio, asserted that the southern states were still in the Union but not entitled to representation in Congress without certain conditions. *Congressional Globe*, 39 Cong., 1 Sess., Appendix, pp. 85–91.

3. Daniel S. Dickinson, New York War Democrat.

4. Samuel Shellabarger.

5. William Dennison, postmaster general.

From Enoch T. Carson
Private

Cincinnati   Feb. 20, 1866.

Dear Sir.

Your Veto message has produced a most profound Sensation here, among the Republicans. It is too Soon yet to form an opinion as to what will follow. This however I am sure of the Cincinnati Gazette, heads the radical wing and will undoubtedly assail you and your policy, in front and rear.[1] The Commercial will support you. I have seen the editor[2] to day, and he most unquallifiedly endorses your message, and regards it as a very able document in which you have stated matters clearly, and he says he would be glad if it were possible to submit your Message and the Freedmans Bill to the popular vote of the people at once. The Commercial you know wields an immense influence on Western politics. Your friends and admirers in this city are not the leading men of the Republican party, they have long since been thrown overboard for "disloyalty," but it begins to look now as though their services may soon be required again, to hold the Jacobins to their place. I dont mean the Buternuts— but the Sober Staid thinking men of the Union party—that portion that beleives we have some fragments of our old organic law still left—from the ruins and so beleiving the want to support & maintain them.

I have taken this opportunity to drop you a note to assure you of my confidence in Your integrity, statesmanship, and honesty of purpose to restore this Union so far as it can be done to something approximating to what it was when given us by our fathers. You will undoubtedly be assaulted in the most venomous manner, and I feel as one of your friends that a word of approbation even from the most humble of your friends at such a time may not be ungrateful to you.

                                                    E. T. Carson.

ALS, DLC-JP.
    1. On this date a correspondent to the newspaper blasted Johnson's veto of the Freedmen's Bureau bill, considering it a "complete withdrawal from the great party which elected him and a union with conservative Copperheads and rebels." The next few days found numerous articles published in the paper critical of the veto. *Cincinnati Gazette*, Feb. 20, 21, 23, 1866.
    2. Martin D. Potter (1819–1866), who began his newspaper career as a journeyman printer in Jackson, Mississippi, had served as editor and senior proprietor of the *Commercial* since 1854. See Potter's editorial support of Johnson's veto message in the February 21 issue of the *Cincinnati Commercial. Chicago Tribune*, Apr. 7, 1866; *Cincinnati Enquirer*, Apr. 5, 1866.

From John F. Coyle[1]

                        Editorial Department National Intelligencer,
                            Washington, February 20th 1865[1866][2]
    Will you allow us to call your attention to a matter, so small in comparison with great events transpiring around us, that we apologize to your Excellency for trespassing on your time.

    The Department of State sent to the Ministers abroad some 60 (sixty) copies of the Daily Chronicle and to the Publishers of the Laws about 60 (sixty) more of the same. I submit, in view of the Editorial in to-days Chronicle,[3] whether *that* is the proper paper to be sent to our Ministers abroad or to be circulated among the Press at home, from that or any other Dept of the Government. Under the ban of the War Dept,[4] while that creature Stanton remains, who loses no opportunity of striking at your friends and the friends of the Constitution and the Country, I respectfully ask that *you will direct* Mr Seward to place us on that list where we were for many years under all administrations, until removed from it by his order for some fancied discourtesy, which displeasure he might with justice transfer to the Chronicle in view of the very offensive article to your Excellency which appear this morning.[5]

John F. Coyle
for Snow,[6] Coyle & Co.

ALS, DNA-RG59, Entry 149, Lets. Recd. *re* Publishers of Laws.

1. Prior to purchasing the *Intelligencer* from William Seaton in late 1864, Coyle (*c*1822–*fl*1875) had been a clerk and bookkeeper at the offices of the newspaper. The *Intelligencer* ceased publication at the end of the decade. 1860 Census, D.C., Washington, 4th Ward, 266; Washington, D.C., directories (1858–68); Coyle to Johnson, Feb. 26, 1875, Johnson Papers, LC; William E. Ames, *A History of the National Intelligencer* (Chapel Hill, 1972), 336–37, 338.

2. Internal evidence makes obvious that the date is actually 1866, instead of 1865.

3. The editorial referred to was quite critical of Johnson's veto of the Freedmen's Bureau bill, declaring at one point that the President's message "will fall like the cold hand of death upon the warm impulses of the American people who have given so much of their treasure and their blood to the cause of the Republic." *Washington Morning Chronicle*, Feb. 20, 1866.

4. This "ban" probably stemmed from the newspaper's break with Lincoln and the Republican party under the *Intelligencer*'s former management. When several cabinet members and Johnson discussed the issue of public printing in the spring of 1866, Stanton recalled that President Lincoln had "ordered him to publish in the *Chronicle*." Robert S. Harper, *Lincoln and the Press* (New York, 1951), 182–84; Beale, *Welles Diary*, 2: 490.

5. Johnson referred the letter to Secretary Seward, who had dropped the *Intelligencer* from the list of publishers of the laws for the second session of the Thirty-eighth Congress. The *Intelligencer* was placed back on the State Department's list and the *Chronicle* was temporarily removed. Moreover, according to newspaper accounts, the President directed his department heads to stop advertising in the *Chronicle*. *U.S. Off. Reg.* (1865–67); *Cincinnati Enquirer*, Mar. 1, 1866.

6. Chauncey H. Snow (*fl*1874) teamed up with Coyle to establish the publishing company that bought the *Intelligencer* from Seaton. Washington, D.C., directories (1866–75); Ames, *National Intelligencer*, 336.

From David W. Lafollette[1]

New Albany, Ind   Feb 20th/66

Dear Sir,

I beg your pardon humble individual as I am, of troubling you amidst your weighty and fearful responsibility, with an indorsement of your veto message of the Freedman's Bureau which I most heartily endorse. I am forty years of age, and am a Republican, and had to battle manfully recently in our county convention to get resolutions passed endorsing your administration, over the head and opposition of all the principal office holders of the Government, among whom were the Collector of Internal

Revenue of this district (2nd) and the Post master of this city.[2] But the
mass of the People endorse you, and will ever do So while you Stand by
the Constitution, as you are now doing, and they respectfully ask of you
to only retain Such men in Office as do not endorse your administration.
That however you are to determine not us.

I Saw Sometime Since a Bill was before the Senate, authorizing you to
District the U.S. for the Purpose of appointing Pension Agents.[3] If that
Bill has become a Law, I respectfully in behalf of a large number of Pen-
sioners, request that you will examine the Propriety of establishing an
agency in this City, all Southern Indiana, being compelled to draw their
Pensions at Indianapolis.[4] I beg leave to refer you in relation to this matter to Hon. W. T. Otto, Acting Secretary of the Interior, with whom I was
personally and well acquainted for more than 18 years past.[5]

David W. Lafollette,

ALS, DNA-RG48, Patents and Misc. Div., Lets. Recd.

1. Lafollette (1825–*fl*1882) was an attorney, judge, and law professor. *History of the
Ohio Falls Cities and Their Counties* (2 vols., Cleveland, 1882), 2: 217.

2. Benjamin F. Scribner and John M. Wilson, respectively. Scribner (1825–1900), a
Mexican War veteran and author, had commanded an Indiana infantry regiment before
Lincoln appointed him in 1865 as revenue collector in which capacity he served for six
years. He continued his profession as a druggist until his move to Alaska, where he served
as a treasury agent. Wilson (*c*1819–*fl*1871), an unsuccessful Republican candidate for
Congress in 1858 and an attorney, was New Albany's postmaster from April 1861 to May
1869. 1870 Census, Ind., Floyd, New Albany, 2nd Ward, 21; Richard E. Banta and
Donald E. Thompson, comps., *Indiana Authors and Their Books, 1816–1916* (3 vols.,
Crawfordsville, 1949–81), 1: 286; *NUC*; *Louisville Courier-Journal*, May 2, 1871;
Charles Zimmerman, "The Origin and Rise of the Republican Party in Indiana from 1854
to 1860," *InMH*, 13 (1917): 367–68; *U.S. Off. Reg.* (1861–69).

3. Probably a reference to the resolution submitted by James H. Lane of Kansas, on
December 18, 1865, instructing the Senate Committee on Pensions to consider the expediency of having the President appoint pension agents. No further action regarding Lane's
resolution has been found. *Congressional Globe*, 39 Cong., 1 Sess., p. 67.

4. Pension agencies were also located in Madison and Fort Wayne. *U.S. Off. Reg.*
(1861–81).

5. The letter was referred to the secretary of the interior and answered on February 27.

From William M. Lowry

New York, Feb 20th 1866

Dear Sir

I have been in this city a few days. Came by way of Nashville Cincin-
natti Pittsburg &c. Spent two days at Nashville where I met many of our
old friends among them Judge Milligan who I am proud to state stands
very high in the confidence of the people and the head of the court. My
object more particularly in dropping you this hasty note is so far as my
humble opinion will go to commend your efforts to restore us a great National Union. Your late veto is being handsomely sustained here, by all
loyal lovers of the Union and they look to you as the only man now able to
defeat the extreme bad men both North & South. I will remain here some

8 or 10 days when I will leave for home by way of Washington where I hope to have the pleasure of seeing you. Trusting that your noble efforts may restore us a great National Union of fraternal feelings and community of interest. . . .

Wm. M Lowry.

ALS, DLC-JP.

From William Marvin

New York   16 Exchange Place
Feby 20. 1866.

Sir,

As the late provisional Governor of Florida and the Senator elect from that state, I cannot forbear to express to you my thanks for the honest fair and able defence of the constitution of the United and of the *Union*, contained in your message to congress returning the freedmens bureau bill. I have faith to believe that the sober second thought of the people, north as well as south, will sustain you in the position you have taken. I know, that in Florida neither the interests of the people, black or white, nor the cause of humanity requires any such legislation by congress.

Wm. Marvin

ALS, DLC-JP.

From Sam Milligan

Greeneville Ten   Feb. 20. 1866

Dear Sir:

Since I reached home, and rested a little, I have endeavored to post myself up in relation to National affairs. I feel I am far behind the current events of the day, but enough is apparent for the most ignorant to see you are having a hard time. Tied hand and foot by a dominant majority in Congress, who seem not to have scarcely a National pulsation; and with all an infatuation in relation to the negro, which is wholly impracticable, and absolutely delusive. I *know* that you are their friend, and in your heart of hearts always have been opposed to the accursed institution. But it does not follow, that all those who labored and fought for their emancipation, must deify them, or even imperil the safety of the Government, for their sake. They have as yet no appreciation even of the family relation, much less of the form or spirit of our government. What they may hereafter become, is left to be seen, but surely, they are not now as a race capable of self-government.

But enough of the negro. There are higher questions pressing hard upon you. The very hope of the republic emphatically rests on your shoulders. No man in Europe or America, in my humble opinion, ever had so heavy a burden. The danger of centralization is eminent. If the policy of the Stephens-Sumner school prevails, republican institutions are lost. Ten years, even without a foreign war, will not elapse, before every vestage of popular liberty will be gone. And with a foreign war, the whole South and much of the North, will unite with the foreign enemy, especially if the war shall be waged on our own soil. There is no hope outside of your policy: and I trust in God, you will stand firm. I know your faith in the people, as well as your distrut of politicians. Now, if ever is the time, earnestly & perseveringly to appeal to the source of all power. The people are with you, and a firm and unwavering course, guided by principle, must and will prevail. The selfish, sectional policy of the leader's of the opposition, I have no doubt, is founded in *political corruption*. I do not know the truth of this statement, but a little attention to this subject, I feel sure, will develope facts enough to damn, in public estimation, every one of them. Spring the triggers on them at the proper time! Added to this, be sure, and advocate the policy of which you spoke when I saw you,[1] of locating the burdens of taxation on the *rich minority*, and leave the *voting majority* to hold it firmly there. The rebel news papers are acting the fool. They are too impatient, and utterly insensible that they have acted a dishonorable part in the rebellion. They are mainly responsible for all the troubles the country labors under, & ought to be held in with a tight rein. I think if Mr Speed, under your directions, could find a sufficient apology to deliver an official opinion in relation to the violation of their Amnesty, and pardons, I am satisfied some of them have violated their obligations, and ought to be indicted. It would do you & them good. Old Mr Fogg[2] & I looked into it at Nashville, and became satisfied such was the law. Mr Fogg is your firm friend and great admirer. He is down on Brownlow & Fletcher—says the latter has no sense. My wife sends her regards to you & family.

                                                                  Sam Milligan

ALS, DLC-JP.
    1. Probably a reference to Milligan's Washington visit in November 1865. See Elizabeth R. Milligan to Johnson, Nov. 29, 1865, *Johnson Papers*, 9: 444–45.
    2. Francis B. Fogg.

From Edward P. Pitts[1]

                                                          Accomac Ct. House Va.
                                                                Feby. 20th 1866
Sir;
    I take the liberty of introducing to your favourable notice, my friend Jno. B. Ailworth Esqr.[2] of this county who visits Washington in the hope of obtaining through your kindly aid, an office, to enable him to support a

large and dependent family. Mr. Ailworth has been a firm and consistent supporter of the Union Cause from the commencement of our late struggle; and has occupied, as all Union men in Va. did occupy, a most trying position and now is even more trying than before. A Union man in Va. and in all of the Southern States, as all, who are informed on the subject, know and if candid will say, occupies a more unfortunate position than any other person either white or black.

The secessionist has the favor of all around him and of the State Government; the negro has the protection of the Genl. Government but the Union man in the South is without succor from any quarter and I had almost said without safety. Look at the Legislature of Va. where Mr. Ailworth had a right to expect aid and had the promise from the Gov. of the State, that he would not forget him, all the offices have been bestowed exclusively upon a party which we might have supposed would have been satisfied with a share, when in fact not entitled to any.

I commend Mr. Ailworth to your favorable notice; he is a *true* friend of the Government and of yours; he needs and deserves aid from the Government he has served with a fidelity which will be his ruin if left to depend upon the present rulers of his native State. I hope it may be your pleasure to give him an office[3] that will enable him to support and rear in credit a family of eight children and a feeble wife.

E. P. Pitts
Judge of the 5th Judicial Circuit of Va.

ALS, DNA-RG56, Appts., Internal Revenue Service, Assessor, Va., 1st Dist., John B. Ailworth.

1. Pitts (c1817–fl1870) was a lawyer and circuit court judge (1852–69) in Accomack County. After stepping down from the bench he practiced law in Norfolk. 1850 Census, Va., Accomack, St. George's Parish, 156; (1870), Norfolk, Norfolk, 4th Ward, 7; Nora M. Turman, *The Eastern Shore of Virginia, 1603–1964* (Onancock, Va., 1964), 272.

2. Ailworth (c1808–fl1870), a merchant before the war, was clerk of the court of Accomack County (1862–65). In the 1860 presidential campaign he was a Douglas elector. Ibid., 274; 1860 Census, Va., Accomack, St. George's Parish, Pungoteague, 186; (1870), Locust Mount, 234; William H.B. Custis to Johnson, Feb. 21, 1866, Appts., Internal Revenue Service, Assessor, Va., 1st Dist., John B. Ailworth, RG56, NA.

3. In May Johnson appointed Ailworth as assessor for the First District of Virginia; he held this position at least through 1867. *U.S. Off. Reg.* (1867); Ser. 6B, Vol. 4: 117, Johnson Papers, LC.

From Orville H. Browning

Washington D.C.   Feby 21, 1866

Sir

I desire to thank you for your able, patriotic and statesmanlike veto of the Freedman's Bureau bill. Had that bill received your sanction, and been put into operation, the restoration of the unity and harmony of our unhappy Country would, thereby, have been made impossible.

Its effect would have been to subvert the constitution, and substitute, in the places where it operated, a military despotism for constitutional government; and I cannot doubt that you will be sustained, by the people, in your efforts to preserve to them the guarantees, privileges, and blessings of the institutions founded by the sages and patriots of the revolution.[1]

O. H. Browning

ALS, DLC-JP.
1. Two days after writing this letter Browning and Thomas Ewing called on Johnson and expressed their approval of "his veto of the Freedmans Bureau bill, and of his measures of restoration generally." They also discussed possible changes in the cabinet. James G. Randall, ed., *The Diary of Orville Hickman Browning* (2 vols., Springfield, Ill., 1925–33), 2: 62–63.

From Oliver O. Howard

Washington, Feby 22d 1866.

Sir:

The subject of the land set apart by General Sherman's Special Field Order No. 15, series of 1865,[1] now presses upon me for immediate settlement. The crop for the present year, turns upon the decision of the Government.

The orders under which I am now acting, are to make an arrangement mutually satisfactory between the land-owners and the resident freedmen. Many places have been restored under these instructions. In order not to break faith with these freedmen, who had received possessory titles, or who occupied lands under General Sherman's order, I had hoped to render them some equivalent or indemnity; possibly this may yet be afforded them by some future action of Congress.

With a most earnest desire to do everything I can, to promote a satisfactory settlement of all the conflicting claims, I still feell unwilling to make any sweeping restoration of the lands above named to their former owners without more definite instructions than I have yet received either from yourself or the Sec'y of War. In your recent message to Congress,[2] with reference to this very matter, it is claimed by the agents of these land-owners, that your orders are sufficiently clear, to require me to make an immediate restoration putting their lands on precisely the same footing, as other lands held by the bureau. I may be mistaken, but I do regard the question as one of the greatest importance, and requiring for the interest of all parties concerned, the most speedy solution.[3]

O. O. Howard
Maj. Gen'l. Commissioner

LS, DLC-JP.
1. See William T. Sherman to Johnson, Feb. 2, 1866.
2. Freedmen's Bureau Veto Message, Feb. 19, 1866. Johnson objected, on constitutional grounds, to taking "land from its former owners . . . without due process of law."

3. On July 16, 1866, Congress overrode Johnson's veto and extended the life of the Bureau. Blacks who still held possessory titles were allowed to harvest their crops, claim compensation for improvements, and exchange their Georgia grants for the right to buy twenty-acre plots along coastal South Carolina from land owned by the Federal government. Implementation of this plan, with many local variations, took years. See Paul A. Cimbala, "The Freedmen's Bureau, the Freedmen, and Sherman's Grant in Reconstruction Georgia, 1865–1867," *JSH*, 55 (1989): 597–632.

From Illinois Editors and Publishers[1]

February 22d. 1866
Peoria, Ill.,

The undersigned Editors and Publishers of the Democratic Newspapers of Illinois, in Convention assembled at Peoria, Illinois, on the 22d day of February 1866, respectfully represent unto your Excellency that they are now rendering a cordial and zealous support to your Administration; that they remember with pleasure your early and long career as a Democrat and a Statesman; that your restoration policy meets their unqualified approbation, and that they hail with delight your late message vetoing the Freedmen's Bureau Bill;[2] that the Democratic party of Illinois is prepared to support you in the good work you have begun; that there should be a community of action and opinion between the Executive and his subordinates in office; that sound policy would recommend that the great Democratic party should be officially recognized by the appointment of one of their number to a position in your Cabinet; that Major General John A. McClernand of Illinois, your old personal and political friend and supporter would be acceptable to the Democracy and Conservative Republicans of Illinois and the Northwest, and that we earnestly recommend that he be placed in a situation which will make his name, influence and talents available to the Administration. And therefore, in case of a vacancy in the position of Secretary of War, by removal of the present incumbent or otherwise, we earnestly and respectfully recommend unto your Excellency the appointment of Gen. McClernand to that position.[3]

Pet, DLC-JP.
1. There were twenty-three signatories, headed by convention president John W. Merritt (1806–1878), editor of the *Illinois State Register* and an "uncompromising Democrat," who enclosed this memorial in his letter to Johnson's son-in-law. *History of Sangamon County, Illinois* (Chicago, 1881), 228; Merritt to David T. Patterson, Feb. 26, 1866, Johnson Papers, LC.
2. During a mass meeting held in Peoria several days later, upwards of two thousand people endorsed the President's veto message, praising Johnson as the "defender of the Constitution—the champion of the people & the savior of the country." Isaac Underhill and W. T. Dow[d]ell to Johnson, Feb. 26, 1866, Johnson Papers, LC.
3. A position for McClernand during Johnson's administration was not forthcoming, despite Merritt's repeated urging. Merritt to Johnson, June 21, 1867, Tels. Recd., President, Vol. 6 (1867–68), RG107, NA.

From James A. Rogers

Brownsville Tenn.   22nd Feby, 1866

Dr. Sir,

On the 7th of last Decr. I wrote a letter to you,[1] giving you a true and correct Statement of the condition of affairs in our country. In this letter I had occasion to refer to the operations of the F. Bureau, believing that in all cases justice was not awarded to those who deserved. It seems that this letter of mine, was placed in the hands of Genl. Grant, by him to Genl Howard, from Genl. Howard to Genl Fisk and by him it was sent to R. C. Scott[2] Superintendent here: by this letter I have drawn down upon my self the ire of the *unerring* Bureau. He has written a letter to Genl. Fisk, endeavoring to make him beleive that I am a traitor to the United States Government, that I had been an inhuman master &c. I herewith enclose a copy of my letter to Genl. Fisk and the accompanying certificates[3] and I could get hundreds more, were I to take the time to do so.

It seems that we are committing high treason if a citizen but modestly adverts to any of the acts of the uncorruptible & undefiled Bureau. It is a perfect money machine, as managed and conducted in this country. I ask it of you as a favor from one of your old friends that you read my statement.

Edward J. Read Esqr. of this place Attorney at Law, a good Union man says he wants the appointment of U.S. D. Attorney for this District in the place of Mr. Williamson who has been appointed chancellor.[4] Please give it to him as he is fully qualified.

James A. Rogers

ALS, DLC-JP.

1. We have not located a December letter from Rogers to Johnson.

2. Robert C. Scott (*c*1823–*fl*1870), a native of Virginia, was a resident of Haywood County, where he had served as sheriff in the 1850s and would subsequently serve as constable. 1860 Census, Tenn., Haywood, Brownsville, 37; (1870), 7; Goodspeed's *Lauderdale, Tipton, Haywood, and Crockett*, 822.

3. As indicated, Rogers's letter to Fisk and the "certificates" are enclosed. Rogers emphasized that he was "one of the original union men of this unfortunate country." Moreover, he stressed that "Every raiding party, from Genl Forrest down to the lowest thieving guerrilla that came through our country, were set on me." The accompanying statements from friends in Haywood County attest to Rogers's unionism and to his benign treatment of slaves.

4. John L. Williamson, who had received a recess appointment as district attorney, was nominated by Johnson in December 1865 and commissioned in late January 1866. Evidently the President next attempted to have Judge Marland L. Perkins of Memphis appointed; but after his nomination in December 1866, Perkins was rejected by the Senate. Johnson then nominated Stanford L. Warren, who took the post later in 1867. Ser. 6B, Vol. 4: 227–28, Johnson Papers, LC; *U.S. Off. Reg.* (1865–67).

Speech to Washington Monument Association[1]

[Washington, February 22, 1866][2]

Gentlemen of the Association:

It is no ordinary pleasure to me to have it in my power to meet you here on this occasion, and participate in your proceedings, intended to resume and progress in the completion of a monument, if I may speak in the language of his eulogist, to him who was "the first in war, the first in peace, and the first in the hearts of his countrymen." I repeat, it is no ordinary pleasure to me to meet you here on this occasion, on the birthday of the Father of his Country, and participate with you in your efforts to complete the monument intended to commemorate his name. I was only in expectation of meeting the society, and not an audience so large as this, and of remaining but a few moments for the purpose of giving whatever little aid or influence I could toward the completion of a monument which every American citizen ought not only to feel proud of but earnestly help forward. I hope and trust the work will soon be completed; I hope and trust that if there are any States which have not yet contributed and placed their pledges in that monument of the Union bearing their inscription, it will go on until all the States have done so. I will here remark, it will continue to go on notwithstanding we have disturbed relations of some of the States to the Federal Government—that it will continue to go on until those relations are harmonized and our Union again be complete. ⟨Applause.⟩ Let us restore the Union, and let us proceed with the monument founded as its symbol until it shall contain the pledges of all the States of the Union. Let us go on with this great work; let us complete it at the earliest moment practicable, and in its progress it will serve to stimulate and encourage the restoration of the States to the Union. Instead of throwing impediments and difficulties in the way, it should be the highest ambition of all to remove every impediment and give every facility that would restore the Union of these States in their original relations to the Federal Government. ⟨Applause.⟩ Then let us restore the Union, and let it stand in perpetuity as it was designed by the fathers who founded the Government. Let your monument rise—if I may be permitted to speak in the language of that celebrated and distinguished statesman who made the greatest effort of his life in vindication of the Union of these States—let the monument of Washington rise higher and higher until it shall meet the sun in his coming, and his last parting ray shall linger and play on its summit. ⟨Applause.⟩

I thank you, gentlemen, for the compliment you have conferred upon me in inviting me to attend on this, the birthday of the Father of his Country, to participate with you in your proceedings, and I hope and trust your noble efforts will be crowned with success. ⟨Applause.⟩

National Intelligencer, Feb. 24, 1866.

1. This organization assembled at the City Hall for its annual meeting. After the election of officers, it was announced that Johnson had arrived and would address the group. Washington lawyer Philip R. Fendall welcomed the President and gave a brief address prior to Johnson's speech. *National Intelligencer*, Feb. 24, 1866; *Washington Evening Star*, Feb. 22, 1866.

2. Internal evidence as well as corroborating evidence establish the date and place for this document.

From Richard Sutton

Washington D C   Feby 22, 1866

My dear Sir

Your Speech of this Evening[1] is in many respects a remarkable one and perhaps it will excite a more intense feeling throughout the U S than any other of Modern days. Its argumentation and its reasoning it was very important to get before the people. Its personal allusions were very caustic and will excite violent indignation, & here again was a reason why it should be given a wide circulation in its entirety as soon as possible. It is admirable in style, cogent in argument, and keenly biting in its personal reflections, and withal heroically bold and true to principle.

I found that there were various reporters for Newspapers taking notes of your Speech, & I know that the large newspapers of the important Cities *will not publish another report after publishing one of their own however imperfect*: I therefore availed myself of a fortunate opportunity to have it telegraphed to a prominent paper in Philadelphia, one in New York City, and one in Boston. The Philadelphia paper will be back before Congress meets tomorrow and the others will give a wide circulation to the Speech in important sections of the Country. I was prompted to do this because I found the N Y Herald had reporters employed that I am Satisfied cannot do it justice. I make this explanation because I have deviated from what I understood was your wish that it should appear in the Intelligencer.

The parties with whom I made the arrangement could only publish it by having it early and I thought their large circulation was of more importance than the Small circulation of the Intelligencer.

I hope you will approve of the course I have taken. The papers to which it has been sent are the *Pha Inquirer*, *NY Times*, and *Boston Journal*.

R Sutton.

ALS, DLC-JP.

1. Sutton, the official reporter of the United States Senate, refers to the address Johnson gave at the White House during the evening of the same date. See Washington's Birthday Address, Feb. 22, 1866.

From William Henry Trescot

[Washington, February 22, 1866][1]

Sir

Permit me in delvering the accompanying letter from Gen Howard[2] to ask your attention to the following considerations

1.   That the number of estates on the Sea Islands of South Carolina which have not been restored under the provisions of Circular No 15 are few—and have not been restored simply by the delay in the Freedmans Bureau in that state in order to wait for the expected passage of the Freedmans Bureau Bill lately vetoed—and that they stand now in precisely the same position as those already restored and now worked by their owners.

2.   That this restoration can work no possible injustice to the freedmen who are occupants under Gen Shermans order because the Order No 1 of Gen Sickles[3] has regulated the whole subject. The old and infirm are to be provided with homes and the able bodied cannot be removed without an opportunity given to make such contracts as the Military authorities may approve.

3.   That owing to the advance of the planting season it is absolutely necessary that within the next ten days the owners should be able to make definite arrangements for the agricultural labors of the year.

I would most earnestly ask that such instructions may be given to Gen Howard as would effect an immediate restoration of these estates.[4]

Wm Henry Trescot
Executive Agent   State So. Ca—

ALS, DLC-JP.
1. A clerk's notation on the cover sheet provides this date and Washington as the place of origin.
2. Oliver O. Howard to Johnson, Feb. 22, 1866.
3. Issued at Charleston on January 1, 1866. Johnson Papers, LC.
4. See Trescot to Johnson, Mar. 12, 1866.

Washington's Birthday Address[1]

Washington, Thursday, Feb. 22. [1866]

Fellow-citizens:

For I presume I have a right to address you as such, I come to tender to you my sincere thanks for the approbation expressed by your Committee in their personal address, and in the resolutions submitted by them, as having been adopted by the meeting which has been held in this city to-day.[2] These resolutions, as I understand them, are complimentary to the policy which has been adopted by the Administration, and which has been steadily pursued since it came into power. I am free to say to you on this occasion, that it is extremely gratifying to me to know that so large a portion of my fellow-citizens approve and indorse the policy which has been adopted, and which it is my intention shall be carried out. ⟨Great applause.⟩ That policy is one which is intended to restore all the States to their original relations to the Federal Government of the United States. ⟨Renewed applause.⟩ This seems to be a day peculiarly appropriate for such a manifestation. It is the day that gave birth to that man who, more perhaps, that any other, founded this Government. It is the day that gave birth to the Father of our Country. It is the day that gave birth to him who presided over that body which framed the Constitution under which all the States entered, and to this glorious Confederacy such a day is peculiarly appropriate for the indorsement of a policy whose object is the restoration of the union of the States as it was designed by the Father of his Country. ⟨Applause.⟩ WASHINGTON, whose name this city bears, is emblemed in the hearts of all who love free government. WASHINGTON, in the language of his eulogist, was first in war, first in peace and first in the hearts of his countrymen. No people can claim him, no nation can appropriate him. His reputation is commensurate with the civilized world, and his name is the common property of all those who love free government. To-day I had the pleasure of a visit from those persons who have been devoting their efforts to the completion of the monument which is being erected to his name.[3] I was proud to meet them, and, so far as I could, to give them my influence and countenance in aid of the work they have undertaken. That monument, which is being erected to him whom I may say founded the Government, is almost within a stone's throw of the spot from which I address you. Let it be completed. ⟨Applause.⟩ Let those various blocks which the States and individuals and associations and corporations have put in that monument as pledges of their love for this Union be preserved, and let the work be accomplished. In this connection let me refer to the block from my own State, God bless her! ⟨applause⟩ which has struggled for the preservation of this Union, in the field and in the councils of the nation, and which is now struggling to renew her relations with this Government that were interrupted by a fearful rebellion. She is now struggling to renew these relations, and to take her stand where she had ever stood since 1796 until this rebellion broke out. ⟨Great applause.⟩ Let me repeat the sentiment that that State has inscribed upon the stone which she has deposited in that monument of freedom which is being raised in commemoration of Washington. She is struggling to get back into the Union, and to stand by the sentiment which is thereon inscribed, and she is willing to sustain it.

What is it? It is the sentiment which was enunciated by her distinguished son, the immortal, the illustrious JACKSON, "The Federal Union —it must be preserved." ⟨Great applause.⟩ If it were possible for that old man, whose statue stands before me and whose portrait is behind me, in the Executive Mansion, and whose sentiment is thus preserved in that monument in your vicinity to be called forth from the grave; or if it were possible to communicate with the spirit of the illustrious dead, and make him understand the progress of faction and of rebellion and treason, he would turn over in his coffin, and shaking off the habiliments of the tomb, would again stand erect, and reiterate that sentiment originally expressed by him on a memorable occasion, "The Federal Union, it must be preserved." ⟨Great applause.⟩ We have witnessed what has transpired since his day. In 1833, when treason and treachery, and infidelity to the Government and the Constitution of the United States, stalked forth in the land,[4] it was his power and influence that crushed the serpent in its incipiency. The movement was then stopped, but only for a time. The same spirit of disaffection continued. There were men disaffected to the Government both in the North and in the South. There was in a portion of the Union a peculiar institution of which some complained, and to which others were attached. One portion of our countrymen in the South sustained that institution, while another portion in the North opposed it. The result was the formation of extreme parties, one especially in the South which reached a point at which it was prepared to dissolve the union of the States for the purpose, as was said, of securing and preserving that peculiar institution. There was another portion of our countrymen who were opposed to it, and who went to such an extreme that they were willing to break up the Government in order to get rid of that institution which was peculiar to the South. I say these things because I desire to talk plainly and in familiar phraseology. I assume nothing here to-day beyond the position of a citizen—one who has been pleading for his country and the preservation of the Constitution. ⟨Immense cheering.⟩ These two portions were arrayed against each other, and I stand here before you for the Union to-day, as I stood in the Senate of the United States for the Union in 1860 and 1861. I met there those who were making war upon the Constitution—those who wanted to break and destroy the Government—and I denounced them in my place, then and there, and exposed their true character. I said that these men who were engaged in the work of breaking up the Government, were traitors. I have never ceased on all proper occasions to repeat that sentiment, and, as far as my efforts could go, I have endeavored to carry it out. ⟨Great applause.⟩ I have just remarked that there were two parties, one of which was for destroying the Government and separating the Union in order to preserve Slavery and the other for breaking up the Government in order to destroy Slavery. True, the objects which they sought to accomplish were different, so far as Slavery was concerned, but they agreed in the desire to break up the Government, the thing to which I have always been opposed, and whether disunionists come from the South or from the North, I stand now, as I did then, vindicating the union of the States and the Constitution of my country. ⟨Tremendous applause.⟩ When rebellion and treason manifested themselves in the South I stood by the Government. I said then that I was for the Union with Slavery—or I was for the Union without Slavery. In either alternative I was for my Government and its Constitution. The Government has stretched forth its strong arm, and with its physical power it has put down treason in the field. The section of the country which then arrayed itself against the National Government has been put down by the strong arm. What did we say when this treason originated? We said, "No compromise." You yourselves in the South can settle this question in eight and forty hours. I said again and again, and I repeat it now—disband your armies in the South, acknowledge the supremacy of the Constitution of the United States, acknowledge the duty of obedience to the laws, and the whole question is settled. ⟨Great applause.⟩ What has been done since their armies have been disbanded, and they come forward now in a proper spirit and say, "We were mistaken; we made an effort to carry out the doctrine of secession and to dissolve this Union, and we have failed. We have carried this doctrine to its logical results, and we find that we were mistaken. We acknowledge the flag of our country, and are willing to obey the Constitution and to yield to the supremacy of the laws." ⟨Great applause.⟩ Coming in that spirit I say to them "When you have complied with the requirements of the Constitution, when you have yielded to the law, when you have acknowledged your allegiance to the Constitution, I will, so far as I can, open the door of the Union to those who had erred and strayed from the fold of their fathers for a time." ⟨Great applause.⟩ Who has suffered more by the rebellion than I have? I shall not repeat the story of the wrongs and sufferings inflicted upon me; but the spirit of revenge is not the spirit in which to deal with a whole people. I know there has been a great deal said about the exercise of the pardoning power. So far as your Executive is concerned there is no one who has labored with more earnestness than myself to have the principal, intelligent and conscious traitors brought to justice, the law vindicated, and the great fact judicially established that *treason is a crime*. ⟨Applause.⟩ But while anxious that leading and intelligent traitors should be punished, should whole communities and States and people be made to submit to the penalty of death? No, no. I have perhaps as much asperity and as much resentment in my nature as men ought to have; but we must reason in great matters of government about man as he is. We must conform our actions and our conduct to the example of Him who founded our holy religion. Not that I would make such a comparison on this occasion in any personal aspect. I came into this place under the Constitution of the country and by the approbation of the people, and what did I find? I found eight millions of people who were in fact condemned under the law, and the penalty was death. Was I to yield to the spirit of revenge and resentment, and declare that they should all be annihilated and destroyed? How different would this have been from the example set by the holy founder of our religion, the extreme points of whose divine arch rests upon the horizon, and whose span embraces the universe;—he who founded this great scheme came into the world and found man condemned under the law, and his sentence was death. What was his example? Instead of condemning the world or even a nation to death, he died upon the cross, attesting by his wounds and his blood that he died that mankind might live? Let those who have erred repent—let them acknowledge their allegiance—let them become loyal, willing supporters and defenders of our glorious stripes and stars, and of the Constitution of our country—let the leaders, the conscious, intelligent traitors, be punished and subjected to the penalties of the law; ⟨applause;⟩ but to the great mass, who have been forced into this rebellion, in many instances, and in others have been misled, I say extend leniency, kindness, trust and confidence. ⟨Great applause.⟩ My countrymen, when I look back over the history of the rebellion, I trust I am not vain when I ask you if I have not given as much evidence of my devotion to the Union as some who croak a great deal about it. When I look back over the battle-fields of the rebellion, I think of the many brave men in whose company I was. I cannot but recollect that I was some times in places where the contest was most difficult and the result most doubtful. But almost before the smoke has passed away, almost before the blood that has been shed has sunk into the earth—before the bodies of the slain have passed to their native dust—what do we now find? The rebellion has been put down by the strong arm of the Government in the field, but is that the only way in which you can have rebellion? One struggle was against an attempt to dissever the Union; but almost before the smoke of the battle-field has passed away—before our brave men have all returned to their homes, and renewed the ties of affection and love to their wives and their children, we find almost another rebellion inaugurated. We put down the former rebellion in order to prevent the separation of the States, to prevent them from flying off, and thereby changing the character of our Government and weakening its power. But when that struggle on our part has been successful, and that attempt has been put down, we find now an effort to concentrate all power in the hands of a few at the Federal head, and thereby bring about a consolidation of the Government, which is equally objectionable with a separation. ⟨Vociferous applause.⟩ We find that powers are assumed and attempted to be exercised of a most extraordinary character. It seems that Governments may be revolutionized—Governments at least may be changed without going through the strife of battle. I believe it is a fact attested in history that sometimes revolutions most disastrous to a people are affected without the shedding of blood. The substance of your Government may be taken away while the form and the shadow remain to you. What is now being proposed? We find that in point of fact nearly all the powers of the Government are assumed by an irresponsible central directory, which does not even consult the legislative or the executive departments of the Government. By resolutions reported from a committee in whom it seems that practically the legislative power of the Government is now vested, that great principle of the Constitution which authorizes and empowers each branch of the legislative department, the Senate and the House of Representatives, to judge for itself of the elections, returns and qualifications of its own members, has been virtually taken away from the two branches of the legislative department of the Government, and conferred upon a joint committee, who must report before either House can act under the Constitution as to accepting the members who are to take their seats as component parts of the respective bodies. By this rule it is assumed that there must be laws passed recognizing a State as being in the Union; or its practical relations to the Union as restored, before the respective Houses under the Constitution can judge of the elections, returns and qualifications of their own members. What a position is that! You struggled for four years to put down a rebellion. You denied in the beginning of the struggle that any State could go out of the Union. You said that it had neither the right nor the power to do so. The issue was made and it has been settled that the States had neither the right nor the power to go out of the Union. With what consistency, after it has been settled by the military arm of the Government and by the public judgment that the States had no right to go out of the Union, can any one now turn round and assume that they are out, and that they shall not come in? I am free to say to you as your Executive that I am not prepared to take any such position. ⟨Great applause.⟩ I said in the Senate in the very inception of this rebellion that the States had no right to go out. I asserted, too, that they had no power to go out. That question has been settled, and it being settled, I cannot turn around now and give the lie direct to all that I have professed, and all I have done for the last five years. ⟨Applause.⟩ When those who rebelled comply with the Constitution, when they give sufficient evidence of loyalty, when they show that they can be trusted, when they yield obedience to the law that you and I acknowledge, I say extend to them the right hand of fellowship, and let peace and union be restored. ⟨Tremendous applause.⟩ I fought traitors and treason in the South; I opposed the Davises, the Toombes, the Slidells,[5] and a long list of others, which you can readily fill without my repeating the names. Now, when I turn round and at the other end of the line find men—I care not by what name you call them—who still stand opposed to the restoration of the Union of these States, I am free to say to you that I am still in the field. ⟨Great applause.⟩ I am still for the preservation of the Union. I am still in favor of this great Government of ours going on and filling out its destiny. ⟨Great applause.⟩

VOICES—Give us three of these names at the other end.

THE PRESIDENT—I am called upon to name three at the other end of the line. I am talking to my friends and fellow-citizens who are interested with me in this Government, and I presume I am free to mention to you the names of those whom I look upon, as being opposed to the fundamental principles of this Government, and who are laboring to destroy it.

VOICES—"Name them—who are they?"

THE PRESIDENT—You ask me who they are? I say, THADDEUS STEVENS, of Pennsylvania, is one; I say Mr. SUMNER, of the Senate, is another, and WENDELL PHILLIPS is another. ⟨Long continued applause.⟩

VOICES—"Give it to Forney."[6]

THE PRESIDENT—In reply to that I will simply say I do not waste my ammunition upon dead ducks. ⟨Great laughter and applause.⟩ I stand for my country. I stand for the Constitution. There I have always placed myself from my advent in public life. They may traduce, they may slander, they may vituperate me, but let me say to you all this has no influence upon me. ⟨Great applause.⟩ Let me say further, that I do not intend to be overawed by real or pretended friends, nor do I mean to be bullied by my enemies. ⟨Tremendous applause.⟩ Honest conviction is my courage. The Constitution is my guide. I know, my countrymen, that it has been insinuated, it has been said directly in high places, that if such a usurpation of power as I am charged with had been exercised some 200 years ago, in a particular reign, it would have cost an individual his head.[7] ⟨Great laughter.⟩ Of what usurpation has ANDREW JOHNSON been guilty? None; none. Is it a usurpation to stand between the people and the encroachments of power? Because, in a conversation with a fellow-citizen, who happened to be a Senator,[8] I said that I thought amendments to the Constitution ought not to be so frequent; that if it was continually tampered with, it would lose its prestige and dignity, and the old instrument would be lost sight of altogether in a short time, and because in the same conversation I happened to say that if it were amended at all, such and such an amendment ought to [be] adopted, it was charged that I was guilty of an assumption of power that would have cost a king his head in a certain period of English history. ⟨Great laughter.⟩ From the same source the exclamation has gone forth that they were in the midst of earthquakes, that they were trembling and could not yield. ⟨Laughter.⟩ Yes, fellow-citizens, there is an earthquake coming; there is a grand swelling of popular judgment and indignation. ⟨Great applause.⟩ The American people will speak, and by their instinct, if not otherwise, they will know who are their friends and who are their enemies. I have endeavored to be true to the people in all the positions which I have occupied, and there is hardly a position in this Government which I have not at some time filled. I suppose it will be said that this is vanity; ⟨laughter;⟩ but I may say that I have been all of them, and I have been in both branches of the State Legislature.

A VOICE—You commenced a tailor.

THE PRESIDENT—A gentleman behind me says that I began a tailor. Yes, I did begin a tailor ⟨applause⟩, and that suggestion does not disturb me in the least, for when I was a tailor I had the reputation of being a good one, and of making close fits. ⟨Laughter.⟩ And I was always punctual to my customers and did good work. ⟨Applause.⟩

VOICES—We will patch up the Union yet.

THE PRESIDENT—No! I do not want any patchwork of it. I want the original article restored. ⟨Great applause.⟩ But enough of this raillery. I know it may be said, You are President, and you must not talk about these things; but, my fellow-citizens, I intend to talk the truth, and when principle is involved, when the existence of my country is in peril, I hold it to be my duty to speak what I think and what I feel, as I have always done on former occasions. ⟨Great applause.⟩ I have said it has been declared elsewhere that I was guilty of usurpation which would have cost a king his head, and in another place I have been denounced for "whitewashing." When and where did I ever whitewash anything or anybody? I have been an Alderman of a town; I have been in both branches of the Legislature of my State; I have been in both Houses of the National Congress; I have been at the head of the Executive Department of my State; I have been Vice-President of the United States; and I am now in the position which I occupy before you, and during all this time where is the man and where is any portion of the people who can say that ANDREW JOHNSON ever made a pledge which he did not redeem, or that he ever made a promise which he violated. None! none! Point me to the man who can say that ANDREW JOHNSON ever acted with infidelity to the great mass of the people. ⟨Great applause.⟩ Men may talk about beheading and about usurpation, but when I am beheaded I want the American people to be the witness. I do not want it done by inuendoes and indirect remarks, in high places to be suggested to men who have assassination brooding in their bosoms. Others have exclaimed that the presidential obstacle must be gotten out of the many. What is that but (I make use of a strong word) inciting to assassination? Are the opponents of the Government not yet satisfied? Are those who want to destroy our institutions, and to change the character of the Government, not yet satisfied with the quantity of blood that has been shed? Are they not satisfied with one martyr in this place? Does not the blood of LINCOLN appease their vengeance and their wrath? Is their thirst still unsatisfied? Do they still want more blood? Have they not honor and courage enough to seek to obtain the end other wise than by the hand of an assassin? I am not afraid of an assassin attacking me where alone brave and courages men will attack another? I only dread him when in disguise and where his footsteps is noiseless. If they want blood let them have the courage to strike like men. I know they are "willing to wound yet afraid to strike."[9] If my blood is to be shed because I vindicate the Union and insist on the preservation of this Government in its original purity, let it be shed out; let an altar to the Union be first erected and then, if necessary, take me and lay me upon it, and the blood that now warms and animates my existence shall be poured out as the last libation as a tribute to the union of the States. ⟨Great applause.⟩ But let the opponents of this Government remember when it is found out that the blood of the martyrs is the seed of the Church.[10] This Union will grow and it will continue to increase in strength and power though it may be cemented and cleansed in blood. I have already spoken to you longer than I intended when I came out. ⟨"Go on."⟩ I merely intended to make my acknowledgments for the honor you have done me, but before I close allow me to say a word in regard to the question of amendings to the Constitution of the United States. Shortly after I reached Washington for the purpose of being inaugurated as Vice-President of the United States, I had a conversation with Mr. LINCOLN[11] in regard to the condition of affairs; we talked particularly in reference to matters in my own State. I told him that we called a convention, that we had amended the Constitution; that we had abolished slavery in that State, which was not included in his Emancipation Proclamation. All these things met his approbation, and he gave me words of encouragement; we talked then about affairs generally, and upon the subject of amendments to the Constitution of the United States; he said to me "When the amendment of the Constitution now proposed is adopted by three-fourths of the States, I am pretty near done, or, indeed, quite done, in favor of amending the Constitution, if there was one other adopted." I asked him—"What is that, Mr. President?" He said—"I have labored to preserve this Union. I have toiled during the four years I have been subjected to calumny and misrepresentation. My great and sole desire has been to presume these States intact under the Constitution as they were before.["] I asked him again, Mr. President, what amendment is that which you would propose? Why, said he, it is that there should be an amendment added to the Constitution which would compel the States to send their Senators and Representatives to the Congress of the United States. ⟨Great applause.⟩ The idea was in his mind that as a part of the doctrine of secession, one of the means to break up this Government was that the States, if they saw fit, might withdraw their Senators and Representatives, or refuse to elect them. He wanted even to remove that difficulty by a constitutional amendment compelling the States to send Senators and Representatives to Congress. But what do we now find? The Constitution of the country, even that portion of it which allows amendment to the organic law, expressly provides that no State, without its consent, shall be deprived of its suffrage and it also provides that each State shall have at least one representative in the House of Representatives; but yet the position is taken that certain States cannot be represented. We impose taxes upon them, we send our tax gatherers into every region and portion of the States. The people are fit subjects of Government for the collection of taxes, but when they ask to participate in the legislation of the country they are met at the door and told, no you must pay taxes you must bear the burdens of Government but not participate in its legislation, that legislation which is to affect you through all time to come. Is this just? Is it fair? No! no!! I repeat, I am for the Union; I am for preserving all the States. I am for admitting into the counsels of the nation all their representatives *who are unmistakeably and unquestionably loyal.* A man who acknowledges allegiance to the Government and who swears to support the Constitution must necessarily be loyal. A man cannot take that oath in good faith unless he is loyal. A mere amplification of the oath makes no difference as to the principle. Whatever test is thought proper as evidence and as proof of loyalty is a mere matter of detail, about which I care nothing but let a man be unmistakeably and unquestionably loyal, let him acknowledge allegiance to the Constitution of the United States, and be willing to support the Government in its hour of peril and its hour of need and I am willing to trust him. ⟨Applause.⟩ I know that some do not attach as much importance to this point as I do, but I regard it as fundamental. One principle that carried us through the Revolution was that there should be no taxation without representation. I hold to that principle, which was laid down as fundamental by our fathers. If it was good then it is good now. If it was worth standing by then it is worth standing by now. It is fundamental, and should be observed as long as free government lasts. I am aware that in the midst of the rebellion it was said by some that the Constitution had been rolled up as a piece of parchment and laid away; that in time of war and rebellion there was no constitution. We know that sometimes in great necessities under great emergencies unconstitutional things must sometimes necessarily be done in order to preserve the Constitution itself. But if, while the rebellion was going on the Constitution was rolled up and laid away; if it was violated in some particulars in order to save the Government, and all may be excused and justified, because in saving the Government you really saved the Constitution; now that peace has come, now that the war is over, we want again the benefit of a written Constitution, and I say the time has come to take the Constitution down, to unroll it—to re-read it to understand its provisions thoroughly. And now, in order to save the Government, we must preserve the Constitution. Our only safety is in a strict adherence to and preservation of the Constitution of our fathers. It is now unfolded. It must now be read—it must now be digested and understood by the American people. I am here to-day, then, in making these remarks, to vindicate the Constitution and to save it, as I believe, for it does seem as if encroachment after encroachment is proposed upon it. As far as I can, I have ever resisted encroachments upon the Constitution, and I stand prepared to resist them to-day, and thereby to preserve the Constitution and Government of the United States. ⟨Great applause.⟩ It is now a time of peace, and let us have peace; let us enforce the Constitution; let us live under and according to its provisions. Let it be published and printed in blazing characters, as though it were in the heavens and punctuated by the stars, so that all can read and all can understand it. Let us consult that instrument and be guided by its provisions. Let us understand them, and understanding them abide by them.

I tell the opposers of this Government, I care not from what quarter they come, East or West, North or South, "You that are engaged in the work of breaking up the Government are mistaken. The Constitution of the United States and the principles of free Government are deeply rooted in the American heart, and all the powers combined cannot destroy that great instrument—that great chart of freedom.["] Their attempts, though they may seem to succeed for a time, will be futile. They might as well undertake to lock up the winds or chain the waves of the ocean and confine them within limits; they might as well undertake to repeal the Constitution, and, indeed, it seems now to be supposed that can be repealed by a concurrent resolution, ⟨laughter;⟩ but when the question is submitted to popular judgment and to the most of the people, these men will find that they might just as well introduce a resolution to repeal the law of gravitation; the attempt to keep this Union from being restored is just about as feasible as would be resistance to the great law of gravitation, which binds all to a common centre. The great law of political gravitation will bring back these States, and replace them in all their relations to the Federal Government. Cliques and cabals and conspiracies and machinations, North or South, cannot prevent this great consummation. ⟨Tremendous applause.⟩ All that is wanted is time. Let the American people get to understand what is going on, and they will soon manifest their determination. By way of exclamation, let me say that I would to God the whole American people could be assembled here to-day as you are. I wish there were a vast amphitheatre here capacious enough to sustain the whole thirty millions, and they could witness the great struggle going on to preserve the Constitution of their fathers. They would soon settle the question if they could once see how things are; if they could see the kind of spirit that is manifested in the effort to break up the real principles of free government. When they come to understand who was for them and who against them; who was for ameliorating their condition and who for elevating them by preserving their Government, if the combatants could stand before them, and there could be a regular set-to between the respective gladiators, in the first tilt that might be made you would find that the enemies of the country would be crushed, and the people would sustain its friends and the friends of Constitutional liberty. ⟨Great cheering.⟩ My fellow-citizens, I have detained you much longer than I intended. ⟨"Go on, go on."⟩ But we are in a great struggle, and I am your instrument, and I have thought it best to express myself frankly. When I ask you have, I usurped authority? Who is there in this country I have not toiled and labored for? Where is the man or the woman, either in private life or public life, that has not always received my attention and my time? Sometimes it has been said, Pardon me for being a little egotistical, but we are engaged in a friendly and familiar conversation. That that JOHNSON is a lucky man. ⟨Laughter.⟩ They can never defeat him. ⟨Laughter.⟩ Now I will tell you what constitutes my good luck. It is in doing right and being for the people. ⟨Great applause.⟩ The people somehow or other, although their sagacity and good judgment are very frequently underrated and underestimated, generally get to find out and understand who is for them and who is against them. They do it by instinct, if in no other way. They know who is the friend; they know in whom they can confide. So far, thank God, I can lay my hand upon my bosom, and state with heartfelt satisfaction that in all the positions in which I have been placed—and I have been placed in many that were as trying as any in which mortal man has ever been placed—I have never deserted them, nor do I believe they will desert me. ⟨No, no, and applause.⟩ Whom have I betrayed, what principle have I violated, what sentiment have I swerved from, can those who assail me put their finger upon any one. No, no; in all the speeches that have been made, no one has dared to put his finger upon a single principle I ever asserted from which I have deviated. Have you not heard some of them at some time attempt to quote my predecessor who fell a martyr to his country's cause, but they can give no sentiment of his that is in opposition or in contradiction to anything that I have done. The very policy that I am now pursuing was pursued by me under his administration—I having been appointed by him in a particular position for that very purpose. An inscrutable Providence saw proper to remove him from this to, I trust, a better world, and I came into his place, and there is not a principle of his in reference to the restoration of the Union from which I have departed. None. Then the war is not simply upon me, but it is upon my predecessor also. I have tried to do my duty. I know that some are envious and jealous, and speak of the White House as having attractions for the President. Let me say to you, the charms of the White House have as little influence upon me as upon any individual in this country, and much less upon me than upon those who are talking about it. The little that I eat and wear does not amount to much, and the difference between what is enough to sustain me and my little family. It is very small, for I am not kin to many folks by consanguinity, though by affinity I am akin to everybody. The difference between the little that suffices for my stomach and back, and more than enough, has no charms for me. The proud and conscious satisfaction of having performed my duty to my country, to my children and to the inner man is all the reward that I ask. ⟨Great applause.⟩

In conclusion, let me ask this vast concourse here to-day, this sea of upturned faces, to come with me, or I will go with you, and stand around the Constitution of our country. It is again unfolded. The people are invited to read and understand, to sustain and maintain its provisions. Let us stand by the Constitution of our fathers, though the heavens themselves should fall, though faction should rage, though taunts and jeers may come, though abuse and vituperation may be poured out in the most virulent form. I mean to be found standing by the Constitution of my country. Stand by the Constitution as the chief ark of our safety, as the palladium of our civil and our religious liberty. Yes, let us cling to it as a mariner clings to the last plank when the night and the tempest close around him. Accept my thanks, my countrymen, for the indulgence you have extended to me while submitting to you extemporaneously and, perhaps, incoherently the remarks which I have now made. Let us go away forgetting the past and looking to the future, resolved to endeavor to restore our Government to its pristine purity, trusting in Him who is on high, but who controls all here below, that ere long our Union will be restored, and that we shall have peace not only with all the nations of the earth, but peace and good will among all parts of the people of the United States. I thank you for the respect you have manifested to me on this occasion, and if the time shall come during the period of my existence when this country is to be destroyed and its Government overturned, if you will look out you will find the humble individual who stands before you there with you endeavoring to avert its final destruction.

The President retired amidst a storm of applause.

New York Times, February 23, 1866.

1. A crowd assembled outside the White House on the night of February 22, evidently to demonstrate its support of the President just three days after the issuance of his Freedmen's Bureau veto. Two or three of Johnson's advisers, knowing in advance that a group would be coming to the White House, urged the President not to address the crowd. Although Johnson accepted their advice, once the supporters arrived that evening, he could not restrain himself. See Castel, *Presidency of Johnson*, 68–70; Trefousse, *Johnson*, 243–44.

2. On the afternoon of February 22, a crowd of non-partisan unionists held a meeting at Grover's Theatre in Washington. There they heard speeches and adopted resolutions which opposed punishment for the southern states, supported the admission of southern representatives to Congress, opposed black suffrage in the District of Columbia and elsewhere, opposed government aid to individuals, particularly freedmen, and supported Johnson's course, including his veto of the Freedmen's Bureau bill. Afterwards, the participants took their resolutions to Johnson at the White House. *National Intelligencer*, Feb. 23, 1866.

3. Another version of this address has Johnson "attending" the meeting of the association. See *New York Tribune*, Feb. 24, 1866.

4. This is a reference to South Carolina's nullification crisis.

5. Jefferson Davis, Robert Toombs, and John Slidell.

6. John W. Forney.

7. A reference to a speech given by Thaddeus Stevens to the House of Representatives, January 31, 1866. *Congressional Globe*, 39 Cong., 1 Sess., pp. 535–38. Stevens was not as specific as Johnson attributes.

8. See Interview with James Dixon, Jan. 28, 1866, *Johnson Papers*, 9: 647–49.

9. From Alexander Pope's *Epistle to Dr. Arbuthnot, Prologue to the Satires*, line 201.

10. Tertullian in *Apologeticus*, "Blood of the martyrs is the seed of the Church."

11. No evidence can be found to substantiate this meeting. Johnson did meet with Lincoln on April 14, the day the President was shot, and urged Lincoln not to be too lenient with the former Confederates. This is the only meeting on record. Earl Schenck Miers, ed., *Lincoln Day by Day: A Chronology, 1809–1865* (3 vols., Washington, 1960), 3: 329; Trefousse, *Johnson*, 192.

From Joseph S. Fullerton

Washington, Feby. 23d 1866.

I have the honor to inclose herewith a copy of a Washington telegram which appeared in the "New-York Daily Tribune" of the 21st inst., and to make the following remarks concerning the same.

Johnson addressing the Washington crowd, February 22
Harper's Weekly, March 10, 1866

This telegram is headed "The President and the Louisiana Freedmen." Then follows the statement that "It has now come to light that the instructions under which the Freedmens Bureau in Louisiana was so completely disrupted in November, its 300 schools brought to a close soon afterwards, the freedmen and discharged colored soldiers arrested as vagrants in the streets of New-Orleans without trial or process of law, and the orphans of freedmen returned to former slave holders as apprentices, were imparted by the President himself, and that Genl. Fullerton acted in accordance with Executive instructions."[1]

First: The statements contained in this telegram in reference to my administration of freedmens affairs while temporarily acting as Assistant Commissioner of the Bureau of Refugees, Freedmen & Abandoned Lands for the State of Louisiana in November last are wholly untrue. After relieving my predecessor[2] from duty with the Bureau I did make some changes in the manner of conducting freedmens affairs in said State, and did correct some abuses. This was done in order to comply with and carry out the general orders and instructions that had been previously issued to his Agents by the Commissioner of the Bureau, and in order to place the freedmen of the State in such a position as to enable them, by their own Exertions, to take care of themselves and to be relieved from Government assistance and support.

I have the honor to inclose herewith, for your information, a copy of an official report of my administration of freedmens affairs while in Louisiana.[3] This report was made and forwarded to the Commissioner of the Bureau on the 3d of December last, and it contains a full and complete statement of my official action.

Second: I did not receive any instructions whatever from you in reference to the matters mentioned in this telegram. The only instructions that I did receive, were joint instructions from you and the Commissioner of the Bureau directing me to proceed to New Orleans, and relieve Chaplain Conway from duty with the Bureau, then to act as Assistant Commissioner of the Bureau for Louisiana until the arrival in New Orleans of Bvt. Maj. Genl. Baird,[4] who had previously been appointed Assistant Commissioner for that State. Also to try and create harmony between the Bureau and other Departments in the State: to carry out the published orders of the Commissioner of the Bureau; and to do whatever might be best for the interest of the freedmen. Under these instructions I acted, and I alone am responsible for what was done by me as Asst. Commr. of the Bureau.

J. S. Fullerton,
Bvt Brig. Genl. Vols.

ALS, DLC-JP.
1. See Howard A. White, *The Freedmen's Bureau in Louisiana* (Baton Rouge, 1970), 23–24, 80, 112; and Fullerton to Johnson, Oct. 28, 1865, *Johnson Papers*, 9: 298.
2. Thomas W. Conway.

3. Not found. For a copy of Fullerton's report, see *House Ex. Docs.*, 39 Cong., 1 Sess., No. 70, pp. 393–403 (Ser. 1256).

4. Absalom Baird.

From Hugh McCulloch

Treasury Department.
February 23d 1866.

Sir:

I have the honor to submit for your consideration the accompanying copies of papers and correspondence relative to the State Works, so called, situated in Greenville, S.C. and claimed by the State as its property.

The history of the property and the facts affecting its *status* are believed to be substantially as follows. The buildings were erected by the State in the spring of 1862, on land given for the purpose by a citizen; and soon after the machinery, tools, materials, &c, for the manufacture of arms and ordinance were procured and placed therein by the State. A part of the machinery originally belonged to the State of Tennessee; and having been removed from that State early in the war to Atlanta, Ga. for greater security, was turned over to an agent of South Carolina by order of Gov. Harris[1] in the spring of 1862, "subject to future settlement," but has never been paid for. Certain of the articles were borrowed from the Confederate States Government.

The buildings and machinery were afterwards used for the manufacture of arms, ordinance, &c. Some of the arms were issued to troops in the State service, and others were deposited in the State Arsenal at Columbia, where they are said to have been destroyed by Genl. Sherman's army. Articles of ordinance were supplied to some extent to the Confederate States arsenal at Charleston in the spring of 1864; which were paid for.

It does not appear that the so called Confederate States ever had any interest in, or claim upon, this establishment, or furnished any of the material manufactured there; and it is stated by the Superintendent[2] of the works that the Governor refused to allow the *arms* made therein to go into the Confederate service. After the fall of 1864 the works were largely engaged by order of the Legislature in supplying the country with necessary farming implements; and this was the principal business doing, when, in May, 1865, the greater part of the materials, stock, and arms then on the premises were plundered and destroyed by the Union forces, and by citizens.

The articles of machinery borrowed from the Confederate States have been turned over by the Superintendent to the Special Agent of the Treasury Department;[3] who also refused to allow the Commissioners, appointed under a resolution of the late General Assembly of the State to sell the remainder of the property, to dispose of the same, until the decision of the Secretary of the Treasury should permit them to do so.

A statement of the facts as above set forth having been submitted to me, by my letter under date of Jan'y 27th, 1866, a copy of which is enclosed herewith,[4] I directed the Supervising Specl. Agent of the Treas'y Dept. for the District comprising South Carolina, to regard the machinery, tools, and other personal estate belonging to the premises in question as captured property, and to dispose of the same in the manner provided by law; as, for the reasons stated in the letter, I regarded the property as confiscable, and forfeited to the United States under the provisions of the Act of Congress approved—August 6th, 1861, and entitled, "An Act to confiscate property used for insurrectionary purposes."

Against my decision and order arguments have been submitted by Hon. James L. Orr. Gov. of South Carolina, and W. H. Trescott[5] Esq. Executive Agent; and by their desire the subject is referred to your consideration and decision.[6]

H McCulloch   Secretary of the Treasury

LS, DNA-RG56, Misc. Div., Claims for Cotton and Captured and Abandoned Property.
1. Isham G. Harris of Tennessee.
2. Probably David Lopez (b. c1809), a Charleston carpenter, who became superintendent in early 1862. 1860 Census, S.C., Charleston, Charleston, 6th Ward, 33; *Report of W. H. Gist, Chief of the Department of Construction and Manufacture, To His Excellency, Governor Pickens* (Columbia, 1862), 13–16.
3. Theophilus C. Callicot.
4. Not found, although accompanying documentation indicates the letter was addressed to Callicot.
5. In his letter Trescot argued that the munitions works belonged to the state of South Carolina because they had been built at the state's expense and had manufactured farming implements solely beginning in 1864. Therefore, he said, the munition works were not liable to be confiscated as Confederate property. Moreover, Governor Perry, acting under the authority of the President, had taken possession of the property and the legislature had approved its sale long before the Treasury Department ordered its seizure. Trescot to McCulloch, Feb. 12, 1866, Misc. Div., Claims for Cotton and Captured and Abandoned Property, RG56, NA.
6. Johnson in turn referred the matter to Seward, who was asked to determine whether "it would be equitable and advisable to allow" the state to sell the property "on account of the expenses of the provisional government," as North Carolina had been allowed to do. Seward recommended that if the net proceeds to the United States from a sale were under $60,000, the property might be relinquished, after appraisal, to the state government. Consequently, on March 14, 1866, Johnson ordered McCulloch to have the works appraised. This was done the next month and the value was estimated at nearly $34,000. The works were put up for sale in October; for a reported amount of $10,000, Dr. S. S. Marshall and others bought the property in November 1866 with the intention of converting it to a cotton factory. Johnson endorsement, ca. Mar. 1866, Seward to McCulloch, Mar. 8, 1866, McCulloch to Johnson, Mar. 10, 1866, Johnson to McCulloch, Mar. 14, 1866, ibid.; *House Reports*, 40 Cong., 1 Sess., No. 7, "Impeachment Investigation," pt. 2, p. 870 (Ser. 1314); *Charleston Courier*, Oct. 13, 1866; *The Carolina Spartan* (Spartanburg), Nov. 29, 1866.

From Nathaniel B. Meade[1]

Senate Chamber,
Richmond, 23 Feb 1866

Dear Sir,

Your friends propose to come out in an address to the People of Va, endorsing your administration & calling for County Meetings to do the same thing. Our object is to form a "Johnson" or "Administration party." The radical Union party, "so called" at the head of which is *John M Botts* will sooner or later be *against you*. I am unwilling to organize this movement at this time, as our support although *honest* & *sincere* might embarrass you, without *knowing your views*, as to the *propriety* of it at *this time*—might not *"Wade"*[2] and his party use it against you with the Radicals. Your views would oblige. . . .

Nathl B Meade
State Senator from Winchester   *Va*

ALS, DLC-JP.

1. Meade (c1828–1888) began an active career as a newspaper editor after his one term in the state senate. In the early 1870s he became editor of the *Richmond Whig*, and in 1876 he served as chairman of the state Democratic committee. Subsequently, he was appointed judge of the corporation court of Alexandria, a post he held until his death. 1860 Census, Va., Clarke, White Post, 669; Frederic Morton, *The Story of Winchester in Virginia: The Oldest Town in the Shenandoah Valley* (Strasburg, Va., 1925), 200, 224–25; *Religious Herald* (Richmond), June 7, 1888.

2. Benjamin F. Wade.

From William B. Phillips[1]

Confidential.

87 East 26h Street   N. York, Feby 23d/66.

Dear Sir,

I enclose you the leading editorial in the Herald of this morning, from my pen.[2] You will see the character of it. I think it is proper that I should explain to you confidentially the motive that prompted and the object of the article. I do this not knowing what your views are as to the succession to the presidency. As far as I am concerned or have any control in the matter I wish only to serve you and sustain your policy.

Mr. Bennett, who had not been to the office for some days, sent for me to Washington Heights, where he resides, on Thursday last, for the purpose of giving me his views on this new programme for the paper and of requesting me to initiate it by this leading article. His idea is that the opposition in Congress to your admirable and patriotic restoration policy is so formidable that it is likely to be a long and fierce contest; that the grounds of opposition are really political, and with a view chiefly to the next presidential election; and that the true way to aid you in the work of restoration and bring peace to the country is to take the course he is now taking. That is, he believes it is calculated to take the wind out of the sails of the politicians and presidential aspirants, to allay hostility and rivalry to you, and to put forth an idea as to the future upon which the people can dwell and hope for peace.

Mr. Bennett has a very high opinion of General Grant, and has for some time thought he would be a worthy successor to yourself. He has not, however, a less exalted opinion of you. The great ability, statesmanship, firmness, patriotism, and inflexible honesty, you have shown commands his admiration. He would be as ready, and, perhaps, more ready to go for you as a candidate for the next term, when the proper time shall arrive if the political condition of the country should in his opinion be then favorable. At present he thinks the proper course to keep Grant attached to you and your policy, to defeat a disorganizing Congress, to checkmate the politician president makers, and to inspire in the people confidence in the future, is to bring the General prominently forward as the candidate for the next term.[3] This is really the motive of the article and the course the paper will now take. Besides there is something sensational, new, and striking in the idea, which is always in keeping with the manner of conducting the Herald. By and by another course may be taken. As to your administration and your patriotic policy for restoring the country there will be no change. The paper will heartily support you in the great and good work.[4]

Had I the control of the Herald I might not have taken this course, and certainly not if I thought it were in opposition to your views or aspirations; but though I have some influence with Mr. Bennett and my advice is often taken, he takes a start sometimes entirely independent of the opinions of any one.

As to General Grant I think he is getting into a fair way of damaging his prospects, if he wishes to be president, by suffering himself to be handled and trotted about by the Loyal League politicians and other politicians. If he be not careful the fate of General Scott, a much less sagacious man, will be his.[5]

I need not say how much I am delighted with your veto and speech. And I am sure the heart of the American people is with you however much a certain set of politicians may be against you.

I hope you are well and may live long to be a blessing to the country.

W. B. Phillips.

ALS, DLC-JP.

1. Editorial writer for the *New York Herald*.

2. The editorial was entitled, "The Succession—the President and General Grant—Schemes of the Politicians." *New York Herald*, Feb. 23, 1866.

3. Although initially considering supporting Grant's candidacy in 1868, Bennett's preference for the Democratic nomination in 1868 was Salmon P. Chase. But when the latter was rejected in favor of Horatio Seymour, the *Herald* ultimately endorsed the Republican nominee, Grant. James L. Crouthamel, *Bennett's New York Herald and the Rise of the Popular Press* (Syracuse, 1989), 153–54.

4. This resolve had weakened considerably by the fall of 1866. Ibid., 152–53.

5. A reference to Winfield Scott's inability to reach the presidency, despite his military successes and enormous popularity.

From William H. Seward

New York   Feby 23 1866

Dear President

It is all right and all Safe. The Union is restored and the Country Safe.[1]

Your Speech[2] is triumphant and the Country will be happy. I Come back on Monday.

Wm H Seward

Tel, DLC-JP.

1. According to Van Deusen, an issue of the *Nation* declared that Seward's statement would "always remain among the curiosities of telegraphic literature." Van Deusen, *Seward*, 446.

2. Washington's Birthday Address, Feb. 22, 1866.

From Thurlow Weed

New York, Feby 23d 1866

Dear Sir

I want to thank you with my whole grateful heart for that glorious speech of yesterday. It vindicates and saves our Government and Union.[1] The People will rally to the support of the Administration. Faction is rebuked, and traitors will seek hiding places.

We had a splendid demonstration here.[2]

Thurlow Weed

LS, DLC-JP.

1. In a telegram to Johnson, Weed proclaimed: "The Union is now a fixed fact." Weed to Johnson, Feb. 23, 1866, Johnson Papers, LC.

2. Resolutions and a speech made during the Washington's birthday meeting at the Cooper Institute were later forwarded to Johnson. New York City Citizens to Johnson, Feb. 28, 1866, ibid.; Van Deusen, *Seward*, 443; *New York Times*, Feb. 22, 1866.

From Thomas W. Bartley[1]

Cincinnati O   Feb. 24 '66

Permit me to express to you my full & most cordial approval of your Veto of the "Freedman's Bureau Bill," & my deep sense of the obligations of the people of the Country to you for the high & noble position taken by you in support of the constitution. Be assured, Sir, that the party trammels in the hands of partizan leaders cannot smother the popular voice, & prevent the great body of the people from standing by you, & sustaining you. Three classes of men will oppose you, & create all the trouble they can. The first & foremost is the distructive abolitionists; second, the consolidationists; & third, the drivelling partizans who would sacrifice the Constitution in order to preserve the mere party organization of the Republican party. The partizan & radical leaders in Cincinnati, who control the news paper organs & cliques of the Republican party, have laboured for the last few days to keep down & smother the public feeling which has been struggling with the masses for a public manifestation. But in a short time it will burst forth with overwhelming force.

There can be no half way about this matter. The Republicans, who oppose you, will be compelled to follow Sumner, Stevens, Phillips, & that class of politicians, as their leaders. The issue is unavoidable— inevitable. The constitution as it is, & the federal relations as they were; or a revolution & distruction of our government as our forefathers made it, & a repudiation of the doctrine of delegated power by the people, who have fought in this war to maintain, not distroy the government.

The radical leaders are determined, & have the power, to make *negro suffrage* a test of party fidelity. Let this issue be fairly & boldly made, & it is the end of their power in this country. I have the means of knowing the real sentiments of the masses of the people on this question. The feeling is intense. Even in Ohio they will be beaten on that question by more than one hundred thousand votes.[2] Negro Suffrage is one of the main instrumentalities, which they seek to use, to distroy our government.

Your speech of the 22d of Feby. comes like an avalanche upon the radicals among the masses of the people. The malignant criticism attempted only give it greater point & more extended influence with the masses. Had it been on their side of the question, it would have been all right, dignified, & proper.

The same men, who now denounce you, declared here in Cincinnati last spring, that Abraham Lincoln's death was Providential, for as the war was just over, he would have been in favour of showing too much favour to the South, & of allowing the Southern States to come back to their former place in the Union &c.

Excuse this intrusion upon your time, & believe me. . . .

T. W Bartley

ALS, DLC-JP.

1. A Democrat, Bartley (1812–1885) was a former Ohio attorney general, state representative and senator, and briefly served as acting governor. A state supreme court justice prior to the war, he continued to practice law in Ohio until 1869, when he removed to Washington, D.C. *DAB*; William Coyle, ed., *Ohio Authors and Their Books* (Cleveland, 1962), 37; *Biographical Cyclopaedia of Ohio*, 1: 94.

2. Bartley was prophetically correct. When the question of black suffrage after the Civil War was finally submitted to a popular referendum in Ohio in 1874, voters rejected by a 2–1 margin a proposed constitution that would have deleted the word "white" in reference to elector qualifications. Although the Republican-controlled legislature of 1867 passed an amendment to the state constitution which would permit black voting rights, black suffrage was not legally established in Ohio as far as the national government was concerned until after the state's ratification of the Fifteenth Amendment in 1870. Ohio's discriminatory elective franchise clause remained unchanged until well into the twentieth century. Bonadio, *North of Reconstruction*, 94–97, 103, 105–6; William Gillette, *The Right to Vote: Politics and the Passage of the Fifteenth Amendment* (Baltimore, 1965), 143–44; C. B. Galbreath, *Constitutional Conventions of Ohio* (Columbus, 1911), 41–43.

From Albert G. Brown

Terry Hinds Co Missi.   Febr 24 1866.

Dear Sir

There was a day whin You and I were friends. At least I thought so. This was the time when we Struggled together for the Success of the Homestead proposition. We were then alike the friends of the humble and the lowly. Circumstances have thrown us wide apart. You are President of the U States and I am a proscribed Citizen. May we not admit that each has been acting from pure motives. I admit it for You and claim it for myself.

I do not propose to address You now as President but as plain Andrew Johnson—the Andrew Johnson whom I used to know as a Democrat and the friend of the people. For myself I have nothing to ask From the President. I *have* asked pardon for the part I took in the Struggle for "Southern Independence."[1] Whenever the President thinks the time has come to grant that pardon he will grant it. If that time should never come I am content to remain under the ban. It is not of this matter that I wish to speak—but of matters that concern, deeply concern the whole people. When the people of the South took up arms they did it with an earnest conviction that their cause was right. It is simple folly to say the politicians *led* the people—the truth is the people *drove* the politicians. The people took up arms with wonderful unanimity in what they regarded as thier own cause. They did it honestly. After four Years of carnage they with wonderful unanimity laid down their arms & *they did it honestly*. It gratifies us all to hear that such men as Grant & Sherman do justice to the fortitude of our people and the courage of our soldiers. We know that we struggled manfully for what we thought was right. We know that we were beaten, and when we surrendered we *know* that we did so in good faith. Here and there may have been heard a discordant murmer. But it was the babbling of rivulets soon to be lost in the great current of the Mississippi. When we laid down our arms we laid them at the feet of an overpowering force and surrendered to what we thought a generous foe, a foe as generous in peace as he had shown himself formidable in War. So far as the men at arms are concerned from Lt Genl Grant down to the humblest private (of course there are exceptions) we have not been disappointed. Your own course has been all that any of us could have desired. If Your counsels & those of Genls Grant Sherman and men like You and they had been followed I do not believe there would in all the South to day have been a whisper of discontent. It is galling to an honest man to have his integrity called in question. The Southern people know the sincerity of thier own professions and when that sincerity is questioned it is natural that irritation should find expression in words of passion. Sumner Stevens Fred Douglas *et id omni genus* have no right to expect of the Southern people to submit quietly to be told that they are hypocrits and liars as well as traitors and cowards.

But all this is not what I set out to say. I wanted simply to say that all who have in view the restoration of peace and quiet law and order and the greatest amount of prosperity in the South to white people and black people ought to espouse and earnestly advocate Your policy. Those who seek discord and strife and long for more blood had better follow the lead of Sumner & Stevens.

It may be fun for miscreants who revel in human gore and gloat over human woes to drive a beaten but Yet a gallant people to desperation. But wise men, good and patriotic men will accept the honorable pledge of honorable men and cease to pursue them. I hope in any contingency we shall have peace, Universal and all pervading peace. But if it be otherwise, If there is to be perpetual Strife—a guerrilla warfare, and a war of races costing more blood and more treasure than the "War of the rebellion" let it not be said it is Your fault—and if You pursue Your present line of policy I am very sure it will not.

Your policy gives us peace and all the prosperity we can now hope for. The Sumner Stevens policy gives us perpetual Strife and never ending misery.

A. G. Brown

ALS, DLC-JP.
1. See Brown to Johnson, July 4, 1865, *Johnson Papers*, 8: 348. Johnson did not finally grant a pardon to Brown until October 1, 1866. *House Ex. Docs.*, 39 Cong., 2 Sess., No. 31, p. 19 (Ser. 1289).

From William W. Duffield

Woodside, Schuylkill Co., Pa.   February 24th 1866

My Dear Sir

I do not know whether you recollect me or not, but I had command of a brigade for a long time stationed at Murfreesboro, under your administration as Military Governor of Tennessee, and received two severe gunshot wounds at the battle of Murfreesboro where I was made prisoner, and from this disability was rendered unfit for active service and therefore resigned, and have accepted my present post of Resident Manager of the above named company.[1] I never was a politician and never allowed myself to run for any office in the gift of the people, and God helping me I never will. But my present post brings me in contact with "all sorts and conditions of men" and fearing that yours occupying the high position which you now hold did not afford you the same opportunities of learning the temper of the people I write you thus freely, so as to aid you in the great work you have undertaken. Sympathizing with you most heartilly as I do I give you all the information in my power, to aid you. If you can find time from other more pressing duties to answer this letter I shall be most happy to hear from you.[2] But if not I am equally content. Rest assured of one thing however that no answer you may send me will under any circumstances be made public or find its way into the public journals. But to the point.

Your views as laid down in your recent message on the Freedmans Bureau Bill and as still here clearly and fully ennuciatiated in your recent speech to the people Feby 22 are the opinions of the great mass of the American People. They like you wish for peace and Union, and your policy for accomplishing these great ends meets with their hearty approval. If there is any one great cardinal principle in which the American people all unite most heartilly and cordially it is in the firm belief of the permanence of the Union of states under the constitution. This principle carried them safely through the rebellion, defeated McClellan, although their confidence in Mr Lincoln was not very strong in either his military or executive ability, and any men who array themselves against this principle will be swept from power, as the dry leaves are driven before the hurricane. The great mass of the people are strongly conservative, and they have had to contend with two radical elements. The first was the radical element of secession. This was a bold and dangerous element. It had been opposed by the puritain abolition, radical, element of New England, and feeling secure of its military strength, and relying upon the moral aid of the Northern Democratic party, it broke out in open rebellion. But in this it reckoned without its host. The Democratic leaders would have given them aid if they dared to do so, but the people firm in the belief that the Union of states under the constitution must and should be preserved deprived the Democrats of all political power. It was the people who fought out this war, who furnished the money, girded on the sabre and shouldered the musket and who crushed out secession, and crushed it out forever. Did Charles Sumner or Thadeus Stevens, or Benjamin Wade or Zachariah Chandler aid in this great work? Did they ever show themselves to the enemy, or head a column in the many thousand charges that have been made upon the rebel lines? Not they. The whole influence and legislative ability of these men was given to a policy which strengthened the rebellion, which fired the southern heart, and made the war for the preservation of the Union one of four years when the rebellion should have been crushed out in two. But crushed out it is thank God, and now that secession radicalism is dead, you have the New England radicalism still to crush out. This is an element equally dangerous with secession. It is equally extreme, equally disunionist, equally revolutionary, and fanatical and has been so from the first. Ever since the original "Liberty Party" broke ground at a political organization under James G. Birney in 1844, they made war upon the constitution. It recognized slavery and therefore they made war upon it. It was in their language "a covenant with death and a league with hell." They were disunionists because they would have "no fellowship with slavery." The great vital principle that actuated them was not so much the opposition to slavery, as that of bitter and uncompromising hatred to the south. This was the motive power and regulator, the main spring and pendulum of their whole machinery.

To restore the union would be to develope the south with all its wonderful resources, and this they will never permit. They control the legislative branch of our Government but they wish to control, yourself as the chief executive, and as the recent decision of the supreme court differs from them,[3] therefore both you and it must be swept out of the way. Poor simple minded politicians they are rushing headlong to their own destruction—they are sowing the wind from which will spring the whirlwind that will sweep them from the power they love so well, and the sooner this whirlwind comes the better.

Go on then in the course you have marked out and may God aid you to accomplish it. If you are ambitious, (which I will not believe) this course will make you the favored head of the Nation, and will certainly return you for another term to the position you now hold in the councils of the Nation. But if (as I sincerely believe) you have at heart solely the welfare of the Nation, you have a brilliant future before you. Your policy rigidly carried out—sternly adhered to will restore the union in its former pristine vigor and integrity, and before your present term of office expires you will have brought back to us again the prosperity of former years, and both North and South will once more kneel together at the same altar, and the prayer addressed our common Father for the peace and welfare of our whole country will be answered in all hearts with the sincere amen of a grateful and united people.

W. W. Duffield

ALS, DLC-JP.
1. The New York and Schuylkill Coal Company, which was among the earliest of such firms to operate in the rich anthracite coal region of Pennsylvania. *History of Schuylkill County, Pa. with Illustrations and Biographical Sketches* (New York, 1881), 44–45.
2. There is no record of a reply from the President. Nevertheless, Duffield wrote Johnson the following month applauding his veto of the Civil Rights bill, and again several weeks later assuring Johnson of his continued support in the "battle" against the Radicals until they are "defeated and surrender." Duffield to Johnson, Mar. 31, Apr. 18, 1866, Johnson Papers, LC.
3. A reference to the Dred Scott decision which Congress overturned through the passage of the Civil Rights Act of 1866 and the Fourteenth Amendment. Don E. Fehrenbacher, *The Dred Scott Case: Its Significance in American Law and Politics* (New York, 1978), 580.

From Pitser Miller

Memphis   Feby 24, 1866

My Dear Sir

Your Veto message of the Freedmans Bureau Bill was read in our City yesterday & so far as I saw or heard your Course is applauded.

Your Speech to the Committee[1] was Read this morning. Your friends say you done Right but there are a good many who want to Complain and say it was undignified & you will find a great many Papers will be down on you. But I assure you I with a great majority of the People applaud your Conduct throughout and I say to you go on in your well doeing & we will sustain you.

Pitser Miller

ALS, DLC-JP.
1. A reference to Johnson's Washington's Birthday Address on February 22 at the White House.

From The Unconditional Union Men of Frederick County, Md.[1]

Frederick, Md.   Feby: 24, 1866.

Sir:

The undersigned have the honor to transmit herewith, in compliance with a resolution contained therein, the enclosed copy of the Preamble and Resolutions[2] adopted at a Mass Meeting of the Unconditional Union men of Frederick County, Maryland, which convened at this place on the 22nd, instant, endorsing your Excellency and Hon *William H. Seward*, Secretary of State.

We deem it proper to inform your Excellency of the peculiar circumstances under which the meeting assembled, that you may more fully understand the nature and character of its proceedings.

A call, signed by only a few of the supporters of your election, and by several known to be hostile to your administration, was cautiously circulated with the knowledge of but few of the prominent Union men of the County, until two or three days before the meeting was to assemble; and professing for its object the approval and endorsement of your constitutional policy, as enunciated in your Message to Congress, and as expressed in your interviews with Senator Dixon, the Montana Delegation, Committee of Colored Persons, and the Committee of the Virginia Legislature.[3]

The meeting assembled at the appointed time, and large numbers of avowed disloyalists and returned rebel soldiers from various parts of the County were in attendance, and their conduct was boisterous, turbulent and arrogant.

The meeting was organized by calling Hon Madison Nelson,[4] to the chair. Judge Nelson acted with the union men of the County during the rebellion, but grew indifferent towards the close of the war, and has always denounced with great bitterness the emancipation of the slaves, and is decidedly hostile in his feelings to "Freedmen," insisting that they are suited only to the condition of slavery.

It soon became manifest that there had been a preconcerted arrangement to place the loyal men of the County in a false position. The presiding officer recognizing the shouts and clamor of rebels and rebel sympathizers, and rejecting all propositions offered by prominent union men, thus evinced beyond all doubt the real purpose of the meeting, which was to betray the Union men of the County into the hands of a few designing men, professing to be loyal, supported by rebel sympathizers and returned rebel soldiers, for local or other sinister purposes.

The excitement became so great that no proposition could be entertained, and the chair finding it impossible to restore order, at length declared the meeting adjourned amidst the wildest confusion, without obtaining any satisfactory expression of its views.

It being apparent that the loyal men greatly outnumbered those in opposition to them, notwithstanding the efforts of some of those who were connected with the call to convene persons of opposite sentiments only, the union men (your original and constant supporters), organized a meeting at once, in which the greatest unanimity prevailed, and which reflected the real sentiments of a vast majority of the people of the County, and adopted the accompanying Preamble and Resolutions.[5]

Assuring Your Excellency of our cordial support in your efforts to restore to the nation by your wise policy, unity & harmony, and to our common country the inestimable blessings of "Life, Liberty and the pursuit of Happines."

LS, DLC-JP.

1. Among the five persons who signed the letter to Johnson was Thomas Gorsuch (1819–1896), who was designated as president of the group. Gorsuch held the post of assessor of internal revenue. Jacob M. Holdcraft, *Names in Stone: 75,000 Cemetery Inscriptions from Frederick County, Maryland* (2 vols., Baltimore, 1985), 1: 476; *U.S. Off. Reg.* (1865).

2. The enclosed resolutions endorsed the Johnson administration and pledged support in sustaining the President "in all proper measures looking to the reconstruction and restoration of the States lately in rebellion," and added other specific pleas. The resolutions also expressed sympathy for William Seward for "the brutal attempt upon his life" and confidence in the Secretary's "ability, patriotism, and statesmanship."

3. See Message to Congress, Dec. 4, 1865, *Johnson Papers*, 9: 466–85; Interview with James Dixon, Jan. 28, 1866, ibid., 647–49; Remarks to Citizens of Montana, Feb. 7, 1866; Interview with Delegation of Blacks, Feb. 7, 1866; Response to Virginia Legislative Delegation, Feb. 10, 1866.

4. Nelson (c1803–1870) held several judicial posts, including the court of appeals in Maryland and chief judge of the sixth circuit. After being elected president of the Union meeting, he made a brief speech in which he declared the purpose to be support of the President and the Constitution. Holdcraft, *Names in Stone*, 2: 842; T.J.C. Williams and Folger McKinsey, *History of Frederick County, Maryland* (2 vols., Baltimore, 1967 [1910]), 1: 132; 2: 1329; *National Intelligencer*, Mar. 2, 1866.

5. This first meeting also produced a second series of resolutions that were forwarded to the President by Reverdy Johnson. These urged the restoration of the ex-Confederate states and the discharge of the public debt; furthermore, the resolutions claimed that the government existed exclusively for the white race. They commended Johnson's veto of the Freedmen's Bureau bill, his opposition to black suffrage, and his resistance to changes in the Constitution. Reverdy Johnson to Johnson, Feb. 27, 1866, Johnson Papers, LC; *National Intelligencer*, Mar. 2, 1866. For a different view of the meeting, see ibid., Mar. 15, 1866.

From Fernando Wood

Confidential

New York   Feby 24/66

My Dear Sir

By the enclosed from the Daily News of this City[1] you will see that the Peace Democracy are well disposed. Myself and friends are desirous of upholding your administration and are of course anxious that its policy shall conform to that already announced & acted upon. I also enclose slip of a correspondence between Govr. Wise of Va & myself.[2] Please read both enclosures. As yet no person authorized to represent the Peace Democracy have visited Washington, and you will please therefore not to consider that interest of the Democratic party as having made any application for favors or as having sent any person authorized to speak for them.

I shall do myself the honour to visit Washington for the purpose of an interview at an early day.[3]

Fernando Wood

ALS, DLC-JP.

1. Not found. The newspaper, a Peace Democrat organ, was owned by Wood and his brother, Benjamin. Jerome Mushkat, *Fernando Wood: A Political Biography* (Kent, Ohio, 1990), 84.

2. Not found. The exchange between Wood and Henry A. Wise, an old friend and political ally, was reprinted in various newspapers. See, for example, the *Cincinnati Enquirer*, Mar. 1, 1866.

3. There is no evidence that Wood saw Johnson anytime soon.

From Ezra J. Bantz[1]

Conkey Store
Vermilion County Illinois   feb the 25th 66

Mr president Johnson

As a farmer of Illinois I am Well pleased With your reply to fred douglass and party.[2]

The Majority of the people of this Stait is opposed to negro Equality.

The negro dont know What he asks for When he asks for the Elective franchise. It is paramount to his destruction.

Here is the talk of the returned Soldiers and it is almost unanimos With them

["]by god I Will di be fore a negro Shal put a ballet in the box on mine.["]

Those ar facts and beyond despute.

E "J" Bantz

ALS, DLC-JP.
    1. A native Ohioan, Mexican War era veteran, and Democrat since 1848, Bantz (1827–*fl*1889) had migrated from Indiana to near Oakwood, Illinois, where he later served as township trustee and district school director. H. H. Beckwith, *History of Vermilion County* (Chicago, 1879), 871; *Portrait and Biographical Album of Vermilion County, Illinois* (Chicago, 1889), 429–30.
    2. See Interview with Delegation of Blacks, Feb. 7, 1866.

From Thomas H. Benton, Jr.

Marshalltown, Iowa.   February 25th 1866

Dear Sir

Pardon me for embracing this method of thanking you for your speech of the 22d inst. I think you have covered the whole ground & have impartially presented the whole issue now before the country. I wish it could be placed in the hands of every man in the land, especially those who have served in the army. In fact if the great questions now before us could be left to the men who conquered the enemy on the battle field, *unawed by official power* & *party drill*, I believe they would all be settled & the whole machinery of government, State & Federal, put into successful operation within sixty days.

    I think your veto message unanswerable. The constitutional objection is alone sufficient to justify your action, & so would be either the military feature or the concentration of Executive power, both at variance with the genius of our institutions & obnoxious to the liberties of the people. The truth is, the whole bill is simply a *sectional, party* machine, which looses sight of the interests of the whole country & the great fundamental principles of free government. We have thousands of returned soldiers in our midst, with families to support, who are dependent upon their daily labor for the means of support, and do not know to day where the supply for to morrow is to come from: but for such the *radicals* in the Halls of Legislation propose no Bureau, no special means of relief.

    I am a Republican, & have fought three years in the army for the preservation of the Union, & believe that we have attained the glorious end for which we struggled; but because I cannot endorse the suicidal policy of Chase, Sumner & Philips, I am told that the Union has not been preserved, that eleven of the States *by their own act* have severed their connection with it, & that I am a "copperhead." Very well. Such idle assertions, however, will not change my views, nor deter me from performing my duty to my country and my country's friends.

    I trust that Providence will preserve & guide you, and that under your administration, based as I believe it is upon the Constitution & the eternal principles of right, the nation may be safely delivered from its perils.

Thomas H Benton Jr.

ALS, DLC-JP.

From George H. Locey[1]

La Salle, Illinois   Feby 25, 1866

Sir.

I have watched the course, wh you have pursued, & are still pursuing with feelings of mingled pride & pleasure. Having been a resident of Nashville for some six years prior to the rebellion, & for a length of time Proffessor in the University of Nashville, by the side of Bushrod R. Johnson[2] who espoused the Cause of the South at the moment the rebellion took its inception—it is but natural that I should take some pride, that yourself, hailing from the same locality, should be the humble instrument in the restoration of our distracted Country. I felt certain that the Freedmen's Bureau Bill, would meet with the Executive veto. I was not disappointed. The Government has never before taken upon itself to Espouse the cause of a Class, at the expense of the many.

Having left Nashville on the very night of the day on which the Secession Ordinance was passed, I have naturally enough experienced, some of the deprivations, which such a course entailed—all of which, by hard work & Providential aid, I have been able to surmount.

Together with the sacrifices which I have made I have also borne cheerfully, the taxation, necessary to an earnest prosecution of the war, to a successful termination—but I am unwilling to be taxed for the support of the Negro. His freedom has Cost us enough & if the Abolition leaders, believed what they said before the war, to wit—that the Negro, was capable of exercising all the rights of freemen, among which prominently was the idea, that he could maintain support himself, & those dependent upon him, I say let them stand or fall by their favorite dogma now. I pity the negro, but after bearing the burdens of the war—which was made the instrument for his liberation—I am unwilling to be taxed for his support. We have soldiers, their widows & orphans & multitudes of the poor white population among us, who are legitimate subjects of Charity. Congress has presented no Bill for their relief. Nor has any been asked, for like the pure Anglo Saxon, they had rather starve than beg—or have their wants, & poverty paraded before the public. Let the negro take his chances on the battlefield of life—& accept the issue wh. he has sought. The result, sooner or later must be a practical service of apprenticeship. Let that be as it may—the people are standing by the veto of our President—& hope we have got one man the radical element can neither bend nor break.

I have long since given up any idea of party. The Union of these States, one & inseparable—upon the basis of equal rights to every loyal man North or South—is the item of great moment now. We look to you to see this accomplished—& the integrity of this White Man's Government sustained. I see that Neill S. Brown, Andrew Ewing R. J. Meigs & Russell Houston—are now & some of them always have been, firm supporters of your Administration. The vessel is tempet-tossed just now, but a firm hand at the rudder will moor her safely in port. After this is accomplished, there is one thing which seems to me, more than another to demand the earnest attention of Congress, to wit—the National finances—& the laws governing distribution. I enclose a resolution on that subject, passed at a Convention recently held at Ottawa Illinois[3]—to which I ask yr careful attention. The producing interests of the Country are suffering from onerous taxation, & they are beginning to inquire into the Cause—& they find one of them, to be an unjustly constituted money power. However highly you may esteem Secy Chase Sir—I regard his financial Career, as any thing but able—& his policy in the interests of Capital at the expense of Labor, Continually.

He was the tool of Wall Street—when he should have been Master of the field. The present circulating medium of the country—amounts to about $1,000,000,000. of wh about $300,000,000. are Legal tender Treasury Notes. Secy. McCullough now asks, to have this legal tender, retired & National Bonds, issued in its stead.[4] Suppose this to be done the interest upon the Bonds, standing behind the circulation wd be about $60,000,000. annually, wh the producing interests, (for they at last bear all these burdens) have to pay into the Coffers of these so Constituted National Banks, & for what?—that is the question wh the people want answered. The Treasury Notes, are a legal tender in the payment of both public & private debts. While the National Cy is only a tender in the payment of private debts.

The Treasury Notes bear no interest, while the National Cy. being secured by the Bonds of the Govt bearing 6% per annum, obliges us to pay $60,000,000. of taxes annually. One half of the amt. necessary to support the Govt, annually goes into the hands of the Shylocks of the Govt, for which they get no value received in return, but are aiding to establish a system of Revenue Espionage wh tends to make the people distrustful of the Government. What is this, but a scheme sanctioned by the Govt. by wh Capital is enabled to *rob* labor of $60,000,000. annually?

As one of the people, Sir, allow me to express the opinion, honestly entertained that it is a system of *legalized robbery* & nothing short of National repudiation must follow in the train of such interested legislation. If you will take the trouble to ascertain, you will find that the leading spirits in & out of Congress were Bankers, who originated & carried to a successful issue this National Bkg System—& that these very Banks are to-day making in the money of trade, from 15 to 40 per cent upon the Capital invested. I ask, is this not a Centralizing power to be dreaded? The statistics of the Country prove that the increase in National wealth by natural production is only 3 1/3 per cent per annum. How, then, can the labor interests of the Country meet this Continual drain upon their resources without not only exhausting their income, but also a portion of the principal annually?

Is it not a system wh tends to make the poor poorer & the rich richer? Is it not a Centralizing power—which is undemocratic—& subversive of the great principles upon wh our Govt. was founded—& is it not tending to a practical vassalage of the producing classes? Is not the Treasury Note, made a legal tender, the True American System of Finance & adapted to the genius of our institutions? The people prefer it & never asked for a change. Much more I wd like to say, but I do not know that this will even reach you.

The people think they have a friend in you—& from my knowledge of yr antecedents, I know they have. This is the peoples measure—& they will sooner or later triumph. If you should deem it politic or practicable, I would very like to know yr views upon the Enclosed Resolution passed at Ottawa.[5]

Geo H Locey

ALS, DLC-JP.
1. Originally from New York, Locey (1834–*fl* 1886) graduated from Genesee College before accepting a position in the Literary Department of the University of Nashville. Shortly afterwards he reportedly served as principal of an academy in Goodlettsville, Tennessee, before moving to Dixon and finally La Salle, Illinois, where he practiced law and later held the office of city court judge (1879–82) and mayor. *The United States Biographical Dictionary and Portrait Gallery of Eminent and Self-Made Men, Illinois Volume* (Chicago, 1883), 44–45; *History of La Salle County, Illinois* (2 vols., Chicago, 1886), 1: 786.
2. Johnson (1817–1880) headed the Literary Department during Locey's tenure, in addition to serving as superintendent of the Military College and as professor of natural philosophy and engineering. For a summary of Johnson's Confederate military experiences, see Bushrod Johnson to Johnson, Sept. 14, 1865, *Johnson Papers*, 9: 78; Warner, *Gray*; H. W. Crew, *History of Nashville, Tennessee* (Nashville, 1890), 393–94.
3. Not found, but the resolutions of the "Anti-Monopoly" meeting held at Ottawa on February 20 were printed in the *Chicago Tribune*, February 21, 1866. The delegates demanded improvements in river and canal navigation, legislation regulating railroad freight rates and grain storage fees, a reduction in excise and import duties on cotton goods and woollens; furthermore, they criticized the national banking system.
4. The secretary of the treasury had been empowered to do this by an act of Congress approved on March 3, 1865. *Congressional Globe*, 38 Cong., 2 Sess., Appendix, p. 128.
5. There is no evidence of a reply by Johnson.

From Joseph A. Cooper

Knoxville Ten   Feb 26th/66

Sir

I take this opportunity to inform you that i am as ever sins your senet speach against treason[1] your devoted frend and supporter. I fully endors your *restoration policy* as I hav seen nothing beter proposed and as I hav nothing beter to offer also your veto mesage of the *Bureau bill*. The people here will sustain you in the act. Wee are on the gaining hand. Ther are some of the Mcclelan party that are *Loud* in ther prais of you now. How

Long they may continue wood be hard for mee to say as they hav changed from three to five times in the last five years. Ther is a bad state of feeling at Nashville both partys to bleame. The rebels are verry bold and defiant. The union men are stuborn and no feeling of forgivness mainly East Tennessee so fore as I know as ever all most a unit. Ther is a hard feeling in regard to the rejection of our members so long from ther seats. Mr Maynard & your self war members after the state was declared to be in surection. What is the mater now is the right of secession to be acknowled after the south is whiped. Is congress going to make you and I traitors by ther act? I trust they will not doo so.

I still hold to the old doctrin the union the constitution the enforement of the law. Do your duty the people will stand by you.

Joseph A Cooper
Lat Bev Maj Gen Vols

ALS, DLC-JP.
    1. Probably a reference to Johnson's Speech on Secession, Dec. 18–19, 1860, *Johnson Papers*, 4: 3–51.

From William J. Hilton[1]

Albany [N.Y.]   Feb. 26, 1866.

Dear Sir

In the very short interview I had with you, when I was in Washington some three or four weeks ago, I said to you that the People generally were getting tired of further agitating the Negro question; and would not sustain those who did. The spontaneous outburst of approval of your Veto Message,[2] and still more recently your Speech, I think proves the correctness of my statement. Your denunciation of Sumner & co[3] appears to please everybody here but the friends of Senator Harris, and Gov Fenton[4] who are extremely abusive. However they can be easily corrected, and even they are beginning to show the white feather.[5] In denouncing Sumner & co, you should have added the Chief Justice, who I think is the most dangerous man in the Country to day. He has ability and cunning sufficient to stimulate men in high places to concoct Evil; without the manliness or courage to face consequences. It has recently been his office to stimulate the weak and the fanatic people of the North by statements of this kind "I have reliable information from the South that, about twenty union, and Freedmen are murdered every day, by the Rebels" "And that the only safety of the Country is through Negro Suffrage," Ergo, Salmon P Chase President.[6] No man in the Country could possibly have had a worse opinion of him as a public man than our much lamented late friend Preston King whose loss the Country feels, and every one must deplore.[7] Since his death, evil and distracting counsels, have been on the rampage with us in New York; stimulating the *underbrush* to a fresh growth;

which I do not think will last beyond one season; that is longer than it should be.

Be of good cheer, fear not. The People are with you.[8]

W. J Hilton

ALS, DLC-JP.

1. Hilton (*fl*1882) was an attorney. Albany directories (1857–83).

2. About a week earlier Hilton had informed Johnson that he and other conservative Republicans of New York reacted favorably to the veto of the Freedmen's Bureau bill. Hilton to Johnson, Feb. 21, 1866, Johnson Papers, LC.

3. See Washington's Birthday Address, Feb. 22, 1866.

4. Republicans Ira Harris and Reuben E. Fenton, respectively.

5. "To show oneself a coward." Eric Partridge, *A Dictionary of Historical Slang* (Harmondsworth, Middlesex, England, 1972), 310.

6. These statements, if actually uttered by Chase, would not have surprised Johnson, who in the early days of his administration had learned firsthand of the chief justice's firm support for black voting rights. There was good reason for critics to suspect that Chase, as a possible candidate for the presidency in 1868, would push for black suffrage. Frederick J. Blue, *Salmon P. Chase: A Life in Politics* (Kent, Ohio 1987), 250–55, 283. See also Chase to Johnson, Apr. 30, 1865, *Johnson Papers*, 7: 672–73.

7. Hilton considered himself as King's "long life personal and political bosom friend." Hilton to Johnson, Nov. 20, 1865, Johnson Papers, LC.

8. In a follow-up letter Hilton further assured Johnson that New York's "influential men & Republicans of democratic Antecedents, are rallying to your support." Hilton to Johnson, Mar. 7, 1866, Johnson Papers, LC.

From Ward H. Lamon

Washington D.C   Feb 26th. 1866

Mr. President

Among the numerous allegations made against you by the ultra Abolitionists, I hear none repeated so often as this; That you have deserted the principles upon which you were elected and turned aside from the path in which your lamented predecessor would have walked if he had lived. It seems to be believed by some that Mr. Lincoln could have been used by the radicals for all their purposes including the destruction of the Government, the overthrow of the Constitution and the indefinite postponement of Union or harmony among the States.

I need not say to you or to any well informed man that the masses of that powerful party which supported Mr. Lincoln & you in the canvass of 1864 were sincerely attached to the Union and devoted believers in the Constitution.

They every where asserted that the object of the War was to reestablish the Union with the least possible delay and one of the resolutions of the Baltimore Convention pledged you both to restore the paramount authority of the Constitution in all the states. It is true that the party included some malignants who hated the Union and tried to destroy it before the War began and their pretended love of the Union during the War was more than suspected to be insincere and hypocritical. But they kept prudently silent. Mr. Thaddeus Stephens was to the best of my knowledge the only leading man in the party shameless and imprudent enough to avow his hostility to the Union. He was not the exponent of our views and he represented not even a fractional part of the honest millions who cast their votes, spent their money and shed their blood to bring back the Government of their fathers.

All this you know. I write now to tell you what I know concerning the personal sentiments of Mr. Lincoln himself. I was his partner in the practice of the law for a number of years. I came here with him as his special friend, and was Marshal of this District during his whole Administration. Down to the day of his death I was in the most confidential and intimate relations with him. I knew him as well as one man can be known to another; I had many and free conversations with him on this very subject of restoration. I was made entirely certain by his own repeated declarations to me that he would exert all his authority, power and influence to bring about an immediate and perfect reconciliation between the two sections of the Country. As far as depended upon him he would have had the southern states represented in both houses of congress within the shortest possible time.

All the energies of his nature were given to a "Vigorous prosecution of the War" while the rebellion lasted, but he was equally determined upon a "Vigerous prosecution of peace," as soon as armed hostility should be ended.

He knew the base designs of the radicals to keep up the strife for their own advantage and he was determined to thwart them as he himself told me very often. If any corroberation of this statement is needed it may be found in the fact that the Ultra Abolitionists had actually begun the out cry against him, before his death, and the moderate men every where North & South sincerely mourned his fall as a calamity which deprived them of their best friend. If that inscrutible Providence whose ways are past finding out had permitted his life to continue until this time, there can be no doubt that the Northern Disunionists would now be as loud in their denunciation of his policy as they are of yours. Mr. Stephen's demand for the head of "that man at the other end of the Avenue,"[1] would not have been a whit less ferocious. Of course he could not and did not anticipate the precise shape of the measures which the radicals might adopt to prevent reconstruction. The ["]Freedman's Bureau Bill" which recently met its death at your hands was not born in his life time. But I pronounce it a foul slander upon his memory to assert that he would have signed a bill so palpably in conflict with the Constitution and so plainly intended to promote the one bad purpose of perpetual disunion.

I did love Mr. Lincoln with a sincere and faithful affection; and my reverence for his memory is intensified by the horrible circumstances in which his high career was closed. Now that death has disarmed him of the power to defend himself, his true friends should stand forth to vindicate his good name. If there be any insult upon his reputation which they should resent more indignantly than another it is the assertion that he would have been a tool and an instrument in the hands of such men as those who now lead the heartless and unprincipled contest against you.

Ward H Lamon

ALS, DLC-JP.
1. A slightly inaccurate quotation from Thaddeus Stevens's speech in the House of Representatives, January 31, 1866. *Congressional Globe*, 39 Cong., 1 Sess., pp. 535–38.

From John L. Moses[1]

Exeter, N.H., Feb. 26, 1866.

Sir:

Will you allow me, a citizen, like yourself, of glorious East Tennessee, (temporarily here for the educational advantage of my children,) to express my approval, however feebly, of the policy which is marking your Administration?

I feel profoundly thankful that your confidence in the people, and your firmness in the right, as God gives you to see the right, are no less conspicuous than they were in former years, before secession was attempted, under the old political organizations in Tennessee, when we did not see the right alike.

Months ago, I wrote to my friend, Col. N.G. Taylor,[2] that, since the death and burial (beyond the hope of resurrection,) of the venerated Whig party, I had been identified with no other; that I had but little disposition to affiliate either with the extreme Democracy or radical Republicanism; and that I was awaiting the formation of a Johnson party, which I confidently believed would combine the best elements of all others, would sustain the Administration through the present term of its existence, and declare, by an overwhelming popular verdict for its continuance. I congratulate myself upon the fact that I am under the necessity of waiting no longer, and that I now know where to go and find my place.

Without a particle of sympathy for the rebellion, I cannot refrain from sympathizing with my neighbors, friends and fellow-countrymen of the South, or from earnestly desiring their restoration—for their own sake and the nation's—to harmonious relations with the people of the North and the West. I can have no toleration for the spirit which, more brutal than that of the champion of the prize-ring, would stamp the life out of a prostrate antagonist.

If the papers have given us a correct version of Mr. Seward's New-York telegram of the 23d,[3] it would seem that his latter years will be characterized not less by political soundness than by ripeness of scholarship and fullness of wisdom.

Jno. L. Moses.

ALS, DLC-JP.
    1. A Knoxville resident who subsequently returned to that city.
    2. Nathaniel G. Taylor.
    3. See William H. Seward to Johnson, Feb. 23, 1866.

From Albert B. Sloanaker[1]

No. 819 Arch street
Phila.   Feby. 26/66

My Dear Sir:

In view of the fact that I was your first and only supporter in the late Baltimore Convention among the Pennsylvania Delegation I, therefore, take the liberty of congratulating you upon your Freedmen's Veto-Message and speech of the 22nd inst.—the sentiments of which I heartily endorse, for upon such principles alone can this Government be administered and the Union restored. While I regretted your recent surrender of my claims to that political whelp John W. Forney, I will, nevertheless, let the past now be forgotten, and I earnestly assure you that in the future you will find in me as in days past, first among your personal and political supporters, for I am still loved and respected "among the lower classes"—to use the Forney stigma.[2]

A B Sloanaker

ALS, DNA-RG56, Appts., Internal Revenue Service, Collector, Pa., 1st Dist.
    1. Sloanaker wrote a somewhat identical letter to Secretary McCulloch who, in forwarding the letter to Johnson, assured the President that "I think that you will like the spirit of the letter." On the jacket of Sloanaker's letter to Johnson the President indicated that "Something must be done for" him. Months later, the President attached a note, "Let Sloanaker be appointed at once," to a July letter he received from George H. Williams. Concerning the post as internal revenue collector at Philadelphia, Sloanaker was subjected to a succession of events between April 1866 and February 1867 that involved nomination, confirmation, and rejection. Sloanaker to McCulloch, Feb. 26, 1866; McCulloch to Johnson, Mar. 1, 1866, Johnson Papers, LC; Senate Ex. Proceedings, Vol. 14, pt. 2: 727, 812, 814, 888, 906; Vol. 15, pt. 1: 189, 238, 268; George H. Williams to Johnson, July 27, 1866, Appts., Internal Revenue Service, Collector, Pa., 1st Dist., RG56, NA.
    2. See Sloanaker to Johnson, Nov. 2, 1865, Johnson Papers, 9: 338–39.

To Alexander H. Stephens

Washington, D.C., Feby 26th 1866

Your letter of the 5th instant just received.[1] The parole heretofore granted you[2] is hereby amended so as to permit you to visit Washington, D.C., and such other places in the United States as your business may render necessary, subject to the conditions imposed in said parole.[3]

Andrew Johnson   President United States.

TelS, DNA-RG107, Tels. Sent, President, Vol. 3 (1865–68).
    1. Stephens requested an enlargement of his parole and permission to come to Washington and confer with Johnson. Stephens to Johnson, Feb. 5, 1866, in Myrta L. Avary,

ed., *Recollections of Alexander H. Stephens* (New York, 1910), 543–44. See also Stephens to Johnson, Jan. 31, 1866, *Johnson Papers*, 9: 656–57.

2. For the terms of his original parole, see Order *re* Release of Prominent Confederate Prisoners, Oct. 11, 1865, ibid., 227.

3. Johnson was notified by the War Department on March 2 that his telegram to Stephens at Crawfordville, Georgia, had to be mailed to Stephens from Augusta and from Union Point, "there being no telegraph station at Crawfordsville." Thomas T. Eckert to Johnson, Mar. 2, 1866, Johnson Papers, LC. For further developments, see Stephens to Johnson, Mar. 23, 1866.

From Charles H. Thornton

Mobile   Feby 26 1866

Your veto message and reply to the Grovers Theatre resolutions[1] have reached here. Thousands of Loyal hearts beat responsive to the bold & noble sentiments therein contained. The people know their interests & will sustain you.

C. H. Thornton
Formerly of Memphis   of St Louis Mo

Tel, DLC-JP.
1. See Washington's Birthday Address, Feb. 22, 1866.

From Robert B. Warden[1]

Columbus, [Ohio]   Feb. 26, '66.

His Excellency, the President, has received and entertained a great variety of "deputations," more or less self-authorised. Will he receive and entertain this note, from one who voted for him, and expects to vote for him again?

It is authorised at least by some experience and observation of affairs, some knowledge of the constitution and the laws, and an unaffected desire to do the state some service. And, if these credentials seem not quite enough, these lines may ask attention in the name and in memory of one, who gave his life for the constitution as the President appears to understand it—to whom the writer of this note gave a father's leave to peril his precious young life for the sake of the cause which the President appears determined to maintain, for I will write herein not a single word that may not be dedicated to the memory of that young soldier,[2] whom I always see when I devote attention to the cause for which he died.

Mr. President, I trust I understand your objects and desires. But, proceeding at once to that part of my present task which will, perhaps, most interest you, I must say, that many certainly do not quite understand your wishes and your drift. The number of your avowed direct supporters, as against the radicals, is not large, within the organization of the Union party, here in Columbus. I am writing by request; but if this letter were signed by all who are known fully to agree with me, the signatures would not be very numerous. I know a sufficient number of representative men, here, who approve the veto while they disapprove the speech that followed, to warrant me in reporting that, but for the latter, the former would have speedily become quite popular. But it does not follow, that those who would have aided in settling the popular mind in favor of the veto, would, in any case, have gone as far as this letter goes, in approbation of the drift of your administration, as the writer has discerned that drift. Of course, the so-called democrats would not sign a letter which contains not only an acceptance of your veto, but full approbation of the preference you made at the beginning of the rebellion of country to party. On the other hand, the strictly partisan "Union men" would sign no letter of the kind of which this will presently appear to be. While, therefore, this note is not the mere expression of my own opinions, it is certainly not precisely expressive of the views at present entertained by any large division of the people.

Some, who quite agree with me, give me to understand that they are constrained to silence for the present. But the great, important fact is, that there prevails imperfect understanding of your policy and drift—in other words, of your designs and your undesigned, unconscious tendency.

It is in your power to conduct the country to repose. Perhaps, that power is in you alone, at present. If you will but patiently resume and preserve the tone from which you certainly departed in a recent exhibition of your temper under grievous provocation—if you will thus enable the few who at once comprehend and accept your policy, to cooperate effectively with you, the people can be brought ere long to embrace as well as to understand your policy. Perhaps, in a sense, all understand that policy already. It is simple, and, to all whose minds are free and ready to comprehend it, it is of easy comprehension. Many, however keep away from it, because they do not find their customary leaders with you, and because mischievous faction undermines you with the people, and mischievous democratic politicians damage you by an offensive demonstration of their unwholesome approbation of your course.

It is a strange sight! You have both patronage and principle with you; and yet there are war men, not fanatics, who appear to side with Congress as against your present policy.

I said, I think I understand your objects and desires. Permit me to explain. I may be mistaken; but if I am not, this is "the way of it":

Like you, I was politically educated by the democratic party when that name had real application. Like yourself, I am unalterably attached to a few cardinal ideas of the constitution, as interpreted of old by democrats. Like you, tho' in a different department and in less degree, I have been bound by gratitude to that party for official trusts. But, like you, I know that there can be no real obligation to party which more than apparently conflicts with what is due to the country at large. I am, therefore, not at a puzzle, when I see that you consider that whatever was at any time good in the democratic principles and policy, has not become evil because that party as an organised entity has, unhappily, preferred a section of the country to the whole, and the prospect of party prosperity to the principles and policy once precious to all democrats. Again, I do not wonder that you do not seem to think, that whatever was at any time pernicious in the ideas and the agitations of the abolitionists, became innocent because for a little while those ultras merged their special objects in those of the balanced loyal mind. Leaving out of view the ultimate analysis of motives; leaving to the Eye all-seeing the excuses which any one may allege when finally required to answer for misconduct or mistake; you can perceive whatever is not evil in the *party within a party* constituted by the radicals, as well as all that is positively good in the so-called "Union party" as a comprehensive whole.

I think, therefore, that I can comprehend at least how you *ought* to be disposed in order to be alike right and self-consistent. But perhaps only a few can at once attain to such a comprehension. The spectacle is novel. Yours is a peculiar, almost the only case, of a distinguished democrat remembering and honoring his principles, after leaving his party to become a member of the "Union party." Nearly all of the democrats who have derived positions from the new party hastened to out-Herod all the radical Herods, pseudo as well as real, of the day. Perhaps, the President himself is the only democrat in present eminence, who has the wisdom, the courage, in a word, the virtue, to respect the fixed ideas of his political life—ideas often sanctioned by the people, and expressly authorised by the writings of the political factions. The patristic love of some of these converted democrats was never very great, perhaps; but so much of it as they had, they surrendered without a summons.

They were wrong: whether foolish or base, they were surely wrong. Grant that their former views were false; they deemed them true; and it was at least a sad mistake to give up, without ryhme or reason, their established principles. In every view, the country needed and was entitled to, the honest adherence of every war democrat to his deliberately formed opinions. Some of us adhered; but you alone of those who did adhere were called to high position. For a time, indeed, it seemed questionable whether any one distinguished by position, had been true to his old ideas. You, sir, did some acts, and said some things, which superficial criticism might pronounce irreconcilable with your democracy. Substantially, however, you have the credit and the country has the benefit, of your adherence to its fundamental principles of democratic politics. If you are wrong in whole or in part, the country can at least discover how and to what extent you are in error; and if you are right in whole or in part, the country can adopt your views.

And this the country certainly will do, if you will but avoid all needless contest with the radicals and all evitable contact with the managers of the so-called democratic party. This, I own, is plain language; but it is respectful as it is earnest. It is full of regard for all that is worthy of regard in that division of the voters to which I once belonged; and it is not unmindful of your office and your dignity. The time has come for every man to do his duty, painful or pleasant. It is time for some one to insist that the President shall contribute to the public service all that he can give, in the nature of action, in the nature of self-restraint, by words and by silence, till he comes to be well understood by the body of the people.

Think of it! The body of the people have seen that Stanton and the rest incontinently rushed to the extreme of radical contempt for the few cardinal ideas, mentioned in a former paragraph. How could they be ready to appreciate your loyalty to principle, when loyalty to principle in Stanton seemed to make him a new man, on his abandoning his old political associates? Your unprecedented course surprises them, confounds them, can but slowly though it can not fail to make itself acceptable to them—subject as it hourly is, to malignant misrepresentation, and the blind and blinding criticism of a set of public characters who cannot look into public things "with thinking eyes."

But you are right, and President.

On your side, are patronage and principle. Patience, moderation, firmness, *must* command the situation.

We who are direct approvers of your policy are, therefore, hopeful. We are no poor flatterers; and we do not conceal that we were deeply pained by your latest unofficial public utterance. But we are just, and therefore we acknowledge that you were most grievously provoked. Without wasting time about any thing that is irrevocable, we implore you to be careful to the utmost henceforth to be not only right but evidently right—as much of an angel as you can—while you continue to possess your present power over reconstruction. Democratic politicians ought to be prevented from abusing such consideration as you find their due. Of course, all men have the right *to be* right. But who can fail to see, that if the President do but carefully avoid all needless contact with the democratic leaders—certain, that their party will, at the proper instant, come to you, because it must, if it have any virtue left—and if the President will but make clearly manifest that, unlike those democratic leaders, he is able to discern whatever is not evil in and of the radicals—he will encourage all who wish him well to do him service, and enable them to serve him with the effect of real benefit to him and to the country?

R. B. Warden.

Feb. 27.

A Postscript seems to be required. The above letter has been submitted to a number of your friends, who thoroughly approve of it. But we all rejoice in the evidences, that the letter of Gov. Cox[3] has brightened wonderfully the face of things, and I have doubted whether it was proper to send the foregoing. After consultation, I conclude to let it go just as it was composed before the letter of the Governor appeared.

ALS, DLC-JP.

1. A former presiding judge of the common pleas court in Cincinnati, Warden (1824–1888) later removed to Washington, D.C., where he practiced law and wrote a biography of his longtime friend, Salmon P. Chase. *DAB*; Blue, *Chase*, 318; J. W. Denver to Johnson, June 22, 1868, Appts. Div., Misc. Lets. Recd., RG48, NA.

2. Probably William E. Warden (b. *c*1845). 1860 Census, Ohio, Franklin, Columbus, 3rd Ward, 203.

3. See Jacob D. Cox to George B. Wright, Feb. 26, 1866, as reprinted in the *New York Times*, Feb. 27, 1866. Cox discussed a recent conversation he had had with the President.

From Gustave F. Weisse et al.

[February 26, 1866][1]

The petition of Gustave F. Weisse, L. A. Levy testamentary Executor of the last will of Samuel Harby, deceased, both loyal citizens of the United States, and of Felix Limet,[2] a bona fide neutral alien subject of the French Empire, all domiciliated in the city of New Orleans

Respectfully represents that they are now, and have constantly been, for many years past, the sole proprietors of the daily Newspaper published in this city, called "The New Orleans Bee";[3] That in the month of May 1864, said Newspaper was libelled and proceeded against in the Hon. the Circuit court of the U.S. of the 6th Judicial Circuit, under and by virtue of the Act of Congress of 6th August 1861, on the ground that from the 17th August 1861 to 1st May 1862, articles were published "in that newspaper, insurrectionary, rebellious and treasonable in character &c."

Now your petitioners respectfully represent that they are now and have always been loyal citizens of the United States and a bona fide neutral alien; that from the beginning they were opposed to secession; and that said newspaper was one of the few newspapers in this city and throughout the southern states which strenuously opposed secession and supported the union down to the time when further opposition would have been extremely dangerous to their persons and property and liberty; that in submitting to the prevailing opinions, they consulted personal safety, and only published such military orders, correspondence and advertisements as was necessary to protect them from suspicion; that said newspaper has always been recognized to be one of the most conservative journal in the southern states;[4] and your petitioners respectfully ask your Excellency to extend the same clemency heretofore granted to "The New Orleans daily Picayune" to the said "New Orleans Bee," by suggesting a discontinuance of said proceedings in confiscation, upon your petitioners paying all necessary costs.[5]

G. F. Weisse
Felix Limet
L A Levy Jr
Testy Exr. Heirs Saml Harby

Pet, DNA-RG60, Office of Atty. Gen., Lets. Recd., President.

1. This date is based on the date the petition was endorsed by Generals Philip H. Sheridan and Edward R.S. Canby.

2. Weisse (b. c1810), a native of France, was a co-proprietor of the *Bee* as early as 1842. His name was associated with the paper until 1868. Levi A. Levy, Jr. (c1817–fl1890) held positions as auctioneer, commission merchant, bookkeeper, and cotton press proprietor. During the 1850s he was a neighbor of Dr. Samuel Harby (c1814–fl1861), who was a co-editor of the *Bee* by 1846. Harby had a substantial personal estate of $30,000 in 1860, was married, and had three teenage daughters living at home, who were probably among his heirs. Felix Limet (fl1881) was in New Orleans working for a rival paper, *L'Union*, as early as 1858. He began working for the *Bee* about 1860. In 1878 he was one of the American delegates who travelled to Paris to discuss a potential Franco-American commerce treaty. 1860 Census, La., Orleans, New Orleans, 5th Ward, 177; 1st Ward, 134; (1870), 1st Ward, 136; New Orleans directories (1841–91); Fayette Copeland, "The New Orleans Press and the Reconstruction," *LHQ*, 30 (1947): 314–30; Conrad, *La. Biography*; *New Orleans Picayune*, Nov. 30, 1878.

3. The *Bee* was established September 1, 1827, and was published in both French and English until 1872–73, when it became exclusively a French-language paper. Goodspeed's *Biographical and Historical Memoirs of Louisiana* (2 vols., Chicago, 1892), 2: 155; *Newspapers in Microform: United States, 1948–1972* (Washington, D.C., 1973), 271–72.

4. First a Whig, then a Know-Nothing paper, the *Bee* supported Stephen A. Douglas in the 1860 campaign but joined the secessionists in December 1860. In May 1862 the *Bee* and several other papers were temporarily closed by Gen. Benjamin F. Butler because they printed editorials which he found offensive. On May 29 the *Bee* resumed publication after making a formal apology. Peyton McCrary, *Abraham Lincoln and Reconstruction: The Louisiana Experiment* (Princeton, 1978), 52, 53, 57; Gerald M. Capers, *Occupied City: New Orleans Under the Federals, 1862–1865* (Lexington, 1965), 92, 176–79; Copeland, "New Orleans Press," 301.

5. Endorsements by Governor Wells, Generals Sheridan and Canby, and others all recommended clemency for the *Bee*. In early May 1866 the court dismissed the libel proceedings against the *Bee* provided the owners paid all costs plus a district attorney's fee of $1,000. Presumably they did so, since the paper continued to be published until 1917. *New Orleans Picayune*, May 6, 1866; *Newspapers in Microform*, 271–72.

From Harvey Dunlavy[1]

Near Bloomfield Iowa   Feb 27' 1866.

Honored Sir,

May the Good Lord bless and sustain you in your efforts to restore the Union of these States upon republican principles. You sir are undergoing greater trials, then any of your predecessors ever did.

For many years there have been men in positions from the North and from the South, who were in fact enemies to Republican Government. The extreme men of the South have been put down by the *people* of the North and South, much the larger portion of the people being of the North. The *people* of the North without distinction of parties, united to crush out the rebellion, having but one object in view, and that object was the restoration of the Union of the States. We have succeded in crushing out the rebellion at the South, And all hoped that the reunited States of America, would mount as it were upon Eagles wings and sore higher in grandure than any nation on earth. We felt that we had decided the long mooted question whether the people could govern themselves in the affirmative. We felt we had set an example to the people of Europe that would one day, cause their Kingdoms to totter and their Kings to quail. A large majority of the Northern men could feel that *he* himself had contributed to bring about this pleasing state of affairs. I confess that I felt this as to myself. I had sent my first born son[2] at the tender age of 17 and again at 19 years of age he had done more than any other private, in battle singlely and alone although crippled by a shell shot; had captured Major Gen Marmaduke.[3] I was proud of the act, not only because he was my son, But because I felt that such heroism would soon convince our deluded brethren of the South that our people were in deep earnest to preserve their Government and could not fail. It is true that I felt wounded when the Government did not recognize the prowes of the boy, simply because he was *white* and his Father a Democrat.[4] I was not only wounded, but in fact alarmed to see that a political party would under such circumstances do violence to every principle of their profession. But the negligence of that boy was not my chief concern. I soon saw what I had feared that the radical portion of the self styled Union party, never intended that this union should be restored under a Republican form of Government. There is Sumner of the Senate & Stevens of the house as you know the leaders of the party. These men are consolidationists, and to cary out their end they pretend to favor Negro equality or as they say equal rights. Your vetoe of the Freedmans buro. was right for the reasons you give, but in my humble opinion the strongest argument against that infamous bill is its destruction of a Republican form of Government. We the Democracy sustain you not for the hope or expectation of place, but because we think you are right, and feel it to be both a pleasure & a duty to stand by the man who stands by our Country. I sincerely hope that no Democrat will except position under your administration unless it be because those who elected you will not support your administration. I am clear of the opinion that the Country demands that none but true men should hold office under you, I mean those who sustain your restoration policy. In many localities it will be a hard matter to find such, Because the great idea of Sumner and company is centralization of power in the hands of New England men. And when this idea is baffled they denounce those who opposes them in unmeasured terms. In this immediately vicinity, Their followers are now wishing you were dead. They call you a *traitor* a coperhead, and Andy the Drunken Taylor. But have no fears the masses of the people are with you, and will sustain you if you stand firm.

If it should become necessary to use extraordinary measures to subdue disunionism at the North We and our children are at your service.

H Dunlavy.

P S If Generals Grant and Sherman were to write a letter in favor of your restoration policy it would cause a number of disunionists of the North to couer.

H D

ALS, DLC-JP.
  1. Dunlavy (*c*1815–*fl*1870), a lawyer and farmer, served two terms in the Iowa state legislature and held several other local offices. 1870 Census, Iowa, Davis, Lick Creek Twp., Bloomfield, 14; Thomas J. Bryant, "The Capture of General Marmaduke by James Dunlavy an Iowa Private Cavalryman," *IaJHP*, 11 (1913): 249; Edward H. Stiles, *Recollections and Sketches of Early Lawyers and Public Men of Iowa* (Des Moines, 1916), 683.
  2. James Dunlavy (1844–*fl*1913), the oldest of at least seven children, enlisted as a private in the 3rd Iowa Inf. in November 1863 and was mustered out at Atlanta on August 9, 1865. He graduated from Keokuk Medical College in 1870 and practiced medicine in Stiles, Iowa, until he moved to Maramec, Oklahoma, in 1892. 1870 Census, Iowa, Davis, Lick Creek Twp., Bloomfield, 14; Bryant, "The Capture," 249–50.
  3. Missourian John S. Marmaduke (1833–1887) graduated from West Point in 1857. A colonel in the 3rd Confederate Inf., he was promoted to brigadier general in late 1862 and participated in several raids into Missouri. On October 25, 1864, Private Dunlavy captured Marmaduke, who was commanding the rear guard protecting Sterling Price's retreating troops at Mine Creek, Kansas. While in prison Marmaduke was promoted to major general. He was not released until July 1865, at which time he returned to Missouri where, after various business ventures, he was elected governor in 1884. Warner, *Gray*; Mark A. Plummer, "Missouri and Kansas and the Capture of General Marmaduke," *MoHR*, 59 (1964): 90–94.
  4. Actually Dunlavy received a medal of honor in the spring of 1865. Ibid., 94.

From Jean W. Freund[1]

New Haven [Conn.]   Febr: 27/66.

Sir

Your veto of the Freedmans Bill, so far as I am a judge, made me feel drawn closer towards you, but your speech before the *crowd*, when I read it, made me feel mortified.

Had not your name appeared at the head of the report I would have taken it for a rant of some of our low ward politicians.

I think all your *real* friends, feel mortified.

This is the opinion of one who loves you, who voted for you and prays for you.

Jean. W. Freund
Pastor of the German M.E. Church.

ALS, DLC-JP.
  1. Not otherwise identified.

From Francis H. Gordon

Lebanon Te   27. Feby 1866.

Sir.

You will recognize the author of this note as a citizen of Tennessee, who has been politically opposed to you most of the time for twenty five years.

  I was sincere in my opposition. But it is just to tell you, that (like thousands of others) I am as honestly and earnestly the advocate of your present policy. That policy alone can transmit our wise Constitution and the blessings of Liberty to our children. It alone can make us again one people. Therefore your Veto & your two speeches of the 22d have sent a thrill of joy over the land. Here in Tennessee, we are conquered—subdued— submissive. The sword has forced us to obey the laws, which were formerly agreeable to us, and the Constitution which we all venerated. Now that all are whipped, it needs no force to make us love & obey the Constitution, which we have ever regarded the best workmanship of man. The cruel war is over. Peace has come. We are again sober; and our lifelong love for that Constitution springs up in us so powerfully (when we see its perils) that we regard him as a benefactor, who will preserve it from change, corruption or overthrow. We have trembled of fear for its safety. But now, we have hope, and rejoice in that hope.

Here in Tennessee, all is peace, friendship and harmony, save that Sumner & Co have a handfull of friends, who yet thirst for blood & dominion. But that little faction grows less daily, and will soon die out. Cruel & unusual punishments will have no advocates here.

This day I was in Lebanon Wilson County. Talked with Dr Barr,[1] Sub Agent of Freedman's Bureau. Learned from him that five or six hundred negroes live in and around that town. Of that number (18) eighteen died last week. This is a fearful mortality. At this rate, the whole population of over 600 would perish in about eight months. It is the more remarkable, because the white population in town and Country are unusually healthy. One of the reported cases died of Small Pox. The other 17 died of the effects of cold. Can the Bureau save the Africans from speedy extermination?

While in Lebanon, I observed another fact which ought to be reported to you. In that town is a literary institution—the Abby Institute,[2] long the theatre of Female Education, and therefore the pride of the town. In passing, I saw in this venerated building some *Negro Soldiers quartered in some of the rooms while* I saw *their Horses & Mules stabled in other rooms, of the building, which were used as Government Stables.* It was strangely constitutional, to see Negro Soldiers & Mules thus quartered in times of profound peace; & that too when the whole population were rejoicing in the newly inspired hope of saving the Constitution from over throw.

F H Gordon M.D.

ALS, DLC-JP.

1. Dr. Samuel B.F.C. Barr (b. c1830) was a native of Kentucky and practiced medicine in the Big Springs area of Wilson County, Tennessee, before receiving the Freedmen's Bureau appointment. Dixon Merritt, *The History of Wilson County* (Nashville, 1961), 154; 1860 Census, Tenn., Wilson, 6th Dist., Lockport, 110.

2. In the 1830s Harriet Abbe and her sister moved to Lebanon to open a school for females, located near the already-existing Campbell Academy for boys in the town. For a time the Abbe Institute operated as the Female Department of the boys school, but eventually received its own charter. Although affected by the Civil War, the Abbe Institute remained in operation. Merritt, *Wilson County*, 96–97.

From Martin Igoe[1]

Indianapolis   Feb. 27th 1866

Dear Sir

This is the Second time I have written you, once before while you were a Senator; you were then right, and I am now proud to Say to you, that I think you have grown in your rightousness, and in that rightousness maintain the Position you have taken at whatever cost.

The people are with you, and are proud to look upon you as a modern edition (unabridged) of Andrew Jackson bound in Calf. In view of which they will Support and maintain you to the bitter end.

If you can possibly furnish transportation for Stevens, Sumner & Co. to the realms of eternal Shades, for the Sake of the Republic do not fail to do it.

In the cause of the Union, I have the honor to be most truly and faithfully yours.

Martin Igoe

ALS, DLC-JP.
1. A prewar attorney and former regimental quartermaster of the 35th Ind. (Irish) Inf., Igoe (c1831–1903) was given a recess appointment in 1866 as an internal revenue assessor and was subsequently nominated as a district land sales receiver but failed to win Senate confirmation for either post. Meanwhile, he continued practicing law in Indianapolis, as well as serving as an insurance and real estate agent and investing in mining. Indianapolis directories (1861–81); Pension Records, Martin Igoe, RG15, NA; W. E. Chandler to W. G. Moore, Aug. 11, 1866, Appts., Internal Revenue Service, Assessor, Ind., 6th Dist., RG56, NA; Ser. 6B, Vol. 3: 553, Vol. 4: 286–87, Johnson Papers, LC.

From A.O.P. Nicholson

(Private)

Columbia Tenn.   Feby 27, 1866

Dear Sir:

May I venture so far upon our *ante-bellum* relations as to write you a frank, familiar and sociable letter—not as an applicant for executive favor but as a friend, personal and political. If you object, just put your *veto* on it, and hand it over to the flames. If not, then read on and charge the loss of your time to old friendships. I attended the Mass Convention at Nashville—a delegate but on a back-seat.[1] I suppose you have read the proceedings. I am confident that they speak truly the voice of nine-tenths of the people of the State. If I were called before Steven's committee[2] I should testify that the people of Tennessee have never been more loyal during my knowledge of them than they are now—that is, provided loyalty consists in an honest devotion to the Constitution and the Union as understood and maintained by you. But if loyalty means an approval of the action and sentiments of the majority in Congress, then the people of Tennessee are quite as disloyal as Brownlow represents them to be. By the way, if it were not for Brownlow the people of Tennessee would be a *unit*. I have sometimes asked myself if it were possible that this obstacle to the perfect restoration of peace and unanimity cannot be removed before Oct 1867, but I have not got any answer—so I conclude there is no remedy except in patient waiting. But to the Convention—it was made up mainly of gray-headed men from every portion of the State. I am sure I never looked upon a body of men who were more truly representative men than they were. The most out-spoken were old-line Whigs but they were not more earnest and zealous than were the old democrats present. If you could have looked in upon the assemblage, you could not have been otherwise than highly gratified. I was content to occupy a back-seat, as were the democrats present—but if it had been deemed politic I felt that I could have made a speech in vindication of your policy which would have done some good. Upon the whole I was highly pleased with the proceedings and with the feeling which pervaded the meeting. The letter of Maynard[3] and the movement of W B. Stokes[4] were looked upon as emanations from radicalism, and as designed to produce distraction and division. They were met with dignity and without excitement, and failed to disturb the harmony of the Convention.

But our Convention dwindles to comparative insignificance in view of your late Veto Message and your 22 Feby Speech. These two documents are now engaging the earnest attention of all our people and I can assure you that with a *radical* exception, here and there, they are receiving the most unbounded commendation. My individual opinion is that the argument of the Veto message is the most conclusive and triumphant ever made by you, whilst I regard your 22 Feby speech as fully equal to any of your best popular addresses. I am not sure that I fully agree with you in your designation of Stevens, Sumner and Philips as the worst of the radical conspirators. I confess that I have more respect for them, on account of their outspoken boldness, than for many who are following them but protesting that they have full confidence in the President. We have some such in Tennessee but you cannot fail to know them. They are hypocrites, without the courage to strike openly. Such men will continue to hang on your skirts and to embarrass your progress, until the issue is distinctly made. I trust it will be fully made by your veto and speech. What we now want, is, a new political party, made up of the true men from the old parties. If I had been authorised to advise in our Convention I should there have proposed to organize such a party. We must organize our forces into a party. I visited Nashville a few weeks ago for no other purpose than to see and talk with your old friend Milligan. I was glad to meet him once more. I was glad to see him sustaining himself so honorably on the bench. He is the main stay of our Supreme Court and is warmly approved by the bar. I have long regarded him as one of the best and truest of men and as a Judge he is proving that he possesses eminent legal abilities. But for him the Supreme Court would command but little confidence.

Our people are displaying more energy and industry in preparing for a crop than I have ever before witnessed. For a time the negroes were backward about hiring but for the last month there has been a marked change. I must say that they are conducting themselves, as a general thing, with unexpected propriety. The idle and worthless portion of them will soon die out or get into the prisons. The race is doomed to an early extinction, but in the mean time they will perform a great deal of valuable work. I dont think the Bureau is doing any good with us nor is it doing very much harm. I look upon it as a useless institution. With civil law fully restored we should have no need for either Bureau or military. My health is good—so is that of my family. I am getting a pretty fair law business. If you will now pardon this trespass I will subscribe my self. . . .

A.O.P. Nicholson

ALS, DLC-JP.
1. The February 22 convention.
2. A reference to the Joint Committee on Reconstruction, which, although headed by Sen. William P. Fessenden, had been pushed by Thaddeus Stevens who also served on the committee. The committee had begun conducting hearings a few weeks prior to Nicholson's letter. Castel, *Presidency of Johnson*, 55, 62, 66, 73.
3. In response to an invitation from the planners of the February mass meeting, Horace Maynard wrote a letter from Washington on February 10 in which he expressed his regrets at being unable to attend the Nashville event. His letter praised President Johnson and concluded with a plea that the unionists in the state remain united. Maynard's letter was printed in full in the *Nashville Press and Times*, Feb. 22, 1866.
4. Stokes, having traveled from Washington to Nashville, addressed the convention at length on the night of February 22. He chided the delegates for their failure to display the U.S. flag at the hall and for their neglect of Abraham Lincoln and Gen. George Thomas. He also spoke about his relationship with Andrew Johnson, past and present. Stokes's speech is printed in full in ibid., Feb. 24, 1866.

From Arden R. Smith[1]

St Louis, Feby 27th 66

Sir

I enclose a translation from the "Westliche Post" of 26th inst published in the Republican of this date.[2] While I regret that such a package of billingsgate should of necessity be brought under your personal observation, I deem it just and proper that you should know of it. I have from time to time forwarded to Mr Noell[3] translations from the same German paper, teeming with violent personal and political abuse of yourself, but this is perhaps the most violent, but yet not very much so.

The point to which I desire to direct your attention is this Sir. This same paper enjoys and has since 1864 enjoyed very extensive government patronage, from the War Dept. Mr Stanton took the patronage from sound Lincoln and Johnson journals and gave it to the Democrat[4] and Post in the interest of Mr Chase. *There is no doubt of this*. The facts are beyond all doubt that this was done in order to aid in defeating Mr Lincoln for the nomination. The result has been a bitter hatred to Mr Lincoln, living and dead, and attacking you not less bitterly and unrelentingly as his successor and heir to his grand constitutional ideas. This paper has villified and abused you in the most shameless style, and it does seem extraordinary to your friends here, that you should permit it to retain the Govt patronage it is fattening on while it is daily stabbing at you. Of course, we fully understand that it is a delicate matter to interfere with the internal machinery of a Department,—yet this abuse of you by his protegé must be known to Mr Stanton, your Cabinet officer. The Democrat is no less hostile to you, but is so in a manner as to language more in conformity with a civilized community. In feeling however, its hatred to you is unextinguishable, while its manner makes it the more dangerous.

I have spoken plainly and without any regard to etiquette perhaps, but I feel in common with thousands here the degradation of extending to this paper a patronage which should be enjoyed by your friends, and which is used now but as a means of support to attack you. The same is to be said unqualifiedly of the Democrat.[5]

Arden R Smith
Sec'y of State Cen Comte. of Conser. Union Party

ALS, DLC-JP.

1. Smith (*c*1828–*fl*1879), a native of England, had arrived in St. Louis by 1860. A captain and brevet major of U.S. volunteers and staff officer under Gen. Francis P. Blair, Jr., during the war, he later worked as an auctioneer and commission merchant, as well as a collector of water rates. In February 1867 Johnson nominated Smith to be surveyor of customs at St. Louis, but the Senate rejected his nomination. 1870 Census, Mo., St. Louis, St. Louis, 6th Ward, E Div., 181; Heitman, *Register*, 1: 894; St. Louis directories (1860–80); Ser. 6B, Vol. 4: 316, Johnson Papers, LC; Francis P. Blair to Montgomery Blair, July 26, 1866, Appts., Customs Service, Surveyor, St. Louis, Arden R. Smith, RG56, NA.

2. Not found enclosed. The article, headed "Spirit of the German Press," contained excerpts from the *Post*'s criticism of Johnson's Washington's Birthday address. The *Westliche Post* of St. Louis, an important German-American antislavery paper, was edited by German immigrant and Unionist Emil Preetorius. *Missouri Republican* (St. Louis), Feb. 27, 1866; Frank L. Mott, *American Journalism: A History of Newspapers in the United States through 250 Years, 1690 to 1940* (New York, 1947), 362, 431; *DAB*.

3. Thomas E. Noell (1839–1867), a Missouri lawyer, served as an officer in the state militia and the U.S. infantry until he resigned in February 1865 to take his seat as a Radical Republican in Congress. *BDAC*.

4. Founded by Francis P. Blair, Jr., in the early 1850s, the *Missouri Democrat*, a Republican paper, had supported Lincoln in 1860 but with the *Post* opposed Lincoln's reelection and conservative reconstruction policies and became a mouthpiece for the Radicals. Its longtime editor, B. Gratz Brown, was currently serving in the U.S. Senate. Harper, *Lincoln and the Press*, 69, 141, 145–46; Smith, *Blair Family*, 2: 147, 166–67, 266; *BDAC*.

5. Johnson referred Smith's letter to Secretary of War Stanton who immediately removed the *Westliche Post* from the War Department's publication list. Edwin M. Stanton to Johnson, Mar. 10, 1866, Johnson Papers, LC; Thomas T. Eckert to Edward D. Townsend, Mar. 14, 1866, Lets. Recd. (Main Ser.), File W-191-1866, (M619, Roll 525), RG94, NA.

From Tighlman G. Compton[1]

Office Southern Sentinel
Opelousas La   Feb 28th 1866

Honored Sir

Believing that it is gratifying to your Excellency to receive intelligence direct from the people, it is my grateful task to inform you of the heart felt gratitude and devotion which your late action on the Freedman's Bureau bill has excited in the breasts of the people of this section. They feel now, as they believed before that in your Excellency they have a friend who will save them from the dreadful fate which seemed inevitable from Northern fanaticism & are now hopeful & confident in the future. Governor Wells' action in vetoing the Election bills lately passed,[2] created a deep feeling of alarm & distrust. I have as perhaps your Excellency will recollect always been a warm supporter of the Governor & regret exceedingly his course which however may have justifications of which I am ignorant. I take the liberty of sending you one of my papers the Southern Sentinel, & would do oftener did I not fear to encroach on your valuable time.

T. G. Compton

ALS, DLC-JP.
    1. Compton (c1815–fl1870), a native of Maryland, was a planter in Rapides Parish with substantial property holdings before the war. He was also an unsuccessful applicant for several federal posts. 1860 Census, La., Rapides, Alexandria, 217; (1870), Lamourie, 183; Compton to Johnson, July 10, 1865, Appts., Internal Revenue Service, Assessor, La., 3rd Dist., RG56, NA; Compton to Johnson, Mar. 1, 1866, Johnson Papers, LC; Ser. 6A, Vol. B: 35, 37, 46, 50; Vol. C: 31, 32, 36, ibid.
    2. See Wells to Johnson, Jan. 29, 1866, and Johnson to Wells, Jan. 30, 1866, *Johnson Papers*, 9: 652, 654. See also the *New Orleans Picayune*, Feb. 13–16, 1866; Johnson to Wells, Mar. 2, 1866.

From Henry W. Hilliard

Woodlawn, Near Augusta, Ga.
Feb: 28th, 1866.

My dear Sir,

Our long acquaintance—and I trust I may say friendship, will account for the frankness with which I write to you. Since my return from my visit to Washington last Fall,[1] I have observed your course closely, and it has afforded me a gratification that I will not attempt to express. Its manliness, its wisdom, its high courage, illustrate the great position that you fill. I was prepared to witness your course, for I *knew* you. The very formidable opposition that confronts you, does not intimidate you. Your speech on the 22d of Feb, has exhibited your qualities in a way to win for you the admiration and confidence of all true men North—South—East, and West. You will be triumphantly sustained. I trust that nothing will impel you to express a purpose, on any occasion, to decline a re-election. Your enemies will try to prvoke you to make such a declaration. I trust that you will be guarded against it. The ground taken by you in one or two of your late speeches, is the true position.

One of the Radical leaders is well known to me—Thaddeus Stevens. You will remember that we served in Congress with him. Like a celebrated personage described by Milton, he is "on a *bad* eminence."[2] But like that hero, he is destined to *sure defeat*.

Allow me to suggest that every one in the South, who in *good faith* supports the Constitution and the Government, should be regarded as loyal. Thousands of true Union men—intensely loyal, were swept into the vortex of revolutionary madness by circumstances: and they profoundly rejoice at the restoration of the Union. I have a right to speak on this subject. A more loyal man than I am does not breathe the air of this American Continent.

I have been strongly urged to return to Alabama. But I like my residence here: My Wife[3] likes it, and my practice pays well. You know my taste for political life;—but I shall trust to my good fortune in Georgia. I am a sincere believer in Providence, and shall put forth my energy when the time comes.

I am sure that you will appreciate the frankness with which I write.

With my best wishes for your personal happiness, and your political success. . . .

Henry W. Hilliard.

ALS, DLC-JP.
1. Hilliard had an interview with the President while in Washington. See Hilliard to Johnson, Oct. 16, 1865, *Johnson Papers*, 9: 250–51.
2. A reference to Satan from *Paradise Lost*, bk. 2, line 1.
3. Eliza Ann Glascock (*c*1814–*fl*1873), the widow of Montgomery attorney Thomas S. Mays, became Hilliard's second wife in August 1862. 1850 Census, Ala., Montgomery, Montgomery, 1st Ward, 249; Charles C. Jones, Jr., and Salem Dutcher, *Memorial History of Augusta, Georgia* (Spartanburg, 1980 [1890]), 181; Evans C. Johnson, "Henry W. Hilliard and the Civil War Years," *AR*, 17 (1964): 109.

From Ephraim Lewis[1]

Como Panola Co Miss   Feby 28t/66

Respected Sir

Permit me to present to you this slip, cut from our County paper,[2] to show to you the opinion of the people generally in regard to your Veto of the Freedman's Bureau bill. I regard the remarks of the Editor[3] as the Exponent of the feelings of the people at large. It may be some gratification to you. Know that your method of disposing of said bill, meets the approbation of a portion of the Union at least.

We of the South thought we were treated badly. Driven from the

Union by repeated violations of the Constitution in the way of Personal Liberty bills &c—Then compulsorily driven back—And then last but by no means least—refused admission into the Union, Alone by the descendants of those Puritans, who burned Old women for witches—And those Pious Traitors who held the treasonable Hartford Convention, Called for the purpose of arranging matters for annexing themselves to the Canadas; taking protection from Great Britian, rather than have their Cod Fish trade, or Commerce interrupted by British Cruisers. The same Pious ones burned Blue Lights on the shores of New England, during the war as tokens of Friendships and protection to the Cruisers. Unfortunately for us, Genl Jackson whipped the British at New Orleans, before the Yankees had time to annex themselves, to the Canadas under the protection of England. The infamous proceedings of that villianous convention, were hushed from the world, when they learned the news of the Battle. And now they pretend to say that we are not good enough to come back into the Union. We are sorry to see that many of the same stock are disposed to show that they are not too good to settle among us—But are doing so. They dont wait for us to call on them either, but they call and say they want to be sociable. We think they can afford it. They *have generally got what we had*.

They dont hesitate to ask us, to bring the Ladies over to see their wives &—we usually reply, we have no way of getting about, since the Yankees stole or burned our Carriages. We sometimes tell them we are waiting for Sumner to admit us into the Union, befor we begin any social intercourse. We think we understand the Yankee pretty well here. And we dont altogether admire his ways. We would to be honest with you, Have prefered to have gotten along without having anything more to do, with the Yankee, in Congress or anywhere else. But since we could not get rid of them—and now in good faith and honest intention ask to be received into the Union again, we think it very hard, to see such Gentlemen as Sharkey, Alcorn[4] & refused their seats by such trash as Sumner, Stevens &c.

However we all with one accord feel thankful and Kindly towards you for your efforts to see justice done us now. Excuse this letter.

Ephraim Lewis—

ALS, DLC-JP.
   1. Not identified.
   2. Not found.
   3. Unidentified.
   4. Senators-elect William L. Sharkey and James L. Alcorn.

Remarks to Philadelphia Library Committee[1]

[Washington, February 28, 1866][2]

I beg leave simply to thank you for the kindness you have shown toward me, and the encouragement you have given me by your approbation of my public policy as it has been presented to the consideration of the country. I can only say that I trust your confidence has not been misplaced, and I can but point you to my past course and to my public promulgation of the principles by which I am guided as an evidence of what my future course will be. It now behooves every man to apply himself diligently to the task of understanding the real condition of the country, and, understanding it, to apply the true remedy for all existing evils by the faithful observance and enforcement of the Constitution and the laws made in pursuance thereof. It has been an object to find a healing plaster co-extensive with the wounds that are inflicted on the body politic—the nation. We thought we had found it, and, still thinking so, we shall pursue and persist in our policy until the great result is accomplished or it shall be defeated by a power over which we have no control. I thank you, gentlemen, for the approbation and encouragement you have extended to me on this occasion, and I repeat that I hope and trust your confidence has not been misplaced.[3]

Philadelphia Press, Mar. 1, 1866.

1. A committee representing the James Page Library Company presented resolutions from a meeting held on Washington's birthday. Speaking on behalf of the committee, John A. Marshall (*fl*1872), an attorney, informed the President that the resolutions had been drafted entirely "without distinction of party." Philadelphia directories (1865–72); Philadelphia Library Co. to Johnson, Feb. 27, 1866, Johnson Papers, LC; *Philadelphia Press*, Mar. 1, 1866.

2. Date and place are suggested by ibid. and by the *New York Times*, Mar. 1, 1866.

3. After the committee members were introduced to Johnson, the interview terminated. Johnson was later elected an honorary member of the Company. See Philadelphia Library Co. to Johnson, Feb. 21, 1867, Johnson Papers, LC.

From Jonathan Worth

Raleigh, N.C., February 28th, 1866

Sir:

In obedience to resolutions passed by the General Assembly of this State, on the 24th day of this month, a copy of which I herewith enclose,[1] I hereby signify to you that North Carolina accepts the benefits of the Act of Congress of July 2nd 1862,[2] entitled "An Act donating Public Lands to the several States and territories, which may provide colleges for the benefit of Agriculture and the Mechanic Arts."[3]

Jonathan Worth   Govr of N C

ALS, DNA-RG48, Lands and Railroads Div., Misc. Lets. Recd. (1840–80).

1. The North Carolina legislature's resolutions authorized the governor to accept "land scrip to the amount of two hundred and seventy thousand acres."

2. The Morrill Act of 1862 allowed each state 30,000 acres per senator and representative then in Congress, and an April 14, 1864, act extended for two years the time for the states to accept such a grant. *Senate Misc. Docs.*, 39 Cong., 1 Sess., No. 76 (Ser. 1239).

3. In early April 1866 Johnson authorized the delivery of the land scrip as claimed by North Carolina. *U.S. Statutes at Large*, 15: 25–26; *House Reports*, 42 Cong., 2 Sess., No. 83, p. 6 (Ser. 1542); Kemp P. Battle, *History of the University of North Carolina* (2 vols., Raleigh, 1907), 1: 757.

March 1866

From Washington Citizens[1]

[Washington, ca. March 1866][2]

Sir.

We respectfully petition Your Excellency that you would cause the Buildings located on East Capitol Street between 2nd and 3rd Sts East to be removed—or at least to make some change as it regards the Occupants. They are now occupied by a mixed mass of colored persons, without any regard to Cleanliness or decency. They are located in a thickly settled portion of the Community, and unless properly cleansed they must engender sickness of the worst character.[3]

Pet, DNA-RG105, Records of the Commr., Lets. Recd. (M752, Roll 30).
1. The petition contained seventeen signatures, including that of Benjamin B. French, commissioner of public buildings for the District of Columbia.
2. This date is based on the March 2 endorsement on the petition by Richard Wallach, mayor of Washington.
3. There is much doubt that Johnson saw this petition which Wallach referred to Maj. Gen. Christopher C. Augur, commander of the Department of Washington, with a request for "his immediate intervention to abate this nuisance." An investigation of the building in question found it "in a good state of cleanliness," a condition that could be maintained with "a little supervision." A copy of the report was forwarded to Wallach. Robert Reyburn to C. H. Howard with Endorsements, Mar. 9, 1866, Records of the Commr., Lets. Recd. (M752, Roll 30), RG105, NA.

From Joseph E. Davis

Vicksburg   March 1st 1866

I have the honor to make application to your Excellency for the restoration of my property which from its position of safety from attacks of the forces, was taken possession of by the Freedman's Bureau for the use of the U.S. I am still excluded from the use of my property by the occupancy of the Freedman's Bureau, the injustice of which I feel that your Excellency will acknowledge, as by this act I am deprived of my property without 'Law' & without compensation.

From your late able, just and Statesman-like message; in 'vetoing' the unjust & unconstitutional Freedman's Bureau Bill,[1] I feel the more ready to again address you & claim at your hands an impartial consideration of my case.

I did not think that it would be necessary for me to make this application for the restoration of my lands, for I took no part in the war. I did not bear arms. I was not a member the Legislature nor of the Convention nor attended any Public Meetings. I contributed nothing, subscribed nothing, made no investments in Confederate Bonds or Securities.

Under the assurance that those would not be molested, who staid quietly at home, I remained at my place until almost all of my property was carried off, my cotton burned and an order was Secured from Genl. Osterhaus[2] to burn my house, giving me with my family half an hour to get out.

The profoundly peaceful condition of the Southern people both in temper, feelings, & actions have made themselves known to your Excellency, not with[stand]ing the abundance of reports to the contrary & the mistatements of facts which have been sent forward to you & to Congress.

The Southern people accepted the terms of the adjustment quietly & we abide by the change in the constitution which is now the law the Land honestly, as men who have pledged their words & who keep their pledges, & we feel that we have a right to be trusted by the Government & to receive justice.

Knowing the numerous & weighty cares that press upon your Excellency, I feel unwilling to ask your attention to the claims of an individual, but I hope the pressure of circumstances will excuse me & that your Excellency will make such orders in the premises as may agree with your sense of justice.[3]

[Joseph E. Davis]

Draft, Ms-Ar, Joseph E. Davis Papers.
1. In a separate letter written to Johnson on the previous day, Davis sent his "thanks" for vetoing the bill. Davis and W. T. Sawyer to Johnson, Feb. 28, 1866, Johnson Papers, LC.
2. Peter J. Osterhaus. For an account of the devastation at his plantation, see Joseph E. Davis to Johnson, Sept. 22, 1865, *Johnson Papers*, 9: 110–13.
3. Davis did not apply for pardon until March 12, 1866, claiming that he believed "the twenty thousand Dollar clause excpted such as had not voluntarily participated" in the rebellion. His pardon was ordered March 28, but he did not receive it for several months. In late April he wrote to Johnson again asking for pardon. A printed copy of the letter, along with numerous endorsements recommending Davis's pardon and the return of his property, were presented in May to the President. Johnson referred the papers in Davis's case to General Howard to report "By what terms is the property held" by the Bureau, and "Why has it not been restored upon application of the owner?" Howard responded on May 23 that Davis "never received this property, because he refused to make application for pardon." The story of Davis's property continued on for several months before finally being resolved. Janet Sharp Hermann, *Joseph E. Davis: Pioneer Patriarch* (Jackson, 1990), 152–57; Davis to Johnson, Mar. 12, 13, 1866, Amnesty Papers (M1003, Roll 32), Miss., Joseph E. Davis, RG94, NA; Davis to Johnson, ca. Apr. 21, 1866, Joseph E. Davis Papers, Ms-Ar; N. B. Moulton to Johnson, May 9, 1866, Land Div., Lets. Recd., RG105, NA; *House Reports*, 40 Cong., 1 Sess., No. 7, p. 25 (Ser. 1314).

From Francis C. Dunnington

Union & Am. Office
Nashville   March 1, /66

Dear Sir—

I received by last mail a letter from Eugene Harris,[1] son of Ex-Gov. Isham G. Harris, asking me in behalf of his mother and her children[2] to make application to you for whatever paper may be necessary to enable them to leave the country free from interruption. She desires to join her husband in Mexico. He says he is informed that a passport from Washington is necessary. I believe that he is mistaken, but in compliance with his request I write you this letter. I am sure you will take pleasure in rendering Mrs. Harris any assistance that may be necessary to further her wishes in this respect. Her family consists of herself and five children. I am informed that two negroes, formerly her slaves, to whom she is attached and who are equally attached to her, desire to accompany her. To this I suppose there will be no objection if the application was made directly by them. I will advise them to make their application, if deemed necessary, through the agent of the Freedmens Bureau. I intended to have enclosed young Harris' letter to me in this, but have mislaid it.[3] They are impatient to get off, as they can secure company by doing so early and I will be thankful if you will have me answered promptly.[4]

F C Dunnington

N B   I trust you have found time to give an occasional glance at our paper. I have been laboring faithfully to advance the true interests of the country, and to properly educate and influence the minds of the people of Tennessee to the new order of things. I would be very glad if I had some friend at Washington who was prepared and would advise me occasionally upon the various points as they come up. I am as sincere in my present desire to advance the good of the government, as I was during the revolution to secure a permanent seperation.

Your policy excites the admiration of every body in Tennessee, without regard to past differences, except Brownlow, Fletcher, Fowler, Maynard, Stokes, Mercer, the radical members of the legislature,[5] &, I was going to say, those under their influence, but I really don't know of any such. Tell Bob[6] to write to me. I know you have not the time.[7]

D.

ALS, DNA-RG59, Misc. Lets., 1789–1906 (M179, Roll 234).

1. Harris (c1844–fl1881), the oldest son of Isham G. Harris, served as a captain in the Confederate army and later lived for a time in Memphis. 1850 Census, Tenn., Henry, 1st Civil Dist., 494; *Memphis Appeal*, Apr. 13, 1866; *List of Staff Officers of the Confederate States Army, 1861–1865* (Washington, 1891), 70; Memphis directories (1876–81).

2. Martha M. Travis Harris (c1822–1897), a native of Henry County, had married Isham in 1843 in Paris, Tennessee. She and her husband eventually had eight children. Mrs. Harris died in January of the same year as her husband; she was buried in Memphis. 1850 Census, Tenn., Henry, 1st Civil Dist., 494; *BDTA*, 1: 336; Jill K. Garrett, comp., *Obituaries from Tennessee Newspapers* (Easley, S.C., 1980), 157; *Memphis Commercial Appeal*, Jan. 21, 1897.

3. The Eugene Harris letter referred to here is doubtless the one reported as having been received by the Executive Department on March 8, 1866. The clerk noted that the letter requested permission for the Harris family to travel to Mexico to join their father. This cover file accompanies the Dunnington letter in Misc. Lets., 1789–1906 (M179, Roll 234), RG59, NA.

4. According to newspaper accounts, the Harris family left for Mexico from Memphis in early April; they went by way of New Orleans. Upon arrival in Mexico, they were questioned by authorities; Mrs. Harris told them that she had a letter from President Johnson

stipulating that no passport or special permission would be required of her. Eugene Harris returned to Memphis in early June and reported that his father and other family members were "in excellent health and spirits, and bearing their exile with the utmost cheerfulness." *Memphis Appeal*, Apr. 13, 1866; *Little Rock Arkansas State Gazette*, May 12, 1866; *Nashville Union and American*, June 9, 1866.

5. William G. Brownlow, Andrew J. Fletcher, Joseph S. Fowler, Horace Maynard, William B. Stokes, and Samuel C. Mercer.

6. Presumably Robert Johnson, the President's son.

7. Johnson referred Dunnington's letter to the State Department.

From Andrew J. Hamilton

Austin Texas   1st March 1866.

Mr President

I have the honor to enclose herewith a certified Copy of preamble and resolution adopted by the Convention of Texas now in session, in relation to our Indian frontier.[1] You will observe that I am therein requested to transmit to your Excellency a copy with such approval and recommendation as the facts will warrant.

It is unquestionably true that numbers of persons have been murdered and many Horses driven away by Indians aided by desperate white men from Missouri and Arkansas in the frontier Counties during the past six months. Indeed in a few Counties the Citizens have for the most part abandoned their homes for safer localities in the interior. I have done what was in my power by organizing Minute Companies in most of the exposed Counties, who serve without pay and have undoubtedly done much good. But now that the season for planting has arrived these people who are for the most part poor will be unable to give their time to this service without compensation.

I believe that two mounted Regiments would be sufficient to give protection to whole Indian frontier from the Rio Grande to Red River. Such a force would give a feeling of security and confidence that would be a great relief to the people of our Northwestern border. I trust that it may be practicable to afford such relief at an early day.[2] Many are desireous for the organization of a State force for this purpose. To this I am opposed— 1st because I have no authority to organize it and 2nd If I had, past experience has fully demonstrated the impolicy of such a course.

Mr. Trueman will give you a full account of the proceedings of the Convention up to this date.[3] They move slowly and a majority come up reluctantly to the full measure of their duty upon several important matters—but there is a steady improvement which will, I doubt not, result in final action as near or even nearer your views than any Convention in the South. The condition of the State in many respects is very hopeful —even cheering. The people generally white and black are at *work*. It is conceded on all hands that a larger Cotton Crop will be planted this season than ever before in the State. The same may be said of the Wheat Crop. Food is abundant and we have no paupers and will have none unless in case of an entire failure of Crop. The great body of the people are quiet and orderly. There are some localities in the State where there exists disorder and turbulence beyond the power of the local civil authorities to suppress and is causing much uneasiness and apprehension on the part of the peaceable and quiet citizens. I may mention particularly the Counties bordering on Red River and the Indian Territory. The worst characters from Missouri Arkansas & from the Indian Territory when driven from thence take refuge in Texas and become a scourge and terror to the good citizens. A small military force is greatly needed in that section—in fact I deem it indispensable to the restoration quiet order and the security of life and property. In this connection I will say further that while it is true as I have said that the great body of the people of the State are quiet and engaged in active and honorable labor still there is such a percentum of desperate Characters througout the Country who have been thrown to the surface and emboldened by the events of the last four Years, as in my judgment, to make it altogether inexpedient to withdraw the military force now. In fact in view of our immense territory the force now here is entirely inadequate to meet the demands upon it. But of this you have doubtless been properly and fully informed by your Military Officers in command in this Department.

Judging from the accounts which meet my eye from the other states that engaged in rebellion I have no hesitation in saying that the condition of Texas is, in every respect, far better than any one of them.

As fast as the Convention matures their work I will promptly report by telegram.[4]

A J Hamilton

ALS, DLC-JP.
1. On February 21, 1866, the convention passed the preamble and resolutions, which requested Johnson "to take into immediate consideration the present deplorable condition of the frontier people of Texas, and to render to them that early and efficient protection, of which they are in so much need." Johnson Papers, LC.
2. Hamilton also had appealed for more troops to Gen. Horatio G. Wright, federal commander in Texas, and Gen. Philip H. Sheridan, but without success. Indian difficulties continued for some years. Waller, *Hamilton of Texas*, 74–75; Ramsdell, *Reconstruction in Texas*, 83–84.
3. Benjamin C. Truman hand carried this letter to Johnson and arrived in Washington, D.C., on or before March 24. *Advice*, 197–98.
4. See Hamilton to Johnson, Mar. 17, 1866.

Interview with Iron and Steel Manufacturers[1]

March 1, 1866

GENTLEMEN:

All I can say, and all, perhaps that is prudent for me to say at this time, is that I am very much obliged to you for calling upon me, and thank you for the compliment. I sympathize with you to the utmost extent in what you purpose to undertake and to perform, and I might say that my whole life has been directed toward ameliorating the condition of the masses of the people. Every effort of my life has tended in that direction. Whether I have been correct or not is for others to determine, and must be left with time. I am gratified to meet you here, and I sympathize in the labors of your undertaking; but while you are engaged in adopting plans and schemes that may result in building up and strengthening the manufacturing interests of the country, you should be equally engaged and interested in developing and restoring the principles of the Union and the Government, which I think should be the precursor of what you are undertaking.

The restoration of our people would be one of the greatest protections to our home industry that could be given. Our currency has reached a point of great inflation. Many are apprehensive that we cannot stand under such an enormous circulation of currency, and yet are fearful that if we attempt to contract we shall be reduced to bankruptcy. All of our nerves should be directed to preserving the currency and preventing expansion on the one hand, and bankruptcy and revulsion on the other.

It seems to me that in this work, which affects the manufacturing, agricultural, and mining interests of the country, the first thing to be done is to labor for a restoration of the Government.

If we could enlarge the area in which our currency is to circulate—increase the number of hands in which it is to pass—we should correspondingly give it a sounder basis without taking out one dollar from the circulation. By restoring the Government and the industrial products of the South, we thereby widen the area of circulation, and along with it bring into the markets of the country millions of tobacco and cotton.

This is a very important item, and would strengthen the country and increase the demand for all manufacturing productions. It seems to me that the most powerful stimulus that could be given to these interests would be to restore our Government. It would increase the demand for manufactured articles of all kinds. By restoring the country you increase its ability to pay taxes. You could leave the present rate of tariff as it is, if you could take away this internal revenue tax. By getting rid of this internal revenue tax, you would correspondingly increase your protection to manufacturing and agricultural interests. I think that as fast as we can we should get away from these internal taxes that now rest so heavily upon the industrial products of the country. Anything I can do I will do that will tend to strengthen the resources of our country. I sympathize with you, and I trust and hope your efforts will succeed and extend as our country is restored and peace returns.

To these remarks Captain Ward responded:

We believe, Mr. President, that the constant drain upon us and our resources is the vast importations that come from England. We believe that that drain will produce very disastrous results unless the present tariff is increased. So far as the currency is concerned, if it is greatly reduced we believe it will result in disaster and bankruptcy.

Mr. Johnson: As I have remarked, if we restore the Government, and thus increase the demand for articles, our currency will be placed upon a firmer basis. I think this does away with all argument for a diminution of the amount of circulation.

But there is one thing of paramount consideration. Let us have a Government. Let us have a united people; then we have got a Government.

Mr. E. B. Ward. Mr. President, *we are all laboring under the belief that we have a Government.*

Mr. Johnson. Then let us have a whole Government. Then we have got a wider area for everything to be carried on in.[2]

Washington Morning Chronicle, Mar. 2, 1866.

1. The American Iron and Steel Association appointed a delegation to wait upon the President. Speaking on behalf of the delegation, Eber B. Ward, Michigan industrialist and first president of the association, indicated to Johnson that the reason for their visit to Washington was to induce Congress to enact legislation protecting American metal manufacturers against European competitors. *NCAB,* 13: 125; *Washington Morning Chronicle,* Mar. 2, 1866.

2. Ward then introduced the other members of the delegation to Johnson.

Remarks to Baltimore Committee[1]

Washington, March 1, 1866

GENTLEMEN:

I cannot make any speech in reply; but in response to what has been said I will simply remark that my policy, to which you have alluded as before the country, was not announced as the result of impulse, nor was it thrown out for any *ad captandum* purpose. It was announced as the result of conviction, of mature consideration, as a necessary consequence of the principles upon which this Government rests. That policy, which I honestly regard as being the best for the country, will continue before the people without the slightest deviation, and without being swerved from on my part. I do not say this in a spirit of menace or threat to anybody, but simply to give assurance that there will be no abandonment of, and no shirking from, that policy; because it is believed that the very existence and perpetuity of the Government depend upon the maintenance of the principles which have thus been enunciated.

I am not insensible to the remarks which have been made accompanying the presentation of these resolutions. The mind and soul of a man who would not feel more or less inspired and impressed by what you have said must be extremely dull and barren. I feel the full force of what you have said, and I think I know how to appreciate it; and so feeling, I am impressed with the conviction that my duty must be performed without regard to consequences.

Your encouragement at this particular time seems peculiarly appropriate. Your countenance and proffers of support under the present circumstances inspire me with a confidence and strength and a hope that the country will ultimately triumph, and those great principles will be sustained. It is not necessary for me to remark to you that I entered this contest at its very incipiency, and I have not deviated a single hair's breadth from the line of policy I then laid down. I stand now precisely on the same ground I stood on in the Senate on the 18th and 19th days of December, 1860.[2]

I know that it has been said, and no doubt by many designedly said, that here is a President who was elected by a party, and who, on coming into power, abandoned that party, that he has "Tylerized" his Administration, that he has joined the Copperheads, and things of that kind. These things have no influence upon me; they fail wholly to drive me from the discharge of my duty. But if you and I have been employed for four years in resisting a separation and dissolution of the Union, and now have reached a point where resistance has ceased; if we can be instrumental in reconciling, in conciliating and bringing back all the people to an honest and loyal and thorough support of the Government, it seems to me we are doing a great deal, and accomplishing the work we undertook.

It happens sometimes in the best of families—if I may be permitted to use the illustration—that there are differences and feuds; but when those differences are understood and arranged, and when the feuds subside, the parties can approach each other feeling more kindly toward those from whom they had been estranged than they did before. Then I do not think we are doing wrong if, while maintaining principle, while trying to preserve the Government, we have succeeded in convincing of their error and bring back to the fold of their fathers those who strayed. I think this is a result of which all should be proud, and for which we should not be taunted. If I know myself, my only object is to preserve the Government. I want it to continue in loyal hands and none others. I hope that the time will soon come when the country will be thoroughly reconciled; but to secure all that is necessary for this purpose will require a severe struggle, for I am free to say to you—it is not worth while to disguise it—that the very same spirit which animated the rebellion at one end of the line now exists at the other to some extent. Before the recent rebellion there were one set of gentlemen who were trying to break up and dissolve the Government for the purpose of preserving the institution of slavery, and another set of gentlemen were willing to break up the Government for the purpose of destroying slavery, and they so avowed. Though these respective parties disagreed in the object they wished to accomplish they agreed in one thing, and that was the destruction of the Government, and so far as that point is concerned the one was as culpable as the other. The blow was first struck at the Southern end of the line. It being struck there, the spirit which was making war upon the principles of the Government must have something to vent itself upon, and it joined with those who were for the Union against those who were for rebellion; but now when rebellion is put down, if we find an attempt to change the character of the Government, we must equally resist it. The attempt now is to consolidate, to concentrate absolute power here. It is a destruction of the Government, and it is a manifestation of the same spirit which attempted to break up the Government. I stand with you for the Government, for the Constitution, for the supremacy of the law, and for obedience to the law and the Constitution.

Let it be understood that, so far as making candidates for the future is concerned, I have nothing to do with it. If I can be instrumental in accomplishing the great work we have undertaken—to bring about peace and harmony and reconciliation among all our people, and again place this Government upon its firm basis—I shall feel that I have reached the summit of my ambition. I have no other object in view, if I know my own heart and my own feelings.

Gentlemen, permit me to thank you most sincerely for the encouragement you have given me and for the countenance you have shown by timely coming forward in this great struggle for the first principles of free Government.

Washington Morning Chronicle, Mar. 3, 1866.
1. A committee of Maryland leaders assembled at the White House on the morning of March 1. Lt. Gov. Christopher C. Cox served as the group's spokesman, offering a brief speech in which he told of the Democrat-Conservative Republican meeting in Baltimore on February 26 supportive of the President's policy. *Washington Evening Star*, Mar. 1, 1866; *Washington Morning Chronicle*, Mar. 3, 1866; *History of Baltimore, Maryland, from Its Founding as a Town to the Current Year, 1729–1898* (n.p., 1898), 557–58.
2. See Speech on Secession, Dec. 18–19, 1860, *Johnson Papers*, 4: 3–51.

From Oscar Stephenson[1]

St Paul [Minn.]   March 1, 1866.

My dear Sir.

I take the liberty of enclosing you the series of resolutions—passed by the *Black* Republican Legislature of this State yesterday.[2] They were gotten up—& passed through by the influence of *office-holders*—appointed under the auspices of Morton S Wilkinson[3] who was here in person *manipulating*, and *Ramsey*, and *Donnelly*.[4] The only way to reach such fellows is to cut off their heads. When ever the fight comes—the *people* of this state will uphold, stand by and sustain the man who has the independence in these days to be a patriot, and such we all recognize our noble President—Through storm and sunshine.[5]

Oscar Stephenson

ALS, DLC-JP.
1. A native of Virginia who took his law practice to the Northwest in the 1850s, Stephenson (1830–1881) served in the Minnesota legislature (1859–60) and later as a

probate judge. Edward D. Neill, *History of Ramsey County and the City of St. Paul* (Minneapolis, 1881), 616; W. F. Toensing, comp., *Minnesota Congressmen, Legislators, and Other Elected Officials: An Alphabetical Check List, 1849–1971* (St. Paul, 1971).

2. Not found, but the resolutions, as reported in newspapers across the country, embraced the "true reconstruction policy" of Congress and called for steps to be taken in securing voting and civil rights for all, "irrespective of color." *Chicago Tribune*, Mar. 2, 1866; *New York Tribune*, Mar. 3, 1866.

3. Former Republican senator and Johnson antagonist over the Homestead bill.

4. Alexander Ramsey and Ignatius Donnelly, Republican senator and congressman, respectively. Donnelly (1831–1901), considered by one of his biographers as "the most vigorous Radical Republican in Minnesota" at the time, eventually abandoned the Republican party and championed successively the Grange, Greenback, Farmers' Alliance, and Populist causes. He also achieved renown as a reformer and writer. Martin Ridge, *Ignatius Donnelly: The Portrait of a Politician* (Chicago, 1962), 95; *DAB*.

5. In his letter written about a week earlier, Stephenson assured Johnson that "here there are faithful hearts and true arms that beat for you." Stephenson to Johnson, Feb. 24, 1866, Johnson Papers, LC.

From Samuel S. Marshall[1]

Washington, D.C.   March 2 1866

Mr President

A number of prominent gentlemen residing at the state capitol of Illinois have requested me to urge the enclosed communication upon the attention of your Excellency.[2] I am confidant that this is done, in perfect good faith by gentlemen who desire that your administration shall be triumphantly sustained by the People. In the war that is now waged with unexampled ferocity against your Excellency it would be suicidal to permit your enemies, and the enemies of the Union to retain the patronage of the Government in their hands. The Democracy of Illinois unite cordially, with extraordinary enthusiasm, in the support of your administration in the measures you have inaugurated for the restoration of the Union under the constitution of our fathers. Their admiration of your statesmanship as displayed in this crisis, and of the extraordinary courage with which you defend the constitution against all its assailants is unbounded. They ask nothing but that you will strengthen your own noble cause, which is the cause of union and good government, by withdrawing patronage from those who are your bitterest enemies and slanderers. One of the editors of the Illinois State Journal is, I believe, the Marshall, of the Southern District of Illinois,[3] and the paper is the recipient of the Government printing. The "State Register"[4] is a Democratic Journal but is a strong supporter of your administration. I submit these Statements with no view or wish but that your Excellency may, in the premises, do what is best for the cause of which you are the recognized champion.[5]

S. S. Marshall

ALS, DLC-JP.

1. Marshall (1821–1890), a Democratic congressman from Illinois before and after the

war, served as a state representative, state attorney for the Third Judicial District, and a circuit court judge before entering Congress in 1855. *BDAC*.

2. Enclosed was a letter from John A. McClernand and six others who, in addition to praising Johnson's veto of the Freedmen's Bureau bill and his Washington's Birthday speech, sought Marshall's influence in substituting the pro-Johnson *Illinois State Register* for the anti-administration *Illinois State Journal* as recipient of government patronage. McClernand et al. to Marshall, Feb. 24, 1866, Johnson Papers, LC.

3. David L. Phillips had been reappointed marshal by Johnson and had pledged his newspaper's support of the President. Phillips to Johnson, July 14, 1865, Johnson Papers, LC. See also Richard Yates to Johnson, May 20, 1865, *Johnson Papers*, 8: 100.

4. Edited by John W. Merritt. See Illinois Editors and Publishers to Johnson, Feb. 22, 1866.

5. By May 1866 Phillips had been removed from office; the *Journal* was soon replaced by the *Quincy Herald*. Ser. 6B, Vol. 4: 299, Johnson Papers, LC; *U.S. Off. Reg.* (1867). See also Richard J. Oglesby to Johnson, June 28, 1865, *Johnson Papers*, 8: 307.

From William L.G. Smith[1]

Buffalo [N.Y.]   March 2, 1866

Dear Sir

I beg to add my humble approval of your restoration policy and in company with thousands of others tender you my thanks. The smiling faces and elastic step of our Merchants and business men indicate also their approval. Your remarks to the Baltimore Committee yesterday is regarded as decisive even by those who had lingering doubts.

We are to have a mass meeting to-morrow evening[2] in our largest Hall irrespective of party. Although the democrats are active and in earnest, the Chairmanship and lead of the meeting was offered to the Collector of the Port[3] and others who enjoy official position, and declined.

Indeed, the Express this morning throws cold water.[4] But we have arranged with true Conservative Union men outside of office to conduct the meeting and they will stand firm I think in spite of the pressure.[5]

For myself I recal many pleasant interviews with you in other days at the United States Hotel. But I have not had the pleasure of seeing you since nine years next month when you was Kind enough to wish me a safe journey to Shanghai China whither I went as Consul General at the instance of my friend Gen. Cass.[6]

W.L.G. Smith

ALS, DLC-JP.
1. A former Buffalo attorney and city official, as well as a published author, Smith (1814–1878) had served as consul at Shanghai (1857–63). Buffalo directories (1861–65); S. Austin Allibone, *A Critical Dictionary of English Literature and British and American Authors* (3 vols., Philadelphia, 1874), 2: 2164; *NUC*; Truman C. White, ed., *Our County and Its People: A Descriptive Work on Erie County New York* (2 vols., Boston, 1898), 1: 475–76; *U.S. Off. Reg.* (1859–63).
2. Resolutions of the meeting endorsing Johnson were later forwarded to the Executive Mansion. See Buffalo Citizens to Johnson, Mar. 3, 1866, Johnson Papers, LC.
3. Charles D. Norton (1820–1867), a former Whig attorney, was commissioned as collector of the port at Buffalo on February 20, 1866. H. Perry Smith, ed., *History of the City of Buffalo and Erie County* (2 vols., Syracuse, 1884), 2: 60; Ser. 6B, Vol. 4: 49, Johnson Pa-

pers, LC. See also E. D. Morgan to Hugh McCulloch, May 12, 1865, Appts., Customs Service, Collector, Buffalo, Charles D. Norton, RG56, NA.

4. The local newspaper objected to the proposed meeting on the ground that it appeared to be "entirely a Democratic affair, and we do not see that Union men have anything whatever to do with it." *Buffalo Express*, Mar. 3, 1866.

5. For an account of the meeting, see ibid., Mar. 6, 1866.

6. Lewis Cass.

From Alexander A. Stokes[1]

NewGarden Indiana.   March the 2nd 1866

Deare Sir

I have Just Read youre objections to the Freedmens Bureau Bill. And in my oppinion you are correct. I can indorse it all, word for word. You need not think that I am not a Copperhead, as Som would like to mak it appieare that all who indorce your corse is. But I amnot going to be Switched off in this kind of a Style. It youst to be Said by the Democrats that all who voted with the Republickans was Abolishians hopeing there by to Draw Some away from that Party. So it is now Said by the Radicals. All who is opposed to the Freedmens Bureau Bill, he is a copperhead. But I will not Switch worth a Cent. I am for the Constitution. And the President. I do not Write to Display my Self as you Se but to throw in my little mite. Two incurage you to go on in the way you have gon So fare. And I will be youre man to the End. My vote helped to put you where you are and I intend while you Stick to the Constitution to Stick two you. I Served 18 monthes in the Defence of our union with Gun in hand, and I am for the union Still. You must Excuse me for my formiluarity, for I love the name of Andrew Johnson. When I think that he was onst a Poore Boy, as my Self, but I will come to a Close.

Alex. A. Stokes.

N.B.   I want the President to See this.

ALS, DLC-JP.

1. Stokes (b. c1834), a North Carolina-born cabinetmaker, enlisted in Co. I, 124th Ind. Inf., in February 1864 but spent most of the war in various hospitals in Georgia and Tennessee. CSR, Alexander A. Stokes, RG94, NA.

To J. Madison Wells

Executive Mansion Washington City,
March 2d. 1866.

It is deemed expedient that the Mayor of New Orleans and the other Municipal Officers should be elected by the people as provided by law, and it is hoped therefore that without delay you will order an election for Mayor and other Municipal Officers in the City of New Orleans, to be held on the Second Monday of this month, in conformity with a law providing for such election. And in the event of your failure or refusal to do so within a reasonable time, Major General Sheridan has been directed by me[1] to cause such order to be issued by the proper military authority for such election, and to put the persons elected into possession of the respective offices for which they were elected and maintain them therein until further order.[2]

L, DLC-JP.
    1. See Edwin M. Stanton to Philip H. Sheridan, Mar. 2, 1866, Johnson Papers, LC.
    2. Wells responded, "Although I do not approve I will order the election for the 12th inst." Wells to Johnson, Mar. 6, 1866, Johnson Papers, LC. Wells's proclamation calling the election, dated March 6, appeared in the *New Orleans Picayune* of March 10, 1866. See also T. G. Compton to Johnson, Feb. 28, 1866; Johnson to Hugh Kennedy, Mar. 16, 1866; John T. Monroe to Johnson, Mar. 17, 1866.

From Ulysses S. Grant

Washington D.C.   March 3d 1866

Sir:
    In connection with the subject upon which I had a conversation with you this morning, that of permitting the sale of Arms and Ammunition to the "Liberal Government of Mexico," without which aid their cause is in great danger, and an ultimate war of great magnitude between this Government and the usurpers of that iminent, I would respectfully ask if it would not be advisable for you to send for the accredited Minister of Mexico[1] to get for yourself the information of the present situation? I ask this because I think the confidence of the Sec. of State is much more sanguine than mine in that the whole "Mexican" question will settle itself if not interrupted, and because the Minister refered to cannot see you except by invitation or through the Authority of the Sec. of State.[2]

U. S. Grant   Lt. Gen.

ALS, DLC-JP.
    1. Matías Romero (1837–1898) served as the Mexican ambassador to Washington (1862–67) and held various positions in the Mexican government during his long career. In 1865 Romero developed a long and lasting friendship with Grant, who supported the idea of sending troops and supplies to be utilized against the French-controlled Maximilian regime in Mexico. *Enciclopedia de México* (12 vols., Mexico City, 1978), 11: 179; Thomas D. Schoonover, ed., *Mexican Lobby: Matías Romero in Washington, 1861–1867* (Lexington, Ky., 1986), 50.
    2. On July 2, 1865, Seward issued the so-called Romero circular that forbid foreign diplomats from seeing the President without first going through the secretary of state. Seward believed that a diplomatic solution to the Mexican situation could be found. Romero, however, communicated with Johnson through Grant and several other political figures, behind Seward's back, hoping to secure U.S. military intervention. Grant helped to arrange an April 8, 1866, meeting between the President and Romero, from which an arms deal resulted. An American merchant could buy weapons from the government and then in a private transaction resell the arms to the Mexicans, thus avoiding any violation of American neutrality. Schoonover, *Mexican Lobby*, passim; Simon, *Grant Papers*, 16: 87–88.

From Andrew Johnson, Jr.

Nashville   March 3d 1866.

Dear Uncle

I trust that the circumstances hereinafter named will apologise for my intrusion upon your time. Your and my friend Mr Fowler the Senator elect from Tennessee, the bearer of this will further than I can write explain the circumstances which prompt me to address you. You no doubt are acquainted with the distracted state of our State government. Such a situation of affairs and the condition in which the Penitentiary is involved render my tenure as agent of that institution doubtful and very harrassing.[1] Under the uncertain prospect of affairs I respectfully solicit your assistance and favor if it is consistent with your judgment and powers. I think that past experience justifies me in saying that I am competent to fill the position of Surveyor of Customs at some post that will be remunerative. My salary at present Considering all things amounts to about $3,000 per Annum. If you could bestow the position named at Mobile or some post where the salary would aproximate this I can promise that by my close attention to the duties incumbent and my official conduct justify you in the appointment and merit the favor of your confidence.[2] With my best wishes for your future.

Andrew Johnson Jr

Copy, OFH.

1. Johnson was removed from his position with the state penitentiary in May 1866 under the new mandate from the legislature to restructure the institution and make new appointments. "Report of the Directors of the Tennessee Penitentiary," *Tenn. House Journal, 1866–1867*, Appendix, p. 93; *Zanesville Courier*, May 26, 1866.

2. The surveyor's position at Mobile was not offered to Johnson. Moreover, no confirmation of his claim in August 1866 that he was to take over the direct tax commissioner's appointment, previously held by Edward P. Cone, has been found. Instead, it has been established only that he became a mail agent at Goodlettsville in the late 1860s and continued in that job for quite a number of years. 1880 Census, Tenn., Davidson, 20th Dist., Goodlettsville, 11; *Clarksville Chronicle*, Sept. 11, 1868; *U.S. Off. Reg.* (1877–79); Johnson, Jr., to Johnson, Aug. 20, 1866, Johnson Papers, LC.

To William W. Holden

Washington D.C.   March 4" 1866.

Did you, when you were appointed Provisional Governor, take the oath of office here or after your return to Raleigh? We have no record here of what was done in your case in regard to your qualifications as Provisional Governor. Please state also whether you took the amnesty oath, as well as the oath of office? Be good enough to answer immediately.[1]

Andrew Johnson

Tel, DNA-RG107, Tels. Sent, President, Vol. 3 (1865–68).

1. This telegram was a follow-up to the January 5 and February 27 Senate resolutions

requesting Johnson to furnish data about the appointment of provisional governors, their salaries, and oaths taken, as well as Secretary of State Seward's observation that the lack of a requirement of an oath in Holden's case had been "entirely accidental." But Seward did note that Holden had taken the amnesty oath. On the same day Holden confirmed that he "took no oath of office either in Washington or Raleigh" except to comply with the Amnesty Proclamation. Seward to Johnson, Mar. 1, 1866, *Senate Ex. Docs.*, 39 Cong., 1 Sess., No. 26, pp. 1–2 (Ser. 1237); Holden to Johnson, Mar. 4, 1866, Johnson Papers, LC.

From Jonathan Worth

Raleigh N.C.   March 4, 1866

Sir:—

An engrossed bill "allowing persons of color to testify in all controversies at law or in equity where the right of persons or of property of persons of color shall be put in issue, & also the pleas of the State where the violence fraud or injury alleged shall be charged to have been done by or to persons of color" has passed its second reading the Senate with this proviso:—

"That this section shall not go into effect until Jurisdiction in matters relating to freedmen shall be fully committed to the courts of this State."[1] Many of the friends of this bill believe this proviso highly inexpedient. It has been much debated and sustained by taking votes in both houses. The advocates of the proviso insist that it does not conflict with your views.

I think it will be stricken out if you disapprove it. Will you express your approval or disapproval with permission to me to show your answer to the individual members of the general assembly but not for the press. The bill comes up for its final reading next Tuesday.[2]

Jonathan Worth   Governor of N.C.

Tel, DLC-JP.

1. This testimony bill was part of the new North Carolina "black code," and the proviso was a protest by some of the legislators against trying former slaves by agents of the Freedmen's Bureau. Worth, fearing repercussions from the Radicals, now sought the President's advice. Zuber, *Worth*, 216–17.

2. Two days later Johnson telegraphed: "Policy at this time would suggest the passage of the bill without the proviso." However, the legislature could not be swayed to drop it. Worth then vainly attempted through prominent North Carolinians visiting Washington to have the proviso nullified by obtaining an order from the President to return to civil courts the jurisdiction over freedmen. The matter was finally settled in May 1866 when the North Carolina convention struck down the proviso. Johnson to Worth, Mar. 6, 1866, Tels. Sent, President, Vol. 3 (1865–68), RG107, NA; Zuber, *Worth*, 217.

From Edmund Burke

Private

Newport, N.H.   March 5th 1866.

Sir.

Permit me to express my thanks and gratitude for your noble Veto of the Freedmen's Bureau Bill, and your late timely and patriotic speeches, and especially that of the 22d ult.

If the People shall now stand by you, as I believe they will, the Union will be restored, and the Republic, as founded by the Fathers of the Revolution, preserved. Your mission is full of responsibility, if not of peril, and your reward will be great. It will be that welcome to the niche of immortality which the Genius of History gives to the political Statesman.

I enclose a short editorial from the newspaper published in this village, and a call for a Mass Meeting, in support of the Administration policy, to show you that the people are moving to your support.[1] They are both from my pen.

I am not aware that you desire democratic support. That is the cue now given by the leaders of the Republican Party to the rank and file, to wit, that the President does not want the support of the Democracy. They hold out the idea that it will be perfectly safe for all office-holders and aspirants to vote for candidates who denounce you and your policy and adhere to Thad. Stevens &Co. as the President has announced that he will reward nobody for opinion's sake. And this is having its effect here in this state and elsewhere.

Permit me to say, that, so far as I know the Democracy of this state, they will support your policy of Restoration from principle, without hope or expectation of office. But, you can win but little support from the Republican ranks without making it known, that support of your policy is the condition on which they can hold office under your Administration. With a judicious use of your power in that direction you could secure a majority in this State in favor of your Administration. Without that, the Republicans will act in masse against you in New England.

Our State election takes place on Tuesday the 13th inst. A victory for the Democratic Ticket, is a victory for the Administration. A victory for the Republican Ticket is a victory for Thad. Stevens, Sumner &Co. If the Veto and the Speech of the 22d had been followed up with the announcement, that those in the Republican ranks who supported your policy, should have the favors of the Administration, and those who did not support your policy, should not be recognized as of the Administration Party, we could have carried this State against the Radicals. The result is now doubtful.[2]

I have recently visited Boston, and Manchester, Concord and Other places in this State, and I find the Radicals bitter in denunciation of your course. Even a surrender to their policy would not now restore you to their good opinion. Therefore, I see no other course but to form a great Administration Party composed of the Democrats and conservative Republicans. That can be done only by bringing the power of the Administration to bear on the Republican Party through the instrumentality of the offices. The Democrats will be held by principle.

Pardon the great freedom with which I have written. When I saw you in October last, I then told you I approved your restoration policy and would support it. I desire most earnestly that it should succeed; and hence the boldness of my suggestions.

Edmund Burke

ALS, DLC-JP.
1. Although not found, the editorial probably appeared in the *Argus and Spectator*, a Democratic organ founded in 1823. *Biographical Review: Volume 22 Containing Life Sketches of Leading Citizens of Merrimack and Sullivan Counties, New Hampshire* (Boston, 1897), 288.
2. See Burke to Johnson, Mar. 12, 1866.

From Henry Simpson[1]

Philadelphia, No. 1304 Green St:
March 5th 1866.

My Dear Sir,

I am known to [be] your *true* friend, and voted for you for vice President & I now take the liberty to declare to you my sincere approval of your late course. Our late friend Preston King, & myself were always good friends, & I deplore his loss. Mr. Raymond, the member from N.Y. knows who I am, so that you may have confidence in what I write. My brother *Stephen Simpson*[2] now dec'd & myself were always great Jackson Democrats & he wrote the enclosed lines,[3] which I now make applicable to you. I hope you will continue to show yourself true to the people, for the radicals *now* are as bad as the rebels were before the surrender. Forney has missed his aim and cannot recover the lost ground. *Stevens* is done for in this state, and Sumner and *negro suffrage* will not succeed. No man can be elected governor of this state, who is opposed to your administration.[4] Be of good cheer, you have gained a glory and renown, that will give you the support of—14,000 *loyal* Democrats in this city, who have heretofore voted the Republican ticket, at both the last Election for President & Vice President.

Henry Simpson

ALS, DLC-JP.
1. An acquaintance of Johnson's as early as Van Buren's campaign of 1840, Simpson (1790–1868) was a former member of the state legislature, appraiser of the port of Philadelphia, city alderman, and historian. *Appleton's Cyclopaedia*; Simpson to Johnson, June 5, 1865, Johnson Papers, LC.
2. Simpson (1789–1854) was a Philadelphia author, newspaper editor, and workingman's political advocate. *DAB*.
3. Two full stanzas from "A Patriotic Song" were enclosed.
4. Not everyone was as confident as Simpson. See, for example, Joseph R. Flanigen to Johnson, Mar. 26, 1866. In fact, the Radical Republican candidate, John W. Geary, was elected governor in October 1866 by a majority of 17,000 votes, and the Republicans captured eighteen out of the state's twenty-four congressional seats—for a net gain of three seats. Bradley, *Militant Republicanism*, 249.

From Henry Wilson

Washington   March, 5th, 1866.

Dear Sir,

Our friend Rice[1] will see you this morning in regard to Mr Mallory.[2] He has seen him within a few days and states his condition to be very bad. I hope you will allow Mr Mallory out of prison, and let him go to his family in Connecticut. It seems to me nothing can be lost by doing so.[3]

H. Wilson

ALS, DNA-RG94, Lets. Recd. (Main Ser.), File M-1209-1866 (M619, Roll 496).

1. Probably Henry M. Rice (1817–1894), a former Democratic senator from Minnesota (1858–63) and unsuccessful candidate for governor in 1865. *BDAC*.

2. Stephen R. Mallory, ex-Confederate navy secretary.

3. Wilson's letter was endorsed by Senators Edgar Cowan and Thomas A. Hendricks, as well as by "H M Rice" for Senator Lane of Indiana. On March 10 Mallory was released from confinement at Fort Lafayette, New York, and ordered to go to and remain in Connecticut until further notice. In June he obtained permission to see Johnson and to travel to his home in Florida. He was not pardoned, however, until the following summer, on July 5, 1867. Johnson granted Mallory a second pardon in mid-September 1867, after the directive authorizing his first pardon had been misplaced. Joseph T. Durkin, *Stephen R. Mallory: Confederate Navy Chief* (Chapel Hill, 1954), 379–80, 383–84; Amnesty Papers (M1003, Roll 15), Fla., Stephen R. Mallory, RG94, NA. See also Mallory to Johnson, June 21, 1865, *Johnson Papers*, 8: 268–69; Horace Greeley to Johnson, Nov. 16, 1865, ibid., 9: 395.

From Benjamin G. Humphreys

Jackson, Miss., March 6th 1866.

Sir—

I have the honor herewith to transmit to Your Excellency, the proceedings of a meeting of the citizens of Jackson Mississippi, held at the Capitol on the 3d inst.[1]

Your Message to the Senate, returning the bill passed by Congress, to amend the act to establish the Freedman's Bureau, and for other purposes —together with your speech to the people of Washington City on the 22d of February, have been published and read throughout this state. The principles, and policy of reconstruction indicated therein, meet with the unqualified approval of the people of Mississippi. Meetings are being held in various portions of the state, expressive of their gratitude to you, for this timely exercise of executive power—of their loyalty to the Union and the Constitution, and of their firm purpose, to support and sustain the Administration of the President that can "afford to do right"—that dares to be the President of the whole nation—and extend to all sections and all classes of our citizens the securities of Constitutional liberty.

It is gratifying to find, that so many conservative men, and Statesmen of all parties in the North have so nobly sustained your effort to restore the Southern States to their Constitutional rights in the Union—and that the obloquy, and insulting misrepresentations of the loyal and conservative Sentiments of our people, will fail to perpetuate the estrangement, produced by the civil disturbances of the past.

To deny that vicious and designing men can be found in the North and South, is saying too much for poor human nature. But to deny that enough good men can be found in the U. States, to restore the three great "estates of the Nation"—the Union—the States—and the People, to the rights and powers, so justly balanced and established by our fathers—is saying but little for the virtue, patriotism, and civilization of their descendants.

It is known that the purest, and most steadfast friendship, between individuals often ensues, on *acquaintance* made by "a big fight and bloody noses."

That such friendship between the various sections of our distracted country, may result from the acquaintance made by the Civil War just closed—must be the fervent prayer of Every true friend of human liberty.

Benj G. Humphreys
Gov of Mississippi

ALS, DLC-JP.
1. Enclosed was a handwritten report of the preamble and resolutions adopted at the March 3 meeting in Jackson. The document expressed strong support for and admiration of President Johnson. Among other things the resolutions asked for the seating of the Mississippi congressmen at Washington so that taxation and representation would be united.

From John C. Keener and Samuel Henderson[1]

New Orleans   6h March 1866

Sir,

On the 16h of August last you were pleased personally to state to the undersigned that the Southern Methodist Churches in New Orleans, which had been placed in the hands of the Northern Methodist Church by Special order of the Secretary of War, Mr. Stanton, Jan. 18th 1864, should be restored.

By telegram on the 10th of November last you ordered them to be restored.[2]

By an order of Gen. Canby dated 18h of Nov. herewith sent,[3] our Churches were restored *excepting three—worth $25,000*, built by us exclusively for our Colored people and used by them for the past 20 to 30 years.

Immediately thereupon, we addressed your Excellency a letter[4] protesting against this exception of Gen. Canby: from which as yet we have not heard.

Recently—the 7h of February—Gen. Canby has issued a new order[5] the purport of which is to force Trustees who have held these Churches from the beginning to transfer to colored Trustees of the Northern Methodist Church their right & title to the said houses, which order we enclose.

What makes this more intolerable is the fact *that we have not shown the least intention of disturbing these Colored Congregations which now occupy these Churches, nor have we any such purpose.* The Churches are for the benefit of the Colored Members of the M.E. Church South. Two of them were built expressly for them, & the third built for a white congregation but presented to them, subsequently.

We do not believe that it is the wish of your Excellency that the Government should first by military force put the Northern Methodist in possession of our pulpits and People, keep them for two years, & then force the transfer of titles, which have vested in us for 30 years, to Trustees elected by another Church.

We pray your Excellency to order that Wesley Chapel, Soule Chapel & Winans Chapel of the M.E. Church South in the City of New Orleans be restored to the said Church & the Trustees of said Chapels be relieved from the force of Order No 32 of Gen Canby dated February 7, 1866.[6]

J. C. Keener

Sam. Henderson

in behalf of the Louisiana Conference &

The Trustees of the M.E Church South in N. Orleans.

ALS (Keener), DNA-RG107, Lets. Recd., Executive (M494, Roll 85).

1. Keener (1819–1906) was a Methodist minister who had served several different churches in Alabama before moving to New Orleans in 1848. He served several terms as presiding elder of the New Orleans district, both before and after the war. Eventually he was elected bishop in 1870, from which post he retired in 1898. Henderson (c1825–fl1892) was a New Orleans cotton factor and merchant. 1870 Census, La., Orleans, New Orleans, 1st Ward, 13; New Orleans directories (1859–1893); John H. Brown, ed., *The Cyclopaedia of American Biographies* (7 vols., Boston, 1897–1903), 4: 485; *NUC*.

2. Johnson's telegram was in direct response to one sent to the President by Keener and Henderson in which they asked him to restore the New Orleans churches. Keener and Henderson to Johnson, Nov. 9, 1865, Tels. Recd., President, Vol. 4 (1865–66), RG107, NA.

3. Canby's order stipulated that the Methodist churches should be turned over to Keener. It then spelled out the conditions of the transfer: if there were no claims for compensation for prior use, then the surrender could be done at once; procedures to be followed if there were claims for use or damages; all church property under control of the Freedmen's Bureau would be turned over as soon as the assistant commissioner could make arrangements. In response to Canby's November order, Keener and Henderson protested against his exclusion of churches used by or in possession of black congregations. Copy of the Canby Nov. 18, 1865, order is attached to the Keener and Henderson letter of Mar. 6, 1866.

4. See Keener and Henderson to Johnson, Nov. 20, 1865, Lets. Recd., Executive (M494, Roll 75), RG107, NA.

5. A copy of Canby's February order is also attached to the Keener and Henderson letter of March 6. It authorized members of the black Methodist congregations to exercise complete control over the church property. The avowed intent of the order was to enable the black congregations to remain free of denominational control until such time as they wished to affiliate with a denomination.

6. In mid-March John Hogan forwarded the Keener and Henderson letter of March 6

to President Johnson. Hogan urged the President to consider the case presented and to take steps to have executive orders followed "and not permit subordinates and interested parties to contravene them at their pleasure." The letter was referred to the secretary of war. Hogan to Johnson, Mar. 17, 1866, Lets. Recd., Executive (M494, Roll 85), RG107, NA.

From Sackfield Maclin

San Antonio Texas   March 6th 1866

Mr President

I have just returned from the Convention.[1] It is with pleasure I can say, that the convention will ultimately do right. They will pass the Amendment to the constitution Abolishing slavery—Abolish the ordnance of secession of 1861; and repudiate the war debt. I exerted myself to induce the convention to act upon those measures looking directly to a restoration of the state before taking up the constitution generally for revision. But the leaders told me frankly, that they were afraid to do so—that it was of vital importance the constitution should be amended in many particulars, and if they completed the Ordnances looking to a restoration, the convention would adjourn at once. Hence they were compelled to suspend final action upon those subjects until they completed other parts of the constitution. I deeply regret this delay, as it is important you should have the assistence of all the influences in your present contest with the Radicals in Congress. It is a pleasure to know that the convention is nearly a unit upon those measures that called them together. It is understood, that ten or twelve members belong to the Hamilton, Sumner and Stevens party, but they will be unable to do anything. They were opposed to Secession—What was called union men, but I entertain no doubt of their hostility to you and your policy. But I can repeat what I said to you in Washington,[2] that there is not a secessionist in the state of Texas who is opposed to you or your policy, but ardently anxious for your success.

I found Col G. W. White at the convention exerting himself to induce prompt action upon those great measures looking to a restoration of the state. The convention will continue in session at least three weeks longer.

Mrs Maclin joins me in our best wishes for your prosperity and happiness.

Sackfield Maclin

ALS, DLC-JP.
    1. The Texas constitutional convention.
    2. Maclin joined his wife in Washington in December 1865 for a talk with Johnson that culminated with his being paroled. *New Orleans Picayune*, Dec. 9, 1865; Parole for Sackfield Maclin, Dec. 21, 1865, Johnson Papers, LC.

From William R. Nofsinger[1]

(Private)

Indianapolis   March 6t/66

Dear Sir,

Being too unwell this afternoon to be out, I have been thinking much about our President, and the critical condition of the country. And without any special reason, I have concluded to communicate some of my thoughts.

Perhaps, before I make any observations, it would be proper, as a key to a correct construction of what I may say, not to leave you in doubt as to my own politics. I was a democrat from education and conviction. In fact, much of my political views, were learned from my Father-in-law, Tillghman A. Howard,[2] who formerly lived in your state, (and if I remember rightly he was personally acquainted with you. I know during his life time, I heard him speak of you with great kindness and regard.) I lost confidence in the democratic organization, when it gave its aid in repealing the Missouri Compromise line, and I predicted, at that time, the consequences of that ill-advised measure. I voted for President Lincoln in 60 & 64—was in favor of the "Critenden compromise," to avert war. But when war came, was warmly in favor of its vigerous prosecution to the end.

As I am but a private citizen, and my views not fully orthodox with any party, it may seem presumptious for me to say any thing. Yet I feel, that I have as much right to be heard, as many of those politicians, rebels, negroes, and blustering humbug committees, with which you are almost daily besieged. Besides, I think, the quiet perusal of a few lines would not be so intrusive to you, as if I were to present myself in *propria personae*, and the former will save me some expense, and a great deal of embarrassment! I never was in the white house but once in my life, (a good many years ago) and I was then scared, much more, than was comfortable to me!

During the progress of the war, I much admired your conspicuous patriotism and gallantry in defence of the union, and at the sacrifize of what seemd to be your personal interest, and your most cherished social ties. Since your occupancy of the presidential chair, my admiration has been much increasd, to witness the generosity, wisdom and statesmanship, with which you have met and treated those difficult and complicated questions, which pressd upon your administration from its commencement down to the present time. Your annual message, in my judgement, was most admirable, both in style and doctrine; and in fact your whole policy down to, and inclusive of your Beauro Bill veto, must be approved by the "sober second thought" of the whole people. Yet, you seem to have met a crisis in your administration. I deeply regret to see a display of opposition in congress, by those who ought to be your friends, and I regret still more, that this opposition is, to a great extent, founded upon the prejudices of the Northren states. The union party of the western states, will part with you, with great reluctance; for they know that a withdrawal of their support from your administration presages inevitable defeat, in a large portion of the west, in their next elections. The defeat of the union party, would be a triumph for the secessionists of the South, and the party North who sympathised with them, and who opposed the prosecution of the war for the preservation of the union. Would it not be a very great calamity to place the legislative powers of the government, in the hands of those who have been so recently its enemies? Admitting that they might in some manner preserve the union, would not national degredation be likely to follow? I know that the party North who opposed the war are at least, in favor of the repudiation of the national war debt. Give them the power in conjunction with the rebels of the South (who have already, properly, repudiated their own war debt) would they not, if they did not by positive enactment, so alter and repeal tax laws, so cripple and embarrass the finances of the country, as to amount to, at least, practical repudiation? The crazy and fanatical views of Sumner and his party, are out of the question—not one man in twenty would endorse them unless as a dernier resort. But are the differences between the executive and the majority in Congress irreconcilable? Cannot, at least, the conservative portion of the union party, and the President harmonize without the sacrifice of principle, and save the country from falling into the hands of the extremists?

This winter I spent some 8 or 10 days in Southren Tennessee and Northren Alabama. My observation convinced me that in several localities the Southren union men are not safe without the protection of the Government of the United States. I do not think, however, it is as bad as Gov. Brownlow represented in a conversation I had with him in Nashvill. He thinks they would hang him instantly were it not for the federal Army. I heard a good deal of bitterness expressd toward him in his state. But much of this is owing to the peculiar Character of the man. He indulges in a good deal of denunciation against those who differ with him, and it is but natural that they retaliate. On the other hand, I am satisfied that the Soutren people are most grossly misrepresented in regard to their treatment of the negroes. In fact, they uniformly spoke most kindly of the negro, and seemd to be specially anxious to court thier favor—but they generally expressd the opionion that the negro would not work unless *forced to do so*. And I have strong reason to believe, that the cotton states proper, unless restrained in some way, will ultimately reduce their negro population to a system somewhat similar to Mexican peonage. The southren people are incapable of conceiving of the existence of a large negro population without its being reduced to some system of subordination. I trust, that one or two years experiment may demonstrate their conjectures to be erroneous, and convince them of the feasibility of negro free labor—and I also trust, that the mutual feelings of bitterness and want of confidence, which generally prevails between the north & south, will soon give way to mutual feelings of kindness and concord. But if a permanent antagonism ensue between the President and the union party, it would greatly aggravate the present irritation. The first effect of an irreconcilable difference between the President and the majority of Congress, would be to elect this year a majority of Anti-war Democrats to Congress, and defeat the union party in most of the State elections. And the next effect would be, to force upon the country a sectional contest for the next presidency, in which the Northren Union Candidate, would be most likely to triumph. Yet he would be check-mated by a democratic majority, at least, in the lower house of Congress, and thus the peace of the country would be indefinitely postponed by the continued agitation of sectional questions. I had hoped, that under your wise and conciliary administration such a calamity would be avoided, and that the whole country would soon have become pacified, and that all sections would become united, into one great brotherhood. The miserable conduct of the democratic party during our struggle for national unity, placed it upon the flat of its back, where I think it is best for the country it should remain, at least for the present. Yet, I do not feel unkindly toward it—neither do I wish to see the republican party resuscitated as a distinctive party. What I desire is that all good men of all parties should unite to restore peace to the country.

I cannot but doubt the sincerity of the democratic party, as a party, in their pretended support of your administration. They doubtless, feel favorable to all measures of your administration, of a conciliatory nature toward the south, for their hopes of ultimate elevation to power is through the aid of the South. But any measures of yours which may demand restraint upon the action of the South, or which would require force to be employd upon the South they would oppose. But I imagine among the attributes of your administration, by which the south may be affected, will be found "*fortier in re*," as well as "*suaviter in modo*,"[3] and while the democrats would sustain you in the latter, they would abandon you in the former.

The fact should not be conceald, that there are strong prejudices in the North against the people of the south; and equally as strong prejudices in the south against the people of the North. It is unreasonable in the North to expect the people of the south, in a few months, to change the education of a whole life time. Great allowance should be made for them. Their entire domestic and industrial systems have just been subverted. They stand paralized and amazed—unable, as yet, to comprehend their real condition. They should have time to adapt themselves to the new order of things. And on the other hand, the people of the South should not feel hurt at the people of the North, because they, as yet, are unwilling to repose full confidence in those who so recently were engaged in a desperate conflict to destroy our Union, and who occasioned such a fearful expenditure of blood and treasure. The mass of the people are not influenced by philosophical views as much as they are by their feelings. But their tendicies are toward the right after a while—and in clusion I will say that, I have flatterd myself, that your administration by discountenancing the radicals of both sections, would be eminently calculated to establish a homogeniousness of sentiment throughout the whole country which is so essential to its lasting peace and prosperity.

W. R. Nofsinger

Enclosed please find an editorial cliptd from the Daily Journal of this place.[4] It pretty correctly expresses the feelings, at least of the many politicians who have an eye to the ensuing state elections.

ALS, DLC-JP.
1. After serving as state treasurer, Nofsinger (c1815–fl1876) worked variously as a physician, bank cashier, and sewing machine dealer. 1860 Census, Ind., Marion, W ½ Centre Twp., Indianapolis, 2; Indianapolis directories (1861–77); B. R. Sulgrove, *History of Indianapolis and Marion County, Indiana* (Philadelphia, 1884), 224, 494.
2. Former Indiana congressman.
3. Strongly in deed; gently in manner.
4. Not found.

From Sylvanus Cobb, Sr.[1]

Boston   March 7, 1866.

Will your Excellency receive a kind word from an humble fellow citizen who has for many years held free intercourse with the ablest Statesmen of our country, including the sainted Lincoln; who has Thanked God for the gift to our Republic of Andrew Johnson; & who has with a lawful pride, quoted from your noble speeches of past years in my public addresses on the philosophy of our government, & the basis of our country's future and permanent peace, prosperity & glory. The matter of fact to which I invite your particu[lar] attention in the manner of review, is your classification of the Republican majority of Congress, & their constituents, the controling majority of the American people of the North & West, with the secessionists of the South, as *disunionists*. You affirm, in your speech of Feb. 22d, & astonish me the more by reiterating after having had time for reflection, that the two sectional parties sought the dissolution of the Union for different objects,—the *Southern*, for the perpetuation & extension of *Slavery*, & the *Northern* for its destruction; both parties, however, being alike in that they sought the dissolution of the union.

Now it is extremely mortifying to your many friends, to witness, from the exalted position to which they & an inscrutable Providence have elevated you, this unhappy misapprehension of the facts of the late political history the Republic. There has been no political party in the North in favor of the dissolution of the Union, either for the extinction of Slavery, or for any other purpose. There have been here a few men & women, not more than a dozen prominent enough to be known to the public, prating for a dissolution of the Union for the overthrow of Slavery. But they were anti-political, the men refusing to vote at our political elections for the alleged reason that it would imply an acceptance of the Federal Constitution, with its practical sanction of Slavery. It is granted, to be sure, that the pseudo-democracy, or "Copperhead" politicians of the North, were disunionists in the times of the rebellion, justifying and encouraging the secession of the South, & violently opposing the policy of the government in their "coersion," or in the maintenance of the Union by force of arms. And this is the rabble that are shouting themselves hoarse over your present war upon the Union party of the country, & your espousal of a policy which will result, as they hope, in the restoration of the governments of the Southern States to the authors of the murderous rebellion, & the government of the country to a coalition of those blood-stained traitors & themselves the Northern accessories to the treason.

Disunionists! The liberty-loving men whose banner has always displayed, in letters of light, *Union & Liberty*, & *Liberty & Union forever*; who have opposed the extension of Slavery over free territory, & its aggrandisement as the pet & pride of the nation,—because of its criminality, & its tendency to national destruction; who have persistently contended, by constitutional means, for securing predominance to the principle of universal liberty & right as the basis of everlasting national Union & greatness & glory, who, in this line of duty, elected Abraham Lincoln to the Presidency; &, when the slave tyranny made this achievement their occasion for throttling the government that they might break up the Union, did, with an immense sacrifice of life & treasure, grapple the aggressive tyranny, suppress the insurrection & save the Union; & who, as a decisive deathblow to the wicked conspiracy, re-elected Abraham Lincoln to the Presidency, & elevated by his side Andrew Johnson as Vice President of the United States;—is this great party of freedom on a level with the secessionists of the South? You must have spoken, Sir, in some strange hallucination, from a bewildering outburst of passion. I trust you will see, on reflection, with what disgust the wise & good of future ages will read this defamatory onslaught upon your friends in the history of the Republic, if you permit it to go without honorable amendment or recall.

With regard to the members of Congress whom you disparage by name, I will say of *Charles Sumner*, who is my neighbor, that his speeches in the Senate in the discharge of his duties under different exigences of the country, & his political orations & essays, will be read by enlightened Statesmen, philosophers & Christian moralists, of all future ages, as expositions of wise & true Statesmanship, & sound moral philosophy. With an enlightened comprehension of human nature, & the mutual hu[man] relations, obligations & dependencies, he bases his theories of political economy on the great principle of moral right, the principal which is eternal, & will abide the test of experience, the scrutiny of the Divine Judgment, & the shocks of the revolutions of ages. It invalues that community of interests, in which the highest good of each is seen to consist with the highest good of all, & the highest good of all with that of each. Had Mr. Sumner's doctrine of reconstruction, based upon this high Christian principle, been adopted by all branches of the government in quick succession to the collapse of the rebellion, & vigorously prosecuted, probably most if not all the seceded States would ere this have been in full operation, with State governments fostering general education, free enterprise, & equal rights; & represented in the national Legislature by delegates reflecting their own loyal & patriotic sentiments. If you begin by placing the supreme power in the hands of known corrupt & oppressive tyrants, you know that peace & safety in the communities so reconstructed will be impossible; & that those tyrants will never either surrender or divide their power to others, until they are forced to do so by the decision of another bloody strife. Surely it is unjust & mischievous to denounce members of Congress as opposed to the restoration of the entire Union, because they are earnestly desirous of effecting a reconstruction upon a basis which shall preclude the necessity of yet another reconstruction through another bloody civil war.

Sylvanus Cobb.

ALS, DLC-JP.
    1. Cobb (1798–1866), a Universalist theologian and clergyman, formerly edited an antislavery newspaper in Waltham, Massachusetts. *DAB*.

From Andrew J. Hamilton

Austin Texas   Mch 17 [7] 1866[1]

The convention has now been in session one (1) month & nothing matured. The struggle is now in reference to the ordinance of secession, whether it shall be declared null & void from the beginning or repealed. The Union men insist on the former and the late rebels on the latter. I think something like the Alabama ordinance[2] will be adopted. The delay [is] in the least discouraging not to say inexcusable. They ought to have completed their labor in ten (10) days.

There will be no trouble upon the debt created by the war[3] and the action upon the state of the freedmen is more satisfactory than that of most of the other conventions.[4]

A J Hamilton   Gov

Tel, DLC-JP.
    1. Although the telegrapher clearly dated this document as March 17, internal evidence indicates that actually the date is March 7.
    2. From the outset the convention evidently had been divided over the question of the

secession ordinance. On March 12 the convention adopted a resolution that simply declared the act of secession null and void and made no reference to its status from the beginning—a position that paralleled the one taken earlier by Alabama. Ramsdell, *Reconstruction in Texas*, 96; Waller, *Hamilton of Texas*, 89; Walter L. Fleming, *Civil War and Reconstruction in Alabama* (New York, 1905), 360–61.

3. On March 15 the convention repudiated the state's public debt. Ramsdell, *Reconstruction in Texas*, 102.

4. The convention abolished slavery in Texas, protected personal and property rights of blacks, and permitted blacks to testify in court cases involving other blacks. Some claimed that Texas had been more generous than other Southern states on the matter of rights for blacks. Ibid., 99–101.

From William C. Dunlap

March 8th 1866. Near Memphis—

My dear Friend,—

It may not be unacceptable in these trying times of our country, to receive a letter from an old and tried friend, giving you the opinion of the citizens of this section of the State. I go to Memphis, very frequently, and from my general acquaintance, meet with gentleman from almost every county in West Tennessee—in full and free conversations with them. I find but *one opinion* in the *country*, and that is—it is the duty of every citizen to *support the President*. I have never seen in the palmiest days of Gen. Jackson, such a universal opinion in favor of a man and his measures; all the Whigs are for you, and trying to do more than the Democrats. The only opposition to you is in Memphis. They are what we call abolishionists or radicals—about three hundred, mostly new citizens, such as have come here, during the War—have been filling most of the offices during that time, and State & Federal since. There is not in this section of the country, a Rebel-officer or Soldier, who is not in favor of Peace and the Union, and are behaving themselves, as good & peaceable citizens.

The freedmen are generally doing well and working in the country; there are a large number in Memphis, collected from different States that refuse to go to the country to work, and live mostly by stealing. It is with difficulty we who live near the city can save our stock of any kind; they come out from the city at night, steal your mules, horses—cows and hogs. Before morning the cows and hogs are in a butcher's pen and slaughtered—and the mules and horses are sold to some white man, who keeps them secreted until he has an opportunity to sell them to some one to take to Arkansas or Missippi. As long as the Government supports them, they will not work; if the Government would do away with the Freedmen's Bureau, the county courts would take care of the old and young, who are unable to support themselves;—they would send the old to the Poor-house, and bind out the children as they do white children. The tax to support the old and infirm would be but small when compared with their losses by theft.

This is the general opinion of the citizens.

Your Veto Message gave more universal satisfaction than any Message ever sent to Congress. I ardently hope for your speedy triumph over your enemies; as to your final triumph, I have no doubt.

Please send me a pamphlet-copy of your Veto Message; it is more convenient for preservation than the news-paper copy I have, and such other public-documents, as may be convenient.

W. C. Dunlap.

ALS, DLC-JP.

From Millard Fillmore

Pau, France   March 8th 1866.

My Dear Sir,

I am in a strange land, but my affections are in the land of my birth watching with intense solicitude the struggle now going on there between those who would restore the Union and those who would prevent it; and I have just risen from the perusal of your noble and statesman like veto of the Bill to establish a Bureau for the relief of Freedmen and Refugees, and I can not forbear to express to you my gratification at the stand you have taken, and my entire approval of the arguments by which it is sustained.

I hail with delight the auspicious day that looks like restoring the Constitution of the United States to its legitimate objects, and terminating with the war the arbitrary powers that endangered the liberty of the citizen and threatened to usurp the powers properly and wisely confided to the states. I can not doubt that the sober second thought of the country will sustain your views, and that we shall soon have the satisfaction of seeing a united people settling down in quiet and harmony and by their common efforts cheerfully engaged in restoring the land to its wonted prosperity and happiness.

That God may prosper and sustain you in your patriotic endeavors is the sincere prayer. . . .

Millard Fillmore

ALS, DLC-JP.

Remarks to Kentucky Delegation[1]

[Washington, March 8, 1866][2]

It is not needful that a formal or extended reply to what you have said should be made. I tender you, and, through you, the people whom you represent, and of the State, my unfeigned thanks for these kind expressions and manifestations of confidence in me personally, and the endorsement of the policy which shall control my administration. It is peculiarly gratifying to receive these assurances at this particular time. I trust the results will show that the confidence thus reposed is not misplaced, and will never become a matter of regret upon the part of those who give expression thereto. The present is regarded as a most critical juncture in the affairs of the nation—scarcely less so than when an armed and organized force sought to overthrow the Government. To attack and attempt the disruption of the Government by armed combination and military force is no more dangerous to the life of the nation than an attempt to revolutionize and undermine it by a disregard and destruction of the safeguards thrown around the liberties of the people in the Constitution. Our stand has been taken; our course is marked out. We shall stand by and defend the Constitution against all who may attack it, from whatever quarter it may come. We shall take no step backward in this matter. No other or higher evidence of our purpose in this regard can be given than has already been furnished. In the future, as in the past, we shall endeavor, in good faith, to make the administration of the affairs of the Government conform to the Constitution in its letter and spirit; therein is the only guaranty to the liberties of the people. It is hoped by an adherence to this rule to remedy ere long all the irregularities and annoyances to which the people have been subjected.

Again we do assure you that these demonstrations of confidence and assurances of support upon the part of the people are exceedingly cheering to us; that we are grateful for and properly appreciate them, and that our wish is to so discharge the trusts confided to us as to merit them. I need hardly say more at present.

Washington Evening Star, Mar. 9, 1866.

1. A delegation of Kentucky citizens, led by James A. Dawson (1834–*fl*1876), register of the land office for that state, and composed of congressional members and others, met with Johnson to report on a meeting held at the state capital. Dawson spoke about the Unionist sentiment in his state and also about the grievances that some felt there: the failure to restore habeas corpus, the continued presence of military forces, and the activity of the Freedmen's Bureau within the state's borders. Dawson, who had served in Kentucky Union regiments during the war, had earlier been a county court clerk. Following the war he served as Kentucky's adjutant general and editor of the *Louisville Daily Ledger* before resuming his law practice. *Washington Evening Star*, Mar. 9, 1866; *The Biographical Encyclopaedia of Kentucky of the Dead and Living Men of the Nineteenth Century* (Cincinnati, 1878), 300.

2. The place and date are based upon information contained in the newspaper account. *Washington Evening Star*, Mar. 9, 1866.

Remarks to Maryland Legislators[1]

[Washington, March 8, 1866][2]

I have no reply to make, gentlemen, more than to thank you for the encouragement and countenance you have given on the present occasion, and the confidence you have indicated as placing in me as an executive

officer, and in my public acts. All that I can say in connection with the
subject has been said. And I trust and hope, so far as concerns my prior
acts, that your confidence has not been misplaced, and that you may not
be mistaken in your approbation. It is unnecessary for me to repeat the
principles I have already laid down. They are understood, and there can
be no mistake when they are read and understood, as to the position I
occupy. Persons who understand principles, and who agree upon principles, have come together, and act together, without any previous concert
or comparison of notions or ideas. We find them involuntarily approaching each other. And the converse of the proposition is just as true. Where
they disagree and do not harmonize in their thoughts and actions, they
early commence a divergent course. The most gratifying thing to me in
this, is, after all, that I am one of those who rely upon principle. From my
earliest advent into public life, there has been some fundamental notion
about this nation that I have entertained and never depart from. But, as I
said, one of the gratifying things to me is, that after we have passed
through the ordeal that has marked our very recent history—that chaotic
state that had characterized the public mind—that when we see these
principles enunciated, there is still an apprehension and a comprehension of them around which and about which there seems to commence a
crystalization and a formation of men, that will, in the end, I believe, sustain the country. As to myself individually, that is a very small affair. It
amounts to but very little. But, so far as that goes, if I have given no evidence of sincerity, or that I can be confided in and relied upon, in the past,
there is nothing I could say now—no profession that I could make, that
would show, that, as it has been in the past, so in the future, the Constitution is my guide. The public good has been my aim. And sink or swim,
live or die, upon that principle and upon that line I shall go through with
it. All that I ask is an honest and confiding public to stand by me, and say
in the future whether I am sincere in what I profess, and whether the
principles upon which we rely are right in themselves. There is one thing
which I have relied upon in early life, and which has become a part of my
very nature. The principles, the great principles, of free government,
never yet failed. In the possession of these great principles we cannot
reach a wrong conclusion. If we are right—if the principles are right in
themselves and we pursue them rightfully—though there may be gloom
gathering around our pathway, though we may not see our way entirely
clear, yet in the pursuit of principle, if we follow it, it will take us triumphantly through, without regard to what may be upon the right hand or
upon the left. But I trust and hope that in this struggle in the Government, as it were, we may be encouraged to commence a new career, and
that we will commence it upon principle. And though so far as I am concerned, I repeat, I am a very small part of this thing, yet, now is a time for
patriots who love principles and who want to preserve the Constitution
intact—now is a time to come forward without regard to any future, so

far as I am concerned, for I am looking to none—now is a time to make a basis and form a combination upon this great question and manifest that it can be successfully demonstrated. Now is a time to make a basis; now is a time to gather the material; now is a time to rally around principle, and law a basis upon which our Government can proceed. And that being done, and this Union being restored, the summit of my ambition has been reached, the measure of my ambition has been fulfilled, and I could now say, as Simeon did of old—if I had it in my power to pronounce that this Union was restored, and the Constitution intact, and the Government had commenced its career anew—if all these things were established I could exclaim:—"The glory of Thy salvation, O God, has been seen and manifested, and now let Thy servant depart in peace!"[3] I thank you, gentlemen, for the encouragement you have given me. I think I know how to appreciate and feel it. I hope and trust in the end to deserve your support.

Washington Evening Star, Mar. 9, 1866.
   1. A group of Maryland legislators, with Speaker John M. Frazier as the leader, met with the President at the White House. He and others presented to Johnson the resolution adopted by the legislature before its adjournment in February. Frazier offered some very brief remarks in which he noted the support of the President's policies found in Maryland. Although Johnson's Freedmen's Bureau veto occurred after the adjournment of the Maryland legislature, Frazier assured the President of endorsement from his state. *Washington Evening Star*, Mar. 9, 1866.
   2. The place and date are based upon the newspaper account. Ibid.
   3. See the account of Simeon in Luke 2: 25–34.

From Thomas Cottman

Washington   March 9th 1866

Mr. President
   There can I presume be no doubt of the passage by the Senate of the House bill *admitting* Tennessee as a State of the Union.[1] This bill assumes that Tennessee is not now a State of the Union and cannot be until admitted by Congress. If this bill becomes a law it declares the Union dissolved & that eleven States are Territories only. Thus is it that secession which failed at the South, is to succeed by Congressional action. Upon the principles announced in your last message, that no State ever was out of this Union the country expects you to veto this bill—this raises distinctly the issue of Union or Disunion. On this issue there will arise a Constitutional Union Party embracing *all* who support the doctrines of your veto messages. An overwhelming majority of the people of the United States concur with you in the opinion that the Union is indissoluble, that every ordinance of Secession was always absolutely void, the Rebellion having failed each State now is & always has been in the Union & is entitled to be represented by loyal men in both Houses of Congress. The case of Tennessee rests not only upon the act of Congress admitting

her into the Union, but a compact for that purpose with the State of North Carolina. That act of Congress is unrepealed & is irrepealable. That compact with North Carolina has not been revoked & is irrevocable. The disunion doctrine rests upon a void ordinance & an unsuccessful rebellion.

The organization of a new party can be effected by the nomination in Pennsylvania of Edgar Cowan (the Senator) for Governor, by those who sustain his course in the Senate which being done, there is scarcely a doubt of the withdrawal of Clymer & the cordial support of those who nominated him to secure the election of Cowan by a triumphant majority.[2] I make these suggestions after a pretty free conference with leading Pennsylvanians, who have differed politically in the last few years both Republicans & Democrats.

Thos Cottman

ALS, DLC-JP.
1. The question of the admission of Tennessee troubled the houses of Congress for some time in the early months of the 1865–66 session. Although there was considerable sentiment in favor of admitting Tennessee, Stevens and others were determined to block it. Indeed, the whole matter would be postponed until July. Patton, *Unionism and Reconstruction*, 209–14.
2. The complex Pennsylvania political situation became increasingly so during 1866. On March 3, for example, the legislature passed a resolution calling for the resignation of Edgar Cowan from the U.S. Senate, and five days later the Union state convention expressed its disappointment in the pro-Johnson Cowan. The Democratic convention on March 5 chose Hiester Clymer to be its gubernatorial candidate. The Republican contender, John W. Geary, defeated Clymer in the October elections. Bradley, *Militant Republicanism*, 234, 249, 260–61, 274.

From John McClelland

Nashville   March 9th/66

Dear Sir & Friend

We are all well. Your friends, and they are numerous, are well.

Old Mr White and his Daughter, Mattie,[1] Started yesterday morning on a visit to Kentucky.

Jno White and family are well. Burns[2] and family are well. These are true friends.

Mr Burns is deeply, and Constantly, engaged in the Management of His Rail Roads, and is really doing more for that Interest, the interests of the state; and the interest of the Citizens & Merchants of Nashville than any single individual in the state.

His position, also, enables him to do an immense amount of good, in the way of transporting indigent persons to their homes—giving employment to those who desire it; and dispensing Charity generally.

A few days previous to the meeting at the Capitol, held on the 22 February, he issued orders for the free Transportation of all Delegates and persons authorised to represent thier Districts on that occasion, to and from Nashville.

The Stevenson faction,[3] as it is called, are in my opinion acting very ungenerously toward Mr Burns. The head of that faction here, is Mr N E Alloway, the Son in law of Col Stevenson, whose vindictiveness, is really Snakish, & is manifested on the Street Corners and private Circles, in the indulgence of Criticisms on Burns Management of the Road. All this, however, has no effect upon Burns, who pursues the even tenor of his Way, confident of his own integrity of purpose, and of the Support of the people, who are with him in all that he does.

I tell you, My Dear Sir, this thing of always doing right, and of getting the People to believe that all our intentions, at least, are honest, will enable a man to remove difficulties, which would otherwise be insuperable, if not end in Blood shed. I honestly believe, my dear sir, that your speech on the 22d has sealed the devotion of the people to you, and they are with you in all your efforts.[4]

                                                                Jno McClelland
PS   Any thing you want to have done, that requires Prudence, secrecy, or dispatch, you can safely confide to M Burns Jno P White or George W Jones. They are all your friends, in foul weather as well as fair.

                                                                        J McC

ALS, DLC-JP.
    1. Presumably Richard White and his youngest daughter, Martha Ann White (b. c1843), who was listed in the 1860 Census as Mattie. 1850 Census, Tenn., Lincoln, 8th Dist., 220; (1860), Davidson, Edgefield, 5.
    2. Michael Burns.
    3. Persons who were looking to Vernon K. Stevenson for leadership in opposition to that of Michael Burns.
    4. In an earlier letter, McClelland had also praised Johnson's veto of the Freedmen's Bureau bill as having revived "the hopes of the friends of Civil and religious liberty through out the land." McClelland to Johnson, Feb. 27, 1866, Johnson Papers, LC.

From Administration Friend

                                      Washington. D.C.   March 10th 1866.
Sir:

I wish to call your attention to a particular fact. There is a party of clerks in the Third Auditors Office & other Bureaus, who have invited Fred Douglas to come on here to give lectures against your administration and excite the negroes to rebel.[1]

I give you a list of names of the following parties who are actuately engaged in this.[2]

    Mr. Gangway   Chief Clk
     "   Fishback—Clerk
     "   Jones   "
     "   Nichols   "

```
"    Slay          "
"    Allen         "
"    Tyler         "
```
Clerks of the Third Auditor's Office
Hoping this will meet your favorable attention.[3]

A friend of your Administration.

L, DNA-RG56, Lets. Recd. from President.

1. An enclosed broadside announced the planned Frederick Douglass lecture for the evening of March 10 at the Assembly Rooms on Louisiana Avenue. The announcement stated that Douglass would speak about Johnson's policy.

2. The full names of the clerks were: Allen M. Gangewer, James Fishback, Danforth B. Nichols, Luther E. Sleigh, James F. Allen, and Henry D. Tyler. During the 1865–66 period at least four different men named Jones were employed in the third auditor's office, making it impossible to know the one referred to in this letter. Gangewer (1818–1904) was a former editor of the *Columbus Ohio State Journal*; Fishback (*c*1828–*fl*1891) of Alton, Illinois, continued in government employ as assessor in Jacksonville, Illinois, and a clerk in the internal revenue and adjutant general's offices in Washington, D.C.; Nichols (*c*1816–*fl*1895), who left the third auditor's office on November 12, 1866, was a Bureau of Statistics clerk before becoming librarian and a trustee of Howard University; Sleigh (*fl*1879) became a Freedmen's Bureau agent and afterwards an examiner in the Patent Office; Allen (*c*1843–*fl*1901), a lawyer during the 1870s, subsequently was a clerk in the Office of Indian Affairs; and Tyler (1834–*fl*1901), a New York City lawyer, by 1870 returned north where, after a stint at selling insurance and merchandising, he resumed his legal practice. 1850 Census, Ill., Madison, Alton, 2nd Dist., 680; (1870), D.C., Subdiv. E. of 7th St. Road, 3; West Part, 22; Washington, D.C., directories (1864–1901); New York City directories (1860–61, 1870–1901); *U.S. Off. Reg.* (1865–91); *NUC*; *Columbus Ohio State Journal*, July 22, 1871; *House Ex. Docs.*, 39 Cong., 2 Sess., No. 100, p. 26 (Ser. 1293); Rayford W. Logan, *Howard University: The First Hundred Years, 1867–1967* (New York, 1969), 13, 605.

3. The President referred this letter to the secretary of the treasury "for his special attention." See his endorsement attached to the March 10 letter.

From Joseph R. Dillin

Nashville   March 10 1866

Through Mellen at Mobile or New Orleans Gen Wood, through Tomeny,[1] who is without doubt in with Mellen, the Sumner Stevens & Phillips branch of the Government ordered my arrest with other friends of yours.[2] It is an attack upon the Administration. I cannot submit to be tried by Hunter Brook Provost Marshal Genl of Alabama without your order. I have stood by you & shall look to you for protection so as far as justice goes. I want to come to Washington unmolested. Answer to E. H. East.[3]

J. R. Dillin

Tel, DLC-JP.

1. William P. Mellen, Charles R. Woods, and James M. Tomeny.

2. Several months earlier Johnson had authorized General Woods to arrest any federal employee within the Department of Alabama who was suspected of stealing government cotton and to try him by court-martial. Evidently Dillin had been implicated as a possible suspect in the investigation of the scandal-ridden ninth special agency which resulted in the

FREDERICK
DOUGLASS
ON
THE PRESIDENT'S
POLICY!
AT THE
ASSEMBLY ROOMS,
Louisiana Avenue, between 4 1-2 and 6th Streets,
THIS EVENING,
Saturday, March 10th, 1866.

TICKETS, ▪ ▪ FIFTY CENTS

At Parker's Book Stand, Post Office.

Broadside announcing Frederick Douglass lecture
Enclosed in Administration Friend to Johnson, March 10, 1866

arrest of Treasury Agent Tomeny. See James M. Tomeny to Johnson, Dec. 20, 1865, *Johnson Papers*, 9: 526; and Tomeny to Johnson, May 15, 1866.

3. The President sent a telegram to East in which he ordered Dillin to report to Washington immediately; and "If he has been arrested, he will be paroled for the purpose of enabling him to report." Johnson to East, Mar. 11, 1866, Tels. Sent, President, Vol. 3 (1865–68), RG107, NA.

From John Hogan[1]

Washington D C   Mar 10th 1866

Mr. President.

I have been anxious to see you about that Church trouble in the Valley of Va and Md.[2] Bishop Ames[3] still issues orders (derived from the War Dept) and Soldiers are still executing them, dispossessing Preachers & People, causing great excitement. The Ministers from the Alexandria Conference have published their conversation with you.[4] The people felt relief, but the continued interference of the Militiary notwithstanding your promise has given them new apprehensions.

I know, you are pressed. You cannot get time fully to examine this matter.

Now will you please do me & the distressed people the favour, just to issue an order to the Millitary commander in the District embracing Loudon County & vicinage Winchester, Harpers Ferry The Valley of Virginia & the region round, *to cease removing* from Churches & Parsonages, the people and Ministers heretofore in possession, until you can have time to examine the questions and have final orders issued.

I enclose letter from Dr Bond[5] one of the Gentlemen of the Alexandria (Va) Conference, who waited on you some time since on this matter.[6]

John Hogan

ALS, DNA-RG107, Lets. Recd., Executive (M494, Roll 85).

1. Hogan (1805–1892), a Methodist minister, served Illinois on the board of public works, as a state representative, and as register of the land office in Dixon before taking up the grocery business and moving to St. Louis. There he served as postmaster before the war and was a Democratic congressman afterwards. *BDAC*.

2. Concern about the status of Methodist churches in Virginia is indicated in additional documents, such as the letter from A. M. Simpson et al. to Johnson, ca. Mar. 14, 1866, Lets. Recd., Executive (M494, Roll 85), RG107, NA; and E. W. Farley to John Hogan, Mar. 19, 1866, ibid. (Roll 84).

3. Edward R. Ames.

4. On February 13 Hogan and a delegation of Methodist ministers met with Johnson at the White House; they were attending the meeting of the conference of the Methodist Church, South, being held at Alexandria. The ministers assured the President of their support, while also registering their complaints about military interference with their churches in Virginia. Johnson promised that the matter would be investigated and that relief would be forthcoming. *Washington Evening Star*, Feb. 13, 1866; *Cincinnati Commercial*, Feb. 15, 1866.

5. Thomas E. Bond (1813–1872) was a physician as well as a Methodist minister. He edited several different religious publications including *The Episcopal Methodist*. *Appleton's Cyclopaedia*, 1: 312; *Richmond Dispatch*, Mar. 22, 1866. The letter referred to here is Bond to Hogan, Mar. 9, 1866, Lets. Recd., Executive (M494, Roll 85), RG107, NA.

6. The President endorsed Hogan's March 10 letter: "Refer to the Sec of War for consideration and report. AJ." Several days later, Hogan wrote another letter to the President in which he offered a lengthy review of the situation concerning the Methodist churches and the seizure of property in several places. Hogan urged Johnson to take steps to halt military interference with the churches. Hogan to Johnson, Mar. 19, 1866, Lets. Recd., Executive (M494, Roll 84), RG107, NA.

From London Committee[1]

32 Nicholas Lane
London [England]   10th March 1866

Sir,

The admiration your patriotic and Statesmanlike policy towards the Southern States has created in England cannot perhaps be more strongly exemplified than by the fact of your receiving a letter from those who have been so deeply injured as ourselves, congratulating you upon your noble efforts to restore the Union of the States, and urging you to persevere in every manner in order to accomplish that object. We represent a large financial interest in this Country, but in our capacity of a Committee we particularly represent the unfortunate purchasers of the Cotton Bonds issued under the loan contracted by Messrs. Erlanger & Co. of Paris with the Southern States lately confederated. We are content to leave the settlement of our claims to the magnanimity of the United States, but our desire now is to assist the Southern States with Capital for the express purpose of re-developing the resources of those States and thus promoting the prosperity of all the United States.

Under the circumstances however in which you have placed us we hesitate in running any further risk; unless we first obtain the concurrence of the Federal Government.[2] At the present time owing to the Financial discredit that overh[angs] the Southern States in consequence of repudiation, there would be no market value for any loan made to th[ose] States. We therefore wish to remove that obstacle [by] proclaiming to the world that our confidence in the integrity and in the future prosperity of the Southern States and of course of the United States is such that we have with your assent furnished them with Money to promote their agricultural industry. We have requested Mr. McHenry[3] to offer the Governors of the several States a much higher rate for a new loan than the ante-war unrepudiated loans of any of these States now command in the market. We feel warranted in doing this, as we believe that when our present claims against the States are surrendered and the taint of repudiation cleared away the credit of the Southern States in Europe will be restored and that of the Federal States augment[ed].

Whereas if nothing be done the United States, t[he] Southern States and ourselves must all continue to be sufferers by the existing state of affairs.

We look at this question in a purely business light. The interests we represent are largely concerned in the Bonds of the States, North and South as well as those issued by the United States.

We purchased these now repudiated Cotton Bonds solely as a commercial speculation, in order to obtain cotton at six pence per pound just as we purchased 5/20 Bonds when Gold was at 200, under the conviction that when peace was restored, it would turn out profitable operations.

We have now to add that in supporting Southern credit at this trying juncture that in the course of a few years we hope a portion of our losses will thus be made up, but we cannot again run the risk of repudiation. We deem it alike fortunate for the States that we alone in this Metropolis can restore to the South her financial position in this community. We feel greatly obliged to Mr. McHenry for his suggestions in reference to these matters. His views are eminently patriotic and at the same time he appears to have grappled with the difficulties presented on both sides of the Atlantic, and as far as we are concerned he has smoothed the way for a complete return of Southern Credit. We entirely approve of the plans presented by him, and we shall be exceedingly glad if they are concurred in by yourself and by the Federal and State authorities.

We pray for your Excellency's health and wish every success in restoring by your wisdom & patriotism, peace and prosperity in the United States.

LS, DNA-RG59, Misc. Lets., 1789–1906 (M179, Roll 236).

1. Six persons signed this document; the list was headed by Sir Provo William Parry Wallis (1791–1892), who had already enjoyed a long and distinguished career in the British navy. In the 1850s he was promoted to rear admiral and then in 1863 to admiral, and in 1860 he had become a Knight Commander of the Order of Bath. *DNB*.

2. In early April Secretary McCulloch forwarded a letter to Johnson from holders of Confederate cotton bonds; it is not clear if that letter was the one here published from the London Committee. In any event, McCulloch indicated that the bond-holders' agent was in Washington but advised the President not to have an interview with him. McCulloch to Johnson, Apr. 10, 1866, Hugh McCulloch Papers, LC.

3. Not identified.

From Julia Peyton[1]

Richmond.   March 10th 1866

Dear Sir,

Mr George W. Randolph,[2] a citizen of Richmond Va.; is now in Pau, in France, where he went in September 1864, in search of health. Having failed to find it there, and being despondent of recovery (as well as wrecked in fortune) he has expressed a desire to come home, that he may be among his friends and relatives. Having been a General in the Confederate Army, and a member of the Cabinet of the Executive of that Government (Sec. of War) he belongs to a class excepted from the general grant of pardon. As he is amenable to prosecution by the United States authorities, and is entirely unable to endure the confinement and excitement incident to a trial, he is deterred from returning to the country.

His friends and medical advisers think imprisonment would be fatal to him.

Under these circumstances, he has made inquiries if his application for pardon, and the oath which must accompany it, cannot be made in France, and be transmitted to Washington, to be acted on before his return.[3]

He is, and has been, from the date of becoming acquainted with the terms on which pardon was to be secured, anxious to comply with the prescribed conditions—but has been prevented from doing so by intelligence that his application would not be considered while he was absent from the country, and his apprehension of arrest if he returned to make it.[4]

Knowing no other way in which the desired information could be obtained, I have thought it not unbecoming (connected with him as I am, and deeply sympathising with him and his wife[5] in their distressed condition) to address to your Excellency the inquiry whether Mr Randolph will be indulged with the consideration of his petition for pardon, if sent from abroad, and to add my respectful and earnest request that he may be.[6]

With the hope of being favored with your early consideration, and with some notification of that indulgence—I have the honor to remain. . . .

Julia Peyton

ALS, DNA-RG94, Amnesty Papers (M1003, Roll 67), Va., G. W. Randolph.
    1. Peyton (b. c1831) was the daughter of Gen. Bernard Peyton and Julia Amanda Green. She married John C. Washington evidently at some date subsequent to her 1866 letter. 1860 Census, Va., Henrico, Richmond, 3rd Ward, 65; *The Peytons of Virginia* (Stafford, 1976), 194.
    2. Randolph (1818–1867), formerly a Richmond lawyer, rose to the rank of brigadier general in the Confederate army before assuming the post of secretary of war for the Richmond government in 1862. Randolph resigned in November of that same year and subsequently went to France. Warner, *Gray; DAB.*
    3. In April one of Randolph's friends, John B. Baldwin, wrote to Johnson in behalf of presidential pardon and gave assurances that Randolph would take the amnesty oath. Subsequently, Randolph himself wrote to Johnson to indicate that he had taken the oath and to pledge his position in support of the government: "I have entirely renounced all wishes or intentions of engaging in any enterprise against the Union of the States." Randolph's oath is enclosed in his pardon files; taken in Pau, it was dated April 19, 1866. Baldwin to Johnson, Apr. 20, 1866; Randolph to Johnson, [May 1866], Amnesty Papers (M1003, Roll 67), Va., G. W. Randolph, RG94, NA.
    4. According to a later letter from Randolph, Johnson had told his brother, Thomas J. Randolph, that he, Johnson, could not act upon a petition from a person not in the United States. See Randolph to Johnson, Sept. 29, 1866, ibid.
    5. Randolph had married Mary E. Pope (c1824–fl1870), a widow, in 1852. 1860 Census, Va., Henrico, Richmond, 2nd Ward, 233; (1870), Madison Ward, 145; *DAB.*
    6. No record of an individual presidential pardon for Randolph has been located.

From Edwin M. Stanton

Washington City, March 11 1866

Mr President

According to your request I had an interview with the Louisiana gentlemen referred to me.[1] Their views as explained by them, do not appear to conflict with any measure of yours for restoration, or to be in any respect objectionable. A convention[2] called by the joint action of the Governor and Legislature with your assent, and fairly representing the people, seems to be the only means of curing the existing evils of which they complain.[3]

Edwin M Stanton

ALS, DLC-JP.

1. The three Louisianans, all members of the state legislature, who already had met with Johnson, probably on March 8, were: William B.G. Egan (1824–1878), appointed an associate justice of the Louisiana Supreme Court by Francis T. Nicholls in 1877; Duncan S. Cage (c1836–fl1874), a planter with large holdings in Terrebonne Parish who lost heavily as a result of the war, during which he served as a Confederate colonel; and James B. Eustis (1834–1899), a New Orleans lawyer who served as a judge advocate in the Confederate army and later as U.S. senator and ambassador to France. *Philadelphia Press*, Mar. 9, 1866; *New Orleans Picayune*, Mar. 10, 1866, Aug. 21, 1874, Nov. 30, 1878; Conrad, *La. Biography*, 1: 282; Hilda M. McDaniel, "Francis Tillou Nicholls and the End of Reconstruction," *LHQ*, 32 (1949): 403; Irene S. and Norman E. Gillis, comps., *Abstract of Goodspeed's Mississippi* (Baton Rouge, 1962), 86; Ritter and Wakelyn, *Legislative Leaders*; Amnesty Papers (M1003, Roll 27), La., Duncan S. and Albert G. Cage, RG94, NA; *BDAC*. For Egan's account of the interview with Johnson, see *American Annual Cyclopaedia* (1866), 450. See also Johnson to Three Louisiana Delegates, Mar. 16, 1866.

2. Persons who opposed the Louisiana Constitution of 1864 proposed to call a convention to devise a new constitution. The Louisiana house considered but tabled a bill for this purpose. *New Orleans Picayune*, Mar. 9, 10, 1866; Taylor, *La. Reconstructed*, 82–83.

3. After talking with the Louisianans, Secretary of State Seward on March 13 endorsed the Stanton letter, saying that he believed that "the proceeding would not conflict with the policy of restoration." However, he thought, "the opponents of the policy would undoubtedly find in the movement an opportunity to make trouble and embarassmt greater than all the benefits to be derived from it."

From Edmund Burke

Private

Newport, N.H.   March 12 186[6][1]

Sir.

By request I enclose you a copy of the Resolutions adopted at a Mass Meeting,[2] held in this town, on Friday, the 9th inst to express the sentiments of the people with regard to your policy of Reconstruction.

The meeting was largely attended by the people. It was called without distinction of party, but much the largest portion who attended were democrats, and they alone took part in the meeting. Candor requires me to say that the Democratic Party approve your policy without exception.

But perhaps that fact may not be pleasing to you to know. The late letter of the Postmaster General, Dennison, to Mr. Patterson,[3] Representative from this State, seems to imply that you do not desire the support of the Democracy. But, if that be your real feeling, that Party will, notwithstanding, give you their support upon principle, although they may withhold that cordial personal support which they were prepared to tender to you, if they had not been repelled by Mr. Dennison. His letter will cost the Democratic Party in this State a loss of 3000 votes tomorow. And if Mr. Smyth shall be re-elected Governor, as he doubtless will be,[4] it will be hailed as a victory for Thad Stevens and Sumner, and a condemnation of your policy. All the office-holders now give their support to the Radical faction.

Our Mass Meeting was called as an *Administration* Meeting, and you will perceive that the resolutions adopted by it ignore party and pledge support to your policy. A great and triumphant party can be reard upon that basis; and it cannot be done without the known countenance and support of the Administration.

In October last, I said to you that I would support you in your policy of Reconstruction.[5] I intend to do so, because I believe your policy is constitutional and patriotic, and must be sustained if we would preserve the Republic. I am willing to rally on the ground of an *Administration Union Party* with all other true men who will array themselves on that ground. And I do it from patriotic motives.[6] I want no offices nor government favors. I only desire to see the Union restored, and this dangerous element North and South put down.

Edmund Burke

ALS, DLC-JP.

1. The document's internal evidence supports this date.

2. The resolutions of the Sullivan County meeting proclaimed the Freedmen's Bureau bill not only "unjust and inexpedient, but unconstitutional," and called for every "true patriot" to "give his earnest and active support to the President."

3. See William Dennison to James W. Patterson, Mar. 3, 1866, as reprinted in the *Washington Morning Chronicle*. Dennison indicated to Patterson (1823–1893), who was later a Republican senator (1867–73), that if he were a citizen of New Hampshire, he would vote "the whole Union Republican ticket." *Washington Morning Chronicle*, Mar. 6, 1866; *BDAC*.

4. Frederick Smyth (1819–1899), the Republican incumbent, defeated the Democratic candidate, John G. Sinclair, by a margin of less than four thousand votes. Sobel and Raimo, *Governors*, 3: 965.

5. Possibly Burke is referring here to his letter of mid-September in which he offered support and advice to the President. See Burke to Johnson, Sept. 18, 1865, *Johnson Papers*, 9: 93–94.

6. Burke also enclosed a newspaper clipping of an editorial he had written in which he appealed to Republicans of New Hampshire to "stand by the President" and join with the Democrats in forming a "great and triumphant ADMINISTRATION PARTY."

From Virginia C. Clay

Washington city—March 12th 1866.

My dear Sir,

Months since, learning of the death of my husband's mother,[1] I addressed you a letter, begging Mr. Clay's release on his parole, to visit his home to see his aged and honored father, and comfort & cheer him for the breif span of Life yet allotted him. You were kind enough to write me that my letter was a "most powerful appeal," & other complimentary words.[2] Hope rose on strong & eager wing for the speedy accomplishment of my object, but alas! to perish! The time has dragged by, and matters remain, as far as my noble husband is concerned, in "statu quo." A late letter from home announces the serious illness of Gov. Clay, who feeble & frail as Autumn's last leaf, trembles at every gale. I know that he cannot live more than a few weeks or months, & he *must not* die without seeing his idolized son! I have troubled you so often & so long, that I fear you are alike weary of my presence & my prayer; but you must bear with me & hear it yet again. I am unwilling to liken you to the "unjust Judge,"— (for you have *ever* been to me, not only patient & polite but kind,)—but I am resolved with God's help, to fully illustrate the woman who was heard for her "much importunity."[3] I am robbed & unjustly, of *all* left me now in this world,—*my husband*, & I will not cease to cry for Justice while wrong maintains, & you are President. My last communication to you was from a sorrowing heart,—this, is from an indignant one! My patience is fled & I am outraged that Mr. Clay should be still, *denied the right of trial*, & *yet refused a parole*! If the Gov: thinks him guilty, why does it not try him & *prove* his guilt? If he be innocent, (as he protests,) is it so lost to every sense of Honor & Justice as to desire to murder by inches an innocent man,—"one who has done the state Some Service,"[4] by long-continued, rigorous & solitary imprisonment?

Altho' not a lawyer Mr. Johnson, or accustomed to analyzing testimony in order to elicit the truth,—or possessed of any of the arts of the forum, or the schools by wh. falsehood is detected, I saw at a glance, more than one bold & atrocious calumny against my husband in the testimony of at least three witnesses as published pending, & shortly subsequent to the trial of those convicted of conspiring the assassination of Mr. Lincoln.[5] I *knew* thier falsehood, & *thought* I could establish it, without my husband's aid or counsel. But in my interviews with him during my recent visit, after informing him as far as in my power of the facts charged on oath, tending; however remotely, to implicate him in that infamous crime,—(which he heard for the first time after Eight month's imprisonment,) I, saw, & am now satisfied, that "proof as strong as Holy Writ"[6] can be produced to convict those witnesses of *perjury*.

Now is it magnanimous, or just or fair Mr. President, to deny Mr. Clay the usual means allowed accused persons of obtaining such proof? Will this Government, with all its power & prestige, take advantage of the trust & confidence in its integrity & justice which he exhibited in promptly & voluntarily surrendering himself a prisoner to confront it & answer its charges, by flatly refusing to permit employment of the mean's of establishing his innocence?

Is he to be kept mute & motionless until his prosecutors gather from *self-confessed* accomplices in crime, or *hired* informers & spies, who live on lies: brazen fronted villians, who unblushingly avow their baseness, & claim credit for it,—I repeat, shall he be kept in "durance vile," until they shall collect Enough shreds & patches of testimony, with wh. to frame & fashion a plausible prosecution? And will no chance be given, to expose these unholy perjurers and their suborners, & bring *them* to judgment? Oh! Justice, where art thou fled?

With the faith & courage of conscious innocence, Mr. Clay delivered himself into the hands of his enemies, to be tried by them, according to their laws & Constitution for an infamous crime with wh. they charge him. He sought refuge from an atrocious calumny in a sanctuary of Justice among them. He has found a cheerless prison, where for ten long dreary months he has been treated as a convicted & condemned felon: denied all communication with the outside world; the consolation of friend or acquaintance; the aid of counsel, or even a knowledge of the grounds of accusation, or the names of his accusers! If he can claim no right as a *citizen*, has he lost those of a *man*?

Shall a brave but fallen foe be trampled & crushed without a hearing? —a foe who staked his life & liberty—in *your* hands Mr. President that he might be given the opportunity to vindicate his honor & his innocence?

And Sir he will yet do it—I feel it, believe it! Truth & Innocence, (as I wrote Judge Holt) are strong champions, & Error is fool-hardy to battle against them. My noble husband is the embodiment of both, & in God's own good time will forcibly & triumphantly illustrate the oft-quoted but immortal lines;

> Truth, crushed to Earth will rise again,
> The immortal years of *God's* are hers;
> But Error wounded,—writhes in pain,
> And *dies* amid her worshippers![7]

I am confident that he cannot only vindicate himself, but satisfy even those who are fond to believe him guilty—that the witnesses on trial here in May & June last, did commit perjury in their statements tending to implicate him in the assassination.

Only allow him the aid of counsel, & the privilege of conferring with Mr. Davis, Mr. Holcombe,[8] & one or two others, & my husband will fully expose the atrocious falsehood of his accusers, & explode beneath *them*, the mine so laboriously prepared for *his* destruction.

He is neither afraid or ashamed to tell you for what purposes he went to Canada, nor what he accomplished while there. Let him come to you, Mr. President, if necessary, like St. Paul, in fetters, in chains,—& he will speak forth such "words of soberness & truth,"[9] as will make his accusers, tho' clad in panoply of official power, quail beneath his indignant glance & eloquent tongue.

Or if this be too great a liberty for him to enjoy, give *me* the privilege of free correspondence with my husband, & free conference with Mr. Davis, not subject to the surveillance of the Govt: & its officials,—thro' whom hired witnesses may learn to fit thier testimony to an altered state of case:—give this precious privilege to me, & even I, a feeble woman, (no,—thank God, not a feeble but *strong* woman, one who is *able* & *resolved* to do what is *possible*, & *right*,) and, I will lay bare as diabolical a plot as was ever concieved to compass the judicial murder of an innocent man.

Time, my dear Mr. Presidt. is rapidly removing from my hands & beyond reach the memorials of the Past,—and each day's departure lessens the probabilities of securing them;—& thus is my precious husband's life, & what he values more, his good name daily more imperilled by this denial of the right of appeal,—the means of defence.

Many accusations in the testimony relate more to Mr. Davis than Mr. Clay, of which my husband, having never heard, can only learn the truth by conference or communication with Mr. D. Hence I so earnestly prefer this request.

And now in conclusion, may I not most respectfully implore that *you*, will no longer *seem* to consent to such gross injustice as has been shown but graciously, without more delay, give me the order for Mr. Clay's release? Your personal knowledge & intimate acquaintance with Mr. C. preclude the possibility of even a *suspicion* of guilt in your mind;—and should he die in prison (not at any time improbable,) on *you*, and *you* alone Sir, wd. fall the odium of the fearful tragedy. *His* & *your* cowardly accusers or persecutors wd. instantly exclaim, "Why did not the President release him,—*we* have nought to do with it!"

Will you not my kind friend do this noble & just deed *now*, and thereby rally to you, the great conservative heart, of this nation,—those who, even thro' the lurid fires of War, can yet discern the unstained robes of Innocence & Purity. You are a man with a *heart*, as well as mind & body, & I appeal to you by every instinct of your nature, not longer to keep me thus tortured beyond power of endurance.

I await your reply with a faith & confidence that refuses to waver—until you strike the blow![10]

V. C. Clay.

ALS, DLC-JP.

1. Susanna Claiborne Withers (1798–1866), wife of Clement C. Clay, Sr., since 1815, died on January 2. Nuermberger, *Clays*, 67, 272.

2. In reaction to her letter of January 11, 1866, Johnson wrote: "It does your head and heart great Credit. It is a most powerful apeal. You have excelled your self in its production." Clay to Johnson, Jan. 11, 1866, Johnson Papers, LC; Johnson to Clay, n.d., C. C. Clay Papers, NcD. See also Virginia C. Clay to Johnson, Jan. 14, 1866, *Johnson Papers*, 9: 600.

3. A reference to the parable of the unrighteous judge found in Luke 18: 1–8.

4. A variation from Shakespeare's *Othello*, act 5, sc. 2, line 338.

5. Mrs. Clay here refers to the testimony presented in Benn Pitman, comp., *The Assassination of President Lincoln and the Trial of the Conspirators* (Cincinnati, 1865), implicating Jefferson Davis, C. C. Clay, Jr., Jacob Thompson, and others in a general conspiracy. In July 1866, following retractions of several witnesses, the Committee on the Judiciary discarded all doubtful evidence obtained from perjurers or suspect men, whereby the conspiracy charge collapsed. *House Reports*, 39 Cong., 1 Sess., No. 104, pp. 28–29, 33–41 (Ser. 1272).

6. Likely a variation of Shakespeare, *Othello*, act 3, sc. 3, line 323.

7. A slightly inaccurate rendering of William Cullen Bryant's "The Battle-Field," stanza 9.

8. James P. Holcombe (1820–1883), lawyer, professor, and Confederate congressman (1862–64), late in the war served in Canada with C. C. Clay, Jr. Wakelyn, *BDC*.

9. A variation of Acts 26: 25.

10. See Virginia C. Clay to Johnson, Mar. 16, 1866.

From Cave Johnson

Clarksville [Tenn.]   12 March 1866

Dear Sir,

I have been urged to write you a line in behalf of W Drane,[1] who is an applicant for Marshal of Southern Mississippi. He was the brother of the late Docr. Walter Drane,[2] who resided in this vicinity. I knew him as an active energetic, well informed young man befor his removal to Mississippi. Since that time I have known but little of him except occasional reports among his relations, of his success & prosperity in his new home.

He is reported among us to have been always a Union man until the secession of Mississippi, when he felt it his duty to acquiesce in the action adopted by his State. His friends in Mississippi will give you more reliable information as to his present status.

The citizens of Robertson, Montgomery Stewart, have again made me their candidate for the Senate,[3] for the avowed object of sustaining your policy of reconstruction & your message & veto of the Freedmans bureau —which meets the undivided support of the people in this section. I am as yet without opposition.

C Johnson

ALS, DLC-JP.

1. Wesley Drane (b. *c*1810) of Canton, Mississippi, wrote a letter to Johnson probably in early March requesting appointment as marshal of the southern district. Received at the White House on March 13, it was referred to the attorney general's office two days later. But in mid-April the President nominated Duff Green for the post; in late June 1866

Green was confirmed and commissioned for the appointment. Drane had applied for a presidential pardon in July 1865 and received it that same month. 1860 Census, Miss., Madison, Canton, 22; Drane to Johnson, ca. July 1, 1865, Amnesty Papers (M1003, Roll 32), Miss., Wesley Drane, RG94, NA; *House Ex. Docs.*, 40 Cong., 1 Sess., No. 32, p. 67 (Ser. 1311); Ser. 6A, Vol. B: 66; Ser. 6B, Vol. 4: 193, Johnson Papers, LC.

2. Drane (1798–1865), a longtime resident of Montgomery County, had practiced medicine for a time but abandoned that in order to devote full time to tobacco farming and other economic endeavors. William P. Titus, ed., *Picturesque Clarksville: Past and Present* (Clarksville, 1887), 181.

3. Having no opposition, Johnson successfully ran for the state senate seat in March. But he was not permitted to serve, because of his earlier Confederate sympathies and support. Robert H. White et al., *Messages of the Governors of Tennessee* (10 vols., Nashville, 1952–90), 5: 493.

From William Henry Trescot

Washington   March 12. 1866—

Sir

I would most earnestly entreat your immediate consideration of the instructions from Gen Howard and the Order No 9 of Gen Scott[1] Asst Commr. of the Freedmens Bureau in S.C, which I enclose and copies of which have been also sent by Gen Howard to the Secretary at War.

By Circular No 15 issued from the Bureau in the fall of 1865, the restoration of the lands occupied under Gen Shermans Special Field Order, was ordered to such owners as had received a special pardon or had taken the oath of allegiance under the provisions of your Amnesty Proclamation upon the obligation of said owners to make satisfactory contracts with the occupying Freedmen. Gen Howard went down to South Carolina and himself initiated this policy of restoration, a policy based upon the principle of a just conciliation and which secured the speedy resumption of the agricultural industry of the State and restored both employed and employers to relations of mutual kindness and mutual profit. But scarcely had this wise policy been initiated than it was abandoned by the Bureau for the express and avowed purpose of allowing the passage of a Bill which should confirm the possession of these Sea Island lands in the hands of the occupying Freedmen. It is sufficient to say that in the exercise of your judgment and by the use of your Executive power, that Bill was vetoed. Under this condition of things I asked of Gen Howard an order for the continuation of those restorations which as an Executive Agent of your Government he never had the right to suspend for the purpose of waiting for Congressional legislation which he deemed proper and possible. This order he declined to give on the ground that he did not know what other legislation Congress might pass and that he deemed it proper to receive special instructions from you. He applied to you for those instructions[2] and I have before this asked your attention to the same subject,[3] not I trust, with undue importunity. In the meantime Gen Howard has sent to Gen Scott the instructions which I enclose and in which he says under date of March 8th 1866 "Being unable to obtain positive instructions and there being much delay in legislation with regard to the lands set apart under Gen Shermans order, I deem it best to locate definitely those who occupy land rightfully under authority of the above named order, holding them in possession until some definite action is had by the Government."

And on the 7" March 1866, Gen Scott, the Asst. Commr. of the Bureau in South Carolina issued orders in entire conformity with these instructions which however had not then reached him. In paragraph III of these orders he declares

"III Grants of land made to the free people in compliance with Gen Shermans Special Field Orders No 15, dated January 16 1865, will be regarded as good and valid. But Major Cornelius,[4] Acting Sub Asst Commissioner for the Sea Islands, may set apart and consolidate them contiguous to each other, on one portion of the plantations upon which grants have been given in such manner as to give the freed people a part possessing average fertility and other advantages and at the same time place no unnecessary obstacles in the way of the owners occupying and cultivating the remaining portion of the plantation."

I submit that this order completely alters the former status of these lands and is equivalent to an absolute revocation of Circular No 15 and your consequent instructions to Gen Howard. When the Freedmans Bureau Bill was vetoed, even the suspension of those instructions which had been permitted in order to this decision, could no longer be maintained. The grant of Gen Sherman, temporiy in its purpose as he himself declares was not confirmed by legislative action and every owner who had received general or special pardon was entitled under your orders to restoration upon entering into obligation to offer just and reasonable contracts to the occupying Freedmen. This all were and are willing to do. Indeed by the Order No 1[5] of Gen Sickles universally accepted and approved by the planters of the State, they are bound to provide for the old and the infirm resident upon their estates until the State shall make some just provision for its Coloured poor and to offer to the able bodied a fair opportunity to make reasonable contracts for their labour.

Without dwelling upon other points which I have brought to your Excellencys attention in conversation I would now simply submit that the scheme embraced in Gen Howards instruction and Gen Scotts order is perhaps of all devised the most mischievous in its consequences to both white and black, owner and freedman.

1.   In the first place to assign forty acres to each Freedman would be [in] most cases to assign the whole estate for twenty five freedmen would absorb more land than is fit for cultivation on any estate upon the Islands. Of these forty acres not one fourth would or could be cultivated. Four acres of cotton and as many of provisions to each worker is as much as could be successfully worked under the old system when every advan-

tage that capital could give was liberally used. The freedman without capital, without animal force, with no surplus labour and no manures, could not attempt the cultivation of ten and this system therefore condemns to barrenness three fourths of the most fruitful and most profitable soil of the country.

2.   This attempted division multiplies the points of difference between the freedmen and the owner. As you know on all southern plantations the negro quarters are built in small villages together. The land then must either be assigned around the quarters or at a distance with the right of way across, cutting up the fields assigned to the owner. Then there would be the right to and right of way for, wood, water and manures, then the provocations from the breaking in of stock and the keeping up of fences. Add to this agents of the Freedmans Bureau vested with a little brief authority and the certain confusion, annoyance and loss attending such a condition will prevent any man of sense from wasting either his time, his temper or his capital on such an experiment.

3.   In the third place it will be utterly impossible for the owner to find labour that will work contentedly for wages along side of these free colonies. The Freedmen do not understand and cannot be made to understand the reasons for this difference of treatment. Those who receive and those who are denied this Government charity will be in perpetual antagonism and the discontent and disaffection will react most injuriously upon the general labour of the State. I do not press the consideration of the general welfare of the State, the increased difficulty in the way of all its local legislation the enormous loss to its resources which the destruction of the whole Sea Island crop the sure consequence of this scheme, will inflict for they have been urged by Governor Orr in his letter to you.[6]

I am painfully unwilling to consume your time with questions of interest merely to the State, questions which I am aware can scarcely be settled without injustice on one side or cruel and mischievous misrepresentation on the other. I feel more strongly than you would permit me to express how much we owe you and how important it is to our interests that you should not be embarrassed with issues that in the distempered feeling of the country, will add to the bitterness of our present controversies. But the action of the Bureau leaves me no alternative. If it is permitted there can be but one result. Nobody believes that this occupation of the Sea Island lands will be permanent but this course consistently pursued will render them utterly valueless to the owners while the uncertain tenure of the Freedman will neither stimulate his industry nor permit the enterprise of others and this whole property will at its point of lowest depression pass into the hands of shrewd speculators who are even now contriving the process which is to work out the profitable result.

And in conclusion I would submit to you that if this action of the Bureau is not revoked, the word of promise, as far as the State of So. Ca. is concerned will indeed have been kept to the ear and broken to the hope[7] for as far as these lands are affected, the action of the Bureau will be precisely that which it would have been if you had not by your veto of the Freedmans Bureau Bill won the confidence and the gratitude of the whole Nation.[8]

Wm Henry Trescot
Executive Agent of State of S.C

ALS, DNA-RG105, Records of the Commr., Lets. Recd. from Executive Mansion.

1. Robert K. Scott (1826–1890), doctor, real estate investor, and brigadier general of volunteers, became South Carolina's governor in 1868. Warner, *Blue*.

2. See Oliver O. Howard to Johnson, Feb. 22, 1866. Howard also had an interview with Johnson on February 21 and a week later. *Washington Morning Chronicle*, Feb. 22, Mar. 1, 1866.

3. See Trescot to Johnson, Feb. 22, 1866. In addition, Trescot had discussed the fate of the Sea Islands with Johnson at the White House on February 28. *Washington Morning Chronicle*, Mar. 1, 1866.

4. James E. Cornelius (c1833–1881), a carpenter and former captain, 100th Pa. Inf., was currently major, 15th Vet. Res. Corps, on duty at Rockville, Wadmalaw Island. After his muster out in 1867 he resumed his trade at Brunswick, Georgia. 1860 Census, Pa., Butler, Muddy Creek Twp., 20; *Charleston Courier*, Mar. 9, 1866; Pension Records, Harriet H. Cornelius, RG15, NA.

5. See Trescot to Johnson, Feb. 22, 1866.

6. Orr's January 19, 1866, letter to Johnson blamed the government for the failure to resolve the question of labor by "encouraging the belief that the sea coast . . . is to be confiscated for the purpose of establishing a system of independent colonization for the freedmen." He predicted that the provision of the proposed Freedmen's Bureau bill, whereby titles granted under Sherman's order would be "confirmed for three years," would have one of two effects. Either, after a few years of "mischievous vagabondage," the freedmen would disappear from the land, or "if these lands are restored, their capabilities [will] insure the certain remuneration of successful cultivation." *Charleston Courier*, Feb. 3, 1866.

7. "That keep the word of promise to our ear, and break it to our hope." Shakespeare, *Macbeth*, act 5, sc. 7, line 48.

8. For the temporary resolution of this issue, see Martin Abbott, *The Freedmen's Bureau in South Carolina, 1865–1872* (Chapel Hill, 1967), 61–62.

From Joseph Holt

War Department   Bureau of Mil. Justice
March 13. 1866.

The accompanying record of the trial of Saml. O. Berry, alias one-armed Berry, citizen of Ky. is respectfully referred to the President of the United States for his action.[1]

The said Berry was found guilty by a Military Commission convened at Louisville Ky., by order of General Palmer Comdg. the Department in Jany. last, of three acts of robbery accompanied with violence, of eleven distinct murders, perpetrated upon white and colored citizens either with his own hand or in conjunction with others, and of the general charge of being a guerrilla.

By General Court Martial Order No. 11, from Hdqrs. Dept. of Ky. the proceedings, findings, and death-sentence were approved, and the sentence was ordered by General Palmer to be carried into execution on the 2d. day of the present month.

The sentence was not executed on the day appointed, and on the seventh (7th) of March, 1866, General Order No. 21. Hdqrs. Dept. of Ky., was published,[2] a copy of which is appended to the record now submitted, of which order the 3d section is in the following words:—

"Subject to the approval of the President of the United States, the sentence of death in the case of Samuel O. Berry, as promulgated in General Court Martial Orders No. 11. Febry. 10 1866, from these Head Quarters, is commuted to ten (10) years confinement at hard labor, in Penitentiary at Albany, New York."

In view of the atrocious character of the prisoner's acts during the recent rebellion, and the number as well as the enormity of the crimes which, in the judgment of the officers composing the Commission and of the Dept. Commander himself, were fully proven by the testimony offered at his trial, this Bureau fails to discover any adequate grounds for the commutation of sentence submitted for the approval of the President by General Palmer.[3]

It is, therefore, respectfully reccommended that the action of General Palmer in commuting the sentence to penitentiary confinement for ten years, be disapproved, and that the original sentence be ordered to be carried into execution.[4]

J. Holt   Judge Advocate General.

Lbcopy, DNA-RG153, Lets. Sent (Record Books), Vol. 19.

1. Berry (b. c1816), a Lexington trader and Mercer County teacher, had been a sergeant in the 6th Ky. Cav., CSA. Reports of his January-February trial are found in various issues of the Louisville newspapers. 1860 Census, Ky., Fayette, Lexington, 3rd Ward, 117; *Report of the Adjutant General of the State of Kentucky Confederate Kentucky Volunteers War 1861–65* (2 vols., Hartford, Ky., 1979–80 [1915–18]), 1: 672; *Louisville Journal*, Jan. 16, 18, 19, 26, 31, Feb. 1, 14, 1866; *Louisville Courier*, Feb. 8, 1866.

2. Palmer's commutation of Berry's sentence was reported in the *Washington Evening Star*, Mar. 8, 1866.

3. Three days after Holt's letter, Johnson approved the Palmer decision to sentence Berry to ten years' imprisonment instead of execution. But the orders approving Palmer's mitigation were not issued by the War Department until early May. Johnson to Holt, Mar. 16, 1866, Orders and Endorsements (M444, Roll 10), RG107, NA; General Court Martial Orders, No. 128, *Index of General Court Martial Orders. Adjutant General's Office 1866* (Washington, D.C., 1867); Holt to Johnson, Apr. 27, 1866, Lets. Sent (Record Books), Vol. 19, RG153, NA.

4. Louisville newspaper editor Charles O. Faxon made a plea for clemency in behalf of Berry, asserting that he spoke in behalf of others who shared his views. However, in the summer of 1867, after other requests for the pardon of Samuel Berry reached Washington, Holt proceeded to review the matter at some length for Johnson and to urge that Berry's imprisonment be continued and no pardon be granted. Berry apparently died in prison after some seven years' incarceration. See Faxon to Johnson, Feb. 26, 1866, Johnson Papers, LC; Holt to Johnson, July 23, 1867, Lets. Sent (Record Books), Vol. 23, RG153, NA; Thomas F. Berry, *Four Years with Morgan and Forrest* (Oklahoma City, 1914), n.p.

From William R. McFerran[1]

Glasgow Kentucky   March 13" 1866

Dear Sir

Permit one personally unknown to You: a citizen of this once happy Government who has never sought political preferment—to Congratulate you on the Noble and patriotic Stand you have taken to Save the Constitution of our Fathers, from the traitors of the North, in their Mad effort to distroy the best Government ever Vouched Safe to man. We have indeed fallen on perilous times, and nothing but patriotic firmness can possably Save us as a Nation from anarchy and ruin. That Stand you have nobly taken. God and the people will I doubt not, Sustain you in your important and desperate Struggle to hand our glorious Constitution down to our Children as our Fathers handed it down to us. I am now one of the oldest Citizens born in the dark and Bloody ground, and have a right to Speak for my native State to Some extent. Our people are a loyal Constitution loving people, as a Mass. The Majority of the people is now, and has ever been true Union Men opposed to rebellion in all its forms. I am of the number that Suffered much for my loyalty like yourself, have been driven from my home, and made a houseless and homeless wanderer for months, because of my opposition to Secession, which I looked upon as a remedy for no evil, but an aggravation for evry immaginary one. I never believed a State legally Could go out of the Union by Secession, and now concur in your opinion, that all the States that went into rebellion are Still States of the Union under the Constitution, and entitled to all the privalidges of States under that Constitution. Although Kentucky has been much Slandered and Maligned by Citizens of Northern States, for whome in the war of 1812 She Shed torrents of her best Blood to Save their infants Settlements from the tomaw hock and Scalping Knife. Yet we have borne it, trusting the time would come when we as a people, and State; would get Justice. That time we believe has come. All eyes are turned to you, as our beloved Chief Magistrate, our hopes are all Centered in You—to relieve us from the worst of tyrants. I mean the Freedmans Bureau. It is a great curse to the Freedman of this State. Our Citizens will risk evrything to protect their former Servants in all their rights of person and property and the persuit of happiness without the aid of a Freedmans Bureau or the Military despotism of the General Commanding this department. I mean General Palmer. I will give you the working of this Bureau. The Negro having just received his freedom, he finds he cannot live without labor. He makes a contract with a citisen to labor for him. He is apprised before hand that the Bureau will protect him. Either for a real or an immaginary Cause, he quits. His imployer has him arraigned before one of the FAITHFUL, he hears the Negroes Statement—fines his employer—Acts as Judge Jury and executioner. No appeal can be taken, the fine has to be paid. No other man will imploy that negro, for fear of the Same treatment. Here the poor Negro must Steal or Starve. If the Bureau was removed, the Civil Courts would redress all the wrongs of the Negro. This is the practical working of the System.

I hope Soon to See this matter given to the Civil Courts and the General now in Command of our State Sent to some more general Clime.

There is an other Suggestion I desire to make to you, that I think important.

It is this. Agents of evry degree are as thick as Backbirds through this State and other border States—from Yankee land and of the deepest Rebel, from the Sunny South, getting up evry character of Claims against the government, proving anything necessary to filch money from the government whether just or not. This Should not be allowed. There is but one remedy that I can conceive of and that is to have a commission appointed by Your Excellency, for at least the border States. Composed of one Civillian of known integrity & loyalty and two faithful officers of the Old Regular Army one of them, an experienced Quartermaster, whose business it Shall be to hold at least one Session in each Congressional district in the State. Before whome all Claims against the Government Should be presented and proof made, and no claim Should be presented for payment that had not passed that Boad & approved by them. In this way millions of dollars would be Saved, to the Government that is now taxed allmost insufferable. The Commission Should have power to Compell the Commanders Quartermasters and Paymasters and Commanders of the Colored Regiments to appear before them and Settle their accounts and Show that they have acted faithfully and honestly with the Soldiers. I Make this last Suggestion from the consideration that Many of the Colored Soldiers, have returned home without Money and no insurance of any coming to them. The Negro informs me that the officers are going to have a Bank established and their Money placed in it for Safe Keeping.[2] This is another Yankee trick to filch their money—all ready there are agents to get Negro *Claims*. The poor Negro is ignorant, he has fought the Battles of his Country & Justice Should be done him. One other Suggestion. That is this. To enable you to Successfully carry out your patriotic pollicy to serve this Government You would do well I think to get clear of all Radical Civil officers of any degree as Soon as possable —and fill their places with honest and Conservative ones Capable of discharging the duties of the various officers. I have written thus plainly because the honor and Stability of My Government requires it.

Mr President the Strength of a Government consists in the affection the people have for their rulers. My ardent prayer is that you may be enabled to so administer the laws, that the people will Call You by the endearing name of Father. Although I am a Stranger to you, I refer you to General Rusaw Hons H. Grider A Harding J Guthrey.[3] They can give you my character and antecedents.

Wm. R. McFerren [*sic*]

ALS, DLC-JP.

1. McFerran (c1794–1871), an attorney, served two terms as a county judge in Kentucky. In September 1866 Johnson appointed McFerran to serve as postmaster of Glasgow, which position he held until May 1869. 1860 Census, Ky., Barren, 1st Dist., Glasgow, 16; William H. Perrin et al., *Kentucky: A History of the State* (Easley, S.C., 1979 [1885–88]),

Edition 3: 1013; Ser. 6B, Vol. 3: 459, Johnson Papers, LC; *U.S. Off. Reg.* (1867–69). There is an eight-year discrepancy regarding McFerran's birthdate as found in the census and in the Perrin book.

2. Probably a reference to the Freedman's Savings Bank, a branch of which opened in Louisville in August 1865. Ross A. Webb, *Kentucky in the Reconstruction Era* (Lexington, 1979), 51.

3. Lovell H. Rousseau, Henry Grider, Aaron Harding, and James Guthrie. Harding (1805–1875) earlier served in the state assembly and during the war was a Union Democrat in Congress (1861–67). *BDAC*.

From Edwards Pierrepont

103 Fifth Avenue   New York   March 13 1866

Dr Sir.

As you are about to make the very important appointment of Collector of this Port, as a friend who will speak truth to you I say one more word.

The leading men & the great body of the Republican Party are not with you and the never will be. They may pretend to be for the retention of offices & for the sake of power until after the fall elections. If they carry them, no further pretense will be needed—their enmity will be open. We can bring the loyal Democrats & conservituve Republicans to your cordial support if you give us the nucleus about which to form. We *cannot* bring Democrats in any considerable numbers over to the President's earnest support unless you give us a bridge over which we can lead the mass of the party. The appointment of a Democrat of high standing who zealously worked for Lincoln & Johnson makes a *safe* bridge. Gen. John A. Dix Col. Henry G. Stebbins[1] both well known & either will fit. If some such man; some loyal War Democrat does not receive this appointment, Democrats will not generally believe that the President relies upon their support. I commit this prediction to your consideration & to the unerring test of time and I am ever *truly* yours.[2]

Edwards Pierrepont

ALS, DLC-JP.

1. Both men had been suggested to Johnson earlier. See Dix to Johnson, Nov. 15, 1865, and John W. Forney to Johnson, Jan. 2, 1866, *Johnson Papers*, 9: 390–91, 562. See also Robert J. Hilton to Johnson, July 5, 1866, Appts., Customs Service, Naval Officer, New York, John A. Dix, RG56, NA.

2. In a follow-up letter Pierrepont reiterated the expediency of appointing as collector a "Lincoln & Johnson Democrat or else a Republican *with whom we can coalesce.*" Pierrepont to Johnson, Mar. 24, 1866, Johnson Papers, LC. See Henry A. Smythe to Johnson, Apr. 13, 1866.

To J. Madison Wells

Washington City D.C.

March 13, 1866

Is there any objection to the Legislature calling a Convention to revise the State Constitution?

There is a Committee[1] here who are anxious that one should be called. Answer immediately.[2]

Andrew Johnson   President U.S.

Tel, DNA-RG107, Tels. Sent, President, Vol. 3 (1865–68).
1. Duncan S. Cage, James B. Eustis, and William B.G. Egan. See Edwin M. Stanton to Johnson, Mar. 11, 1866.
2. See Wells to Johnson, Mar. 15, 1866.

From John Bigler[1]

Sacramento (Cal)   March 14 1866

D Sir

Yesterday we had a fiercely contested election for first Trustee or Mayor of this City. Wm F Knox,[2] Esqr. a worthy Mechanic was supported by the Democrats & Conservatives—Your friends—and C. H. Swift,[3] one of the Vice Presidents and principal actors in the Radical meeting recently held in this city—which meeting, in bitter terms denounced your conduct and policy generally, was the candidate of the Radicals. Swift is a very wealthy man, and has two sons-in-law also wealthy,[4] and thousands of dollars were expended to secure a Radical triumph. We had great odds to contend against, but we struggled gallantly and although defeated have reduced their majority from 1575 to 406. Radical loss 1,169. Although defeated by a comparatively small majority the result was so cheering to your friends that it was followed by a regular jollification. If the Postmaster[5] and U.S. Revenue Assessor[6] had not opposed us with their votes and money, we would have been able to make a much better showing, and perhaps have triumphed.

I am the Brother of Ex Senator Bigler of Penna[7] and had the pleasure of making your acquaintance some years ago in Washington City.

John Bigler

ALS, DLC-JP.
1. In 1849 Bigler (1805–1871), a Pennsylvania lawyer and editor, migrated to California, where he served two terms in the state assembly and two terms as Democratic governor (1852–56). Defeated for a third term, Bigler served four years as minister to Chile, returning to California in 1861, where he was an unsuccessful candidate for Congress. Sobel and Raimo, *Governors*, 1: 102–3.
2. Knox (c1827–fl1881), a native of Virginia, was already in California by the time of the 1850 Census. A builder and contractor, he eventually held minor local public offices. 1870 Census, Calif., Sacramento, Sacramento, 3rd Ward, 54; Alan P. Bowman, comp., *Index to the 1850 Census of the State of California* (Baltimore, 1972), 367; Sacramento directories (1855–81).
3. Vermont-born Charles H. Swift (c1801–fl1881), a "capitalist," grain merchant, and president of the Sacramento Savings Bank, had earlier served as justice of the peace and treasurer of Sacramento County before his election as first trustee or mayor of Sacramento, a post he held by 1863 and retained until at least 1871. Ibid.; 1870 Census, Calif., Sacramento, Sacramento, 2nd Ward, 97.
4. The 1870 census shows Swift with $6,000 real estate, $2,000 personal estate, and Knox with $10,000 and $1,000 respectively. The sons-in-law have not been identified. Ibid., 3rd Ward, 54.

5. George Rowland (*c*1814–*fl*1875), who served as postmaster from 1863 to 1875, came to California from New York or Connecticut by 1850. Also, he dealt in stoves, tin, and hardware and served on the Sacramento city council. Bowman, *Index to Census of Calif.*, 383; Sacramento directories (1856–71); *U.S. Off. Reg.* (1863–75).

6. John M. Avery (*c*1834–*fl*1880), a lawyer and native of Maine, became internal revenue assessor for the Fourth District of California in 1863 and held the position until the fall of 1866, when John Bigler received a commission to succeed him. However, Avery refused to surrender his office, and Bigler was forced to bring suit against Avery to cause his removal. The Senate rejected Bigler's nomination in January 1867. 1870 Census, Calif., Sacramento, Sacramento, 3rd Ward, 55; Sacramento directories (1863–80); John Bigler to Johnson, Oct. 22, Dec. 1, 1866, Appts., Internal Revenue Service, Assessor, Calif., 4th Dist., John Bigler, RG56, NA; Ser. 6A, Vol. D: 22, Vol. 4: 347, Johnson Papers, LC; Berwanger, *West and Reconstruction*, 75–76.

7. William Bigler.

From Ulysses S. Grant

Washington, March 14th 1866.

Sir:

I have the honor to submit herewith for your information reports from the Department of Alabama of outrages committed by Whites against Blacks and by Blacks against Whites, made in pursuance of previous telegraphic instructions.

The following tabulated statement presents a resume of the papers, which papers also contain much other matter relating to the feeling and condition of society in Alabama.

Whites against Blacks.

assault and battery	larceny	assault with deadly weapon	murder	driven off without compensation for labor	retaining freedmen without compensation	arson
42	2	11	14	14	15	1

Blacks against Whites.

assault	larceny	assault with deadly weapon	murder	assaulting ladies	arson	rape
7	7	3	1	2	1	2

Assault and battery excess committed by Whites   43
Murder excess by Whites   13
Larceny excess by Blacks   5

U. S. Grant   Lieutenant General.

LS, DLC-JP.

From Davidson M. Leatherman

St Louis Hotel   New Orleans La
14th March 1866

Since writing you a few days ago, I am only confirmed in what is there stated.[1] There would have been here immense gatherings of the People expressive of their gratitude, and endorsing your every act and policy, but for fear of inflaming opposition. They feel the time is not come when they can act without being injurious, and disapprobated by you.

All that has been, or may be said, or written about the disloyalty of the South, is purely nonsense. There is not one man in a thousand whose head & heart is not for the restoration of the Government upon the principles of your Policy.

The friends of Gen Morgan L. Smith as I am informed intend presenting his name to you for the position of "Collector of Customs" at Mobile.[2]

Those who will urge his appointment from this region, do so from a knowledge of his unyielding position for you and your policy. He is well known to me, is a conservative man and was so when in the Army of the Government fighting for the preservation of the Union, and is so now.

He was badly wounded at Vicksburg, in the first seige of that place. It is well known to me that He has the full confidence & friendship of both Generals Grant & Sherman.[3] I regard him in all respects competent and true. His appointment would give great satisfaction to the people who knew him in this section during his connection with the Army and conservative course. The office is temporarilly filled by Tominy[4] who is also Treasury Agent at Mobile. I have much to say to you when it is proper to encumber your mind, about the *Frauds* upon the Government in this region.

D. M. Leatherman

ALS, DNA-RG56, Appts., Customs Service, Collector, Mobile, Morgan Smith.

1. This is perhaps a reference to Leatherman's letter of late February, also written from New Orleans, in which he depicted widespread and enthusiastic support for the President in that city and surrounding areas. Leatherman to Johnson, Feb. 26, 1866, Johnson Papers, LC.

2. Smith (1821–1874), a native of New York but subsequently a resident of several states, recruited and organized the 8th Mo. Inf., USA, when war broke out. Smith was actively involved in a number of campaigns in the western theater and ended his career as commander of the District of Vicksburg (1864–65). Although he did not receive the appointment at Mobile, Smith was named as consul general at Honolulu by President Johnson. *DAB*; Warner, *Blue*.

3. For their opinions of Smith, see Grant to Johnson, Aug. 20, 1866, Simon, *Grant Papers*, 16: 301; and William T. Sherman to Johnson, Aug. 13, 1866, Lets. of Appl. and Recomm., 1861–69 (M650, Roll 45), Morgan L. Smith, RG59, NA.

4. James M. Tomeny.

From Thomas Cottman

Washington   March 15th 1866

Mr. President

No one can regret more than I do, the abuse of the confidence, you have so generously reposed in our people, evinced in the recent Municipal election in New Orleans.[1] If my Southern friends had premeditated, the design to furnish your enemies, pretexts & arguments to be used against you they could not by any possibility have been more successful than they have been, in the selection of officers for high trust & responsibility in New Orleans. The Mayor[2] & Recorder[3] are as well known to the different Commanders of the Department as they are to the *poor Dutch* & *Irish* they have permitted to live on the condition of keeping away from the polls or casting their obligatory suffrage for the *Thugs*, who stood by as wolves ready to devour them. This fellow Lucien Adam, who has been chosen to fill the most responsible office in the City of New Orleans (Recorder 4th Dis) is as notorious in New Orleans as ever Murril[4] was in your State. He was arraigned before Mr. Sewards friend Judge Peabody[5] for such crimes as to preclude bail. Judge Peabody is here now & ready to furnish such legal evidence regarding him as would either consign him to the halter or Penitentiary for life. Generals Butler & Banks can give you a history of these men, from which I refrain as I prefer, the evidence of their character to come from a diferent quarter. Governor Wells used every exertion in his power to a void this humiliation, which our Secession friends, had prepared for him with the cooperation of the Commander of the Department. Neither the Governor or Mayor can be held accountable for this disgrace, which must attach to such disreputable expressions of public sentiment. It is a stigma upon the Legislature & Genl Canby. It pains me immeasurably to be compelled to bring this to your notice, but however disagreeable I feel it my duty. Mr. Seward had Judge Peabody appointed Provisional Judge for the State of Louisiana—as a special friend of his, he will be responsible for his statement. Lucien Adam was before him & he can give his character & the chance a Dutchman or Irishman has for protection from his gang of slung shot & brass knuckled gentry. I have said more than I intended as I only desired to call your attention to the class of men that the party of the *three* commissioners[6] who have just left here elevate to position for the purpose of doing their dirty work. With such men in power Kennedy (The Ex Mayor) could no more live in Louisiana than in the jungles of Africa. It is very unfortunate just at this time that such things should occur; but you know best how to remedy them.

Thos Cottman

ALS, DLC-JP.
1. The election was held March 12, 1866. *New Orleans Picayune*, Mar. 13, 1866.

2. The new mayor, Democrat John T. Monroe (1822–1871), a former stevedore and New Orleans alderman, had previously served as mayor from 1860 until he was ousted by Gen. Benjamin Butler in 1862. Monroe refused to take the oath of allegiance to the Union. After some months of imprisonment, he spent the rest of the war in Mobile, Alabama. Monroe had not applied for a pardon from Johnson prior to his reelection as mayor. He was later removed from his position as mayor in March 1867 by Gen. Philip Sheridan. Conrad, *La. Biography*; *New Orleans Picayune*, Mar. 11, 1866; Taylor, *La. Reconstructed*, 81. See also Johnson to Hugh Kennedy, Mar. 16, 1866; Monroe to Johnson, Mar. 17, 1866; and John Purcell to Johnson, Mar. 22, 1866.

3. Lucien Adams, Sr. (c1821–fl1900), now a Democrat, had been a Know-Nothing politician in the 1850s. Previously recorder for the Fourth District, Adams was not, contrary to Cottman's belief, elected. Out of six candidates for the office, Adams ran third with 244 votes, outpolled by the National Union candidate H. T. Vennard (350) and independent J. H. Jackson (334). Following his defeat, Adams served as a port warden, stock inspector, municipal judge, and lawyer. 1860 Census, La., Orleans, New Orleans, 11th Ward, 405; New Orleans directories (1861–1901); Ted Tunnell, *Crucible of Reconstruction: War, Radicalism and Race in Louisiana, 1862–1877* (Baton Rouge, 1984), 103; *New Orleans Picayune*, Mar. 13, 20, 1866.

4. John A. Murrell.

5. Charles A. Peabody.

6. William B.G. Egan, Duncan S. Cage, and James B. Eustis. See Edwin M. Stanton to Johnson, Mar. 11, 1866; Johnson to J. Madison Wells, Mar. 13, 1866; Wells to Johnson, Mar. 15, 1866; Johnson to Three Louisiana Delegates, Mar. 16, 1866.

From Thomas Ewing

Strictly Confidential

Washington   March 15. 1866.
No. 12 North. A. St.

Dear Sir:

I was ill last night, and do not get off to day.[1] Among the multiplicity of things of which we spoke last night, I forgot to mention the Atty General. It is of the utmost importance that you have a stronger man in that place. It is due to yourself and also to the Court—for Mr. Speed is not a competent legal adviser, especially in the present critical condition of affairs; and I know that the Court does not rely on him. I beleive he is loyal; and you ought not to turn him adrift, but make him District Judge somewhere, say in Mississippi. Henry Stanbery[2] of Kentucky has been named to you for Attorney General. It is sufficient for me to say of him that he stands with the head of the Bar in the West—"if not first, in the very first line."[3] He is also entirely reliable, and would, I think, be more generally acceptable than any one you could name. I do not think the Senate would reject him, knowing as they do that his appointment would be most acceptable to the Supreme Court.

Mr. O. H. Browning is, perhaps, his equal in legal capacity, and with some more political experience—has better health, more capable of labor with great energy of character. He would make an admirable Secretary of the Interior, if you should not select him for Attorney General. He is distinguished as a land Lawyer. He is a strictly honest man; and that Department, which has been a den of plunderers since 1861, requires a man like him to purify it and correct its abuses. His energy and decision of character might be very useful to you in case of emergency.

I throw out these suggestions by way of giving you such information as I have, which may or may not be useful to you. I have nothing to ask for anyone, & my only wish is that the best and most efficient men should fill these important offices. It will be well to make an early change in the office of Attorney General, as you want the intellect of another strong man in your Cabinet.

As to Mr Delano,[4] you may rely on him fully. He knows as much of the men of Ohio, as any one you can consult.

T. Ewing

ALS, DLC-JP.
    1. The next morning Ewing left for Ohio. Randall, *Browning Diary*, 66.
    2. Stanbery (1803–1881), an Ohio lawyer, practiced law with Ewing early in his career. After serving as Ohio's attorney general and a member of the state's constitutional convention of 1850, Stanbery continued his law practice until 1866, when Johnson appointed him to replace Speed. Stanbery resigned in March 1868 to serve as Johnson's chief counsel in the impeachment trial. *DAB*.
    3. From Oliver Goldsmith, *Retaliation*, line 93.
    4. Columbus Delano.

From Benjamin F. Perry

Greenville S.C   March 15th 1866

My dear Sir

I have been requested by Govnor Orr, to write you in reference to an order of General Sickles, which if carried out will produce incalculable distress & ruin to the Freedmen & their employers in Laurens & Newberry districts.

It seems that an officer or employee of the Federal Government, by the name of Coan,[1] has made a report to General Ames,[2] who commands Western South Carolina, that the Freedmen are constantly shot down & killed for leaving their former owners & making contracts with other persons, that there is a combination amongst the planters in those districts not to hire or contract with Freedmen who did not formerly belong to them, & that there is a regular band of bushwhackers who roam over those districts to kill all freedmen who have left their former owners.

On this Report, which is filled with attrocious falsehoods, General Sickles has issued an order[3] for the removal of all the negroes in Laurens & Newberry districts (thirty thousand in number) at the expense of those districts for transportation & support. If this order is enforced it will ruin & make desolate a rich & beautiful portion of South Carolina. The crops will be lost, the negroes will be unwilling to leave & take to the woods, and those who are removed will be subjected to exposure, suffering & disease.

There may have been a few acts of violence in those districts, and all communities are liable to them. There are also a parcel of marauders in the upper country, from Texas, Maryland & other States, who have been robbing, stealing & killing. We now have a cavalry force sent here for the purpose of arresting them or running them out of the country. But that the citizens generally of Laurens and Newberry are concerned with them is absurd & preposterous.[4]

I am sorry to say Mr President that the military force in this section of the State do not behave well. Yesterday a Federal Soldier shot & killed in a cold blooded manner a negro man who had not disturbed him. The Soldier was drunk.

It would be a great relief to the country if the military was removed. They do no good. The negroes would be better protected without them than with them. Generally & almost universally there is a kind feeling on the part of the former owners for their freedmen. The presence of the military authorities excites and disturbs the community. Our laws & courts are set aside by them. We feel that we have no law & no freedom whilst they remain amongst us. They are fining our citizens for every little petty offence & pocketing the money. A fine of one hundred dollars was imposed the other day on a quiet honorable citizen because he did not obey the summons of the Provost marshal & appear before him promptly. Misrepresentations are made by negroes & the most respectable citizens are arrested & lodged in jail—and on investigation the charges are proved to be utterly false.

There are good people enough in every district to protect the Freedmen & suppress maurauders if they could be permitted to do so. Where there has been no military force there has been less disturbance. I can assure your Excellency that the people of South Carolina are truly & sincerely loyal and determined henceforth to stand by the U. States & obey the laws.

If we could only have civil law fully restored & our courts not interferred with & the military removed we should be once more quiet happy & prosperous.

B. F. Perry

ALS, DNA-RG94, Lets. Recd. (Main Ser.), File P-772-1866 (M619, Roll 505).

1. Alonzo Coan (1842–1921), captain, 15th Maine Inf., lived in Massachusetts, Maine, and Missouri before permanently settling in Boulder, Colorado, where he engaged in mining. Pension Records, Alonzo Coan, RG15, NA.

2. Adelbert Ames. For the report see Alonzo Coan to Joseph A. Clark, Feb. 10, 1866, Lets. Recd. (Main Ser.), File S-412-1866 (M619, Roll 512), RG94, NA.

3. Not found, but it apparently accompanied the February 20, 1866, instructions from Sickles's Charleston headquarters to have the freedmen's conditions in Newberry and Laurens Districts investigated. Henry A. Shorey and George H. Ziegler to Joseph A. Clark, Mar. 19, 1866, ibid.

4. On March 8, 1866, Capt. Henry A. Shorey, on behalf of the army, and Lt. George H. Ziegler, on behalf of the Freedmen's Bureau, were ordered to investigate Captain Coan's allegations. Their findings substantiated the charges, with conditions being worse in Newberry than in Laurens. However, in both districts disturbances had decreased significantly since early February. They recommended that detachments of cavalry be sent to both dis-

tricts and that in Newberry at least a thousand freedmen be removed. General Ames believed that part of the trouble in Newberry District was due to the "inefficiency" of the army officer there, whom he proposed to relieve. Moreover, Ames was not convinced that removal was the best policy. Ibid.; Ames to John W. Clous, Mar. 24, 1866, ibid.

From Albert Pike

Memphis, Tennessee   15th March 1866.

Sir & Bro∴

The Supreme Council of the 33d Degree for the Southern jurisdiction of the United States, in which all the States west of the Mississippi River are included, convenes at the City of Washington on the 16th of April,[1] for purposes strictly Masonic, as Bros∴ B. B. French and George C. Whiting, 33d can assure you.

One of its members is Bro∴ Howell Cobb of Georgia.

I hope it will not be considered improper for me to ask that special permission may be sent him to attend that meeting.[2] We seek to heal the wounds of the Country by re-uniting the Brethren so long separated by the impediments of war, to honour the memory of our dead on both sides, and to work for the good of the order.

I make this respectful request, because it is understood that the parole of Ill∴ Bro∴ Cobb confines him to the State of Georgia: and I can safely assure you that the favour, if granted, will neither be abused or forgotten.

Albert Pike, 33d
Gr∴ Commander of the Sup∴ Council

ALS, DLC-JP.
1. A brief report of the Supreme Council meeting in Washington may be found in the Washington Evening Star, Apr. 16, 1866.
2. No evidence to indicate that the President responded to the request that Cobb be permitted to attend the Masonic conclave has been found. French also asked Johnson to allow Cobb to attend the Washington meeting. B. B. French to Johnson, Mar. 23, 1866, Johnson Papers, LC.

From J. Madison Wells

New Orleans La   Mch 15 1866

Nine tenths members of Legislature show daily by acts they are unrepentant if pardoned rebels. Madam Jeff Davis was yesterday admitted to the honors of the House.[1] They want a convention for reactionary objects. Any bill they pass for the object will be vetoed.[2]

J Madison Wells   Gov La

Tel, DLC-JP.
1. Mrs. Davis was passing through New Orleans on her way to join other members of her family then in Canada. New Orleans Picayune, Mar. 13, 1866; Eron Rowland, Varina Howell, Wife of Jefferson Davis (2 vols., New York, 1931), 2: 472.
2. Wells is responding to Johnson's telegram of March 13, 1866.

From Robert B. Carnahan[1]

Pittsburgh, March 16th 1866

Dear Sir,

I had intended to send you a brief account of the proceedings of the late Union State Convention of Penna,[2] but have hitherto been prevented by an attack of sickness. I had been confined to my bed for several days before the meeting of the Convention by an attack of Catarrh Fever, and was physically unable to take a very active part in the deliberations of that body.

You have, no doubt, seen a copy of the Resolutions which were adopted. The fourth of the series relates to you.[3] Being a member of the Committee on resolutions, when the 4th one was read in Committee, I offerred a substitute hastily prepared, substantially the same as that afterwards moved by me in Convention.[4] In the Committee composed of 33 members, and 31 being actually present, my substitute received 9 votes. It gave rise to a controversy which was quite acrimonious. Opposition was made by myself alone to the 5th, which claims absolute powers for Congress over the States lately in rebellion, and the 17th requesting Senator Cowan to resign.[5]

When the report of the Committee had been made the first, second third and fourth resolutions were seperately considered. When the 4th was read I offered the Resolution, marked in the accompanying newspaper[6] as a substitute, and called the yeas and nays.

What then took place is reported with more accuracy in the inclosed copy of the Pittsburgh Commercial than in any newspaper which I have seen. The substance of my remarks is correctly given, striking out the words erased in pencil, which are not mine. The scene was one of the wildest confusion. I was at once attacked, taunted with being an office-holder, having sympathies with Copperheads &c but defended by my radical colleague Mr Marshall,[7] as being as good a Republican as any on the floor. I was appealed to and entreated to withdraw my resolution but declined. It is not the truth, that I was shamed or bullied into withdrawing it, as stated in several newspapers.[8] Hon George V Lawrence[9] a member of the present Congress from this State, and a half a dozen of others friendly to the resolution, and who told me on the floor that they would vote for it, if pressed, suggested that it would not be wise, to take a vote as it was manifest that, it could not be carried. There were about 20 members of the Convention, who would have voted with me. Forney's statement in the "Press" and "Washington Chronicle" that I stood alone is wholly untrue. The leading merchants and manufacturers in this place, were amazed at the temper of the Convention, and cannot comprehend why so mild and conciliatory an endorsement should fail to receive the support of the Convention.

The remaining 13 resolutions including the one requesting Cowan to resign were passed in a body, notwithstanding a division of the question was called for. The chairman (John Covode) recognized no body, but one of the majority, and neither a division of the question nor yeas and nays could be obtained. There were about two hundred persons not members of the Convention on the floor, who cheered, yelled and voted, and hissed every body they did not want to hear.

I have written much more at length than I intended, and will conclude by saying that a majority of the Republicans of this County are friendly to the policy of your Administration; and among those who think differently I know very few who are not willing to accord to you the merit of good intentions and undoubted patriotism.

R B Carnahan

P.S   For the purpose of showing the malignity of some of the members of the late Convention, I inclose a copy of the "Franklin Repository" edited by Col A K McClure. He was the delegate from Franklin Co.

R B Carnahan

ALS, DLC-JP.
1. A former Whig state representative and early Republican stalwart, Carnahan (1826–1890) served as U.S. attorney for the western district of Pennsylvania under Presidents Lincoln, Johnson, and Grant, before returning to his private practice in Pittsburgh. *The Biographical Encyclopaedia of Pennsylvania of the Nineteenth Century* (Philadelphia, 1874), 579; *Memoirs of Allegheny County Pennsylvania* (2 vols., Madison, 1904), 1: 36.
2. The state's Republicans had convened on March 7 in Harrisburg for the purpose of naming a gubernatorial candidate and adopting the party's platform. Erwin S. Bradley, *Simon Cameron, Lincoln's Secretary of War: A Political Biography* (Philadelphia, 1966), 260; *Pittsburgh Gazette*, Mar. 8, 1866.
3. Although a draft copy of the resolutions has not been located in the Johnson Papers, the platform was reprinted in various newspapers. The resolution referred to commended Johnson for his "bold, outspoken denunciation of the crime of treason," pledged the future support of the "loyal masses" in punishing "traitors and their sympathizers" and restoring the Union, and expressed "entire confidence" in his "character and principles." *Washington Morning Chronicle*, Mar. 9, 1866.
4. Carnahan's substitute plank declared "full confidence" in the President's "ability, integrity, and patriotism." *Philadelphia Press*, Mar. 8, 1866.
5. Four days earlier the state legislature had also demanded Edgar Cowan's resignation. Bradley, *Militant Republicanism*, 234.
6. No enclosures have been found.
7. Thomas M. Marshall (1819–*fl*1881), a Pittsburgh attorney and former city councilman, later allied with Greeley's Liberal Republicans. *Biographical Encyclopaedia of Pa.*, 657; *Diffenbacher's Directory of Pittsburgh and Allegheny Cities (1881–82)*, 490; Bradley, *Militant Republicanism*, 407.
8. One newspaper reported that, after Carnahan withdrew his amendment, the original fourth resolution was approved by a 109 to 21 vote. *Pittsburgh Gazette*, Mar. 9, 1866.
9. Lawrence (1818–1904) was a veteran Republican politician, serving numerous terms in the state legislature as well as in Congress (1865–69, 1883–85). *BDAC*.

From Virginia C. Clay

Fortress Monroe, [Va.]   March 16th 1866.

My dear Sir,

The order which was sent me the evening of the 14th[1] has resulted exactly as I feared, in accomplishing nothing. General Miles is unwilling to assume a responsibility—which he thinks should be taken by the Govmt. He does not feel it *just*, to require of *him* to become the guarantor of Mr. Clay's parole. While he does not hesitate declareing *his entire* trust & confidence in my husbands honor. He therefore refuses to let him come out save under guard, as usual unless *you* order his parole. I *beg* you will do it. It is ambiguous & equivocal & whether intended or not, is susceptible of two constructions & calculated to embarrass a man not trained at the bar to special pleading.

After Mr. Clay's proof of integrity, it is humiliating & painful in the extreme, to be thus treated, & I hope you will remedy matters without delay. I am now locked in with him, nor will we move, save as usual, with officer & guard until further orders. The consequence is, I cannot walk with him nor will he be permitted any extension of liberty in the Fort. He cannot escape if he *wd*. & wd. not if he could.

Gen. Miles telegraphed for explanation[2] on receiving the order & the *reply*[3] is even more embarrassing than the order. The orders, taken together are tantamount to this: Let him out but at *your* peril, *your* risk, wh. the Gen'l. thinks unjust to him, & so do I. Please explicitly send the liberty—of the fort, during my stay, or refuse.[4]

Draft, NcD-C. C. Clay Papers.

1. Before leaving Washington, Mrs. Clay, having obtained permission from Johnson on the 13th to go to Fortress Monroe, also probably received a copy of the President's order, via a wire from the War Department to Gen. Nelson A. Miles, whereby her husband's limits, while taking "exercise in the open air," were expanded "to such extent within the walls of the Fort as may be consistent with his safe custody." Johnson to [Miles], Mar. 13, 1866, Johnson Papers, LC; Edward D. Townsend to Miles, Mar. 14, 1866, Tels. Sent, Sec. of War (M473, Roll 90), RG107, NA; Virginia C. Clay to Johnson, Mar. 14, 1866, C. C. Clay Papers, NcD.

2. Miles inquired whether the armed guard which usually accompanied Mr. Clay on his daily walks ought to be continued, or should he be granted a limited parole and free exercise within the fort. Miles to Townsend, Mar. 14, 1866, Lets. Recd. (Main Ser.), File M-398-1866 (M619, Roll 493), RG94, NA.

3. Townsend advised Miles to "exercise your own discretion as to the surveillance over him while taking out door exercise." Townsend to Miles, Mar. 15, 1866, Tels. Sent, Sec. of War (M473, Roll 90), RG107, NA.

4. On this same date Mrs. Clay also sent a telegram to Johnson imploring him to issue a more "explicit order." Receiving no reply, she wrote the President again three days later. Clay to Johnson, Mar. 16, 1866, Johnson Papers, LC; Clay to Johnson, Mar. 19, 1866, C. C. Clay Papers, NcD. See Johnson to Lorenzo Thomas, Mar. 19, 1866.

To Hugh Kennedy

Washington, D.C., March 16", 1866

I have no instructions to give in regard to surrendering the mayoralty of New Orleans to the person who has been elected to fill that position.[1] We have no information showing that the election was not regular, or that the individual who has been elected cannot qualify. In the absence of such information, the presumption is that the election has been according to law, and that the person elected can take the oath of allegiance and loyalty required.[2]

Andrew Johnson

Tel, DNA-RG107, Tels. Sent, President, Vol. 3 (1865–68).
1. Kennedy had telegraphed Johnson requesting instructions about turning over his mayoral responsibilities to John T. Monroe. Kennedy to Johnson, Mar. 14, 1866, Johnson Papers, LC.
2. Kennedy replied, "The Mayor Elect was Mayor under the Confederate authorities imprisoned by Gen Butler for aggravated hostility to the re-establishment of the National authority & finally voluntarily left Union lines for the Confederacy, persistently refusing to take oath of allegiance. Is not specially pardoned and the Union sentiment is unanimous against him." Kennedy to Johnson, Mar. 17, 1866, Johnson Papers, LC. See Monroe to Johnson, Mar. 17, 1866.

To Three Louisiana Delegates[1]

Washington, D.C., March 16' 1866.

Developments since you left Washington and the answer from New Orleans[2] induce me to advise against calling a Convention at the present time. Those here who oppose the restoration of the States to all their relations with the Federal Government seem determined to interpose every possible obstacle in the way, both at the seat of government and in the States. I therefore think that it would be the best policy to defer for the present any call for a Convention.[3]

Andrew Johnson

Tel, DNA-RG107, Tels. Sent, President, Vol. 3 (1865–68).
1. The delegates were: Duncan S. Cage, James B. Eustis, and William B.G. Egan. See Johnson to Wells, Mar. 13, 1866.
2. See J. Madison Wells to Johnson, Mar. 15, 1866.
3. The Louisiana legislature adjourned on March 22 without calling for an election of delegates to a new convention. *American Annual Cyclopaedia* (1866), 450.

From Henry Ward Beecher

Brooklyn   March 17, 1866.
Dear Sir.

Unless withheld by the most substantial reason, it is exceedingly to be desired that you should sign the Civil Rights Bill.[1] The *thing itself*, is desirable. But, aside from that, I am persuaded that it would go far to *harmonize the feelings* of men who should never have differed, or permitted a difference. I am in a situation to *feel*, in the north, the deep tide of moral feeling. It has been sought for several months, to detatch from you the sober and reflecting class of men.

The passage of this bill will, in a great degree, frustrate the influence of those who have sought to produce the impression that you had proved untrue to the cause of liberty & loyalty.

It would, also, strengthen your friends hands. I have strongly and to my own personal inconvenience, (for the present) defended both your *wisdom*, in most things, and your *motives*[2]—and I feel most profoundly, how the signing of this bill will strengthen the position that I have defended in your behalf; and weaken the influence of men who have been deceived, or who have wilfully Sought to mislead the *community*.

I do not enter upon any question of the constitutionality of this Bill. Assuming that it is constitutional, I only say that it will strengthen all the north & west, give great strength to you, to sign it.[3]

I pray you not to consider me as intruding upon your sphere in thus writing. Having suffered, as being a friend of President Johnson, I felt a liberty of speech, which I should not have done, had I been opposed to you, or even lukewarm.

H. W. Beecher

ALS, DLC-JP.
1. Introduced by Sen. Lyman Trumbull on January 5, 1866, the measure as amended had passed both houses of Congress by March 15 and was the following day delivered to a committee to be presented to the President. *Senate Journal*, 39 Cong., 1 Sess., pp. 62, 237, 241 (Ser. 1236). For a text of the bill, see *New York Times*, Mar. 16, 1866.
2. Beecher, for example, had defended the vetoing of the Freedmen's Bureau bill, claiming that there was "no man in the land . . . more in favor of efficient legislation for the black man than President Johnson himself." *National Intelligencer*, Feb. 22, 1866.
3. See Veto of Civil Rights Bill, Mar. 27, 1866.

From Maryland Blacks[1]

[Baltimore, March 17, 1866][2]

The undersigned, a portion of the loyal colored men of Maryland, who during the National struggle for liberty sent eight regiments of their brothers and sons to the field,[3] respectfully ask the President in behalf of the colored people of Maryland to sign the bill guaranteeing civil rights to the inhabitants of the United States and for the following reasons.

1st. Because since the war they have undertaken to establish schools for their children throughout the State in the various school-houses and churches which they have usually occupied, eight or ten have been burned to ground for no other reason than that they were used for this purpose, and because in no instance has the law of Maryland been efficient to bring a single incendiary to punishment or even to trial, though a large reward was offered by the Governor[4] for the arrest and conviction of the guilty persons, because the testimony of colored persons who know the facts, and in some instances saw the arson perpetrated, is not allowed to be received in the State Courts.

2nd. Because the teachers who are sent to us are brutally assaulted, shot at, and maltreated, without the power or right of appeal to any Court of Justice in the State for protection or redress, and our only hope is in the effort of Congress to guarantee us the fact of freedom, which till now has proved an illusion and a dream.[5]

3rd. Because even in the State of Maryland where Christianity has been preached two hundred years, we have not the out-spoken sympathy or practical assistance of Christian people themselves, and our only protection against the baser sort till the followers of a common Master shall cease to be corrupted or overawed by treason must be the strong arm of Law, a poor substitute indeed for the warmth of Christian sympathy, but rightly exercised, a sufficient barrier to gross outrages and wrongs.

4th. Because everywhere throughout the State our homes are invaded and our little ones seized at the family fireside, and forcibly bound to masters who are by law expressly released from any obligation to educate them either in secular or religious knowledge; and because the Legislature of Maryland would not by the repeal of these laws give us the right to a home, or guarantee to us the safety of our children around the hearth while we were at labor or their support in old age.

We hope the President will see from these reasons abundant causes for signing this Bill, and we promise him so doing the silent it may be, but still heartfelt affection of all our people.[6]

Pet, DLC-JP.

1. Two hundred and forty-nine signatures appeared on the petition.

2. This is the date of Lyman Trumbull's endorsement. In all probability the document was written at Baltimore since many of the signers were from there.

3. According to John W. Blassingame, 8,718 Maryland blacks volunteered to serve in six Union regiments during the war. "The Recruitment of Negro Troops in Maryland," *MdHM*, 58 (1963): 29.

4. Thomas Swann.

5. O. O. Howard briefly recounts the plight of education for blacks in Maryland during this period. *Autobiography of Oliver Otis Howard Major General United States Army* (2 vols., New York, 1908), 2: 273–74.

6. The petition carried the endorsement of Lyman Trumbull, who wrote: "I have recd & been requested to lay the within before the President." No evidence could be found to suggest that Trumbull helped to draft the petition.

From John T. Monroe

New Orleans La   Mar. 17" 1866

I have been elected Mayor by the people.[1] An effort is making by the Present incumbent Hugh Kennedy to keep me from my position.[2] I am as fully determined in my sincere loyalty to the union and as strong in my support of your noble policy as any man living. Please answer in time to reach me before Monday.[3]

J.M.T. Monroe

Tel, DLC-JP.

1. Monroe received 3,469 votes to Joseph H. Moore's 3,158. *New Orleans Picayune,* Mar. 13, 1866.

2. Hugh Kennedy to Johnson, Mar. 17, 1866. Tels. Recd., President, Vol. 5 (1866–67), RG107, NA.

3. Johnson responded with a copy to Monroe of his telegram to Hugh Kennedy of March 16. Monroe was inaugurated as mayor on Monday, March 19, and then promptly suspended from office by order of Gen. Edward R.S. Canby. Johnson to Monroe, Mar. 17, 1866, Tels. Sent, President, Vol. 3 (1865–68), RG107, NA; *New Orleans Picayune,* Mar. 20, 1866. See John Purcell to Johnson, Mar. 22, 1866.

From Eli Thayer

Private

17th March 1866
1 Park Place   New York City.

Dear Sir:

I wish to say a word to you in this crisis of our country.

It is needless for me to say that I have always been & am now your friend.

I desire no office & could take none if offered, but I do most earnestly wish to see the policy which you have inaugurated carried out & the country again in state of harmony & prosperity.[1]

In favor of this policy I have spoken three times in the State of Conn. & shall speak every evening till the close of the Campaign.[2] I am for the democratic party as the *only union party*.

I have had ample opportunity to know that about three fourths of the Republican Party are your bitter personal & political enemies.

The Democrats are honest disinterested in the support they give you. They desire no offices but they are ardent in the support of your views.

But here as in N.H. the Bureau party are using the patronage of the government to destroy your policy & to sustain your bitterest enemies.

It is now there fore a matter of the greatest importance to the country that your administration should not be longer embarrassed by such enemies as derive all their vitality & power from the government which they are attempting to ruin.

There should be some speedy removals in the state of Conn. You cannot fail to be aware of the importance of the success of the only party in this state which sustains your policy. If that party be defeated here Thad. Stevens will be very likely to triumph in Pennsylvania.

I need say no more. A few words from yourself will at once secure the triumph of your policy & the admission of the excluded states.

Eli Thayer

P.S.   It seems to me that Mr. Doolittle's proposed amendment to the Constitution[3] will operate very much against the negroes.

The South will not admit them to the ballot but instead will try to supply their places with white laborers. Many negroes will there fore either be compelled to leave or to suffer. If they come North where they can vote they will be even worse off, for we do not want them & would not endure them.

ALS, DLC-JP.

1. About a month earlier, Thayer had telegraphed the President: "You are gloriously right and the country will sustain you." Thayer to Johnson, Feb. 20, 1866, Johnson Papers, LC.

2. Thayer spoke at Norwich on the 18th and at Hartford the following evening. Thayer to Johnson, Mar. 19, 1866, ibid.

3. On March 9, 1866, Senator Doolittle had proposed apportioning representation in Congress on the basis of the number of adult male voters in each state. *Congressional Globe*, 39 Cong., 1 Sess., p. 1287.

From James W. Wall[1]

Burlington New Jersey
March 17th 1866

My Dear Sir

I called in company with Hon Saml J Randall of Pennsylvania to see you on Thursday eveg. but found you engaged with the Secry of the Treasury. My object in calling was to assure you of the support of the *true* Union men of New Jersey in your great and patriotic policy of the restoration of the southren states to the Union. I regard this now as the paramount issue before the country, that like Aarons rod, swallows up all the others.[2] I would fling all party prejudices and predelections to the winds, and under the banner of a great Constitutional Union party, unite the patriotic men every where in a struggle against the Radicals. The claims of country are now superior to the claims of party. We have been separated for four years, at the swords point, at the cannons mouth along the dividing line. At war, there has been for a time a northern and a southren Union. On two sides of a boundary of blood, we have been for a season two nations nominally but now that the exhaustion of war has compelled to peace, with states naturally and providentially connected, it must necessarily end in re-union, or the destruction of the government established by our Fathers. With a sublime courage, you have declared for reunion. The blessings of those who were ready to perish will be yours, and the consciousness of a high duty nobly performed, your best reward. I feel profoundly impressed with the consciousness that providence has raised you up for the performance of this great work. This [is] Gods work, and will triumph.

James W. Wall

ALS, DLC-JP.
1. Wall (1820–1872), a Princeton graduate and an attorney, had been elected in 1863 as a Democrat to the Senate, serving only three months. *BDAC*.
2. A reference to Exodus 7: 12.
3. In a previous letter Wall had praised Johnson's veto of the Freedmen's Bureau bill as "overwhelming in its logic, and unassailable in its constitutional position." Wall to Johnson, Feb. 20, 1866, Johnson Papers, LC.

From Francis P. Blair, Sr.

Wash   18 March, '66

My Dear Mr. President

It seems to me that the civil rights Bill is the revival of the Freedmans Bureau, in both its civil & military aspects, but is expanded into a wider authority over the municipal rights of the State Govts.

Under this Bill the Municipal regulation of the States, are to be so cramped, that there shall be no discrimination between *Whites* & *Black* and that the latter are *"to be entitled to the full & equal benefit of all* laws & proceedings for the security of *person and property as is enjoyed by White citizens & shall be subject to like punishment, pains & penalties, & to none other, any law ordinance, statute, regulation or custom to the contrary notwithstanding"* &c.[1]

Now in the South there is a Negro nation within a white nation, the two contradistinguished in a thousand particulars. The latter holds dominance of the Soil, is charged with the business of the Govt. Their well-being as a nation & as individuals in their personal & social concerns are dependent upon their municipal regulations; and yet another inferior caste without the myriad of interests attached to this superior caste is to have the laws & regulation of society accomodated to it, without consideration of the vital differences between them! See what effect follows from denial of a right to discriminate between the races on matters of the highest concern, now subject to State municipal regulation.

We have seen insurrections of Freedmen in St. Domingo—on Jamaica & we have had insurrections of the Blacks in our country even when the condition of the hostile race was such as to render success hopeless. Will not the South feel itself called on to provide against danger, now that the race is manumitted, and thousands of disbanded negro soldiers are in their midst to organize insurrection and thousands of fanatic whites with hostile feelings ready to instigate it? The Southern Govts. will certainly mass and discipline & arm its militia & make laws & regulations to keep down the negroes. They will exclude them from the benefit of instruction and training & the use of arms as military bodies. They will not be allowed "the equal benefit of all laws & proceedings for the security of person & property as is enjoyed by white citizens" for the reason, that the negroes are in no danger of an insurrection against them on the part of the Whites, & because they have no property of sufficient value to tempt its conquest.

By the late Military Bill[2] it is provided that there shall be no discrimination between blacks & whites who are to fill the Regiments of the Regular Army. So many black regiments, so many white. Will not the South enquire why are there any black regiments? The Govts. of the South will surely enact that no black troops shall form a part of their militia. If the Genl. Govt. discriminates & provides there shall be black troops in our army to threaten the South, may it not discriminate in return and say, we will educate no black troops within our bosom to join their fellows of the black cockade, if they should ever come to aid a negro insurrection.

The late Military Bill provides that an officer of the United States army may be detailed to the Schools & Colleges as to impart a military education to the youth of the Country.[3] The South will gladly avail itself of this provision; but if it does, can it indulge a race which covered St. Domingo in blood and which might conclude the sad tragedy of the late war with a similar catastrophe, with an education to tempt them to the trial?

There are other differences of race which must control the policy of the South & require a legislation from the benefits of which the negro will be excluded. No man can advocate an amalgamation of the white & black races and so create a mongrel nation—a nation of bastards, for the laws forbid the marriage of blacks & whites. The policy of the country must therefore be a gradual Segregation of the races. This will be attempted by the legislation of the States now filled by negroes. Immigration of the whites will be invited from the north & from Europe by the tender of Homesteads & other allurements. Negroes from Africa & the neighboring Islands, will be excluded by penalties and the emigration of our native born blacks, will be urged by enactments which the pressure of the white immigration will prompt. A land of refuge will be provided for the superflow of the inferior Race. Great Britain has her penal colonies for such of her own white race as imperil her safety and prosperity. May not the South have its penal colony? May it not send its black convicts away, while its white convicts—especially the young & unfortunate class driven to crime by misfortunes—may be retained & reformed in work houses & penitentiaries & converted into useful citizens? Can an act of Congress interpose & deprive the States of this right of discrimination? The Bill of civil rights says it cant. "Like punishments, pains & penalties" are to apply to all persons, however different in their condition & their relations to the State, & the Govt. of the State is powerless to adapt its legislation to the various classes of the people however benevolent they may be in design & in operation.

Another great policy may be brought to the aid of the suffering Southern States, if not shorn of their powers of municipal legislation. The northern States are built up on their maratime power by the fishing bounties accorded by Congress.[4] Might not the Southern States by *a bonus* to chartered companies bring the manufacture of cottons, woollens, flax & silks to take root in their borders and then rising generations of the white race be educated in the system excluding the blacks & addicting the latter to the ruder trades & to the producing of the raw material? Has Congress the right to arrest any such fostering legislation in any useful pursuit, to promote the culture & superiority of their white kindred, because it subordinates the negroes?

An infinite variety of municipal regulations grow up in the economy of States to advance the interest of the Race who made the Govt. & to whom it belongs by making the discrimination congress forbids. Has it the right to do it?

F P. Blair

ALS, DLC-JP.
    1. Here Blair is objecting to the first section of the Civil Rights bill, as introduced by Trumbull. The Senate approved it initially on February 2 and the House on March 13; the

Senate approved it a second time as amended on March 15. *Congressional Globe*, 39 Cong., 1 Sess., p. 474; McKitrick, *Johnson and Reconstruction*, 305; Castel, *Presidency of Johnson*, 70; *Senate Journal*, 39 Cong., 1 Sess., p. 237 (Ser. 1236).

2. A reference to a bill "to increase and fix the military peace establishment of the United States," which the Senate passed and referred to the House on March 14, and which was ultimately approved by both the Congress and the President in July 1866. Ibid., pp. 233–34; *Congressional Globe*, 39 Cong., 1 Sess., Appendix, pp. 420–22.

3. See Section 26, ibid., p. 421.

4. In the margin Blair wrote: "I am against bounties—fishing & other." Congress repealed the laws allowing fishing bounties by an act approved on July 28, 1866. Ibid., p. 419.

From Henry T. Blow

Washington   Mch 19 66

Sir:

I relied so implicitly on your proposal not to act in the case of Mr Taussig,[1] Coll of St Louis, until you had sent for me and afforded me an opportunity of refuting all the charges made against him, as well as showing the injustice to the Public interests if he was removed, that I am both grieved & disappointed at the course you have seen fit to pursue,[2] but I cannot think Sir that you will deny his representative the privilege you had voluntarily extended and presume that you had forgotten what occurred on the occasion referr'd to. I write therefore to request that you will carry out your original proposal and allow me time (say next week) to prove all that I asserted in my conversation with you on this subject.[3]

Henry T Blow.

ALS, DLC-JP.

1. William Taussig (1826–1913) had a distinguished career in Missouri as a medical doctor and a county court member before being appointed by Lincoln in January 1865 as collector. Following his removal in the summer of 1866 and replacement by Barton Able, Taussig turned his efforts to banking and transportation. *DAB*; Ser. 6B, Vol. 3: 633; Vol. 4: 316, Johnson Papers, LC.

2. Three days earlier Johnson's nomination of Francis P. Blair, Jr., to Missouri's First District collectorship was presented to the Senate. *Senate Ex. Proceedings*, Vol. 14, pt. 2: 677.

3. A record of an interview between Johnson and Blow before the latter left Washington has not been located. For further developments in this story, see Francis P. Blair, Jr. to Johnson, May 5, 1866.

From Robert B. Carnahan

Pittsburgh, March 19th 1866

Sir:

A meeting is called for Tuesday the 20th inst. to sustain you and the policy of your Administration.[1] The circumstances under which the movement was commenced and is now prosecuted are not very favorable to its success. Three weeks ago, after the publication of your veto message, a meeting was called to denounce you and the principles of the message. A call was immediately circulated, for a meeting to sustain the President and was quite numerously signed. As the "indignation meeting" did not go on owing to the prevalence of the counsels of moderate men, it was thought best to go no further with the counter movement, and it was considered at an end. On Saturday last, however, the call was published, and contains the names of some parties a good many, perhaps in number, who signed it for the purpose of check-mating the other meeting and who now think it unwise, to hold any meeting at all. Others object greatly to the parties who are at the head of the movement. N P Sawyer Esq[2] who leads in the matter, was a delegate to the Convention which nominated Fremont and Cochran in 1864, and was far from being friendly to the Administration, or reelection of President Lincoln. He has somewhat of the reputation of a disorganizer, and although, personally a highly respected man, has not in my opinion, the Confidence of the Union Party here. A rumor is also abroad that one object of the meeting to-morrow night is to denounce Hon J K Moorhead[3] our member of Congress from this District. General Moorhead is personally very popular with his Constituents, and an attempt of the kind referred to, would be, in my opinion, very unwise and meet with little favor.

The facts referred to will probably operate largely against the success of the meeting of to morrow night, and I regret that the movement is in the hands which appear to Control it. Still some of the very best men here will be at the meeting, and I hope will be able to give it, the weight and character which ought to attend the demonstration. Distinguished Speakers from Washington are expected, and others of this city will be present to address the meeting. If opportunity offers I shall myself have some thing to say in favour of the policy of your Administration, which I fully approve.[4] I cannot, however withold the expression of my regret, that the movement had not been inaugurated, under circumstances more favorable to success, than the present indications seem to warrant. I also regret to see in the printed call the names of a number of McClellan Democrats. The meeting should in my opinion, have been confined to the Union Party. You have as warm friends here as in any part of the country, and I shall be much mistaken if their sentiments are not signally manifested notwithstanding the unfavorable surroundings referred to above.

R B Carnahan

ALS, DLC-JP.

1. The President had already been notified of the meeting. See N. P. Sawyer to Johnson, Mar. 15, 1866, Johnson Papers, LC.

2. A longtime "admirer & friend" of Johnson's, Nathaniel P. Sawyer (c1828–1903), a former postmaster of Pittsburgh, worked variously as a banker, soap and candle manufacturer, and real estate agent. Ibid.; *New York Times*, Nov. 25, 1903; Pittsburgh directories (1872–92); William F. Johnston to Johnson, Nov. 19, 1866, Appts., Heads of Treasury Offices, N. P. Sawyer, RG56, NA.

3. A former president of a canal and a telegraph company, James K. Moorehead (1806–1884) served a full decade as a Republican in Congress (1859–69). *BDAC*.

4. As Carnahan explained two days later, owing to the failure of the two speakers from

Washington to attend, he ended up giving the only speech that evening, but the meeting was a "decided success." Sawyer telegraphed Johnson that "Resolutions thoroughly endorsing your policy [were] unanimously adopted." Nevertheless, a newspaper account reported that not only were the resolutions endorsing the President "about equally divided in yeas and nays," but also when the meeting's speaker asked the crowd of some four thousand " 'which is right, President or Congress?' " the people responded "largely in favor of the latter." Carnahan to Johnson, Mar. 21, 1866; Sawyer to Johnson, Mar. 20, 1866, Johnson Papers, LC; *Philadelphia Press*, Mar. 21, 1866.

From Joshua Hill

Madison, Ga.   March 19, 1866.

Sir.

At the hazard of being troublesome, I call your attention to the enclosed editorial[1] of the American Union printed at Griffin, Ga. by an old and devoted Union man, Alexr. G. Murray, Esquire.[2] During the war Mr. Murray's paper was suppressed by a mob, for his opposition to the war. I know no man more sincere in his opposition to the origin and conduct of the struggle. You will oblige "a good man and true" by reading his comment on Mr. Raymonds speech.[3] He sent me the paper, with a request that I should say whether I thought Mr Raymond reflected accurately your views, and desired to publish, what I might write. I, of course, declined to speak for you, of that of which, I was no better informed than was he. I wrote him "confidentially" that I had no right to doubt that Mr Raymond properly represented you.

If not asking too much of you, I would be glad for the Government to aid Mr. Murray, by such patronage as it might be convenient to bestow upon him. He has not intimated a wish of the sort, but he is so deserving and so poor, that I undertake to plead for him. Genl. Slocum[4] did me the honor to say of me, that I forgot my own interests in trying to serve others. I am sensible of having spent much of my life, in that sort of service. But it does not become me to speak of it.

It is known in Georgia—that an effort was made by certain persons to depreciate me in your esteem. I was aware of it, but was too proud to refute it—and suffered it to go on unresisted. I wanted nothing, but to be understood, *as not being a hypocrite*.

I am fully aware of the propriety of one in your position, refraining from the every day declaration of opinions on important subjects—but feel that I have the claim on you, to ask *confidentially*, whether your line of policy is properly indicated by Mr. Raymond?

It may be very well for you to understand, that in the recent election for Senators, Govs. Brown, Cobb & Judge Jackson,[5] openly advocated the election of Provl. Gov. Johnson, and myself—on ground of expediency and propriety. Jefferson Davis is to day more popular in Georgia, than any other man. James Johnson, is unpopular, because of having accepted the office of Governor. I say these things in sorrow,—but I know they are true. James Johnson, knows it too.

I have been written to by some friends, who desire to serve me, offering to apply for a government appointment for me. There are very few, that I could afford to accept. None that would not support a large family, genteely. Should such a suggestion be made, it was originated without the slightest knowledge on my part—and yet, I hope, would be kindly entertained.

I should be pleased to get a line from you in reply. No man ever suffered by placing confidence in me—so will testify Aleck Stephens, Toombs, Howell Cobb, Gov. Brown—and everybody else, that knows me.

Joshua Hill.

P.S. You would be surprised to know, how general, the idea and hope is, that the contest between the ultraists and yourself—will eventuate in civil strife—in less than six months. I hear it continually, from ultra secessionists, and particularly from soldiers. It takes a long time, for passion to cool, and reason to resume its sway. I am only tolerated myself by thousands, because of my supposed influence with government officials. The mails bring me many bitter and denunciatory anonymous letters. I have tried to win men back to a sense of duty and obligation to country—but I find poor encouragement from many. No man desires more than I, the speedy and genuine restoration of patriotic regard for the Union—and yet knaves and fools try to teach the people that I would injure them— and perpetuate military rule in the State. This would be to war against my own peace—and is therefore absurd.

ALS, DLC-JP.
    1. Not found.
    2. Murray (b. c1808) was a Virginia native. 1860 Census, Ga., Spalding, 1001st Dist., Griffen, 159.
    3. Murray's editorial regarding Henry J. Raymond's speech, probably the one on February 22, 1866, at New York City's Cooper Institute in support of Johnson's policy, has not been found.
    4. Henry W. Slocum.
    5. Joseph E. Brown, Howell Cobb, and Henry R. Jackson.

To Lorenzo Thomas

[Washington]   March 19, 1866.
General:
Immediately upon the receipt of this order, you will please send to Major General Miles, by telegraph[1] & by mail, instructions to permit Clement C. Clay jr. to have the liberty of Fort Monroe, daily from sunrise to sunset, upon his giving his parole of honor in writing, not to leave the limits of the said Fort, or to make any attempt to escape from custody, or to do or perform any act that may be hostile or detrimental to the interests of the Government of the U.S.[2]

Andrew Johnson.

Tel draft, DLC-JP.
    1. See Edward D. Townsend to Nelson A. Miles, Mar. 19, 1866, Tels. Sent, Sec. of War (M473, Roll 90), RG107, NA.
    2. On the following day Virginia Clay responded: "Your order is received. Accept my thanks." On April 17 Johnson ordered Clay's release from confinement, permitting him to return to Alabama and visit other places until further notice. Clay to Johnson, Mar. 20, 1866, Tels. Recd., President, Vol. 5 (1866–67), RG107, NA; Townsend to Miles, Apr. 17, 1866, Tels. Sent, Sec. of War (M473, Roll 90), RG107, NA.

From Charles G. Halpine[1]

Private and Confidential.

Office N.Y. Citizen, New York
March 20th, 1866.

My dear Sir:

I address you on a matter only to-day brought to my knowledge, and which strikes me as of great interest both to you and the country.

I had today a long interview with my old friend Surgeon John J. Craven,[2] late of the U.S. Vols., and assigned to duty with Jefferson Davis at Fort Monroe, from which he has only recently been relieved.

His statements in regard to the views of Mr. Davis impress me as of profound interest to the whole country; and as further likely to strengthen the sound, constitutional and conservative opinion of the country in support of your policy and views.

Dr. Craven kept a minute diary of his attendance on Mr. Davis,[3] noting down in it his physical condition, the effects of different therapeutic agents, & also the conversations of the prisoner on all subjects of public interest.

He (the Doctor) is a gentleman of rare & high intelligence, eminent as a scientific man amongst the most eminent, and an old & active member of the Republican party—I believe—So that his evidence in the case will be less likely to be impugned.

These conversations, from such brief disclosures of their contents as I have had, are of absorbing importance, and could not but modify the rampant passions and hatreds on which such men as Sumner and Stevens make their trade. In my judgment their disclosure would make the most powerful campaign-document ever issued in this country—a document that could not but abate the fanaticism of the radicals (meaning such of them as do not follow that "ism" for a living,) & strengthen & rally the conservative opinion of the country to your increased support.

Dr. Craven has as yet but spoken on this subject to two persons—to Gen Grant who appeared curious & asked for information; and to myself with whom former intimacy has accustomed him to consult.

Gen. Grant declared the doctor's disclosures of absorbing interest, and begged him to refrain from giving them the slightest publicity at present, adding that "only to the President and himself should such matters be revealed." *Perhaps* the Lieut. Gen. has conversed with you on this point; & if so my labors are thrown away.

If not, I think you might with profit give Surg. Craven an audience, in order to judge for yourself & with your larger experience what wd. be the probable effect of his disclosures, if published, on the general mind. Mr. Davis formed for him the tenderest & even most pathetic attachment during the time he was Craven's patient; and the doctor's chief wish at present is to be given an opportunity of visiting Fort Monroe & calling on Mr. Davis—a not unnatural wish to the former medical attendant of so eminent a person.

General Miles, commanding the fort, as you are doubtless aware, is "a Boston boy" par excellence—the special pet & protegè of Senators Sumner and Wilson, Gen. Butler, Gov. Andrew and so forth; and that some of the facilities furnished by his position in regard to Mr. Davis will be converted by his friends into political capital for next November and further on, there can be no doubt.

I write this believing Dr. Craven's disclosures might be of public service, though perhaps not helpful to some of the military authorities. He as yet has only spoken of them to Gen. Grant & myself; and I shall never mention to any one save yourself, or by your orders, what general views he has given me.

Should you desire to see him, or should you think his request for liberty to visit his former patient reasonable & grant it,—he would either go on to Washn. at once, or visit Fortress Monroe, as you might be pleased to indicate.[4]

Pardon the roughness & haste of this letter. I intended this as a draft & to copy it; but time presses on me & the matter seems urgent.

Chas. G. Halpine

LS, DLC-JP.

1. An Irish immigrant, Halpine (1829–1868) wrote for several New York City and Boston newspapers, before joining the 69th N.Y. Inf., serving as a staff officer for Generals Dix and David Hunter and gaining renown as a wartime journalist under the pseudonym of "Miles O'Reilly." Soon after the war Halpine became editor of the *Citizen*, a reform organ for New York Democrats. *DAB*; Hunt and Brown, *Brigadier Generals*; Edward K. Eckert, *"Fiction Distorting Fact"* (Macon, 1987), xliv.

2. A former telegraph construction worker and California "forty-niner" who taught himself medicine, Craven (1822–1893), as medical director of the Department of the South, had met Halpine while both were stationed on the Sea Islands. In March 1867 Johnson appointed him as postmaster of his native Newark, New Jersey, but the Senate rejected Craven's nomination. Ibid.; *DAB*; Ser. 6B, Vol. 4: 75, Johnson Papers, LC.

3. Spanning from May to December 1865, the daily account formed the basis of Craven's unauthorized and controversial book, *Prison Life of Jefferson Davis*, ghostwritten and grossly fabricated by Halpine, which first appeared in print in June 1866. William Hanchett, *Irish: Charles G. Halpine in Civil War America* (Syracuse, 1970), 144–50; Eckert, *"Fiction Distorting Fact"*, xlii.

4. There is no evidence that Johnson ever conferred personally with Craven nor does there seem to be any substantiation of the claim that the President was "decidedly interested" in the scheme, as one of Halpine's biographers has suggested. Hanchett, *Halpine*, 144.

From George B. McClellan[1]

Personal

Dresden [Saxony]   March 20 1866

Sir:

I am confident that you will receive, in the same spirit as that by which I am actuated in addressing you, my sincere congratulations upon the course you have seen fit to pursue in regard to the vital questions now at issue in America.

I believe that you will succeed in effecting a real and durable reconstruction of the Union, for I cannot doubt that the great mass of the people will sustain you in the appeal you have made to them. But, whether you succeed or fail, you have earned the everlasting gratitude of those who love their country for the manly & statesmanlike attitude you have assumed in defence of the Constitution, the welfare, the very existence of the Nation.

The gratitude which I, in common with every true patriot, feel towards you will not permit me to be silent at such a juncture as the present, and I trust, Mr. President, that you will not deem me intrusive in thus expressing to you the gratification I have derived from your policy, the satisfaction it affords me to observe how well it is appreciated by intelligent Europeans, and my earnest wishes for your complete and early success in the restoration of the Union.

With the firm conviction that the blessing of God will attend your labours in behalf of the country, and with the hope that He will long preserve a life so valuable to the Nation. . . .

Geo B McClellan

ALS, DLC-JP.
1. The letter was enclosed in Reverdy Johnson to Johnson, Apr. 5, 1866, Johnson Papers, LC.

To Sam Milligan

Washington, D.C., Mch. 20th 1866

Do you feel at liberty to make any recommendation in the case of McCann?[1] There is a strong pressure here for his release by the Military authorities.[2] Has the case been disposed of by the Court? Please answer by telegraph.[3]

Andrew Johnson.

Tel, DNA-RG107, Tels. Sent, President, Vol. 3 (1865–68).
1. J. Richard McCann and three other ex-Confederate officers had been incarcerated in Knoxville for some time on charges of murder, stemming from the late 1861 execution of three East Tennessee bridge-burners. The trial did not finally get underway until June 1866. See William G. Brownlow to Johnson, June 25, 1865, *Johnson Papers*, 8: 287–88.

2. As early as December 1865 the prisoners wrote to Stanton concerning their situation; and on March 10 General Grant endorsed their letter with the "recommendation that the prisoners J. R. McCann, W. C. Kain and Reuben Rodie be unconditionally released." These stirrings are perhaps the "strong pressure" that Johnson mentioned. The following month, on April 16, McCann, Kain, and Roddie wrote to Grant in reference to his recommendation of March 10; they noted in particular Governor Brownlow's refusal to comply with Stanton's request for their release and therefore their continuing imprisonment in Knoxville. Once again they entreated Grant's intervention with the President. See Simon, *Grant Papers*, 16: 490–91. For a convenient reprinting of the Stanton to Brownlow, Mar. 27, 1866, and the Brownlow to Stanton, Apr. 6, 1866, letters *re* the McCann, Kain, and Roddie case, see the *Chicago Tribune*, Apr. 11, 1866.

3. Milligan responded immediately to indicate that he had not heard of McCann's trial and to testify that McCann "may be a bad man but good faith and respect to belligerant rights justify his discharge." As noted earlier, McCann was put on trial in June; apparently the President did not intervene in the matter. Sam Milligan to Johnson, Mar. 22, 1866, Johnson Papers, LC. See J. Richard McCann et al. to Johnson, June 20, 1866.

From James C. Moses[1]

Knoxville, Tennessee, March 20th, 1866.

I take the liberty of addressing you on a subject of interest to myself and family, though possessed of but little for any one else.

My son, Frank A. Moses,[2] was a private in the Confederate services 63d Reg't Tennessee Infantry. He was paroled at the time of Lee's surrender, returned home, applied to take the Amnesty Oath, but at that particular juncture there was no one here who would administer it. He took the oath of allegiance administered by the military authorities, in its stead,[3] and as soon as the Federal Court appointed Col. Heiskell its Commissioner, he took the Oath of Amnesty.[4] In the meantime, however, he was indicted for Treason, which places him among the excepted classes, as is understood here.

There are no *Special Charges* against him—he has no personal enemies—in fact, he is a mere lad, and was at College, when through the influence probably of his Professor, Capt. Blair,[5] since deceased, he was induced to join Blair's Company.

He has made two applications for Pardon—one of them recommended by Rev. T. W Humes, Thos. A.R. Nelson, Wm. Heiskell & others[6]—to any of whom I would refer you for my character and standing, if you shall have forgotten me yourself. The other was endorsed by Governor Brownlow, and forwarded by him from Nashville to the State Department at Washington city, some months ago.[7]

From neither of these applications have we heard, nor can we hear, though repeated efforts have been made to ascertain what has become of them.

Will you do me the favor to grant the petition, if not inconsistent with duty?

My son is detained here, when I should have had him elsewhere. The suit is still pending in his as in other similar cases. His personal attendance is required at the sittings of the Court,—lawyers fees, witness fees, and other expenses accumulate unnecessarily,—and I trust by the interposition of your clemency the lad may be relieved from further anxiety annoyance and suspense.[9]

Excuse the liberty I have taken in thus addressing you, in behalf of my son.

I would refer you to Col. Jno. Williams, Hon N. G Taylor, Rev. Thos W Humes, Col. Wm. Heiskell, F. S. Heiskell, G. M. Hazen, A. G. Jackson,[10] Col Jno Netherland, or O P Temple, for information as to myself.

I cannot refrain from saying in conclusion that your humane and magnanimous and wise policy for the restoration of the National authority throughout the land is almost unanimously approved here.

Jas. C. Moses

ALS, DNA-RG94, Amnesty Papers (M1003, Roll 50), Tenn., Frank A. Moses.

1. Moses (1818–1870), a native of New Hampshire, moved to Knoxville to enter the newspaper business, first as a printer, and then in the 1840s as owner and editor of the *Knoxville Times* and the *Knoxville Register*. Afterwards, he became involved in the hardware business. He served on the boards of both the Tennessee School for the Deaf and East Tennessee University. Rothrock, *French Broad-Holston Country*, 460–61.

2. After military service in the Confederate army, Moses (1845–1918) completed his education at East Tennessee University and entered the hardware and banking business in Knoxville. He served in the 1870s as a member of the board of railroad tax assessors and subsequently from 1891 until death as a member of the state board of pensions. *Knoxville Journal and Tribune*, May 10, 1918; *Con Vet*, 26 (1918): 364.

3. According to documents in Moses' amnesty files, he took the oath of allegiance at the office of the provost marshal in Knoxville on May 3, 1865. Amnesty Papers (M1003, Roll 50), Tenn., Frank A. Moses, RG94, NA.

4. Moses took the oath before William Heiskell on June 19, 1865. Ibid.

5. Alexander A. Blair (1829–1865) was an ordained Presbyterian clergyman who taught chemistry and natural history at East Tennessee University before resigning in 1862 to become a captain in the Confederate army. In the closing weeks of the war it was recommended that Blair be appointed chaplain. E. C. Scott, comp., *Ministerial Directory of the Presbyterian Church, U.S., 1861–1941* (Austin, 1942), 60; Stanley J. Folmsbee, "East Tennessee University, 1840–1879," The University of Tennessee *Record*, 62 (1959): 29n, 45; CSR, A. A. Blair, RG109, NA.

6. Moses' first request for pardon was a letter to Johnson, June 19, 1865, which was endorsed by a number of prominent citizens from the Knoxville area. Thomas W. Humes (1815–1892) was an Episcopal priest who served as rector of St. John's in Knoxville, beginning in the 1840s and continuing until the end of the 1860s. In 1865 he accepted the presidency of East Tennessee University, a post which he held until his resignation in 1883. *DAB*; Amnesty Papers (M1003, Roll 50), Tenn., Frank A. Moses, RG94, NA.

7. On November 4 Brownlow endorsed Moses' request for pardon and forwarded the document to Washington, where it was received a few days later. Ibid.

8. According to one of the cover sheets in Moses' file, he was pardoned on November 13, 1865. This pardon date is also given in *House Ex. Docs.*, 39 Cong., 2 Sess., No. 116, p. 45 (Ser. 1293). For some unknown reason, notification of this pardon did not reach Moses.

9. Although on March 31 the President requested that a pardon be issued to Moses, it apparently was delayed until April 10, 1866; but then this second pardon was forwarded to him. Amnesty Papers (M1003, Roll 50), Tenn., Frank A. Moses, RG94, NA.

10. Gideon M. Hazen (1810–1880) served on Knoxville's board of aldermen in the 1830s and 1840s and was a well-known businessman, particularly for his operation of the Middlebrook Paper Mills. Abner G. Jackson (1807–1869) was a businessman who dealt in mercantile goods and also agricultural implements. Knoxville directories (1859–69); Lucile Deaderick, ed., *Heart of the Valley: A History of Knoxville, Tennessee* (Knoxville,

1976), 636–37; WPA, Knox County Tennessee Tombstone Records Old Gray Cemetery (Apr. 22, 1938), 14, 120; *Knoxville Chronicle*, Jan. 18, 1880; *Knoxville Press and Herald*, Dec. 15, 1869.

From John B. Haskin[1]

Fordham, Westchester Co. N.Y.
March 21, 1866.

Dear Sir—

I have just read in the New York Herald an extract from the London Times[2] commending your 22d of February speech, and I am impelled to offer you my congratulations upon the fact that your course has been so straight forward and your patriotism so plain, as to compel even the praise of the selfish organ of the British government. I have never troubled you heretofore and shall not trouble you hereafter with any personal applications, and I feel therefore that I can speak frankly without fear of my motives being misund stood. The Constitutional statesmanship with which you have administered the government, has won my admiration. I have watched the development of your policy with anxiety and I have not been disappointed by any of your acts. If I know myself, I have no wish other than my country's good and by this standard I have measured you. When I saw that it was your design to admit the Southern states to full fellowship in the Union at as early a day as possible, and thus to restore peace and harmony to the country, I feared and felt that you would not have the support of those who controlled the organization which elected you. Actuated by this feeling, as Chairman of the Committee on Resolutions, in the Democratic state Convention in this state last fall, I made a platform upon which the Conservative union men of the state would have rallied to your support, had the Republican state convention held soon after, avowed the hostility, which its leaders have since developed against your policy. But those leaders gave you the Judas kiss. They were then ardent in support of your Administration and loud in their denunciations of the "Copperhead" Democracy and they deceived the masses. My attempt to organize a successful party in your behalf failed. Events have since proved that something must be done to rescue the country from the hands of the radicals in Congress, and I know of no way but by the organization of a party in support of your Administration which will assuredly become the party of the people. Sometime ago I wrote you suggesting delay in the appointment of a Collector for this port,[3] and I think the necessity for such delay still continues. You know the political power attached to the office and the importance of keeping it out of the hands of those who are either openly or secretly antagonizing you, or at best are but lukewarm friends. The man who holds that office should be bound to *you* by "hooks of steel." I would not take the liberty of naming any one, but as I write the thought occurs to me that it would be poetic justice if Major General Henry W. Slocum should yet occupy the position.[4]

Among the first to strike with an armed hand at rebellion he returned home only at the close of the war. He forgot politics as you did when treason showed its head, and no taint of the "Copperhead" attaches to him. Foreseeing the attempt that would be made to overthrow your labors for the union, he joined hands with the Union loving Democrats of the state who were trying to raise the old flag in your support and became their standard bearer. It was through no fault of his that we failed. The bad management of John Van Buren and other rotten timber, of which the organization could not rid itself, had something to do with our defeat but the deceit and "false pretences" of the Republican leaders in claiming to be the particular and trusted supporters of your policy had more to do with it. The people now see how their confidence was abused and an election tomorrow would, I believe, give Gen. Slocum an overwhelming majority in the state. His appointment as Collector would be a proper rebuke of the treachery of the Republican leaders. It is time that the handwriting should appear on the wall to these Radicals. Even now they are stealing your strength in the different state elections. Fighting you in Congress they dare not carry the question before the people but rely on your neutrality and still make their fight against the "Copperhead" Democracy. Each victory is a victory for Congress and a defeat for you. They make the Canvass and they claim the glory. I hope the time will soon come when like Jackson you will have a party as well as a policy and when you will show the world that those who are not for you are against you and must suffer the consequences.

John B Haskin.

LS, DLC-JP.

1. Enclosed in Haskin to Robert Johnson, Mar. 22, 1866, "with the anxious hope" that the President "*will read* my letter." Johnson Papers, LC.

2. The *Times's* editorial was dated March 8. *New York Herald*, Mar. 21, 1866.

3. Not found, but his letter recommending Moses F. Odell for the same post has been located. Haskin to Johnson, Nov. 15, 1865, Appts., Customs Service, Collector, New York City, Moses F. Odell, RG56, NA.

4. Slocum, who had resigned from the army on September 28, 1865, was not Johnson's choice for collector, but he was nominated to replace Moses Odell as naval officer after John A. Dix declined serving. The Senate, however, rejected Slocum in March 1867, as well as three others subsequently appointed by Johnson, and the position continued to be held by Odell's former deputy, Cornell S. Franklin, when Grant took office. Powell, *Army List*, 590; *BDAC*; Ser. 6B, Vol. 4: 49, 54–58, Johnson Papers, LC; Hendrick B. Wright to Johnson, Aug. 14, 1866, Appts., Customs Service, Naval Officer, New York City, Henry W. Slocum, RG56, NA; Hugh McCulloch to Johnson, Mar. 27, 1867, Lets. Sent *re* Customs Service Employees (QC Ser.), Vol. 6, RG56, NA; *U.S. Off. Reg.* (1867–69). See Abel R. Corbin to Johnson, June 25, 1866.

From Russell Houston

Louisville   March 21, 1866

My Dear Friend—

This letter will be handed to you by our friend Capt. Shirley[1] of this City, who has spent the last four months in Texas & who is better posted

as to the condition of affairs in that state than any one you will probably meet. On the question of the negro he is free from all prejudice, as
Attorney General Speed, well knows: & as to the working of the *Bureau* &
its effect upon black & white he will be able to give you much information. He is the precise character of man, to be examined by the "Reconstruction Committee." Cannot Mr. Doolittle, Morgan or Harris,[2]
have it done? The *expressed* design of the Committee is fairness & impar-
tiality, & the testimony of such a man as Capt Shirley is worth that of
scores of Bureau Agents. He was four months with & in the midst of the
people & is authorized to speak from his knowledge of the *people* & not by
hearing only a half dozen idle persons speak for & pretend to represent
whole communities.

I have seen many good people here since my return—have conversed

   It does not seem to me that our friends have yet taken the true view of
the matter. An expressed dislike of classes of Northern people by the
South, or the failure by the South to express a love for the North, the "Old
Flag" & the Yankees generally seem to be conceded as sufficient grounds
for the charge of disloyalty. This is not the true issue. But the real fact to
be ascertained, is whether the people of the South are disposed to submit,
& to submit to the authority of the Constitution & laws of the United
States & intend to obey & are obeying the same. It is not a question of
love, but of obedience. And if the South were to profess an affection for
the northern people or the Flag of the United States, I should deem it
unnatural & therefore not to be believed. All the loyalty that we can now
ask, is obedience, in good faith, to law & this we now have. The good
wishes are to be won by good treatment. We never will be able to win the
affections of our fellow citizens of the South, by Act of Congress. As well
might we expect to win & secure the love of husband & wife or of parents
& child by legislative enactment. The "Re-construction Committee" will
never devise a law that will or can change the order of nature.

   I have seen many good people here since my return—have conversed
with many & made many enquiries as to the State of feeling generally & I
have heard of no man worthy of the name who is not your friend & the
advocate of your political measures.

   As soon as it is possible for you to do so, with safety to *all the points*,
you ought to dispense with the "Bureau" to the extent of your lawful
authority.

   Although its workings have created a good deal of disturbance, yet I
am not prepared to say that the good has not predominated. It is a poor
invention at best, & it has been so badly managed by the "Assistants,"
that you need not be at all surprised to find, in a few months, that it is a
very unpopular "institution" with a majority of the negroes themselves. I
think it is even now so with the *respectable & well raised* negroes of the
South; & this is quite natural. They never go to it nor near it. They feel
that the white race is obliged to predominate in this Country—that they
(the negroes) are obliged to live here & be supported by the employment

furnished to them by the predominent race & they wish to be on good terms with them; & in this they are wise. I believe that if a fair expression of the opinion of the negroes of the South could be ascertained, it would be found that three fourths of them are in favor of the withdrawal of the Freedman's Bureau. And I think, further, that all the cases, (with very rare exceptions) that come before the Agents of the Bureau are of the lowest & most worthless class of negroes, & the Agents are not much better. Would it not surprise our radical friends, to find, before long, accounts of large & enthusiastic meetings of their colored friends in the South, asking a withdrawal of the Bureau?

But I return to the original purpose of this letter, which is, to suggest the propriety of having Capt. Shirley's testimony taken before the Committee of Fifteen.[3]

Russell Houston

ALS, DLC-JP.
1. Zachary M. Sherley (1811–1879) was a well known and successful entrepreneur in the steamship business, operating several lines on the Ohio River and elsewhere. During the war he helped provide transportation for Union troops. *Ohio Falls Cities*, 1: 496k-m.
2. James Doolittle, Edwin D. Morgan, and Ira Harris.
3. There is no evidence to suggest that Sherley gave testimony before the Joint Committee on Reconstruction.

From George Howland[1]

Providence R.I.   March 21, 66

Sir,

I enclose you a hurriedly written synopsis of a part of my address to the state democratic Convention this day at 4. P.M.[2] We passed resolutions sustaining your policy, but made no nominations for a state ticket, which I was sorry for, and did all I could to effect. But the S. P. Chase Sprague[3] money I am sorry to say was the cause and Burnside and the radical Conventions nominations will be carried without opposition.[4] I well remember that 13 of us only voted for Genl. Jackson at first in Newport and we were hooted at evry corner of the streets, but in the two succeeding campains we put him in by an overwhelming majority. We are crouched down now by the money power, of Sprague and Senator Anthony[5] and his clique are under its influence and making inroads upon the democratic leaders, which prevented a nomination of state officers, so I suppose the other party will try to make it appear they elected Burnside unanimously throughout the state, the democratic party voting for him, but be not deceived, no true democrat will vote for him. We yet keep up an organization, and are yet again destined to go with the majority of the democratic states in our next presidential campain.

Pleas excuse the presumption of an old sailor thus addressing you. I love my *whole* Country, and though born in Rhode Island I fought throughout the war of 1812 under Com Joshua Barney in his Flotilla on the Chesepeak at the Pawtuxent, Bladensburg and Baltimore,[6] and hope you may favor our pension bill[7] so long before Congress, as there are but few of the veterans of that war left and their average ages is 75. I am 70, and yet hale and hearty, and if any chance offers hope you may remember me for the collectorship of Newport in place of the present radical incumbent[8] I can be highly recommended and though a poor old Shipmaster my brothers[9] are wealthy and would give bonds for me.

George Howland of Newport.

ALS, DLC-JP.

1. Howland (c1796–fl1870) was probably the same "Retired Sea Captain" whose total estate was assessed at nearly $10,000 in 1870. 1870 Census, R.I., Newport, 3rd Ward, Newport, 12.

2. His proposed speech, dated March 21, is enclosed. For a report of the convention which was attended by about one hundred delegates, see New York Herald, Mar. 22, 1866.

3. Rhode Island's war governor and former aide to Gen. Ambrose E. Burnside, as well as a Democratic senator (1863–75), William Sprague (1830–1915) was also Salmon P. Chase's son-in-law and a textile entrepreneur. DAB.

4. Nominated during the convention held at Providence on the previous day, Burnside soundly defeated his Democratic rival in the April election. American Annual Cyclopaedia (1866), 670; New York Herald, Mar. 21, 1866.

5. Henry B. Anthony.

6. While in Newport during the summer of 1813, Captain Barney (1759–1818) was summoned to Washington to assume command of a flotilla of barge-gunboats at Baltimore in an attempt to block a suspected British advance up Chesapeake Bay. In June 1814 Barney's forces succeeded in repulsing the British near the mouth of the Patuxent River, but on August 24, at the Battle of Bladensburg, Barney's sailors and marines were routed. DAB; Mary Barney, ed., A Biographical Memoir of the Late Commodore Joshua Barney (Boston, 1832), 253; John K. Mahon, The War of 1812 (Gainesville, 1972), 289–90, 299–301; Donald R. Hickey, The War of 1812: A Forgotten Conflict (Urbana, 1989), 197–98.

7. Invalid pensions had been awarded to disabled veterans of the War of 1812 as early as 1816, but an 1858 House measure granting service pensions to all veterans of the second war with Great Britain had failed in the Senate, despite Johnson's support. When Howland wrote, there were two separate pension bills being considered by Congress, but no such federal entitlement was approved and signed into law until February 1871. William H. Glasson, Federal Military Pensions in the United States (New York, 1918), 108–9; House Journal, 39 Cong., 1 Sess., pp. 13, 122, 823, 928, 958–60 (Ser. 1243); Johnson to Robert Johnson, Dec. 23, 1858; Samuel Rhea to Johnson, Apr. 13, 1859, Johnson Papers, 3: 203, 271.

8. Appointed in 1861 and recently reappointed by Johnson, Seth W. Macy (c1804–fl1875) continued serving as collector of customs at Newport at least through September 1875. U.S. Off. Reg. (1861–75); Ser. 6B, Vol. 4: 37, Johnson Papers, LC; 1870 Census, R.I., Newport, 4th Ward, Newport, 14.

9. Probably Benjamin B. Howland (1787–1877), who served as city clerk of Newport for fifty years, and perhaps John B. Howland (c1804–fl1870), a farmer. 1870 Census, R.I., Newport, Little Compton, 8; Thomas W. Bicknell, The History of the State of Rhode Island and Providence Plantations (5 vols., New York, 1920), 4: 23–24.

From Lucius P. Walker[1]

Louisville, Ky, Mar 21st 1866.

Hon. Sir.

I write to solicit your attention to the familiar institution in this state called the Freedman's Bureau, which of late, has been conducted very badly, and which will not be improved unless some action is taken on the subject by Congress, or by yourself. In the first place I will state to you that I am a New Yorker, have served in the Union Army, and am a friend of the negro. I believe something is necessary to be done to protect freedman from abuse, but I also think that the white man should be cared for also. The agents of the Bureau in this city will take a negro's oath before they will a number of white men's affidavit.

An example of this kind occurred the other day, when a colored groom claimed to have been in the service of his employer three months, when he had only been in service for about two weeks. He demanded pay for three months, & on the refusal of his employer to pay for that length of time, went to the agent of the Bureau, who had the white man arrested & on the statement of the negro, compelled him to pay for three months service, although a large number of respectable white people testified that the groom had served but two weeks. I would respectfully call your attention to this subject, & although I can not expect the "Bureau" in this state to be abolished, still I would like to see a white man's word, taken as soon as a darkey's.

Hoping that you will take measures to mitigate this evil as soon as convenient. . . .

L. P. Walker.

ALS, DLC-JP.
1. Walker (c1848–fl1872) was involved in the newspaper advertisement business in Louisville. 1870 Census, Ky., Jefferson, Louisville, 8th Ward, 69; Louisville directories (1866–72).

From Edward R. Chase

Austin Nevada   March 22 1866

Sir

The entire federal patronage of this state is in the hands of your enemies. The masses here I know to be your friends; they will scarcely remain so if the patronage continues to be used against them. Stewart[1] is incapable of keeping faith with a straight forward man. He is an Intriguant, dangerous and unprincipled. He possesses great powers for mischief.

Hon. A C Bradford[2] the first Democratic candidate for Congress, is now somewhere in the East, dealing in mining claims. He would be eminently fit to advise with in relation to Nevada Matters; he is able loyal & candid.

I have no axes to grind and only desire to serve your interests.

E R Chase

ALS, DLC-JP.
1. William M. Stewart (1827–1909), migrant to California during the gold rush, put his early mining and legal experience to work as a specialist in mining litigation first in California, where he also served as state attorney general in 1854, and then in Virginia City,

Nevada, beginning in 1860. Deeply involved in Nevada politics and representing major banking and mining interests, Stewart served as U.S. senator (1864–75, 1887–1905). *BDAC; DAB*.

2. In 1864 A. C. Bradford was defeated for congressional delegate by Independent Union party candidate John Cradlebaugh, who won by 65 votes. Since Nevada became a state in 1864, this vote was nullified and Bradford ran for congressman. He lost again. Hubert H. Bancroft, *History of California. Vol. 6: 1848–1859* (San Francisco, 1888), 675, 682; *History of Nevada With Illustrations and Biographical Sketches of Prominent Men and Pioneers* (Oakland, 1881), 86–87.

From Jacob D. Cox

Columbus, O.   22 March 1866.

My dear Sir:

I trust I am not mistaken in assuming that you will not regard it an impertinence if I endeavor to give you, as clearly & briefly as I can, the judgment my own mind has formed of the general tone of sentiment amongst our western Union men in regard to the present juncture in public affairs, and especially in reference to the "civil rights bill" recently passed by Congress. I desire to be as far as possible from obtruding upon you my opinions, unasked, but your kindness & cordiality in my personal interviews with you have made me think you would not take amiss an attempt to lay before you the appearance of things as viewed from this standpoint. If honestly and frankly given, such views must assist in some degree in forming one's own conclusions, and I trust I need not assure you that whether you agree or disagree with me, the cordial friendliness of my own attitude toward yourself & your administration will not be changed.

The characteristic of our western loyal people which it is most difficult to deal with just now is a sensitive jealousy lest in some way the advantages of the war should be lost by mistaken statesmanship. Not having the responsibilities of government directly upon them, even our intelligent people fail in great measure to appreciate the wisdom and necessity of handling the Southern States kindly as well as firmly, and of smoothing down difference & avoiding exasperating measures. Men who have hated and fought rebels as you and I have done, can understand this feeling, and if we ourselves see the propriety of refusing to let this hatred be the ruling principle in establishing a policy of restoration, we can still feel kindly toward & sympathize with the intense loyalty of the masses of our people which makes even their error appear an excess of patriotism.

I think therefore that it is wise to conciliate this loyal spirit, wherever it can be done without a plain sacrifice of principle. I feel this the more deeply, because since my return from Washington I have been impressed with the belief that the leaders of the Democracy are hypocritical in their pretense of supporting your policy. In their private & more unguarded talk, and in many of their newspapers, they show that they are acting on the policy of applauding everything which is a diminution of the extreme

radical programme, but the *principle* on which they do it, is that the war
& Everything pertaining to it was illegal & wrong and they condemn as
fiercely and sweepingly as ever all that we have done hitherto in support
of the government. They show no disposition here to abandon their organization as a party, and I am convinced that we shall get no help from
them except as we convert *individuals* of their party & bring them into an
organization of which the bulk must be our true & loyal union men.

This outline sketch of the condition of the people and of parties seemed
to me necessary to explain the attitude of the people in reference to the
civil rights bill. Few people have read it through. They judge of it by
synopses of its provisions which have been published very briefly in the
country papers. They fasten their minds upon the fact that the bill declares that the freedmen shall have the same rights of property and person, the same remedies for injuries received & the same penalties for
wrongs committed, as other men. This they approve, and they know that
you and I and all true Union men have constantly desired this result.
They do not look much at the means employed to enforce the provisions
of the bill—they do not care much about or very well understand them.
In fact, the prevailing *mood*, as I have above indicated, rather inclines
them to be pleased with Everything which looks like severity.

Under these circumstances, and especially in view of the fact that the
persistent efforts which have been made by the extremists to create distrust of your motives and intentions are recoiling, and Every day add to
the strength of your position before the country, I believe it will be well to
sustain a point in order to meet the popular spirit and impulse rather than
to make a strict construction of duty the other way.

My own view of the negro problem has been & still is, that *ultimately* it
will be found that the separation of the races will become a necessity; but
as no one can tell how long it will take the natural causes which are at
work to bring about that result, I recognize the necessity and propriety in
the meantime of giving to the freedmen a large measure of kindness and
protection, rather than in any way to stint the justice they have a right to
expect.

The provisions for enforcing this civil rights bill, are many of them objectionable, but they are *civil* provisions, under the checks of civil law &
legal responsibility, and are not the unrestrained despotism of military
power which was embodied in the Freedmans bureau bill. It must be executed by the ordinary judicial & executive officers of the United States
Courts, appointed by yourself, resident among the people of whom they
will be a part and whose public sentiment will surely modify their own
disposition to be arrogant or tyrannical in its enforcement.

If the Southern people will act upon the motives you have heretofore
presented to them, and do right themselves, by legislation of their own
which shall break down the distinctions between classes in the matters
specified in the bill, as I hope they will do, the law itself would become
of little practical moment, for cases under it could rarely arise, and a

very short time would make it practically a dead letter—not because the rights of the blacks would be disregarded, but because they would be respected by the community and protected by the State Courts. In this case it would prove a mere tub to the radical whale. The clause giving exclusive jurisdiction to the U.S. Courts applies only, (as I read it) to cases where it is violated "under color of any law, statute, or ordinance, regulation or custom." If then the Southern legislature will remove such laws, statutes, ordinances &c (as I hope we shall persuade them to do), I should not fear any troublesome conflict of jurisdictions. The *bark* of the law would, I think, be infinitely worse than its *bite*, and it seems to me that sensible Southerners could easily be brought to see this, and to see further that in yielding to this measure, all conservative Union men at the North would gain vantage ground with the people which will make us far more powerful for good in other matters & other directions. I sincerely believe that if you can find it in accordance with your sense of duty to sign the bill, it will with our Western people make you fully master of the situation, & remove the possibility of any such opposition in the Union ranks on other measures as would prove at all embarrassing to your administration. For similar reasons I believe it would assist us greatly in holding together our State organizations, but this is a consideration I would not feel like urging upon you.

My own views of Executive responsibility for bills signed is that signature by no means implies full assent to a measure, but only that its objectionable features are not so gross and so necessarily injurious as to make it an executive *duty* to interpose. On my theory therefore a bill could be signed which was not regarded as wise in *any* respect, provided it was not regarded certain to work great & real mischief.

I have thus, my dear Sir, given my thoughts as freely as if spoken to myself, and I have mistaken the frankness of your own character, if you do not receive them kindly. I should not have said a word, had I not believed you would wish to know honestly & exactly how these public matters strike those who are the true friends of your administration. Whatever be your conclusions I shall have great faith that they are wiser than mine, and shall only claim the credit of being sincerely and disinterestedly desirous of being of real service to you.

J. D. Cox

ALS, DLC-JP.

From Ulysses S. Grant

Washington, D.C., March 22d 1866.

I would respectfully recommend the release, on parole, of D. L. Yulee,[1] late of the United States Senate. I make this recommendation on the supposition that no special charges have been made against him.

In making this recommendation I would give it as my opinion that no good is to be accomplished by confinement, without trial, or at least the prospect of a trial, and legal conviction, of conspirators against the Government, who are not directly charged with heinous offences, or with holding positions of great power or influence in the rebellion.

Mr. Yulee has already been long confined. I would urge this in his behalf unless, as before stated, charges exist against him of which I know nothing.[2]

sd   U. S. Grant
Lieutenant General.

LS, DNA-RG94, Lets. Recd. (Main Ser.), File W-210-1866, (M619, Roll 525).
1. David L. Yulee, a political prisoner incarcerated in Fort Pulaski, Georgia, since June 1865.
2. In addition to Grant, Senator-elect William Marvin and other prominent Floridians appealed to Johnson for Yulee's parole from prison. The President endorsed Grant's letter: "Referred to the Secretary of War for consideration and action. Andrew Johnson." Later in the day, on March 22, Stanton directed that Yulee be released from custody upon giving his parole of honor to go to Florida and remain there until further orders. Apparently owing to problems in the telegraph line between Washington and Augusta, a second wire had to be sent before Yulee was actually released on or about March 27. Less than two weeks later Johnson extended the limits of Yulee's parole, permitting him to travel outside of Florida. William Marvin et al. to Johnson, Mar. 11, 1866, Amnesty Papers (M1003, Roll 15), Fla., D. L. Yulee, RG94, NA; Edward D. Townsend to John M. Brannan, Mar. 22, 1866, Lets. Recd. (Main Ser.), File W-210-1866, (M619, Roll 525), RG94, NA; Townsend to Brannan, Mar. 25, Apr. 7, 1866, Tels. Sent, Sec. of War (M473, Roll 90), RG107, NA; *National Intelligencer*, Apr. 5, 1866.

From Alvin P. Hovey

Legation of The United States
Lima, March 22d. 1866.

Sir:

I have read, with great pleasure, your speeches announcing your policy of reconstruction. Situated at a great distance from the scene of Political action, I look down on the contest now raging in The States with an impartial eye.

The day was, when, fighting Rebels, South and North, that I felt as bitter and radical as the most radical of the Stevens party. But, now, when I calmly and dispassionately view the condition of affairs at home, I am thankful that the reins of Government are in the hands of one, who fully comprehends the issue, and knows by long experience in the South what the best destinies of our Government demand.

The fault of The Radicals is, that many of them are merely honest abstractionists, who are really ignorant of the true condition of the Black Man in the South. If Sumner, or Stevens, could live in their midst three months, many of their fine theories and abstractions would melt into thin air. Grant to the radical party their full requests, and in less than four years, a war of races would inevitably follow. Black men, both Negroes and Indians deserve our commiseration, but, the philanthropy of the Radicals would prove, "Such Protection as Vultures give to lambs,—covering, but devouring them."[1]

I assure you that the Americans here, many of whom are intelligent and well posted in the history and policy of our Government, view your course with sincere and strong approval.

The admixture of races is a problem solved in South America, and, I trust that the good sense of the people of the United States will shun the rocks which have all but wrecked these Republics. In my opinion, the separation of the Races is the most desirable of all results. Even though it cost a sum equal to the national debt incurred by the late rebellion, the money would be well spent. Man, cannot do by his wisdom, that which God's providence never designed. You cannot mix oil and water nor break down the barriers of Nature between the Black man and the Caucassian. Thad. Stevens may try it either by theory or practise and he will find all his labors (or pleasures) result in—nothing!

I read Mr. Seward's speech with great satisfaction.[2] He is a statesman who can rise above the storms of the hour, and take a comprehensive view of the future of our Great nation. Depend upon it, you will triumph over your enemies, and the next Congress will leave the Stevens-Sumner party in a sad minority. Although, my antecedents, like yours, are Democratic, I have but *little, little—little*—faith in many of our old comrades and friends of the north. Do not trust that wing that fought against us, too far. They will betray you, as they attempted to betray our country. Do right as you have done, and a clear conscience, at least, if not a complete success will reward you. I believe in the sober second thought, and feel sure that your triumph is near at hand.

Alvin P. Hovey

LS, DLC-JP.
    1. From Richard B. Sheridan's *Pizarro*, act 2, sc. 2.
    2. Probably a reference to Seward's Washington's Birthday address. Van Deusen, *Seward*, 443–44.

From John Purcell[1]

Private

New Orleans, March 22, 1866.

Mr. President—

Your letter of the 21st January last,[2] was received by me just at the proper time. Its contents were hailed with delight by nearly all classes.

An election has been held for city officers, under the charter, and although *all* the parties elected are not such as we desired, still the tax payers and citizens are generally pleased with the result.

Gen. Canby has, I think, very properly suspended, John T. Monroe, Mayor elect, and J. O. Nixon,[3] an Alderman elect, for the present.

This suspension will have a salutary influence on a large class here. It is absolutely necessary to show them that we have a government magnanimous and forgiving to the penitent, but able and determined to punish the contumacious.[4]

John Purcell   La Senator.

ALS, DLC-JP.

1. A delegate to the 1864 Louisiana constitutional convention before his election to the state senate, Purcell (*c*1818–*fl*1887), a resident of New Orleans since about 1831, worked variously as a real estate agent, lumber dealer, street commissioner, attorney, and insurance inspector. Applying to Johnson in late March 1866 for a treasury post, he was not appointed. New Orleans directories (1857–87); McCrary, *Lincoln and Reconstruction*, 248; Purcell to Johnson, Mar. 29, 1866, Appts., Internal Revenue Service, Assessor, La., 1st Dist., RG56, NA.

2. Johnson, answering Purcell's letter of January 19, stated "that the military authorities will not interfere in any way with an election for city officer in New Orleans, which may take place in accordance with existing laws, or in conformity with regulations prescribed by the State Legislature, and which will insure the election of loyal men to the office referred to in your letter." Johnson to Purcell, Jan. 21, 1866, Johnson Papers, LC.

3. New Jersey native James O. Nixon (1822–1891) moved to New Orleans (*c*1840) and worked with an uncle in a clothing business. In 1854 Nixon bought the *New Orleans Crescent* and edited it (1854–61, 1865–69). As lieutenant colonel, 1st La. Cav., Nixon was captured in July 1863 and imprisoned until 1865. At two different times he was chairman of the New Orleans board of aldermen. Conrad, *La. Biography*.

4. Monroe and Nixon were suspended because General Canby believed that they required special pardons from Johnson. Monroe came under the tenth exception because he had left Union lines to go into the Confederacy (Monroe claimed Gen. Benjamin F. Butler had forced him to do so). The eleventh exception applied to Nixon because he had owned an interest in a privateer. Johnson directed that both men should continue to be suspended until they were pardoned, which occurred on April 26, 1866. Monroe resumed his office on May 15, 1866. *New Orleans Picayune*, Mar. 20, 1866; Edwin M. Stanton to E.R.S. Canby, Apr. 11, 1866, Tels. Sent, Sec. of War (M473, Roll 90), RG107, NA; Amnesty Papers (M1003, Rolls 28 and 29), La., John T. Monroe and J. O. Nixon, RG94, NA; Joseph G. Dawson, III, *Army Generals and Reconstruction: Louisiana, 1862–1877* (Baton Rouge, 1982), 32.

From Edgar Cowan

Senate Chamber   23" March 1866

Mr. President.

My Letters Show today that a very favorable change is going on in Penna. I am informed that we can carry the regular organisations in most of the localities in a month or So.

Don't hesitate for a moment to veto the "*Civil Rights Bill.*" To do otherwise will be fatal—and no argument will remain to us. They will then be able to claim power to do any thing—even to conferring the right of suffrage upon people of the States—negroes or any body.

Be careful to put it distinctly as a question of *power*—not of policy. Indeed it might be recommended to the States with propriety. In my State athiests are not allowed to testify[1]—and no one ever dreamt Congress could change our law.

Edgar Cowan

ALS, DLC-JP.
1. The same restriction applied to officeholders, who were required to believe in the "being of God and a future state of rewards and punishments." J. William Frost, *A Perfect Freedom: Religious Liberty in Pennsylvania* (Cambridge, 1990), 75, 77, 102.

From John C. Gaut

Nashville Tennessee   March 23d 1866

Dr Sir.

I have been a close observer of the political movements, and the public feeling and sentiments in the State of Tennessee. And it may be, that you at Washington, do not understand the sentiments of the people in this state, as well as we do. I have been twice to East Tennessee recently. Whatever interested partizans may say, I do know, that nearly the entire population of this state, cordially and sincerely endorse your policy and administration. And they will stand by you to the last. You may ask why it is that the radical majority in the legislature pursue the course they do? The answer is, that they are led on by those in the interest of Sumner Stevens & Co, to overthow you, and your policy, against the will and wish of the people whom they represent. If the Radicals of this state were to go before the people, they could not be elected to any office, in any county in the state. I do not believe that a radical could get fifty votes to the county in East Tennessee. They know that they are misrepresenting their constituents. History affords no parallel of such wanton disregard of the will and wishes; and such reckless disregard of the liberties of the people, as is now manifested by the dominent majority in the legislature, and those who control them. The great body of our people throughout the state are peacible, law abiding & loyal to the Government of the United states and can be trusted.

The great source of troubles and discontent in the state, is the Franchise Bill, as it is called, now pending before the legislature, which if passed puts the whole power of the state in the hands of the Governor and his Eighty four commissioners.[1] The Commissioners determine who shall vote and who shall not. There is no appeal. My belief is, that the Franchise Bill is pressed with such persistant pertinacity, to not only affect the next state elections, but the Presidential election of 1868. The Franchise bill violates the Bill of Rights & Constitution of the state, and also that provision of the Constitution of the United States, which declares that no state shall pass any Bill of Attainder, or *ex post facto* Law or Law impairing the obligation of contracts. The Franchise Bill is intended to take from all those who have voluntarily aided and abetted the rebelion, the right of Suffrage and the right to hold office, as a penalty and punishment for past offences. Those who have taken the oath of Amnesty and have been pardoned by the Government of the United States, and show by their conduct and votes that they are true to the U S government ought to be allowed the right of suffrage.

If they manifested a disposition to oppose your administration and policy, and to sustain Sumner, Stevens & Co, I doubt very much, if the new Franchise Bill would have been introduced. In this I may be in error. At no time during the history of the state, do I believe that there has been so much disposition in our people to yield implicit obediance to the laws of the land, as they now do. They see and acknowledge the errors of the past. Justice will be done to the Colored people as well as to the white race. And the Courts of justice are the proper forums for all. The *constitution*, the *Union* and the *enforcement* of the laws are what the people now most desire.

I sometimes almost dispair. But still I hope it will all come right in the end. Your veto of the Freedmens Bureau bill is universally approved, except by a very few radicals. I am glad that you made those speeches on the 22n of February. The people understand them and approve them.

John C. Gaut.

ALS, DLC-JP.
1. After much controversy in the General Assembly the new franchise bill was enacted in early May 1866. It was, as desired by Brownlow, a much more restrictive voting measure and gave the governor the right to appoint commissioners to supervise registration and suffrage. Patton, *Unionism and Reconstruction*, 114–18; Alexander, *Reconstruction*, 101, 106–9.

Interview with Burr and Ingersoll[1]

[March 23, 1866][2]

MR. BURR—We have come, Mr. President, as loyal citizens of the State of Connecticut to have a talk with you concerning the pending election in our State.

The President—That is a matter gentlemen, which I do not propose to interfere with. Your local politics should be decided among yourselves.

MR. BURR—But we sustain your restoration policy, your veto message, &c., and our candidate, Mr. ENGLISH,[3] indorses your position unequivocally, while Gen. HAWLEY[4] and those who support him are opposed to you and your policy.

The President—The personal opinions of candidates will make little difference. The platform of both parties express clearly political positions, and I understand that my political friends—those who sustain my policy—in the Union party, are satisfied with their party platform. Indeed I believe the resolutions of the Union Convention[5] were reported by a personal friend of mine—Mr. BABCOCK.[6] But as I have said to you, it is a local election, and I have no desire to interfere one way or another.

Mr. INGERSOLL—But the issue in the State is between the friends of your policy and its opponents. Party lines have been drawn on that issue.

The President—I don't so understand it. But if it were true, that would not affect my conduct. I can conceive how such an issue might be forced by designing politicians for the purpose of securing political advantage; and if it has been so forced, it has been done on the sole responsibility of your men, without any sanction or intimation from my administration.

Mr. BURR—M. Cleveland,[7] postmaster at Hartford, has openly avowed his intention to support Mr. English.

The President—I know he has, but he does it on his own responsibility. I tell you it is not my purpose to interfere one way of the other. I refused to interfere with the election in New-York State last Fall,[8] and also with the recent New-Hampshire election.[9] I am President of the United States; whatever policy I maintain is of a national character, and it would poorly become me to take sides in the local elections of the country. My political position is understood. I stand here to defend the Constitution, as I took an oath to do, and when great public measures, which are under my control, require my sanction or disapproval, it is my duty and privilege to act; but to step down in to the local contests of a State is not part of my business.

Mr. BURR—You have not accepted Mr. CLEVELAND's resignation?[10]

The President—No, I have not. I approve of his political action in upholding my measures and policy, as I approve of other men, who may entertain different views as to their duty to party. I would not remove him because he supports one man for Governor, any more than I would remove another man for supporting a different candidate. Let me make this plain. Taking the ground, first, that I will not meddle with local elections, I follow it up consistently by making no tests in the political conduct of any man who receives his appointment from me. I prefer men, of course, to sustain my policy; but if they do not sustain it I shall not ostracise them.

Mr. BURR—Gen. HAWLEY and the gentlemen who were here the other day report that you declared yourself in favor of "the success of the Union party," intimating that you desired Gen. HAWLEY to succeed.

The President—I did tell them so, and I frankly stated that while I preferred men to adopt my policy, there was no necessity of going outside of our party organization, in cases of difference of opinion, to fight out battles. I told them that I stood upon the platform of principles adopted by the last Union National Convention.[11]

Mr. BURR—(insinuatingly.) Then you didn't mean the last Union National Convention, the Democratic Convention?

Mr. President—Hardly. If I remember correctly that Convention pronounced the war a failure, and cried for peace when armed treason stood defiant and sought the life of the nation.

Mr. BURR—But, Mr. President, you seem to forget that your restoration policy is the one great issue in our State.

The President—No, I do not. I have already told you my views on the subject. I take party platforms, not the individual opinions of men.

Mr. BURR—We sustain your policy unequivocally.

Mr. INGERSOLL—Yes, that's the point.

The President—Perhaps you do; but do you mean to tell me that this is not done, as I have already intimated, for partisan effect—to deceive the people, in order that you may thereby obtain power? I cannot yet forget the record of the Democratic Party. It opposed the war; it placed obstacles in the way of the Government, while we were grappling with the enemies of the Union; it denounced my lamented predecessor as a usurper, and classed me as an enemy of my country because I gave up all to crush the wicked rebellion; and it hardly seems possible to me that such a party could become converted so suddenly into lovers of the Union, professing to be its best friends.

Mr. BURR—(Aside to INGERSOLL) What time is it Colin?

Mr. INGERSOLL—It is about time to go.

The President—Hold on, gentlemen; don't be in a hurry. I wish to have you understand this matter. I was speaking about the sudden conversion of the Democratic party. I have been in public life too long to be deceived, by having men who violently opposed and denounced me during the war, now come forward and profess to be my special champions! I was elected by the Union party of the country—the party which sustained the war and crushed out the rebellion, in spite of the opposition of Northern copperheads!

New York Times, Mar. 31, 1866.

1. Connecticut Democrats Alfred E. Burr (1815–1900), longtime editor and proprietor of the Hartford *Daily Times*, and Colin M. Ingersoll (1819–1903), a former diplomat and two-term congressman, met with the President on the evening of March 23, accompanied by Rep. Lovell H. Rousseau of Kentucky, who introduced the two men to Johnson. *DAB*; *BDAC*; *National Intelligencer*, Mar. 28, 1866.

2. Both internal evidence and other newspaper accounts suggest this date.

3. James E. English, who eventually lost the April gubernatorial election by some five hundred votes, had been nominated by a Democratic convention which denied the right of Congress to grant suffrage to blacks, affirmed the principle that the southern states were still in the Union, and endorsed the President's policies generally. *American Annual Cyclopaedia* (1866), 252–53, 255.

4. A former attorney, newspaper editor, Free Soiler, and Republican organizer, Joseph R. Hawley (1826–1905) had served throughout the war, advancing in rank from captain to brevet major general, before becoming Connecticut's governor in 1866 and afterward representing the state in Congress for nearly thirty years. Heading a delegation of Connecticut Republicans who had met with the President on March 21, Hawley was reportedly assured by Johnson that, contrary to rumors, he had made no pledges to support English, but instead favored the "Union nominee" in the Connecticut election. Ibid., 253; Warner, *Blue*; *Chicago Tribune*, Mar. 22, 1866.

5. The Republicans met at Hartford on February 14. *American Annual Cyclopaedia* (1866), 253.

6. A Conservative Republican, James F. Babcock, collector of customs at New Haven under both Lincoln and Johnson and editor of the *New Haven Palladium*, was among the

Connecticut delegation which saw Johnson on March 21. Ibid., 253–54; Beale, *Welles Diary*, 1: 81; 2: 457–58, 508; *Chicago Tribune*, Mar. 22, 1866; *U.S. Off. Reg.* (1861–67).

7. The nephew of a former Democratic governor and congressional colleague of Johnson's, Edward S. Cleveland (1825–*fl*1891) served in the state legislature as an Independent and was the Democratic candidate for governor in 1886, prior to his term as postmaster at Hartford (1861–69). *Encyclopedia of Connecticut Biography: Genealogical—Memorial, Representative Citizens* (Boston, 1917), 239–40; J. A. Spalding, comp., *Illustrated Popular Biography of Connecticut* (Hartford, 1891), 93–94.

8. As a result of this election, New York Democrats, who had endorsed Johnson's policies in their convention in early September 1865, were soundly defeated, with the Republicans adding to their majority in the legislature and capturing the governor's office. James C. Mohr, *The Radical Republicans and Reform in New York During Reconstruction* (Ithaca, 1973), 88–89; *American Annual Cyclopaedia* (1865), 614–15.

9. See Edmund Burke to Johnson, Mar. 12, 1866.

10. According to other newspaper accounts, supposedly, at this point during the interview, Burr and Ingersoll handed Johnson Cleveland's resignation letter of March 22, in which he stated he was supporting English for governor. After reading it, Johnson stated: "I this morning read in the INTELLIGENCER Mr. Cleveland's late speech at Hartford. It is a good speech. He takes the right ground." Thereupon, the President endorsed the letter in this manner: "Your political action in upholding my measures and policy *is approved*. Your resignation is therefore not accepted, but is herewith returned." In a private letter written the following day, Johnson asked James Dixon whether his handling of Cleveland's resignation had met with the senator's approval. No answer from Dixon has been found, but Secretary Welles, for one, worried that the President's action would be "misconstrued and misunderstood" as an endorsement of English's candidacy. Beale, *Welles Diary*, 2: 461; *National Intelligencer*, Mar. 24, 28, 1866; Johnson to Dixon, Mar. 24, 1866, Wellington Coll., CtHi.

11. Another version of the interview has Johnson stating emphatically that by "Union Party" he had meant "*the party which supports his Union restoration policy*," not necessarily the Republican party of Connecticut. *National Intelligencer*, Mar. 28, 1866.

From James W. Singleton[1]

Washington City   March 23 1866

Mr President

I have the honor in compliance with your request to enclose a copy of Judge Pecks letter[2] read to you last evening. I regret that the presence of a person with whom I had no previous acquaintance, forbid my Communicating as freely as I desired—especially such facts as related to you *personally* coming to my knowledge from the lips of Mr. Lincoln himself the night previous to his death. You *may* have the same information from another source—if not—it is proper you should know the facts, as well as the kind feelings and confidence of Mr. Lincoln expressed at the recital —and his utter disapprobation of a policy at *that time determined upon against you.*

For this I refer you to our mutual friend Judge Hughes[3] who was present during the most and *material* part of the conversation.

Jas. W. Singleton

ALS, DLC-JP.

1. Singleton (1811–1892) had practiced law and medicine in Illinois and had gained some notoriety as brigadier general of the state militia during its involvement in the so-

called Mormon War. He enjoyed frequent contact with Lincoln and in fact was married to one of Mary Todd Lincoln's cousins. After the war, Singleton served as president of two different railroad companies in Illinois and subsequently was elected to two terms in the U.S. House of Representatives. *BDAC*; Philip Van Doren Stern, *An End to Valor: The Last Days of the Civil War* (Boston, 1958), 33.

2. Singleton enclosed a copy of the October 14, 1864, letter from Ebenezer Peck to Singleton. In this letter Peck recounted a conversation that had taken place between Lincoln and him in which the President voiced his willingness to admit a Southern state that ceased hostilities, elected senators and representatives, and asked for such recognition. Lincoln expressed a reluctance, however, to announce such a position in advance because of possible political ramifications.

3. James Hughes, Washington lawyer.

From Edwin M. Stanton

Washington City   March 23d 1866

Sir;

Your reference of a Memorial dated at Fredericksburg Virginia February 20th 1866, and addressed to the Chairman of the Committee of Military affairs[1] by A. Watson[2] in relation to the field in which the remains of Union Soldiers who were Killed in the Battle of Fredericksburg are interred, has just been received, and in accordance with your directions to give it my immediate attention and such suggestions as I may desire to make I would respectfully recommend:

1st   That the Military Commander of the Department of Virginia[3] be instructed to take possession of said field, and turn it over to the care and custody of the Quarter Master's Department.

2'd   That the Quarter Masters Department be instructed to take charge of, and enclose the field, if it be not already done, and, hold the same as a National Cemetery, and adopt proper measures to secure the graves from desecration.[4]

Edwin M Stanton
Secretary of War

LS, DNA-RG94, Lets. Recd. (Main Ser.), File P-150-1866 (M619, Roll 501).

1. The letter to Robert C. Schenck expressed great concern that the mayor and council of Fredericksburg were "about to turn over to the Agricultural Soceity the very grounds on which our soldiers fought and died, and on which we intend to erect a monument to their memory." The letter was referred back and forth between Johnson and the War Department. The President asked Stanton for suggestions and advice. A. Watson to [Schenck], Feb. 20, 1866, Lets. Recd. (Main Ser.), File P-150-1866 (M619, Roll 501), RG94, NA.

2. Probably Augustus Watson (*fl*1873) who had served as a postal clerk in the dead letter office. Washington, D.C., directories (1863–73); *U.S. Off. Reg.* (1863).

3. Gen. Alfred H. Terry.

4. The Fredericksburg National Cemetery was established in 1866 with the reinterment of soldiers from the battlefields of Fredericksburg, Chancellorsville, The Wilderness, and Spotsylvania. Situated one mile west of Fredericksburg, the cemetery was completed in 1869 at a cost of about $180,000. *Washington Evening Star*, June 13, 1866; *Senate Ex. Docs.*, 43 Cong., 2 Sess., No. 28, pp. 36–38 (Ser. 1629); *Roll of Honor: Names of Soldiers Who Died in Defense of the Union Interred in the National Cemeteries* (Washington, D.C., 1870), 11.

From Alexander H. Stephens

Private

Crawfordville Ga   23 March 1866.

Dear Sir—

I expected to be in Washington before this time to return you my thanks in person for the enlargement of my parole[1] and to do whatever I could in the advancement of your policy for restoration peace and harmony in the country. But the State of my health & the weather besides the difficulty in raising the means to bear expenses &c have delayed the execution of my purpose. I had made all arrangements to get off tomorrow and may do so yet but the sudden change in the weather this morning excites apprehensions that I may not prudently encounter the exposure until the present spell shall pass.[2] I rush you this line barely for the purpose of explaining why you have not heard from me since the enlargement of the parole and to let you know that it has not arisen from any want of due appreciation of it. I will also take the occasion to say to you that our Legislature before adjournment passed an act in accordance with my advice to them amply I think securing the rights of the Freedmen. They not only have the right by our law now to contract and be contracted with and to sue and be sued but to *testify* in our courts in all cases under the same rule that white people are and they are amenable to the same punishments for like offences as the Whites are.[3] No distinctions are made in any of these respects on account of race or color. This it does seem to me should be sufficient. So far as suffrage is concerned that Should be left where the Constitution leaves it with the States. But enough. You will please pardon this. I hope in all events at no distant day to be in Washington.

Alexander H. Stephens

ALS, DLC-JP.

1. See Johnson to Stephens, Feb. 26, 1866.

2. Stephens had been summoned to the national capital to testify before the reconstruction committee. He arrived April 2 and took up board at his old residence, Mrs. Crutchett's, corner of 6th and D Streets. On April 5 he had an interview with Johnson and on April 11–12 gave his testimony. Thomas E. Schott, *Alexander H. Stephens of Georgia: A Biography* (Baton Rouge, 1988), 465; *National Intelligencer*, Apr. 3, 1866; *Washington Evening Star*, Apr. 3, 5, 12, 1866; *Richmond Dispatch*, Apr. 12, 1866.

3. Although most civil rights were accorded to Georgia blacks, they could only testify when the case involved another black person, they could not serve on a jury, nor could they intermarry with whites. C. Mildred Thompson, *Reconstruction in Georgia: Economic, Social, Political, 1865–1872* (Savannah, 1972 [1915]), 144.

From Three Mississippi Fathers

[Hinds County, ca. March 23, 1866][1]

Your petitioners, Rawley Sivley, John A. Edwards and John Shelton,[2] all of the County of Hinds in the State of Mississippi, respectfully pray your Excellency to grant to their Sons, William R. Sivley, Oliver S. Edwards and John M. Shelton,[3] full pardon, so far as the National Government is concerned, for an offense with which they are charged, though candor requires us to say that neither our Sons or ourselves beleive they have committed any offense whatever in the premises.

That the matter may be understood however, we will now give as full and as fair an account of the whole affair, as we can. About the end of November last, a volunteer Militia Company was formed in the Town of Raymond, near to which we live, under an act of our Legislature, and the steps taken by the Governor of Our State, for the purpose of aiding the Civil authorities in the suppression of crime, of disarming the colored population, who, in some vicinities at least, were thought to be arming themselves for unlawful and violent purposes, and of performing police duties generally. On the organisation of this Company, William R. Sivley was elected a Lieutenant, while Oliver S. Edwards and John M. Shelton were only privates.

For a day or two previous to the 20th day of December 1865., three colored persons dressed in the garb of Federal Soldiers, but not armed except as herein after stated, so far as we know, and furnishing no evidence besides their dress that they belonged to the Army, had been about the Town of Raymond. And the mere uniform surely furnished little, if any evidence of the fact, in this region, where so many colored persons, who never did belong to the Army, are seen dressed up in the complete uniform of the Federal Soldiers. These three colored persons were known to very few, if to any of our white population, and certainly unknown to our Sons and ourselves. One of the number wore a large sized Army Pistol in a very bold and defiant way, and this too at the very time, the colored people were being disarmed generally.

On the morning of the 20th day of December last, Lieut. Sivley was ordered by the Captain of his company[4] to call upon the man last referred to, to ascertain who he was, his authority to be here, &c.

When politely asked by Lieut Sivley for his papers, he rudely replied that he did not have any thing to do with him, and when the request was repeated, in the same manner, he defiantly threw open his Coat, thus exhibiting the large Pistol he wore, saying that it was his papers, and went on to indulge in most violent and profane language.

He then started off, along the street, continuing his defiant language and manner, drawing his Pistol, and keeping it in his right hand and ready for use, before any Pistol or other weapon was drawn upon him. He was followed by Lieut. Sivley and privates Edwards and Shelton, as well as by some others, who continued, without provocation or violence, to try to get him to show his papers. After going some distance along the Street, all the while continuing his noisy and profane language, none of which was returned, he purposely, as is supposed, dropped some papers, which were picked up and examined by Lieut. Sivley. Some persons say that among these papers, was his pass or leave of absence from his command, and that Lieut. Sivley, after looking at it, called out to him that it was all right, and to come back and get it, which he did. While others, whose opportunities, for seeing, hearing and knowing how the fact was, from their positions at this point of time, were equally good, say that the papers dropped were only a fragment of a newspaper and a small note of the Fractional currency, that there was no pass or leave of absence among them, and that Lieut. Sivley, after looking at the papers, only called out to him to come back and get them, and that he did so.

Neither of us was present, we have no personal knowledge on this point, and we are unable to say with certainty how the fact was, but certain it is that on the examination of this person's pocket Book, after his death, and in the presence of a Federal Officer, Lieut. P. S. Jacobs[5] of the same Regiment, his pass, or leave of absence was found carefully folded up in it. We do not consider it material how the fact was, or whether or not it was then ascertained that this colored person, was in fact a soldier, and a private in the 50th Regiment of United States Colored Infantry, and that his name was perhaps Judge Norman,[6] for just at this point of time one of our Justices of the peace[7] (and he has recently died) who had witnessed the whole affair, from its very inception, came up and ordered Lieut. Sivley and men to arrest this colored person, for his violence and misbehavior on the Streets.

Of course, even supposing that Lieut. Sivley had seen the pass or leave of absence, he and his men, undertook to perform the additional duty, thus legally, as they beleived as well as ourselves, imposed upon them, by this order of arrest from a well known and recognised civil officer and Justice of the peace. But while Judge Norman still maintained his manner of defiance and resistance, Lieut. Sivley and men were so unwilling to use violence, and encounter the risk of bloodshed in his arrest, that instead of at once insisting upon his submitting to the arrest they were ordered to make, they followed him several hundred yards farther, trying to persuade him to yeild without force. And when at last he was fired upon, it was only after he had twice or three times tried to fire upon the party, pulling the trigger of his pistol that often, every barrel of which was afterwards found to be loaded, and which no doubt failed to go off, only from some defect in the loading, and when his pistol was still actually presented upon some of them. When the only ball, that struck him, was fired, he was still facing the party, and his pistol was raised and aimed at some one of them. He fell with it grasped in his right hand. He died the same day, from the wound he had thus received, and Lieut. Sivley and privates Edwards and Shelton, without delay, surrendered themselves voluntarily to our peace officers. These are the facts of the case, as we understand them.[8]

The Mayor of Raymond[9] began an investigation of this affair, on the next ensuing day, the 21st of December, and at night fall adjourned it over to the following day. All further progress in it by him was arrested, by the appearance in Raymond, from the military post at Jackson in this County, during the nights of the 21st. and 22nd. of December, of parts of *four* Companies of Colored Infantry, nominally, to arrest the parties implicated, and this was no doubt the only purpose of all the commissioned officers, but in our opinion, which is concurred in by nearly every person here, they could not have restrained their men, from shooting down, on sight, our three sons, had they been found. Indeed many of the colored soldiers openly avowed their purpose to do so.

But they were not found. They at once left this region, and are absent yet, refugees from their homes, for the reason that they are now, and all along have been, threatened with arrest and trial by Military Commissions, the result of which were it to take place, from our experience in this section of Country, is as well known to us now, as it could be after the trial was over. They have thus evaded Military arrest, not from a sense of guilt, but from the fear that they would not get justice. They do not seek to avoid a full investigation and a fair trial by a Jury of their peers, and we pledge ourselves that if your Excellency will pardon them of the offence with which they are charged, only as against the National Government, they will at once return to their homes, and meet any charge made, or Indictment found, against them, in the Courts of the State, certainly much more appropriate, if not the only consitutional, tribunals for the trial of such an offence as is charged, when committed by any one other than a Soldier in actual service in the Army.

In conclusion, Your Excellency will allow us to recognise the fact that you too are a parent, as ourselves, and can understand our feelings, and sympathise with us in this enforced absence of our children from their homes, and excuse us for appealing to your kindness of heart as well as to your good sense, to grant us the boon we ask.[10]

R Sivley
J A Edwards
John Shelton.

ALS (Shelton), DLC-JP.

1. Internal and external evidence indicates that this letter was written in Hinds County. The date of the letter is suggested by the attached endorsement from Benjamin G. Humphreys which is dated March 23, 1866, and by the reference in the letter to the recent death of Justice of the Peace Phillip M. Alston, who died on March 16 (see note 7 below).

2. Sivley (1806–1887), Edwards (b. c1803), and Shelton (c1815–fl1880) were, respectively, a planter, farmer, and lawyer. Gillis, *Goodspeed's Mississippi*, 560; 1860 Census, Miss., Hinds, Raymond, 153, 155, 188; (1880), Raymond, 12th Enum. Dist., 49.

3. Little has been learned about the younger Sivley (1843–fl1871), Edwards (b. c1845), and Shelton (c1850–fl1880) except that Sivley was a Confederate veteran and Shelton later became a lawyer. Dunbar Rowland, *Mississippi* (4 vols., Spartanburg, 1976 [1907]), 3: 779; 1860 Census, Miss., Hinds, Raymond, 153, 155, 188; (1880), Raymond, 12th Enum. Dist., 49.

4. B. S. White (c1837–fl1880), a former Confederate lieutenant of scouts, had recently been elected as one of the selectmen of Raymond. Later he was a deputy sheriff. 1880 Census, Miss., Hinds, Raymond, 12th Enum. Dist., 55; *OR*, Ser. 4, Vol. 3: 650; *Hinds County Gazette*, Jan. 13, 1866.

5. Peter S. Jacobs (1838–1907), an Illinois resident, in 1863 transferred from the 10th Mo. Inf., USA, to the 50th USCT where he rose from first sergeant to first lieutenant. Mustered out March 20, 1866, he became a farmer and traveling salesman, living variously in Adams County, Illinois, Kansas City, Missouri, and Chicago. CSR, Peter S. Jacobs, RG94, NA; Pension File, Victoria A. Jacobs, RG15, NA.

6. Norman (c1838–1865), private, Co. A, 50th USCT, had been born in Sumter District, South Carolina, and was listed as a "farmer" near Hickory Station, Mississippi, upon his late 1864 enlistment. CSR, Judge Norman, RG94, NA.

7. Philip M. Alston (1804–1866) was a farmer who for several years held the post of county ranger. 1860 Census, Miss., Hinds, Raymond, 151; Hinds County Gazette, Sept. 10, 1862, Oct. 14, 1865, Mar. 23, 1866.

8. A contemporary account of the incident and editorial comment may be found in ibid., Dec. 23, 30, 1865.

9. Thomas I. Hunter (c1815–fl1870), a carpenter, had been mayor since before the war. He was also an undertaker. 1860 Census, Miss., Hinds, Raymond, 146; (1870), 8; Hinds County Gazette, Dec. 28, 1859, Dec. 30, 1865, Jan. 13, 1866.

10. Several residents of Raymond and vicinity signed an endorsement which testified to the correctness of the letter from Sivley, Edwards, and Shelton. The signers included the mayor of Raymond, county sheriff, judges, court clerks, physicians, and legislator. In a separate attached note, Governor Humphreys admitted that he had no direct knowledge of the incident dealt with in the letter but declared that he had known the fathers who had written the letter for some time and vouched for their integrity and character. Judge William Yerger also endorsed the fathers' letter and testified in behalf of John Shelton. He entreated Johnson for assistance and clemency. The President's response is not known.

From Francis P. Blair, Jr.[1]

Washington City   March 24, '66

I know both the persons named by Genl Vaughn.[2]

Wallace[3] is a firm consistent & original union man whose entire fortune has been sacrificed in the rebellion. Schofield[4] is a malignant Radical of the very worst type. A rebel until the rebellion failed and a radical now for the sake of office.[5]

Frank P Blair

ES, DNA-RG60, Appt. Files for Judicial Dists., Mo., Thomas B. Wallace.

1. Blair wrote his comments on a letter of March 12, 1866, which he received from Richard C. Vaughan of Lexington, Missouri, urging the removal of Smith O. Scofield as marshal for the western district of Missouri and his replacement with Thomas B. Wallace.

2. Vaughan (b. c1813), a Virginia native, lost his Missouri property as a result of a Rebel raid during the war. After a brief clerical stint in Washington, D.C., Vaughan returned home to command some of the Missouri state militia. In September 1866 he was appointed assessor for the Sixth Congressional District of Missouri but resigned in December when he was driven from office and his life was threatened by unruly troops quartered in his district by the governor. 1850 Census, Mo., Saline, 90th Dist., 29; Edward Bates to Johnson, July 12, 1866; OR, Ser. 1, Vol. 13: 693; Vol. 34, Pt. 2: 130; Missouri Democrat (St. Louis), Sept. 20, 1866; Vaughan to Hugh McCulloch, Dec. 17, 27, 1866, Appts., Internal Revenue Service, Assessor, Mo., 6th Dist., Richard C. Vaughn, RG56, NA; Ser. 6B, Vol. 4: 316, Johnson Papers, LC.

3. Wallace (1813–fl1881) moved to Missouri from Kentucky in 1819. Initially trained as a carpenter, he became a successful merchant, but lost most of his effects in the Battle of Lexington in 1861. He served as marshal for the western district of Missouri (1862–65, 1866–69). After 1871 he sold insurance. History of Lafayette County, Mo. (St. Louis, 1881), 624–25; Senate Ex. Proceedings, Vol. 14, pt. 2: 714–15; Vol. 15, pt. 1: 84, 156, 180.

4. Scofield, a native of North Carolina, was a former assistant assessor and elector-at-large from Missouri for Lincoln and Johnson. He served as marshal from March 1865 to late August 1866. Vaughan characterized him as "an unscrupulous tool of [Congressman] Ben. Loan and among the most hostile men in the state to the policy of the administration." Rep. Thomas E. Noell claimed that Scofield was "instituting proceedings . . . against the property of all persons who have been in any way involved in the secession movement," charging "exhorbitant fees" to file charges and investigate titles and then dropping the matter. Edward Bates insisted that Wallace was removed and Scofield appointed to the office strictly for partisan reasons. *U.S. Off. Reg.* (1865); Smith O. Scofield to Benjamin F. Loan, June 18, 1864, and Scofield to Abraham Lincoln, ca. June 18, 1864, Lincoln Papers, LC; Vaughan to Blair, Mar. 12, 1866; Noell to Johnson, Aug. 9, 1866, Appt. Files for Judicial Dists., Mo., Thomas B. Wallace, RG60, NA; Bates to Johnson, July 12, 1866; *Senate Ex. Proceedings*, Vol. 14, pt. 1: 287; Ser. 6B, Vol. 3: 633, Johnson Papers, LC.

5. Johnson endorsed the Vaughan/Blair letter: "The Especial attention of the Atty Genl is Called to this case." Wallace was reappointed.

From Henry L. Burnett[1]

Cincinnati, Ohio, 24th March, 1866.

Mr. President:—

In accordance with the understanding arrived at in the consultation between yourself, Mr. Campbell and myself, in our recent interview,[2] I have, since my return here, endeavored to ascertain how matters stand here, so as to be able to report to you what in my opinion ought to be done.

First, then—as to the U.S. Marshalship—I don't think it necessary nor for your interests or the public good to remove Mr. Sands.[3] He is Chairman of the Union Executive Committee of this County, and wields as such Chairman, and personally, a vast local and State influence, is a man of enthusiastic, earnest character, warm in his friendship and bitter in his hates; of great mental and physical energy, and possessed of a good deal more than ordinary brain-power and capacity,—a good man to have in your ranks and sealed to your support, and a dangerous man to have in the ranks of the opposition. He is, by nature, conservative and moderate in his notions, has always, since the days of the old Free Soil Party, fought with all his might the Western Reserve Wade-Giddings Abolition fanatics.[4] He believes in you, and will give you his honest, earnest support. He has no interest in the "Gazette"[5]—is not tied to it nor attached to it in any way, and gave it the public printing—he controlled—solely because the Court by its order had directed him so to do. I enclose you a leaf from our "Rules of the U.S. District Court."[6]

Soon after your veto of the "Freedmen's Bureau Bill," the long-haired gentry of the Radical school sought through the Union Executive Committee to get up a meeting of the extreme men of the Union Party—to denounce your action and support Congress. Sands put his heel upon the movement and crushed it. If he is let alone in his position, and you extend to him your confidence, he will give your Administration most faithful and efficient support—will be of far greater service than any new man that could be put in his place. Aside from all this, he has stood consistently and firmly by you, your policy and measures, through all the fight.[7]

Second—there is a change here that ought to be made at once. Col. R. Brinkerhoff,[8] Depot Quartermaster at this Depot, ought to be relieved and sent to some interesting frontier post where he could exercise his proselyting radical notions upon "ye red men of the forest." He is not fitted for this atmosphere; is a very good, conscientious and efficient officer, I have no doubt,—but he has yet to learn that it is his sole duty to look after and attend to his duties, and not to assail and malign the Commander-in-Chief of the Armies. He *does* believe in Congress, and does *not* believe in Andrew Johnson. He believes that Congress is right and that the President is wrong,—and shows his faith by his works. He is a "Gazette" man all over—gives it all the Government patronage he can control—supports it in every way, and it is the only city paper, I believe, that he takes or reads. That paper, as you know, is the most bitter and unqualified in its denunciation and personal abuse of you, of all papers, perhaps, in the west.[9] He should be relieved at once and some man who will conscientiously support your administration and measures, sent here to take his place: say Col. Geo. P. Webster, A.Q.M., a resident of Newport, Ky., now on duty at St. Louis, a man of sound judgment and wide influence; or Major C. E. Bliven,[10] A.Q.M. here,—either of whom could be relied upon. The Depot Quartermaster has a very large influence here—more, perhaps, than any other one official. He has a large number of employees, his expenditures and purchases are very heavy, and his printing and patronage more than any other one official. During the Campaign of 1864, Mr. Lincoln and the Sec'y of War did not hesitate to relieve any officer from any influential position who supported McClellan, or did not give the Administration his earnest, hearty support.

Why should you not save and protect yourself by the same means? If these officials cannot and will not support you and your measures, it is but just that they should give place to those who will.

H. L. Burnett

LS, DLC-JP.
1. Burnett (1838–1916) saw some minor military service prior to becoming judge advocate of the Ohio Department in 1863. Afterwards he went to Indiana where he prosecuted members of the Knights of the Golden Circle; still later he assisted in the trial against the Lincoln assassins. Eventually in 1872 Burnett removed to New York, where he worked as a railroad and federal district attorney. *DAB.*
2. The exact date of his meeting with Lewis D. Campbell and the President is unknown.
3. Alexander C. Sands.
4. Benjamin F. Wade and Joshua R. Giddings.
5. Editor Richard Smith's *Cincinnati Gazette* was a staunch Republican organ that championed equal rights for blacks, congressional reconstruction, and later Johnson's impeachment. T. Harry Williams, *Lincoln and the Radicals* (Madison, 1941), 321–22; Bonadio, *North of Reconstruction*, 51, 88–89, 154.

6. Not found.

7. Despite this and several other recommendations, Sands was removed from the marshalship and replaced in July 1866 by a candidate endorsed by Generals O. O. Howard and Grant. Howard to Johnson, June 14, 1866, Hickenlooper Coll., OCHP; Ser. 6B, Vol. 4: 256, Johnson Papers, LC; *U.S. Off. Reg.* (1867–69).

8. An Ohio lawyer and newspaper editor, Roeliff Brinkerhoff (1828–1911) served in the army quartermaster service for five years before being mustered out in September 1866 with the rank of brevet brigadier. Afterwards he became involved in banking and politics. *DAB*; *Biographical Cyclopaedia of Ohio*, 3: 749–50; Powell, *Army List*, 777; Hunt and Brown, *Brigadier Generals*.

9. Marginalia written in Johnson's hand and appearing at this juncture read: "Do not let this portion of the letter be forgotten."

10. Neither man succeeded Brinkerhoff. Webster (b. *c*1828), a lawyer in civilian life, remained at his St. Louis post until September 1866 and was mustered out a short time later. After Charles E. Bliven (*fl*1892) left the army in May 1866, he went into business and worked briefly as an attorney in Cincinnati. 1860 Census, Ky., Campbell, Newport, 190; Cincinnati directories (1866–68); Powell, *Army List*, 775, 826; CSR, Staff Officers Files, George P. Webster, C. E. Bliven, RG94, NA; *Cincinnati Daily Enquirer*, Mar. 16, 1866.

From Charles H. Hildreth[1]

District of Gloucester [Mass.].
Surveyor's Office, March 24 1866

Sir.

I hold, by your commission, the office of Surveyor of Customs for this District, and believing in your policy of reconstruction I have sustained it in public and private.

I enclose the earliest of several editorial articles which I have written upon the subject for the Republican paper published here as proof of this statement.[2]

My removal from office is sought by Hon. John B. Alley,[3] the ultra radical representative of this District, and I am informed that by means of his influence another name has been sent to the Senate for confirmation, in place of mine.[4] But as no one can be commissioned without your approval, and as we have an abundance of ultra radical office holders in Massachusetts, I respectfully request that I may not be sacrificed to increase the number.

The proprietor of the "Telegraph," John S.E Rogers Esq.[5] has lately been removed from the office of Inspector of Customs, by the present Collector,[6] an appointee of Mr. Alley's for the same reasons for which my removal is sought, namely want of sympathy with ultra radical ideas. We are both active Republicans but have been so unfortunate as to incur radical enmity for "supporting the President," in which course, nevertheless, in company with a large and increasing number of Republicans, we intend to persist.[7]

Chas. H. Hildreth, Surveyor

ALS, DNA-RG56, Appts., Customs Service, Surveyor, Gloucester, Charles H. Hildreth.

1. A graduate of Harvard Medical School, Hildreth (1825–1884) had been appointed surveyor at Gloucester by Lincoln and had received a temporary appointment from Johnson in July 1865. *Biographical Review: Volume 28 Containing Life Sketches of Leading Citizens of Essex County Massachusetts* (Boston, 1898), 598; Hildreth to Johnson, Dec. 23, 1865, Appts., Customs Service, Surveyor, Gloucester, Charles H. Hildreth, RG56, NA.

2. Enclosed is an editorial entitled, "Reconstruction," clipped from the *Gloucester Telegraph*, Jan. 17, 1866. The essay was strongly supportive of the President and his policies.

3. Alley (1817–1896) served in Congress for about eight years (1859–67) and earlier in local offices. In his letter to the treasury secretary, Alley warned: "I think if the President desires to gratify those who support him & his policy he will not appoint Mr Hildreth." *BDAC*; Alley to Hugh McCulloch, Apr. 12, 1866, Appts., Customs Service, Surveyor, Gloucester, George W. Adams, RG56, NA.

4. The nomination of George W. Adams (c1838–1869), a fish dealer and late acting master of the U.S. Navy, had been sent to the Senate in January 1866. The following September he resumed his naval career. McCulloch to Johnson, Jan. 22, 1866; Adams to Johnson, Apr. 2, May 7, 1866, ibid.; Pension Records, Annette B. Wonson, RG15, NA.

5. Rogers (c1824–fl1870) ran the newspaper from 1843 to 1874. Benjamin F. Arrington, ed., *Municipal History of Essex County in Massachusetts* (4 vols., New York, 1922), 2: 751; 1870 Census, Mass., Essex, Gloucester, 41.

6. Billed as "not a radical party man" but rather a "warm friend" of Johnson's, William A. Pew (c1832–1912), who had received a temporary commission as collector in April 1865, was reappointed to a full four-year term beginning in July 1866. Afterwards he served in the legislature (1870–72) and went into the banking business. F. W. Choate to Johnson, June 4, 1866, Appts., Customs Service, Collector, Gloucester, Wm. A. Pew, RG56, NA; *New York Times*, Aug. 25, 1912; Ser. 6B, Vol. 4: 22, Johnson Papers, LC.

7. Johnson referred the letter to McCulloch, with the recommendation that it was both "just and proper" that Hildreth "should be retained," and he instructed that Adams's name be withdrawn and Hildreth's nomination be sent to the Senate. On June 4 and again on December 13, 1866, Hildreth's nomination was presented, but it was rejected in favor of a third nominee. Johnson to McCulloch, Apr. 7, 1866, Appts., Customs Service, Surveyor, Gloucester, Charles H. Hildreth, RG56, NA; McCulloch to Johnson, Mar. 9, 1867, Lets. Sent *re* Customs Service Employees (QC Ser.), Vol. 6, RG56, NA; Ser. 6B, Vol. 4: 22, 24–25, Johnson Papers, LC.

From Privates of the 35th Regiment, USCT[1]

Summerville [S.C.]   March 24th 66

Dear Sir

We the undersigned, Privates, in the 35th Regt Col Troops under the Command of B. B. Gel Beecher,[2] beg leave to bring to your notice the fact, that we were Court Martialed for having the Vineal Deseas, and Sentenced to a deduction of one months pay. We therefore appeal to you for redress. We wish to know if we are to be so delt with. We have done our duty as Men & Soldiers, but Sir we appeal to you and will abide your decision.[3]

Edmond Nickson Co B. 35 Regt
Andrew Lafenhous "   "   "
Alfred Blunt
Jack Sharp Co B
Jackson Filmore Co A.

L, DNA-RG94, USCT Div., Lets. Recd., File P-111-1866.

1. Nickson [or Nickerson] (c1845–1897), a "driver" before his 1863 enlistment in Co.

I, 35th USCT, later lived in Norfolk and Hampton, Virginia. Laffinhouse [sometimes Grise] (c1840–1893) had been a slave in Beaufort County, North Carolina. Blunt (c1841–1867) had also been a slave in Beaufort County. Sharp has not been identified. Fillmore (c1845–1873), also a North Carolina slave, after his discharge was a laborer in Wadmalaw and Edisto Island, South Carolina. CSR, Edmund Nickerson, Andrew Laffinhouse, Alfred Blunt, Jackson Fillmore, RG94, NA; Pension Records, Edmund Nickerson, Mary A. Laffinhouse, Mary J. Blunt, Tyra B. Fillmore, RG15, NA.

2. James C. Beecher (1828–1886), a Congregational minister and brother of Henry Ward Beecher, had been chaplain, 67th N.Y. Inf., and lieutenant colonel, 141st N.Y. Inf., before assuming command of the 35th USCT. Hunt and Brown, *Brigadier Generals*.

3. Received on April 2, the letter was referred to the war office. Apparently, no action was taken, since all the men were mustered out with their regiment on June 1, 1866. Ser. 4A, Vol. 4: 567, Johnson Papers, LC; USCT Div., Lets. Recd., File P-111-1866, RG94, NA; CSR, Nickerson, Laffinhouse, Blunt, Fillmore, RG94, NA.

From James R. Rogers[1]

Chunnenuggee Ala   March 24th. 1866

During the latter part of last summer I made application to your Excellency for special pardon. I state now, as I did then, that the application was made from prudential motives alone, to avoid future annoyance by agents and possible loss. At that time I was trying to form a copartnership with a gentleman of capital for the purpose of purchasing cotton on speculation. I was afraid the cotton thus purchased would be estimated &c. Through the want of mail facilities and ignorance, and the dread of evil impending, felt generally throughout the community, I was led to commit a blunder which has already cost me more money & trouble than was ever contemplated by your Excellency, for those who availed themselves of the amnesty proclamation. I have made a showing to the U.S. Attorney, at Montgomery[2] that my property was not worth $8,000. The list of all my taxable property presented, sworn to by myself & two of my near neighbours; men of fine business capacity and good moral character, as clever men as any in this (Macon) county. They have been living near me ever since I commenced business, thirteen year ago. He refused to let me off unless I would pay him one per cent on $20,000 = 200$ because for the "sake of application I admitted my property to be worth $20,000." Two of my neighbours were in his office the same day represented by Hon" David Clopton,[3] one worth $11,000.00 the other $14,000. He charged each 50$. Two others paid under similar circumstances 75$ & 125$ respectively. Neither of them had ever made application for pardon. Clopton & Ligon[4] were my attourney's also. Mr Smith now makes all pay *one* per cent on $20,000, ³/₄ of one per cent, on all over $20,000 and under 30,000; ¹/₂ of one per ct on all over 30,000 & under 40,000 &c. There were *eleven hundred* cases of libeled property in this District (Montgomery). Should Mr Smith collect one per cent on 1,000 cases worth $20,000 the am't collected would be $200,000. Is there no way to prevent this extortion? The people cannot afford to defend themselves in the Courts, for with but few exceptions the men have nothing left except real estate. Besides the cost of defense would be more than the am't unjustly demanded by J. Q. Smith.

Inclosed I send you a copy of the acceptance I sent to Hon William H Seward on the next day after I received the warrant of pardon signed by your Excellency. I have never received any acknowledgement of its reception at Washington City. The U.S. Attourney requires a copy of the acknowledgment signed by the Honl W. H. Seward to be placed on file in his office before he will dismiss the case. I went to Montgomery in Jan'y & again in February for the express purpose of paying the 200$ demanded by Mr Smith. He was absent in Washington city, his clerk had resigned and there was no one to attend to his business in the city. I live 52 miles from Montgomery. He wrote to a neighbour of mine that all who had not paid by the 15th of March should pay additional cost. I did not know that he had returned to Ala until after the fifteenth. If men like myself who have to sell real estate to meet current expenses have to pay these sort of charges, fee-lawyers, bribe clerks at Washington to present your petition then bribe to present your acceptance of Warrant of Pardon, pay travelling expenses & still not accomplish business &c &c It will not take long to bankrupt all the 8 to $15,000 men whose property has been libelled.[5]

J. R. Rogers.

ALS, DNA-RG60, Office of Atty. Gen., Lets. Recd., President.

1. Rogers (b. c1831), whose prewar property was valued at $66,000, had been pardoned October 7, 1865. 1860 Census, Ala., Macon, Southern Div., 22; Rogers to Johnson, ca. Sept. 8, 1865, Amnesty Papers (M1003, Roll 9), Ala., James R. Rogers, RG94, NA.

2. James Q. Smith.

3. Clopton (1820–1892), a Tuskegee, Alabama, attorney who served in both the U.S. and Confederate congresses, later resided in Montgomery where he was a legislator and judge of the state supreme court. His third wife was Virginia, widow of Clement C. Clay, Jr. *DAB*.

4. Robert F. Ligon (1823–1901), Clopton's brother-in-law, Mexican War veteran, and state legislator, was later lieutenant governor and U.S. representative. He too moved from Tuskegee to Montgomery. Ibid.; Owen, *History of Ala.*, 4: 1046–47.

5. The letter was routinely forwarded to the attorney general.

From Sterling R. Cockrill

Pine Bluff Ark   Mar. 26th 66

Mr President.

I have from necessity located in this village, near what was my planting interest before the War. By virtue of your Pardon,[1] I have recovered possession of my lands in this State, and am endeavouring to grow a crop of Cotton this year; with the aid of borrowed Capital. The negroes in their altered condition are doing pretty well in this immediate valley.

It is a generous soil, and yields well, and is a fine "Cotton region." My family are here. I have mention this fact merely to advise you of my local-

ity, and to say that I will at anytime give you any information which you
may wish, relative to the State, or individuals thereof.

The Military force has been reduced here, but not sufficiently to meet
the wishes of the citizens of the country. Some officers posted here, are
quiet, well behaved men; others are burdened with self importance, and a
tendency to interfere with matters which should belong exclusively to
civil officers. They seem inclined to take advantage of the *fact* that the
President has never issued a Proclamation, affirming that "Peace" *existed*
in the Country; and until that was done they had a right to presume that
war existed still, and of course *War remedies*. As the garrisons are reduced, Officers of *lower rank* are left in Command, and the lower the *rank*
of Officers, the more liability there is, to exercise authority improperly.
At some of the Garrisons Lieuts are in command. If it can be done, Officers of higher rank; (and the higher the better), than Lieuts should
command Posts and garrisons; an *Order* from the Secy. of War to Department Commanders could effect this.

My own opinion is, that the necessity for any Military Command, in
this part of the State, does not exist.

Your policy, as set forth in your Messages, Speeches, and actions, is
highly approved in Arkansas, and you may rely on a generous support,
by a very large majority of the voters thereof.

I see that *"Brother Brownlow,"* has taken ground against you again.[2]
The better opinion is, that this will only add to your strength. I think
there is very little doubt of this.

The Negroes here are doing pretty well, better than was supposed at
the beginning of the year. The front lands of the river will be generally
cultivated, but the back lands and uplands will not be. The Cotton crop
will be small this year.

Wages paid men on the plantations in this valley is $20 per mo; and
women $15, besides substantial rations, and good Quarters and Medical
attention, and garden lands attached to Quarters. A few contracts, give a
portion of the Crop.

The Negro Soldiers when disbanded, are rather turbulent and noisy,
with this exception they are generally well behaved.

I have 150 *work hands* employed, and no disturbance of any Kind has
occurred, and I have no misconduct to complain of. The land here yields
about 400 lbs of "ginned Cotton"; hence wages are better, than on any
uplands; where the yield generally is 150 to 200 lbs of ginned Cotton;
labor in production about the same.

We need Capital very much in the Cotton growing Districts, and we
are ready to form an *"Alliance"* with the Cotton Spinners North of the
Ohio River, if they will furnish us capital. You are authorized to assure
them, that there is no danger in the South now. We regard the war closed,
and *peace made*; notwithstanding you have not issued a proclamation on
that subject.[3] There is no Law requiring such a proclamation, as I am

advised and therefore not really necessary, but many think it is necessary. I do not.

Capital is needed among us, and the "*Cotton Spinners*" have been very prosperous during the War. The "Cotton growing" labor is *free*, and an "alliance" among growers & Spinners, might soften the asperities of the extremes (North & South).

S. R. Cockrill

ALS, DLC-JP.

1. Johnson had pardoned Cockrill in October 1865. See Cockrill to Johnson, Sept. 18, 1865, *Johnson Papers*, 9: 95–97.

2. It is next to impossible to determine exactly what Cockrill is referring to here. The rift between Brownlow and Johnson steadily became more apparent once the new year of 1866 began. Brownlow was publicly very critical of the President's veto of the Freedmen's Bureau bill. See Coulter, *Brownlow*, 309–10.

3. On April 2, 1866, Johnson issued a proclamation declaring the official end of the war everywhere except in Texas.

From Joseph R. Flanigen[1]

Philadelphia, Mch 26 1866

My dr Sir

Please examine the enclosed slip which is the leading article in the news of this morning.[2] It is designed as you will doubtless observe as a sort of "skirmisher" for the purpose of preparing the public mind for events that should occur in the near future.

If it meets your approbation, and you agree with me as to the policy that should be adopted and persued in Pennsylvania I will follow it up with a veiw to reach the desired position by gradual but not too tardy approaches.

Altho I was of opinion some time back, that Geary[3] could be made to endorse and approve your policy I do not now beleive that he will be allowed to do so, and hence there will be a neccesity for holding another Convention. Of Course we can have nothing to do with Clymer.[4] Please say to me immediately wether or not you think it adviseable to persue the matter in this way.

I enclose you also the leading articles from the *Sunday Times* of this city. I have no doubt we can rely on it for support when the emergency arises. The Times is thoroughly independent and its owner Mr Robert C. Smith[5] is my warm personel freind and alltogether free from Radical influence altho allways a Union man.

J R Flanigen

ALS, DLC-JP.

1. The editor and proprietor of the *Philadelphia News* and a Conservative Republican, Flanigen (*fl*1897) was mentioned as a possible candidate for the lucrative Philadelphia collectorship. Although appointed by Johnson on September 18, 1866, as the naval officer of that port, he was rejected by the Senate, but continued serving at least through March

1867. Philadelphia directories (1865–98); J. L. Husband to Johnson, May 22, 1866; Henry Simpson to Johnson, Aug. 4, 1866, Appts., Customs Service, Naval Officer, Joseph R. Flanigan [sic], RG56, NA; Ser. 6B, Vol. 4: 84, Johnson Papers, LC; Flanigen to Johnson, Apr. 3, 1867, Johnson Papers, LC; *House Reports*, 40 Cong., 1 Sess., No. 7, "Impeachment Investigation," pt. 2, p. 84 (Ser. 1314).
    2. No enclosures have been found.
    3. Republican gubernatorial candidate John W. Geary.
    4. Democratic rival Hiester Clymer.
    5. Smith (*fl*1869), a native of Princeton, New Jersey, and a former printer with the *New York Herald* and *Philadelphia Ledger*, sold the *Sunday Times* in 1869. Philadelphia directories (1850–69); J. Thomas Scharf and Thompson Westcott, *History of Philadelphia, 1609–1884* (3 vols., Philadelphia, 1884), 3: 2033.

From Osborne A. Lochrane

Macon [Ga.]   March 26 1866

The warmest friends of the Govt here anxiously ask the removal of colored troops. If they are not removed there will be collisions, not from any disloyalty of feeling but the relative position each occupy antagonism is certain and has been with difficulty thus far avoided. I urge earnestly but respectfully the necessity of this measure.[1]

O. A. Lochrane

Tel, DLC-JP.
    1. Over a week earlier Stanton had ordered that black troops in Gen. George H. Thomas's Military Division of the Tennessee be reduced to thirteen regiments, only one of which was to be in Georgia. Lochrane's telegram was referred to General Grant who soon wired Thomas: "Orders were long since given for the withdrawel of Colored troops from the interior of the Southern states. . . . How far it is practicable to carry out that order in Georgia you will have to be the judge." Charles W. Foster to Thomas, Mar. 15, 1866, Tels. Sent, Sec. of War (M473, Roll 90), RG107, NA; Grant to Thomas, Mar. 28, 1866, Simon, *Grant Papers*, 16: 139–41.

To William S. Huntington[1]

Washington, D.C., March 27th 1866

I have just received your despatch,[2] and must state in reply what I have said again and again, that in reference to the elections in Connecticut or elsewhere, that I am for the candidate who is for the general policy, and the specific measures promulgated, of my administration in my regular message, veto message, Speech on 22d of February, and the veto message sent in this day. There can be no mistake in this. I presume it is known, or can be ascertained, what candidates favor or oppose my policy, or measures as promulgated to the Country.[3]

Andrew Johnson.

Tel, DNA-RG107, Tels. Sent, President, Vol. 3 (1865–68).
    1. A native of New York, Huntington (*c*1838–*fl*1872) was cashier of the First National Bank of Washington, one of Jay Cooke's establishments, where Johnson frequently conducted his financial transactions while president. 1870 Census, D.C., Washington,

Georgetown, 156; Washington, D.C., directories (1869–74); Ellis P. Oberholtzer, *Jay Cooke: Financier of the Civil War* (2 vols., Philadelphia, 1907), 1: 341; *House Reports*, 40 Cong., 1 Sess., No. 7, "Impeachment Investigation," pt. 2, pp. 178–83 (Ser. 1314).

2. Huntington had wired earlier that afternoon from New York City seeking clarification whether Johnson desired the election of James English as governor of Connecticut. Huntington to Johnson, Mar. 27, 1866, Johnson Papers, LC.

3. Huntington replied the following morning that the President's dispatch was "very satisfactory," as was his veto of the Civil Rights bill. Huntington to Johnson, Mar. 28, 1866, ibid.

Veto of Civil Rights Bill

WASHINGTON, D.C., March 27, 1866.

To the Senate of the United States:

I regret that the bill, which has passed both Houses of Congress, entitled "An act to protect all persons in the United States in their civil rights and furnish the means of their vindication," contains provisions which I can not approve consistently with my sense of duty to the whole people and my obligations to the Constitution of the United States. I am therefore constrained to return it to the Senate, the House in which it originated, with my objections to its becoming a law.

By the first section of the bill all persons born in the United States and not subject to any foreign power, excluding Indians not taxed, are declared to be citizens of the United States. This provision comprehends the Chinese of the Pacific States, Indians subject to taxation, the people called gypsies, as well as the entire race designated as blacks, people of color, negroes, mulattoes, and persons of African blood. Every individual of these races born in the United States is by the bill made a citizen of the United States. It does not purport to declare or confer any other right of citizenship than Federal citizenship. It does not purport to give these classes of persons any status as citizens of States, except that which may result from their status as citizens of the United States. The power to confer the right of State citizenship is just as exclusively with the several States as the power to confer the right of Federal citizenship is with Congress.

The right of Federal citizenship thus to be conferred on the several excepted races before mentioned is now for the first time proposed to be given by law. If, as is claimed by many, all persons who are native born already are, by virtue of the Constitution, citizens of the United States, the passage of the pending bill can not be necessary to make them such. If, on the other hand, such persons are not citizens, as may be assumed from the proposed legislation to make them such, the grave question presents itself whether, when eleven of the thirty-six States are unrepresented in Congress at the present time, it is sound policy to make our entire colored population and all other excepted classes citizens of the

United States. Four millions of them have just emerged from slavery into freedom. Can it be reasonably supposed that they possess the requisite qualifications to entitle them to all the privileges and immunities of citizens of the United States? Have the people of the several States expressed such a conviction? It may also be asked whether it is necessary that they should be declared citizens in order that they may be secured in the enjoyment of the civil rights proposed to be conferred by the bill. Those rights are, by Federal as well as State laws, secured to all domiciled aliens and foreigners, even before the completion of the process of naturalization; and it may safely be assumed that the same enactments are sufficient to give like protection and benefits to those for whom this bill provides special legislation. Besides, the policy of the Government from its origin to the present time seems to have been that persons who are strangers to and unfamiliar with our institutions and our laws should pass through a certain probation, at the end of which, before attaining the coveted prize, they must give evidence of their fitness to receive and to exercise the rights of citizens as contemplated by the Constitution of the United States. The bill in effect proposes a discrimination against large numbers of intelligent, worthy, and patriotic foreigners, and in favor of the negro, to whom, after long years of bondage, the avenues to freedom and intelligence have just now been suddenly opened. He must of necessity, from his previous unfortunate condition of servitude, be less informed as to the nature and character of our institutions than he who, coming from abroad, has, to some extent at least, familiarized himself with the principles of a Government to which he voluntarily intrusts "life, liberty, and the pursuit of happiness." Yet it is now proposed, by a single legislative enactment, to confer the rights of citizens upon all persons of African descent born within the extended limits of the United States, while persons of foreign birth who make our land their home must undergo a probation of five years, and can only then become citizens upon proof that they are "of good moral character, attached to the principles of the Constitution of the United States, and well disposed to the good order and happiness of the same."

The first section of the bill also contains an enumeration of the rights to be enjoyed by these classes so made citizens "in every State and Territory in the United States." These rights are "to make and enforce contracts; to sue, be parties, and give evidence; to inherit, purchase, lease, sell, hold, and convey real and personal property," and to have "full and equal benefit of all laws and proceedings for the security of person and property as is enjoyed by white citizens." So, too, they are made subject to the same punishment, pains, and penalties in common with white citizens, and to none other. Thus a perfect equality of the white and colored races is attempted to be fixed by Federal law in every State of the Union over the vast field of State jurisdiction covered by these enumerated rights. In no one of these can any State ever exercise any power of discrimination between the different races. In the exercise of State policy over matters exclusively affecting the people of each State it has frequently been thought expedient to discriminate between the two races. By the statutes of some of the States, Northern as well as Southern, it is enacted, for instance, that no white person shall intermarry with a negro or mulatto. Chancellor Kent[1] says, speaking of the blacks, that—

> Marriages between them and the whites are forbidden in some of the States where slavery does not exist, and they are prohibited in all the slaveholding States; and when not absolutely contrary to law, they are revolting, and regarded as an offense against public decorum.

I do not say that this bill repeals State laws on the subject of marriage between the two races, for as the whites are forbidden to intermarry with the blacks, the blacks can only make such contracts as the whites themselves are allowed to make, and therefore can not under this bill enter into the marriage contract with the whites. I cite this discrimination, however, as an instance of the State policy as to discrimination, and to inquire whether if Congress can abrogate all State laws of discrimination between the two races in the matter of real estate, of suits, and of contracts generally Congress may not also repeal the State laws as to the contract of marriage between the two races. Hitherto every subject embraced in the enumeration of rights contained in this bill has been considered as exclusively belonging to the States. They all relate to the internal police and economy of the respective States. They are matters which in each State concern the domestic condition of its people, varying in each according to its own peculiar circumstances and the safety and well-being of its own citizens. I do not mean to say that upon all these subjects there are not Federal restraints—as, for instance, in the State power of legislation over contracts there is a Federal limitation that no State shall pass a law impairing the obligations of contracts; and, as to crimes, that no State shall pass an *ex post facto* law; and, as to money, that no State shall make anything but gold and silver a legal tender; but where can we find a Federal prohibition against the power of any State to discriminate, as do most of them, between aliens and citizens, between artificial persons, called corporations, and natural persons, in the right to hold real estate? If it be granted that Congress can repeal all State laws discriminating between whites and blacks in the subjects covered by this bill, why, it may be asked, may not Congress repeal in the same way all State laws discriminating between the two races on the subjects of suffrage and office? If Congress can declare by law who shall hold lands, who shall testify, who shall have capacity to make a contract in a State, then Congress can by law also declare who, without regard to color or race, shall have the right to sit as a juror or as a judge, to hold any office, and, finally, to vote "in every State and Territory of the United States." As respects the Territories, they come within the power of Congress, for as to them the lawmaking power is the Federal power; but as to the States no similar provision exists vesting in Congress the power "to make rules and regulations" for them.

The object of the second section of the bill is to afford discriminating protection to colored persons in the full enjoyment of all the rights secured to them by the preceding section. It declares—

> That any person who, under color of any law, statute, ordinance, regulation, or custom, shall subject, or cause to be subjected, any inhabitant of any State or Territory to the deprivation of any right secured or protected by this act, or to different punishment, pains, or penalties on account of such person having at any time been held in a condition of slavery or involuntary servitude, except as a punishment for crime whereof the party shall have been duly convicted, or by reason of his color or race, than is prescribed for the punishment of white persons, shall be deemed guilty of a misdemeanor, and on conviction shall be punished by fine not exceeding $1,000, or imprisonment not exceeding one year, or both, in the discretion of the court.

This section seems to be designed to apply to some existing or future law of a State or Territory which may conflict with the provisions of the bill now under consideration. It provides for counteracting such forbidden legislation by imposing fine and imprisonment upon the legislators who may pass such conflicting laws, or upon the officers or agents who shall put or attempt to put them into execution. It means an official offense, not a common crime committed against law upon the persons or property of the black race. Such an act may deprive the black man of his property, but not of the *right* to hold property. It means a deprivation of the right itself, either by the State judiciary or the State legislature. It is therefore assumed that under this section members of State legislatures who should vote for laws conflicting with the provisions of the bill, that judges of the State courts who should render judgments in antagonism with its terms, and that marshals and sheriffs who should, as ministerial officers, execute processes sanctioned by State laws and issued by State judges in execution of their judgments could be brought before other tribunals and there subjected to fine and imprisonment for the performance of the duties which such State laws might impose. The legislation thus proposed invades the judicial power of the State. It says to every State court or judge, If you decide that this act is unconstitutional; if you refuse, under the prohibition of a State law, to allow a negro to testify; if you hold that over such a subject-matter the State law is paramount, and "under color" of a State law refuse the exercise of the right to the negro, your error of judgment, however conscientious, shall subject you to fine and imprisonment. I do not apprehend that the conflicting legislation which the bill seems to contemplate is so likely to occur as to render it necessary at this time to adopt a measure of such doubtful constitutionality.

In the next place, this provision of the bill seems to be unnecessary, as adequate judicial remedies could be adopted to secure the desired end without invading the immunities of legislators, always important to be preserved in the interest of public liberty; without assailing the independence of the judiciary, always essential to the preservation of individual rights; and without impairing the efficiency of ministerial officers, always necessary for the maintenance of public peace and order. The remedy proposed by this section seems to be in this respect not only anomalous, but unconstitutional; for the Constitution guarantees nothing with certainty if it does not insure to the several States the right of making and executing laws in regard to all matters arising within their jurisdiction, subject only to the restriction that in cases of conflict with the Constitution and constitutional laws of the United States the latter should be held to be the supreme law of the land.

The third section gives the district courts of the United States exclusive "cognizance of all crimes and offenses committed against the provisions of this act," and concurrent jurisdiction with the circuit courts of the United States of all civil and criminal cases "affecting persons who are denied or can not enforce in the courts or judicial tribunals of the State or locality where they may be any of the rights secured to them by the first section." The construction which I have given to the second section is strengthened by this third section, for it makes clear what kind of denial or deprivation of the rights secured by the first section was in contemplation. It is a denial or deprivation of such rights "in the courts or judicial tribunals of the State." It stands, therefore, clear of doubt that the offense and penalties provided in the second section are intended for the State judge who, in the clear exercise of his functions as a judge, not acting ministerially but judicially, shall decide contrary to this Federal law. In other words, when a State judge, acting upon a question involving a conflict between a State law and a Federal law, and bound, according to his own judgment and responsibility, to give an impartial decision between the two, comes to the conclusion that the State law is valid and the Federal law is invalid, he must not follow the dictates of his own judgment, at the peril of fine and imprisonment. The legislative departure of the Government of the United States thus takes from the judicial department of the States the sacred and exclusive duty of judicial decision, and converts the State judge into a mere ministerial officer, bound to decide according to the will of Congress.

It is clear that in States which deny to persons whose rights are secured by the first section of the bill any one of those rights all criminal and civil cases affecting them will, by the provisions of the third section, come under the exclusive cognizance of the Federal tribunals. It follows that if, in any State which denies to a colored person any one of all those rights, that person should commit a crime against the laws of a State—murder, arson, rape, or any other crime—all protection and punishment through the courts of the State are taken away, and he can only be tried and punished in the Federal courts. How is the criminal to be tried? If the offense is provided for and punished by Federal law, that law, and not the State law, is to govern. It is only when the offense does not happen to be within the purview of Federal law that the Federal courts are to try and punish him under any other law. Then resort is to be had to "the common law, as modified and changed" by State legislation, "so far as the same is not inconsistent with the Constitution and laws of the United States." So that over this vast domain of criminal jurisprudence provided by each State for the protection of its own citizens and for the punishment of all persons who violate its criminal laws, Federal law, whenever it can be made to apply, displaces State law. The question here naturally arises, from what source Congress derives the power to transfer to Federal tribunals certain classes of cases embraced in this section. The Constitution expressly declares that the judicial power of the United States "shall extend to all cases, in law and equity, arising under this Constitution, the laws of the United States, and treaties made or which shall be made under their authority; to all cases affecting ambassadors, other public ministers, and consuls; to all cases of admiralty and maritime jurisdiction; to controversies to which the United States shall be a party; to controversies between two or more States, between a State and citizens of another State, between citizens of different States, between citizens of the same State claiming lands under grants of different States, and between a State, or the citizens thereof, and foreign states, citizens, or subjects." Here the judicial power of the United States is expressly set forth and defined; and the act of September 24, 1789, establishing the judicial courts of the United States, in conferring upon the Federal courts jurisdiction over cases originating in State tribunals, is careful to confine them to the classes enumerated in the above-recited clause of the Constitution. This section of the bill undoubtedly comprehends cases and authorizes the exercise of powers that are not, by the Constitution, within the jurisdiction of the courts of the United States. To transfer them to those courts would be an exercise of authority well calculated to excite distrust and alarm on the part of all the States, for the bill applies alike to all of them—as well to those that have as to those that have not been engaged in rebellion.

It may be assumed that this authority is incident to the power granted to Congress by the Constitution, as recently amended, to enforce, by appropriate legislation, the article declaring that—

Neither slavery nor involuntary servitude, except as a punishment for crime whereof the party shall have been duly convicted, shall exist within the United States or any place subject to their jurisdiction.

It can not, however, be justly claimed that, with a view to the enforcement of this article of the Constitution, there is at present any necessity for the exercise of all the powers which this bill confers. Slavery has been abolished, and at present nowhere exists within the jurisdiction of the United States; nor has there been, nor is it likely there will be, any attempt to revive it by the people or the States. If, however, any such attempt shall be made, it will then become the duty of the General Government to exercise any and all incidental powers necessary and proper to maintain inviolate this great constitutional law of freedom.

The fourth section of the bill provides that officers and agents of the Freedmen's Bureau shall be empowered to make arrests, and also that other officers may be specially commissioned for that purpose by the President of the United States. It also authorizes circuit courts of the United States and the superior courts of the Territories to appoint, without limitation, commissioners, who are to be charged with the performance of *quasi* judicial duties. The fifth section empowers the commissioners so to be selected by the courts to appoint in writing, under their hands, one or more suitable persons from time to time to execute warrants and other processes described by the bill. These numerous official agents are made to constitute a sort of police, in addition to the military, and are authorized to summon a *posse comitatus*, and even to call to their aid such portion of the land and naval forces of the United States, or of the militia, "as may be necessary to the performance of the duty with which they are charged." This extraordinary power is to be conferred upon agents irresponsible to the Government and to the people, to whose number the discretion of the commissioners is the only limit, and in whose hands such authority might be made a terrible engine of wrong, oppression, and fraud. The general statutes regulating the land and naval forces of the United States, the militia, and the execution of the laws are believed to be adequate for every emergency which can occur in time of peace. If it should prove otherwise, Congress can at any time amend those laws in such manner as, while subserving the public welfare, not to jeopard the rights, interests, and liberties of the people.

The seventh section provides that a fee of $10 shall be paid to each commissioner in every case brought before him, and a fee of $5 to his deputy or deputies "for each person he or they may arrest and take before any such commissioner," "with such other fees as may be deemed reasonable by such commissioner," "in general for performing such other duties as may be required in the premises." All these fees are to be "paid out of the Treasury of the United States," whether there is a conviction or not; but in case of conviction they are to be recoverable from the defendant. It seems to me that under the influence of such temptations bad men might convert any law, however beneficent, into an instrument of persecution and fraud.

By the eighth section of the bill the United States courts, which sit only in one place for white citizens, must migrate with the marshal and district attorney (and necessarily with the clerk, although he is not mentioned) to any part of the district upon the order of the President, and there hold a court, "for the purpose of the more speedy arrest and trial of persons charged with a violation of this act;" and there the judge and officers of the court must remain, upon the order of the President, "for the time therein designated."

The ninth section authorizes the President, or such person as he may empower for that purpose, "to employ such part of the land or naval forces of the United States, or of the militia, as shall be necessary to prevent the violation and enforce the due execution of this act." This language seems to imply a permanent military force, that is to be always at hand, and whose only business is to be the enforcement of this measure over the vast region where it is intended to operate.

I do not propose to consider the policy of this bill. To me the details of the bill seem fraught with evil. The white race and the black race of the South have hitherto lived together under the relation of master and slave—capital owning labor. Now, suddenly, that relation is changed, and as to ownership capital and labor are divorced. They stand now each master of itself. In this new relation, one being necessary to the other, there will be a new adjustment, which both are deeply interested in making harmonious. Each has equal power in settling the terms, and if left to the laws that regulate capital and labor it is confidently believed that they will satisfactorily work out the problem. Capital, it is true, has more intelligence, but labor is never so ignorant as not to understand its own interests, not to know its own value, and not to see that capital must pay that value.

This bill frustrates this adjustment. It intervenes between capital and labor and attempts to settle questions of political economy through the agency of numerous officials whose interest it will be to foment discord between the two races, for as the breach widens their employment will continue, and when it is closed their occupation will terminate.

In all our history, in all our experience as a people living under Federal and State law, no such system as that contemplated by the details of this bill has ever before been proposed or adopted. They establish for the security of the colored race safeguards which go infinitely beyond any that the General Government has ever provided for the white race. In fact, the distinction of race and color is by the bill made to operate in favor of the colored and against the white race. They interfere with the municipal legislation of the States, with the relations existing exclusively between a State and its citizens, or between inhabitants of the same State—an absorption and assumption of power by the General Government which, if acquiesced in, must sap and destroy our federative system of limited powers and break down the barriers which preserve the rights of the States. It is another step, or rather stride, toward centralization and the concentration of all legislative powers in the National Government. The tendency of the bill must be to resuscitate the spirit of rebellion and to arrest the progress of those influences which are more closely drawing around the States the bonds of union and peace.

My lamented predecessor, in his proclamation of the 1st of January, 1863, ordered and declared that all persons held as slaves within certain States and parts of States therein designated were and thenceforward should be free; and further, that the executive government of the United States, including the military and naval authorities thereof, would recognize and maintain the freedom of such persons. This guaranty has been rendered especially obligatory and sacred by the amendment of the Constitution abolishing slavery throughout the United States. I therefore fully recognize the obligation to protect and defend that class of our people whenever and wherever it shall become necessary, and to the full extent compatible with the Constitution of the United States.

Entertaining these sentiments, it only remains for me to say that I will cheerfully cooperate with Congress in any measure that may be necessary for the protection of the civil rights of the freedmen, as well as those of all other classes of persons throughout the United States, by judicial process, under equal and impartial laws, in conformity with the provisions of the Federal Constitution.

I now return the bill to the Senate, and regret that in considering the bills and joint resolutions—forty-two in number—which have been thus far submitted for my approval I am compelled to withhold my assent from a second measure that has received the sanction of both Houses of Congress.

ANDREW JOHNSON.

Richardson, *Messages*, 405–13.

1. James Kent (1763–1847) was three times elected to the New York Assembly. In 1798 he was appointed a New York supreme court judge, becoming chief justice in 1804, and chancellor of the New York court of chancery in 1814. He retired as chancellor in 1823 and briefly taught at Columbia before writing his *Commentaries on American Law*, the foremost American institutional legal treatise. The following statement in Johnson's veto message comes from Kent's *Commentaries* (4 vols., New York, 1832 [1826]), 2: 258n. *DAB*.

From Thomas H. Williams[1]

"Private"

Virginia [City] Nev.   Mar. 27, 1866

Dear Sir

My only apology for tresspassing upon your valuable time is a supposition that you would like to know something concerning the state of affairs in this remote part of your Dominion, and a pressumption that no one else has taken the trouble to give you a truthful statement of the political status of our People. The People of this region are too go-aheadative and money loving to pay much attention to politics, or any state matters which do not affect them directly. They have felt much concern on the mint question and a branch here will certainly be of great advantage to them.[2] The sooner it is constructed the better, and the greater the hold of the Administration upon the hearts and affections of this People ⟨which seems to argue that their vital part is to be reached through the pocket; granted⟩. Nye[3] is trying to make personal capital out of the mint matter &, claims to be the Father of the institution. It may be well to take some of the wind out of his sails on that point. Julians Mineral land bill[4] excites much attention. It is unpopular. Our miners—like "our wayward sisters"—wish to [be] let alone. The popular measure will be to give the mines to the locators and workers of them absolutely; and it is just. Without the application of capital and labor they are worthless, and after their developement through private enterprise by tacit permission of the Government, it is wrong to interfere with their enjoyment. Government will be fully compensated by the incidents resulting from the increased wealth of the country.[5]

In your efforts to restore Peace to our distracted Country you are opposed by a very large majority of the—so called Union party. The Democracy here, as elsewhere, sustain you. I think however with judicious management you will be sustained at the next election. Fortunately the election is a great ways off, and there will be ample time for reflection. The second sober thought is all that is needed to bring the masses right. Unfortunately there is no man of ability belonging to the Union Party fully competent to take the lead. Ex Judge Ex Col Cradlebaugh[6] is the most prominent man of that stripe who supports your policy. But he lacks most of the characteristics necessary to constitute a good leader in perilous times. We are fortunate however in not having heavy timber opposed to us. Stewart[7] & Nye stand most prominent. You know and can measure them. Baldwin,[8] Mr Lincolns U.S. Dist Judge comes next. He aspires to the Gubernatorial nomination on the Radical side. Whitman[9] an aspirant to Nye's place may be ranked next. He succeeded to Stewarts law business and is remarkable only for having the greater part of his *brain below* his ears. There is some ability among the Democrats,—more than the other side—But good policy dictates that "Union" men take the lead.

Nye has but little personal strength and is generally regarded as very dishonest.

Stewart—as you have discovered—is of small calibre and very unreliable. He lacks back-bone. You cant count on him. He is not governed by principle either as a man, a lawyer or politician, but watches for the tide and tries to drift with it. His proclivities are all against the radicals yet he will not hesitate to act with them if his personal interest seems to so dictate. I have no doubt he meant to support your policy. But a few dozen telegrams and letters frightened him off. The consequence is that he will fall between the parties. The fact is that the People never did have confidence in him, and he was only elected through and by influences which may never occur again, and it is to be hoped never will.[10] His Father in law[11] is too well known in this country to add to his strength. On the contrary he is a down right cipher. I have no axes to grind, But hope that the Federal patronage of this state may be very carefully used and so as not to add to the strength of the enemies of our Country. I was not among your supporters for the Vice Presidency and witnessed your ascent to the Presidential chair with fear and trembling. I regarded you as far more vindictive and dangerous to the southern People than your predecessor. I am now happy to acknowledge my error, and am proud of the privilege of enrolling myself under your banner in the great battle for the constitution as made by our Fathers which you are so nobly fighting.

Thomas H. Williams

P.S.   The senators and members from this state[12] and California[13] know me. Judge Feild[14] also. He was on the Supreme Bench of California during both of my terms as Attorney General of that state.[15]

T.H.W

ALS, DLC-JP.

1. Attracted by the Comstock Lode, Williams (1828–*fl*1881), a California lawyer, moved to Nevada in the early 1860s, serving in the Nevada legislature in 1864. A Democrat, he was twice defeated for the U.S. Senate; subsequently he moved back to California. Bancroft, *California*, 6: 683, 723; Hubert H. Bancroft, *History of Nevada, Colorado, and Wyoming, 1540–1888* (San Francisco, 1890), 189, 191; Oakland directories (1879–81).

2. In 1863 Congress authorized the establishment of a branch mint in Carson City. Ground was not broken for the building, however, until July 18, 1866, and the mint did not actually begin production until January 1870. *U.S. Statutes at Large*, 12: 770–71; WPA, *Nevada: A Guide to the Silver State* (1940), 205; Russell R. Elliott and William D. Rowley, *History of Nevada* (Lincoln, Nebr., 1987 [1973]), 127.

3. In 1861 Lincoln appointed James W. Nye (1814–1876), a New York lawyer, the first, and only, governor of the Nevada Territory. Upon statehood in 1864, the Nevada legislature elected Nye, a Republican, to the U.S. Senate, a position he held until 1873. *DAB*; *BDAC*.

4. George W. Julian of Indiana was chairman of the House Committee on Public Lands. Originally introduced by Julian in February 1865 and reintroduced in December, the measure "provided for the subdivision and sale of gold and silver lands of the United States." Westerners strongly opposed the bill and it was not passed. Russell R. Elliott, *Servant of Power: A Political Biography of Senator William M. Stewart* (Reno, 1983), 51–53.

5. The western-sponsored act which was eventually passed in July 1866 and deviously titled, "Act granting the right of way to ditch and canal owners," recognized "free mining" and "gave legal status to local mining district regulations that were initially based on squatter sovereignty." Ibid., 53–55.

6. In 1858 John Cradlebaugh (1819–1872), an Ohio lawyer, was appointed an associate U.S. justice for the Utah Territory, which then included Nevada. When the Nevada Territory was formed, he was elected territorial delegate to Congress, but instead from April 1862 to October 1863 he served as colonel of the 114th Ohio Vol. Inf. and was wounded at Vicksburg. He returned to Nevada in 1863 and engaged in mining activities. *BDAC*.

7. Sen. William M. Stewart.

8. Alexander W. Baldwin (1835–1869), son of California Supreme Court Justice Joseph G. Baldwin, was Stewart's law partner before being appointed in 1865 as U.S. district judge for Nevada, a post he held until he was killed in a railway accident. *NCAB*, 13: 472; *U.S. Off. Reg.* (1865–69); Elliott, *Servant of Power*, 14.

9. Bernard C. Whitman (1827–1885) moved in 1850 to California where he practiced law and politics until his move to Virginia City, Nevada, in 1864. In 1868 he was appointed a Nevada Supreme Court justice and served as chief justice (1873–74). Whitman returned to California in 1882. *NCAB*, 12: 188.

10. Williams served as attorney for the accusing party in a slander suit against Stewart in 1864–65, which may account for his animosity. Elliott, *Servant of Power*, 43.

11. Henry S. Foote.

12. Stewart and Nye were the Nevada senators. Rep. Delos R. Ashley (1828–1873), a lawyer who had moved to California in 1850 and held various state offices there, relocated to Nevada in 1864. He served in the House as a Republican from 1865 to 1869. *BDAC*.

13. California senators were John Conness and James A. McDougall. California had three representatives. John Bidwell (1819–1900) arrived there in 1841, engaging in state politics and serving as brigadier general of California militia during the Civil War, before serving a single term in the House (1865–67). Vermont lawyer William Higby (1813–1887) moved to California in 1850 and held several state offices before being elected to three terms in the House (1863–69). Donald C. McRuer (1826–1898), a commission merchant who removed to California in 1851 and engaged in various political and educational activities, served one term in Congress (1865–67). *BDAC*.

14. Lawyer Stephen J. Field (1816–1899) migrated to California in 1849. After involvement in local politics and the state legislature, Field was elected to the California Supreme Court in 1857. Lincoln appointed him in 1863 to the U.S. Supreme Court where he served until 1897. *DAB*.

15. Williams held no state office before 1858. In 1859 he was nominated for California attorney general by "Lecomptonite" Democrats. Bancroft, *California*, 6: 700, 723.

From Andrew J. Hamilton

Executive Office
Austin Texas   28th March 1866.

Mr President.

This will be handed to you by Col Robert H Taylor[1] a loyal citizen of this State and a member of the Convention now in Session[2] (but which will adjourn in a day or two) who I present to your acquaintance, and commend to your Excellency's usual courteous and respectful attention to all who seek your presence upon legitimate business. He is a firm and devoted Union man—an old and highly influential citizen of the State, for many years connected with public affairs as a Representative & Senator in the Legislature. He visits the Capitol of the Nation on public business for the State being charged with two Missions; to wit, 1st To arrange with the Treasury Department the terms upon which the State can assume the direct tax apportioned to her by act of Congress. The Convention having passed an Ordinance for this purpose which required the Comptroller of the State to proceed to Washington to adjust the terms assumption and there being a vacancy in that Office by reason of the resignation of A H Latimer,[3] the late incumbent, I prevailed upon Col

Taylor to accept the Office at least long enough to discharge this important duty. 2nd He bears with him and will present to Your Excellency resolutions passed by the Convention upon the subject of the suffering condition of our Indian frontier.[4] Col Taylor himself lives near this frontier and will be able to give you all necessary information touching the subject. I will also remark that there are few men in the State better able to give correct information upon the condition of the State politically or whose opinions are entitled to more weight. You will doubtless hear many contradictory reports, as many in fact as there are shades of opinion. There will even be differences between those who are in perfect political accord, each judgeing of the actual condition of things from his own individual stand point. It is perhaps not possable for any one to give a complete and perfect analysis of the political feelings, purposes, hopes and intentions of the people of this State. My own opinion is that no one can fully comprehend the State of the public mind for the reason that I do not believe there is at this moment such a thing as a settled public mind. There is every shade of feeling, of opinion, of expression and of hope, from the most exalted patriotism down to a determined spirit of anarchy —and from the highest hopes for a glorious future to utter despondency.

Union men have been so long depressed that many of them are not hopeful of the future—while the secessionists are only depressed at the prospect of a final settlement of our troubles on the basis of a permanent Union precluding another fair oppertunity to attempt to effect its overthrow.

I have watched vigilantly and scrutinzed closely to ascertain their feelings and purposes; and the result is that in my opinion without any well defined or settled plan of future action they do as a class (I mean leading original Secessionists and the young men of the party who are led by them and have learned to love War rather than peace) cherish the hope that some turn of political affairs may again involve the Govt in War with England or France in which case they would promptly declare against this Govt. This may be considered an uncharitable opinion, but it is justified by both acts and expressions. Many do not scruple openly to declare such sentiments, and it is quite common, I am informed, in every part of the Country to hear epithets of hatred to the Govt and hopes expressed that it will yet go to pieces. It [is] still more common to hear men openly declare their belief that republican Govt is a failure and that soon or late a Monarchy or Imperial dynasty will supercede ours. This I regard as the most dangerous feature of the whole. The hatred of the Govt, if confined to those who conspired to overthrow it would create in my mind no alarms for the future—for their present feelings can be accounted for upon a principle of our nature well understood. The man who wantonly injures or wrongs another without cause will never be reconciled to the party wronged. So those who so deeply injured the Govt without cause

—who abused it and sought its destruction (the leaders I mean) will never be, in heart, at peace with it. The mere bitterness of heart which they feel consequent upon disappointed hopes would work no ill effects in the future if indulged in without producing its influence upon others —especially the young men of the Country. We all admit that the bullwork of republican institutions is the affection for and the confidence which the Citizens feel in their justice and stability. If this be so it is most certainly not to be regarded without apprehension that any considerable number of our people manifest a total want of affection for the Govt but an apparent assured belief in its speedy overthrow in such manner as day by day to familiarise the public mind with and impress upon the young men of the Country with sentiments and opinions the very opposite of those which you and I were taught to believe essential to the preservation of liberty. The work of revolution first, anarchy it may be at last, is more than half accomplished when the body of the people learn to speak doubtingly or disparageingly of our institutions or even to hear others so speak with indifference. I trust however that this will be corrected in time by such agencies as will convince the disloyal element that their hopes are vain. I do not pretend to know precisely how this change in this section is to be brought about, but I have an abiding faith that even if we are destined to have more trouble at last when it is over our Govt will rest upon a firmer base than ever before. While all this mixed and strange medley of feeling and opinion exists among us the great body of the people in most sections of the State are orderly and quiet and the material interests prospering beyond what I had any reason to hope when I first returned to the State. I think I can affirm that there is a larger crop planted this season than in any previous year. If it is seasonable there will be a larger Cotton crop raised this year ever than in any previous year. To a casual observer things are going on in our State very much as in former years. But I should fail in my duty to your Excellency if I did not in the most emphatic and earnest manner entreat you not to listen to the representations of those who insist upon the troops being withdrawn from the State. There are many very good men who doubtless believe that this could be done with safety and with advantage to the Country. I know the contrary. I have information from every portion of the State and am I doubt not better prepared to judge upon this subject than any one man in it. I cannot say how long it will be before they can be safely withdrawn but I know the time has not yet arrived. Col Taylor will give you all needful information touching the action of the Convention including details. I may say of the action upon the subject of the Ordinance of Secession—The Status of the freedmen in respect of personal and civil rights—And the rebel state debt, it is perhaps better than that of any of the other states. This is entirely due to the determined efforts of the Union men. The conflict was long and the fight well contested and although the Unionists did not secure all they wanted they certainly defeated the secessionists in having what they wanted.[5]

I will in a few days (as soon as printed) forward to you the entire action of the Convention. Our election for State Officers will come off the fourth Monday in June. I look forward to the time with impatience for indeed I am anxious for the time to come when I can rest. I have not had one days or hours respite from labour since my return to the state. I have not given satisfaction to all but I am happy to know that the Union men of the State do fully endorse my course.

I may have been too indulgent and forgiving but if so I can only plead in excuse that it was my constant aim to reflect the magnanimous and liberal spirit of the Govt of the U S which I represented.

I have I must confess recommended parties for special pardon who, if it were not done, I would not recommend, but these cases are few and I think scarcely worthy of troubling you about.

You will have a deputation of four members of the Convention to visit you as soon as the Convention adjourns. They are nominally two Union & two disunion.[6]

They will present to you their views of the present condition of the State. I know not what they will say; but I do know that the views of a majority of them differ materially from mine.

I have dispatched to your Excellency four telegrams[7] without having any thing in reply and our mails are so uncertain that we have no late news from Washington and are in ignorance of what is going on.

Wishing you continued health and success in all your efforts for the restoration and perpetuity of the Govt. . . .

A. J. Hamilton

ALS, DLC-JP.

1. South Carolina lawyer Taylor (1825–fl1888) moved to Texas in 1844. A cavalry commander in the Mexican War, he served two terms in the Texas house in the early 1850s and later one term in the senate. Although opposed to secession, Taylor raised three regiments for the Confederacy. After the war he served as a judge and a member of the state house of representatives. Webb et al., *Handbook of Texas*, 2: 716.

2. The Texas constitutional convention.

3. Albert H. Latimer (1808–1877) moved to Texas in 1833 and became involved in the struggle for Texas independence. He later served in the Texas house of representatives (two terms) and as senator. Although Latimer was a Unionist, some of his sons fought for the Confederacy. He was nominated in February 1866 to be one of three direct tax commissioners for the state of Texas. The Senate confirmed his nomination in March. The following year he was appointed to the Texas Supreme Court. Ramsdell, *Reconstruction in Texas*, 94; Webb et al., *Handbook of Texas*, 2: 34; Ser. 6B, Vol. 4: 211, Johnson Papers, LC.

4. See also Hamilton to Johnson, Mar. 1, 1866.

5. Johnson's observer Benjamin C. Truman agreed with Hamilton's observations. See Truman to Johnson, Mar. 24, [1866], *Advice*, 197.

6. Johnson met with the Texas delegation on May 3. The Unionists were Judge John Hancock and Robert H. Lane. Lane (c1815–fl1870), a lawyer from Fannin County, was later elected in June 1866 to the state legislature. The following month Johnson nomi-

nated and the Senate confirmed Lane as internal revenue collector for the Second District of Texas. James W. Henderson (1817–1880), a disunionist, had served in the house of representatives for both the Republic of Texas and the state of Texas, as well as held the post of lieutenant governor and, briefly, that of governor. He was a captain in the Confederate army. J. S. Porter (*c*1835–*fl*1870) may have been a lawyer who lived in Sherman, Grayson County, by 1870. 1860 Census, Tex., Fannin, Bonham, 179; Kaufman, Kaufman, 25; (1870), Fannin, Bonham, Precinct No. 2, 174; Grayson, Sherman, 13; *National Intelligencer*, May 4, 1866; Webb et al., *Handbook of Texas*, 1: 796; Robert Shook, "Toward a List of Reconstruction Loyalists," *SWHQ*, 76 (1973): 318; Hamilton et al. to Johnson, Mar. 24, 1866; George W. White et al. to Johnson, Aug. 23, 1866, Appts., Customs Service, Collector, Brownsville, Tex., R. H. Lane, RG56, NA; Ser. 6B, Vol. 4: 211, Johnson Papers, LC.

7. See Hamilton to Johnson, Feb. 16, Mar. 7, 1866, in this volume, as well as Hamilton to Johnson, Feb. 20, 1866, Tels. Recd., President, Vol. 5 (1866–67), RG107, NA; and Hamilton to Johnson, Feb. 26, 1866, Johnson Papers, LC.

From Richard P.L. Baber

Columbus, O., March 29t 1866.[1]

I deem it my duty in the present state of Public affairs as a steadfast friend of your Restoration policy, to make a few suggestions as to what should be done to insure success. From my position as a member of the Union State Central Committee of Ohio, I have had ample opportunity to watch the working of politics here. The Radicals must be satisfied by this time that you are not to be swerved from the platform, upon which you were elected, to their impracticable scheme of Universal Suffrage and Universal Amnesty, and the people will be with you on this issue, as they were with Lincoln as against the Wade-Davis plan. But a great effort will be made to conceal the true issue under the cry of "Johnson has gone over to the Copperheads, wishes to admit unwashed rebels to Congress and won't hang Davis." These accusations I have endeavored to refute in two articles, signed, Ohio, in the Cincinnati Commercial of the 24 and 26th Inst.[2] which I send you, and think if the New York Times would copy, it could find material in the Resolutions cited of the Union State Conventions, to show that your action, has been in strict conformity, to the party platform. I offered, myself in the Republican State Central Committee the resolutions in 1861, upon which the Union organization was formed. I had a long conversation with our mutual friend Gov Cox, yesterday, and can assure you that your Ohio friends stand firm. We desire some basis on which to arrange the coming campaign and think that the following would put you in a winning position. *1st* Some effective and Constitutional law to enable the Freedmen to enforce in the Federal Courts, rights denied them in the State Courts, as to the protection of person and property. *2nd* A move to compel the Radicals in Congress to act on Senator Doolittle's bill for the trial of treason cases and the arraigning of Jefferson Davis for trial[3] as soon as practicable in Tennessee, so as to get rid of Chase's sitting in Virginia, and at the same time by writ of error forcing to deliver himself in the Supreme Court of his Ohio, Oberlin Secessionism. And we think Henry Stanberry would be a much safer lawyer in the case than Speed, who sympathizes with the Radicals. *3rd.* Force a vote on the admission of the Tennessee members, so as to compel individual Congressmen to show their hands. *4th* Have a vote on the voting basis amendment[4] as to representatives which will show the country that New England selfishness is not willing to accept any basis of representation that diminishes her political power. The object of the Radicals is to pass a Constitutional Amendment, as a mere pretext to keep Southern representation out, but if New England rejects the voting basis, as she will do, if it is proposed, it will *shut their mouths*. Lastly—. The patronage of the Government must be put in every Congressional district, in the hands of men who know how to wield it in the next elections. A Radical Senator, sent me under frank Forney's Weekly Chronicle,[5] with a programme for the election of all the present Congress—this will be a good weapon to wield against them. The combination amongst these stay at home politicians, to hold on to their lease of office, against the men, who have been in the Army will be fiercely contested in every Congressional District in this State, and if you will throw your patronage so as to deprive the present Radical incumbents of its use, your friends will make it *count*. Already candidates are springing up against the present Radical incumbents, and Genl Schenck[6] is put at the head of a Congressional Committee, to circulate documents for the re-election of the clique—he can be beaten at if you only will send in the name of Col William Miner as assessor in stead of Dunlevy.[7] You recollect Judge Swayne[8] and my self called you attention to this case and I remarked, Secretary McCullough would not do it on account of certain influences. You know he is not posted on Ohio politics. The Hon Lewis D. Campbell who is from Schencks district, will coroborate my views in this matter. As I told you in Washington I ask nothing for my self except that power be given to place the friends of your policy in effective positions, where they can work. Our State Central Committee will probably call a State Convention, about August 1st,[9] and in the mean time your friends don't want to have to fight in that body the whole pack of collectors and assessors with which Chase and Radical Congressmen have stocked the State. I hope to be in Washington next month[10] and then desire after consultation here to have these things reformed. I hope you will have time to note the articles I have sent you.

R P L Baber

ALS, DLC-JP.

1. On this same date Baber addressed a letter to Robert Johnson, directing him to "be sure and see that, the President *gets* the documents, I thus mailed to him." Johnson Papers, LC.

2. Baber also sent copies of the articles to Robert Johnson and to Secretary Seward, but no enclosures have been found in either this or those letters. Ibid.; Baber to Seward, Mar. 30, 1866, Johnson Papers, LC. The articles, "The Union Party, President Johnson and Congress," appeared in the *Commercial*, March 24, 26, 1866.

3. Of the several congressional resolutions proposed thus far, none had been introduced by James R. Doolittle, although he had indicated to Johnson his qualified support for giving Davis a speedy trial. *House Journal*, 39 Cong., 1 Sess., pp. 97–98, 198 (Ser. 1243); *Senate Journal*, 39 Cong., 1 Sess., pp. 58, 84 (Ser. 1236); Doolittle to Johnson, Sept. 23, 1865, *Johnson Papers*, 9: 118, 120.

4. Perhaps a reference to Doolittle's proposal concerning the basis of congressional representation. See Eli Thayer to Johnson, Mar. 17, 1866.

5. John W. Forney's *Washington Chronicle*.

6. Robert C. Schenck.

7. Neither Miner nor John C. Dunlevy received the appointment. See Robert C. Schenck to Johnson, Dec. 7, 1865, *Johnson Papers*, 9: 494–95.

8. Noah H. Swayne.

9. The National Union party convention was held at Columbus on August 7. Bonadio, *North of Reconstruction*, 169; Joseph H. Geiger to Johnson, Aug. 2, 1866, Johnson Papers, LC.

10. Baber visited with Johnson in June. See Baber to Johnson, June 28, 1866.

From James Brooks[1]

Washington D.C.   March 29 1866

Dear Sir

Why, I cannot say, but, the old Whig Constitutionl Union Com'e of the City of New York, sent me the enclosed and desired me to lay the facts before you.[2]

This Commitee after your 22 speech sent a formal Delegation to congratulate you, (whom I presented in the East Room) and they represent a great New York party, the living remembrances of the life & practice of Henry Clay & Danl. Webster.[3]

James Brooks

ALS, DLC-JP.

1. Editor-in-chief of the *New York Express*, Brooks (1810–1873) also represented the Eighth District of New York in Congress as a Democrat. *BDAC*.

2. Enclosed was a series of resolutions disapproving of the majority report recently submitted by the congressional Committee of Elections which determined after months of investigation that Brooks had been elected by fraudulent means in 1865 and was therefore no longer entitled to his seat. Daniel B. Northrup et al. to Johnson, Mar. 28, 1866, Johnson Papers, LC. For both the majority and minority reports of the contested election, see *House Reports*, 39 Cong., 1 Sess., No. 41 (Ser. 1272).

3. Johnson was powerless to prevent Brooks's expulsion from the House on April 6, 1866. In the fall elections later that year, however, Brooks regained his seat in Congress and continued serving from March 1867 until his death. *BDAC*; *House Journal*, 39 Cong., 1 Sess., p. 516 (Ser. 1243).

From Sarah F. Mason[1]

Yanceyville N C   March 29th/66.

President Johnson:—

Will you sir pardon me for this intrusion and trespass upon your time every moment of which is precious? I want to ask you a question and it is this, whether the Government will make provision for the education of the colored race? If so I would ask for an appointment as teacher of a female school. I know this in the eyes of many women at the South would be considered degrading; But why should it be so esteemed? Why not benefit those around you as much as possible? I acknowledge that my motive is two-fold. 1st I would like to be engaged in some thing to make a comfortable support, and at the same time feel that my time is not thrown away upon money alone. My husband Rev S. G. Mason[2] has been preaching to two heretofore wealthy churches now reduced to poverty as all the churches are South, and I see but little prospect of their being able to sustain him fully, and the thought occured to me that perhaps I might do some thing in the way above mentioned. Other schools are so numerous it is not worth while to think of that. And why not I set an example to the women of our country as any one else?

I refer you to Dr Bedford Brown,[3] formerly of this county, now a resident of Washington City, and son of Col. Bedford Brown of this state whome you very well know. And if need be to Rev G. W. Sampson D.D. Pres. Columbian Col.

Any information in regard to this matter will be greatfully received.[4] I cannot bear the idea of my name being mentioned in public so please withold it.

Sarah F. Mason

ALS, DNA-RG105, Records of the Commr., Lets. Recd. (M752, Roll 29).

1. Sarah Frances Davidson (c1824–fl1870), formerly of Charlotte County, Virginia, had married Samuel G. Mason in 1841. 1870 Census, N.C., Caswell, Yanceyville Twp., 36; Joanne L. Nance, comp. and ed., *Charlotte County, Virginia, 1816–1850: Marriage Bonds and Ministers' Returns (with Additions to Marriages, 1764–1815)* (Charlottesville, 1987), 171.

2. Mason (c1813–fl1890), a Bedford County, Virginia, native, was pastor of the Providence Baptist Church, northwest of Yanceyville. 1850 Census, Va., Charlotte, Charlotte Div., 77; William S. Powell, *When the Past Refused to Die: A History of Caswell County North Carolina 1777–1977* (Durham, 1977), 453–54.

3. Brown (1825–1897), a graduate of Philadelphia's Jefferson Medical College (1855), during the war was inspector of Confederate hospitals and camps. Afterwards, he practiced his profession in Alexandria, Virginia. Howard A. Kelly and Walter L. Burrage, *Dictionary of American Medical Biography* (New York, 1928), 152.

4. Johnson had his secretary refer Mason's letter to General Howard of the Freedmen's Bureau.

From Sam Milligan

Greeneville Ten.   March 29, 1866

Dear Sir:

I start to Jackson in the morning to hold the court at that place, and before I go I thought I would say a word or two in relation to political affairs in this region. It is now apparent that Gov Brownlow and his influence is to be counted against your policy; and failing to make satisfactory headway in the State, he has tacked about, and we are to have a struggle to devide the State, and thereby perpetuate his power. I understand, circulars are in course of preparation, to be sent broad-cast over this end of the State, to influence the people to speedy action.

Brownlow was posted to speak at Jonesboro, I believe it was saturday, but failed to attend. His place was however filled by his son John and some other man,[1] whose name I did not learn; but Mr Deaderic[2] writes to one of his friends here, the fruits of the discussion, are already being developed by the renewal of notices to Rebels to leave the country. Were it not for the evil influence of such men the country would be at peace.

I see you have a hard time, but it is so absurd, after a war to restore the Union, that a few fanatical Members of Congress, should attempt to defeat the judgement of the sword. It is impossible, and only requires a little time, and the action of the people to set it right. It has occurred to me, and I will venture to suggest it, that you would make your reconstruction policy more impregnable by letting it appear a little more distinctly, that after the principle that the States are in the Union, shall be recognized, that it would be the duty of Congress to see that none but true & loyal men, be admitted to seats. This I know is your position, and it is the right of Congress to judge of the election, qualifycation &c of its members; but what I am driving at, is, that it should fully appear as a part of your programe, that in the reconstruction, Congress must be kept pure and loyal.

John Baxter, is a very ardent supporter of your administration, and as I learn, he is saying many foolish things, which like the State Convention under his control,[3] did more harm than good. The Whigs never had any sense in the management of political assemblies, and the war has made them no wiser.

In my disultoy reading I have come across a decision of the Supreme Court of the United [States] that substantially settles the doctrine of Secessions as you have allways contended for it. See Dodge vs Woolsey 18—Howard page 351—middle of the opinion.[4]

I have bored you long enough. Good night.

Sam Milligan

ALS, DLC-JP.

1. Since there were several speakers at the March 24 meeting in Jonesborough, it is difficult to know exactly to whom Milligan refers here. Quite likely he means Timothy R. Stanley of Chattanooga, who with John B. Brownlow addressed the convention while the committee on preamble and resolutions retired to complete its work. Governor Brownlow had earlier indicated that, because of health reasons and other commitments, he would be unable to attend the Jonesborough convention. *Jonesborough Union Flag*, Mar. 23, 30, 1866.

2. Possibly James W. Deaderick of Jonesborough.

3. Probably a reference to the meeting held at the state capital in late February at which John Baxter took an active role. One of the Nashville papers labelled it "the Disorganizers' Convention." *Nashville Press and Times*, Feb. 23, 1866.

4. The case, heard by the Court in 1855, concerned taxes levied upon banks in the state of Ohio. As Milligan indicated, there were statements in the Court's decision that were wide-ranging in their ramifications and possible application. An example of one such statement is this: "In such a union, the States are bound by all of those principles of justice which bind individuals to their contracts. They are bound by their mutual acquiescence in the powers of the constitution, that neither of them should be the judge, or should be allowed to be the final judge of the powers of the constitution, or of the interpretation of the laws of congress." *Dodge v. Woolsey*, 18 Howard 351 (1855).

From Robert W. Bates[1]

Washington   March 30th 1866

Sir.

My long acquaintance with, and my warm feeling of friendship for you personally, as well as the principles and Policy of your Administration is my only apology for addressing you at this time.

On the 9th of June 1863 I received through the Hon Mr Sargeant[2] of California a Clerkship in the Office of Internal Revenue Treasury Department, at the Sallary of $1200 per annum, from which time to the present I have been *persistently kept without any advance*, and have been compelled to endure the mortification of seeing *young men and boys* without experience placed over my head at Sallaries ranging from Fourteen to Eighteen hundred dollars, and my family consisting of a wife grown daughter and two small boys have been almost deprived of the necessaries of life, and for no other reason (as I stated to you in the Hall of the Treasury Building about the 1st of April last[)], than that I could not concienciously beleive in all the Radical Measures now being aggitated by the present Congress.

Since your accession to the Presidency I have been obliged to sit from day to day and hear *you denounced* as *a Traitor* to your Country and an enemy to the human race, and because I have had the spirit to resent such language, I have been dismissed from the petty position held by me,[3] while the very men who thus denounce you, *have been* and are *still being retained and promoted* to the best positions—for the fact is notorious that within the last few weeks, nearly all of your real friends have been dismissed, under the plea that the public interest demands a reduction of the present force. There are men in this Office who are gratuitously circulating papers that openly denounce you in the *most bitter unmeasured terms*, and these very men are receiving favours at the hands of the Commissioner,[4] in fact, there is no earthly chance for the retention or promotion of any firm and outspoken friend of Andrew Johnson.

I do *not beleive* that the Hon Sec of the Treasury has any just conception of the character of the opposition existing in this Office to your Administration, *nor* do I beleive that he would sanction the course persued by the Comr. of Int Revenue.

I beg leave most respectfully *now to make my appeal to your Excellency*, beleiving that justice to yourself as well as the great principles and policy of which you are the exponent, demands that you should be surrounded by your *friends*, and *not* your enemies and that you will see that I receive such a position as my long experience in public office should entitle me to, and the necessities of a large family demand.[5]

R. W. Bates

ALS, DNA-RG56, Appls., Positions in Washington, D.C., Treasury Offices, R. W. Bates.

1. Bates (*c*1812–*fl*1882), a Virginia native and longtime resident of Washington, was at various times a tailor, clerk in the Treasury Department, Post Office, and Pension Office, wood and coal dealer, furniture salesman, and real estate and insurance agent. 1860 Census, D.C., Washington, 1st Ward, 148; Washington, D.C., directories (1846, 1858–84).

2. Aaron Sargent (1827–1887) moved from Massachusetts to Washington in 1847 and became secretary to a member of Congress. Two years later he moved to California where he established a career in newspaper work and law. He became active in state politics, eventually being elected as a Republican to one term in the U.S. Senate. After the war Sargent served two terms in the House (1868–72) and then was elected again to the Senate. *DAB*.

3. In early March, Assistant Secretary of the Treasury William E. Chandler notified Bates that his services with the department would "cease and terminate with the 31st instant." Despite letters of support from Sen. James H. Lane and Washington mayor Richard Wallach, Bates was removed. Chandler to Bates, Mar. 8, 1866; Lane to Johnson, Apr. 30, 1866; Wallach to Johnson, May 2, 1866, Appls., Positions in Washington, D.C., Treasury Offices, R. W. Bates, RG56, NA

4. Edward A. Rollins.

5. An applicant for the post of warden of the District of Columbia jail, Bates was not appointed but by 1867 did receive a clerkship in the Pension Office in Washington. William H. Ball to Johnson, Aug. 16, 1866; Joseph H. Bradley to Johnson, Aug. 24, 1866, Appts. Div., Lets. Recd., RG48, NA; *U.S. Off. Reg.* (1867). For more on Bates, see John W. Leftwich and Nathaniel G. Taylor to Johnson, May 18, 1866.

From Francis P. Blair, Sr.

Wash   30 March '66

My Dear Mr. President

Gen Bartlett[1] has served country bravely in battle throughout the War rising from a volunteer captaincy to the Major Generalship, commanding a division in the closing scenes before Richmond. He has been most effecient in the efforts since your accession to blend the Democrats with the conservative Republicans and will contrive to exert himself in your service as long as he remains in the country. I asked of you personally a foreign appointment that he might have means and leisure refit himself for his profession. Mr. F. Seward[2] tells him that the Hague is an *unpromised* place[3] that might suit him. I beg you to give it to him.[4]

F P. Blair

ALS, DLC-JP.

1. A veteran of most every major engagement in the East from Bull Run to Appomattox, Joseph J. Bartlett (1834–1893) later served as deputy commissioner of pensions for President Cleveland. Warner, *Blue*.

2. Frederick W. Seward (1830–1915) worked as a newspaper editor in Albany before moving in 1861 to Washington to become assistant secretary of state under his father and remained through Johnson's administration. Afterwards he served in the New York Assembly and again in the State Department (1877–79). *DAB*; *New York Times*, Apr. 26, 1915.

3. Hugh Ewing was appointed minister to The Hague in December 1866 in place of Gen. Daniel E. Sickles, who had declined serving. *DAB*; Ser. 6B, Vol. 2: 75, Johnson Papers, LC.

4. Recommended also by his former commanding officers and influential political leaders, Bartlett was appointed in February 1867 as U.S. minister to Sweden and Norway. Ibid., 31, 34. See Samuel L.M. Barlow to Johnson, Nov. 27, 1865, Johnson Papers, LC; and Lets. of Appl. and Recomm., 1861–69 (M650, Roll 3), Joseph J. Bartlett, RG59, NA.

From George L. Curry[1]

New York, March 30th, 1866.

Mr President,

May I say a kind word in behalf of my friend Col. William B. Thomas, the present Collector of the Port of Philadelphia. He held this position under your lamented predecessor, and has since been reappointed under your administration,[2] without having been as yet confirmed by the Senate, as I understand. Permit me to say that the confirmation of the appointment, in my judgment, would subserve the public interest and be eminently proper and satisfactory.[3] Col. Thomas is a faithful and popular official, and brings to the discharge of his public duties integrity, capacity and fidelity. Added to this, which pleases me the more, he believes as your friends believe in reference to the political measures of the day. He is decidedly conservative, in contradistinction to the radical element which seeks to control, through Congress, the politics of the country. He is earnest and sincere in his political faith without being obtrusive in defence of it.[4]

I know that I can assure you, that on the Pacific slope of the continent, you will be sustained by a very large majority of our people. As you may not be aware of the fact I incidently mention that I was Governor of Oregon for a period of six years, and, therefore, feel that I ought to know, with some certainty, the sentiment of our people in regard to the present condition of public affairs. I had the pleasure of being presented to you the other day by our mutual friend Senator Nesmith,[5] and was exceedingly gratified with the very candid and intelligent expression of your views which you were pleased to give us on that occasion. You have my most cordial wishes for the complete success of your policy, as I am firmly convinced it is for the best interests of our beloved country.

Geo. L. Curry

ALS, DLC-JP.

1. A native Philadelphian, Curry (1820–1878) edited newspapers in St. Louis and Oregon before becoming secretary, acting governor, and finally governor of the Oregon Territory prior to statehood in 1859. Afterwards he was involved with the Northern Pacific Rail Road and served briefly as a state land commissioner. *Appleton's Cyclopaedia.*

2. Thomas had been granted a temporary commission beginning July 29, 1865. Benjamin Huckel to Hugh McCulloch, July 22, 1865; Thomas to Johnson, Aug. 3, 1865, Appts., Customs Service, Collector, Philadelphia., Wm. B. Thomas, RG56, NA.

3. Thomas's tenure as collector was controversial in 1865 as several persons wrote to Johnson about either retaining or removing him. See, for example, Joseph R. Flanigen to Johnson, July 18, 1865; Thaddeus Stevens to Johnson, July 20, 1865; Solomon E. Cohen to Johnson, July 27, 1865; and Edward G. Webb to Johnson, July 28, 1865, *Johnson Papers*, 8: 425–26, 439, 482, 497.

4. On July 26, 1866, the President nominated William F. Johnston to replace Thomas, who refused to vacate his office and publicly challenged Johnson's right to have him removed. Within a few weeks, however, Thomas apparently agreed to step down "peaceably and quietly," and Johnston assumed the duties of collector until the Senate rejected his nomination in January 1867. As many as three other candidates were presented to the Senate before the fourth, Joseph W. Cake, won confirmation and was commissioned on April 18, 1867. McCulloch to Johnson, July 26, 1866, Lets. Sent *re* Customs Service Employees (QC Ser.), Vol. 4, RG56, NA; Charles W. Carrigan to Johnson, Aug. 2, 1866, Appts., Customs Service, Collector, Philadelphia, Wm. B. Thomas, RG56, NA; Johnston to Johnson, Aug. 21, 1866, Johnson Papers, LC; Ser. 6B, Vol. 4: 83–84, 87, 89, ibid.; Bradley, *Militant Republicanism*, 242.

5. James W. Nesmith (1820–1885) represented Oregon in the Senate (1861–67) and in the House (1873–75) as a Democrat. *BDAC.*

From Ulysses S. Grant

Washington   March 30th 1866.

I understood from *Bradley T. Johnson* late of the Southern Army and who was included in the paroled officers under the convention between General *W. T. Sherman* and General *Joe E Johnston* has been arrested in the State of Maryland on the charge of treason for acts committed at the Battle of Gettysburg, Pa. in 1863.[1] I have noticed the same thing from the newspapers. There is nothing clearer in my mind than that the terms of the parole given by officers and soldiers who were arrayed against the authority of the General Government of the United States prior to their surrender exempts them from trial or punishment for acts of legal warfare so long as they observe the conditions of their paroles.[2]

General *Johnson* was in Maryland by express authority from these Headquarters.[3] I would now ask as a point of faith on the part of the Government, that proper steps be taken to relieve *B. T. Johnson* from the obligation of the bonds which he has been forced to give in the State of Maryland.[4]

sgd   U S Grant   Lieutenant General

LBcopy, DNA-RG108, Lets. Sent, Let. Bk. C, No. 23 (1866–69).

1. In late August 1865 a grand jury in Maryland returned an indictment against the former Confederate general "for Levying war, with others, against the United States, especially on the 18th of June, 1863, in Washington county, Md., and in capturing and taking possession of Gettysburg." Johnson was arrested on March 26, 1866, and released after paying bail. Johnson reportedly went to Washington to talk with Grant about his arrest and the terms of his parole. *National Intelligencer*, Sept. 5, 1865, Mar. 28, 1866; *Philadelphia Evening Bulletin*, Apr. 5, 1866; *New Orleans Picayune*, Apr. 5, 1866.

2. Johnson made the same argument at his arraignment, but to no avail. *National Intelligencer*, Mar. 28, 1866.

3. In mid-February one of Grant's staff officers had authorized the extension of Johnson's army parole so as to allow him to travel freely throughout the United States. Simon, *Grant Papers*, 16: 144.

4. Received on March 31, Grant's letter was immediately forwarded to the attorney general "for his early consideration." On April 2 Grant sent a second letter to the President requesting that he move to have charges against Bradley Johnson dropped. The President also forwarded that letter to Speed with the endorsement: "Comply with this request." Bradley Johnson was released and charges dropped on April 5. *National Intelligencer*, Apr. 6, 1866; Ser. 4A, Vol. 4: 391, Johnson Papers, LC; Grant to Johnson, Apr. 2, 1866, Office of Atty. Gen., Lets. Recd., President, RG60, NA; James Speed to William J. Jones, Apr. 2, 1866, Office of Atty. Gen., Lets. Sent, (M699, Roll 10), RG60, NA.

From Robert J. Walker

Clarendon Hotel
N. York, March 30/66

Dear Sir

When I left Washn. the contest for the collectorship, *seemed* to be narrowed down between my friend Mr. Smythe[1] & Mr. Davies,[2] the Anti Seward Republican candidate. Mr. McCulloch has *no objection* to Mr. Smythe, altho he may not be his first choice. Rest assured, in the present aspect of our political affairs, you should appoint to the collectorship, a Johnson *Republican*. You have already appointed an excellent War Democrat to the second best office here.[3] You cannot *now* go farther *in this line* without weakening the true Union party. Mr. Smythe is a Republican, who went for you, and your Union policy, *before* there was any vacancy in the collectorship.

I do not speak too strongly when I say that his appointment would render *certain* the triumph of the Union Johnson party in this state. The appointment of a democrat, will keep back wavering Republicans.[4]

We have strong hopes of English's election in Connecticut.[5] I have been quite unwell for several weeks, but will be soon well enough to commence over my signature a review of the great issue—*Union or no Union —Constitution or no Constitution* now pending.

R. J. Walker

ALS, DLC-JP.

1. Walker had been among the first to recommend Henry A. Smythe, "a conservative *Union* Republican" who "voted for Lincoln in 1860—and (like myself) for Lincoln & Johnson in 1864." Walker to Hugh McCulloch, Nov. 21, 1865, Appts., Customs Service, Collector, New York, Henry A. Smythe, RG56, NA.

2. Henry E. Davies. See James Dixon to Johnson, Apr. 12, 1866.

3. Naval officer Moses F. Odell, who had been reappointed in January. Ser. 6B, Vol. 4: 49, Johnson Papers, LC.

4. Walker several weeks later sent a dispatch reiterating the "importance" of appointing Smythe. Walker to Johnson, Apr. 14, 1866, ibid. See Henry A. Smythe to Johnson, Apr. 13, 1866.

5. James E. English ran unsuccessfully for governor. See Interview with Burr and Ingersoll, Mar. 23, 1866.

From John H. Gilmer

Richmond Va   March 31, 1866

Fatal results apprehended if Celebration allowed to proceed Tuesday. Answer.[1]

John H. Gilmore[*sic*]   City Senator

Confidential.

Tel, DLC-JP.

1. Gilmer refers to the celebration planned for April 3 by blacks in Richmond in honor of the first anniversary of the fall of that city. The plans raised much fear and anxiety among both the white population of the city and Federal military officials. Maj. Gen. Alfred H. Terry advised the planners not to carry out the celebration; Grant ordered Terry not to leave Richmond until after the third, and gave him permission to "put a stop to it [the celebration] or take steps to suppress the disorder" that may result. On the morning of the third, Grant ordered all drinking establishments to be closed and the use of "patrols to arrest . . . all parties black or white, who are threatening in their manner, or who are intoxicated." That evening Terry reported that "The celebration today passed off in peace & quiet except a dubious report that the procession was fired upon by a white man from a window —I have heard of no disorders." *Washington Evening Star*, Mar. 23, 30, Apr. 4, 1866; *Washington Morning Chronicle*, Apr. 6, 1866; *Richmond Dispatch*, Apr. 9, 1866; Simon, *Grant Papers*, 16: 142–43.

From Theodore Miller[1]

Hudson (N Y)   March 31st 1866

Dear Sir

Although removed from any active participation in politics, being one of the Justices of the Supreme Court of this State, I cannot refrain from expressing my cordial approval of your patriotic efforts to restore the Union & to maintain the Constitution & the laws of the land.

Allow me to say, that your veto of the "Freedman's Bureau Bill" one of the ablest and most statesmanlike papers which has emanated from the Executive office since the days of Andrew Jackson; your eloquent and most excellent speech of the 22d of February, so replete with truth and sound views, which have fired the popular heart; and last but not least and I am inclined to think above all; your veto message on the "Civil Rights Bill" are worthy of the Chief Magistrate of a great nation and cannot in my judgment fail to command the approbation and earnest support of every loyal heart and of every true lover of our common country.

As a State Judicial officer, I feel greatly indebted to you and thank you for your firmness, courage and determined resistance to such an unconstitutional invasion of the judicial power of a state, as the provisions of this act contemplated and for your vindication of the independence of this class of public officers in the discharge of their duties. Unless I much mistake the character, intelligence & patriotism of the masses of the American People, they will stand by you in the present eventful crisis.

Trusting that you will excuse me, a stranger to you personally, for the liberty which I have taken in addressing you; with my earnest desire for your success, in the efforts which you are making to work out the deliverance of the country from the impending evils which threaten it and with my best wishes for your prosperity and happiness. . . .

Theodore Miller

ALS, DLC-JP.
1. After serving thirteen years on the New York Supreme Court, Miller (1816–*fl*1894) commenced a twelve-year stint as an associate justice of the state court of appeals. *Biographical Review: The Leading Citizens of Columbia County, New York* (Boston, 1894), 416–23.

From David L. Swain

University of North Carolina,
Chapel Hill, 31 March 1866

Dear Sir,

I have just read your Veto Message returning the Civil Rights Bill to the Senate and concur with you fully and heartily in all the positions assumed. I can assure you most confidently that the measures of no administration in my day, General Jacksons, inclusive, have been more universally acceptable to the great body of the people of North Carolina, and so they would pronounce most emphatically, if they considered themselves at liberty to speak at home when they are not permitted to be heard at Washington.

The enclosed newspaper[1] contains what I do not remember to have seen elsewhere, a condensed historical sketch of American Rebellions. It is from the pen of a lady,[2] who is one of my nearest neighbours and most intimate friends. It has occurred to me that if placed in the hands of some one of your friends in Congress, it might suggest a new line of defence for your policy of reconstruction, and therefore I send it.

D. L. Swain

ALS, DLC-JP.
1. Not found.
2. Cornelia Ann Phillips Spencer (1825–1908), daughter of a University of North Carolina professor and widow of an Alabama lawyer, was a prolific postwar writer and educational crusader. Her series of articles for a New York magazine were later published as *The Last Ninety Days of the War in North Carolina* (1866). During the 1870s she wrote

numerous times for the *North Carolina Presbyterian* in support of education for women. Edward T. James et al., eds., *Notable American Women 1607–1950: A Biographical Dictionary* (3 vols., Cambridge, 1971), 3: 333–34.

From Fred Tate[1]

St. Charles Hotel, New Orleans,
March 31, 1866.

My Dear Sir—

I feel assured that you will pardon me for trespassing upon your valuable time, when my motives for so doing are made known to you. I am now a resident citizen of the State of Texas, formerly resided in Huntsville, Ala., and have frequently listened with pleasure to your eloquent appeals, in behalf of the Democracy, before the mass meetings held in Tennessee, in days long past and gone by.

It was with pain, mortification and regret, that I read the testimony of Gen. Custar, before the Reconstruction Committee, in reference to the feelings of the people of Texas.[2]

I have lived in Texas for fourteen years; have mingled with her people in all the various relations of life—as lawyer, as planter, as politician—and I think I know their feelings far better than Gen. Custar, if I may be allowed to judge of his knowledge by his statement made before the committee.

You are well aware, Mr. President, that there are fanatics, North and South, who have nothing to care for, nothing to lose, "nothing to gain," and that there may be individual instances in Texas, as there are, doubtless, men who are perverse and obstinate, unwilling to go backward or forward, I am free to confess; but, I am sure, with your long experience in political affairs, you will not allow yourself to take individual isolated cases to be the exponents of the sentiments of the great mass of the people. Allow me to assure you, in all candor and sincerity, that the people of Texas have "accepted the situation" in good faith, and are now ready, willing and anxious, to do everything in their power (except to confer the right of suffrage upon the Freedmen) to restore their former relations to the Federal Government.

I know you will agree with me, when I say it is not a matter of astonishment or surprise to find Southern gentlemen aroused with indignation, when they have been arraigned, tried, condemned, and fined, by irresponsible agents connected with the Freedmen's Bureau, for a violation of the laws of their State—knowing, as they do, that, under the act of Congress organizing the bureau, no such jurisdiction was conferred. Allow me in this connection to remark, that the Freedmen's Bureau is based upon a false presumption, viz: that their former owners will wrong, cheat and defraud them. Such is not the case; and until the Federal soldiers were quartered in our midst, no one ever heard of a poor negro being knocked down and robbed of his pitiful earnings; but now it is of frequent occurrence.

The ostensible, the pretended object of the Freedmen's Bureau was, and is now, to protect the freedmen; the real object, however, was, and is now, to organize a Department in the several Southern States, with a legion of attachés, who may fill their coffers and grow rich out of the hard earnings of the Southern people, including the freedmen. I speak plainly, Mr. President, but I speak truth (although it may be frequently an unwelcomed messenger).

There are cases in law in which the plaintiff is allowed to testify in his own behalf, ex necessitate rei;[3] but while his competency is established by law, the jury or the Court passes upon his credibility. How many officers in the Freedmen's Bureau, and other military departments, who are directly and pecuniarily interested in the continuation of their respective departments, have been called upon to give testimony? "Verb. sat. sap."[4]

It does seem to me, that those who have seized, and are endeavoring to hold in their own hands the reins of the Government, (and against whom you are waging a manful warfare,) have forgotten (if they really ever knew) a fundamental principle and axiom in political economy, viz: The wealth of a nation depends upon the products of her soil.

Until the Freedmen's Bureau is withdrawn, and we are allowed to make our own contracts with the freedmen, to be enforced by the laws of the States, respectively, (which are now, or will be made amply sufficient for their protection,) the agricultural interest of the South will continue to languish, and languishing may die.

Allow me to say, in conclusion, Mr. President, that your veto messages, upon the Freedmen's Bureau and civil rights bills, have been hailed everywhere as master pieces of statesmanship, that we now look to you as the great champion of constitutional liberty, and that prayers ascend by day and by night asking that you may be enabled to stand by and preserve the constitution in its original purity, and when you have departed to that "bourne whence no travelers returns," be assured that you will have left in the hearts of your countrymen a monument more lasting, more enduring, than one of brass or gold.

Fred. Tate.

New Orleans Picayune, May 27, 1866.

1. Tate (*c*1826–*fl*1868) was a prosperous attorney in Fayette County, Texas. He ran unsuccessfully for the Confederate Congress in 1861 and during the war years served as an aide to General Van Dorn. 1860 Census, Tex., Fayette, Oso, 196; *Austin State Gazette*, Oct. 12, Dec. 21, 1861; *Confederate Staff Officers*, 161; Tate to Johnson, Oct. 9, 1868, Johnson Papers, LC.

2. George A. Custer (1839–1876), an 1861 graduate of West Point, rose up through the ranks during the war and saw considerable action, especially in Virginia late in the war. Custer remained in the army after mustering out of the volunteers in early 1866. His military exploits in the West against the Indians are well known; he met his death at the Battle of

the Little Big Horn. On March 10, 1866, Custer testified before the congressional committee and asserted the lack of Union support in Texas and therefore warned against the withdrawal of federal troops. He also noted the hostility towards freedmen in that state. Custer
warned that only ex-Rebels could be elected to congressional seats from Texas. *DAB*; *House
Reports*, 39 Cong., 1 Sess., No. 30, pt. 4, pp. 72–78 (Ser. 1273).

3. From the necessity of the case.
4. *Verbum sat sapienti est.* A word to the wise is sufficient.

April 1866

From J. Madison Wells

New Orleans, [April 1866][1]

President

Both duty and inclination prompt me to solicit your views upon a subject fraught with general interest. The times are parturient of events relative to which your opinion should be ascertained previous to the necessity of my action with them as actual entities. A party styling it self "Constitutional Union" are making arrangements for the Calling of a Convention based upon "universal Suffrage" Suffrigans and dellegates unrestricted to race of[or] Color. This party professes both talent and money. Another party, the one which framed the Constitution of 1864 and under which the present State Government is conducted propose to reconvoke its convention as provided for by that body its adjournment being only temporary. It is quite probable this is contemplated as a Check move and if conducted wisely good result may be hand and quiet all clamor for any other change of the present constitution by the party who are designingly revolutionary and will be for some time to come quite hostile to the Government of the United States. Three of its most prominent leaders acting as a committee of the State Legislature[2] visited you recently to obtain your saction or views for the Calling of thier Convention. They too by oath bound and secret assosiations are thoroughly organized and if they are permited to hold power will cause in some future day, much trouble to the Government of the United States. The constitution party of 1864 I presume will take midle grounds. I cannot however undertake to devine the action of this body when assembled. The tone of Sentiment among such of its members as I have had an opportunity of seeing is one of direct antagonism to the Legislature which adjourned here on the 22nd of march last the feeling between the two bodies being reciprocal. The Legislature having evinced a disposition to enforce ostricism upon all those who have [been] supporting the Government of the United States for the last four years, must naturally expect retaliation. It is not my intention to Justify the one or complain of the other. But especially wish to confine my action strictly to the superior Judgement and settled policy of the executive of the United States whose eminent position enables him to survey the ground and effect of action at different points upon the general course to be persued for the final settlement of these expected troubles. I am apprehensive the Parochial elections which are ordered for the seventh of May next will be but the enregistration edict of the rebel sentiment of the State. I shall anxiously await your views as to the proper policy to be persued.

J Madison Wells   Gov Louisiana

ALS, DLC-JP.
1. The date is based upon Wells's references to "the 22nd of march last" and "the seventh of May next."
2. Duncan S. Cage, William B.G. Egan, and James B. Eustis. See Edwin M. Stanton to Johnson, March 11, 1866.

From Larkin T. McKenzie[1]

at home Aprile 1st 1866
Tippah County Mississippi.

Dear Sir

Accept my heart Felt thanks For your Love of Justice and right in arresting the mostrous attempt of Wm. J Smith[2] to crush the Citizens of Grand Junction and Vicinity by Collecting $9938.18, which would have utterly ruind us to enrich him *self*. He has on a previous military assesment Collected off the Citizens $3300[3] a portion of which I paid. I am assessed again. We then had no one to protect us. In you sir we the People have a Friend. Allow me Sir to say that you are to day as Dear to the people of the south as was Andrew Jacks in his pammiest days. The peopl of the south as far I know are as Loyal as you would have them be. And if we could have the Goverment that you would and will give us a more devoted and Loyal Commutiy than the south are not in Existance than we are. For we accept the results of the war in good Faith. Evry Boddy is at home and at work trying to resusitate our once prosperous but now Devastated country and if we can be permitted we will in a short time have our Broad Fields in a prosperous state of Cultivation.

The Freedmen are Laboring with a zeal that no one hoped for or expected.

May god spare your Life that we may again have a republican Goverment that will give to evry Citizen Equal rights under the Law.

Accept sir again my thanks For the bold stand you have taken For the people.

L. T. McKenzie

ALS, DLC-JP.
1. McKenzie (b. c1812), a farmer near the Tennessee line, had once been county tax collector. 1850 Census, Miss., Tippah, 3rd Div., 24; (1860), Northern Div., 161; Andrew Brown, *History of Tippah County, Mississippi: The First Century* (Fulton, Miss., 1976), 23.
2. Smith (1823–1913), currently a state legislator, was a Mexican War veteran, Grand Junction, Tennessee, farmer, and Civil War colonel of the 6th Tenn. Cav., USA. After the war he served as a state senator (1867–69, 1885–87) and U.S. congressman (1869–71). *BDTA*, 2: 844–45.
3. In September 1863 a military commission found that Smith had sustained losses amounting to $9,938.18. By orders of June 25, 1865, December 13, 1865, and January 27, 1866, this amount was to be assessed against the citizens of Grand Junction and

vicinity "who were lately in rebellion." On March 24, 1866, by Johnson's direction, Secretary Stanton had ordered Gen. George H. Thomas to suspend collection of Colonel Smith's assessment of damages against Grand Junction citizens. *Memphis Post*, Feb. 27, 1866; Tels. Sent, Sec. of War (M473, Roll 90), RG107, NA.

From Ralph Ely[1]

HEADQUARTERS B.R.F. & A.L.,
WESTERN DISTRICT S.C.,
COLUMBIA, S.C., APRIL 2, 1866.

MR. PRESIDENT:

As a representative of this Bureau, I respectfully beg leave to submit personally to you a communication upon the subject of the condition of this section of our country, involving the interests of the freed people, as well as the interests of their former masters, and of the country at large.

I have been in this Department on duty since July, 1865, during which time I have endeavored to discharge my duty toward all parties in a just and humane manner, and, as I believe, with general satisfaction to all concerned. The system of free labor has been universally established, and the freed people are at work with honest energy, holding high anticipations of future success. This, with very few exceptions incident to localities having surplus labor.

There is no doubt from the present prospect that the freed people will become self-sustaining. If, as is likely, they obtain remunerative yield for their labor this year, to effect which aid from the Government need only be extended until the first of September of this year, and after which date there will not exist any necessity for this Bureau, excepting a few officers or agents to act as attorneys for the freedmen before the Courts. This is a necessity which I am firm to believe is of vital importance. At this time there is great destitution with all classes of people which must exist and increase until the crops of the season mature.

This city, I may say, is the depot for the whole Western district of the State, embracing fifteen districts, (or counties) and into it I often think is gathered all the infirm and helpless who live as the type of oppression and rebellion. They are fed in the strictest economy by this Bureau, and the city government, the latter confining its offices to the poor of the city entirely. Through benificent Northern aid Societies these poor people have depended for clothing during the winter. They number less than a thousand souls.

To properly facilitate and economize this charity by and with the advice of proper authority, I rented a plantation adjacent to the city as a rendezvous for the homeless and friendless. It is now in operation upon the principle of a "poor-house and farm," and, I verily believe that after the first of September of this year, even this place will be entirely self-sustaining, and might pass into the hands and management of local authority, as in the event of complete restoration the State would, doubt-less, receive and assume.[2]

Therefore, as a citizen, soldier and officer of this Bureau, I offer for your acceptance my hearty endorsement of your veto and the subject-matter of your official message thereon.

I firmly believe that the sooner the freed people are thrown upon their own resources, the better. Give to them the aid needful for this season, and teach them that they must then take care of themselves, will prove by far more beneficial to all concerned than to have them taught that this Government is to provide for them for years to come, &c.

There are desperados still in organization in the upper sections of this State committing depredations upon all classes of people.[3] I believe the temporary presence of a small garrison of regular troops would be salutary—for how long this state of things may exist time only will deter-mine. And from my observation and knowledge, I can but conclude that the sooner the responsibility is thrown upon the people and civil law is fully established, the sooner all complaints will cease, and the people properly govern themselves.

                    Ralph Ely, Brevet Brigadier-General and A. A. Com.

Charleston Courier, June 26, 1866.

1. Ely (1820–1883), a farmer-lumberman, commanded the 8th Mich. Inf. Later he was state auditor. Hunt and Brown, *Brigadier Generals*.

2. Generals Joseph S. Fullerton and James B. Steedman undertook a review of Ely's work and activities in South Carolina and subsequently charged that his endeavors in oper-ating plantations caused Ely to neglect his duties. Particularly disturbing were the claims made by blacks that Ely had crowded freedmen suffering from smallpox into quarters that caused further problems, even death. Since Ely subsequently resigned his position, Gen-eral Howard saw no reason to pursue the allegations further. *New York Herald*, June 13, 1866; *Charleston Courier*, June 23, 1866.

3. One such band, consisting of former Confederate soldiers from Texas, Kentucky, and Tennessee, reportedly was operating in Edgefield District "stealing horses from white peo-ple and robbing and murdering colored men." *New York Herald*, June 13, 1866.

From Ransom H. Gillet

New Lebanon Springs N.Y.
2 April 1866

Dear Sir:

Since my return home, your second veto has been recieved. The first was strong with the people, but this is stronger. A republican said to me last week, that if the civil rights' Bill had become a law, it would have repealed, in effect, our state constitution, which requires negroes to own $250. worth of real estate before they can vote, while no such condition is imposed upon the white man. And if he should challenge a negro, be-cause not a voter under it, & the inspectors of election should reject it, all would be liable to indictment, & to be punished by fine & imprisonment.

He was not for allowing congress to interfere with & defeat the constitution & laws of his state. This, he could not stand.[1]

When I changed my residence from Washington to this, my native town, I did not intend to engage again in political matters. But the course of events renders it an apparent duty to meet & repel the present assault upon the constitution & rights of the people; & I intend to go before the people & discuss the issues before us. I have no doubt you will be sustained, if the under currents from some of your own cabinet do not defeat it.

R. H. Gillet

ALS, DLC-JP.
1. The drive to eliminate discriminatory property qualifications in New York through a constitutional convention failed in 1867. When black suffrage was finally submitted to a popular referendum in November 1869, New Yorkers rejected it. Mushkat, *New York Democracy*, 119, 127, 155; Mohr, *Radical Republicans*, 223–35, 269; Gillette, *Right to Vote*, 26.

From Henry C. Myers[1]

Springfield Illinois   April 2nd/66

President Johnson,

I presume to write you on the state of public sentiments here, in regard to your vetoes, and the reasons why we are not permitted to reach the people, on the noble stand you have seen proper to persue, in regard to the reconstuction of the Union.

When your first vetoe message reached us many of your friends who voted for you, made a call for a public demonstration in support of the noble stand you assumed in your first vetoe message. I am safe in saying that a large majority of the people here were with you. But the radical wing of our union party became alarmed and they called a meeting at which Gov Oglesby[2] became the champion of Radicals & by personal abuse of you and Scared the timid & those who do not think for themselves.

Again your Second vetoe comes and we who had taken our stand for your policy, at once determined to take our position and organize a "Johnson Club," composed of those who supported Lincoln & Johnson in 1864. We called a public meeting at the Court House for the 30th and had engaged two Republican speakers to address the club. The morning of the meeting, Mr D. L. Philips, U.S. Marshall, called to see me, to know if we would not abandon the meeting that night and try to support you inside the Radical party. I told him emphatically no. As for the Johnson men, we assumed the responsibility of going for your policy and it could not be supported inside the Radical wing. Then he remarked in a pet "*You are going off with the Jeff Davis party*." I replied as he was going out of my store, No Mr Philips we are right and in the language of

Clay, "I would rather be right, than be President." An a hour later in the morning, Marshall Philips office had a caucus in Session, composed of Philips, John W. Smith, Collector,[3] Lawence Weldon, District Attorney[4] & other officials. An hour later, and the political machinery was in working order, and this city was canvassed by these tools, and men who had Joined our club and others who were coming in that night, were *abused* & tampered with to remain from our club. And they partialy succeeded,—I took occassion in that meeting, after calling the club to order, to *denounce* these officials as guilty of tyrany worse than was used in any age, to deter white men from coming up to the support of you, whom we had elected.

The "State Journal" to whom we at least expected fair treatment, inserted our call for the meeting in an obscure as an advertisment, for which they charge to me. That was all right. This morning they call upon the Radicals to stand firm &c.

Allow me to assure you, as plain man, one who daily mixes with the masses, that the people are for and with you in your reconstruction policy. And your officials and Radicals only are against you. And they are determined to keep the people from giving expression to their honest sentiments.

Our township election comes off here to morrow[5] & our city election a week later and these Radicals are moving heaven & earth to defeat the expression of the people will, in sustaining you in your patriot course. If they succeed, your officials here will have done it. But I think now we will be able to defeat them.[6]

Pardon my intrusion upon your precious time. But being beset by wirey politicians I for one want you to know the people are for President Johnson and his reconstruction policy.

                                                     Henry C. Myers   President of the Club
P.S.   Allow me to add in Sincerity, that I am no office Seeker or politician, have lived here almost 30 years and am of and for the people, and there constitu[tion]al rights.

                                                                                    H C Myers

ALS, DLC-JP.
    1. Myers (*c*1815–1871), a confectioner and fruit dealer, had just completed a three-year term as Springfield city alderman. 1860 Census, Ill., Sangamon, Springfield, 16th Dist., 137; Springfield directories (1857–61); *History of Sangamon County*, 567, 698; Myers to Johnson, Apr. 19, 1866, Johnson Papers, LC.
    2. Richard J. Oglesby (1824–1899) served as Illinois governor from 1865 to 1869, again in 1873, and finally in the late 1880s. In the 1870s he represented the state as a Republican senator. *DAB*. For an account of the meeting which featured speeches by Oglesby and other "Union men," see *Chicago Tribune*, Feb. 27, 1866.
    3. In addition to serving as an internal revenue collector, Smith (*c*1820–*fl*1881) worked variously as a farmer, state representative, census commissioner, deputy sheriff, and Springfield mayor and alderman. 1860 Census, Ill., Sangamon, Springfield, 16th Dist., 126; Springfield directories (1857–58); Basler, *Works of Lincoln*, 2: 425; *Sangamon County*, 567–68. See Springfield Johnson Club to Johnson, June 19, 1866.

4. Appointed district attorney by his friend President Lincoln in 1861 and reappointed by Johnson four years later, Weldon (1829–1905) resigned from office sometime before the end of 1866 and was replaced by John E. Rosette. Afterwards Weldon moved to Bloomington, Illinois, where he practiced law until 1883, when he was appointed an associate justice of the U.S. Court of Claims in Washington. Newton Bateman and Paul Selby, eds., *Historical Encyclopedia of Illinois and History of Sangamon County* (2 vols., Chicago, 1912), 2: 582; Ser. 6B, Vol. 4: 300, Johnson Papers, LC. See also Richard J. Oglesby to Johnson, July 1, 1865, *Johnson Papers*, 8: 336.

5. For reaction to this election, see John A. McClernand's dispatch from Springfield to Johnson which read: "This town revolutionized. Johnson ticket elected." See also the *Chicago Tribune* of April 4 which noted: "The township election has gone Copperhead." McClernand to Johnson, Apr. 4, 1866, Tels. Recd., President, Vol. 5 (1866–67), RG107, NA.

6. In a follow-up letter Myers, as president of the Springfield Johnson Club, assured the President that the city election results had proven "that a majority of the Union men who voted for Lincoln & Johnson here, are with you." Myers to Johnson, Apr. 19, 1866, Johnson Papers, LC.

From Edwin A. Parrott[1]

Columbus, O, April 2nd 1866

Mr President—

A friend just from Washington this morning tells me that a re-organization of your Cabinet is talked of and I take advantage of the information/whether well or ill-founded to say that if Ohio is to have a Representative in the new cabinet Lewis D. Campbell should be the man.[2] It is superfluous for me to speak of his abilities or fitness to you who know him so well, but it is proper to say that his appointment would be very satisfactory to the Union men who are with you. Of course no appointment you could make would satisfy the Radicals who are blinded with bad passion.

Ed. A Parrott
Speaker House Reps—

ALS, DLC-JP.

1. Parrott (1830–1931) at this date was serving his second term as a Republican in the Ohio legislature. A former brigade commander and head of the Provost Marshal's Bureau in Ohio, Parrott soon withdrew from politics and engaged in iron manufacturing at Dayton. Ritter and Wakelyn, *Legislative Leaders*.

2. Campbell's appointment as minister to Mexico was still being considered by the Senate. See Campbell to Johnson, Apr. 25, 1866.

Proclamation re End of Insurrection

[April 2, 1866]

A PROCLAMATION.

Whereas, by proclamations of the fifteenth and nineteenth of April, one thousand eight hundred and sixty-one, the President of the United States, in virtue of the power vested in him by the Constitution and the laws, declared that the laws of the United States were opposed, and the execution thereof obstructed, in the States of South Carolina, Georgia, Alabama, Florida, Mississippi, Louisiana, and Texas, by combinations too powerful to be suppressed by the ordinary course of judicial proceedings, or by the powers vested in the marshals by law;

And whereas, by another proclamation, made on the sixteenth day of August, in the same year, in pursuance of an act of Congress approved July thirteen, one thousand eight hundred and sixty-one, the inhabitants of the States of Georgia, South Carolina, Virginia, North Carolina, Tennessee, Alabama, Louisiana, Texas, Arkansas, Mississippi, and Florida (except the inhabitants of that part of the State of Virginia lying west of the Alleghany Mountains, and of such other parts of that State and other States before named as might maintain a loyal adhesion to the Union and the Constitution, or might be from time to time occupied and controlled by forces of the United States engaged in the dispersion of insurgents), were declared to be in a state of insurrection against the United States;

And whereas, by another proclamation of the first day of July, one thousand eight hundred and sixty-two, issued in pursuance of an act of Congress approved June seven, in the same year, the insurrection was declared to be still existing in the States aforesaid, with the exception of the certain specified counties in the State of Virginia;

And whereas, by another proclamation, made on the second day of April, one thousand eight hundred and sixty-three, in pursuance of the act of Congress of July thirteen, one thousand eight hundred and sixty-one, the exceptions named in the proclamation of August sixteen, one thousand eight hundred and sixty-one, were revoked, and the inhabitants of the States of Georgia, South Carolina, North Carolina, Tennessee, Alabama, Louisiana, Texas, Arkansas, Mississippi, Florida, and Virginia (except the forty-eight counties of Virginia designated as West Virginia, and the ports of New Orleans, Key West, Port Royal, and Beaufort, in North Carolina), were declared to be still in a state of insurrection against the United States;

And whereas, the House of Representatives, on the twenty-second day of July, one thousand eight hundred and sixty-one, adopted a resolution in the words following, namely:

"*Resolved by the House of Representatives of the Congress of the United States*, That the present deplorable civil war has been forced upon the country by the disunionists of the Southern States, now in revolt against the constitutional Government and in arms around the capital; that in this national emergency Congress, banishing all feelings of mere passion or resentment, will recollect only its duty to the whole country; that this war is not waged upon our part in any spirit of oppression nor for any purpose of conquest or subjugation, nor purpose of overthrowing or interfering with the rights or established institutions of those States, but to defend and maintain the supremacy of the Constitution, and to preserve the Union with all the dignity, equality, and rights of the several States unimpaired; and that as soon as these objects are accomplished the war ought to cease."

And whereas, the Senate of the United States, on the twenty-fifth day of July, one thousand eight hundred and sixty-one, adopted a resolution in the words following, to wit:

"*Resolved,* That the present deplorable civil war has been forced upon the country by the disunionists of the Southern States, now in revolt against the constitutional Government and in arms around the capital; that in this national emergency Congress, banishing all feeling of mere passion or resentment, will recollect only its duty to the whole country; that this war is not prosecuted upon our part with any spirit of oppression nor for any purpose of conquest or subjugation, nor purpose of over-throwing or interfering with the rights or established institutions of those States, but to defend and maintain the supremacy of the Constitution and all laws made in pursuance thereof, and to preserve the Union with all the dignity, equality, and rights of the several States unimpaired; that as soon as these objects are accomplished the war ought to cease."

And whereas, these resolutions, though not joint or concurrent in form, are substantially identical, and as such may be regarded as having expressed the sense of Congress upon the subject to which they relate;

And whereas, by my proclamation of the thirteenth day of June last, the insurrection in the State of Tennessee was declared to have been suppressed, the authority of the United States therein to be undisputed, and such United States officers as had been duly commissioned to be in the undisturbed exercise of their official functions;

And whereas, there now exists no organized armed resistance of misguided citizens or others to the authority of the United States in the States of Georgia, South Carolina, Virginia, North Carolina, Tennessee, Alabama, Louisiana, Arkansas, Mississippi, and Florida, and the laws can be sustained and enforced therein by the proper civil authority, State or Federal, and the people of said States are well and loyally disposed, and have conformed, or will conform, in their legislation to the condition of affairs growing out of the amendment to the Constitution of the United States prohibiting slavery within the limits and jurisdiction of the United States;

And whereas, in view of the before-recited premises, it is the manifest determination of the American people that no State, of its own will, has the right or the power to go out of, or separate itself from, or be separated from, the American Union, and that therefore each State ought to remain and constitute an integral part of the United States;

And whereas, the people of the several before-mentioned States have, in the manner aforesaid, given satisfactory evidence that they acquiesce in this sovereign and important resolution of national unity;

And whereas, it is believed to be a fundamental principle of government that the people who have revolted, and who have been overcome and subdued, must either be dealt with so as to induce them voluntarily to become friends, or else they must be held by absolute military power, or devastated so as to prevent them from ever again doing harm as enemies, which last-named policy is abhorrent to humanity and to freedom;

And whereas, the Constitution of the United States provides for constituent communities only as States, and not as Territories, dependencies, provinces, or protectorates;

And whereas, such constituent States must necessarily be, and by the Constitution and laws of the United States are made equals, and placed upon a like footing as to political rights, immunities, dignity, and power with the several States with which they are united;

And whereas, the observance of political equality as a principle of right and justice is well calculated to encourage the people of the aforesaid States to be and become more and more constant and persevering in their renewed allegiance;

And whereas, standing armies, military occupation, martial law, military tribunals, and the suspension of the privilege of the writ of habeas corpus are, in time of peace, dangerous to public liberty, incompatible with the individual rights of the citizens, contrary to the genius and spirit of our free institutions, and exhaustive of the national resources, and ought not, therefore, to be sanctioned or allowed, except in cases of actual necessity, for repelling invasion or suppressing insurrection or rebellion;

And whereas, the policy of the Government of the United States, from the beginning of the insurrection to its overthrow and final suppression, has been in conformity with the principles herein set forth and enumerated:

Now, therefore, I, Andrew Johnson, President of the United States, do hereby proclaim and declare that the insurrection which heretofore existed in the States of Georgia, South Carolina, Virginia, North Carolina, Tennessee, Alabama, Louisiana, Arkansas, Mississippi, and Florida is at an end, and is henceforth to be so regarded.

In testimony whereof I have hereunto set my hand and caused the seal of the United States to be affixed.

Done at the city of Washington this second day of April, in the year of our Lord one thousand eight hundred and sixty-six, and of the Independence of the United States of America the ninetieth.

Andrew Johnson.

OR, Ser. 3, Vol. 5: 1007–9.

From Ulysses S. Grant

Washington, D.C.   Apl. 3d 1866

Sir:

Whilst in conversation with you this morning I forgot to mention a subject which I promised to speak to you upon the first opportunity. It is in relation to a Cadet's appointment for Steven A. Douglas, Jr.[1] son of the late Senator Douglas. The boy is very desirous of entering West Point in September next. The claims the lad has upon this Govt. through the services of his father, it is not necessary for me to speak of.

It was not my intention to make a formal application for this appointment but to say to you that it was desired by the boy, and his stepmother,[2] and if it could be given then it could be sent to him as a compliment due his family.[3]

U. S. Grant, Lt. Gen.

ALS, DNA-RG94, USMA Appls. (M688, Roll 241).

1. Following his graduation from Georgetown College, D.C., Stephen A. Douglas, Jr., (1850–1908) studied and practiced law in North Carolina before removing to Chicago. *Who Was Who in America* (5 vols., Chicago, 1943–73), 1: 335.

2. Adèle Cutts Douglas (1835–1899) had married the Illinois senator in 1856. She actively participated in Washington society and in Douglas's political career. James, *Notable American Women*, 1: 509–10.

3. In early June Douglas wrote Johnson declining the "conditional" appointment he had received because he was under the required age of sixteen. Douglas to Johnson, June 9, 1866, USMA Appls. (M688, Roll 241), RG94, NA.

From Francis P. Blair, Sr.

Wash. 4 Apl. 66

My Dear Mr. President

I wish you would take Genl. Fullerton to your confidence & give him employment near you.[1] His knowledge of the Freedmen's Bureau business and its Agents & the confidence of the army in him & his knowledge of the feelings of its officers, will I think enable him to render you invaluable service.[2] I know this gentleman & have great faith in his capacity & honor. I hope you will decide the matter for him soon.

F. P. Blair

ALS, DLC-JP.

1. While serving as acting assistant commissioner of the Freedmen's Bureau in Louisiana, Joseph S. Fullerton wrote to Blair in November 1865 indicating his support of the President's "wise and liberal" reconstruction policy. He also told Blair that he intended to visit Washington shortly and tender his resignation from the army. On February 28, 1866, however, Johnson had directed Secretary Stanton to revoke his department's orders mustering Fullerton out of the service. Fullerton to Blair, Nov. 4, 1865, Johnson Papers, LC; Johnson to Stanton, Feb. 28, 1866, ACP Branch, File F-51-CB-1866, J. S. Fullerton, RG94, NA.

2. During the impeachment investigation a year later, Fullerton testified to having conversed with Johnson on at least two occasions prior to April 7, when he and General Steedman received orders from the secretary of war to conduct an inspection tour and report on the conditions of the Freedmen's Bureau in various southern states. In January 1867 Fullerton was rewarded with the postmastership of St. Louis, where he resided during part of the war and practiced law after leaving the army in September 1866. *House Reports*, 40 Cong., 1 Sess., No. 7, pp. 99–100, 110–11 (Ser. 1314); Fullerton to E. D. Townsend, Aug. 25, 1866, ACP Branch, File F-51-CB-1866, RG94, NA; Ser. 6B, Vol. 4: 316, Johnson Papers, LC; Brown, *Am. Biographies*, 3: 206. See James B. Steedman and Joseph S. Fullerton to Johnson, June 14, 1866.

From David M. Fleming

Piqua [Ohio], April 4th 1866

Sir:

I have just been informed by a note from Judge Lawrence,[1] Representative in Congress from this District, that a petition[2] has been sent you through him asking for my removal from the position of Assessor of this District, which you were kind enough to give me at the instance and recommendation of Rev. Col. Moody and others of this city.[3]

I am not advised as to the charges they prefer against me, and therefore cannot speak on the subject. I have endeavored to do my whole duty faithfully and honestly, and so far as I know I have given very general satisfaction. The increased amount of taxes collected since my induction into the office over corresponding months of last year, under my predecessor,[4] is the best evidence I can give of my fidelity to the trust and fitness for the position. The actual reasons of the petitioners, how ever, are not based on the manner in which I have discharged the duties. The project originated through malice, on the part of the Representative in the Ohio Legislature from this county,[5] a Sumnerite, because I opposed his nomination last fall, and the feeling has been intensified by my advocacy of your measures for a restoration of the Southern States to the Union in my paper the Piqua Journal. The other parties signed the paper because of my friendship for you. The vote in the Legislature of Ohio sustaining Congress as against your Veto of the Freedman's Bureau Bill[6] is an evidence of their feelings towards yourself and your policy.

Being the first to present your name to the American people for the high position to which you were elected, I very naturally felt a deep interest in your prosperity and the success of your Administration. Believing that your loyalty and patriotism were only equalled by your ability and statesmanship, I felt a confidence that with the reins of power in your hands the country would be equally as safe as in those of the lamented Lincoln, and I am glad that I have not been disappointed. Your desire to see our distracted country once more united in the bonds of peace and concord, each section vieing with the other to restore the scattered fragments to their original positions in the Temple of Liberty, is shared in by your true friends through out the land, and prayers for the adoption of your policy, which is believed in by the great mass of the Union party, as the best method to produce the glorious result, ascend daily from true and loyal hearts. Honestly coinciding in your measures I have given my feeble efforts to sustain you in your trying position.

Under these circumstances, having stood by you when others were defaming your good name, and defended you against your enemies and slanderers, I respectfully ask that I be not sacrificed without a hearing and an opportunity to meet my enemies and yours face to face with yourself, and I will cheerfully abide the result.[7]

D. M. Fleming   Assr 4th Dist O.

ALS, DNA-RG56, Appts., Internal Revenue Service, Assessor, Ohio, 4th Dist., David M. Fleming.

1. William Lawrence (1819–1899) served in the state legislature and as district court judge, and was colonel of the 84th Ohio Vol. Inf., before his terms as a Republican congressman (1865–71, 1873–77). *BDAC*.

2. See Donn Piatt et al. to Johnson, Mar. 5, 1866, Appts., Internal Revenue Service, Assessor, Ohio, 4th Dist., James Harvey, RG56, NA. The petitioners lambasted Fleming, calling him an "unreliable Politician" and a "notorious *liar*," and urged Johnson to "remove this stench in the nostrils of all loyal citizens."

3. See Granville Moody to Johnson, Nov. 17, 1865, *Johnson Papers*, 9: 398–99. Moody also endorsed Fleming's letter of April 4 and shortly afterwards wrote Johnson a separate letter in Fleming's behalf. Moody to Johnson, Apr. 5, 1866, Appts., Internal Revenue Service, Assessor, Ohio, 4th Dist., D. M. Fleming, RG56, NA; Moody to Johnson, Apr. 6, 1866, Johnson Papers, LC.

4. Fleming had been appointed in July 1865 in place of James Walker (1826–1885), who had held the assessor's office since 1862. A former prosecuting attorney of Logan County and a local Republican party organizer, Walker was later elected mayor of Bellefontaine (1868–79) and afterwards served in the Ohio legislature. Ser. 6B, Vol. 1: 107, Johnson Papers, LC; Robert P. Kennedy, *The Historical Review of Logan County, Ohio* (Chicago, 1903), 736–38.

5. William D. Alexander (c1829–1899), formerly captain, 110th Ohio Vol. Inf., whose name appeared on at least two petitions requesting Fleming's removal, moved to Topeka, Kansas, in the 1870s. Pension Records, William D. Alexander, RG15, NA; Donn Piatt et al. to Johnson, ca. Mar. and Mar. 5, 1866, Appts., Internal Revenue Service, Assessor, Ohio, 4th Dist., D. M. Fleming, RG56, NA.

6. Apparently in late February a caucus of the Union members of the legislature adopted a resolution supporting Congress. *Cincinnati Gazette*, Feb. 28, 1866.

7. The hostile petitions notwithstanding, Fleming was reappointed on May 31 and confirmed by the Senate on June 18. Before the end of August, however, he was removed and John E. Cummins, the Ohio senator who represented Miami County in the legislature, was given the commission for Fleming's post. Convinced that Fleming had been "improperly removed," Johnson directed Secretary McCulloch on September 20 to "do Mr. Fleming justice without delay." For whatever reasons, Cummins's appointment, which the Senate would ultimately reject in February 1867, was not rescinded. Meanwhile, Johnson wrote Fleming a letter of apology, promising some future "evidence of my association of your friendliness." The assessorship was finally restored to Fleming in July 1868, following the death of incumbent James H. Hart. Ser. 6B, Vol. 4: 256–57, 259, 262, Johnson Papers, LC; Johnson endorsement of Sept. 20, 1866, on McCulloch to Fleming, Sept. 5, 1866; W. G. Moore to McCulloch, Sept. 24, 1866, Mar. 12, 1867, Appts., Internal Revenue Service, Assessor, Ohio, 4th Dist., D. M. Fleming, RG56, NA; Johnson to Fleming, Oct. 15, 1866, Johnson Papers, LC.

From Phineas W. Hitchcock[1]

Washington D.C.   April 4, '66

I respectfully ask that Captain James M. Bradshaw,[2] late of the Volunteer service be appointed Sutler at Fort Kearney, Nebraska. It has been the custom with the War Department to make these appointments, generally, in compliance with the suggestions of the Delegates from the Territories in which the Posts were located. Mr. Stanton has seen fit to make me an exception in this case. In a frontier country like mine the position of Sutler at a Post is important politically because, having the exclusive right to trade there, he is necessarily brought into contact personally with the farmers for miles around, they being dependent on him for a market. I know of no reason why the usual courtesy should not be shown me, and I respectfully and confidently appeal to the President to make the matter right.[3]

P. W. Hitchcock

ALS, DNA-RG107, Lets. Recd, Executive (M494, Roll 84).

1. Hitchcock (1831–1881), a native of New York, moved to Nebraska in 1857 where he practiced law. A staunch Republican, he was appointed U.S. marshal for the territory in 1861, resigning the position in 1864 when he was elected territorial delegate to Congress (1865–67). With the coming of statehood, Hitchcock was appointed surveyor general of Nebraska and Iowa (1867–69) and later served in the U.S. Senate (1871–77). *BDAC*; *DAB*.

2. After three years as steward of the Indiana Hospital for the Insane in the 1840s, Bradshaw (1821–1890) engaged in a mercantile business until he joined the U.S. Army as a captain in the Quartermaster Department in 1861. He served at various stations in the Midwest before being mustered out in 1865. Pension Records, James M. Bradshaw, RG15, NA; Staff Officers Files, J. M. Bradshaw, RG94, NA; Powell, *Army List*, 776.

3. An endorsement by Stanton attached to Hitchcock's letter offered the explanation that the sutlership at Fort Kearney had already been filled by a person recommended by General Grant. According to Stanton, Hitchcock wanted a friend in that post to help with his political aspirations, not a justifiable reason for removing the incumbent.

From R. Weakley Brown
Tennessee Affairs (PRIVATE)

Nashville Tenn   April 5th 1866

My Dear friend—

With the exception of the members of your immediate family I do not believe you have a friend in this Broad Land who feels a deeper interest in the success of your Administration and in your personal welfare (temporal and eternal) than myself.

Though the Political Heavens look dark and angry, yet I have great faith in the final triumph of justice and right—which I believe can only be secured by the success of your Restoration policy—for all others so far are utterly impracticable. You are for the Restoration of the union and preservation of Constitutional Liberty as opposed to the Sumner, Stevens and Tenn. Radical policy of a *Consolidated Military Despotism*. For many months I have seen that the troubles with our state Executive and Majority of the Legislature were inevitable. From the beginning I had little or no confidence in the political sagacity of a Majority of them. I used all my efforts with the Govenor (as a Peac-Maker.) but in vain. Some weeks since my Kinsman Gov Patton[1] of Ala. urged me to have a second interview with Gov B. but I declined feeling that no good result could be accomplished. These men will yet find there is virtue in the second, sober thought of the people—and thank God they now Know "*who* is *their real* and *best friend*." Nine tenths of the people of Tennessee are with Andrew Johnson—their favorite leader and they believe he is looking to the good of the whole country & people.

There is nothing like standing on *correct principles* and you have proved by your acts (which speak for themselves) that you are for the preservation of Constitutional liberty—the restoration of Union, law and order—of Peace to the Nation—good will among the People, and you too are the founder and leader of the "*Restoration Party.*"

I regret Gov Brownlow and others think you are trying to reestablish the old Democratic Party. He entirely mistakes your aims and ends. Your great mission is higher and nobler than subserviency to any party. You are like Washington for your whole Country and the restoring of Peace and good feeling among the people. Your mission is to heal the Nations wounds. We sometimes hear long and empty professions of Christianity. "But not every one that saith unto me Lord-Lord! shall enter the Kingdom of Heaven—but he that doeth the will of my Father in Heaven."[2] Toward your unfortunate misguided Countrymen of the south you are acting the part of the good Samaritan, and you have God's blessings in the proud consciousness of doing right, and this course will continue to you the blessings of Heaven and the support, gratitude and prayers of the people. Gov. B. thinks you will loose every state in the North but let him remember that Rev Henry Ward Beecher has ten times the influence in New York he has in Tenn. I wonder if Gov B. has changed his opinion of Mr Seward. Well if he has not many Tennesseeans have. We think he is now acting the part of the true patriot and Statesman. Gov B. forgets that Raymond Senator Morgan Dix Dickerson[3] and many other gallant spirits are cordially supporting you. If he is determined to go with Stevens, Sumner and the "*Destruction Party*" he will find his journey a rough one—before he gets to the end.

I will use no harsh epithets. I trust in reason justice, mercy and truth and have no unkind feelings towards Gov B. I only regret the course he is pursuing. In the last interview I had with him some 5 or 6 weeks since he spoke very kindly of you—and I regard you above all living men as the *special instrument* of *Divine Providence*. Your grand mission is to save what Washington founded and like Washington look to Isreal's God & you will never fall.

I wrote you last fall that many people were impressed with the opinion that you were Pardoning some very solid original Democratic Secessionists and passing by some Whigs—who were far less guilty.[4] I mentioned to you the propriety of pardoning Ex Gov. Neill S. Brown, and wrote you how cordially he approved your policy. As an evidence of his good faith I enclosed you his speech delivered 22nd Feb. last at the Capitol which speaks for itself.[5] The Radicals here will do every thing in their power to create divisions among the people and produce the impression that you will only *favor Democrats*. I am satisfied that the pardoning of some more

Johnson's strongest supporters in the Cabinet, Seward, *top*, and Welles, *bottom*
Courtesy National Archives

prominent Whigs will make fast friends of them and *produce* a most *salutary effect*. A few evenings since I rode out seven miles in the Country with my friend and Kinsman Judge R. L. Caruthers and returned the next morning. He gave me quite an interesting sketch of his early struggles when a poor boy, making his way in the world. He launched out on the state of the Country and said if you succeed in your Restoration Policy (and he has great faith in your final success) your name in History will only be second to Washington. But even were you to fail and Despotism triumph your name like Cato's would be historical and "History would consecrate it to immortality."

I do not believe you will fail as I believe in the final triumph of right over wrong. If Judge Caruthers was pardoned immediately he *could* and *would* become an active supporter of your policy.[6] (I *know what* I *say*.) At present his hands are tied. The Federal Court meets the 3rd Monday in this month—and his trial would produce no good here but probably evil. I dont believe any Jury that might be selected here or from Wilson County would convict him.

Some say "Treason must be punished &ct." He has already been severely punished. He has lost a large estate and has to toil hard in his old age for a support. Last Summer the Att. Genl.[7] had him arrested and placed in the Penitentiary. He went there quietly with me in my buggy and gave the Marshall[8] no trouble. Judge C. was a poor young man and is self made like yourself. He has a great deal of *influence* and *personal popularity* which will be most cordially and actively used to increase your influence and popularity with the People. I know he has been represented to you as one of the getters up of this Rebellion. I know some of the facts in his case. In Dec 1860—I had a long conversation with him on the state of the Country and he thought there would be no war and our difficulties would be adjusted or Compromised. When he went on to the Peace Congress his great desire & hope was that there would be a peaceable settlement of all the difficulties. He thought then there would be no war—and that if the North & South in this *christian* and *enlightened* age—could not agree, that they would seperate in Peace.

After the failure of the Peace Congress and the fall of Fort Sumpter he believed that the Republican Party would attempt to overthrow the constitution—and wage war upon slavery—the peculiar institution of the South, and thereby abolish it. He believed that the people of a state had the right to exercise their reserved rights for their own protection & safety. And when Tenn united her destiny with the Gulf states he believed that she was acting for the best and good of her people. He has taken the *Amnesty* Oath in good faith and desires to see a return of peace & order and humbly submits to the *results* of the *war*. He was not a believer in the doctrine of Secession and condemned the action of the Gulf states. He believed slavery to be a Divine institution and that it could not be abolished. He now sees that *God's directing* or *permissive providence* is different from what he then supposed it would be, and being *honestly mistaken* and *misguided* he is I think a fit subject for executive Clemency. I will vouch for his loyalty in the future. You have pardoned such men as Leroy Pope Walker. W. C. Whitthorne Judge A Wright[9] and other original secessionists and I pray for Judge Caruthers your pardoning power. His wife[10] is my cousin—a good devoted christian lady—and I feel much interest in her—& am satisfied that this instance of clemency would do much good—and still increase your number of friends—and defeat no demand of justice.

God works by human instrumentalities and if it was his will that slavery should be abolished, I do not see how it could have been done in any other manner or way except by that in which it was done.

In Dec 1860 you predicted the effect war would have upon slavery, but a great many other talented and patriotic men were not as foreseeing and yet honestly desired to do their duty.

I ask as a personal favor that Judge Caruthers be immediately pardoned and you will only increase the larger the debt of gratitude, I owe you for many favors.

R. W. Brown

P.S.[11] In the last interview I had with Gov. B. I found him in very feeble health. He treated me with marked courtesy as he has ever done. I have no unkind feelings towards him and only regret the course he and others are pursuing—but in the end he will probably injure himself more than any one else. As Gov B nominated you for Vice President—you can well afford to be very forbearing towards him. His prejudices against democracy—warp and blind his judgment. But in your greatness of soul—you can overlook his frailties and at the same time act alone for the good of the whole American people. Charity or love is the great law that should govern us all.

R. W. B—

LS, DLC-JP.

1. Robert M. Patton had become governor of Alabama in December 1865.
2. Matthew 7: 21.
3. Henry J. Raymond, Edwin D. Morgan, John A. Dix, and Daniel S. Dickinson, all of New York.
4. Brown to Johnson, Oct. 16, 1865, *Johnson Papers*, 9: 244–47.
5. No letter from Brown regarding the February 22, 1866, Union meeting at Nashville has been located. Neill S. Brown apparently did make a brief speech at that conclave. See *Nashville Press and Times*, Feb. 24, 1866.
6. Despite several direct and indirect appeals on behalf of Caruthers's pardon, he was not granted amnesty until August 1866. See *Johnson Papers*, 8: 386n.
7. Possibly Thomas H. Coldwell, state attorney general.
8. Edwin R. Glascock, U.S. marshal for the middle district.
9. Archibald Wright (1809–1884) was originally from Middle Tennessee but had moved to Memphis in the 1850s. He served on the state supreme court prior to the outbreak of the Civil War. Earlier he had served one term in the General Assembly. Johnson pardoned Wright on July 26, 1865. *BDTA*, 1: 821; *House Ex. Docs.*, 39 Cong., 2 Sess., No. 116, p. 53 (Ser. 1293).
10. Sarah Saunders Caruthers.

11. This postscript is written in Brown's handwriting, whereas the text of the letter is not.

From John Campbell

Phila   April 6th 66

The first thing for me to do is to tell you who I am. I am by birth Irish. Some 15 or 16 years ago I was Secretary of the Land Reform Society of this City and then had some correspondence with you. I sent you petitions &. you usualy sent me your speeches. I admired [you] then. I admire you now. You must know that I do not want any offer of patronage at your hands. My business precludes me from this. Independent of my own views I can only repeat the expressed opinions of many of the leading lawyers of Penna. You will see from the enclosed circular[1] that Lawyers constitute a large portion of my customers. From them I hear evey conflicting opinion. I give as correctly as I can the concentration of this opinion. As a general thing the Republicans are against you except those who have voted that ticket but who have no poltics say 2 per cent. Then you have the entire Democracy of Penna who stand by you to the bitter end. Courage Courage Courage is the great desideratum you must have. Let me iterate that to me you cannot give office because I wish your Policy to succeed therefore it is that I willnot embarrass your action. So far I have written and have read it to an ex state senator Charles Lamberton[2] who said your true remark is Courage. You are Commander in chief of the Army and Navy of the U S—and for what purpose to see the laws faithfully executed—are there not traitors in the free states so called? Are not Sumner Forney Stevens and Kelley[3] as much traitors as any southern rebel? When great principles are at stake those who have power must see them enforced. Are you aware that there is a deliberate plot to impeach you? I do not believe that you are not already informed of this villanous plot. I am I suppose 55 years old about your age but so help me God I will shoulder my rifle in your behalf sooner than see the disunites and enemies of the County succeed in destroying you and per consequence this Govrment. I have written to E G Asay[4] a Lawyer of Chicago who sent me the Chicago Tribune with the impeachment article.[5] He and I will write a letter each in which we will review the entire conduct of the present Congress.[6]

The victory rests with you and with you alone. You must send for or cause to be seen every office holder in Penna and say to him that Gearys ticket is the DISUNION *Ticket.* You must say clearly that it must be defeated. Cowan (whom I do not know and have never seen and more shame for him—He a book worm and I having the best collection of Books either in N Y or Phila) must go back to the senate—where you do not have an office holder who will sustain your policy. Appoint a Conservative Republican but in no instance appoint a Democrat. See Buckalew Cowan and Randall[7] who I am sure will say as I do.

Col Wm C Patterson born in Tenn approves of this letter. He and his have alway been supporters of you in Tennessee. Bye the bye I see that that old blaguard Brownlow wants to send you and the state of Kentucky to Hell. If you desire to see me I will go to Washington if you choose but I do not think that I Can give you more information.

John Campbell

ALS, DLC-JP.
1. No enclosure has been found.
2. A former Peace Democrat, Lamberton (1829–fl1885) had served in the state senate during much of the war (1862–64) and afterwards practiced law in Wilkes-Barre. George B. Kulp, *Families of the Wyoming Valley: Sketches of the Bench and Bar of Luzerne County, Pennsylvania* (3 vols., Wilkes-Barre, Pa., 1885–90), 1: 25, 265–82 passim.
3. William D. Kelley.
4. A Philadelphia native, Edward G. Asay (1825–fl1899) was a Methodist minister for several years before being admitted to the bar of New York City and commencing the practice of criminal law in Chicago in 1856. *The Bench and Bar of Chicago: Biographical Sketches* (Chicago, 1883), 636–37; John M. Palmer, ed., *The Bench and Bar of Illinois: Historical and Reminiscent* (2 vols., Chicago, 1899), 2: 638.
5. The newspaper reasoned that Johnson ought to be impeached for and convicted of high treason. *Chicago Tribune*, Mar. 31, 1866.
6. Not found.
7. Charles R. Buckalew, Edgar Cowan, Samuel J. Randall.

From William B. Campbell

Lebanon Tennessee   April 6th 1866

Dear Sir

Your time is too valuable to be occupied in reading my poor effusions, yet I cannot longer refrain from offering you my warmest congratulations on your patriotic endeavors to restore the Union and save the constitution from further abrasion. We entered political life together in the Legislature of 1835 and although for many years arrayed on oposite sides, yet have I ever regarded you as honest, patriotic, faithful and true to the people. In all your public employment you have been above suspicion of having subserved your private interests at the public expense. Your whole public carrer has been exemplified by unusual ability without the display of pomp or pride. Firm and brave, without cruelty or vindictiveness—earnest, sympathetic and active for the wealfare of your fellowmen. Jackson was idolized by our people, but he had it not in his power to do for the Country what you have done, and should you succeed in maintaining the principles enunciated in your messages & speeches since you succeeded to the Presidency, your name will go down to posterity more venerated than that great hero.

"That there is a God all nature cries aloud," and that Almighty has raised you up for great and special purposes, I most devoutly believe. Our country is too youthful and vigorous yet to lapse into despotism and although difficulties may crowd thickly around you and danger environ your path, you will successfully lead this people safely through the deep waters, and restore the Union of these States and *Constitutional liberty*. You are now the true high priest bearing the "Ark" of our deliverance.

Brownlow, Fletcher and the radical Legislature are goading the people of this state into madness & desperation but they will bear many grevious outrages while you are at the *helm*. The time is not far distant when you will be obliged to interpose against their tyrrany & oppression. A most ignorant and unprincipled set of fanatics, without kindness, mercy, forgiveness, charity or justice in the heart of any one of them. They are determined to *rule* or *ruin*. You cannot be blind to the fact that if they can perpetuate their power, they will use it to the utmost extent against you and your policy. Like Stokes, Fowler & Maynard, these home radicals make professions of friendship only to decieve. Thad Stevens & Charles Sumner are not more bitterly your enemies. The time is at hand when none but true and trustworthy friends should be placed on guard. I confide most implicitly in your discretion and patiently await your action.

Most heartily do I approve your speech on the 22nd of Feby and that you maintained your manhood by giving Stevens Sumner &c. blow for blow. No concessions will conciliate them—give them an inch & they will take an ell. The contest they have sought and their purpose is to kill you off, so that you will not be in the way of their aspirations. The contest must be fought out by hard blows. You have the best weapons and the skill and ability to use them potentially and you will come off conquorer.

My heart is with you and in your cause.

W B Campbell

ALS, DLC-JP.

From Kenneth Rayner

Raleigh, No. Ca.   April 6th 1866.

Confidential

My Dear Sir,

Through the kind interposition of a friend—Mr. Mar[sh]all O. Roberts of New-York—the Mess: Appleton[1] agreed to undertake the publication of the *work*,[2] which I casually mentioned to you last Fall— and about which, Judge Patterson and myself have been corresponding. I requested the Mess: Appleton, to forward the advance proof-sheets to Judge Patterson, every two or three days; that he might read them, and make such corrections, as in his judgment, he may think proper. If it is worth publishing at all, why then, it is necessary, it shall be all *right*. Owing to the circumstances of the case, the book will probably be very extensively read. There is, at this time, a morbid anxiety, to know all about your character, your antecedents &c. If I know myself, my object was to do good—to prove, that the interests of the north and the south were identified—and that, through the force of circumstances, you occupied the position of a mediator, to bring about harmony and concord between the sections.

I felt it was to be regretted, that owing to the pressure on your time, you could not possibly look over the manuscript, before it went to press. I was particularly anxious to say nothing, that might be imprudent for, of course any thing said in your vindication or advocacy, will be closely criticized, in certain quarters.

In regard to that portion, referring to the events of your personal life—and also that, referring to your Congressional life—I hope you will see but little to disapprove of. It is mostly narrative, followed by such comments as the occasion called for. A large part of the work is a *disquisition*, on your scheme of policy for the restoration of the union. I have discussed it from the stand-point of your own argument—and have been very cautious to try and avoid all inadvertence or imprudence, which might possibly compromise your position before the country. I have urged it upon Judge Patterson, to modify, amend, or leave out, any portion, that he may think good policy would require, should be done. This I hope he will not fail to do; and when his own judgment is at fault, I hope he will request your opinion.

I have endeavored to avoid harshness, bitterness, and severity. 'Tis true, I have been severe on the originall plotters and conspirators of disunion and secession—also on Prest. Buchannan's shortcomings in 1860–'61—and on the London Quarterly review, for its Jesuitical article in regard to the war, and its ungenerous assault on yourself.[3] In the main I have consulted a feeling of conciliation, between the North & the South—and between your friends and the republicans, who are disposed to find fault with you.

The style of the composition in regard to yourself personally—is that of high panegyric, of course. No one is expected to write a memoir of any distinguished man, unless he has something good to say of him. In this regard, I must beg your pardon—one thing is certain, I have said nothing more, than what I believed and felt, under the circumstances, to be just and true.

I am almost afraid I have made the work too large. It will make 500 pages of large duodecimo size. I sent on to the publishers, two days sinsce, some 60 pages of additional manuscript—but owing to my fears, that the book might be too large, I had to leave it to the discretion of the publishers, as to whether they would include it in the book. This last is a calm and unprejudiced review, of the influences acting on the minds of the Southern people, through which they blundered into that most woful and tragical of all mistakes (to call it by no worse name) that a sane people ever committed. I shall regret it, if this last cannot appear in the body of the work; for I am rather pleased with the exposition I have presented—and I believe, it will find an approving response from the great conservative body of the Southern people, themselves.

Of course, I feel a deep interest in the fate of my book. I expect nothing else, than to be roundly abused by the extreme and radical men, both North and South. The work is written from a high national stand-point. If it meets with the approval of moderate, conservative, and national men, in both sections—I shall have an assurance, that its tone, temper, and style are what they ought to be.

I can only repeat, what I stated to you, last Fall—that if ever there was a people, who looked up to any man, as their friend and father—as their only hope in their day of despondency and gloom, such is the Southern people, at the present time, and you are the man. It is not, that they regard you as *Southern* in your proclivities and feelings—but as a *national* man, and as a *national* President. And yet, the Southern people feel, that it would not be prudent, to give expression to any thing like jubilation and triumph. With calm and quiet hope and resignation, they await the developments of the future. I really wish the ultra radical element of the North, could see the Southern people, just as they are, ruined, crushed, and broken-spirited. As I told many Northern men, in my late trip to the North—if they could see the real and true condition of the South, as it is—their resentments would be disarmed—there would be nothing to feed resentment on—sympathy would take the place of every thing like unkindness. I wish the day could arrive, when the Southern people could give expression, through the ballot-box, to those feelings of unalloyed confidence and hope, which they entertain for yourself.

I beg pardon, Mr. President, for annoying you with this long letter. I have duly appreciated the constant engagements on your time. I am aware, that your onerous duties monopolise all your time. I have abstained from troubling you—anxious as I was, to secure an interest by you, in the forthcoming work. If I shall have done any thing, towards promoting harmony between the two sections—if I shall have done any thing, towards awakening the public mind, to a proper appreciation of your sacrifices, your trials difficulties and labors, in your embarrassing position—I shall be more than gratified at the reflection, that I have effected some little of good, for my country.

K. Rayner
April 10—

Your second veto has been received and read by our people—followed by the depressing news, that the bill had passed the Senate, by a majority of more than two thirds, on the question of reconsideration. The state of feeling among our people, is difficult to describe. It is not excitement—not at all. The days of *excitement* are at an end, in the South. The predominant feeling is one of deep and despondent anxiety. There is nothing seen or heard, of any thing like a definite hope or prospect of our future.

You and you alone are on every lip, and in every heart. We feel that our destiny, is, under providential dispensation, in your hands; and that all we can do, in our present, poor, unfortunate, and powerless condition, is to wait calmly and resignedly; and to pray that you may be sustained, by a Higher Power, in your efforts to preserve the constitution, and save the institutions of our fathers, from overthrow and ruin. This point, I have kept constantly in view throughout the work I have written—viz: that your efforts to restore and preserve the union, were in perfect consistency and harmony with the views you had enunciated, from the beginning of the struggle—that you had been governed *by system*, perfectly in accord with the recorded sentiments of your past life. This portion of the work, I indulge the hope, will meet with your approbation. And herein, is the great moral strength of your position. Your enemies can not charge you with inconsistency—or with having misled any one, in regard to your course.

There is one feeling, that seems to prevail, with almost entire unanimity, among the Southern people. And that is a strong and abiding *faith*, in your ultimate triumph and success. This is all that sustains them against almost absolute despair. They have no definite plans, purposes, or calculations, as to the future. "President Johnson is our only hope"—is the only comment indulged in, in reference to the startling events, developed from day to day.

Unless there is some *special* cause for the influences operating on public opinion, in Connecticut—the result of the election in that state is most cheering.[4] If we are allowed to hope, that a similar condition of affairs prevails in the other Northern States, there is great chance for the success of constitutional principles, when the people shall have reflected, and spoken through the ballot-box. If there be any men of *national* views and feelings, I know I belong to that class. And yet when I reflect on the sad, and suffering, and disconsolate condition of the South (wrong and misguided as it has been) I can only exclaim—"May God in his mercy save my poor native land, from ruin!"

K. R.

ALS, DLC-JP.
    1. The publishing firm of D. Appleton & Co., composed of the sons of its founder, Daniel Appleton: William H. (1814–1899), John A. (1817–1881), George S. (1821–1878), Samuel F. (1821–1883), and Daniel S. (1824–1890). John Tebbel, *A History of Book Publishing in the United States* (2 vols., New York, 1972–75), 1: 287–88.
    2. Rayner's book, *Life and Times of Andrew Johnson . . .*, was published anonymously later in 1866.
    3. See *Life and Times of Andrew Johnson*, 248–50, 330–53. *The London Quarterly Review* (American edition) article which offended Rayner was "The Close of the American War," Vol. 118 (1865): 55–72.
    4. Evidently Rayner refers here to the April 2 gubernatorial election in Connecticut which was narrowly carried by Republican candidate Joseph R. Hawley over the Democratic contender James E. English. Much controversy had surrounded the question of Johnson's preference in that contest. It is admittedly unclear why Rayner would find the election returns to be "most cheering." *American Annual Cyclopaedia* (1865), 252–55.

From Robert F. Stockton
Private

Phila   April 6th 66

On my return[1] to New Jersey; I thought it best to have the Legislature adjourn without appointing a Senator.[2] It *hung too long*—and as *secured safety* was so desireable—and as it could only be had by getting rid of doubtful persons I consented to it.

As far as N.J. is concerned for the future—be wary—don't seem to be a democrat or radical nothing but a "*Johnson Man*." If you are *troubled* by the aspiring to render you service, or to take office you can refer to me. I am entered into the arena, as a Johnson Man to stand by your principles policy and courage. Dont give office to *democrats* at present.

R. F. Stockton

The Legislature have just adjourned *sine die*. In haste.[3]

R. F S

ALS, DLC-JP.
1. He had been in Washington a few days earlier and may have seen Johnson then. Stockton to Johnson, Apr. 2, 1866, Johnson Papers, LC.
2. The attempt to elect a U.S. senator in place of Stockton's son, John P. Stockton, a Democrat whose seat had been declared vacant on March 27, failed when the Democratic minority of the New Jersey legislature refused to recognize that a vacancy existed. It was not until September 19, when the legislature reassembled during a special session, that Republican Alexander G. Cattell was chosen senator by a strictly partisan vote (the Democrats again protesting). *BDAC*; *DAB*; *American Annual Cyclopaedia* (1866), 539–40.
3. Earlier that morning Theodore F. Randolph, a Democratic state senator at Trenton, had informed the President by telegraph that the legislature would adjourn at midday, "thus defeating the sending of an anti-Administration senator in Mr Stocktons place." *DAB*; Randolph to Johnson, Apr. 6, 1866, Johnson Papers, LC.

From Cuthbert Bullitt

New Orleans, April 7th 1866

My Dear Sir

I have the honor to enclose you a copy of the resolutions passed by the "*Andrew Johnson Club of Louisiana*" on the evening of the 5th Instant[1] —from which you will perceive that the Union party have planted themselves upon your messages to Congress, as the platform of their principles.

I hope that in giving to the party a personal complexion, devoted to the maintenance of the doctrines of your most timely vetoes of the two bills, which encountered your disapproval will not be displeasing to you. I confess that so doing gave me the liveliest satisfaction.

You are aware that a large majority of the voters of this city, & a yet greater majority of the voters of the parishes, is composed of returned confederates within the relief of the amnesty proclamation, or especially pardoned.

Many of these express sincere gratitude for the resistance you have made to the Freedmens Bureau Bill, & to the civil rights bill, & avow themselves entirely content with your restoration policy.

In framing our resolutions, it was thought best to say nothing that would offend these supporters of your policy, who will be found, I hope, in the ranks of your personal supporters.

It gives me great pleasure to add, that the executive committee,[2] stand preeminently high in this community, as gentlemen of loyalty & integrity & that they will exert an influence that will be felt & appreciated throughout the state.

Cuthbert Bullitt

ALS, DLC-JP.

1. Although not found enclosed, a copy of the resolutions is readily available in the New Orleans newspapers. At its meeting on April 5, the group took a stand in compliance with Johnson's policies and principles. See *New Orleans Picayune*, Apr. 3, 7, 1866.

2. Among the members of the executive committee were Thomas Cottman, Christian Roselius, Thomas P. May, and John S. Whitaker. Ibid., Apr. 7, 1866.

Circular re *Appointments to Office*

Executive Mansion, April 7th, 1866.

It is eminently right and proper that the Government of the United States should give earnest and substantial evidence of its just appreciation of the services of the patriotic men who, when the life of the Nation was imperilled, entered the Army and Navy to preserve the integrity of the Union, defend the Government, and maintain and perpetuate, unimpaired, its free institutions. It is therefore directed—

First—That in appointments to office in the several Executive Departments of the General Government, and the various branches of the public service connected with said Departments, preference shall be given to such meritorious and honorably discharged soldiers and sailors— particularly those who have been disabled by wounds received or diseases contracted in the line of duty—as may possess the proper qualifications.

Second—That in all promotions in said Departments, and the several branches of the public service connected therewith, such persons shall have preference, when equally eligible and qualified, over those who have not faithfully and honorably served in the land or naval forces of the United States.[1]

Andrew Johnson

DS, DLC-JP, Ser. 7A, Vol. 1.

1. In response to this circular Johnson received many petitions from or in favor of veterans seeking appointments. See, for instance, Henry L. Potter to Johnson, Apr. 9, 1866. See also James Wood, Jr., to Johnson, Apr. 10, 1866, Appts., Customs Service, Collector, New York, James Wood, Jr., RG56, NA; Newburyport, Mass., Veterans Petition, May

1866, Lets. Recd. (Main Ser.), File M-1600-1866 (M619, Roll 498), RG94, NA; Citizens of Armstrong County, Penn., to Johnson, ca. Apr. 7, 1866, Johnson Papers, LC.

From James H. Lane

Washington, April 7 1866.

Dear Sir

This will introduce to you Keokuk, Chief of the Sac & Fox Indians,[1] and Mr. William Whistler,[2] his interpreter, who desire to have a conversation with you relative to the Agency of that Tribe, in which they naturally feel an absorbing interest.

I share in the extreme anxiety which they feel for the retention of Maj. Martin[3] as their Agent, and would be very glad if you can yield to their request, and withdraw the nomination of Henry Shanklin,[4] which has not yet been acted upon by the Senate Committee. By granting them an early personal interview on this subject, you will much oblige.[5]

J. H. Lane

LS, DNA-RG48, Patents and Misc. Div., Lets. Recd.

1. Moses Keokuk (1824–1903) became principal chief upon the death of his father. He was designated by the other chiefs to go to Washington to confer with Johnson about several matters. Ida M. Ferris, "The Sauks and Foxes in Franklin and Osage Counties," KSHS *Collections*, 11 (1909–10): 385; Blackmar, *Kansas*, 2: 68; Chiefs to Johnson, Mar. 20, 1866, Misc. Lets. Recd., 1849–1884, RG48, NA.

2. Whistler (c1837–1872), the son of Gen. John Whistler, kept the post office in Osage County and was a trader. He served in the Kansas legislature a year before his death. 1860 Census, Kans., Franklin, Ohio Twp., 294; Ferris, "Sauks and Foxes," 387.

3. Henry W. Martin (1817–1901) was a native of Kentucky who lived in Illinois for several years before moving to Kansas. He was in the mercantile business, served in the Kansas legislature in 1862, and was appointed as Indian agent that same year, a post he held for approximately five years. Several years later he moved to Arkansas and eventually back to Illinois. Ibid., 360n, 361n; *U.S. Off. Reg.* (1865).

4. Originally nominated by Johnson on March 2, 1866, Shanklin (*fl*1869) did not become the agent for the Sauks and Foxes, no doubt because of Johnson's handwritten endorsement on the Lane letter: "Let Shanklin be withdrawn. AJ." His nomination withdrawn on April 10, Shanklin was, however, nominated and confirmed later in the month as Indian agent for the Wichita agency; a post he held until his resignation in 1869. *Senate Ex. Proceedings*, Vol. 14, pt. 2: 579, 714, 729, 755; Shanklin to Johnson, Jan. 9, 1869, Gen. Records, Lets. Recd. (M234, Roll 929), RG75, NA.

5. Keokuk and Whistler met with Johnson on April 9. *Washington Evening Star*, Apr. 9, 1866.

From Benjamin F. Perry

Greenville S C   April 8th 1866

My Dear Sir

I am in receipt of Major Long's[1] telegram of the 31st ult directing me not to issue the Pardons for South Carolina until I received his letter.[2] Last evening I received his letter requesting me to inform Mr Elford[3] "that he must either deliver the Pardons free of charge or return them to this office without delay."[4]

I have shown these communications to Mr Elford & he is perfectly willing to do as directed. He prefers returning the Pardons as the delivery of them to four or five hundred persons would cause him to incur considerable expense & trouble in corresponding with the various parties.

I deem it due Mr Elford to make the following explanation in reference to the course he has pursued.

The applicants for Pardon were writing to me every mail to enquire about their Pardons & I could give them no information except that their applications had been duly forwarded. In consequence of these constant applications to me, I suggested to Mr Elford, who had drawn over a hundred of the applications for Pardon, to go on with me to Washington & look them up & that I had no doubt the parties would be willing to compensate him liberally for his trouble. I stated that I would render him all the service I could whilst in Washington. I spoke to you in reference to this matter, and you kindly permitted the Pardons to issue. Mr Elford procured lists & hunted them up in the Secretary of States office & had them signed, sealed & executed & remained in Washington several days after I left there attending to this matter.

Mr Elford thought he was doing the parties a great service, & that they would generously compensate him for his service. I thought so too. The Pardons had been delayed a great while & the parties were very anxious to get them. Mr Elford knew that he had no right & could not "*force*" the parties to pay him. He, now, will return the Pardons & let them git them themselves. If he retained them for distribution, it would be a considerable annoyance to him in writing letters & paying postage.

I hope it is not necessary to say to you that I had no pecuniary interest in the matter & what I did was gratuitiously & generously done to oblige the parties.

B F. Perry

P.S.   Since writing the above Col Elford has agreed to turn the Pardons over to me & I will deliver them all free of any charge when called for. I have given public notice of this[5] & it will save the applicants trouble in sending for the Pardons to Washington.

B F. Perry

ALS, DLC-JP.

1. Andrew K. Long. See Long to Perry, Mar. 31, 1866, Tels. Sent, President, Vol. 3 (1865–68), RG107, NA.

2. Not found.

3. Charles J. Elford (1820–1867), a lawyer and former co-editor with B. F. Perry of the *Greenville Southern Patriot*, had been a Confederate commissioner and colonel of the 16th S.C. Inf., CSA. During the summer of 1865 Johnson appointed him assessor of the Third Internal Revenue District, a position he held about a year before being replaced because he "declined taking the oath of office." *Greenville County, South Carolina Cemetery Survey* (5 vols., Greenville, 1977–83), 3: 42; Lillian A. Kibler, *Benjamin F. Perry: South Carolina*

Unionist (Durham, 1946), 248–50; Charles J. Elford to Johnson, July 18, 1865, Amnesty Papers (M1003, Roll 45), S.C., Charles J. Elford, RG94, NA; *OR*, Ser. 1, Vol. 6: 348; Ser. 4, Vol. 2: 899; *U.S. Off. Reg.* (1865), 57; Ser. 6B, Vol. 1: 97, Johnson Papers, LC; *Spartanburg Carolina Spartan*, Aug. 30, 1866.

    4. Early in March 1866 Elford advertised that he had been in Washington, D.C., "investigating and prosecuting the applications for PARDON from South Carolina," and listed a fee schedule: five dollars for information, twenty-five dollars for "procuring the warrant of pardon and final certificate," and ten dollars for obtaining just the certificate. *Charleston Courier*, Mar. 5, 1866.

    5. Not located.

From Joseph A. LaRue[1]

Washington   April 9th 1866

Sir—

On the 19th of March 1863, I was chosen by the council of Administration[2] at Fort Sumner New Mexico,[3] Sutler at that Post for three years and the selection was approved by the Secretary of War.[4] I acted as sutler under the appointment to the entire satisfaction of the Garrison and of the Generals commanding the District & Department—and before the expiration of my term was unanimously re-elected by the Council of Administration for another term of three years. The papers showing my second election were approved and forwarded by Maj & Bvt Lt Col Wm. McCleave[5] commanding the Post, through Bvt Maj Genl Carleton[6] to the Secretary of War on the 10th of February last.

Supposing that in conformity with the invariable usage of the service, my second election would be approved by the Secretary of War, I made purchases of goods to the amount of over $25,000. and have been proceeding with the erection of a large Store & warehouse on which I have already expended over $10,000.[7]

About the 15th of March last and probably before the record of my second election had reached the war Dept. the Secretary of War as I am informed at your request appointed Oscar M Brown of Calafornia[8] Sutler in my stead.

I enclose herewith a certified copy of the proceedings of the Council of administration, in which they say that in selecting me again for the place "they have been influenced by the satisfactory manner in which Mr LaRue has conducted his affairs as sutler during the past three years— the large amount of money lately expended by him to facilitate the business, & because his removal would entail upon him undeserved losses without in any manner adding to the interests of the Govt. or the good of the troops serving at Fort Sumner."

I beg leave also to call your attention to the enclosed letter from Maj Genl Pope[9] Comg Dept of New Mexico, expressing his regrets at my removal and certifying from personal knowledge to my character "as an honest upright & honorable man." In urging the revocation of Mr

Browns appointment & the approval of the selection of myself by the council of Administration he says "it is but reasonable that the Officers & Soldiers of Military Posts on the Frontier should have some voice in the choice of the sutler upon whose character & knowledge of the business so much of their comfort at these remote stations depends. It has always been the custom of service to select sutlers by the voice of those whom he is to supply & with whom his relations must be friendly & satisfactory."

Supposing that this appointment of Mr Brown was suggested by you without knowledge of the custom of the service or of my election by the Council of Administration and feeling sure that you would be unwilling to inflict so great an injury as this unexpected removal will be to me—I respectfully request that you will refer these papers to the Secretary of War with a request that he will reconsider the appointment of Mr Brown and act on the election of the Council of Administration, as the good of the service and a fair consideration of my interests may dictate.[10]

J A LaRue

P.S.—In this connection I would also state that I have for the last eleven years been a resident of New Mexico and that all my interests are identified with that country while my successor Mr Brown is a citizen of Calafornia and in no way identified with New Mexico.

J A LaRue

ALS, DNA-RG94, ACP Branch, File L-170-CB-1866, J. A. LaRue.

1. A native of New Jersey, LaRue (c1831–fl1882) ran a dry goods store in Lincoln, New Mexico, in the early 1880s, served as Lincoln County treasurer, and was otherwise involved in Democratic politics. 1880 Census, N.M., Lincoln, Lincoln, 5; *Business Directory of New Mexico* (1882), 90; Leon C. Metz, *Pat Garrett: The Story of a Western Lawman* (Norman, 1974), 55, 134.

2. The council of administration consisted of the second through fourth ranking officers at the post. Darlis A. Miller, *Soldiers and Settlers: Military Supply in the Southwest, 1861–1865* (Albuquerque, 1989), 346.

3. Brig. Gen. James H. Carleton established the post of Fort Sumner in late 1862 and named it for Maj. Gen. Edwin V. Sumner, his former commander in New Mexico. The fort guarded the Bosque Redondo Reservation for Navajo and Mescallero Apache Indians until it was abandoned at the end of the decade. Thompson, *Navajo*, 12, 157, passim.

4. Edwin M. Stanton.

5. McCleave (1823–1904), a native of Ireland, spent ten years in the U.S. Army (1850–60). Beginning in 1861 McCleave served as captain and then major in the 1st Calif. Vol. Cav., commanding Fort Sumner from March 1865 until August 1866. Following his discharge from the volunteers, he served in the regular army until retired for disability in 1879. Powell, *Army List*, 461; Thompson, *Navajo*, 77, 167; Pension Records, Mary C. McCleave, RG15, NA.

6. James H. Carleton (1814–1873), born in Maine, joined the U.S. Army in 1839. In 1862 he recruited the "California Column" and, as brigadier general of volunteers, relieved Gen. Edward R.S. Canby as commander of the Department of New Mexico. Frequent controversies plagued Carleton as commander. Removed from duty with the volunteers in September 1866, Carleton served with the regular U.S. cavalry until his death. Warner, *Blue*.

7. About December 1866 LaRue sold his old store building to the army for $9,000 to be used as a hospital for the soldiers. Thompson, *Navajo*, 129.

8. Brown (d. 1889), a native of Petersburg, Virginia, and a veteran of the Mexican War, enlisted in the 1st Calif. Cav. in late 1863. Brown had applied for the sutlership February 2,

1866, recommended by Sen. John Conness and Rep. John Bidwell of California, as well as Jose Francisco Chaves, delegate from New Mexico, among others. His appointment was ordered and issued by Stanton on March 1, to take effect on May 18, the expiration date of LaRue's appointment. Brown experienced personal tragedy during his stint as sutler when his wife and his brother, who helped run the store, both died. Brown moved to Texas, then practiced law in Globe, Arizona, and finally settled in New Mexico. Statement of E. D. Townsend, May 4, 1866, ACP Branch, File A-302-CB-1866, O. M. Brown, RG94, NA; Richard H. Orton, comp., *Records of California Men in the War of the Rebellion, 1861–1867* (Detroit, 1979 [1890]), 87; Darlis A. Miller, *The California Column in New Mexico* (Albuquerque, 1982), xi, 9, 20, 148–49, 270.

9. John Pope. The letter is not found with this document.

10. Johnson referred LaRue's letter to the secretary of war "for special attention. It appears that this man is the choice of the Council of Administration, and that he has an excellent record." Colonel Brown's order was not revoked, however, despite a plea to that effect from Sen. James H. Lane. The dispute between LaRue and Brown eventually involved General Grant, who permitted LaRue to remain at Fort Sumner for awhile to dispose of his goods for cash to avoid causing too great a sacrifice of his investment. Soon Brown complained vehemently that LaRue's continued presence had severely injured his business as LaRue undercut his prices. Eventually LaRue was reinstated. Statement of E. D. Townsend, May 4, 1866, ACP Branch, File A-302-CB-1866, O. M. Brown, RG94, NA; Lane to Johnson, Apr. 12, 1866, ACP Branch, File L-170-CB-1866, J. A. LaRue, RG94, NA; Simon, *Grant Papers*, 16: 183–86; Frank McNitt, *The Indian Traders* (Norman, 1962), 46.

From William A. Newell[1]

Washington, D.C.   9 April 1866

Dear Sir.

I trust your Excellency will not infer from my vote on the "civil rights" bill that I design or desire to desert your Administration.[2] Whilst a different course would not have sustained you practically it would have been in violation of my own sense of right, and, in decided contravention of the will of our friends whose opinion I have ascertained, by personal observation during my stay at Trenton last week. They strongly desire protection to the freedmen and fear the States would be slow to accord it. I am confident they entertain for you the best feeling and desire to support you. I trust that your Excellency will confide in me as earnestly desiring your personal and political success. I have supported you hitherto and still have confidence in you, as much as I could repose in any living man.[3]

Wm. A Newell

ALS, DLC-JP.

1. Elected as a Republican to the Thirty-ninth Congress, Newell (1817–1901), a prewar Whig congressman and governor of New Jersey, failed in his bid for reelection in 1866 and took up the practice of medicine. He later served as territorial governor of Washington. *BDAC*.

2. Newell was no "Johnson man," later warned Andrew J. Rogers, a New Jersey Democrat and colleague. Newell "votes and acts with the radicals," Rogers complained, citing specific examples. Rogers to Johnson, Apr. 21, 1866, Johnson Papers, LC; *BDAC*.

3. A few days later at Horace Maynard's urging, Newell forwarded Johnson a copy of a recent speech in which he defended Johnson against the accusation that the President had committed treason. Newell to Johnson, Apr. 13, 1866, Johnson Papers, LC.

From Henry L. Potter[1]

New Marlboro Mass. April 9th 1866.

Sir

Your circular order of 7th inst.—in reference to the appointing of disabled and meritorious veterans of the War—is most commendable—but with all due deference and respect to your Excellency—why not commence by setting the example yourself?

For over four months past, the politicians have been wrangling over the collectorship of the Port of New York. Why not cut their jealousies and differencies short—and give example to all other dispensers of Federal patronage, by appointing to that position the gallant, patriotic, able and *disabled* veteran—Major Genl. Daniel E. Sickles—truly the man for that position.[2]

The Senate—surely cannot refuse to confirm one so eminently entitled to the position as him.

Except on principle of "giving earnest and substantial evidence of the Govts. just appreciation"—to those patriotic men who gave their health or limbs a willing sacrifice "when the life of the nation was imperiled," I repeat—except on this principle—so nobly promulgated in your circular above referd. to—I would be glad to see Mr Wakeman, the present Surveyor of the Port of N.Y. elevated to the collectorship—a most worthy man—and a hearty supporter of your policy and administration; but give the gallant Daniel the collectorship—(whether he is an applicant or not) and let the "radicals" howl. The people are with you, and will hold up your hands. Continue as you have commenced, and there is a bright future for our country.

H. L. Potter
late Col 71st N.Y. Vs

ALS, DNA-RG56, Appts., Customs Service, Collector, N.Y., Daniel E. Sickles.
1. Potter (1828–1907), a brewer before the war, served as colonel of the 71st N.Y. Inf. during the conflict. He later became a lawyer. Pension File, Henry L. Potter, RG15, NA.
2. Sickles, who lost his right leg at Gettysburg, was also recommended by others. *DAB*. See Charles G. Halpine to Johnson, July 24, 1866.

From Benjamin C. Truman

Washington City. D.C. April 9, 1866.

Sir.

I have the honor to make the following report of my observations in the south, and my information concerning affairs and the people in that section.

I arrived at Montgomery, Ala. about the first of September, 1865, and remained in the south 31 weeks, or nearly eight months, during which time I travelled over nearly every portion of eight of the eleven seceded states, viz: Alabama, Georgia, Florida, Tennessee, Arkansas, Mississippi, Louisiana, and Texas. I remained in Alabama from the first of September, 1865, until the 15th day of October, of the same year. From there I went to Georgia, where I remained until the 7th of December, when I left that State for Florida, where I remained until the 20th. Subsequently I spent two weeks in Tennessee, one week in Arkansas, one week in Mississippi, two weeks in Louisiana, and four weeks in Texas. In this time I visited all of the large and important cities of the south, and made frequent and extended stops upon many of the largest plantations. I passed over nearly all of the Railroads in the above named states, was upon all of the navigable rivers, and travelled seven hundred odd miles in stage coaches.

I called upon all of the general officers commanding posts, districts, and departments in the eight states above mentioned, and also upon all of the Commissioners of Freedmen, except Gen. Fisk, and many other officers connected with the Freedmen's Bureau. I also conversed with at least one-third of the ex-generals of the late Confederate army, and large numbers of southern politicians and southern people, including ministers of the gospel, editors of newspapers, and others in professional capacities.

From my close and careful observation, in addition to what seems to me to have been my correct and varied sources of information, I derived the impressions which, with entire candor and frankness, I will endeavor briefly to set forth.

I will speak, first, of the sentiments of the people, touching their relations with the General Government and the people of the North.

I distinguish between *Loyalty* and *Patriotism*, and I believe the distinction not ill-grounded. That glorious spontaneous burst of popular enthusiasm with which the North responded as one man to the echoing thunders of Sumpter was the most splendid exhibition of *Patriotism* the world has yet witnessed; the quietness, and even cheerfulness, with which the same people once yielded obedience to the rule of James Buchanan, whose administration they despised, and hated, was an instance of *Loyalty*, such as only American citizens could have furnished.

The North never rebelled against James Buchanan, it is true, nor seriously proposed to; but I assert without hesitation that, now the war has swept over the South, there is no more disposition in that section of the country to rebel against the National Government, than there then was in the North at the time above referred to.

If any general assertion can be made that will apply to the masses of the people of the south, it is that they are, at the present time, indifferent toward the General Government. For four years of eventful life as a Nation, they were accustomed to speak of, and regard, "our government" as the one which had its seat in Richmond, and thousands who, at first looked upon that government with great suspicion and distrust, gradually, from the mere lapse of time, and the force of example, came to admit it into their ideas as *their* government. The great body of the people, in any country always move slowly—the transfer of allegiance from one *de facto* government to another is not effected in a day, whatever oaths of loyalty may be taken; and I have witnessed many amusing instances of mistakes on the part of those of whose attachment to the Government there could be no question. Ignorance and prejudice always lay furthest behind any radical change, and no person can forget that the violent changes of the past few years have left the ideas of the populace greatly unsettled, and increased their indifference. Fully one-half of the southern people never cherished an educated and active attachment to any government that was over them, and the war has left them very much as it found them.

The rank and file of the disbanded Southern army—those who remained in it to the end—are the back-bone and sinew of the South. Long before the surrender, corps, divisions, brigades and regiments had been thoroughly purged of the worthless class—the skulkers; those of whom the south, as well as any other country, would be best rid, and these it is that are now prolonging past bitternesses. These are they, in great part, as I abundantly learned, by personal observation, that are now editing reckless newspapers, and that put forth those pernicious utterances that so little represent the thinking, substantial people, and are so eagerly seized out and paraded by certain Northern journalists, who, themselves, as little represent the great North. To the disbanded regiments of the rebel army, both officers and men, I look with great confidence as the best and altogether most hopeful element of the south—the real basis of reconstruction and the material of worthy citizenship. On a thousand battle-fields they have bested the invincible power of that Government they vainly sought to overthrow, and along a thousand picket lines, and under the friendly flag of truce they have learned that the soldiers of the Union bore them no hatred, and shared with them the common attributes of humanity. Around the returned soldier of the south gathers the same circle of admiring friends that we see around the millions of hearthstones in our own section, and from him they are slowly learning the lesson of charity and of brotherhood. I know of very few more potent influences at work in promoting real and lasting reconciliation and reconstruction than the influence of the returned Southern soldier.

The question above all others that our people are anxious to ask is, in case of a war with a foreign nation, what would be the action of the South? Of course, all answers to this must be founded chiefly in speculation, since a great deal would depend upon the character of the nation with whom we were at war, and much upon the action of the Government between now and any such event. I need hardly say that, whatever might be their sympathies, in case of a war with England, not a regiment of men could be recruited in the south in her support, even if it were freely permitted. In other cases it would be different. There is a certain loose floating population in the south, as everywhere, and largely disproportionate to that of the North, in consequence of the more complete disruption caused by the war, that would be eager to enlist in any army, whether for or against the United States. It would be necessary, then, as things are at present, to keep a strict surveillance over the harbors of the principal ports to prevent them from sailing to join the common enemy, if such an object was desired, though I am far from certain that the class spoken of would not be well gotten rid of in foreign camps. They would consist almost entirely of that class of persons who are preparing to emigrate to Mexico and Brazil—men whose reputations in the rebel army were greatly overdone, or men who never did any service at the front, but who were valorous with words alone. If a large foreign army were to invade the south, and march uninterruptedly through the country—a very improbable contingency—without doubt it would receive many recruits. In Texas it would probably get eight thousand recruits—discontented, roving men, who are not engaged in any profitable employment, and are adding nothing to the state's productive capacity. I estimate that there are five thousand men in that state—deserters principally, and rebel refugees from Arkansas and Missouri—that are to-day depending entirely upon robbery and murder for a precarious subsistence. These would, of course rejoice at such an opportunity. In other states the proportion would be very much less. But if no invasion were accomplished, the substantial assistance that a foreign enemy would receive at the hands of the late insurgents would be quite insignificant; and the fears that many otherwise well-informed persons entertain in this regard are highly absurd. Naturally the American people, as a nation are devoted to the arts of peace. The soldiers of the late rebel army are if possible, infinitely more wearied and disgusted with war and all its works, than those of our army, and long for nothing so much as quiet. The best proof of this, is the fact that our noble volunteers, though crowned with the honors of almost limitless success and victory, are clamorous and even mutinous to be discharged from military duty. Therefore, I am constrained to believe that, with few exceptions, the great masses of those who have been in the rebel army will never again seek to enter the lists. If there is anything that I certainly learned in the south, it was that its people are tired of war and are anxious to establish and perpetuate peace.

If a war should arise against Great Britain, I do not believe that one-fourth of the people would even sympathize with that power; thousands would, of course; but not to an extent that would lead them to make any sacrifices in her interest. Those who did not join or sympathize with the Federal army, would maintain a "neutrality," which would be observed more strictly than that of England during the existence of the rebellion. The South to-day hates England more rigorously than the North does; and the country may rest assured of this much, at least, that the south, as a

people, is no more anxious for a war with any foreign power than we ourselves are. Besides, there is a deep and steadily-growing conviction, in
the minds of many of the most intelligent and thoughtful of the South—
a conviction that a stranger would seldom discover in the journals or
public speeches of prominent men, but only in the still under-currents of
private conversation—that in the late war the hand of Providence, the
decrees of destiny, were against them—are steadfastly averse to any separation of the Union. I confess that this discovery gave me an unfeigned
satisfaction, such as no other I have made in the South. A prominent
member of the Alabama Convention, a Railroad President in Florida,
three different Texas editors and scores of nameless private individuals all
over the south, have spoken to me in a tone of deep earnestness on this
subject, citing the numerous instances that had come under their observation, showing an almost Providential interference—a balancing of the
scales of fate against them. Nor were they persons who had been luke-
ware in "the cause," and who had been on the lookout for such inclinations. I am not mistaken. I know that there is a profound and abiding
conviction gradually gaining ground in the southern mind that their late
struggle was hopeless from the outset—that it was contrary to the will of
the Infinite.

More than that I know, from actual observation, that thousands of the
rank and file, and hundreds of their officers would gladly enlist in the
United States armies against any and all foreigners, particularly if they
could be allowed to serve under their old officers. I have conversed personally with hundreds of the ex-officers and soldiers of the late Confederate army, and I only repeat what I have from their own lips when I say
that a majority of them assured me they would enter our army in such an
event, in great part to give the Government a convincing proof that they
meant to be good and loyal citizens hereafter. I recall at present the names
of Gen's Hardie, McLaws, Forrest, Nichols and Jeff Thompson[1]—and
there are some others whose names have escaped my memory who told
me that in case a foreign war should grow up, they would offer their services to the United States Government in *any* capacity, even as a private.

The opinion has gained wide-spread acceptance in the North, through
the medium of letter-writers, Southern editorials, and other vehicles of
rumor and information, that the south is to-day more disloyal toward the
Government than at the conclusion of the war. Various reasons are urged
to account for this, chief among which is that this people have been
brought to this State by an ill-timed, ill-advised leniency. What are the
facts? When the war ended it left the south prostrated, stricken, helpless. Even many of the most intelligent looked for general confiscation,
proscription, and the reign of the scaffold, the news of the successive surrender of those armies that they had looked upon as standing alone between themselves and the direct calamities of history threw the minds of
the people into a state of the most abject terror. For many days, and even

weeks, so I have been informed in a thousand instances, the wretched frightened women and children, deprived of their former protectors lived in a state of the most fearful suspense, in hourly apprehension of the beginning of all that their fruitful imaginations, and those of their editors, had been able to conceive of Northern vandalism and hideous butchery. The old men and the youths, and even the adult citizens shared largely in this fearful looking for of judgement. This was not loyalty, though, in my opinion. It was silence—the silence of submission, of terror, of defeat. At this juncture, any terms, including even negro suffrage, might have been imposed so far as they were concerned. This feeling however, almost immediately after passed away, and the combined delay of anticipated retribution restored them to their wonted equanimity. Immediately succeeding this there sprang up what many conscientious people are prone to term an increase of disloyalty. But was it such? I give it another solution. What then, is the sentiment that has inspired these noisy and reckless utterances of late, which have given so much color to the charge? It is simply the returning wave that followed the depression of defeat—the inevitable and wholesome reaction from despair. It was to have been expected, and in my humble opinion, could not well have been avoided, and is not indicative of any deep-seated malady, but rather the contrary. The wise and skilful physician watches with well founded apprehension the progress of one of the most fatal diseases with which his art is acquainted, so long as its ragings are confined in the secret recesses of the body; but so soon as he beholds it assuming the form of violent and troublesome cutaneous eruptions, his confidence returns and he predicts for the patient a speedy convalescence. The boisterous demagogues, and especially the reckless editors, whom not even the iron despotism of Davis had been able to awe into silence, were for the moment, appalled and stricken dumb in the presence of the gigantic calamity that had overtaken them, and in the near prospect of impending ruin; but soon they became reassured by the moderation of the Government, and finding their lives still in their hands, have not ceased to pour forth those obnoxious utterances which are taken as evidence and proof of an increase of disloyalty. It is with diffidence that I venture to dissent from the published opinions of many distinguished witnesses who have taken this vew; but I am free to declare my firm conviction that it is altogether supercial and not founded in fact.

It is my belief that the south—the great, substantial and prevailing element is more loyal now, than it was at the end of the war—more loyal today than yesterday, and that it will be more loyal tomorrow than today. It would be impossible to present the numerous and scattered evidences upon which I base this belief; but I entertain it in all sincerity, and believe it to be consonant with the facts. "No revolution ever goes backward," is a convenient, but shallow truism; or, rather, expressive of no truth whatever, since every revolution has its ultimate revulsion, partially, at least;

and just as certainly as for four years the mass of popular sentiment in the south was slowly solidifying and strengthening in favor of the bogus Confederacy, just so certain it is that, from the date of its downfall, that opinion has been slowly returning to its old attachments. For many years the dream of independence had been increasingly cherished and nurtured in the breasts of thousands; for four years that dream was a living fact, penetrating the consciousness of all, and receiving the sympathies of scarcely less than all; and then came the sudden and appalling crash—the awakening from this dream, to the unwelcome but inexorable truth that the pleasing vision had vanished. As weeks, months, and years steadily accumulate, and the remembrances of the brief happiness vanish in the distance, the yearning for it will grow weak and inconstant. That dream will never be revived, in my opinion, never; and if I am satisfied of anything in relation to the South it is that the great majority of its leading men have forever renounced all expectations of a separate nationality.

If I were asked to reconcile the above statements with the grossly palpable appearances that argue to the contrary, especially as seen in some of the late Constitutional Conventions, I would simply answer that this apparent contradiction is an inevitable product of human inconsistency; or rather, the "consistency of politicians." For four years they found themselves required—most of them by preference, all of them by circumstances which they could not, if they would, control—to argue in favor of the right of secession and independent government. It is strange how soon and how inevitably, defence leads to conviction. I cannot say that when the Confederacy went down, there was not in all its borders a citizen who did not yield it so much of allegiance as he ever gave to any government; but I do not hesitate to declare that there were not five prominent politicians, *still remaining* within it, who could truly and conscientiously declare that they had not given it, first or last their sympathy. It has furnished me an interesting branch of historical study to look up the antecedents of those men who, when our troops made their appearance, were forward in their professions of unwavering Unionism. Alas; for political human nature! Scarcely one of them but had either accepted an office under the Confederacy, or signified his willingness to do so.

There comes now, a sudden and imperious necessity, that they cannot blink, to declare by their acts at least, that they were wrong in all this, but who could expect politicians and editors, before they had been reduced to a condition of absolute vassalage, to reverse their "records" *ab initio* and declare freely and without hesitation that all their utterances of the past four years had been mistaken. But this unwillingness does not necessarily involve a corresponding sluggishness of belief. I record it as my profound conviction, gathered from hundreds of intimate and friendly conversations with leading men in the south, that there are not fifty respectable politicians who still believe in the constitutional right of secesspeeches or published articles. Our conversations generally ended with the confession—which to me was entirely satisfactory, as meaning much more than was intended. "Whatever may be said about the *right* of secession, the thing itself may as well be laid aside, for it is certainly not *practicable*, and probably never will be." I believe there is the most charity, and by far the most correctness, in that reasoning which accounts in this way for the extreme reluctance that has been exhibited in most of the Conventions against declaring the act of secession null and void from the beginning. They will willingly concede that the *right* of secession does not now exist, provided only they are allowed to assert that it *did* at that time, which is simply a petty device of sorely humbled and defeated men to save their wounded pride. Said Gov. Hamilton, (of Texas) the most nobly and earnestly loyal man I met in all the South, in conversation with me one day, "After all, our people are doing about as well as a reasonable man ought to expect. Politicians must have their 'explanations' and their records; they must be allowed to retreat gracefully and to fall gently; but the vast majority of them are all right at heart. They must have time." And I will here add that I found in Texas more genuine and honest loyalty and patriotism than in any other of the cotton states. There are 54,000 Germans 8,000 Norwegians, 9,000 Mexicans, and 70,000 Americans in that State who have remained loyal all the time, and they have in Gov. Hamilton the noblest leader in any Southern State. There were thirty-four men in the Texas Convention who voted for the most loyal measures, and in favor of the most enlarged civil rights to the negro, seven of whom favored universal suffrage.

There is a prevalent disposition not to associate too freely with Northern men, or to receive them into the circles of society; but it is far from insurmountable. Over Southern society, as over every other, woman reigns supreme, and they are more embittered against those whom they deem the authors of all their calamities than are their brothers sons and husbands. It is a note worthy ethnological fact, and one I have often observed that, of the younger generation, the southern women are much superior to the southern men, both in intellect and energy; and their ascendancy over society is correspondingly great. However this disparity is to be accounted for, whether by the enormous wastage of the war among the males, or otherwise, it nevertheless exists, and to its existence is greatly due the exclusiveness of southern society.

But the stories and rumors to the effect that Northern men are bitterly persecuted and compelled to abandon the country I pronounce false. If Northern men go south they must expect for a while to be treated with neglect, and sometimes with contempt; but if they refrain from bitter political discussions and conduct themselves with ordinary discretion, they soon overcome these prejudices, and are treated with respect. The accounts that are from time to time flooded over the country in regard to Southern cruelty and intolerance toward Northerners are mostly false. I could select many districts, particularly in Northern Texas and portions of Mississippi, where Northern men could not at present live with any degree of self-respect. There are also localities in many of the Southern States where it would be dangerous for a Northern man to live; but they are exceptional, and are about equally unsafe for any man who possesses attractive property. For some unknown cause, a large number of persons are engaged in writing and circulating falsehoods. For some unpatriotic purpose, or other, reports of an incendiary character concerning the southern people are transmitted North. To learn the falseness of these reports one needs only to obtain the facts. I am personally acquainted with most of the officers of a hundred odd regiments of volunteers, and out of these I could name thirty regiments, and half of whose officers and many of the men have returned to the south, and as many more that have left large numbers there upon being disbanded. Hundreds, even, of the officers of colored regiments—the most offensive to the south—have remained there and entered into business, the most of them having rented plantations and employing their old soldiers. Large numbers of ex Federal and ex Confederate officers are engaged together in mercantile pursuits and in cotton planting. Nearly all of the cotton plantations in Florida are being run by such parties. The banks of the Mississippi are lined with plantations which have been leased by Northern men and Federal officers. Arkansas and White river plantations are generally being run by officers who have served under Gen. Reynolds, while a large number of the Red river plantations have been placed under cultivation by ex officers of Gen. A. J. Smith's command. Fourteen officers of a colored (Kentucky) regiment are engaged in planting and raising cotton near Victoria, Texas. The First National Bank of Texas, at Galveston, has for President ex Major Gen. Nichols of the late Confederate army, and ten of its directors are also ex rebel officers, while the cashier is ex Major Genl Clark[2] of the Union army, and who formerly commanded a division of colored troops. In all of these connections the utmost harmony prevails. Notwithstanding the above facts, and I could multiply them, I maintain that in many sections of the south there is a wide-spread hostility to Northern men, which however, in nine cases out of ten, is speedily dispelled by individual contact, and the exercise of a generous regard for private opinions. In fine, I will say that all who can be spared from the industry of the North to go South can readily find places of business where they can live in quiet and prosperity.

I have already alluded to the loyal Germans of Texas. I visited their colony and settlements, and was most favorably impressed. They are the most thrifty, industrious and prosperous citizens of that State; and, now that the rebellion is over, are living in comparative security, though their sufferings during the war were more dreadful than any that the history of this country has before afforded. They were ably represented in the late Convention by five men, three of whom favored negro suffrage with certain educational qualifications. The loyal Norwegians, and the loyal

Americans of the Red river district—men whose loyalty was fearless and unwavering throughout the rebellion—I did not have time to see. Their delegates in the Convention, however, were among the ablest, as well as the most patriotic in that body, and far superior to those loyalists of North Alabama, who were generally men of moderate capacity. Though there is no district in Florida than can strictly be called loyal, in contradistinction to all others, yet I found the feeling of the people in that state much better and more encouraging than in Georgia, which is overrun with politicians, many of whom seem to defy the Government and its authority. Alabama is in a much better condition than Georgia, and its state of affairs are extremely encouraging. Mississippi, from one end to the other, of all the states which I visited, is far behind hand in her tokens of loyalty. There is an unmistakable flow of ill-feeling in that State, although I witnessed no exhibitions of unmitigated disloyalty. On the whole, the people of that state fear the authority of the United States more than they respect it. In Louisiana there is an encouraging element of loyalty, which is experiencing a healthy increase. Tennessee evidenced in a great degree, the most flourishing signs of loyalty. I do not think there are ten men in that State at present who could be induced to favor a dissolution of the Union, not, even indeed, if such a thing should be peacably permitted. There is a healthy intercourse between all classes in Arkansas, and it seemed to me to occupy nearly the identical position of Tennessee.

I will now proceed to the second great topic, to wit "The Freedmen and their affairs." Almost the only key that furnishes a satisfactory solution to the southern question in its relations to the negro, that gives a reasonable explanation to the treatment which he receives, and the estimation in which he is held, is found in the fact too often forgotten in considering this matter—that the people from their earliest days have regarded slavery as his proper estate, and emancipation as a bane to his happiness. That a vast majority of the southern people honestly entertains this opinion, no one who travels among them for eight months can doubt.

To one who looks out from this stand-point of theory, and can see no other that is rational, the question presents itself in a different aspect. Every one who conscientiously seeks to know the whole truth should not ignore their beliefs, while he censures the revolting practices. Holding that the negro occupies a middle ground between the human race and the animal, they regard it as a real misfortune to him that he should be stripped of a protector, and that the immortal Proclamation of President Lincoln was wicked, or at least mistaken, and a scourge to society. The persistency and honesty with which many, even of the greatest men of the south, hold to this opinion is almost unaccountable to a Northern man, and is an element of such magnitude that it cannot well be omitted from the consideration.

Resulting as a proper corrollary from these premises, we have seen various laws passed in some of the States, but more particulary Mississippi

—which state I am bound to say has displayed the most illiberal spirit toward the freedmen of all the south—imposing heavy taxes on negroes engaged in the various trades, amounting to a virtual prohibition. Petty, unjust, and discriminating licenses are levied in this State upon mechanics store-keepers and various artisans. Following the same absurd train of argument that one will hear in the North in regard to the "proper sphere of woman," their legislature and their common councils contend that in these pursuits the negro is out of his place; that he is not adapted to such labors, but only to the ruder tasks of the fields. What are known as the "poor whites" sustain, in fact originate this legislation, upon the insane dread they share in common with certain skilled laborers at the North, of competition and an overcrowding of the supply. This folly and injustice on the part of the lawmakers is being corrected in many sections. The negro, however, has not been discouraged, even in Mississippi. His industry and his thrifts are over-leaping all obstacles, and in Jackson there are at least, two colored craftsmen of most kinds to one of the whites.

From the surrender of the rebel armies up to the Christmas Holidays, and more especially for a few weeks preceding the latter, there was a nervousness exhibited throughout the south in relation to their late slaves that was little consonant to their former professions of trust in them. There were vague and terrible fears of a servile insurrection—a thing which the simple-minded negroes scarcely dreamed of. In consequence of this there were extensive seizures of arms and ammunition, which the negroes had foolishly collected, and strict precautions were taken to avoid any outbreak. Pistols, old muskets and shot-guns were taken away from them as such weapons would be wrested from the hands of lunatics. Since the holidays however, there has been a great improvement in this matter, many of the whites appear to be ashamed of their former distrust, and the negroes are seldom molested now in carrying the firearms, of which they make such a vain display. In one way or another they have procured great numbers of old army muskets and revolvers, particularly in Texas, and I have, in a few instances, been amused at the vigor and audacity with which they have employed them to protect themselves against the robbers and murderers that infest that state.

Another result of the above mentioned settled belief in the negro's inferiority, and in the necessity that he should not be left to himself without a guardian, is that in some sections, he is discouraged from leaving his old master. I have known of planters who considered it an offence against neighborhood courtesy for another to hire their old hands, and in two instances that were refuted the disputants came to blows over the breach of etiquette. It is only, however, in the most remote regions, where our troops have seldom or never penetrated, that the negroes have not perfect liberty to rove where they choose. Even the attempt is made to restrain them by a system of passes from their employers, or from police patrols, it is of little avail; for the negroes, in their ignorance and darkness of understanding, are penetrated with a singularly-strong conviction that they "are not free as long as they stay at the old place;" and all last summer and fall they pretty thoroughly demonstrated their freedom by changing their places of residence. Such a thorough chaos and commingling of population has seldom been seen since the great barbarian invasion of the Roman Empire. In this general upheaval, thousands of long-scattered families were joyously reunited. It is a strange fact, however, and one which I have abundantly established by the testimony of hundreds of the negroes themselves, that a large majority of them have finally returned voluntarily and settled down in the old cabins of their former quarters. The negro clings to old associations—it was only a temporary impulse of their new found freedom to wander away from them; and at last, they returned, generally wearied, hungry and forlorn. In most cases, or at least in many cases, it was not so much from any affection toward their former masters, as it was from a mere instinctive attachment to the homes of their youth—the familiar scenes in the midst of which they were born and reared. When I was in Selma. Ala. last fall, a constant stream of them, of all ages and conditions, were pouring through that city, on their way, as they always told me, to Mississippi or Tennessee. Many were transported free by our Government, while many were on foot, trudging hopefully but painfully forward toward their old homes, from which they had been taken to escape our armies.

I believe that, in some of the most interior districts, especially in Texas, the substance of slavery still remains, in the form of the bondage of custom, of fear, and of inferiority; but nowhere are there any negroes so ignorant of the great change that has taken place to submit to the lash. In no place did I hear the slightest allusion to any punishment of this sort having been inflicted since the rebellion ended. In every case it was violent stabbing or shooting, resulting from a personal encounter. The negro was aware of his rights and was defending them. His friends need never fear his reenslavement—it never can, never will take place. His head is filled with the idea of freedom, and anything but the most insidious and blandishing encroachments upon his freedom he will perceive and resist. The planters everywhere complain of his "demoralization" in this respect.

As to the personal treatment received by the negro at the hands of the southern people, there is wide-spread misapprehension. It is not his former master, as a general thing, that is his worst enemy, but quite the contrary. I have talked earnestly with hundreds of old slave owners, and seen them move among their former "chattels." and I am not mistaken. The feeling with which a very large majority of them regard the negro is one of genuine commiseration, although it is not a sentiment much elevated above that with which they would look upon a suffering animal for which they had formed an attachment. Last summer the negroes, exulting in their new-found freedom, as was to have been expected, were gay, thoughtless and improvident; and, as a consequence, when the winter came, hundreds of them felt the pinchings of want, and many perished. The old planters have often pointed out to me numerous instances of calamity that had come under their own observation, in the case of their former slaves and others.

It was one of the most pernicious effects of slavery that it confined the attention of the owner entirely to the present bodily condition of his slaves, and ignored all calculations upon his future mental or moral growth; it gave him that mean opinion of the negroes' capacity that he still retains. The planter reasoned only from the actual facts, and never from possibilities. Inheriting his slaves, and finding them always brutish, stupid, and slow of understanding, he committed the logical inaccuracy of preventing them from ever becoming anything else, and proceeded to argue that they never could become so. To a certain extent it is true, as it has been forcibly said, that "those who have seen most of the negro know least of him," though the assertion should be reduced to this,—that they know far less of him as a human being than we of the North, but much more respecting his mere animal characteristics. Notwithstanding all this, I insist that there was in most cases a real attachment between master and slave, and still is, especially between the family and house servants.

It is the former slave-owners who are the best friends the negro has in the south; those who, heretofore, have provided for his mere physical comfort, generally with sufficient means, though entirely neglecting his better nature, while it is the "poor whites" that are his enemies. It is from these he suffers most. In a state of slavery they hated him; and now that he is free, there is no striking abatement of this sentiment, and the former master no longer feels called by the instincts of interest to extend that protection that he once did. On the streets, by the roadside, in his wretched hut, in the field of labor—everywhere, the unoffensive negro is exposed to their petty and contemptible persecutions; while, on the other hand, I have known instances where the respectable, substantial people of a community have united together to keep guard over a house in which the negroes were taking their amusement, and from which, a few nights before, they had been rudely driven by white vagabonds, who found pleasure in their fright and suffering. I reiterate that the former owners, as a class, are the negroes' best friends in the south, although many of this class diligently strive to discourage the freedmen from any earnest efforts to promote their higher welfare. When one believes that a certain race of beings are incapable of advancement, he is very prone to withhold the means of that advancement. And it is in this form that a species of slavery will longest be perpetuated—it is in these strongholds that it will last die out. I am pretty sure that there is not a single negro in the whole south who is not receiving pay for his labor according to his own contract; but as a general thing the freedmen are encouraged to collect about the old mansion in their little quarters, labor for their former master for set terms, receiving, besides his pay, food, quarters, and medical attendance, and thus continuing on in his former state of dependence. The cruelties of slavery, and all of its outward forms, have entirely passed away; but, as might have been expected, glimmerings of its vassalage, its subserviency, and its helplessness linger.

It is the result of my observation, also, not only that the planters, generally, are better friends to the negro than the poor whites, but also better than a majority of Northern men who go south to rent plantations—at least, they show more patience in dealing with him. The Northerner is practical, energetic, economical, and thrifty—the negro is slow, awkward, wasteful and slovenly, he causes his new employer to lose his patience, and to seize hold and attempt to perform himself, what he sees so badly executed. The Southerner is accustomed to the ways of slaves from his youth up, hence he is languidly and good naturedly indifferent; or at most, vents his displeasure in empty fuming. The Northern employer is accustomed to see laborers who are vigorous and industrious; he knows the extent of a full day's labor, and he expects all to perform the amount; the Southern man has always been compelled to employ two or three to do the work of one, and is more indulgent. It is the almost universal testimony of the negroes themselves, who have been under the supervision of both classes—and I have talked with many with a view to this point— that they prefer to labor for a Southern employer. This is not by any means to be construed to mean that they desire to return to slavery—not by any consideration; for the thought of freedom is dearer to their hearts than to any other people of like intelligence in the world; but that, being once assured of their liberty to go and come at will, they generally return to the service of the Southerner.

The negro has far less to apprehend in my judgment, from organized oppression by the courts than from sudden and violent outbursts of passion on the part of employers, or from the petty and malicious persecutions of mean whites. He has less to fear from the perversion of law than from the absence of it; and the same is true of the whites, and has always been. It might almost be said of some interior counties in Texas that there never has been any executed law there for white or black; for it is a recorded fact that, before the war, even, 450 murders per year were committed in that State, while there never were half a dozen formal convictions and executions for manslaughter. The others were acquitted on the ground of self-defense. The point is, then, that there have not been and are not now, more colored people murdered in proportion to their whole number, than whites.

On the great question of negro suffrage I have seen no occasion, in presence of the facts, to change materially the belief I entertained eight months ago. To say that the south is opposed to it, almost to a man, is simply to utter that of which every one already is aware; to say that it is simply a question of time is to give it no satisfactory solution. The pith and substance of the whole matter lies in the answer to this single question. "Will the immediate conferring of suffrage on the blacks put them in possession of any substantial good which they are now denied, or avert from them any evil that threatens their welfare?" So general and so bitter is the opposition of the whites to this measure, that I am fully persuaded that to confer suffrage forcibly by national enactment, upon the blacks at this time, would result to their serious detriment. I do not believe it would beget a war of races; but from the manner in which negro schools and other similar institutions have been treated in some sections, by ignorant and malicious persons, I am constrained to believe that the negro would be the recipient of more wrongs and injuries than he now is if he was found at the polls voting. It is the truth of history, that, when classes of population are opposed in feeling and unequal in power and influence, the dominating class is oppressive and intolerant toward the inferior in reverse proportion as it is elevated above it. The southern poor whites, conscious as they are, of only a slight superiority over the negro, and knowing that the suffrage, and a few minor factitious distinctions, are the chief points of their superiority, are jealous over them accordingly. It is they that will resist most stubbornly the negroes enfranchisement as it will remove the most marked of the few slight barriers that separate them from the blacks, and it is they that will hail his advent to the polls with the most unrelenting and senseless abuse.

The proper avenues of approach to these unreasoning minds is through the wealthy and powerful land-owners of the south—the politicians— who are lords and masters over the peasantry to almost as great an extent as they are over the negroes. Through these let the parallels be constructed upon this strong castle of prejudice. If the politicians of the south have the absolute certainty laid before them that in 1870 their representation in Congress will be diminished largely in consequence of the nonenfranchisement of the negro, they will see to it before that time that the proper [reform] is introduced. They will convince their constituents that it is necessary and proper to allow the negro to vote, and he will be allowed so to do. At present it seems to me that it would be a misfortune to the negro himself to thrust this privelege upon him. There is a popular tradition that a certain very humble, and useful, but unsightly animal carries in its head a precious pearl, and it is often killed in the vain search for it, so it would be, substantially, with the helpless, inoffensive negro, if this valuable prerogative was at once put into his hands.

The southern negro is far less concerned in the result of elections at present than he is in the decisions of the local courts, and far less interested in these than in the general temper of society. The negro always has been and always must remain associated with the people of the south in a thousand intimate relations—relations over which legislation can have little control, whatever attempts are made to the contrary. Even before the courts of the country I have little fear but that he will secure substantial justice. These courts are generally in the hands of the more intelligent and reasonable classes, among whom there is a sentiment of real pity toward the negro, as being now left to contend on his own resources against the stronger white man. Legislatures and common councils may frame mean-spirited and discriminating laws against him, but when he is brought to actual trial, and his helplessness is made apparent, the practice of his jurors, his judges and his lawyers is much better than their professions. Especially is it true when the suit is, as it often happens, between a negro and a mean white. The old slave-owners always felt a preference for their negroes over this class, and even had a positive dislike toward the latter, and they entertain the same feelings still; and let a suit be brought between one of them and a respectable negro, and I have no fears for the result on the part of the negro.

The treatment which the negroes receive at the hands of the people is a quick and accurate theomometer, guaging southern loyalty—the temper of the whites toward the General Government. Closely following the conclusion of the war were witnessed far more outrages upon the blacks than have been known since. In the exasperation and bitterness resulting from fresh defeat, they in many cases vented their wrath on the head of the unoffending negro. Since then there has been a steady improvement under the fostering influences of hope and returning loyalty. The South always has been, and always must be, to a great extent, the guardians of the negro; for the time will never come, so long as he remains a part of our society, when from the very nature of his inferiority, he will not require a certain guardianship.

As an evidence of the most encouraging growth of public sentiment in the south, conforming to the great onward march of events, I may mention the advance that has taken place in relation to the question of negro testimony. Eight months ago, when I first went South, the subject was one that scarcely engaged the serious attention of public men, much less their favorable consideration; but when the Texas Convention, the last in the South, and only very recently assembled, came together, so much had popular sentiment advanced in this subject, that only eight members of that body offered any opposition to a measure proposing to allow the negro to testify in cases of his own concern, and nearly one half the delegates favored giving him the most unrestricted right. A tremendous struggle was made over this last point—a struggle not for partial rights but for universal privileges. The opponents of the measure strongly argued that, if the negro was admitted to testify in all cases in which he or any of his race might be interested, his own rights were secured beyond peradventure, and he was legally placed on a better foundation than the white man, which is true, since, in Texas, a colored man can now subpoena witnesses both from whites and blacks, while a white man can summon only those of his own color. I know of no state among all that

I visited in which either the Constitution or statutes do not authorize the negro to testify in all cases in which he or any of his race may be interested.

The Freedmen's Bureau is an institution that was highly necessary in the months immediately following the close of the war, and which is still needed in all of the States but Tennessee, and will continue to be for some time, especially in Mississippi, Alabama and Georgia. Except for the aid furnished by the Bureau last summer, fall and winter, thousands of freedmen and refugees as well, would have perished from starvation. The Bureau also performed a highly useful office late in the fall, and early last winter, in assisting both planters and laborers to make mutually profitable arrangements, securing the latter against fraud and the former partially against the negroes fickleness. When the Christmas holidays came and passed, and brought around no Government agents, as the freedmen had fondly trusted, to divide out the property of their late masters, they were sorely disappointed, and for a brief space were naturally despondent, but very soon their wonted buoyancy returned, and they entered in earnest upon preparations for the coming year. Then it was that the Bureau was instrumental in accomplishing more good than it had at any previous time, the task of settling hundreds of thousands of improvident and disappointed people into situations with those who were distrustful and discouraged, was one of great magnitude and importance. Thanks, however to the unexpected kindness with which these discordant elements assimilated, the Bureau performed its task well, vast numbers of the freedmen were provided with good situations, and the planters received a new impetus of hopefulness. In the great state of Texas the reports of the Bureau show that there are three hundred thousand laborers at work, happy, contented and prosperous. There is not a single colored pauper in the State, and less than a dozen at any one time in the Government hospital. Auspicious result! In other States Tennessee, Florida and Arkansas, especially, I found an admirable condition of affairs—the negroes industriously at work, receiving fair pay, and a demand for thousands more of them to till the waiting plantations. In other states either more desolated by the war, or more densely populated by freedmen, the condition was not so abounding in present good, but was equally full of promise. In Texas, Florida, Tennessee, Arkansas, Louisiana, Mississippi and Georgia, together, I think am not mistaken in saying that nearly a half a million more laborers than are now there could secure situations and good wages if they were there today. Nowhere does the plantation hand get less than $10. per month, in addition to rations and quarters; many of them get $15 and $18, some even $25, while those who are renting get from a quarter to three-quarters of the crop. These extreme bargains are rare, except in Texas. The usual bargain is for one-third, or one-half the crop, the planters furnishing seed, implements and beams. I estimate that there will be ten thousand negroes renting small lots of ground this year who never did before.

The Bureau, in my respectful opinion, has nearly accomplished the work for which it was created, and the necessity that called it into existence is rapidly passing away. If it shall have looked faithfully after the interests of the freedmen during the coming season, and especially in the division of the crops next fall, and after that, succeeds in again locating them on the plantations in favorable situations for the year 1867, as it did last winter, then I think the negro can be released from its bonds and will be able to go forth alone. It is surprising and electrifying to the steadfast believer in the inherent capacity of all men for self-government, to witness the rapid strides in advance which the late slaves have taken. They as well as their white fellow-citizens, both North and south, learned much from the late war. Its teachings were fruitful to them in lessons of self-reliance and self-helpfulness. They have purchased and secreted arms; they hold little meetings together in which they consult with much sageness concerning their common safety; they feel a dignity and an independence becoming their relations as freemen, and I am convinced that in nine months from this time the longer presence and assistance of the Bureau will be unnecessary and superfluous.

Regarding the military establishment south. I will respectfully submit a few words. Taking everything into consideration, there is every reason to believe that it would be extremely injudicious to remove from the south the force now stationed there. Troops are required in the Red river counties in Texas to protect loyal men, who are being continually outraged by some thousand or more rebel refugees from Missouri and Arkansas, who, on account of their atrocities during the war, dare not return to their homes. Troops are also required in the loyal German counties in Texas, whose people are suffering considerably from the depredations of nomadic bands of Indians. Regarding the colored soldiers, I only agree with all of our officers in the South, including those connected with the Freedmen's Bureau, that they should be removed as speedily as possible. To a great extent they incite the freedmen to deeds of violence, and encourage them in indolence. There has been a great improvement in this respect, however, during the past three months. Further, there is the most bitter feeling existing between white and colored soldiers, and many of the latter have been cruelly treated by the former. Volunteer regiments are gradually wasting away by desertion—desertion officially encouraged. The demoralizing effects of this wholesale desertion is felt in the Regular army, which is also suffering in like manner. The Fourth and Sixth Cavalry and the Nineteenth Infantry Regiments, are losing hundreds of men by desertion.

Emigration, both from the North and abroad is almost everywhere encouraged, but, particularly in Texas, Florida and Tennessee.

If the season is good, cotton will be raised in large quantities all over the South. Texas will make a larger crop than ever before. I studied this matter with a good deal of care, and am of the opinion that the eight states above mentioned will make this season nineteen hundred bales. Two-thirds of the sugar plantations in Louisiana have been destroyed, or from neglect gone to ruin, while but a few of those in good order are being worked. The rice fields are quiet, and the chances are that very little rice will ever again be raised in the United States.

In conclusion I must say that I bespeak for the south a glorious future. I predict that peace, prosperity, wealth and happiness will be her lot. Her rich lands will come rapidly under cultivation, and increase ten-fold in value; her noble waters will be thronged with the appliances of commerce; population, such as she desires, will flow steadily into her borders; cities and villages will dot her landscapes; schools and churches and public institutions will be her boast, and a refined society will grace the land. What may we not expect of her now that *Freedom* is her guiding star?

(Signed)   Benjamin C. Truman

Copy, DLC-JP.

1. William J. Hardee, Lafayette McLaws, Nathan Bedford Forrest, Francis Redding Tillou Nicholls, and Meriwether Jeff Thompson. McLaws (1821–1897), an 1852 West Point graduate, resigned his commission in March 1861 and entered the Confederate army as colonel of the 10th Ga. Inf. He attained the rank of major general in May 1862 and served under both Longstreet and Johnston. Following the war he was in the insurance business in Augusta, Georgia, and served as an internal revenue collector and postmaster of Savannah. Nicholls (1834–1912) graduated from West Point in 1855, but resigned the next year to study law at the University of Louisiana (Tulane). He became a Confederate brigadier general in October 1862 following the loss of his left arm in Jackson's Valley campaign and his left foot at Chancellorsville. For the rest of the war he headed the Volunteer and Conscript Bureau of the Trans-Mississippi Department. Following the war he served as governor of Louisiana (1876–80, 88–92) and as a justice of the Louisiana Supreme Court (1892–1911). Thompson (1826–1876) was an engineer and railroad president before the war. He entered the Confederate army in July 1861 and was soon made brigadier general of the 1st Military District of Missouri. Nicknamed the "Swamp Fox" for his actions in the swamps of southern Missouri, he was captured in August 1863 but returned to command following his exchange. After the war he had business interests in New York, Memphis, and New Orleans before retiring to St. Joseph, Missouri. Warner, *Gray;* Howard I. McKee, "The 'Swamp Fox,' Meriwether Jeff Thompson," *Bulletin of the Missouri Historical Society* 13 (Jan., 1957 [1956–57]): 118–34.

2. William Thomas Clark (1831–1905) was admitted to the New York bar in 1854 and began practice two years later in Davenport, Iowa. In 1861 he recruited the 13th Iowa Inf., of which he was first lieutenant and adjutant. By May 1865 he was brigadier general of volunteers. He was brevetted brigadier general and major general. Following the war he went to Texas where he organized the Galveston bank and eventually, with the support of the black leaders, was elected to the U.S. House of Representatives in 1869. In 1871, though defeated for reelection, he was certified by the Republican governor who threw out thousands of opposing votes; but by a unanimous vote of both parties, Clark was expelled from the House. He then spent his remaining years working for the Bureau of Internal Revenue. Warner, *Blue.*

From Russell Houston

Louisville   April 10, 1866

My Dear Friend.

I see that the Radicals have passed their bill over your veto. I regret it of course, but do not know that I ought. I have often grieved over events as evil & great misfortunes, that finally ended in the greatest possible good.

The great matter for the American people, is, first, that pending questions should be settled correctly; & then, that they be settled speedily, that the minds of men may be quieted. Now, the men who oppose you, the better for you & for those who sympathize with you. They present the questions not simply with rashness & haste, but with all their defects & deformities, & therefore we may expect a more speedy, & a more correct solution.

Moreover, these controversies will not be settled until they go before the American people; & hence, it is important, that they be not insidiously put, but fairly presented. For myself, I prefer an extreme radical, to one of moderation. There is more stubbornness in moderation, than in extremes. There is delay in one & haste in the other. If death is to be, to this Country, within any short time, let it be hasty & not lingering.

I know you too well, to feel for a moment, that you are seriously disturbed by recent events. We cannot hope for a smooth sea always, or for a perpetual sunshine. It is not unusual, to have first, "a Bull Run" & still a final & complete conquest & surrender of the early victors. The people in this part of the Country, will sustain you almost unanimously. There is no ground for fear as to that fact. But the great political battle is to be fought in the Northern, Middle & Western States & let the issues so be made. Nothing will be done for your measures until after the people have spoken. The other side know this & their great effort is & will be, to get the advantage in shaping & coloring, the issues. What you should desire & what your friends desire, is, to have your measures of restoration presented to the people, in their plain simplicity. But your opponents will present this if they can. They will attempt to obscure & disfigure them & present you in a false light to show, if possible, inconsistencies, in your course & make that an issue, & not the merits of the questions. Hence we see Mr Trumbull,[1] when arguing a great national & constitutional question, attempt to dodge the true issue & to make the great points your inconsistency, as if that matter had any thing to do with the merits of the question. That question is, what are the merits of your measures, & not whether you have been a consistent politician. Your friends in Congress should see to this thing. It is only skirmishing that is now going on—a contest merely for position, & not the great battle. Let not your skirmishers be deceived, nor yourself be cheated out of your true position, by the strategy of your opponents.

The struggle is to make it appear that you are the enemy of the freedmen & of universal freedom; & after all you have done & said on these matters in the South in behalf of the negroes, would it not be most strange, if the Northern people should be made to believe that you are a pro-slavery man? Your enemies are now attempting to induce this belief.

You very much need, in Congress, a few bold friends, who when your fidelity to the Country is "*insinuated against*" can fearlessly present the contrast between you & any member of Congress. You have a better record for true faith to the Government than any of them. You lived in a Section where loyalty was a disgrace—where it endangered all you had, even your very life. They lived where to be disloyal was to jeopardize all they had, even to the loss of life—where to be loyal, was an honor & a passport to power & position. But I will not trouble you further now. All things will come out right yet.[2]

Russell Houston

ALS, DLC-JP.
    1. Lyman Trumbull.
    2. Houston had written to Johnson five days earlier suggesting that if the override of the Civil Rights bill veto failed, Johnson should initiate legislation of his own through Edgar Cowan "or some other friend." By vetoing the Civil Rights bill, Houston argued, Johnson only showed what he was against, and not what he was for, leaving the President open for misrepresentation. Houston's proposed bill called for a recapitulation of the fact of the abolition of slavery and the provision of "heavy fine & imprisonment" for individuals "found guilty of the offence of enslaving any person within the United States." Houston to Johnson, Apr. 5, 1866, Johnson Papers, LC.

From Albert Voorhies[1]

New Orleans   Apl 10th 1866

Sir,

It is made my duty as President of the Senate of this State to transmit to you by telegraph a copy of a joint resolution relative to the collection of taxes by the Freedmens Bureau for purposes of education. This resolution reads as follows—

Whereas, We are informed that a Superintendent of the Freedmens Bureau for the State of Louisiana[2] is proceeding to enforce the collection of a tax levied by Military Order in the State of Louisiana to refund monies expended or provide a fund to be expended by the Federal authorities in the education of Freedmen in the State, And Whereas—Sufficient provision is made by the Constitution & laws of the State without any resort to this extraordinary & oppressive mode of taxation in the present exhausted & impoverished condition of the country—and Whereas we are informed that the collector of this tax on a former occasion was suspended by Gen Fullerton[3] when acting as Superintendent of Freedmen for Louisiana under instructions from President Johnson— Therefore, Section One —Be it Resolved—by the Senate, the House of Representatives of the General Assembly concurring, that Gen'l Howard—General Supt of the Freedmens Bureau for the U S., or in his default, the President of the U S, be respectfully requested to suspend the further collection of said taxes[4] & to procure or make a revocation of the order upon which they rest & that the President of the Senate & the Speaker of the House of Reps be requested, immediately to communicate this resolution by telegraph to Washington & to draw upon their warrants the actual expenses incurred out of the contingent funds of the two houses.

Duncan S. Cage   Speaker of the H of Reps.
Alfred Partins   Lt Gov & Prest of the Senate

Approved March 22nd 1866

G.[sic] Madison Wells   Gov of the State of La

The people of this State are in expectation that some relief be extended to them in this instance more especially since your Excellencys procla-

mation declaring Martial law at an end & recognizing the complete restoration of peace. The fact that the Freedmens Bureau is to be kept in
operation for the coming twelve months does not necessarily, we opine,
authorize the Bureau to continue to exercise the high prerogative of taxation, especially as it is believed that the remedy is no more needed for
present purposes. In this connection I may well refer to the present status
of the freedmen under our State law. Practically as well as in theory they
are on the same footing of equality before the tribunals with the whites.
They can sue & be sued, prosecute & be prosecuted and testify in all the
courts without discrimination as to color, indeed such were the privileges enjoyed by the free colored population of Louisiana as at all times
previous to the late war & such today are the rights recognized to all
freedmen.

Albert Voorhies

Tel, DNA-RG107, Tels. Recd., President, Vol. 5 (1866–67).
    1. Voorhies (1829–1913) became a justice on the state supreme court in 1859 and
then, during the war years, Confederate judge advocate general in the Trans-Mississippi
Department. Voorhies served as lieutenant governor (1865–67) and in the state legislature
during the 1870s. Conrad, *La. Biography*.
    2. Absalom Baird served in this capacity for approximately one year (1865–66). White,
Freedmen's Bureau, 22–26.
    3. On November 7, 1865, Gen. Joseph S. Fullerton had issued an order to halt the col-
lection of the school tax. A few days later General Howard ordered Baird to resume collection of the controversial tax. *New Orleans Picayune*, Nov. 8, 1865; Bentley, *Freedmen's Bureau*, 123. See also Fullerton to Johnson, Oct. 28, 1865, *Johnson Papers*, 9: 298.
    4. On April 12, Secretary Stanton notified Johnson that he had ordered the suspension
of the collection of the school tax; General Howard ordered Baird to halt collection; and the
President himself informed Voorhies that tax collection had been suspended. Stanton
to Johnson, Apr. 12, 1866, Lets. Sent, Mil. Bks., Executive, 57-C, RG107, NA; Howard
to Baird, Apr. 12, 1866, Tels. Sent, Sec. of War (M473, Roll 90), RG107, NA; Johnson to
Voorhies, Apr. 12, 1866, Johnson Papers, LC.

From Montgomery Blair

Wash   Apl 11, 66

My dear Mr. President,
    I failed to show you my address as I had asked the liberty to do because
upon reflection I felt that a portion of it, & that in my view a material
portion of it, reflected upon persons holding such relations with you for
the present as made it embarrassing to discuss the parts in question with
you. I will beg your indulgence having referred to the subject to make a
Single remark. You have no doubt been told that I have some personal
grudge against Mr. Seward. I assure you that I have not & that I have no
reason to have any that I am aware of. He has assured my friends that he
recommended me for the place of Chief Justice to President Lincoln & he
tendered me a foreign mission since I left the Cabinet. My strenuous opposition to his continuance in position arises Solely from the conviction
that he more than any one else is responsible for the late civil war & that

he is doing all that he can to involve us in another by Striving to keep the so called Union party consolidated.[1]

He knows that the democrats will never Support him. He tried to induce them to do so in the late Elections. Hence tho he is making an effort to keep up a Conservative faction within the Republican party, it is the avowed purpose of his associates not to break with the party. But while he knows the Democrats will not support him, he knows they are anxious to support you & hence that it is of the first importance to unite the Republicans who agree with you & the masses of the Democratic party in order to restore the Union. But he will not even allow Mr. Pomeroy[2] the Representative of the Auburn District who is known to do nothing he does not sanction to sustain you.

My judgment is that there is no reason for your retaining this gentleman in your confidence more than for keeping Mr. Stanton & others generally mentioned as opposing you. Mr. Stanton is acting in concert with Mr. Seward. The Radical press are restrained through Mr. Stantons influence from attacking Mr. Seward whilst pouring out their wrath upon you. Mr. Stanton indeed was bought at the Cabinet by Mr. Seward & his policy presented by Mr. Seward I have no doubt in order to undercut Mr. Chase. This mode of operating is characteristic of Mr. Seward. He was Elected to the Senate from New York by men who pretended to be Know-nothings & as such got the Know nothing nominations but voted for Seward in betrayal of their associates. So he prompted Mr. Dixon[3] of Ky a Whig, to move the repeal of the Missouri Compromise urging the Southern Whigs to outdo the Democrats as pro slavery men whilst he covered the North as an anti Slavery man.

If when you change any portion of your Cabinet you should turn Mr. Seward out the Rads will not have the same ground to object to your invidious discrimination against their friends. It may then be argued that you have a right to a new cabinet & it can not be replied that by the change you propose you are striking down the Radical members whilst keeping the Conservatives.[4]

M Blair

ALS, DLC-JP.
    1. Since the summer of 1865 Blair had been publicly speaking out against Seward, although it is not clear in this letter which address he wanted to show Johnson. The Blair family wanted Johnson to replace Seward; they first hoped that Montgomery would take over the State Department but by the spring of 1866 were advocating David Dudley Field for the position. Van Deusen, *Seward*, 422, 434; Smith, *Blair Family*, 2: 340–41, 352.
    2. Theodore M. Pomeroy.
    3. Blair's contention regarding Seward's role in influencing Sen. Archibald Dixon is questionable. Seward's biographer claims that Seward boasted of pushing Dixon to insist upon the repeal of the old Missouri line; another scholar indicates that Dixon "arrived independently at the conclusion" that repeal must be done directly, not solely by inference. Van Deusen, *Seward*, 209; David M. Potter, *The Impending Crisis, 1848–1861* (New York, 1976), 160.
    4. What appears to be an early draft of this letter, dated April 9, 1866, has been located. In the draft Blair is harsher in his attack on Seward, calling him a more dangerous man than

Thaddeus Stevens and Charles Sumner together. Blair to Johnson, Apr. 9, 1866, Blair Family Papers, LC.

From Hugh McCulloch

Treasury Department.   April 11, 1866.

Sir:

It appearing to my satisfaction that persons heretofore or now Agents of this Department, as well as private individuals not in any official position, have been engaged in defrauding the Government, by unlawfully appropriating cotton belonging to it, and in other ways, I have from time to time given instructions, general and specific, to have such cases investigated, with a view to securing restitution of property or proceeds, and bringing the guilty parties to justice.

Since the date of your proclamation declaring the insurrection lately existing in certain States to be at an end, an officer of the Department to whom some of the matters above referred to were entrusted, submits the question, whether "a former Agent of the Treasury Department, or one still in office, or any other person, can ⟨now⟩ be arraigned and tried by a military commission, except as provided by the rules or articles of war, or be placed in arrest by the military authorities?"[1]

I have the honor to respectfully request that you will indicate your views on this subject to me, in order that the necessary and proper instructions in the premises may be given.

H McCulloch   Secretary of the Treasury.

LS, DLC-JP.

1. Following the April 2 proclamation, all military commanders were notified by the adjutant general's office on April 9, 1866, with the President's approval, that the proclamation did not supersede martial law nor relieve commanders of the responsibility of arresting persons committing crimes against freedmen. Furthermore, on May 1, 1866, the War Department issued General Orders No. 26 in response to uncertainty expressed by military commanders over the effect of the proclamation in regard to the arrest and trial of civilians. The order directed that civilians be turned over to the civil authorities for trial where civil courts were in existence. *House Reports*, 39 Cong., 2 Sess., No. 23, p. 18 (Ser. 1305); James E. Sefton, *The United States Army and Reconstruction, 1865–1877* (Baton Rouge, 1967), 75, 78.

From John M. Orr[1]

Mayor's Office   Leesburg Loudoun Co Va.

April 11 1866

Sir

I beg leave, respectfully to submit to you a statement of facts and to ask such information pertinent to the rights and interests of our citizens in the matter as you may think proper to afford.

A detachment of the 7th Veteran Reserves under Captain McCauley[2] has been on duty here for some time.

On monday morning last Col Jno S Mosby[3] came here to attend our Court, in which he practices. Soon after his arrival a squad of soldiers belonging to the detachment, came to arrest him. He refused to submit to the arrest and they left him—He stating as a reason (among others) for refusing that since Your proclamation of April   inst[4] military arrests of citizens were unauthorized.

Later in the day, by several hours, the entire force was ordered out—loaded their muskets & started at double quick through the streets after Col Mosby who had left town, hearing of the intention and desiring to avoid the inconvenience of detention or the risk of a disturbance if he resisted an unwarrantable arrest.

The pursuing party did not take him but fired on him repeatedly.

The only reason which I heard, for the proceeding was that Col Mosby had some Virginia buttons on his overcoat. It has been the practice here by this detachment to stop all persons having any buttons with a military device and to cut off the buttons—even negroes on foot—not excepted. Carriages containing ladies have been stopped and the negro driver taken off & his buttons cut off of ordinary negro clothing.[5]

We had hoped that these annoyances were at an end.

Col Mosby comes here only in his character as a lawyer pursuing his profession. He has uniformly conducted himself as a quiet and orderly citizen though he has been constantly subjected to annoyance & irritation of arrest.

I do not write on behalf of Col Mosby nor as his advocate—but on behalf of our people.

They have not the slightest idea of disregarding the law and they have every disposition to fulfill their present duties and undertakings with the Government as faithfully and as honestly as they sustained the South in the war.

They fully believe that the supremacy of civil law is restored by Your proclamation—and it is of importance to them—while troops are stationed here to know whether they or any one is liable to military arrest—or to the authority of a provost marshall.

Any information as to this which can be afforded them, will be respectfully & thankfully received.[6]

Jno. M. Orr   Mayor

LS, DNA-RG107, Lets. Recd., Executive (M494, Roll 85).

1. Orr (1820–fl1900), a graduate of the University of Pennsylvania, was a lawyer who became quite affluent after the war. 1860 Census, Va., Loudon, Leesburg, 362; (1870), Southern Dist., Leesburg, 157; (1900), Leesburg, 49th Enum. Dist., A5; *NUC*; *Con Vet*, 22 (1914): 334.

2. Levi G. McCauley (1837–1920) was a successful businessman and active Republican from Chester County, Pennsylvania. He enlisted in June 1861 in a Pennsylvania regiment but was wounded and captured in 1862. After his exchange as a prisoner in January 1863, he was assigned duty in the Washington and northern Virginia area, where he remained in service until his discharge in June 1866. Wiley, *Chester County, Pa.*, 213–15; Pension Records, Levi G. McCauley, RG15, NA.

3. Mosby (1833–1916), a lawyer by profession, was one of the most famous and flamboyant Confederate Partisan Rangers. He served under J.E.B. Stuart as a scout before organizing his band of rangers in January 1863. Mosby's Rangers operated in northern Virginia throughout the remainder of the war, after which Mosby became a Republican and avid supporter of U. S. Grant. *DAB.*

4. Proclamation *re* End of Insurrection, Apr. 2, 1866. Orr left a blank space for the day's date.

5. In February 1866 Gen. Alfred Terry, military commander of the Department of Virginia, forbade the wearing of any portion of the Confederate uniform, including buttons. *Louisville Journal*, Feb. 15, 1866.

6. No response from Johnson has been found.

From John Walz et al.[1]

Washington. D.C.
April the 11th 1866.

President!

Pardon us for the liberty, we have taken to address you.

We are members of that party who captured "Booth and Herald"[2] and the reward offered by the Government[3] has not yet been paid to us, nor does it seem, as if the resp: Officers of the Government connected with the case, do try to do us justice.

We have gone into great expenses we lay here and we can not earn money sufficient to go to our home.

If you will have the kindness to order an official acknowledgement that we are entitled to so and so much money (whatever our share in the reward is) we could easily get money and help ourselves.

We hope you will see that justice is done to us.[4]

John Walz, late Corpl Co "H" 16 N Y. Cy.
Joseph Zisgen, late Privat. Co "M" 16 N Y. Cy.
Adolph Singer late Co "M" 16" N Y. Cavy.
pr. Chateaubriand

ALS (Singer), DNA-RG107, Lets. Recd., Executive (M494, Roll 84).

1. Walz (*c*1843–1904) was a grocery clerk before the war and a carpenter after; he resided in New York City and Jersey City. Zisgen (1833–1914) was a laborer and lived in New York City and Togus, Maine, dying in the soldiers' home at the latter location. Singer (b. *c*1839) listed his occupation as soldier at the time of his enlistment. All three were Prussian immigrants. Pension File, John Walz, Joseph Zisgen, RG15, NA; CSR, John Adolph Singer, Joseph Zisgen, RG94, NA.

2. John Wilkes Booth and David Herold.

3. On April 20, 1865, the War Department offered rewards for the capture of Booth and his accomplices. The rewards for Booth and Herold totalled $75,000, to be divided by those involved in the capture. *National Intelligencer*, Apr. 20, 1865.

4. On March 1, 1866, Edwin Stanton informed Johnson that as of yet no reward money had been distributed so as to give claimants ample time to present their claims. Congress authorized payment of the rewards on July 28; Walz, Zisgen, and Singer each received $1,653. Stanton to Johnson, Mar. 1, 1866, Lets. Sent, Mil. Bks., Executive, 57-C, RG107, NA; *Congressional Globe*, 39 Cong., 1 Sess., Appendix, p. 423.

From James B. Bingham

Private

Bulletin Office, [Memphis] April 12, 1866.

Dear Sir—

In response to my letter of the 19th of February,[1] I have received a letter of inquiry from Secretary McCulloch, in reference to "the roving commissioner" of which I made brief mention. I have been very feeble, not able to do a full day's work, since I last wrote. But in a few days I hope to be well enough to write up the whole cotton business, or at least to give you a bird's eye view of the "loose" manner in which it has been conducted.

I write now to say that I am gratified at the noble stand you have taken, in behalf of the Constitution and the Union. There has never been a day, since I made your acquaintance in the Capitol at Nashville, in the fall of '62, that I have not been a firm, steadfast and consistent supporter of your administration—first, Military Governor, then as Vice Presidential candidate, and since as President of the United States. I have not been able to support Brownlow in his extraordinary course, and I am glad that he has at last come out boldly against you. He was doing you more harm, as a *pretended friend*, than he can ever do as an open enemy. He did not take position against you *openly*, until decency and self-respect alike required it, and since he has done so, he is shorne of his powers for mischief. You will have seen from the *Bulletin* which I send regularly to Senator *Patterson*, that I have exposed his false assertion that "*he* nominated you for Vice President." He did no such thing. I worked as much as he did to bring about that result, and when he had a chance to make a powerful impression in your favor, he only mentioned you as a man whom he had been fruitlessly fighting all his life, and then intimated that he would have to quit to go to the "back-house," but I know that he did no such thing for one or two hours after, for Maynard, Brownlow and myself talked with members of the New York delegation for fully an hour afterwards, and it was fully another hour before I left him at his hotel. When Brownlow broke down, so suddenly, old Thad Stevens remarked to those around him, and I was sitting near, that "he didn't think he had sense enough to finish so soon." Now, he thinks old Thad is a purer patriot than you are. But it may interest you to know that Brownlow has gone to the other side for a purpose. That purpose is, to be "*nominated as Vice President on the Radical Ticket.*" This is now the goal of his ambition. Failing in that, he is for achieving immortality as the divider of the State of Tennessee. I am perfectly willing, if by that means we shall get rid of Brownlow. I regret to inform you that Cooper, assessor, Hough, collector, Ryder, marshal, Mitchell, clerk,[2]—all office-holders under your administration—are spending their money to try and establish a negro-suffrage paper here, *in opposition to your administration.* The editor is Gen. Eaton,[3] formerly of the Freedmen's Bureau. When the telegraph first brought the news of your veto and 22d of February speech, this paper—the *Post*—said you were drunk or you would never have made such an exhibition of yourself.[4] I pitched into them and they have been less out-spoken in opposition to your acts, *but they oppose every thing you do.* Wallace,[5] whom you appointed to Attorney Generalship, is also among the number of joint-stock owners of the *Post.* Tomeny,[6] who is here from Mobile, is a subscriber to the amount of $2,500! They have sunk, in the three months they have been under way, as they report themselves, just $23,000. They are in debt about $5000, and owe $4000 on their office. They are trying to get additional subscribers of stock, to continue it longer at $150 per week loss! I am watching the ungrateful course of all these office holders, to the end that when you get over your *larger* difficulties, you may speak into nothingness the men—pensioners upon your bounty—who would sell you into the hands of your enemies!

John Loague, whom I recommended for Post-Master, and subsequently for surveyor of the Port,[7] was treated so shamefully by the Treasury Department that he had to resign, and since he has been elected to the lucrative office of county clerk. Carlton, who was the pet of Mellen,[8] while surveyor here, became defaulter, or squandered some 556,000 dollars of government money, and Risley[9] came here and *whitewashed* it over. Loague succeeded, and they refused to allow him a salary of over *three hundred and fifty dollars a year*, and he had to quit. It was intimated to him, by Asst. Sec. Chandler,[10] when here, that if he would remain in the position his salary would be *three thousand dollars a year*! But he was disgusted with their meanness and quit. I hope before you allow a permanent appointment, you will allow me to say, that I would like to see a *friend of yours in the office.*

I hear that the new programme is, to hold new elections for congressmen in the Southern States, under your peace proclamation. I wish I could divine some way to divine your programmes, for I mean to rally the Bulletin under your policy until peace is restored and the rights of the Southern States are recognised.

I will only say that though Gallaway and Dill[11]—the latter now dead —have revived their *Avalanche* and *Appeal*, that the Bulletin—the firm and consistent supporter of Andrew Johnson—is ahead of all competitors and is "a power" in West Tennessee, North Alabama, North Mississippi, and in all Arkansas. The *Argus*, whom Dennison[12] sent his patronage to, and which opposed your gubernatorial course, is no where, also, Rolfe Saunders paper—the *Commercial.*

J B Bingham

ALS, DLC-JP.
1. A Bingham letter of this date has not been found.
2. Halsey F. Cooper, Reuel Hough, Martin T. Ryder, and Abram S. Mitchell. Cooper

(c1831–1885) was editor of the *Chattanooga Advertiser* in 1861 before returning to his native New York. In 1863 he moved back to the South as an internal revenue assessor in Memphis before going to California in 1869. Ryder (1831–1894) was a sign and ornamental painter in Memphis both before and after his appointment as marshal. His career as marshal was short-lived. Byron and Barbara Sistler, trs., *1860 Census-Tennessee* (5 vols., Nashville, 1981–82), 1: 423; 1860 Census, Tenn., Shelby, 8th Ward, Memphis, 147; (1870), 6th Ward, Memphis, 74; Memphis directories (1865–67); James, *Notable American Women*, 1: 380; *BDTA*, 2: 792–93.

3. John Eaton (1829–1906), brevetted brigadier general in 1865, had had supervision of the freedmen in the Department of Tennessee during the Civil War. At the war's end he became assistant commissioner of the Freedmen's Bureau in the District of Columbia, Maryland, and parts of Virginia. In 1866 he moved to Memphis to establish a newspaper, the *Memphis Post*, and in the following year was elected state superintendent of education. Eventually, in 1870, President Grant named him commissioner of education. *DAB*.

4. Bingham correctly reported the position of his rival newspaper, the *Memphis Post*. It declared that evidently the President "was suffering from an attack of the same malady that beset him on the occasion of his inauguration, last spring." The paper repeated essentially the same interpretation on the following day. How else, it asked, could one explain "such an undignified speech; so unworthy in style and sentiment of the Chief Magistrate of this great nation?" *Memphis Post*, Feb. 24, 25, 1866.

5. William Wallace.

6. James M. Tomeny.

7. See Bingham to Johnson, May 28, June 6, 1865, *Johnson Papers*, 8: 122–24, 188; Bingham to Johnson, July 13, 1865, Johnson Papers, LC.

8. George N. Carlton and William P. Mellen. See Bingham to Johnson, May 28, 1865, *Johnson Papers*, 8: 122–24.

9. Probably a reference to Hanson A. Risley, Treasury Department official.

10. William E. Chandler.

11. Matthew C. Gallaway and Benjamin F. Dill. Dill (1814–1866) had died in early January. He served as a banker and newspaper man in Memphis, Mississippi, and Missouri before returning to Memphis in the mid-1850s to help establish the *Memphis Appeal*. Dill moved around the South with the *Appeal* during the war years but eventually returned to Memphis where the newspaper resumed publication in November 1865. Thomas H. Baker, *The Memphis Commercial Appeal: The History of a Southern Newspaper* (Baton Rouge, 1971), 26–115 passim; *Memphis Appeal*, Jan. 7, 1866; Amnesty Papers (M1003, Roll 48), Tenn., B. F. Dill, RG94, NA.

12. William Dennison, postmaster general (1864–66).

From James Dixon

Washington   April 12th 1866.
407 N.Y. Avenue

My dear Sir,

Judge Davies came in town this morning to consult with you in regard to the Collectorship of New York.

He is more anxious to have that appointment made which will most contribute to the support of your administration and the success of your policy, than to obtain the place for himself.[1]

I have as you well know regarded his appointment, from an early day, as promising to give you great strength in New York and in the country generally, and have not therefore, listened to the suggestions of Judge Davies' friends to withdraw his name; but yet hope that you may see your way clear to appoint him.

You will confer a special favor on me, by giving Judge Davies an opportunity of explaining the present aspects of the case personally, which will, I am sure relieve, and not add to present embarrassments.[2]

James Dixon

ALS, DLC-JP.
    1. Senator Lane of Kansas also favored Henry E. Davies's appointment, urging Johnson to "give us Davies as Collector of New York & the death knell of your enimies & ours will begin to toll with the announcement." James H. Lane to Johnson, Apr. 13, 1866, Johnson Papers, LC.
    2. Dixon wrote Johnson on the following day, thanking him for agreeing to see Davies later that evening. Whether the interview actually transpired is unknown. Nevertheless, Davies was not appointed. Dixon to Johnson, Apr. 13, 1866, ibid.

From David J. Godwin et al.[1]

Portsmouth Va.   Apl: 12th, 1866.

Dear Sir:

We are on the eve of a municipal election. We regret to say that there are here two parties. One that has endorsed & fully identified itself with your policy. The other which has failed to endorse your policy. The latter party, is however small. But this latter party derives its main strength from the impression that has been *studiously* made that every one who votes for the administration party, will be excluded from work in the Navy Yard.

You will do the public & your administration good service by giving us the assurance that no one shall be proscribed, or excluded from work in the Navy Yard for the reason of having voted with the party that *supports your* administration.[2]

An early reply will very much oblige. . . .

D. J. Godwin
J. F. Crocker
Virginius A Haynes

ALS (Godwin), DLC-JP.
    1. Godwin (1829–*fl*1890) was a lawyer and had served in the Confederate army. After the war he was judge of the Corporation Court of Norfolk and in the 1880s he went to Washington to work on the compilation of the *Official Records*. James F. Crocker (1828–1917), a lawyer and graduate of Pennsylvania College at Gettysburg, served in the 14th Va. Inf. during the war and was captured during Pickett's charge at Gettysburg. Haynes (1836–*fl*1870) was a sailmaker. 1860 Census, Va., Norfolk, Jackson Ward, Portsmouth, 169; (1870), 92; *Boyd's Directory of the District of Columbia* (1890); Robert K. Krick, *Lee's Colonels* (Dayton, 1979), 143; "The Godwins and Borlands," *VMHB*, 17 (1909): 97; James F. Crocker, "Prison Reminiscences," *Con Vet*, 14 (1906): 503–4; *NUC*.
    2. No reply from Johnson has been found. According to newspaper accounts the "JOHNSON party triumphed by an overwhelming majority" in the Portsmouth election. James C. White was elected mayor of the city and David Godwin was chosen the Commonwealth's attorney. *Richmond Dispatch*, Apr. 12, 24, 1866. See also James C. White to Johnson, June 2, 1866.

From Joseph Holt

Bureau of Mily. Justice
April 12. 1866.

In accordance with your desire, expressed through Col. Wright Rives in a letter of this date,[1] I have the honor to submit the conclusions reached by this Bureau in regard to the trial by Military Commission of T.C.A. Dexter, late supervising special agent of The Treasury Dept.

He was convicted of "Fraud upon the U.S. government"—in combining with certain parties to appropriate to his and their use cotton belonging to the government,—and of "malfeasance in office,"—in accepting a consideration of twenty five thousand dollars for the appointment of a deputy.

He was sentenced to be fined in the sum of two hundred and fifty thousand dollars, ($250000) to be confined in some penitentiary for the term of one year, and be forever disqualified from holding any office of honor, trust or profit under the U.S. Government.

After a careful examination of the voluminous record in this case, it is believed that the findings of the Commission are not sustained by the testimony, much of which was incompetent and inadmissible, and that the evidence does not warrant the enforcement of the sentence.

A report setting forth an abstract of the proofs as a basis of these conclusions, is being prepared, and will be submitted in a few days.[2]

J. Holt, Judge Adv. General.

LBcopy, DNA-RG153, Lets. Sent (Record Books), Vol. 17.
1. Following Johnson's request, Rives had asked the judge advocate general to submit "*as soon as possible*" his "conclusions in the Dexter case." Rives to Joseph Holt, Apr. 12, 1866, Lets. Recd. (1854–94), File 1765, RG153, NA.
2. Five days later, Holt's twenty-one page report "recommended that the proceedings be disapproved." Johnson subsequently ordered Dexter discharged from custody. Holt to Stanton "for the President," Apr. 17, 1866, Lets. Sent (Record Books), Vol. 17, RG153, NA; *Memphis Post*, May 26, 1866.

From John Hosley[1]

City of Manchester, N.H.
Mayor's Office, City Hall, Apr. 12, 1866.

Dear Sir,

The death of Judge Harvey[2] of this state which occurred at Concord N.H. on the 7th inst. has undoubtedly been brought to your notice.[3] This leaves a vacancy in the office of Judge of the U.S. District Court for the District of New Hampshire. The importance of this office to which an appointment is to be made by yourself will, I trust, be deemed a sufficient excuse for my addressing you at this time.

I desire to recommend to you as a most suitable person for the appointment Edward S. Cutter[4] Esqr. a lawyer in this city. Mr Cutter is at present our city Solicitor, and previously he was Clerk of the Supreme Judicial Court of this state for Hillsborough County. In both situations he has proved a most excellent officer. He is a gentleman of irreproachable character, a learned lawyer and a good citizen, he has been a supporter of the Republican party in politics and of the administration in suppressing the Rebellion. But since the controversy has arisen between the Radicals in Congress and your present Administration he has from the very first been an ardent advocate of your policy of reconstruction while a large portion of the Republican party in this State support the Radicals.[5]

The appointment to so important an office in this State of a Republican lawyer who supports your views will surely strengthen the Administration. By encouraging those conservitive Republicans to hold on to their views and unite with those Democrats who entertain similar views a party will be formed which will hold a majority.

I hope you will give Mr. Cutter the appointment, as I know it will give general satisfaction to the friends of your administration.[6]

The appointment I suppose will not be made at present and in the meantime Mr. Cutters friends will furnish you with ample recommendations of his fitness for the office.

John Hosley   Mayor of Manchester

ALS, DNA-RG60, Appt. Files for Judicial Dists., N.H., Edward S. Cutter.

1. Hosley (1826–fl1885) held a variety of occupations—textile manufacturer, grocer, realtor, and farmer—in addition to serving in the state legislature and as city alderman, tax collector, and mayor of Manchester. He was a delegate to the National Union Convention at Philadelphia. D. Hamilton Hurd, comp., *History of Hillsborough County, New Hampshire* (Philadelphia, 1885), 135–36.

2. A former Democratic congressman and New Hampshire governor, Matthew Harvey (1781–1866) had been appointed to the federal bench by Andrew Jackson. *BDAC*.

3. Two earlier letters from New Hampshire, both of which recommended John P. Hale as a possible replacement for Harvey, may have reached Johnson before Hosley's. James T. Brady to Johnson, Apr. 9, 1866, Johnson Papers, LC; C. W. Woodman to Johnson, Apr. 9, 1866, Appt. Files for Judicial Dists., N.H., John P. Hale, RG60, NA.

4. Cutter (b. 1822) taught at an academy before commencing the practice of law in 1849. George T. Chapman, *Sketches of the Alumni of Dartmouth College* (Cambridge, 1867), 348.

5. A conservative Democrat who was himself an applicant for Harvey's seat wrote Johnson: "I do not know a Republican in the state that is qualified . . . who is not a radical." Ira A. Eastman to Johnson, Apr. 13, 1866, Johnson Papers, LC. See also William Butterfield to Johnson, June 15, 1866, and Edmund Burke to Johnson, July 5, 1866.

6. Later in the month, Chief Justice Chase recommended Judge Asa Fowler of Concord to succeed Harvey. But neither Fowler nor Cutter received the appointment. Samuel P. Chase to Johnson, Apr. 24, 1866, Appt. Files for Judicial Dists., N.H., Asa Fowler, RG60, NA. See William C. Clarke to Johnson, June 25, 1866.

Interview with The Times (London) Correspondent[1]

[April 12, 1866][2]

The President first adverted to the condition in which he found the country on his accession to office, and pointed out that ever since that time the Radical party, which now has the control over Congress, had been preparing for the issue forced upon him. Their object was manifest, and it was one which, from their point of view, they could scarcely be blamed for pursuing so eagerly. They knew perfectly well that when the South came back into Congress their day of power would be over—the Southern representatives would stand as a unit; they would probably fall into alliance again with the Democratic party, the old issues of slavery and State sovereignty would be dead and buried, and the party which now ruled would be stripped of its power. Their talk about philanthropy and benevolence to the negro meant nothing more than a desire to work upon the feelings of the North, so that they might be enabled to carry everything their own way. It was a renewal of an old conflict. The two sections of the country were ready to go to war before the rebellion broke out—the one to preserve slavery, the other to destroy it. Each side was willing to sacrifice the Government in order to gain its object. The South struck first; the rebellion was subdued at the Southern end of the line, and now it is swinging round to the other end. "These men," continued the President,—and he always used these words to denote the Radical party,—"are almost ready to go into rebellion again rather than have their supremacy destroyed by the re-introduction of the South. They know nothing practically of the real state of the South. The very man who had drawn up the Civil Rights Bill,[3] what are his means of judging? I left him in the Senate during the war, and went out to Tennessee and saw it all, and bore my share of the troubles. He stopped at home, and now endeavors to make his theories square into the events of the war, and legislate on ideas which he has never put to the test."

The President then went on to speak of slavery and the negro. He had been brought up, he said, under the very shadow of the institution of slavery. He had bought and owned slaves, but still he had always been for abolishing slavery upon any basis which could be adopted with safety to the country. When it came to the question whether slavery should be abolished or the Government broken up, he never had a doubt as to the course which he ought to pursue: he decided to give up slavery, and he abided by that decision. But the South now would treat the negro with greater kindness than the North if it were let alone and not exasperated. "They talk of justice to the negro," continued the President. "God knows my heart yearns towards him when I think of the end which these men are preparing for him. I see that end clearly enough,—they are going the way for a conflict of races. When that occurs we all know how it will fare with the negro. How has such a contest always ended? When the time comes there will be no *struggle*. The result will be decided without that. Now, then, what do we find? The very thing which we said these Southern States could never do, which we fought these four years to prevent them doing, these men affirm that they have actually done—namely, been out of the Union. The Southern States are ready to come back upon our terms, take loyal oaths, and acknowledge their allegiance, but these men say they shall not. Why, if they had offered to come back, or any of them, during the rebellion, should we have turned them away on the ground that they had placed themselves out of the Union? Mr. Lincoln offered to receive the whole Legislature of Richmond—a rebel Legislature, and would have welcomed them with open arms. Would he have refused to receive these States now that they have fully submitted?"

The President next referred to the misrepresentations of his policy which have been so industriously spread abroad. "These men" had for months past had the public mind open to them, and had poured into it whatever they pleased. Now it had become incrusted, as it were; but once let that incrustation be broken through, and the truth would begin to find its way. "I am not discouraged," added the President; "either these States must be brought back, or they must be kept out. It is like doing a sum in addition—some sums want figuring up more than others before you can get the answer, but I believe it will all come out right in the end."

Mr. Johnson then enlarged with considerable detail upon the operations of the Freedmen's Bureau, and said that its machinery was now being used to get negroes conveyed *from* the North *back* to the South by the very men who were asserting that the lives of the freedmen were not safe in the South. They had hired or bought lands, they wanted labour, and they got their negroes transported at the expense of the Government. The Freedmen's Bureau compelled the negroes to go, or they stopped their subsistence allowance. It was little better than another form of slavery, only that it was solely conducted by Abolitionists; for the Freedmen's Bureau would not assist a Southern man in getting negroes from the North, where many thousands of them have taken refuge during the war. A gentleman from Falkland County, Virginia,[4] had been to him, the President said, only a few days ago, saying that he had sent 300 negroes to the district (of Columbia) for security during the war. He now wished to hire them, but the Freedmen's Bureau interposed obstacles, and would give him no help in transporting them; whereas the Government railroads were placed at the service of other speculators. In all that he said it was evident that the President approved some plan for protecting the negro and giving him succour, but that he considered the administration of the Freedmen's Bureau was not all that could be desired. It did not accomplish the true object for which it was founded.

Passing from this subject, the President said that the Radical party in

Congress talked to the people as if they had to fear some act of oppression on the part of the Executive because the Civil Rights Bill had been vetoed. "But the Veto power," he said, "could never be made an engine of oppression. It has only a negative force—it originates nothing. It can only say when it sees unwise or unconstitutional legislation attempted, 'Now stop. Consider this thing a little further. Pass the Bill if you will by your constitutional two-thirds majority, but I think it well to give you an opportunity to think over it again.' They have passed the Civil Rights Bill, and it will not be long before a judge is arrested for carrying out the laws of his State. Then the case will be brought to the Supreme Court, and the people will soon see which was right—Congress in insisting upon having it, or I in endeavouring to dissuade them from it." Here, again, the President distinguished between the principle on which the Bill is professedly based, and the Bill itself; the former he was anxious to see carried out, but the means proposed he considered objectionable and hazardous.

"Congress," the President further said, "represents the States, but the men who voted for them individually *all* voted in my election. I am like the Tribunes elected by the Roman people—I am to stand and represent their interests. And what other object can I have but to represent those interests—the interests of my country? *I* have no party objects to serve— no selfish interests to promote. If I were a man of ambition, I do not know what I could desire more than I have gained. I have gone the whole giddy round, from alderman upwards, and I do not value this office (here the President spoke with great earnestness and feeling) except for the good which it may enable me to do. I want but a corner of this house to live in, and I do not care a bawbee, as the Scotch say, for all the rest. Let me but see the country at harmony and peace, and how gladly would I give up all! I suppose I may say that I have done enough to satisfy any reasonable ambition, and feel that my race is wellnigh run. These men want power; I have enough, and am indifferent to what I have. We think"—he said these words with a smile—"we think this a great position, with our ideas —we are educated to do so; but I can assure you that I am often here twelve hours a day without it ever occurring to me that I am President." He evidently meant, without the *pride* of power occurring to him.

"These men," he also said, "have raised the cry of 'mad dog' at me, and the people seem to be getting afraid. They will understand me better by-and-by, and understand these men too. I could not expect to get through without a struggle." Yet it was most extraordinary, he continued, to think of the course which "these men" were pursuing. By being united again the country would stand respected in the eyes of the world. It was now labouring under the evils of an inflated currency, and while trade is restricted by the South being kept in uncertainty—an element of danger in the State—such evils could not be corrected. Yet there were signs that people were beginning to be alive to the truth. "Look at Peoria"—and he mentioned several other towns where meetings in support of the President's policy have lately been held since the passage of the Civil Rights Bill. "It is like water trickling along the ground," said Mr. Johnson. "You can see the *damp places* here and there, and you know that it will gradually spread. It will take time; but, after all, what good can be accomplished without trial and difficulty? If I fail, my regret will not be for myself. I will hope that some one wiser will rise up to do the work." The President uttered these words in a somewhat weary and sad, but very earnest tone. He continued with greater animation:—"My convictions are firm and strong, and strong convictions are a great source—the best source—of courage to a man. I have fought disunion nearly all round the circle, and if I am called upon to complete the circle I will. Then I could say most heartily that I would that I could depart in peace."

Such, so far as I feel myself at liberty to repeat them, were the remarks made by the President. I believe that I have repeated his very words in most instances, but there were many illustrations which he employed which I am unable to recall, and in a conversation of nearly two hours there must necessarily be a great deal which I cannot pretend to remember with sufficient accuracy to repeat. That the President is as firm and unshaken as ever it was impossible to doubt after listening to him. He relies upon the good sense of the people to bring the present crisis to a favourable end; but it is clear that he has no personal objects to serve. He told one of the most distinguished of American politicians only yesterday, as he told me on Thursday, that he will never consent to be a candidate for the Presidency again. I will only add that the President looked better in health than when I saw him some months ago, and that he speaks with great clearness, force, and ability, and brings to bear on the subject upon which he is talking many very suggestive and felicitous figures and illustrations.

The Times (London), May 1, 1866.
1. This account also appeared in the *New York Times*, May 14, 1866.
2. The date of the interview is based on the date the correspondent wrote the report and internal evidence.
3. Lyman Trumbull.
4. Not otherwise identified. The only Virginia counties beginning with "F" are Fairfax, Fauquier, Floyd, Fluvanna, Franklin, and Frederick of which Fairfax is closest to Washington, D.C.

From G. W. Williams[1]

Claiborne Co. Missi   April 12th 1866
Dr. Sir

An old man and friend takes the liberty of addressing you in a plain & frank manner. My knowledge of your character makes me know this, in preference to any other will be appreciated by you.

By birth I am a Tennessean and lived in the same County with you for a number of years, and voted for you for every office for which you ran, up to ten years ago when I moved to this state. I mention this simply to let you know that I am an old friend and not a new one.

We have just heard of your proclamation, declaring the war at an end, and that the writ of Habeas Corpus is again restored, & that for the future we are to be governed by the Civil instead of Military laws, thank God for it.[2] We are tired of Military. We are tired of War, and wish to be again as we were before the late terrible and calamitous rebellion.

I do assure you it is the wish and desire of all good men in this State to be once more in the glorious old Union, And we all know and see that to your patriotic and firm action, we are indebted for the blessings we are now enjoying.

My object in writing this is to say that your noble efforts in our behalf are appreciated by us. You will ever be looked upon as our truest and best friend. These are not my sentiments alone, but of all sensible men whom I have heard speak on the subject.

My old friend and neighbor Gov Ben. G. Humphreys has just expressed himself to me in similar terms, & *he says* they are the sentiments of the people. He is a man of sound sense, good judgment *and is honest* mixes with the people, & knows more of them than any public man in the state. In making appointments to fill offices in this state, if you will be governed by his recommendations you will be certain to have good officers, and gentlemen he will recommend no others—which I am sorry to say is not the case with all of our public men in high positions. They are too often influenced by their own personal interest.

Again thanking you for your efforts in our behalf, and wishing you a long & happy life. . . .

G. W. Williams

Our post offices have not as yet been established. My address for the present is care J. S Vicksburg Miss.

ALS, DLC-JP.
1. Not identified.
2. See Proclamation *re* End of Insurrection, Apr. 2, 1866.

From George V. Moody

Port Gibson, Mississippi   April 13th 1866

Sir

The undersigned had the pleasure to receive from your Excellency, in October last, a pardon.[1] He had been a colonel of artillery in The Confederate Army, under Genl. Robt. E. Lee.

Judging from public State papers & debates in Congress, Your Excellency may shortly find it needful to sustain the authority of The United States Govt. & the Constitution thereof by, & with such armies, as by the said immortal instrument are legitimate. In the event of such necessity, I tender my services & can raise in thirty days 1000 trained men, of the late Confederate army, as artillerists, who will bear the banner of the Union, to sustain the constitution, wherever you will direct.

Govr. B. G. Humphreys will *cheerfully* give his official & personal (if needed) services on any field you may indicate & to him & Judge W. L. Sharkey and Revd. Granville Moody of Ohio (my brother) I refer you sir, for testimony, as to my sincerity & competency. I do confidently assert that all the *men* of Miss. will sustain the Govt. & Constitution under your authority.

Geo. V. Moody

ALS, DLC-JP.
1. See Moody to Johnson, Aug. 20, 1865, *Johnson Papers*, 8: 623–25.

From J. McClary Perkins[1]

Washington   April 13" 1866.

The New Hampshire School is a free-colored school, consisting of about 100 pupils, on G street between 6th and 7th streets (Island), Washington City, under the auspices of the American Baptist Home Mission Society, and has been under the supervision of Mrs. M. C. Milligan.[2]

Thus far this school has been held in a barrack building belonging to a colored church, but located on ground leased for that purpose. The owner of the land has notified this church that this building must be removed. There is no place for the school when this building is taken down.

The Freedmen's Bureau, and also the Principal of this school, made application, last fall, for the use of the Chapel at Armory Square Hospital. But the War Department did not grant it to any one. It is now only used for the same purpose that the hospital barrack buildings on Armory Square are used—the storage of clothing.

Filed with the applications above named is the written evidence of the following facts:

That this Chapel was built without a cent of expense to the United States Government—that the money spent in its erection was contributed by parties principally from Boston and vicinity—that these donors desire that this Chapel may be used for a colored school.

It is so disconnected from the hospital buildings that its use for a colored school could not interfere with or cause inconvenience to the quartermaster's department in using the main hospital buildings for storage purposes.

In using this Chapel for this school, the same neatness, care, and order would be observed both in regard to the building & the ground as has hitherto been used.[3]

J. McClary Perkins for Home Mission Society.

ALS, DNA-RG107, Lets. Recd., Executive (M494, Roll 84).

1. Perkins (c1839–fl1899) established and for a short time operated an evening school and Sabbath school in Washington in 1864. In mid-1864 he became one of three trustees of the Colored Schools for Washington and Georgetown, but was removed by the middle of 1867. He then acted as principal for Wayland Normal School for a while before pursuing a legal practice in Washington. 1870 Census, D.C., Washington, 3rd Ward, 593; Washington directories (1866–84); *NUC*; *History of Schools for the Colored Population* (New York, 1969 [1871]), 240, 257; *Washington Morning Chronicle*, Aug. 28, 1865.

2. Matilda C. Mulligan also opened a school for white students in Morgan County, Alabama, in June 1866. Joe M. Richardson, *Christian Reconstruction: The American Missionary Association and Southern Blacks, 1861–1890* (Athens, 1986), 231–32; Lillian G. Dabney, *The History of Schools for Negroes in the District of Columbia, 1807–1947* (Washington, 1949), 65n.

3. Johnson referred the petition to Edwin Stanton "for his examination and action." Stanton reported back that he did not deem it expedient to grant Perkins's request. Stanton to Johnson, Apr. 23, 1866, Lets. Recd., Executive (M494, Roll 84), RG107, NA.

From Franklin Pierce

Concord N.H.   Apl. 13, 1866

My dear Sir

I know, of course, the annoyances which are inseparable from your position, and depart from a rule which I have observed ever since I left Washington, when I hand to Mr J. McCleary Hill[1] this note of introduction. He is one of our most estimable and distinguished citizens—a Gentleman whose high manhood and true probity have never been questioned by any man of any party. You can rely with entire confidence upon his fidelity and prudence, as well as upon his good sense & patriotism. Patronage in this State is, as he will explain to you, really of no consequence, except so far as it may be used to sustain or to strike you down in the great cause in which you are engaged. You need no expression of the thanks, which my heart acknowledges for your brave devotion to the Constitution and the Union and for the unanswered & unanswerable arguments with which you have confounded the Enemies of both.

Franklin Pierce

ALS, DLC-JP.

1. The son of a former Democratic senator and New Hampshire governor, Hill (1821–1900) was for several years before and after the war engaged in the newspaper business in Concord. As chairman of the Democratic State Committee, he had earlier forwarded to Johnson a resolution passed at a meeting in Concord which endorsed the Freedmen's Bureau bill veto and presidential reconstruction. Ezra S. Stearns et al., comps., *Genealogical and Family History of the State of New Hampshire* (4 vols., New York, 1908), 4: 1982–83; *DAB*; Hill to Johnson, Mar. 6, 1866, Johnson Papers, LC.

From Henry A. Smythe

No 46 & 48 Willard   April 13th 1866

My dear Sir.

I trust your Excellency has *fully determined* to appoint me & that *it may be done today*.[1] My reasons being many & strong, which I will explain, when I see you, must be my excuse for troubling you with a note early in the day.

Three Senators have endeavored to see you since yesterday— recommendg this course.[2]

Should you still feel any doubt or hesitation, I would suggest that I retain my Presidency of the bank, & other offices of trust held by me, for a month, or two, till you are either satisfied I am "the one of all others," you should have selected, or that some one else might bring more strength— or popularity to the place—*in that case*—I could resign with propriety, & in justice to other duties, while you would possess the good will & support of the Merchants.[3]

H. A. Smythe

ALS, DLC-JP.

1. Smythe had originally applied for the New York collectorship on November 15, only two days after the incumbent, Preston King, committed suicide. Numerous recommendations in support of Smythe's candidacy were shortly thereafter sent to Washington, helping him to gain an interview with the President in mid-December. These developments were followed in March 1866 by Smythe's own letter to Johnson's son-in-law, in which Smythe reiterated his desire to serve the President. Smythe to Hugh McCulloch, Nov. 15, 1865, Appts., Customs Service, Collector, New York City, Henry A. Smythe, RG56, NA. See also the dozens of letters written on Smythe's behalf between November 1865 and January 1866 in ibid. Smythe to Johnson, Dec. 18, 1865, *Johnson Papers*, 9: 520; Smythe to David T. Patterson, Mar. 20, 1866, Johnson Papers, LC.

2. There was reportedly a large number of persons unable to obtain an interview on April 12. As Smythe later indicated to Johnson, senators and other members of Congress "complain of having to wait many hours" only to be denied the opportunity of speaking with the President. *Washington Evening Star*, Apr. 12, 13, 1866; Smythe to Johnson, Apr. 19, 1866, Johnson Papers, LC.

3. Smythe was tendered the appointment sometime between Johnson's receipt of this note and the afternoon of the 15th, when James Gordon Bennett, Jr., was sent a "strictly confidential" dispatch requesting the *Herald* to "take ground in favor" of Smythe's nomination. Smythe met with Johnson at the Executive Mansion on April 16, and later that day his appointment papers were forwarded to the Senate. Winning confirmation on May 11, Smythe assumed his duties as collector five days later. Robert Morrow to Bennett, Apr. 15, 1866, Tels. Sent, President, Vol. 3 (1866), RG107, NA; Beale, *Welles Diary*, 2: 484; Ser. 6B, Vol. 2: 295, Johnson Papers, LC; *National Intelligencer*, May 18, 1866.

From Reverdy Johnson

Washn.   15 Apl '66.

My Dear Sir,

The appointment of the N. York Collector is, in a political vein, to important & especially at this time, that one who is not a resident of that City, may be pardoned for writing you in regard to it.

Letters from there, & conversations with many well judging men, who are your friends, & friends of those in public life, who support your Administration satisfies, me that the best, the very best, solution you can make for the place, is Mr Smythe, the President of one of the largest Banks of the City.

A zealous supporter of the war, his appointment in a political view, would be popular, whilst for his well known business habits, & unspotted integrity, it would be approved by the merchants. Let me earnestly therefore, recommend it to you. Such a nomination too, would receive I am sure, the sanction of the Senate.

Reverdy Johnson

ALS, DLC-JP.

From Sam Milligan
Private

Jackson M. [*sic*] Ten.   April 15, 1866

Dear Sir:

Here I am "in these low grounds of Sorrow," where the dinge and dust of the battle, is not off the population. Their sin-tanned faces, and sun-scorched beards, tell on which side they fought. They think they have done no wrong, but rather feel a Conscious pride, that they have made a manly struggle for their "independence." They do not like the "North" —the yankee-population, but the war is over, and they patiently acquiesce in its results. They are at work, and have no idea of renewing the Contest. Their over anxiety to be restored to their former rights & privileges, embarrass your action, and retard the consumation of their desires. I have told them so, and endeavored to induce them to check the imprudence of their journals.

The hostility to Governor Brownlow, and the Tennessee Legislature, is, irreconsilable. They feel that the action of these departments of the State Government, are the greatest obstacles in the way of their "reconstruction"; and I doubt whether, the late Franchise law, if passed as now propsed, can be executed in this end of the State without military force.

I tell the Rebels to forget the past, and not attempt to make their efforts to brake up the Government, the ground of promotion to office in that same Government. It would have been applicable, had they succeded, but as they failed, it is a reward for their treason, and wrong. They must rise or fall on the new issues.

You are having an awful time. I really sympathize with you with all my heart. Have you blockaded the radicals, or have they you? If you are correct, (and there can be no doubt of that,) that the States are still in the Union, then there ought to be seventy two Senators in their seats, and all being present, no less than 37 could pass a bill. Say—then there are 35 radical votes in the Senate now, and 15 Conservative votes. The 15 added to the 22 seceded states, makes 37. Can a less number pass a Constitutional law? It is not like the state of things that existed during the rebellion. Then the doors of the Senate were open, and the States voluntarily refused to send their Senators; now they are closed, and they elect their senators, according to the forms of law, and their credentials are not even examined. The cases are wholly dissimilar. If improper men are sent up, or proper men with improper credentials, the Senate has the right to reject all such. But its action must be on individuals, and not upon whole delegations, or States, and that without examination. Could you not make a case, on the Constitutionality of a law, thus passed, for the action of the Supreme Court?

I think I could make "an able paper" on this idea; and hope you will not regard it impertinent to suggest it. There is some thing in it, and I have no doubt you have often thought of it.

The negros here are in many instances *strong "rebel sympathizers."* It is a fact, and if they could vote to day, they would vote with the South.

I have many things to say, but I have wearied you. Go on & God & the country will reward you.

Sam Milligan

ALS, DLC-JP.

From John D. Phelan[1]

Montgomery Alabama   Sunday April 15th 1866

Mr. President:

I have been meditating this Sunday morning upon you, and your position, and I feel so impressed with the conviction, that you have been called, in the providence of God, to save this noble and glorious form of Government which the men of '76 set up to be a light to the nations, that I cannot forbear to indulge the wish to hold communion with you, altho' personally to me a stranger.

And, first, let me tell you in a brief, plain way, who and what I am, politically and otherwise, that I may gain, it may be, some attention, or even favor, to what I have to say.

I am a native born American, the son of an Irishman,[2] born like yourself to poverty, but who by industry, general propriety of conduct, an ardent temperament, and good talents have achieved in my time these respectable and responsible positions in this State of Alabama; Attorney General, Speaker of the H of Reps, Circuit Judge, Judge of the Supreme Court. In politics I was always an unwavering Democrat; a Jackson, Anti Banks, Union Democrat; and refined, in due time, into an earnest and decided secessionist; to which cause I gave all the sons I had grown, four in number, two of whom now sleep beneath the battle fields of the war.[3] While the war lasted I was what would be called an extreme man. When we were exhausted, and forced to surrender I made my surrender full and entire, as I had made my effort to cast off the Govt of the U.S. and establish an independent nationality. I found, as a man always desirous to act on broad and well defined principles, that I had but two courses to pursue; one was to quit this country; the other to renew my allegiance *bona fide* to the Government of the U.S. For many reasons I decided to take the latter course; and to the surprise of many, who cannot fully understand what it is to act upon a principle, I rapidly became an open and active coworker with those men whom I had formerly opposed, in favor of the South's resuming in perfect submission, and good faith, her position in the Union. My friend Gov. Parsons, if you think it worth while to bring my name to his notice, will coroborate the body of these statements.

At first Mr. President I accepted you somewhat doubtingly and distrustfully. I had not taken the right measure, I am now satisfied, either of your leading characteristics, or of your abilities as a ruler. I hope I do not offend you by my plainess. I wish to be above both rudeness and flattery, because if I get to be heard with any favor, in what I shall have to prefer in the conclusion, it will be because you, as a prudent ruler, wish to know the *individual experiences* of men of sense and candor; and because you may conclude that I am worthy to be placed in that category.

Your success so far in the work of conserving our great and glorious form of Govt.—the "Representative Republic"—has been great, and to my mind gives assurance of your ultimate triumph. You are *holding your position*; and that is enough until the reserves come up; as come they will. Had Congress been in a frame to have shewn even a respectful deference for your views and opinions, we should probably have had (it is the experience of history) some halfway measure—some compromise. They have determined in their supposed might to *ignore* you—to set the third estate of the Government aside. This is judicial blindness. They have made you the *champion* for the Constitution of the U.S., that grand charter which embodies all the true political wisdom that has been refined in the crucible of experience from the days of King John and the old Bishops and Barons down to the day in which it was framed by Washington and his compatriots. But, what is more, they have made you the champion of this Constitution when the question concerns, not the *right of property* in *black slaves*, but the ancient *right* coupled with the high and solemn *duty* of the *white* man to *govern* the State and *preserve* his own race from *taint* and *deterioration*. Unless God has given over this people to destruction this surely can be no doubtful contest. All you have to do is to hold your position in the fear of God, with a positive determination never to yield, or compromise the great principles upon which you have planted yourself. The American people, nurtured in the principles of the English Common Law; inheritors of the high type of civilization belonging to their language and Religion will sustain you, because it will be sustaining themselves, and their posterity.

I come now to what has been in my mind all along. It is to beg of you, Mr. President, as you value your own fame, and true greatness, and the future happiness and glory of this country, in making our whole people once more united and fraternal; do nothing, and let nothing be done in relation to your most distinguished prisoner, and the other prominent men still detained as prisoners, which may plant a thorn in the heart of the South that can never be removed. Mr. Davis is our representative man. Impute to him whatever errors, or, in your mind, whatever delinquencies you may, nothing earthly can alter the relation he bears to the South, and the South to him.

I pray, as I have done nightly since I accepted you as my President, that "God will give you his grace to govern in wisdom, justice, and *Charity.*"

Jno. D Phelan of Montgomery Alabama.

ALS, DNA-RG94, Amnesty Papers, Jefferson Davis, Pets. to A. Johnson.
    1. Phelan (1809–1879) afterwards taught law at the University of the South, Sewanee, Tennessee. Willis Brewer, *Alabama: Her History, Resources, War Record, and Public Men From 1542–1872* (Tuscaloosa, 1964 [1872]), 471–72; *NCAB*, 36: 504.
    2. John Phelan (c1769–1850) immigrated to America in 1793 and was a bank employee in New York City and New Jersey before moving to Huntsville, Alabama, in 1818. Ibid.; *Huntsville Southern Advocate*, June 5, 1850.
    3. Thomas (c1836–1862) and Watkins (c1837–1865) Phelan, captains in the 8th and 3rd Ala. Inf., CSA, respectively, were killed in Virginia at Gaines' Mill and in front of Petersburg. Both the younger brothers, John (1842–1890), captain of an artillery battery, and Ellis Phelan (1843–1897), major of the 45th Ala. Inf., CSA, survived and became lawyers. In addition, John was a Birmingham cotton exchange manager, and Ellis was state secretary, clerk of the Alabama house; and after his move to Connecticut in about 1890, he was elected to a judgeship there. CSR, Thomas Phelan, RG109, NA; 1850 Census, Ala., Perry, Marion Beat, 742; Clement A. Evans, ed., *Confederate Military History Extended Edition* (12 vols., Wilmington, 1987 [1899]), 8: 744; Owen, *History of Ala.*, 4: 1355–56.

From Benjamin W. Penick

April 16, 1866, Greensburg, Ky.; ALS, DNA-RG94, USCT Div., Lets. Recd., File A-111–1866.

Penick petitions for the release of "an old servant of mine," Shelton Penick, who ran away and became a soldier and is now serving eighteen months at hard labor in Fort Pickens, Florida, as a punishment for "cutting loose, of a fellow soldier, who was *tied* by command of an officer, full exposed, to the fire, of the enemy, near Richmond." The writer intervenes because "there was a strong affection between master, and slave." [On June 7, 1866, Johnson remitted the unexecuted portion of the sentence and ordered Penick's release from confinement.]

From Henry Grider

Washington, D.C.   17. April 1866

I beg leave to state that Mr   Keenan[1] a citizen of Frankfort Ky not in (my) *third* district, was appointed Assessor at Bowling Green, without my knowledge, or the request or knowledge of the people of the district. All of which I aver to be wrong & without precedent, especially as many competent men & soldiers are ready & anxious to accept the office who live in the district. I therefore ask this matter to be reconsidered & corrected as it can now be done without injustice to any or violating the usage of *districts* filling their *own offices*. I therefore present you, the petition & testimonials of Coln Campbell,[2] who is fully qualified as is shewn by his petition (drawn by himself) & the testimonials accompanying it, manifesting most clearly his clerical business habits, as well as his successful, long patriotic services as a soldier & officer. So I must most earnestly request, this matter be reconsidered & the question refered to the appropriate department for the consideration of Coln Campbell's claims & that he be appointed to sd office &c.[3]

H. Grider

ALS, DNA-RG56, Appts., Internal Revenue Service, Assessor, 3rd Dist., Ky., Thomas W. Campbell.

1. Edgar A. Keenan (c1834–fl1866) was a Franklin County merchant. At one time he had served as chief assistant in the auditor's office for the state of Kentucky. During the war Keenan commanded a regiment of state militia. Johnson had appointed Keenan assessor in February 1866; the Senate confirmed his nomination on February 16. Grider left a blank space in front of Keenan's last name. 1860 Census, Ky., Franklin, Frankfort, 105; Citizens of Frankfort to Johnson, May 30, 1866; James A. Dawson to Johnson, May 28, 1866, Appts., Internal Revenue Service, Assessor, Ky., 3rd Dist., Edgar Keenan, RG56, NA; Ser. 6B, Vol. 1: 192; Vol. 5, Johnson Papers, LC.

2. Thomas W. Campbell (1830–1903) was a lawyer and Mexican War veteran. During the Civil War he attained the rank of lieutenant colonel while serving in the 25th Ky. Inf. and the 17th Ky. Cav., USA. Grider also wrote to Secretary McCulloch regarding the appointment of Campbell. On the envelope of the latter which Grider wrote to Johnson, the President placed a handwritten note: "Referred to the Sec. of the Treasury. A reconsideration is desired in this Case by the Hon Henry Grider of Ky." Then, on April 18, the President's secretary affixed the following message to the file cover sheet: "Respectfully referred to The Secretary of the Treasury and attention called the endorsement on the envelope." He added that it appeared that Keenan did not reside in the district, whereas the applicant (Campbell) "was a gallant soldier in the War and is competent." Pension Files, Thomas W. Campbell, RG15, NA; CSR, Thomas W. Campbell, RG94, NA; Grider to McCulloch, Apr. 23, 1866, Appts., Internal Revenue Service, Assessor, Ky., 3rd Dist., Thomas W. Campbell, RG56, NA.

3. Johnson received numerous petitions in Campbell's behalf; this drive also prompted Keenan supporters to respond for their candidate. On May 8 Johnson nominated Campbell for the assessor's post; ten days later the Senate confirmed the nomination and Campbell was commissioned. He held the position through at least 1869. Ser. 6B, Vol. 2: 40, Johnson Papers, LC; U.S. Off. Reg. (1867–69).

From Alexander H. Stephens

(Private not official)

Washington D C　　17 April 1866

Mr. President

You will please allow me to express my deep regret at not being able to wait longer last night for the desired interview with you[1] for a few minutes only before my leaving the city on my return home. My object was mainly to present to your consideration some views upon the subject of the present condition of the Country so far as relates to the writ of Habeas Corpus and the effect of the late Proclamation on the restoration of that writ.[2] That view however will doubtless be presented in a short time to you by Judge Wayne[3] as we have conferred together upon the subject and I had not seen them here. I wished also to say something about the appointment of a District Attorney for Georgia—that is an important office—And I wished to present the name of Hon. J. R. Parrot[4] of Cartersville for it—and also the name of Hon. Garnett Andrews for the Bench in case the Judiciary system should be revised as proposed.

Allow me to say I deeply sympathize with you in the heavy press upon your time. I do not see how you can stand it. With hope, that you may be sustained in your physical strength to bear you through your Herculean work and that your patriotic efforts at restoration of union harmony & prosperity throughout the Country may be successful. I need not repeat the assurance of my cordial and earnest cooperation with you in your exertions whether here or at home. I can remain here no longer at present. I must return. With sentiments of the highest consideration and esteem for you personally and officially and best wishes for our Common Country. . . .

Alexander H Stephens

ALS, DLC-JP.
1. Stephens had an appointment to see the President at 8 p.m., April 16. Wright Rives to Stephens, Apr. 16, 1866, Alexander H. Stephens Papers, LC.
2. See Proclamation *re* End of Insurrection, Apr. 2, 1866.
3. James M. Wayne.
4. Josiah R. Parrott (1826–1872), a lawyer who briefly served as a Confederate quartermaster, was currently solicitor general and subsequently (1868–72) judge of Georgia's Cherokee District. A few months earlier, Stephens had recommended Andrews for the district attorney position. Stephens to Johnson, Dec. 12, 1865, *Johnson Papers*, 9: 505; Lucy J. Cunyus, *The History of Bartow County Formerly Cass* (Easley, S.C., 1971 [1933]), 86.

From Joseph E. Brown

Atlanta Ga   Apl 18th 1866

One hundred and ten (110) bales cotton the property of John Billingsley and Nicholas Hutchinson[1] have been seized upon the charge that they are subscribers to the Confederate cotton loans. They are able to prove beyond a doubt that they were not subscribers. The Chancellor[2] has granted bills of injunction prohibiting the shipment of the cotton. The cotton is now in possession of the Sheriff,[3] safely stored, by order of the court. An order has arrived from Genl Thomas through R W Johnson Bvt Brig Genl to ship the cotton.[4] Under the order of the court Billingsley and Hutchinson have given bonds for twenty thousand dollars ($20,000) to save harmless the defendants and the Government of the United States. The shipment of the cotton would be cruel injustice to the parties. I appeal to your known sense of justice for an order stopping the shipment till the evidence under oath can be laid before you, or the judgement of the court can be had upon the hearing as you may direct.

Please reply promptly or the cotton will be shipped. I am satisfied Genl Thomas has not been correctly informed as to the facts.[5]

Joseph E Brown

Tel, DNA-RG107, Tels. Recd., President, Vol. 5 (1866–67).

1. Because Billingsley and Hutchinson were not prewar Atlanta or Macon residents, their identification is speculative. Possibly they were both from south Georgia. A John Billingslew [Billingslea] (b. c1821) lived near Albany on the plantation of a brother[?]; and a Nicholas Hutchenson (b. c1809) was a well-to-do farmer near Whitesville. 1860 Census, Ga., Dougherty, 15; Harris, 781st Dist., 132.

2. No such official has been located.

3. Possibly Benjamin N. Williford (d. 1903), former Atlanta city marshal, who became Fulton County sheriff in January 1866. Franklin M. Garrett, *Atlanta and Environs* (2 vols., Athens, 1969 [1954]), 1: 353, 546, 701; 2: 447.

4. Not found.

5. The telegram was referred to Secretary of the Treasury McCulloch, who two days later suggested that "Gen. Thomas' proposed action be approved, or not interfered with," since McCulloch had promised that shipping the cotton would not damage the interests of the claimants. McCulloch to Johnson, Apr. 20, 1866, Misc. Div., Claims for Cotton and Captured and Abandoned Property, RG56, NA.

From W. M. Poisson[1]

Wilmington N.C.   April 18th 1866.

Dear Sir

When the United States Troops took possession of this city about twelve months ago under a false statement made by negroes in reference to the owners of the property Genl. Schofield issued orders[2] that the negroes be allowed the use of the Front Street Methodist E. Church of this city one half of each day.

At that time in consequence of the County records having been removed to a place of safety & the destruction of our Rail Roads it was impossible for us at that time to produce copies of our deeds to show that the church property belonged to the whites & has belonged to them for 40 or more years.

Since this the records were removed back to the city and one of our *best* Lawyers[3] employed by the negroes to ascertain if they had any claim to the church property and after a thorough search he decided they had no claim to the church property whatever. After Genl. Schofields order was issued 5/6ths of the negroes withdrew from our church refusing to attend the preaching of the regular white Pastor[4] and connected themselves with the African Methodist church of the United States of which there were one or two colored ministers[5] here from the north who principally occasioned all of the trouble. Some of the negroes have since admitted that they have no claim to the church property. We had copies made of the deeds from the records and certified to by the proper officer. A Provost Marshall here[6] also examined into this matter & endorsed upon the papers that he was satisfied that the church property belonged to the whites but in the face of this & the copies of the deeds Genl. Schofields order has not yet been countermanded & the negroes still use the church under his order.

For one year & over the whites have been using it *only* about 2½ hours every sabbath morning for sunday school and preaching notwithstanding they are the real owners of the church. We have been frequently disturbed by the bad behavior of the blacks, by their frequent attempts to sit with the whites and by the use of our church for conventions and other meetings not religious and which was strictly prohibited by a resolution of our official Board some 10 years ago.

We have *quietly* submitted to these unjust things and at the last meeting of our conference notice was taken of it & Bishop Early was sent to Washington to lay the matter before you.[7] The Ladies of the city I believe also sent a petition in reference to it.[8] We have great confidence in you & your good & wise administration and although we know you are pressed with cares &c of more importance yet we would again call your attention to the matter & ask that justice be done and our church property restored to us its proper owners. Does your order restoring property to the M. E. Church south embrace our church? Our superior court will meet in a week or two & I would ask if your peace proclamation would give us authority to sue the negroes for our property? As we are willing to submit our deeds & claims to the inspection and decision of 12 honest men. We are perfectly willing for the negroes to come and sit in the gallery as they have been accustomed to do and listen to the word of truth as preached by our Pastor who has been placed in charge of the church by our Conference & in accordance with the discipline of our church. And we are willing for our Pastor to preach one sermon for the exclusive benefit of the negro every Sabbath afternoon when he is able if they remain in his charge & conform to the rules of the church as we have been in the habit of doing for years. A *few* colored members still remain true to the church & whites and we are disposed to do all we can for their spiritual welfare.

Your early attention to this matter will greatly oblige.[9]

W. M. Poisson

Please answer.

ALS, DNA-RG105, Asst. Commr., N.C., Lets. Recd.
   1. Poisson was a steward of the Front Street Methodist Church.
   2. Special Order No. 22, Department of North Carolina, March 5, 1865. L. S. Burkhead, "History of the Difficulties of the Pastorate of the Front Street Methodist Church, Wilmington, N.C., for the Year 1865," *An Annual Publication of Historical Papers Published by the Historical Society of Trinity College Durham, N.C.* (1908–09), Series 8: 56.
   3. Not identified.
   4. Liryum S. Burkhead (1824–1887), a Methodist minister since 1849, during his career had appointments in most of North Carolina's larger towns, from Charlotte to Wilmington. He was a member of the board of missions (1872–87) and in 1876 edited the *Centennial of Methodism in North Carolina. NCAB*, 7: 315.
   5. Chaplain William H. Hunter (1831–1908), 4th USCT, a former North Carolina slave, whose primary residence after the war was Washington, D.C. A Rev. Mr. Brown was temporarily pastor of the black congregation which had withdrawn from the Front Street Church. He was succeeded by Rev. James A. Hardy. Burkhead, "Difficulties of Front Street Methodist Church," 50; Pension Records, Henrietta J. Hunter, RG15, NA; Endorsement of Lt. Col. Allan Rutherford, May 28, 1866, Lets. Recd., Asst. Commr., N.C., RG105, NA.

6. Abial G. Chamberlain (1831–1890), captain, 1st Mass. Inf., and subsequently lieutenant colonel, 37th USCT, was actually commander of the post of Wilmington. His report in favor of the white members of the church was dated July 1, 1865. Pension Records, Ellen R.B. Chamberlain, RG15, NA; Burkhead, "Difficulties of Front Street Methodist Church," 91.

7. John Early (1786–1873) of Virginia, a Methodist minister since the early 1800s, had become a presiding elder in 1813 and a bishop in 1854. *DAB*.

8. Not found.

9. Endorsements show that Johnson referred the letter to Stanton, who referred it to O. O. Howard, who sent it to the Raleigh office of the Freedmen's Bureau. Bvt. Col. Allan Rutherford responded that the church had never been under Bureau control and gave a brief account of the controversy.

Speech to Soldiers and Sailors

[Washington, April 18, 1866][1]

It is not affectation in me to say that language is inadequate to convey the heartfelt feelings produced on this occasion by your presence here, and the presentation of your sentiments, as expressed by your representative in his address, and in the resolutions which you have thought proper to adopt.[2] I confess that, in the peculiar posture of public affairs, your presence and address give encouragement and confidence to me in my efforts to discharge the duties incumbent upon me as Chief Magistrate of the Republic; and in what I have to say I shall address you in the character of citizens, sailors and soldiers. I shall speak to you on those terms, and on none others.

I repeat my thanks for this manifestation of your approbation and of your encouragement. ⟨Applause.⟩ We are to-day involved in one of the most critical and trying struggles that have occurred since this Government was spoken into existence. Nations, like individuals, must have a beginning, must have a birth. In struggling into existence a nation passes through its first trying ordeal. It is not necessary for me now to carry your minds back to the struggle when this nation was born. It is not necessary for me to allude to the privations and hardships of those who were engaged in that struggle to achieve the national birth. It is not necessary to point to the blood shed and the lives sacrificed in accomplishing that result. The next ordeal through which a nation has to pass is when it is called upon to give evidence that it has strength, capacity and power to maintain itself among the nations of the earth. In giving such evidence, we passed through the war of 1812 and through the war with Mexico, and we passed through all the struggles that have since occurred, up to the beginning of the rebellion. This was our second ordeal. But a nation has another test still to undergo, and that is, to give evidence to the nations of the earth, and to its own citizens, that it has power to resist internal foes, that it has strength enough to put down treachery at home and treason within its own borders. ⟨Cheers.⟩ We have commenced that ordeal, and I trust in God we will pass through it successfully. ⟨Cheers.⟩ I feel complimented by the allusion of your representative to the fact that I stood in the Senate in 1860 and 1861, when the nation was entering on this third ordeal, and raised my voice and hand against treason, treachery, and traitors at home. ⟨Cheers and cries of "Good."⟩ I stand here to-day holding to and maintaining the same principles which I then enunciated. ⟨Cheers.⟩ I stand here to-day opposing traitors and treason, whether they be in the South or in the North. ⟨Loud cheers.⟩ I stand here to-day, as I then stood, using all my powers, mental and physical, to preserve this nation in passing through the third phase of its existence. The organized forces and combined powers that recently stood arrayed against us are disbanded and driven from the field, but it does not follow that there are still no enemies against our present form of Government and our free institutions. ⟨Applause.⟩ I then stood in the Senate of the United States denying the doctrine of separation and secession. I denied then, as I deny now, that any State has the right, of its own will, to separate itself from the other States, and thereby to destroy the Union and break up the Government. And I think I have given some evidence that I have been sincere and in earnest. And now I want to know why it is that the whole train of slanderers, calumniators and traducers have been barking and snapping at my heels.[3] ⟨Cheers.⟩ Why is it that they array themselves against me? Is it because I stand on the side of the people? And when I say the people, I include the sailors and soldiers. ⟨Cheers.⟩ Why is it that they are arrayed in traducing and vilifying and calumniating me? Where were they during the rebellion? ⟨A voice, "Home in bed." Laughter.⟩ In the Senate I raised my voice against it; and when it was believed that it would be to the interest of the nation, and would assist in putting down the rebellion, did I not leave my place in the Senate—a place of emolument, ease and distinction—and take my position where the enemy could be reached, and where men's lives were in danger? ⟨Cheers and cries of "That's so."⟩ While I was thus exposed, personally and publicly, and in every way, some of my present traducers and calumniators were far removed from the foe, and were enjoying ease and comfort. ⟨Cheers and laughter.⟩ But I care not for them. I care not that slander, the foul whelp of sin, has been turned loose against me. I care not for all that; and let me tell you here to-day, that although pretty well advanced in life, I feel that I shall live long enough to live down the whole pack of traducers and slanderers. ⟨Applause.⟩ They have turned the whole pack loose to lower me in your estimation. ⟨Voices, "They cannot do it."⟩ Tray, Blanch and Sweetheart —little dogs and all—come along snapping and snarling at my heels;[3] but I heed them not. ⟨Cheers.⟩ The American people—citizens, soldiers and sailors—know that, from my advent into public life to the present moment, I have always stood, unyieldingly and unwaveringly, the advocate and defender of their rights and interests. ⟨Cheers.⟩ We are now in the nation's third ordeal. We are not yet through it. We said that States could not go out of the Union. We denied the doctrine of secession; and we have demonstrated that we were right. We demonstrated it by the strong arm. Yes, the soldiers and the sailors—God bless them—have demonstrated by their patriotic hearts and strong arms that States have not the power to leave the Union. ⟨Applause.⟩ What followed? The Confederate armies were overpowered and disbanded, and there was a willingness on the part of the people of those States to come back, be obedient to the laws, and acknowledge the supremacy of the Constitution of our fathers. For what have we passed through this third ordeal? It was to establish the principle that no States had the power to break up the Government. It was to put down the rebellion. The rebellion has been put down; and for what? Was it to destroy the States? ⟨Voices, "Never."⟩ For what have all these lives been sacrificed, and all this treasure expended? Was it for the purpose of destroying the States? No! it was for the purpose of preserving the States in the Union of our fathers. ⟨Cheers.⟩ It was for that you fought. It was for that I toiled—not to break up the Government, but to put down the rebellion and preserve the Union of the States. That is what we have been contending for; and to establish the fact that the nation can lift itself above and beyond intestine foes, and treason and traitors at home. When the rebellion in Massachusetts was put down, did that put Massachusetts out of the Union and destroy the State?[4] When the rebellion in Pennsylvania was put down, did that destroy the State and put it out of the Union?[5] So when the recent great rebellion was put down, and the Constitution and laws of the country restored, the States engaged in it stood as part of the Union. The rebellion being crushed, the law being restored, the Constitution being acknowledged, those States stand in the Union constituting a part of this glorious and bright galaxy of States. ⟨Loud cheers.⟩ In passing through this ordeal what has been done? In Tennessee, under the direction of my lamented predecessor, we commenced the work of restoration. We had succeeded, before I came here, in restoring the relations which had existed between Tennessee and the rest of the Union—with one exception, and that was the relation of representation. I came to Washington, and, under extraordinary circumstances, succeeded to the Presidential chair. What then? The Congress of the United States had adjourned without prescribing any plan—I then proceeded—as I had done in my own State under the direction of the Government—to restore the other States. And how did we begin? We found that the people had no courts, and we said to the judges, the district attorneys and the marshals, "Go down and hold your courts; the people need the tribunals of justice to be opened." Was there anything wrong in that? The courts were opened. What else? We looked out and saw that the people down there had no mails. They had been interrupted and cut off by the operations of the rebellion. We said to the Postmaster General, "Let the people have facilities for mail communication, and let them begin again to understand—what we all feel and think—that we are one people." We looked out again and saw that there was a blockade, that the custom-houses were all closed. We said, "Open the doors of the custom-houses, and remove the blockade. Let trade and commerce, and the pursuits of peace be restored." And it was done. We thus traveled on, step by step, opening up custom-houses, appointing collectors, establishing mail facilities, and restoring all the relations that had been interrupted by the rebellion. Was there anything undertaken to be done here that was not authorized by the Constitution; that was not justified by the great necessities of the case; that has not been clearly consonant with the Constitution, and with the genius and theory of our Government? ⟨Cheers.⟩ What remained to be done? One other thing remained—to demonstrate to the civilized and pagan world that we had passed successfully through the third ordeal of our national existence, and proved that our Government was perpetual. A great principle was to be restored, which was established in our Revolution. When our fathers were contending against the power of Great Britain, what was one of the principal causes of their complaint? It was that they were denied representation. They complained of taxation without representation. ⟨Cheers.⟩ One of the great principles laid down by our fathers, and which fired their hearts, was that there should be no taxation without representation. How, then, does the matter stand? Who has been usurping power; who has been defeating the operations of the Constitution? And what now remains to be done to complete the restoration of those States to all their former relations under the Federal Government, and to finish the great ordeal through which we have been passing? It is to admit representation. ⟨Cheers.⟩ And when we say "admit representation," what do we mean? We mean representation in the constitutional and law-abiding sense, as was intended at the beginning of the Government. And where does that power lie? The Constitution declares, in express terms, that each House—the Senate and House of Representatives, each acting for itself—shall be the judge of the returns, elections, and qualifications of its own members. It is for each House to settle that question, under the Constitution, and under the solemn sanction of an oath. And can we believe that either House would admit any member into its body, to participate in the legislation of the country, who was not qualified and fit to sit in that body and participate in its proceedings? They have the power—not the two Houses, but each House for itself. The Constitution further declares that no State shall be deprived of its equal suffrage in the Senate of the United States without its consent. Then, where do we stand? All that is needed to finish this great work of restoration is for the two Houses, respectively, to determine these questions. Oh, but, some will say, "a traitor might come in." The answer to that is, each House must be the judge, and if a traitor presents himself cannot either House know that he is a traitor. ⟨Applause.⟩ And if he is a traitor can they not kick him out of the door, and send him back, saying to the people who sent him, "you must send us a loyal man?" ⟨Cheers and a voice, "That is logic."⟩ Is there any difficulty about that? ⟨"No, no," and cheers.⟩ If a traitor presents himself to either House, cannot that House say to him, "No, you cannot be admitted into this body; go back. We will not deny your people the right of representation, but they must send a loyal representative?" ⟨Cheers.⟩ And when the States do send loyal representatives, can you have any better evidence of their fidelity to the Constitution and laws? There is no one learned in the Constitution and the laws who will say that if a traitor happens to get into Congress the body cannot expel him after he gets in. That "makes assurance doubly sure," and conforms the action of the Government to the Constitution of our fathers. Hence I say, let us stand by that Constitution; and, in standing by it, the covenant will be preserved. While I have been contending against traitors, and treason, and secession, and the dissolution of the Union, I have been contending, at the same time, against the consolidation of power here. ⟨Cries of "Good."⟩ I think the consolidation of power here is equally dangerous with the separation of the States. ⟨Cheers.⟩ The one would weaken us, and might run us into anarchy, while the other would concentrate and run into monarchy. ⟨Cheers, and cries of "Can't do it."⟩ Oh! but there is an idea abroad that one man can be a despot—that one man can be a usurper—but that a hundred or two hundred men cannot. Mr. Jefferson, the apostle of liberty, tells us, and so does common sense, that tyranny and despotism can be exercised by many more rigorously, more vigorously, and more tyrannically, than by one. What power has your President to be a tyrant? What can he do? What can he originate? Why, they say, he exercises the veto power. ⟨Laughter.⟩ What is the veto power? ⟨A voice, "To put down the nigger." Laughter.⟩ Who is your President? ⟨Several voices, "Andy Johnson."⟩ Is he not elected by the people through the Electoral Colleges? The President is nothing more than the Tribune of the people. His office is tribunitial in its character. In olden times, when Tribunes were first elected in the Roman Republic, they stood at the door of the Roman Senate, which was then encroaching on the popular rights, and putting the heel of power on the necks of the people. The people chose a Tribune and placed him at the door of the Senate, so that, when that body ventured on oppressive acts, he was clothed with power to say "*Veto*," I forbid. Your President is now the Tribune of the people, and, thank God, I am, and I intend to assert the power which the people have placed in me. ⟨Cheers.⟩ Your President, standing here day after day and discharging his duty, is like a horse on the treadwheel; and because he dare differ in opinion in regard to public measures, he must be denounced as a usurper and a tyrant. Can he originate anything under the veto power? Think. The veto power is conservative in its character, not affirmative. All that can be done by the veto power is to say when legislation is improper, hasty, unwise, unconstitutional, "Stay; stop action; wait till this can be submitted to the people, and let them consider whether it is right or wrong." ⟨Applause.⟩ That is all there is in it. Hence I say that tyranny and power can be exercised somewhere else than by the Executive. He is powerless. All that he can do is to check legislation, to hold it in a state of abeyance till the people can consider and understand what is being done. Then, what has been done? I have done what I believed the Constitution required me to do. ⟨Applause.⟩ I have done what I believe duty and conscience required me to do. ⟨Cheers.⟩ So believing I intend to stick to my position, relying on the judgment, the integrity and the intelligence of the masses of the American people—the soldiers and sailors expressly. ⟨Cheers.⟩ Then, for my life, I cannot see where there is any tyranny. It is very easy to impugn motives, and suspect the purest and best acts of a man's life. If you come forward and propose a certain theory, your motives are suspected and condemned; and if you withhold your opinion you are regarded as being opposed to the matter; so that it is very hard to move one way or the other, so far as certain persons are concerned. On all questions pertaining to the interests of the great masses of the American people—for in them is my hope and the salvation of the country—I am with you, citizens, soldiers and sailors. Who has sacrificed or perilled more than the humble individual who addresses you? Has not my all been put upon it? My life, my property, everything sacred and dear to man has been staked upon it. And can I now be suspected of faltering, at the close of this third ordeal of the nation? Where is he, in public or in private life, who has sacrificed more, or who has devoted more of his time and energies to the accomplishment of the great end than I. And I have done it from the promptings of my own heart and conscience. I believe it was right, and with your help and your countenance and your encouragement, I shall get through on that line. ⟨Cheers and laughter.⟩ And when I come to talk about sailors and soldiers, about this to be done and that to be done, all I want is for you to wait and see, so far as the future is concerned. Wait and see if I do not stand by you, although every other may falter and fail. ⟨Cheers.⟩ I want to see measures of policy brought forward that will advance the interests of the people, and that portion of the people who have constituted the gallant and brave men who, in both branches of the service, have upheld the national flag and sustained the country in the recent struggle. I thank you, gentlemen, for this encouragement. I thank you for your countenance on this occasion. It cheers me on, and gives me strength to perform the work before me. If we are true to ourselves, if we are true to the Constitution, the day is not far distant when this Government will be restored. Let us go on and restore the Government. Let us enlarge the area of our commerce and trade. Let us not only inspire confidence at home, but respect abroad, by letting the nation resume its career of prosperity and greatness. I know that some will find fault with me, and say I am too lenient, too kind, and all that. If we were all to be put to death, or punished, or thrown away for one offence, or for the second offence, and were to be lost and excluded from society and communion with our fellow-men, how many of us would be left? I have felt when I have done wrong and have repented of it, that I was as sincere and honest as he who had done no wrong at all. Then we must reason with each other, and understand our nature. And what is necessary to restore peace, and harmony, and concord to a distracted and divided people? In time of war it is right to burn villages, sack cities, and devastate fields, to lay waste a country, and cripple and reduce the enemy; but in time of peace the converse of that course is precisely the right one, and the true policy of a nation is to rebuild its cities, restore its villages, renew its fields of agriculture, and let all the avocations of peace and prosperity be restored. I know there are some who have been at home calculating during the war, and who bring now to the consideration of questions of peace and harmony, and the avocations of civil life, all the feelings of resentment which animated us when the excitement was up and running high. But take the brave men who sustained the flag on the field and on the wave, and you will find better feelings and better judgment on these questions than you will find with those who have been sitting in the closet and never smelled gunpowder. ⟨Cheers.⟩ Yes, from the private up to the commanding general, they know better how to treat the present circumstances than any of these closet patriots and humanitarians.

Then, my countrymen, fellow-citizens, soldiers and sailors, let us rejoice that peace has come. Let us rejoice that the relations of the States are about being restored. Let us make every effort that we can, on proper principles, to restore the relations which existed between the Federal Government and the States. I thank God that peace is restored. I thank God that our brave men can return to their families and homes, and resume their peaceful avocations. I thank God that the baleful planet of fire and blood, which a short time ago was in the ascendant, has been cleared away by the benignant star of peace. Now that the bow of peace is suspended in the heavens, let us cultivate the arts and relations of peace, and all those associations which appertain to men in peace. The time is not distant when we can have a political millenium, a political jubilee, and when we can proclaim to all the nations of the earth that we are again a united people, and that we have triumphantly passed through our third ordeal—having peace at home and power to bid defiance to all the world. ⟨Loud cheers.⟩ Remember one thing, gentlemen, that in my past life—though slanderers may misrepresent—no man can say that I ever deceived or betrayed him. It will be for you to see, in the future, who will redeem all his promises, and who will be most faithful. I thank you, gentlemen, for the compliment you have paid me.

Washington Evening Star, April 19, 1866.
    1. Newspaper accounts make clear that the speech took place at the White House on the evening of April 18. A procession of sailors and soldiers, accompanied by the Marine Band, formed at Willard's Hotel and marched to the White House, where it was greeted by several

congressmen and the President himself. After first being addressed by one of the military procession, Johnson then spoke to the group out of doors at the north front of the Executive Mansion. See *Washington Evening Star*, Apr. 19, 1866; *New York Times*, Apr. 19, 1866.

2. The previous night a mass meeting of soldiers and sailors adopted a series of resolutions concerning pensions, military bounties, and civil appointments for qualified veterans. The soldiers and sailors requested that any benefits conferred on them be done so without regard to color. The resolutions also called for severe punishment for the former leaders of the Confederacy, the exclusion of former Rebels from Congress, and a delay in permitting former Confederate states back into the Union. The organizers of the meeting had invited Johnson to attend but the President declined. *National Intelligencer*, Apr. 18, 1866.

3. Variation of William Shakespeare, "King Lear," act 3, sc. 6, line 65.

4. Shay's Rebellion of 1786–87.

5. The Whiskey Rebellion of 1794.

From Gordon Granger

Washington, D.C.   Apr 19th 1866

Dear Sir.

When I last Saw you,[1] you requested me to call & See you before Starting on my Southern tour. I am now on my way to New Orleans & other points South.[2] If I can be of any Service it will afford me pleasure to receive your instructions, orders &c as to what you may wish me to attend to.[3]

G. Granger

ALS, DLC-JP.

1. Mustered out of volunteer service in January 1866, Granger is known to have been in Washington in early March seeking nomination for the lucrative New York collectorship. Although not appointed, he did manage to secure recommendations from a number of Johnson's supporters. Later Granger sought appointment as naval officer at New York. Powell, *Army List*, 337; Granger to Johnson, Mar. 1, July 25, 1866, and letters of recommendation, all in Appts., Customs Service, Collector and Naval Officer, New York, Gordon Granger, RG56, NA.

2. For his reports written from Knoxville and New Orleans, see Granger to Edmund Cooper, May 13, June 11, 12, 1866, Johnson Papers, LC. For a summary of his tour, see Granger to Johnson, Aug. 24, 1866, published in *New York Herald*, Aug. 28, 1866.

3. The instructions issued by the President's secretary authorized Granger to report on the operations of the Freedmen's Bureau and to ascertain the attitude of southerners toward the federal government. Cooper to Granger, May 9, 1866, Johnson Papers, LC.

From Cave Johnson

Nashville   April 19th 1866

Dear Sir

We think it necessary to keep you advised of the movements in Tennessee. I have had a good opportunity for the last two weeks here, of seeing citizens from the different parts and your position for a restoration of the Government may be truly said to meet the approbation of every body. The few who are in opposition to it are silent & not worth counting, and the country is as quiet & as peacable as at any former period of our history, with the solitary exception of the course of Governor Brownlow, & his friends in the Legislature. Their course would have produced great excitement if not bloodshed at any other time. Now however they have remained quiet & bore much, from an apprehension, that any movement here, to right themselves however peaceble & orderly, might be so construed at the North as to militate against your policy. If any means could be adopted to get rid of them, every thing would be at once quieted in the state. Their first Bill in June last disfranchised more than half of our people.[1] The March elections[2] showed that even among those entitled to vote the radicals as they call themselves were defeated almost every where & in my section mainly on the ground of better qualifications. When the Radical Legislature discovered that to be [the] case, they introduced a new law repealing the former & recalling the certificates given to voters making new & more stringent restrictions, that will exclude from the polls, nineteen-twentieths of the people, disregarding the oath of allegiance and amnesty & pardon, & introducing a new machinery which substantially compels every one to submit to the decision of a County Commissioner, the right of every citizen to vote, under such rules of evidence as enables no one to vote except those who will vote with them. The best & most reliable citizens are thus driven from polls. The Bill has passed the House & is now in the Senate & will probably pass that body before you receive this letter.[3]

It is a complete subversion of our State institutions & the places the negro upon a footing of equality with the disfranchised citizen. I have been excluded from voting under the first law & now here as a Senator unanimously elected in my district & excluded from my seat[4] by sending my credentials all regular & according to law to the Com. of election where it is supposed they will sleep until the new disfranchising act shall pass the Senate. There has been much talk of calling a new convention & has been & is now delayed from an apprehension that it might be seized hold of & used to the injury of the policy of the administration. This with some other measures give a good deal of disquietude to the country and I think there is great danger of blood shed, whenever an election takes place under the new Law, if it is attempted to be enforced. Give us a Military Governor or any thing else, would be better than what we now have.

C Johnson

ALS, DLC-JP.

1. A reference to the controversial franchise law passed by the General Assembly on June 5, 1865.

2. Special elections were held in Tennessee in March in an attempt to fill legislative vacancies caused by resignations. For a brief discussion of these contests, see Alexander, *Reconstruction*, 108–9.

3. The franchise law of 1866 had indeed passed the house on April 12 and would subsequently clear the senate on May 3. Patton, *Unionism and Reconstruction*, 116–118.

4. See Cave Johnson to Johnson, Mar. 12, 1866.

From William B. Scott

Davis House 19 St bet 17 & 18   Washington City
[April 19, 1866][1]

I have been in the city a week and have made several effort to See you. My Friends in the City of Nashville desired that I would See you and Speake these Sentiments to you and apprise you of the fact you have there highest regards while many of your white Friends are for condeming your pressent coarse. All of the intelligent Colored people highly approve the veto of Bureau bill and regard it as one of the Noblest act you ever did.[2]

I would be much please to See you a few moment on other buisiness if I can. Please let me know and at what time.[3]

W. B. Scott   Editor Colored Tennessean
Nashville Tenn

ALS, DLC-JP.

1. The date is supplied here, based upon the file cover sheet which shows April 19, 1866, as the date the letter was received at the White House.

2. Scott and his son wrote an earlier friendly letter to Johnson, May 27, 1865, *Johnson Papers*, 8: 120.

3. No information about an actual visit between Scott and the President has been uncovered.

Speech to Washington Blacks[1]

[April 19, 1866][2]

I have nothing more to say to you on this occasion than to thank you for this compliment you have paid me in presenting yourselves before me on this your day of celebration. I come forward for the purpose of indicating my approbation, and manifesting the appreciation of the respect thus offered or conferred.

I thank you for the compliment, and I mean what I say. And I will remark in this connection to this vast concourse that the time will come, and that, too, before a great while, when the colored population of the United States will find out who have selected them as a hobby and a pretence by which they can be successful in obtaining and maintaining power, and who have been their true friends, and wanted them to participate in and enjoy the blessings of freedom.

The time will come when it will be made known who contributed as much as any other man, and who, without being considered egotistic, I may say contributed more, in procuring the great national guarantee of the abolition of slavery in all the States, by the ratification of the amendment to the Constitution of the United States—giving a national guarantee that slavery shall no longer be permitted to exist or be re-established in any State or jurisdiction of the United States.

I know how easy it is to cater to prejudice, and how easy it is to excite feelings of prejudice and unkindness. I care not for that. I have been engaged in this work in which my all has been periled. I was not engaged in it as a hobby, nor did I ride the colored man for the sake of gaining power. What I did was for the purpose of establishing the great principles of freedom. And, thank God, I feel and know it to be so, that my efforts have contributed as much, if not more, in accomplishing this great national guarantee, than those of any other living man in the United States. ⟨Applause.⟩

It is very easy for colored men to have pretended friends, ensconsed in high places, and far removed from danger—whose eyes have only abstractedly gazed on freedom; who have never exposed their limbs or property, and who never contributed a sixpence in furtherance of the great cause; while another periled his all, and put up everything sacred and dear to man, and those whom he raised and who lived with him now enjoy his property with his consent, and receive his aid and assistance; yet some who assume, and others who have done nothing are considered, the great defenders and protectors of the colored man.

I repeat, my colored friends, here to-day, the time will come, and that not far distant, when it will be proved who is practically your best friend.

My friendship, as far as it has gone, has not been for place or power, for I had these already. It has been a principle with me, and I thank God the great principle has been established that wherever any individual, in the language of a distinguished orator and statesman, treads American soil, his soul swells within him beyond the power of chains to bind him in appreciation of the great truth that he stands forth redeemed, regenerated and disenthralled by the genius of universal emancipation! ⟨Applause.⟩

Then let me mingle with you in celebration of the day which commenced your freedom. I do it in sincerity and truth, and trust in God the blessings which have been conferred may be enjoyed and appreciated by you, and that you may give them a proper direction.

There is something for all to do. You have high and solemn duties to perform, and you ought to remember that freedom is not a mere idea. It must be reduced to practical reality. Men in being free have to deny themselves many things which seem to be embraced in the idea of universal freedom.

It is with you to give evidence to the world, and the people of the United States whether you are going to appreciate this great boon as it should be, and that you are worthy of being freemen. Then let me thank you with sincerity for the compliment you have paid me by passing through here to-day and paying your respects to me. I repeat again, the time will come when you will know who has been your best friend, and who has not been your friend from mercenary considerations. Accept my thanks.[3]

Washington Evening Star, Apr. 19, 1866.

1. This speech was occasioned by the celebration of the fourth anniversary of emancipation in the District of Columbia. The celebration was initially scheduled for April 12, but inclement weather caused a postponement of one week. *Washington Evening Star*, Apr. 19, 1866.

2. The date is given by the newspaper.

3. After the speech Johnson remained to shake hands with participants in the celebration. *Washington Evening Star*, Apr. 19, 1866.

From Benjamin F. Perry

Greenville S C   April 20th 1866

My Dear Sir

I take the liberty of enclosing you, two or three Editorials,[1] which I wrote for the Paper, at this place, during the illness of its Editor Col Townes.[2]

I have inplicit confidence in the success of your wise & patriotic policy. It may not be however till after an other election.

The Southern States must bide their time patiently, & I am sure they will do so most loyally. We are all quiet & hard at work. The "freed men & women" are behaving well & working well. There is no use whatever for any military force in the upper part of South Carolina. They are drinking, and behaving badly, both to whites & blacks. Fines are imposed on the humble people & pocketed. The soldiers are having frequent fights with the citizens & negroes. The only disturbance we have is from the garrisons. A negro was killed in this place the other day by a drunken soldier in cold blood!

Our State Courts are open, & all the Judges except one rode their Circuits & tried the business, civil and criminal, which was ready. They were not interfered with by the military out of Charleston.

The order of General Sickles, which I wrote you about some time since, removing the negroes from Laurens & Newberry districts has been suspended. He sent a commission to examine in to the reports & found them all false.[3]

We are anxious to get rid of Military commissions, which we think now unnecessary & unconstitutional as well as dangerous to liberty & justice.

B. F. Perry

ALS, DLC-JP.

1. Not found but, according to notations on the file cover sheet, the editorials were entitled "The Civil Rights Bill" and "The Signs of the Times." Johnson Papers, LC.

2. George F. Townes (1809–1891), the editor of the *Greenville Mountaineer* and a state senator. Emily B. Reynolds and Joan R. Faunt, comps., *Biographical Directory of the Senate of the State of South Carolina, 1776–1964* (Columbus, 1964), 323.

3. Perry's assessment of the commission's findings is an apparent contradiction of the army's report. See Perry to Johnson, Mar. 15, 1866.

From George S. Shanklin[1]

Washington D C   April 20th 1866

D Sir

I am informed that it is in contemplation, to present the name of Benj Gratts[2] Esqr. of Lexington Ky. to your Excy for appointment, to the office of Assessor in the 7th District of Ky. I can state to your Excy. that I have a personal acquaintance with Mr. Gratts, and know him to be a Gentman of high carracter, possessing business qualifications & habits and I believe he would be acceptable to the people of the District, and would faithfully discharge the dutys of his office, if appointed.

I also know the present incumbent of that office Col. D S Goodloe,[3] and I think I do him no injustice when I state that I do not believe he either possesses the capacity, or integrity, to discharge the dutys of that office well or faithfully.

He is not only unpopular with the people, but justly odious to three fourths of those that know him. I do not believe he could or ought to be elected, to the most insignificant, office in any precink in the district. I have no information as to his present political status; formerly he was considered an extream ultra Radical of the Sumner Stephens school and no doubt would coopperate with them now if he thought he could promote his own selfish purposes, thereby. Perhaps it would be well if that is his position, for I am well satisfied that he would greatly, injury any party or cause that he might espouse in that District. Certainly he could not promote it. In a word I do not believe a more unfortunat, appointment than his could have been made, in the District.[4]

G. S. Shanklin

ALS, DNA-RG56, Appts., Internal Revenue Service, Assessor, Ky., 7th Dist., Benjamin Gratz.

1. Shanklin (1807–1883), a lawyer, served in the Kentucky legislature for several terms and as commonwealth attorney (1854). A presidential elector on the McClellan ticket in 1864, Shanklin was elected to Congress that year and served one term. *BDAC.*

2. Gratz (1792–1884), a graduate of the University of Pennsylvania and veteran of the War of 1812, operated a successful hemp manufacturing business in Lexington. He also participated in railroading and banking. Temple Bodley, *History of Kentucky* (4 vols., Chicago, 1928), 4: 171; "The Lexington Cemetery Map," (Lexington, n.d.).

3. A farmer and merchant by trade, David S. Goodloe (1811–1881) served for a while as deputy sheriff of Madison County, Kentucky. Through his activity in the state militia before the war, Goodloe attained the rank of major general. In 1864 Abraham Lincoln appointed him assessor. Johnson reappointed Goodloe in early February 1866; his nomination was approved by the Senate on February 15. Robert Peter, *History of Fayette County, Kentucky, with an Outline Sketch of the Bluegrass Region* (Chicago, 1882), 607; *U.S. Off. Reg.*, (1865); Ser. 6B, Vol. 4: 241, Johnson Papers, LC.

4. Shanklin's letter was forwarded to Johnson by Montgomery Blair, who seconded the recommendation. Johnson nominated Gratz for assessor on July 17 and the Senate confirmed the nomination a week later. Blair to Johnson, Apr. 23, 1866, Appts., Internal Revenue Service, Assessor, Ky., 7th Dist., D. S. Goodloe, RG56, NA; *U.S. Off. Reg.* (1867);

From Henry Stanbery

Cincinnati   April 20, 1866

Mr. President,

I have seen by the despatches from Washington that you have been pleased to nominate me to the vacancy on the bench of The Supreme Court.[1]

Whatever may be the fate of this nomination, I am not the less indebted to you for the confidence in, and favorable opinion of me, which it implies. I feel it to be a high honor—especially as it was conferred spontaneously, and without the pressure of political or personal influences. Allow me Mr. President to express my thanks, and appreciation of this signal evidence of your esteem.

Henry Stanbery

ALS, DLC-JP.

1. Stanbery had been nominated on April 16, but the Senate apparently never acted upon his nomination, for Congress was in the process of enacting a bill to reduce the number of Supreme Court justices. On July 23, the date of the final approval of that measure, Stanbery's nomination as attorney general (which Johnson had sent to the Senate on July 20) was confirmed. Ser. 6B, Vol. 2: 295, 299, Johnson Papers, LC; *Congressional Globe*, 39 Cong., 1 Sess., Appendix, p. 378; *National Intelligencer*, July 24, 1866; Beale, *Welles Diary*, 2: 558, 560. See Johnson to Stanbery, July 13, 1866.

From Washington County Citizens[1]

Jonesboro [Tenn.]   April 20 1866

The undersigned most, if not all of whom, are personally known to you, would respectfully represent—that they are citizens of Washington County and union men. Incurring the risque of occupying more space than is desirable they beg leave to state a few preliminary facts. Soon after the permanent occupation of this county by the Federal troops a system was inaugurated by which the union soldiers, taking the law into thier own hands, avenged the wrongs they had suffered during the rebellion by beating and in some instances killing the men who had wronged them. Like all similar movements, It soon became progressive and in short culminated in Rape, Robbery and Murders Extending to citizens indiscriminately without regard to party. In one day several houses were plundered, assaulted and Josiah Conley who was a rebel, but an aged, quiet, law abiding man, and Jeremiah Keyes[2] a consistent union man inoffensive and kind whose sons were in the union army and a soldier of the War of 1812 and an invalid pensioner were brutally murdered.[3]

The most of the men engaged in this violence have been in both armies but are classed as union men (all).

After the occurrence of the above accompanied by other outrages upon the liberty of the citizens and social order and in the re-organization of the Courts of Justice, these things in a measure subsided, the mob became quiescent and we fondly hoped that the worst was over.

After it became manifest that a breach was imminent between the Legislative and Executive departments of the government an order (we infer) from head quarters in Tennessee to organise Loyal or Union Leagues—a secret organization who meet weekly and issue orders—resulted in organization. Some Conservative men accidentally, became acquainted with the subject matter of their deliberations. They have a gang of the sort of union soldiers herein before described who execute thier decrees, and it is decided at each meeting what "rebels" shall be notified to leave the Country. For the last two weeks violence to person, pillage, of property, assaulting of Houses and almost all kinds of disorder are perpetrated in the night. Notices emanate from the Post Office to Rebels to leave, in so many days signed *Vox Populi*. Our townsman James W. Deaderick was notified some two weeks ago. He paid no attention to it. Night before last a mob variously estimated at from 20 to fifty armed and mounted as cavalry entered his dwelling to execute the decrees of the *"secret tribunal."* But on his solemn assurance that he would leave on the day after he was released—They allow him two weeks to remove his family.[4] He is gone and our best citizens are leaving every day and herewith you will find the comment of a Federal Office holder on thier melancholy exodus. The Sheriff who signs this petition is utterly powerless. Death is the certain fate of any man who prosecutes or appeals to the Law. The civil power cannot reach this social insurrection. We are in a state of Anarchy and we implore the goverment to send us a force here to protect its citizens. With it to sustain us we can enforce the civil Laws without it, it is impossible. The members of the "secret tribunal" are known and we can point them out—men of *semi* social consideration, thrown up amid the convulsions of Revolt, who hiss on the mob until murder Rape and Robbery are the rule. Our citizens are driven off into those states in which after a while we must rely for sale of our entire surplus from which our traders will in turn be driven and we wholly cut off from the use of our productive power— while new immigrants coming to our borders with thier enterprise and capital turn away to quieter and more inviting localities. If it is in the power of the government send us help or we are *lost*. We transmit this by a commission who will relate facts more in detail. Every fact herein presented can be *proved*.

Pet, DLC-JP.
    1. The document was signed by eleven citizens, including William Henry Maxwell, Shelby T. Shipley, and Seth J.W. Lucky.
    2. Conley [Conly] (1804–1865) and his wife had at least eight children. Keys (c1794–

1865) had married Mary Ferguson in 1826 and they had at least seven children. 1850 Census, Tenn., Washington, Eastern Dist., 4th Subdiv., 471; Charles M. Bennett and Loraine Bennett Rae, eds., *Washington County, Tennessee, Tombstone Inscriptions Plus Genealogical Notes* (3 vols., Nashville, 1977–79), 3: 252; Goldene F. Burgner, *Washington County, Tennessee Marriages, 1780–1870* (Easley, S.C., 1985), 27.

3. The Jonesborough newspaper reported the atrocities in Washington County in early December that resulted in the murder of both Conly and Keys. The former had been shot, whereas Keys had been beaten with clubs. *Jonesborough East Tennessee Union Flag*, Dec. 8, 1865.

4. In late April Deaderick wrote from Bristol to David Patterson to inform him of additional misdeeds in Washington County and to plead with Patterson to have something done to quiet the region. According to Deaderick, "This state of things is the legitimate result of the teachings of Gov. Brownlow & his party." Considering the situation in the county, Deaderick declared that "I never expect to live in Jonesboro again." Deaderick to Patterson, Apr. 28, 1866, Johnson Papers, LC.

From Benjamin B. French

[Washington] April 21, 1866

Sir,

I have the honor to acknowledge the receipt from you this day, of a letter addressed to you by W. H. Stanford,[1] enclosing an extract from a letter from me, to Mr. Stephen C. Wailes,[2] evidently intended, by omitting a portion of my letter, to lead you to believe that I had dismissed Mr. Wailes from the public service. A manifest attempt, as it appears to me, to *deceive you*, and injure me.

On the envelope of the letter sent to me by your direction, is the following endorsement "Respectfully referred to Hon. B. B. French, Commissioner Pub. Buildings for report as to who made the pressure for the removal, and what were the opinions of the man removed, and those of the person appointed. By order of the President."

The first, and most urgent request made for the appointment of the successor of Mr. Wailes, was made by Hon. Columbus Delano, and Hon. James R. Hubell,[3] both members of the House of Representatives from Ohio. These gentlemen called on me many times and pressed upon me the appointment of Mr. Walter G. Berry[4] of Maryland. I told them there was no vacancy. The fact was then argued to me, if not by them by other friends of Mr. Berry, that there were several members on the Police force from the District of Columbia, and not one from Maryland. And my own rule established four years ago, that in my appointments of the Police I would distribute them, as much as possible, among the States, was brought up. Finally I told these gentlemen, that by removing one of the Policemen from the District I could appoint Mr. Berry, and they expressed the desire that I should do so.

I then addressed to Mr. Wailes the letter, an extract of which was sent to you. I unfortunately, kept no copy of that letter, but after using the words with which the extract closes, "I must vacate your place on the police"—I added that I should transfer Mr. Wailes to the carpenters' shop, and pay him the highest wages given to a journeyman carpenter; which I did and he is now employed, at, I think $3 per day, as a carpenter, he being one of the very best of workmen. Those who pressed upon me for the appointment of Mr. Berry, as a *right* to the State of Maryland, were

Messrs. Delano, Hubbell, Reverdy Johnson, Creswell,[5] Francis Thomas,[6] Phelps,[7] John L. Thomas jr.[8] R. W. Hall[9] (Register of Deeds) D. L. Gooding,[10] (Marshal of the Dist.) Ward H. Lamon, and several others.

I do not know what were the opinions of the man removed. I only know that, from pure and honest friendship toward him, I have kept him in office for years, when complaints were made to me that he was opposed to the Administration of Mr. Lincoln, and they came, at last so strong, that I had to remove him, in Jan. 1864. He was an excellent Police officer, and upon the strong representations of his friends that he was a loyal and true man, and from a feeling of warm personal friendship toward him, I again appointed him, in Jan. 1865.

At the time I transferred him to the carpenters shop, on the 1st. of March last, I did it most reluctantly, but with a perfect understanding with him, and with the assurance from me that, whenever the pressure from the States should cease, and an opportunity offer, I would restore him to the Police. I confess I did not suppose that he would persue the ungrateful course he has, toward me, and I now almost believe that this application has been made to you without his knowledge.

Mr. Stanford says, in his letter to you, "Mr. Wailes was one (if not the only one) of the whole force who fully endorsed you, and your policy of reconstruction."

This may be true, as regards Mr. Wailes, but I have never heard him express an opinion on the subject either one way or the other.

You well know that most of my policemen were appointed before it was customary to express opinions on the subject of reconstruction, and it has not fallen in my way to know what are the opinions generally, of the Policemen under me. I do know, however, that Philip H. Rohrer,[11] appointed at your special request, Elisha Owens,[12] and some others of the Police, are warmly the supporters of your policy, and you have not a warmer friend and supporter any where, than Warren G. Berry, the man appointed in place of Stephen C. Wailes!

As for myself, Mr. President, I take this occasion to place upon record the fact, that I have been, for twenty years, and am now, as ardent a friend as you ever had, or have, and your policy of reconstruction has been sustained and defended by me from the start, and will be to the end.

I return, herewith, all the papers sent.

(Signed)   B. B. French   Com. of P. B.

April 22d.   Mr. Wailes, having heard of the letter of Mr. Stanford, and that you had referred it to me, has just called, to assure me, on his honor, that he knew nothing of the sending of that letter. At his earnest request

I have written a note, dictated by him, which he has signed, and I enclose it.[13]

B.B.F.

Copy, DNA-RG42, Lets. Sent, Vol. 16.
1. William H. Stanford (c1811–fl1884) was a merchant tailor in Washington. 1870 Census, D.C., Washington, 5th Ward, 37; Washington, D.C., directories (1860–85).
2. A policeman at the Capitol since 1861, Wailes (c1828–c1885) subsequently worked as a carpenter. Ibid. (1867–87); 1870 Census, D.C., Washington, 5th Ward, 55; U.S. Off. Reg. (1861–65).
3. Hubbell (1824–1890) served in the Ohio legislature before his election to Congress (1865–67) as a Republican. After the Senate rejected his nomination by Johnson to be minister to Portugal, Hubbell resumed his law practice and served one term in the Ohio state senate in 1869. BDAC.
4. Berry (c1827–fl1869) was a carpenter and for a short time a member of the Capitol Police force. 1860 Census, D.C., Washington, 3rd Ward, 65; Washington, D.C., directories (1866–69).
5. John A. J. Creswell, senator from Maryland.
6. Thomas (1799–1876) entered the bar in 1820 and served in the Maryland legislature before his years in Congress (1830–41). Afterwards governor of Maryland, Thomas returned to Congress as a Union Republican in 1861 and served through most of that decade. BDAC.
7. Charles E. Phelps (1833–1908) became a member of the Maryland bar in 1855. Later an officer in the 7th Rgt. Md. Vol., he attained the rank of brevet brigadier general. Afterwards Phelps served in Congress (1865–69). He resumed his law practice in the latter year. BDAC.
8. Thomas (1835–1893) practiced law after entering the bar in 1856 and served as city solicitor of Baltimore (1860–62) and state attorney (1863–65). Elected to one term in Congress (1865–67), he later was collector of the port of Baltimore for a number of years. BDAC.
9. Richard M. Hall (c1834–fl1880) was a real estate broker in Washington, and from 1866 to early 1867 he served as recorder of deeds. 1870 Census, D.C., Washington, 4th Ward, 475; Washington, D.C., directories (1872–81); Wilhelmus B. Bryan, A History of the National Capital (2 vols., Norwood, Mass., 1914–16), 2: 521n.
10. David S. Gooding (1824–fl1895) served in both houses of Indiana's legislature and on several judicial benches. In June 1865 President Johnson offered Gooding the appointment of U.S. marshal for the District of Columbia, a post he held for approximately four years. Gooding lost two bids for Congress (1870, 1872) but remained active in Indiana Democratic politics throughout the rest of his career. Charles W. Taylor, Biographical Sketches and Review of the Bench and Bar of Indiana (Indianapolis, 1895), 507–11.
11. Rohrer, who has not been further identified, apparently served as a policeman for only a short time. Boyd's Washington and Georgetown Directory (1867); U.S. Off. Reg. (1867).
12. Owens (c1805–fl1871) was a member of the Capitol Police force (1865–66) and messenger for the House of Representatives (1870). 1870 Census, D.C., Washington, 5th Ward, 3; Washington, D.C., directories (1869–71); U.S. Off. Reg. (1865).
13. The note has not been located.

From William D. Wallach[1]

Star office, [Washington]   April 21st, 1866

Dr Sir

I beg leave to be permitted to apply to you to appoint my nephew, Richard Wallach,[2] to the naval school from this district, of which he is a resident. He is the son of Mr. C P Wallach,[3] a pay master in the service, whose record at the department is as satisfactory to its heads as that of any other officer. The boy has been carefully educated with the view of putting him in the Navy, and is in all respects correct in his character and deserving: besides being a youth of fine intelligence and much energy.

I have to apologize to you for not visiting you more frequently. I have abstained from doing so because of my reluctance to occupy your time on which there are so many demands, public and private. While so doing I have given you a steady and zealous support through the columns of the *Star*. That it has been an effective one, I know from the fact that whatever eminates from it in your support, is more generally copied by the press of the country, than similar articles published in any other newspaper in the United States. I state these facts that you may know that while refraining from occupying your time with personal calls, I do my whole duty to my old personal relations towards you and to my country in its present condition.

                                                                    W D Wallach

ALS, DLC-JP.
    1. Wallach (1812–1871), brother of Washington's mayor Richard Wallach, became a civil engineer and worked for various railroad companies in Massachusetts and Virginia before moving to Texas. There he published the *Matagorda Gazette* for several years. Subsequently, he returned to the District of Columbia, and in 1852 he and an associate purchased the *Washington Evening Star*. Within a few months Wallach became the paper's sole proprietor and continued as such until 1867. *Washington Evening Star*, Dec. 1, 1871.
    2. Richard Wallach (c1849–fl1902) received an appointment to the Naval Academy and in 1869 was commissioned a second lieutenant in the Marine Corps. He retired in 1899 with the rank of major. 1860 Census, D.C., Washington, 4th Ward, 151; Douglass Zerely, "Old Residences and Family in the City Hall Neighborhood," *Records CHS*, 6 (1903): 108; Callahan, *List of Navy and Marine Corps*, 699.
    3. Cuthbert P. Wallach (c1829–1895) was a deputy with the District of Columbia's marshal's office before entering the Pay Corps of the Navy in 1861. Over the years he received several promotions before finally retiring in 1889. 1860 Census, D.C., Washington, 4th Ward, 151; Callahan, *List of Navy and Marine Corps*, 566; *U.S. Off. Reg.* (1881).

From Colorado Grand Jury

                                                                    [April 23, 1866]

The Grand Jury of the County of Gilpin Territory of Colorado April Term 1866 respectfully Call the attention to the Evidence and statements hereto annexed and request their Careful Consideration—Constituting as they appear to them to do, sufficient reason for the removal from office of Chas F. Holley Associate Justice of the United States Court for the Territory of Colorado.[1]

Upon what appears to them as Convincing and damning Evidence said Grand Jury have at this term presented true bills of indictment against

    Charles F Holly   )   For Adultery
        and   )   and Fornication
    Mary Hooper[2])

The letters hereto annexed are a part of this testimony which have forced the Grand Jury to find the above mentioned bill of indictment.[3]

Being fully impressed with the importance in any land of a wise, virtuous, respected and respectable judiciary; and the still greater importance in a new and growing Territory of Judges beyond Even the suspicion of guilt, having a just and proper pride in and veneration for the Government under which we live, an abiding respect for law and a genuine love of order, they, desire that the judicial representatives of the Government in the Territory of Colorado may be men who by legal knowledge and attainment & by personal probity virtuous living and due respect the laws of the land and to the acknowledged ordinances of God and man shall deserve and receive the respect to which officers holding such responsible position should be Entitled.

And inasmuch as Charles F Holley has forfeited the respect of this Jury and this Community we respectfully request his removal and the appoint of some good man and good lawyer as his successor.[4]

Signed at the Grand Jury room Gilpin County Colorado Territory this twenty third day of April A D 1866.

Geo E. Randolph[5]
Foreman

DS, DNA-RG60, Appt. Files for Judicial Dists., Colorado, Charles F. Holly.

1. Holly (b. 1819), a native of Connecticut, graduated from Kenyon College in Ohio and studied law with Henry Stanbery and Thomas Ewing, Sr. In 1842 he moved to Missouri where he practiced law and served as judge of the probate court, after which he practiced law in the Nebraska Territory (1857–60). Moving to the Colorado Territory in 1860, Holly was a member of the first territorial legislature and first speaker of the territorial house of representatives. In 1862 he recruited a company for the 2nd Colo. Vols., USA, and served as captain of Co. H until his health broke in 1864. He was appointed associate justice of the supreme court of the Colorado Territory in June 1865 and reappointed in January 1866 for a four-year term. Allen A. Bradford, List of C. F. Holly's qualifications, Apr. 1865; Bradford to Johnson, June 5, 1865; Holly to Stanbery, July 30, 1866, Appt. Files for Judicial Dists., Colo., Charles F. Holly, RG60, NA.

2. Mary Hooper, a twenty-five-year-old alleged god-daughter of Holly's, was married to Thomas Hooper, a sixty-year-old physician. Holly to Henry Stanbery, July 30, 1866, ibid.

3. Thomas Hooper alleged that while Holly was boarding with the Hoopers in Central City, Colorado, Holly and Mary Hooper actively engaged in an illicit relationship over a considerable period of time. Two letters were presented as evidence. One purported to be from Mary to Holly, March 20, 1866, in which she said she had settled some unspecific arrangement with Thomas. The other, supposedly from Holly to Dr. Hooper, undated, urged a continuation of the arrangement whereby the three of them lived together with the two men sharing Mary. Holly was married, but, obviously, his wife did not live in Central City. Deposition of Thomas Hooper, ibid.

4. Holly claimed that he was innocent of any wrongdoing. Supposedly Thomas Hooper was jealous of the attention Holly paid to his god-daughter (Hooper's wife). Members of the Colorado bar signed a petition attesting to the excellence of Holly's official character and urged that he be retained in office. When the case came to trial in July 1866, Holly was acquitted because the prosecutor refused to prosecute the case any further. Apparently no witness against Holly appeared. Despite this exoneration, Holly, who had already been removed from office, was not reinstated. Holly to Henry Stanbery, July 30, 1866; Petition from Members of the Colorado Bar, June 15, 1866; Copy of record People v. Chas. F. Holly, July 1866, ibid.; John D.W. Guice, *The Rocky Mountain Bench: The Territorial Supreme Courts of Colorado, Montana, and Wyoming, 1861–1890* (New Haven, 1972), 65–66.

5. Randolph (1840–1911), a resident of Rhode Island at the time of the Civil War, served in the 1st R.I. Lgt. Art. from 1861 to 1864, attaining the rank of captain and being

wounded at Bull Run in July 1861 and Gettysburg in July 1863. Soon after his resignation from the army he moved to Colorado and lived there for the rest of his life. Pension File, Harriet P. Randolph, RG15, NA; CSR, George E. Randolph, RG94, NA.

To Daniel E. Sickles

Washington, D.C., April 23d 1866.

The execution of the sentence in the cases of Stowers, Elisha Byrem, Crawford Keyes, and his son whose name is not known,[1] convicted of the murder of some soldiers[2] of the 1st Maine Batallion at Brown's Ferry Anderson District South Carolina is hereby suspended until further orders. The proceedings will be forwarded to the Judge Advocate General for examination and report to the President.[3]

Acknowledge the receipt and execution of this order.[4]

Andrew Johnson   President U S

Tel, DNA-RG107, Tels. Sent, President, Vol. 3 (1865–68).

1. Francis Gaines Stowers ($c1820$–$fl1870$) of Hart County, Georgia, Elisha W. Byrem (b. $c1838$), and James Crawford Keys ($c1814$–$fl1873$) were farmers. In addition, Stowers was a boatman, licensed distiller, and past state senator; Byrem was an ex-Confederate soldier in the 2nd S.C. Rifles; and Keys was a former railroad contractor and agent to collect the Confederate tax-in-kind. Robert L. Keys ($c1838$–$fl1868$), a soldier in the 4th S.C. Inf., CSA, and Palmetto Sharpshooters, had surrendered at Appomattox. *Charleston Courier*, Jan. 23, 27, 29, Feb. 24, Mar. 5, 12, 20, 1866; 1860 Census, S.C., Anderson, 4th Regiment, 1; (1870), Ga., Hart, Dooley's Dist., 135; CSR, Elisha W. Byram, Robert L. Keys, RG109, NA; Tom C. Wilkinson, abs., *Early Anderson County, South Carolina Newspapers, Marriages and Obituaries, 1841–1882* (Easley, S.C., 1978), 86, 141.

2. Corporal William C. Corbett ($c1843$–1865) and Privates Emery N. Smith ($c1847$–1865) and Mason J. Brown ($c1845$–1865), all of Co. A, who were guards at the ferry on October 8, 1865. CSR, William C. Corbett, Emery N. Smith, and Mason J. Brown, RG94, NA; *Charleston Courier*, July 6, 1866.

3. On May 17, 1866, Joseph Holt reported that he believed the prisoners were guilty and that their sentences, hanging for Stowers and the senior Keys and life imprisonment for the others, should be enforced. Holt to Stanton "for the President," May 17, 1866, Lets. Sent (Record Books), Vol. 15 (M218, Roll 6), RG153, NA.

4. Due to an interruption in the telegraph line, Sickles did not receive Johnson's orders until April 24. The prisoners were held in Castle Pinckney in Charleston Harbor, but Stowers applied for a writ of habeas corpus. Sickles refused, however, and a controversy followed. On July 23, 1866, Johnson commuted the death sentences and ordered all four men to be held at Dry Tortugas; eight days later the place of imprisonment was changed to Fort Delaware. The transfer was delayed for some time; after it was accomplished, the commander of the fort was served with a writ of habeas corpus. This time the War Department allowed it to be obeyed; a hearing was held before Judge Willard Hall; and the prisoners were discharged about November 17, 1866, and dispersed to their homes. Thomas T. Eckert to Johnson, Apr. 24, 1866, Lets. Sent, Mil. Bks., Executive, 57-C, RG107, NA; Sickles to Johnson, Apr. 24, 1866, Johnson Papers, LC; *Charleston Courier*, July 6, 7, 10, 14, 1866; E. D. Townsend to Sickles, July 31, 1866, Tels. Sent, Sec. of War (M473, Roll 91), RG107, NA; *House Reports*, 39 Cong., 2 Sess., No. 23, pp. 3–4 (Ser. 1305); Charles Fairman, *Reconstruction and Reunion, 1864–88, Part One* (New York, 1971) [Vol. 6 of *History of the Supreme Court of the United States*], 149.

From J. Rutherford Worster

Washington   Apr. 24" 1866.

My dear President—

Knowing the multitudinous cares by which you are constantly surrounded, I have conformed to my judgment, more than my inclination, in
not calling upon you more frequently; as you know, I'm a Johnson man,
all over, and need no whitewashing. I have watched with surprise and
deep concern, the wild and bewildering doings of Congress; and have,
with the most unqualified gratification and delight, observed the cool
and unflinching integrity, firmness and determination with which, this
ultra and irrationl legislation has been met by you. You know—that
being so long connected with Congress, I can pretty well comprehend
the pulsations of that *august* body, which of late have been above fever
heat, especially when a veto-message would arrive. I have recently been
travelling considerably, & during my sojourn in N.Y. had ample opportunity to hear the sentiments of the multitudes relative to the policy of the
President and his rupture with Congress; and you could hardly think it
possible, how universal was the expression, *the people will sustain him*; &
the same sentiments were prevalent in Phila. and Baltimore, of course. I
have never heard more general approval and enthusiasm, than was evinced,
on the receipt of your first Veto-message. That veto was seen and read, by
every body,—and was the first intimation, the majority, I might say nineteen twentieths, of the reading-public had, of the monstrous provisions
and consequences, of the Freed-men's-Bureau Bill, had *it* become a Law.
Your skilful dissection of the Hydra, exposing, as you did, its every feature and bearing, was unlooked for by the adroit framers and friends of
the monster;—they expected a simple veto on constitutional grounds,
and that so curtly and insultingly written, as to give impetus to its passage over your head; in this, they were sadly disappointed and chagrined,
as the language of the paper, was as modest and respectful, as the reasoning was cogent and conclusive. The timid frequently ask me the question, do you think the President will be sustained by the people? Of
course you can easily guess my reply, by an overwhelming majority; but
the people must have time for reflection, and their action will astonish
you.

These are almost stereotyped expressions, from every quarter & I can
perceive a visible paralysis in Congress; you have bothered them exceedingly, & what mischief they have now in contemplation, remains to be
seen.

Mr. President—I beg to call your attention to the Riot, in Alexandria,
on Christmas day[1]—as I am certain that the citizens of that town, have
suffered grievously, at the hands of the negroes, and the "Star-chamber"

trials, by the Military-Court-Martial, have been, to a great extent, an ex-parte affair no doubt.

I have had a very ample opportunity of knowing all the circumstances connected with the riot, and the trial of the Prisoners.

On Christmas-eve the negroes commenced parading through the town, with music & firearms, curses and imprecations, making night hidious with the yells, and insulting every respectable citizen they met, in many cases kicking-in the doors of respectable citizens, & smashing their windows, till the small hours of midnight, and many of them continued their revels, throughout the night. They overawed the town completely, for a time, and acted like demons, let loose from the bottomless pits. In the morning they renewed the scene, and as they imbibed, they became more stormy and turbulent, till it culminated in the shooting, &c.

The term, d--d, white livered-sons o' b-c's and such epithets were the watchwords of the negroes, who outnumbered the whites ten to one, on the streets. Men of respectability were taken and thrown into the slave-pen indiscriminately, and kept there for weeks & then permitted to go at large without any explanation or satisfaction whatever.

On the trials none but Radical Lawyers, of the Stevens-Sumner, congressional School, were allowed, in the defence and gentlemen, who were of the most unquestionable character, & cognizant to the whole affair, dare not come forward as witnesses, for fear of being accused of complication & thrown into the Slave-Pen, as others had been, who came forward, as witnesses. The main testimony, on which the convictions were predicated, was that of three notorious, negro strumpets—(this especially applies to the case of the two Mankins.[2] One of the most remarkable features of all is the case of the younger Mankin, who was coolly condemned to death, and the fact carefully concealed from you, no doubt, for fear your clemency might be enlisted, in his behalf, & they would bring the gallows so near, that no time would be afforded his family to solicit your interposition. The young man had a hint of his fate, from a kind-hearted soldier, while some odd-looking lumber was being deposited in the Prison-yard, and in a paroxysm of dispair, he escaped from custody, chuseing to risque a less ignominious death, in his attempt to escape, than that which awaited him if he remained. To you the case is—clear and comment is unnecessary; hanging, under the circumstances, would have been downright murder, to gratify the insatiate appetite of negro-worshipers.

The case of the elder Mankin, is a hard one: he having incur'd the displeasure of the wenches, who testified, & who lived in the neighborhood, & kept a horrible den & he having had them up before the Mayor,[3] on several occasions, and they had as often declared vengeance against him, made this occasion, a favorable one for revenge.

Mankin was a Painter by trade, and has contracted that species of consumption, peculiar to his art. His character was unblemished, as a citizen. He was quiet, never carried firearms nor had them. His door was perforated by 7 bullets,—his windows smashed, and his wife was threatened with instant death, if she dared to shut her door, by a huge bully-brute of a negro, who had kicked it open: so far from participating in the riot, he kept out of the way, and his wife exposed herself to prevent them getting hold of him, as they had expressed a determination to take his life. He being extremely feeble, could not defend himself, and no doubt but his prison-life will soon terminate, in his demise. The others convicted, are unknown to me, but I feel a deep interest in this family and hope you will not lose sight of the great wrong that has been done them.[4] No truer friends of the Executive, & his policy, are found in this Union, than the citizens of Alexa. If you have any enemies there, they are most likely, of those who are employees of the Govt.

I notice the Washington correspondent of the Balto. Sun of this date shadows forth, the Senatorial curtailment of Executive power, as a substitute for Impeachment.[5] Dont you tremble, Mr. President,—for consequences, such as might result from the Fiat, of the Sumner-Club & Co.

Now let me beg of you, not to trouble yourself to read this lengthy letter, but catch enough, to understand, that you have in me, a devoted and untiring friend, through evil and good report;—whose only regret is, that he cant serve you better.

God bless the President and his family.

J. Rutherford Worster

ALS, DLC-JP.

1. For newspaper accounts of the Alexandria riot, see the *Washington Evening Star*, Dec. 27, 28, 30, 1865; *National Intelligencer*, Dec. 27, 1865; *Washington Morning Chronicle*, Dec. 27, 29, 1865.

2. John W. Mankin (*c*1836–*fl*1874) and his younger brother Oscar Mankin (b. *c*1844). The extensive trial of the Mankins and others resulted in convictions and sentences: hanging for Oscar Mankin and fifteen years' imprisonment for John Mankin. 1850 Census, Va., Alexandria, Alexandria, 142; (1860), 41; Washington, D.C., directories (1860–74); Holt to Stanton, Mar. 12, Apr. 17, 1866, Court-Martial Records, MM3654, RG153, NA.

3. Mayor Charles A. Ware received the complaints which John Mankin registered against his neighbors. These women subsequently testified against Mankin in his murder trial. *National Intelligencer*, Feb. 13, 19, 1866.

4. In early April the President ordered the reduction of John Mankin's sentence from fifteen years to five years' imprisonment. In the middle of the month Judge Advocate General Holt informed Johnson that there were no grounds to modify the earlier execution sentencing of Oscar Mankin, but Oscar appears to have successfully escaped from jail. John evidently served a portion of his sentence and was released in late May 1866. See Stanton endorsement, Apr. 3, 1866, Holt to Stanton, Apr. 17, 1866, and Holt to Johnson, Apr. 23, 1866, all in Court-Martial Records, MM3654, RG153, NA. There are a number of other documents regarding the Mankins in ibid.; *New Orleans Picayune*, June 14, 1866.

5. The correspondent discussed amendments to the Post Office bill which would prevent payment of officials whose nomination had not been confirmed by the Senate and predicted the passage of a bill prohibiting removal from office without Senate approval, a prognostication fulfilled by the Tenure of Office Act. *Baltimore Sun*, April 24, 25, 1866.

From Lewis D. Campbell

Hamilton O.   April 25, 1866.

My Dear Sir—

On Sunday last receiving information from home that Kate[1] was quite ill; also that an important business matter required my immediate attention which involved several thousand Dollars, I left Washington unexpectedly and in haste. I told Hanscom[2] to tell you the reason of my leaving *without orders*—also one of your messengers whom I saw at the Depot. Fearing they may have forgotten to tell you I write this. I arrived here much wearied yesterday and found Kate better though quite delicate. My business matters I will have arranged in a day or two, and then if you think I can be of any earthly account to you, telegraph me and I will go on again. Still, as the Senate have had me *on their anvil* pounding away for lo! these four months, I think they will probably botch the job at last, and perhaps spoil some good raw material in their d----d bungling way of doing things.[3]

I have scarcely been here long enough to see how things are working. I already perceive that your most bitter foes are among those who read the "New York Independent" Gen. Howards paper "the Right way"[4] and similar precious sheets of the same stripe that are being freely circulated by your post Masters and Revenue officers all over the Country. The *preachers* are also acting as agents and Colporteurs for these sheets.

I see it announced that since I left Washington you have nominated Gen. S. F. Carey as Collector for the 2nd District.[5] Not knowing who recommended him, permit me to say that I doubt the propriety of it. I am reliably told to-day that since his return from W- he has represented you and your family as drunkards and sots.[6] His brother[7] who lives a few miles below this, and is a very active and talkative man and *spreads* himself at prayer meetings and temperance societies is active *in saying these things and quoting* the General as one who having been at Washington ought to know. I incline to believe you owe it to yourself to revoke his nomination until at least this matter is cleared up. I may learn more about it in a few days.

From reliable information I am satisfied that every Revenue Collector in Ohio except perhaps one or two, are bitterly opposing you. Your Assessors and Post Masters ditto.

You have long since won all the reputation that is desirable as a *forbearing* Chief Magistrate. Your *real* friends ask me imploringly "*when* will he raise his battle axe" and let it fall heavily. I can only answer as echo might "*When?*"

Lewis D Campbell

There will probably be a mass meeting called here early next week to be addressed by myself on the subject of *your policy.*[8]

L.D.C.

ALS, DLC-JP.

1. His daughter, Catherine, who would soon marry Oscar Minor. See Campbell to Johnson, June 22, 1866.

2. Probably Simon P. Hanscom (*c*1821–*fl*1869), a Boston reporter, who was briefly the *New York Herald*'s Washington "bureau chief" before becoming proprietor and editor of the District of Columbia's *National Republican*. 1860 Census, Mass., Suffolk, Boston, 11th Ward, 63; Emmet Crozier, *Yankee Reporters 1861–65* (New York, 1956), 181, 185; Washington, D.C., directories (1862–69); Beale, *Welles Diary*, 2: 653; 3: 325.

3. Appointed by Johnson as minister to Mexico in December 1865, Campbell was finally confirmed by the Senate and commissioned on May 4, 1866. Ser. 6B, Vol. 5, Johnson Papers, LC. See Campbell to Johnson, May 1, 1866.

4. Edited by George Luther Stearns of Boston, the *Right Way* supported radical Republican policies, especially negro suffrage. *DAB*.

5. Recommended by the postmaster general, Rep. Rutherford B. Hayes, and the governors of Ohio, Indiana, and New York, among others, and claiming that Lincoln had promised him the position, Cary was nominated on April 23 and confirmed by the Senate on July 13, 1866. Within six months, however, Cary had been removed and replaced by Stephen J. McGroarty. Ser. 6B, Vol. 4: 256–57, Johnson Papers, LC; Cary to Johnson, Mar. 2, 1866, Appts., Internal Revenue Service, Collector, Ohio, 2nd Dist., Samuel F. Cary, RG56, NA; McGroarty to Johnson, Oct. 16, 1866, ibid., Stephen J. McGroarty, RG56, NA.

6. Cary was a temperance advocate who had written to Johnson on the subject shortly after the latter's unfortunate performance at his vice-presidential inauguration. See Cary to Johnson, Mar. 14, 1865, *Johnson Papers*, 7: 517.

7. Freeman G. Cary (1810–1888) was a college president, agricultural reformer, and devout Presbyterian. Bert S. Bartlow et al., eds., *Centennial History of Butler County, Ohio* (Indianapolis, 1905), 923–24.

8. No account of such a meeting has been found.

From Joseph H. Geiger[1]

Private

Columbus Ohio   April 25th 1866

My Dr Sir

I have delayed writing because I know how much you are beset and annoyed. Since my return to Ohio[2] I have observed the state of public sentiment. The Republican branch of the Union party is decidedly radical and a large majority thereof opposed to you. The "Silver Gray" old Whigs[3] are loyal to your doctrines. The Conservative democrats, comprising a majority of the party sustain your policy and you. The Officers of the Genl. Govt. in all its Depts. are the representatives of radicals. I know of but one leading officer in the Treasury Dept. who sincerely advocates your views and that is B F Martin[4] Collector of the 7th Ohio District. Please send his name soon to the Senate or he will be rejected. A large majority of the people are with you *without doubt*. We have however strong forces to contend against. The socalled Union press has generally turned its batteries on you and your officers are giving you no support. The only way to show your confidence in your views is to employ Agents to strengthen them. No President can maintain himself when his apptees labor for his destruction. Appoint your own friends from the Union party and their rejection by the Senate will re-act. If the Senate keeps Stanbery from the Supreme Bench it will be remembered. I have talked to many of your friends and all are anxious that you should protect yourself by displacing your foes. They say "how shall we fight those who the President nourishes, beg him to clean the ditch.["] I can only say

> "Theres a good time coming boys."
> ["] Wait a *little longer*."

One word in regard to myself. Since my appointment I went to Western Penna. to investigate a fraud and by my report the Govt. ought to be $42000.00 richer.[5] I have reported, and asked to be ordered to Washington to enable me more fully to understand my duties. I have not been ordered there or any where else. I am not allowed to travel only under orders and the game will be to keep me all the time in Columbus. I want authority to go over the State and see the Collectors Assessors &c *at will.* I took the place to render the Govt. and your administration, which I believe is right, a vigorous support. I want the chance to do it and do not wish to draw a salary and render no service. *I should like to come to Washington* and have a full understanding with the revenue department.[6]

Your speech to the soldiers and sailors[7] did good. The doctrines in it strengthened us all. Your policy will be triumphant, all it needs is your friends in the places to back it. Your past history is the best assurance that can be given that there will be no step backward. Gov. Cox is all right and if he has not written you lately will do so soon. He feels modest about writing because he thinks you are so harassed by correspondence.

Jos. H. Geiger

ALS, DNA-RG56, Lets. Recd. from Executive Officers (AB Ser.), President.

1. A former Whig attorney and state senator, Geiger (*c*1818–*fl*1901), who had worked as circuit court clerk and U.S. mail agent in Ohio during the war, had recently been appointed by Secretary McCulloch as a special investigator within the Treasury Department. *Franklin and Pickaway Counties*, 79; *Franklin County at the Beginning of the Twentieth Century* (Columbus, 1901), 274; *OR*, Ser. 2, Vol. 3: 400; Vol. 5: 574; *House Reports*, 40 Cong., 1 Sess., No. 7, "Impeachment Investigation," pt. 2, pp. 264–65 (Ser. 1314).

2. Geiger had been in Washington several weeks earlier, vying for the Mobile collectorship. J. D. Cox to Johnson, Mar. 12, 1866; Lewis D. Campbell to Johnson, Mar. 15, 1866; Johnson Papers, LC.

3. A faction of Conservative Whigs which had favored compromising with the South over the slavery issue during the 1850s. Hendrik Booraem, *The Formation of the Republican Party in New York: Politics and Conscience in the Antebellum North* (New York, 1983), 14.

4. Benjamin Franklin Martin (1819–*fl*1881), a former city clerk of Columbus and prosecuting attorney of Franklin County, had received a temporary appointment as collector in 1865. He was reappointed in May 1866 and served throughout Johnson's administration. Columbus directories (1876–81); *Biographical Encyclopaedia of Ohio of the Nineteenth Century* (Cincinnati, 1876), 206; Ser. 6B, Vol. 4: 256, Johnson Papers, LC; *U.S. Off. Reg.* (1863–69).

5. His report alleging fraud in the Twenty-fourth Internal Revenue District of Pennsylvania, as Geiger recalled during the impeachment investigation months later, was greeted in the Treasury Department "with scoffs and ridicule, more than anything else." *House Reports*, 40 Cong., 1 Sess., No. 7, "Impeachment Investigation," pt. 2, pp. 265, 267–68 (Ser. 1314).

6. On April 30 Johnson referred Geiger's letter to Secretary McCulloch, who was instructed to allow the Ohioan to proceed to Washington. McCulloch replied that Geiger's travel request had been approved several days earlier. McCulloch to Johnson, Apr. 30, 1866, Lets. Recd. from Executive Officers (AB Ser.), President, RG56, NA.

7. See Speech to Soldiers and Sailors, Apr. 18, 1866.

From John Orcutt[1]

private

Washington D.C.   April 25/66

Dear Sir,

I have the honor and the pleasure in accordance with your request to hand you herewith a statement covering the facts you desire. I obtained them from responsible parties and from personal knowledge. Before stating them, allow me to say that after spending four weeks in Virginia— visiting most of the large towns in the State, and extensive intercourse with Southern men of intelligence and controlling influence, I have not a doubt that the people of the South generally are ready and willing to give their *adherence to the organic law of the land as interpretted by the Supreme Court, and administered accordingly*; and, Sir, it gives me much pleasure to add the people of the South so far as my knowledge extends have confidence in the ability and disposition of the president to restore the Union on the basis of the Constitution in all its integrity and provisions.

John Orcutt

I visited Norfolk the day after the celebration of the passage of the Civil Rights Bill in that City, where I made special inquiry in regard to the riot that occurred on the occasion. The facts are in substance as follows:

The Negroes were allowed to carry loaded *arms*—one of whom in a state of intoxication and standing or lying in the street discharged his pistol. The cry was immediately raised the procession had been fired on by citizens, and calling for retaliation. Being told or supposing that the pistol shot came from the house of a respectable white family near by, a rush was at once made upon it, and two or three members of the family killed by being shot by negroes. There was no provocation whatever on the part of the injured family or any other citizen. So I had it from persons who had investigated the matter.[2] The next morning the City was put under martial law, and I left. The following Thursday a like celebration was held at Hampton, which, though it passed off without blood shed at the time, made a very undesirable not to say fearful impression on the vast concourse of colored people present. After marching through the streets, the assembly was addressed by Col. D. B. White[3]—editor of an inflamitory sheet at Norfolk, Genl. Armstrong[4]—Supt. of Freedmen's Bureau, and Genl. Miles[5] commanding the District. In order to hear what might by said, I was present to hear Col. White's speech of near an hour in which he undertook to expound to the listening throng the Civil Rights Bill. He informed them that it was made and passed by their friends— that in his opinion it secured to them the right of suffrage, but if not they were sure to have it—that their former oppressors would oppress them again if they had the power, and that foreseeing this the Bill takes the power to oppress them out of the State Courts and places it where they would be safe—that President Johnson had professed great sympathy for them, but he (White) had never seen him shed tears over it [on] their behalf—that the President had forfeited their confidence and respect—should be forgotten in their families, and would be despised and forgotten by the nation. He expressed regret that he had not time to consider the objections made to the Bill in the president's veto: but said he—they may be all summed up in a sentence—"He (the President) didn't like it."

I have no knowledge of the character of the speakers who followed Col. White, as I was not present and have heard nothing in regard to it.

I have no hesitation in saying that I firmly believe the freedmen's Bureau *on the whole*, is undesirable and mischievous. And I can say the same of the system of teaching the freedmen by northern teachers and organizations.

Some—perhaps most of the teachers employed in the business come with benevolent motives; but some of them are naive and otherwise—especially in the new circumstances in which they are placed. I saw two female teachers who, finding themselves in a false position, had resolved to quit the business and go home. A male teacher—a general superintendent of certain schools said to one of these teachers—"I am going to stay long enough to curse the South." I prefer not to mention his name, though I had conversation with him.

Pardon me, Sir, for repeating what was said to me by Clement C. Clay on his passage up the James river from fortress Monroe on Friday last:

You are aware that one Mosgomery[6] testified that he was the bearer of letters written in Cypher from Mr. Clay in Canada to Jefferson Davis in Richmond.

Mr. Clay affirms that he never wrote a letter in Cypher to any person in his life, and that he was gone from Canada when it was said of him that he sent such communication.

I send you a copy of Col. Whites paper[7] referred to in the above statement.

ALS, DLC-JP.

1. Orcutt (1807–1879) was a traveling secretary for the American Colonization Society. *NUC*; *Boyd's Washington and Georgetown Directory* (1869).

2. According to the report of the board of inquiry that investigated the April 16 riot, the incident began when a black celebrator fired his rifle, which may have been loaded with a blank cartridge. An intoxicated police officer mistakenly attempted to arrest another black man for firing the shot. The suspect resisted while other blacks assisted. The officer was attempting to flee to his nearby home when a neighbor, John Whitehurst, came to his aid, firing several pistol shots into the crowd of pursuers. Whitehurst then retreated to his home and unintentionally shot and killed his stepmother upon entering the house. He then fled from the dwelling and soon after was fatally wounded. Racial disturbances continued throughout the day and night before order was restored through the intercession of Maj. Philip Stanhope, military commander of Norfolk. *House Ex. Docs.*, 39 Cong., 2 Sess., No. 72, pp. 64–66 (Ser. 1293).

3. David B. White (1831–1886), an antebellum Methodist preacher from upstate New York, joined the 81st N.Y. Vols. in the fall of 1861 and remained in the army until August 1865. He then moved his family to Hampton, Virginia, where he pursued farming and established the *True Southerner*, a newspaper that advocated equality for blacks. The publication, which he moved to Norfolk in February 1866, discontinued in June 1866 when a mob of whites broke into the editor's office and destroyed his press. Hunt and Brown, *Brig-*

adier Generals; Gladys A. Blair, "Northerners in the Reconstruction of Hampton, Virginia, 1865–1870," (M.A. thesis, Old Dominion University, 1975), 2, 33, 66–67, 70, 72.

4. Samuel Chapman Armstrong (1839–1893) was attending Williams College when the war began, at which time he received a captain's commission in the 125th N.Y. Rgt. Later he was commissioned as colonel in the 9th Rgt. USCT. Near the end of the war he was breveted brigadier general and then served in the Freedmen's Bureau. Armstrong founded Hampton Institute and devoted the rest of his life to advancing educational opportunities for blacks. *DAB*.

5. Nelson A. Miles.

6. Richard Montgomery had served in a New York volunteer regiment before his discharge for fraud. He then went to Canada, where he associated with Confederate agents. He was one of the first witnesses to testify in the Lincoln assassination conspiracy trial. Nuermberger, *Clays*, 261, 283, 285.

7. Not found.

From Albert F. Pike[1]

Washington, April 25 1866

Hearing that circumstances have arisen which prevents Your Excellency from giving me the Cadet Appointment I had reason to expect,[2] I have the honor to apply for a commission as Second Lieutenant in the Army of the United States.[3]

Albert Field Pike

ALS, DNA-RG94, ACP Branch, File P-2351-CB-1875, Albert F. Pike.

1. Pike (*c*1847–1875) of Massachusetts held an appointment in the Department of Agriculture before entering the army. *Boston Advertiser*, May 24, 1875; Isaac Newton to Edward Schriver, June 7, 1866, ACP Branch, File P-2351-CB-1875, RG94, NA.

2. Because Mary Todd Lincoln, nearly a year earlier, had recommended Pike for appointment to West Point, Pike doubtless "had reason to expect" success with his request. Mary Lincoln to Johnson, May 3, 1865, Cadet Application Papers (M688, Roll 231), RG94, NA.

3. In June Johnson wrote to Inspector General Edward Schriver requesting that Pike be appointed second lieutenant "if there is a vacancy" and if he "can stand an examiation as required by the order." Pike was commissioned a second lieutenant in the 5th Rgt. Art. on July 31, 1866. Johnson to Schriver, ca. June 1866, ACP Branch, File P-2351-CB-1875, RG94, NA; *Washington Evening Star*, Aug. 14, 1866; Ser. 6B, Vol 2: 255, Johnson Papers, LC.

From Joseph W. McCorkle[1]

Virginia City State of Nevada
April 26th 1866.

Sir

It has been made my pleasant and agreeable duty, to transmit to you, the enclosed resolution, unanimously adopted by the Democratic State Central Committee of the State of Nevada, endorsing the principles contained in your Messages, vetoing the Freedmans Bureau and Civil Rights Bils &c &c.[2]

Permit me to embrace this opportunity, of resuming an acquaintance I had the honor to make with you in 1852, when I represented the people of the state of California in Congress;[3] and to assure you personally, of my humble, though cordial support of your Administration, especially as regards your policy of "reconstruction," and the gloriously bold, decided and patriotic stand you have taken for the Constitution and Union.

I have no hesitation in assuring you, that a large majority of the people this state, approve of your policy of restoration, and your administration.

Your messages and speeches have struck deep into the great American heart, in the impulses and instincts of which, you can place implicite confidence and reliance; while educated "loyalty" is always in the market, or controlled by prejudice or hope of plunder. Genl. Jackson had not in the zenith of his greatness, more the confidence of the masses of the people, than you have inspired, by the bold and patriotic stand you have taken, to protect the constitution and the reserved rights of the people, from the mad assaults and usurpations of the mob of tyrants in Congress.

In regard to the local politics of this State, while I am satisfied a large majority of the people are with you; it is by no means certain that we can carry the State this fall, and elect a Congressman and a U.S. Senator who will support you; for the reason that we have a most iniquitous registry law, which requires every voter, not only to register, but to pay a poll tax of *four dollars* before he can vote. In this, as in all mining countries, the mass of the people are poor, and we have hundreds of voters who can not afford to pay the four dollars. Last year, out of a voting population of fifteen thousand, only five thousand eight hundred votes were registered. Your enemies in this State, the friends of Stewart and Nye[4] can command money, and if we are defeated in this state, it will be for the want of funds, with which to register and pay the poll tax of our friends and not from want of honest effort.

We will do all that we can to secure success, and sustain you.

I pray that God may sustain you, and that you may be able to crush out, the mad schemes of a tyranical majority in Congress—"One tyrant is dangerous to Liberty; but a multitude of Tyrants is certain death."

Jos. W. McCorkle, Esqr.

ALS, DLC-JP.

1. McCorkle (1819–1884), an Ohio-born lawyer, moved in 1850 to California where he served in the state assembly and as a judge. In 1860 he moved to Virginia City, Nevada, to practice law. Ten years later he moved his legal practice to Washington, D.C. *BDAC*.

2. The resolution, passed on April 21, also supported the admission to Congress of representatives from the former Confederate states.

3. McCorkle served only one term (1851–53). *BDAC*.

4. Nevada's Republican senators William M. Stewart and James W. Nye.

From Humphrey Marshall[1]

(Confidential)

New Orleans   26 April 1866

Dear Sir.

The Enclosed Statement is from a gentleman[2] whose acquaintance I made at Abingdon Va. where he called on me during the war. He was then a Colonel in the C.S. Army, or had authority to raise a regiment and was engaged in the work. I know that, while so engaged, he was captured, and served through a long imprisonment at Johnson's Island, and was only exchanged a short time before the fall of Richmond. He is now in one of the largest commercial houses of New Orleans. I cannot doubt the truth of the statement; for I can conceive of no interest that Greenwood could have to lie in the matter, even were he capable of uttering falsehoods. He does not feel that Davis treated him well or properly during the struggle, I happen to have known long since. He communicated the facts to me only to day, and *I requested him* to let me reduce them to writing and to place them before you privately and confidentially; for I thought *you ought to know it.* I know, were I in your place and such facts were connected with me or a crisis of my life and he who had so served me was situated as Davis is, I should like to know the facts.[3] I write this, then, more in kindness to you than to your state-prisoner. It is curious as a romance. I am desired by Mr. Greenwood to request that you will regard the communication as confidential. He seems to shrink from all appearance of officiousness—and says he would not have this get to the newspapers for any money.

I hope, Sir, you will appreciate my own motive in sending you this paper.

                                                    Humphrey Marshall

ALS, DLC-JP.
    1. Marshall, a Kentuckian who had served as a Confederate brigadier general and, from June 1864 to April 1865, as a member of the Confederate House of Representatives, was himself still on parole for these offenses. He was not pardoned until October 1, 1866. Wakelyn, *BDC*, 311–12; Amnesty Papers (M1003, Roll 26), Ky., Humphrey Marshall, RG94, NA.
    2. Alexander G. Greenwood (*c*1835–*fl*1873), a native of Virginia, was a cotton factor and commission merchant in New Orleans after the war. 1870 Census, La., Orleans, New Orleans, 2nd Ward, 15; New Orleans directories (1861–73).
    3. In the enclosed statement Greenwood related that in 1861, as a Confederate officer in Bristol, Tennessee, he learned of a conspiracy to waylay Johnson and harm him as his train passed through Bristol en route from Washington. He "was warned by Jefferson Davis President C.S.A. to move the Cars by Bristol so as to avoid the danger that threatened the life of Mr. Johnson." Greenwood obeyed Davis's order and sent the train directly on to Jonesborough. Thus he credited Jefferson Davis with saving Johnson's life.

From J. Sterling Morton[1]

                                    Omaha City Nebraska   April 26th 1866
Sir
    Permit me to call your attention to the enclosed Platforms of the two parties in Nebraska together with the nominees that stand upon them respectively.[2] It gives me great pleasure to inform your Excellency that the masses of the People are flocking to our standard. The principal opposition to our Platform and ticket in Nebraska comes from federal officials. The Governor of this territory, Alvin Saunders,[3] is a Nephew of

Secretary Harlan[4] and a candidate for the Senate under the State Constitution, if the same be adopted. As a Sumner-ite Saunders is doing us much harm and if he should succeed would be a detriment to the Country by going against your policies of reconstruction.

We hope to carry the Territory, to organize the new State and to Stand our people squarely and fairly upon your platform by a handsome majority.[5]

Wm. A. Richardson of Illinois, Senator Saulsbury of Del, Voorhees of Ind and Eldridge of Wisconsin[6] can inform you upon the *personel* of a part of the Democratic ticket.

J. Sterling Morton   Dem Candidate for Governor

ALS, DLC-JP.
1. New York-born Morton (1832–1902) grew up in Michigan and moved in 1854 to Nebraska where he engaged in newspaper editing and territorial politics, serving in the legislature and as territorial secretary (1858–61). A Democrat, Morton was a perennial and unsuccessful candidate for office. He made his mark as an agriculturalist, serving as secretary of agriculture during Cleveland's second term. *DAB*.
2. Not found. The platforms and nominees can be found in the *Omaha Herald*, Apr. 20, 27, May 4, 1866.
3. Born in Kentucky and raised in Illinois, Saunders (1817–1899) moved to Iowa in 1836. There he served as postmaster of Mount Pleasant and later was elected to the Iowa state senate. Lincoln appointed him territorial governor in March 1861, a position he retained until statehood. Saunders became an Omaha businessman involved in banking, real estate, and public utilities, and served a term in the U.S. Senate (1877–83). McMullin and Walker, *Territorial Governors*, 228–30.
4. Secretary of the Interior James Harlan.
5. In contrast to Morton's Democratic hopes, the Republicans narrowly won the June 2, 1866, election. David Butler defeated Morton for governor by 145 votes. James C. Olson, *History of Nebraska* (Lincoln, 1955), 127, 131. See also James M. Woolworth to Johnson, July 30, 1866.
6. Willard Saulsbury, Daniel W. Voorhees, and Charles A. Eldredge. Vermont-born Eldredge (1820–1896) moved to Wisconsin in 1848 and practiced law. At the conclusion of his terms in the U.S. House (1863–75) he resumed his law practice. All of the named individuals were Democrats. *BDAC*.

To William H. Snyder[1]

Washington, D.C.   April 26' 1866.

Sir:

I duly received, by Express, your letter of the 17th instant, and also a volume entitled "Our Living Representative Men," which formerly belonged to my library at Greenville, Tennessee.[2] I beg now to return the volume, with the request that you will accept it as an evidence of my appreciation of the kind feeling which induced you to restore it to my possession.[3]

A J

Tel, DLC-JP.
1. Snyder (b. c1836), a clerk and former private, 2nd Va. Cav., CSA, had been detailed as a courier and ordnance sergeant at General Longstreet's headquarters. CSR, William H. Snyder, RG109, NA.

2. Snyder returned the book after having received it under unknown circumstances from "some one who was with the Army of Genl. Longstreet when it marched through 'East Tenn' during the Winter of -63." Snyder to Johnson, Apr. 17, 1866, Johnson Papers, LC.

3. The book, an 1860 publication written by John Savage, and the original copy of Johnson's letter to Snyder were offered for sale in 1982.

From William H. Allen[1]

Washington, D.C.   April 27 1866

Sir

In accordance with youre Desire to Senator McDougall,[2] I Reduced To writeing the Subject matter, To which I Aluded in my note of Sunday Last, but Thus far not haveing reported The matter To you I deem it proper To do So without Delay.

The Information I have recived and of which Their Can be no Doubt, is That a most Dangereous Conspiriacey is Existing in this City, To Deprive you Sir of youre Personal Liberty, under assumed Charges of youre Corsepondeance with many Prominent Rebels of North Carolina and Other Southern States.

In One of those Letters writen Three days after the Death of Mr Lincoln you are made To Say, "I will Soon have Things my Own Way. You Shall have all you want as before The War, and back in the Union as you ware." This with Other Expressions in other Letters theay Count upon as Certain To Secure a Conviction before the People.

Theay have also arranged To Surround youre House with Guards Dureing The Debate on the Bill, if you attempt To arrest Them as Theay belive you will. Theay have also Provided a force at hand East of the Captiol, To Protect Them in Debate if required. This arrangement is made by Mr Stanton with the approval of "Genl Grant" who has attended one of the *Secreet* Meetings Nightley heald.

The Letters in question, ware obtained by the Orders of Mr Stanton, To L. C. Baker and his assistants who went South and returned with Eight or Ten in all. Capt McArthur[3] Editor of the Troy whig is now here. Can give The Names of Parties, Places of Meeting, and Such Matters as has Transpired Scince Friday Last.

Wm. H. Allen
Late Col 1ist & 145th regts   New York Volunteers.

ALS, DLC-JP.

1. A former bridge constructor and civil engineer, Allen (c1823–fl1868), who enjoyed something of a checkered career during the Civil War, was evidently in Washington at this time in an effort to induce Congress to pay him for expenses incurred in raising troops in New York. He had been tried by a court-martial in 1861 and dismissed as colonel of the 1st N.Y. Inf., and had never mustered into the 145th N.Y. Inf. Secretary Stanton cautioned Johnson against any favorable action in Allen's case. A year earlier, Allen had gained some notoriety in an alleged attempt to raise volunteers to assist Gen. Jésus González Ortega of Mexico. Brooklyn directories (1861–68); Charles A. Smart, *Viva Juarez!: A Biography*

(Philadelphia, 1963), 352; Robert R. Miller, "Gaspar Sánchez Ochoa: A Mexican Secret Agent in the U.S.," *The Historian*, 23 (1961): 323–25; *Senate Journal*, 39 Cong., 1 Sess., p. 335 (Ser. 1236); CSR, William H. Allen, RG94, NA; Allen to Abraham Lincoln, Apr. 25, 1862, Lincoln Papers, LC; Stanton to Johnson, June 4, 1866, Lets. Sent, Mil. Bks., Executive, 57-C, RG107, NA.
2. James A. McDougall of California.
3. Charles L. MacArthur (1824–*fl*1897) had a long career in newspaper work, including Detroit and Milwaukee as well as New York papers before the Civil War. After a variety of service and experiences in the war, he returned to Troy where, in 1864, he established the *Troy News*. In 1866 he served briefly as editor of the *Troy Whig*. Long active in politics, MacArthur switched from the Democratic to the Republican party with the election of Lincoln. In the 1880s he served in the New York state senate. George B. Anderson, *Landmarks of Rensselaer County, New York* (Syracuse, 1897), 728–29; Nathaniel B. Sylvester, *History of Rensselaer County, New York* (Philadelphia, 1880), 151.

From Aaron A. Bradley

Washington   April 27th 1866

Will the President please let me *Return Hone* to Savannah Ga. I have been away by your order 9 Weeks, and my business brought me in $58 per week and when I attended to law cases one hundred dollars, & I am here without a $1. I have commited no Offence against the laws of the United States nor the State of Georgia for which I could be tried and convicted.

On the 5th day of December last I call a public meeting of all the Citizens without distinction of color or race, to Sign a Petition to Congress for Equal rights before the law: towit The Elective Franchise, Honesteads in lands belonging to the United States, the Right to Testify in State courts, and to strike out the word White from the Naturalization laws. And this I suposed we had the legal right to do, under the U S Con Art 1 of the amendment: "Congress shall make no law abridging the freedom of Speech or of the Press; or the right of the People peaceably to assemble, and to Petition the Government for a redress of grievance. And congress alone shall have the Power to make all laws to regulate every Department of the Government or Officer thereof." Art 1 Sec 8 at the end.

The State of Georgia was under Civil and not Military Government Dec 5th 1865 and the Writ of *habeas corpus* had nothing to do with the matter as the law read that the President may in his judgment *suspend* the Writ of Habeas Corpus in any *case* DURING the *Present Rellian* act passed in Mark 3 1863 and not after it had been declared that it had ended: then it was a general *Suspention* but each case had to be named.

I was charge and convicted of and with advising and counselling the Loyal Negros to do unlawful acts which were never done, or attempted to be done as it appears in the Complaint, Therefore found guilty as accesory before the Fact and the *fact never took place*.

I would call your Excellency's attention to the Truth of the *Fact*; that a

Parole does not exist under the laws of the United Stats after a *Verdict* and a prejudgment.

If the Convict is relieced he can not be legally retaken. Therefore I submit to your Excellency that Ordering me away from Savannah was a Retaking and Void in law.[1]

Aaron A Bradley

ALS, DNA-RG94, Amnesty Papers (M1003, Roll 16), Ga., Aaron A. Bradley.
    1. For the outcome of Bradley's appeal, see Bradley to Johnson, Dec. 7, 1865, *Johnson Papers*, 9: 491n.

From John W. Wright

Private

Washington, April 27" 1866

Dear Sir,

I am very anxious to go home. For an act of yours in removing an able-bodied rich man from the Post office in my town and appointing the widow of a brave soldier in his place,[1] I am published as a "copperhead" and rebel. This is more than I can suffer; I, who was a John Brown democrat, and had my children[2] in the army; who spent my time in visiting the sick soldiers; to be thus slandered,—I feel that I must go and take the stump and defend my character.

All that detains me is my case of the "Indian bounty."[3] I know it is right and I have conversed with several eminent men and they all say it is legally and morally right. Do not compel me to go to Congress with it; to get justice there, for myself or for a client, is impossible; if you think my case is just, send a note to Maj: Genl. Brice[4] and he will pay it. I will call tomorrow and see you.

The U.S. Court in Indiana, is now in session and I am anxious to go there and thence to Northern Indiana, and as soon as I open "fire in the rear" you will find some distinguished Indiana Congressman anxious to adjourn and go home—which I believe would be a blessing to the country.

John W Wright

ALS, DLC-JP.
    1. Mrs. Elizabeth P. Brown (c1830–*fl*1874), a mother of six and the widow of Lt. Col. William L. Brown (1817–1862) who had been killed during the second battle at Manassas, was commissioned postmaster of Logansport, Indiana, on April 26, in place of incumbent William Wilson (1818–1889), a former pork packer whom Lincoln had appointed in 1861. 1860 Census, Ind., Cass, Eel Twp., Logansport, S & E of Broadway St., 28; Thomas B. Helm, ed., *History of Cass County, Indiana, from the Earliest Time to the Present* (Chicago, 1886), 705–6; Jehu Z. Powell, ed., *History of Cass County, Indiana* (2 vols., Chicago, 1913), 1: 385, 536; 2: 1204; Ser. 6B, Vol. 4: 285, Johnson Papers, LC.
    2. Probably Irwin B. Wright (c1841–1905), first lieutenant, 11th U.S. Inf., who had been brevetted a captain for gallantry at Gettysburg, and John Brown Wright (c1838–*fl*1871). Both were lawyers and lived in Washington, D.C., immediately after the war. By

the early 1870s, however, the former had set up practice in Cincinnati. 1860 Census, Ind., Cass, Eel Twp., Logansport, S & E of Broadway St., 23; Washington, D.C., directories (1866–68); Cincinnati directories (1873–75); *House Reports*, 42 Cong., 2 Sess., No. 96, p. 17 (Ser. 1543); Powell, *Army List*, 691; Pension Records, Irvin B. Wright, RG15, NA.

3. For some time Wright had been serving as an attorney on behalf of Cherokee, Creek, Seminole, and other members of the three Kansas Indian Home Guard units who sought back pay, pensions, and bounties for their services rendered during the war. On June 18 Congress authorized the payment of a bounty of $100 and on July 11 Wright was appointed as a claims agent by the secretary of the interior. By late 1871 allegations of fraud and embezzlement prompted a congressional and criminal investigation into Wright's agency, eventually resulting in his conviction and prison term. *House Reports*, 42 Cong., 2 Sess., No. 96, pp. 1–5 (Ser. 1543); *Congressional Globe*, 39 Cong., 1 Sess., Appendix, 429; Bailey, *Indian Territory*, 86–87.

4. Benjamin W. Brice (1806–1892), an 1829 graduate of West Point, had a long career in the army interspersed with a lengthy stint as a lawyer. He served as paymaster general from 1866 until his retirement from the regular army in 1872. Hunt and Brown, *Brigadier Generals*; Powell, *Army List*, 210.

From Bland Ballard

Louisville, Ky, Apr. 28th 1866.

Dear sir,

Accompanying this communication you will find a transcript of the record of certain proceedings which have been had before the circuit court of the United States for this circuit.

You will see that, on the petition of Isham Henderson,[1] showing that he is imprisoned by Brevt. Maj. Gen. Jeff. C. Davis and Lieut Col. W. H. Coyle[2] under color of authority of the United States, and that he is in no wise subject to military jurisdiction—the court issued a writ of *habeas corpus* directed to said Davis & Coyle requiring them to bring said Henderson before the court with the cause of his detention and then to abide by such order as should be made in the premises.

You will also see that, Gen. Davis declined to obey the writ, and simply certified to the court under oath that Henderson was detained by him as a prisoner, under authority of the President of the United States as would appear by certain orders of Maj. Gen. Thomas, copies of which orders accompany the certificate.[3]

Neither the certificate nor the orders of Gen. Thomas show any cause for the arrest or detention of Henderson, nor that he is guilty of any offence subject to military jurisdiction—nor, indeed, that, he is guilty of any offence whatever. Gen Davis assumes to decide that the writ of *habeas corpus*, which was suspended by virtue of the Act of Congress of March 3d 1863 and the President's proclamation of 15th Sept 1863, still remains suspended in this state notwithstanding your proclamation of the 2d April 1866—nay more, he undertakes to decide for himself and in opposition to the opinion of the court, that the writ is yet suspended, and, when the court adjugded his return insufficient, that he was in contempt and ordered his arrest, he resisted by force the arrest and still resists it with such force that it cannot be made.

From the foregoing statement your excellency will see that, the question is not whether Henderson is or is not subject to military jurisdiction, is or is not probably guilty of any offence for which he may be tried before a Court Martial, or, is or is not guilty of an offence for which he is subject to be tried by any court. The simple question is, does the writ of *habeas corpus* remain suspended in this District? Or, rather, must not the opinion and decision of the court respecting this matter be respected and obeyed by all persons whether soldiers or citizens?

If Gen Davis, instead of assuming that the writ of *habeas corpus* remains suspended, had, in obedience to the command of the writ, made a return showing that the prisoner is subject to military jurisdiction, that he is subject under the rules & articles of war to be tried by a court martial and that he was arrested & is held for trial before such court, the circuit court would undoubtedly have adjudged such a return sufficient and remanded the prisoner. On the other hand, if a return had been made showing that Henderson is held for trial before a Court Martial, but also showing he is not a prisoner, who, in the opinion of the court is subject to be tried by a military court, you know Sir, the decision must have been that the prisoner be eithe[r] charged or held for trial before a civil court accordingly as the evidence offered might have established his probable innocence or guilt. But, I could not hold the return, (in the nature of a certificate) which was made, sufficient without holding that insurrection still continues—contrary to the knowledge of all mankind and to your formal declaration of April 2d 1866. If the effect of this proclamation be not to restore the right of the citizen to the writ of *habeas corpus* and to resort to the civil courts for protection it is impossible to conceive what its effect is, and, if any citizen or soldier can disregard with impunity the judgement of the courts at this time of peace then have we a Government not of law but of arbitrary power. If the courts are not to espound the laws of the land and their exposition be not submitted to or enforced then are all the safeguards which the constitution throws around the citizen for the protection of his life and liberty a delusion, then have we no constitutional government at all.

The Marshal[4] has undoubtedly, under well known laws, "power to command, all necessary assistance for the execution of the writs and orders in his hands," but, as Gen. Davis has announced his purpose to resist the Marshal with the military forces under his command, and as such a contest would be not only deplorable but probably fruitless in exacting obedience, I have advised the Marshal not to push matters to this extreme issue for the present. In adopting this course I have been influenced not alone by the considerations above mentioned, but also by the consideration that Gen Davis and the forces under his command, whom I am obliged to denominate "*insurgents*" assume to act under your authority, and will, I suppose, at once, submit to your directions. Relying with confidence that your Excellency fully appreciates your constitutional obligation to "take care that the laws be faithfully executed" and that Gen Davis erroneously assumes to act under your authority, I shall certainly expect that he and Gen Thomas, likewise, be promptly directed to submit to the orders of the court.[5]

Bland Ballard

ALS, DNA-RG94, Lets. Recd. (Main Ser.), File A-392-1866 (M619, Roll 446).

1. Henderson (c1824–1876) was co-owner of the *Louisville Journal* with George D. Prentice until he bought out Prentice's interest in the paper. Henderson invested in the Citizens Passenger Railway Company and the Louisville and Portland Railroad Company. During the war years he had contracted with the U.S. Army to supply mules and other materials. The alleged failure to fulfill the terms of his 1864 contract was the issue that brought Henderson before the courts in 1866. *Louisville Courier-Journal*, Nov. 15, 1876; J. Stoddard Johnston, ed., *Memorial History of Louisville: From Its First Settlement to the Year 1896* (2 vols., Chicago, 1896), 1: 327, 2: 65; *Louisville Journal*, Apr. 30, May 2, 8, 1866; *National Intelligencer*, May 4, 1866.

2. William H. Coyl (c1841–1866), formerly of Decorah, Iowa, served as major and lieutenant colonel, 9th Iowa Inf., and major and judge advocate of volunteers. *American Annual Cyclopaedia* (1866), 581; *The History of Dubuque County, Iowa* (Chicago, 1880), 235; Heitman, *Register*, 1: 332.

3. By the time Ballard wrote his letter to Johnson, Henderson had already been whisked away to Nashville to be tried there before a court-martial. At this point President Johnson had concurred with the decision to try Henderson before a military rather than civilian tribunal. *Louisville Journal*, Apr. 27, May 9, 1866; *National Intelligencer*, Apr. 28, 30, 1866; Stanton to George H. Thomas, Apr. 27, 1866, Stanton to George D. Prentice, Apr. 27, 1866, Tels. Sent, Sec. of War (M473, Roll 90), RG107, NA; Prentice to Johnson, Apr. 25, 1866, Tels. Recd., President, Vol. 5 (1866–67), RG107, NA.

4. William A. Merriwether (1825–*fl*1901), a Mexican War veteran and real estate agent, was successively deputy U.S. marshal, U.S. marshal, and clerk of the U.S. Court, District of Kentucky. Perrin et al., *Kentucky*, Edition 8A: 847; Louisville directories (1865–1901).

5. In mid-May Johnson directed General Davis and Colonel Coyl to amend their earlier responses to the writ of habeas corpus request and by early June General Thomas ordered the temporary suspension of the court-martial proceedings and the transfer of Henderson to Louisville to appear before Judge Ballard. Eventually Ballard ruled that Henderson was entitled to a civilian court trial, that the court-martial was without jurisdiction, and that Henderson should be discharged. *Louisville Journal*, June 6, 9, 21, 1866; *Louisville Courier*, June 7, 22, 1866.

From William Murphy[1]

Salisbury North Carolina
April 28th 1866

I take the liberty of addressing your Excellency upon the subject of my pardon, an application for which was forwarded by me to Governor Holden early last fall. I am not able to state what action, if any, Governor Holden took in the case, but as I have not heard from it, I am becoming very solicitous about the matter.[2] The only ground upon which I am excluded from the General Amnesty Proclamation of your Excellency issued on the 29th of May 1865 is the $20,000 exception. I was always opposed to secession, I was opposed to the war of rebelion, I was opposed to the Confederate Government, and for these reasons I was badly used by the Confederate authorities who impressed my property for their use without compensating me. Such was the State of affairs when the Federal forces reached here, and they at once seized my property because it had been in the use of the Confederates, and they have continued to use it from their arrival here until the present time and they are still using it, to my great injury, under the plea that they have a right to use any buildings or property formerly used by the rebels, and for this long detention and use of my property I have never been paid a dollar, and I am told, when I apply for reasonable compensation, that I am an unpardoned rebel and can not get any thing. These are the hardships I am subjected to for being a union man while the most obdurate rebels here have not only received their pardons but have never been disturbed in the possession of their property, the property of some of the original secessionists being now rented by government officers at full prices and paid for regularly,—and the excuse given is that my property was used by the Confederate Government, and the property rented from the secessionists was not.

This is all true, but I am not to blame for it, for my property was seized by the Confederate Government because I was a Union man. This may be just, but I can not so understand it, for it is paying a high premium for disloyalty.

I feel that I have no recourse but to your Excellency to whom as the head of the Nation and the Father of the people I have a right to come. My complaint is not a frivolous one, for my condition is a grievous one. If there is any reason why my pardon should not be granted, I am not aware of it. No man will say that I have not been a union man during all the hardships and trials of the last six years, and to have been a Union man here during the war was, as your Excellency well knows, something more than being a Union man in a place of safety.

With these views I respectfully submit my case to your Excellency's discretion, confidently hoping that I will receive my pardon and trusting that if any relief can be extended to me for the past, present or future occupation of my property by the Federal authorities it will be done.[3]

William, Murphy,

LS, NcD-Benjamin Sherwood Hedrick Papers.

1. Murphy (b. c1812) was a merchant and banker. 1850 Census, N.C., Rowan, Salisbury, 290; James S. Brawley, *The Rowan Story, 1753–1953* (Salisbury, 1953), 274.

2. On October 28, 1865, Governor Holden favorably endorsed Murphy's application and on November 15 the President ordered a pardon which apparently did not reach Murphy. Amnesty Papers (M1003, Roll 41), N.C., William Murphy, RG94, NA; *House Ex. Docs.*, 40 Cong., 1 Sess., No. 32, p. 29 (Ser. 1311).

3. No other pardon date has been found. In mid-May Governor Worth informed Murphy that his pardon had been located and was being forwarded to him. Worth to Murphy, May 16, 1866, J. G. deRoulhac Hamilton, ed., *The Correspondence of Jonathan Worth* (2 vols., Raleigh, 1909), 1: 587.

From J. J. Papy[1]

San Francisco Cal   April 28th 1866

Sir:

I address this note to you at the solicitation of many prominent citizens of this state, friendly to your administration.

I was solicited to write because from the Commencement I took decided stand against the rebellion: and since your Presidency, have advocated, and made converts to, all your acts. I have written to Senator McDougal[2] on this subject, and to him I refer for my political and social status. If there were any old representatives from Florida, I would refer to them also.

The prupose of this note is to invite your attention to the condition of the Pacific Coast—especially California.

With a few, if any, exceptions, all the office holders are violently opposed to your reconstruction policy, and also denounce your vetoes. We wish to carry this state in your favor. With the entire federal patronage against you, we apprehend defeat unless a division can be made in the opposition ranks. Our radical Legislature were so fearful of defeat, that they postponed our municipal election until next September— apprehensive that you would be endorsed, and influence, thereby, exercised on the eastern side of the Rocky Mountains.

Give us Somebody, any body but a radical congress supporting, anti Johnson man. Two or three changes will accomplish much. It will unite our people in a solid body, and they will contest with confidence.

We tried to get some of the Office holders with large patronage to unite with us in our great mass meeting indorsing your first veto and policy, but they declined to lend us their aid or countenance. They will not cooperate with us in our organization of Johnson Clubs.

I do not refer to the balance of our delegation in congress[3] for my Union proclivities, because they are radicals. I have no political simpathy with them other than their desire to maintain, intact, the integrity of the Union.

You will please pardon me for thus writing you; but it is done at the urgent solicitation of many of your supporters in this state, because my political status is not liable to impeachment by any of our delegation.

J. J. Papy

ALS, DLC-JP.

1. Papy (fl1868) was a lawyer in San Francisco about 1856–68. San Francisco directories (1856–68).

2. James A. McDougall of California.

3. Senator John Conness and Representatives John Bidwell, William Higby, and Donald C. McRuer.

From David G. Rose[1]

Indianapolis   April 29th 66

Since I last wrote you[2] I have been into Colfax—the 9th District. There the people read only, the Chicago Tribune, and have for the last twelve years been under the teaching of the present member of congress.[3] Of course the radical element is in the ascendency. Yet I was delighted to meet many whose sympathy was decidedly with you. But they knew not how, best, to develope it. I showed them! Clubs will be formed[4] and independent tickets put in the field when the latter is deemed best. On the whole matters look more cheering. In regard to the appointments to be made in that part of the state I would like to suggest when *the time comes*, that PROPER ones should be made no one knows better than you.

In this connection permit me to say that the appointment of Henry Nelson[5] as disbursing agent for the Govt. improvements here, was not the best. Not that he is not a good man and every way fit. But because at that *point* your enemies make their chief attack. Indeed there are many who have abandoned all other objections and charge only that you have left the Union party. This appointment, such men regard as a God-send. My suggistions have been to build up inside of the Union organization (*cementing close*) and claim you as the "Head Centre," and never yield that point—this will not drive the Democrats fom us, and will tie many weak brothers to us. We need more labourers in the vineyard. We need more display of Executive *power*. The best, shall be done with the means we have to work with. I should like orders from HeadQuarters. There is too much Federal power wielded in this state against you. This should be *changed but with care*.

I have written to friends in different parts of the state to get themselves "in shape" to attend a call of your friends to meet on the 30th of May or about that time.[6] We shall need some help from the centre, (where I presume there is a reserve) for that occasion, about two good speakers. With the best wishes for your triumph, in your patriotic efforts, and a continuance in good health. . . .

D. G. Rose

ALS, DLC-JP.

1. A former U.S. marshal and commander of the 54th Ind. Inf., Rose (c1818–fl1869) was appointed on August 20, 1866, as postmaster of Indianapolis and confirmed by the Senate in February 1867. 1860 Census, Ind., LaPorte, LaPorte, 70; *U.S. Off. Reg.* (1861–63); Ser. 6B, Vol. 3: 553, Vol. 4: 286, Johnson Papers, LC; Indianapolis directories (1865–69); Jacob P. Dunn, *Indiana and Indianans: A History of Aboriginal and Territorial Indiana and the Century of Statehood* (5 vols., Chicago, 1919), 2: 615; W. G. Moore to Rose, Oct. 1, 1866, Tels. Sent, President, Vol. 3 (1865–68), RG107, NA.

2. No prior correspondence from Rose to Johnson has been located. At the close of 1865, however, Johnson did acknowledge receipt of Rose's letter of December 27. Johnson to Rose, Dec. 30, 1865, Johnson Papers, LC.

3. Schuyler Colfax.

4. On May 1 Rose reportedly began organizing a Johnson Club of Indianapolis, with Martin Igoe serving as secretary. *Louisville Journal*, May 3, 1866.

5. Nelson (*c*1812–*fl*1872), who had served as sheriff of the Indiana Supreme Court for several years, recently had been appointed by Secretary McCulloch to supervise and complete the furnishing of the U.S. Court House and Post Office at Indianapolis. It is unclear whether he kept the appointment. 1870 Census, Ind., Marion, Indianapolis, 3rd Ward, 145; Indianapolis directories (1857–72); *Chicago Tribune*, Apr. 27, May 2, 1866.

6. A pro-Johnson meeting did take place in Indianapolis at the end of May, but it was in preparation for a "Johnson State Convention" held in mid-July. At the latter meeting Rose was appointed a state-at-large delegate to the forthcoming National Union Convention at Philadelphia. *Chicago Tribune*, May 30, 31, July 19, 20, 1866; David S. Gooding to Johnson, July 19, 1866, Johnson Papers, LC.

May 1866

From Lewis D. Campbell

(*Private*)

Hamilton, O.   May 1st, 1866.

Dear Sir—

I have this moment received a letter from a friend in Washington who recently had a conversation with Senator Harris about my nomination &c. It was upon his motion that it was recommitted to the Committee on Foreign Affairs. My friend writes me that Senator H. told him the main objection to me in the Senate was that I had been "*instrumental in fomenting the misunderstanding between the President and Congress.*" Now, I think the honorable Senator does me too much honor. That I have concurred in your policy since you assumed the Presidential chair is most true, and known to all men with whom I have talked; but he does not know you as well as I do, or he would not credit me with having any influence in swerving you from your fixed convictions of duty. That I have sometimes, in my warmth, said that certain Radicals in Congress were acting like d---d fools, is quite true,[1] and, confirmation or no confirmation, I still stick to it. Ere many months the people will *confirm* my declaration at the ballot-box. I mention the fact as to Senator Harris, so that, if you see fit, you can avail yourself of an early opportunity to disabuse his mind on this point. This impression doubtless grows out of that ever-memorable interview with Senator Sumner in which you sunk your gaffs into his flanks with some severity.[2] Little did I suppose that in occasionally and most innocently putting in my little oar on that interesting occasion, I was incurring the eternal displeasure of that Senator who was shedding his crocodile tears over the poor freedmen of *Alabawma*! Little did I suppose, when, years ago, I stripped off and washed the blood out of his eyes, ears and nose, and brought him to consciousness, on the occasion of the little hammering that Brooks gave him,[3] that I was restoring to life one who would use his Senatorial power, in *Secret Session* to degrade me and humiliate my family. Be it so. The next time he is pounded to death he may stay dead, and d---d too, before the stains of his cold blood shall be on my hands again.

The Senate may refuse me a permit to hunt up our Republican friend Juarez on the banks of the *Rio Grande* and to have his amiable daughter[4] teach me to *talk* Spanish and "walk Spanish" too, according to her contract; but thank God they cant prevent me from looking after my young colts, my fast trotters and my stud horses on the banks of the *Rio del Miami*! Neither can they prevent me from defending your course, before the people, which, God willing, at the proper time, I mean to do.

Through a political career of thirty-five years—somewhat eventful, if not distinguished—I have never made a *commercial commodity of my political principles*, and the Senate shall learn that I am now too old, if not too honest, to change my fixed system in that respect.

Lewis D. Campbell

ALS, DLC-JP.
    1. For example, see Campbell to Johnson, Apr. 25, 1866.
    2. For a more descriptive reminiscence by Campbell of the Sumner-Johnson interview of December 2, 1865, see Campbell to Johnson, Mar. 9, 1868, Johnson Papers, LC.
    3. A reference to the May 22, 1856, assault on Sumner in the Senate chamber by Preston S. Brooks (1819–1857), a States' Rights Democrat from South Carolina. Brooks resigned following his attack on Sumner but was reelected to finish out his own term. He died the following January. *BDAC*.
    4. Probably Margarita Juárez y Maza (*fl*1872), who accompanied her mother to Washington and attended a reception at the White House on the evening of March 26. Campbell was seen at the President's levee with a "Mexican lady on his arm." Smart, *Juárez!*, 70, 363; *New York Herald*, Mar. 27, 1866.

From J. George Harris
Unofficial.

U.S. Navy Yard, Boston.
Paymaster's Office, May 1st 1866.

My Dear Sir—

The Hon. Sec. of the Navy has been pleased to communicate to me your decision in the case of Mr. Latham,[1] of Texas. I thank you for it. It accords exactly with the advice I had given Mr. Latham by letter before receiving it. There is manifest justice and propriety in contrite *personal* overture by those who have offended the Majorty of our Constitution and Laws. But I believe him to be sincerely repentant, and of loyal intentions —nor could I, for these and other reasons, refrain from asking for his pardon, as he had desired me to do so.[2] And then when I heard his aged father[3] in Connecticut the other day—a man who voted for Jefferson and Jackson—so cordially and enthusiastically defending you and your great and generous policy of Restoration, I really warmed up with him and resolved to ask the favor which I did for his son.

I feel as though this apology or explanation were due to you for having troubled you as I have through the Hon. Sec. of the Navy.

My greatest regret in these times is that our noble old friend President Jackson is not still in the land of the living that his patriotic heart might be made glad by your magnanimous national policy and your gallant defence of the Constitution and popular rights from the inroads of intemperate legislation.

J. Geo. Harris

ALS, DLC-JP.
    1. Francis W. Latham (*c*1818–*fl*1880), a native of Connecticut, by the 1850s had moved to Texas where he raised livestock and served as collector of customs at Point Isabel.

He was also a delegate to the Texas secession convention. During the war Latham collected customs for the Confederacy and served as an unofficial Confederate consul at Matamoros, Mexico. 1860 Census, Tex., Cameron, Point Isabel, 105; (1880), 33rd Enum. Dist., 453; Amnesty Papers (M1003, Roll 53), Tex., Francis W. Latham, RG94, NA; *U.S. Off. Reg.* (1859); Ralph A. Wooster, "An Analysis of the Membership of the Texas Secession Convention," *SWHQ*, 62 (1959): 359; W. J. Hughes, *Rebellious Ranger: Rip Ford and the Old Southwest* (Norman, 1964), 191, 208, 219, 225.

2. Apparently Harris had been making preliminary inquiries about a pardon for Latham who visited Washington for that purpose in the fall of 1866. He took the oath at Providence, Rhode Island, on October 22 and was pardoned November 19, 1866. J. George Harris to Johnson, Sept. 22, 1866; Latham oath, Oct. 22, 1866; File Cover, Amnesty Papers (M1003, Roll 53), Tex., Francis W. Latham, RG94, NA.

3. Not identified.

From Joseph Smith[1]

Boston   May 1st 1866.

Sir—

Permit me as one of the humblest of your fellow citizens, to tender you my sincere thanks for the noble & manly efforts you are making for the preservation of the Constitution, & the genius of our government. These latter seem to be regarded by your antagonists in Congress as of no more importance than a last year's almanac.

In my customary devotions, I have prayed for this Congress ever since it has been in session, "that all things may be settled by its endeavors upon the best & surest foundations that truth & justice may be established among us." But it is so regardless of both that I begin to despair. I endeavor always to be reverent but this Congress continually forces upon my mind the case of the Connecticut parson of primitive days, notwithstanding my efforts to avert it. He was in the habit of going over his grounds at seed time to ask a blessing on them, that they might bring forth an abundant harvest. On one occasion he was attended by his negro servant, when, coming to a piece of land uncommonly sterile, the negro looked at the land, & then at the parson & exclaimed "by gingo I guess you better manure this." He probably considered it beyond praying for. I very much fear that Congress is in a like condition. The servant evidently saw the difference between faith & works. I think conservative Republicans begin to see it also.

I am sure, Sir, that in your efforts to preserve the Constitution under which we have lived so long & flourished so well, the majority, even here, is with you. I was bred a mechanic & my associations have been mainly with that class of our citizens, & I *know* that they agree with you in sentiment.

The great question of constitutional liberty in this country, liberty regulated & controlled by law, it seems to me, depends largely on the complexion of the next Congress to be elected the ensuing autumn, & there is a fair chance that a majority of your friends may be returned thereto. However that may be in other sections of the country, I am constrained to believe that by a judicious distribution here of the offices in your gift among your friends, they will be enabled to elect conservatives in both of the two districts made up mainly of this city. In 1862 a conservative was fairly elected in the district now represented by Mr Rice.[2] The votes "counted & declared in open town meeting," in conformity with our law so decided it, but in one ward in this city the clerk of the ward[3] took the ballots home, having no more control over them than any other citizen. *One week* after he managed to get another count & enough votes were found changed to elect Mr. Rice. That clerk was at once appointed P.M. at South Boston which office he now holds.

The other district represented by Mr. Hooper is very evenly balanced, & with proper effort, can be carried by your friends.[4] Previous to the election of Mr. H. it was represented by a conservative—Hon. Wm. Appleton.[5]

What I mean by your friends touching the distribution of offices, is, conservative Republicans, not democrats—of which I am one—*they* will sustain you in any event. The most relentless of your opponents here is the federal office holders, & the moral effect is damaging. Their opposition was to be expected. When the Republicans came into power they filled the offices here with the most radical of their number, malignant Sumner satellites, original abolitionists.

There is however a strong reserve of conservative Republicans, formerly democrats or Whigs, who have no sympathy, & very little respect for Sumner or his satellites. These, together with your democratic friends, can with proper encouragement, elect your friends triumphantly in these districts.

Senator Wilson, one of the shrewdest political engineers in the country understands this, & is anxious to avoid it. I beg you to excuse the liberty I have taken in these suggestions. The facts I state are as evident as the sun at high noon.

I have witnessed with profound gratitude & admiration the noble stand you have taken & the struggle in which you are engaged has aroused in your behalf all the sympathies of. . . .[6]

Joseph Smith

ALS, DLC-JP.

1. A former navy agent at Boston during the Pierce administration, Smith (1809–1878) was in the gaslight fixture business and later served as a city street commissioner. Smith to Johnson, Jan. 16, 1867, Appts., Customs Service, Naval Officer, Boston, Joseph Smith, RG56, NA; Boston directories (1864–79); *U.S. Off. Reg.* (1855); *Boston Advertiser*, Dec. 28, 1878.

2. John S. Sleeper (1794–1878), a longtime merchant shipmaster, Boston newspaper editor, and mayor of Roxbury, protested the 1862 election results, but the incumbent, Alexander H. Rice (1818–1895), retained his seat and afterwards served one term as governor (1876–78). Not seeking reelection in November 1866, Rice was replaced by Ginery Twichell, also a Republican. *NCAB*, 13: 206; *BDAC*.

3. Appointed as a "letter-carrier" for South Boston, George W. Bail (*c*1833–*fl*1881)

later worked as a furniture dealer and coal and wood supplier. Boston directories (1864–81); *House Misc. Docs.*, 38 Cong., 1 Sess., No. 14, pp. 9, 24, 32, 51 (Ser. 1198).

4. Republican Samuel Hooper was reelected to the Fourth District seat.

5. A former Whig, Appleton (1786–1862) had served only a few months of his third term in Congress before resigning in September 1861 on account of his declining health. *BDAC*.

6. Johnson personally thanked Smith for his letter, assuring him of his "appreciation of and gratitude for" his "friendship and confidence." However, when Smith applied several months later to become naval officer of the port of Boston, he was not appointed. Johnson to Smith, May 16, 1866, Johnson Papers, LC; Smith to Johnson, Jan. 16, 1867, Appt., Customs Service, Naval Officer, Boston, Joseph Smith, RG56, NA.

From James P. Sullivan[1]

New Orleans La   May 1st 1866

The conflict between the United States authorities and Genl Canby[2] arose thus: certain cottons admitted to belong to Mr. Tweed[3] were placed in his possession by the written order of the Treasury Agent;[4] then to compel Mr. Tweed to withdraw his claim to other cottons, Flanders gets Canby to seize that which all admit is Mr. Tweeds. The pretended capture is a seizure in New Orleans warehouses on the twenty sixth 26th April Eighteen hundred sixty six (1866) of the private property of a loyal citizen. Unless Gen Canby is ordered to cease obstructions to the United States Courts process, there will be no United States Courts held here, and the Government and your policy will be fatally injured. We have had enough of Arbitrary rule. Will you not let the case be settled by the United States Court when an appeal can be had to the United States Supreme Court?[5]

J P Sullivan

Tel, DNA-RG107, Tels. Recd., President, Vol. 5 (1866–67).

1. Sullivan (*fl*1869) was one of the lawyers representing Tweed. *New Orleans Picayune*, Apr. 28, 1866; New Orleans directories (1866–70).

2. E.R.S. Canby.

3. John P. Tweed (b. *c*1819) was a produce dealer who spent part of his time in New Orleans. 1860 Census, Orleans, New Orleans, 3rd Ward, 248; *Louisville Journal*, May 8, 1866.

4. Benjamin F. Flanders.

5. Tweed had made a contract with the U.S. government to purchase government cotton in the Red River country, giving the government one quarter of the amount purchased. When Tweed arrived at Shreveport he found that there was too much competition from other government contractors and that his contract had been annulled. Tweed then bought non-government cotton for himself. However, when he shipped it to New Orleans, Flanders claimed one quarter of it as though the contract were still in effect. When Tweed sued Flanders, Flanders had Canby seize the three quarters which were unquestionably Tweed's. Tweed got a writ of sequestration from the court but Canby refused to let it be executed, claiming that he had seized the cotton as captured property. On April 28, 1866, Judge Durrell ruled that Canby was in contempt of court and threatened to adjourn the court indefinitely. In response to Sullivan's telegram, Johnson told Stanton to order Canby not to interfere with the U.S. courts without first submitting the case to Washington. On May 5 Stanton directed Canby to have nothing to do with Treasury agents, to let their cases

be judged in civil courts, and to restrict military proceedings to persons in the military. In mid-June the court ruled that Tweed was the lawful owner of the three-quarters of the shipment seized by Canby. *Louisville Journal*, May 8, 1866; *New Orleans Picayune*, June 12, 1866; J. P. Sullivan to Johnson, Apr. 28, 1866, Johnson Papers, LC; Edmund Cooper to Sullivan, Apr. 30, 1866; William G. Moore to Sullivan, May 2, 1866, Tels. Sent, President, Vol. 3 (1865–68), RG107, NA; Stanton to Canby, May 5, 1866, Tels. Sent, Sec. of War (M473, Roll 90), RG107, NA.

From Humphrey Marshall

Private

New Orleans La   2d May 1866.

My client M. D. Miller[1] had addressed to you the accompanying memorial, which I hope, very fervently, will arrest your attention and induce your immediate action in the case.[2]

I shall not venture to write what I feel: suffice it, that I say *the existing condition of things is perfectly anomalous*; no man knows what to think— no one feels that the citizen has any rights, and your friends *are perfectly nonplused*.

This case will test a principle. If one unoffending citizen can be held in durance vile *without due process of law—without affidavit—*in *another state than that in which the crime is alledged to have been committed—*deprived of liberty—habeas corpus & rights before the law of the country, it will be proof positive that the vitality of the Constitution has not survived the late struggle, and will justify a remark I hear frequently— "the war has closed, and the Revolution just begun." I need not say with what exultant hearts the people hailed the coming of your peace proclamation but the reason for their glowing anticipation of it was that they supposed it was to be the knell of martial law and the era of resuscitation, the Habeas Corpus and all the privileges collated in the bill of rights. If in this they are deceived a fatal despondency will sieze them from which you will find it hard to rouse them. Ah! My dear Sir, would that I could write effectively all I feel—but I write no more than is necessary to urge you to act on this case *telegraphically and energetically* and *decisively.*[3]

Humphrey Marshall
Atto. for M D Miller

ALS, DNA-RG94, Lets. Recd. (Main Ser.), File M-751-1866 (M619, Roll 495).

1. Michael D. Miller (b. *c*1839), a native of Athens, Ohio, had been a banker and exchange broker at Vicksburg, Mississippi, but as a result of wartime losses, had moved to Brownsville, Texas, in 1865 to follow a similar occupation. Miller to Johnson, May 2, 1866, Lets. Recd. (Main Ser.), File M-751-1866 (M619, Roll 495), RG94, NA.

2. In March 1866 the Southern Express Company at Brownsville was robbed of about $90,000. The civil authorities arrested Miller at Galveston for complicity in the robbery but discharged him after further investigation. After charging his accuser with false arrest, Miller traveled to New Orleans where he was arrested on April 1 by order of General Sheridan and imprisoned for four days. Miller was permitted to leave the jail after furnishing $10,000 bail. At no time after his arrest had Miller, or his counsel, Humphrey Marshall, ever been informed of the charges nor had they been permitted to speak with General Sher-

idan. Miller supposed that the charges related to the Southern Express Company case but believed that Sheridan had no jurisdiction in such a civil case. Ibid.; P. H. Sheridan to E. D. Townsend, May 25, 1866, ibid.

3. On May 23 Johnson referred the letter to the secretary of war, who referred it to the adjutant general with instructions to inquire into the case by telegraph. Sheridan replied on May 25 that "Miller is a party to the robbery . . . . He made his way to New Orleans to escape justice and was arrested by me and returned to Brownsville for an investigation and trial where he now is." No information on the outcome of this case has been found. Ibid.

From Joseph A. Wright

Berlin   May 2nd 1866—

My Dear President,

I have not written you for sometime, knowing your time is so fully occupied, that you must feel pressed with weightier matters.

But do allow me to say, that, from my standpoint, the positions & principles set forth in your two veto messages, are *correct* & *true*, and *will stand the test of time*, & *must be approved by the people*. If this Congress adjourns without admitting the loyal men, now demanding seats in the National Congress, not one in five of the present number will be returned to the next Congress.

The most flagrant abuse of the Constitution and of power, ever occuring in any age, was the adoption of the Stevens Resolutions, by which a Joint Committee of both Houses was given virtually the power to pass upon the right of Senators and Representatives to a seat in Congress.

How any intelligent man could vote for such a proposition with the solemn language of the Constitution before him, reading thus, "Each House shall be the Judge of the Electors returns and qualifications of its own members," *is*, to *me* perfectly inexplicable. It is said by some of the papers that "You have no party." I *thank them* for *this assertion*, and more thankful that *you* have a *Country*, and a country that will ever remember you and the trials you are passing through. "Bide your *time*." Be *patient*. Exercise your well known confidence in the people, and by next fall you will hear the voice of approval.

Pardon me for suggesting to you the names of Col Needham of Vermont, and Austin Baldwin of New York as most suitable persons to represent us at the great Exhibition at Paris next year.[1] They are your friends, and can fill most worthily any position you may have in connection with this Exhibition. Gov Dyer of Rhode Island is anxious to come abroad.[2] I know him to be a gentleman, *your friend* and worthy of your Confidence. He would like to fill the place made vacant at the Hague, by the resignation of Hon Mr Pike.[3]

We are having a stormy time in Prussia, great commotion, and rumours of War. I do not believe any collision will occur between Prussia & Austria.[4] Napoleon is not yet ready to change "the Map of Europe." He holds in his hand the peace of Europe. I wish I was with you, you will see me most likely before the contest of 1868 is over. I trust friend Seward keeps you posted with my efforts to adjust and settle this vexed question of Military Service which has been exacted from time immemorial of returning American Citizens to their native Land. If I can be instrumental (under your instruction) in effecting its settlement, *it will be* one of the brightest land marks of your administration.⁵ Mrs Wright unites with me in kindest regards, praying your health and strength may be suffisent to sustain you in your arduous duties.

Accept therefore the assurances of your friend.

J A Wright

ALS, DLC-JP.

1. Daniel Needham (1822–*fl*1893), usually a Massachusetts resident but for nine years a citizen of Hartford, Vermont, had a varied career as a lawyer, farmer, state legislator, inventor, and bank examiner. He acquired his title as colonel from an 1851 governor's appointment, and served as secretary of the Vermont and New England Agricultural Societies. Baldwin (1807–1886), a New York City shipper, for many years lived in Connecticut where he too had been a legislator. Neither man was among the thirty paid and unpaid U.S. commissioners to the Universal Exhibition held at Paris in April 1867. D. Hamilton Hurd, comp., *History of Middlesex County, Massachusetts* (3 vols., Philadelphia, 1890), 1: xlviii-l; *NUC*; Ritter and Wakelyn, *Legislative Leaders*; *U.S. Off. Reg.* (1867).

2. Elisha Dyer (1811–1890), who served as adjutant general of Rhode Island and later governor for two successive terms (1857–59), received another recommendation for The Hague post, but was not chosen by Johnson. Sobel and Raimo, *Governors*, 4: 1347; James Y. Smith to Johnson, Apr. 16, 1866, Lets. of Appl. and Recomm., 1861–69 (M650, Roll 15), RG59, NA.

3. Prior to being appointed minister resident in 1861, James S. Pike (1811–1882) gained national prominence as a correspondent for the *Boston Courier* and the *New York Tribune*. Following his return to the United States in mid-May 1866, he initially sided with the Radicals. However, by the end of Grant's first term he had moved into the Liberal Republican camp. *DAB*; James S. Pike, *The Prostrate State: South Carolina under Negro Government* (New York, 1968 [1874]), xii-xvii.

4. Wright's prediction proved inaccurate as Prussia's premier, Otto von Bismarck, attempting to overcome Austrian control of the German states and unite them under Prussia, provoked war with Austria in late June, thus beginning the Seven Weeks' or Austro-Prussian War. George C. Kohn, *Dictionary of Wars* (New York, 1986), 417.

5. George Bancroft, Wright's replacement, succeeded in negotiating naturalization and citizenship treaties with Prussia and other German principalities by 1868. However, interpretation and implementation proved to be troublesome. Lillian Handlin, *George Bancroft: The Intellectual as Democrat* (New York, 1984), 296–98.

From Francis P. Blair, Jr.

St Louis   May 5 1866.

I would most respectfully ask the appointment of Captain Barton Able of this city as Collector of Internal revenue for the 1st Dis of Missouri.¹ Captain Able is a gentleman of very high character & standing and a firm supporter of your political policy. His appointment would give unqualified satisfaction to your friends in Missouri.

I would beg leave to suggest to your Excellency that the factious course of the senate in the rejection of your nominations for this & other positions justifies you in dismissing the present incumbents who are hostile to your policy. This might be done in the case of the Collector of Internal Revenue in this District[2] & the appt of Captain Able as Special agt. of the Treasury Dept to take charge of the office. His nomination as Collector would in that case meet with less opposition as he would be in the office & they could not by rejecting him, retain their Radical friend in the position. The same object might easily be attained by a change of the Collection Districts of Missouri, so as to make them correspond with the congressional Districts. This would throw out the present incumbents and allow you to make the appointments & issue commissions which the parties who received them would hold until their successors are appointed & qualified.

Under all circumstances Capt Able should be appointed. The office is one of great political influence & should be in the hands of one of your friends.[3]

Papine the assessor for this District[4] is your friend & should be retained.

Frank P Blair

ALS, DNA-56, Appts., Internal Revenue Service, Collector, Mo., 1st Dist., Barton Able.

1. The Senate had just rejected Johnson's nomination of Blair for this same post. *Senate Ex. Proceedings*, Vol. 14, pt. 2: 777.

2. William Taussig. See Henry T. Blow to Johnson, Mar. 19, 1866.

3. In August Able was given a recess appointment as collector, then was nominated in January and received approval by the Senate and his commission on February 6, 1867. Ser. 6B, Vol. 3: 633; Vol. 4: 316, Johnson Papers, LC. See also Blair, Sr., to Johnson, May 19, 1866, Appts., Internal Revenue Service, Collector, Mo., 1st Dist., Barton Able, RG56, NA.

4. Theophile Papin (1827–1902), a native of St. Louis and initially a journalist and editor, joined his brother's real estate firm in the 1850s. Appointed assessor by Lincoln and reappointed by Johnson, Papin held the position for six-and-a- half years, until he resigned for business reasons. St. Louis directories (1854–81); William Hyde and H. L. Conrad, eds., *Encyclopedia of the History of St. Louis* (4 vols., St. Louis, 1899), 3: 1693–95; Walter B. Stevens, *St. Louis: The Fourth City, 1764–1909* (3 vols., St. Louis, 1909), 2: 153–55.

From Virginia C. Clay

Huntsville, Ala.   May 5th 1866.

My dear Sir:

Your patient attention to my appeals in my distress & your sympathy and kind deeds, embolden me to again trouble you, & beg a redress of grievances.

The U.S. District Attorney for this State, has libelled the property, real & personal, of almost every one able to pay his fees, whether worth 20,000 or $20., whether pardoned or unpardoned,—and, among them, my husband's, his father's, C. C. Clay Sr., & his brother Withers Clay's[1] property. To defend the libel vs. my father's property, there is needed, from the office of the Secretary of State, *a certified copy of C. C. Clay Sr.'s letter of acceptance, and certificate that his oath of allegiance has been duly filed.* Mr. Beirne,[2] father's Atty:, forwarded his oath & duplicate letter of acceptance more than *five weeks ago*, but has not yet received the certified copies required. As the Court will sit on Monday, 21st May, only 16 days hence, I earnestly beg, as a great favor to me, as well as our feeble & aged father, that you will order the papers sent *forthwith, without delay*, to Beirne & Gordon,[3] Attys: At Law, Huntsville, Ala. If Gov. Clay should die, (at any moment probable,) before the Suit is terminated, it will be necessarily protracted, at great additional cost to his heirs or legatees, besides aggravating the bitterness of his last hours on earth.

I must, also, entreat your aid in my *own* behalf. All the property of my husband (part, obtained by marriage with me) has been destroyed, or seized by the U.S. Gov'mt., or by individuals. Our dwelling was robbed before being burned, & my furniture, books &c. are now in the hands of *sojourners* here, *so-called* citizens, who deny our title, and rejoice and exult over their ill-gotten plunder. The only tenement we owned, which has not been destroyed, is a brick building of six rooms, on the public square, which could not be burned without destroying the adjoining building. In it was my husband's office, containing a very large & costly library. This building is now occupied by two Northern men,[4] called lawyers, whose chief business, I am told, is catering to the rapacity of the U.S. District Atty. and the Chief of the Freedman's Bureau,[5] who, also, holds his office in the said building. If the U.S. *Gov'mt.* was realizing the property we purchased with our toil, I might bear it with more resignation & philosophy, but to see it appropriated to their own use by Camp followers & vampires who feed & fatten upon the blood of others is too much for the stoic or Christian; especially when living, as we are, on the bounty of others. It would not support us, but would furnish Mr. Clay a place to deposite what books he may recover, & a roof under which he may labor. Most of his costly books are now missing, stolen at different times, & *all* will shortly follow unless possession is restored to us.

I need not remind a statesman who understands & venerates the U.S. Constitution, that it allows no forfeiture or confiscation of property until conviction of crime, and, that, therefore, this Seizure & appropriation of our property, by real, or pretended agents or friends of the Govm't. is the exercise of *might* without *right*. How long, Mr. President, shall the sword reign in defiance of the Constitution,—since, *Peace* has been restored. Now, you know, better than I, how to relieve me,—but my legal friends suggest that a *mere order* from you to J Q. Smith, District Atty: to *dismiss the libel* against the property of C.C.C. Jr. will suffice.[6] It may, but I fear he can never *make claim* to anything until *pardoned.* As you are my only "friend at court," and all sufficient for my wants there, I am constrained to trespass on yr time & beg your help. Hope it will not be in vain.

V. C. Clay.

ALS, DLC-JP.

1. John Withers Clay (1820–1896) was a lawyer and former editor of the *Huntsville Confederate*. Nuermberger, *Clays*, 68, 216.

2. George P. Beirne (1809–1881), was a large landholder and farmer as well as attorney. At one time or another he was a director of the Memphis and Charleston Railroad and a bank director. For a very brief period he had served as a Confederate treasury agent. Pauline J. Gandrud, comp., *Marriage, Death and Legal Notices From Early Alabama Newspapers, 1819–1893* (Easley, S.C., 1981), 538; 1860 Census, Ala., Madison, Huntsville, 43; Amnesty Papers (M1003, Roll 1), Ala., George P. Beirne, RG94, NA.

3. Beirne's son-in-law, George A. Gordon (c1831–1872), was formerly of Savannah and colonel of the 63rd Ga. Inf., CSA. Gandrud, *Early Alabama Newspapers*, 261, 538; 1860 Census, Ga., Chatham, Savannah, 1st Dist., 76; *OR*, Ser. 1, Vol. 14: 824.

4. Not identified.

5. John B. Callis (1828–1898), a Lancaster, Wisconsin, merchant, who during the war was breveted brigadier general, was subassistant commissioner of the Freedmen's Bureau in Huntsville from January 1866 to January 1868. Afterwards, he served as an Alabama congressman before returning North. *BDAC*; Elaine Everly and Willna Pacheli, *Preliminary Inventory of Records of the Field Offices of the Bureau of Refugees, Freedmen, and Abandoned Lands* (3 parts, Washington, D.C., 1973), 1: 22.

6. On November 25, 1866, Johnson authorized the release of C. C. Clay, Jr.'s property. But when Clay tried to obtain possession, officials of the district court refused, intending to force a court action so they could collect the costs. In January 1867 Attorney General Stanbery ordered the suit dismissed and soon proceedings against Clay's property as well as his indictment for treason were suspended. On April 11, 1867, the Freedmen's Bureau began paying about a hundred dollars a month rent for use of Clay's Huntsville office, the first payment covering the period from the previous November 25. Nuermberger, *Clays*, 302–3.

From John Conness

Washington   May 5th 1866

Sir

Circumstances which may be briefly stated will I trust be sufficient apology for this letter. First I have of late occupied much of you valuable time and may thus present more briefly what I have now to say. Next the subject matter.

William M Gwin formerly a Senator from California is a prisoner in one of the southern forts of the United States.[1] I need not recapitulate to you any of the antecedent facts upon which his last arrest and imprisonment was based.[2] With a view to have them go before the country I called by resolution of the Senate a long time since for all correspondence implicating him, which was furnished and published.[3] He has been long in prison without trial[4] or other warrant for holding him beyond the inexorable necessity of upholding the national authority and preserving the public safety. This I acknowledge to have been sufficient. You will pardon me if I say that now I think the public safety and national authority are vindicated as against him. He is in "the sere and yellow leaf."[5] Few years are left for him upon earth and I propose and ask that they be left to him with his personal liberty.[6] I do most firmly believe that common justice demands that in his case the bond should be free. I do not plead for him as a political, or even personal friend of his, but on the ground of a common justice to which we all at one time or another are amenable. If there be any responsibility attaching to the act of giving Mr Gwin his freedom do I pray let it rest upon me.[7]

John Conness

ALS, DNA-RG94, Lets. Recd. (Main Ser.), File G-216-1866 (M619, Roll 474).

1. Fort Jackson, Louisiana. Amnesty Papers (M1003, Roll 28), La., William M. Gwin, RG94, NA.

2. Gwin had been imprisoned in Fort Lafayette, New York, from November 18 to December 2, 1861, for southern sympathies. His later imprisonment was the result of a plan he had discussed with Napoleon III to settle Confederate refugees in northern Mexico. This scheme collapsed during the summer of 1865 when the Mexican emperor, Maximilian, refused to permit Gwin to put his plan into action. *DAB*; W. C. Nunn, *Escape from Reconstruction* (Fort Worth, 1956), 27–29; Andrew F. Rolle, *The Lost Cause: The Confederate Exodus to Mexico* (Norman, 1965), 62–64. See also Grant to Johnson, June 19, 1865, *Johnson Papers*, 8: 258–59.

3. Conness's resolution can be found in the *Congressional Globe*, 39 Cong., 1 Sess., p. 77. Three letters, two allegedly from Gwin but not signed, and one from his son, were printed with other documents pertaining to Confederate activities in Mexico, many of them not related to Gwin. *Senate Ex. Docs.*, 39 Cong., 1 Sess., No. 8 (Ser. 1237).

4. Gwin was apparently imprisoned in October 1865 and remained there for eight months. *DAB*.

5. From Shakespeare's *Macbeth*, act 5, sc. 3, line 24.

6. Gwin was sixty years old, but he lived until 1885. *DAB*.

7. The endorsement on the document indicates that on May 5, 1866, as a result of Conness's appeal, Johnson ordered Gwin released "on the parole usually required in such cases."

From Varina Davis

Fortress Monroe Va   May 5th 1866.

My dear Sir.

I had the honor, upon the receipt of the Adjt. Genls telegraphic permission to visit my Husband, to send you a telegraphic message of thanks,[1] a very feeble expression of my gratitude for this to me inestimable boon. Please allow me now to add his to mine, and to assure you that it will long be remembered by us both as a kindly effort upon your part to ameliorate our very wretched condition.

The first day of my arrival here, the excitement of my coming gave Mr Davis an apparent strength and vivacity which were unfortunately very illusory.

I find him fearfully changed, exceedingly weak, and to my horror the Surg. in charge Dr Cooper[2] agrees with me in the beleif than he can not bear a slight attack of malaria. Will you not invite an opinion from Dr Cooper?[3] You are the only person to whom I can appeal, and it is so shocking to sit still and see my Husband die by inches, powerless to help him.

The manner of his confinement is the most wearing that you could imagine. He is in effect still in solitary confinement except the limited time which I can spend with him. Would to God you could see with your own eyes his condition. I am exceedingly anxious not to annoy you by any wordy complaints to others, after your very generous conditioning in my parole. I feel that you sought to give me the leest possible annoyance or embarrassment, and thank you very sincerely for your consideration. I therefore refrain from seeking any assistance from others in the matter certain of your desire to oblige me so far as is consistent with your ideas of your duties. I have refrained from coming to Washington[4] from an opinion which has been expressed to me repeatedly that my doing so might give you some annoyance, and a certainty which I feel that you do not need importunity to urge you to do what you can for us.

Will you not take Mr Davis' case in your own hands and give him the freedom of the post—*both of night and day*, so that his mind and body may have *natural rest*? I think you know that his parole would secure to you his person even if the gates were wide open—and the world invited his exit.

Will you not grant me this? I ask it for a man who is really dying, though the death is coming gradually. Will you not put it into our power to ask our people to love you for his sake, as well as for all your care for them?

Please Mr President do not refuse me. It is far more than life to me for which I plead. Will you not grant it? If Mr Davis could be in a quiet dark room at night, releived of the agony of knowing that so many watch around him, with power to walk about at will all day, he would I think in a few months be better. Will you not have quarters assigned to him, and let us try the experiment? Upon further consideration I have concluded to send you the copy of my note, and Dr Coopers answer (which I must say was intended for my eye alone) and which I enclose to you in the same confidential manner.[5] I shall dear Sir rest with confidence upon the certainty that I feel that you will cooperate with the Dr and with me and thus by your powerful intervention ensure success.

Varina Davis.

P.S.   Will you not invite an opinion from Dr Cooper in the case? Will please do this.

ALS, DLC-JP.
1. On April 25, 1866, Varina Davis telegraphed Johnson for permission to visit her husband. Johnson referred the matter to Stanton, who had no objection. Johnson then gave his permission on April 26 and the order was telegraphed. Varina Davis telegraphed her thanks the same day. On May 3, 1866, she visited her husband for the first time in a year. Davis to Johnson, Apr. 26, 1866, Tels. Recd., President, Vol. 5 (1866–67), RG107, NA; *OR*, Ser. 2, Vol. 8: 900, 902; Hudson Strode, *Jefferson Davis* (3 vols., New York, 1955–64), 3: 280; *New Orleans Picayune*, May 13, 1866.
2. George E. Cooper (1824–1881), born in Pennsylvania, entered the army in 1847 as a first lieutenant and assistant surgeon. Subsequently he was made major/surgeon in May 1861 and brevet lieutenant colonel in September 1864, at which time he was medical director of the Army of the Cumberland. After Christmas 1865 Cooper, now a brevet colonel, replaced Dr. Craven as post surgeon of Fortress Monroe and assumed primary responsibility for Jefferson Davis. Powell, *Army List*, 256–7; Strode, *Jefferson Davis*, 3: 272; ACP File, George E. Cooper, RG94, NA; Pension Records, Elvira M. Cooper, RG15, NA.
3. Johnson did request a report on the health of Davis, which Cooper supplied in detail. Johnson to Stanton, May 9, 1866, *OR*, Ser. 2, Vol. 8: 906; *National Intelligencer*, May 15, 1866; Cooper to Lorenzo Thomas, May 9, 1866, Johnson Papers, LC.
4. Varina Davis went to Washington May 24, 1866, to speak with Johnson. Granted an audience on the evening of the 25th, she pleaded for better conditions for her husband. Johnson informed her that Davis had already been given the liberty of the entire fort with-

Jefferson Davis enjoying the comforts of Fortress Monroe
Harper's Weekly, June 30, 1866

out the strict surveillance previously required. *New York Herald*, May 26, 1866. See also
Varina Davis to Johnson, May 12, 1866, Johnson Papers, LC.
    5. Enclosures not found.

From Rush R. Sloane[1]

Sandusky, O., May 5th 1866.

Dear Sir

I hand you herewith our call for the State convention in Ohio and trust
it may meet your approval.[2] Those who may favor the propositions of
Congress as well as those who sustain your policy can meet together and
if *discretion* and patriotism controls our convention we may *agree* upon a
platform. *I hope* for this result but am not *confident.* The majority of our
Union party in Ohio are strongly against your polacy and sustain Congress, yet we hope that conservative counsels will prevail and all pass off
satisfactory. I succeeded in getting the size of the convention small and
therefore the hope of moderation is greater. We shall have a conference of
our friends a day or two before the convention and if we do not accomplish what we wish it shall not be on account of the proper efforts not
being put forth.

Rush R. Sloane

ALS, DLC-JP.
    1. Chairman of the State Union (Republican) Committee, Sloane (1828–1908), a for-
mer Sandusky city clerk and probate judge for Erie County, had served throughout the war
as a special agent for the U.S. Post Office in Ohio, prior to his removal in 1866. Afterwards
he was president of the Cincinnati, Dayton, and Eastern Railroad and mayor of Sandusky.
Sloane had met with Johnson on April 2 and would have several more interviews regarding
the Fourteenth Amendment. Harriet T. Upton, *History of the Western Reserve* (3 vols., Chicago, 1910), 3: 1580–81; Sloane to Johnson, Apr. 2, 1866, Johnson Papers, LC; *House
Reports*, 40 Cong., 1 Sess., "Impeachment Investigation," pt. 2: 268–70 (Ser. 1314).
    2. No enclosures have been found. For reports of the convention held on June 20 at
Columbus, see James D. Cox to Johnson, June 21, 1866, and Richard P.L. Baber to Johnson, June 28, 1866.

To J. Madison Wells

Washington, D.C., May 5th 1866

    The paroles heretofore granted G. T. Beauregard, and Wirt Adams,[1]
have this day been extended by me as requested in your telegram of the
3rd[2]—and the orders of extension will be forwarded to your address by
mail, or elsewhere, or retained here subject to their call as you or they
may desire and designate. Answer by telegraph.[3]

Andrew Johnson   Prest U.S.

Tel, DNA-RG107, Tels. Sent, President, Vol. 3 (1865–68).
    1. William Wirt Adams (1819–1888), a native of Kentucky, served in the army of the
Republic of Texas and then became a planter, banker, and state legislator in Mississippi.

Initially the colonel of the 1st Miss. Cav., Adams was promoted to brigadier general in September 1863. Warner, *Gray*.

2. Wells to Johnson, May 3, 1866, Johnson Papers, LC.

3. Beauregard and Adams needed their paroles extended so they could go to Europe as agents for the New Orleans, Jackson, and Great Northern Railroad. They requested that the papers be sent to them in New York. Wells to Johnson, May 6, 1866, Johnson Papers, LC; Beauregard to Johnson, May 7, 1866, ibid.; *Arkansas State Gazette* (Little Rock), May 26, 1866.

From Sterling R. Cockrill

Pine Bluff   May 7th 1866.

Dear Sir,

There is a rumor on the streets this evening, that the House had resolved to proceed with "*Articles of Impeachment*" against you, as Presidt.[1] It came by passengers from Little Rock, on a Steamboat. I can scarcely credit it, still it may be so. I hope not however.

The thinking portion of the people, have a *deep feeling* about it, and I have been requested to give you the substance of what they think.

They say the Senate as now organized, with 22 members excluded from their Seats, is not "*the Court*" which the Constitution provides for the trial of the Prest; and therefore you ought not to allow yourself to be arraigned before that body. You can say, "admit the absent members and you are ready for trial; whilst they are excluded you dont intend to be tried." If they undertake to proceed with it, disperse them, by Military force, & issue a Proclamation for a "National Convention" to adjust the pending difficulties.

It would be no trial. The decision would be made before the Articles are written. The people here know you have not usurped authority or power, or committed any high crime or misdemeanor, and therefore you ought not to allow, a *part* of the Senate thus to Stigmatize and defame your character: for it must so read in history.

They think *here* that you should make your Cabinet a "*unit*," a reliable "unit." The Secy of *War*, should be especially reliable; as you may have to rely for a moment on the protection of a guard to execute an important order about the Capitol. It is not intended to be Revolutionary, far from it, but to prevent Congress from deposing the President and thus usurping power which by the Constitution belongs to the President. That is, if the rumor has any foundation in fact.

The people here, wish you to know that they are not willing to see you defamed and deposed by a "*Senate*" which refuses to allow 22 Members to take their Seats. Their finding must go to the world as *true*, when they know it is "*not true*."

The "*Executive Department*," as provided for in the Constitution, must be preserved unimpaired, and they hereby pledge you their support, in all lawful, modes of resisting its destruction. Tennessee had her Jackson, who never surrendered to any combination of forces and he allowed no discord in his Cabinet; and held his "*own forces*," well in hand ready for action. Warning from such an example may not be amiss.

Hoping the *rumor* may be unfounded *now*, and for the future. I subscribe myself, as representing the sentiments of the masses, who desire that they shall be communicated to you.

S. R. Cockrill

ALS, DLC-JP.
1. There was some mention of impeachment of the President as early as October 1865. Though the rumor Cockrill heard was without foundation, Johnson's vetoes of the Freedmen's Bureau and Civil Rights bills caused increased discussion of the possibility in the spring of 1866. Widespread consideration of impeachment did not begin until that fall. Hans L. Trefousse, *Impeachment of a President: Andrew Johnson, the Blacks, and Reconstruction* (Knoxville, 1975), 48.

From James R. Doolittle

Senate Chamber   May 7, 1866.

Dear Sir

Enclosed I send you some very important papers in relation to Colorado.[1] The letter to Mr Grimes[2] is private But you can I think rely with the utmost certainty upon its statements.

The other paper shows that the allegations made by some that in their late election there were 7500 votes is false.

The whole idea of Colorado being now able or fit to be a state is a grand farce.[3]

J R Doolittle

ALS, DLC-JP.
1. Congress had just passed legislation making Colorado a state. Doolittle enclosed a clipping from the *Baltimore Sun*, Apr. 27, 1866, opposing statehood because of insufficient population in the territory, and one from the *Rochester Union & Advertiser* (N.Y.), May 5, 1866, urging Johnson to veto the bill because it passed the Senate without a quorum being present.
2. James W. Grimes (1816–1872), a lawyer and farmer active in Iowa politics in both the territorial and state legislatures and as governor, was first elected to the U.S. Senate in 1858. The letter was from future territorial governor Alexander Cameron Hunt, who opposed statehood because the Colorado population was declining rather than growing. Hunt was convinced the territory contained no more than 21,000 persons, even less than the official estimate of 25,000, and no more than 3,000 taxpayers, who would be unable to pay state expenses. Hunt to Grimes, Apr. 19, 1866, Johnson Papers, LC; *DAB*.
3. Hunt's letter may have influenced Johnson, since he mentioned the issue of taxation and support of government functions in his veto message. See Colorado Statehood Veto, May 15, 1866. For a communication from a Colorado official who urged statehood, see George W. Chamberlain to Johnson, May 14, 1866, Johnson Papers, LC.

From Newton B. Lord[1]

Milwaukee Wis   May. 7, 1866

Sir.

I have this moment finished reading Mr. Ingersolls speech on reconstruction in the House of Representatives[2] and I cannot refrain from writing you to express to you my endorsement of your course. Such speeches as those of Mr. Ingersoll do you no dishonor but rather redound to your credit with sound conservative men—rich men who would not destroy their country for an idea.

Has Mr Ingersoll ever been in battle—ever smelled gun powder—ever camped in the snows of winter?[3] Men of his stripe have not been in the army the last four years, at least I never saw or heard of one in it. Such men as he create war but do not take part in it.

Sir I joined the army in Apl 1861 and left it in Apl 1865 after the capture of Richmond. I raised in Jeff. Co N.Y (my native county) a Regiment of Infantry and fought it two years. I then raised the 20th NY Cavly and fought that two years, and carried on my shoulders eagles[4] only for four years because I dared be a conservative, because I dared sustain such men as you. I raised those two Regiments at my own expense to maintain the Union. I would have given my life to that cause. If necessary I can raise another Regiment to sustain your administration and will do it if the emergency requires.

I have been in thirteen battles. I have smelled gunpowder. I have camped in the snows of mid winter. I have sustained my country by hand and purse during her hour of trial instead of drawing from its purse salary for a political office and I heartily sustain you. All men of my stamp sustain you. Go on in the course you are pursuing. Restore the Union. Do right to all. Be not governed by the one idea of a radical party, and trust to the discord sure to follow such a course.

I think (without egotism) I may say the support of one such man as myself counts for more than the opposition of a dozen such partisan blackguards as Mr. Ingersoll.

Newton B. Lord   Late Col 35th NY Infanty
1st Divn. 1st Army Corps   Army of the Potomac &
Late Col 20th NY Cavly   Cavly Divn. Army of the Pomc.

ALS, DLC-JP.

1. Lord (1832–1890) entered the war in 1861 and eventually commanded the 35th N.Y. Vol. Inf. and the 20th N.Y. ("McClellan") Vol. Cav. until his forced resignation by Gen. Benjamin F. Butler in March 1865. After the war his work as a railroad contractor carried him to Chile, where he died. John A. Haddock, *The Growth of a Century: As Illustrated in the History of Jefferson County, New York, from 1793 to 1894* (Philadelphia, 1894), 475.

2. In his impassioned oration of May 5, Ebon C. Ingersoll (1831–1879), a moderate Illinois Republican, attacked presidential reconstruction as being too lenient and accused Johnson of secretly plotting to curry the favor of the southern people as a means of getting reelected in 1868. *BDAC*; *Congressional Globe*, 39 Cong., 1 Sess., pp. 2399–2404.

3. Here Lord borrows wording directly from Ingersoll's May 5 speech in which the congressman declared that Johnson had never fought in battle. Ibid., 2404.

4. A federal colonel's insignia.

From Lawrence Worrall[1]

Mobile Ala   9 P M   May 7th 1866

I am already informed that a Steamer is fitting out at New Orleans to take a cargo of Negroes from near Pensacola to Cuba. It is the *Virgin*, formerly a blockade runner. Sails on friday, and is reported to be the fleetest vessel in these waters. Another vessel will follow in a day or two if the first one is allowed to sail without being intercepted.[2] The facts have been fully disclosed to me by a person employed as Engineer on the first vessel to sail. Instructions are requested.[3]

Lawrence Worrall   U S Dist Atty

Tel, DLC-JP.

1. Worrall (*fl*1897), an attorney formerly in Richard Busteed's New York City law office, was clerk and acting district attorney for the southern district of Alabama. Subsequently, he was "register in bankruptcy" before returning to New York City during the late 1870s. New York City directories (1860–64, 1879–97); Mobile directories (1866–72); Hugh McCulloch to Johnson, May 9, 1866, Lets. Sent *re* Restricted Commercial Intercourse (BE Ser.), Vol. 13, RG56, NA.

2. The English-built *Virgin*, trapped in Mobile Bay by Admiral Farragut's fleet, was impressed by the Confederate army for picket duty. After the war the Treasury Department possessed the boat until early 1866, when it was turned over to the Freedmen's Bureau and offered for sale. On April 12, the *Virgin* was moved to Pensacola, presumably by her new owners, and within a few days continued to New Orleans. This development, plus Worrall's alarming telegram, as well as one from A. R. Nininger, prompted the War Office to wire Generals Philip H. Sheridan at New Orleans and John G. Foster in Tallahassee to "intercept the steamer and prevent her design from being accomplished." On May 11 Sheridan reported that he had seized the vessel and there was "no evidence of a design to carry slaves to Cuba." Consequently, eight days later, the War Department ordered the *Virgin*'s release. *OR-Navy*, Ser. 1, Vol. 10: 395; Impressment Certificate, Aug. 16, 1864; Stanton to Johnson, Apr. 5, 1866, Lets. Recd., Executive (M494, Roll 84), RG107, NA; E. C. Woodruff to Charles Mundee, May [June] 9, 1866; Sheridan to E. D. Townsend, May 11, 1866, Lets. Recd. (Main Ser.), Files G-342-1866 and G-282-1866 (M619, Roll 474), RG94, NA; Nininger to Townsend, May 7, 1866; Townsend to Sheridan and John G. Foster, May 8, 1866; Townsend to Sheridan, May 19, 1866, Tels. Sent, Sec. of War (M473, Roll 90), RG107, NA.

3. Two days later, one of the President's secretaries responded that action by Worrall "may become necessary." If that was the case, "no person, either white or black" was to be "sent out of the country contrary to his own consent." Edmund Cooper to Worrall, May 9, 1866, Tels. Sent, President, Vol. 3 (1865–68), RG107, NA.

From Walter A. Burleigh

Washington   May. 8th 1866

I have recently learned with much surprise that the Commissioner of Indian Affairs[1] has ordered the removal of the Sioux Indians now in Dakota Territory who were the perpetrators of the Minnesota Massacre in 1862[2] from their present location at Crow Creek down into one of the Settled Counties of Nebraska and directly opposite our white settlements in Dakota.

You are aware that these Indians at that time murdered more than a thousand defenceless men women & children in that State. In the conflict which followed some four or five hundred Indians were taken and incarcerated in Iowa while the ballance of the hostile bands were forced from Minnesota into Dakota Territory where they now are.

In 1863 the Goverment ordered and effected the removal of all the Sioux from Minnesota and located them at Crow Creek a place about one Hundred and fifty miles above Yankton the capital of Said Territory.

Within a few weeks past and order has been issued for the release of these hostile Savages who have been so long in confinement and their Transportation to our Territory where they too are to be turned loose to seek revenge by a system of robery rapine and murder upon our unprotected citizens only known to barbarians.

The place which I learn is selected for their location is upon the opposite side of the Missouri and but a short distance above my own residence.

This act of the Government endangering the lives of our people and damaging our Territory has been determined upon without a word of consultation with the citizens of Dakota that I am aware of and has been concealed from their Representative here by the Commissioner of Indian Affairs.

If this order is carried into effect—if these Indians are located thus near our settlements—our citizens will be compelled either to—abandon their homes for the security of their lives & property or wage a war of extermination against them.

If the officers of your Administration having these important matters in charge would consult the feelings and interests of our people and take counsel from them in the disposal and management of the Indian Tribes with whom they are compelled to live as neighbors it would relieve the Government of much embarrassment and save the lives and property of many of our citizens.

In behalf of the citizens of Dakota whose interests it is my duty to look after I beg to say, with all due respect, that I enter my solemn protest against the removeal & location of these Savages any nearer to our white population than they now are.[3]

W A Burleigh
Delegate in Congress from Dakota Territory

ALS, DLC-JP.
1. Dennis N. Cooley.
2. The massacre had been precipitated by the near starvation of the Indians as the result of a crop failure and the federal government's delay in paying the tribal annuity. David A. Nichols, *Lincoln and the Indians: Civil War Policy and Politics* (Columbia, Mo., 1978), 76–77.
3. Johnson apparently referred Burleigh's letter to Secretary of the Interior James Harlan, who, in turn, forwarded it to Commissioner Cooley. Cooley explained that the Indians being moved to the Niobrara reservation were peaceable. Because the Crow Creek reservation had proven unsuccessful with repeated crop failures, the Indians were nearing

starvation. A five-member commission recommended the removal of the Sioux. Cooley to
Harlan, May 18, 1866, *National Intelligencer*, June 1, 1866.

From Salmon P. Chase

Washington   May 9th 1866.

Dear Sir,

I enclose, according to promise, my Report of December 10th 1863.[1]
On pages 13, 14, & 15, you will find the ideas to which I invited your
attention.

The bill lately introduced into the Senate[2] provides for what is called a
consolidated loan, intended to be substituted for all existing loans and of
course to be of equal amount to our whole existing debt.

It proposes 5 per cent interest; no payment of principal till after 30
years; exemption from taxation by the Nation or the States; and 2 per
cent for expences of negotiation.

The debt amounts say to two thousand seven hundred millions. The
loan, if the theory of the bill is carried out, will be for the same amount.
The cost of negotiation will then be 54 millions of dollars, or twenty
thousand dollars for every million; all possibility of payment, till after 30
years, will be excluded; and the holders, who will become fewer and
fewer as the loan gradually passes, as all loans in time do pass, into the
hands of rich individuals and corporations, will be exempted from contribution to the public burdens both of the Nation and the States. The
interest to be paid by the people to the bond holders, during the thirty
years will be four thousand and five hundred millions of dollars.

The cost of the negotiation of the loan of 514 millions of 5–20s was
3/10ths of one per cent, or $3000 on every million. I think, though I
cannot speak positively, that no other loan, negotiated by me, cost more.

It is true that I do not think it wise to subject loans, redeemable after
short periods, to State taxes; and as all the loans, made during the war,
were made so redeemable, they were by law exempted from such taxes.
But never, even in the hardest times, did I suggest or did Congress consent to exemption from national taxes; nor, in my judgment, should any
such exemptions from State taxes be allowed, if the loan is to be put beyond the control of the Government for many years.

It seems to me to be a point of prime importance to keep the debt
within easy reach of payment. We paid at first, as high as 7.30 per cent;
but no such loans were made for a period longer than three years; then
came loans at 6 per cent, but only for 5 years; then at 5 per cent but only
for 10 years. The 7.30 bonds were convertible into 6 per cent bonds. The
first 7.30 was convertible after the three years into bonds redeemable after 1881, that is after 15 years from last January, the last, and much the
greatest part, into bonds redeemable after 5 years. These last bonds and

all other 6 per cent bonds, except those redeemable after 1881, *may* be paid at any time redeemable after five years, until the end of twenty when they *must* be paid. The 5 per cent bonds are redeemable at any time after two years, until the end of forty years, when they also must be paid.

You will see what I say on the subject of controllability of debt on the 14th and 15th pages of the Report, and I think you and every other Statesman, who does not believe that a national debt is a national blessing, will agree with me.

I have not the slightest doubt that, with judicious management, all the temporary debt can now be funded at very small cost, in bonds at 5 per cent interest, redeemable at any time after ten years, and payable forty years from date,—that is to say, in the bonds commonly known as the Ten Forty bonds. My idea in issuing those bonds was, that the Nation should not tie its hands beyond ten years at most, even in 5 per cent loans; and that it should be understood that within forty years at farthest, the whole debt will be paid off. I believed and still believe that under this plan it may be paid much sooner. I have no doubt that within ten years this Nation will be able to borrow money as cheaply as Great Britain, which pays nominally 3 but really about 4 per cent, and that the benefits of cheap interest may be secured to the whole industry of the Country. It can then pay its debt, whenever and in whatever amounts may be convenient, or make a new ten forty loan at 4 per cent or less.

I have not had time to look into the old documents to ascertain what time the earliest loans had to run; but it is safe to say that no loan made irredeemable for a longer period than twenty years has been negotiated this last half century; while most loans have been made redeemable after much shorter periods. Under Jackson, as you well know, the former national debt was paid off. You will hardly allow your administration to be distinguished from his by the postponement of the payment of the present debt for thirty years.

The practical effect of tying the nation's hands in this matter of payment was strikingly illustrated during the administration of Mr Pierce. There were then outstanding six principal descriptions of debt, namely, the loans of 1842, 1843, 1846, 1847, 1848, and the Texan Indemnity; redeemable respectively after 1862, 1853, 1856, 1868, and 1865; that is to say two of them during Mr Pierce's administration and the other four after five years, eight years, and eleven years from its close. They all carried interest at 6 percent except the Texan Indemnity which carried five per cent. The whole amount of the debt was $79,032,897.00. The Government desired to anticipate payment, but the holders of the loans preferred to keep their bonds; and the Government was obliged to pay heavy premiums in order to redeem a part. The total amount redeemed was $48,060,787.37, for which, in addition to the principal the Government paid premiums amounting to $4,609,882.31, or nearly ten per cent.

If our whole debt could be converted to day, without a cent of expense, into a thirty year 5 per cent loan, it may be confidently asserted that the bonds would be at a premium within thirty days, if not from the start, and that it would cost the Government hundreds of millions, by way of premiums, before it could be paid off.

My recent relations to the Government as Secretary of the Treasury seem to impose on me the duty of making these observations; and I hope that they may receive your thoughtful consideration.

S. P. Chase

LS, DLC-JP.

1. See *House Ex. Docs.*, 38 Cong., 1 Sess., No. 3, "Report of the Secretary of the Treasury on the State of the Finances," pp. 1–27 (Ser. 1186).

2. The bill in question was Senate bill No. 300, proposed by John Sherman on May 2, 1866. The bill passed in the Senate on July 19 but died in the House. *Congressional Globe*, 39 Cong., 1 Sess., pp. 2331, 3927, 4156.

From Lewis D. Campbell

Hamilton O.   May 10th, 1866.

My Dear Sir—

I see it stated that the rumor in Washington is that you will veto the Habeas Corpus bill.[1] I know full well that there should be little reliance placed on *Washington* rumors, still I venture to suggest that it would probably be better for our cause if you could approve the bill, unless you find that it clearly conflicts with the cardinal principles laid down in your annual message. I have not seen the bill as it passed and therefore could give no opinion upon it, even if it were desired. I have, however, had a conference with Stanbury who *has examined it* and who seems very anxious that you should approve it.

I have thought and still think that the vetos of the Bureau and civil rights bills stand upon clear Constitutional grounds; but I think it questionable whether this could be said of a veto of the Habeas Corpus bill, if it passed as it was reported to the House. I gave the bill reported to the House a cursory examination when I was in Washington. There is beyond doubt a necessity for some such law to protect Union Soldiers, offices and private citizens, and I incline to the opinion that its constitutionality could be sustained under that clause of the Constitution extending the Judicial power to all cases in law and equity, arising under the laws of the U. States,—as this clause is construed by the Supreme Court in the case of Osborn & the Bank of the United States—9th Wheatons Reports.

I fear the veto of the Bill would give the Radicals great Capital and alienate many of our cherished friends. But you will of couse give the subject ample deliberation and discharge your duty consciensciously. My views are merely suggestive.

If you give the Colorado bill[2] "*fits*" your friends out here will shed no tears.

Since I returned home I have been busy on my farms—and am about finishing planting 250 acres of corn. As they have done hammering me in the senate and have taken me from their anvil, I think something of making a flying rip to the Capitol to see what sort of a Job boss Sumner has made of it.

Lewis D. Campbell

P.S.   Last eving a large Crowd gave me a Congratulatory serenade. Following in the footsteps of my illustrious friends in your region I made a speech of Course. I cannot say that it was a good speech, but I do know that it was well received and that my defence of your policy was heartily cheered—particularly by the *soldiers*.

L.D.C.

ALS, DLC-JP.
1. Signed by the President on May 11, the bill amended the habeas corpus act of March 3, 1863, by relieving all persons who had acted under legitimate military authority from responsibility for acts allegedly perpetrated during the war and guaranteeing said persons when sued the right to be tried in federal rather than state courts. The amendment stemmed from the thousands of such cases involving federal officers in Kentucky and other border states. *House Journal*, 39 Cong., 1 Sess., pp. 682, 705 (Ser. 1243); *Congressional Globe*, 39 Cong., 1 Sess., p. 1387; *New York Herald*, Mar. 21, 1866.
2. See Colorado Statehood Veto, May 15, 1866.

From James Lyons

Richmond   May 10 1866

My dear Mr. President
In the month of December last, I addressed you a letter[1] stating that Mr. Davis and myself were personal friends, and requesting that I might be permitted to act as one of his Counsel in the event of his trial.

As I have not the honor of a reply to that letter, and the news papers say that he has been Indicted at Norfolk, and is to be tried in June, I hope you will pardon me for respectfully repeating my request.[2]

James Lyons

ALS, DNA-RG60, Office of Atty. Gen., Misc. Papers *re* Imprisonment and Trial of Jefferson Davis.
1. See Lyons to Johnson, Dec. 9, 1865, Amnesty Papers, Jefferson Davis, Pets. to A. Johnson, RG94, NA.
2. Johnson referred the letter to Attorney General James Speed, who responded on May 24, informing Lyons that Davis would be allowed to select his own counsel; the President had no say in the matter. Lyons did act as one of Davis's attorneys. Speed to Lyons, May 24, 1866, Office of Atty. Gen., Lets. Sent, Vol. F (M699, Roll 11), RG60, NA; Warner and Yearns, *BRCC*.

From Benjamin Robinson[1]

Fayetteville N.C.   May 10th 1866

On the 13th Decr last I was arrested in my office in the town of Fayetteville N.C. by a guard of Federal soldiers on an order which emanated from Genl. Ruger[2] Comdg. the Military Department of N.C. I was carried to Raleigh where after being imprisoned I was permitted to give bail to appear before a Military Commission to answer any charges which might be preferred. No such charges were then preferred, nor have I ever been furnished with any such charges since. I understood that the course of the Fayetteville News, of which I was senior editor, was offensive to the General, and while no particular article was regarded as disloyal, the general tone of the paper was such as to induce this action. A criticism of general Grant, and some animadversions in the Congress being particularly alluded to in this connection.

The best evidence that Genl. Ruger's action was premature is to be found in the fact that you denounced the course of the members of Congress who had excited my wrath & induced my animadversions, in your 22d Feby speech, and that I had been misinformed & was mistaken concerning the reasons of Genl. Grant's visit to Raleigh,[3] which was rather, as I afterwards learned, in the interests of Conservatism, than for the purpose of receiving an ovation as I thought.

I am still under bond; but as you have ordered that civilians be no longer tried by Military Courts, & as Genl. Ruger seems to have no desire to prosecute the case, and as I can not leave the state, I would like to have an issue of an order for my release, from you; or at least have the matter investigated before a Civil tribunal.[4]

I am not disloyal, but am now, and have been since the taking of an oath under your amnesty proclamation, a warm supporter of your administration. I was a Confederate soldier and to the cause to which my faith was plighted was true till the last. I cannot do more now than to abide by the laws and in an humble sphere work with you for the preservation of the Constitution, which under existing circumstances is the single hope for Southern prosperity.

This letter is transmitted through Hon J. W. Chanler[5] of New York that it may the more surely reach you.

I have the honor to be with the highest respect & the assurance that I shall be earnestly your supporter in the policy of reconstruction which you have inaugurated. . . .

Benj. Robinson
Editor   "Fayetteville News"

ALS, DNA-RG94, Amnesty Papers (M1003, Roll 42), N.C., Benjamin Robinson.
1. Robinson (c1843–fl1868), a captain in the 5th N.C. Inf., CSA, had been wounded at Spotsylvania. During the summer of 1866 he became the senior editor of the *Wilmington Dispatch*, and two years later he published a novel. He was a law associate of Roger A. Pryor in New York City. Louis Manarin et al., comps., *North Carolina Troops, 1861–1865: A Roster* (11 vols., Raleigh, 1966-), 4: 130; *NUC*; *Fayetteville News*, Aug. 14, 1866, June 25, 1867; *Warrenton Courier*, Mar. 5, 1868.
2. Thomas H. Ruger (1833–1907), a West Point graduate and brigadier general of volunteers since 1862, remained in the army until 1897. Warner, *Blue*.
3. This is probably a reference to Grant's tour of the South, November-December

1865, during which he visited Raleigh, North Carolina, on November 28–29 and appeared before the state's legislature. See Simon, *Grant Papers*, 15: 423–24; *Advice*, 207.

4. By May 18 Robinson had been released through the influence of Gov. Jonathan Worth. Hamilton, *Worth Correspondence*, 1: 590.

5. Rep. John W. Chanler.

From Edwin M. Stanton

Washington City, May 10th 1866.

Sir:

In compliance with your communication of the 27th ultimo,[1] requesting a report showing the number of free persons of color that have been removed from the District of Columbia under contracts approved by the Bureau of Refugees Freedmen and Abandoned Lands, and certain other information concerning the same, I have the honor to submit the accompanying report of the Commissioner of said Bureau, containing the information called for.[2]

Edwin M Stanton   Secretary of War.

LS, DNA-RG105, Records of the Commr., Lets. Recd. (M752, Roll 26).

1. Edmund Cooper to Stanton, Apr. 27, 1866, Records of the Commr., Lets. Recd. (M752, Roll 26), RG105, NA.

2. Although the accompanying report has not been found, subsequent correspondence between the War Department, Freedmen's Bureau, and Quartermaster Department sheds some light on this subject. General Howard reported 1,145 freedmen removed from the District of Columbia under contracts approved by the Bureau. Later correspondence with the Quartermaster Department, however, indicated 2,262 freedmen transported from the District of Columbia as of May 1, 1866, at a cost of $29,158.69, or 1,247 as of April 11, 1866 (the date of Howard's report), at a cost of $15,372.25. Various officials deemed it impossible to separate Howard's figure of 1,145 from the aggregate numbers. Spurgin to Rogers, May 2, 1866, ibid.; Moore to Stanton, May 14, 1866; Payne to Rucker, May 23, 1866; Rucker to Meigs, May 24, 1866; Stanton to Johnson, May 28, 1866, Johnson Papers, LC; Stanton to Johnson, May 26, 1866, Lets. Sent, Mil. Bks., Executive, 57-C, RG107, NA.

From Alexander H. Stephens

Private and official—

Crawfordville Ga.   10 May 1866

Dear Sir—

Since my return I have been through the State from Dalton to Augusta and met with people from other sections. I find all things in as good condition—politically—as could be expected. There is evidently a disposition on the part of Some Northern people to Stir up Strife between the blacks and whites by urging the former on to set up Conventions &c but such things are to be expected and upon the whole our people are acting with great forbearance. The prospect of the planting interest at this time is very bad—the continued rains and the failure to get a good stand of cotton are casting a Shadow just at this time over the hopes of the planters generally. The people are watching with deep interest the progress of events at Washington. I need not assure you that they all look to you as the only hope for a restoration of perfect peace in the union with a preservation of Constitutional liberty. Enclosed I send you a newspaper Slip which speaks for itself[1] and which I Suppose you may take some interest in reading.

Alexander H. Stephens

ALS, DLC-JP.
   1. Not found.

From Lorenzo Thomas

Washington, D.C   May 11, 1866

Sir
   During the month of January last I accidentally made the acquaintance in Louisiana of General Z. York[1] who has been in the rebel service. On a subsequent occasion meeting him on a steamer at Natchez he took me aside and told me in confidence that a person in or near Vidalia in the parish of Concordia had sworn to take my life because I am a member of the Commission which tried Wirz. He asked me if I carried arms, and on my replying in the negative advised me to do so, which advice I followed. I found afterward that he had imparted the same information to two of my friends in Natchez that they might put me on my guard, in case he should not see me.
   In march last whilst descending the Mississippi river I again saw General York and on stating that I was proceeding to this city he requested me to ask your Excellency for his pardon, for which he had made application,[2] assuring me that he would be a peacable law abiding citizen of the United States. I believe him sincere in his professions, and as he certainly rendered me an officer of the United States almost a stranger to him, a most important service I earnestly request that your Excellency will grant him a pardon.

L. Thomas   Adjt. Genl.

ALS, DNA-RG94, Amnesty Papers (M1003, Roll 29), La., Zebulon York.
   1. Zebulon York (1819–1900), a Confederate brigadier general, was raised in Maine and studied law at the University of Louisiana. While practicing law in Vidalia, he and his partner accumulated a large fortune. By 1861 they owned six plantations with 1700 slaves producing an annual 4500 bales of cotton. York organized a company of the 14th La. Inf. at the outset of the war and fought in almost every major campaign in the eastern theatre. Warner, *Gray*.
   2. York began the process of pardon application as early as June 1865, but evidently communications and documents went astray. His amnesty files are filled with letters written by him and in his behalf over a period of months. York was finally pardoned on May 11, 1866, eleven months after he first sought presidential absolution. Later that same month, York informed General Thomas that he had received a copy of his pardon in the mail and that through S. R. Maltby he had paid Maj. Andrew K. Long, the President's secretary, a fee of $300 to assist with the matter of York's pardon. See Amnesty Papers (M1003, Roll

29), La., Zebulon York, RG94, NA; *House Ex. Docs.*, 39 Cong., 2 Sess., No. 31, p. 13 (Ser. 1289); York to Thomas, May 22, 1866, Johnson Papers, LC.

From David F. Caldwell

Greensboro N C   May 12 66

Will you pardon your old *Bank Corrospondent* to say one word to your Exelency? I have ever been an ultra union man, and for opposing secession *was mobed* before the war and twice since. Have been shot at wounded & beten with clubs & I blush to say it pelted by a crowd of boys and *ladies* with rotten eggs for my union principals &c. Yet I am no black Republican & never shall be I will add. I was held up in the papers as the "*Andy Johnston of N C.*" I want nor ask for no office—and when I say I suport your administration policy I assure you I do so because I think it best for our country. And for this reason I desire to see you sustained & will do all I can to secure it success. I have been 18 years a member of our Stat Legislature twice Presidential Elector & am now a member of our State convention and have some little influence. I have had three especal corrospondents of the fanatical press to call upon me, who have indeavored to persuad me to take sides against your policy. I have been assured if I would do so I would be genaly the gainer in a political point of view. And as an old line Whig I should not hesitate for a moment, when Holden a Secession Democrat was doing all he could for them &c &c. These gentel hints I treated in the way I thought they deserved.

Now in 1848 Van Buren & Adams[1] ran on a platform in which were the resolutions of 98–99 so Fremont & Daton[2] ran on a platform in which was the same Resolution of 98, 99. All the antislavery resolutions of the free states has been based on States Rights doctrine—First acted upon by the Hartfert Convention &c &c. So New England is the author of Secession The author of slave importation & exportation Authors of Abolition & insurection & exterminity 212 emancipation & colinasation sosits in the South—& consequenly all our rigorous laws on the subject of slavery. Also the authors of *Anti Masonry.* But the point I wish to bring to your notice & press upon you is this—Sumner, Wilson, Banks, Stephens &c—are all, not only oposed to the Union now, but have always been ready to *let it slide.* They were united on the No Nothing Anti Catholic platform But now go for Negroes sufferage & equality *instantum* whether the states will or not. Now it seems to me all your friends would but post themselves thoroughly as to the past Anti Mason No Nothing Record of thes ultras—and simultaenously in Congress & throgh the press open upon them & keep up the fires upon them, we could do much to sustain your administration & policy and perpetuate our form of Goverment & free institutions. These men are for pulig up the negroes at once & forevr above the poor union white men of the South—who are now degraded and oppressed by their poverty. In short I assure you that the ultra course taken by Sumner Wilson Stevens & others is fast rendering the *union men odious* instead of *Traitors odious*. For the reason that these worthies are taking precisely the course the disunionist predicted they would if they conquered or we submitted—while the union men declared we would be welcomed back and the fated calf would be killed. Had we all gone back at once Republicans & the party would have been enthroned in power & the harts of the people. But Alas this was not done and if maters progress in the way proposed—I know the masses will become confirmed in their prejudices. Pardon all I may have said amiss.

D. F. Caldwell

ALS, DLC-JP.
   1. Martin Van Buren and Charles Francis Adams were Free Soil candidates.
   2. John Charles Fremont and William L. Dayton were the Republican party's candidates in 1856.

From Francis P. Blair, Sr.

Silver Spring   13th May 1866

My Dear Mr. President

In reply to my application to you for redress of the wrong done my son-in-law Capt Lee[1] you were so good as to refer me to Mr. Secy. Welles intimating, that having had a conversation with him you hoped he would make some satisfactory arrangement. I immediately went to his office and laid before him my wishes and the grounds which seemed to me to sustain them as reasonable.[2] He recieved me very kindly, assured me of his willingness to give effect to the object you had in view in sending me to him as well as to oblige me as his friend of many years and one, whom he was pleased to recognize as having some claims from continued public service. I then frankly explained my complaint—the cause of it, and proposed various modes in which he might exert his official power properly for remedy.

I told him Mr. Fox[3] had years ago when under Lee's command concieved that an affront was intended him in some order of his superior and that I knew the hostility he entertained had been on the increase since he obtained power in the Department and Lee's importance had grown up with the war—that I had opportunity to observe his aversion and a multitude of official acts in the Department marked with injustice to Lee and calculated to degrade him, which as I could not impute to ill-feeling on the part of his principal, I felt must proceed from the sinister influence of the Assistant who was charged as a naval man for the most part with the personel of the navy.

He is the Functionary most conversant with the officers—with their aptitude & deserts and is permitted therefore to some extent to control appointment and confer honors and advancement. It was in this way that Mr. Fox "fed fat the grudge" he bore Lee. He overslaughed him by appointing his juniors & inferiors over him only one of whom (Porter)[4] deserved such promotion for the enterprize, skill & value of service exhibited. Mr. Welles attributed this view to the partiality which naturally arose from my relations with Lee. I admitted that great abatement ought to be made from my estimate on this score, but I besought him to look at the Records the Department itself had made on which he founded the promotions of inferiors over Lee, and compare the recorded services of the latter with them. The gallant achievement for which Rowan[5] was put over his senior was the affair at Newbern. There the land force took the place Rowan firing at long range recieving no injury from the enemys fire either to his vessels or those on board of them. Dalghren[6] was appointed Rear Admiral over him because he had invented a useful gun and deserved remuneration. Mr. Welles admitted Dalghren's promotion to be against the principle & rule of promotion in the Dept. and ascribed it to Mr. Lincolns over ruling authority. Rogers,[7] another of inferior grade, promoted over Lee, is a very brave & very useful officer. His exploit was the taking of the Atlanta with two Monitors. From the invulnerable turret of one of his Iron-clad Monitors he fired four shots, at the Atlanta two of which took effect and disabled her. The Rebel Boar did not fire a shot at him—made no resistance, but hung out its Flag of Surrender. Rogers deserved promotion for this prompt, decisive exhibition of skill and as the records states truly, for other and long continued exertions evincing his zeal, activity and capacity.

Capt Winslow[8] of the Kearsage that sunk the Alabama is another junior promoted over Lee. He certainly deserved promotion for his triumph —but why should not Lee be also promoted, who destroyed more of the enemy's ships in battle than all of those who had superceded him? These brilliant attractive points which they have won in high commands have drawn down rays of glory on the heads of those of lower grade—*the commodores*—from which Lee is excluded. They now alone are eligible to become admirals unless the President interposes. I asked if it would not be glaring injustice to deny promotion to a man who had showed like courage in conflict & destroyed more of the enemys ships in battle and more of thier blockade runners than any of his justly rewarded Rivals And who besides was the first man in the Navy to abjure President Buchanan's scheme of Treason and *non coercion policy*[9]—who when he had been sent away to the East Indies to carry the Vandalia beyond the reach of the nations authority that might use her, to suppress the rebellion the moment he got the news of the Southern treason, himself revolted against the authority that betrayed the Govt and was the only man who took the initiative and the responsibility of disobedience of orders to a faithless Executive. He turned the prow of his ship homeward to confront the enemies of his country in the South though himself of Southern origin. When he reported himself at the Department Mr. Fox who was then installed in it, recieved him coldly saying "he did not know how Secy. Welles would consider the violation of orders on his part." Secy. Welles however, soon made it manifest that he construed disobedience to a treacherous Executive though clothed with the authority of the Govt into loyalty to the Government itself. Lee was sent to blockade the Harbor of Charleston with the Vandalia that those at the heart of Secession might know that the lineal heir of the man who first proposed the Resolution to make the country one nation[10]—a unit—by the Declaration of Independence was there to enforce the Union. For months he was employed maintaining the blockade of Charleston. He was next under the Command of Farragut[11] associated in the great enterprize of opening the Mississippi with his wooden vessels, against Forts—ironclads & ram fitted gun boats. How does the part he bore there in his wooden steamer compare with the exploits of those I have named who were afterwards put over him. Porter extols him in his letters to the Department, and to Mr. Fox which he read to me, for his skills and bravery in fighting Forts St Philip & Jackson relieving Porters mortar fleet for the time from its arduous duty of keeping them constantly under fire. The casualties on Lees vessel were greater than any other ship so engaged. Porter also gave Lee great credit for good service connected with the difficult passage of the bars by one, or more of the large ships for which Farragut waited to attack the Forts. Bailey[12] who commanded the division where Lee fought, gives him credit for the alacrity with which lee came to the rescue of two ships, first of his flag ship and then of the Veruna sinking under the power of two vessels of the enemy—saving the Veruna's crew —destroying both of her assailants—driving them ashore where they were burnt, and capturing the Captain[13] and men attempting to escape from one of them—the only naval capture made in this fight. In ascending the River he was engaged with Fort Chalmette—which surrendered. He was twice engaged with the batteries of Vicksburg.

Lee was then given the separate command of the Atlantic Squadron making the blockade of the Atlantic Coast, and also maintaining the communications of the Army of the Potomac & its cooperating forces along the coast. This duty accomplished with great success during several campaigns, Lee was detached to take command of the Mississippi Squadron rendering the same support to the Armies of the West. His service in the East, met the entire approbation of Genl Grant (as his letter shows),[14] with whom he cooperated—his effective blockade astonished all who understood the difficulty and the extent of the coast, & his limited means to give it effectiveness—and The Government justified his measures against the domestic contraband trade in our harbors, though involving collision with the Genl commanding at Fortress Monroe.[15] In the West when controlling the whole naval force and administering its power over the Mississippi & all its tributaries, all his acts had the sanction of the Government—and, Genl Thomas with whom he cooperated, in a public letter[16] gave him thanks for the able & important support he had afforded throughout his final struggle.

After adverting to Lee's uninterrupted success in all his labors from the opening to the close of the War, embracing the management of its two great fleets East and West, I asked Mr. Welles to say what Naval Commander had rendered greater service during the contest with the exception of Farragut & Porter than Lee? He named no one—and now I appeal to you to say whether the success of Winslow over the Alabama, of Rogers over the Atlanta, or the cooperation of Rowan with the Army that took Newbern, however properly recommending these commanders to promotion justify the overslaughing the Officer, who, as Rear Admiral had the responsibility of managing the two great Squadrons cooperating with two great armies of the Union and did it thoroughly to the satisfaction of the illustrious Generals who conquered the Rebellion and a Peace? Ought the Officer who independently of this service in connection with the armies, also carried on a system of blockade & made it so effective as to cut the sinews of war of the Confederacy, and to drive it almost to destitution—Keeping its money power—*its cotton*—at home, destroying its credit abroad—and siezing supplies however contributed & wherever presented on the Rivers or the coast,—to be degraded from his position of Rear Admiral and sent back behind those whom he had ranked in the Service and put under them on the peace establishment? I told Mr. Welles that it looked like injustice to See Rowan, the junior of Lee put over his head for participating in the taking of Newbern, while Lee, who had taken an active and important share in the operations & successes of our great armies by maintaining their bases of communications was not only remitted to the humble rank he held before the war, but by artful legislative organization in his Department was precluded from rising during his life to the rank in which he served during war. Mr. Welles replied that Lee had no greater right to complain than other Captains whom Rowan's advancement as a junior had overslaughed? I told him I thought differently. Lee had earned promotion by greater services than Rowan & had therefore right to complain. But the other captains whom Rowan overslaughed had never rendered even the partial services on which his pretensions were founded. They fell from no eminence to which active and efficient capacity had raised them as Lee did, & now they find themselves advanced by the peace principle of graduating by Seniority to a position to obstruct his rise to the higher honors of his profession which he earned and showed his fitness for, by the actual discharge of their functions in the most trying times that ever tested the qualifications of a commanding officer—not only do the junior officers put over him unjustly, stand between him and preferment, but all the other captains whom they superseded because they were held to be less competent, now rise by the specific gravity of seniority (in despite of the laws of nature) to take the position he occupied, in turns, & thus exclude him while one of them remains. This is the artful contrivance of Mr. Fox to depress a man whose merit he was obliged to admit while the exigency of the service required, but whom his malignity would now punish by degradation because he discharged his duty so well as to add Envy to his hatred. He urged a law through Congress confining eligibility for promotion to the grade of Admiral, to the list of Commodores.[17] As the Secretary has been induced to refuse Lee all promotion for his services during the war, he is excluded from this list & this excludes all hope of reaching the destinction which he held during the war to enable him to serve the country and which is now withdrawn to gratify the ambition of those who did not serve it & whom the appointment of Rowan & other juniors over them, proves the Dept did not consider competent to serve in the command of squadrons. Mr. Welles's excuse to me for this flagrant injustice was, that all those interested officers exclaimed against the promotion of Lee because he had made so much prize money[18]—imputing the opportunity given by his appointment to a squadron to enable him to obtain it, to partiality in the Dept—to influence of the Blairs, & insisting that he had been paid for his services (and in that the Secy. seemed to concur) by the prize money. Surely there never was a more shameful confession on the part of those seeking to sacrifice a meritorious officer.

The whole class of officers who would disparage him on the score of prize money, Know that the amount of it wrested from the enemy, is a strong proof of effective aid given in suppressing the rebellion. It not only cut off the resources of the enemy, in preventing Europe from giving them its aid, but it shut up in thier own coffers, all the money they had— their cotton—so that they could pay their own people & their army in nothing but blank paper. To accomplish this great object was to crush the rebellion—and hence to Stimulate the highest effort in this direction, prize money is given by the Government to all officers & crews engaged in this most important service. It is meant to impart sleepless vigilance and unwearied exertion, by adding individual interest to the higher inspirations of ambition & patriotism. But if the officers of the Navy are given to understand that what they gain by prizes is to be detracted from the honors of their profession gained in battle, in carrying on the war for their country, they are turned instantly into mere pirates. Farragut and Porter gained prizes, by seizing the blockade runners of the enemy but they were not off-set against thier claims for promotion—why should such a rule be applied to Lee who was Still more successful in this most fatal sort of warfare against the enemy—which put millions into our own Treasury while it gave mites only to the brave & much enduring men who wore out their lives in their patient, perilous & exhaustive labor?

Mr. Welles ought to have made this reply to the interested class who threw up the prize money as an obstruction to the recognition of Lee's merits in this as in every other avenue of the service in all of which he had acted his part well. He ought to have told these complainers too, that niether Lee himself nor any of the Blairs asked for him, the position in which the Navy Department placed him, solely because they wanted his service and considered him the best suited to perform it. He should have defended himself against the charge of favoritism by stating bluntly the truth the Lee was no favorite at the Dept. Instead of doing this Mr. Welles in effect admits the imputation by acceding to the purposes of the Cabal who make use of them to degrade Lee as one having recieved unmerited favors already, and undeserving to wear the honors of the Station to which he was [illegible] without solicitation, and the duties of which all associated with him, even the highest in the Service bear ample testimony, he performed with distinguished success. These clamorers who beseige Mr. Welles, by Mr. Fox's Bill are made a close corporation of commodores like the conclave of cardinals from which the pope the admiral is chosen, give us our admiral. The President has no choices. Mr. Welles told me that the Admirals as well as the privileged order out of which Admirals are hereafter to be made are all against Lee. I hope this is not so—generous natures which I know belong to such men as Porter would not kick down the ladder on which they reached their eminence while those were on it who helped them to rise on it. I found Mr. Welles set against Lee's promotion as I found him at an earlier day. I therefore requested as he was forbidden to hope for the higher honors of his profession, that his war services might at least be requited by some humble place at his home where he might be useful to his country & enjoy the comfort of his family. I suggested that you had issued a notice in the papers that war service was to give preference to competent persons who sought suitable employment under the Govt. at Washington & elsewhere,[19] and I told Mr. Welles that I would apply to you for a place in some of the Naval Bureaus & observed that as Adl. Smith[20] the elder, was on the retired list, had enjoyed a plurality of official honors and emoluments, having a son[21] also in a Bureau—an heir in advance)—to eke out the father's lifetime in civil office by another lifetime, I would if he, consented make application for Lee as his successor. Mr. Welles objected, and insisted that he should go to Mare's Island in California. I told him this was looked to by me not only as exile for Lee & his little family but for me & mine, for I had resolved that I would not give up during the few years remaining of my life, my daughter & grandchild[22]—that I would not detain them from the father & husband or stay myself in a home made a solitude. He insisted that he was sure I would find it much better for me that he should go, assuming that I would subject myself to the charge of using improper influence if he remained. I saw that his purpose was that Lee should have no employment in the city, for I proposed several other places in his gift, which he declined, saying at the sametime that I deserved so much from the country and he was much my friend that he would do any thing in his power to oblige me! I then proposed to him that as Rowan had been out of service & waiting orders for 18 months, that he would give the place which he thought so eligible to re-quite Lee for his war services & make amends for the injustice of which I thought he had a right to complain, to the gentleman who had super-seded him in the career of naval honors. He replied that he could not ap-point him (Rowan) to the care of the California Navy yard—that he was entirely unfit for it & on looking over his list of unemployed officers, he declared that he could find no one fit for the place but Lee. The result of my long interview with the Secy. was, the conviction that he was resolved *that Lee should quit the city or the Navy.* This whole series of official op-pression I do not attribute to the ill will of the Secretary but to the cold blooded persecuting temper of his Subaltern.

I hope on examining the whole case that you will find it the interest of the public to do the justice to Lee of nominating him to the Senate for promotion with a vote of Thanks. If this is not Suitable in your opinion, I would ask for a Bureau for him in connexion with the Navy. None can doubt his fitness. If this cannot be granted, I would ask for the indul-gence, the Department has given, to the gentleman who supplanted him, —a *leave of absence.* Rowan's leave & waiting orders has now reached 18 months. Lee's affairs requires his attention for a year at home.[23]

F P. Blair

ALS, DLC-JP.

1. Samuel Phillips Lee.

2. Blair met with Welles on May 12, 1866, concerning the passing over of Lee for pro-motion and the orders for him to proceed to the Navy Yard at Mare Island on the west coast. (The President's private secretary had conferred with Welles on May 9 regarding Lee.) Blair requested, as a favor to an old friend, a change of orders that would provide Lee a Washington post. Beale, *Welles Diary*, 2: 504–7.

3. Gustavus V. Fox (1821–1883), assistant secretary of the navy, graduated from the U.S. Naval Academy in 1841. After serving in the Mexican War and attaining the rank of lieutenant, he resigned. In 1861 Lincoln asked Fox to devise a plan for the relief of Fort Sumter, and in April he sailed south from New York with a squadron, but arrived too late. In May of 1861 he was appointed chief clerk of the Navy Department and then assistant secretary in August. Fox resigned near the end of May 1866 and at Johnson's behest he led an official delegation to Russia. *DAB*; Beale, *Welles Diary*, 2: 512, 514.

4. David D. Porter (1813–1891), a naval officer who had a long career in various as-pects of the navy before the Civil War. In April 1861 he led the relief expedition of Fort Pickens, began the blockade of Mobile, and attained the rank of commander. Subsequent service saw him commanding a flotilla under Farragut in the New Orleans expedition, com-manding the Mississippi Squadron as an acting rear admiral, and aiding in the capture of Vicksburg. In 1865 he was appointed superintendent of the Naval Academy and vice ad-miral the following year. *DAB*.

5. Stephen C. Rowan (1808–1890) was a naval officer who served in a variety of posts and capacities, including duty in the Mexican War. When the Civil War began he was com-mander of the steam-sloop *Pawnee* defending Washington, D.C., and unsuccessfully at-tempted the relief of Fort Sumter. During the war he served primarily off the North Carolina coast, becoming a captain and commodore in 1862. In 1866 he was promoted to rear admiral in command of the Norfolk Navy Yard, and later served with the Asiatic Squadron, becoming vice admiral in 1870. *DAB*.

6. John A. Dahlgren (1809–1870) entered the navy in 1826 and in the 1850s devel-oped the Dahlgren gun. When the Civil War began he was in command of the Washington

Navy Yard, and in 1862 became captain and also chief of the Bureau of Ordnance. In 1863 he became rear admiral and was given command of the South Atlantic Squadron, from which he resigned in 1865. The next year he was appointed commander of the South Pacific Squadron. *NCAB*, 9: 377–80.

7. John Rodgers (1812–1882) entered the navy in 1828. A commander since 1855, he was sent at the outbreak of the Civil War to superintend the ironclads in the West and to command the *Galena* of the North Atlantic Squadron. Between 1864 and 1867 he held various ship commands before becoming commandant of the Boston Navy Yard. Ibid., 5: 14.

8. John A. Winslow (1811–1873) was a career naval officer who served in the Pacific, Mediterranean, and along the Brazilian and Mexican coast prior to the Civil War. Winslow served on the Mississippi River in 1862 and was promoted to captain. For the next two years, however, he saw duty off the European coast. Because of his victory over the *Alabama*, he became a commodore. Following the war he commanded the Gulf Squadron (1866–67) and, when promoted to rear admiral in 1870, took command of the Pacific Fleet. *DAB*.

9. In Buchanan's last message to Congress in December 1860, he denied the right of secession, but he declared that he could do nothing to stop secession, because the Constitution did not give the national government the power "to coerce a state into submission." James M. McPherson, *Battle Cry of Freedom: The Civil War Era* (New York, 1988), 246, 248; Richardson, *Messages*, 5: 628–37.

10. Samuel Phillips Lee was the grandson of Richard Henry Lee (1732–1794), a prominent Virginian, who proposed a resolution "that these United Colonies are, and of right ought to be, free and independent states . . . ." Smith, *Blair Family*, 18; *Who Was Who in America 1607–1896* (Chicago, 1963), 309; George B. Tindall, *America: A Narrative History* (New York, 1984), 200–201.

11. David G. Farragut (1801–1870) directed the construction of the Navy Yard at Mare Island in the 1850s. The outbreak of the Civil War in 1861 forced the removal of him and his family from Norfolk because of their Unionist sentiment. The following year he was appointed to command the West Gulf Blockading Squadron and led the successful campaign at New Orleans. In July 1862 he was promoted the first rear admiral, a position created for him, and two years later he commanded the victorious capture of Mobile Bay. In his honor the President approved a bill creating the office of vice admiral, to which Farragut was immediately named. In 1866 the position of admiral was created specifically for him. *DAB*.

12. By 1861 Theodorus Baily (1805–1877) was a naval commander who served in the blockade of Pensacola and was second-in-command to Farragut in the New Orleans campaign. In late 1862 he assumed command of the East Gulf Blockading Squadron. He was named rear admiral in 1866 and soon thereafter retired. Mark M. Boatner, III, *The Civil War Dictionary* (New York, 1959).

13. Beverly Kennon (1830–1890) resigned from the U.S. Navy in April 1861 to serve the Confederacy. He was the leading figure in torpedo and mine warfare and commanded the *Governor Moore* in the naval battle at New Orleans. Kennon torched his ship in order to avoid surrendering her. Picked up by men from Lee's *Oneida*, he was later denied parole because he had burned his ship. *NCAB*, 4: Index; Beverly Kennon, "Fighting Farragut Below New Orleans," in Robert U. Johnson and Clarence C. Buel, eds., *Battles and Leaders of the Civil War* (4 vols., New York, 1887), 2: 88; J. Thomas Scharf, *History of the Confederate States Navy* (New York, 1887), 279; John D. Hayes, ed., *Samuel Francis Du Pont: A Selection From His Civil War Letters* (3 vols., Ithaca, 1969), 2: 86; Robert Carse, *Blockade: The Civil War at Sea* (New York, 1958), 31; Milton F. Perry, *Infernal Machines: The Story of Confederate Submarine and Mine Warfare* (Baton Rouge, 1965), 11; Callahan, *List of Navy and Marine Corps*, 311.

14. Not found.

15. Benjamin F. Butler. Strode, *Jefferson Davis*, 37.

16. Not found.

17. Blair refers to a Senate bill which proposed "to define the number and regulate the appointment of officers in the Navy." Presented by Sen. James Grimes in April 1866 at the request of the Navy Department, the bill stipulated an increase in the number of line officers. The new positions were to be filled from the grade immediately below, however; and,

while Lee had been a rear admiral during wartime, he was only a peacetime captain. Lee therefore could not yet be made admiral. Senator Trumbull unsuccessfully proposed an amendment allowing advancement to the rank one had held during the war. Johnson signed the Grimes bill in July 1866. *Congressional Globe*, 39 Cong., 1 Sess., pp. 1982, 3151–54, 4116.

18. Over $150,000 according to Welles. Beale, *Welles Diary*, 2: 504–5.

19. In early April 1866 Johnson issued such a proclamation. See Circular *re* Appointments to Office, Apr. 7, 1866.

20. Joseph Smith (1790–1877), a lifelong naval officer, who in 1846 was named chief of the Bureau of Navy Yards and Docks and continued as such until 1869. *DAB*.

21. Albert N. Smith (c1822–1866), also a longtime naval officer, commanded the *Wissahickon* at New Orleans in April 1862. He was then appointed to the Bureau of Equipment and Recruiting upon the death of Admiral Forte, having been promoted to lieutenant commander and then commander in 1862. Callahan, *List of Navy and Marine Corps*, 502; *National Intelligencer*, Sept. 11, 1866.

22. Elizabeth Blair (1818–1906) married S. P. Lee in April 1843. Before the Civil War she was known as "Little Democrat." Their only child was Francis Preston Blair Lee (1857–1944), a lawyer who later served as a Maryland state senator and then as U.S. senator from Maryland (1913–17). *BDAC*, 1204; Elbert B. Smith, *Francis Preston Blair* (New York, 1980), 10, 18, 181, 183, 439–40; *DAB*.

23. Not found.

From Caleb Greene[1]

North Kingston   May 13th 1866

To the Chief Magistrate of our Nation. May his *name* be blended with that of Lincoln and Washington in this world, and his Soul with theirs in immortal Glory in the world to come, is the wish of very many this way as well as the humble servant that ventures to intrude on your Majesties most fully occupied time.

I served my Country three years in the Fourth Regiment of Rhode Island Volunteers, who had for bounty only fifteen dollars when they went out and when honorably discharged one hundred more, This was readily paid to me.

There is much rumor as to their being made equal to those who went out on large bounties, the last talk is, I am told that I with some others am to have some one hundred and fifty or sixty acres of government land, but the truth as to whether it is so, or where it is, I have never yet been able to ascertain. If your Majesty will have the condescention to set some of your penmen to inform me as to the truth of it, and where located & to whon to apply to know how to find it. I will feel under many obligations as a good and faithful Subject and Servant.

Caleb Greene *formerly* Caleb Greene Jr.

P.S.   Allow me to say I have been, as is often termed, an iron constitutioned man, but 3 years in the United states service tore that constitution in pieces, and laid the strong man weak.

I am subject to attacks of fever and ague. Badly affected lungs, at times I think cant stand it long, (when a colon irritates;) Heart complaint, dis-

MAY 1866

pepsy dreadfully. I shall be very thankful if there be something for me. I have a dependent family.

I lost one noble son at the battle of Fredericksberg. (R.B.G.)[2] If he had lived he might have been good help to me. My next son's[3] abilities of body and mind are ruined by fits; consumptive wife,[4] &c.

I hope I have not worn very hard on your patience by the liberty taken. But I thought if it would not be too much trouble to you, If I could get information from head quarters I could rely on it.[5]

Caleb Greene.

If you do write please direct to Caleb Greene Allenton P.O. North Kingston R.I. Thousand thanks, to you.

ALS, DNA-RG48, Lands and Railroads Div., Misc. Lets. Recd. (1840–80).

1. On the eve of the war, Greene (b. c1821) owned a farm valued at $800. 1860 Census, R.I., Washington, North Kingstown, Lafayette, 75.

2. Robert B. Greene (c1843–1863), a mariner and private, 7th R.I. Inf., whose left foot had been amputated, died nearly three weeks after the battle. Ibid., 76; CSR, Robert B. Green, RG94, NA.

3. Probably Caleb Greene (b. c1849). 1860 Census, R.I., Washington, North Kingstown, Lafayette, 75.

4. Sarah Greene (b. c1809). Ibid.

5. Greene's letter was referred to the Department of the Interior, where it was routinely handled. Bounty land warrants for honorably discharged Union veterans and their dependents were not authorized by Congress until 1872. James Harlan to Greene, May 25, 1866, Lands and Railroads Div., Misc. Lets. Sent (1840–80), RG48, NA; *Senate Journal*, 42 Cong., 2 Sess., p. 495 (Ser. 1477).

From Virginia C. Clay

Huntsville, Ala.   May 14th/66.

My dear friend,

I know you will pardon this letter when handed you by our mutual lovely friend Mrs. Bouligny.[1]

I write to acknowledge receipt of my father's pardon papers from Mr. Seward. Mr. *Joseph C. Bradley*, had them, to our surprise. He is a bitter Enemy of *yours*, & my husband. He belongs to the D.C. Humphries wing. Please order *all* Communications for us, to "Beirne & Gordon," who are our lawyers.

I trust you will not give the Mobile Collectorship to *Ben: Jolly*.[2] It is but a short time since he *damned you*, on the public street, while hurrahing for the Union. He is *totally untrustworthy. Humphries* is finding lucrative employment, as *pardon*-broker & universal agent for rebels. It is said that poor old *Gurley*[3] paid him 3000$ to get his son Frank released!

I hope you will soon send me some relief for my husband. His office, now the Freedman's Bureau, was *never abandoned* property. Our tenant[4] *was forced* out of it, at the bayonet's point.

And now, a *secret*.

Is it possible for you to send me my husband's pardon without any one knowing it beside yourself?

I will keep it silent as the grave, until Gov. Clay's death. He fears his son cannot inherit his patrimony, small as it will now be, & the tho't Embitters his last hours. He is so feeble he may die any moment. Mr. Clay's hands are tied, until we hear from you. Meantime, strangers are consuming what we really need for our daily bread. We buy milk, while Yankees keep dozens of our cows.

Write me if only a *Card*-letter. Mrs. B. will enclose anything to me.
V.C.C.

AL, DLC-JP.
1. Mary E. Bouligny (*c*1839–*fl*1875) was a daughter of Washington merchant George Parker, with whom Virginia Clay was a guest while visiting in Washington, and the widow of Louisiana Congressman John E. Bouligny. Subsequently, she was an author and, after a second marriage, moved to England. 1860 Census, D.C., Washington, 4th Ward, 290; Washington directories (1875–76); Nuermberger, *Clays*, 292; Conrad, *La. Biography*; *NUC*.
2. Jolley (*c*1810–1873), a Huntsville farmer who claimed to have been "an unqualified Union man," did not become the Mobile collector. 1860 Census, Ala., Madison, Huntsville, 46; Jolley to Johnson, Aug. 21, 1865, Amnesty Papers (M1003, Roll 6), Ala., Benjamin Jolley, RG94, NA; Pauline J. Gandrud, comp., *Alabama Records* (245 vols., Easley, S.C., 1981), 131: 38.
3. John Gurley (*c*1788–1868), a well-to-do farmer who had served under Andrew Jackson during the War of 1812. Ibid., 38: 65; 1860 Census, Ala., Madison, SE Div., 77.
4. Not identified.

From William Y. Leader[1]

Philadelphia   May 14th 1866

Respected Sir

I herewith present you my application[2] for the position of assessor of Internal Revenue for the 5th Congressional District of Pennsylvania. In doing so I deem it proper to state that I have never been a Democrat. My first Presidential vote was cast for Fillmore & Donnelson, my next for Bell & Everett. When Mr Lincoln was elected I gave his administration my hearty support. As the Editor of a public journal in Philadelphia, *The National Guard*, with my pen, and with my voice upon the stump I earnestly and with all my power sustained the government in suppressing the rebellion. I earnestly supported Mr Lincoln and yourself for the Presidency and Vice Presidency.[3] From the day that you gave your instructions to the first Provisional Governor you appointed to this time I have honestly supported the policy you have adopted. I have used my best efforts and exerted all my influence to sustain and defend you and shall continue to do so whether I get the appointment or not. I hereby submit a copy of the paper I published[4] which you will perceive was recommended and endorsed by the first men of the State. I also submit a letter from Governor Curtin.[5] There is not a Republican in Philadelphia who would not be compelled endorse every word in the letter of Gov. Curtin. Mr Glossbrenner and Mr B. M. Boyer[6] Democratic members from our State also endorse me. Should you be pleased to confer this appointment

upon me I pledge myself to discharge the duties with honesty and fidelity, and will use the entire influence of the position to promote the success
of the principles of the Union Party of which you are the acknowledged
head. With my best wishes for your health and trusting that Providence
may spare you to finish the work of restoring our beloved country to
peace and prosperity. . . .[7]

Wm. Y. Leader

ALS, DNA-RG56, Appts., Internal Revenue Service, Assessor, Pa., 5th Dist., William Y.
Leader.
    1. Beginning in 1870, Leader (*c*1836–*fl*1880), an attorney and real estate agent, also
coedited a weekly Philadelphia journal, *The National Independent*. Later he moved to Austin, Texas, where he continued his journalistic endeavors. 1880 Census, Tex., Travis, Austin, 7th Ward, 135th Enum. Dist., 23; Philadelphia directories (1863–71); Scharf and
Westcott, *Philadelphia*, 3: 2044.
    2. Supporting documentation indicates that Leader personally submitted his applica-
tion to Johnson on May 21. Adam J. Glossbrenner to Johnson, June 8, 1866, Appts.,
Internal Revenue Service, Assessor, Pa., 5th Dist., William Y. Leader, RG56, NA; Ser.
6A, Vol. B: 159, Johnson Papers, LC.
    3. On the eve of the war, Leader, as a member of the Union Club of Philadelphia, had
declared to Johnson that, "Although not a Democrat . . . I hope my next vote may be cast
for you as the candidate of a great union party." Leader to Johnson, Jan. 31, 1861, Johnson
Papers, LC.
    4. Not found.
    5. The Governor described Leader as being "an intelligent active and useful member of
the Union party of Penna." Andrew G. Curtin to "whom it may concern," Feb. 16, 1866,
Appts., Internal Revenue Service, Assessor, Pa., 5th Dist., William Y. Leader, RG56, NA.
    6. Adam J. Glossbrenner (1810–1889), a Philadelphia newspaperman who had
served as one of President Buchanan's secretaries before his election to Congress in 1865,
actively promoted Leader's candidacy. Benjamin M. Boyer (1823–1887), like his colleague Glossbrenner, served in the Thirty-ninth and Fortieth Congresses. Glossbrenner to
Johnson, June 8, 1866, ibid.; *BDAC*.
    7. Leader's file was referred by Johnson to Secretary McCulloch for his "Special atten-
tion." However, a temporary commission for the post was later given to Henry R. Coggshall, "By order of the President." William L. Elkins et al. to Hugh McCulloch, June 25,
1866, Appts., Assessor, Pa., 5th Dist., Henry Coggshall, RG56, NA.

From Oliver Wood[1]

Private

Baltimore, May, 14,/66

I beg leave respectfully to say to your Excellency, that I have been
an active union man from the first out brakeing of the rebellion, and I
am supporting you in your good work to restore our unhappy Country. I
was Sergeant At Arms to the first union Legeslature that met in Maryland, and at the close of the Session went before the Postmaster General
endosed by all the union members of boath houses. Hon Revedy Johnson
went with me in person. I was also endorsed by every member of Congress from my state, and it was understood that I was to be appointed to
the first vacency that occured in the Special Agency's department, but
very much to my Supprise and through what influence I cannot say the
appoint was given to Mr. Wm. B. Kimball.[2] Mr K is now opposeing

your Administration, and is a member of the executive committee with Hon. J. L. Thomas and Others. Now I would respectfully cergest, is it right to exspect men to leave their buisness and spend their money going to the different Counties and makeing Speeches to elect Congressmen to Sustain your Excellency in your good work, and then to be met by Special Agents from the Post office department, who get pay and charge Mileage to travel around the Country to oppose your Excellency in your good Just and Glorious work—for the truth of what I Say I respectfully refer you to my friend Hon. Reverdy Johnson. Please do not refer this letter to the department, for it would Injure me. I do not want Mr Kimball place. My object is to post you on a matter I presume your Excellency knows nothing about.

                                                         Oliver Wood

ALS, DLC-JP.
    1. Wood (c1822–fl1886), a real estate broker and former customs inspector (c1853–c60), served as a special agent of the Post Office Department at Baltimore in 1867. 1860 Census, Md., Baltimore, Baltimore, 1st Ward, 234; Baltimore directories (1858–1886); U.S. Off. Reg.(1853–59).
    2. William P. Kimball (fl1901), a machinist, served as an inspector for the Customs House in Baltimore in 1864 and 1884–85 and as a mail agent from 1871 to 1874. Baltimore directories (1858–1901).

From Albert T. Bledsoe[1]

                                    Greenwood Depot, Albemarle, Co. Va.
                                                        May 15th 1866
Sir,
    In submitting this applicatin for a pardon, it will be necessary, as your petioner trusts, to state only a few facts. Your petioner, then, not believing in the constitutional right of secessin, voted for Bell and Everett, whom he considered the Union candidates; though he had previously voted for the democratic nomination for Presidet & Vice Presidet of the United States. He deprecated disunin as the greatest of calamities.
    On the other hand, he could not, in his own humble opinin, approv the scheme of co-ercion; and, consequetly, when Virginia determined to resist co-ercion, he felt it to be his duty to go with Virginia. He acted in confomity with his conviction of duty; and if he erred, he has paid the severest penalities which human power could inflict.
    He took the oath of allegiance to the Govent of the United States in London, and returned to this country a short time since, with the disposition, founded on a sense of duty, to act the part of a faithful and law-abiding citizen; doing all in his power to promote peace & good will among all men; especially among all the people of the United States.
    He comes, in one respect only, under the excepted classes; that is, he held for a short period,—for abut a year,—a subordinate positin in the late Confederate Govermt. He resigned that positin, & returned to the

his duties as professor of Mathematics in the University of Virginia; resolvg never more to hav any connexin with it; a resolution which he freely expressed to many persons.

He went abroad after being at the University one year; he did not go as an aget of the Confederate Govermnt; he was not in its pay, either directly nor indirectly. Indeed, he culd not have been induced to take any place under it; and while abroad, he had no sort of intercourse with that Govermnt whatever. He went to England as a private citizen; & with a view to publish certain literary & scientific works, which he had spent many years in preparing for the press.

His whole life has been devoted to science & letters; & he is now most desirus to obtain a pardon from your Excellency, in order that he may publish a series of mathematical text books for schools and colleges, as well as, in other ways, devote the remainder of his life to the educatin and prosperity of the people among whom he was born, & whom he loves infinitely more than any other on earth. He certainly desires no more war; he loves peace abov all things, except truth & duty. And with this, his prayer for pardon, he unites also the prayer, that your Excellency may be sustained, to the end, in the noble & magnanimous policy on which you have so bravely entered, and which has so justly won for your Excellency the highest ferver in all parts of Europe. And, as in duty bound, your petioner will evr humbly pray, &c.

A. T. Bledsoe

P.S.   Your petitiner forgot to state, that he is moved to seek his pardon by no desire to sav his property; for he has no property, except in the labor of his brain, as any one might conclude from the fact that his life has been devoted to science & letters.[2]

A. T. Bledsoe

ALS, DNA-RG94, Amnesty Papers (M1003, Roll 56), Va., Albert T. Bledsoe.

1. Bledsoe (1808–1877), an 1830 graduate of West Point, taught mathematics at Kenyon College and at Miami University and then practiced law for ten years. He returned to academics in 1848 as professor of mathematics at the University of Mississippi and then at the University of Virginia. His West Point training earned him a commission as colonel in the Confederate army in 1861, but he soon was made assistant secretary of war. In 1864 Bledsoe ran the Union blockade and traveled to London to prepare a legal defense of the right of secession, returning to the South shortly before the war ended. His finished product, *Is Davis a Traitor?, or Was Secession a Constitutional Right Previous to the War of 1861* (1866), was used by Jefferson Davis's defense lawyers. After the war Bledsoe founded and edited the *Southern Review*, a magazine that romanticized the Lost Cause. *DAB*.

2. On the recommendation of O. H. Browning, who discussed the matter with Johnson on June 24 and wrote to him the next day concerning the same, the President pardoned Bledsoe on June 26, 1866. Browning to Johnson, June 25; A. K. Long to James Speed, June 26, 1866, Amnesty Papers (M1003, Roll 56), Va., Albert T. Bledsoe, RG94, NA; *Washington Evening Chronicle*, June 27, 1866.

Colorado Statehood Veto

WASHINGTON, D.C., *May 15, 1866*.

I return to the Senate, in which House it originated, the bill, which has passed both Houses of Congress,[1] entitled "An act for the admission of the State of Colorado into the Union," with my objections to its becoming a law at this time.

First.   From the best information which I have been able to obtain I do not consider the establishment of a State government at present necessary for the welfare of the people of Colorado. Under the existing Territorial government all the rights, privileges, and interests of the citizens are protected and secured. The qualified voters choose their own legislators and their own local officers, and are represented in Congress by a Delegate of their own selection. They make and execute their own municipal laws, subject only to revision by Congress—an authority not likely to be exercised unless in extreme or extraordinary cases. The population is small, some estimating it so low as 25,000, while advocates of the bill reckon the number at from 35,000 to 40,000 souls. The people are principally recent settlers, many of whom are understood to be ready for removal to other mining districts beyond the limits of the Territory if circumstances shall render them more inviting. Such a population can not but find relief from excessive taxation if the Territorial system, which devolves the expenses of the executive, legislative, and judicial departments upon the United States, is for the present continued. They can not but find the security of person and property increased by their reliance upon the national executive power for the maintenance of law and order against the disturbances necessarily incident to all newly organized communities.

Second.   It is not satisfactorily established that a majority of the citizens of Colorado desire or are prepared for an exchange of a Territorial for a State government. In September, 1864, under the authority of Congress, an election was lawfully appointed and held for the purpose of ascertaining the views of the people upon this particular question. Six thousand one hundred and ninety-two votes were cast, and of this number a majority of 3,152 was given against the proposed change. In September, 1865, without any legal authority, the question was again presented to the people of the Territory, with the view of obtaining a reconsideration of the result of the election held in compliance with the act of Congress approved March 21, 1864. At this second election 5,905 votes were polled, and a majority of 155 was given in favor of a State organization. It does not seem to me entirely safe to receive this, the last-mentioned, result, so irregularly obtained, as sufficient to outweigh the one which had been legally obtained in the first election. Regularity and conformity to law are essential to the preservation of order and stable government, and should, as far as practicable, always be observed, in the formation of new States.

Third.   The admission of Colorado at this time as a State into the Federal Union appears to me to be incompatible with the public interests of the country. While it is desirable that Territories, when sufficiently matured, should be organized as States, yet the spirit of the Constitution seems to require that there should be an approximation toward equality among the several States composing the Union. No State can have less or more than two Senators in Congress. The largest State has a population of 4,000,000; several of the States have a population exceeding 2,000,000, and many others have a population exceeding 1,000,000. A population of 127,000 is the ratio of apportionment of Representatives among the several States.

If this bill should become a law, the people of Colorado, 30,000 in number, would have in the House of Representatives one member, while New York, with a population of 4,000,000, has but thirty-one; Colorado would have in the electoral college three votes, while New York has only thirty-three; Colorado would have in the Senate two votes, while New York has no more.

Inequalities of this character have already occurred, but it is believed that none have happened where the inequality was so great. When such inequality has been allowed, Congress is supposed to have permitted it on the ground of some high public necessity and under circumstances which promised that it would rapidly disappear through the growth and development of the newly admitted State. Thus, in regard to the several States in what was formerly called the "Northwest Territory," lying east of the Mississippi, their rapid advancement in population rendered it certain that States admitted with only one or two Representatives in Congress would in a very short period be entitled to a great increase of representation. So, when California was admitted, on the ground of commercial and political exigencies, it was well forseen that that State was destined rapidly to become a great, prosperous, and important mining and commercial community. In the case of Colorado, I am not aware that any national exigency, either of a political or commercial nature, requires a departure from the law of equality which has been so generally adhered to in our history.

If information submitted in connection with this bill is reliable, Colorado, instead of increasing, has declined in population. At an election for members of a Territorial legislature held in 1861, 10,580 votes were cast; at the election before mentioned, in 1864, the number of votes cast was 6,192; while at the irregular election held in 1865, which is assumed as a basis for legislative action at this time, the aggregate of votes was 5,905. Sincerely anxious for the welfare and prosperity of every Territory and State, as well as for the prosperity and welfare of the whole Union, I regret this apparent decline of population in Colorado; but it is manifest that it is due to emigration which is going on from that Territory into other regions within the United States, which either are in fact or are believed by the inhabitants of Colorado to be richer in mineral wealth and agricultural resources. If, however, Colorado has not really declined in population, another census or another election under the authority of Congress would place the question beyond doubt, and cause but little delay in the ultimate admission of the Territory as a State if desired by the people.

The tenor of these objections furnishes the reply which may be expected to an argument in favor of the measure derived from the enabling act which was passed by Congress on the 21st day of March, 1864. Although Congress then supposed that the condition of the Territory was such as to warrant its admission as a State, the result of two years' experience shows that every reason which existed for the institution of a Territorial instead of a State government in Colorado at its first organization still continues in force.

The condition of the Union at the present moment is calculated to inspire caution in regard to the admission of new States. Eleven of the old States have been for some time, and still remain, unrepresented in Congress. It is a common interest of all the States, as well those represented as those unrepresented, that the integrity and harmony of the Union should be restored as completely as possible, so that all those who are expected to bear the burdens of the Federal Government shall be consulted concerning the admission of new States; and that in the meantime no new State shall be prematurely and unnecessarily admitted to a participation in the political power which the Federal Government wields, not for the benefit of any individual State or section, but for the common safety, welfare, and happiness of the whole country.

ANDREW JOHNSON.

Richardson, *Messages*, 413–16.
1. The Colorado statehood bill passed the Senate on April 25 and the House on May 3, 1866. *Congressional Globe*, 39 Cong., 1 Sess., pp. 2179–80, 2373–74.

From Theodore Cook and Henry L. Burnett

Cincinnati   May 15, 1866

At a meeting of the "Constitutional Union Club" it was resolved

That we recommend Col. Len. A. Harris,[1] Mayor of Cincinnati, for one of the Collectorships of Internal Revenue in the First or Second Congressional Districts of Ohio.

Col. Harris commanded the Ninth Brigade in Rousseau's Division of the Army of the Cumberland, at the battle of Perryville, and was recommended by Genls. Buell, McCook & Rousseau for promotion for gallant conduct on that day.[2] Compelled, finally, by loss of health, to resign,[3] he was elected Mayor of Cincinnati. Having served his first term, he was nominated by acclamation by the Union Party for re-election, and was elected by the unprecedented municipal majority of Eight Thousand. We believe him to be eminently qualified for the position, and know that his appointment would give great satisfaction to his fellow citizens, without reference to party. We also believe that honest & fearless advocates of President Johnson's policy of reconstruction should occupy positions of trust, rather than those who oppose that policy, or are afraid to proclaim their sentiments. We therefore earnestly request the appointment of Col. Harris.[4]

Theo Cook.   V—Prest

H. L. Burnett   Secy.

LS, DNA-RG56, Appts., Internal Revenue Service, Collector, Ohio, 1st Dist., L. A. Harris.

1. In addition to holding military and civil offices, Leonard A. Harris (1824–1890) served on the National Board of Soldiers' Homes and as principal founder and longtime president of an organization devoted to the advancement of ornithology and other natural sciences. Melvin G. Holli and Peter d'A. Jones, eds., *Biographical Dictionary of American Mayors, 1820–1980* (Westport, 1981); *Biographical Cyclopaedia of Ohio*, 3: 728–29.

2. For Don Carlos Buell's recommendation, see his letter to Lorenzo Thomas, Oct. 26, 1862, *OR*, Ser. 1, Vol. 16, Pt. 1: 645. Alexander McD. McCook and Lovell H. Rousseau were Harris's corps and division commanders, respectively.

3. Harris resigned in December 1862, but later served with the 137th Ohio Vol. Inf., 100-days men, and the 7th Rgt. of the Ohio National Guard. *Biographical Cyclopaedia of Ohio*, 3: 728–29; *Off. Army Reg.: Vols.*, 5: 48, 366.

4. Johnson referred the matter of Harris's nomination for a collectorship to Secretary McCulloch, commenting: "This is a good Case and the attention of the Sec is especially Called to it." On May 23 William G. Moore, one of Johnson's secretaries, directed Mc-Culloch to submit Harris's nomination for the First District to the Senate. However, the nomination was held up until the first week of July when it was finally submitted to the Senate. The Senate confirmed his appointment on July 13. Moore to McCulloch, May 23, 1866, Appts., Internal Revenue Service, Collector, Ohio, 1st Dist., L. A. Harris, RG56, NA; Theodore Cook to Johnson, Oct. 12, 1866, Appls., Heads of Treasury Offices, RG56, NA; Ser. 6B, Vol. 2: 127; Vol. 4: 256, Johnson Papers, LC.

From James M. Tomeny

Mobile Ala, May 15, 1866

The indictment was this morning read in District Court. It charges that I received from Government ten 10 dollars per bale freight on nine hundred bales cotton and only paid seven. I was required to plead immediately, and my trial set for Friday next.

My witnesses cannot be there. These are the facts.

In November last, I employed an agent to go for this cotton coming on flat boats, to stop it at Demopolis and have it brought on steamers to prevent its capture by raiders then infesting the river. Gen'l Woods[1] gave the necessary orders, and strong guard. I agreed to pay, and did pay the employee who went, as an Express agent, ten 10 dollars per bale. He probably paid seven 7 dollars freight, receiving three 3 dollars a bale for all other Expenses, his time and services, which were great and valuable.

He got every bale of the cotton through safely while thousands had previously been lost by guerrilla raids. These facts were long ago given in my reports. I was often threatened with this prosecution unless I would allow Gen'l Roddy[2] 15 fifteen dollars a bale freight on this same cotton from Gainsville to Demopolis instead of five 5 as recommended in my report April twenty seventh 27th. I am unquestionably the victim of a conspiracy and will not have a fair trial or a continuance. Will you not interpose your authority and give me relief?[3]

J. M. Tomeny   Acting Collector

Tel, DNA-RG60, Office of Atty. Gen., Lets. Recd., President.
1. Charles R. Woods.
2. Philip D. Roddey.
3. The next day Tomeny complained that the U.S. district judge (Richard Busteed) would require "another bond so large that I cannot give it" and again asked Johnson's intercession. On May 20 Tomeny complained again about the required bond. Attorney General Speed was directed "to suspend further proceedings against J. M. Tomeney, until further orders" and to see that bail "for his future appearance shall not be excessive." On May 22 the grand jury at Mobile indicted Thomas C.A. Dexter and his successor, Tomeny, as "guilty of false, fraudulent and felonious practices," all of which Tomeny denied. The charges were later dismissed. Tomeny to Johnson, May 16, 1866, Tels. Recd., President, Vol. 5 (1866–67), RG107, NA; Edmund Cooper to James Speed, May 17, 1866, Office of Atty. Gen., Lets. Recd., President, RG60, NA; *New York Times*, June 2, 1866; Tomeny to Johnson, May 20, 1866; Tomeny to Johnson, Apr. 16, 1866, Appt. Files for Judicial Dists., Ky., James M. Tomeny, RG60, NA.

To Lawrence Worrall

Washington, D.C., May 15th 1866.

You will please without delay, forward to the Secretary of the Treasury the proof referred to in your despatch respecting Turner's cotton;[1] also, copies of the letters upon which you rely, and a statement of the names and character of the witnesses, so that the case can be submitted to the Attorney General. I would suggest that, unless the proof is clear in regard to the seizure of the cotton, you follow the instructions of the Secretary of the Treasury,[2] relative thereto, and make special report of all the facts to the Attorney General. Answer by telegraph.[3]

Andrew Johnson

Tel, DNA-RG107, Tels. Sent, President, Vol. 3 (1865–68).
1. Four hundred thirty-eight bales of cotton probably belonging to William F. Turner (c1821–1877) of Sumter County, Alabama, had been seized by treasury agents. *Senate Ex. Docs.*, 39 Cong., 2 Sess., No. 37, p. 10 (Ser. 1277); 1860 Census, Ala., Sumter, Southern Div., 5; Gandrud, *Alabama Records*, 70: 72.
2. Both the attorney general and treasury offices had already decided that detention of Turner's cotton in Mobile, "on the strength of certain letters . . . which are palpable forgeries," was ill advised and that proceedings against it should stop. On May 9 Johnson asked Worrall if there was "any other evidence," to which the next day Worrall responded that "two witnesses will prove Turner's admissions that he had subscribed the cotton . . . to Confederate loan:—also that letters were received from him in their present form and are all genuine." J. Hubley Ashton to Worrall, May 3, 1866, Office of Atty. Gen., Lets. Sent, Vol. E (M699, Roll 10), RG60, NA; McCulloch to Johnson, May 9, 1866, Lets. Sent *re* Restricted Commercial Intercourse (BE Ser.), Vol. 13, RG56, NA; Johnson to Worrall, May 9, 1866, Tels. Sent, President, Vol. 3 (1865–68), RG107, NA; Worrall to Johnson, May 10, 1866, Johnson Papers, LC.
3. The next day Worrall informed Johnson that the "Turner cotton was released on the fourteenth 14th instant to Withers Adams & Co." Worrall to Johnson, May 16, 1866, Johnson Papers, LC.

From David King[1]

L'aunce Houghton County, Lake Superior[2]
May 16th 1866

Your red children wish to come and see you. And I ask your permision to come.

We have number of importent things to lay before you, and also to state our grievieance to you. For I am shure no Agent can sattisfy us.

Often Agents come to us, and say, *this*, and *that*, to us. This is what your great Father says to you. *Now*, I dont know wether it is so, or not. I find to often the promises that are made to us are not carried out. For this reason your red children of superior wish to come, to hear for themselves, &c. An immediate answer will be a faviour.[3]

his
David   X   King, chief[4]
mark

P.S.   Should you think favourable of our coming to Washington I hope you will send us means to come with or direct us how to get means, &c.

his
David   X   King
mark

LS(X), DNA-RG75, Gen. Records, Lets. Recd. (M234, Roll 407).

1. King had been principal chief of the L'Anse band of Chippewa Indians since about 1842. Bernard J. Lambert, *Shepherd of the Wilderness: A Biography of Bishop Frederic Baraga* (L'anse, Mich, 1967), 152.

2. The L'Anse band, which numbered about 600 in the mid-1850s, was relatively "civilized," living in houses, wearing "white" clothing, farming, and attending a Catholic mission church and school. By a treaty of 1854 the band shared a ninety-square-mile reservation on the Upper Peninsula of Michigan at the head of Keweenaw Bay with the Vieux de Sert. Edmund J. Danziger, Jr., "They Would Not Be Moved: The Chippewa Treaty of 1854," *Minn. Hist.*, 43 (1973): 176, 179.

3. Probably King was concerned about the same difficulties which eventually motivated the Chippewa chiefs to seek a conference, with equal lack of success, in 1867: desiring "compensation due for Civil War annuities paid in devalued greenbacks rather than specie or coin, as required by the terms of their treaties," and the Indian office's defaulting on payments specified by treaty Article IX. The commissioner of Indian affairs refused to allow the chiefs to come to Washington and the problems dragged on into the 1890s when the federal government appears to have acknowledged its debt to the Chippewas but not paid it. Ibid., 182.

4. The letter was also signed by "George Blaker, missionary," who apparently wrote the missive. A Methodist, Blaker was expelled from the church at the Detroit conference in 1869. *Minutes of the Detroit Conference of the Methodist Episcopal Church, 1869*, 198.

From James B. Bingham

Memphis, Tenn., May 17th 1866.

Dear Sir—

I have recently returned from Nashville, whither I went to dispose of my interest in the *Union* newspaper. I got there just in time to squelch a most iniquitous revolution. After the decapitation of certain Conservative members of the legislature, a meeting was held, or rather a legislative caucus, to determine a future policy. At that meeting, they resolved to send you a delegation from their own body to ask you to permit them to get up meetings and send delegates to Nashville to form *another State government*, and upturn or overthrow the present State government. After this policy had been agreed upon and a committee of three—consisting of Col. Garritt, A J. Steele and H. Brown of Madison[1]—had been appointed to wait upon you, another meeting was held to approve the written address or petition they were to bring with them. Judge J. C. Gaut and myself were invited to this last caucus. Both of us opposed the plan as revolutionary and disorganizing—as asking you to stultify yourself and to disregard your oath of office—and as calculated to lose your friends a hundred thousand votes in the fall elections in the Northern States. After speaking against it until near eleven o'clock, the vote was taken on an indefinite postponement, and it was carried in the affirmative by only *one* dissenting vote—that of Brown of Madison, who is yet unreconstructed. We then proposed, and the caucus sanctioned this plan: That we would make a vigorous fight against the franchise act and Brownlow's administration—that we would advise the people to hold on to their certificates of registration—to offer to vote whenever an opportunity offered, and if the Judges of election refused them, to bring suit for damages, appeal to the Supreme Court on the constitutionality of the act. This is a lawful, constitutional mode of obtaining relief from unconstitutional action, and we can afford to wait until the highest Judicial authorities can pronounce in our favor. I regret to see that Gallaway[2] and other malcontents are still after the revolutionary process. They have already held one meeting in Memphis in favor of their Scheme, but I have directed such specific attention to their course, that I think it is arrested. If it is not, I shall follow it up till the thing is *dead*. It must be Killed. We must have *peace*, and no more revolutions, either State or National. The former "rebels" in this latitude are not conducting themselves with the modesty which becomes them. I mean the *leaders*, such as Gallaway, Cluskey[3] & Co., who are moving in this matter. They will die if they can't get office, and the prospect is rather blank for them at present.

I did not get home till the riots were over.[4] I have investigated the matter sufficiently to learn that the difficulty had its origin in an impromptu difficulty between a negro and white driver. Their teams collided, and from words they fell to blows. The police (all Irish) interfered, and one was Killed. This incensed the Irish police, and the difficulties became more general. It was a literal verification of your prophecy to Fred. Douglas, when he waited on you for universal suffrage for the negro.[5] You then told him that the measure would beget an irrepressible conflict between the non-slaveholding whites of the South and the blacks. This is the real cause of our difficulties here. Our police are all Irish. The negro soldiers are particularly down on the poor whites and Irish. Several skirmishes have occurred between them, and when the negro soldier no longer had an officer *to obey*, he was betrayed into unusual violence. The better class of citizens had nothing to do with the "muss." The ex-rebels were particularly *not engaged*. They had nothing to do with it. I was called upon by Gen. Fisk, at my house, the night he arrived. I told him the substantial facts, as above detailed, and characterized it as a verification of your Douglas argument—all which he admitted; but whether he will say so in his report remains to see. He professed to be a friend of yours in his conversation with me.

I understand Frank Blair is making arrangements to become a candidate for President *in your interest*.[6] He is now canvassing to get Missouri right, and overtures have been made looking to his getting an *organ*, or newspaper, in this city. I have informed all parties that the *Bulletin* is for Andrew Johnson, first, last and all the time, and is not for sale. Though my health is so shattered from long and continuous application, that if I could get a good fat berth I would like to retire from severe duties for a while. Tell Ed. Cooper than when he wants to reach the people of Tennessee, Mississippi, Alabama, and particularly Arkansas, he can reach more readers through the *Bulletin* than the *Union* or any other paper. I have had an interest in both, and know. I hope you will gain in the approaching elections. You can if the southern "blowhards" will only keep their foolish tongues quiet. Brownlow and the legislature hate you, but fear you, nevertheless.

J B Bingham

ALS, DLC-JP.

1. Abraham E. Garrett, Abner A. Steele, and Hervey Brown. Brown (1817–1870), a Jackson, Tennessee, lawyer, had served one term in the antebellum as well as in the postwar legislature. *BDTA*, 1: 85.

2. Matthew C. Gallaway.

3. Michael W. Cluskey (1832–1873) had moved to Memphis in the late 1850s to become associated with the *Avalanche*. During the war he held several different military positions until his resignation in 1864 to serve in the Confederate Congress. He returned to Memphis where he resumed his editorial work with the *Avalanche*. Subsequently, he moved to Louisville, Kentucky, to serve as editor of the *Ledger*. Warner and Yearns, *BRCC*; Wakelyn, *BDC*; *Confederate Staff Officers*, 34.

4. A reference to the infamous Memphis race riot which broke out at the end of April and first of May 1866. See George Stoneman to Grant, May 12, 1866, *House Ex. Docs.*, 39 Cong., 1 Sess., No. 122, "Riot at Memphis," pp. 1–3 (Ser. 1263); Bobby L. Lovett, "Memphis Riots: White Reaction to Blacks in Memphis, May 1865-July 1866," *THQ*, 38 (1979): 9–33; Speed to Johnson, July 13, 1866.

5. See Interview with Delegation of Blacks, Feb. 7, 1866.

6. Francis P. Blair, Jr., busied himself in the spring and summer months of 1866 making speeches throughout Missouri in behalf of Johnson and the forthcoming National Union Convention. Smith, *Blair Family*, 362–64.

From Robert B. Carnahan

Pittsburgh, May 18th 1866

Dear Sir:

I inclose a copy of the "Pittsburgh Commercial" of this date Containing an article written by me on the Colorado Veto Message and published as editorial matter. The Article was so much altered by the editor[1] before it was adopted, as to materialy change it's tone and spirit, and to some extent defeat the purpose of the publication. When these alterations were indicated to me by the editor I consented that it should appear simply as an exposition of your views, rather than have it entirely suppressed. I inclose a copy of the Article as written, for the purpose of showing the extent of the editor's changes.

The Commercial is a Republican paper of highly Conservative Character. It has said much in Commendation of your policy and Administration, without being committed unqualifiedly, to the support of either. I have done what I could to bring the paper up to a higher standard. I have written for it's columns many articles and procured others to be written in defence of your policy and in condemnation of the Course of Congress. I have written several articles which were suppressed for the reason, that, in the opinion of the editor, they took too high Administration ground. I have supported your policy from Conviction, openly and publicly in Speeches, in Conversation, and through the newspapers. It is more than four years since I first gave my views to the public on the leading principle of your present policy,[2] and I have not hitherto seen reason to change my opinions. I beleive that your system of Administration is the only one that can give peace, security and prosperity to the country, and it will have my feeble support whether in or out of office. I beg you to beleive that this support is not in any way Contingent, on my holding the Official position which I have under your Administration. I should dispise myself if I thought it were so. The office of U S. Attorney is this District has no great value for me either pecuniarily or otherwise. I make these observations, because it is very extensively reported by parties in this city that I am about to be removed, and that they have assurances from you to that effect. These rumors have not made any impression on my mind of an unpleasant character, other than the disagreeable notoriety which such reports always give to a man in a public position. I have given them no credence notwithstanding the apparent confidence with which they are promulgated. I have only to request, that, if any part of my course and conduct, official or personal, does not meet with your approbation, or if any reason of policy, connected with the holding of office under your Administration should make it desirable to your Excellency that the office I hold should be filled by another, Your Excellency will be good enough to communicate to me such wish. I would not have your Excellency beleive that I attach any credit whatever, to the rumors referred to; but a letter received this morning from Senator Cowan has led me to think, that some reason such as that indicated above may exist making my resignation desirable to you. Senator Cowan has not said so in direct terms, nor perhaps by fair inference; but his letter seems to shadow forth something of the kind and I wish to releive you from embarrassment on the subject in that contingency.[3]

R B Carnahan

ALS, DLC-JP.

1. Charles D. Brigham (1819–1894) began editing a newspaper at the age of eighteen and spent most of the remainder of his life in that business. During the war he served for a year as correspondent at the front, part of that time occupying a tent with General Grant. He began editing the *Commercial* in 1862, soon acquiring controlling interest in the paper, and made himself famous in the newspaper business by getting news of the battle of The Wilderness twenty-four hours before any other editor. *NCAB*, 9: 280–81.

2. Here Carnahan may be alluding to an article, the "Subject of Reconstruction," originally published in April 1862, which he had recently forwarded to the President. Carnahan to Johnson, Mar. 27, 1866, Johnson Papers, LC.

3. Carnahan later identified the "friends" of Heister Clymer, the Democratic gubernatorial candidate, as the persons seeking his removal. Carnahan offered to resign if Johnson considered his views to have been at variance with the President's. But Carnahan was neither removed nor requested to resign by Johnson. Carnahan to Johnson, Aug. 7, 1866, Johnson Papers, LC.

From John W. Leftwich and Nathaniel G. Taylor

Washington City D.C.   May 18th '66

Sir

If you will remove Edward Tompkins,[1] a 1600$ per Annum Clerk, in the Int. Rev Bureau; and put R W Bates[2] in his place at the same salery; we are, from reliable information, fully justified in saying; You will remove a young man of ample means and no family and a *bitter* opponent of your Administration; and will substitute an old man of excellent moral character with limited means and a family and an *able earnest* and *active* friend of your administration on which account evidently, he has just lost his position in the same Bureau.

Jno. W. Leftwich

N. G. Taylor

ALS (Leftwich), DNA-RG56, Appls., Positions in Washington, D.C., Treasury Offices, R. W. Bates.

1. Tompkins (*fl*1876) had held the post of clerk for several years in the Washington office of internal revenue and continued to hold it for several more years, despite the active attempts to have him removed. Washington, D.C., directories (1869–77); *U.S. Off. Reg.* (1863–71).

2. See Robert W. Bates to Johnson, Mar. 30, 1866.

From William H. McCartney

[ca. May 18, 1866, Boston, Mass.]; LS, DNA-RG56, Appts., Internal Revenue Service, Collector, Mass., 3rd Dist., William H. McCartney.

An applicant for the post of collector of Internal Revenue for the Third Congressional District of Massachusetts bases his claim on his extended wartime service as captain, 1st Massachusetts Battery, part of the 6th Corps of the Army of the Potomac. As early as April 19, 1861, he gave up his lucrative legal practice ($4,600 net income during the preceding year) to enlist in a "three months" company, after which he immediately recruited, "in less than twenty four hours," his company and went on to win numerous commendations for participation in many engagements, extending from West Point and Antietam to Winchester, and including Fredericksburg, Gettysburg, The Wilderness, and Petersburg. Moreover, he stumped the 3rd and 4th Districts of Massachusetts in the Lincoln and Johnson campaign, as well as the state of Connecticut "for the Union Candidate Jos. R. Hawley, making twelve Speeches in support of Your Administration," in the last election. [Johnson's endorsement, "Let this appointmt be made and sent in for nomination confirmation," resulted in his receiving the office. He was confirmed by the Senate on June 5.]

From Ohio Citizens[1]

Hamilton Ohio   May 18, 1866.

We respectfully represent that John L. Martin[2] now the Collector of Internal Revenue for this the 3d District of Ohio, for many years prior to the breaking out of the Rebellion held in the state a lucrative office, to wit: Member of the Board of Public Works. Although a man in the prime of life and of vigorous constitution he did not deem it expedient to Volunteer to defend the Union in the National Army. When the Internal Revenue system was inaugurated he was appointed Collector for this district and has ever since held and still holds the office, notwithstanding he is a man of wealth.

When the rebellion commenced, Ferdinand Van Derveer Esqr.,[3] resided in Hamilton, a poor man with a family of young children, which he supported by his profession as a lawyer.

Abandoning his practice he entered the service in the summer of 1861 and organized the 35th Regiment O.V.I. In Sept 1861 he took the field and reported to Genl. Thomas at Somerset Ky. He continued to serve until the war was over. He was with Buells army in the Shiloh campaign —was at the investment of, and in the fights before Corinth—was at the Battle of Perryville—in the fights preceeding the taking of Tullahoma in 1863,—was with Rosencrans through the Chicamagua campaign, fighting both days at Chicamagua and was the last to leave the field after repulsing the enemy. He was engaged in several fights in front of Chattanooga and in the battle of Mission Ridge. He was also at the battles of Ringgold, Buzzard Roost, Tunnel Hill, Dalton, Kenesaw, and in several fights of the Atlanta Campaign. In October 1864 he was promoted to Brigadier General and served in the 4th Army Corps until June 1865, when, the fighting being over he resigned.

The Cavalry Regiment of Col. Robt. Johnson of Tennessee, was sometime a part of Genl. Van Derveers command.

After the Battle of Chicamagua Maj. Genls. Thomas, Rosencrans, and Brannan all urgently recommended the promotion of Col VanDerveer.

On his return home after a service of four years in the Army—Genl. Van Derveer finds himself impoverished and his practice at the bar, gone into other hands.

He is a gentleman of good moral character, a supporter of the restoration policy of the Administration and well qualified to discharge the duties of Revenue Collector.

We therefore members of the Union Party, approving cordially of your general policy, and especially of the circular of your Excellency declaring that preference should be given to the Soldier over the Civilian,[4] qualifications being equal, in the appointments to Civil Office, respectfully but earnestly ask that Genl. Van Derveer may be appointed Collector of Internal Revenue for the 3d District of Ohio in the place of John L. Martin. Genl. V. is in every respect as well qualified as Mr. Martin. As we see no reason why civilians should enjoy the emoluments of office *for life* to the exclusion of our gallant Union Soldiers, who perilled their all, we ask that Mr. Martin may be *rotated out* and Genl. Van Derveer *rotated in.*[5]

Pet, DNA-RG56, Appts., Internal Revenue Service, Collector, Ohio, 3rd Dist., Ferdinand Van Derveer.

1. Among the eight signatories were Thomas Millikin, Alexander F. Hume, and Isaac Robertson, all prominent Democratic attorneys. Lewis D. Campbell wrote a long endorsement for Van Derveer on the petition.

2. Martin (1814–*fl*1882) had worked as a civil engineer and served as a Republican member on the state board of public works, prior to his appointment in 1862 as collector of the 3rd district. Following his removal from the internal revenue post in 1866, he engaged in banking and later farming. *A History and Biographical Cyclopaedia of Butler County, Ohio, with Illustrations and Sketches of Its Representative Men and Pioneers* (Cincinnati, 1882), 326–28.

3. A native of Butler County, Van Derveer (1823–1892) also served after the war as sheriff and judge of the court of common pleas. Warner, *Blue.*

4. See Circular *re* Appointments to Office, Apr. 7, 1866.

5. Johnson nominated Van Derveer on July 13 and ten days later he was commissioned as collector. Ser. 6B, Vol. 4: 256, Johnson Papers, LC.

From John M. Parkman

Selma   May 18th 1866.

Sir.

The undersigned a citizen of this city received in August last at your hands a full pardon dated 25th July[1] & accepted the conditions of the same in a letter to Hon W. H. Seward receipt of which he acknowledged & at the same time took the required oath, in fact conformed with every requirement of the pardon. On my return home in Septr from New York I was served with notice of libel against all my property dated 8th Sept 1865 by J Q Smith U.S. District Attorney through the U S Marshall John Hardy. My real estate was advertized & my cotton in the several warehouses seized. The U S Marshall refused to permit me to ship my cotton although I exhibited to him my pardon, the permit of the Treasury Agent[2] & the receipt of the Internal Revenue Collector.[3] He (the U S Marshall) ridiculed my pardon, failed to recognize the highest authority in the Nation and refused to give me any information as to when my cotton would be released. Doubting the authority of the Marshall I con-

sulted the Commander of this Post[4] to whom I exhibited all my papers &
to whom I communicated all the facts. The said Commander gave me a
guard under a Lieutenant[5] whose orders were to aid me in shipping my
cotton. I proceeded to make the shipment but before I had gotten all of
the cotton on board of the Steamer, the Marshall hearing of my proceedings called upon the Post Commander & made him reverse his orders &
place the guard over the cotton to prevent my shipping until I had complied with the requirements of the Marshall, which were that I should
give bond for twice the value of the cotton, which I did. This was the first
intimation I had received that the Marshall would permit the cotton to be
removed at all. After having complied with the Marshalls demands you
can imagine my surprize & indignation the next day (Sunday) on being
arrested by him for resisting the U S Marshall & held to appear by bond
of $7000—before the U S Commissioner[6] here whenever it would suit
the Marshall to appear. The case up to this time has not been called, nor
has the bond been returned to me. My opinion is that the Marshall was
desirous of securing (*personal*) pay to release the cotton, whereby he
might dismiss my case before the U S Commissioner.

It was not my intention to resist the Marshall nor do I think I did it. If
you remember I communicated some of my greivances to you by telegraph at the time,[7] & ought to have made this statement sooner, but as
my property was released by the Disct Attorney soon after, I deemed it
unnecessary. However the Attorney has my case still in hand & hesitates
to dismiss the libel because I refuse to pay him $200—which he calls
"costs." I have my pardon & a duplicate of oath taken in Washington both
dated 25th July & the libel bears date of Sept 8th 1865.

The U S Disct Attny James. Q. Smith & the U S Marshall John
Hardy unfortunately are not as well known in Washington as they are
here. Hon F W Kellogg Collr at Mobile knows something of Mr Hardy
and his conduct in this section.

These facts are presented to your Excellency with the hope that you
will take such action as will relieve not only myself but others from
the continued annoyances & impositions of both the U S Attorney &
Marshall.[8]

Jno. M. Parkman

References.
D R Martin Prest Ocean NlB N.Y.
David Wagstaff 76 & 78 Cortlandt St. N.Y.[9]
F W Kellogg Collector Mobile Ala.

LS, DNA-RG60, Office of Atty. Gen., Lets. Recd., President.
1. The President did in fact grant Parkman a pardon on July 25 under the thirteenth
exception. *House Ex. Docs.*, 40 Cong., 2 Sess., No. 16, p. 29 (Ser. 1330).
2. Probably James P. Nimmo.
3. Francis W. Kellogg.
4. Not identified.
5. Not identified.

6. William Q. Smith was currently a nominee for surveyor of customs at Selma. Amnesty Papers (M1003, Roll 1), Ala., A. W. Arnold, RG94, NA; Hugh McCulloch to Johnson, May 11, 1866, Appts., Customs Service, Surveyor, Selma, William Q. Smith, RG56, NA.

7. See Parkman to Johnson, Sept. 30, 1865, *Johnson Papers*, 9: 157.

8. Parkman's letter was referred to Attorney General Speed who asked James Q. Smith about the case. Smith replied that because Parkman had reportedly been pardoned his property had been released. But, in order to "have the proceedings dismissed," Parkman was required to show "his pardon, letter of acceptance and oath, or produce the same in court," which Parkman "an original precipitating fireeater of the Yancey school, could not stoop to do." Speed agreed with Smith that Parkman should plead his pardon in open court and comply with all its conditions. Speed to Smith, June 7, 18, 1866, Office of Atty. Gen., Lets. Sent, Vol. F (M699, Roll 11), RG60, NA; Smith to Speed, June 11, 1866, *House Reports*, 40 Cong., 1 Sess., No. 7, p. 445 (Ser. 1314).

9. David Randolph Martin (c1811–fl1870), president of Ocean National Bank, and Wagstaff (fl1878), a grocer, later respectively became residents of Englewood, New Jersey, and Long Island. New York City directories (1858–78); 1860 Census, N.Y., New York, 21st Ward, 1st Div., 28.

From Wyoming County, N.Y., Citizens[1]

Dated May 18th, 1866

The undersigned Citizens of the County of Wyoming in the 29th Collection district of New York, respectfully represent that they are informed that a petition is in Circulation for the Appointment of Thomas. M. Webster Esq.[2] of Lockport, Assessor of Internal Revenue for said 29th Dist.

And whereas if such an Appointment shall be made it will involve the necessity of removing the present incumbent James P. Murphy,[3] who since September 1862, has creditably and efficiently performed the arduous and difficult duties pertaining to said Office.

Such removel in our judgment should only be made for *Cause*, And so far as we are informed and beleive, no Cause, or shadow of a Cause exists, but on the contrary there are many reasons why the present incumbent should not be removed, and Chief among others is the fact—that to understand practically the Internal Revenue law requires the experience of many months, so that all parties and the government may be justly and lawfully dealt with. It is important in this respect to all parties—all are equally interested—and the undersigned beleive the present incumbent has mastered the many difficulties, and is thoroughly informed on all the numerous points of the law and the rulings and decisions of the Commissioners. His removal would in this respect be a public loss. And we would respectfully submit that the rule should prevail in this branch of the public service, which prevails in many others—that so long as the incumbent Administers the duties of his Office fairly and Aceptably, he should not be removed and an inexperienced person Appointed.

We therefore most respectfully & earnestly remonstrate against any removal and such Appointment.[4]

Pet, DNA-RG56, Appts., Internal Revenue Service, Assessor, N.Y., 29th Dist., James P. Murphy.

1. The petition was signed by more than eighty citizens.

2. A lawyer, Webster (c1820–fl1870) served as surrogate of Niagara County, New York, from 1851 to 1854. Hamilton Child, comp., *Gazetteer and Business Directory of Niagara County, N.Y., for 1869* (Syracuse, 1869), 219; Samuel T. Wiley and W. Scott Garner, eds., *Biographical and Portrait Cyclopedia of Niagara County, New York* (Philadelphia, 1892), 61; 1870 Census, N.Y., Niagara, Lockport, 3rd Ward, 238.

3. A cabinet maker several years prior to his appointment as revenue assessor, Murphy (1816–fl1892) later owned and operated a grocery business in Lockport. Wiley and Garner, *Niagara County, N.Y.*, 517.

4. Murphy retained his post until 1871. Ibid.

From Varina Davis

May 19 1866.   Fortress Monroe

Sir,

I had the honor to write you a petition which Mr McCullough[1] very kindly bore to you in person, in which I plead for the parole of the Fort for my Husband, who under the unnescessarily strict, and exhausting confinement under which he has languished for more than twelve months is not slowly, but surely, and swiftly failing. Having received no answer, and the modification of the removal of the sentinels to a greater distance thus securing a more unbroken sleep being the only one—I again write to urge you to offer him the parole of the Fort. I do not mean in partial trust, but free him from sentinels, and surveillance. He will surely die in the course of another month if some such change is not made. He is now suffering from the premonitory symptoms of his spring attack which he cannot stand in his present emeciated exhausted condition. I plead with you for the life of my Husband, and it is hard to see him die by inches, the victim of tortures inflicted by a man as cruel as he is ignorant, and unmanly. I gave you through Genl Taylor[2] an implied assurance that I would not seek to make public at present any of the cruelties practiced upon him, and I am satisfied that you were not aware of the horrible means which were taken to torture him, by starvation, and other modes too horrible to mention. I shall strictly adhere to my implied promise as you were generous enough to trust my [arriving?]. Your conditions of parole to me were in fact no requirements at all, and I thank you for your generous consideration with all my heart. You thus prevented Genl Miles[3] from adding my agonies to those which he cherishes the memory of having inflicted upon Mr Davis. I am authorised to say that every officer on duty at this post will pledge their lives, or their commissions upon Mr Davis' faith if you will grant him the free parole of the Fort. If you do not desire that he should speak to strangers, I will pledge myself that he shall sign such an agreement. If you could see him, too weak to walk without tottering, emeciated to the lest degree—you would realise that he is dying, and that not slowly. A release, or a trial deferred until the last of June will find him released by a greater than man, and though it may be better for him, for his little helpless impoverished children, and for me it is bitterer than death. He is locked up now in a small room—guarded on three sides by barred windows—outside of which are sentinels, and an officer. The nescessary motion and bustle are oppressive in the extreme. Then a light streams into his room—& one burns within his room turned low it is true, but burning all night. When he walks, he goes only around the ramparts, be it rainy, or muddy he walks in the saturated grass—followed by two sentinels accompanied by an officer of the Guard. The Com Genl, refuses me the priviledge of walking with him, or him the advantage of walking in the Fort—because "the newspapers will talk."

No one doubts his honorable observance of a parole but the Com. Genl. I refrain from drawing any deductions. I do not know that his health can be recruited by your granting my request, but I pray God you may receive my simple statement and petition as it is intended. I think my friends will tell you that I am outspoken and sincere—and in this metter of more than life to me, I have not exaggereted anything for effect. Twenty-two years of devotion have taught me to foresee every danger in small symptoms—and these twenty two years have convinced me that no man in government would risk anything by trusting to this man whose life has been one of strictest good faith. The accordance of my petition a month, or even two weeks hence my dear Sir, I fear will be of little avail. I therefore urge it on you while I hope by care to recruit his health before the first warm week of June. I believe you will not refuse me. I pray that you may not.

In the life of this feeble man are bound up the hearts of thousands and they will pray for you with their whole souls if you save it. And with your cares, and sorrows which I know are many sweet sympathies and hopes will be mingled by those who love him, and only are prevented from entirely loving you by these bonds.

Varina Davis.

ALS, DLC-JP.
  1. Secretary McCulloch visited Jefferson Davis at Fortress Monroe on May 6. McCulloch had been given permission in advance by President Johnson to have an interview with Davis. Presumably the petition to which Varina Davis refers here is her letter of May 5, 1866. *National Intelligencer*, May 10, 1866; Johnson to General Miles, May 5, 1866, Johnson Papers, LC.
  2. This is probably a reference to Gen. Richard Taylor with whom Varina Davis had earlier visited in New York City. Taylor (1826–1879), the son of President Zachary Taylor and the brother of Jefferson Davis's first wife, was a Louisiana sugar planter and politician. During the Civil War he commanded troops in both the eastern and western theatres, surrendering the last Confederate forces east of the Mississippi River in May 1865. Warner, *Gray*.
  3. Nelson A. Miles, commanding general of the fort.

From Adam J. Glossbrenner

House of Representatives, May 19, 1866.

My dear Sir:

I beg now to submit, for your consideration, the application and testimonials of Col. *Andrew J. Fulton*,[1] of York county, Penna. whom I had the honor of introducing to you some three weeks since, and whom your friends, of both political parties, earnestly recommend for the position of Assessor of Internal Revenue for the 15th Congressional District of Penna. The present incumbent,[2] against whose official conduct I have nothing to say, uses the influence which his official position gives him to oppose the policy of your Administration; and his subordinates, I regret to say, are of those who are most bitter and unjust in opposition to you personally. In accordance with my promise to you, as well as with my sense of what was due to you, I have been most careful in obtaining from the best sources, ample testimony as to the political status of Col. Fulton —I am entirely satisfied that he heartily endorses your views—and although I have been directly opposed to him in partisan politics for many years, I cannot but feel that it is due to you to urge his appointment as the best means of promoting, in my district, the success of your policy, with which, in common with the entire body of Democrats whom I represent, I feel identified. When I had an interview with you in which this application was discussed, I was, as you may perhaps remember, opposed to immediate action upon it. I felt that it was an appointment too pregnant with important consequences to be lightly or incautiously made. But having taken every possible care to assure myself that it is right and expedient, I now adopt your own language in regard to it, i.e. "the sooner it is done the better."

I have indicated, in the body of the petition, and in the letters herewith enclosed, the political character of the signers and writers.

Allow me, Mr. President, to express the hope that you will act promptly in this matter, so that we may have, at the earliest possible day, the advantage of the excellent effect which I am sure will be produced by this appointment throughout the counties of York, Cumberland and Perry.[3]

A. J. Glossbrenner.

ALS, DNA-RG56, Appts., Internal Revenue Service, Assessor, Pa., 15th Dist., Andrew J. Fulton.

1. A prewar surveyor, Republican, and "a firm & influential Union man," Fulton (c1834–1872) of Stewartstown, Pa., had risen in rank from private to colonel while serving in three different regiments. Adam Ebaugh to Johnson, May 7, 1866; J. Y. Cowhick to Johnson, May 7, 1866, Appts., Internal Revenue Service, Assessor, Pa., 15th Dist., Andrew J. Fulton, RG56, NA; 1870 Census, Pa., York, Stewartstown, 500; Pension Records, Elizabeth A. Fulton, RG15, NA.

2. Horace Bonham (1835–1892) was described by a detractor as "extremely Radical in his views" and "extremely odious and unpopular in the Union party." George C. Groce and David H. Wallace, *The New-York Historical Society's Dictionary of Artists in America, 1564–*

1860 (New Haven, 1957), 64; William Griffith to Johnson, May 7, 1866, Appts., Internal Revenue Service, Assessor, Pa., 15th Dist., Andrew J. Fulton, RG56, NA; 1860 Census, Pa., York, 1st Div. York Borough, 1091.

3. Senator Cowan also recommended the appointment. Referring Fulton's file and Representative Glossbrenner to the secretary of the treasury, Johnson advised McCulloch: "It would be best to make the appoint as he suggests." Fulton was indeed nominated on May 31, but some three weeks later the Senate refused confirmation. Nevertheless, Fulton was given a temporary commission as assessor of the Fifteenth District after Congress had adjourned, and he acted in that capacity for several months before the Senate rejected his nomination for a second time in February 1867. Ser. 6B, Vol. 4: 82, 84, Johnson Papers, LC; *Philadelphia Evening Bulletin*, May 31, 1866; Fulton to McCulloch, Feb. 25, 1867, Appts., Internal Revenue Service, Assessor, Pa., 15th Dist., Andrew J. Fulton, RG56, NA.

From Benjamin G. Humphreys

Jackson, Miss., May 19th 1866.

Sir

I have the honor to transmit to your Excellency a letter from the Hon Wm. Yerger dated Jackson May 16th 1866—Also a letter from the Attornies of certain citizens of Mississipp, dated Columbus Miss May 8th 1866[1]—complaining of the unwarrantable interference of the Military authorities of this Department, with certain suits brought in the state courts, against Harrison Johnson[2] Asst Treasury Agent of the U. States, for private wrongs suffered by these citizens, at the hands of said Johnson under cover of authority conferred on him as special Treasury Agent.

These papers and the documents accompanying them, exhibit the conduct of Johnson as a flagatious, and tyrannical exercise of power not warranted by the circumstances of the case, or his duty to the Government —but used for his own private and selfish ends and aims.[3]

It is difficult to understand how the Military domination, assumed over the civil Courts of Mississippi, can be sustained by the Genl. Orders of the Govt., issued for the protection of its officers in the discharge of their legal duties.

The Loyal citizens of Mississippi have exhibited every disposition to yield implicit obedience to a just administration of all the laws passed and Genl. Orders issued for their guidance, but when oppressed by the Agents of the Government, they deem it but right and just to seek redress through the Courts of the Country. This redress is now denied them, by the interference of the Military power placed over them. The wrong doer is screened from legal investigation of his usurpations, and responsibility to the injured citizen—and goes unwhipt of justice.

These citizens now appeal to your Excellency as the Cheif Executive of the Nation, for protection—and only ask for such peaceable remedies, as the laws of the land afford them.

I hope your Excellency will give the documents herewith enclosed (marked *A. B. C.* & *D*) a perusal, and I feel assured you will decide the matter justly—and require the Military authorities to abstain from any interference, with the investigation by the Courts of the wrongs complained of.

If the Agent of the Treasury has acted honestly and faithfully, in the discharge of his duties to the Government, he need fear no danger from the Courts. It is justice only that he need fear. If he has used the power with which he is clothed, which has been too often the Case to extort, and plunder the Citizens of Mississippi, it is but right and just that he should be made to disgorge his ill gotten gains, and be punished for his crimes and villainies.

Relying upon your sense of justice, and known disposition to protect our citizens in all their constitutional rights, I submit their case to your decision, and await your action[4]—and respectfully request an answer at your earliest convenience.

Benj. G. Humphreys   Gov. of Mississippi

ALS, DLC-JP.
1. Both of these letters are in the Johnson Papers, LC.
2. Harrison Johnston.
3. The "accompanying" documentation included a copy of the charges against Harrison Johnston for offenses committed in Lowndes County, Mississippi, in July 1865: false imprisonment of John K. Portwood and seizure of cotton belonging to Robert Stinson.
4. On June 7, 1866, Secretary of War Stanton reported that the general commanding in Mississippi, Thomas J. Wood, had been directed "to abstain from interfering with the Civil tribunals in the case of Porterwood v Johnson." Stanton to Johnson, June 7, 1866, Johnson Papers, LC.

From Patrick Ford[1]

Office of S.C. Leader,
Charleston, May 20, 1866.

Your Excellency:

I take the liberty herewith to transmit to you the three last numbers of the *South Carolina Leader*,[2] a journal in the interest of the colored people of this State, but one hitherto under the control of extreme Radicals from New England. I believe, Your Excellency, the *Leader* is *the only conservative paper in the country that is avowedly in the interest of the negro*; and it is a source of much satisfaction to me that I have been mainly instrumental in placing it upon the platform on which it now stands, and, thereby, virtually endorsing your policy of restoration.

It is but proper to state here to your Excellency who I am. I am a compositor in the *Leader* office; but, for the three or four weeks back, have furnished the paper with the leading articles. During the day I support myself laboring at the case with my hands, and a part of the night I devote to the service of the black man. For this extra service I ask and desire no pecuniary recompense. I belong to no party, and intend to have nothing to do with politicians; and, in undertaking this Task, I have been actuated solely with a desire to aid in promoting peace and harmony among all classes, and help to *withdraw the bone of contention from out of the mouths of the Radicals, the disturbers of the Country*.

The extracts marked in the *Leaders* have been copied almost universally by the Southern press, and the sentiments contained therein endorsed. This is the first time the paper has received any recognition.

It would afford me much pleasure should Your Excellency be pleased to send a brief acknowledgment, either private or public, as you may desire.[3] I believe it would tend to strengthen the influence of the *Leader*, and extend its sphere of usefulness.

Patrick Ford

ALS, DLC-JP.

1. Ford (1837–1913), an Irishman and Boston newspaperman, whose former associations included William Lloyd Garrison, came South as a soldier in the 9th Mass. Inf. He later moved to New York City where for many years he championed his native country's cause as editor of the *Irish World*. *New York Times*, Sept. 24, 1913.

2. Not found.

3. There is no record of a response from Johnson to Ford.

From William B. Phillips

Confidential.

87 East 26h. Street.
New York, May 20h/66

Dear Sir,

I enclose you three of my articles in to-day's paper. The two last are on financial matters and the financial condition of the country.[1] The leader on "the irrepressible war of the radicals on the president"[2] was written some days ago and laid over till to-day. I hope they will accord with your views.

You may remember, perhaps, that I made some remarks to you when I was in Washington, and I think also in a letter,[3] about the course of the Herald, Mr. Bennett's views with regard to your policy, and the chances of the paper continuing to support you. I wish now to recall that to your mind and to say something more in confidence on the subject.

Mr. Bennett has manifested lately a good deal of impatience with regard to your course with the cabinet and radical office-holders. He came down to the office on yesterday and discussed the matter pretty fully with us. The leading editorial in yesterday's paper will give you an idea of the views he entertains.[4] But he was more emphatic in conversation than that. He is firmly convinced that you can not sustain yourself in any other way than by a bold, striking, and prompt action with the opponents of your administration. His arguments are that the radicals are able to carry the timid and wavering conservatives with them because you are not decisive and bold enough in using the patronage in your hands against them and in favor of those who do support you. You "are gone," he says unless you take the boldest and most decisive course, and thus rally all the conservatives to you. He maintains that the issue is clearly defined, and you must draw the line so distinctly that there can be no middle course left for politicians to take, that they must be decidedly for you or decidedly against you. The country he argues is impatient and tired of the present unsatisfactory state of things.

The indications were yesterday and have been for some days past that the paper may take a turn unfavorable to you unless you take the course mentioned. The Herald, as you are aware, goes with the strongest, or with the party it beleives to be the strongest, and Hercules like it will help those who do and can help themselves. Mr. Bennett beleives your policy, as to reconstruction and in general, a good one, and he is satisfied the sentiment of the country is with you, but he thinks you may lose all the advantage of this by the persistency, tact, and ability of the radicals if you do not disarm them and seperate the wavering conservatives from them.[5]

I know your situation is a very difficult one, and I think I see this better than Mr. Bennett, still there is much force in what he says. As far as my influence goes it shall be exerted, as it has been all along, in your support, but the paper takes a strange jump sometimes, and then the influence of any individual has to give way for the time.

I write very freely and frankly to you, beleiving you will both excuse the liberty and appreciate the motive. I make no argument, but simply give you a little information which I think you ought to know.

W. B. Phillips.

ALS, DLC-JP.
1. Although no longer found enclosed, the articles are readily available in the *Herald*. Entitled "Modest Demand of the National Banks," the first article opposed Congress's granting tax exemptions to U.S. banks, while the second, "False Alarms About a Revulsion," attempted to allay widespread concerns about an impending financial panic. *New York Herald*, May 20, 1866.
2. This article criticized recent legislation submitted in Congress which would place severe limitations upon the President's legal and constitutional power of removal. Ibid.
3. See Phillips to Johnson, Feb. 23, 1866.
4. "President Johnson's Policy—What's to be Done?" advised the President to dismiss his entire cabinet, "root and branch," appoint a new one consisting of war heroes, and then "let the Senate reject them if they dare." *New York Herald*, May 19, 1866.
5. A few weeks earlier Phillips had warned Johnson of the negative consequences of appearing too timid and careful, stressing that "the people are very sensitive to anything like a want of courage in their chief magistrate." In short, "They admire pluck." Phillips to Johnson, Apr. 13, 1866, Johnson Papers, LC.

From Alvin L. Robinson[1]

Fillmore City   May 20th 1866

Most honored Sir

Being a citizen of Utah, a union man, a lover of law and order, and a well wisher of mankind, I take the liberty to address a few lines to you, as the national executive, in relation to the state of society and existing affairs in this territory. That the laws are frequently disregarded here or totally annuled; and that religious heresies, which cause men to disregard and violate the laws, which degrade society and brutalize mankind, which cause men, innocent in the eyes of the law, to be assassinated and butchered in cold blood, in the streets of our towns and cities, is a fact that no one knowing the ways of society here can honestly deny, and that many of the "saints" honestly believe they are doing the will of the Lord, in upholding and practicing such things, is a fact equally true.

Now Sir, If better ways can be introduced and maintained for the benefit of the people here, and the numerous posterity which is to follow after them, I, as a humble, citizen appeal to you to introduce those ways, and enforce the laws with equity justice.

Alvin L Robinson

ALS, DNA-RG59, Misc. Lets., 1789–1906 (M179, Roll 238).
    1. Perhaps the Fillmore farmer listed in the 1870 census as Almon Robison (b. c1845), a native of Illinois who possessed $5,000 real estate and $5,000 personal estate. J. R. Kearl et al., comps., *Index to the 1850, 1860 and 1870 Censuses of Utah* (Baltimore, 1981), 307.

From James M. Tomeny

Mobile Ala.   May 20th 1866.

I have again been indicted & another bond for $25,000 required.[1] I am not allowed to see this indictment but am informed it is for alleged frauds. The bonds was given & approved by the judge[2] & not-withstanding I am now under bonds for $150,000 the Judge forbids me to leave Mobile. I desire to go to Washington & lay the whole matter before your Excellency.[3] Cannot Attorney General telegraph an order to the District Attorney[4] here to Continue the cases against me till October or November to send all books, vouchers & records seized from me to Washington and permit me to go in person and to furnish me with a copy of the indictment? This will secure me justice which is all I ask. I am satisfied the purpose here is to press the cases to immediate trial.

J. M Tomeny   Actg Collector &c

Tel, DLC-JP.
    1. See Tomeny's earlier complaint about indictment and bond. Tomeny to Johnson, May 15, 1866.
    2. Richard Busteed.
    3. Within a few weeks, Tomeny did go to Washington and attain relief from the attorney general. See Tomeny to Johnson, June 12, 1866.
    4. Lawrence Worrall.

From John Campbell

Phila.   May 21st 66

Sir

You are engaged in a great patriotic work in endeavouring to save the Union. Your name is inevitably involved with its reconstruction. Your character will be transmitted to the distant future second to no patriots that ever existed if you can succeed in your sublime undertaking. Courage Courage Courage is one of the elements that must sustain you—you have the prayers of every good citizen for your success. I suppose that Congress intends not to adjourn until its term will have expired and I presume it is resolved that you shall be shorn of that portion of your Ex Power which enables you to remove from office incompetent and obstructive Federal office holder. You have the means to neutralise every such revolutionary proceeding. Send for Republican Gentlemen of character and such are to be found in every state. Tell them that you desire them to accept such and such offices but that until after the meeting of next Congress they cannot be paid as the Radical Faction in the present Congress will not permit it. You can get Gentlemen of wealth and of high character in the Republican ranks who will deem themselves honored by your confidence and who will consent to administer the duties of the offices to which you may appoint them irrespective of payment. I am sure there are honor and patriotism enough in the Republican party to make such sacrifices. In no instance appoint an old broken down unprincipled hack. Do not hesitate or delay. If you do you are a doomed man. If the Radicals beat you in the forthcoming elections they will impeach try and remove you from office as certain as your name is Andrew Johnson. In districts of Pa. where Democrats can be elected let them be, in districts where your supporters can be elected let the Democrats manfully vote for them. I can speak plainly for the Pa. Democracy that it will truly and faithfully act upon this policy but the work must begin soon if this distracted Union is to be saved. Let me here state that you know me of old. I am and have ever been a Democrat but I say to you in your changes of Federal office holder appoint no Democrat indeed the Democracy do not expect it. Hon Edgar A Cowen will be sent back to the Senate if my party can carry Pa. in the fall. You see therefore the absolute necessity of John W Geary being defeated in October. His defeat will be your victory.[1]

There is one other thing among many that you must do. Cause all the members of both Houses of Congress from the excluded states to attend in Washington in December next to take their seats. Should any Revolutionary and bloody faction attempt by violance to oust them you have the power to see that the law shall be vindicated and the Constitution obeyed.

Had I an hours conversation with you I might be able to give you some useful information but I have not the time to go nor you the time to spare to listen. I have no axe to grind. I want no office. I have written this because I admire your bravery fortitude and patriotism. May God in his providence enable you to restore this Union and to triumph over all your enemies. . . .

John Campbell

ALS, DLC-JP.
1. The Democrats won only six out of twenty-four congressional seats in the fall elections (for a net loss of three seats, compared to 1864), Cowan was unsuccessful in his bid for

reelection, and Geary won by a convincing majority. Bradley, *Militant Republicanism*, 249; *BDAC*.

From Nathan Johnson

Nashville Tenn   May 21st 1866

Dear Uncle

You will, no doubt be surprised when you peruse this, my first Epistle and see with what impertinence I address you, the Chief Magistrate of this mighty nation! I hope however you will forgive me, and attribute it to my extreme youth, and to the dificulties of an early education. I feel myself very deficient, and am fully determined to remedy it by hard application to study.

But in the mean time, I must have money and clothing, and other necessary articles, and I appeal to you for advise in the matter, and ask at your hands some assistance. Could you not give me some *comon position* that would afford me an opportunity of both learning and excercise?[1] You have many places of profit at your disposal, and I feel as though I ought to have some encouragement, as I am cast upon this cold and uncharitable world with none to advise me, and then I feel as though I should do something for myself, and not always be dependent on my Brothers.

I will be satisfied with anything you may see proper to give me, and will strive dilligently to make myself worthy of your confidence, and try in my humble way to please you in every respect.

I am Young, very Young, but have determined to no longer remain idle; but push forward for myself, and I think with your assistance I will be able to succeed.

All the family is well. Bro Andrew will soon give up the Agency of Tenn Penitentiary.[2] The Legislature is still *quarrelling* and doing but little business, in fact everything seems to at a deadlock, nothing for a poor man I can assure you. Give my respects to all, and please answer this on reciept. Direct to Care Box 180 Nashville Tenn. The *masses* endorse your policy. *Radical* party on the *dicline*.

Nathan Johnson

ALS, DLC-JP.
    1. Available evidence does not reveal whether Nathan Johnson received a federal appointment from the President.
    2. See Andrew Johnson, Jr., to Johnson, Mar. 3, 1866.

From William W. Mills

Metropolitan Hotel
Washington D.C.   May 21st 1866

Sir:

I beg leave to call Your attention to the enclosed papers[1] from Gentlemen well Known to Yourself and to the country recommending R. L.

Robertson Esq[2] for the Office of Collector of Customs at Brownsville Texas District of Brasos Santiago. This District is on the Mexican frontier adjoining the one where I have been Collector for the four Years last past. The District is large and the temptations for smuggling very great which renders the employment of a large number of subordinate Offices necessary at points distant from the Office of the Collector.

Many of the Merchants who import goods there are Mexicans who do not understand our language. Considering these facts the Office there is an important one, and one which few men are competent to fill efficiently.

In my opinion Mr Robertson has peculiar qualifications for this office. His business qualifications are of the very highest order and having lived since 1857 on the frontier where the office is situated he perfectly understands the business and language of the people there. He is well Known and highly esteemed by the people of the frontier, and his appointment would give general satisfaction, and inspire confidence. Mr. Robertsons claims to the favorable consideration of the government are certainly not second to those of any other man; at the out-break of the Rebellion he was forced to leave his home and business in Texas and abandon his property. He came immediately to Washington City and entered the Military service and has been in the service of the government in different capacities ever since. He wishes now to return to Texas, and I am sure that in giving him this appointment the government will reward a faithful man and secure the services of an efficient Officer.[3]

Wm. W. Mills   Collector Customs
El Paso Texas

We respectfully refer to the enclosed recommendations from Senator Doolittle. Hon F W. Kellogg. Hon Montgomery Blair. Hon John S Watts. S. S. Andros Esq Richard Busted Esq and Major Anson Mills.[4]

LS, DNA-RG56, Appts., Customs Service, Collector, Brownsville, R. L. Robertson.

1. Not found.

2. New York-born Richard L. Robertson (c1837–fl1867), a clerk in El Paso in 1860, was nominated and confirmed consul at Mazatlan, Mexico, in July 1861. He was appointed from California. 1860 Census, Tex., El Paso, El Paso, 7; McCulloch to Johnson, Jan. 11, 1868, Lets. Sent re Customs Service Employees (QC Ser.), Vol. 8, RG56, NA; Basler, Works of Lincoln, 4: 445.

3. Eleven days before Mills wrote this letter Johnson had withdrawn a nomination for the collectorship and made another, which he also withdrew. In July 1866 Johnson nominated Robertson, who served until his death sometime before January 11, 1868. Ser. 6B, Vol. 4: 211, Johnson Papers, LC; Johnson to Senate, May 10, 1866 (with endorsement, July 19, 1866), Appts., Customs Service, Collector, Tex., R. L. Robertson, RG56, NA; McCulloch to Johnson, July 19, 1866, Jan. 11, 1868, Lets. Sent re Customs Service Employees (QC Ser.), Vols. 4, 8, RG56, NA.

4. James R. Doolittle, Francis W. Kellogg, Richard S.S. Andros, and Richard Busteed. Anson Mills (1834–1924), brother of William W. Mills, spent four years in El Paso as a surveyor, then joined the Union army at the outbreak of the war. He remained in the military, serving on the frontier until 1893. In his old age he made a fortune from the invention and manufacture of an improved cartridge belt. DAB; Mills, El Paso, xi.

From James S. Odle[1]

[ca. May 21, 1866][2]

Your Petitioner James S Odle would respectfully Shew that he is and has been for several years a resident citizen of this State,[3] that his age is thirty four years and that his occupation is a farmer.

That in politics he is Conservative, and would gladly have avoided any participancy in the late war that his friends being on the Side of the Rebellion his feelings were with them, but that he did not take up arms against the United States until the time hereinafter mentioned. That in the month of December 1862 at Said County of Washington his place of residence he was forced into against his will and in order to Sav his life into Co F, 1 Arks Cav United States Army and remained and Served therein for three months and as Soon as an opportunity offered he left Such Service and Said Company and departed South, where he joined a company in the So Called Confederate States Army, where he remained until the final Surrender, and since in Said Company.[4] That such is the extent of his paticipancy in the late rebellion.

He is advised that on account of his Conduct aforesaid that he is debarred from taking the Amnesty Oath and liable to Heavy pains and penalties.

He therefore prays your Excellency granting him special Amnesty and pardon, that he may be permitted to take the oath of Amnesty and that he be restored to all the privileges of a citizen of the United States.[5]

And he will ever pray &c.

James S Odle

ALS, DNA-RG94, Amnesty Papers (M1003, Roll 14), Ark., James S. Odle.

1. Odle could not be further identified other than that his place of birth may have been Washington County, Arkansas, and he deserted the Federal army on March 17, 1863. CSR, James S. Odle, RG94, NA.

2. This is the date he appeared before the county clerk to swear to the truth of his statements.

3. Arkansas.

4. The designation of this military unit has not been determined.

5. Odle was not pardoned until May 1, 1867.

From Robert M. Patton

Montgomery, Ala, May 21st 1866.

My Dear Sir

Raphael Semmes[1] the Judge of Probate, elect, for the County of Mobille has filed regularly in the office of Secretary of State;[2] his application for Commission, as Said Judge of Probate, and the return having been made by the proper offices of his election—And having consulted the Atty General of the State,[3] I have felt it my duty to issue to him the Commission of Office. I am also advised of the disabilities under which the party elect, is labouring, and without the removal of which he cannot consistantly exercise the functions of his office. His election to the responsible, and Lucrative office of Judge of Probate by the people of the City and County of Mobille without opposition, is Satisfactory evidence that he is in theie, entire confidence for honesty, integrity, and Capacity.

I cannot be insensible of the very heavy weight of responsibility, and the unprecedented embarrassments, with which you are surrounded at the present time, as well as your great anxiety for restoration of the recently discordant states to there former harmonious relations to the Union. If however it will not be inconsistant with your policy of Reconstruction (so hastily approved by all true National Men) it will be highly gratifying to me as well as to the people of Alabama if you can extend to Judge Semmes that Executive Clemency which will fully restore him to Citizenship and authorize his to exercise the functions of the office to which the people have called him.[4]

I think I hazard nothing in saying, Judge Semmes has in good faith sunk the Soldier into the Citizen, and will in time to come prove true to the National Government, and the Constitution of the United States.

R M Patton   Gov. of Alabama

ALS, DNA-RG94, Amnesty Papers (M1003, Roll 10), Ala., Raphael Semmes.

1. Semmes (1809–1877), a former U.S. naval officer, attained widespread notoriety as commander of the Confederate commerce cruisers *Sumter* and *Alabama*. After the debate over his election to the Mobile probate court, he was a professor in Louisiana and a lawyer and newspaper editor in Memphis. Wakelyn, *BDC*, 380.

2. Albert O. Elmore.

3. John W.A. Sanford (1825–1913), a Montgomery lawyer and colonel of the 60th Ala. Inf., CSA, twice served as Alabama's attorney general (1865–68, 1870–78). Marie B. Owen, *The Story of Alabama: A History of the State* (5 vols., New York, 1949), 5: 1192–93.

4. Johnson had already determined that Semmes would not be permitted to act as probate judge or in "any other civil or political office" until he was pardoned. However, when Semmes did apply for pardon, accompanied by memorials signed by over 400 citizens of Mobile, it was denied. Semmes did not receive an individual pardon, but was included in Johnson's general amnesty proclamation of July 4, 1868. Edwin M. Stanton to George H. Thomas, May 15, 1866, Tels. Sent, Sec. of War (M473, Roll 90), RG107, NA; Edmund Cooper to Semmes, June 3, 1866, Johnson Papers, LC; *Louisville Courier*, May 19, 1866; Patton to Johnson, May 22, 1866, Tels. Recd., President, Vol. 5 (1866–67), RG107, NA; Jonathan T. Dorris, *Pardon and Amnesty Under Lincoln and Johnson* (Chapel Hill, 1953), 185.

From Richard C. Mason[1]

Near Alexandria Va.   22d May 1866

Sir,

In compliance with the Suggestion your Excellency made on Saturday last 19th inst,[2] I beg leave to respectfully present the following facts of my case, to which I desired to ask your attention. vidzt.

My farm, in the County of Fairfax va. was confiscated and sold in July

1864 upon the alledged ground that it was "abandoned land," whilst in fact, I was driven from my home, (where I had predetermined to remain, being then 69 years of age and in very bad health,) by an armed force of ten men, whose avowed purpose was to arest me.

The farm was sold by the Marshall,[3] and he himself became the purchaser, or in other words he sold to himself and at his own price.

The Judge,[4] as I learn, gave the Marshall a deed for my property, altho' he had not a shadow of claim to such a deed, nor do I suppose the judge can with propriety make a deed to one not entitled to receive it.

The Marshall, by his agent,[5] very soon commenced a vigorous cutting of timber and wood off the premises, & have continued it for three seasons —and to a most destructive extent. I obtained a Bill of injunction to stay the enormous waste being made and had it duly served. The process was disregarded and the work continued. When about to take steps to enforce the injunction, according to law, I was told that the Military would not allow me to proceed. I saw Genl. Auger[6] & asked him whether he would interfere to prevent the action of the injunction.

He said "we held a meeting a few days ago and determined to uphold *all* confiscation sales." I asked if he would do so in the case of a violation of law, in making the sale? or of manifest fraud. He said in reply that he could not be troubled by trying cases, in taking testimony &c.

Our circuit Superior Court will sit on Monday the 4th of June prox., when I hope to have the validity of the sale made of my property, determined upon by a court of law. But, that I may expect a military interference to prevent my obtaining Justice, I beg, in addition to what I have stated on that subject, to enclose herewith a Copy of General Orders No. 9 5th March 1865.[7] The constitution of U. States, allows citizens of different states to resort to federal courts, but not citizens of the same states. Mr. Duncan and I are of the same state.

In fine, I ask leave to add, that I am now in my 74th year and have seven children, and have not the strenth to enable me to labor—am entirely destitute, and therefore most respectfully but earnestly beg that you will exert your Constitutional power to control the military in their purpose to prevent my attainment of Justice.[8]

R C Mason

ALS, DNA-RG60, Office of Atty. Gen., Lets. Recd., President.

1. Mason (c1793–1868), a grandson of George Mason, was for many years a successful physician in Alexandria, Virginia. His estate of 800 acres was located near Mount Vernon. Tyler, *Va. Biography*, 4: 24; Mason to Johnson, Sept. 20, 1865, Amnesty Papers (M1003, Roll 65), Va., Richard C. Mason, RG94, NA.

2. Evidence of a May 19 meeting between Mason and Johnson has not been found. Mason had previously written to Johnson about the fate of his farm; the President routinely forwarded that letter to the attorney general. A letter from Mason's son finally elicited in September 1866 the opinion of the new attorney general, Henry Stanbery, that the farm could not be restored to his father and that the "question of title belongs exclusively to the civil tribunals." Mason to Johnson, Mar. 15, 1866, Office of Atty. Gen., Lets. Recd., President, RG60, NA; *Official Opinions of the Attorneys General of the United States* (42 vols., Washington, D.C., 1852–1974), 12: 54.

3. William A. Duncan (c1821–fl1870) was deputy marshal for the U.S. District Court of eastern Virginia. He later pursued farming in Fairfax County, Virginia. 1870 Census, Va., Fairfax, Falls Church Twp., 314; *OR*, Ser. 1, Vol. 37, Pt. 1: 475; Ser. 2, Vol. 8: 984; *Boyd's Washington and Georgetown Directory* (1867).

4. John C. Underwood.

5. Not otherwise identified.

6. Christopher C. Augur (1821–1898), a West Point graduate and veteran of the Mexican War, served on the frontier and then as commandant of cadets at West Point. During the war he fought in the eastern theater before being transferred to the Department of the Gulf in November 1862, where he commanded the District of Baton Rouge. After the Port Hudson campaign Augur returned to Washington, where he performed various administrative duties and commanded the XXII Corps and the Department of Washington. He remained in the regular army until 1885, retiring as a brigadier general. Boatner, *CWD*.

7. General Augur's order directed that persons who obtained title to confiscated property by U.S. government sales were not to be disturbed by state or local courts. Only the "action of the Federal Courts . . . would be regarded." Office of Atty. Gen., Lets. Recd., President, RG60, NA.

8. Johnson forwarded this letter to James Speed. There is no evidence that Mason regained his farm. In 1870 William Duncan owned a $16,000 farm in Fairfax County in the vicinity of the location of Mason's farm. 1870 Census, Va., Fairfax, Falls Church Twp., 314.

From James L. Orr

Columbia   22d May 1866

Dear Sir:

I beg leave respectfully to represent to you that there no longer exists any necessity whatever for the continuance of garrisons throughout all the districts of this State and the peace and quiet of the whole community would be promoted by mustering out all the volunteer troops now on duty here.

The 6th Regt. U.S. Infantry under command of Col. J. D. Greene[1] is a sufficient military force to do all necessary garrison duty.

A Small garrison in Columbia and garrisons in Charleston and at three other points on the Coast would be entirely adequate to the preservation of order.

You may be assured that there is less disposition in this State to oppose antagonize or destroy the federal government than has existed at any previous time for Thirty Six Years.

Our people feel very Keenly the injustice being done them by excluding them from all participation in the government by the radicals and requiring them to bear all the burthens imposed upon them without consulting their interests or feelings but are very hopeful that your wise just and constitutional policy will very soon be indorsed by the great body of the constituents of the radicals themselves, and that restoration will be speedily accomplished.

As Genl. Sickles is understood to have accepted the Mission to the Hague[2] and will vacate his command of the department of S.C. I think that Col. Greene of the 6th U.S Infantry would make an excellent department commander especially if his troops only are retained to garrison the State. This suggestion is made without the Knowledge of Col. G. and is predicated upon my desire to see the place filled by a regular officer of the army rather than by a politician.

James L. Orr   Gov of S.C

ALS, DLC-JP.
1. James D. Greene (1828–1902), a firearms manufacturer and inventor, resigned from the army in 1867 with the brevet rank of brigadier general. Hunt and Brown, *Brigadier Generals*.
2. The President nominated Daniel E. Sickles as minister to The Hague in late April 1866; the Senate confirmed the appointment on May 11. However, Sickles declined the post. Ser. 6B, Vol. 2: 295, Johnson Papers, LC.

From Wilmington, N.C., Freedmen[1]

[ca. May 22, 1866][2]

We your humble petitioners whose names are hereunto affixed, are Freedmen of the city of Wilmington and state of North Carolina with regret and pain learn you have placed in arrest those officers entrusted to the care of the Bureau who are engaged in the cultivation of plantations in this district.[3]

We are confident that these gentlemen have engaged in these operations for the purpose of promoting the interests of the freedmen instead of a pecuniary benefit to themselves.

It is a fact susceptible of the clearest proof, that Mass Mann and Wickersham[4] were urgently solicited by the owners of the lands, to undertake the cultivation of them, with the urgent request of Freedmen who belonged and were owned by these their former masters, and desired employment on lands they were acquainted with. We beg leave to assure your Excellency that the actions of the aforesaid officers Mass. Mann and Wickersham have been beneficial to the Freedman, have furnished them labor and sustenance, taught them the value and sacredness of Contract, and the importance of economy and industry and afforded them books and schools.

We are not aware the cultivation of these lands has interfered with their prompt and faithful discharge of their official duties. We have been so much indebted to the Bureau for protection and vindication of our rights, in the past, and are still so dependent upon it for security in the future and also are under a great debt of gratitude to Mass. Mann and Wickersham for their official and personal efforts in our behalf and have such confidence in their honor and integrity that we pray your Excellency to scrutinize well the accusations which are made against them by our enemies, and withhold condemnation until the truth can be developed. We pray you not to let our stronghold of defence be stricken down.

And we will ever pray.[5]

Pet, DNA-RG105, Records of the Commr., Lets. Recd. (M752, Roll 29).
1. There were 133 signatories.

2. This date is given because at 8 p.m., May 22, 1866, G. P. Rourk, who on his "own volition" had drawn up the petition, forwarded it to General O. O. Howard, with the notation that all the signatures had been obtained "since two O clock P.M." Rourk to Howard, May 22, 1866, Records of the Commr., Lets. Recd. (M752, Roll 29), RG105, NA.

3. Johnson was responding to the report of Generals James B. Steedman and Joseph S. Fullerton when on May 15, 1866, he ordered the arrest of a number of Bureau officers, agents, and associates in North Carolina. Bentley, *Freedmen's Bureau*, 125–28; *House Ex. Docs.*, 39 Cong., 1 Sess., No. 120, pp. 2–3 (Ser. 1263).

4. James C. Mann (c1834–1897), a former lieutenant, 1st Wis. Cav., was currently a captain, assistant quartermaster of volunteers. Mustered out at the end of 1866, he subsequently resided in Wilmington, North Carolina, San Francisco, California, and Denver, Colorado, ultimately becoming a bookkeeper. Charles I. Wickersham (c1837–1905) had been a captain, 8th Pa. Inf., before serving with the same rank as assistant adjutant general of volunteers. Much of his later life was spent in Chicago. Pension Records, Fannie J. Mann, Anna C. Wickersham, RG15, NA.

5. Steedman and Fullerton complained that Freedmen's Bureau officers had personally invested money in plantations near Wilmington. After General Howard's own investigation, on June 7, 1866, a general court martial was ordered to convene in Raleigh to try Mann, Wickersham, and others, on the charge of "Conduct to the prejudice of good order and military discipline." Only Eliphalet Whittlesey and George O. Glavis were found guilty, the former to be reprimanded and the latter to be dismissed from the service. By the time the trials were over, Congress had overridden Johnson's veto of the Freedmen's Bureau bill. *House Ex. Docs.*, 39 Cong., 1 Sess., No. 120, pp. 67–68, 70–71 (Ser. 1263); *Louisville Journal*, June 14, 1866; Gen. Court-Martial Order Nos. 211–16, Nov. 17, 1866, RG94, NA; Bentley, *Freedmen's Bureau*, 132–33.

To Sarah C. Polk

Washington, D.C.   May 23d 1866.

Your despatch this moment received.[1] The release of Mr. John Porterfield has been ordered, upon his giving parole.[2] I will be glad to see you in Washington during this summer.[3]

Andrew Johnson.

Tel, DNA-RG107, Tels. Sent, President, Vol. 3 (1865–68).

1. As a favor, Sarah Polk had asked the President to release or parole Porterfield, a friend and family associate. Newspapers and General Thomas had conveyed the news that Porterfield had been arrested in Nashville on May 17. Thomas had asked Johnson, "what disposition is to be made" of Porterfield, and Secretary Stanton, who transmitted Thomas's telegram to the President, had encouraged Johnson to provide "any instructions you may be pleased to give." Polk to Johnson, May 23, 1866; Thomas to Stanton, May 18, 1866, Johnson Papers, LC; *Louisville Courier*, May 18, 1866.

2. See Stanton to Johnson, May 24, 1866, Lets. Sent, Mil. Bks., Executive, 57-C, RG107, NA; *Louisville Courier*, May 25, 1866. For an earlier document dealing with the Porterfield case, see Holt to Johnson, Dec. 16, 1865, *Johnson Papers*, 9: 515–16.

3. Mrs. Polk's telegram of May 23 makes no mention of a possible summer visit to Washington.

From Edwin M. Stanton

Washington City, May 23rd 1866

Sir,

I have the honor to acknowledge the receipt of S.[sic] A. Irwin's[1] application for the appointment of 1st Lieutenant of U.S. Cavalry, recommended by *Senator Cowan*,[2] and your direction that the appointment be made, endorsed thereon—in reference to which I beg to inform you that there are no vacancies of that grade in any arm of the service. In the Cavalry there are but seven Second Lieutenancies vacant, and they are, according to the established usage of the service, retained for the class of cadets which is to graduate in the coming month of June. If an Army Bill should pass there will then be a vacancy or if with the information here given you are pleased to order the appointment a nomination will be submitted.[3]

Edwin M. Stanton, Secretary of War.

LBcopy, DNA-RG107, Lets. Sent, Mil. Bks., Executive, 57-C.

1. David A. Irwin (*c*1840–1901) served in the 12th Pa. Cav. during the war, eventually attaining the rank of captain before being mustered out in July 1865. CSR, David A. Irwin, RG94, NA; Pension Records, Adelle D. Irwin, RG15, NA.

2. Edgar Cowan's recommendation stated that he had "the best evidence of [Irwin's] worth and gallantry as a soldier." Another recommendation from Charles H. Shriner, a Pennsylvania internal revenue collector, claimed that Irwin had killed a Confederate major with his bare hands in a skirmish the day after the battle of Gettysburg. Irwin to Johnson, with endorsements, May 14, 1866, ACP Branch, File I-23-CB-1866, D. A. Irwin, RG94, NA.

3. Although the army bill did not pass Congress until July, Johnson did not wait for it and instead ordered the appointment to be made and forwarded the May 14 application to the War Department, eliciting the above response from Stanton. On May 28 Johnson returned the application to Stanton, requesting that Irwin be nominated as second lieutenant in the cavalry service of the regular army. Irwin received the appointment and served until 1879, retiring as a captain. Ibid.; Heitman, *Register*, 1: 564.

From John McCarty

May 24, 1866, Parish Prison, New Orleans, La.; LS, DNA-RG45, Subj. File N, Subsec. NO, Courts-Martial, John McCarty.

An eighteen-year-old, who at sixteen had enlisted in the Navy at Boston in April 1864, seeks release from prison. He was court martialed as a deserter because he left his ship in April 1865 to join "the 1st Louisiana (Union) cavalry in which regiment he had an older brother serving." Arrested as a deserter from the Navy, he was subsequently returned to his original ship. Tried and sentenced to five years imprisonment, later reduced to one, he now pleads that "he was decoyed away from his home in Lawrence Mass and induced to join the service under false pretences," that when he deserted "he was ignorant of the enormity of the offence and thought that it could make little difference whether he was in the military or naval service of the Government," and that for his mother, "in very delicate health," to know he is in prison would kill her. He can not believe that the President will "refuse that priceless boon of liberty to a young thoughtless though perhaps erring boy thereby restoring him to his afflicted parents." [Endorsed in Johnson's pencilled note: "Let the prisone be released. A.J."]

From Abner L. Gilstrap[1]

Macon Mo.   May 26th 1866.

Difficult indeed is the task before you; and is rendered more difficult in the border States by the Selfishness of men who assume to advise as committees in the large Cities. The State Central Committee at St Louis is composed of men formerly called Claybanks,[2] or supporters of the Schofield-Gamble[3] policy of carrying on a war upon a peace basis, and Democrats. Radical Union men, who have supported you in the Baltimore Convention, and support your Administration now, are either ignored entirely, which is the *general rule*, or subordinated in such a manner as that they are completely ostracised. The Committee, at St Louis, before the present political Status was developed, went to work without consulting any of your original friends, and parceled out all your official patronage, of any consideration, among their own political friends. These facts are just now coming to light, as the people begin to move, they find themselves forestalled by the action of that Committee. Members of the Radical party who were your true friends from the beginning, and not only stand by you now, but were the first men to forecast the bitter assault upon you by the faction in Congress, and meet the issues in that assault, and defend you, now find themselves as completely ignored as if they were of, and belonged to your bitter enemies. These facts are accomplished under various disguises, and will be denied in detail; but they are nevertheless true. The special reason given in detail, in each case, were *prepared in advance for the occasion.* The City of Macon, the most important in the State, next to St Louis, made the first contest and won the first contested victory in behalf of the policy of Abraham Lincoln as carried out by Andrew Johnson and his Cabinet.

And now, in North Missouri, we are completely ignored by that Committee. Recommendations are made for all the important positions without consulting us. The only success we have had was in the appointment of Col. C. H. Green, Pension Agent vice Maj. Clemens;[4] and this measure was carried *without the Committee* as Col. Green informs me. The Post Office at Macon is still in the hands of your enemies the efforts of the Committee to the Contrary Notwithstanding.

Now there is no doubt of the Patriotism, or sincerity of the members of the Committee, in support of the Government and your Administration; but their policy, as indicated above, will soon produce bad results.

On the other hand the many letters written and published in this District by the Hon. J. F. Benjamin,[5] in connection with a new secret organization, called the "advanced guard," *among your political enemies*, proves conclusively that a Revolutionary conspiracy is being hatched in Congress, and is being organized in the country also. Its first general movement, in my opinion, will be the assassination of Andrew Johnson, in order to get the control of the Army and Navy. It is boldly declared that "the Contest has to be fought over again." And secret military organizations are now going on in that Secret Organization, in many parts of this State. I would direct your attention to the late Speech of Gov. Fletcher[6] at St. Louis. For boldness of design and flimsiness of disguise I regard that Speech as unrivaled.

Abner L. Gilstrap.
late member Baltimore Convention

ALS, DLC-JP.
1. Gilstrap (1814–*fl*1890) served briefly with the Missouri state militia and then as a state senator from Macon County. He was also a member of the Missouri convention of 1865. *Off. Army Reg.: Vols,* 7: 40; *OR,* Ser. 3, Vol. 4: 90; *NUC;* Walter Williams, ed., *A History of Northeast Missouri* (3 vols., Chicago, 1913), 1: 430–31; Bryon Lee Dilts, comp., *1890 Missouri Census Index of Civil War Veterans or Their Widows* (Salt Lake City, 1985), 98.
2. There were two major political groups in Missouri beginning about the fall of 1862. The "Charcoals" were Radicals who favored immediate emancipation and the enlistment of black troops. "Claybanks," so called "because of their supposedly colorless middle ground," were Conservatives who favored gradual, compensated emancipation and were appalled at the idea of black troops. A third, smaller, group, the "Snowflakes," also Conservatives, did not believe the war would end slavery. William E. Parrish, *A History of Missouri, 1860 to 1875* (3 vols., Columbia, Mo., 1973), 3: 93–94.
3. Gen. John M. Schofield, military commander of the district (May 1862-January 1864), and Provisional Governor Hamilton R. Gamble (1861-January 1864). Ibid., 106; James L. McDonough, *Schofield: Union General in the Civil War and Reconstruction* (Tallahassee, 1972), 46, 68.
4. Clark H. Green (*c*1820–*fl*1868) and John T. Clements (1836–1914) apparently were rival newspaper editors. During the war Green served as a colonel in the Missouri militia while Clements returned to his native Washington, D.C., and became a private in the 3rd Btn. D.C. Inf. and a captain, commissary subsistance of volunteers. After Clements's stint as pension agent in Missouri, he worked in the Pension Department in Washington, D.C., the remainder of his life. Green's appointment as pension agent in 1867 was very brief for he "was removed on a forged letter of an insulting character addressed to the President." Despite being reinstated, all pension agents were soon legislated out of office. Reappointed, he was rejected by the Senate. In 1868 he was recommended, apparently without success, for the post of collector for the Third District of Missouri. 1860 Census, Mo., Howard, Glasgow, 82; Pension Records, Mary S. Clements, RG15, NA; *General History of Macon County, Missouri* (Chicago, 1910), 274–75; *U.S. Off. Reg.* (1865–69, 1881–1913); Heitman, *Register,* 2: 105; "Missouri History Not Found in Textbooks," *MoHR* 27 (1933): 213; William F. Switzler to Johnson, July 13, 1868, Appts., Internal Revenue Service, Collector, Mo., 3rd Dist., Clark H. Green, RG56, NA.
5. At this time a Radical Republican congressman (1865–71), John F. Benjamin (1817–1877) came to Missouri in 1848, practicing law and serving in the state house of representatives. During the war he became a brigadier general and provost marshal of the Eighth District of Missouri. *BDAC.*
6. Thomas C. Fletcher.

From J. Madison Wells

New Orleans, May 26th 1866

Mr President.

This will be handed you by Messrs Duralde and Claiborne,[1] both well known Citizens of our State and highly intelligent Gentlemen, who are charged with the important trust of presenting to Congress, a memorial on behalf of the people of the State of Louisiana, praying for national relief and assistance in restoring the Levees on the Mississippi River. This measure is one involving the life and existence of the State and unless the Federal Government comes to our relief, I fear there is no alternative, but to abandon the cultivation of the alluvial lands and thus allow, the most fertile lands on the Globe to become a desert and waste.[2]

I feel assured Mr President that it is not necessary for me to appeal to your Sympathies in behalf of the distressed condition of the people of my

State to induce you to give them all the aid and assistance in your power in accomplishing the objects of the memorial.

While Congress seems to be afflicted with the Mania of "*reconstruction*" so far as the South is concerned, if they will only take the work of *reconstructing* our destroyed Levees in the hands of the Federal Government, or give us the means of doing so, they will I am sure have accomplished a work of *reconstruction* that will receive the approbation of all parties.

Commending Messrs Claiborne & Duralde to your favorable attention, and invoking your continued paternal care and protection in behalf of the rights and interests of the whole people and particularly of the once erring but now repentant population of the Southern States.[3]

J Madison Wells   Governor of Louisiana

ALS, DLC-JP.

1. Col. J. V. Duralde (b. *c*1817) was the president of the Board of Levee Commissioners and a prewar railroad president. Col. Ferdinand L. Claiborne (*c*1814–*fl*1892), a planter in Pointe Coupee Parish since 1855, served as its legislative representative on a number of occasions, as well as its delegate to the 1879 state constitutional convention. 1850 Census, Miss., Adams, 74; 1850 Census, La., West Baton Rouge, 488; (1870), Pointe Coupee, Pointe Coupee, 6th Ward, 47; *New Orleans Picayune*, May 26, 31, June 14, 1866; Lawrence E. Estaville, Jr., "A Small Contribution: Louisiana's Short Rural Railroads in the Civil War," *La. Hist.*, 18 (1977): 91; Goodspeed's *Louisiana*, 1: 349.

2. The levee system had deteriorated during the Civil War as a result of neglect and military destruction and thus was not prepared to withstand the severe flooding in the spring of 1866 which "almost entirely desolated" thirteen parishes and threatened thirty-six others. Taylor, *La. Reconstructed*, 86; Robert W. Harrison, *Alluvial Empire* (Little Rock, 1961), 96–97; *New Orleans Picayune*, May 26, 1866. For an earlier version of the levee problem see Wells to Johnson, July 5, 1865, *Johnson Papers*, 8: 360–61.

3. Duralde and Claiborne arrived in Washington on June 7 and promptly met with Johnson, Secretary of War Stanton, and Gen. O. O. Howard of the Freedmen's Bureau, as well as two commissioners from Mississippi who were in the city on the same errand. Sen. Daniel Clark of New Hampshire presented a levee aid bill on July 2, 1866; despite positive encouragement from various people, including Johnson, the proposed appropriation of $1,500,000, which passed the Senate, was defeated in the House. In fact, the federal government did not provide any flood control aid until 1882. *New Orleans Picayune*, June 14, 15, 17, July 26, 28, 29, 1866; *Congressional Globe*, 39 Cong., 1 Sess., p. 3522; Walter Prichard, "The Effects of the Civil War on the Louisiana Sugar Industry," *JSH*, 5 (1939): 329–30.

From William M. Daily

New Orleans, Louisiana.
May 28th, 1866

Mr. President:

My confidential relations to you, and your Administration make it my duty to state a fact.[1]

The most positive evidence is laid before me this morning that *Mr. Murphy*[2] the *Acting U.S. Assessor* at New Orleans, has committed himself "*soul and body*" to the most extreme "*Sumner Radicals*," and in opposition to the Administration with the view of securing his confirmation by the Senate. Your friends are very indignant towards him. He has been rejected by the Senate once, on other grounds—and now by the very extreme of *radicalism* he hopes to *"cover a multitude of sins."* I simply state the facts on the honor of a gentleman, feeling assured that if you and *Secretary McCulloch*, only knew the facts, as they are known here, you never could be induced to renominate him, or consent to his re-appointment, in any way—as *all your friends here, without an exception*, would regard it as a great outrage, for your Administration to be thus imposed upon.

I write in haste, under a sense of duty to you. You know my desires. I rely with confidence on your favor. *"Naval Officer,"* or *"U.S. Assessor,"* at New Orleans, will satisfy me.[3]

Wm. M. Daily

ALS, DNA-RG56, Appts., Internal Revenue Service, Assessor, La., 1st Dist., Edmund Murphy.

1. Daily was special agent of the Post Office Department for Louisiana and Texas. *National Intelligencer*, May 1, 1866.

2. Edmund Murphy (*c*1837–*fl*1868), a native of Louisiana, was appointed assessor of internal revenue for the First District of Louisiana by Johnson in May 1865, but Secretary of the Treasury McCulloch opposed the nomination and the Senate did not confirm it. Murphy then applied for the position of U.S. marshal for the state, but he did not receive that post either. *U.S. Off. Reg.* (1865–69); 1860 Census, La., Orleans, New Orleans, 7th Ward, 543; New Orleans directories (1861–69); Murphy to Johnson, Oct. 1866, Mar. 6, 1867, Appt. Files for Judicial Dists., La., Edmund Murphy, RG60, NA.

3. Daily, a perennial office seeker, did not receive either of these appointments. See Daily to Johnson, Sept. 11, 1865, *Johnson Papers*, 9:62.

From Horatio King

Washington, May 28, 1866.

Dear Sir:

I believe it is no assumption to say that I possess one characteristic in common with yourself, namely, that of never flinching from the performance of a *clear duty*; and as, unexpectedly, it still devolves on me to speak for G. M. Delaney,[1]—and as I firmly believe he is being unjustly punished, I feel that I should be guilty of dereliction did I not continue to do all in my power to effect his release.

1. All who know him best, say he is not guilty and ask that he be pardoned.

2. He was dragged six hundred miles from home and friends and *violently* prosecuted by a personal enemy, whose overbearing and vindictive course stands *approved*, so long as Delaney is kept in prison.

3. Many of the witnesses against him were *scamps*, whom he had had convicted for desertion, and who were *let out* of prison to *swear him in*.

4. Both witness and counsel for him were threatened with the "Old Capitol," if they were not cautious in the defence.

5. One or more members of the Commission before whom he was

tried, I have been assured, were a part of the time *so drunk* as to be incapacitated to sit on the trial.

6. The prosecuting attornies of the Government admit that the defence was badly conducted, and there is good reason to believe that, *for a fee*, they would cheerfully advocate his release.

7. There is no longer occasion to "make an example" of poor Delaney; and if I am not mistaken, Gen. Holt clearly intimates as much in his last Report. In fine, if you still entertain doubt, may I not ask that you will send for Gen. Holt (as I know President Lincoln was in the habit of doing in similar cases) and hold a free conversation with him on the subject?

I am either *right*, or *wrong*, in pressing this matter. If I am *right*, I ask to be heard; and if *wrong*, I pray it may be made plain to me, that I may dismiss the thing from my mind and cease to trouble you.

Horatio King

ALS, NHi-Misc., Horatio King.
1. George M. Delaney had been tried in the spring of 1865 by a court-martial and found guilty of all charges—falsely assuming to be a government officer, aiding and abetting desertion, obtaining money under false pretenses, procuring false and fraudulent enlistments. Sentenced to ten years of imprisonment and a fine of $45,000, Delaney was sent to the state prison at Concord, New Hampshire. Mrs. Delaney's attempts in the fall of 1865 to secure executive clemency for her husband were unsuccessful. *Index of General Court Martial Orders. Adjutant General's Office, 1865* (Washington, D.C., 1866), No. 284; *Washington Morning Chronicle*, May 6, June 15, 1865; Joseph Holt to Mrs. G. M. Delaney, Oct. 13, 1865, Lets. Recd. (1854–94), File 1570, RG153, NA.

From Hugh McCulloch

Treasury Department
May 28th 1866.

Dear Sir,

I enclose a copy of an endorsement[1] made by your authority on the papers of Dennis Lineham.[2]

Mr. Hamlin[3] wishes to know if you feel an especial interest in Mr. Lineham. He has no vacancy at present, but will, of course, endeavor to meet your wishes. Please advise me in regard to the matter.[4]

H McCulloch

ALS, DNA-RG56, Appts., Customs Service, Sub-officers, Boston, Dennis Lineham.
1. Not found.
2. Dennis Lineham (c1844–fl1901), born in Ireland, was appointed a night inspector for the Customs House in Boston in 1867 and served until 1901. 1870 Census, Mass., Suffolk, 1st Ward (East Boston), 7; *U.S. Off. Reg.* (1867–1901).
3. Hannibal Hamlin served as customs collector for Boston officially from his confirmation in February 1866 until his resignation in September of that same year. However, he had actually performed the duty since September 1, 1865. Ser. 6B, Vol. 3: 35; Vol. 4: 22; Vol. 5, Johnson Papers, LC; *Baltimore American*, Sept. 4, 1865.
4. Johnson believed Lineham's case to be a good one and directed that "he be provided

for in the Custom House at Boston." Endorsement, McCulloch to Johnson, May 28, 1866, Appts., Customs Service, Sub-officers, Boston, Dennis Lineham, RG56, NA.

From Memphis Citizens Committee[1]

Memphis, Tenn.   May 28th 1866.

The undersigned, a portion of your fellow citizens of Memphis, have been appointed a committee to memorialize you upon the subject discussed in the preamble and resolutions which we have the honor herewith to forward.[2] We discharge this duty the more cheerfully, as your past history justifies the conviction that they will recieve from you that calm & dispassionate consideration always bestowed by you upon all questions touching the rights & liberties of your fellow citizens in any and every portion of the Union.

The Legislature of Tennessee has lately disfranchised nine-tenths of the adult male population of the Middle & Western portions of the State.[3] In good faith, they had accepted all the issues of the late war; and they were influenced to do this more through the kind suggestions & advice of your Excellency than by any other consideration. They had yielded all that true magnanimity could demand of them; and they had then hoped to be restored to the rights of a free people in a free country, under the provisions of the amnesty proclaimed by your Excellency in 1865. But in this we have been cruelly deceived; and an accidental majority of a Legislature representing a small minority of the people of the State, has usurped despotic power & set aside, as of no value, the representative feature of our Government. This despotism has disfranchised nine out of every ten of the qualified voters of this State; and the pretext for this is, that those thus disfranchised, have been engaged, at some time or in some way, in the late attempt to dissolve the Union.

Many of the very members voting for this odious law, were themselves once engaged in this same scheme, as we learn; but they were early seized with a desire to save their property; & they soon deserted a cause so ardently espoused at first. But, in the provisions of the law, they have especially provided that, as they returned to their allegiance a year or two sooner than their more unfortunate friend, and as they have since voted, the franchise act shall not affect them. Their legislation towards us is based upon an odious tyranny. While refusing the privilege of participating in the legislation of the State, they do not hesitate to tax us to the extent of three fourths of the means requisite to conduct & defray the expenses of the very Government which thus oppresses & degrades us.

Is this disfranchisement one of the legitimate results of the late war? Is it calculated to heal wounds still bleeding? Is it at all in harmony with that kind, conciliatory policy so happily inaugurated by your Excillency? Is there any justice or manliness in the hate which would thus pursue, us even unto death? Can this hatred engender any thing but continued discord and alienation between those who once were & who should still be equals & friends? Our people are weary of war. They have had enough of its horrors. They are firmly resolved to abide by & obey all the laws of their State or of the Union, until some peaceable plan shall be presented through which they may remedy the wrongs under which they now live. They do not invoke the agency of any doubtful power. But that clause of the Constitution of the United States, quoted in the preamble herewith forwarded, is one from which some of our people have been induced to hope relief. Tennessee has no republican form of Government now. That form is the government of majorities, under proper, written checks. Our present Government in this State, is one of a *small minority* which denies to an overwhelming majority as loyal as themselves, the right to participate in the legislation governing all. The usual mode of redress is denied us, with the knowledge that if the State Government be transferred to our hands, & the hands of four fifths of the population of the State, radicalism would be extinct in Tennessee, & the support of the state given to sustain the conciliatory policy of your Excellency.

All we desire is a restoration of a republican, representative form of Government; and with this view, we ask Your Excellency, to aid us if you can rightly do so, in obtaining the redress we seek.

J. T. Trezevant
G. A. Hanson
Wm. K. Poston

ALS (Trezevant), DLC-JP.

1. The three members of the committee were: John T. Trezevant; Gustavus A. Hanson (b. c1833), a lawyer who later served one term in the state senate; and William K. Poston (1819–1866), a lawyer and Memphis bank director who served briefly in the legislature in 1866. *BDTA*, 2: 380, 741; 1860 Census, Tenn., Shelby, 7th Dist., 204.

2. The copy of the preamble and resolutions has not been located with this letter or Trezevant's June letter.

3. This is a reference to the franchise law of 1866 which passed the legislature in early May.

From Sam Milligan

Private

Greeneville Ten.   May 28, 1866

Dear Sir:

When I was at Jackson Tennessee, I promised Judge A.W.O. Totton to write to you on the subject of his pardon.[1] I had a fair opportunity to judge of his feelings towards the Government of the U.S., and I was unable to discover in him any thing worse than I found in the great majority of the population in that part of the state. He feels disappointed at the defeat of the Southern Confederacy; but he declairs it to be his purpose to conform to the state of things imposed by the war. I saw or heard of no disposition on his part to do otherwise. It is true, he has been a bad rebel, and in turn, he has been a great sufferer by the war. His pecuniary losses are said to be little short of $200,000, including his negros. He appears cordial in the support of your administration; and all I can say, is, that if you can pardon him consistently with your sense of duty, it would tend, I think to harmonize things in that locality.

This is all I really need say, as it redeems my promise, and calles your attention to his application heretofore made. But I can not forbear offering my earnest congratulations for the comparative harmony, which the recent speeches and letters of your Cabinet officers, have manifested between you and them, on the great questions of the day. The public avowal of their concurrence in your policy of reconstruction, will doubtlessly be of great service to you; and hasten very much its ratification by the people. It is a heavy blow, struck at the right time, and by the right men.

I have long since been satisfied that there was no other Constitutional mode of reorganizing the insurgent states, and if it failed, the Government itself would have to be changed. Without change it has been sufficient to put down the rebellion; and it can, certainly, without alteration, restore the country to peace again.

It is true, I do not like the conduct of many of the rebels. They still cling to the fallen fortunes of the "Confederate States," and by evey means in their power, endeavor to honor & dignify their own treason. This is absurd, if they are sincere in their professions of loyalty to the U.S. They can not serve both God, and Mammon: nor can they love the Government of the U.S., and honor their treason against it. But it is human nature to attempt to justify our own errors and crimes; but I do not think they should be allowed to carry it too far.

The Government has demonstrated its military power; and the rebels dread it. They tremble at it, and are silent in its presence. What we now need, as it seems to me, is, an equally clear demonstration of the *Civil power of the Government*. No man has, at any period of its history, felt its power, acting purely through its civil officers, to punish any of the higher crimes against the Government. Its ability, without the intervention of the military, to protect itself, by its own civil power, and its fixed determination to do so, once demonstrated, will do more to rebuild the Government than any or all other things that could be done. The rebels feel now, and so do I am sorry to say, some of the Northern politicians, that they can not be punished except by the military—that a war must be inaugurated before they can be reached, and that is too slow, expensive, & dreadful in its consequences to be resorted to in order to effect individual cases. I think this idea ought to be exploded, and if we have no laws adequate to accomplish this object, they ought to be at once passed. To this end, I would try and execute Davis—if convicted on a fair trial. I would arrest try & certainly hang Hen[r]y A Wise if convicted. I think I would try Gus Hen[r]y, simply for being a fool. I might pardon him on the ground of imbicility after conviction and others of that class—north &

south. Such a course is right—it will make you immortal, and the Government perpetual and the people happy.

I write as familliar to you as I think to myself.

God bless & prosper you.

Sam Milligan

ALS, DLC-JP.
1. Totten had applied for presidential pardon as early as September 1865 but was not granted a pardon until January 18, 1866. It is not clear why Milligan was writing to Johnson about Totten's pardon in late May 1866. See Archibald W.O. Totten to Johnson, Sept. 13, 1865, Amnesty Papers (M1003, Roll 51), Tenn., Archibald W.O. Totten, RG94, NA; *House Ex. Docs.*, 39 Cong., 2 Sess., No. 116, p. 51 (Ser. 1293).

From Fernando Wood
Private

New York   May 28 1866

Dear Sir

A few days ago I had the honour to address you,[1] and now beg to call your attention to the enclosed[2] from the "World" of this City. This paper is the special organ of the Albany Regency Branch of the Democratic Party in this state; therefore its utterances are prompted by that source.

You can rely on no support from that quarter. These men are now making every effort to prevent the rank & file from endorsing the late Veto message.

Fernando Wood

ALS, DLC-JP.
1. No letter from Wood for May 1866 has been located.
2. The enclosed clipping from the *New York World* has not been found.

From J. Jay Buck[1]

Clarksville, Tenn.   May 29, 1866.

I send you the enclosed informal payer coming up from a poor colored worman asking on behalf of an injured child of a deceased sister, protection from her "friends" as well as enemies.[2]

The Bureau as administered in this state is a Humbug & the civil courts of Kentucky no place for a Negro to get redress.

As the true friend of this race, I appeal to you to overlook this informality & grant the applicant the protection of the child in question.[3]

To refer this matter either to the Bureau or the courts is a practical denial of redress. I speak from personal knowledge as a resident lawyer here.

J. Jay Buck
late 1st Lt 101st U.S.C. Inf & Judge Adv. Dist Mid. Tenn

ALS, DNA-RG105, Records of the Commr., Lets. Recd. (M752, Roll 35).

1. Buck (1835–1917), a native of New York, served an earlier enlistment as a private in the 32nd Wis. Inf. He resided in Clarksville until 1870 when he permanently moved to Emporia, Kansas, where he continued to practice law. Pension Records, J. Jay Buck, RG15, NA.

2. Attached is a sworn document from Lethia Ship, sister of the late Dora Ship of Kentucky and aunt of the child, Louisa Ship (b. c1858). According to Lethia Ship's statement, her sister had wanted her to have custody of Louisa; but John B. Gowen, superintendent of the Freedmen's Bureau in Christian County, Kentucky, had had Louisa bound out to a William Withers of that same county. Lethia Ship entreated the President to have Louisa sent to her in Clarksville.

3. When the documents arrived at the White House, they were forwarded to General Howard of the Freedmen's Bureau, who in turn sent them to General Fisk at Nashville. On June 13, Fisk forwarded the materials to Gowen at Hopkinsville, Kentucky. A week later Gowen returned the Ship files to Fisk, saying that he had made a personal investigation of the whole matter and that Buck's letter and Lethia Ship's statement "are false from bigining to end." On July 3, Fisk returned the Buck-Ship materials to General Howard in Washington with a strongly-worded condemnation of Buck as "a shyster lawyer who is swindling the Freedmen most shamefully." According to Fisk, Buck charged Lethia Ship some $6.75 to write the "scandalous letter & preparing an oath for her nearly every word of which is perjury." All of these documents accompany the Buck to Johnson letter and are found in Records of the Commr., Lets. Recd. (M752, Roll 35), RG105, NA.

From Mary Stuart

Waynesboro, Burke Co. Georgia.   May 29th 1866

Sir,—

Having understood that the Confiscation Act of 1862, exempted the property of widows,—I trust you will excuse my intruding upon your valuable time, by presenting a petition for the restoration of my plantation, situated on Port Royal Island, 10 miles from the town of Beaufort, South Carolina, and described in official papers, as the "Middleton Stuart plantation." It consists of 750 acres of land, and is considered as the finest on the island.

Since the cessation of hostilities, being considered as "abandoned land," (though left in *charge* of one I considered responsible) it passed into the hands of the "Freedmen's Bureau," and by them, a portion was sold to my former slaves, (who have informed me though, that they bought it to prevent its falling into the hands of strangers) a portion, considered as a "*school farm*," tho' no school has been established, and a portion, leased (by the Government, I suppose) by Capt. Judd[1] of the "Freedmen's Bureau," who advised my not applying last fall, a former application of mine had been acknowledged, as he was sure my rights would be restored. Since then, I have ascertained that through *his* instrumentality, it was disposed of as above-mentioned.

Now, Sir, as a homeless, penniless, widow, a refugee in Georgia, I appeal to your justice and clemency, to be restored to my property,—to my *all*. With the United South, I look to *you*, for justice,[2] and pray, as our Chief Magistrate, God may bless you, and yours.

Mary Stuart.

ALS, DNA-RG107, Lets. Recd., Executive (M494, Roll, 84).

1. Henry G. Judd (*c*1822–*fl*1872) of Connecticut became superintendent of Port Royal Island, South Carolina, contrabands in 1862. After the war he was briefly (September 1865-January 1866) a Freedmen's Bureau agent and later county court clerk. 1870 Census, S.C., Beaufort, Beaufort Twp., 35; *NUC*; Willie Lee Rose, *Rehearsal for Reconstruction: The Port Royal Experiment* (Indianapolis, 1964), 177–78; Everly and Pacheli, *Records of Field Officers*, pt. 2: 384.

2. Mrs. Stuart's letter was referred to the War Department and subsequently to Howard and subordinate officers of the Freedmen's Bureau as well as the direct tax commissioner in South Carolina. In mid-August 1866 Stanton reported that title to the property was vested in the United States and that his "Department has no power over the subject." One hundred sixty acres of the property had been reserved for educational purposes under presidential instructions dated September 16, 1863, and had been rented for four years, starting January 1, 1865, to H. G. Judd and by him in turn to Nathaniel Page. The remainder either had been or was to be sold to blacks "in parcels not to exceed twenty acres each." Endorsements, Stuart to Johnson, May 29, 1866; Stanton to Johnson, Aug. 16, 1866, Lets. Recd., Executive (M494, Roll 84), RG107, NA. See also Emily H. Barnwell to Johnson, Sept. 22, 1865, *Johnson Papers*, 9: 109–10.

From G. E. Stanford et al.

May 30, 1866, White's Ranch, Tex.; L, DNA-RG94, USCT Div., Lets. Recd., File P-163-1866.

Six members of the 116th U.S. Cld. Inf. Rgt. (a captain, 2 sergeants, 2 corporals, a private), express dissatisfaction with their lot. Among their complaints: they worry about their families back home—"I Know that my own Famuley is Liven in old Kentucky under just as much Slave as She was When I left her or before the war broke out"; although they have done their duty, they have not had a fair share of furloughs—"it is Very true thire has ben ferlowes easherd, but a Mighty few of them. What has ben easherd they was easherd to the Men that the Officers Like the best"; they had no safe way to get money home to their needy families—"I larns that thire is a Number of Our famuleys has ben turned out of Doors . . . and we has no Way to healp them." Protesting that they do not blame the President or the army regulations for their treatment, but rather their immediate superiors, they ask: "Mr President is it Law-ful for a Company Officers to Detail Men Soldiers out of thire Companys to Waite upon them as a Servent, and Boot-blacker or a cook and Keep them. I dont think thire is any Such law as that, in the regerlations, and then at the same time Gave them the Power to Punish them at the ful Extent as if a Genel cort marshel might Punish a Soldier when he has don a grat crime."

To George W. Morgan[1]

Washington, D.C., May 31st 1866

Our desire is to appoint good and honest men who are capable, faithful to the Constitution, and for the preservation of the Union.[2] Any suggestions made by you, which will aid in carrying out this objict will be thankfully received.[3]

Andrew Johnson

Tel, DNA-RG107, Tels. Sent, President, Vol. 3 (1865–68).

1. This is in reply to Morgan's dispatch received earlier in the evening requesting the President to refrain from making any appointments in the Thirteenth Congressional Dis-

trict of Ohio until "your friends . . . are heard from." Morgan to Johnson, May 31, 1866, Johnson Papers, LC.

2. Johnson's draft of this sentence, written on the lower half of Morgan's telegram, was somewhat different, reading: "Our desire is to appoint good faithful and correct men who are honest capable and for the preservation of the Union." Ibid.

3. Within a week Morgan was in Washington urging the appointment of a new Thirteenth District revenue collector and an assessor, as well as postmaster of Mount Vernon, in place of the incumbents. Morgan to Johnson, June 5, 6, 1866, OFH.

June 1866

From Alabama Citizens

[ca. June 1866][1]

The undersigned Tax payers, Merchants and Planters, residing in the first Internal Revenue District of Alabama,[2] having reason to believe that the present Senate will not confirm any of your nominations of Revenue officers, who are unable to take the Test Oath, beg leave to suggest, if the Senate should reject your nomination of A. M. McDowell,[3] as the Assessor of this District, for no other reason than his unwillingness to take that oath without modification, that after the adjournment of this Congress, you re-nominate him for the same office.[4] We are all friendly to your Administration, and are deeply anxious to see its policy sustained, and we make this recommendation for the following reasons:

Mr. McDowell has held the office under your appointment from the beginning; is thoroughly acquainted with its duties and details; is diligent and faithful, and has discharged his duties not only without complaint, but with great satisfaction to the people. He has been a resident of the State for thirty five years; has a high reputation for business capacity and integrity, and is thoroughly acquainted with the Country and people; and we know of no man who can take the Test Oath, who can be as acceptable to the Tax-payers in this District, and can perform the duties of the office as advantageously to the public. He has taken the Amnesty Oath, is not liable in any of the exceptions in your Proclamation, and is as loyal to the Constitution and the Union as any man we know.[5]

And your Petitioners will ever pray &c.

Pet., DNA-RG56, Appts., Internal Revenue Service, Assessor, Ala., 1st Dist., A. M. McDowell.

1. This date is based on a notation on the file cover sheet.
2. There were twenty-four signatures of individual Mobile citizens or business firms.
3. Alexander M. McDowell (b. c1807) was a civil engineer from Demopolis. 1860 Census, Ala., Marengo, Demopolis, 66.
4. Johnson referred this petition to Secretary McCulloch with the endorsement, "Special attention is called to this case."
5. McDowell was replaced as assessor by William D. Mann, who was confirmed by the Senate on July 27, 1866. Ser. 6B, Vol. 4: 180, Johnson Papers, LC; *U.S. Off. Reg.* (1867).

From Sarah Juliana Maria Gales[1]

Washington   June 1st 1866.

Dear Sir,

I beg to offer to you for rent as a summer residence my Country Seat of Eckington.[2] The House is a capacious one, well arranged for domestic comfort, and also adapted for Entertaining, three of the rooms on the first floor measuring 18 by 26 and 21 by 27 feet. It is well lighted and airy, and has been put in order by the Govt since vacated by it last August, painted and papered within, while I have had it newly painted without. It has good water arrangements, and bricks the main building. There are two out buildings suitable for Laundry and Servants rooms with accommodations for a large household and *Guard* if required. I venture to enclose a statement of the rooms on each floor,[3] and call your attention to the extensive apartment on the first floor so admirably suited to the convenience of an invalid, as I regret to believe Mrs. Johnson to be. The situation is a very beautiful one, noted for its salubrity. It borders upon the City Boundary line and County Road, and though less than a quarter of a mile from North Capitol street, it is sufficiently retired to be out of sight, and intrusion from passengers on that thoroughfare, and it is within a brisk 20 minutes drive of the Presidents House—Post office or Capitol. The house and place are well known to Mr. W. Seward, and others of your near friends, to whom I confidently refer to endorse my recommendation of Eckington as a suitable, convenient, and healthful abode for yr. Excellency and family during the Summer months.

Praying yr. careful and favorable consideration of this my proposition, and that you will drive out and look at the house before giving a decision.[4] I have the honor to remain, with sincere respect and most friendly regard.

S.J.M. Gales

ALS, DLC-JP.

1. Gales (*fl*1870) was the daughter of Theodoric Lee of Virginia, and first cousin to Robert E. Lee. In 1813 she married Joseph Gales, Jr., editor of the *National Intelligencer* and several term mayor of Washington. Her date of birth remains a mystery because her age was consistently represented to census takers as a generation too young. Edward Jennings Lee, *Lee of Virginia 1642–1872* (Philadelphia, 1895), 372–73; *DAB*; 1850 Census, D.C., Washington, 505; (1870), Subdiv. East 7th St. Road, 48.

2. At this time the President and Congress were considering the possibility of a private residence for the President away from the White House during the summer months. Eckington was one of several sites proposed. It had been acquired and named by the late Joseph Gales, Jr., in 1815. The main house was built in 1830 and by 1866 the estate consisted of 130 acres. Harold D. Eberlain and Cortlandt Van Dyke Hubbard, *Historical Houses of George-Town and Washington City* (Richmond, 1958), 472–73; *Sen. Ex. Docs.*, 39 Cong., 1 Sess., No. 22, pp. 4–7 (Ser. 1278); *National Intelligencer*, June 22, 1866. See also Jonathan M. Foltz, Aug. 2, 1865, *Johnson Papers*, 8: 529.

3. Sarah Gales enclosed her handwritten, detailed description of the house and grounds at Eckington. At the conclusion of said enclosure she wrote: "Should the President or the ladies of his family think proper to look at the Eckington house, and will intimate to me the day and hour they will chance to go there, I will have a person there to open and show the house." Another but much briefer description of Eckington is found in the rental announcement that appeared in Washington newspapers. See the *National Intelligencer*, June 11, 1866.

4. On June 30 the House and Senate committees charged with finding a new presidential mansion visited Eckington, along with other possible residences in the area. Apparently Johnson remained at the White House for the summer, however. *Washington Evening Star*, July 2, 1866; *National Intelligencer*, July 3, 1866.

From Absalom A. Kyle

Rogersville Ten   1st June 1866

My Dear Sir,

Allow me to present to your consideration, the claims of my friend Col. Samuel M. Letcher,[1] of Lexington Ky. for the office of Internal Revenue Collector of said District. I made the acquaintance of Col Letcher at Knoxville in the Fall of 1863, when a soldier in the Federal Army, & knew him intimately, for more than 12 months, when he was ordered to another field of duty; during this whole time, we boarded at the same boarding house, & I had every opportunity to know him *well*, and I take pleasure in recommending him to you, as a gentleman in every way qualified for the position herein referred to, & who most heartily endorses your Rstoration Policy.

Col Letcher is honest, full of energy, & capable, & I should rejoice to see him receive the appointment.

I understand that Willard Davis[2] the present incumbent of the office is not only an incompetent man, but that he is a radical, doing every thing in his power against your policy and administration. Is it not time, to bring to bear upon these fellows, the policy of Genl Jackson? I think your administration would have been much stronger, if you had have adopted this policy immediately after your Speech of the 22d. of Feby last.

I do not desire to be importunate, but I do hope, if at all consistent with duty, you will give this appointment to Col Letcher, as he richly merits it, both on account of arduous services to the Govt. & upon the score of competency.[3]

A. A. Kyle

ALS, DNA-RG56, Appts., Internal Revenue Service, Collector, Ky., 7th Dist., Samuel M. Letcher.

1. Letcher (*fl*1866) entered the military as a private and eventually attained the brevet rank of lieutenant colonel. He served on the staff of both Gen. George H. Thomas and Gen. John M. Schofield and was at one point the chief mustering officer of the 23rd Corps. *Off. Army Reg.: Vols.*, 4: 1259; Letcher to Johnson, June 1, 1866; Jacob D. Cox to Johnson, May 9, 1866, Appts., Internal Revenue Service, Collector, Ky., 7th Dist., Samuel M. Letcher, RG56, NA.

2. Davis (b. *c*1833) had held the post of collector for the old Fifth District of Kentucky for a while, but with the post-war restructuring of districts, his district became the Seventh. President Johnson nominated Davis for the collectorship of the Seventh District in February 1866; Davis was confirmed by the Senate and commissioned in March 1866. *U.S. Off. Reg.* (1865); Ser. 6B, Vol. 4: 241, Johnson Papers, LC; 1870 Census, Ky., Fayette, 2nd Ward, Lexington, 248.

3. Oddly enough, the newly-reappointed Davis lost his job in the summer of 1866 when the President decided to name Robert M. Kelly (and not Samuel Letcher) to the collectorship of the Seventh District. Kelly held the position for several years. *U.S. Off. Reg.* (1867–69); Ser. 6B, Vol. 4: 242, Johnson Papers, LC.

From Samuel S. Cox[1]

N.Y   June 2/66.

Mr. President:

I would not presume to make any suggestions to you in reference to Mexico and our relations to that unhappy and lacerated country,—had I not given the subject more than usual study. I enclose to you, a speech of mine in Congress,[2] in 1860, not so much for its intrinsic merits, with a view to the present situation in Mexico, as to show you that I have studied the problem which seems so insolulable; and that my judgment then, is prophecy *now*. Gen. Cass[3] did me the honor to say, he would base his Mexican policy on my premises & conclusions. You cannot do less than consider them, even if they are not worthy of adoption. It was wise in 1860, & is now,—for us to assure to Republican Mexico, "an erect & orderly independency."[4]

If it were wise then, to avert English, Spanish or French intervention, by adopting the McLane treaty,[5] as I urged; it is surely wise now, to rid Mexico of such intervention, by our action and without war with France or trouble with Austria. How can this be done?

The present situation in Mexico is a hard knot for Mexico, France & U.S. The sword ought not to be used, if it can be untied.

France cannot very well treat with the Juarez government, which we recognize. We do not recognize the French arrangement with Maximillian. That Maximillian has no business there in our view, is just as true, as that Juarez has no business there in the French view; and in both views, —taken together the whole Mexican nation agree. What is the solution?

Be so kind as to remember that when in Feb. '57, the present Constitution was adopted, Comonfort became President.[6] He vacated the post in a year. By the 79th Art. of the Constitution, the "President of the Supreme Court of Justice" became *dejure* President of the Republic. This office of Supreme Justice was held then by Juarez. He could not be inaugurated, as Executive *de facto*; Zuloaga, & finally Miramon held the Capitol.[7] The war raged between the Constitutionalists under Juarez & the usurpers until the former held the Capital, & became in fact & in law, the Executive. Then the French came; & the result is known. Juarez has been elected President; & his term has expired. He is no longer, *de facto* or *de jure* Chief Magistrate. He holds no provinces, scarcely any seaports and is just on the border of his Republic. He has not been reelected, *but there is a Constitutional President, by virtue of the same clauses of the Constitution, which gave Juarez the reins of power.* That man is *Jesus G. Ortega;*[8] by virtue of his office as President of the Supreme Court. I do not know him. Gen Frémont can tell you about him, and his disposition toward this country.

If, as is alleged, the Emperor of France, would withdraw Maximillian from Mexico, in Ortega's favor; and our sanction could be given;—Monarchy is dethroned in that country, without a blow of violence, and what is more, *Constitutional* Republicanism is established. Mexico is erect & independent, by the consent of all parties.

It seems to me that this solution is feasible; and if so, does it not save your administration infinite embarassment,—if not war with France?

With great respect, I submit these views; hoping that you will glance at the facts succinctly gathered in the enclosed speech, to show the magnitude of the interests, to which we are bound by our neighborhood to Mexico.

S. S. Cox

ALS, DLC-JP.
1. The former Ohio congressman was at this time practicing law in New York City.
2. The enclosure has not been found. The discourse to which Cox refers was given on March 19, 1860, when he argued that it was "absolutely necessary" for the United States to intervene in Mexican affairs by ratifying the McLane-Ocampo treaty. *Congressional Globe*, 36 Cong., 1 Sess., pp. 1238–39.
3. Lewis Cass.
4. Here Cox quotes directly from his earlier appeal for "Territorial Expansion" which he delivered before the House on January 18, 1859. Ibid., 35 Cong., 2 Sess., pp. 430–35.
5. Negotiated by Buchanan's minister to Mexico, Robert M. McLane (1815–1898), and Benito Juárez's foreign minister, the McLane-Ocampo treaty of December 14, 1859, stipulated that Mexico would cede to the United States perpetual transit rights across the Isthmus of Tehuantepec and along two other routes in northern Mexico, in return for the payment of $4 million. The most controversial aspect of the treaty, however, provided for the United States to support the Juárez government militarily. The treaty was rejected on May 21, 1860. *DAB*; Samuel F. Bemis, *The Latin American Policy of the United States: An Historical Interpretation* (New York, 1943), 110; James M. Callahan, *American Foreign Policy in Mexican Relations* (New York, 1967), 271.
6. Among the leaders in the Liberal revolt against Santa Anna, Ignacio Comonfort (1812–1863) had been killed by Mexican troops loyal to the French. *Enciclopedia de Mexico*.
7. Two of Comonfort's generals. Félix María Zuloaga (1813–1898) served as interim president (*ipso facto* military dictator) of the Mexican Republic from January 1858 until the end of February 1859, when Miguel Miramón (1832–1867) deposed Zuloaga and assumed the presidency. By the time of Cox's writing, however, both men were political emigrés from Mexico. Ibid.
8. A former commander-in-chief of Juárez's army, General Ortega (c1822–1881) had had an interview with Johnson in May 1865 while he was on an unauthorized mission in the United States recruiting American mercenaries and money in the war against Maximilian's forces. In July 1866 he again went to Washington and met with Secretary Seward in an unsuccessful attempt to gain recognition as the constitutionally-elected president of Mexico. Ivie E. Cadenhead, Jr., *Jésus González Ortega and Mexican National Politics* (Fort Worth, 1972), 1, 42, 91–92, 110, 136.

From James C. White[1]

Portsmouth Virginia June 2 1866

Sir

I have the honor to enclose copy of a communication from the Commandant of the Military Post at Norfolk, Virginia,[2] to me, by which it will be seen that I am forbidden "to excersise the functions of my office, as

Mayor of this City, until such time as I am pardoned by the President of the United States, for my participation in the Rebellion."

I beg leave to state that, having been elected by my fellow citizens of this City to the Office of Mayor, I took the Oath of Office on the 8th day of May 1866, and entered at once upon the discharge of its duties until the afternoon of the 31st, when I was suspended by the Order of Major Stanhope, above referred to. I desire respectfully to state that, acting under the advice, and proceeding upon information received from the United States District Attorney, L H Chandler Esq., I felt no hesitation whatever in assuming the duties of the Office in question; having previously complied with all the requirements under the Amnesty Proclamation of your Excellency dated 29th of May 1865, as well as the Proclamation of the late President Lincoln.

The District Attorney Mr Chandler, was and now is of opinion that not one of the exceptions in the Proclamation of the 29th of May 1865 applies to my case; and I am therefore ignorant of the grounds upon which a special Pardon is required.

It is however suggested that the 10th Section may be construed to apply to my case, inasmuch as I left this City for the County of Brunswick in this State in October 1862; at which time the City was within the jurisdiction and under the protection of the United States. But I did not leave "for the purpose of aiding the Rebellion."

I left Portsmouth to join my Children[3] who were then domiciled and at school in that County, and for no other purpose or intent.

I did not at any time bear Arms, hold any Office or position of any kind, or perform any duty of any kind connected with the War.[4]

Therefore at the close of the war, acting as before stated under the advice and Counsel of the U States Law Officer for this District, as well as in accordance with my own judgement, I did all that was deemed requisite by taking and subscribing to the Oaths of Amnesty; Having in view no other object than that of strictly fulfilling my Obligations to the United States Government.

It appears however that a special Pardon in my case is necessary, I therefore Respectfully make application to your Excellency for a special Pardon.[5]

Referring you to the foregoing Statement of facts and to the accompanying documents relative thereto. . . .

James C. White

ALS, DNA-RG94, Amnesty Papers (M1003, Roll 70), Va., James C. White.

1. James C. White (c1811–fl1870), ferry proprietor, was elected mayor of Portsmouth, Virginia, in April on the "Citizens ticket" and was purported to be a strong advocate of Johnson's policies. 1860 Census, Va., Portsmouth, Jackson Ward, 112; (1870), Norfolk, 365; *Richmond Dispatch*, Apr. 12, 24, 1866.

2. Philip W. Stanhope (c1829–1895) of Cincinnati served as a captain and brevet major and lieutenant colonel during the Civil War, after which he was military commander of

Norfolk. He left the service in 1871 but was advanced one rank on the retired list eight years later. Pension Records, Mary S.B. Stanhope, RG15, NA; Powell, *Army List*, 604.

3. Eight children are listed in the census prior to the war: Mattie C., Sallie, James, Thomas B., Argyra, Mortimer, India, and Luke. 1860 Census, Va., Portsmouth, Jackson Ward, 112.

4. According to one newspaper account, White held a "petit" office under the Confederate government. *Washington Evening Star*, June 7, 1866.

5. Johnson pardoned White on June 7, 1866. Ibid.

From James K. Chappell[1]

Rochester N.Y.   June 3.d/66

Sir:

Your friends in this Section, all of them, desire a Change in the federal offices here. They are now, perhaps excepting the Post Master,[2] filled by the worst kind of malignants, who proscribe all administration men, and patronize and sustain the most scuralous dirty and libelious sheet in the Country, the Rochester Democrat. The collector[3] has a large interest in said paper & was before being made Collector its Editor, and Continues to write for it semi-occasionally gives it all the printing from his office, uses it to promulgate orders of the Dpt. and answer personal attacks. He got into his possession our Call for a Johnson meeting and suppressed it for four months, telling his radical friends that *he had squelched the thing* and it was only by intimidation and working on his fears that he was made to yield it into proper hands.[4]

The Collector & Assessor[5] are creations of our present mem of Congress Mr Hart.[6] Their character you can guess from that fact. If you expect your friends here to accomplish any thing; you must not allow all the federal offices to be filled against them. The facts I state you can have verifyed by asking our Mayor Amon Bronson[7] Genl I. F Quinby[8] late of the Army and now a professor in our university, or Genl. H S. Fairchild[9] late of the army. That you may have some idea of the proscribtion of administration here I enclose a slip cut from one of our daily papers.[10] I understand that Genl Quinby will be a candidate for the Collectorship of Int Rev.[11] The Genl is a Johnson man out & out with no reservations. Pardon me for the liberty I take in penning this but you know it is a characteristic of administration men to be bold as well as frank.[12]

J K Chappell

ALS, DNA-56, Appts., Internal Revenue Service, Assessor, N.Y., 28th Dist., John W. Graves.

1. Formerly a coal and iron dealer, Chappell (*c*1830–*fl*1881) worked as an inspector of wines and liquors prior to serving as an assistant internal revenue assessor under John W. Graves and his successor. Rochester directories (1859–81); 1870 Census, N.Y., Monroe, Rochester, 3rd Ward, 32.

2. Scott W. Updike (*c*1819–*fl*1881) had served as postmaster of Rochester since 1861. After failing to win Senate confirmation for his reappointment in July 1866, Updike was for many years a pickle and sauce manufacturer. *Landmarks of Monroe County, New York*

(Boston, 1895), 109; Ser. 6B, Vol. 4: 50, 52, 54; Rochester directories (1859–81); 1870 Census, N.Y., Monroe, Rochester, 10th Ward, 33.

3. Samuel P. Allen (c1815–fl1870), who had served as collector for several years, co-owned and edited the *Monroe Democrat* from 1846 to 1864 and the *Democrat and American* from 1857 to April 1864, when both papers were purchased by William S. King & Co. and Allen resigned. Ibid., 7th Ward, 27; *Landmarks of Monroe County*, 114; *History of Monroe County, New York* (Philadelphia, 1877), 135; *U.S. Off. Reg.* (1863).

4. Allen did attend the Johnson meeting held later in June 1866, and he was in fact appointed to serve on the committee of resolutions; all of which was evidence, as Allen himself claimed, of his sincere support of Johnson's policies. Allen to Hugh McCulloch, Sept. 26, 1866, Appts., Internal Revenue Service, Collector, N.Y., 28th Dist., Samuel P. Allen, RG56, NA.

5. Assessor John W. Graves (c1837–fl1881), whose office was located in Medina, also dealt in fish and oysters and later ran a confectionary in Rochester. *U.S. Off. Reg.* (1863–67); Rochester directories (1866–81); 1870 Census, N.Y., Monroe, Rochester, 4th Ward, 70.

6. Roswell Hart (1824–1883) was a Rochester businessman and attorney before his election to Congress in 1864 as a Republican. Serving only one term, Hart afterwards was superintendent of a railroad mail service for several years. *BDAC*.

7. A War Democrat, Bronson (1807–1876) for many years owned and operated a lumber dealership in Rochester. *Monroe County*, 148.

8. Isaac F. Quinby (1821–1891) had taught math and science at the University of Rochester for nine years prior to the war, during which he commanded a regiment at First Manassas and afterwards served as a brigadier general during the Vicksburg campaign. Resigning from the army at the end of 1863, Quinby was later U.S. marshal for the northern district of New York (1869–77), while continuing his teaching at the University of Rochester. Warner, *Blue*.

9. Harrison S. Fairchild (1820–1901) worked after the war in Rochester as a stockbroker, realtor, and U.S. pension claims agent. Hunt and Brown, *Brigadier Generals*.

10. Entitled "Proscription of Johnson Republicans—How is This?," the attached article questioned Assessor John W. Graves's authority and judgment in dismissing an assistant, John J. Bowen, who was an honored veteran who happened to support Johnson's policies.

11. Quinby apparently did not apply for any position in the Johnson administration.

12. Both Allen and Graves retained their offices and withstood at least two other attempts at removal prior to their retirement from government service at or near the end of Johnson's term. Allen to Johnson, Apr. 15, 1867, Appts., Internal Revenue Service, Collector, N.Y., 28th Dist., Samuel P. Allen, RG56, NA; S.E. Church to Johnson, May 28, 1868; Church to Hugh McCulloch, Nov. 18, 1868, ibid., Assessor, John W. Graves.

From Samuel Newberry[1]

Plymouth N.C.   June 4th 1866,

My dear Sir

This communication is addressed to you for the purpose of calling your attention to the acts of the convention, of the said State in 1865, which convention is now again in session. We would not by any means trouble, you were it not from the fact, it was convened by your directions, as the commander in chief of the Army and navy of the U.S. and therefore wholy military and being such we ask whether any act done by said Convention, at varience with civil Liberty and the plain letter of the constitution of the U. S. cannot be by you abrogated, and we further ask whether said Convention being of the character above, can now have any validity, after it was made known to the citizens of said State that there was peace in said State, by your Proclamation, unless reelected, by the people, as it is fair to presume civil Law reigned from the publication of your Peace Proclamation. These are as we consider grave considerations and of vital importance to many Citizens of the State whose rights we think have been trampled under foot by said Convention in palpable violation of the constitution of the U. S. which warrants to every Person obedient to the Laws the right of Life Liberty and a republican form of Goverment, as well as property. Now the Convention passed an Ordinance Last Oct declaring every Civil officer of the State, out of office,[2] without regard to the rights of any Person whatever no matter how Loyal they may have been and how much they have Suffered in the defence of the Constitution of the U. S. Now Sir there are officers and particularly Justices of the Peace, who are and always have been Long defenders of the Constitution of the U. S. Scattered over the Country, who are by this unhallowed act declared out of office and Rebels whose hands are Stained with innocent Blood filling Said offices. We therefore ask whether you will tolerate such an act of monstrous injustice towards any one who can Show he has always been Loyal to the Government of the U. S. and we further ask that if any power is vested in you in relation to this grave matter that you will in justice toward the oppressed proceed to inform it, and further dissolve said Convention, as we think as good and Loyal Union men, that the Convention afsd would have as much right to take the House and Land of a Loyal man as his office as a man has the right of Property in each, a portion of these oppressed men, are men, who have taken arms and defended the flag of the U. S. during the war through which we have just passed. I would not have you think that I mean to point out any course for you to pursue but leave it to you, that if no distinction can be had between Loyal, and disloyal, men, what inducement could any one have to defend the Government, when that Government refused to defend him. I hope you will not think it treason in me, when I tell you I am and always have been a Union man, and Served my Tour in Richmond Prison, that amenable place Castle Thunder, and should you require any proof of my integrity, you can be furnished with any amount.

Saml Newberry

N B   This embodies the Sense of every Union man, I do not mean those made so by the Amnesty oath.

S. N.

ALS, DNA-RG59, Misc. Lets., 1789–1906 (M179, Roll 239).

    1. Newberry (c1806–fl1870), variously listed as a farmer, surveyor, and teacher, had been an outspoken Washington County, North Carolina, unionist. 1860 Census, N.C., Washington, Mackeys Ferry, 48; (1870), Skinnersville Twp., 22; Wayne K. Durrill, *War of Another Kind: A Southern Community in the Great Rebellion* (New York, 1990), 3, 118, 228.

    2. Dated October 19, 1865, this ordinance indeed declared vacant all state offices in existence on April 26, the date of Gen. Joseph E. Johnston's surrender. All "offices should be filled anew" and no state official who took an oath to support the Confederate Constitu-

tion would "be capable" of holding a position "until he may be reappointed or reelected to the same." *Senate Ex. Docs.*, 39 Cong., 1 Sess., No. 26, pp. 37–38 (Ser. 1237).

From James Harlan

Department of the Interior
Washington D.C.   June 5 1866

Sir,

I have the honor to submit for your consideration a letter of the 2d inst. from the Commissioner of Indian Affairs,[1] representing the urgent necessity which exists for an early appropriation by Congress of the means which the Government requires to enable it to fulfil existing treaty stipulations and to prosecute negotiations with sundry Indian tribes.[2]

I entirely concur with the Commissioner in the statements and views he presents, and respectfully recommend that the attention of Congress be invited to the subject.

Jas Harlan

ALS, DLC-JP.
1. The letter from Dennis N. Cooley has not been found.
2. The war profoundly affected the Indian Nations. Following a preliminary conference at Fort Smith in September 1865 that reestablished their allegiance to the U.S., delegates from various Indian groups convened in Washington in January 1866 for negotiation of new treaties required by the government and to press for fulfillment of existing treaties and promises. The Seminoles were the first to conclude negotiations on March 21, 1866, followed by the Choctaw/Chickasaw on April 28, Creeks on June 14, and Cherokees on July 18. By August 1866 all the treaties had been proclaimed. Bailey, *Indian Territory*, 41–79 passim; Moulton, *John Ross*, 193–94.

From Samuel J. Randall

Washington D.C.   June 5, 1866

Mr President.

Your equanimity was wonderful. Do not despair. They all felt easy after they had releived themselves. We shall move steadily on. The result will prove our determination and the propriety of our efforts. Success will come to you and us. More when an opportunity to see and converse with you is presented.[1]

Sam J. Randall

ALS, DLC-JP.
1. A notation on the document reads: "In reference to interview with Democratic members, House of Reps held the previous evening." No other reference to such a meeting has been found.

From Landon C. Haynes

Memphis, Tennessee, June 6th, 1866.

Sir:

In pursuance of the parole which you had the goodness to order to be sent me to North Carolina, I returned to Tennessee, in February last. I had hoped the parole would have protected me from further trouble, by the Federal authorities. But having been indicted for treason, in the Federal Court at Knoxville, a *capias* has been recently sent to the marshal of West Tennessee,[1] in whose custody I am now held.

Judge Trigg[2] is of opinion, that the parole affords no legal protection, and that nothing but the pardon of the President of the United States, will secure me from the impending prosecution. The promise of the parole is, that I go to Memphis Tennessee, or elsewhere; and attend to my business, on the conditions therein named; (all of which have been faithfully performed) until ordered by the President to report, at such time and place as he may direct, to answer any charges that may *hereafter* be preferred against me by direction of the President. It follows that my arrest and detention are in contravention of the terms of the parole. This I feared, would be the result, when I called on you at Washington, and I then drew your Excellencys attention to that probability: you had the goodness to say to me, if I was interfered with, to telagraph you. I am under the necessity of informing you, that I will be put on trial, on the indictment alluded to, unless your Excellency releives me by granting the special pardon, for which I have long since applied.[3]

Having filed my application, now nearly one year ago, and having duly taken the oaths required; I trust the President may now feel it to be consistent with a sense of public duty to grant the application, and relieve me from the embarrassments which now surround me.[4]

That I am already ruined in fortune, I need not inform you; and that my life and professional exertions are all that are now left to my family, for their livelihood and support, is equally true. These facts make it my duty to request the interposition of the Executive amnesty; which I feel I may do, on the intimations of the proclamation of the 29th of May 1865. The pledges of loyalty made, the oaths taken, and the faithful performance thereof, must be the guaranty of my fidelity in the future.

In the conflicts of life now past, that I have not at all times agreed with you on all questions, and differed with you in respect to the events which led to the late war is true; but that I have often agreed with, and often sustained your Excellency is equally true. To me these differences have passed away together with the momentory excitements which they produced; and I now feel that they were the transient interruptions of the good understandings, which sometimes transpire between those who ought to be friends, and, often, come and go without leaving any lasting trace behind.

I cordially approve your policy as announced in your messages, speeches and official acts to restore the Southern States to their rights of representation in the Federal Congress, and to reinvest them with all their ancient constitutional privileges, as members of the Union. And I may be allowed to say, that I cannot express, the gratitude I feel, for the determined resolution you have shown, by Executive influence and by the Presidential negative, to guard the Southern people against persecutions, and the

States against Congressional legislation, frought with ruin to them. I have not felt stronger sympathy with any public man, than I do with your Excellency, in your struggle for the Constitution of the Country, the existence of the States, and the liberties of the people. And I not only express my own, but the unanimous sentiments of the Southern people, "to the manor born," when I say, that in you, the President, is their hope of safety, against faction and against all the calamities of present and future ruin.

Born without early advantages, fortune, powerful friends, or family influence, you have ascended through all the grades of official station, State and Federal, to the first honors of the Republic. And I for one am ready and frank to acknowledge, that neither I, nor the world at large, have ever heretofore done justice to the heart, which events have shown, large enough to overlook all personal dislikes, and to embrace the whole country; and to an understanding which has proved equal to any situation to which you have been called. Your Excellency cannot afford to do, what others may, whose insignificance will exempt them from the censure of future ages. You will allow me to say that your character is now historic. And it is before the Tribunal of History, that public men of generous ambition pause to consider, what shall be the judgment of posterity on their conduct; to which, no mind animated by sentiments of dignity can, for a moment, be indifferent. When the voice of faction shall have been silenced, the reward which awaits the generosity of your behavior, to a vanquished people, will be the approbation of the virtuous and enlightened portions of mankind.

It would have afforded me pleasure to have done you the justice, which I have in this letter expressed, and publicly and more fully to have defended the principles and policy of your administration, as announced in your annual message, veto messages, and your public utterances on the 22nd of February last; but considering the situation in which I am placed, I thought that delicacy and personal propriety forbid me, on the one hand, while on the other, I have not thoughts that an over-zealous advocacy of your administration, by leading Southern men however much approved, was the way, best to serve you, or the country at such a time as the present. Because such a course, serves in some degree to give rise to false issues, and to furnish the elements of prejudice, for the use of faction and jealous aspirants to power. But it cannot long be so. And I trust, the time is not far distant, when I may make those utterances in defence of your policy of restoration, and your claims to the gratitude of the Southern people, which a sense of honor will surely prompt us all to make.

You know personally my relations to Mr. Brownlow. I have reason to believe, that he does not love me, with that tenderness of sensibility which his pious profession and Christian duties require him to do. I have some reasons to suppose, that his hostile influence, the bitterness of personal hates, and the violence of party feeling, at Knoxville, ever stirred afresh by some means or other, might make my appearance and trial there, unsafe beyond any legal danger that attaches to my situation.

If I must be tried, I should prefer that it should occur at a time and place, when and where I would be exempted from personal insults and indignities, and would have some guaranty, that passion and faction would not exert their influence on results.

In his Honor, Judge Trigg, in common with the people of the State, I repose the fullest confidence, and feel that he would do all in the premises, that might become an upright and enlightened judge. I have thus, Mr. President, frankly opened my heart to you, foregoing all false delicacy and personal pride. I long since elected to remain in the country and to meet my fate. And having heretofore made my application to you for amnesty, as I promised if interfered with by the authorities to telegraph you, I have written this letter instead thereof. If your Excellency grant the application, it will relieve me from the prosecution and place me under obligations to be greatfully remembered. Please have the goodness to order such response to this note as will give me to understand what I may expect.

Landon C. Haynes

LS, DNA-RG94, Amnesty Papers (M1003, Roll 39), N.C., Landon C. Haynes.

1. Martin T. Ryder.
2. Connally F. Trigg.
3. Haynes had initially applied for special pardon in August 1865. See Haynes to Johnson, Aug. 20, 1865, *Johnson Papers*, 8: 622.
4. This time Johnson responded immediately and granted a pardon to Haynes on June 11, 1866. Ibid.

From Henry W. Hilliard

Augusta, Georgia   June 6. 1866

My dear Sir,

Some days since I telegraphed you,[1] requesting a respite of two weeks for *Burns*[2] sentenced to death by a Military Commission, upon the charge of murder.[3] The respite was ordered. Some *delay* has occurred in taking the testimony to which I referred. It is now forwarded, and I trust it will satisfy your mind that Burns was improperly convicted: that he is the victim of a conspiracy between the wretches who actually committed the murder. One of our best men learning the facts of the case appealed to me to interpose, and save Burns if possible. I was not his counsel when he was tried. I am not now his counsel. I have not the slightest pecuniary interest in the result. I simply wish from motives of humanity to save the life of a man improperly convicted.

The examination of the witnesses was conducted with the most perfect fairness. The Government was represented by Capt: Deane[4] of Genl.

Tilson's Staff: & Capt: Dykous,[5] Commandant of this Post, assisted by A. D. Picquet,[6] Esq. of the Augusta Bar. I examined the witnesses in Chief. Judge McLaws[7] presided. The deputy Clerk of the Superior Court of Richmond County[8] took down the testimony. The witnesses were subjected to a searching cross Examination. They were sequestered strictly and they corroborated each other: The first two Townsend and Beall[9] proving that in *advance* of the trial, the two negreos agreed that they must "put it on Burns to save themselves; " & the other witness[10] testifying that some two weeks *after* the trial: the negro Jackson stated that they had "sworn it on Burns to save themselves."

The idea of the negroes seems to have been that if they swore the *white* man committed the act, they might escape.

My own settled conviction is, that these witnesses, Townsend, Beall, & Pinkard testify to the exact truth. If this be so, Burns ought to be pardoned. I repeat I have no interest whatever in the case: I would not *take* a fee in it, if it were offered to me.

The consciousness of helping to save the life of a human being, is all that I desire in such a case. It is for your Excellency to decide the matter. The time is too short to protract this statement. It must go by tonight's mail.[11]

Henry W. Hilliard

ALS, DNA-RG94, Lets. Recd. (Main Ser.), File B-403-1866 (M619, Roll 460).
  1. Hillyard [*sic*] to Johnson, May 30, 1866, Tels. Recd., President, Vol. 5 (1866–67), RG107, NA.
  2. William Burns (d. 1866) may have been a twenty-two-year-old overseer working for a farmer in Monroe County, Georgia, or a forty-five-year-old resident of Paulding County, Georgia, in 1860. 1860 Census, Ga., Forsyth, Brantly's Dist. No. 554, 22; Paulding, 1080th Dist., 793.
  3. Burns and two freedmen, John Jackson and John Brumly (or Brumby), were employed by former Confederate Capt. Charles H. Tew. While they were helping Tew move his belongings on October 6, 1865, near Marietta, Georgia, they allegedly killed him with an axe. The court-martial, which began March 16, 1866, at Augusta, Georgia, found Burns and Jackson guilty and sentenced them to be hanged. Brumly was found guilty of assault and being an accessory to the murder and sentenced to life imprisonment at hard labor in the Albany, New York, penitentiary. General Court-Martial Order No. 131, May 12, 1866, RG94, NA; *Augusta Constitutionalist*, June 23, 1866.
  4. A native of Maine, William W. Deane (1832–1870) joined the 12th Maine Vols. as first lieutenant in November 1861 and rose to the rank of brevet lieutenant colonel after the war. Mustered out of the volunteers in November 1866, he then served in the regular army. Powell, *Army List*, 277; Washington, D.C., directories (1869–70); 1870 Census, D.C., Washington, 5th Ward, 150; *Washington Evening Star*, July 23, 1870.
  5. Davis Tillson. Newton L. Dykeman (*c*1829–*fl*1869), a New York native who joined the 2nd Iowa Inf. as first lieutenant in May 1861, became captain of regulars in February 1862. He resigned from the service in July 1867. Commission Branch: 1867-D307, Newton L. Dykeman, RG94, NA; *Des Moines City Directory* (1869); *Augusta Constitutionalist*, Sept. 28, 1866.
  6. Picquet (b. *c*1820), a long-time justice of the peace in Augusta, apparently resigned from that position in May 1866 to run for county judge. 1860 Census, Ga., Richmond, Augusta, 3rd Ward, 97; *Augusta Constitutionalist*, Mar. 20, May 5, 1866; *Directory for the City of Augusta, and Business Advertiser* (1859).
  7. Newly-elected county judge in May 1866, William R. McLaws (b. *c*1819), a lawyer and former solicitor general of Augusta, had served as a lieutenant colonel with Georgia

troops in the Confederate forces. Ibid.; 1860 Census, Ga., Richmond, Augusta, 119th Dist., Bel Air, 14; *Augusta Constitutionalist*, Mar. 20, May 15, 1866; Jones and Dutcher, *Augusta, Ga.*, 246; *OR*, Ser. 1, Vol. 44: 875; Vol. 47, Pt. 3: 732, 786.

8. Not identified.

9. Joseph B. Townsend and William Henry Beall (or Beal) were both privates in Co. E of the 16th U.S. Inf. who had been jailed for desertion. They claimed to have overheard Jackson and Brumly discussing their conspiracy in the jail. Lets. Recd. (Main Ser.), File B-403-1866 (M619, Roll 460), RG94, NA.

10. Preston Pinkard (or Pinckard) (b. c1849), a Monroe County, Georgia, teenager charged with horse theft, had overheard a conversation between Jackson and another man. Ibid.; 1850 Census, Ga., Monroe, 60th Div., 160; (1860), Monroe, Forsyth, 480th Dist., 12.

11. Burns and Jackson, scheduled to be executed on June 15, 1866, received a reprieve of another week. Apparently no one in authority was convinced by the testimony of Townsend, Beall, and Pinkard, so Burns and Jackson were hanged on June 22. Davis Tillson to W. A. Nichols, June 12, 1866, Lets. Recd. (Main Ser.), File T-390-1866 (M619, Roll 520), RG94, NA; *Augusta Constitutionalist*, June 23, 1866.

Speech at National Union Fair[1]

[June 6, 1866][2]

The President remarked that he came here to night merely to say a word in the cause of humanity, and to unite in the expression of the gratitude of the nation for the nation's defenders. ⟨Applause⟩ He did not come prepared to make a speech, but simply to give his countenance and encouragement in aid of the enterprise which the ladies had so nobly undertaken. He appeared here with no set phrase of speech and nicely rounded periods, to play upon the ear and to please but for a moment. If there was a cause which more than another should engage their sympathies, it was that of orphans, especially of those who lost their all and perilled their lives to save the Government. What nobler and better work could you be engaged in? He was proud that this great move should have its origin here at the seat of the National Government. Woman, God bless her! has been instrumental in the performance of great and noble acts in all periods of history, and it is not less becoming to them now than in the time gone by. But is was not his intention to invite his hearers to go back and review the new made graves of the nefarious rebellion, nor to excite angry feelings in connection with the contest; nor to revive the scenes of the battle-field, where brother was arrayed against brother. No, no; God forbid, and relieve us from the repetition of such calamities. We now rejoice that the land is no longer to be drenched by fratricidal blood. He would not reopen the wounds and make them bleed afresh. That was the work of war and contest and struggle, growing out of mistaken apprehensions.

Yours, he said, is the work of peace, to pour the balm that the healing may take place; and what is more proper to that end than to take up the destitute orphans, and educate and guide them, thus laying a solid moral basis which may control them throughout their future lives? You will find in these caskets precious gems, though now dimmed by poverty. Talents and genius are not confined to particular localities and places.

Let them be provided for and educated, and you can not fail to accomplish the great end you have undertaken.

You all remember the story of Cornelia, the mother of the Gracchi, the two greatest Romans who ever lived, and who lost their lives in vindicating the great cause of the people. A number of distinguished ladies, in whose company she was, expatiated on their fine dresses and accomplishments and the jewelry they wore, and other articles with which they were decorated and adorned. Cornelia attentively listened to each in turn, and then, looking out at the door, saw her two boys running homeward from school. Her cheeks flushed with matronly pride, and clasping them, one on each side, she exclaimed: "These are my jewels!" You, ladies, can gather around you the orphans, the little boys and girls, and say, these are our jewels. This is your work, and no doubt it will be well accomplished. Let woman be engaged in this noble work; God bless her! Yes, woman can accomplish it if she will.

> "None, none on earth's above her,
> As pure as thought as angels are,
> To see her is to love her."[3]

⟨Applause.⟩ Go on, your efforts will be crowned with success.

One view is of war, the other of peace—yes, peace. The other day near this city—and not only once, but several times—he walked among the graves of the dead; and when he passed along and looked at the headboards he saw the names of soldiers from New York, Indiana, and other State regiments of the Federal army. There they sleep in peace, the green sward growing upon their graves. They were Federal soldiers. He looked next on the other side, and what did he see? A. B., rebel soldier, belonging to such a regiment. The strife had ended—the contest closed. That was peace. When they were in the field, engaged in strife, it was war. Now they sleep in alternate graves while it is peace. ⟨Applause.⟩ And let peace do its work.

He trusted our country and Government would be blessed with peace, and that confidence and respect for one another everywhere would be restored. ⟨Applause.⟩ And that those warring and disturbing elements which separated and divided us in the sanguinary conflict through which we passed may pass away. He trusted, too, that the asylum which it was proposed to establish might be extensive enough to bless all orphans. We should not inquire what made them orphans. Charity doth not thus behave. They are human beings, and deserve your protection, kindness, and instruction.

The President thanked the ladies and gentlemen for the compliment of inviting him to be present. He should not have liked to come as an intruder; but in an association of this kind he was not sure that he would be an intruder. This was a cause in which he had a large amount of stock and interest. ⟨Laughter.⟩ He knew how to appreciate and admire the efforts and motives of the friends of organizations of this kind, and so far as in him lay, physically, mentally, pecuniarily, and intellectually, he would give this great work his aid. ⟨Applause.⟩

It was not his purpose to make any allusion to politics or the condition of the country; but as this asylum had been convened at the seat of the General Government, at the metropolis of the nation, he trusted it would take the character of a national orphan asylum. If it is a misfortune to be an orphan, it ought to be our pride, as it is our duty, to care for him. He wished a great national church could be provided, not by law, but by the consent of the American people, so that in this church there could be a pew for every orphan and a pew for every loyal man from every State. Let our religion be national, and this orphan asylum be national. Let them be the controlling and supreme idea which runs through all our national institutions.

The President thanked the ladies and gentlemen for indulging him in his desultory and crude remarks. Under no circumstances, though he had long been in the habit of public speaking, had it been his custom to prepare written addresses. He had always thrown them off without preparation. He always tried to address himself to the brains and sense of males and females, and not merely to please the fancy. The work in which they were engaged was a reality, and should have a lodgment in their minds and hearts. It was not a mere idea. It was something which would bear thinking about and acting on; something requiring effort and not mere profession. We know what can be done in a great work of this kind. Then let us consult our hearts free from anger, which has existed in them too long. Let the breach be healed, and let difficulties be done away, that we may become a great and happy people. ⟨Applause.⟩

National Intelligencer, June 7, 1866.

1. The National Union Fair was held for the benefit of the orphans of soldiers and sailors killed during the war. The building erected for the purpose of housing the fair later caused much controversy. See Washington Merchants and Property Holders to Johnson, July 24, 1866.

2. This date is provided by text in the June 7 article referring to the fair opening the previous night.

3. Samuel Rogers, *Jacqueline*, Stanza 1. Johnson misquoted the last line which should have been, "To know her was to love her."

To Edwin M. Stanton

Washington, D. C.   June 6th 1866.

Sir

The Honorable, the Attorney General desires that the following named gentlemen be permitted to visit Jefferson Davis, as his counsel. Will the Secretary of War please direct General Miles to allow

Thos. G. Pratt, James T. Brady, W. B. Read, William George Brown,

Edwin A. Vansicle, Thos. H. Edrall, Burton N. Harrison[1] to see Jefferson Davis in that capacity.

Andrew Johnson

LS, DNA-RG107, Lets. Recd., Executive (M494, Roll 84).
    1. Pratt (1804–1869), former Maryland governor and U.S. senator, had been a Confederate sympathizer; William B. Reed; George William Brown (1812–1890), mayor of Baltimore during the troop riot of April 1861, subsequently was incarcerated by the Federals; Vansickle (*fl*1868) and Edsall (d. 1897) were Wall Street attorneys, the latter usually a New Jersey resident and the publisher of several minor histories; Harrison (1836–1904), a Yale graduate and University of Mississippi mathematics professor, served as Jefferson Davis's private secretary before becoming a New York City lawyer. *DAB*; New York City directories (1866–87); *NUC*; *New York Tribune*, Mar. 30, 1904.

From R. C. Anderson and Robert W. McNeil[1]

Nevada City, Vernon Co. Mo.
June 7th 1866.

Sir,

I have the honor to transmit you the enclosed resolutions which were unanimously adopted by a "Johnson mass meeting" of the citizens of Vernon County Mo. held at Nevada City, on the 4th inst.

Resolutions.

Whereas, In a government like ours, where the people are the source of all power it is always their privilege and often their imperative duty—as in a crisis like the present—to assemble together, consult about the public welfare, and fearlessly and frankly express their views and sentiments on all questions touching the general interests of the Country—

Therefore Resolved,

1st. That the citizens of Vernon County do most emphatically approve the just, wise, benevolent and Constitutional policy of President Johnson as indicated by his proclamations, speeches and vetoes.

2nd. That we do hereby pledge ourselves to sustain and uphold the President in his humane and noble efforts to heal the wounds caused by the late terrible civil war, and to restore the Union of the States on the broad principles of the Constitution and on a basis alike honorable to both sections of the Country.

3rd That we condemn and denounce the narrow, vindictive and sectional policy of the fanatical radical majority in congress as calculated to destroy all fraternal feeling between the two sections of the Country—to alienate the friendly relations that now again happily exist, and if persisted in to finally destroy all hope of that real and substantial union which all conservative men of every section of the country now so ardently desire.

4th That it is alike the duty and the interest of the late Slave States to do all in their power to elevate and enlighten the Freedmen, to protect them in their persons and property and by wise and liberal legislation to render them prosperous and happy—but all attempts to elevate them to the level of the White Man by making them politically and socially his equal, we will resist by all constitutional and honorable means.

5th. That we declare the present tariff unjust, unequal, burdensome and oppressive to the South and West, while it is pouring immense wealth into the pockets of the men of the North and East. We cannot believe that mode of taxation that fills their pockets at the expense of the poor laborer of West, honest, much less just. We therefore call upon our Western members of Congress to wake up in our defense—and especially do we most respectfully ask our own *mis*representative the Hon. Mc-Cluy[2] to devote *one* day in each week to the "White trash" and bid his "American brethren of African descent" to be satisfied with the remaining five.

6th. That we thank God and congratulate our fellow citizens of Missouri that one of the most odious provisions of the new Constitution is, like its father "Drake" a "Dead duck"[3]—and that we trust the time is not far distant, when upon the whole of that monstrous iniquity will be written "Mene Mena Tekel Uphursin."[4]

7th That it is the opinion of this meeting that immediate steps should be taken to organize a "Johnson Club" in this County.

8th That the secretary be instructed to forward a copy of these resolutions to his Excellency the President of the United States.

After an eloquent speech from Gen. Blair[5] of Ft Scott the meeting adjourned with *three rousing cheers for "Andy Johnson"*

R C Anderson sec.
R. W. McNeil Pres.

LS, DLC-JP.
1. Possibly Randolph Anderson (b. c1837), a Maryland native, who was a well-to-do farmer by 1870. Robert W. McNeil (1816–1900) moved to Missouri in 1843 after which he first farmed and raised stock and then bought a mill and store at Balltown. After the war he held several local offices. 1870 Census, Mo., Vernon, Osage Twp., Nevada City, 630; *History of Vernon County, Missouri* (St. Louis, 1887), 346, 348, 606, 665–66; J. B. Johnson, ed., *History of Vernon County, Missouri Past and Present* (2 vols., Chicago, 1911), 1: 311, 313, 351; 2: 910–11.
2. Joseph W. McClurg (1818–1900), a Missouri native, taught school and practiced law before the Civil War. During the conflict he served as a colonel of cavalry in the U.S. Army and afterwards was elected as a radical to the U.S. Congress (1865-68). After a term as governor of Missouri (1869–71), McClurg engaged in mercantile, steamboating, and lead mining ventures. *BDAC*.
3. Charles D. Drake had been the major motivating force behind the Missouri constitutional convention of 1865. One of the most controversial features of the new constitution was a stringent "Iron-clad" test oath which had to be taken not only by those registering to vote, but also by lawyers, teachers, and ministers before they could practice their profession. In mid-March 1866 the case of Father John A. Cummings, a Roman Catholic priest who refused to take the oath, came before the U.S. Supreme Court. Although the Court did not decide the case before it adjourned in May, rumors spread that the majority favored Cummings and opposed the test oath. This is presumably why the petitioners could refer to this provision as a "dead duck." The case was eventually decided in favor of Cummings on January 14, 1867. Parrish, *Missouri, 1860–1875*, 3: 131–34.

4. "Mene, Mene, Tekel, Upharsin." Daniel 5: 25–28.
5. Probably Francis P. Blair, Jr.

From George Bancroft

New York, June 7, 1866.

Dear Mr President,

In writing to let you know that I leave New York for Newport R.I. today, to remain there four months, I flatter myself your regard for me warrants the act.

The sentiment of this city is altogether with you in wishing for the representation of the South by loyal men. Anxiety is now turned to the finances. Happily we have a president who favors a hard money system. Heavy taxation & rigid economy can alone carry the country through.

I am very glad to see that the bill facilitating commerce between the states, has passed both houses.[1] Adopted on your recommendation,[2] it will long be remembered in history, as one of the most important & universally popular measures of our day; a safeguard to union, & an obstacle to monopoly. The country will be grateful to you for it. Had a weak man been in the chair, the monopolists might have striven to overawe him; happily for us all, on this and on former occasions, your firmness is beyond their reach. Moreover, the *universal* public opinion is with you for the measure.

I am sorry to add, that the health of Mrs Bancroft[3] is not very firm.

Give our best regards to Mrs Johnson & to your daughters: I remember my visit with such pleasure, that I wish them not to forget, their & your faithful friend.

George Bancroft

ALS, DLC-JP.
1. Introduced on December 11, 1865, by Ohio Rep. James A. Garfield, the legislation authorizing "continuous lines" of interstate railroad transportation was presented to the President on June 11 and approved four days later. *House Journal*, 39 Cong., 1 Sess., p. 39 (Ser. 1243); *Senate Journal*, 39 Cong., 1 Sess., p. 507 (Ser. 1236); *U.S. Statutes at Large*, 14: 66.
2. See Message to Congress, Dec. 4, 1865, *Johnson Papers*, 9: 475–76.
3. Elizabeth Davis Bliss (c1804–1886) had married Bancroft in 1838. *DAB*; *New York Tribune*, Mar. 17, 1886.

From Silas D. Wood

Marshall Texas   June 7th 1866

Dear Sir

Presuming upon our former acquaintance[1] I beg leave to request your attention and interposition in behalf of my friend Mr. C. E. Bolls[2] who seeks a pardon from your Excellency, he having come under the 13th exception of your Amnesty Proclamation of May 1865 by holding a sub-ordinate office under the so called Confederate Government, of Confederate Tax assessor. Mr. Bolls has used the proper diligence by forwarding his application to Gov Hamilton who approved the same and it has been duly forwarded to Washington City to the proper officer. From some cause it has not been attended to and he is very anxious to be again reinstated to citizenship. I have known Mr. Bolles for several years and have found him to be a good orderly man never extreme in any views that he has entertained. So far as I know the loyal union men of the county are anxious that he should recieve his pardon.

Your early attention to this matter will place me under renewed obligations.[3]

As you are a ware our state election comes off on the 25 of this month. I thank unless I am much mistaken that your policy will be very heatily sustaned by the voters of the state. Politicians may differ in this matter but the feelings of the masses are with you and if they have a fair chance they will sustain your plan of reconstruction. I have not time to write more.

S. D. Wood

ALS, DNA-RG94, Amnesty Papers (M1003, Roll 52), Tex., Charles E. Bolles.

1. See Wood to Johnson, Sept. 22, 1865, *Johnson Papers* 9: 116–17.

2. Charles E. Bolles (*c*1819–*fl*1880), a farmer and native of Virginia, was drafted into the Texas militia in 1863, served as Confederate tax assessor in 1864, and by 1870 was county clerk of Harrison County, Texas. 1870 Census, Tex., Harrison, Marshall, 24; (1880), McLennan, Enum. Dist. 112, 178; Amnesty Papers (M1003, Roll 52), Tex., Charles E. Bolles, RG94, NA.

3. Bolles initially applied for pardon about August 28, 1865. On September 7, 1865, A. J. Hamilton recommended pardon for Bolles, but nothing happened until after Silas Wood wrote to the President. Johnson ordered Bolles pardoned on June 28, 1866. Ibid.

From Andrew G. Magrath

Charleston S. C.   8th June 1866.

Sir.

I respectfully ask of you, my pardon, with the hope, that in so doing, you will not consider me, ungrateful for the clemency you have already extended to me, or unmindful of the high duties & responsibilities which constantly press upon you. When released from Fort Pulaski, the oath I then took, was the clear, precise, distinct guide for me in conduct & opinion, in all the rest of my life. Whatever hitherto have been either theory or opinion as to the paramount allegiance of the Citizen, now & in all time herafter, it is plain. To the Government of the United States it is due; & to it, obedience must be given. Whatever hitherto may have been theory or opinion, upon the subject of Slavery; now & in all time hereafter, that question is settled. Slavery has ceased; it cannot, it should not be restored. These two great sources of doubt, of disquietude, & ultimately of unmeasured misery to the States; whose public policy has been affected & controlled by the opinions which were adopted in relation to these questions; have been absolutely & forever settled. With these questions at rest & finally disposed of; and in that I do freely & fully acquiesce, I feel it to be the duty of all; I know it to be mine; to discharge with unquestionable fidelity my obligations to the Government, the Constitution, & the laws of the United States.

Since by your clemency I was liberated from imprisonment at Fort Pulaski, I have endeavored faithfully & fully to discharge all the duties of a Citizen of the United States. In public & in private, with the pen & in discourse, I have given all the aid I can to banish the recollections of past bitterness; to establish the ample recognition of all the duties which now devolve upon the people of this State; to stimulate the efforts of all, to renew & repair the sources of prosperity, the development of which is so essential to the general welfare; and to give to the Freedmen of the State, the fullest measure of Civil Rights, & the most complete protection for their enjoyment of such Rights. In any & in all respects I have endeavoured to do & to have done, all that will produce reconciliation with the people; & restoration of the States, of this Union.

I shall ask General Sickles to transmit for me, this application for Executive Clemency; & will also ask him, who is fully informed of my conduct & opinions, since my liberation from Fort Pulaski, to say how far I have discharged the duties to which I have referred: with what efforts I have tried to accomplish what I have stated: & how far, as one thoroughly cognizant of all I have written said or done, he will add the weight of his recommendation to my application.

Respectfully asking your favorable consideration of the matter,[1] I am, with the highest respect, Your obedient Servant.

A. G. Magrath

ALS, DNA-RG94, Amnesty Papers (M1003, Roll 46), S.C., A. G. Magrath.

1. Upon Sickles's recommendation, Johnson on June 14, 1866, enlarged Magrath's parole to the boundaries of the United States. Not until the end of the year, however, did the general favor Magrath's pardon, which was granted early in 1867. Sickles to Cooper, June 13, 1866, Tels. Recd., President, Vol. 5 (1866–67), RG107, NA; Johnson to Magrath, June 14, 1866, Johnson Papers, LC; Sickles to Johnson, Dec. 15, 1866, Amnesty Papers (M1003, Roll 46), S.C., A. G. Magrath, RG94, NA.

From William B. Phillips

Private

87 East 26h Street,
New York, June 8h./66

Dear Sir,

The enclosed editorials[1] are in to-day's paper. The one on your proclamation,[2] which was made "the leader," does not endorse your action as strongly as I thought and felt upon the subject.[3] You have done your duty, and have done it in the right way and at the right time. But there was a manifest disposition in our editorial conference yesterday to find fault with the government. Seeing this not only in the writers, but in young Mr. Bennett[4] himself, who presides in the absence of his father, I requested the privilege of writing the article myself. Consequently I have done the best I could under the circumstances.

You may remember I informed you a short time ago that the paper was disposed to waver somewhat from the very earnest support it had been giving you.[5] There is still that disposition, particularly in young Mr. Bennett, who has a great deal to do with the paper since Mr. Hudson[6] left, and who is self-willed and not very steady or comprehensive in his views. I do not think the Herald will oppose your conservative policy under any circumstances, though it is true it sometimes makes extraordinary somersaults, but it is strongly inclined to take a new start. I need hardly say to you that as far as my influence goes and as long as I can exercise any influence in the matter you and your patriotic policy shall be sustained.[7]

The Weekly Herald commenced publishing my book[8] last week. I should like you to read it if you had the time. Although it is a novel or romance, it contains a vast deal of information with regard to our political and social life. I can hardly expect you to spare the time to read it, particularly as it comes out in a serial form. After it has run through the Herald, which will take four or five months, I shall publish it in a volume; and, then, I shall have the honor to send you a copy.

I hope you are in good health and may long be so.

W. B. Phillips

ALS, DLC-JP.

1. Not found.

2. In his June 6 proclamation of neutrality the President declared the recent Fenian invasion of Canada as having constituted "a high misdemeanor, forbidden by the laws of the United States as well as by the laws of nations," and he warned all citizens "against taking part in or in any wise aiding, countenancing, or abetting said unlawful proceedings." Richardson, *Messages*, 6: 433.

3. While noting that Johnson's proclamation was not universally accepted and that some would "gladly seize the opportunity . . . to condemn" the President's course, the *Herald* also suggested that there was no better time than now for demanding a settlement of the *Alabama* claims. *New York Herald*, June 8, 1866. For more on the Fenian issue, see Phillips to Johnson, Aug. 23, 1866, Johnson Papers, LC.

4. James Gordon Bennett, Jr. (1841–1918), who had been made managing editor of the *Herald* several months earlier, practically assumed full control of the newspaper the following year. *DAB*; Oliver Carlson, *The Man Who Made News: James Gordon Bennett* (New York, 1942), 383–84.

5. See Phillips to Johnson, May 20, 1866.

6. Frederick Hudson (1819–1875) had been with the *Herald* for nearly thirty years before taking a year's leave of absence in the spring of 1866. Officially resigning his position as managing editor in July 1867, Hudson later wrote a history of American journalism. *NCAB*, 11: 163; Crouthamel, *New York Herald*, 152.

7. Perhaps Johnson wanted to hear the same assurances from the Bennetts themselves, prompting him to request Bennett, Jr., to come to Washington and to "Confer freely with you father before you leave." He obliged the President. Johnson to Bennett, Jr., June 13,

1866, Tels. Sent, President, Vol. 3 (1865–68), RG107, NA; Phillips to Johnson, June 25, 1866.

8. *The Diamond Cross; a Tale of American Society* was published by both a New York and a Philadelphia firm in 1866. *NUC.*

From William Seawell[1]

Greenville Alabama   June 8th 1866

Sir,

The enclosed communication from Genl. Swayne, is in reply to one from me to him, suggesting the necessity of his providing Medicine and Medical aid to sick Freedmen, in this place, who were too poor to provide them at their own cost.[2]

An appeal to the County Commissioners for this assistance, as suggested by the Genl., would be vain—because this class of the White population they are not only unable to furnish with Medicine—but they would starve for the want of necessary food, but for the bounty of the US. Government.

The refusal of Genl. Swayne to take care of the Freedmen in sickness is in effect to abandon them to perish by disease, of which, in many cases, they might be cured.

Simply in behalf of humanity, I beg leave to lay this matter before your Excellency, in the hope, that the relief desired, may be afforded to a very destitute class of human beings.[3]

Wm. Seawell

ALS, DNA-RG105, Records of the Commr., Lets. Recd. (M752, Roll 35).

1. Seawell (b. *c*1808), a former Selma lawyer, more recently had been a Butler County planter. Seawell to Johnson, July 26, 1865;, Seawell to A. J. Smith, July 26, 1865, Office of Atty. Gen., Lets. Recd., President, RG60, NA; William Garrett, *Reminiscences of Public Men in Alabama* (Spartanburg, 1975 [1872]), 789.

2. The "enclosed communication" was a letter from Charles J. Kipp, surgeon-in-chief of the Freedmen's Bureau in Alabama, who, on May 28, 1866, at the direction of Gen. Wager Swayne, responded to Seawell's letter of May 26. He said that since the Bureau could not provide a physician, Seawell should apply to the county commissioners for medical aid. Kipp to Seawell, May 28, 1866, Records of the Commr., Lets. Recd. (M752, Roll 35), RG105, NA.

3. Seawell's letter was also referred to General Howard's office and in turn to General Swayne, who on July 13, 1866, noted, "The writer Seawell is conspicious in his neighborhood for having persistently denounced the presence of the Bureau. Arrangements are on foot for doing what can be done at Greenville." Endorsements, Seawell to Johnson, June 8, 1866, Records of the Commr., Lets. Recd. (M752, Roll 35), RG105, NA.

From Charles H. Shriner[1]

(Private)

Mifflinburg, Union Co. [Penn.], June 9th, 1866

Dr Sir

Although I know your time is precious, I take the liberty of sending you here-with, proceedings of a large meeting in Beaver,[2] in which I think you will take an interest.

The Resolutions pass'd *unanimously*, although when I came there, the politicians told me, "there was but *one* Johnson man in the County, who voted for him in 1864"—in that district. The politicians & office-holders are all against you, except 2 or 3,—but the *people* are for you, as the meeting shows,—all they want is *light*. The papers try to keep them in the dark in the interest of Stevens Sumner & Wade.

I spoke over 2 hours, and although a very poor speaker, the *subject*, so interested, the people, I am sure they would have listen'd 2 hours longer. Ex Senator Robertson,[3] who presided, should be taken care of—he is a noble man & asks nothing.

Mr Sankey,[4] Collector in that district is against you, presided at an anti-Johnson meeting, as I was informed. Thinks ⟨like Orwig⟩[5] you can't put him out &c. I think if you would give Mr. Robertson his place, it would do the '['] State some Service."[6]

Last year certain strong men in this state, demanded my removal. You refus'd, for which accept my very best thanks. But I want to say now, in all sincerity, if my holding this place, is a hindrance to you in any way—if there are certain interests in this state—that could help you, but will not, because this humble "Mordecia sits at the kings gate"[7]—please tell me, and I will resign.

Born & bred a democrat,—taught to believe that each state has, a right to make her own laws,—and that without that, right liberty must perish, —I am for your policy, with all my heart.—if I had been removed last year,—I would stump the state, for this "Lincoln Johnson policy."

I will do all, I can, in that direction any how—and in any event.

Chas. H Shriner

ALS, DLC-JP.
1. A miller by trade and a former Democrat, Shriner (c1824–fl1886), who served as collector of the Fourteenth District under both Lincoln and Johnson, left Pennsylvania in 1875 and eventually settled in Dixon, Illinois. *History of that Part of the Susquehanna and Juniata Valleys, Embraced in the Counties of Mifflin, Juniata, Perry, Union and Snyder, in the Commonwealth of Pennsylvania* (2 vols., Philadelphia, 1886), 2: 1308, 1382; *History of Butler County, Pennsylvania* (n.p., 1895), 123; Shriner to Johnson, Oct. 30, 1869, Johnson Papers, LC; 1870 Census, Pa., Union, Mifflinburg, 22.
2. Not found. The meeting was held on June 5. Shriner et al. to Johnson, Aug. 16, 1866, Appts., Internal Revenue Service, Collector, 24th Dist., Archie Robertson, RG56, NA.
3. Archibald Robertson (1805–1871), a paper mill owner and operator, had been a Whig state senator (1851–52) and a Lincoln-Johnson supporter. Ibid.; Joseph H. Bausman, *History of Beaver County Pennsylvania and its Centennial Celebration* (2 vols., New York, 1904), 1: 230.
4. Appointed by Lincoln as collector of the Twenty-fourth District, David Sankey (b. c1808), a farmer and former bank president, had been the previous occupant of the senate seat won by Robertson in 1850. *U.S. Off. Reg.* (1863–65); *History of Mercer County, Pennsylvania: Its Past and Present* (Chicago, 1888), 164–65; *DAB*; 1860 Census, Pa., Lawrence, Union Twp, New Castle, 17.
5. Possibly Mifflinburg native Samuel H. Orwig (1836–fl1886), who was at this time a Republican member of the state assembly. *Susquehanna and Juniata Valleys*, 2: 1216–17.
6. Recommended shortly afterwards by his fellow delegates to the National Union Convention in Philadelphia, Robertson was appointed in place of Sankey on August 28 and confirmed by the Senate in February 1867. Charles H. Shriner et al. to Johnson, Aug. 16, 1866; William F. Johnston to Johnson, Aug. 17, 1866, Appts., Internal Revenue Service,

Collector, Pa., 24th Dist., Archie Robertson, RG56, NA; Ser. 6B, Vol. 4: 84, Johnson Papers, LC.
7. Mordecai. From Esther 2: 19 and 21.

From Frederick J. Stanton[1]

Gazette Office   Denver, Colorado   June 9th 1866.

Revered Sir

No doubt ere this, most strenuous efforts have been made by the enemies of Mr Cummings[2] to remove him from the Governorship of Colorado, and no doubt you have been pertinaciously approached for that purpose. Many reasons actuate these men, some are his personal, some his political enemies and some wish him removed to make room for their own political friends. My object is thus dropping you a few lines is simply to inform you apart from all these considerations and interested motives what the *People* want. They are a strictly loyal people, are the people of Colorado, and they are, (the majority of them) warm supporters of your Administration and eschew the unconstitutional arbitrary measures of the Congress and Senate.[3]

The People are terribly opposed to foreign appointees to Territorial offices outside their own people, and this is the cause of their opposition to Cummings as Governor and Gale as Justice.[4] They want a man of their own, and three fourths of the people hope you will appoint Gov. Wm. Gilpin[5] if you conclude to remove Cummings. Though a Democrat, I have no hesitation in saying, that Gilpin, tho' a Republican will give great satisfaction. It was the antagonism of Frank Blair and Ed. Stanton, which caused his removal, by your lamented predecessor, for private personal reasons; but the people have elected him by a large majority as Governor in case the State had been admitted, and they hope he will be endorsed by you as the Governor of the Territory. I have no apologies to ask for this communication as I am well aware you will duly appreciate it. I need only say, that the personal enemies of Gilpin are Evans, Chaffee & Chivington[6] who have so outrageously ostracized all the wishes of their constituents as to work and manoeuvre for the Radical Junta at Washington. Excuse these rambling and desultory scratchings, and hoping you may shortly ride triumphantly over your enemies.[7]

Fredk. J. Stanton

LS, DLC-JP.
1. Frederick J. Stanton (c1828–fl1881), a native of England who had previously resided in Iowa, was variously a publisher of Democratic newspapers, notary public, surveyor, draftsman, land claim agent, florist, and assayer in Denver. 1870 Census, Colo., Arapahoe, 74; Denver directories (1859–81).
2. Alexander Cummings (1810–1879), a Philadelphia newspaper publisher, commanded Pennsylvania cavalry and black troops during the Civil War. Johnson appointed him governor of the Colorado Territory in 1865. Some people wanted him removed because he opposed Colorado statehood. McMullin and Walker, *Territorial Governors*, 69–70.

3. Admitting Colorado to statehood.

4. Colorado Associate Justice William H. Gale was appointed from New York in 1865. He resigned his office in July 1866 allegedly because of an inadequate salary. Pomeroy, *The Territories*, 126; Guice, *Rocky Mountain Bench*, 43.

5. Gilpin (1815–1894), a lawyer and Missouri newspaper editor, participated in John Charles Frémont's second exploring expedition and served in the Mexican War. Briefly territorial governor of Colorado (July 1861-March 1862), Gilpin remained in the territory afterwards and achieved wealth through land deals. Johnson did not reappoint him governor. McMullin and Walker, *Territorial Governors*, 65–66; *DAB*.

6. John Evans, Jerome B. Chaffee, and John M. Chivington. Chivington (1821–1894), a Methodist preacher in Nebraska and Missouri, moved to Colorado in 1860. He commanded Colorado troops as they helped drive the Confederates out of New Mexico and also led the soldiers who perpetrated the infamous Sand Creek massacre of 1864. Subsequently, he lived in Nebraska, California, and Ohio before returning to Colorado in the 1880s. Dan L. Thrapp, *Encyclopedia of Frontier Biography* (3 vols., Spokane, 1990), 1: 264–66.

7. Johnson did not remove Cummings but the governor resigned in April 1867 to become collector of internal revenue for the Fourth District of Pennsylvania, whereupon Johnson replaced him with A. Cameron Hunt. Frank Hall, *History of Colorado* (4 vols., Chicago, 1889), 1: 391–92; McMullin and Walker, *Territorial Governors*, 70.

From William J. Vason[1]

Augusta Ga.   9th June 1866

Mr. President;

I appeal to you for Justice from a refusal of Genl A. Baird Asst. Comr. of the Bureau of R. F. & A. L. for the State of Louisiana, to surrender to me, my property situated in the City of New Orleans, which withheld by the said Bureau as "abandoned property" from me.

I herein submit to your consideration, the original papers[2] which I filed in the office of the said Bureau—and which were withdrawn therefrom by permission of Genl. A. Baird for the purpose of laying them before Majr. Genl O. O. Howard who advises me to lay them before you for your opinion.

1st.   It appears from these papers; that on the 1st of February 1860, I departed from the city of New Orleans with my family with the intention of changing my domicil to the city of Augusta, where I arrived on the fourth day of that month, and where I have resided ever since; that previous to my departure I appointed L. E. Simonds Esqr.[3] a resident of New Orleans my agent in fact to manage and control my property in said City—who accepted the trust, and managed and controlled my said property by paying the taxes and collecting the rent, until prevented by orders from Majr. B. F. Butler issued in 1862; and that he is still acting as my agent; and that the tenants who occupy one of the tenements, rented the same from me, more than ten years ago. I respectfully submit that these facts prove that I have never abandoned my property in the City of New Orleans.

2nd.   It appears from the duly certified copy of my oath of Amnesty and Allegiance, that on the 19th day of May 1865—I took and subscribed the oath prescribed by the Proclamation of Pres. A. Lincoln &c. &c.

I respectfully submit that by taking and subscribing the said oath I became entitled to the restoration of all my rights of property except my property in slaves; and that the asst comr. of said Bureau should have surrendered to me, my property in the city of New Orleans on filing my application with the proof these facts, above stated.

3rd.   It will appear from the papers, that Genl. A Baird refused to inquire into the question of the abandonment of my property, or to investigate the fact, whether it was rightfully or wrongfully seized; but insisted that I should answer under oath the 24 Interrogatories herein enclosed marked D.[4] I respectfully submit that Genl. Baird erred in refusing to inquire into the fact whether my property was abandoned. The obvious meaning and intent of the 5th paragraph of the Circular No. 15[5] approved by your Excellency, make it his duty to receive proof of the fact, that the property was not *abandoned.* If not, then the said paragraph is a deception calculated to dupe and mislead applicants for a restoration of their property. Majr. Genl. Howard in his reply to me of the 5th inst. states, that "he does not DESIRE to go behind the fact, that the Treasury and other Departments of Government have turned property over to him as abandoned." The indulgence of his desire annuls the said 5th paragraph, and leaves parties whose property has been seized as abandoned, against whom no judicial proceedings have been instituted, as in this case, REMEDILESS. I can not admit, nor recognize the right or authority of an asst. Comr. of said Bureau, to require me to answer under oath the Interrogatories; because I have complied with the requirements prescribed by his *superior*—your predecessor, Prest. A. Lincoln, by taking and subscribing the oath of Amnesty & allegiance, which precludes all further inquiry as to my status. Majr. Genl. Howard, further states, "the conditions imposed by Genl. Baird are undoubtedly for the purpose of carrying out in good faith the provisions of the enclosed circular." There is no provision in that circular which authorizes an asst Comr. of said Bureau, to require applicants for the surrender of their property to answer interrogatories under oath, or to sign a release, for the rents of, or damages done to the property, during the possession thereof by the officers of the said Bureau. I therefore decline to comply with those conditions, and insists that the said asst. commissioner has no right nor authority to prescribe such terms as a condition precedent to the surrender of my property.

In conclusion, Mr President, I will frankly state, that I have not taken and subscribed the oath of Amnesty and Allegiance prescribed by your Proclamation of the 29" day May 1865—because ten days previous to that date, I took and subscribed the one prescribed by the Proclamation of your predecessor which entitles me to the restoration of my all my rights of property, except to my property in slaves—as fully and effectively as if taken and subscribed under your Proclamation.

I have not applied to you for a special pardon, because I did not consider that I had done any act during the last four years, which made it necessary or proper for me to ask a pardon from you after taking and subscribing the oath prescribed by Prest. Lincoln's Proclamation. I am now in the fifty ninth year of my age. I was exempt by reason of my age, and took no active part, in the late war. I held no office civil or military either State or Confederate during the war.

Believing that I was entitled to the restoration of my property in the City of New Orleans—of which I had received no benefit since 1861—I applied to Majr. Genl. Howard on the 10" of Octr. last past for it. He refferred my application, with out notice to me, to the asst. comr. of the Bureau in New Orleans where it has been until 19" of last month, when I went to New Orleans to inquire into the reasons why my property was not restored to me. The reasons assigned, herein stated—that I must answer the 24" interrogatories under oath, and sign a release for the rents &c. &c.

I decline to comply with the terms prescribed; and now appeal to you for an order directing the asst. comr. Genl. A. Baird of the Bureau &c &c, to deliver to me my property and to pay to me the rents received therefrom, since it has been under the control of the officers of said Bureau.[6]

All of which is respectfully submitted by your humble Servt.

Wm. J. Vason
Augusta Georgia

ALS, DNA-RG107, Lets. Recd., Executive (M494, Roll 84).
1. Vason (c1807–fl1870), a former New Orleans lawyer, in 1861 was Georgia's commissioner to Louisiana for the encouragement of secession. He claimed to still own "a double tenement brick House" on the Crescent City's Tchoupitoulus Street. 1860 Census, Ga., Richmond, Augusta, 4th Ward, 863; (1870), 2nd Ward, 34; New Orleans directories (1850, 1859); Avery, Georgia, 165, 166; Vason to O. O. Howard, October 10, 1865, Lets. Recd., Executive (M494, Roll 84), RG107, NA.
2. The papers included Vason's October 10, 1865, and May 28, 1866, letters to Gen. Oliver O. Howard; a copy of his May 19, 1865, amnesty oath; a December 16, 1865, sworn statement by Lewis E. Simonds; and a copy of the twenty-four "interrogatories" to be answered by claimants for the release of Louisiana real estate. Ibid.
3. Lewis E. Simonds (fl1884) was Vason's former law partner. New Orleans directories (1850–84).
4. The twenty-four questions accompanied an August 16, 1865, Freedmen's Bureau memorandum by the Louisiana assistant commissioner Thomas W. Conway, whereby rules for the release of real property were enumerated. The questions were so stringent that, if answered honestly, only consistent unionists could expect the return of their estates. Lets. Recd., Executive (M494, Roll 84), RG107, NA.
5. The exact wording of the paragraph was, "Upon its appearing satisfactorily to any Assistant Commissioner that any property under his control is not abandoned as above defined, and that the United States has acquired no title to it, by confiscation, sale, or otherwise, he will formally surrender it to the authorized claimant or claimants, promptly reporting his action to the Commissioner." Ibid.
6. Vason's papers were referred to General Baird, who reported that Vason was "obsti-

nate." Shortly thereafter, on August 21, 1866, General E.R.S. Canby held that the amnesty oath taken by Vason May 19, 1865, "neither pardons the past nor returns any forfeited rights." He ruled that Vason, by refusing to take Johnson's amnesty oath and to answer the questions, demonstrated "that he is still unrepentant," and should not have his property restored. Secretary Stanton forwarded the reports of the two generals to Johnson and also concluded that Vason had forfeited his rights "by his failure to return to his allegiance." Vason was not immediately informed and, in early November 1866, again presented his case to Johnson, who then ordered that an "Official copy" of Canby's decision be sent to him. Absalom Baird to Townsend, Aug. 6, 1866; Canby to Townsend, Aug. 21, 1866, Lets. Recd. (Main Ser.) File V-175-1866 (M619, Roll 523), RG94, NA; Stanton to Johnson, Aug. 23, 1866, Lets. Recd., Executive (M494, Roll 84), RG107, NA; Vason to Johnson, Nov. 3, 1866, Records of the Commr., Lets. Recd. from Executive Mansion, RG105, NA.

From John T. Trezevant

Private.

Memphis, June 11/66

The accompanying document & preamble are the opinions of an overwhelming majority of our people.[1] As may possibly be known to your Excellency, I was opposed to the movement made by the Southern States. By speech & pen, I did all I could to prevent it. But, when the contest began, I felt I owed enough to my State & my fellow citizens to attempt to repel the invasion that followed. The effort failed, and, in good faith, I accepted the consequences. But let me say to your Excellency, in honest candor, that I did not think the South would find a friend in you when you succeeded Mr. Lincoln. I have always been a democrat, but I never voted for you. I thought you a radical in politics, & I feared you would be a fanatic in power. Let me use this occasion to acknowledge how much I have been mistaken; and how deeply gratified I am that I can now say so to you without creating a suspicion in your mind that I am making this Confession from interested motives. I am no office seeker; never sought office but twice in my life, & was then rewarded with the generous support of my fellow citizens. I could not hold office, even if I sought it; and I do not seek it. The better years of my life have been devoted to building up my country, in inducing my fellow citizens of West Tenn. Ark & Miss. to build Rail Road; and my chief ambition now, is to see these completed which will contribute most to the welfare of our State. But we labour without heart. Our people feel that a foul injustice has been done them in disfranchising them; and they naturally look around for comfort. We do not know what to do, while unwilling to do any thing rash or impolitic. We think that a word of encouragement from you would induce public meetings in every county in the State; & that through these, there might be such a change effected as to inaugurate a new state of things entirely. The resolutions are lost;[2] but they were but two—one requesting you to aid us in our wishes, if it be in your power to do so—the other asking other counties to move. The course of the present Congress has engendered in the public mind an *indifference* to our conditions that is alarming. It is teaching us all to lose all respect or affection for a Government that has not one word of kindness for us. Powerless for evil as we are, it would seem that the plain policy of Congress would be to conciliate, & make us feel that the North is our friend rather than our conqueror.

I know the valuable time of your Excellency, and I will no longer trespass, save to ask you to read the accompanying petition & let us hear from you at your earliest convenience.

J. T. Trezevant

ALS, DLC-JP.
    1. The accompanying documents have not been found. See also Memphis Citizens Committee to Johnson, May 28, 1866.
    2. Trezevant's meaning here is unclear.

From James M. Tomeny
Personal

Washington   June 12, 1866

Sir:

Although I have been here several days I have not been able to see you. My business has received prompt attention from the Hon. Sec. of the Treasury and the Atty General. They have done all I asked.[1] At my earnest request the Hon. Sec. of the Treasury will cause to be made a thorough investigation of my accounts and official acts. Knowing that they will bear the closest scrutiny I rest easy. What I feared was a corrupt court and a set of common informers who would swear to anything. No proceedings were taken by the Court against Dexter. It is said Rufus F. Andrews[2] his Counsel, who went out from New York with Judge Busteed, and lives with him received a fee of $50,000. The intention was to put me in prison and let Dexter go.[3] This was probably the contract. They made a bold strike for it anyhow. Judge Busteed has done enough since he went to Mobile to impeach half a dozen better Judges. He is the worst curse brought by the war upon the people of Alabama. The Atty. Genl. pronounces his order to seize my official records, books and papers, "unwarranted, illegal oppressive and contrary to the usages of Courts and of law."

I regret that I could not see you, simply to express to you my unbounded gratitude for your many kindnesses, and to say that come what may I shall stand by you. With unwavering faith in your patriotism and statesmanship I pledge my self to support and defend your Administration, and to go with your friends whatever shape parties may take. When the contest comes I will find your banner and fight under it; and I pray that God will give your friends, (who are the true friends of the Union[)], the victory. I go to New York tonight and will return in a few days, when I hope to have the pleasure of seeing you,

J M Tomeny

ALS, DLC-JP.

1. See Tomeny to Johnson, May 20, 1866.

2. Andrews (*fl*1894), Richard Busteed's New York City law partner, had served under Lincoln as surveyor of that port. New York City directories (1860–94); *NUC*.

3. After reviewing the case against Thomas Dexter, Johnson ordered him discharged. Similarly, charges brought against Tomeny were dismissed; indeed it was established that the government owed Tomeny money. *Memphis Post*, May 26, Oct. 2, 1866.

From Zebulon B. Vance

Charlotte N. Ca   12th June 1866

I would be greatly obliged if you would give me permission to visit Washington City.[1]

Z. B. Vance

ALS, DNA-RG94, Lets. Recd. (Main Ser.) File V-164-1866 [filed with V-382-1865] (M619, Roll 431).

1. At the end of the war, May 13, 1865, Governor Vance was arrested and incarcerated at Old Capitol Prison, Washington, D.C. In July he was paroled to his home at Statesville, North Carolina, and in mid-December his limits were enlarged to the entire state of North Carolina. Vance's request to visit Washington was referred to the War Department and granted June 25, 1866, Johnson being so informed the next day. However, there is no evidence that Vance actually journeyed to Washington during the summer of 1866. Clement Dowd, *Life of Zebulon B. Vance* (Charlotte, 1897), 95, 97, 100–101; Thomas T. Eckert to Johnson, June 26, 1866, Lets. Recd., Executive (M494, Roll 85), RG107, NA.

From Gideon Welles

June 12, 1866, Washington, D.C.; LBcopy, DNA-RG45, Lets. Sent to Pres., Vol. 21 (M472, Roll 11).

In reply to the President's submission of a petition from the agents of the Columbia Rolling Mills requesting the return of property captured by General Sherman's forces at Charlotte, North Carolina, Welles asserts that "the machinery . . . was employed by the rebel organization in the construction and fitting out of vessels of war"; therefore, there is "no ground for making a distinction between this and other property belonging to the public enemy and used by him for purposes of war." Welles is about to advertise the "rapidly deteriorating" property for sale at public auction, but he will suspend action "until your further pleasure be known."

From Varnum S. Mills[1]

New York, June 13 1866

My dear Sir

I being one of the oldest Citizens of this City I am Solicited and Requested by a large majority to inform you that all the Loyal and all the Union people of this City would be highly pleased to have you as the Chief Magistrate of our Common Country to make us a visit during this beautifull month. We are all anxious to see and Shake hands with you and if you will answer this and let us know at what time you can make it Convenient I will be highly pleased to proceed to Washington and Escort you to this City and I will prepare a Suit of Rooms at any Hotel you may name or Select.[2] The inhabitants not only of this City but of the Union are highly pleased with your administration and while the people for the last year having been Sorrowing and Mourning for the loss of President Lincoln they have at the same time been Rejoicing and Congratulating one another at having so worthy a Successor. My advice to you is not to put any more Confidence in the Fanatics than you would in any Rebels. You are situated in a position which Requires great Caution and if you place your whole trust and Confidence in our Heavenly Protector the same as Washington you may then have the fullest assurance then the different Politicians that take such delight in Calling themselves fireaters, Copperheads, Hard Shells, half Shells, Soft Shells, Shedders, Snappers, Niggerheads, and Fanatics will hide their hideous heads and Shells, in Confusion Shame and despair and in your Success not only through your administration but likewise through you Natural life you have my best wishes. Nb I am an old man and have always put my trust in my Heavenly Maker and the Result is that my memory my intelect and my talent has improved with my age and I have never seen a sick day in my life.

Varnum S. Mills

Nb   Please Respond and inform me at what time you make it Convenient to make us the desired visit.[3]

V. S. M

ALS, DLC-JP.
   1. Mills (*fl*1869) worked variously as a marshal, constable, auctioneer, and collector. New York City directories (1838–69).
   2. Although Johnson did go to New York City in late August, it is not known whether Mills was among the thousands who cheered the President. Trefousse, *Johnson*, 262–63.
   3. A reply from Johnson has not been found.

From Charles O'Conor and Thomas G. Pratt

[Washington]   13 June 1866

The Undersigned as Counsel for Jefferson Davis now a Prisoner at Fortress Monroe, repectfully show that the State of Mr. Davis' health renders his further inprisonment detrimental, and probably dangerous to his life, in whatever form it may be continued. That every alleviation of its severity tends so far to diminish just apprehension. That the measures prescribed by military rule in reference to his custody during the night are attended with many pernicious results by depriving him of regular & undisturbed sleep.

Feeling confident that no possible hazard as to his safe detention could result & willing to pledge ourselves for his honorable observance thereof as is hereby done; we earnestly solicit that your Excellency will be pleased to direct that the parol which has been granted to him within the Fort during the day time be extended to the whole twenty four hours.[1] As in reference to this relief every hour is deemed precious we beg that you will be pleased to give this direction as soon as may be consistant with your Convenience.

Ch. O'Conor
Thomas G. Pratt

ALS (Pratt), DNA-RG94, Amnesty Papers, Jefferson Davis, Pets. to A. Johnson.

1. After Davis had been granted the freedom of the fort during daylight hours, his counsel had petitioned Judge John C. Underwood on June 11 for his release from the fort on bail. That same day the judge ruled that, as Davis was a military prisoner in a state where military jurisdiction and martial law were still in effect, the civil court had no power to intervene. The lawyers then made this plea for a twenty-four hour parole. Attorney General Henry Stanbery, who replaced Speed, advised the lawyers later that it had been decided that Davis would remain at Fortress Monroe. Underwood opinion, June 11, 1866, Johnson Papers, LC; *National Intelligencer*, June 13, 1866; Stanbery to O'Conor, August 21, 1866, Lets. Sent, Atty. Gen. (M699, Roll 11), RG60, NA. See Speed to Johnson, May 21, 1866, Jefferson Davis Papers, RG109, NA.

From J. Ross Browne[1]

Washington, D. C.   June 14 1866.

Sir:

I am sure you feel an interest in whatever tends to develope the resources of the Pacific Coast. As a citizen of California, proud of our young State, I take the liberty of sending you a specimen of our native wine, just received from San Francisco.

You will find it a pure article. No foreign wine, of a similar grade, can in my opinion, compare with it. The "Angelica" is especially adapted to the use of the ladies, as you may judge from its name. It is made at Los Angeles, and is expressly designed as a beverage for the angels. Hebe used it—or something like it—as nectar for the gods; and if it should come into general [use] I have no doubt the smallest infants would cry for it.[2] The "Mound Vineyard" is an exceedingly fine dinner wine, light and mellow, with just sufficient acidity to render it appetizing. For invalids it is invaluable.[3]

In 1849, when I first landed on the shores of California, there were within the boundaries of the territory 150,000 vines. At this time, (June 1866), there are within the limits of the State 12,000,000 vines. In ten years more, the wine-growing interests of California will be of greater national importance than its gold products.

Those who are engaged in the culture of the grape, have had many difficulties to encounter. It is an experiment which has cost them many losses and much labor. They now ask that this infant branch of domestic industry shall not be too heavily taxed. It requires a long time and a heavy outlay of money to bring a vineyard into a paying condition. All branches of agriculture especially on our remote frontiers, deserve to be encouraged. Native wines, I think, should be entirely free from taxation, if for no other reason than to exclude adulterated foreign wines and promote the cause of temperance.

The settlement of public lands cannot fail to be advanced by a liberal course of legislation toward the wine-growing interest; and in that way, together with a general increase of taxable property, government will derive an ultimate advantage without imposing an unnecessary burden upon the products of labor.

J. Ross Browne

ALS, DNA-RG56, Lets. Recd. from Executive Officers (AB Ser.), President.

1. Browne (1821–1875), a prolific author of humorous and travel books, served as the official reporter for the first California state convention. Evidently, Secretary McCulloch appointed Browne in August 1866 as a special commissioner to collect mining statistics in the states and districts west of the Rocky Mountains. Two years later the President appointed Browne as minister to China, from which post he was subsequently recalled. *DAB*; *Louisville Courier*, Aug. 4, 1866.

2. The drink, actually a fortified grape juice, was named for Los Angeles where it was "once the most famous produce of the . . . county vineyards." Thomas Pinney, *A History of Wine in America: From the Beginnings to Prohibition* (Berkeley, 1989), 240–41.

3. Mound Vineyard was apparently another name for Lake Vineyard, a large establishment in the San Gabriel Valley near Los Angeles, which was owned by Benjamin D. Wilson. Ibid., 294–96, 300.

From Asahel N. Cole[1]

Custom House, New York, June 14, 1866.

My Dear Sir:-

Pardon me for addressing you this line. I am holding, or have been holding the office of Weigher in the revenue service of this Port.

My name has been sent to Washington for removal, and, I find I am charged with the authorship of certain most indecent articles which recently appeared in my old paper, the *Genesee Valley Free Press*.

Were I the author of anything of the kind, I should expect to be removed, and should not have respect for the appointing power if my political head failed to pay the penalty.

I established the paper in 1852, and it was the pioneer of Republicanism in this State. I sold it out a year ago to a brave and gallant young soldier,[2] who did better with the sword than he seems to with the pen, since he went out a private and came back Colonel. My only connection with the paper for a year past was the allowance of the continuance of my name as associate Editor.

The removal of a few Post-Masters in Allegany[3] awakened the ire of the young Colonel, and he wrote and published one or two articles which were utterly shocking to me. I wrote, a private note to the Editor directing him to drop my name from the paper, and, in a temperate and yet firm letter which I asked him to publish, I censured his course in conducting the paper.

But enough of this. I expect I shall be decapitated, or, rather, I *fear* I shall, as the Collector, Mr. Smythe, as I understand, adhering to the nomination in my place, does not incline to withdraw that portion of his message referring to me.[4] He exhonerates me from all blame, but persists in my removal.

The Secretary of the Treasury has kindly deferred action, and I would be very glad to continue in office, but dare not hope for continuance.

I should not have written you at all on this matter except that, from a letter received from Mr. Raymond, I found, that the attention of the appointing had been directed to the scurrilous articles referred to, and their authorship attributed to me.

Presuming that your own attention had been possibly called to the subject,[5] I did not want you to feel that I would be guilty of writing such things of any man, much less of yourself, for whose success as a candidate I labored, and whose whole course has been such as to much more frequently elicit my approval than disapproval.

Neither publicly or privately did I ever attack anybody with the vocabulary of the fishmonger, and hope to never be guilty of such folly. If I am to be removed from office, I wish to go out like a gentleman and not for indecency and vulgarity.[6]

A. N. Cole

ALS, DNA-RG56, Appts., Customs Service, Sub-officers, New York, A. N. Cole.

1. A teacher, Methodist minister, and lumber dealer who later turned to editing, Cole (1821–*fl*1877) had been employed in the New York City customs office first as a measurer and then as a weigher since 1861. John S. Minard, *Allegany County and Its People: A Centennial Memorial History of Allegany County, New York* (Alfred, N.Y., 1896), 383–84; *U.S. Off. Reg.* (1861–65).

2. Probably Henry C. Fisk (1838–1918) of Wellsville, New York, who entered the volunteers as a sergeant and left as a colonel and brevet brigadier general. After the war he had a varied career. Until the early 1880s he was an editor, lawyer, and clerk of a congressional committee. Pension Records, Mary E. Fisk, RG15, NA.

3. As many as a dozen Allegany County postmasters serving in September 1865 were not subsequently reappointed. But the exact removals Cole refers to are unknown. *U.S. Off. Reg.* (1865–67).

4. Henry A. Smythe's "message" has not been found.

5. No other letters regarding Cole's removal have been uncovered.

6. Received on June 27, the letter was routinely forwarded by Edmund Cooper to the Treasury Department. Evidently Cole retained his post at least through September 1867. *U.S. Off. Reg.* (1867).

From George W. Paschal

June 14, 1866, Washington, D.C.; ALS, DNA-RG94, Amnesty Papers (M1003, Roll 55), Tex., J. S. Sullivan.

A pardon broker asks that several pardon warrants for Texans, whose applications he had submitted and which Johnson has approved, be sent to them. He assures the President, who he understands "does not allow the interference of any third persons in the matter of pardons," that he has "never asked the pardon of but one man, who acted with the rebels," and regrets his "part in the matter." He also reports having inquired at the office of the attorney general on behalf of the pardon of Judge Garnett Andrews and other Georgians whose applications had been submitted by Andrews. The latter complained to Paschal "that although he had forwarded his own affidavit as to their and his loyalty before, during and since the war, yet he could get no action, while the worst of rebels amongst their neighbors were pardoned, from which he was 'compelled to infer that the union men are as poor dogs at Washington as they are at home.' " He concludes by praising Johnson for his "goodness of heart in the exercise of executive clemency" and expressing his "deep regret that any unrepentant secessionist rebel has ever been permitted to share it."

From James B. Steedman and Joseph S. Fullerton

Montgomery, Alabama, June 14, 1866.

Dear Sir,

In pursuing the investigation we have been directed by yourself to make of the operations and mode of administration of the Freedman's Bureau, and the conduct of its officers &c.[1] we have received information sufficient to satisfy as beyond all doubt, that many of the present officers of the Bureau, but perhaps, a greater number of the predecessors of those now in office than of the present incumbents, have appropriated considerable sums of money collected from fines and forfeitures to their own use. To thoroughly investigate and expose these peculations, will require at least one energetic, sharp, inspector for each State. If we were to take the time necessary to do this, we could not complete our inspection within the present year, and we have therefore omitted investigation of this class of offenses, except where embezzlement has been brought directly to our attention.

We respectfully suggest that an Inspector be sent to each State, with power to send for persons and papers, to administer oaths; to investigate the accounts of all Agents of the Bureau—those who have been agents, as well as those now serving—who have collected money, whether from fines or otherwise. By publishing in a newspaper at each of the points where these agents have been or are now located, a request that all persons who have paid money to an Agent of the Bureau, come forward and state the amount so paid, the sums collected can be ascertained, and when ascertained, comparison with the amount returned, will show the *stealings*, which in our opinion are very large.

James B. Steedman.   Maj. Genl. Vols.

J.S. Fullerton   Bvt. Brig. Genl. Vols.

ALS (Steedman), DLC-JP.

1. See Francis P. Blair, Sr., to Johnson, Apr. 4, 1866, and Wilmington, N.C., Freedmen to Johnson, ca. May 22, 1866.

From William Butterfield[1]

Concord, N.H.   June 15, 1866.

I respectfully recommend the appointment of Hon Josiah Minot[2] to the vacant District Judgeship in this State. He is a gentleman of irreproachable personal character and high professional standing, and of his eminent fitness for the position there is no question. The only possible objection to his appointment, to my mind, is his political character. He is a Democrat and an earnest supporter of your policy from the Start. If that objection is fatal, then you must appoint an opponent of your policy; for I risk nothing in asserting that there is not within the borders of the State a Republican fit for the position, who is not an opponent of your Administration.

The appointment of Judge Minot, I feel very sure, would give great satisfaction to the people of the State.[3]

W M Butterfield.

ALS, DNA-RG60, Appt. Files for Judicial Dists., N.H., Josiah Minot.

1. Butterfield (1815–1884) was for more than twenty-five years (1847–73) editor and co-proprietor of the *New Hampshire Patriot* at Concord. James O. Lyford, ed., *History of Concord, New Hampshire* (2 vols., Concord, 1903), 1: 410; 2: 1036.

2. An ex-circuit justice of the court of common pleas, Minot (1819–1891) had served in the U.S. Interior Department as commissioner of the Pension Office under the presidential administration of Franklin Pierce, his former law partner and business associate. Ibid., 1: 438; 2: 974, 985–86, 1357; Roy F. Nichols, *Franklin Pierce: Young Hickory of the Granite Hills* (Philadelphia, 1958 [1931]), 176; *U.S. Off. Reg.* (1855).

3. Although recommended by several other prominent New Hampshire Democrats, Minot did not receive the appointment. See Appt. Files for Judicial Dists., N.H., Josiah Minot, RG60, NA; William C. Clarke to Johnson, June 25, 1866.

From James L. Orr

Columbia S.C.   June 15, 1866.

James Eagan[1] a citizen of this state was tried here by a military Commission in December for killing a negro, was convicted of murder & sentenced to imprisonment for life in the Albany N.Y. State Prison. He was sent there under guard & delivered to the Keeper. Soon afterwards a habeas corpus was sued out before Judge Nelson[2] of the Supreme Court. Judge Nelson heard the case & decided that the war was ended when the trial proceeded & that the trial & sentence of the military Commission were illegal & void, & ordered Eagan's release. The old man eighty three 83 years old, returned home where he remained but a day or two when Genl. Sickles ordered him to be re-arrested as an Escaped Convict. He was arrested last Saturday, sent to Charleston on Sunday & is now in prison by order of Gen. Sickles. This order nullifies the solemn decision of a Judge of the Supreme Court & I earnestly appeal to you to

peremptorily revoke Genl. Sickles' order.[3] Send answer to 'Mills House
Charleston.

                                        James L. Orr, Governor of S.C.

Tel, DNA-RG94, Lets. Recd., (Main Ser.), File E-261-1866 (M619, Roll 470).
    1. Egan (b. c1783), a Lexington County planter, shot his victim on September 24,
1865, reportedly in self-defense. *National Intelligencer*, June 1, 1866; Charles Goodyear to
Johnson, June 25, 1866, Lets. Recd. (Main Ser.), File E-261-1866 (M619, Roll 470),
RG94, NA; Amasa J. Parker to Johnson, June 25, 1866, ibid., File P-767-1866.
    2. Samuel Nelson.
    3. By Johnson's direction, the next day Stanton again ordered Sickles to release Egan
and to "report the reason for arresting him after his discharge." Sickles immediately complied and on June 17 sent a lengthy explanation to the adjutant general. The re-arrest of
Egan was based on the continued suspension of the writ of *habeas corpus*, the belief that he
"was not authorized to permit an adjudication of a court at Albany to supercede the authority of the President in South Carolina," and he still had authority to arrest those who committed outrages upon blacks. Stanton to Sickles, June 16, 1866, Tels. Sent, Sec. of War
(M473, Roll 90), RG107, NA; Sickles to Lorenzo Thomas, June 17, 1866, *House Reports*,
39 Cong., 2 Sess., No. 23, pp. 16–19 (Ser. 1305); *Charleston Courier*, June 13, 21, 1866.

From Robert M. Patton

                                        Montgomery, Ala   June 15th 1866.
My Dear Sir
    I beleave I have not been troublesome in pressing the claims of persons
for Your Executive clemency, and dont think I would in any case do so
when it would in the least conflict with or embarrass Your wise policy of
restoring our once distracted country to peace, order and prosperity.

    I have, however, two very worthy and respected friends, whose appli-
cations for pardon are, as I am advised, filed at Washington; and as far as I
know, these are the only two Gentlemen who were prominent officers in
the Rebellion from this State whose embarrassments have not been removed. Genls H D Clayton and Alpheus Baker[1], of Barbour County, this
State, both Lawyers of high respectability, and character; the former was,
at the last election, chosen by the people of the 7th Judical district, Circuit Judge of that District; but declines to take his commission until I can
hear from You or until next month. I have no hesitation in saying, as a
true and loyal man, to the country, and to Your policy of restoration, he is
much preferable to his predecessor or the present incumbent,[2] who will
discharge under the Constitution the functions of the office until Judge
Clayton receaves his commission.

    Majr Genl Swayne Agent of the Freedmans, Beaureau, and com-
manding in this State, fully agrees with me in this; and may write You on
the subject.[3] I will regard it a special favour if You will, at as early a day as
may seem wise to You, extend to him pardon for past offences. I have no
hesitation in saying he, and indeed both the Gentlemen will in all time to
come prove true to the National Govt.; and the Constitution of the U
States,[4] I enclose hearwith letters to me from these Gentlemen.[5]

                                        R. M. Patton   Gov. of Alabama

ALS, DNA-RG94, Amnesty Papers (M1003, Roll 1), Ala., Alpheus Baker.

1. Both Henry D. Clayton (1827–1889) and Baker (1828–1891) held field commands during the Georgia and Carolinas campaigns. Warner, *Gray*. See also Baker to Johnson, Aug. 2, 1865, *Johnson Papers*, 8: 529.

2. J. McCaleb Wiley (1806–1878) returned to Alabama after a sojourn in the 1830s in Mexico and lived in several locations before moving to Troy. Wiley was grand master of the Masonic Lodge of Alabama before the war; in 1865 Governor Parsons appointed him to be judge of the eighth circuit but he lost to Clayton in the 1866 elections. Subsequently, Wiley was elected judge of the state circuit court. Garrett, *Reminiscences*, 351–52; Henry S. Marks, comp., *Who Was Who in Alabama* (Huntsville, 1972), 192.

3. On that very day, Gen. Wager T. Swayne wrote recommendations for each of the generals in question. Swayne to Johnson (two letters), June 15, 1866, Amnesty Papers (M1003, Rolls 1 and 2), Ala., Alpheus Baker and Henry D. Clayton, RG94, NA.

4. Both men were pardoned July 11, 1866. Ibid.

5. Not found.

To Alexander T. Stewart

Washington DC   June 15 1866.

Dear Sir—

Your letter dated June 12 1866—addressed to Honl Hugh McCulloch Secretary of the Treasury has been read to me.[1]

I need not say to you that in the midst of political convulsions which surround me that the approval of my course by one who occupies such a prominent position in the Commercial history of the Country, greatly encourages me, to persevere in the course of political conduct which has heretofore guided my official actions.[2] It is upon the aid of such true men that my administration must rely and I feel deeply gratified for the frank and sincere manner in which you have expressed your encouragement and your earnest wish for its success.

It is true that the position which I occupy is an embarassing one, yet trusting in the patriotism of the people I firmly believe that the details of an informed civilization will be brought out by the peaceful operation of a restored and united government.

Andrew Johnson

LBcopy, DLC-JP.

1. Stewart's letter had been prompted by McCulloch's earlier invitation to go along with him "and a few friends" on a visit to Richmond. Stewart to Johnson, June 18, 1866, Johnson Papers, LC.

2. In his June 12 letter Stewart had evidently been supportive of Johnson and had indicated that the views of many "leading citizens" would be similarly favorable. Ibid.

From John Binny

545 Broome St.
New York   16th June 1866.

Dear Sir

I am gratified to find that the extreme Radicals Mr Sumner, Mr Stevens & others have at length been induced to cooperate on a judicious scheme of Reconstruction with the Conservative Republicans. The national Union party in Congress by a solid & overwhelming vote have passed the series of Constitutional Amendments in both Houses and I understand propose to send them as speedily as possible to the State Legislatures for their concurrence.[1] This scheme leaves out the question of the franchise for the present—and—I have full confidence that it will meet with the approbation of the great mass of the loyal American people.

It would be deeply gratifying to the nation if you would cooperate with the majority in Congress in carrying forward this important measure.[2] After the enormous sacrifice of life and the vast expenditure of money during the past four years the people would not be satisfied with a less satisfactory adjustment than the one passed through Congress. I earnestly trust you will cooperate with the majority in Congress in this wise & practical scheme. You have it in your power to gain glorious renown by lending your countenance to this measure. *Under your Controlling influence* the Congress has been led to moderate its reckless impetuosity and to decide at last on a scheme so wise & Statesmanlike that it is highly worthy of your Countenance & Cooperation.

Should you allow this golden opportunity to pass unimproved and leave the scheme to be adjusted by the Congress & the State Legislatures you will fall in public estimation & be condemned by the verdict of history as incompetent for the momentous work entrusted to you. But should you on the other hand, cordially cooperate in this judicious scheme *you will rise in immortal renown as one of the greatest Statesmen in the world*. It is in your power to have my words as recorded in a former letter to you verified. "George Washington Abraham Lincoln & Andrew Johnston will shine in a Constellation apart the three greatest & most honored names in American history.["][3]

There is no man in this Continent I should like to see the President of the reUnited States during the next four years better than yourself. If you are faithful & true to the mission which God has given you the culminating honor of your life is possibly still to come.

I expect Tennessee will be admitted into Congressional relations before the session closes.

John Binny

ALS, DLC-JP.
    1. An obvious reference to the recently passed Fourteenth Amendment.
    2. Johnson immediately raised objections to the Fourteenth Amendment. See his letter to the Senate and House of Representatives, June 22, 1866.
    3. See Binny to Johnson, Jan. 10, 1866, Johnson Papers, LC.

From Amos Kendall

Kendall Green [Washington, D.C.]   June 16th 1866

Dear Sir,

When, during my last call upon you, I mentioned my purpose of visiting with my family the eastern continent, you were kind enough to suggest that you might be able to facilitate our movements, as I supposed through the public agents abroad and perhaps by some testimonial from yourself.[1]

The object of this note is to express my desire to avail myself of your kindness in such way as you may deem proper. Our excursion will probably embrace Great Britain France, Switzerland and Italy, possibly Constantinople, Egypt and Palestine.

I shall look back, my Dear Sir, with great interest, to the progress of your patriotic efforts to restore unity, kind feeling, constitutional government, moral reform and material prosperity to our distracted country.

Amos Kendall

ALS, DLC-JP.
1. Johnson wrote a letter of introduction for Kendall to U.S. consuls and ministers. See his letter of June 16, 1866, Johnson Papers, LC.

From Maria Grundy Masterson[1]

Nashville   June 18th 1866.

Dear Sir

I wrote to you some time ago,[2] but presume it miscarried. Or amid so many cares, you had not an opportunity to answer. Presuming upon the old intimacy that has existed between you—and my family, particularly my Father F Grundy,[3] I ask your influence to get either of my Sons—16 & 18 years of age—to obtain a place in the Army or Navy.[4] As you know my husband[5] was a planter. And all he left me was mostly in negroes. I am not able to Educate my Sons—As the descendants of Felix Grundy should be. Do assist me—I need it. And soon. Excuse me—but a widowed mothers anxiety, must be my apology. Mrs Porter and Mrs Winder[6] —(my sisters) were delighted with their visit to you. That encourages me greatly in addressing you.

If possible let me hear from you.[7]

Present me kindly to Mrs Johnson.

I write in haste Being in the country And anxious to send this to town to be mailed.

So please excuse errors.

Mrs. M. Grundy Masterson.

ALS, DLC-JP.
1. Masterson (1815–1880), who had married in 1838, was usually a resident of the Green Hill community in Wilson County, Tennessee. Edythe R. Whitney, comp., *Marriages of Davidson County, Tennessee 1789–1847* (Baltimore, 1981), 171; Jill K. Garrett and Iris H. McClain, comps., *Old City Cemetery: Nashville, Tennessee Tombstone Inscriptions* (Columbia, 1971), 62; 1860 Census, Tenn., Wilson, 1st Dist., 48; (1870), 10.
2. No earlier correspondence between Masterson and Johnson has been located.
3. Felix Grundy (1777–1840), a lawyer, jurist, and politician, served in both the Kentucky and Tennessee state legislatures, the U.S. House and Senate, and as U.S. attorney general under Van Buren. *DAB.*

4. She probably refers here to her sons, John B. (*c*1848–*fl*1872) and William E. (*c*1851–*fl*1872). 1860 Census, Tenn., Wilson, 1st Dist., 48; *Nashville City Directory* (1872).

5. William W. Masterson (*c*1812–*fl*1860) also served as Green Hill's postmaster (1841–60). 1860 Census, Tenn., Wilson, 1st Dist., 48; Naomi M. Hailey, comp., *West Wilson County Neighbors* (Nashville, 1986), 163.

6. Felicia Ann Grundy Porter. Her sister, Martha (1812–1891), was the widow of Van Perkins Winder of Louisiana. 1860 Census, Tenn., Davidson, Nashville, 4th Ward, 165; Nashville directories (1859–89); Whitney, *Davidson County Marriages*, 190; *Nashville Republican Banner*, Nov. 10, 1861; Garrett and McClain, *Old City Cemetery*, 101.

7. There is no record of Johnson's response. By 1870 John Masterson was a farmer and William was a farm laborer. 1870 Census, Tenn., Wilson, 1st Dist., Green Hill, 10.

From J. R. Swift[1]

Washington, D.C   June 18th 1866.

Sir

I have the honour to present to your favourable notice Col J.C. De Gress formerly on duty in Texas on Genl. Mower's[2] Staff, from personal observation and from positive knowledge I know that Col De Gress has done good service both to our Country and also to your Brothers family. At the death of your Brother Col DeGress performed many acts of kindness to his family and also done all he could to save his life[3] and if you could consistently put him in the regular army I think it would be of great service to the Country.[4] I was in Texas during the time of your Brother's death, and knowing to [of] the many acts of kindness shown your Brothers family by the Col.

J. R. Swift

ALS, DLC-JP.

1. Not further identified.

2. Joseph A. Mower (1827–1870), under whom DeGress had served as an aide-de-camp, had displayed considerable boldness and gallantry in the western theatre and during Sherman's Georgia campaign. After the war he commanded black troops in the regular army. Warner, *Blue*; Mower to Johnson, June 6, 1865, ACP Branch, File D-1729-CB-1871, J. C. DeGress, RG94, NA; *OR*, Ser. 1, Vol. 39, Pt. 3: 481; Vol. 47, Pt. 1: 388–89; Vol. 48, Pt. 2: 840.

3. See John Adriance to Johnson, Oct. 26, 1865, *Johnson Papers*, 9: 287.

4. Appointed under the military reorganization act on July 28, 1866, as first lieutenant, 9th U.S. Cav., DeGress was subsequently nominated to that post by Johnson in February 1867. After having been confirmed and commissioned, DeGress then was appointed as captain in July 1867, nominated by Johnson in December, confirmed by the Senate in February 1868, and commissioned four months later. Powell, *Army List*, 278; Ser. 6B, Vol. 2: 61, 65, Johnson Papers, LC.

From Annie L. Ash[1]

Phil.   June 19. 1866.
222 South Fourth Street

Mr. President

I have had the honor to address you several times,[2] as I would a Father and the Head of our Nation, in reference to the Statement I sent you of our position;—but I have reason to fear none of my communications have reached you, as I have not received any acknowledgment, altho' I have waited with intense anxiety.

My Mother[3] desires me to ask you to do her the very great kindness, in her extreme weakness and loneliness, to have her Pension granted immediately. She is in great need of it. She has indeed suffered for it, during the two said years which have elapsed since her only and invaluable son,[4] who filled my Father's place was killed.

My Mother would ask the kind favor of an early answer to relieve her.

Annie L. Ash.

ALS, DNA-RG48, Patents and Misc. Div., Lets. Recd.

1. Ash (c1843–fl1900) lived for many years at the family residence in Philadelphia. 1870 Census, Pa., Philadelphia, Philadelphia, 5th Ward, 51; Philadelphia directories (1869–1900).

2. From the extant documents it is believed that Annie Ash was a rather regular correspondent with Johnson. See, for example, Ash to Johnson, May 16, July 31, Aug. 2, 26, 1865, Johnson Papers, LC; Ash to Johnson, May 1, 1866, Lets. Recd., Patents and Misc. Div., RG48, NA.

3. Bella Maria Ash (c1820–fl1895) was the widow of Caleb L. Ash, a Philadelphia attorney. 1870 Census, Pa., Philadelphia, Philadelphia, 5th Ward, 51; Philadelphia directories (1853–1895).

4. Joseph P. Ash (c1840–fl1864) enlisted in 1861, became a first lieutenant, 5th Cav., the next year and a captain in 1863. Powell, *Army List*, 167; Annie L. Ash to Johnson, July 31, 1865, Johnson Papers, LC.

From James Atkins[1]

Knoxville   June 19th 1866.

Dear Sir,

A few weeks since I visited Washington, for the purpose of asking you if you pleased to make an order putting us in possession of our Church Houses in E. Tenn the use of which, we have been deprived of, in consequence of a military order on that subject.[2] Among the papers you referred to Col. Morrow for examination was a request from the Trustees and people of *Athens*.[3] Also, one from Mr A.G. Jackson of *Knoxville* on behalf of that Congregation.[4] That Church is simply held by the Freedmen. Others have been taken by the Methodist of the north, under Mr Stanton's order and they still hold them. All we ask is, that you order these Churches into the possession of the Denomination that owned and occupied them in 1860, leaving disputes about Titles, if there should be any, to the adjustment of the Courts. About the same as was ordered in reference to the Virginia Churches. I ask for *Athens* and *Knoxville* especially, but hope your order will cover all that have been taken in like manner.[5] We are anxious to hear.

Jas. Atkins.

(P.S.)   In some parts of E. Tenn the radical Methodists do not, try to take our property, but in others they do. A word from you will put this question to rest, and my opinion is that they will not contend for it. There is a strong public sentiment in E. Tenn in favor of the Churches that have been taken from their original and rightful owners being returned. I am glad to say to you that E. Tenn is strongly Conservative to day—& for your administration.

J.A.

ALS, DNA-RG107, Lets. Recd., Executive (M494, Roll 85).
1. Atkins (1817–1886) was a Methodist minister who was very much involved in the affairs of the Holston Conference of the southern branch of the Methodist Church before transferring in 1879 to the Florida Conference. R. N. Price, *Holston Methodism: From Its Origin to the Present Time* (5 vols., Nashville, 1904–14), 4: 400–445 passim; 5: 229–31.
2. Probably a reference to the circular issued by Stanton in November 1863 which authorized federal troops to place Methodist churches of the South into the hands of Northern Methodist officials. See ibid., 4: 478.
3. Not located.
4. Not located.
5. No record of such an order issued by Johnson has been found. The President's attached endorsement simply states that he referred the matter to the secretary of war.

From Edmund Burke

Newport, N.H.   June 19, 1866.

Private

Sir,

I have today addressed a letter to you recommending William W. Taylor Esq.[1] to fill the vacancy in the office of Postmaster at Concord, N H. occasioned by the death of Gen. Corning.[2]

It is proper that I should advise you that Mr Taylor is, and has been, a democrat in his politics, but a moderate one. Notwithstanding his politics he was kept in the office of Chief Clerk by Gen. Corning, a republican. But, in conference recently with Judge Ira A. Eastman,[3] and other prominent democrats, and true friends of your policy, it was deemed important that, in the present crisis of national affairs, you should have a true friend and supporter in so important an office as Postmaster of the Capital of this State. And no person of republican antecedents fit for the office, and friendly to your Administration, can be found in that city. The Candidates for the office except Mr Taylor, I am informed, are all radical republicans, supporting the Thad. Stevens policy of restoration.[4]

Permit me to say that the Democracy of this State are the firm supporters of your policy. It is the only party which supports it. The Republican Party is in opposition supporting the schemes of Congress. Let me speak frankly. Without the Democracy you would have no supporters in this State. There are many republicans who would ally themselves with the Democratic Party in support of the Administration, if they could be sure of support from the Administration. At present, so far as the patronage is concerned, in this State, they see it all conferred on the enemies of the Administration policy. They, therefore, hesitate to take ground in favor of

the Administration, which would be a separation from the present dominant party.

I know the sentiments of the leaders of the Democratic Party in this
State, including Ex-President Pierce, is, that you should recognize the
Democratic Party as an ally, and that your supporters of the Republican
Party (Conservatives) should openly co-operate with the Democracy,—
that the position of the Administration on this point should not be equivocal, but open and decided. And we believe that, with such co-operation,
we can redeem this State from Radicalism next March, and send you new
Representatives, either Johnson Republicans, or democrats, who will
give a cordial support to your Administration.

The democrats do not expect office from you, if sound and reliable
Johnson men can be found to fill them. But, I know it is the sentiment of
the leaders of our party, that, in no event, should a Radical be appointed
to office, or to remain in one, where a Johnson Republican or a democrat
can be found to fill it. We know that, whatever may now be the pretensions of the Abolitionists to loyalty and patriotism, they were the original
traitors here in the North, and true to the instincts of rebellion, they are
opposed to the reconstruction of the Union except upon terms that will
forever perpetuate the hatred and hostility of the lately belligerent sections. These men are as bitterly hostile to you today, as they are to Jeff.
Davis. And they comprise a large majority of the Republican Party.

Pardon the frankness with which I have written, because I desire to
impress upon you a correct view of the state of things here in the North,
and especially in N.H. and because I desire most heartily that you may be
the victor in the noble and heroic battle which you are waging against the
consolidationists, for the constitution and the Union.

Business will require me to visit Washington next week, and then, if it
be your pleasure, I should be glad to confer with you more fully touching
the matters referred to in this letter.[5]

Edmund Burke

ALS, DLC-JP.
    1. The June 19 recommendation of Taylor (c1827–fl1870), a former jeweler who
clerked at the post office at Concord from the mid-1850s through at least 1867, is enclosed.
U.S. Off. Reg. (1853–67); Concord directories (1853–56); 1860 Census, N.H., Merrimack, Concord, 5th Ward, 158; (1870), 36.
    2. A militia brigadier general and former Republican legislator (1854–55), Robert N.
Corning (1818–1866) had been appointed postmaster at Concord by Lincoln and renominated in May 1866 by Johnson. Stearns, *History of New Hampshire*, 2: 539; Ser. 6B, Vol. 4:
10, Johnson Papers, LC.
    3. Eastman (1809–1881) had served as a Democrat in Congress (1839–43) and after-
wards held a succession of judicial posts in New Hampshire. He sought a U.S. Senate seat
in 1866 but was not successful. *BDAC*. See also Burke to Johnson, July 5, 1866.
    4. Taylor was eventually nominated by Johnson in March 1867, but failed to receive
Senate confirmation. Ser. 6B, Vol. 4: 10, Johnson Papers, LC. See Burke to Johnson, July
30, 1866.
    5. Johnson's note accompanying Burke's letters of June 19 read: "Post Master at Con-
cord N.H. Letter of Edmund Burk—File for reference. A.J."

From John A. Dix[1]

New York, 19. June 1866.

Sir:

Colonel Wm. H. Ludlow,[2] whom I take pleasure in introducing to you, served on my staff from the Year 1861 to the close of the war, and discharged all his duties with zeal, efficiency and fidelity. In addition to his services as a staff officer, he was entrusted by the government with the responsible and delicate duty of exchanging prisoners of war, and as long as he acted as Commissioner, no difficulty of any importance occurred between the government and the rebel authorities in regard to these exchanges. In all Col. Ludlow has done he has been able and efficient.

Before the war he was Speaker of the House of Assembly in the Legislature of this State. He was always a Democrat, and was one of the first to take part in sustaining the government against the efforts of the secessionists to overthrow it. He has been long known in political & public life in this State, and is capable of discharging intelligently and efficiently any public trust.[3]

John A. Dix

ALS, DNA-RG56, Appts., Customs Service, Naval Officers, New York, William H. Ludlow.

1. This letter was enclosed in Ludlow's application of the previous day. Ludlow to Johnson, June 18, 1866, Appts., Customs Service, Naval Officer, New York, William H. Ludlow, RG56, NA. Dix also had been recommended for the same post of naval officer. See John J. Cisco to James R. Doolittle, June 15, 1866, which was referred to the President. Ibid., John A. Dix.

2. Ludlow (1821–1890) later received brevet commissions of brigadier and major general. Hunt and Brown, *Brigadier Generals*; *Senate Ex. Proceedings*, Vol. 15, pt. 2: 548–49, 572.

3. Although also recommended by the "majority of the Democratic and Conservative Representatives from New York," as well as a host of others, Ludlow was not appointed. Ludlow to Johnson, June 26, 1866, Appts., Customs Service, Naval Officer, New York, William H. Ludlow, RG56, NA. See Abel R. Corbin to Johnson, June 25, 1866.

From James Hughes

Washington, June 19, 1866.

Mr. President:—

Out of many matters which it has been my duty as an attorney to present to you for decision, in my last interview, I selected the following as most important and pressing:—

1. Major Burn's[1] case.

An application for relief from an unjust and tyrannical order of *Mr. Cameron* Secy. of War, in violation of a contract with an executive Department, and which is a peculiar subject of executive relief.

2. The case of Col. Jno. S. Williams,[2] in which your action is entirely satisfactory.

3. The case of *Mr. Cook* for restoration of property at Athens Ga.[3]

4th   Mr. Corcoran's application for restoration of his property.[4]

Many other very urgent and important cases, I have refrained from pressing on your attention.

The *only personal favor* I have ever asked, the matter of employment as counsel to recover money belonging to the government resulting from the rebellion, I withdrew because I found it was misapprehended or misconstrued.

I wish to say, that your manner, in our two last interviews, indicated great impatience and irritation, perhaps personal dislike.

I am unconscious of any reason for this.

I have barely done my duty to clients, who if I had not represented them would have applied to you in person, or through some other channel.

My object now is to request action on the cases presented, and to express regret that I should have been the innocent means of disturbing your equanimity, and to promise you that I will trouble you no more.

James Hughes

ALS, DLC-JP.

1. William Wallace Burns (1825–1892), a career army officer, was a brigadier general of volunteers just after the start of the war. He later served with the commissary service, retiring in 1889. Warner, *Blue*; Heitman, *Register*, 1: 266.

2. Williams (1825–1900), a lawyer, served two terms as mayor of Lafayette, Indiana, before becoming colonel of the 63rd Ind. Vols. Forced to resign because of ill health, he later was appointed collector of internal revenue for the Eighth District of Indiana (1866–69). In 1885 he was appointed an auditor for the U.S. Treasury. *NCAB*, 2: 330–31; Pension Records, Mary J. Williams, RG15, NA; Washington, D.C., directories (1885–89).

3. Francis L. Cook (b. *c*1819) operated an armory in New Orleans with his brother Ferdinand W.C. Cook. Under contract with the Confederacy to produce Enfield rifles, they moved their business to Athens, Georgia, when New Orleans was captured. They operated there until the property was seized in May 1865 by federal troops. Cook was pardoned by Johnson in December 1865 and afterwards applied for restoration of his property. The case was referred to the U.S. district court in Georgia which ruled in Cook's favor, but as late as June 1868 the army was still in possession. Kenneth Coleman, *Confederate Athens* (Athens, 1967), 96–99; Amnesty Papers (M1003, Roll 17), Ga., Francis L. Cook, RG94, NA; *Opinions of the Attorneys General*, 11: 480–81; Lets. Recd. (Main Ser.), File C-581-1866 (M619, Roll 465), RG94, NA; 1860 Census, La., Orleans, New Orleans, 3rd Ward, 248.

4. William W. Corcoran. He went to Europe in 1862 and remained there until war's end. His Washington residence was used as a military hospital and another hospital was built on the grounds of his summer residence. His art gallery, later given to the city, served as an army clothing depot. Margaret Leech, *Reveille in Washington, 1860–1865* (New York, 1941), 435–36.

From Cydson Lee[1]

Newbern NC   June 19 1866

Sir

You have Been Givengs us aWhat Belong To us all and will you please to have the papers [illegible] Look our the 1st N.C and after We Came to

Folly Island SC near Charleston SC and then moved to Jackville, Florida and my Son John, Tiler Lee[2] Co I 35th[3] Died Folly Island SC and I Would like to Draw his money if the is any Belong to him for he Was all the Child that I Ever had and I thinks that you Will Grant me the preveyledg of Drawing his money if the So [go?] owes him any.[4] He Was Born in Elizbet City the Steate of north Carolina.

Cydson Lee

ALS, DNA-RG94, USCT Div., Lets. Recd., File P-176-1866.
1. Sidney Lee (c1810–fl1893), a former slave of James Lee, is probably the black woman recorded in the 1870 Census as Cydia, a housekeeper. Pension Records, Lydia Henley, RG15, NA; 1870 Census, N.C., Craven, 7th Twp., New Bern, 5.
2. John Tyler Lee (c1844–1864), a farmer, had enlisted as a private in May 1863 and died of "Consumption" some eight months later. CSR, John Tyler Lee, RG94, NA.
3. The 35th USCT had been organized from the 1st N.C. Colored Inf. in early 1864. After being attached to a Florida brigade, it was stationed in Jacksonville and in late 1864 was sent to South Carolina, where it saw action. Subsequently, the unit returned to Florida and then was ordered to Charleston. Dyer, *Compendium*, 1729.
4. A few days later the adjutant general's office in Washington informed "Mr. Cydson Lee" that he would have to send his application for payment to the second auditor's office. Finally, in December 1868, "arrears" of John Tyler Lee's pay plus a $200 bounty were issued to Sidney Lee. C. W. Foster to Lee, June 23, 1866, Lets. Recd., USCT Div., File P-176-1866, RG94, NA; Pension Records, Lydia Henley, RG15, NA.

From John Letcher

Lexington Virginia: June 19th: 1866:

Dear Sir:

Your letter of the 13th inst[1] granting me permission, to participate in public meetings held for the purpose of developing the resources of the State of Virginia, has been received. Accept my thanks for the prompt and favorable reply to my request.

John Letcher

ALS, DLC-JP.
1. Edmund Cooper to Letcher, June 13, 1866, Johnson Papers, LC.

From Springfield, Ill., Johnson Club[1]

Springfield Illinois   19th June 1866.

We the undersigned who voted the Republican ticket in 1864, and who now have full confidence, in the reconstruction and general policy of Your Excellency, would beg leave to represent that because of our adherences to your policy and expressing confidence in your honesty of purpose, and that you have been carrying out the same policy that would have been pursued by Mr Lincoln, had he lived, we are now, and have been subject to all manner of slander and vituperation, (which was shared largly by yourself) because we still beleive and assert that such is your position and policy. The radicals sneer, and jeer, because of the appointment of Mr Smith,[2] Collector of this district, and say the President does not support *his* friends, does not recognize them, and repudiates their pretentions, and the supporters of "My policy." Now all we desire and wish, if we are to be recognized at al, is, that we should be heard by Your Excellency as your friends, that no appointments shall be made until such time as some of us can see your Excellency and have a full and perfect Conferance on the subject, as to what is to be done, and how we are to build up out of the Republican party friends that recognize Your Excellency as an honest and faithfull representative of the principles upon which you were elected. There is no question about the fact, that when the dificulty first arose between yourself and the radicals, but that a large portion of the Republican party, received your policy as the right and the one that ought to be adopted. But at once the charge was made that you were not a true man, and used with that of John Tyler, the charge was publicly proclaimed by Gov Oglesby[3] and others in this City, and such a terror inaugurated over the party, that it required a bold man to stand up and say that the President was right. From the first we have stood firm for you, supported, and still support your Excellency, because of our *faith*, not for a moment thinking that a man who had been tried as you were, could or would depart, from principles he had been ready to lay down his life for. We are still of the same opinion and still stand and support your views and policy, because of faith in your purposes and intentions. We have seen nothing to shake our confidence, nothing to make us think that we were mistaken in our voting as we did in 1864. We therefore have formed what we call a Johnson Club composed *exclusively* of those who voted for you in 1864. That Club now numbers over one hundred and fifty members in this City, it is regularly organized, has had, and still has its stated meetings, and the radicals are doing all in their power to break it down and destroy its influence. With such appointments as that of Smith, it will have the desired effect and the "Club["] become a matter of ridicule in the eyes of the radicals and of no practical benefit to us or to your Excellency. In view of these facts, it is the unanimous opinion and voice of all members of the Club, and all your friends, here, that it would be wise policy for the present not to make any appointments until such time as some of the members of the "Club["] fully recognized and authorized as such have a Conference with Your Excellency.[4]

LS, DLC-JP.

1. There were seven signatories.

2. John W. Smith was nominated as collector of the Eighth District of Illinois on May 30 and confirmed by the Senate six days later. Ser. 6B, Vol. 4: 299, Johnson Papers, LC.

3. Richard J. Oglesby.

4. By the time this petition was received, Johnson had already directed the secretary of the treasury to withhold the issuance of Smith's commission until McCulloch had received further orders. Several other groups of citizens from Springfield and surrounding areas had earlier written Johnson requesting the removal of Smith and the appointment of David T. Littler, a Conservative Republican. Before the end of 1866, Smith had been removed and Littler was nominated. McCulloch to Johnson, June 12, 21, 1866, Appts., Internal Revenue Service, Collector, Ill., 8th Dist., John W. Smith, RG56, NA; see documents in ibid., David Littler, RG56, NA; Ser. 6B, Vol. 4: 300, Johnson Papers, LC.

From J. Richard McCann et al.

Knoxville Tenn   June 20th 1866

The Court on our trial yesterday utterly refused to regard or even to allow us to read our paroles or pardons under your amnesty proclamation[1] saying in the words of the prosecuting officers, they wanted no such stuff. We accepted your amnesty in good faith & have kept it on our side. We appeal to you to enforce its observance on yours.[2]

J.R. McCann
Reuben Roddie[3]
W.C. Kain - J.C. Ramsey

Tel, DLC-JP.

1. Despite this and earlier assertions that they had been pardoned by the President, no evidence to confirm such claims for McCann, Kain, and Roddie has been located. Ramsey, on the other hand, appears to have been issued a pardon on November 10, 1865. McCann to Johnson, Sept. 19, 1865, Lets. Recd. (Main Ser.), File M-475-1866 (M619, Roll 494), RG94, NA; John M. Fleming to Edwin M. Stanton, Mar. 21, 1866, ibid., File F-357-1866 (Roll 472); Kain to Johnson, Sept. 19, 1865, Governors' Papers, TSLA; Ramsey to Johnson, ca. July 20, 1865, Amnesty Papers (M1003, Roll 50), Tenn., J. C. Ramsey, RG94, NA; *House Ex. Docs.*, 39 Cong., 2 Sess., No. 116, p. 48 (Ser. 1293).

2. No indication that Johnson responded to this last-minute plea from the prisoners has been found. As a matter of fact, the trial ended the day after this telegram was sent and all of the accused were acquitted of the murder charge. *National Intelligencer*, June 25, 1866.

3. Roddie (b. *c*1814), a farmer and Jonesboro merchant, had been a captain in the 37th Tenn. Inf., CSA. Resigning in 1862, he was subsequently a private in a local defense company. *Washington Evening Star*, June 27, 1866; *Brownlow's Knoxville Whig*, July 4, 1866; 1850 Census, Tenn., Carter, Elizabethton, 385; (1860), Washington, Jonesboro, 141; CSR, Reuben Roddie, RG109, NA.

From Thomas McElrath[1]

New York   June 20, 1866.

Dr Sir,

Some two or three weeks since the Hon. H.J. Raymond presented to you an application[2] for the app't of my son Lieut T.P. McElrath[3] to a captaincy in the Quarter M. Depar't. His record I presume is all that could be asked—at least so I am informed at the War Department, and I trust that you will find it consistent with the interests of the service to grant the application.[4]

It will be the more gratifying to me just at this time from the fact that having identified myself with your general policy I can hardly expect the influence of influential parties with whom I heretofore acted in concert.

But the truth is I always found in Governor Seward a safe guide. My children were all instructed to love him—they now all revere him. I never desert a friend.

Thomas McElrath
late of *"The Tribune"*

ALS, DNA-RG94, Lets. Recd., ACP Branch, File M-261-CB-1869, T.P. McElrath.

1. McElrath (1807–1888) had served both before and during the war as business manager and co-publisher with Horace Greeley of the *New York Tribune*. He had also held several state and city offices, and was later involved with sponsoring and promoting various world fairs. *DAB*. See also Kenneth Rayner to Johnson, July 2, 1866.

2. Congressman Raymond had endorsed and forwarded young McElrath's application of early April to the President, and in mid-June he had written a recommendation accompanied by a "memorandum" of the lieutenant's military service, as submitted by McElrath's father. Thomson P. McElrath to Johnson, Apr. 4, 1866; Raymond to Johnson, June 13, 1866; Thomas McElrath to Johnson, June 12, 1866, ACP Branch, File M-261-CB-1869, T. P. McElrath, RG94, NA.

3. Currently stationed at Fortress Monroe as post quartermaster, Thomson P. McElrath (c1837–1898) was a veteran of the Peninsular Campaign and a former regimental staff officer under Gen. John A. Dix. During later years he wrote a handbook of Yellowstone Valley and edited the periodical, "The American Analyst." Ibid.; Pension Records, Thomson P. McElrath, RG15, NA; *NUC*.

4. Although unsuccessful in getting a transfer from the artillery to the Quartermaster's Corps, McElrath was promoted to captain and also awarded the brevet ranks of captain and major (with Johnson's approval) before he resigned from the army in January 1870. Ibid.; *Senate Ex. Proceedings*, Vol. 15, pt. 1: 27, 337; Vol. 16: 11, 168; Ser. 6B, Vol. 2: 218, Johnson Papers, LC; Heitman, *Register*, 1: 664.

From Mrs. L. E. Potts[1]

Paris, Lamar County   Texas
[ca. June 20, 1866][2]

Dear Sir

In addressing you, I do not address you as the Cheif Magistrate *only*, but as the Father of our beloved country, one to whome we all look more or less for Protection, but most especially the *poor* negros. I wish that my poor pen could tell you of their persecutions here. They are now just out of slavery only a few months, and their masters are so angry to have to loose them, that they are trying to persecute them back into slavery. It is not considered crime here to kill a negro, they are often murdered by bloodhounds and shot because they do not do precisely as *the* white man says.[3] I have been in Nashville Tennessee all the winter and I am constantly being reminded of the difference in thier condition here and thier. Thier has never been any Federal troops in here and every thing savors of Rebellion. I wish that we could have a few soldier here for a while just to let these rebels know that they have been whiped. The Confederacy has destroyed and ruined mine and my childrens property. In 1858 I took my two children and went to California with the hope of restoring the health of my daughter who was in a deep decline, and in 61 I was ready to return home when the rebellion broke, out and fearing that my son a youth only 13 years of age might be forced into the war I remained there untill peace. We left a large estate here which they confiscated and distroyed all that they could. The land is all that is left to us. They striped it of all the timber and distroyed my houses, had my notes and claims turned over to the Confederate receiver who has them yet. But it is not to my wrongs that I wish to call your attention: but for humanity sake I implore you to send protection in some form to these suffering freedmen. Your good heart and wise head know best what to do. I have stated only facts. The negroes need protection here. When they work they scarcely ever get any pay, and what are they to do?

I am a plain woman from your own State, and hope that this appeal may not be made in vain.[4] I have never had the pleasure of your acquaintance but as a Tennessean I am proud of you, and as a President I approve your course, and hope that bright laurels may forever crown your brow.

Mrs. L. E. Potts

ALS, DNA-RG94, Lets. Recd. (Main Ser.), File G-726-1866 (M619, Roll 479).

1. Not identified.

2. The first endorsement on this document showed that it had been received in Washington, D.C., on June 28, 1866. It is assumed that it would have taken at least a week for the letter to travel from Texas.

3. Similar conditions were reported in other counties. James M. Smallwood, *Time of Hope, Time of Despair: Black Texans During Reconstruction* (Port Washington, N.Y., 1981), 32–35.

4. Johnson referred the letter to O. O. Howard, who sent it first to Grant. By a circuitous route, the well traveled letter finally reached Gen. Philip H. Sheridan. He returned it to Washington, along with a letter from Gen. H. G. Wright to Bvt. Lt. Col. George Lee, assistant adjutant general of the Department of the Gulf, dated July 21, 1866, explaining that, "I get frequent complaints from the N.E section of the state [the location of Lamar County] regarding the condition of that part of the country, of the barbarities practiced toward refugees and freedmen, but owing to the want of force for the purpose nothing could be done in the matter." General Howard requested Texas authorities to investigate the situation and take steps to provide protection. All of the endorsements and the letters are found attached to the Potts letter.

From John H. Reagan

Fort Houston, near Palestine, Texas
June 20th 1866.

I feel the full weight of my obligations for your generous kindness in granting me a parol last fall, to return to my home and the care of my family. On my return home I engaged in farming, and in the improvement of my home, endeavouring to render it in some degree comfortable. Situated as I was I did not think it advisable or agreeable to myself to take any part in public affairs, further than in my humble and quiet walks and amongst my neighbors and friends to urge the importance of sustaining you in the policy you are pursuing for the reconciliation of a lately belligerent people and for the restoration of constitutional government and order and prosperity to the country. In this country your course has the general and I believe I may say universal approval of all; and all admire that exalted mind and character which has enabled you to unite in you action in so noble a degree wise policy and justice and mercy. And you have the united prayers of our people for the success of your policy.

Mr. President I came home to find myself impoverished by the losses which resulted from the war. My home, in bad condition, and some wild lands is all that was left me. I have four children to support and educate.[1] And on the 31st of last month I married the daughter of one of my near neighbours,[2] who is as poor as myself. I have this additional inducement to desire repose and security for the future. I have been and shall continue to be faithful in my duty to the government and the oath I have taken. And I would respectfully ask if you cannot now extend to me a full pardon, and restore me to my rights as a citizen. I have avoided all solicitation on this subject since I saw you, knowing how you were involved in great public cares; and if I were willing to pursue that course I am unable to employ counsel to intercede for me. But I prefer coming frankly and directly to you. You know my case and the grounds I have heretofore set forth to support my application for pardon. I do not now wish to ask you to do anything which would in any way embarass you when you are beset by so many difficulties. But if you can, without embarassment, extend to me pardon without further delay I shall ever recognise it as the greatest earthly favour you could bestow on me, and shall be ever grateful to you for it. And I believe if you knew my heart and feelings and course of action as they are you would not hesitate to do so.[3]

John H. Reagan

ALS, DNA-RG94, Amnesty Papers (M1003, Roll 54), Tex., John H. Reagan.

1. Reagan had one twelve-year old son and three daughters, the youngest of whom was five, all by his second wife, Edwina. John H. Reagan to Johnson, June 2, 1865, Amnesty Papers (M1003, Roll 54), Tex., John H. Reagan, RG94, NA.

2. Molly Ford Taylor (c1847–1916), Reagan's third wife, was the daughter of John F. and Rebecca Walker Taylor. Ben H. Proctor, *Not Without Honor: The Life of John H. Reagan* (Austin, 1962), 181; *Con Vet*, 24 (1916): 532.

3. Reagan did not receive a pardon until April 29, 1867. Amnesty Papers (M1003, Roll 54), Tex., John H. Reagan, RG94, NA.

From George W. Samson

Columbian College
Washington DC.   June 20th 1866

Dear Sir

A year since on my return from a Missionary Convention at Richmond Va. you kindly considered the cases of three or four gentlemen, excepted from the general amnesty, whose Christian devotion made them a special reliance for the sustaining of Missionary & Educational interests at the South.

At a similar meeting at Russellville Kentucky,[1] held about three weeks since, at which some of the truest representatives of Christian sentiment in the South were present from all the Southern & border states except Arkansas, the Case of Genl. C.H. Battle[2] was spoken of with special interest, as an applicant for pardon from Alabama.

Mr. Battle at the opening of the war was a private citizen, who never had held office, known as conservative in politics, never a secessionist *per se*. At the Call of his State he accepted office as Major; & his generous nature & Christian integrity raised him, though but a youth, to the rank of Brig. Genl. In Tennessee & other States he is reported as ever magnanimous & a protector of Union men; some instances of which are made known to the Attorney Genl. No stain rests on the Character of Genl. Battle in his private or official Character known to hundreds of his Christian friends; except the common error of the South in the late resort to arms.

Genl. Battle's application for amnesty, duly endorsed by Gov. Parsons,[3] has been on file in the office of Attorney General for some months; without any desire on his part to give you annoyance by pressing it. He is strongly commended by Rev. Dr. Henderson, his pastor, by Gov. Shorter his brother-in-law,[4] & other gentlemen. In the assurance that your Clemency in his Case will be both worthily bestowed & widely & highly appreciated, his name is respectfully laid before you.[5]

G.W. Samson

ALS, DNA, RG94, Amnesty Papers (M1003, Roll 1), Ala., Cullen A. Battle.

1. The Southern Baptist Convention, May 22–26, 1866, had an attendance of 244, "representing every Southern State," including Arkansas. *Louisville Journal*, May 27, June 2, 1866; Robert A. Baker, *The Southern Baptist Convention and Its People, 1607–1972* (Nashville, 1974), 458.

2. Cullen A. Battle.

3. Parsons had recommended Battle's pardon on August 15, 1865. Amnesty Papers (M1003, Roll 1), Ala., Cullen A. Battle, RG94, NA.

4. Samuel Henderson and John G. Shorter. Henderson (1817–1890) was pastor for twenty-one years of the First Baptist Church in Tuskegee, Alabama, and was editor of the *South Western Baptist*. He was also a delegate to the Alabama secession convention, voting for immediate secession. *Encyclopedia of Southern Baptists* (4 vols., Nashville, 1958–82), 3: 1754.

5. Battle was pardoned June 30, 1866. Amnesty Papers (M1003, Roll 1), Ala., Cullen A. Battle, RG94, NA.

From Virginia C. Clay

Huntsville, Ala.   June 21st/66

My dear Sir:

At the request of a valued citizen & my friend, Robt. W. Coltarl,[1] I write to ask, that certified copies may be Sent me of his pardon, acceptance of the same, and amnesty oath,—which, it seems, are necessary to defend him against an indictment for treason—found, notwithstanding his pardon!

It appears that your Executive shield is no longer a protection from the peculation & plunder of those official cormorants, the Federal officers, who now hover like buzzards over the murdered carcass of the South. Your District Judge, Marshals & Attorneys,[2] confederates in robbery & spoliation, like the horse leech never cry, "*enough*." They pursue with libels & indictments for treason, those, who they are *well informed*, have pardons in their pockets! I speak by authority & can *establish all I say*. How long, my dear friend, how long are these alien enemies to glut themselves upon our blood & sweat? Will you not, without delay, muzzle them, by a *General Amnesty*, & save at least bread & water to the Empoverished South? Except the names of Mr. Davis, Mr. Clay or any body else, but relieve the *masses* for Humanity's, Mercy's & Justice's sakes.

The promised letter thro' Mr. Speed has *never reached me*. What does it mean? The blood-suckers will never let go till *you* choke them off. Two weeks have passed since your letter to me, thro' *Moore* [3] & yet no tidings! Shall I appeal to Mr. Speed, or will *you* be so Kind as to investigate the matter?

Please pardon me if I have written too strongly, but I *know* that *crimes* are committed in *your name* of which you have never heard & they keep me always indignant. I enclose to *our friend*, the lovely widow,[4] for safe delivery. I hope you are well & have not forgotten your true friend.[5]

V.C.C.

ALS, DLC-JP.

1. Coltart (c1822–1879), a merchant, had been Confederate marshal for northern Alabama. Pardoned September 29, 1865, he subsequently served several terms as Huntsville's mayor. 1850 Census, Ala., Madison, Huntsville, 919; Owen, *History of Ala.*, 3: 383; Amnesty Papers (M1003, Roll 2), Ala., Robert W. Coltart, RG94, NA.

2. Judge Richard Busteed, Marshals Edward E. Douglass and John Hardy, and District Attorney James Q. Smith.

3. Johnson's secretary, major, and assistant adjutant general of volunteers William G. Moore (1829–1898). Remaining in the army until 1870, he was later superintendent of the District of Columbia police. St. George L. Sioussat, "Notes of Colonel W.G. Moore, Private Secretary to President Johnson, 1866–1868," *AHR*, 19 (1913): 98–99.

4. Mary E. Bouligny. See Bouligny to Johnson, June 25, 1866, Johnson Papers, LC.

5. Johnson requested the State Department to "furnish duplicates" of Coltart's pardon, letter of acceptance, and amnesty oath. The department supplied a copy of the pardon but claimed the letter and oath had never been received. Coltart stated that he had received "an acknowledgement of the receipt of his letter of acceptance and amnesty oath;" it was hoped that "upon further examiniation" the papers would be found. Robert Morrow to William Hunter, July 20, 1866, Misc. Lets., 1789–1906 (M179, Roll 242), RG59, NA.

From Committee of Atchison and Pikes Peak Railroad Company

June 21, 1866, New York, N.Y.; DS, DLC-JP.

Effingham H. Nichols, treasurer, and Samuel C. Pomeroy, U.S. senator, on behalf of their fellow board members (of whom seventeen are listed) object to the pending bill before Congress to amend the Pacific Railroad Act "so as to enable the Kansas Branch, now known as the 'Union Pacific Railway, Eastern Division' to *re-file* the map by which their route is to be *determined* and *fixed* ANEW." They point out that they "have acted on the *faith* of this location and expended a million of dollars," and sold bonds and stock "on this *Supposition*;" that they "have graded their road for over *Sixty miles*, and there has been built and equipped and *accepted, twenty miles* by the Commissioners appointed by the President"; and that "the change of the line of the Eastern Division would take away the *westerly terminus* of the Atchison and Pikes Peak Railroad and would thus *materially injure* and damage the enterprise." The document concludes with a proposed amendment to "the Bill now awaiting the President's signature" which would give the Atchison Road authority to continue its line "westerly" from the point specified in the preceding Acts "to a connection with the Union Pacific Rail Road at some point east of the one hundredth meridian of Longitude."

From Jacob D. Cox

(Confidential)

Columbus, 21 June 1866

My dear Sir:

I enclose to you a copy of the Resolutions passed at our Union Party Convention yesterday,[1] and take the liberty of explaining very briefly my own view of the action of the Convention.

My strong efforts have been making for some time to ensure a declaration by the Party Convention of full & complete support of Congress as against yourself in the matter of reconstruction. I have constantly said to our more radical friends here that I would be content to abide by the teachings of *time* to prove which policy is the true one for the country, and that if they would confine themselves in the state platform to a simple enunciation of the necessity & propriety of protecting the civil rights of the freedmen, of reducing Southern Representation to a fair equality with ours, of repudiating the rebel war debt, *without* demanding of any Union man the abandonment of the doctrine of the right of immediate representation through loyal representatives, I would willingly waive all contest as to the specific endorsement of the policy of the administration. My belief has been that time has already worked so great changes in the policy if not the opinions of extreme men, that we can easily afford to let the same great causes work a little longer, provided these men would not insist upon platforms which should distinctly condemn the views we uphold.

The platform adopted here is the result of this compromise, and is as I believe the best attainable at the present moment. It is better for what it omits than for what it contains. You will notice that it does *not* affirm that the acceptance of the Constitutional amendment shall be a condition precedent to representation. It does not endorse any *expected* measures which Congress may add to its programme. It does not advocate or advise negro suffrage. It does not endorse any specific *act* of Congress whatever, but simply & solely the *amendment as it stands* & makes it a party measure *in Ohio* to vote for it.

For myself I heartily approve of all parts & sections of the amendment except the disqualifying clause substituted for the original third section. I believe that is unnecessary & impolitic—tending to exasperate the disease it professes to cure. But as in all such measures there must be some yielding of opinions, I cheerfully support the amendment, keeping myself entirely free from any pledges or trammels which would prevent my insisting upon the true policy in regard to representation at all times.

In the several Congressional Districts each Candidate must stand on his own record or his own platform, & I cannot help feeling sure that the result of the fall elections will be to teach the party what the country really demands, & that the crisis of our struggle with extremeism will have ended with the present session of Congress.

The action of this Convention justifies my prediction of what it would do, communicated to Gov. Dennison about a month since and strengthens my belief that with a little further exercise of patience we shall see the logic of events bringing the whole Union Party to the support of the true theory & practice of restoration. I feel that such a result is worth much calm & patient labor, and that the friends of your administration can well afford to make no quarrel with the action of the Convention, & to cooperate cheerfully in the State canvass, making meanwhile earnest & strenuous efforts to have the voice of the Congressional Districts what it should be in the election of new representatives.

I believe I coincide thoroughly in your plan of restoration, and have been deeply grieved at every obstacle which has been thrown in its way. I would not willingly go too slow in urging it upon the people, but after carefully viewing the ground here, it is my deliberate opinion that we have gained all we could reasonably hope from our State Convention, & that considering the opposing influences, the result is a real & substantial victory, which assures the final triumph.

Campbell & Geiger[2] doubted whether it was not best to force a direct issue upon the endorsement of your policy, but I am sure the result would have been unsatisfactory in every way.

Assuring you of my determination to continue a firm support of what I agree with you in regarding the true theory of restoration, asking only what is the most truly wise mode of reaching the desired end. . . .

                                                                    J.D. Cox

ALS, DLC-JP.
    1. Not found with this letter, the trio of resolutions passed during the Republican convention at Columbus may be found in *American Annual Cyclopaedia* (1866), 603–4. For a somewhat more negative report of the proceedings, see *Cincinnati Enquirer*, June 21, 1866. See also Lewis D. Campbell to Johnson, June 22, 1866, and Richard P.L. Baber to Johnson, June 28, 1866.
    2. Lewis D. Campbell and Joseph H. Geiger.

From Edmund H. Martin[1]

                                        Columbus [Ga.]   21st June 1866—

Sir

    In August last I sent on to Washington my petition for pardon[2] & have never heard from it since until within a few weeks, when I was notified by a Lawyer of Washington City that it was lying upon a table in some of your offices, and that if I would enclose him One hundred Dollars he would return it to me in ten days signed by your Excellency. I write simply to represent to your Excellency that I am unable to pay this fee & to make the request that I shall not be forced to do so. My petition shews that I have never borne arms nor taken any part in the late rebellion. Will your Excellency be pleased to examine this matter & return my petition signed to the Ordinary of Muscogee County.[3]

E.H. Martin

ALS, DLC-JP.

1. Martin (b. c1824), a former slave-holding planter in Meriwether County, Georgia, had applied for pardon under the thirteenth exception. Amnesty Papers (M1003, Roll 21), Ga., Edmund H. Martin, RG94, NA.

2. This petition apparently was lost, for Martin's earliest surviving pardon application was dated December 9, 1865. Ibid.

3. Martin was pardoned July 5, 1866. Muscogee County's ordinary was John Johnson, whose exact identity is unclear since at least three residents bore that name: a tailor (b. c1825), a farmer (b. c1810), and a factory operator (b. c1818). Ibid.; 1860 Census, Ga., Muscogee, Columbus, 68; New Dist., 34; 8th Dist., 60.

Pardon of Mary Blake

[June 21, 1866]

Whereas, at the March term 1866, of the United States Criminal Court of the District of Columbia one Mary Blake[1] was convicted of "Keeping a bawdy house" and sentenced to pay a fine of five hundred dollars and costs and to be imprisoned until said fine and costs be paid.

And whereas, I am assured by the Jury who convicted her that she is unable to pay the said fine and that the circumstances of her case render her a proper object of Executive clemency;[2]

Now, herefore, be it known, that I, Andrew Johnson, President of the United States of America, in consideration of the premises, divers other good and sufficient reasons me hereunto moving, have granted and do hereby grant to the said Mary Blake a full and unconditional pardon.

In testimony whereof I have hereunto signed my name and caused the Seal of the United States to be affixed. Done at the City of Washington, this Twenty first day of June, 1866 and of the Independence of the United States the Ninetieth.

Andrew Johnson

Copy, DNA-RG59, Pardons and Remissions, Vol. 8 (T967, Roll 3).

1. Mary Blake, a resident of Washington from 1863 to 1866, was arrested in March not only for "keeping a bawdy house" but also for receiving stolen goods. At the time of Johnson's pardon, she was also awaiting trial on a charge of larceny. *Washington Morning Chronicle*, Mar. 14–16, 25, June 5–7, 22, 27, 1866; *Washington Evening Star*, Mar. 15–16, June 5–6, 21, 26, 28, 1866; Washington, D.C., directories (1864–66).

2. Members of the jury and citizens petitioned Johnson that she be pardoned. However, some felt that a deal had been made for Blake to leave town and that some names had been

forged to the petition. Pardon Case File B-220, Mary Blake, RG204, NA; DeWitt C. Williams to Johnson, June 25, 1866, Johnson Papers, LC.

From Nathaniel G. Taylor

Private

Washington D. C.   June 21st 1866

Sir:—

Pardon the necessity which impells me to trouble you with a request for a personal favor.

If you esteem me honest and capable, and worthy I desire at your hands a lucrative appointment.

Commendatory letters, if desired, can be obtained without number, but you know me, and I prefer concentrating my obligations in and to yourself alone.

In the common cause of the Country my personal estate has been swept away: debts contracted in part to protect Union men from the rebel conscription—subsequently nearly all gallant Federal Soldiers—are even now concentrating upon and will absorb my real estate: a wife and nine children look to me for support and education: to meet their just demands, my salary if in hand, would scarcely be adequate, at present inflated prices: but you know even the salary is withheld, and I have been for several months at heavy expense and prevented from making a dollar.[1]

That is briefly my case. I know I have been true and faithful to the Country, and in my devotion I have lost all: it seems to me not unreasonable that in the service of the Government, I might ask some position which will enable me to discharge the duties I owe to my family, and if possible to restore to some little extent my ruined fortunes.

The office of Naval officer at New York—lately made vacant by the death of Hon. M. Odell,[2] I would most respectfully ask for. For it there are doubtless many aspirants—perhaps more capable and more deserving but certainly not more needy that I; and I am sure among them all, there is none more devoted to the principles the policy and the person of the President than I.[3] In this connection—it may not be improper to suggest that there is no point in the limits of the Union where a *vigilant* and *faithful confidential friend* of your Excellency is more needed—than in that great commercial and political centre.

If it is not convenient to assign me to the position indicated, you will excuse me for naming one other place now occupied by a gentleman, who I am informed has no special claims upon the fostering care of the President—namely Commissioner of Indian Affairs—occupied by Mr Cooley.[4] I would not however, by any means request the displacement, for my benefit, of any friend of your administration.

I should not have troubled you Mr President but for the purpose of a *present painful and urgent necessity*—which will compell me to *withdraw* from *Congressional life*—even if *admitted* to my *seat* in the House.

If you have it in your heart to aid me as desired—I believe you have it in your power to do so without detriment to the Country or to yourself.[5]

A response at your earliest convenience will oblige me.

N. G. Taylor

N.B.   If the above is unfavorably considered, please enclose this letter to me.

N. G. T.

ALS, DLC-JP.

1. Taylor had been elected to Congress in the special Tennessee elections held in August 1865, but he, along with all other Southern delegates, had been denied his seat by action of Congress in December. Consequently, Taylor had merely been biding his time for months, hoping to be seated. Ironically, he and all of the Tennessee delegation were permitted to take their places in Congress the month after his letter (upon the admission of Tennessee into the Union).

2. Moses F. Odell had died on June 13, 1866. Samuel Odell to McCulloch, June 13, 1866, Johnson Papers, LC; *BDAC*.

3. Johnson did not bestow the requested office upon Taylor. See Abel R. Corbin to Johnson, June 25, 1866.

4. Dennis N. Cooley had been nominated by Johnson as commissioner of Indian affairs in July 1865 but had not been confirmed by the Senate until April 1866. Cooley, a close ally of Secretary Harlan, resigned in October 1866 after Harlan resigned in the summer months of 1866. Robert M. Kvasnicka and Herman J. Viola, eds., *The Commissioners of Indian Affairs, 1824–1977* (Lincoln, 1979), 99–108.

5. To replace the resigned Cooley, Johnson first appointed Lewis V. Bogy to take office on November 1, 1866, but Congress opposed his nomination. Therefore, in the spring months of 1867, the President turned to Taylor and named him as commissioner of Indian affairs, a post which he held until his departure in April 1869. Ibid., 109–14, 116–22.

From Joseph A. Wright

Berlin [Prussia]   June 21st 66

My Dear President.

You doubtless watch with interest, the great events now transpiring throughout Europe, and I drop you this line, with the view of suggesting the propriety of having an American Man of War cruising near the mouth of the Elbe, looking to the protection of our shipping and trade from Hamburg, and Bremen. At this very *moment*, it would do us *great good*. I have suggested the same in my Despatch this day to friend Seward. Our trade and emigration at these two points, are greater than any other two ports in Europe, and other nations have their ships constantly cruising near these two ports.

You will pardon me for offering another suggestion also, and that is, to appoint as soon as possible, an *American* consul at Hamburg[1] for I do assure you, *at this time*, our interest requires, *not an adopted citizen*, but one who can represent our Country in all its varied interests. I was greatly pleased at the appointment of a (*true American*) Consul at Bremen,[2] and Hamburg is one of the most important positions, also connected as it is, with our commercial interests, and the rights of our adopted Citizens. Emigration &c. all tend to make it the more necessary, that the position of Consul be filled by a *native American*, possessing intelligence of *no ordinary character*. Do my dear President, take one moment to lay this matter before the Secretary, I have not a doubt he will agree with my suggestion.

It looks to day as if we should soon have a terrible battle between Austria & Prussia.[3] Thank heaven, we have escaped from farther struggle of Arms, and tho we may have a contest at home, I have *not a doubt* the fall Elections will settle all disputes, and the rights of *every portion* of our great republic shall be represented in the National Legislature by *loyal men*, sustaining your well known, and oft repeated opinions. I know the value of your time, and will not trespass farther.

Mrs Wright desires to be remembered to yourself & family.

Joseph A. Wright

ALS, DLC-JP.
1. Samuel T. Williams, although nominated in December 1866, was not commissioned for this post until February 1867. Ser. 6B, Vol. 2: 358, Johnson Papers, LC.
2. George S. Dodge (1838–1881), a Vermont-born former merchant and chief quartermaster of the Army of the James, was commissioned consul to Bremen on June 26, replacing Henry Boernstein, a native of Hamburg. Ibid., 57; Hunt and Brown, *Brigadier Generals*; *U.S. Off. Reg.* (1865).
3. After Prussia's defeat of Schleswig-Holstein, Saxony, and Hanover, Prussian and Austrian forces met in Bohemia. The most decisive encounter was the Battle of Sadowa (July 3, 1866), in which the Austrian army was defeated by Prussian forces. With the Treaty of Prague on August 23, 1866, Prussia established the North German Confederation, eventually to become *the* German Empire in 1871, and Austria was excluded from German affairs and formed the Austro-Hungarian Empire. See Wright to Johnson, May 2, 1866; *American Annual Cyclopaedia* (1866), 366; Kohn, *Dictionary of Wars*, 417.

From Lewis D. Campbell

(Private)

Hamilton O.   June 22, 1866.

Dear Sir—

I have been all week at Columbus attending our State Convention and have just returned home. It would be impossible to give you *in a letter* an intelligible account of the doings of that body. You had many friends in the Convention notwithstanding the radical members of Congress had labored to pack it with delegates from the ranks of your enemies. I think, nevertheless, that we should have succeeded in having a resolution approving your official course; but for certain causes which I will state briefly.

1st.   One third at least of the delegates to the Convention was composed of the Revenue Collectors, their assistants and clerks—the Assessors and their horde of assistants (all of whom were originally selected by

Mr. Chase from the most ultra radical element in Ohio). To these were added the Post Masters who are generally of the same class. Marshal Sands,[1] P.M. Myer of Cincinnati,[2] Collector of Customs Stephenson,[3] Pension Agent Davis[4] and all their *subs* were on hand laboring to prevent any expression in your favor, on the *pretext* that it would prevent *harmony*.

2nd.   On the morning of the Convention Col. Burnett[5] arrived at Columbus fresh from Washington, and it was forthwith actively circulated that he had whilst there had a protracted interview with you and that you had expressly stated that you would be *satisfied* if the Convention simply indorsed the Constitutional amendment passed by Congress without any other action. This knocked all the calculations of your friends in the head, and completely disconcerted all the plans which I with others had been laboring for, for many months. Your real friends under such circumstances could do nothing more than temporarily *subside* and conceal, as well as they could, their chagrin and mortification. We held private Conferences and transferred the fight to Congressional Districts, in which we are organized. Your friends, I must however, add, seem greatly *discouraged*, because your most active and *vindictive opponents* are permitted to hold the Federal patronage. If this cannot be remedied, it is my candid opinion we shall make a poor fight in Ohio. Otherwise we may carry several Congressional districts.

Your friend(?) the *Rev.* Gaddis[6] *fell early*. I hope you will remember that *Geiger*[7] *and I declined to recommend him for Assessor*. Well, he was of no earthly benefit to your friends at the Convention. At the ratification meeting in the evening he was called on and made a speech in which he substantially *denied* that he was a *Johnson* man, and expressed himself satisfied with the course of Congress. He said also that there was *no material difference* between you and Congress. Your other friend(?) Gen Carey[8] was not there; but so soon as he is *confirmed* you may expect to hear of his following in the footsteps of the illustrious Gaddis!

Pardon me for obtruding myself upon you with these annoyances. I thought it was right to give you an outline of what has been done. I confess my mortification and am about becoming disgusted with mankind generally.

Kate is to be married on Tuesday next or I should have gone to Washington from Columbus. I may go on in ten days to see you about Mexican affairs &c. and will then if you give me opportunity and desire it, present you with a more detailed account of the condition of things in Ohio.[9] You should be informed, particularly, of the conduct of the men who have betrayed your cause, and mortified your friends.

Lewis D Campbell

ALS, DLC-JP.
1. Alexander C. Sands.
2. A Hamilton County commissioner during most of the war, Frederick J. Mayer

(c1822–fl1881), a saddler, was removed from the postmastership in December 1866 and afterwards returned to the saddle business. 1860 Census, Ohio, Hamilton, Cincinnati, 10th Ward, 46; Cincinnati directories (1861–81); *U.S. Off. Reg.* (1867).

3. Commissioned in February 1866 as surveyor of customs at Cincinnati, Reuben H. Stephenson (1822–fl1881), a former teacher, librarian, and attorney, was removed later in the year and replaced in 1867 by Bvt. Gen. George W. Neff. Early in Grant's administration, however, Stephenson was reappointed as surveyor and served for nearly a decade. Henry A. and Kate B. Ford, comps., *History of Cincinnati, Ohio, with Illustrations and Biographical Sketches* (Cleveland, 1881), 485; Chapman, *Alumni of Dartmouth*, 359; Ser. 6B, Vol. 4: 256–57, Johnson Papers, LC; *U.S. Off. Reg.* (1869–81); Hugh McCulloch to Johnson, Sept. 20, 1866, Lets. Sent *re* Customs Service Employees (QC Ser.), Vol. 4, RG56, NA.

4. A former war correspondent of the *Cincinnati Gazette*, William E. Davis (1831–fl1877) remained a pension agent for several more years, then organized and managed a newspaper publishing company, served as president of a railroad, and was appointed by Grant as a U.S. assistant treasurer at Cincinnati. *Ohio of the Nineteenth Century*, 649–51; Cincinnati directories (1865–79).

5. Henry L. Burnett.

6. Maxwell P. Gaddis (1811–1888), a former Methodist circuit rider, served as assessor of the Second District of Ohio, from his commissioning on June 18, 1866, until his resignation on August 31, 1868. Coyle, *Ohio Authors*, 231; Ser. 6B, Vol. 4: 256, Johnson Papers, LC; Gaddis to Johnson, Aug. 31, 1868, Appts., Internal Revenue Service, Assessor, Ohio, 2nd Dist., M. P. Gaddis, RG56, NA.

7. Joseph H. Geiger.

8. Samuel F. Cary.

9. He did go to Washington. See Campbell to Johnson, July 17, 1866.

Message re *Amending the Constitution*

June 22, 1866

To the Senate and House of Representatives:

I submit to Congress a report[1] of the Secretary of State, to whom was referred the concurrent resolution of the 18th instant,[2] respecting a submission to the legislatures of the States of an additional article to the Constitution of the United States. It will be seen from this report that the Secretary of State had, on the 16th instant, transmitted to the governors of the several States certified copies of the joint resolution passed on the 13th instant, proposing an amendment to the Constitution.

Even in ordinary times any question of amending the Constitution must be justly regarded as of paramount importance. This importance is at the present time enhanced by the fact that the joint resolution was not submitted by the two houses for the approval of the President, and that of the thirty-six States which constitute the Union, eleven are excluded from representation in either House of Congress, although, with the single exception of Texas, they have been entirely restored to all their functions as States, in conformity with the organic law of the land, and have appeared at the national capital by senators and representatives who have applied for and have been refused admission to the vacant seats. Nor have the sovereign people of the nation been afforded an opportunity of expressing their views upon the important questions which the amendment involves. Grave doubts, therefore, may naturally and justly arise as to whether the action of Congress is in harmony with the sentiments of the people, and whether State legislatures, elected without reference to such an issue, should be called upon by Congress to decide respecting the ratification of the proposed amendment.

Waiving the question as to the constitutional validity of the proceedings of Congress upon the joint resolution proposing the amendment, or as to the merits of the article which it submits, through the executive department, to the legislatures of the States, I deem it proper to observe that the steps taken by the Secretary of State, as detailed in the accompanying report, are to be considered as purely ministerial, and in no sense whatever committing the Executive to an approval or a recommendation of the amendment to the State legislatures or to the people. On the contrary, a proper appreciation of the letter and spirit of the Constitution, as well as of the interests of national order, harmony, and union, and a due deference for an enlightened public judgment, may at this time well suggest a doubt whether any amendment to the Constitution ought to be proposed by Congress, and pressed upon the legislatures of the several States for final decision, until after the admission of such loyal senators and representatives of the now unrepresented States as have been or as may hereafter be chosen in conformity with the Constitution and laws of the United States.

Andrew Johnson

PD, *Senate Ex. Docs.*, 39 Cong., 1 Sess., No. 57, pp. 1–2 (Ser. 1238).
    1. See Seward to Johnson, *Senate Ex. Docs.*, 39 Cong., 1 Sess., No. 57, p. 2 (Ser. 1238).
    2. Ibid.

From William L. Sharkey

Jackson   June 22st 1866

Sir

I take the liberty of introducing to your acquaintance my friend and fellow citizen J T Lampkin Esqr,[1] who visits Washington with a view to obtain his pardon, as his condition is somewhat embarrassing in regard to his private matters in consequence of not having been pardoned.

Mr. Lampkin's political anticedents were of the most unexceptionable character. He was decidedly and actively opposed to secession, and did what he could to prevent it. But unfortunately for him his friends I think without any agency of his own, and when the odium of having been a union man had somewhat died out, elected him to the last session of the Confederate Congress; and "this is the head and front of his offending."[2] He is anxious to be restored to his former position as a citizen of the United States, which he never voluntarily abandoned. He is doing what he can to produce harmony in the country, and it will confer a great favor on him if he can be pardoned.[3]

W. L. Sharkey

ALS, DNA-RG94, Amnesty Papers (M1003, Roll 33), Miss., John T. Lamkin.
1. John T. Lamkin (1811–1870), a Holmesville, Mississippi, lawyer, had been a captain in the army before his election to the Second Confederate Congress. Wakelyn, *BDC*, 275–76.
2. From Shakespeare's *Othello*, act 1, sc. 3, line 80.
3. Lamkin's pardon was issued July 3, 1866. Amnesty Papers (M1003, Roll 33), Miss., John T. Lamkin, RG94, NA.

From James Diamond[1]

Toronto Old Jail C. West
June 23rd 1866

Sir,

On the morning of the 2nd Inst I went over from Buffalo to the Cannadian side, hearing of the great excitement being there. There were a great many went over to see what was going on. When we were returning we would not be allowed by a Cannadian guard. I went to the U.S. Council at Fort Erie. and got a pass from him to cross but when I presented it to the Corporal of the guard he took it and went to a higher officer. and I did not see it from that forth. They arrested me afterwards as prisoner (in the name of the Queen) searched me thoroughly but found nothing on me but 4 likenesses of young men & young women—and a 10 dollar bill u. s. money, all of which they kept. They told me they arrested me on suspision of being a Fenian. All I could say would not avail. They sent me to this Place, and here I am since without any trial, and do not know when we will have any. My mother and one brother & 3 sisters[2] are still in Nashville Tennessee. The eldest of them is only a little over 10 years old. I am a moulder by trade and I youst to send them all I could spare. I served in your own Redgment the 10th Tennessee for 3 years & one month. Captain Joyce[3] was my Captain Co. B. Cournal Gilliam[4] our Cournal. and when I was discharged by an Honourable discharge— Cournal Scully[5] was our Cournal. I afterwards got my Citizenship papers. Hoping to your Honour that you will do something for me, to get me out of this Place—

James Diamond

Please write immediately. Direct for James Diamond prisoner. Care of the american Council at Toronto

ALS, DNA-RG59, Misc. Lets., 1789–1906 (M179, Roll 240).
1. Diamond (*c*1843–1898), a native of Galway County, Ireland, was apparently a laborer at Nashville's Claiborne Machine Works before his enlistment. He had been in Buffalo only a month before his arrest, and sometime after his release resumed work as a moulder in Nashville. But because of ill health he later clerked in a dry goods store. CSR, James Diamond, RG94, NA; Pension Records, Julia Diamond, RG15, NA; *New York World*, June 8, 1866; *Williams' Nashville City and Business Directory* (1860–61).

2. Information about Diamond's mother and siblings has not been located.

3. Railroad contractor and farmer Miles Joyce (c1819–1871), also an Irish native, apparently lived in Virginia before coming to Tennessee. After the war he was a Nashville grocer. Pension Records, Margaret J. Joyce, RG15, NA; 1870 Census, Tenn., Davidson, Nashville, 4th Ward, 39.

4. Alvan C. Gillem.

5. James W. Scully.

From Ward H. Lamon

Washington D.C.   June 23rd 1866

Mr. President

Many of your warmest friends, from delicacy, have refrained from troubling you with their views relative to removals from, and appointments to office—considering that you would in due time on your own motion make all needful changes,—and while they have still no wish to influence such appointments, it may be proper for them to place before you facts in regard to those now holding responsible and lucrative positions. There seems to be a determination on the part of some representative men to do that which the Southern people failed to accomplish viz. the destruction of the Country. Mr. Lincoln's Administration as well as his good name suffered much by the men who are now on the corners of the Streets denouncing you as a Traitor.

The reputation and good name of the Executive should be as sacred as his life or his person, and justice to yourself requires that you should know who these office holding Assassins are.

It would enable me to discharge a duty which I owe to my country to call upon you at such time as may suit your convenience, and give you the names of some of your traducers who are holding office—whom I believe should speedily have an opportunity of earning a livelihood in some other way than by traducing the Government which supports them.

I have no one to suggest for their places, but I doubt not many who have done their Country real service in her hour of trial can be found who would be able and willing to fill the places of the present unworthy incumbents.

Ward H Lamon

ALS, DLC-JP.

From Dan Rice[1]

Girard [Pa.]   June 23rd 1866

Respected Sir

Your kind favor was duly recid.[2] I regret that I should have been so *thoughtless* as to put a question to you in relation to the Governorship of Pennsylvania. Now to business. This 19th District needs overhauling.

Judge Scofield[3] the present representative is a *bitter foe*. M. B. Lowry[4] of
the State Senate still worse; by an arrangement between these two *radical worthies* Scofield is to be sent back to Congress. They have their favor-
ites in office who are loud in their denunciations against the President
and his Administration. This District is thoroughly radical and will enter its protest this fall at the ballot box against you, if some thing is not
done to defeat it. The question then is how can it be done?

I will tell you. This Congressional District gives a majority of from
seventeen hundred to two thousand majority against the Democrats, and
this county furnished nearly the whole majority. I propose to bring out a
Candidate for Congress A sort of people's Candidate on a *Johnson Union
Platform* &c &c.[5] Scofield & Lowry have neglected the interest of Soldiers who having fought for their Country are disabled for life, and ought
to have positions which are filled by persons who are time serving tools of
Scofield & Lowry. By turning them out *forth with*, appointing Soldiers in
their places which will carry all the Soldiers votes and they are very
numerous in this county united with the Democrats who will not make a
Nomination which will without doubt defeat Scofield or any other man
who may be nominated by the Radical Convention. The Collector of Internal Revenue of this 19th District John W. Douglass,[6] your Conservative Republican friends as well as Democrats have no love for. You can not
depend on him, although recently he has been "*mum*" and may have seen
you.[7] But he "*will not do to tie to*" and the reason he keeps the position is
from the fact that he is related to the *Hon. M. B. Lowry* and divides
the profits of the office with Judge Scofield[8] or contributes liberaly to
the Freedman's Bureau. *Excuse the joke*. The assistant Assessor T. C.
Wheeler[9] publicly declares you ought to be impeached and then hung.
He denounces Seward, Stanton and yourself as traitors to the party that
elected you &c &c. I have talked with him and found him unworthy of the
position he holds. Daniel Livingston[10] is the head assessor of this District. I shall know more of his views in the course of a few weeks. The
Collector of Customs for the port of Erie and the Post Master[11] are and
have been against you and have no delicacy in denouncing you on all occasions where it will make you enemies. I do not know who to reccomend
to fill their places as yet but when I discover good Johnson Republicans, I
will at once forward their petitions. I should prefer Soldiers who have the
ability to discharge the duties of office with credit to you and honor to
themselves. The whole of North Western Penna are in favor of Soldiers
holding office which disconcerts the politicians very much. It is the most
popular move you can make, besides doing justice to the noble men who
have sacrificed so much for the Republic to put them in office, which I
know you are desirous of doing if you possibly can. Consequently I am
very particular in examining as to qualifications, character and worthi-
ness, which no man would be apt to do if he had a political "ax to grind"
which God knows *I* have not, neither do I want office or money. But I

busy myself in this good work entirely from principles and as far as the interest of the Soldiers is concerned I delight in accomplishing that which will comfort them.

I send you a petition to appoint Andrew F. Swan.[12] A Lieut Col. he is a Republican a brave, noble young man with an unblemished character and perfectly idolized throughout this County but is in bad favor with Scofield who insulted him by intimating that he could secure an appointment for him as Collector of Internal Revenue for this 19th District if Swan would guarantee him one thousand dollars, or some thing to that effect. Now I do hope you will at once appoint him. Do not fail to do so. And then you will have every Soldier in Erie County shouting God bless Andy Johnson. Also appoint as assistant Assessor 19th District in place of T. C. Wheeler, William Hopkins[13] of Erie County who lost a leg at the battle of Gettysburg. He belonged to the 111th Reg't Penna Vol. He is qualified to discharge the duties of the office, has a family dependent upon him and the appointment would be hailed with great joy by every one excepting Lowry, Scofield & Co.

If you have any suggestions to make or instructions to give please write me as soon as convenient.

Dan Rice

ALS, DLC-JP.

1. Rice (1823–1900) was a popular circus entertainer and political humorist who, following his unsuccessful bid for the presidency in 1868 and a long bout with alcoholism, became a temperance lecturer. *DAB*.

2. Nearly two months after a protracted interview with the President in early April, Rice had written Johnson, informing him of his many public appearances on behalf of the administration and asking whether the Chief Executive favored any candidate in the upcoming Pennsylvania gubernatorial contest. Johnson's reply, however, has not been found. Rice to Johnson, June 1, 1866, Johnson Papers, LC; *Washington Evening Star*, Apr. 7, 1866.

3. Glenni W. Scofield (1817–1891) served in Congress for six successive terms (1863–75) before his appointment as register of the treasury (1878–81) and as associate justice of the U.S. court of claims (1881–91). *BDAC*.

4. A Democrat until Buchanan's presidency, when he became a Republican and a Cameron supporter, Morrow B. Lowry (1813–c1876) was later elected to the state senate and aligned himself with the Liberal Republicans. Erie directories (1875–77); *Biographical Encyclopaedia of Pa.*, 559–60; Bradley, *Cameron*, 144, 327; Bradley, *Militant Republicanism*, 366, 379, 418.

5. Perhaps here Rice had himself in mind. Nominated by several citizens of Crawford and Erie counties and endorsed in August 1866 by ex-soldiers residing in the Nineteenth District, Rice styled himself as a "People's" or "Andy Johnson" candidate in the fall election campaign, before he eventually withdrew from the race. Maria W. Brown, *The Life of Dan Rice* (Long Branch, N.J., 1901), 147–48, 417–18, 421–22; Rice to Johnson, ca. Aug. 1866, Johnson Papers, LC.

6. Appointed by Lincoln in 1862 and subsequently reappointed by Johnson, Douglass (1827–1909) continued as revenue collector for the Nineteenth District until the end of Johnson's term. Afterwards he served as Grant's commissioner of internal revenue (1871–75) and practiced law in Washington, D.C. *Who Was Who in America*, 1: 336; Benjamin Whitman, *Historical Reference Book* (Erie, Pa., 1896), 263; *U.S. Off. Reg.* (1865–67).

7. Douglass had reportedly seen Johnson several weeks earlier. *Philadelphia Evening Bulletin*, May 5, 1866.

8. Both Lowry and Scofield had urged Douglass's reappointment. See M. B. Lowry to

Johnson, Aug. 28, 1865, Jan. 1, 1866; G. W. Scofield to Johnson, Aug. 26, 1865, Appts., Internal Revenue Service, Collector, Pa., 19th Dist., J. W. Douglass, RG56, NA.

9. Wheeler co-owned the Girard *Republican,* formerly *Express. History of Erie County, Pennsylvania* (Chicago, 1884), 849.

10. Livingston (b. *c*1820) was a tailor. 1850 Census, Pa., Clearfield, Pike Twp., 574. See Rice to Johnson, July 31, 1866.

11. Thomas Wilkins and Joseph M. Sterrett, respectively. Wilkins (*c*1796–*c*1870) had been recommissioned as customs collector at Erie in February 1866. Sterrett (1800–*fl*1887) was a former newspaper publisher, Whig senator, and associate judge of the county court. Both men remained in office throughout Johnson's administration. Erie directories (1861–87); *Erie County,* 957; Whitman, *Reference Book,* 263; Ser. 6B, Vol. 4: 83, Johnson Papers, LC.

12. A recommendation for Swan (1832–1876), who rose in rank from private to brevet lieutenant colonel during the war and was later elected sheriff of Erie County, is enclosed. Swan had been mentioned as a possible replacement for Douglass for some time. Rice to Johnson, June 23, 1866, Johnson Papers, LC; *Erie County* (Township Biographies), 44; Morrow B. Lowry to Johnson, Jan. 1, 1866, Appts., Internal Revenue Service, Collector, 19th Dist., Pa., J. W. Douglass, RG56, NA. See also Rice to Johnson, July 31, 1866.

13. Rice afterwards changed his mind regarding Hopkins (1838–1923), and nominated him instead for the Girard postmastership and John L. Hart, another veteran, for the assessorship. But Hopkins was not appointed and Hart did not receive Wheeler's post, though Hart did later serve for several months as postmaster of Girard. Rice to Johnson, Sept. 13, 1866, Appts., Internal Revenue Service, Assessor, 19th Dist., Pa., John L. Hart, RG56, NA; Pension Records, William Hopkins, RG15, NA; *U.S. Off. Reg.* (1867).

From Amos Shurtleff[1]

Decaturville, Tenn.   June 23rd 1866

Dr Sir:

You will I trust generously pardon me for addressing you upon the subject of affairs in this portion of Tennessee. Mr. Arnell, congressman elect,[2] is here organizing a "Union League,"[3] which will, I fear, seriously impair usefulness of some of your friends. Thousands of hearts are beating anxiously for you and the cause of the Union. You have a host of political friends here, but we have no organization, and I fear that the Franchise law lately passed[4] will be made to bear as hard upon your friends, as upon rebels, What shall we do? If consistent please advise me.

I am trying, by addressing the people publicly, from time to time, to help along, in my contracted sphere of influence, but wish to do more.

All we ask is a fair show.

We do not like the prospect of having the Franchise Law, employed by the Radicals against *us.*

Pardon this intrusion and believe me faithfully and sincerely Yours.

Amos Shurtleff

ALS, DLC-JP.

1. Not identied.

2. Samuel M. Arnell (1833–1903) was seated in Congress in 1866, along with the other members of the Tennessee delegation, and served until 1871. Afterwards he practiced law in Washington before returning to Tennessee, where he served as Columbia postmaster and subsequently as superintendent of schools. He had gained notoriety in 1865 as the principal author of the controversial franchise law enacted by the Brownlow legislature. *BDAC; BDTA,* 2: 26–27; Alexander, *Reconstruction,* 86–87.

3. The Union League became a political club to which Radical Republicans belonged. Chapters of the Union League spread to Tennessee with Federal occupation during the war years. There was a flurry of organizing activity in 1866 in Tennessee; subsequently when black franchise became a reality, Union Leagues sprouted up to secure blacks more firmly within the Radical Republican ranks. See ibid., 142–44.

4. See Samuel P. Walker to Johnson, Feb. 18, 1866, and Memphis Citizens Committee to Johnson, May 28, 1866.

From H. L. Carrick[1]

Sparta, Tennessee   25 June 1866.

Sir:

I have what I conceive to be an indisputably just claim against the government, originating in acts of Governor Brownlow while he was acting as Treasury Agent, and being unable in consequence of the perverseness of the Governor to present it in shape satisfactory to the Secretary of the Treasury, I take the liberty of addressing you directly although I am aware, that in doing so, I violate the rules governing the business of the departments.

The case is this. In 1863 Gov. B. came across a lot of Cotton yarn, I had at Athens, Tennessee, and at once determined to confiscate it, he had it conveyed to Knoxville there sold it for $1650 (Without libelling it and procuring a decree of a competent court decreeing its sale) and, *as he says*, paid the money into the Treasury.

I have just received a letter from Mr Hughes[2] claim agent for Tennessee informing me that the books of the Treasury department do not show from *what* source the money paid into the Treasury by the Governor was derived and the Governor's son, Col. John Brownlow now having charge of the Custom house books at Knoxville refusing to let my friend at that place, have a copy of the transaction, from all of which, it would seem that I am at the end of my row unless your Excellency will order an investigation of the matter and thereby afford me that relief and justice, which the *Governor* of Tennessee refuses.

I presume an order from the Treasury department requiring the Gov. to furnish a statement of the source from which the money was derived that he paid into the Treasury would be respected and complied with.[3] Mr. Hughs (claim agent) has my claim in his possession, accompanied by such proofs as I deemed necessary to enable me to successfully prosecute my claim.

Mr. F. S. Heiskell of Knox Co who you doubtless well know, has furnished me with the facts of the *seizure & sale* of the yarn in question.

H. L. Carrick

ALS, DNA-RG56, Misc. Div., Claims for Cotton and Captured and Abandoned Property.

1. Carrick (c1810–fl1870) was the court clerk of White County. 1860 Census, Tenn., White, Sparta, 6; (1870), 1st Dist., 25; Goodspeed's *White*, 804.

2. James Hughes.

3. Johnson's response evidently was restricted to forwarding Carrick's letter to the secretary of the treasury for "consideration & action." See file cover sheet accompanying the Carrick letter; Ser. 4A, Vol. 4: 118, Johnson Papers, LC.

From William C. Clarke[1]

Manchester N.H.   June 25, 1866.

I learn that Hon. Daniel Clark, Senator in Congress, is a candidate for the office of U.S. Judge for the District of New Hampshire.

It would be superfluous to speak of his character as known at Washington. I wish simply to say that Mr. Clark occupies a very eminent position in this state as a Lawyer and gentleman and that his appointment to the office would give great satisfaction.[2]

Wm. C. Clarke

ALS, DNA-RG60, Appt. Files for Judicial Dists., N.H., D. Clark.

1. A former War Democrat who helped organize the Union Party of New Hampshire, Clarke (1810–1872) was the state's attorney general from 1863 until his death. Hurd, *Hillsborough County*, 20–22.

2. Also recommended by the New Hampshire governor and various members of the legislature, as well as nearly fifty Congressmen and fellow Senators, Clark was nominated by Johnson on July 27 and confirmed by the Senate on the same day. Shortly afterwards the senator sent Johnson his acceptance of the appointment. See Appt. Files for Judicial Dists., N.H., Daniel Clark, RG60, NA; Ser. 6B, Vol. 4: 10, Johnson Papers, LC.

From Abel R. Corbin[1]

Personal & Private.

No. 37, West 27th Street, New York City,
June 25th 1866.

My Dear Sir:

On the day Gen. Scott was buried[2] you were so good as to favor me with a long interview, during which you clearly explained the immutable principles upon which you have based the excellent and judicious actions of your Presidential life. On my return home next day I called at the office of the N. York Evening Post to see my venerable old friend Wm. C. Bryant,[3] as I *longed* to explain to him your noble act of justice to his Illinois brother[4] whom you had recently restored to his office in the Internal Revenue Service. Unfortunately he was detained at his home in the country by the severe illness of his aged wife.[5] I hope, however, to see him ere long back in his office; for although he differs with you on some points, yet, *at bottom*; he wants *to do right*, and has a sincere respect for both your abilities and your intentions. This is saying much, but not too much. He is your earnest & honest friend.

A few words on *the Policy* of Custom House appointments. You will excuse me, I know, for what I am about to say, even though I may err; for you know I seek to benefit you, and *have no candidates* to thurst on your attention; but I believe you will think me right, and that the following suggestions ought to be *kept in view* when appointing the Naval Officer of the New York Custom House.

The Custom House has three principal officers, each comparatively independent of the others—the Collector; the Surveyor of the Port; the Naval Officer. The first two are residents of this city—Smythe, & Wakeman;[6] the latter is a Connecticut lawyer of many years residence here, and Mr. Smythe is a New York merchant many years connected with the Boston trade.

New York State is very large in territory and has more than 4,000,000 of people. I want the Naval Officer taken from the State, *outside* of the City; I want an honest & capable man, but I also want an *influential man* who knows the State, and who can help *efficiently* in organizing & directing a Johnson party that will have numbers, power, & *vim*.

Again. It is urged upon you, (I am told,) to appoint a *"Gen. Grant man"* (Col. Hillyer) to the Naval Office.[7] How would that *policy* work?

If you desire to *exclude yourself* from the canvass of 1868; if you wish to wield your official power in behalf of Gen. Grant for President in 1868 and *against everybody else*, yourself included, *then* put a "Grant man" into the Naval Office: for if the Collector, & the Surveyor, on *any* occasion, failed to do *anything* for Grant's advancement which his superserviceable friends might choose to dictate they would be denounced by their associate as "an enemy to Grant"! He would be a constant thorn in their side, a spy in the camp.

No, no. All Johnson men, or all radicals; but do not appoint any *from our side* who are for anybody but you: when the time comes should you *then* decline a canvass, it *will be time enough* to appoint men who are looking towards other men than yourself for President. I pray you, my exalted friend, not to overlook the importance of appointing only known friends. Of these you have countless numbers; they are not difficult to find.

Do you not recollect the fact that Gen. Butterfield—a man originally from the middle of this State—on hearing of the pecuniary embarrassments of Gen. Grant, went among our people and raised for him $105,000?[8] This man—a gentleman of rare education & talents, and of very high position *all over the State*—was a candidate for Collector of New York; when the struggle waxed hot, & he feared you would be injured, he promptly went to you & withdrew his name, saying that he was for you, not because he wanted the office, but because you were right, and the interests of the country demanded that you should be thoroughly sustained. He is the sort of "Grant man" to be sustained—one that believes you are as superior in the Cabinet as Grant is in the field. But, my dear Sir, that reliable class of men is not the class being pushed on you—I do not hear him even named—but the Hillyers are being crowded upon you by every little editor in the land. I hope you will be able to avoid one class & to secure the other. Suppose, at the advent of the fall elections, we attempt to raise the necessary means to defray the ordinary expenses. Could Hillyer raise $500 if it would save his life? Who would trust him? Whereas Butterfield could collect a quarter of a million in a week—why is this so? Because everybody knows he is honest, honorable, & *has brains* —he has the confidence of the community. I have said this much, not to censure the one nor to praise the other, but to be able to show clearly to Your Excellency my idea of two large classes of men from whence appointments are likely to come. One class represents *the adventurers* and the other *the solid men* of New York—one is *tolerated* in society, the other *leads* society. The first are pretty sure to fasten on to men like Gen. Grant as the most likely way to achieve success. To show you how they get up papers to *influence you* I send to you a despactch[9] sent to me by a man who had to remind me where I had met him that I might know who he was! As he claimed to be your very ardent friend, he supposed I would be glad to forward any scheme he would recommend! He evidently could see no impolicy in placing a "Grant man" into the "*leader-team*" of the N. York Custom House! Leading officials may be able to drag Grant into the next canvass: but if we treat Grant well, without recognizing distinctive "Grant men", & bringing them forward *as such*, he will not be a candidate; he is too poor and cant afford so soon to give up his present valuable position. If we create a large corps of noisy "Grant men" they will try to perpetuate themselves in office by striving to make him run even against his interest.[10]

A.R. Corbin.

ALS, DLC-JP.

1. Corbin (1808–1880), a former publisher of the St. Louis *Missouri Argus* and clerk of a congressional committee on claims, later married a sister of General Grant. *New York Times*, Mar. 29, 1880.

2. Winfield Scott was buried on June 1, 1866.

3. The editor and co-proprietor of the *New York Post*, Bryant (1794–1878), who was also a renowned lyric poet, favored a liberal postwar policy toward the South. *DAB*.

4. A prominent landowner, Republican legislator, and businessman of Princeton, Illinois, John H. Bryant (1807–1902) had been appointed by Lincoln as collector of the Fifth Illinois District and removed by Johnson in mid-December 1865. Restored to his position in May, Bryant—admitting his profound political differences with Johnson—resigned in September 1866, only to withdraw his resignation in February 1867. Soon afterwards, however, he was removed for the second time and William Kellogg was given his commission. Ibid.; Ser. 6B, Vol. 4: 299, 302, Johnson Papers, LC; Bryant to Hugh McCulloch, Dec. 22, 1865, Feb. 2, 1867; Bryant to Johnson, Sept. 14, 1866, Appts., Internal Revenue Service, Collector, 5th Dist., Ill., John H. Bryant, RG56, NA; *U.S. Off. Reg.* (1863–67).

5. Frances Fairchild Bryant (c1796–1866) died shortly afterwards. *DAB*; *New York Herald*, July 29, 1866.

6. Henry A. Smythe and Abram Wakeman.

7. For General Grant's recommendation of William S. Hillyer, which was later forwarded to the President, see his letter to James R. Doolittle, July 5, 1866, Simon, *Grant Papers*, 16: 227.

8. Daniel Butterfield successfully raised the funds and gave them to Grant in mid-February 1866. *DAB*.

9. Enclosed is J. D. Perryman to Corbin, June 15, 1866. Perryman urged Corbin to telegraph his endorsement of Hillyer to the President and reminded Corbin that they had earlier been introduced by "Doctor Maynard."

10. John A. Dix was Johnson's first choice for the post, but Dix soon resigned in order to accept the French mission which had also been offered to him. In September Hillyer withdrew his application for the appointment as naval officer, in favor of a more "prominent soldier," Gen. Henry W. Slocum, whose nomination the Senate ultimately rejected. Hillyer to Johnson, Sept. 17, 1866; Dix to Johnson, Nov. 21, 1866, Appts., Customs Service, Naval Officer, New York, William S. Hillyer, John A. Dix, RG56, NA; Beale, *Welles Diary*, 2: 602; Ser. 6B, Vol. 2: 58; Vol. 3: 95; Vol. 4: 54, Johnson Papers, LC.

From Thomas Hynes[1]

Mount Joy Prison   Dublin, June 25, 1866.

Honorable Sir—

Having applied in vain to the Representatives of our Government here for that protection, to which as citizens of the Great Republic we feel justly entitled, we call upon you, Mr. President, Knowing that you of all men are the person who has it in his power to aid us.

To me it is incomprehensible why the United States authorities permit us to remain the victims of a foreign despotism. Treated as the vilest criminals—shut up in convict cells, and laughed at if we speak of our adopted country. I have committed no crime, or violated no law, and I am sure that the same is the case with scores of my fellow citizens whom I daily see, but to whom it is a crime to speak. Mr West[2] the U. States Consul here in Dublin, told me, that his position had become a very humiliating one, since *all* the *requests* and demands which he made, were made with the foreknowledge that they would be refused. *This very fact* is enough to make an American blush. We are told plainly, that we are subjects of Her Majesty—documents to the contrary, not withstanding. I am a cripple—never bore arms and never can. Should my imprisonment be prolonged I will be ruined for life. I hope, Mr President, you will do as you have heretofore done—remember the suffering—and at the same time, vindicate our national honor.[3]

Thomas Hynes
Late of Kansas   U.S.

Copy, DNA-RG84, Foreign Service Posts, Instructions, Great Britain, Vol. 17.

1. Hynes (b. *c*1826), who had lived in Chicago prior to his sojourn in Dublin, was arrested in late May 1866 and imprisoned by virtue of the suspension of the writ of habeas corpus by the British government. A number of other Irish-Americans were also arrested in Dublin and held at Mountjoy Prison. At the end of July Hynes's release from prison was ordered with the proviso that he return to the United States. Having been given tickets for passage to America by a Chicago business firm, Hynes left the prison and embarked for the U.S. in early August. *House Ex. Docs.*, 40 Cong., 2 Sess., No. 157, "Trial and Conviction of American Citizens in Great Britain," pp. 286–338 passim (Ser. 1339); R. V. Comerford, *The Fenians in Context: Irish Politics and Society, 1848–82* (Atlantic Highland, N.J., 1985), 133; W. S. Neidhart, *Fenianism in North America* (University Park, Pa., 1975), 36.

2. William B. West (*fl*1869), himself an Irish-American appointed from Wisconsin, served as consul in Galway, and sometimes in Dublin, from 1861 to at least 1869. *U.S. Off. Reg.* (1861–69).

3. The House of Representatives had asked the President on June 18 for information regarding the arrest of Irish-Americans in Ireland. On June 21 Seward provided Johnson

with the names of the persons arrested and imprisoned; he in turn forwarded the information to Congress. Johnson to House, June 22, 26, 1866; Seward to Johnson, June 21, 1866, Foreign Service Posts, Instructions, Great Britain, Vol. 18, RG84, NA; *House Ex. Docs.*, 39 Cong., 1 Sess., No. 139, pp. 1–2 (Ser. 1267).

From William B. Phillips
Confidential

87 East 26h. Street.
New York, June 25h/66

Dear Sir,

I notice in the news from Washington this morning the action of the Committee of the "National Union Club" in calling a convention.[1] I remember this is a matter of which you spoke both to me and to young Mr. Bennett, and which several of your friends mentioned to me when I was in Washington. I had a conversation with Mr. Bennett Sr. upon the subject. He thinks it very well in its way, and may do some good, certainly not any harm, but he says it will be merely a political gathering, like other political conventions, and will have no binding force upon any one; not as much so even as the conventions of strictly organized parties. It may agitate the question of the day and throw light upon it, and so far may do good, but he says he fears it will lack force. He regards the approaching elections for Members of Congress as of the utmost importance. There is but little time to act upon the public mind before they take place, for it takes time to reach the masses of the people with the clear light of Truth where so many and such powerful agencies are at work to deceive. He thinks the slow process of forming a new party or a new political combination will prevent this movement from making much impression upon the next elections. Yet these elections involve momentous consequences not only to your administration but to the future of the country. He still maintains that some striking policy, as to your cabinet or some other matter, that will arouse the public mind is necessary.[2] Whether this should be a striking and popular movement of domestic policy, as a change of cabinet for example or some other bold movement, or some stroke of bold foreign policy, you are best able to judge. This would present a clear and sharply defined issue that would arouse the people in time, and have its influence over the Congressional elections. Perhaps something of this sort may be done to give force to the Convention movement proposed. From present appearances the Herald will throw all its weight for a change in Congress through the next elections. I respectfully submit this information and these views to you for your consideration.

I had not the honor of seeing you again after my interview with Mr. Frederick Seward.[3] The card you were kind enough to give me to him made my visit pleasant. He gave me, however, no positive assurance of the employment I desired; still he held out the hope. He said if there should be war in Europe the Department might employ a special secret agent, provided Congress should appropriate, as usual, a sum for secret service. If you will permit me to presume upon your kindness I would ask the favor of you to bring the matter before Mr. Seward's notice again.[4] I do not like to trouble you with my private wishes or interests when I know you have such weighty and so many other matters to attend to; but I am anxious to go to Europe and feel satisfied I can serve your administration and the public interests by going in the manner I desire.

W. B. Phillips.

ALS, DLC-JP.

1. A June 25 report from Washington announcing the call for the August convention in Philadelphia appeared in the following day's issue of the *New York Herald*, June 26, 1866.

2. See Phillips to Johnson, May 20, 1866.

3. Phillips had been seeking a foreign appointment of some kind since the first of the year. Phillips to Johnson, Jan. 4, 1866, Lets. of Appl. and Recomm., 1861–69 (M650, Roll 38), W. B. Phillips, RG59, NA.

4. Later Johnson did intervene again, personally requesting the secretary of state to offer Phillips a special mission in Europe, but it is not known whether an appointment was in fact conferred. Phillips to Johnson, Apr. 26, 1867, June 7, 1868, NRU.

From James B. Steedman

Jackson, Mississippi, June 26, 1866.

Dear Sir.

I hope the policy we have pursued in looking into the operations of the Bureau and the *conduct of its officers*, will meet your approval.

The strong hold which I knew the institution had upon the religious and sympathetic people of the North—thousands of whom honestly believed the negroes would be butchered, if it were not for the protection afforded them by the Bureau—convinced me we would be more likely to produce effect upon the public mind and secure candid attention, by exposing the abuses and frauds, and peculations of its officers than by attacking the system.

Our investigations have developed to my mind, clearly, that the Bureau officers, with a very few exceptions constitute a Radical close corporation, devoted to the defeat of the policy of your Administration. In Virginia, they were all Radicals. In North Carolina, all we met but one— Brevt Lt Col. Cilley[1]—were of the same stripe—South Carolina the same as the other two States. In Florida, Col. Osborne,[2] the Commissioner is your friend and supporter. Tillson, of Georgia,[3] a good man and an excellent officer, supports your Administration. Genl. Swayne,[4] of Alabama, is a good officer and a man of ability, but he is as fierce a radical as Thad. Stevens himself.

I met Judge Busteed[5] at Mobile, and found him to be your bitter enemy and an unscrupulous demagogue. He is a positive disgrace to the Government in his present position.

Kellog,[6] former Member of Congress from Michigan, is an intelligent excellent man, and *professes* to be your friend. I almost forgot to mention the fact that he is Collector of Internal Revenue, at Mobile.

Genl Woods,[7] Commanding the Department is not as conservative as he ought to be. I met him at Montgomery and discovered that he was disposed to exaggerate and magnify any little thing as evidence of hostility on the part of the people to Government of the U.S. I think he is a *radical witness*.

The Post Master Genl. has a gentleman from Columbus, Ohio,—Mr. Buttles[8]—as Special Agent of the Department, in charge of the Post Office, at Mobile, who thinks he is the only loyal man in that City.

We will report for Georgia, Alabama and Mississippi, from New Orleans.[9] The condition in Miss, is not as favorable as I wish.

I am afraid the officers of the Bureau, on trial at Raleigh,[10] will be acquitted for want of evidence. We have their confessions with us in writing and if either Genl. Fullerton or myself could be present, with Mr. Clink of N.Y. Herald,[11] who took down their statements, they could not escape conviction, if the Court will do its duty—for they are all guilty precisely as charged in our report. We reported nothing but the naked facts as stated by the officers themselves.

We shall complete our investigation and reach N. York, about the first of August.

If we have omitted any point in our reports on the Bureau which you desire to have reported upon we would be glad to have an intimation from you.

I may without exaggeration [say] that nearly all the Bureau officers are in correspondence with radical Senators and radical newspapers. We have found Forney's Chronicle in nearly all their offices, and have scarcely once discovered a paper supporting your Administration in the possession of a Bureau Agent.

James B. Steedman   Maj. Genl.

ALS, DLC-JP.
1. Clinton A. Cilley (*c*1837–1900), formerly sergeant and captain, 2nd Minn. Inf. (1861–64), was subsequently captain, major, and assistant adjutant general of volunteers (1864–66). A lawyer, he permanently settled in North Carolina, living first at Lenoir then Hickory. Pension Records, Emma Sophia Harper Cilley, RG15, NA.
2. Thomas W. Osborn (1836–1898) was a Watertown, New York, lawyer who served as colonel and chief of artillery of the Army of the Tennessee. After heading the Freedmen's Bureau in Florida (1865–66), he settled in Tallahassee and became a U.S. senator (1868–73). During the later 1870s he moved to New York City and renewed his law practice. *BDAC*; Richard Harwell and Philip N. Racine, eds., *The Fiery Trail: A Union Officer's Account of Sherman's Last Campaign* (Knoxville, 1986).
    3. Davis Tillson.
    4. Wager T. Swayne.
    5. Richard Busteed.
    6. Francis W. Kellogg.

7. Charles W. Woods.

8. Lucien D. Buttles (c1821–fl1879) of Columbus, Ohio, served as lieutenant colonel, 24th (1861) and 88th (1862) Ohio Vol. Inf. After the war he was special agent and post-master at Mobile, and gauger of internal revenue at Columbus. CSR, Lucien Buttles, RG94, NA; *Off. Army Reg.: Vols.*, 5: 85, 183; *U.S. Off. Reg.* (1865–67, 1873–79); Columbus directories (1862, 1873–74).

9. Fullerton and Steedman submitted their final report from New Orleans on July 20 after cutting short their visit to Texas and dispensing entirely with visits to Arkansas and Tennessee. Bentley, *Freedmen's Bureau*, 131.

10. Eliphalet Whittlesey, Charles I. Wickersham, James C. Mann, Franklin A. Seely, Isaac A. Rosekrans, and George O. Glavis. Seely (1834–1895), captain, assistant quarter-master of volunteers, was superintendent of the Freedmen's Bureau's eastern district of North Carolina, headquartered at New Bern from January to May 1866. He later worked as an examiner in the Patent Office. Rosekrans (c1835–fl1868), captain, commissary of subsistence of volunteers, was an assistant superintendent of a New Bern subdistrict from October 1865 to April 1866. Glavis (c1819–1898), a Swiss native, Dutch Reformed minister, and editor of the Newark *American Watchman*, was a hospital chaplain of volunteers who from December 1865 to May 1866 was a Freedmen's Bureau subdistrict superintendent near Goldsboro, North Carolina. Afterwards he was a lawyer in Washington, D.C. *Louisville Journal*, June 14, 1866; Pension Records, Delia R. Seely and Loucette E. Glavis, RG15, NA; Commission Branch: 1866-R507, Isaac A. Rosekrans and 1865-G495, George O. Glavis, RG94, NA; Everly and Pacheli, *Records of Field Officers*, pt. 2: 333, 346–47, 359. See Wilmington, N.C., Freedmen to Johnson, ca. May 22, 1866.

11. Not identified.

From Marion C. Taylor[1]

Shelbyville Ky   June 26th, 1866.

President Johnson

Presuming upon between 3 & 4 years service in the U S Army and a canvass last year for Congress in favor of the Constitutional Amendment against Hon A Harding[2] the present Representative from Ky—Who was elected by his denunciation of the Administration that had Crushed the rebellion and who said in a public speech in Elizabethtown in the year 1864 when Speaking of you "that if one drop of your blood could be in-fused into the Vain of a lamb that it would change it to a Hyena," I wish to say that I understand that Mr. Harding has recommended J R Beckley[3] as Collector of U S Revenue for this District. Beckley is an ex-Mail and Government Stock Contractor and speaking of the Govement some months ago said that the Govement had stolen his property meaning his negroes and that he would not support it. His appointment would be doing a great injustice to true Union men. In the name of justice if there is to be a change appoint Col Quin Morton[4] a true and loyal soldier who is an applicant for the appointment. Beckley's rebel Son[5] is in Washington with a Petition for the appointment of his father. Young Beckley kept well out of the way when the Draft made some men do thier duty. I re-spectfully give Hon L H Rousseau as a reference.

M C Taylor

ALS, DNA-RG56, Appts., Internal Revenue Service, Collector, Ky., 4th Dist., J. R. Beckley.

1. Marion C. Taylor (1822–1871) served as county attorney of Shelby County, Kentucky, and was elected to the state legislature in 1853. During the war he organized a company of the 15th Ky. Inf., USA. Promoted to colonel, he was twice wounded during his military service. Following the war, he once more involved himself in state politics. Bodley, *Kentucky*, 3: 121–22.

2. Aaron Harding.

3. John R. Beckley (c1809–fl1870) served as collector of internal revenue for the Fourth District in 1866 and 1867. *Louisville Journal*, Sept. 20, 1866; *U.S. Off. Reg.* (1867); 1870 Census, Ky., Shelby, Jacksonville, 571. For Harding's recommendation, see Harding to Cooper, n.d., Appts., Internal Revenue Service, Collectors, Ky., 4th Dist., John R. Beckley, RG56, NA.

4. Benjamin Quinn Morton (1811–fl1870) of Kentucky served as a Union lieutenant colonel of the 23rd Mo. Rgt. Vols., and was captured with most of his regiment at Shiloh. Mustered out in January 1865, he was a prominent citizen of Shelby County, Kentucky. By July 13, 1866, he had withdrawn his name for collector. Lovell H. Rousseau to Hugh McCulloch, July 13, ibid.; 1870 Census, Ky., Shelby, 7th Dist., Harrisonville, 540; Perrin et al., *Kentucky*, edition 6: 830; *OR*, Ser. 1, Vol. 10, Pt. 1: 290–91; *Off. Army Reg.: Vols.*, 7: 109.

5. Not identified.

From Richard P. L. Baber

Columbus Ohio, June 28t 1866.

Having fully surveyed the field of Politics in Ohio, I write to give you the result of my observations as a sincere friend of your Administration. You recollect when in Washington, the conversation I had with you on the 1st of June, when I told you, there would probably be no open breach at the Union Convention, as the Radicals would dodge the issues in the platform viz: negro Suffrage and the admission of Representatives from the Southern States and the fight must be made on the reelection of the Congressmen who had raised these issues, as against your policy. The Convention did not attempt to make the Constitutional Amendment a condition *precedent* to the admission of Congressmen, but doubtless the nominees presented by the Radicals in the different Congressional districts will represent this Congressional programme and should be defeated at all hazzards by the Union of those opposed to the obstruction policy. Your friends at the Convention as Honorable L. D. Campbell has doubtless informed you[1] constituted a State Central Committee of five, of which I am chairman, with a consulting member in each Congressional District to look after this matter and also by proper concert of action see that in the matter of appointments the right men should be recommended for the right places, so that you might not be misled by misrepresentations from irresponsible sources. I think by judicious management at least 8 or 10 of the radical Congressmen will be defeated, but it partly depends on the co-operation the Democracy may give by allowing independent Johnson candidates to run in this district (Shellabargers) Schencks and Ashleys.[2] There is a disposition to do so among many, but John G.

Thompson[3] the Chairman of the Democratic Central Committee is a Vallangenghan[4] man and obstinately bent on supporting only regular Democratic nominees. Judge A. G. Thurman,[5] and George H. Pendleton of Cincinnati can alone control him and means should be at once taken from influential sources at Washington to effect this. I know the great want is to have a fair and square canvass on the merits of your Restoration Policy unimbarrassed by old issues,—it would tell on the country. In this District the opportunity for Such a fight is admirable—the regular Democracy would be beaten at any rate as Shellabarger was elected by 3000 majority, but a Johnson man could carry the District by 2000, if no Democratic nomination is made. Enclosed I send you a Cincinnati Commercial of June 24th[6] containing an article written by me on June 18th and Sent down for publication before the meeting of the Union State Convention. I discuss and show up the Constitutional Amendment and was anxious to have the facts before the Convention, but I thought we had to make the fight at any rate and was glad to see your message of the 22 Inst disabusing the public mind of the idea that you Supported the Amendment. My information is that Brownlows effort for ratification in Tennessee will fail. The west is tired of being swindled by New England influence and the Soldiers will Show the Radicals, by their votes this fall that they did not fight for negro Suffrage. I see they are determined to send you the District of Columbia Senate Suffrage Bill, to risk another veto.[7] The people in the end will whip the politicians and nothing is more certain than this negro question will progress again from the ballot box to the cartrage box and culminate in a war of races if your policy does not prevail. I will strive with our Committee to look after the interests of the Administration closely, but we have to fight most of the office holders and *half* the Cabinet.[8]

R P L Baber

ALS, DLC-JP.

1. See Campbell to Johnson, June 22, 1866.

2. All three of these incumbent congressmen, Samuel Shellabarger, Robert Schenck, and James Ashley, were reelected in October 1866, defeating their Independent Republican challengers in the Seventh, Third, and Tenth Ohio Districts, respectively. Bonadio, *North of Reconstruction*, 66–68.

3. A Columbus businessman and banker, Thompson (1833–*fl*1883) later served as a Democratic state senator, commissioner of railroads and telegraphs, and as sergeant-at-arms of the House of Representatives. *Biographical Cyclopaedia of Ohio*, 1: 238–39.

4. Clement L. Vallandigham.

5. Allen G. Thurman (1813–1895) was a Democratic congressman (1845–47), senator (1869–81), and Grover Cleveland's running mate in the 1888 election. *BDAC*.

6. No enclosures were found.

7. Sen. Benjamin F. Wade's measure regulating the elective franchise in the District was debated on June 27–28, but postponed until the next session of Congress, when the bill was passed, vetoed, and ultimately passed over Johnson's veto. *Senate Journal*, 39 Cong., 1 Sess., pp. 582, 584 (Ser. 1236); Patrick W. Riddleberger, *1866: The Critical Year Revisited* (Carbondale, 1979), 249.

8. Johnson's endorsement of Baber's letter reads: *"File for reference A.J."*

From Sarah F. Mudd

Rock Hill[1]   June 28th 66

Dear Sir,

It is with regret I am forced again to intrude on your valuable time.[2] I know you have but little to devote to individuals. After long weary weeks watching and waiting I have just received a letter from my Husband, Doctor Mudd.[3] He says he is very weak and nervous and general health yielding to long and close confinement and impproper food. The chains were taken off in December Since the he has been kept under close guard.

Hon Rev Johnson told me an order had been sent to the Island that my Husband should be treated as other Prisoners. The order has never been fulfilled. I was hopeful after the decision of the Supreme Court the trial of Civilians by military Court is illegal.[4] He would be released. So far I have been disappointed.

I was then hopeful after your Proclamation restoring the states to the Union and Civil Law,[5] of getting him out under a writ of Habeas Corpus. The Lawyers I consulted did not know whether your Proclamation restored the Writ and feared military interferance. My last hope for immediate relief is to ask his releas of you. I know dear Sir and appreciate the many difficulties of your position and would not ask this of you did I know how else to act. If you cannot let him return to his home, banish him, anything is preferable to this living death he is now Suffering. But is sending him from his country you could not send a more innocent man and a Citizen who has done less gainst the Laws of his Country.

Mr President the Large rewards offered by the Government for Booths accomplices paced my Husband in his present Suffering Condition. Those witnesses who Swore against my Husband swore falsely and for the sake of the money. I wanted them prosecuted for Pergery but was told by the best Lawyers of Washington that it was useless as they were Government witnesses the Government would protect them. I called on Judge Holt for advice he refused to give it. The papers of yesterday as well as his letter states that his health is failing and he cannot live this summer out in his present condition. My every effort has failed. My only hope now is in you. Grant my petition give back to me and our poor little babys the little of life that remains And Almighty God will bless you and yours.[6]

S. F. Mudd.

ALS, DNA-RG204, Pardon Case File B-596, Samuel A. Mudd.

1. Rock Hill Farm was the name of the Mudds' home near Bryantown, Maryland. Samuel Carter, III, *The Riddle of Dr. Mudd* (New York, 1974), 9, 37.

2. See Mudd to Johnson, Dec. 22, 1865, *Johnson Papers*, 9: 529–31.

3. Samuel A. Mudd.

    4. This was the *ex parte Milligan* decision of April 3, 1866, whereby the Supreme
Court ruled that civilians outside war zones could not be tried by the military authorities.
James M. McPherson, *Ordeal by Fire: The Civil War and Reconstruction* (New York, 1982),
510, 533; *National Intelligencer*, Apr. 5, 1866.
    5. See Proclamation *re* End of Insurrection, Apr. 2, 1866.
    6. At least one Washington, D.C., paper had reprinted the *Memphis Appeal*'s notice of
the pardon and return of William White, who had been Mudd's roommate on Dry Tortugas. It was stated that "The Doctor's health is rapidly failing, and Mr. White believes he
will not live through the summer." *National Intelligencer*, June 27, 1866.

From John Ross[1]

Joys Corner of 8th Penna Ave.

Washington City   June 28th 1866

Hon Sir

From my earliest Boyhood in reading, I was tought to reverance the
Government of the United States.

And after I advanced far enough to understand the beautiful system
under which the Constitution of the United States was established, My
Reverance became more firmly confirmed, which has not and shall never
be changed.

Permit me to say on my arrival at Fort Smith, at the first meeting of
those Southern tribes in the Confederate Service, all in arms.[2] Without
any intimation the Commissioner of Indian Affairs[3] opened the Council
by saying he would read a paper for the information of [the] Council,
which had been agreed upon [by] [t]he Commission,[4] prefering charges
against me.[5] I asked permission to make my defence before the Council,
this being granted I made a verbal defence,[6] which has not appeared in
the report of the Commissioner of Indian Affairs. On the next day my
Nephew W. P. Ross[7] from doucamentary facts, made an able defence.
Upon the close of the delivery, the Commissioner of Indian Affairs (and
others) came up and complimented me that a Cherokee should be so talented as to make so able a Speech.

It was then decided that the Loyal Cherokee Delegation[8] with myself
should return to attend the National Council at Tahlequah.[9] On our arrival there, the Commissioner of Indian Affairs gave instruction to Superintendant Sells directing Agent Harlin[10] to notify the National Council
and myself, That the Indian Department would never recognize me as
Chief of the Nation." Also a letter from Commissioner Cooley to Col
Downing as an apology regretting that he could not comply with the *Protest* of the Delegation requesting them to rescind there action against me.

The Protest of the National Council having been already laid before
you. A Copy of these Charges And a communication of Agent Harlin,
also Commissioner Cooleys letter to Col. Downing copies of which is
herewith laid before you.[11]

Now permit me to say that the charges are altogether false. But proof will establish the facts. I regret to say that the Commissioner of Indian Affairs and the Superintendant have been influenced by mercenary motives through the influence of the great monied Capitalists McDonald and Fuller,[12] Suttlers at Ft. Smith which has been corrupting every thing on that frontier for so long a time.

And have induced them to accept there offer, which of course renders them unfit to hold the offices they now occupy.

That all those who came from the South now in Canadian district, together with the Loyal Citizens of the Nation have *unitedly* Protested against a seperation of the Nation.[13] And it has been agreed upon that all Southern Cherokees shall have the right to come into the Country and occupy there Places at once, And as there are a great many who have left valuable improvements scattered over the Country. And they all desire to come in and occupy them at once, And to enjoy equal privileges.

It is Known that those who may refuse to return to the Nation will be very few.

It is anticipated that peace and *harmony* will once more prevail in the Country.

I thank you and your family for the kindness which has been extended to me.

Jno Ross
Prinl Chief   Chrokee Nation

P.S   Believing that the action against myself and people was brought about by Messrs Cooley and Sells, I do not wish to impugn the other Commissioners.

Jno Ross   Prinl Chief   C N

LS, OkWeaT-Carter Col., Papers of Chief John Ross.

1. As principal chief of the Cherokees for about thirty-eight years, Ross (1790–1866) had been a leading opponent of their removal from Georgia to the Indian Territory. Ross had been in Washington since November 1865 attempting to negotiate a new treaty. Success eventually crowned his efforts a few days after his death in August 1866. *DAB*; Moulton, *John Ross*, passim.

2. The peace council at Fort Smith, Arkansas, met on September 8, 1865, with the goal to bring the disloyal tribal factions of the Indian Territory (not just the Cherokees) back into the Union and unite them with their loyal brethren. The federal commissioners also intended, unbeknownst to the Indians, to ask for various territorial concessions and to organize a unified government for the Indian Territory. Ibid., 185–87; Bailey, *Indian Territory*, 58–65.

3. Dennis N. Cooley.

4. In addition to Cooley, the Commission included five other men. Elijah Sells (1814–1897), former Iowa stoneware manufacturer, legislator, secretary of state, and adjutant general, was the superintendent of Indian affairs for the southern superintendency. He later moved to Kansas, served in its legislature, and then served as Utah territorial secretary. Thomas Wistar (1798–1876), a Philadelphia merchant, was a leader of the Society of Friends in Pennsylvania. The first Indian to serve as commissioner of Indian affairs (1869–71), Col. Ely S. Parker (1828–1895), a Seneca from New York, became a civil engineer after his racial identification prevented his admission to the bar. After confronting this racial obstacle again, Parker became a staff officer and military secretary for U. S. Grant. Gen. William S. Harney (1800–1889), a Tennessean who joined the regular army in 1818, served with distinction in the Mexican War and the Indian-fighting west, achieving the

rank of brigadier general before the Civil War. Because of his southern sympathies, he did not serve in that conflict and retired in 1863. Charles E. Mix (1810–1878), a clerk in the Office of Indian Affairs since about 1837, became chief clerk in 1850 and held the position until 1869, frequently serving as acting commissioner. *NCAB*, 13: 593–94; Bailey, *Indian Territory*, 58; Moulton, *John Ross*, 185; *DAB*; *NUC*; *McElroy's Philadelphia City Directory* (1867); William H. Armstrong, *Warrior in Two Camps: Ely S. Parker, Union General and Seneca Chief* (Syracuse, 1978), passim; Warner, *Blue*; Kvasnicka and Viola, *Commissioners*, 77–79.

5. Claiming that Ross had deliberately plotted to take the Cherokees into the Confederacy and was still disloyal, Cooley refused to recognize him as principal chief of the Cherokees. Moulton, *John Ross*, 185–86.

6. Ross denied that he had ever been disloyal. The Cherokees were forced to make a treaty with the Confederates in self-defense after the Union troops left the Indian Territory. Ross, in fact, spent most of the war in the north. Ibid., 186; David Buice, "Lincoln's Unissued Proclamation," *Prologue*, 10 (1978): 157, 160, 165–66.

7. Son of one of Ross's sisters, William P. Ross (1820–1891) graduated from Princeton before returning to the Indian Territory to serve as secretary to the upper house of the tribal legislative council and editor of the *Cherokee Advocate*. Although opposed to an alliance with the Confederates, Ross was the lieutenant colonel of the Cherokee regiment until it disbanded after the Battle of Pea Ridge. He succeeded John Ross as principal chief. *NCAB*, 19: 227–28; Emmet Star, *History of the Cherokee Indians* (Oklahoma City, 1921), 66.

8. The delegation from the northern-sympathizing Cherokees included Smith Christie, Thomas Pegg, White Catcher, H. D. Reese (not identified) and Lewis Downing (c1825–1872), former lieutenant colonel of the 3rd Indian Home Guards, Kans. Inf., and future principal chief (1867–72). Moulton, *John Ross*, 185; Kenny A. Franks, *Stand Watie and the Agony of the Cherokee Nation* (Memphis, 1979), 194; *New York Times*, Nov. 13, 1872; CSR, Lewis Downing, RG94, NA.

9. The Cherokee governing body met November 7, 1865. Moulton, *John Ross*, 188.

10. Justin Harlan, the Cherokee agent, was appointed September 11, 1862, and replaced in September 1866. Edward E. Hill, *The Office of Indian Affairs, 1824–1880: Historical Sketches* (New York, 1974), 35.

11. Not found.

12. McDonald has not been identified. Perry Fuller (c1827–1871), a controversial merchant and agent for the Sauk and Fox Indians in Kansas before the war, was appointed collector of the port of New Orleans in 1868 and departed in 1869, accused of custom house fraud. Ida M. Ferris, "The Sauks and Foxes in Franklin and Osage Counties, Kansas," KSHS *Collections*, 11 (1909–10): 352n; H. Craig Miner and William E. Unrau, *The End of Indian Kansas: A Study of Cultural Revolution, 1854–1871* (Lawrence, Kans., 1978), 64–65; Perry Fuller to Johnson, Sept. 30, 1868, and James B. Steedman and Perry Fuller to William G. Moore, Jan. 15, 1869, Johnson Papers, LC; 1870 Census, D.C., Washington, 5th Ward, 38; *Washington Evening Star*, Dec. 15, 1870, Jan. 11, 1871; Washington, D.C., directories (1866–72).

13. The desire to divide the Cherokee Nation, a goal espoused by the southern delegation, was an issue dating back to pro- and anti-removal factionalism. Moulton, *John Ross*, 188–89.

From Rosanna C. Taylor[1]

Montgomery   28th June 66

Sir

I reciev'd your answer to my first application for remuniration for losses sustain'd by the Federal Army; and like the importunate widow I again write to request that you will consider my situation. An old woman of 74 accustom'd from infancy to all the comforts and eligancies of life— reduc'd now to penury. I have lost at least 150 thousand dollars by the

war—had no son in the army—did not approve of the rebellion—had to
borrow money to keep from starving and now no prospect of paying. If
Congress would only let me have five thousand dollars to pay for the corn
and mules I was obliged to purchase; I might avoid ruin.

My family have always occupied the highest position in our republic.
My brother John Taylor[2] was Senator in Congress for 20 years and afterwards Governor of So. Carolina. My nephew Franklin Elmore was likewise in Congress for years. I ought to have written by my nephew Albert
Elmore, to whom you have been so very kind, if I had only thought of it,
but now my necessities have press'd upon me and I feel that you alone can
rescue me and mine from ruin.[3]

Rosanna C. Taylor

ALS, DNA-RG92, Consolidated Correspondence File, 1794–1915.
    1. Taylor (b. c1792), neé Theus, was the widow of Jesse Peter Taylor, a planter who had
died in 1852. B. F. Taylor, "John Taylor and His Taylor Descendants," *SCHM*, 8 (1907):
97, 102.
    2. Taylor (1770–1832), Rosanna's brother-in-law, was a lawyer who also served in a
number of lesser political positions. *BDAC*.
    3. So far as it is known, Johnson did not aid Mrs. Taylor. Quartermaster General Mont-
gomery C. Meigs had already ruled that damages to her property were "done by the troops
on the march in a hostile district" and recommended that her claim "be disallowed." [Meigs]
to Stanton, June 5, 1866, Consolidated Correspondence File, 1794–1915, RG92, NA.

From Alvan C. Gillem

Nashville Tenn   June 29, 1866.
Dear Sir.

I have often desired to write you, and have only done so at long intervals from a conviction of the constant annoyance to which you are subjected.

As you no doubt anticipated, the Governor of this state heads a most
bitter party in opposition to you, in this there is nothing strange, nature
custom & habit unite in separating you. The Radical party in this state
contains but a small fraction of the original Union party. The leaders of
this party in Nashville—the head of the concern in the state are Derby,[1]
Manson Brien, E. P. Cone, Dolbear,[2] A. J. Fletcher & Judge Lovering.[3]
The bitterest of these is Cone, whom I should have thought common decency if not gratitude would have prevented assailing you.

Among your most active supporters is to be found nineteen twentieths
of the ability of the Union men of the state. Netherland, Nelson (T.A.R.)
Kyle, Temple, East Houston[4] Francis B. Fogg & a host of others. With
the course of the Tennessee Representatives you are more familiar
than I am.

Not all the Franchise laws on earth nor Universal suffrage can ever return Stokes to Congress.[5] I have seen no person who exactly knows what
Maynards position is.

An Extra session of the Legislature is called for the 4th of July—to act on the Constitutional Amendments or rather to ratify them, for they certainly will be ratified and by the votes of the members from Middle & West Tenn. in the same manner that the Negro Testimony Bill & The Franchise Law were passed, whilst the Representatives of many Districts & counties in East Tenn opposed them. This apparent anomoly is easily explained. The members from East Tenn are the *Representatives* of the people and know they will be held responsible for their conduct at the next election, whilst the members from Middle & West Tenn. know their political lives will expire with their present term, unless they proscribe a majority of their fellow citizens by whose votes they now hold their seats.

After passing the Constitutional amendment, a resolution censuring your course will be introduced,[6] and since the refusal to allow such men as Maj Lewis & Col Garret[7] &c to take their seats I think they have secured the majority necessary to pass any thing. I am satisfied that resolutions similar to those forwarded to you last winter have *already been* prepared.

Genl Thomas thinks that all the inhabitants of the Southern States should be declared by act of Congress aliens that those who could establish their loyalty should be admitted to citizenship at once, that all others with a few designated exceptions should be compeled to take the ordinary course of naturalization in the same manner as foreigners. As by this plan all (with the specified exceptions) would be eventually admitted to the rights of citizenship I can see nothing to recommend it. Why keep a wound open five years that can be sooner healed. Would the southern people of the south come back to their duties with any better feeling after a five years punishment.

Your enemies in this state bring no other charge against your course than that it has the support of the rebels. It is the charge brought against the founder of Christianity—"This man eats with Publicans & Sinners."[8]

I would write oftener, but for the fear of adding to your annoyance. Gratitude impels me to seek every opportunity to serve you.

Alvan C Gillem

ALS, DLC-JP.

1. N. Derby (*fl*1868), a clothier/tailor at 54 N. College Street and a director of the First National Bank, apparently came to Nashville during the war and was gone before 1870. Nashville directories (1865–68); Walter T. Durham, *Reluctant Partners: Nashville and the Union, July 1, 1863, to June 30, 1865* (Nashville, 1987), 65.

2. Jonathan W. Dolbear.

3. Amos Lovering.

4. John Netherland, Thomas A.R. Nelson, Absalom A. Kyle, Oliver P. Temple, Edward H. East, and Russell Houston.

5. Gillem was doing some wishful thinking in this letter, for William B. Stokes was twice re-elected to Congress after his 1865 victory. See Alexander, *Reconstruction*, 83; *BDAC*.

6. No record of such a resolution has been located.

7. William B. Lewis and Abraham E. Garrett. Possibly Gillem is confused here and

meant instead to refer to the problems that Garrett and Cave Johnson, not Lewis, had in the spring of 1866. See White, *Messages of Govs.*, 5: 493.

8. Matthew 9: 11 and Mark 2: 16.

From Richard Sutton

Washington, D. C.   June 29th. 1866.

Sir:

Having learned that the Proprietors of the National Intelligencer Newspaper Establishment[1] have presented a claim to the Government for upwards of $13,000 for printing in that paper a report of the trial of the Assassins of the late President Lincoln.[2] I beg respectfully to submit that I deem myself to have an equitable lien on part of that amount if it should be allowed by the auditing officers, and I appeal to your Excellency to exercise your authority so as to effect a just and equitable division.

The claim is preferred I presume on the ground of the facilities which the Report afforded to the Court in the trial of the case, and that it was thus of service to the Government and to the ends of justice. Your Excellency is aware that there were several reports published of the proceedings of that remarkable trial, for which it is not proposed to pay though each report served to enlighten the Court and the Community; but if the Court derived any special advantage from the Report published in the Intelligencer—and it was highly commended by the Court and by the Counsel as peculiarly able and exact; indeed it was treated as official and authoritative—should not the skill and learning and intellect of the Reporters be deemed more deserving of compensation than the mechanical types and presses of the Intelligencer establishment? The Proprietors of the Intelligencer would be without any pretence for claiming remuneration if the Reporters had not supplied the Report which was found so valuable to the Commission. For that Report the Proprietors of the Intelligencer have refused to pay a dollar and have intimated their intention to resist any attempt to enforce payment to every extremity. I therefore trust your Excellency will not prejudice my just claim by awarding such an amount to them.

I respectfully ask that I may be heard before the officer to whom the claim may be submitted for examination personally or by Counsel.[3]

R Sutton

ALS, DNA-RG94, Lets. Recd. (Main Ser.), File S-1339-1866 (M619, Roll 517).

1. John F. Coyle and Chauncey H. Snow.

2. On May 25, Thomas Pratt, counsel for Coyle and Snow, presented their claim to Stanton. Judge Advocate General Holt denied having requested the article. *National Intelligencer*, May 15, 1866; Holt to Stanton, May 30, 1866; Pratt to Stanton, June 2, 1866, Johnson Papers, LC.

3. Despite Pratt's argument in favor of the claim, Stanton denied the claim. Pratt to Stanton, June 2, 1866; Pratt to Johnson, Sept. 21, 1866, Johnson Papers, LC.

To David L. Swain

June 29th 1866

My dear Sir.

Your kind letter of the 9th instant, informing me of the complimentary action of the Faculty of the University of North Carolina in conferring on me the degree of "Doctor of Laws," has been received.[1]

The motives which prompted this act, and the friendly expression with which it was accompanied, are warmly appreciated by me, and excite sincere gratitude and an honest desire to merit and retain this friendship and confidence you, and they proffer me in the discharge of my public trust.

Andrew Johnson

LBcopy, DLC-JP.

1. This honorary degree was conferred on Johnson by the "Academic Senate" at the June 7th commencement, "in consideration of the eminent services rendered to our native State and our common Country . . . under the most trying circumstances." Swain to Johnson, June 9, 1866, Johnson Papers, LC.

July 1866

From Charles R. Buckalew et al.

[ca. July 1866][1]

We respectfully submit for your consideration the question of conferring the rank of General upon Lieutenant General Grant; the initiation of the measure to be with you and to be consummated by you (with the concurrence of the Senate) under a Resolution to be passed by Congress.

The proposition is, that you address a communication to Congress recommending that the rank of General be established and the President be authorized to nominate and appoint one officer of that rank.

A very extensive system of military promotion has been carried out recently extending to most officers of special merit in the war, who survive. But such recognition of service, such honorary promotion, is not possible under existing laws in the case of the actual head of the army (under the President) because he holds the highest rank established by law.

That rank was not given him merely in recognition of past service but for purposes of future service and command in the war. It was to enable him to control actual operations in the field and was conferred before his great work was done. That work *was* done and well done, and would it not be fit and proper to give him who performed it a testimonial of national appreciation and gratitude similar in character to that given to gallant officers subordinate to him in the service?

Would not this promotion of the chief General of the Army be accepted by all who have seen service under him as a graceful and appropriate tribute to the Army itself? Other promotions have relation, so far as the honor of them extends beyond the officer promoted, only to some *part* of our military force under the immediate command of the officer promoted. Their achievements as well as his own are recognized in his elevation. But the promotion now suggested has relation to the whole army and will be esteemed as doing honor to the whole.

We think also that this measure would be regarded by the people generally as proper, and would receive their cordial approval. It is an unusual expedient to reach a legitimate object, but the case itself is extraordinary and popular sentiment will rise fully up to the demand made upon it by the President. The war was of a magnitude to lift mens thoughts above precedent, and its success was, (so far as military operations were concerned,) so complete and satisfactory that the people of the country, now exultant and grateful, would hail any signal mark of honor conferred upon Gen. Grant as merited and timely.

But this thing if done at all should begin with the President who represents the whole people, and with whom is lodged the power of appointment under the Constitution. Initiated by an individual in either House of Congress, it sinks from its dignity as a national act into the class of private projects, and becomes of very questionable propriety.

This national tribute to our chief soldier, would be peculiarly appropriate at a time when his reputation is assailed by one of the leading though not most meritorious Generals of the War.[2]

The rank assigned to Gen. Washington in prospect of a contest with France, cannot be mentioned as a precedent to control the present question. That rank could not be one of honor, but of service merely, to a great character who had been President of the United States and Constitutional Commander in Chief over all possible officials of the army. Besides, the present extent of the country and the magnitude of our army are out of all comparison with what they were in 1798.[3]

We have thus put Your Excellency in possession of our views upon this interesting question.[4]

C R Buckalew

J. W. Nesmith

Edgar Cowan

LS, DLC-JP.

1. This date has been assigned because the matter of Grant's promotion occurred in July and, furthermore, a clerk wrote July 1866 on the cover sheet of the letter.

2. Probably a reference to Benjamin F. Butler. See Butler to Johnson, Feb. 20, 1866.

3. On July 2, 1798, during the undeclared naval war with France, Congress named George Washington commanding general of the army with the rank of lieutenant general, in case hostilities with France should escalate. After some controversy and political debate, the rank was revived in 1855 and bestowed on Winfield Scott. Scott retired on November 1, 1861, and in March 1864 Ulysses S. Grant became the nation's third lieutenant general. Richard B. Morris, ed., *Encyclopedia of American History* (New York, 1982), 154, 1044, 1148; *DAB*.

4. On July 20, 1866, Congress passed a bill "to revive the Grade of General in the United States Army." According to William G. Moore, one of Johnson's private secretaries, both the President and Stanton were hesitant to create a rank higher than lieutenant general. Nevertheless, on July 25 Johnson signed the bill, Stanton recommended Grant for the rank, and Johnson officially sent Grant's nomination to the Senate. The Senate confirmed the appointment on the following day. Grant, who correctly assumed beforehand that he would receive the promotion, accepted the new rank on July 28. *Congressional Globe*, 39 Cong., 1 Sess., p. 3974, Appendix, p. 383; "Notes of Colonel W. G. Moore, Private Secretary to President Johnson, 1866–1868," *AHR*, 19 (1913): 102; Stanton to Johnson, July 25, 1866, Johnson Papers, LC; Presidential Nominations, Anson McCook Coll. (1837–88), RG46, NA; *Washington Evening Star*, July 27, 1866; Grant to Townsend, July 28, 1866, Simon, *Grant Papers*, 16: 263.

From John J. Goetschius et al.

[Ca. July 1866, Paterson, New Jersey]; ALS (Goetschius), DNA-RG56, Appts., Internal Revenue Service, Collector, N.J., 4th Dist., Daniel Winfield.

Five Paterson, New Jersey, citizens recommend Daniel Winfield, whose "principles are eminently conservative," as collector for the Fourth District of New Jersey. Since his return from five years in military service, "he has been outspoken in favor of Andrew Johnson's policy throughout, denouncing the Radicals in the boldest manner." Moreover, Eugene Ayres, the incumbent, "refused to sign a call for a meeting to sustain Andrew Johnson's policy, and is a Radical of the most uncompromising character, who neither went to war nor permitted any of his family to enlist." [Although nominated for the collector's post, Winfield was rejected by the Senate.]

From William B. Phillips
Confidential.

87 East 26h. Street,
New York   July 1st 1866.

Dear Sir,

The Herald, as I have intimated to you before and as you have probably noticed, is in the habit sometimes of taking a new point of departure. Well, we are about to start afresh on the question of the National Banks— to make a platform, or a plank in a platform, for the approaching elections and as a political issue in the future. We have been decidedly hostile all along to the whole system, and it fell to my lot to wage the war. I must say, too, that I performed my duty con amore, for I am as fully persuaded as Mr. Bennett is that the system of National Banks is a fraud upon the country, a gross monopoly, and dangerous. We have treated the question up to this time, however, only in a financial and an economical point of view. It is thought now that it must be made a political one, that it is of such magnitude that it will enter more prominently into political affairs and political parties than the old United States Bank did. We have broken ground a little in the leading article of to-day's paper. To-morrow there will be a bolder article.[1] These will be followed up. Mr. Bennett thinks the democrats may appropriate this question as a plank in their platform. I think it might be well for the new conservative combination party to look into the matter and see what can be made of it. So much depends upon the next congressional elections, and there is such a short time in which to operate upon public sentiment before they take place, that it seems necessary to wake up the people by some new and striking issue.

The Herald is a little on the fence relative to the proposed Convention. If the movement takes a vigorous start and it looks like being successful the paper will support it. At present there is some doubt. I keep it leaning as strongly in favor of the Convention as I can.[2]

I enclose you an article on the National Banks, pretty much in the same strain I have written before, and a short article on the Impending war in Europe.[3]

W. B. Phillips.

ALS, DLC-JP.
1. "The Evils of the National Bank System" and "Income of the Government," respectively. *New York Herald*, July 1, 2, 1866.
2. Shortly afterward Phillips reassured the President: "I think we are fairly committed

to sustain the Philadelphia Convention movement." Phillips to Johnson, July 17, 1866, Johnson Papers, LC.

3. Not found. The "Impending war" was between Prussia and Austria, with Italy disputing the latter's control of Venetia. *New York Herald*, July 1, 1866. See also Joseph A. Wright to Johnson, May 2, June 21, 1866.

From James H. Bell

Austin Texas   July 2 1866.

Mr. President

The election for state, district & county officers in this state transpired on Monday, twenty fifth ultimo, in accordance with the ordinance of late state Convention. The Conservative union ticket, headed by Gen'l Throckmorton[1] is no doubt elected by very large majority, say three 3 possibly four 4 to one 1.[2] As question arises when the County officers lately elected will qualify, and enter upon the discharge of their duty I have expressed the opinion that the officers of the provisional Government appointed by Gen'l Hamilton ought to hold their respective offices until your Excellency shall signify your Consent to the installation of the officers lately elected.[3]

I would be much pleased to hear from your Excellency.

Jas. H. Bell   Sec'y of State

Tel, DLC-JP.

1. James W. Throckmorton (1825–1894), a physician and lawyer, moved to Texas in 1841 and served as a surgeon in the Mexican War. A member of the prewar Texas house of representatives and senate, he served in the Confederate army and then as a brigadier general of state troops. After his brief gubernatorial term (Gen. Philip Sheridan removed him from office in August 1867), Throckmorton served four terms in the U.S. House of Representatives (1875–79, 1883–87). *BDAC*.

2. The vote was 49,277 for Throckmorton and 12,168 for his opponent Elisha M. Pease. Waller, *Hamilton of Texas*, 93.

3. Secretary of State William H. Seward, by direction of the President, authorized the legislature to assemble on August 6 and Throckmorton to be inaugurated on August 9, but he did not send this authorization until July 28. Seward to Bell, July 28, 1866, Tels. Sent, Sec. of War (M473, Roll 91), RG107, NA.

From John W. Forney

WASHINGTON, D.C., July 2, 1866.

MY DEAR SIR:

Understanding that you are anxious to disclose certain private letters of mine, written to you before and since you became President by the assassination of ABRAHAM LINCOLN, and also that you are troubled with some delicate doubts as to the exact propriety of publishing them, I hereby invite you to print them in one or all of your four organs at the national Capitol, or through a more convenient medium, the club or committee representing the "Bread-and-Butter Brigade." These letters were written without the slightest concealment, and without the slightest suspicion that you were about to betray the party that had placed you where you are. There is a charming consistency between the conscientious promptings that constrained you to separate from that great party and the spirit which now impels you to reveal to the world your private relations with those who still adhere to that organization; and although the practice is somewhat novel, it will serve to shed a rich light upon the pages of the historian when he comes to describe your grateful and virtuous Administration. The following letter, long threatened by your organs is at last given to the world, and I reprint it as well for the purpose of acknowledging it as for the purpose of making some comments upon it.[1]

When this letter was written there was scarcely a Union Republicaan in the United States who did not believe that your restoration policy included impartial suffrage to the colored race, full guarantees before the return of the rebels, and such a change in the basis of representation as would prevent the murderers of American liberty from resuming their former power. The only real difference between you and the radicals was whether the rebellion destroyed the State organizations or not. I write with the files of the Washington *Chronicle* before me; and find that two days after the above letter was written MR. TRUMBULL's two bills one "the enlargement of the powers of the freedmen's bureau," and the other, "for the protection of civil rights," were introduced into the Senate in the full expectation that they would receive your sanction. It was only when the Copperhead and traitor organs here and elsewhere began to speak as if by your authority against the Union majorities in Congress, that the suspicion of the treason, subsequently indicated in your veto of the freedmen's bureau bill, and your disgusting 22d of February speech,[2] began to pervade and finally to possess the loyal mind of the country. So fixed was the belief of the Republican party that you could under no circumstances co-operate with your slanderers and theirs, and so willing were they to overlook your suspicious indifference previous to the coming elections in Ohio, Pennsylvania and New Jersey, that at the period when I wrote the above letter hundreds of thousands cheerfully recognized you as their political leader, and supposed you intended to stand firmly by the substantial principles of their organization. My own conviction was so strong upon this subject that I need only refer to the pages of THE CHRONICLE and THE PRESS to prove how steadily I resisted the idea that you were plotting to betray your friends, and how earnestly I endeavored to convince the country that you had no sympathy with the common enemy. In all my visits to the Presidential mansion, and they were frequent, it was not until late in January that I began clearly to perceive you were conspiring with the Copperheads and traitors. Before that time, not a word had ever fallen from your lips to excite the suspicion that you were preparing to become the persecutor of the colored race, or that you were preparing to bring back into full power the red-handed traitors whom you had so bitterly denounced during four long years. But when, with an amazement that I can never forget or faithfully describe, these facts appeared too plain for doubt, I fearlessly discharged my duty, regardless of, and fully prepared for, all the consequences. I did not stop to calculate whether in denouncing the dangerous conspiracy of which you were then proved to be the chief, I was helping or harming the distinguished gentleman in whose behalf I wrote the above letter.

And now, sir, a word in reference to *your* personal affairs. I know right well the difficulty, if not the danger of the position I occupy. I know that for sternly holding you to your pledges I am assailed and threatened by every Copperhead and traitor between Maine and Mexico, and I know also that, stimulated by the passions that have controlled you since you broke away from those pledges, there is nothing that you would not resort to to demoralize the party that elected you, and ruin those who refuse to follow you into the ranks of the common enemy. It is not the first time I have been thrown into conflict with a faithless and corrupt Executive; but it is the first time I have ever been called upon to contemplate and to expose such perfidy as yours. I will not remind you of my earnest and uncalculating friendship, from the period when you took issue with treason in the Senate, in 1860, down to the Baltimore convention, in 1864, which body, at the request of the lamented Lincoln and such earnest radicals as BENJAMIN F. WADE, of Ohio, I attended alone for the purpose of pressing your nomination for the Vice Presidency, after it became apparent that HANNIBAL HAMLIN, the incorruptible patriot, was willing to give way in order to allow a representative of the War Democracy a position upon the national ticket. That you should have forgotten these facts amounts to nothing in comparison with your heartless ingratitude to the party which placed you in nomination and elected you Vice President. Individual ingratitude and cruelty concern only the person betrayed and injured; but when, as in your case, the betrayal of the whole country is contemplated, the offence becomes national and should be accordingly checked and counteracted.

There is, however, one part of your experience which deserves to be differently considered, especially in view of the new system of revenge you have adopted, viz: that of publishing the private letters of gentlemen who refuse to sustain your attempt to make loyalty odious and treason honorable. Need I tell you that I allude to the disgraceful 4th of March, 1865? *When you resolved to desert the brave and benevolent men who threw over you the cloak of their forgiveness and charity on that day—you consciously or unconsciously prepared for every succeeding treachery.* When you obtained your own consent to do that single act of shame, your intrigues with the Copperheads before the fall elections of 1865, your veto of the freedmen's bureau bill after having almost explicitly promised to sign it, your revolting 22d of February speech, your proscription of the brave white and colored loyalists of the South, and your publication of private letters written to you in unsuspecting confidence, followed naturally and irresistibly. Supposing that any other gentleman could have been guilty, as you were guilty on the 4th of March, 1865, what would such a gentleman have done? You stood before your own country and the world dishonored and degraded.

The ordinary calumnies of the Copperheads and traitors were coined into the most frightful maledictions against you. I know of no scene in history where a public character, for an act of inexcusable weakness, was at the same time so universally execrated by one party and so indulgently and magnanimously treated by another. Any true man, equally unfortunate and equally forgiven and defended, would have turned to the great Republican Union party, and have said: "For this act of noble clemency I am bound to you through life and unto death; that which you have done this day, places me under obligations from which I can never escape, and which I shall forever cherish. I feel that I have disgraced you and dishonored myself, and by a life of gratitude I will prove that, although unworthy of your confidence, and unworthy of your vindication, I can at least do my best to atone for my offence." But as you seem to be made of different metal from such a character, you have not only coolly forgotten the generous men who saved you from disgrace, but are now engaged in the pleasant pastime of slandering them and proscribing their friends. I will postpone a description of my own part in that sad drama, preferring to wait for the other private revelations you promise to lay before the country. It is very certain that, if you have forgotten all shame, you cannot have forgotten my connection with yourself during that unhappy experience. Probably no more graphic and instructive page could be added to the curious history of your Administration than a detailed account of that celebrated day. I have not been as careful in treasuring all the incidents, as you have been in preserving the private letters of the gentlemen whom you intended to betray; but where my own memory fails I shall be able to eke out a complete narrative by turning to the copious and fascinating columns of those traitor and Copperhead newspapers which are now defending your character and your conduct.

J. W. FORNEY.

Philadelphia Press, July 3, 1866.

1. At this point, Forney reprints his January 2 letter to Johnson. For the full text see *Johnson Papers*, 9: 562.

2. See Freedmen's Bureau Veto Message, Feb. 19, 1866, and Washington's Birthday Address, Feb. 22, 1866.

From William Cornell Jewett

Clifton House   Clifton C.W [Canada]
July 2d 1866

President Johnson,

From your non-reply to my last,[1] I should not again address you. I must however do so for an explanation.

My views in telegram herein—are basid upon a belief—you are not, at heart—with the leaders of August Convention—indeed cannot be, as a democrat & defender of the Constitution, for it is plain the design of the Conservative Republicans,—can only be to distroy the radical power, for a rule of their own.

I deem you the sole sustainer to day of American Liberty & I feel under the power of God, you will prove true to the Constitution—the rights of the South—& the Democratic principles upon which, in their patriot spirit—the regeneration of the Republic, must look to, through the independent action of the people of all the States.

The Republican party was founded upon the freedom of the slave, *with that gained it ceases*. As the South are now willing to give up slavery, & to unite, with the North in sustaining a strong & ligetimate government—they should as a party retire from the field & join a movement of the people—simply to restore the Constitution of our fathers & a union of the States in harmonious representation.

Wm. Cornell Jewett

ALS, DLC-JP.
1. Perhaps a reference to his telegram of ten days earlier. See Jewett to Johnson, June 23, 1866, Johnson Papers, LC.

From Kenneth Rayner

New York, July 2nd 1866.

Dear Sir,

I forward to you by to day's mail two copies of "The life and times of Andrew Johnson." One of them you will please accept as an humble testimonial of my high appreciation of your public character as a Statesman and Patriot, and of your private virtues as a man. The other you will present to Mrs. Johnson in my name. I hope she will pardon the liberty I thus take. I have not the honor of personally knowing her, but, having made most respectful mention of her name in the book,[1] I wish to offer this humble tribute to the virtues of her character, as wife, mother, and friend.

It is the impression here, that the work will be in demand and have a wide circulation, as soon as the political canvasses of the Fall are opened. In the mean time, it is to be hoped, your friends will use the necessary appliances, in having the book brought favorably, to the notice of the reading public.

I leave here in a day or two, for my home in Raleigh, there to make arrangements for finally leaving the state, and taking up my abode in the south-west—probably in Mississippi.

May an all-wise and merciful Providence protect and bless you, in your efforts to save the constitutional rights and liberties of your country.

K. Rayner

P.S. My friend, Mr. Thos. McElrath has, at my suggestion, forwarded to you, divers testimonials in his behalf, in reference to the appointment of "naval officer," of this port.[2]

K. R.

ALS, DLC-JP.

1. Rayner portrayed Eliza as being a "lady of fine native intellect, and of considerable cultivation," who was largely responsible for her husband's early education. *Life and Times of Andrew Johnson*, 6.

2. McElrath had secured the endorsement of several business firms of New York City, and on the following day Rayner himself wrote a separate letter to Johnson urging his appointment. Although not chosen for the naval officer post, McElrath was nominated in December 1866 as appraiser of merchandise for the port of New York and confirmed by the Senate shortly afterwards. See letters in Appts., Customs Service, Naval Officer, New York City, Thomas McElrath, RG56, NA; Ser. 6B, Vol. 4: 51, Johnson Papers, LC.

From Thomas P. Collins[1]

Crockett, Texas, 3rd July 1866.

I would not trouble your Excellency at this time, being aware you have more than enough already to attend to, but necessity almost forces me to it. I was appointed Postmaster at this place in March (I think) of last year, merely accepted it for the Convenience of the Community and my own, and never received as much one cent from the emoluments of the office. As soon as Governor Hamilton gave us an opportunity, I made an application to your Excellency for special pardon. I was the third person in this County who took the Oath of amnesty as prescribed in your proclamation. It went forward at once to Austin for Governor Hamilton's approval, but owing to the delays of office it was unattended to, until the representative from this County in the Convention, by my request, had it approved by the Governor, and mailed at once to you. Although months (I think) have elapsed since, yet I have not heard from it, and a week ago I was denied the privilege of voting in a very important election by the Governor's proclamation.

A short time since I observed in the newspapers, that thereafter pardons would not be issued except to applicants in person. If this be correct, I must implore your Excellency to make me an exception, as I am nearly sixty seven years old, and almost ruined by the results of the war.[2]

I trust your Excellency will not give ear to any reports of disloyalty in Texas. It is true, that many have been discouraged by the conduct of the Radicals in Congress, who have not treated us as brothers should, yet we are all determined on being good citizens in future.

Thomas P. Collins

ALS, DLC-JP.

1. Collins (b. *c*1799), a native of Ireland who had been active in the Texas Whig party in the early 1850s, was a merchant of substantial wealth by 1860. 1860 Census, Tex., Houston, Crockett, 209; Randolph Campbell, "The Whig Party of Texas in the Elections of

1848 and 1852," *SWHQ*, 73 (1969): 31; Collins to Johnson, Feb. 23, 1866, Amnesty Papers (M1003, Roll 52), Tex., Thomas P. Collins, RG94, NA.

2. Collins's oath is dated August 30, 1865. Hamilton recommended pardon for him March 5, 1866. In fact, Johnson had already pardoned Collins on April 30, 1866, but, obviously, the news had not yet reached Crockett, Texas. Amnesty Papers (M1003, Roll 52), Tex., Thomas P. Collins, RG94, NA; *House Ex. Docs.*, 39 Cong., 2 Sess., No. 116, p. 57 (Ser. 1293).

From Joseph R. Flanigen

Philadelphia, July 4 1866

My Dr Mr President—

I enclose you the proceedings of our state Convention held yesterday.[1]

It was rather an informal one, but considering the excitement consequent on the return of flags which takes place to day,[2] it was a full success.

Our friends general complained very much that the post offices in the state—nearly all of them—are still in the hands of our enemies. Thes are great engines with which to operate, and they should be put into the hands of *your freinds* at once.

I hope to be in Washington in a few days, and will then take pleasure in suggestg to you some changes that shd be made at once.

J R Flanigen

ALS, DLC-JP.
1. Not found. The resolutions endorsing Johnson's administration and calling for the organization of Johnson Clubs in every school district in the state may be found in the *Philadelphia Press*, July 4, 1866.
2. Battle flags of various Pennsylvania regiments were formally presented to the state as part of Philadelphia's Independence Day celebrations. Ibid., July 5, 1866.

From John B. Henderson[1]

United States Senate Chamber.
Washington, July 4, 1866

Dear Sir—

I have been absent from the City for a week, and regret on my return to hear that you have some doubt about the propriety of signing the bill recently passed by Congress to amend the Pacific R.R. charter.[2]

Had I been in the City I would have called on you before this to express my wish that you might be able to sign the bill. I originally drew and offered the bill myself. It is one in which the people of Missouri are most deeply interested. It does no injustice to any state, while its failure will tend to make Missouri & all states on the same parallel tributary to those on a higher parallel of latitude.

The direct line to the Pacific, and the line now most needed by the Government, and best calculated to subserve all the great interests of a united Country, which must soon be united, is on the line indicated in the bill now before you. I do sincerely hope that your views of public policy will not prevent your approval of the measure.[3]

J. B. Henderson

ALS, DLC-JP.
1. Henderson (1826–1913), a lawyer who had served in the Missouri state legislature, was appointed to the U.S. Senate in 1862 and then elected in 1863. A Democrat, he was especially active on the finance and Indian affairs committees until his term expired in 1869. *BDAC*; *DAB*.
2. An act amending a July 1862 act was passed July 3, 1866, to make provisions for the location and connection of the Union Pacific and Central Pacific tracks. *U.S. Statutes at Large*, 14: 79–80.
3. Johnson had already signed the bill on July 3, but the information was not announced to the Senate until July 6. *Congressional Globe*, 39 Cong., 1 Sess., p. 3612.

From Edmund Burke

July 5, 1866, Newport, N.H.; ALS, DNA-RG60, Appt. Files for Judicial Dists., N.H., Ira A. Eastman.

Having earlier written in support of Henry A. Bellows for the district judge vacancy in New Hampshire, the writer now recommends Ira A. Eastman for the position, explaining "I then supposed that none but a Republican could be appointed," but "understanding now that appointments may be conferred on persons of a different political faith who are patriotic and loyal and who support the Restoration policy of the Administration," he backs Eastman. Former justice of the supreme court of the state, member of Congress, and recently a candidate for the U.S. Senate, Eastman would be "entirely acceptable to the friends of the Administration in this State."

From A. A. Campbell[1]

Nashville   5 July 1866

Sir

It is being reported here that the Hon Horas Manard says you are in favor of the Constitutional amendment being passed by the Leguslature.[2]

A. A. Campbell

ALS, DLC-JP.
1. Not identified.
2. Certainly Campbell was wrong about Johnson's being in favor of the Fourteenth Amendment. Information about Maynard's having declared the President's support of the amendment has not been uncovered.

From Thomas Fitzgerald

Philadelphia   July 5th 1866.

E. G. Webb Assessor for first (1st) District of Pennsylvania is dead. Can I have the place?

Thomas Fitzgerald

Tel, DLC-JP.

From John W. Frazier[1]

Philada   July 5th 1866

Sir:

I hereby respectfully make application for the position of Assessor of Internal Revenue for the 1st Penna. now vacant, Caused by the death of the late incumbent Mr Edward G Webb, and in doing so submit the following claims.

1st   Am thoroughly conversant with the duties of the office.

2nd   I was in the Army under Col E D Baker, was *honorably* discharged "on account of disability resulting from confluent smallpox."

3thd   Have an ordinary share of integrity; had it been otherwise I would have been ousted by Mr Rollins, five months ago.[2]

4th   I am a *union man*, always have been; am as bitterly opposed to the political principles of Thad. Stevens and Chas Sumner and their followers as I was to these of James Buchanan and Jefferson Davis.

5th   Have pluck enough to run the office (if appointed) in the interest of the Government. And hoping for a favorable consideration. . . .[3]

Jno W Frazier
929 So 4th St   Philada Penna.

ALS, DNA-RG56, Appts., Internal Revenue Service, Assessor, Pa., 1st Dist., John W. Frazier.

1. Frazier (*c*1837–*fl*1916), a private in Co. C, 71st Pa. Inf., for a few months in 1861, was employed after 1869 as a carpenter, engraver, author, editor, and publisher. CSR, John W. Frazier, RG94, NA; Philadelphia directories (1870–84); *NUC*.

2. Edward A. Rollins, internal revenue commissioner. Frazier currently worked as a revenue inspector in Philadelphia. *McElroy's Philadelphia City Directory* (1866).

3. Although Johnson was advised to appoint an Irish candidate to the assessorship, he chose Frazier, whose recess appointment became effective in August, but whose nomination was not presented to the Senate until February 1867. Confirmed by the Senate on March 30, Frazier continued serving throughout Johnson's administration. George F. Train to Johnson, endorsement on J. M. Spellissey to Train, July 20, 1866; Spellissey to Johnson, July 5, Aug. 29, 1866, Appts., Internal Revenue Service, Assessor, Pa., 1st Dist., J. M. Spellissey, RG56, NA; Ser. 6B, Vol. 3: 161; Vol. 4: 83–84, 87, Johnson Papers, LC; *Senate Ex. Proceedings*, Vol. 15, pt. 1: 159; pt. 2: 589.

From William Sayles[1]

Browns ville Texas   July the 5 1866

Presen johnson

I am a flicked and i Wold liked to B mousted out of Sufers. My famly is out doose. I in lested in the year 18[6?] and i was in the Hospittel Va 2 mounts in the Hospitel at ringgo 2 mountes and in the Hospitel Browns ville Texas 2 mountes and i am in the Hospitel now and dont think that i Will B fit for Sufes inmore and i am in Bad Steate of healt. I hav got a wife and three Childen. My Wife is Sick and has not got enay place to Stay and thar fore i Wold like to B mousted Out of Suves.[2]

William Sayles
117 Co D uSCT

ALS, DNA-RG94, USCT Div., Lets. Recd., File P-200-1866.
1. Sayles [Sayres, Sayers] (b. c1838), a native of Carroll County, Kentucky, and a "farmer," had enlisted in August 1864 at Covington. He was suffering from syphilis "contracted while on Furlough." CSR, William Sayres, RG94, NA.
2. Johnson forwarded Sayles's application to the adjutant general who in turn sent it to Gen. Philip Sheridan. The application descended through the departmental ranks until it finally reached Lt. Col. Charles H. Morse, commander of the 117th USCT, who, on September 26, related that "an Application for Discharge accompanied by 'Certificates of Disability,' has been made for Private Sayles. This man was Sick in Hospital, or Application for his Discharge would have been made before." On October 19 Sheridan finally returned the application and its numerous endorsements to the War Department with the information that Sayles had been discharged. However, Sayles [Sayres, Sayers] was not actually discharged until November 30, 1866. CSR, William Sayres [Sayers], RG94, NA.

From John A. McClernand

PRIVATE!

Springfield Ill   July 7th A.D. 1866.

My son, Edward J. McClernand,[1] now an active, well grown youth, in his seventeenth year, is very desirous to receive a military education. West Point is the only place in the United States where he can receive a thorough one and obtain rank in the military profession.

Understanding that one or more of the cadets lately appointed by you, have failed, or will fail to pass examination, I venture to solicit, again,[2] the appointment of my son. I suppose such vacancys as may occur will be filled by appointments to made in next August, or September, probably, in September.

My apology for troubling you a second time on this subject is based on information that my request, under existing circumstances, would be likely to receive favorable consideration. I think my son is capable of making himself useful in the profession to which he aspires. Whether my civil and military services justify me in preferring such a request, you will, no doubt, impartially judge. If the concurrence of others in my request should be required it can be furnished to any desired extent.

As I expect to send my son abroad to acquire a military education if he should fail in opportunity to acquire one in his native country, you will oblige me by giving, at your earliest convenience, information; whether it will be in your power, or agreeable to you, to bestow on him the solicited appointment.[3]

After what I have written, I need, hardly, add, that both my son and myself would be profoundly thankful for the favor solicited.

John A. McClernand.

ALS, DLC-JP.
   1. Following his graduation from West Point in 1870, McClernand (1848–1926) saw frontier duty under Custer, during which time he received the congressional medal of honor, and later served in Cuba and the Phillipines, before his retirement from the army as brigadier general in 1912. *Washington Post*, Feb. 10, 1926.
   2. See John A. McClernand to Johnson, Apr. 13, 1866, USMA Appls. (M688, Roll 241), RG94, NA.
   3. Secretary Stanton notified McClernand of his son's appointment later in the month. John A. McClernand to Johnson, July 18, 1866, Johnson Papers, LC.

From George W. Morgan

Mount Vernon, O   July 7 1866

Mr. President

I have not before written, for the reason that I had nothing satisfactory to communicate. Our State Central Committee have called a council to meet in Columbus on the 12 inst. to take action relative to the Philadelphia Convention.[1] We had already agreed upon two delegates for this 13h District—Genl. W. H. Ball[2] and George B. Smythe.[3] The former is a Republican; the latter a Democrat—both are men of standing and ability. However, I will attend the Columbus consultation.

You, I trust, will pardon me for writing with the same frankness that I had the honor to speak to you when in Washington. You have inspired the body of the democracy with confidence; but constant complaints are made at the retention in your cabinet of men who are known to be hostile to you, and your policy. Mr. Stanton is justly more detested than any man in America, and his bad fame would throw a cloud upon any administration to which he might be attached.

The democracy have no favors to ask in the way of offices, but they do respectfully, but earnestly hope that your enemies, and the enemies of the Constitution may be removed, and that conservative republicans may be appointed to fill their places. The office holders are beginning to boast that they cannot be removed, and the public are commencing so to think.

Despite my wishes, and against my will, the Congressional Convention put me in nomination, by acclamation for Congress, and I have reluctantly consented to be a candidate.[4]

I will probably be in Washington during the present month to aid in organizing Ohio Democratic Head Quarters.

George W. Morgan

ALS, DLC-JP.
   1. For his reports of the council at Columbus, see Morgan to Johnson, July 13, 14, 1866, Johnson Papers, LC.
   2. William H. Ball (1818–1907), a former Whig lawyer and commander of the 122nd Ohio Vol. Inf., who had been previously recommended by Morgan for the Thirteenth District collectorship, was given a recess appointment to that post on October 1 before Secretary McCulloch suspended his commission two days later. Afterwards he served one term in the Ohio legislature and five years as a common pleas judge in Zanesville. Hunt and Brown, *Brigadier Generals*; Morgan to Johnson, June 5, 1866, OFH; F. E. Scobey and B. L. McElroy, comps., *The Biographical Annals of Ohio, 1902–1903* (n.p., n.d.), 243, 734;

Morgan to McCulloch, Oct. 16, 1866, Appts., Internal Revenue Service, Collector, Ohio, 13th Dist., William H. Ball, RG56, NA; Ser. 6B, Vol. 3: 495, Johnson Papers, LC.

3. Formerly a militia major general and a War Democrat, Smythe (1807–1898) for more than fifty years practiced law in Newark, Ohio. *Memorial Record of Licking County Ohio* (Chicago, 1894), 188–89; E.M.P. Brister, *Centennial History of the City of Newark and Licking County Ohio* (2 vols., Chicago, 1909), 2: 146.

4. Morgan was elected in 1866 to the 40th Congress.

From James Dixon

Hartford   July 8th 66.

My dear Sir

In the event of the passage of the Education Bill[1] I am very desirous that Henry Barnard[2] of Ct the great apostle of Common schools should be appointed Commissioner or superintendent.[3]

There is not in the United States a man so well fitted for the place.

The Philda. Convention will be the great movement of the day. Never have I been so sure of the salvation of the Country & of your re-election as now. But I do think you ought to do some thing to soothe the Fenians. How would do to pardon all the Fenian Prisoners?[4] I wish you would. The radicals are making some capital on that point.

James Dixon.

ALS, DLC-JP.

1. Introduced by Rep. James Garfield on February 14, the act establishing the Department of Education had passed the House on June 19, but remained tied up in a Senate committee until the next session, when the Senate finally passed the measure at the end of February 1867 and Johnson approved it a few days later. *House Journal*, 39 Cong., 1 Sess., pp. 271, 865 (Ser. 1243); *Senate Journal*, 39 Cong., 1 Sess., p. 548 (Ser. 1236); 2 Sess., pp. 171, 373, 453 (Ser. 1275).

2. Barnard (1811–1900) had been active in education in both Connecticut and Rhode Island, prior to serving as chancellor of the University of Wisconsin (1858–60) and president of St. John's College of Annapolis, Maryland (1866–67). *DAB*.

3. Two days before the Senate passed the education bill, Dixon sent a note to Johnson, reminding him of "the encouragement you gave me" regarding Barnard's appointment. On March 8, 1867, Johnson's secretary requested Secretary Seward to have Barnard's nomination as commissioner of education "sent over early to morrow." Nominated on March 11, he was confirmed three days later. Dixon to Johnson, Feb. 26, 1867, Appts. Div., Misc. Lets. Recd., RG48, NA; Robert Johnson to Seward, Mar. 8, 1867, Lets. of Appl. and Recomm., 1861–69 (M650, Roll 3), Henry Barnard, RG59, NA; Ser. 6B, Vol. 2: 35, Johnson Papers, LC.

4. The Fenian prisoners were not tried. Brian Jenkins, *Fenians and Anglo-American Relations during Reconstruction* (Ithaca, 1969), 189.

From William H.C. King

Important and *Personal* to the *President*

New Orleans, July 8 1866.

Honored President

After our interview, saw the importance of being at home. Left N.Y. on 23d and arrived 1st inst.

Immediately set the ball in motion.

Have considerable trouble to manage schemers who can think of nothing but their own and unworthy purposes—*will manage them somehow*, or I will lash them with a scorpion's whip.

Am to-day to meet the most prominent gentlemen to arrange upon good delegates—men of mark, character, *and from all* PAST parties—your friends.[1]

Please read enclosed articles[2]—you will lose nothing by the time devoted to me, *be sure of that*.

Wrote Senator Doolittle.[3]

I want nothing in the world but for you to strengthen my hands and influence.

Bullitt, U.S. Marshal,[4] is scheming now to be retained. *Do*, I BEG YOU, appoint E. E. Norton[5] to his place.

I ask this, and will prove my sincerity and gratitude. It is important to you and to your friends here.

                                                                Wm. H.C. King

Savage[6] wrote the *best* article. Arranged with him to counsel with you—that I might not get astray.

                                                                              K

ALS, DLC-JP.
    1. King's project was managing the selection of the Louisiana delegates to the National Union Convention at Philadelphia in August. The Democratic Central Committee met in New Orleans on July 7 and 10 and between those dates a subcommittee also met with some of the non-Democratic conservatives. Perhaps King refers to such a sub-committee meeting. Michael Perman, *Reunion Without Compromise: The South and Reconstruction, 1865–1868* (Cambridge, 1973), 211, 219; *New Orleans Picayune*, July 12, 1866. See also King to Johnson, July 10, 1866.
    2. Not found, but probably from King's paper, the *New Orleans Times*.
    3. James R. Doolittle of Wisconsin.
    4. Cuthbert Bullitt.
    5. Emery E. Norton (*fl*1901) was an assignee for bankrupt estates at the U.S. Customs House in New Orleans for several years and a disappointed seeker of a senatorial seat in 1873. New Orleans directories (1866–1901); Agnes Smith Grosz, "The Political Career of Pickney Benton Stewart Pinchback," *LHQ*, 27 (1944): 595.
    6. John Savage (1828–1888) fled his native Ireland because of his revolutionary activities and came to the United States in 1848. He worked as a journalist and in the late 1860s supported the Fenian cause. His *Life and Public Services of Andrew Johnson* was published in 1866. King hired Savage to write pro-Johnson articles as early as June 1865. *DAB*; William H. C. King to Johnson, June 9, 1865, *Johnson Papers*, 8: 207.

From Thurlow Weed

                                                                New York, July 8, '66

Dear Sir,

The Hon Mr Cobb[1] of New Jersey, who will deliver this Letter, was formerly a Democratic member of Congress from N.J. Like yourself, however he preferred his Country to his Party, and was through the war, what he is now, a Loyal man.

Mr Cobb is enlightened and thoughtful. He is capable and efficient. Please take his suggestions as to New Jersey.

Thurlow Weed

ALS, DLC-JP.
    1. George T. Cobb (1813–1870), who served one term in Congress (1861–63), had been elected in 1865 as a Republican to the mayoralty of Morristown, New Jersey. *BDAC*.

From Christopher W. Dudley

Bennettsville S.C.   July 9th 1866.

Dear Sir.

I hope you will pardon the rather too frequente interruptions you may have to endure, from the several communications heretofore sente you by me.[1] I am proud to acknowledge, that I have the very highest regard for your character, both personal & political, & desire to be numbered amongst the humble adherents, who are endeavouring to sustain your administration. The world must know you, *as the friend of your country*, & not the partizan of a section—you have suffered already, very much for the sake of the union—& are suffering still, in the patriotic effort to carry out the principles for which you were so generally denounced, in the early part of the revolution, by the advocates of Secession. Believing this to be the case; I have been impressed under the conviction, that you would be willing to hear, from any one, no matter how humble, whatever pertained to the great interests over which you have been called to preside. I have the honour therefore, to lay before your Excellency, an editorial from the Darlington Southerner,[2] (a paper published in an adjoining district to that in which I reside,) from which you will be enabled to determine, what kind of temper is cultivated by the emissaries from the North, amongst the numerous freedmen, with whom we compelled to live. I offer no comments, but will simply add, that we are now compelled to avoid issues with them, by humiliating appeals to their better natures, even whilst they are imposing upon us, in every way a dishonourable nature can inspire. Contracts are violated, without the least regard whatever to their stipulations—they absent themselves when they please, & lounge lazily about, when they pretend to work—yet we have to accept this return for wages promptly paid, or be left without an operative at all. The consequence is, very little cotton, will be made in this State, the present year—& very little corn—the grass has swept every thing—long rains, heavy grass & negro labour, have left us scarcely any thing to hope for. Had it been possible to urge the freedmen—or persuade them—or stimulate them in any way, we could have done better—but we are entirely at their mercy, & must accept any kind of labour we can get, & pay for it, as for the best.

The effort in Darlington, seems to be, to keep them in a good humour

—they are very numerous over there & under very little control. How long "Sedatives" will keep them quiet, it is difficult to say, but we all know, they must lose their effect before long. What are we to do? Is there to be no peace for us—no relief from continual apprehension—no assurance of protection from a crowd, which has only to consult it's own appetite as to the material with which it is to be gratified?

C. W. Dudley.

ALS, DLC-JP.
1. The only previous Dudley to Johnson correspondence that has been found, August 30 and September 6, 1865, Johnson Papers, LC, both pertained to the freedmen.
2. The "editorial" was a report of a large 4th of July celebration by Darlington freedmen. The part offensive to Dudley was remarks by a black northern minister, Rev. Mr. Hamilton, "well calculated to array the black man against his white neighbor." *Darlington Southerner*, July 5, 1866.

From Harry Gilmor[1]

Washington—D.C.   9th July 1866

Sir

I was released on my parole, (after taking the Oath of Allegiance & the Amnesty Oath) from Fort Warren, where I had been a prisoner of War for more than seven months. I immediately started for my home in Md. but found, on reaching New York City that I had been indicted by the State courts of Pennsylvania & Md.,[2] and was advised by all my friends not to return home. Since that time (a year ago) I have lived in New York City for the most part, but now wish to return to my Fathers[3] Estate in Maryland to engage in some agricultural pursuit. And as the indictments above mentioned, are still pending, and as I am in fear of arrest and imprisonment by the State authorities, I hope your Excellency will take favorable action on my request and grant me a pardon.[4] I am willing & ready to give any security that may be required of me, for the faithful performance of all pledges that I have heretofore given, and which I consider renewed in this application.

Deeming it unnecessary to absorb more of the Valuable time of your Excellency I have the honor to remain. . . .

Harry Gilmor

ALS, DNA-RG94, Amnesty Papers (M1003, Roll 30), Md., Harry Gilmor.
1. Gilmor (1838–1883), Confederate soldier, served with the 12th Va. Cav. and the 2nd Md. Btn. in the Shenandoah Valley and Maryland, proving to be an exceptional raider. He was captured several times, the last being in February 1865. After the war he was a Baltimore businessman and later police commissioner (1874–79). *DAB*.
2. Gilmor was indicted in Maryland as a guerilla. Grant endorsed him when he recommended that paroled officers be exempt from civil trial for acts of civilized warfare. Stitt to Stanbery, July 9, 1866, Amnesty Papers (M1003, Roll 30), Va., Harry Gilmor, RG94, NA.
3. Robert Gilmor (1808–1874), a capitalist, was a Harvard graduate and served as attaché to the U.S. legation in Paris from 1829 to 1832. *NCAB*, 2: 402.

4. Docketing indicates he was pardoned November 12, 1866. See also Gilmor to Stanbery, Oct. 31, 1866, Amnesty Papers (M1003, Roll 30), Va., Harry Gilmor, RG94, NA.

From John Hancock

Austin, Texas   July 9th 1866.

Mr. President:

Genl. M. D. Ector[1] of Rusk County, this State, as I learn, sometime since made application for your special amnesty and pardon. The rank he held in the rebel service[2] constituting an exception which has not been usually relieved by you unless the applicant presented some special cause. I would not trouble you did I not think the facts in this case such as will, in your estimation, readily entitle the applicant to your clemency. I have been well acquainted with Genl. Ector for many years, know him to be an honorable man, moral and orderly in his deportment and rigidly observant of all his undertakings. He was a lawyer in prosperous circumstances at the commencement of the war; he came out empoverished in fortune and with the loss of one leg. For the last year he has obtained a meager support for himself and family by teaching in an institution of learning, exerting himself in the meantime, in his section, in the restoration of social order and the return of all to their allegiance to the U.S. Gov't., obedience to and support of its laws and authority, exerting an extensive and beneficial influence. At the recent election the people of his Judicial district elected him their judge, An office that will comfortably support himself and family. To enable him to avail himself of this boon from the people, and again to comfortably feed, cloth and educate his little children,[3] I have ventured to trespass upon you, and to earnestly request you will extend to him pardon and amnesty, and thereby restore happiness to a sorrow-stricken family and very greatly oblige.[4]

John Hancock

ALS, DNA-RG94, Amnesty Papers (M1003, Roll 52), Tex., M. D. Ector.

1. Matthew D. Ector (1822–1879), a lawyer, served one term in the Georgia legislature before he moved in 1850 to Henderson, Texas, where he was elected to the state legislature in 1855. Warner, *Gray*; Webb et al., *Handbook of Texas*, 1: 541.

2. Ector enlisted as a private in 1861 and speedily rose to colonel of cavalry. Commissioned a brigadier general to rank from August 23, 1862, he commanded infantry in the western theater of the war until he was wounded near Atlanta on July 27, 1864. The wound cost him a leg and terminated his field service. Warner, *Gray*; Ector to Johnson, Dec. 11, 1865, Amnesty Papers (M1003, Roll 52), Tex., M. D. Ector, RG94, NA.

3. Ector claimed a wife and three dependent children. Ibid.

4. Gov. A. J. Hamilton and Gen. U. S. Grant supported Ector's request for pardon. Johnson agreed and endorsed the application "Issue pardon in this case." This was done on August 8, 1866. Ector assumed the office of district judge but was removed with other state officials by Gen. Philip Sheridan in 1867. Again appointed district judge in 1874, Ector was serving on the state court of appeals at his death. Amnesty Papers (M1003, Roll 52), Tex., M. D. Ector, RG94, NA; Webb et al., *Handbook of Texas*, 1: 541; 2: 778.

From Robert M. Martin[1]

55 Beekman Street, N.Y., July 9th, 1866.

Sir:

An applicant for Executive clemency, I beg to submit the following statement and petition for your consideration.

I was Colonel of the 10th Kentucky Cavalry of the (So-called) Confederate States army; and in August, 1864, while serving in that capacity, I was ordered by Mr. Seddon, then Secretary of War, C.S.A., to report to Mr. Benjamin, then Secretary of State, C.S.A., and by him ordered to report to Mr. Thompson, then Secretary of Interior C.S.A.[2] and in Canada West, for the purpose of aiding in a scheme, then on foot, to release a prisoner confined at Johnson's Island, or for such other service as might be beneficial to the Confederate Cause.

Compliance with this order placed me in that class exempted by 11th clause of your amnesty proclamation of May 29th 1865.

On the 27th of September 1865, I was arrested at my home in Kentucky, and carried to New York City, where I was charged with complicity in the attempt to burn that city in October 1864, was tried before Judge Shipman[3] of the Circuit court of the United States for the Southern District of New York, and by him on the 27th day of February last acquitted of the charge.

I am also of the class exempted by 10th clause of the before mentioned proclamation wherefore, I beg that executive clemency be extended me.[4]

R. M. Martin

ALS, DNA-RG94, Amnesty Papers (M1003, Roll 26), Ky., Robert M. Martin.

1. Martin (1840–1901) served under Gen. John H. Morgan in Kentucky before being assigned to secret service behind enemy lines. Returning to his old command just prior to Lee's surrender, he ended the war as part of Jefferson Davis's escort, at which time he surrendered and was paroled. He was later arrested for his participation in the unsuccessful Confederate scheme to burn New York City and spent seven months in jail. He was released when charges were dismissed in February 1866. Nat Brandt, *The Man Who Tried to Burn New York* (Syracuse, 1986), 71, 235–36; Otto A. Rothert, *A History of Muhlenberg County* (Louisville, 1964 [1913]), 318, 324–25; Martin to Johnson, n.d., Amnesty Papers (M1003, Roll 26), Ky., Robert M. Martin, RG94, NA.

2. James A. Seddon, Judah P. Benjamin, and Jacob Thompson.

3. William D. Shipman (1818–1898), jurist, was admitted to the bar in 1850 and went on to serve as U.S. attorney and then as U.S. district judge of Connecticut. During this time he also served on the circuit court of New York City and occasionally sat in the northern district of New York and Vermont. *NCAB*, 11: 262.

4. Martin was pardoned September 19, 1866. Amnesty Papers (M1003, Roll 26), Ky., Robert M. Martin, RG94, NA.

From Thomas Pattinson[1]

Laconia Harrison Co Ind
July 9, 1866

Sir,

I hope you will not think me intruding or meddeling with your pre-rogative, when I state my object in addressing you these lines. It is to inform you that T. C. Slaughter[2] District Assessor of internal Revenue 2nd Congression district is going the rounds making stump speches against you and your Policy and defaming your character and patriotism while he is as I think at your mercy for the Office he holds and I think if you could but hear one of his harangues you certainly would remove him and also B F Scribner the Collector for he is as bitter an enemy as the other and there are men in the District of the same Party *Republicans* who advocate and defend you and your Policy. Allow me to name some which I know are conservative. D. W. Lafollette and Kelso[3] both of New Albany and I think able to fill those offices. They are Republican and has always been but now of course because they sustain you they are abused by these office holders for not endorsing Stevens Sumner & Co. It does seem to me that so long as you keep your bitter enemies in office you cannot succeed in your restoration policy. They tell the people that you and the Radicals are not far apart and that you will come over to them yet. By this means the people will vote for Radicals. They believe that you and these officers must be alike or you would remove them as a house divided against itself cannot stand.

Now Sir my advice is remove all such and fill those places with Conservative Republicans and it would greatly strenghen you.[4] This is my oppinion. Hoping you will not think me dictating, but advising—which every Citizen as a right to do.

Thos. Pattinson

ALS, DNA-RG56, Appts., Internal Revenue Service, Collector, Ind., 2nd Dist., B. F. Scribner.

1. Pattinson (b. c1812) was a successful merchant and farmer, and a native of England. 1860 Census, Ind., Harrison, Boon Twp., Laconia, 113; (1870), Maukport, 5.

2. Appointed as assessor by Lincoln, Thomas C. Slaughter (c1821–fl1876) was also a merchant, attorney, and judge. 1860 Census, Ind., Harrison, Harrison Twp., Corydon, 72; Matilda Gresham, *Life of Walter Quinton Gresham, 1832–1895* (2 vols., Chicago, 1919), 2: 459; Taylor, *Bench and Bar of Indiana*, 192; *U.S. Off. Reg.* (1863–65).

3. Probably James V. Kelso (c1835–fl1882), a New Albany teacher, school trustee, and city attorney. 1860 Census, Ind., Floyd, New Albany, 6th Ward, 106; *Ohio Falls Cities*, 2: 159, 176, 218.

4. Slaughter was removed and replaced on August 6 by Col. William P. Davis, who was highly recommended by three members of Indiana's congressional delegation. After holding office for several months, Davis, however, was not confirmed by the Senate, nor were as many as fourteen others (including James V. Kelso) whom Johnson nominated between March 1867 and July 1868. In fact, the post appears to have remained vacant until the expiration of Johnson's term. Ser. 6B, Vol. 3: 553; Vol. 4: 285, 287–89, Johnson Papers,

LC; *U.S. Off. Reg.* (1867–69); Michael C. Kerr, Thomas A. Hendricks, and William E. Niblack to Johnson, June 20, 1866, Appts., Internal Revenue Service, Assessor, Ind., 2nd Dist., William P. Davis, RG56, NA.

From Thaddeus Stevens

Washington   July 9 1866

Sir

May I be allowed to express the hope that the sentence of Maj. Paulding[1] may be mitigated. I am not acquainted with him but know his relations and connexions to be highly honorable and honest men. I cannot think the evidence makes out a case of corrupt intention, though a great error was committed. Would not the disgrace and early dismissal from the army be sufficient atonement for that?

If not wholly inconsistent with the public good I would most earnestly desire that so much mercy might be shown to this unfortunate man.

Thaddeus Stevens

ALS, DNA-RG94, ACP Branch, File P-640-CB-1866, E. E. Paulding.
1. Edmund E. Paulding, a brevet lieutenant colonel, served as additional paymaster and was charged with disobedience of orders, misappropriation of funds, and neglect of duty in April 1866 while chief paymaster of the District of Washington. He was sentenced on July 9 to a fine of five thousand dollars and a one-year imprisonment. Johnson approved the sentence and designated Fort McHenry as the place of imprisonment. In December 1866 Paulding was released from confinement at Fort McHenry. E.R.S. Canby to Adj. Gen., Dec. 12, 1866, Lets. Recd. (Main Ser.), File P-870-1866, (M619, Roll 529), RG94, NA; Court-Martial Records, MM-3969, RG153, NA; Powell, *Army List*, 811; *Philadelphia Press*, July 19, 1866.

From William B. Thomas[1]

Ionia Michigan   July 9" 1866

My Conservative Friends have requested you to appoint me United States Marshal for the Western District of Michigan.[2]

The Petition States my qualifications and my views on the great questions now agitating the Country.

Although I have always acted with the Republican Party and have felt a Strong attachment to that organization, yet if the views of Congress on the reconstruction of the Southern States is to become a plank in the Party Platform, I cannot act with or Support that Party.

I regard the Southern States as being Still in the Union, and I think that Loyal men elected to represent them in Congress should be addmitted to their seats.

If we expect the Country to be ever restored to a peaceful & prosperous condition the policy which you recommend must be adopted.

While in the army my health was very much impaired and after my discharge I was for a long time unable to perform the labors of my profession.

The appointment of U.S. Marshal for this District I desire, and would therefore respectfully ask the Same.[3]

Wm. B. Thomas

ALS, DNA-RG60, Appt. Files for Judicial Dists., Mich., William B. Thomas.

1. Thomas (*fl*1904) was a surgeon with the 21st Mich. Inf., until his resignation in December 1862. Afterwards he continued the practice of medicine in Ionia. John S. Schenck, *History of Ionia and Montcalm Counties, Michigan* (Philadelphia, 1881), 74, 155; E. E. Branch, ed., *History of Ionia County, Michigan: Her People, Industries and Institutions* (2 vols., Indianapolis, 1916), 1: 426, 428, 430–31.

2. See A. F. Bell et al. to Johnson, July 9, 1866, Appt. Files for Judicial Dist., Mich., William B. Thomas, RG60, NA, which enclosed Thomas's application. The half dozen men requested the President to appoint Thomas in place of the incumbent, Osmond Tower, whom they described as an "active supporter of the Sumner, Wade, and Chandler policy on reconstruction."

3. Thomas was given a recess appointment in August 1866, but his December nomination was rejected in February 1867. Ser. 6B, Vol. 3: 539; Vol. 4: 274, Johnson Papers, LC.

From Elizabeth Hockaday[1]

James City County Va

July 10th 1866

Dear Sir

In March of '63 I had the misfortune to have take from my stable in the night the only horse I owned in the world. It was carried off by a Mr. Doanlly,[2] who clamed at that time to be a soldier belounging to the United States army stationed at Wmsburg. I have tried but in vain to get my horse back again. While others have succeeded in giting their horses, I have certainly failed. I applied to General Terry[3] & he refered my case to the General in command at Fortress Monroe,[4] who ascrtained that my horse had been turned over by the Q.M. department to be used by the Freed mens' bureau & for these reasons the authorities declined to return my horse. Now Tis, I have to appeal to you for, relief. I am a widow with only one child a daughter,[5] who is afflicted & was entirely dependtant upon the work of my little farm upon the service of horse to obtain food for my family. I had neither son or husband engaged in the war, for I have none to be so engaged & why I am refused the property thus taken from me I cannot tell. The other horse which was stolen by a negroe, I do not know that it is a live. I heard that the horse was carried to Yorktown & I believe it as all stolen goods are carried there. President if you will give me any relief be so good as to do it speedily. I have on hand a small crop planted with the assistance of my neighbors, & if I can not get a horse, which I have no means of purchasing I must lose my crop & what my Condition must [be] you can well imagine. I have one of women living with me & the only way we have to live is to gather berries & sell them to purchas bread. If you would exercise your authority you have so that I could get my horse, which has been sold by the *Freed mens bureau* to a negroe at Slab Town & have me compensated for the one Stolen by a negroe to buy bread to keep me from starving, I for I assure you I must starve if I can not get any aide. Please send the order for my horse as soon as possible & by so doing you will confer a great favor on a helpless widow & receive the gratitude of . . . .

Elizabeth Hockaday
Williamsburg Virginia

ALS, DNA-RG92, Claims *re* Services, Horses, and Property, Bk. H 75.

1. Elizabeth Hockaday (*c*1810–*fl*1870), widow of James T. Hockaday, ran the family farm until her daughter took over sometime after the war. 1850 Census, Va., James City, 535; (1860), Burnt Ordinary, 730; (1870), James Town Twp., Williamsburg, 320.

2. Not identified.

3. Alfred H. Terry.

4. Nelson A. Miles.

5. Margaret Hockaday (*c*1845–*fl*1870), who by 1870 had taken over the farm. 1850 Census, Va., James City, 535; (1860), Burnt Ordinary, 730; (1870), James Town Twp., Williamsburg, 320.

From William H.C. King

Private to the President

New Orleans, July 10 1866.

Honored President

Have great trouble to secure the PROPER delegates.[1] The friends of Dick Taylor (Gen.)[2] want him as one. Think I can convince them and him of the great injury may be done thereby.

My name is on the list. I have told them *I will not go, unless the delegation can be a credit to you and serve our cause.*[3]

I worked very hard in this matter which brought me away from my family, post haste, after our interview. I have the whole matter greatly at heart.

Wm. H.C. King

Read the articles on the other side of sheet.[4]

Have had to reconcile a scheming set of politicians calling themselves after you—a Club consisting of about a dozen—will take their most prominent men as a portion of their delegates.[5] *Oh! these politicians!*

Nixon, the Alderman you pardoned,[6] is the man who urged Dick Taylor and others whose names at this time are inappropriate.

After the delegates are selected I advise a mass meeting to endorse them.[7]

ALS, DLC-JP.

1. Delegates to the National Union Convention in Philadelphia in August. See also King to Johnson, July 8, 1866.

2. Taylor was a Democrat and considered an "irreconcilable." He was chosen as a delegate and attended the convention. Perman, *Reunion Without Compromise*, 211, 221; Thomas Wagstaff, "The Arm-in-Arm Convention," *Civil War History*, 14 (1968): 101.

3. King went to Philadelphia. King to Johnson, Aug. 14, 1866, Johnson Papers, LC.

4. Not found, but probably from King's *New Orleans Times*.

5. He refers to the Andrew Johnson Club of Louisiana, headed by Cuthbert Bullitt, U.S. marshal for Louisiana, and enemy of King. Bullitt and his followers, in conjunction with the National Union Association led by Christian Roselius, nominated their own slate of delegates independently of the Democrats. *New Orleans Picayune*, Apr. 3, 7, July 25, 1866. See also Bullitt to Johnson, Apr. 7, 1866.

6. James O. Nixon was pardoned April 26, 1866. See John Purcell to Johnson, Mar. 22, 1866.

7. The nominating sub-committee from the Democratic Central Committee announced its delegate selections on July 10. These were ratified at a mass meeting in Lafayette Square on July 24. *New Orleans Picayune*, July 12, 25, 1866.

From Thomas J. Sorsby[1]

Greensboro Greene County Ala
July the 10th /66

Respected Sir

About the 12th of December last (1865) I forwarded to your Exellency through Hon. R. B. Waller[2] a Member of the Legislature from this County a petition for a Pardon. Mr Waller immediately after the Petition reached Montgomery handed it to the Governors private Secretary.[3] The Secretary informed him he would Send it on immediately to your Exellency at Washington. Nothing further was heard from the Petition until Some time in April last I recvd a letter from a Mr J. H. Speed[4] of Marion Ala. (Mr Speed is an entire Stranger to me.) He writes me he had obtained my Pardon, and that his fee was Two Hundred and Fifty ($250). I did not answer Mr Speeds letter until Seeing Mr Waller to ascertain of him if he had authorized Mr Speed to obtain the Pardon. Mr Waller informed me he had not Seen Mr Speed upon the Subject, and had never Seen him but once. In November last when on his way to Montgomery he was introduced to him on board of the Boat. I then wrote to Mr Speed, that as he had obtained my Pardon without any authority from Mr Waller, or myself I was willing to pay him what I thought was a reasonable compensation for his trouble, (which was certainly unsolicited) as he had no authority from Mr Waller or myself to act in the matter.

Mr Speed states in his letter, (as a reson I presume for acting in the matter and to get a heavy fee) that Coln Wm. M Brooks[5] told him I wished him to obtain a Pardon for me.

The circumstances are these. While on my way to Selma last December to go before an Agent of the Government to take the Oath, I met Coln Brooks on the Cars. And in a conversation with Coln Brooks upon the Subject of obtaining my Pardon, he remarked to me that a Gentleman Mr Speed of his Town Marion, Spoke when he last saw him of going on to Washington in a few days, and that he could ascertain in Selma whether Mr Speed had gone on or not, And Suggested, that he would be a Suitable person to Send on the Petition by. I remarked to Coln. Brooks I would like him would ascertain if Mr Speed had gone on or not as I would like to See him. But I did not Say that I would send on the petition by him. After our arrival in Selma I lost sight of Coln Brooks, and not being able to learn any thing of Mr Speed I expressed the petition to my friend Mr Waller at Montgomery. Mr Speed in his letter States that Coln Brooks told him I wished him Mr Speed to obtain a pardon for me, (which is not the fact,) and that he had done So and charges me $250.00, which I am not willing to pay, if I can prevent it. This is not the first instance in this County of persons going on to Washington and geting Pardons without authority and charging exhorbitant fees.

I regret very much that Mr Speed has forced me to the necessity of troubling you with this business, as I have no doubt you are already over taxed with more important duties, that require your valuable time. But I know of no other Source to apply. And I hope and pray your Excellency will have the goodness to Send me on a duplicate copy of Pardon, to the care of Hon R. B. Waller Greensboro Greene County Ala.[6]

T. J. Sorsby

P.S.   I learn that Mr Speed is a relation of the Attorney General.[7]

ALS, DLC-JP.
    1. Sorsby (b. *c*1814), a planter and supporter of secession, had applied for amnesty under the $20,000 clause. Amnesty Papers (M1003, Roll 10), Ala., Thomas J. Sorsby, RG94, NA.
    2. Robert B. Waller (*c*1805–1877) was also a well-to-do planter and supporter of the Confederacy, who himself had been pardoned September 12, 1865. Ibid. (Roll 11), Ala., Robert B. Waller; Gandrud, *Early Alabama Newspapers*, 46.
    3. Probably one of Governor Parsons's secretaries, his son George W. Parsons (*c*1843–*fl*1879), a former private in the 8th Confederate Cav., or S. H. Dixon, who was possibly Samuel H. (b. *c*1819), a Wetumpka editor. John W. DuBose, *Alabama's Tragic Decade: Ten Years of Alabama, 1865–1874* (Birmingham, 1940), 44, 54; 1860 Census, Ala., Talladega, Northern Div., 190; Coosa, Southern Div., Wetumpka, 61; CSR, George W. Parsons, RG109, NA.
    4. Joseph H. Speed (1834–*fl*1874), a teacher and a captain in the 28th Ala. Inf., CSA, became a prominent "scalawag" and served as U.S. marshal and state superintendent of education. Owen, *History of Ala.*, 4: 1605–6; Sarah W. Wiggins, *The Scalawag in Alabama Politics, 1865–1881* (University, Ala., 1977), 153.
    5. Brooks (1815–1894), a lawyer, had practiced in Linden, Mobile, and Marion, Alabama, in addition to serving terms as district solicitor and circuit judge. President of the state secession convention, he was a colonel of a reserve regiment during the war. In 1866 he moved to Selma and twenty years later to Birmingham. F. W. Teeple and A. Davis Smith, *Jefferson County and Birmingham Alabama* (Birmingham, 1887), 342–46; *NCAB*, 19: 61.
    6. It is not known if Johnson sent a duplicate, but Sorsby's pardon had been issued on December 22, 1865. Amnesty Papers (M1003, Roll 10), Ala., Thomas J. Sorsby, RG94, NA.
    7. Joseph H. Speed was the attorney general's cousin. Wiggins, *Scalawag in Ala.*, 129.

From Richard S. Spofford, Jr.[1]

Boston   10 July 1866

Honored & Dear Sir:

Herewith, I have the honor to enclose a letter of John Quincy Adams[2] wh. should have reached me and been delivered while I was in Washington, but failed to do so. It has reference to the Office of District Attorney,

& will explain itself. I am well pleased that it confirms what I said to you on the same subject.[3]

R. S. Spofford.

ALS, DNA-RG60, Appt. Files for Judicial Dists., Mass., Richard H. Dana.

1. Spofford (1832–1888), a lawyer in Newburyport, Mass., and Washington, D.C., had recently married Harriet Elizabeth Prescott, soon to become a prominent writer. In March 1866 he sent Johnson a copy of a speech he had made in the Massachusetts legislature in support of the President's policies. *DAB*; *American Annual Cyclopaedia* (1888), 652; Spofford to Johnson, Mar. 13, 1866, Johnson Papers, LC.

2. The grandson of the former president and son of Johnson's minister to Great Britain, Adams (1833–1894) later ran on several occasions as the Democratic nominee for Massachusetts governor, but was not elected. Adams wrote Spofford that he regretted the rumored removal of District Attorney Richard H. Dana and saw "nothing but damage from the move." *NCAB*, 11: 173; Adams to Spofford, June 16, 1866, Appt. Files for Judicial Dists., Mass., Richard H. Dana, RG60, NA.

3. In September 1866 Dana resigned his post, and the following month George S. Hillard, at Spofford's urging, was appointed in Dana's place. Hillard was confirmed by the Senate three months later. Ser. 6B, Vol. 3: 35; Vol. 4: 24, Johnson Papers, LC; Spofford et al. to Johnson, Oct. 4, 1866, Appt. Files for Judicial Dists., Mass., G. S. Hillard, RG60, NA.

From Jonathan Worth

Executive Dept. of NC
Raleigh   July 10th 1866

Sir

Being intensely anxious for the success of your policy, because I believe it identified with the well-being of the nation, I venture some suggestions to you at the risk of being deemed obtrusive, in relation to the pardon of three distinguished individuals of this State. I know you have a much wider field of observation than I have, but your conclusions on this wider field must be made up from your knowledge of the parts. I fear, in the multitude of your cares, some inconsistencies, as they appear to the people of North Carolina, in the exercise of the pardoning power, may have escaped your attention. Four members of the Confederate Congress, known here as original Secessionists,—to-wit, Venable, Arrington, Bridgers and Lander[1] have been very properly pardoned. I entertain no doubt as to their purpose to obey the laws and Constitution of the United States and that a Union, worth preserving requires that such men be treated with the generous magnanimity you have exhibited towards them: but while these are pardoned I can conceive of no principle of equity or policy, which warrants the withholding of a pardon from Graham, Dortch and Turner.[2] The discrimination attracts universal attention in this State. Your friends believe they are withheld from legitimate policy or more propitious season. I think that propitious season has arrived. You must be aware that Govr. Graham is by far the most popular man in this State, both on account of the purity of his personal character, his talents and the confidence of our people in his patriotism. He opposed disunion and secession till war had actually commenced. Turner carried his opposition still further. As a Senator he voted against the Ordinance of Secession in May 1861,—and at the same Session Dortch was elected a Senator to the Confederate Congress, the Union members voting for him as less obnoxious than the other candidates from among whom the selection had to be made. It is well known that Graham and Turner, as members of the Confederate Congress, desired and believed Mr. Stephens & his associates invested with power to treat at Fortress Monroe for peace on the basis of restored Union. Those facts being notorious in this State, the opinion is universal and strong, that these gentlemen ought to be pardoned, excepting a very inconsiderable number of personal enemies. Nothing would so warm up the people of this State to be represented in the approaching national Convention at Philadelphia as the pardon of these gentlemen. If pardoned, every body would look to Govr. Graham as our chief representative in that Convention. If still unpardoned it may be held a matter of doubtful expediency to send him. Every body in this State (excepting a handful of radicals) supports your policy. If you would pardon these three men it would give fervor to this support.[3]

I make this communication to you without consultation or conference with any person, and without the knowledge of any body. It springs entirely from my desire to promote the best interest of my country.

The courtesy which the Sec. of State has exhibited towards me in a personal interview last Summer, and in our official correspondence, warranted me, as I conceived, in presenting to him these views in a letter a few days ago,[4] which I authorised him to use as he might deem proper. He informs me he has laid that letter before you. I deem it my duty to reiterate and impress the views therein presented.

Jonathan Worth   Govr. of N. C.

ALS, DLC-JP.
1. Abraham W. Venable, Archibald H. Arrington, Robert R. Bridgers, and William Lander. The latter (1817–1868), a Lincolnton, North Carolina, lawyer, planter, legislator, and solicitor, had been a member of the state secession convention before his election to the Confederate Congress. Wakelyn, *BDC*.
2. William A. Graham, William T. Dortch, and Josiah Turner, Jr.
3. Graham, Dortch, and Turner had been pardoned December 4, 1865, June 18, 1866, and February 17, 1866, respectively. Receipt of official pardon was delayed in Graham's case and apparently in the cases of Dortch and Turner. *Johnson Papers*, 9: 72–73, 260–61, 376.
4. Worth's appeal to Seward in behalf of Josiah Turner was dated sometime during the first three days of July 1866. Hamilton, *Worth Correspondence*, 2: 660–62.

From William Dennison

WASHINGTON, July 11, 1866.

SIR:

I have the honor to tender you herewith my resignation of the office of Postmaster General, to take effect upon your notifying me of its acceptance.[1]

In thus withdrawing from your Cabinet, it is proper to say that I do so chiefly because of the difference of opinion between us in regard to the proposed amendment of the Constitution, which I approve, and the movement for the convention to be held in Philadelphia on the 14th proximo, to which I am opposed.[2]

My confidence in the patriotism of the Union Republican party, and conviction that upon its permanent control of the Government depends in a large measure the peace and happiness of the country, will not permit of my holding any equivocal attitude in respect to it.

Assuring you of my personal regard and appreciation of the uniform courtesy I have received from you . . . .

W. DENNISON.

Philadelphia Press, July 16, 1866.
　1. Johnson accepted Dennison's resignation on July 14. Johnson to Dennison, July 14, 1866, Johnson Papers, LC.
　2. One of the Washington newspapers, skeptical of the reasons offered by Dennison, speculated that his railroad and other interests in the West prompted his resignation from Johnson's cabinet. *Washington Evening Star*, July 12, 1866.

From William W. Holden

Ebbitt House,
Washington, July 11, 1866.

Sir:

You were kind enough to intimate, in the conversation I had the honor to have with you this morning, that if I would reduce the substance of what I had said to writing, you would put your reply in the same shape.

I beg leave to repeat, that under your order I reorganized the government of North Carolina on a thoroughly loyal basis, with men in office who had been opposed to the rebellion, who were devoted to the Union, and who were co-operating cheerfully and heartily with you in the work of restoration. At that time loyalty to the national Union was respectable, and treason and disloyalty were odious. I was relieved of office on the 28th December, 1865, and since that period, under the administration of my successor, a marked change has taken place. Loyal men have been turned out of office, and disloyal men put in, for no other reason than that the latter are the special friends and partizans of the present Governor. The original Union men like yourself, and those who were for peace on the basis of the restoration of the Union before the close of the rebellion, are almost entirely excluded from office by my successor, and are thereby deprived of the opportunity and the pleasure of aiding you, as they desire to do, in the work of restoration; while unpardoned rebels are honored, and places of trust and confidence are filled by leading war men and rebels, who have not, in the opinion of our Union people, sincerely or duly repented of their great crime of seeking deliberately and from choice to destroy the national government.

The President and other political leaders,
including the three Cabinet members who resigned in 1866
An engraving in Horace Greeley,
The American Conflict. . . . Vol. 2. (1866)

This has been done, Sir, under the lead and direction of the present Governor of the State. The Union men have appealed to him in vain for consideration and protection. They have even offered to forget and forgive his defection from the Union cause last October, and support him for re-election, provided he would cast off the influences by which he was elected, would appoint only true Union men to office, and would cooperate with you in good faith in carrying out the work of restoration. But he has rejected this offer, and is now engaged, as he has been from the first, in undoing the work of restoration in our State, in proscribing Union men, and thus obstructing the return of the State to the Union.

Our Union people look to you for sympathy and succor. They are supporting you in good faith, and they are attached to your administration. They cannot forget your sufferings and sacrifices for the Union, at a time when it required extraordinary moral and physical courage to be a Union man, as you were in Tennessee; and this, joined to the fact that you are a native of our State, disposes our people to look to you with peculiar confidence and affection.

Our Union people believe that loyalty will not be estimated as it should, nor your plan for restoring the States be placed on the high ground it deserves to occupy, until the means and instrumentalities which you put in operation in 1865 shall have been restored. They feel that in no other way can the State be made to appear in a truly loyal garb, and thus enforce its claims on Congress and the country for admission into the Union, without further changes in the Constitution until all the States are again represented.

Those public men who have control of affairs in our State, insist that you are opposed to the present Congressional test oath; and that you are in favor of the immediate admission of *all* the members of Congress from the recently insurgent States. When we deny this, and insist that the oath, or some similar oath is necessary, and that the oath is a matter specially with the Congress, they declare it to be unconstitutional; that they do not respect it; and that, if it is to be maintained, it will amount, as recently declared by my successor in his message to the Convention, to the perpetual practical disfranchisement of the State. They thus defiantly set themselves up against one of the laws of the land, and take refuge under your shadow to protect and justify themselves.

The Unionists of our State, so far from desiring to proscribe or persecute their fellow-citizens, are ready to receive into their ranks all who sincerely repent that they deliberately sought to destroy the government, and who give unmistakable proof of their thorough submission to the national authority; but they still think, as they did in 1865, that Justice and sound policy require that such persons should take no active or conspicuous part in the work of restoration, but leave it where it was placed by you in the outset, to wit, in the hands of the loyal Union men.

In conclusion, allow me to say that the cause of restoration is obstructed in our State by those in power; the truly loyal people are depressed and mortified; malcontents and rebels are exultant and defiant; ill feeling is engendered; injustice is perpetrated through the Courts by means of disloyal prosecuting officers, and Juries, and some magistrates, though our Judges are loyal, yet not always able to withstand the pressure of public opinion; treason and disloyalty are promoted and honored, while loyalty is evinced at the hazard of political, social, and pecuniary proscription.

All we ask is, that the truly loyal of our people shall govern until the State is restored to the Union. This is the best, if not the only assurance we can have of Justice to both races, white and black, And in no other way can good feeling, and harmony, and security to life, liberty, and property be secured, and the State be put upon the clear, open road to the completion of the great work of restoration, so auspiciously commenced by you, Sir, in May, 1865.

W. W. Holden, Late Prov. Gov. N.C.

ALS, DLC-JP.

From William W. Holden

Ebbitt House [Washington, D.C.], July 11, 1866.
My dear Mr. President.

I have written hurriedly what you will find enclosed. Please read it carefully, and answer accordingly.[1] I will not presume to say what your reply should be, but I trust you will make it as direct and pointed as you can. You can form no idea of the depression among your real friends in our State, or of the exultant, overbearing manner of our enemies and masters.

If you can enable us to carry the State we can help you, and help the Union cause, now in so much peril. Our friends in the Convention postponed the election until October so as to secure a chance of success. This was all they could do. If you will only help us, we will make a united, determined, and sucessful fight.

I should like much to leave for home to-morrow evening. I would be glad if you could have your reply ready by to-morrow twelve M. I would like to take the correspondence home, and have it appear first in the Standard, if you have no objection.

W. W. Holden.

ALS, DLC-JP.
1. Enclosed was a fairly lengthy statement that expressed both approval of Holden's tenure as provisional governor of North Carolina and regret at his defeat. Next was the claim that Johnson was working to restore the Union and his need for loyal Union men to assist him. Congress would determine who would be admitted to their seats; certainly unpardoned persons or those who could not take the prescribed oath should not expect to be received. The statement concluded with a plea for North Carolinians to seek restoration and return to the Union "at the earliest possible period."

From Jonathan Worth

Raleigh, N.C., July 11th, 1866.

Sir:

I herewith enclose to you a copy of a communication lately made to me by Brevet Major General Robinson,[1] and my answer thereto,[2] for the purpose of inquiring whether it is held that the military has power to decide when a Judge has failed to discharge the duties set forth in this military Order:—and, if such decision be adverse to the action of the Judge, thereupon to *suspend* him from the exercise of his functions.

Such I understand to be the power claimed in the concluding sentence of General Robinson's letter.[3]

Jonathan Worth   Governor of No. Ca.

ALS, DNA-RG94, Lets. Recd. (Main Ser.), File N-113-1866 (M619, Roll 499).

1. John C. Robinson (1817–1897), a division commander of the Army of the Potomac during the war, saw quite a bit of action and many years later received the congressional medal of honor. After the cessation of hostilities, he served as commandant of military forces and also as assistant commissioner of the Freedmen's Bureau in North Carolina. Robinson left military duty in 1869 and served as lieutenant governor of New York in the 1870s. In his letter to Worth, Robinson informed him of his intention to provide protection from prosecution for blacks and Unionists and of his desire that "there will be no clash between the Military and Civil authorities in the State." Warner, *Blue*; Zuber, *Worth*, 223; Robinson to Worth, July 3, 1866, Lets. Recd. (Main Ser.), File N-113-1866 (M619, Roll 499), RG94, NA.

2. Worth informed Robinson that he had distributed the order concerning the protection of certain persons but then declared that he should not have attempted to dictate to the judiciary about carrying out its duties. Like Robinson, Worth did not want conflict between civilian and military authorities; he stated his intention to ask the President about the authority of military officials over the state judiciary. Zuber, *Worth*, 223–24; Worth to Robinson, July 11, 1866, Lets. Recd. (Main Ser.), File N-113-1866 (M619, Roll 499), RG94, NA.

3. Robinson was instructed to consult with the War Department before taking any action "to suspend Civil officers from their functions." Robinson in turn directed Bureau agents to transfer to the civil courts all cases involving blacks, except suits dealing with collection of wages under contracts. The Robinson-Worth correspondence continued through the summer months. Zuber, *Worth*, 223–25; Townsend to Robinson, July 19, 1866, Lets. Recd. (Main Ser.), File N-113-1866 (M619, Roll 499), RG94, NA.

From Samuel J. Baird[1]

Washington, July 12, 66

Dear Sir.

Under the impression that I have information which may be interesting to you, I have sought this opportunity of communicating it.

Eight months ago I went into Virginia as agent of the American Bible Society, for that state. I announced myself openly & uniformly as a union man, who never had nor could have any sympathy with secession, but who, loving the people of the south, wished to extend to them a hand of cordial Christian fellowship, to aid them with the Bible, & to do all in my power to heal the wounds of war, & restore relations of harmony & love among a distracted & divided people.

My approaches were met in an equal spirit. The Virginia Bible Society, which had been, by the war, estranged from the national Society, at once tendered me commission as its general Agent, Correspondence was reopened with the American Society, & the most cordial relations re-established; & for eight months I have been travelling the state as the joint agent of the two societies.

I have thus been placed in relations of the most unreserved confidence with the people, & have been received to their houses & tables every where. With such unsurpassed facilities, it has been my study to ascertain the real sentiments of the people upon the questions involved in the restoration of the Union. I have studied them in cars & steamboats, in the utterances of the platform & the pulpit, in assemblies secular & ecclesiastical, at the family table & fireside, & in the revealings of the family altar. I feel confident in the correctness of the following conclusions:

1.   The doctrine of secession is dead, & the whole people would hail with the utmost satisfaction the restoration of the Union in the fulness of all its normal functions, & would fulfil their duties, & use their privileges, in good faith, for the welfare of all.

2.   Not only do they submit to the abolition of slavery, as an accomplished fact; but accept that result with cordial satisfaction, as a relief from a most perplexing question; & could they tomorrow, by vote, restore the institution, they would reject the proposition.

3.   The feeling of the people generally toward the negro, is that of the most cordial good will, & the better classes are unanimous in recognizing it as their duty to take him by the hand, to protect, instruct, enlighten & elevate him.

4.   The most judicious, impartial & best friends of the negro, all concur in the conviction, that, however, faithful, in some instances, the agents of the Freedmen's Bureau, & however favorably it may work in some cases, its influence, on the whole, is evil & necessarily so, & detrimental to all the interests involved, both of the black & the white.

5.   The restoration policy urged by you, is universally regarded as eminently wise, & calculated to restore harmony, reestablish the authority of the laws, & render the Union beneficent & perpetual. The people of Virginia look to you with trust & love, as a true friend of your country, & their great hope in this day of darkness & distress.

Cordially sharing in those feelings, & praying God's blessing on your administration, I only wish, further, to assure you, how gladly I would serve you in your great work, in any way consistent with my duties as a minister of the Gospel of Christ.[2]

Samuel J. Baird
P.O. "*University of Va.*"

ALS, DLC-JP.

1. Baird (1817–1893), a Presbyterian minister, served as pastor of churches in several different states during his long career. He also compiled the first collection of decisions made by the Presbyterian church's governing body, the General Assembly, and wrote many books on theology and Presbyterianism. *DAB*.

2. On July 14 Johnson replied asking if he could publish Baird's observations, but the minister refused. Baird thought it would be improper to take part in what could be construed as "party politics," and that it could damage his work in healing the wounds between North and South and within the Presbyterian church. Johnson to Baird, July 14, 1866; Baird to Johnson, July 20, 1866, Johnson Papers, LC.

From Edward Bates

St Louis, Mo., July 12, 1866.

Honored Sir,

In the midst of your arduous labors & painful cares, I pray you to pardon me for troubling me you with a few words about the condition of affairs, here in Missouri.

Be assured, Sir, that I would not do it if the condition of Missouri, were *local* & peculiar to us. But it is not so: It is part & parcel of the condition of the nation. We, the constitutional, law-abiding men of Missouri, are enlisted in the same great cause which now demands the exercise of all your energy & courage. We are organizing (& expect soon to be perfectly organised) & fully resolved to fight the great battle for the constitution, against the factious usurpation of a reckless party—and to fight it *under your banner*. We have lately held a "Conservative, Union Convention,"[1] which, for numbers, individual worth, popular estimation and general weight of character, has never been surpassed in this State; and we have "*Johnson Clubs*," zealous & brave in the good cause, in almost every part of the Community.

Under these circumstances, we think it not unreasonable, to ask the countenance & support of our great leader, who is, at the same time, the oath-bound conservator of the Constitution & the Supreme executor of the laws. We ask this, not as a personal favor to any particular man or set of men, but as a part of the great, national duty (in the performance of which you are now so urgently engaged) to restore the Union & rehabilitate the shattered fabric of our *legal* government.

The Radical faction in Missouri is but a part of, & cooperating with that Radical faction in Congress which is, even now, waging fierce war against you & the Constitution. Before that faction would venture to disclose the full proportions of its wicked scheme to usurp the Government & overturn the Constitution, ("wiser in their generation than the children of light")[2] they prudently secured as much patronage & influence as possible, by foisting into office their unscrupulous partizans. I suppose that was done, more or less, every where, but it was disgustingly flagrant here in Missouri. Some of those men (by reason of the character of the offices into which they have been obtruded) are beyond your reach; but others lie open before you, subject to be disposed of as you shall find that the public good requires. For instance, Judge Krekel[3] (*nominally* of the Western District of Missouri) had not the slightest qualification for the place, but only this—he was supposed to have considerable influence with the *German element* of the Radical party in Missouri. And therefore (& only therefore) he was manoeuvered into the judgeship of the Western District, over the heads of far more competent men, both within & without the District, and (as I know personally) against the judgment of President Lincoln, although he lives in the eastern edge of the State.

Such appointments are generally considered by the recipients, as rewards for past partizan services, or as perquisites of the party-position which they have the good fortune to occupy. Hence, Mr. Krekel (who is a Prussian by birth & a Red republican in doctrine) seems to consider the office as a mere personality, due to him as a teacher of German Radical politics. He has enjoyed the honors & emoluments of the judgship, for more than a year; he has removed from his old home in St. Charles (not to his District, as the act of Congress requires, but) to this City of St Louis, the focus of Radical politics for the State—and still lives here. He, however (holding the sacred office of a judge) is beyond the reach of Executive correction. Not so with the Marshal, Mr. Schofield.[4] He was appointed for the sole purpose of filling an office of some popular influence, with a devoted partizan; and the place had to be made vacant for him, by the removal of an efficient, worthy, good man, *Thomas B. Wallace.* Mr. Wallace was appointed Marshal of the Western District of Missouri, by President Lincoln, while I was Attorney General, and at my suggestion; and I fully believe that he has performed all the duties of the office, with activity, zeal & good faith, and to the entire satisfaction of the Courts, and his other official superiors.

And now Sir, I think that, in justice to Mr. Wallace & to our good cause, and in sound policy, on the part of the administration, he ought to be restored. And I, most respectfully request that it be so done.

I desire also to say a word in favor of my excellent friend, Genl. Richard C. Vaughan,[5] of Lexington Mo. He is a man far above mediocrity, in talents & in literary & business attainments; and, in his personal character, stands as well as any man in the State, for truth, honor, courage & patriotism. He was in pretty good circumstances, at the beginning of the war, but when the rebels sacked the beautiful little City of Lexington, his property was destroyed & himself driven into exile. He then went to Washington, and (to get a bare living) served for a time, as a clerk in the Interior. But his services were needed at home, and, returning, Govr. Gamble made him a Brigr. Genl. of enrolled Militia & Clerk of the Circuit Court of Lafayette County. As a Commander of Militia forces, he did service, as long as his services were needed; and as Court Clerk, he did all the duties of his office well, until cast out by the proscribing ordinance of the Radical Convention.[6]

Some of his friends (and he has many) think that it would be eminently proper to make him *Federal Assessor* in his Congressional district (the *Sixth,* I think); And I entreat you sir, to give him the place, for he is worthy & well qualified.[7]

I could say much more about the affairs & men of this State, but I fear to trouble you.

Edw. Bates

ALS, DLC-JP.

1. The convention began on July 3. The delegates listened to speeches, drafted resolutions, and selected representatives to attend the National Union Convention in Philadelphia in August. Beale, *Bates Diary,* 562–63; Parrish, *Radical Rule,* 88.

2. Luke 16: 8.

3. Arnold Krekel (1815–1888) moved to Missouri from Prussia in 1832. A former surveyor, lawyer, justice of the peace, newspaper editor, legislator, and, during the Civil War, militia colonel, Krekel chaired the Missouri state convention of 1865. Bates strongly opposed the constitution promulgated by this convention, which probably affected his perception of Krekel, who continued as judge for the western district of Missouri until his death. *The Bench and Bar of St. Louis, Kansas City, Jefferson City and Other Missouri Cities* (St. Louis, 1884), 288–89; Parrish, *Radical Rule,* 15, 23, 43; *U.S. Off. Reg.* (1865–89); Howard I. McKee, "The School Law of 1853, Its Origin and Authors," *MoHR,* 35 (1941): 560; Pension File, Martha H. Krekel, RG15, NA.

4. Smith O. Scofield.

5. Wallace and Vaughan both attended the Conservative Union Convention. Beale, *Bates Diary,* 562. See also Francis P. Blair, Jr., to Johnson, Mar. 24, 1866.

6. The Radical-dominated state convention of 1865, in order to remove all allegedly disloyal persons from office, passed the so-called "Ouster Ordinance" which provided that as of May 1, 1865, all judges and clerks of the state supreme court, the circuit courts, the county courts, and special courts, as well as all county recorders, circuit attorneys, and sheriffs were to be removed from office. The 842 vacancies which resulted were to be filled by gubernatorial appointment until the next election. Parrish, *Radical Rule,* 32–33, 50.

7. See Francis P. Blair, Jr., to Johnson, Mar. 24, 1866.

From George L. Gillespie[1]

Chattanooga Tenn   July 12th 1866

D Sir

Altho I may be an entire stranger to you, being only a lad of 16 years old when I frequently saw you while Governor of our state at Nashville, where I then resided, I am the son of W. N. Gillespie[2] late of Rhea County Tennessee and one of the unfortunate individuals who was in the late Confederate Army, surrendered with Genl. Jo Johnson in North Carolina. I held the office of Major & I must be candid enough to acknowledge that, altho I did not do anything to bring on the War or Secession of my state, yet when my State went out I entered the service of the Confederate Army, and that my whole sympathy was with the south in the Contest. But the war over, I took the ammesty oath in good faith intending to keep it sacredly—have kept it & will keep it. I now ask Your Excellency to grant me full pardon for all that you may consider that I have done wrong in the premises. At present there is no legal process against me, having heretofore been indicted for Treason & acquitted at Knoxville.[3]

I believe the regulations require that before seeking to obtain a pardon —I should procure from the Governor of our state a recommendation. I trust you will not make this requirement in the present Case, as Governor Brownlow & my self never did agree in anything—hope you will relieve me from such a humiliation.[4] Should your Excellency feel disposed to grant me the pardon I shall always remember with lively gratitude the favor thus Confered & remain your much obliged Humble Servant.

Geo. L. Gillespie

LS, DLC-JP.
1. Gillespie (1836–fl1887) served as a major in the Confederate army; after the war he worked in Chattanooga as a merchant and contractor. Penelope J. Allen, *Leaves from the Family Tree* (Easley, S.C., 1982), 90; Chattanooga directories (1880, 1886–87).
2. William N. Gillespie (1803–1840) had been active in organizing the Masonic lodge in Rhea County. Allen, *Family Tree*, 90.
3. On May 10, 1866, Gillespie had written to the President, seeking an individual pardon, because he was then under indictment for treason. This letter had been forwarded to Congressman-elect William B. Stokes in Washington by one of Gillespie's friends in Chattanooga. Upon receipt, Stokes sent the document over to the White House although, as he said, "I know nothing about the applicant." Gillespie's first attempt to secure a presidential pardon had taken place in mid-December 1865 when he wrote to Johnson. Despite what Gillespie states in his July letter, he had already been pardoned by the President on July 6, 1866; evidently that information had not yet reached him at Chattanooga. See Amnesty Papers (M1003, Roll 49), Tenn., George L. Gillespie, RG94, NA; *House Ex. Docs.*, 39 Cong., 2 Sess., No. 116, p. 41 (Ser. 1293).
4. Ironically, Governor Brownlow had, on December 16, 1865, recommended Gillespie's pardon, apparently in connection with Gillespie's December 14 letter to Johnson. See Amnesty Papers (M1003, Roll 49), Tenn., George L. Gillespie, RG94, NA.

From Edward C. McDonald[1]

Moulton Lawrence County Alabama
July 12th 1866

Sir

I would respectfully ask the indulgence of your clemency to the extent that I may bring to your knowledge a matter which very materially affects my interest and standing as a citizen.

The facts are these. For several years previous to the rebellion I was Post Master at Moulton Ala. and when the offices came into the control of the authorities here after the war broke out I still retained the Post office at this place and by doing so was enabled to stay at home and avoid the service throughout the war. This is the grounds of my having to apply for special pardon.

So soon as an office was opened here for the purpose of administering the amnesty oath by Capt Latty[2] Provost Marshall from the 1st Ala Federal Cavalry I went to him and made out my application for pardon which was promptly forwarded.

I am recently advised by Mr. Jos. H. Sloss[3] of Tuscumbia Ala in an adjoining County that he has my pardon forwarded to him from Washington and 75$ charges against it. I am poor and have not that amount of money am anxious to accept the pardon but am debard by no fault of mine unless to be without money is a fault.

I do not know what to do and wish to know if I can not get the benefit of the pardon without paying 75$. If the money goes into the U S treasury and is a legitimate charge I shall have to ask indulgence until I can get the amount but if it is a charge made with but one party to the contract I do not think I ought to be forced to pay 75$ for what the Government has offered me by complying with her terms. I did not employ any attorney nor authorize any one else to do so.

If in the great press of business you will find time to let me know what course to pursue you will greatly relieve one who desires to heartily conform to any requirements made by the Government in which he desires full citizenship.

E. C. McDonald

ALS, DLC-JP.
    1. McDonald (*c*1837–*fl*1897), a former store employee, later served as the county probate clerk. 1860 Census, Ala., Lawrence, Southern Div., 3; Dorothy Gentry, *Life and Legend of Lawrence County Alabama* (Tuscaloosa, 1962), 81; James E. Saunders and Elizabeth S.B. Stubbs, *Early Settlers of Alabama: With Notes and Genealogies* (New Orleans, 1899), 67.
    2. John Latty [Latta] (1838–1915), a Pennsylvania native, was a private in the 57th Ill. Inf. before becoming captain, Co. C, 1st Ala. Cav., USA. After the war he lived in Illinois, South Dakota, and Iowa. Pension Records, Angeline Latty, RG15, NA.
    3. Sloss (1826–1911), a lawyer and Somerville, Alabama, native, had been an Illinois legislator before the war. After service as a Confederate soldier, he was mayor of Tuscumbia, U.S. congressman (1871–75), and then U.S. marshal. *BDAC*.

From Granville Moody

Piqua Ohio   July 12th/66

Dear Sir

Pardon the intrusion on your precious time.

My sincere regards for you, personally; urge me to give you this *warning of danger*.

The impression—yes the conviction is abroad in the land that the announced Philaa. Convention is designed as the inception and nucleus of a "new party" designing to draw you into its circles, and if possible use you, and your *Official* influence in furtherance of its partisan designs.

The fact that every Copperhead in Congress has rushed into it, and that the *rebels of the South* are *jubilant over it* indicate its composition and its designs.

It doubtless intends *the admission* of the eleven (11) States (which *we have subjugated to the authority of the United States*)—without *indemnity* for the *past* or *security for the future*—aye without *conditions preceedent* of any kind.

Now my honored friend—I affirm that no living man has stood by you more firmly and sincerely than I have; and I cannot think of your being drawn into that *whirlpool*, where you will go down with certainty; without lifting up the warning voice. I am *amongst the people*, day by day. I know their feelings—their *modes* of *thinking*—their *latent* and their *active* patriotism.

And I know that if you identify yourself with *that party* you will be ruined!

I see the end as with a Prophets eye.

The *grave* of every Federal Soldier—The *Ghosts* of our starved Prisoners in Belle Isle—Libby Prison—Anderson Prison Pens. Every *maimed Veteran*—Every *widow* in her weeds—Every *Orphan*—Every *dollar* of extra *taxation* caused by Traitors and their Allies the Copperheads—Every *humiliation* we were compelled to submit to from Foreign Nations enlisted against us by the South. Every recollection of our *past renoun*. Every *battle field* where our glory was won. Every *wrong* visited on the *Freedmen, out of spite* to the *Yankees*, as we are all called by the Southern Traitors and Rebels. Every principle of sound *Statesmanship*. Every cherished hope of the future, for our institutions. Every obligation we owe to the dead, and the living, and those yet to live; and our paramount obligations to the *God of Justice* and of Nations *will be trumpet tongued against* this Union of Copperheads and Traitorous rebels, who combine, like *Herod and Pilate* did, when the hope of humanity was to be sacrificed.

I tell you—President, that the excitement amongst the people is *intense*. And the tide sets in no uncertain direction.

And the greater the elements that gather around that *Philaa. speculation* the greater will be the power aroused to resist it.

"He who of old would rend the oak,
Dreamed not of the rebound["][1]

Ah Sir we have *suffered* too much—*invested* too much in the *integrity* of this Nation to *hazzard* its interests by any maudlin sympathy with the *men* who *would be in arms against* that Flag, that you proudly said should not come down from the Capitol of your native State; when God gave you *infallible* direction, to maintain it, at every hazzard; as you *most nobly did*.

Listen not to the Mermaid song—rather the half Copperhead—half Pelican—that comes from that "Philaa. speculation"—the sunken rocks of ruin *are there* and your noble craft, which has weathered so many a storm and tornado—will go to pieces there "where *two seas meet*."

I assure you that the infallible *instincts of the people* are *against* that concocting of "the party," who at Chicago declared "the war for the maintenance of the Union a *failure*" and advised "the withdrawing of our armies from" the bloody battle fields where our glory was won, and our National life secured.[2]

Let that coalition become an accomplished fact, and in proportion to their prospects of success, is the *gloom* that hangs over our land. Our "*public securities*" given to get money to buy clothing—food and ordnance with which to put down rebellion are hazzarded,—professions to the contrary notwithstanding.

"*Security for the future*"—by accepted amendments to the *organic* and *paramount* law of the Nation, is our only safety; and I assure you *the People* will demand that.

That sentiment is as a flood tide—with a ground swell from the profoundest depths of the national Patriotism and there is no power and can be no combination of powers that can bid those billows back.

> "They roll'd not back
> When Canute gave command."[3]

I fear Wm. H Sewards counsels—he has *brains* but "he has . . . . .—. . . . .—*on the brain.*" I fear like the boatman he is *looking one way* whilst he *rows another*! His repeated prophecies of the ending of the war in 60 or 90 days—his *truckling* to Great Britain his *inordinate ambition*—his remarks about *you* in New York[4]—his *versatility*—all combine to arouse the *fears* of the people that some body will be *sold for nothing* who cannot be redeemed with price.

When I saw you last week you may recollect I urged the Proverb

> "Look before you leap."

The great question, is *yet in your own* hands, and I assure you that the loyal people of America, will *rally around* you with all their former enthusiasm, when they see you standing by your *declarations* in the Senate of 1860–61—Your declarations whilst Governor of Tennessee. Your declarations when in the inscrutable and permissive Providence of Almighty God, the Head of the Nation was laid low by the hand of the assassin, and you assumed the reins of Government with the declaration on your lips that

> "Treason is a *crime*—the *highest*
> And must be made to appear *odious*!["]

Ah Sir to *restore those rebel States* to power WITHOUT—at least the *conditions precedent* presented by Congress—would be the *blunder* and the *crime* of taking the in the wooden horse, within the walls of our Troy—for you cannot *fail to hear the clanking* of *armed men*, within its capacious body. Let the horse in, and the men within will let themselves loose on all the *interests* of our more than Trojan State.

Judge Hueston[5] of Nashville, whom I met at your house, said; on that occassion, that he agreed with me, that there should be *conditions preceedent* to the *restoration* of those States to the places *they vacated* for the purpose of *breaking up* our glorious government.

And that utterance (though he did not specify what conditions) will swell into harsh thunder when the ballott box shall give the authoritative response.

The Country needs a *settlement* a *peace* on a *just* and *understood basis*. The South needs—desires this and must have it.

It is in vain to cry "exclusionist" and "Secessionist" and endeavour to make *Congress* as blame worthy as Southern destructionists.

The South was *self excluded*. Like the rebels in heaven, *they left their first estate*—vacated their thrones of glory, and as far as they could do it—defied the Government of God.

But as the fallen angels could not *get out of God's domain*—nor *dissolve their obligations* to this Throne—so these Southern Rebels have failed in breaking the bonds that bind them to obedience, and subjugated by *our arms* they *should consent* to such *amendments* of our organic laws as will afford a *reasonable assurance of safety for the future*!

This I most religiously believe.

I saw Sherman—Shellabarger—Laurence Bingham—Clark[6] and others and stated your most *urgent objection* to the action of Congress in that—Congress had not said that these amendments shall be a finality or that the States shall be admitted immediately on their ratification by them of the amendment.

Each one of those gentlemen declared in favor of said finality for admission, and told me that they *would see to it* that such a *Declaratory Act* should be passed at the present Congress if that was any obstacle in the way.

I also advised them to call a Caucus of the Union members and appoint a Committee of Confrence to *see you*, and if possible adjust the matter, so that we can again cooperate in the maintenance of the integrity of our glorious Country and *you* have the peerless honor of "Building the waste places—and raising up the foundations of many generations["] and be called "The repairer of the breach, The restorer of paths to dwell in"—Isaiah 58th Chapter—12th verse.

"Then shall thy light break forth as the morning and thine health shall spring forth speedily and thy *righteousness* shall go before thee—the glory of the Lord shall be thy *rereward*.["] Verse 8th.

Then shalt thou *call* and the Lord shall *answer*. Thou shalt cry and *He* shall say *Here I am*. And if thou draw out thy soul to the hungry (the freedman) and satisfy the afflicted soul, then shall thy Light rise in obscurity and thy darkness be as the noon day, and *the Lord shall guide thee* continually and thou shalt delight thyself in God and he will cause thee (*with thy people*) to ride upon the *high places* of the earth and feed thee with the heritage of thy fathers. Verse 14th.

Dear Sir, Pardon the freedom with which I have addressed you. My love to my *Country*—my regards for *you*—and for your *fame*—the assurance in my mind that *you* above *any other man* can lay your right hand on the North—And your *left* hand on the South and be "*the Mediator of the New Covenant founded on better promises.*" And thus serve your Country in this critical hour to better effect than—Jackson or Lincoln, both have done—or could do—(for prevention is better than cure) and such an *opportunity* and responsiby comes but seldom in *Centuries*.

My dear Sir let me beg *you* to *pause* and *think* and *Pray* and decide to abide with the friends who elevated you to power with the assurance of your cooperation, in securing the Nationality of our land on a *just*—and lasting foundation. The eyes of Millions are upon you, and you must *soon pass the Rubicon*!

May our *all wise* God guide your mind, and preserve you from *evil counsels* and fatal decisions.

Granville Moody

ALS, DLC-JP.
   1. Quotation not identified.
   2. Johnson had also decried the so-called "peace plank" which had been drafted at the Democratic National Convention in Chicago, from which Moody extracted these quotations. See Speech at Logansport, Indiana, Oct. 4, 1864, *Johnson Papers*, 7: 225.
   3. Quotation not identified.
   4. Perhaps a reference to Seward's Washington's Birthday Speech. See William S. Hillyer to Johnson, Feb. 10, 1866.
   5. Russell Houston.
   6. John Sherman, Samuel Shellabarger, William Lawrence, John A. Bingham, and Reader W. Clarke were members of the Ohio congressional delegation. Clarke (1812–1872) was a two-term Republican who was later third auditor of the Treasury Department. *BDAC*.

From Samuel J. Randall

Washington D.C.   July 12, 1866

Mr President

Your Cabinet has a vacancy. It ought to be filled by a firm, true man of convictions in favor of your policy.

Pennsylvania is the battle ground, in the October elections. That State is without a member in your Administration. Reflect whether it would strengthen you by taking a Minister from our State. Should you so determine, let me suggest William F. Johnston[1] a man of mind and nerve.

This is written with the most sincerest friendship.

Saml. J. Randall

ALS, DLC-JP.
   1. Johnston (1808–1872) served in the Pennsylvania legislature before he became governor (1848–52). Prior to the war he was involved in various business enterprises; when the war came, he organized troops and superintended the construction of Pittsburgh's defenses. Whether the President actually considered Johnston a viable candidate for the postmaster generalship is not known. However, he did nominate Johnston for the position of collector for the Twenty-third District of Pennsylvania in April 1866, but the nomination was rejected the following month. In late July, the President nominated Johnston as collector at Philadelphia; after some controversy he served a recess appointment until January 1867, when the Senate rejected Johnston's regular appointment. *NCAB*, 2: 288;

Nathaniel P. Sawyer et al. to Johnson, ca. Apr. 1866, Appts., Internal Revenue Service, Collector, Pa., 23rd Dist., RG56, NA; Ser. 6B, Vol. 4: 82–84, Johnson Papers, LC; George L. Curry to Johnson, Mar. 30, 1866.

From Thomas F. Meagher

Virginia city, Montana Territory,
Executive office, July 13th 1866.

My Dear Sir,

Being satisfied that you are desirous of learning, in a familiar and confidential way, of the condition and progress of these new and noble Territories, since that is the way that a clearer and truer knowledge is, generally speaking, obtained in regard to them, I take the liberty of writing you a few lines concerning Montana, with the government of which I am at present, as I have been, for the last ten months, charged, in the absence of a fully-appointed Governor.[1]

As for its' material condition and progress, nothing could be more satisfactory, as most probably you have been some time since assured. The mineral wealth of the Territory is, to speak without exaggeration, incalculable. The gold and silver deposits are everywhere distinctly ascertained. Several of them—especially those located in the gulches or gorges of the mountains—have yielded already hundreds of thousands of the precious metal. The gulche, along which this town is built, has yielded millions. The vaster deposits, however, are to be found in the quartz "leads" or arteries of the mountains. Yet these, owing to the absence of competent machinery, have been, up to this date, very imperfectly and hastily worked. Yet, as the Territory becomes better known, Capital will, assuredly, flow in to supply this want, and give positive and great effect to the spirit of discovery and the manual industry which in a wonderful degree characterizes the mining population of the Territory. The merchants, settled among us and drawing enormous profits from the sale of the very necessaries of life (such as flour and bacon) might, as they have it in their power, do much towards the development of the mineral resources of the country. I regret deeply, however, to say, that they seem animated with little or no spirit above that which stimulates them to the acquisition of prompt and prodigious profits.

The miners derive hardly any assistance from them—hence it is, that after a gulch has been, comparatively speaking, but superficially worked, it has to be abandoned—the practical miners not having the means to extend their operations. The profits of the merchants, for the most part, are spent and invested outside the Territory. This leaves the miners, in the great majority of instances, in a condition little (if anything) better than that of the usual run of day-labourers in the East. A more spirited and generous class of merchants is, however, gradually appearing, and with new discoveries and more assured prospects, such as we are gaining every day, this class will multiply.

Besides gold and silver, copper has been found, and so has coal, lead, and other valuable, though intrinsically inferior, deposits. Coal, very recently discovered within a few miles of Fort Benton, and at other points along the Upper Missouri, lies in remarkably extended and paralel lines with the river. This is most fortunate, as the wood along the Missouri is rapidly disappearing, and steam-boat navigation would be arrested, or, at grievous cost, be prosecuted, were it not for this discovery.

That Montana will heartily and permanently flourish, and its mining operations be conducted on a broad and grand scale, and with no extravagant expense, I feel confident from the fact—that, in all the essentials of life, it will, in a short time, amply sustain itself. Its agricultural resources are abundant—singularly and splendidly abundant. Forage is plentiful to excess, and of the most nutritious character. The prairies of Illinois do not yield a finer description of hay. Oats are being, and have been, raised, all over the Territory, in great quantities, and they are of an excellent quality. Vegetables, likewise, are produced in abundance—not only potatoes and other kinds of the coarser and commoner description—but the more delicate, such as radishes, lettuce, onions, and so forth. As yet, no attempts have been made to grow fruit—but the farmers entertain the firmest hopes, that the hardier kinds of fruit will propagate here admirably and in profusion. Wild strawberries, plums, rasberries, and grapes even, are found all over the lower and more sheltered ranges, and are very palatable and wholesome. You will, I well know, be cordially pleased to learn that farming is becoming a favorite and very profitable business, and that hundreds and hundreds, instead of trusting their fortunes to the precarious pursuit of gold, are availing themselves of the liberal and hospitable provisions of the Homestead Act, with the successful working, as well as with the auspicious origination, of which your name will be almost parentally identified.[2] Thus a healthy, prosperous, and thoroughly independent yeomanry is growing up within our Territory—and thus will Montana assuredly acquire the proportions and the stamina of a vigorous and solid [brave?] young State.

Politically characterized, Montana is Democratic—Democratic not, indeed, in the old and obsolete signification of the term, but in the new, improved, and nobler one. Accepting frankly and sincerely all the issues and conclusions of the war, the people of the Territory (two-thirds of them positively) heartily support the Government, and will support it, in every way they are qualified to give it support, concurring fully, as they do, in the enlightened national policy the President has announced, and to which he has been so resolutely stedfast. Secession sympathies—Nay! out-and-out Rebels—there were here by the score, at the time of my arrival; but I am convinced, that had Governor Edgerton[3] pursued a fairer and kindlier and wiser line of administration, these men would have much sooner merged themselves into the great body of Unionists, and renounced their affinities with the Rebellion.

His administration, however, was one of bitter and relentless exasperation, so far as those politically opposed to him were concerned and affected—and the consequence was, that these sympathizers with the hostile South were embittered and hardened with their pernicious prejudices, instead of being softened, reformed, and reconciled. Sharing the sentiments and spirit which have distinguished the Government, as well as all the great soldiers of the war, I considered it my duty to reverse the action of Governor Edgerton, and in my limited sphere, endeavoured to give full effect to the proclamation of peace. I ignored the existence of Secessionists or their sympathizers, and recognizing every man as a true man who honestly accepted the decision pronounced by our final victory, effaced the sectional lines that had been so rigorously and viciously drawn by the Federal officers up to the day of my appearance in the Territory. The consequence is, that the vast majority of the people are now, and for some months past, have been in thorough harmony with the Government, and devoted to the measures and the policy which would, with wise and magnanimous statesmanship, restore and consolidate the Nation.[4]

But in pursuing the line of conduct I have indicated, I regret to say, that, not only have I not been supported by the other Federal officers of the Territory, but have been very viciously opposed.[5] So much so, that, without any affectation, I may say, that I stand today *alone* in my fidelity to the Government and the policy it has declared. Were these factionists to have their way, the Territory would stand in a repugnant attitude to the Government, all their old and mischievous prejudices and sympathies being kept alive and inflamed by the aggressive treatment they would be sure to experience through the implacable bigotry and partizanship of the men to whom I expressly refer. It would, indeed, in my respectful judgement, be a blessing to Montana were every one of these officials removed, and others of more enlightened minds and more patriotic hearts sent out here to supersede them.

The change would be enthusiastically and most gratefully welcomed, and serve still more strongly and intimately to unite the people of the Territory with the Administration and its friends. For my part, satisfied I am doing what is right, and what will tend to substitute a healthier and nobler public spirit for that which prevailed, previous to my coming, and satisfied, moreover, that, by so doing, I shall all the more effectively and completely discharge my duty to the Government, nothing shall persuade or coerce me to abandon, or by an inch relinquish, the position I have taken up.

Having now written, in a general way, all that occurs to me in connection with the Territory, and have a word or two to say in reference to myself, and having said this, shall not further infringe upon leisure moments, which, snatched from the laborious occupation of the day, should be held sacred, even by the most privileged of friends, for pleasanter relaxation than any communication of mine can afford.

Yesterday I wrote to Mr. Cooley,[6] Commissioner of Indian affairs, strongly urging the appointment of a Superintendent of Indian Affairs for Montana. At present, in conformity with the provisions of the Organic Act, the Governor (or Acting-Governor) of the Territory is ex-officio Superintendent. But, as I have said to Mr. Cooley, it is next to an impossibility for the Governor (or Acting Governor) to discharge the duties of the two offices with the necessary efficiency and completeness—the supervision of the different Agencies requiring him to be constantly in the saddle and performing journeys of from two to three hundred miles at a stretch, whilst his administration of the Territory, as its Chief Executive officer, equally demands his presence at the Capital or in its immediate neighborhood. I have endeavoured to combine and satisfy the two requirements—but in such a country as this is, where such journeys take a week, two weeks, a month, the attempt to do so is futile, or rather involves and necessitates the sacrifice of one class of duties to the other—and this is, of course, highly, if not seriously, disadvantageous, where both classes of duties are equally essential and imperative.[7]

Satisfied that it would be in my power thoroughly to discharge the duties of the Indian Superintendency, whilst the office would be far more in consonance with my predilections than either the Secretaryship or Governorship, I have requested him to be so good as to recommend me to the position, should he think fit to approve and advise the seperation of the Superintendency from the Governorship. I now, my dear sir, repeat the application to you in person, and beg that you will do me the favour of appointing me to the position in question. Nothing delights me so much as being on horseback, and taking long, rough, and adventurous journeys, and as the Superintendency would enable me heartily to indulge in this partiality and perform these services, I should be perfectly at home with that appointment. I respectfully but earnestly beg you will bear this in mind, and grant me the favour I have now asked.[8]

There's a young friend of mine here, Mr. Harry Rainforth,[9] a resident of and property-holder in the Territory, who desires to enter West Point, and who would feel most grateful should you appoint him to the Academy. He is but 19 years of age—is highly intelligent—a perfect little gentleman—high-spirited, and a soldier by nature. I cordially recommend him to you for one of the appointments in your gift. That, and the Indian Superintendency of Montana for myself, is all I ask—and all I shall ask now, or at any future time.

Granting these requests, you will gratify me deeply.

Heartily wishing you, for many years to come, the best health and brightest happiness, which is the most successful termination to your great labours in the Presidency, and with the friendliest regards and best wishes towards all in the White House, in which Mrs. Meagher,[10] who has just reached me, cordially unites with me.

                                                        Thomas Francis Meagher

ALS, DLC-JP.
    1. Meagher was territorial secretary and, thus, acting governor.
    2. See *Johnson Papers*, 1: 598–600, 608–10.
    3. Sidney Edgerton.
    4. Meagher sided with the Democratic majority of the citizens rather than the Republican officeholders, stirring up an "extremely bitter anti-Meagher campaign." Robert G. Athearn, *Thomas Francis Meagher: An Irish Revolutionary in America* (Boulder, 1949), 150–55, 165–66.
    5. The Federal officials consisted of Chief Justice Hezekiah L. Hosmer, Associate Justices Lorenzo P. Williston and Lyman E. Munson, and Marshal George M. Pinney. Munson (c1822–1908), a Yale graduate and New Haven, Connecticut, lawyer, disagreed with Meagher over two major issues, pronouncing the legislature called by Meagher illegal, and sentencing one James Daniels to three years imprisonment, a judgment rendered ineffective when Meagher pardoned Daniels. For their opposition to the legislature, Meagher had Hosmer and Munson "sagebrushed"—sent to virtually uninhabited judicial districts in the territory. Even Pinney opposed Meagher in a letter to Lyman Trumbull of June 10, 1866. Ibid., 149–53; *U.S. Off. Reg.* (1865); Pomeroy, *The Territories*, 139–40; *History of Tioga County, Pennsylvania* (n.p., 1897), 157; Edward L. Munson, "Lyman Ezra Munson," *Contributions to the Historical Society of Montana*, 7 (1910): 199–202; Guice, *Rocky Mountain Bench*, 18, 19, 35, 71–72.
    6. Dennis N. Cooley.
    7. The problems of Meagher and other territorial governors are discussed in William M. Neil, "The Territorial Governor as Indian Superintendent in the Trans-Mississippi West," *MVHR*, 43 (1956–57): 213–37.
    8. Meagher remained secretary under the new governor Green Clay Smith, and was again acting governor at the time of his death in July 1867. No separate superintendent of Indian affairs was appointed in Montana, although some other territories had them before Congress abolished the gubernatorial superintendency in 1871. Ibid., 213; Athearn, *Meagher*, 155.
    9. Not further identified. Rainforth did not attend West Point. *West Point Register*.
    10. Elizabeth Townsend (1830–1906), a New Yorker who married Meagher in 1855, was his second wife. After Meagher's death she was active in various charities in New York City. *DAB*; *New York Times*, July 6, 1906.

From James Speed

                                                        Attorney General's Office,
                                                        July 13th 1866.

Sir—

    Lieutenant General Grant's letter to the Secretary of War, of date July 7, 1866, which you have referred to me, with the papers that accompanied that letter, show that the riots in Memphis, Tenn.,[1] in the early part of May resulted in most disgusting scenes of murder, arson, rape and robbery, in which most of the victims were helpless and unresisting colored citizens. Gen. Grant well remarks that such a scene stamps lasting disgrace upon the civil authorities of Memphis. Inasmuch as the civil authorities have thus far failed to arrest the perpetrators of these wanton outrages, or to do anything towards redressing the injuries and damages sustained, he asks whether the military shall interfere.[2]

Whilst this conduct is so disgraceful to human nature, subversive of good order and peace, and derogatory to the dignity of the laws of the State of Tennessee, it constitutes no offence against the laws and dignity of the United States of America. Under our frame of government, the States are charged with the duty of protecting citizens from outrage, by public prosecutions, and the citizens themselves have the right to appear in the appropriate courts, State or national, for the redress of any private wrongs that they may have sustained. The military stationed at Memphis performed their duty in aiding to suppress the mob violence. Having done that, they have and can have nothing to do with the redress of private grievances, or prosecutions for public wrongs. The Courts, State and national, are open in Tennessee, and there is no war. Under the State laws, as well as United States laws, the injured party may appeal to the courts for redress.

James Speed   Attorney General.

LS, DNA-RG94, Lets. Recd. (Main Ser.), File T-412-1866 (M619, Roll 520).
   1. See James B. Bingham to Johnson, May 17, 1866; *Memphis Appeal*, May 2, 1866; *Nashville Dispatch*, May 3–8, 1866. For results of the House investigation, see *House Reports*, 39 Cong., 1 Sess., No. 101, "Memphis Riots and Massacres" (Ser. 1274).
   2. See Simon, *Grant Papers*, 16: 230–31, 231n-32n, 233–34, 234n–36n.

To Henry Stanbery

Washington, D.C., July 13th 1866

I will be pleased to see you in Washington on a matter of importance. Can you be here immediately? Answer.[1]

Andrew Johnson.

Tel, DNA-RG107, Tels. Sent, President, Vol. 3 (1865–68).
   1. On the following day Stanbery replied that he would "leave for Washington on Tuesday," the 17th. Exactly a week later he was confirmed as attorney general and handed his commission in person. Stanbery to Johnson, July 14, 1866, Tels. Recd., President, Vol. 5 (1866–67), RG107, NA; J. Hubley Ashton to William H. Seward, July 24, 1866, Office of Atty. Gen., Lets. Sent, Vol. F (M699, Roll 11), RG60, NA.

From Anonymous

Washington, D.C.   July 14th 1866.

My dear friend:

In the name of God Almighty, do you intend to let this fellow Harlan remain in your Cabinet? Old Otto,[1] also, his assistant Secretary, who, when the "Veto" was passed over your head[2]—shook hands with the Radicals—in the office (clerks) made FUN OF YOU, &c. I have travelled during the past six months, through fourteen States of the now-*separated Union*, and the only fault found with you is—that you are losing ground by inaction. The people wish that you would go on—remove the damned rascals by whom you are surrounded. *Defy* Congress. Keep up your reputation for steadfastness—and decision. The people will sustain you, by God.

Commence at once and go through the whole business. You will find plenty of men to take places without Salary and rely upon the next Congress and your recommendation for it. Do it, or you are forever gone. Be surrounded by your *friends*—or you are forever gone—I assure you.

L

L, DLC-JP.
   1. William T. Otto.
   2. Evidently a reference to the overturning of Johnson's veto of the Civil Rights bill in early April. Castel, *Presidency of Johnson*, 71.

From Samuel B. Buckley[1]

Austin Texas   July 14/66

Dear Sir

I believe you do not know the true condition of things in this State, because most of the information you receive from here, is from those connected with the Provisional Government, or with the Freedmans Bureau, men, who are personaly interested in continuing the present condition of affairs, & retaining thier offices. Having devoted a large portion of my life, to Scientific pursuits, I have not identified myself with any political party, & only address you as a patriot, who loves the Union, & who sincerely desires peace, harmony, & prosperity to be restored as speedily as possible to the whole country, which I think your Restoration Policy if carried on will soon effect. Having been engaged in the Geological Survey of Texas during the two years immediately preceding the war, traveled through most of its settled region, & mixed freely with its inhabitants, & also having been in the State since the first of last January, I know much about the feelings of its people towards the Union, both before the war, & since. There is no doubt but that a majority of the people of Texas were in favor of the Union at the Commencement of the war, & even while the war prevailed, the Union sentiment was strong, which was evinced by many of its citizens leaving the State to avoid the Conscript laws. Now the Union feeling is almost unanimous, & there never was a more law abiding, & submissive people than those of Texas at the present time. I went North in 1861 & was engaged with the U.S. Sanitary Commission during the war.[2] Reports published in the Northern newspapers about the lawlessness of the people of Texas made me hesitate long before leaving my native State of New York, to return here last December. I assure you I was very much, & very agreeably surprized to find matters as quiet, & orderly as I have found them in this state. There are comparatively no more criminal acts committed here than among an equal number of people in any of the Northern States. The Rev. Mr. Welch,[3] sent here by the Methodist Bishop of Pennsylvania[4] to cooperate with the Freedmans Bureau, who has been in this state since the middle of last January, & who has traveled extensively through the planting counties; last week informed me that he found things much better than he anticipated, & full as good as could be expected under the circumstances. The freedman were working well; & the planters were cooperating quietly, & hopefully. This corresponds with what I have seen, & with what I have learned from others. Not but that there are law breakers, & criminals in Texas but not as many as most persons would expect considering that many thousands of soldiers were suddenly discharged without pay & almost without clothes; circumstances sufficient to make many men desperate. This however applies more to the other Southern States, than to this. Here the officers after the Surrenders of Lee & Johnson were for continuing the struggle; but the soldiers refused & left in crowds for home, & there went to work to provide for themselves, & their families. Texas has suffered less from the effects of the war than the other Confederate States, & there is less cause here for those bitter feelings which were in many instances engendered by destroying the property of the inhabitants of the other Rebel States. Notwithstanding you left Texas in a state of insurrection by your Proclamation declaring a cessation of hostilities in the other Confederate States,[5] I have not the least doubt but that there is more real genuine Union feeling in this state than in any other one of the late Slave States. Unhappily the course which Gov. Hamilton has pursued here has been such as to exasperate the people against him. He has not endeavored in the least to conciliate, but constantly strove to wound their feelings by taunts, & harsh language. He has falsified facts, & where things were bright, cheering, & promising, he has made them dark, & sorrowful, denouncing all those engaged in the rebellion as traitors, & meriting the punishment due to traitors. He has tried to array the Union men of the State against each other, & while openly pretending to favor your Restoration Policy, he has secretly favored the Radical party in Congress. This is now manifest from the public declarations of Judge Bell his Secretary of State[6] & the Inteligencer his party organ in this City;[7] Judge B. in his oration here on the 4th inst., denounced a "One Man Power" asserting that in our Government all power came from the people, that Congress as coming more directly from the people were the true power, & head of the Government, instead, of the President. I do not give his exact words only the meaning. Again in an oration delivered a few days before the late election in the Capitol; he said he did not intend to make a political speech, that no matter how the election went it would have no effect, leaving the people to infer that the Provisional Government would be continued. I enclose you his Proclamation lately issued which shows what he expects.[8] The Inteligencer in commenting on the Report of the Restoration Committee,[9] said that "nothing since the surrender of Genl. Lee had had such an important bearing & gave so much hope for the future of our Country as that document." I think you must have discovered ere this that Hamilton is unfriendly to your Restoration Policy; else why should he, & his party leaders strive by misrepresentation to thwart the will of the people of this State in their choice of Dr. Thrckmorton[10] for Governor, than whom there never was a more pure Patriot, nor now a better friend, of the Union, & of your general, & entire policy. He in the Secession Convention of '61 was in favor of the Union from the beginning to the end. He made frequent, & eloquent appeals in its favor, & when all the other original Union members had been subdued or bought over; he stood alone as the single representative of his party, in that body. The vote was taken viva voce, & when Thrckmorton said No! there was a general hiss among the members throughout the house. He immediately rose & said "When the rabble hiss, patriots may well tremble." All was then Silent, & there were none even in that body who did not respect him.[11] When he was first nominated for Governor there was a split in the caucus which nominated him, & the Secessionists were only deterred from nominating another man by the certainty that they could not command sufficient votes to avail any thing. The Southern Inteligencer of this city of date June 7/66 in an editorial commenting on a letter of Dr. Thrckmorton to Gov. Hamilton says "From this letter it appears that Dr. Thrckmorton never flinched, or wavered in his loyalty to the United States Government. He expresses himself in vigorous Saxon English. He does not say when offered a Brigadier Generalship, I declined it, but "I refused it." He says when the State troops were disbanded and Conscripted into the confederate Service "it had no effect upon me. I was in command of a separate organization, raised by Act of the Legislature for special purposes, & avowedly to keep the frontier men out of the Confederate Service."[12] It would have been an insult to offer pardon to such a man. He may have needed one from Jefferson Davis but never from Andrew Johnson. If in the Chapter of accidents he should chance to be elected Governor, in spite of the bad company in which he is found, so far as he, & we might add, Col. Jones,[13] & Judge Smith[14] are concerned, it would be a triumph of the Union men." Such is the language of the Editor of the Inteligencer the organ of Hamilton & the Radical Party, at a time when it supported Gov. Pease[15] for Governor. Such is the Governor elect of Texas, than whom there is no man living better calculated to make the people of this state quietly & peacefully submit to the Government of the United States, & cause all the inhabitants of Texas both white & black to have the blessings of freedom, & be protected in life property, & the lawful pursuit of happiness. Shall the people of Texas be told by a Governor of your appointment, to choose by ballot a Governor & other state officers, & when they have at great expense, & in good faith elected as good Union men as could possibly be selected, suitable for their respective office after having done all this; shall they be told that the election is void merely because the tools of Hamilton were not chosen? God forbid; & if you will but say *No* then your work of Reconstruction will go bravely on, & soon be brought to a successful termination. Then the whole nation will soon learn to bless & revere the name of Andrew Johnson. Otherwise if a hateful provisional Governor be continued in power here, then your Reconstruction Policy is a failure; & the people of this State will justly feel that they have been shamefully wronged, & decived; which may God avert.

S. B. Buckley

P.S. I am a graduate of the University at Middletown Conn.[16] A Member of the Academy Nat. Sciences Phila. Member of the Entomological Society of the same city, of the Lyceum Nat. His. of New York, Buffalo Nat. His. Socty American Association of Science Phi Beta Kappa Society Etc. Etc. You will find my name as an Author in all recent works on the Botany of the United States. I have written various papers for Sillimans Journal[17] & other Scientific Journals, A sample of which I enclose. Referances James Harlan Secr. Interior with whom I have a slight acquantance, Isaac Newton Agricultural Bureau Comr. Clark Mills Artist Prof. Baird of the Smithsonian Prof. Glover Entomoligist, Agri. Bureau, Mr. Saunders Superintendent Agricult. Garden, all of Washington.[18] With the exception of Harlan all the above know me well.

I give the above because you as a politician never heard of me before. This letter is strictly private in case the Provisional Government is continued here but should Thrckmorton be the Governor, & you think its publication will benefit your Policy, you are at liberty to publish all excepting the postscript. I was Botanist & Assistant Geologist in the survey of this State. The State Geologist died,[19] & it devolved on me to prepare a Geological Report[20] which I have done to submit to the next Legislature of this State hence you will see why if H. should return as Gov. here I wish this to be unknown.

S.B.B.

ALS, DLC-JP.
  1. Buckley (1809–1883), a noted naturalist, collected plant and other specimens in Alabama, Tennessee, North Carolina, and Florida as well as Texas. He was also state geologist of Texas (1866–67, 1874–76). *DAB*; Webb et al., *Handbook of Texas*, 1: 238; George P. Merrill, *The First One Hundred Years of American Geology* (New York, 1969 [1924]), 401–2.
  2. Buckley was chief examiner in the commission's Statistical Department. *DAB*.
  3. Rev. Joseph Welch (1836–1920), Methodist minister and former chaplain of the 91st Penn. Inf., served as a missionary in Texas after the war. He became the second superintendent of freedmen's schools in Texas in mid-1868 and served until early 1870. Thereafter he filled a number of pastorates in Pennsylvania and spent twenty-nine years as chaplain to the prisoners in the Eastern Penitentiary. Claude Elliott, "The Freedmen's Bureau in Texas," *SWHQ*, 56 (1952): 15, 17; Alton Hornsby, Jr., "The Freedmen's Bureau Schools in Texas, 1865–1870," *SWHQ*, 76 (1973): 406, 412–15; *Official Journal and Year Book of the Philadelphia Annual Conference of the Methodist Episcopal Church . . .* (Philadelphia, 1920), 780–81.
  4. Bishop Matthew Simpson.

5. See Proclamation *re* End of Insurrection, Apr. 2, 1866.

6. James H. Bell.

7. The *Southern Intelligencer* was apparently published in Austin from July 1865 to January 1867 by Frank Brown, Austin alderman and court clerk, in association with a James A. Foster. Webb et al., *Handbook of Texas*, 1: 223.

8. This proclamation has not been found.

9. It is not certain to what report Buckley refers.

10. James W. Throckmorton. See also James H. Bell to Johnson, July 2, 1866.

11. For accounts of these proceedings, see Walter L. Buenger, *Secession and the Union in Texas* (Austin, 1984), 63, 148; Claude Elliott, *Leathercoat: The Life History of a Texas Patriot* (San Antonio, 1938), 53–55.

12. Throckmorton's alleged statement does not appear to be quite accurate, for he served with Confederate troops in campaigns in the Indian Territory, Arkansas, and Louisiana, as well as Texas. For a time he was a state brigadier general commanding the Frontier District of Texas. Webb et al., *Handbook of Texas*, 2: 778; Elliott, *Texas Patriot*, 88–92.

13. George W. Jones (1828–1903), who moved to Texas in 1848 and became a lawyer, served as colonel of the Confederate 17th Tex. Cav. Elected lieutenant governor of Texas in June 1866, he was removed by Gen. Philip Sheridan in 1867. Jones served two terms in the U.S. Congress as a representative from Texas (1879–83). *BDAC*.

14. George W. Smith, associate justice of the Texas Supreme Court (June 1866–September 1867), later served in the Texas house of representatives (1873–74), and as Texas secretary of state (1891). Webb et al., *Handbook of Texas*, 2: 623.

15. Elisha M. Pease.

16. Wesleyan University.

17. The *American Journal of Science*, edited by Benjamin Silliman. *DAB*.

18. Sculptor Clark Mills (1810–1883) was noted for his equestrian statue of Andrew Jackson in Lafayette Square, Washington, D.C. (with replicas in New Orleans and Nashville), and his bronze casting of "Liberty" for the Capitol dome. Spencer F. Baird (1823–1887), a zoologist, as assistant secretary (1850–78) and then secretary of the Smithsonian, did much to enlarge its natural history collection. A prolific writer specializing in birds, he was also the first head of the Commission of Fish and Fisheries (1871–87). Townend Glover (1813–1883) was raised in England, received an art education in Germany, and came to the U.S. in 1836, where he became the country's first government-sponsored entomologist. William Saunders (1822–1900), a Scot by birth, came to the U.S. in 1848. Active as a horticulturist and landscape gardener, he designed a number of private estates and cemeteries, including the national cemetery at Gettysburg. From 1862 to 1900 he was superintendent of the Department of Agriculture's experimental gardens and did much to introduce suitable foreign trees into the U.S. *DAB*.

19. Francis Moore, Jr. (1808–1864), a medical doctor, lawyer, and newspaper editor, moved to Texas in 1836. Mayor of Houston (1838, 1843, 1849–52), he was also interested in Texas geography and geology. After studying with the New York Geological Survey, he served as Texas state geologist (1859–60) but went north at the outbreak of the Civil War and died in Minnesota. Webb et al., *Handbook of Texas*, 2: 229; Merrill, *American Geology*, 401–2.

20. *Preliminary Report of the Geological and Agricultural Survey of Texas*, published in 1866. Webb et al., *Handbook of Texas*, 1: 238.

From Alfred D. Evans[1]

Baltimore   July 14th 1866

Sir—

After a long conversation with a mutual friend to day in relation to the present Situation of affairs, I was Struck with a remark "that the friends of President Johnson Should drive the *Radical Congress to the wall*." I asked how it could be done. "He did not know" but certainly there was evidence enough among your friends to bring forward Something that would Strike the people as right, and "Congress would reject" which would at once take the wind out of their Sailes. After one hours reflection I was convinced that my friend was right and now is the time to do the good work an have your reconstruction plan carried out and the Subterfuge that you desire disloyal men to represent the South in Congress will be nailed to the counter as base coin. My plan is for you to have Some brave unquestionable loyal members of Congress to propose Something like the following.

Whereas fifteen months have elapsed Since the Subjection of those who were in armed Rebelion against the united States, and beleving it right and proper that all the States Should be represented in Congress according to the Constitution. Be it therefore

Resolved by both houses of Congress that the President of the United States is hereby instructed to notify the Governors of the State of Georgia [to notify the Governors][2] &c to order the Election of Senators and Congressmen to represent the Several States So notified in the Congress of the United States.

Resolved that the President, be further instructed to notify the Governors of the afforesaid States that congress will not recognise any representative who has been in the Rebel Army or Navy or been in any way connected with the Rebel Governmt or disloyal to the Goverment of U.S.

I think the practical effect of Something like the above would effectively take Some of the Curl out of their hair.

Your Excelency will please pardon me for taxing your time but if you knew how much I prize your good Success you would excuse me as I Shall never forget the thrilling patriotic appeal you made 27 March 1861 in Fredrick City[3] were I had the honor to take a glass of wine with you at Genl E Schrivers.[4] Stand by the old Ship like *Andrew Jackson* and the people will not fail to Stand by you.

A D. Evans

ALS, DLC-JP.

1. Evans (1817–c1883) ran a large wholesale and retail business. He was warden of the Maryland Penitentiary from 1858 to 1862. A Union supporter, he was sergeant-at-arms for the House of Delegates (1863) and the Constitutional Convention (1864). In 1866 he was appointed justice of the peace and later engaged in the practice of law. Baltimore directories (1879–84); *The Biographical Cyclopedia of Representative Men of Maryland and the District of Columbia* (Baltimore, 1879), 171.

2. Evans used ditto marks in the manuscript under the phrase, "to notify the Governors," to indicate that the phrase should be repeated, thereby becoming inclusive of all the governors.

3. Johnson made a strong Union speech at the organizational meeting of the Union party of Maryland in Frederick City. *National Intelligencer*, Mar. 28, 1861. See Frederick (Md.) Committee to Johnson, Mar. 25, 1861, *Johnson Papers*, 4: 426–27.

4. After a career in the army, Edmund Shriver (1812–1899) worked with several railroads. He then served as aide to Governor Morgan of New York with the rank of colonel until the war. Serving in the eastern theater he attained the rank of brevet major general by March 1865. Subsequently he headed the Inspector's Bureau (1865–69, 1871–76), was inspector of West Point, and was inspector general of the Division of the Pacific. *DAB*.

From Jane Nave and Annie B. Ross[1]

[Washington, ca. July 14, 1866][2]

Dear Sir,

Our beloved Father being too ill to write has dictated the letter written by a member of his family.[3]

It will prove to you, sir, how his mind dwells on the unjust and outrageous treatment inflicted on him by the Commission at Ft Smith, in September last.[4] He has been placed by it, in a false and unjust position before the world and before the world he *craves* to have his honor vindicated and exonerated.

The verbal assurances given by your honor, to our Delegation, as well as to myself, (altho' he is still unapprised of my visits to you) was very gratifying to him, and has been a source of relief and comfort, as he lays on his bed of suffering, and *anything* Official from you would indeed remove every thorn from his pillow.

Altho' reduced bodily to a very low and prostrate condition—his Mental faculties, thank God, remain active, clear and vigorous—except in the delirium of fever—then it only lives over that great wrong—dwells on the interests of his people, his reverance for the Government of the U.S, his unshaken confidence in the President, and his firm belief that you will see him righted.

His days on Earth, at best, will be few[5]—his peace is made with his Maker. Then in pity remove from his pathway this *dark cloud*, & let not his Sun Set in *darkness*. Many thanks I owe you, and please Accept, for your Kind indulgence, in permitting me to trespass so much upon your time and patience, and for the interviews, you have favored me. In conclusion I would beg of you a favorable consideration of my Father's documents; and a reply; no matter how brief, will give him so much satisfaction, and be most gratefully Appreciated by his daughters.[6]

Jane Nave

Annie B Ross

P.S.   This was intended to be sent with my Father's but was overlooked.

ALS (Nave), DNA-RG75, Gen. Records, Lets. Recd. (M234, Roll 100).

1. Jane Ross Meigs Nave (1821–1894) was a daughter of John Ross by his first wife, Elizabeth Brown Henley ("Quatie"). Educated at the Moravian Female Academy in Salem, North Carolina, Jane Nave was twice widowed. Annie B. Ross (1845–*fl*1870), the older of John Ross's two children by his second wife, Mary Brian Stapler, was one of the executors of his estate. Moulton, *John Ross*, 12, 13, 162, 177, 194, 242.

2. The file cover sheet carries the date July 14, 1866. Internal evidence indicates that the letter was written in Washington.

3. Probably John Ross to Johnson, June 28, 1866.

4. See ibid.

5. John Ross died on August 1. Moulton, *John Ross*, 195.

6. Johnson referred this letter to Secretary of the Interior James Harlan "for special attention." On July 17 the secretary referred it to Commissioner of Indian Affairs Dennis

N. Cooley. On July 19 Cooley and the northern Cherokees, Ross's faction, signed a treaty, a condition of which was that Ross would still be "Principal Chief of the Cherokees." The Senate ratified the treaty August 11. Ibid., 194.

Freedmen's Bureau Bill Veto

WASHINGTON, D.C., *July 16, 1866.*

To the House of Representatives:

A careful examination of the bill passed by the two Houses of Congress entitled "An act to continue in force and to amend 'An act to establish a bureau for the relief of freedmen and refugees, and for other purposes' " has convinced me that the legislation which it proposes would not be consistent with the welfare of the country, and that it falls clearly within the reasons assigned in my message of the 19th of February last, returning, without my signature, a similar measure which originated in the Senate.[1] It is not my purpose to repeat the objections which I then urged. They are yet fresh in your recollection, and can be readily examined as a part of the records of one branch of the National Legislature. Adhering to the principles set forth in that message, I now reaffirm them and the line of policy therein indicated.

The only ground upon which this kind of legislation can be justified is that of the war-making power. The act of which this bill is intended as amendatory was passed during the existence of the war. By its own provisions it is to terminate within one year from the cessation of hostilities and the declaration of peace. It is therefore yet in existence, and it is likely that it will continue in force as long as the freedmen may require the benefit of its provisions. It will certainly remain in operation as a law until some months subsequent to the meeting of the next session of Congress, when, if experience shall make evident the necessity of additional legislation, the two Houses will have ample time to mature and pass the requisite measures. In the meantime the questions arise, Why should this war measure be continued beyond the period designated in the original act, and why in time of peace should military tribunals be created to continue until each "State shall be fully restored in its constitutional relations to the Government and shall be duly represented in the Congress of the United States?"

It was manifest, with respect to the act approved March 3, 1865, that prudence and wisdom alike required that jurisdiction over all cases concerning the free enjoyment of the immunities and rights of citizenship, as well as the protection of person and property, should be conferred upon some tribunal in every State or district where the ordinary course of judicial proceedings was interrupted by the rebellion, and until the same should be fully restored. At that time, therefore, an urgent necessity existed for the passage of some such law. Now, however, war has substantially ceased; the ordinary course of judicial proceedings is no longer interrupted; the courts, both State and Federal, are in full, complete, and successful operation, and through them every person, regardless of race and color, is entitled to and can be heard. The protection granted to the white citizen is already conferred by law upon the freedman; strong and stringent guards, by way of penalties and punishments, are thrown around his person and property, and it is believed that ample protection will be afforded him by due process of law, without resort to the dangerous expedient of "military tribunals," now that the war has been brought to a close. The necessity no longer existing for such tribunals, which had their origin in the war, grave objections to their continuance must present themselves to the minds of all reflecting and dispassionate men. Independently of the danger, in representative republics, of conferring upon the military, in time of peace, extraordinary powers—so carefully guarded against by the patriots and statesmen of the earlier days of the Republic, so frequently the ruin of governments founded upon the same free principles, and subversive of the rights and liberties of the citizen—the question of practical economy earnestly commends itself to the consideration of the lawmaking power. With an immense debt already burdening the incomes of the industrial and laboring classes, a due regard for their interests, so inseparably connected with the welfare of the country, should prompt us to rigid economy and retrenchment, and influence us to abstain from all legislation that would unnecessarily increase the public indebtedness. Tested by this rule of sound political wisdom, I can see no reason for the establishment of the "military jurisdiction" conferred upon the officials of the Bureau by the fourteenth section of the bill.

By the laws of the United States and of the different States competent courts, Federal and State, have been established and are now in full practical operation. By means of these civil tribunals ample redress is afforded for all private wrongs, whether to the person or the property of the citizen, without denial or unnecessary delay. They are open to all, without regard to color or race. I feel well assured that it will be better to trust the rights, privileges, and immunities of the citizen to tribunals thus established, and presided over by competent and impartial judges, bound by fixed rules of law and evidence, and where the right of trial by jury is guaranteed and secured, than to the caprice or judgment of an officer of the Bureau, who it is possible may be entirely ignorant of the principles that underlie the just administration of the law. There is danger, too, that conflict of jurisdiction will frequently arise between the civil courts and these military tribunals, each having concurrent jurisdiction over the person and the cause of action—the one judicature administered and controlled by civil law, the other by the military. How is the conflict to be settled, and who is to determine between the two tribunals when it arises? In my opinion, it is wise to guard against such conflict by leaving to the courts and juries the protection of all civil rights and the redress of all civil grievances.

The fact can not be denied that since the actual cessation of hostilities many acts of violence, such, perhaps, as had never been witnessed in their previous history, have occurred in the States involved in the recent rebellion. I believe, however, that public sentiment will sustain me in the assertion that such deeds of wrong are not confined to any particular State or section, but are manifested over the entire country, demonstrating that the cause that produced them does not depend upon any particular locality, but is the result of the agitation and derangement incident to a long and bloody civil war. While the prevalence of such disorders must be greatly deplored, their occasional and temporary occurrence would seem to furnish no necessity for the extension of the Bureau beyond the period fixed in the original act.

Besides the objections which I have thus briefly stated, I may urge upon your consideration the additional reason that recent developments in regard to the practical operations of the Bureau in many of the States show that in numerous instances it is used by its agents as a means of promoting their individual advantage, and that the freedmen are employed for the advancement of the personal ends of the officers instead of their own improvement and welfare, thus confirming the fears originally entertained by many that the continuation of such a Bureau for any unnecessary length of time would inevitably result in fraud, corruption, and oppression. It is proper to state that in cases of this character investigations have been promptly ordered, and the offender punished whenever his guilt has been satisfactorily established.

As another reason against the necessity of the legislation contemplated by this measure, reference may be had to the "civil-rights bill," now a law of the land, and which will be faithfully executed so long as it shall remain unrepealed and may not be declared unconstitutional by courts of competent jurisdiction. By that act it is enacted—

That all persons born in the United States and not subject to any foreign power, excluding Indians not taxed, are hereby declared to be citizens of the United States; and such citizens, of every race and color, without regard to any previous condition of slavery or involuntary servitude, except as a punishment for crime whereof the party shall have been duly convicted, shall have the same right in every State and Territory in the United States to make and enforce contracts; to sue, be parties, and give evidence; to inherit, purchase, lease, sell, hold, and convey real and personal property, and to full and equal benefit of all laws and proceedings for the security of person and property, as is enjoyed by white citizens, and shall be subject to like punishment, pains, and penalties, and to none other, any law, statute, ordinance, regulation, or custom to the contrary notwithstanding.

By the provisions of the act full protection is afforded through the district courts of the United States to all persons injured, and whose privileges, as thus declared, are in any way impaired; and heavy penalties are denounced against the person who willfully violates the law. I need not state that that law did not receive my approval; yet its remedies are far more preferable than those proposed in the present bill—the one being civil and the other military.

By the sixth section of the bill herewith returned certain proceedings by which the lands in the "parishes of St. Helena and St. Luke, South Carolina," were sold and bid in, and afterwards disposed of by the tax commissioners, are ratified and confirmed. By the seventh, eighth, ninth, tenth, and eleventh sections provisions by law are made for the disposal of the lands thus acquired to a particular class of citizens. While the quieting of titles is deemed very important and desirable, the discrimination made in the bill seems objectionable, as does also the attempt to confer upon the commissioners judicial powers by which citizens of the United States are to be deprived of their property in a mode contrary to that provision of the Constitution which declares that no person shall "be deprived of life, liberty, or property without due process of law." As a general principle, such legislation is unsafe, unwise, partial, and unconstitutional. It may deprive persons of their property who are equally deserving objects of the nation's bounty as those whom by this legislation Congress seeks to benefit. The title to the land thus to be portioned out to a favored class of citizens must depend upon the regularity of the tax sales under the law as it existed at the time of the sale, and no subsequent legislation can give validity to the right thus acquired as against the original claimants. The attention of Congress is therefore invited to a more mature consideration of the measures proposed in these sections of the bill.

In conclusion I again urge upon Congress the danger of class legislation, so well calculated to keep the public mind in a state of uncertain expectation, disquiet, and restlessness and to encourage interested hopes and fears that the National Government will continue to furnish to classes of citizens in the several States means for support and maintenance regardless of whether they pursue a life of indolence or of labor, and regardless also of the constitutional limitations of the national authority in times of peace and tranquillity.

The bill is herewith returned to the House of Representatives, in which it originated, for its final action.[2]

ANDREW JOHNSON.

Richardson, *Messages*, 6: 422–26.
1. See Freedmen's Bureau Veto Message, Feb. 19, 1866.
2. The same day Johnson returned his veto, both the House and Senate overturned the veto. *Congressional Globe*, 39 Cong., 1 Sess., pp. 3842, 3850.

From Rolfe S. Saunders

Memphis, Tenn., July 16 1866.

To the President:

I would respectfully call your attention to the enclosed two editorials, one from the *Post* & the other from the *Commercial*.[1] You will see who are your friends.

Every federal office holder (*civil*), here, except Col. Gist & Ryder,[2] are your enemies & opposed to your policy. Hough[3] is a *stock holder* in the *Post*, & keeps it up to stab you, partly through the profits of an office he holds at your hands.[4]

Rolfe S. Saunders.[5]

ALS, DLC-JP.
 1. The editorials are not found with the Saunders letter.
 2. Robert C. Gist and Martin T. Ryder.
 3. Reuel Hough.
 4. On July 16, Rep. John W. Leftwich, who was in Washington waiting to be seated in the House, wrote to the President urging the removal of Ryder and the appointment in his place of Samuel H. Jones. As a matter of fact, Jones was nominated for the marshal's post in December 1866 and again in March 1867 but was rejected by the Senate. Leftwich to Johnson, July 16, 1866, Appt. Files for Judicial Dists., Tenn., M. T. Ryder, RG60, NA; Ser. 6B, Vol. 4: 227–28, Johnson Papers, LC.
 5. At the top of the letter Saunders wrote: "Maj. Morrow. Please see the President gets these extracts, especially the one from the *Post*."

From Lewis D. Campbell

(Private)

Washington D.C.   July 17, 1866.

Dear Sir—

On to-morrow, or next day at farthest, I expect to leave for Ohio, and as I may not have another personal interview with you, I deem it proper to address you in this manner.

On Saturday last I expressed to you hastily but perhaps imperfectly my inclinations in regard to the Mexican mission. I find that the peculiar condition of my private affairs and my domestic obligations render it exceedingly doubtful whether I can, without very great sacrifices, go out of the country, in the event of my receiving instructions to proceed on that mission. The disturbance of my business affairs by reason of such an absence, I might overcome; but the somewhat peculiar situation of my family, (which I explained to you) imposes obligations on me of a more sacred character. In the disturbed and unsettled condition of Mexico I could not take my wife and daughters with me, nor could I, consistently with my duty to them, leave them behind during such an absence as a faithful discharge of official duty might require. I feel too, that there are many persons of more merit and superior qualifications for that position, whose surroundings would enable them to find in it a source of both profit and pleasure. Besides I am impressed with the belief that in the fierce and unjust warfare which is being waged against the policy of your administration, I can render better service by remaining in the country.

For these reasons I have seriously contemplated tendering you my resignation at such time as you may be ready to select a successor; and if it should be desirable to you to make a nomination to the *present session of the Senate* it may be best that I create the vacancy before leaving the City. On this point however I desire to adopt such course as will be least embarressing and most acceptable to you.[1]

I wish to assure you that this proposition to resign does not in any degree arise from dissatisfaction with the policy you have pursued. On the contrary, I have from the commencement most fully and cordially, in public and in private, approved your course; and though I may continue in private life, I shall not cease to employ my humble abilities and energy actively, to defend you and advance your cause. And, appreciating highly the compliment your generous confidence has reposed in me, I will cherish in grateful remembrance your acts of official and personal kindness.

I am about returning to Ohio to aid in arranging for a full representation from that state to the Philadelphia Convention. Should a personal interview on the subject of which I have written be desirable before I leave, it will give me very much pleasure to call at any time you may suggest.

Lewis D. Campbell

ALS, DLC-JP.
1. Campbell did go to Mexico, continuing to serve as envoy and minister until June 1867. Campbell to Johnson, June 16, 1867, Johnson Papers, LC.

From Albert Smith[1]

Boston   17 July, 1866

My dear Sir—

I learn from a long interview with Rich S Spofford Esq. who has recently returned from Washington, that you are about to *make a move* in the *right direction*—i.e. to organize a national party which will cordially support your administration. It would have been well had it been done six or eight months ago. But I am well aware of the very great difficulties attending such an undertaking. The most prominent of them is—*the selection of the most suitable* men for office. But, the longer the matter is delayed, the more trouble there will be in making those selections—for there are *now* many of the Republican party who were conservative Johnson men six months ago—and who have since gone over to the radicals. Had they received the least sign of encouragement—it would not have been thus.

Mr. Spofford & myself—who have been long tried friends, have had a full & free interchange of views & agree in every particular as to the course to be pursued. The Republican element should be the basis of the party—embracing as much as possible—those who served in the Army or Navy against the Rebellion.

I flattered myself that I had caused a small beginning to be inaugurated —in the case of the Post Office at *Walpole*—in the removal of *Hartshorne*

& the appointment of *Parkis*[2]—the former being not only your bitter enemy, but the most odious and unpopular man in the town—while the latter was your sworn friend & advocate & popular with all parties. It was a removal and appointment devoutly to be wished by that republican *town*—irrespective of politics—and would never have been assailed. But—unfortunately, you listened to the false representations of your bitterest enemies, & were persuaded to undo what had been so well done.

Now—in every *such* case—where a true friend & a *Soldier* can be found who will accept a post office in any country town—the incumbent being a radical &—*of course*—your enemy—a change should be made— and thus you would form the nucleus of a party which would be more formidable than many *national* conventions. But great caution must be observed (and here is the great thing to be considered in all such cases) to appoint as good—& as capable men in all respects—as those who are removed. These ideas I have heretofore suggested in several missives to Col Cooper.[3] Whether he received them or not—or if so—whether he deemed them worthy of notice, I am not informed.

My worthy friend—Bion Bradbury[4] is doing good service in Maine— my old stomping ground. He agrees with me as to the proper elements of the new party—*circumstances* make it necessary, that old Democrats— who did not contribute of their means to crush the rebellion should stand aside, for the present. Should they push themselves forward as *prominent* members of the Johnson party, it would surely be defeated.

Spofford informs me—confidentially—that you are ready to go ahead —when the proper men are presented for the appointments. This ought to be done—at once. Every days delay is manifestly injurious to the cause.

Now, my dear friend—I trust that you are aware that my advice is wholly disinterested. I would not accept of any office in your gift. My age—as well as my tastes forbid it & I have no relative whom I have the slightest wish to provide for. In tendering to you the counsel of a successful political manager of fifty years, my sole object *is to save my Beloved Country* from destruction—and I can perceive no other way of doing it— but by the success of *your policy* of reconstruction.

I hope you have received the copy of Frank Birds dis-union Resolutions,[5] which I sent you through Judge Blair.[6] I think they may be used with effect in Maryland.

The *Press* in Boston is becoming more & more vindictive against you —personally. The Presidential campaign for 1868 was opened by several of the clergy of this city on the Sunday, preceding the 4th July—by the most low & vulgar abuse yourself & your policy. The Campaign of 1860 was opened in the same disgraceful manner—nearly every pulpit in the State being desecrated by vile political harrangues on the Sabbath. Mr. Lincoln owed his election more to these "Men of God"—(or the D—L)— than to any other single Cause. And, now, let me assure you—sir—that every member of the present Congress from Massachusetts is as deep in the mire of treason as Thad Stevens. Even Spoffords man whom he intended to put forward for Congress in his District—has flown the track —& flunked out! He will have to find a new man. Such is Massachusetts —which raised the *five striped flag* of dis-union in *1814*—inaugurated the *Hartford Convention* & has been a *disunion State ever* since. Those who tell you that she will return more than *one* or *two* true men to the next Congress—deceive you—unless—in the mean time—things change wonderfully for the better. *Nous verrons*.

Albert Smith

ALS, DLC-JP.

1. Smith (1793–1867) had served in the Maine legislature, was a U.S. marshal, and represented the state of Maine as a Democrat for one term in Congress (1839–41). Subsequently he moved to Boston. *BDAC*.

2. James G. Hartshorn (b. *c*1816), a former grocer, was replaced by Ira H. Parkins as postmaster of Walpole, Massachusetts, in October 1866. Parkins has not been further identified. 1860 Census, Mass., Norfolk, Walpole, 287; *U.S. Off. Reg.* (1861–67); Ser. 6A, Vol. C: 207, 210, Johnson Papers, LC.

3. Letters to Edmund Cooper have not been found, but see Smith to Johnson, Feb. 24, Apr. 19, 1866, Johnson Papers, LC.

4. Defeated for the Maine governorship during the war years, Bradbury (1811–1887) was a teacher, attorney, judge, customs collector, state legislator, and delegate to the 1856, 1860, and 1880 Democratic National Conventions. *Biographical Review: This Volume Contains Sketches of the Leading Citizens of Cumberland County, Maine* (Boston, 1896), 422, 425.

5. Francis W. Bird (1809–1894) served both before and after the war in the Massachusetts legislature, first as a Whig, then as a Free-Soiler, and later as a Republican, prior to breaking with the latter party and running unsuccessfully as a Democrat in the 1872 gubernatorial election. The "resolutions" Smith refers to here have not been located. D. Hamilton Hurd, comp., *History of Norfolk County, Massachusetts* (Philadelphia, 1884), 729; *NUC*.

6. Montgomery Blair.

From J. R. Swift[1]

Washington, D.C., July 17 1866.

Sir

I called on Mr H. A. Smythe the Collector at New York and through our Member of Congress Hon Mr Radford[2] solicited a position under him. I was also introduced by Mr Haight[3] the President of the National Bank of the Commonwealth of New York. I laid before Mr Smythe my several recommendations, Endorsed by Yourself, Mr McCullough, Genl W. T. Sherman and other distinguished Gentlemen, and to my surprise Mr Smythe would not notice my papers and from actual observation I found him to be really opposed to your Administration. As I promised you to let you know the result of my interview I do so more for the purpose of letting you know his opposition to you than to complain for myself, for I can get along without any of his help. Mr. Radford, M. C & Mr Winfield[4] M. C. are also convinced of his opposition to you as they had an

interview with him also. It looks strange to me that a man controlling
about ten thousand votes should be in position to oppose you. I hope a
remidy will be applied to prevent him from doing any more mischief. My
solicitude for your welfare alone prompts me to let you know the above.
He also spoke very lightly of Mr Cooper your private Secretary.

J. R. Swift, Peekskill, N.Y.

ALS, DLC-JP.
1. Not identified.
2. William Radford (1814–1870) was born in Poughkeepsie and later moved to New
York City and engaged in business. Following his years in Congress (1863–67), he returned to his business interests. *BDAC*.
3. Edward Haight.
4. Charles H. Winfield (1822–1888) practiced law and was a district attorney in New
York before serving in Congress (1863–67). He resumed his law practice in 1867. *BDAC*.

From Daniel E. Conery

July 18, 1866, Ellenburg, N.Y.; ALS, DNA-RG56, Lets. Recd. from Executive
Officers (AB Ser.), President.

Conery complains of the search and seizure of property in Ellenburg and adjoining towns by order of the internal revenue collector "on the charge of smuggling
goods from Canada." He has represented the aggrieved and secured return of all
but three of the twenty horses seized. "There was no evidence against the parties." Yet, "Houses were searched from cellar to attic without warrant: property
taken and carried away and officers refusing to give their names when requested
to do so, & on a second demand being made, drawing a revolver as an insignia of
office." He can explain this activity only as "a game of the radicals to make you
unpopular in this northern section." When "parties are put to expense for nothing
. . . they learn soon, to 'Dam Andy Johnson.' " The Democrats have endorsed the
principles enunciated by Johnson in his February 22 speech, and the Democrats
are the ones subjected to these seizures, instigated by the collector and the deputy
who oppose Johnson's policy and favor Congress. He urges their removal.

From John S. Brien and John C. Gaut

Nashville Tenn   July 19 1866.

Fifty four members two less than a quorum pretended to pass the Constitutional amendment to-day.[1] Williams & Martin[2] was prisoners under
arrest & not in the house but detained in another room. Judge Frazier[3]
has just decided against the legislature in the writ of Habeas Corpus
Case.

Jno S Brien
Jno C Grant [Gaut]

Tel, DLC-JP.
1. Two days after House approval of ratification, Speaker William Heiskell and John C.
Gaut telegraphed the President that Heiskell had refused to sign the ratification notice be-

cause of the circumstances surrounding its final passage in that chamber. See Heiskell and Gaut to Johnson, July 21, 1866, Tels. Recd., President, Vol. 6 (1866–67), RG107, NA.

2. Pleasant Williams and Andrew J. Martin. Williams (c1821–1890), a native of Carter County, had served in the Union army and in 1865 was elected to the state legislature. Both Williams and Martin had left the special session of the General Assembly in an attempt to block ratification of the Fourteenth Amendment by that body. The House sergeant-at-arms arrested both men and returned them to Nashville and to the legislative chambers. Byron and Barbara Sistler, trs., *1890 Civil War Veteran Census—Tennessee* (Evanston, Ill., 1978), 343; *BDTA*, 2: 982; Patton, *Unionism and Reconstruction*, 220–21.

3. Williams and Martin had applied to Judge Thomas N. Frazier for a writ of habeas corpus which he issued on the 16th of July, but the legislature refused to recognize the jurisdiction of the court. A trial in Judge Frazier's court ensued; Brien and Gaut appeared at the trial in behalf of Williams and Martin and pleaded for their release. Frazier ruled in behalf of Williams and Martin and ordered their release, which was accomplished after some difficulty. But when the actual vote was taken in the House on July 19, Williams and Martin were detained in an adjoining room and not permitted to vote. Ibid., 221–23.

From Abner A. Steele

Lewisburg Tenn.   July 19th 1866.

Dear Sir.

Permit me to thank you for the friendship and confidence shown in nominating me for Assessor of the Fourth Congressional District of this State.[1] I cannot too gratefully appreciate it, as a Tennessean and since my introduction to public life in 1853—your personal and political friend.

I regret that there is a faction (contemptible in numbers) here in Tennessee—under the lead of Brownlow, that are hostile to you and your administration. The leaders of this faction here and in Washington have no doubt induced the Senate to reject your Tennessee friends—under the intention of injuring all of us here at home, and using those offices if they can to promote their own radical schemes. Wormed into positions by your generous favor, in the past, so soon as they have had an opportunity they ungratefully strike—at first covertly—now openly—at you. Rest assured dear President, the people of Tennessee—are overwhelmingly in favor of your administration and the Radical faction here is mainly composed of men who were *rebels* at the beginning, in order to become *radicals* at the end of the war.

If the people of this State ever regain their just rights at the ballot box they intend to wipe out every one of them—; as it is, Tennessee is now in the hands of an oligharchy, selfish—unprincipled—and the right to vote lodged in the hands of Brownlow & his petty Satellites—and this usurped power is actively used against you—and the loyal true men of our own State. We will send a full delegation to Philadelphia[2]—of the very best men.

I hope something will be done by which the Tennessee Radicals can no longer misrepresent Tennessee and her loyal people to the people of the North.

I have had an interview with Joseph Ramsey—and we leave the future of our cases to you[3]—believing that when the Senate has time to think about it again, they will act differently.

A. A. Steele.

ALS, DLC-JP.
    1. Johnson first nominated Steele for the assessor post in May 1866, but the Senate rejected the nomination on June 26, 1866. The President renominated Steele in January 1867, only to have the nomination rejected again by the Senate in February. Ser. 6B, Vol. 4: 227, Johnson Papers, LC.
    2. This is an obvious reference to the forthcoming Philadelphia National Union Convention scheduled to meet in mid-August 1866. See Trefousse, *Johnson*, 258, 260–62.
    3. Ramsey had been nominated as collector of internal revenue for the Fourth District in May 1866 and rejected in June, much like Steele's experience. On January 14, 1867, Johnson renominated Ramsey but the Senate took no action. Finally in March 1867 the President once again submitted Ramsey's nomination and the Senate approved it. Ser. 6B, Vol. 4: 227–28, Johnson Papers, LC. Ramsey's last name was incorrectly rendered as Ramsay in *Johnson Papers*, 5: 299–300, but corrected in subsequent volumes.

From Edward B. Boutwell

Richmond   July 20th 1866

Honored Sir:
    It is due to my character that I should inform you that I am no relation to that rebel, George S. Boutwell,[1] of Massachusetts. I was born in Virginia, and came from different stock. I have never been a rebel in my life, but always a constitutional union man. I have been what was called here in Virginia, "a strict constructionist." While I disagree with you in your leniency, in permitting the friends of those men who are proclaiming you a traitor to your country, to hold office in your administration, yet I do not doubt that you are governed in this, as well as in you reconstruction policy, by patriotic motives.[2]

Edward. B. Boutwell
Late of the Navy and now of Richmond Virginia

ALS, DNA-RG56, Appts., Internal Revenue Service, Collector, Va., 3rd Dist., Edward B. Boutwell.
    1. Boutwell (1818–1905), a lawyer and politician, served Massachusetts as a state representative, governor, U.S. representative (1863–69), and U.S. senator (1873–77). During part of the war he served as the first commissioner of the internal revenue. He later served as one of the House managers of Johnson's impeachment proceedings and as Grant's secretary of the treasury (1869–73). *BDAC*.
    2. In March Boutwell had applied to Johnson for an office in Virginia. He eventually became a Richmond commissioner for the internal revenue in 1869. Boutwell to Johnson, Mar. 25, 1866, Appts., Internal Revenue Service, Collector, Va., 3rd Dist., Edward B. Boutwell, RG56, NA.

From Merrils H. Clark[1]

Grand Rapids, Mich., July 20/'66,

Sir:
    I wish to recommend to your favorable consideration Hon. CHARLES H. TAYLOR,[2] of this city, as a fit person to receive the appointment of Collector for this Collection District, in case of the removal of Mr. TURNER,[3]

the present incumbent. Here it is taken for granted that Mr. T. will be removed as his politics is of the intense radical stripe, and he is the editor and proprietor of the "*Grand Rapids Daily Eagle*," which journal daily opposes your Reconstruction Policy, and attacks you personally in the lowest and most scurrilous manner. His removal ought not to be delayed. We have not in this district a single leading Republican who has had the stamina to break away from his party and give endorsement to your Reconstruction Policy. I know of no soldier who desires the office, and believe there are none who are competent, who would accept it. If a change is made, the appointment, unless you exchange one political opponent for another, must go to a democrat. I assure you there is no appointment which would give more general satisfaction to all classes of citizens than that of Mr. Taylor to this position. He has filled various political positions —always with credit—and his integrity either in public or private affairs has never been questioned. He has much political experience and can render us great aid in the great contests for the Union which are approaching. This office, can exercise more political influence than any other in the district. It is, therefore, very important that the *right* man should have the position. No better and more capable man could be found in this district for this position, and I urgently recommend his appointment.[4]

M. H. Clark,
Editor & Proprietor of Grand Rapids *Democrat*

ALS, DNA-RG56, Appts., Internal Revenue Service, Assessor, Mich., 4th Dist., Charles H. Taylor.

1. Clark (1826–*fl*1881) edited newspapers in Michigan and Nebraska, where he was also a member of the legislature. His affiliation with the *Grand Rapids Democrat* lasted from its founding in 1864 to 1877. *History of Kent County, Michigan* (Chicago, 1881), 423–24.

2. A former Douglas Democrat, Taylor (1813–1889) had served in the Michigan legislature and as secretary of state while editing the *Grand Rapids Enquirer*. Ernest B. Fisher, ed., *Grand Rapids and Kent County Michigan* (2 vols., Chicago, 1918), 1: 506; *Michigan Biographies* (2 vols., Lansing, 1924), 2: 348; Taylor to Johnson, July 20, 1866, Appts., Internal Revenue Service, Assessor, Mich., 4th Dist., Charles H. Taylor, RG56, NA.

3. Described by Taylor as an "uncompromising and bitter Radical," Republican Aaron B. Turner (1822–1903), a former Michigan senate reporter and secretary who established the *Grand Rapids Eagle* in 1856, had been appointed collector in 1862. Turner later served as postmaster of Grand Rapids. Ibid.; *Kent County*, 418, 421; Fisher, *Grand Rapids and Kent County*, 1: 508.

4. Turner was removed and replaced in August 1866 by Col. Robert P. Sinclair, whose nomination the Senate ultimately rejected. Taylor, meanwhile, was nominated as postmaster of Grand Rapids, serving for several months before likewise failing to win Senate confirmation. Ser. 6B, Vol. 3: 539; Vol. 4: 275, Johnson Papers, LC; *U.S. Off. Reg.* (1867); A. T. McReynolds to Johnson, Aug. 13, 1866, Appts., Internal Revenue Service, Collector, Mich., 4th Dist., Robert P. Sinclair, RG56, NA.

From John B. Stoll[1]

Ligonier Ind.   July 20th AD 1866

Dear Sir:

Whereas great dissatisfaction exists in the 10 District of Indiana, in regard to the radical opinions and open manifestations of opposition to your wise and just policy by George D. Copeland,[2] the present Assessor of Internal Revenue of the above District, even so much so, that the people and the good of the country demand his removal. In order to show your excelleny, that Mr Copeland is a violent opposer of your policy, I herewith annex a copy of Resolutions[3] adopted by the Republican Convention of Elkhart County, which was held at Goshen on the 30th of June last. Mr. Copeland was a member of said Convention and voted for their adoption. He says he is "ready to be decapitated" and determined to stand by Congress. Therefore, in consideration of these facts, I would respectfully solicit at your handes the appointment to the Assessorship of the 10th Ind District. In support of this application I would respectfully represent.—

First, That I have always been a firm supporter of the war policy of the Government during the late rebellion.

Second, That I have been a faithful adherent to your policy ever since your accession to the Presidential chair.

Third, That I had control of a Republican paper in Middleburg Penna., and devoted it to the advocacy of your administration, and disposed of the same with the understanding that it should continue to advocate the same (I Submit a copy for your perusal).[4]

Fourth, That I have lately started a new organ in the 10th District (a copy of which is also submitted) to be devoted exclusively to the advocacy of your administration.

Fifth, That this District is now represented by Mr. Defrees[5] who uniformly acts and votes with the Radicals. The District is a close one and it is important that the patronage of your administration be only given to those who are in favor of sending a Union, Conservative man to the national Congress who will sustain you in your laudable purpose and policy of effecting a permanent and speedy restoration of the Union.

All of which is respectfully submitted to your Excellency's consideration.[6]

John B. Stoll

In addition to the above I would respectfully represent that assistant assessor for this county vociferously shouted three "groans for Andy Johnson," waving his hat, at the radical county convention, held at Albion on Saturday last—all of which clearly shows the malignancy of these officers in their denunciation of your policy.

J.B.S.

ALS, DNA-RG56, Internal Revenue Service, Assessor, Ind., 10th Dist., George D. Copeland.

1. Stoll (1843–1926) edited the *Volksfreund* and *Independent Observer* in Middleburg and Johnstown, Pennsylvania, respectively, before removing to Indiana after the war and establishing the *Ligonier National Banner*, a Democratic paper. An unsuccessful Democratic candidate for Congress in 1878, Stoll also edited newspapers in LaPorte and South Bend, Indiana. H.S.K. Bartholomew, "Editor John B. Stoll," *InMH*, 28 (1932): 73–83; Stoll to Johnson, Jan. 22, 1867, Lets. Recd. *re* Publishers of Laws, RG59, NA.

2. Copeland (b. *c*1833), a lawyer, had formerly edited the *Goshen Times*. 1860 Census,

Ind., Elkhart, Elkhart Twp., 234; Anthony Deahl, ed., *A Twentieth Century History and Biographical Record of Elkhart County, Indiana* (Chicago and New York, 1905), 251.

3. The enclosed resolutions endorsed the Fourteenth Amendment and decried Johnson's opposition to that amendment. Furthermore, they lauded the Union soldiers and urged bounties for them. Finally, Congressman Defrees was recognized as "a true and tried supporter of the great principles of the Republican Union party."

4. A copy of neither the *Volksfreund* nor the *National Banner* is found with this letter.

5. Joseph H. Defrees (1812–1885), a Goshen businessman and banker, served only one term as a Republican in Congress (1865–67). He was not a candidate for the ensuing election. *BDAC*.

6. Referring to his "recent visit to Washington" and an interview he had with the President, Stoll on July 23 wrote to Sen. Thomas A. Hendricks and enclosed a copy of his July 20 application, both of which were then forwarded to Secretary McCulloch. Nevertheless, Copeland was not removed, and in fact continued serving as assessor at least through September 1871. One source does indicate, however, that Stoll acted as Copeland's assistant from early 1868 to the end of Johnson's term. *Counties of LaGrange and Noble, Indiana: Historical and Biographical*, (Chicago, 1882), pt. 2: 349–50; Stoll to Hendricks, July 23, 1866, Appts., Internal Revenue Service, Assessor, Ind., 10th Dist., George D. Copeland, RG56, NA; Ser. 6A, Vol. C: 32, Johnson Papers, LC.

From Charles F. Baldwin

July 21, 1866, Mount Vernon, Ohio; ALS, DLC-JP.

Baldwin, a lifelong Democrat who left his party to give full support to preserving the Union during the war, voting for the Lincoln-Johnson ticket in 1864, does now "earnestly and heartily, endorse your reconstruction policy." He "congratulates our people, that we have an executive who regardless of the clamor of corrupt politicians, has the moral courage, to combat, the moneyed aristocracy of the country, and defend the loyal masses, who are eager, for the addoption of such a policy, as shall result in usefullness and harmony." He rejects "the destructive notions" of the majority in Congress. "I cannot approve unqualified Negro Suffrage, but think that question ought to be left, where the constitution leaves it, with the people of the States themselves." He also favors "the immediate admission, of all loyal representatives to Congress," and disagrees with those who "denounced the President, as a tyrant and usurper, and that secession was a right reserved to the States."

Interview with Paschal B. Randolph[1]

[Washington, July 21, 1866][2]

Mr. RANDOLPH said:

"Mr. President, our colored schools in Louisiana, since the suspension of the military tax, and the return of property held by the Freedmen's Bureau to its owners, have gone down, and to-day we have not one-tenth of the pupils, teachers or schools we had a year ago. My mission is to endeavor to raise a public sentiment at the North in behalf of the freedmen of Louisiana and to procure voluntary assistance to establish a school of high grade in New-Orleans, where colored children may be taught and colored men and women may be prepared to become teachers of our people."

Mr. JOHNSON—That, Sir, is a laudable object, and a one which I entirely and heartily approve of; for the more a man knows the better are his chances of being a good and useful member of society. The colored man, like the white, needs education, and the sooner he receives it the better will it be for all concerned. If the professed friends of the colored people would devote more attention to the work of education, and less to politics, it would be greatly to the benefit of your race. I have been accused of being inimical to the true interests of the colored people; but this is not true. I am one of their best friends; and time, which tries and tests all, will demonstrate the fact. I have owned slaves (but never sold one,) and never ill treated them. If I had they would not regard me with the affection and respect they do to this day.

Mr. RANDOLPH—I have just seen a man who was once one of your slaves,[3] and he tells me of your kind treatment to him and his fellows. I was glad to hear that from such testimony; for I had been led to believe, from some whom I now begin to think use the negro question as a political one, that you were not a friend of the colored people.

Mr. JOHNSON—You will find, Sir, that those who try to ride the negro into political power, and use him as a hobby are not the men to stand by him when he wants useful friends. I once said I would be the Moses of your people[4] and lead them on to liberty—liberty they now have; and the responsibility in a large degree is now placed upon your people to make the best use of this newly-acquired position. How must you do that? Not by sitting down in idleness, no, Sir. Liberty means the manly assumption of all the responsibilities devolving upon good citizens, the necessity of labor and the enjoyment of the fruits of labor, to foster education, morality, virtue, self-respect, self-reliance, and every other quality which goes to make up a true man.

Mr. RANDOLPH—I heartily agree with you, Mr. President, and I come here to-day to ask your influence and the use of your name to assist me in my desire to do what I can to elevate my people.

Mr. JOHNSON—Of course, certainly; let me see your paper; *the President took it, read it and appended his signature*, and then continued: I am aware that great abuses have existed in the Southern States since the close of the war, and that in some instances violence has been used toward the recently emancipated slaves. I earnestly regret and deprecate this state of things, but the abuses alluded to follow in the wake of all great civil commotions and revolutions. It cannot be expected that men who have for four years been made familiar with the blood and carnage of war, who have suffered the loss of property, and in so many instances reduced from affluence to poverty, can at once assume the calm demeanor and action of those citizens of the country whose worldly possessions have not been destroyed, and whose political hopes have not been blasted, and the worst view of this subject affords no parallel in violence to similar outrages that have followed all civil commotions, always less in magnitude than ours. But I do not believe that this to-be-regretted state of things will last long. Why? Because capital and labor are mutually dependent upon each other; they are controling powers in the State, and must act harmoniously together, else chaos reigns. Now, the freedmen form the labor-power of the South—they are at perfect liberty to go where they please on the wide domain of the United States; if they leave the South, what then? Why their places will be supplied by immigration, or the land will lie idle, and capital must find new channels elsewhere than the South. Meanwhile, constant loss to both parties is going on. It is therefore the policy and interest of both capital and labor to make the best possible terms with each other, for it is the interest of the freedman to stay at home, and get the best possible pay for his services, and for the planter or capitalist to treat him so that he will have no inducement to emigrate, but remain and become useful as a laborer; and believe me, the freedmen, who are better understood South than they can be at the North, will eventually have but little cause of complaint on account of the treatment by their former masters, provided their educational interests are properly secured. I have been blamed for vetoing the Freedmen's Bureau Bill, and have been also represented to the colored people as having done it because I was their enemy. This is not true. It was upon no hostility to the black man; on the contrary, to put a stop to the temptations for corruption among Federal officials, but more especially to end a constant cause of local irritation between the freedmen and their former masters. Whatever good the Freedmen's Bureau may have accomplished in individual cases, has been overbalanced by the unrecorded evils which have resulted from its action. The question proposed to be solved by the Freedmen's Bureau can only be harmoniously settled by the Southern man and the freedman. They alone can do it, and this without any direct interference of the Federal Government.

In the long desultory conversation that ensued, the President frequently remarked that the colored man would eventually learn that he was their best friend; he seemed desirous that he should be thus esteemed. Incidentally he alluded to the question of suffrage and reiterated that its settlement belonged to the individual States. He said he did not doubt but that the difficult question would be eventually solved justly and satisfactorily by the parties directly interested; that great reforms were never violent, and that States, and the intelligence of the people inhabiting them, were in their growth like trees—gradual in reaching perfection. He remarked that the white man had reached his present position by long ages of suffering and discipline, and that the colored man of the South was now undergoing the first stages of that necessary experience, but with every advantage in his compared with the early advantages of the white race. Unwise advisers seek to place the colored people in a position for which they are not educated, or yet qualified, thus precipitating an unnecessary conflict—inaugurating possibly a war of races, a thing too dreadful to contemplate. The President concluded his general remarks by saying, "I believe with you Mr. RANDOLPH, that education, (moral, social, industrial and intellectual,) is the only hope for your race, and you have my very best wishes for the success of the laudable enterprise in which you are engaged, and I believe that all the assistance you need will be accorded you by the realy true friends of the colored man, and the true friends of the Government."[5]

New York Times, July 26, 1866.
    1. Randolph (1825–1874), a spiritualist and notable doctor and author, worked to provide educational opportunities for freedmen in Louisiana. The aim of his visit to Washington was to obtain the endorsements of leading politicians for his plan to provide educational opportunities for Louisiana freedmen through voluntary contributions. *NUC*; Oscar Fay Adams, *A Dictionary of American Authors* (Detroit, 1969 [1904]), 546; W. Stewart Wallace, comp., *A Dictionary of North American Authors* (Toronto, 1968), 371; *New York Times*, July 26, 1866; *New Orleans Picayune*, July 26, 1866.
    2. The interview took place at the White House on Saturday afternoon, July 21 presumably, since the Washington correspondent to the *Times* filed his report on Sunday, July 22, 1866.
    3. Unknown.
    4. See "The Moses of the Colored Men" Speech, Oct. 24, 1865, *Johnson Papers*, 7: 251–53.
    5. Johnson's support did not end with his words and endorsement. Shortly thereafter, he gave $1,000 to a school for blacks. *National Intelligencer*, Aug. 1, 1866.

From Granville P. Smith

Nashville Tenn., July 21, 1866

Mr President—Sir

You cannot fail to remember our personal and political friendships in years gone by, nor our estrangements during the war, (as I am frank to admit so far as I am concerned we were antipodes) but now things have changed, I submit gracefully, and I say it without the fear of successful contradiction no One in Tennessee is more Loyal than your Obt Servt— and not one has a more longing desire for peace and a ful restoration of the Union than myself. Please be assured that I neither *expect or desire office*, and that at my advanced age I am labouring most assiduously to support my family, having been ruined pecuniarily by the War, and that whilst thousands of your old friends (now all conservative) are anxious to sustain you in your views and policy of restoration, is it right and proper, is it doing justice to your self or friends, to retain in power Federal Officers in our midst that are *at all times*, and *under all circumstances* arraigned *against* the Conservative element of the State! Is their no redress? Can you not find men true & trusty, who were never engaged in the rebellion that can fill their places? If you can and will, it will do much to strengthing the hands of the real friends of the Administration, trambled as the most of them are, by every disability the Rump Legislature of the State could impose upon them. Let the Augean Stables be cleansed.

G. P. Smith

ALS, DLC-JP.

From James A. Stewart

Confidential

Rome Ga   July 22nd 1866

The Secessionists of this State as also appears to be the case in adjoining States—so eager for place and power, are stirring themselves to [select] representation in the proposed Philadelphia [Convention] and yet with all their professed desire for a restorartion of a Constitutional Union in accordance with your policy of reconstruction or restoration we find them bitterly opposed to sending Union men as delegates.[1] A man who firmly and consistently opprossed Secession and Rebellion during the long night of suicidal war has not the Shadow of a chance for a voice in the great work of restoration so much needed.

Although they are to some extent profuse in laudations of your patriotic motives, your Sagacity, and honesty of purpose—yet if they could re-enaugurate rebellion with prospects of success, they would not hesitate to denounce you as a traitor and a tory to the South or to hang you to the first limb.

It is the constant desire of some that civil war should Spring up in the North, so as thereby to paralize the old government and pave the way for the easy achievement of Southern Independance. To foment discord and precipitate this terrible evil upon us, will be the chief purpose of some, whose names are now mentioned as probable delegates to Said convention. I am proud to say however that Hon A. H. Stephens and Hon Herschel V. Johnson whose names have been mentioned are exceptions. But my object in this communication is to post you as to the fact that the old-line Jacksonian Union men of the South in the estimation of some reconstructed and pardoned Secessionists,—are fit Subjects for contumely and insult—and exposed not only to personal violence, but to loss of perishable property by the torch of the incendiary. Yet notwithstanding this dark picture, it is a pleasure to know that a large majority of the citizens generally of the South give no countenance or aid to such fiendish persecutions; but the misfortune is that the reign of terror enaugurated under Davis administration of the affairs of Rebellion, has not yet abated, and hence protection and encouragement to Union men is still held as treason to the South and threatened with punishment.

I am a Union man—was educated in the Jacksonian and Jeffersonian school of politics—was taught to love the Union as I loved my life—was nationalized in feeling and sentiment, and was ever proud of the name of American Citizen. Was never willing to Sacrifice my interest in a great and good government for the sake of party assendancy. Was never influenced by sectional lines or lead astray by local prejudice—and with all was no aspirent for public position. Thus educated and impressed, it was natural to oppose rebellion, and I did opposed it with all the powers I could reasonably bring to bear aginst it, and never even in the full carear of its arbytrary power did I yield the Slightest assent to its revolutionary and bloody purpose. I was not bitter nor vindictive towards those who differed with me in opinion but I appealed to them, and beged and implored them to desist from their bloody and suicidal experiment—pointing out the consequences which all along were vividly impressed upon my mind, and warning them of the certainty of defeat in their vain hopes of Southern Independance.

At the breaking out of war my home was in Atlanta Ga. In—64 I removed to this city to escape the desolation I knew awaited Atlanta. My home is now here—my property is all here. I desire to make this my permanent home. Have many good friends here, and yet I am living in the midst of dangerous and most bitter enemies. Last december my dwelling was fired front and rear during a dry windy night; but fortunately was saved from destruction. Recently, on the night of the 8th inst, my mill destroyed by order of Genl Sherman (now nearly rebuilt) was set on fire, but was discovered by a neighbor in time to save it. The city authorities have done nothing to secure the apprehension of the incendiary, or to discourage a renewal of the attempted arson. No city watch is furnished, and I have to stand guard myself. The citizens generally condemn the deed; but that does not relieve me from the wearing effects of suspense and dread. My mill was destroyed by Genl Sherman for military purpose. Have recieved no pay for the loss. Have strugled to rebuild, and it is now too hard to have it again destroyed, to gratify the malice of some low fiend—probably instigated by contumulous and incautious expressions against Union men by some in higher position.

We the true union men of the South want the privalige once more of living in peace and security and are willing to do all on our part as good citizens to merit protection—but until the fell spirit of rebellion is effectually crushed out we will never enjoy it.

J. A. Stewart

ALS, DNA-RG94, Lets. Recd. (Main Ser.), File S-1346-1866 (M619, Roll 517).

1. Georgia's delegates to the August 1866 National Union Convention in Philadelphia included Alexander H. Stephens (who went but missed the sessions because of illness), Linton Stephens, Herschel V. Johnson, and Hiram Warner, unionist members of the 1861 secession convention, who, with the exception of the latter, held Confederate political or military positions. Many of the other delegates were deemed moderates. Perman, *Reunion without Compromise*, 220; Avery, *Georgia*, 358; Schott, *Stephens*, 469; William J. Northen, *Men of Mark in Georgia* (7 vols., Atlanta, 1907–11), 3: 43–47; Wakelyn, *BDC*; Amnesty Papers (M1003, Roll 24), Ga., Hiram Warner, RG94, NA; *BDAC*.

From James H. Carlton[1]

Haverhill, Mass   July 23. 1866

Sir,

The present condition of political affairs in Mass: is anomalous. The Democracy and a large body of voters hitherto acting with the Republican Party, advocate your policy in the reconstruction of the States. But yet the Administrative party has no official Status; there are no centres of influence and action; its offices are controlled by its enemies, and, necessarily, we are without efficient organization. In this congressional District (Banks' the 6th)[2] I do not recall the name of a single official who is its outspoken and earnest advocate. A change in this respect will enable your friends to give direction to public opinion in this State & in the bordering counties of New-Hampshire. As tending to this, I respectfully recommend Hon. N. S. Howe,[3] of this town, for collector of Internal Revenue, in place of George Cogswell,[4] the present incumbent, also of this town, is a thorough Radical, and, with his appointees, a disciple in full fellowship, of the Sumner School. His personal & official influence is against the Administration. Judge Howe has a large acquaintance and great popularity in this county: was a whig down to the commencement of the war, during which he supported the administration, and the candidates of the Baltimore Convention of 1864. His appointment would be very acceptable to the people of the District, and your Administration would have in him an earnest and active friend. He is a gentleman of honor and integrity and fitted for the position.[5] It may be proper I should say, that though associated politically with Judge Howe during the existence of the whig party, I am now a member of the Democratic State Committee.

James H. Carlton

ALS, DNA-RG56, Appts., Internal Revenue Service, Collector, Mass., 6th Dist., Nathaniel S. Howe.

1. Carlton (1818–*fl*1888) was a Haverhill businessman and Democrat, who ran unsuccessfully for Congress in 1878, but served in the state legislature (1874–75) and was a delegate to the Democratic National Convention in 1876. Hurd, *Essex County*, 2: 2074–76.

2. A reference to Nathaniel P. Banks.

3. Nathaniel S. Howe (b. 1817) was a former attorney and probate judge. M.V.B. Perley, "James Howe of Ipswich and Some of His Descendants," *Historical Collections of the Essex Institute*, 54 (1918): 270; Arrington, *Essex County*, 2: 842, 853.

4. Cogswell (1808–*fl*1888), a former physician and member of the Republican State Executive Council, had been appointed collector in 1862. Hurd, *Essex County*, 2: 2109.

5. Also recommended by Caleb Cushing, Howe was appointed as collector in August 1866 and confirmed by the Senate the following January. Cushing to [Johnson?], Aug. 2, 1866, Appts., Internal Revenue Service, Collector, Mass., 6th Dist., Nathaniel S. Howe, RG56, NA; Ser. 6B, Vol. 3: 35; Vol. 4: 24, Johnson Papers, LC.

From James R. Doolittle

Private

[Washington, July 23, 1866][1]

Dear Sir;

Mr Cowan Mr Hendrix and Mr Guthrie[2] with myself will call to see you at 8" O'clock this evening. I hope you will be able to see us, at that time. We wish specially to consult with you about the Tennessee Resolution.

These gentlemen are of opinion that you can let the resolution take effect and by a message you use up utterly their Preamble, more especially as it is *now absolutely false* in fact that the amendment was adopted.

The trouble anticipated by them is that in case you return the resolution, as well as the preamble and the fact appears that their darling amendment has not been ratified they will lay the matter over and charge upon *you* the non admission of the members from Tennessee.

While if you let the Resolution stand they will be compelled at once to admit the members, and that too when Tennessee has not adopted the Amendment and thus there would be an utter abandonment of their scheme.

J R Doolittle

ALS, DLC-JP.
    1. This is the date on the cover sheet. Internal evidence suggests Washington as the letter's place of origin.
    2. Edgar Cowan, Thomas A. Hendricks, and James Guthrie.

From Greenwood, S.C., Council

Greenwood, S.C.   July 23rd/66.

Sir;

Have the Military Authorities & the Agents of the Freedman's Bureau the right to set aside a Statute law of So. Ca. that makes no distinction on account of color? The penalty for Petit Larceny, in this State, is public whipping. The above cited authorities forbid its execution in the case of Freedmen. Shall we execute the law, or obey these Pro. Tem. authorities?[1]

W. P. McKellar, Clk, of Council.[2]

ALS, DNA-RG60, Office of Atty. Gen., Lets. Recd., President.
    1. Upon receipt at the President's office, the letter was referred to the attorney general. There was evidently no further presidential involvement. Ser. 4A, Vol. 4: 506, Johnson Papers, LC.
    2. William P. McKellar (b. c1832) was a school teacher. 1860 Census, S.C., Abbeville, Greenwood, 109.

From Robert W. Johnson

Private

Pine Bluff   July 23/66

Mr. President

Believing that a letter from myself would be not unwelcome I write you. The great difficulties around you, the relentless factious enmities that beset you, I have observed with constant interest, and though disfranchised, and so completely out of political harness by my condition,[1] I can not refrain from writing you to express the intense sympathy I take in your mighty struggle; and to say that since I left you I have not been able to sit entirely inactive. Arkansas has been and still is perfectly quiet, waiting patiently & relyantly upon your action, and every step thus far on your part has confirmed the hopes & good-will of our people towards you. Your vetoes, your messages, your proclamations, & letters published, have given a degree of satisfaction that no one can feel who has not like the people of the South, *every thing* staked upon the result. You can not yourself Sir appreciate its depth or universality among all that class, who it is only frank to tell you looked upon both yourself & Mr. Seward with neither love for the past, nor hope for the future, during the progress of the war. There has been a freshness & originality, a consistency & vigor, that has confounded the most incredulous & has completely upset, & reversed the currents of both calculation & feeling with the leaders in the act of Secession.

And of all your acts, (one that you perhaps set less store by) your speech of the 22 Feb[2] was the most masterly in its effects, the most perfect surprise of friend & foe & in all elements the greatest piece of practical political generalship.

By its full volume & completeness, rejecting all middle ground, it was established as the result of careful forethought and by its vehemence and very violence of delivery, it established beyond all question its deep sincerity of purpose & your own profoundly fixed will; And by it you rallied to one flag at once all your own & Mr. Sewards portion of the old Union Party, and every other party & element in the land, of opposition to Radicalism. It was a masterly blow!! And just there, if ought could have added to its force & effectiveness short of the palpably supernatural, it was the bold prompt & unequivocal telegram of Mr. Seward, so unlike him in the public opinion, so decisive as to be almost insulting to all who opposed you, when from New York he telegraphed "*he had read your speech*" of the 22nd, "*it was all right*" "*go ahead*" "*the people would sustain you*" "*all was safe.*"[3] My God! how much of wonderful assurance, calm happiness, & of hopeful confidence it imparted, when but a moment before all felt the temerity and audacity of your steps, & that all was dark if not desperate before you.

If all thinking & leading men have not come out to proclaim praise and confidence in both yourself & Mr. Seward, all have and do in this region, feel it; and whilst they feel that you did much, & he most of all, to ruin our cause, revolutionize our Social institutions & destroy our wealth & property, yet you & he by the course & policy you force onward, facing so much of danger & difficulty, & of power and malignity, are doing & have in fact done & achieved the conviction, that no little enmities directed you, no "contracted Utica"[4] bounded your powers; but that a *great Statesmanship* governed your policies whether we believed them wise or not, & that you have pushed them to consummation [illegible] vast ruins in the

South, & will now press them to final triumph not only by the full restoration of the Union, but at the same time by a great redeeming act of magnanimity shielding the crushed & prostrate South & restoring to her broken hearted & despairing people their rights of self government, their liberty & some hopes & objects for which to continue to live. It will in the future, present a most singular fact for history, that there lived two men in this generation, who crushed and ruined a great people to establish a great social revolution & to remove the only remaining great danger to the future of the United States; SLAVERY, and who were hated for years & years violently, yet who having achieved it—,took upon their shoulders the broken fortunes & crushed families & prostrate states of that people and when all was hatred gave them support, all was despotism saved their liberty, all despair & death, secured for them new hopes, & renewed life. A most singular spectacle it will present, two men who will have been hated ardently for years, by millions of their people & yet in less than a year, by great magnanimity of action and glorious statesmanship will have rendered themselves the champions & have commanded the confidence and ardent support of those millions.

You have "taken no step backward" & now that threats are so violent & the recklessness of faction is so regardless of the Constitution, I must express the confidence that yourself & Mr. Seward will know how to defend your policy & rights & display no weakness by yielding up either.

Fearing in the quietude which pervades our state, that no Delegation would be provided to represent us in supporting you at Phila. on the 14th Augt. I took steps to get up a Convention and appoint them, holding myself in the back ground and declining all position for the sake of harmony and your own strength, except the Chairmanship on Resolutions which would show my own people my positions & full committal.

Enclosed I send you a copy of the Resolutions,[5] & must further state that my conviction is fixed that we can support for next President no other man than yourself if you will allow it, & if you will not, then no other than such a man as you will support ardently & determinedly: and any other course for the South would be in 1868 absolute (& to use a forcible phrase) "*judicial blindness*."

As I feared, my letter is too long, & I fear my value is hardly sufficient in your eyes to secure its perusal.

So I will close with the assurance that I am capable of appreciating the noble magnanimity of your course not only to myself but also our unfortunate people & that I am resply your friend.

R W Johnson

ALS, DLC-JP.

1. Johnson, who had worked for secession, had been a delegate to the provisional Confederate Congress in 1862 as well as a member of the Confederate Senate (1862–65). Wakelyn, *BDC*, 256–57.

2. See Washington's Birthday Address, Feb. 22, 1866.
3. See William H. Seward to Johnson, Feb. 23, 1866.
4. Jonathan M. Sewall's "Epilogue to Cato": "No pent-up Utica contracts your powers, But the whole boundless continent is yours."
5. Not found.

From George Park[1]

[Quincy, Ill.][2] July 23rd 1866

Sir

I wish to state to you the situation of thes widows that have Petitioned you to give them the Baracks.[3] If they are turned out of them they have No homes to go to. They have Not Drawn ther Money from goverment. Ther Papers are in the Hands of the lawyers but it does them No good yet Now those that has Charge of the Baracks tell the Blacks that they Do not belong to goverment that they belong to the ladys. They tell them that President Johnson is A Rebel And Donot care for them onley to keep them Down. Now President Johnson I want you to give those Poor Widows the Baracks for too Reasons. First for it will Do them More good than it can any one Ells and would Not Bring anough to do goverment any good. Second Reason is to show the Poor Ignorant Cretures that you Are ther friend which I have labord hard to convince them. I can obtain Consent of Mr Stuart[4] that owens the Land where the Baracks stand to let them Remain where they are for years.[5]

George Park

ALS, DNA-RG105, Records of the Commr., Lets. Recd. (M752, Roll 40).
1. Park (1806–fl1879), a physician and surgeon, moved to Quincy in 1861 after having lived in Ohio and Missouri. Park was a member of the Masonic order. The History of Adams County, Illinois (Chicago, 1879), 673.
2. External evidence points to the probability that Quincy was the place of origin for Park's letter.
3. A group of Quincy blacks who were widows of soldiers killed in the war sent a petition to Johnson which asked that the barracks buildings now slated to be sold be reserved for their use and that George Park be authorized to make assignments of the facilities. Records of the Commr., Lets. Recd. (M752, Roll 40), RG105, NA.
4. Not identified.
5. According to notations on the docket for the Quincy widows' petition, the President referred it to the secretary of war who in turn forwarded it to the quartermaster general for report. Eventually the petition landed at the Freedmen's Bureau office in Washington, but what actions were taken, if any, are not known.

From Abelard Guthrie[1]

Private

Washington City D.C.   July 24th 1866

President Johnson,

There are bills before congress and awaiting your signature appropriating for railroad and other purposes, public lands equal to the area of the states of New York and New Jersey.[2] Is it right that the farmer and the working man should be singled out and taxed thus enormously for the benefit of these speculators? Your record is against it; at the session of Congress when I first met you in 1852,[3] you introduced the following rsolution: "*Resolved* That so much of the Presidents' message as relates to the public lands be, and the same is hereby, referred to the Committee on Agriculture, with instructions to report a bill to the House, graduating and reducing the price of the public lands, and prohibiting the further sale of the same, to all persons than those who shall become actual settlers and cultivators of the soil and only to them in limited quantities." Globe vol. 26 page 122. This was and is the true policy in regard to the public lands and ten years after was embodied in the "Homestead Law" which has been rendered a mere mockery by this system of grants now grown to be a gigantic evil. I trust you will veto all these bills and in doing so you can send to congress the most popular veto message ever written. We need just such a veto message at this time—it will ring through the ears of the people like the voice of salvation.[4]

Abelard Guthrie of Kansas.

ALS, DLC-JP.
1. Guthrie (1814–1873), a native of Ohio, moved to the Kansas area in 1844, working in the U.S. Indian Service and then as an army paymaster during the Mexican War. He married a Wyandot Indian woman and thus became a member of that nation. William E. Connelly, *A Standard History of Kansas and Kansans* (2 vols., Chicago, 1918), 1: 302; William E. Connelly, "Kansas City, Kansas: Its Place in the History of the State," KSHS *Collections*, 15 (1919–22): 188–89; *NUC*; 1860 Census, Kans., Wyandotte, 62.
2. At least five railroad and telegraph bills came before Congress in July 1866 and two of them related specifically to Kansas: one to grant lands to the state to aid in the construction of the Kansas and Neosho Valley Railroad and the other to grant lands to Kansas to assist in the construction of a southern branch of the Union Pacific Railway and Telegraph. *Congressional Globe*, 39 Cong., 1 Sess., Appendix, pp. 387–88, 405–6. The other bills can be found in ibid., pp. 388–89, 406–9, 422.
3. In October 1852 the Wyandot nation, anxious to see the territory of Kansas organized, elected Guthrie as a delegate to Congress to aid in that purpose. Guthrie was not seated but did influence members of Congress to introduce several territorial bills, although none passed both houses of Congress during that session. Connelly, "Kansas City, Kansas," 188–89.
4. All of the bills became law in July 1866. *Congressional Globe*, 39 Cong., 1 Sess., Appendix, pp. 388, 389, 406, 409, 422.

From Charles G. Halpine
PRIVATE

32 Beekman Street, N.Y.
July 24th 1866

Dear Sir:

If Gen. Sickles be on your mind for Naval Officer of this Port I have nothing to say: but if not, I suggest my own name as a candidate.[1]

I have never sought an office, nor do I care to ask endorsements unless reasonably sure they will succeed, or are wanted. But if you DO want them & will tell me so, I can give you the following:

ALL the non-radical Press of the Country, & much of the Radical, including the *Tribune*.

ALL the Army (I believe) except Gen. Grant who is pressing Col. Hillyer,[2] and such officers as are themselves candidates,—enough, even of these, most, I think, would have me as their second choice.

ALL the democratic leaders of the City & State (unless you call the Woods[3] leaders) including Dean Richmond & the whole State Central Democratic Committee. Also the 13 Sachems of Tamy. Hall, of which I am an "Indian in good standing."

ALL the Fenian elements (excluding Stephens,[4] who is reputed a British Agent) & including P. J. Meehan[5] of the *Irish American* President Roberts[6] (I think) & the whole Fenian rank and file.

It is late in the day to make these suggestions, but I do so because I believe you must have heard my name or *nomme de plume a hundred times* for every once you heard that of any of the other candidates—except Gen. Sickles; and never could have heard of it, save in an honorable connection.

I have a tongue & pen, such as they are, which have always commanded good audiences in this paper,[7] & the *Herald*, & elsewhere. And I promise you that whenever I cannot support your policy with my whole heart & strength that I will be man & gentleman enough to tell you so & ask you to accept my resignation.

If I require endorsements from politicians, or soldiers, or journalists at this time of my life, then I must have lived in vain; for it is either true, or my vanity tells me so, that few names in the Country are more widely known—whether well or ill I leave Your Excellency to determine—than that of . . . .

Chas. G. Halpine

P.S.   About Postmaster Kelly[8] & other matters I will write in a few days.[9]

ALS, DLC-JP.
    1. About five weeks earlier Halpine had recommended the acting naval officer, Cornell S. Franklin, for the appointment. Halpine to Johnson, June 16, 1866, Johnson Papers, LC.
    2. William S. Hillyer.
    3. Fernando and his brother Benjamin Wood (1820–1900), newspaper editor, Democratic congressman, and state senator. *BDAC*.
    4. Leader of the pan-Irish nationalist movement, James Stephens (1824–1901) had arrived a few months earlier in New York City to begin a speaking tour in an effort to drum up support for and heal divisions within the American-based Fenian Brotherhood. Leon Leon Ó Broin, *Fenian Fever: An Anglo-American Dilemma* (New York, 1971), 64, 85, 250; Neidhardt, *Fenianism*, 3–5.
    5. Patrick J. Meehan (*c*1832–1906), a member of the Fenian Brotherhood, owned and edited the *New York Irish American* for more than fifty years. Ibid., 113; *New York Times*, Apr. 21, 1906.
    6. President of the Fenian Brotherhood from 1865 to 1867, William R. Roberts (1830–1897) was elected in 1870 as a New York Democrat to Congress and was later appointed by Cleveland as minister to Chile. *DAB*.
    7. The *New York Citizen*.
    8. Republican James Kelly (1812–1871) ended his four-year term as New York City's postmaster on April 30, 1869. *New York Tribune*, Jan. 11, 1871; *U.S. Off. Reg.* (1865–69).

9. In his letter written a few weeks later, Halpine continued to proclaim General Sickles as "the best man" for the job of naval officer, while urging his own appointment in the event that Sickles was not nominated. But neither man was appointed. Halpine to Johnson, Aug. 11, 1866, Johnson Papers, LC.

From Wade H. Hough[1]

Columbia La   July 24. 1866.

Mr. President:

Having recently learned that an act of Congress had been passed or undoubtedly soon would be passed to consolidate the Eastern and Western Districts of the District Courts of the United States for the State of Louisiana, into One District[2] In that event I have been Solicited by some of my Friends to apply to your Excellency for the Appointment of the District Judgeship of this State,—And in accordance with these solicitations and my own desire I hereby make application for the appointment to Said Office. I have been a practicing Attorney at Law in North Louisiana for nearly twenty years and I am well known to the legal profession in Louisiana, particularly in North Louisiana. I have at the risk of my life maintained the character of a Consistent Union man previous to and during the late unfortunate Rebellion against the United States Government believing all the time that the best security we had for the protection of Southern rights and institutions was to be derived from the Government of the United States. You can learn from my friends the political course that I pursued here previously to the Secession of the State of Louisiana from the Federal Union. You can learn from them that I took as strong grounds against that measure as any man in the State,—that I was a member of the State Convention that carried the State or attempted to carry the State out of the Union—That I represented a Senatorial District carrying a larger majority than any other candidate perhaps in the state in opposition to Secession—that in the Convention I opposed and voted against the measure, and that I was one of the "Very few," who refused to sign that Treasonable Ordinance.[3] I deem it unnecessary to present to you a petition numerously signed which thing is in the power of almost any one to obtain but will content myself by referring your excellency to the annexed Documents and letters in support of my claims[4] —premising that if deemed necessary I can furnish any amount of Satisfactory evidence as to good moral Character—my former and present attachment to the Federal Union—even during the late "Rebellion"[5] And as to my Legal qualifications for the Position Sought for.[6]

Wade H. Hough.

P.S.   Any Telegraphing or other communication that your Excellency may be pleased to have with me on this subject can be had through J. B. Bres Esqr. my Commission Merchant at New Orleans La.[7]

W. H. Hough.

ALS, DNA-RG60, Appt. Files for Judicial Dists., La., Wade H. Hough.

1. A native of South Carolina, Hough (1819–*fl*1870) not only practiced law but also owned 700 mostly-unimproved acres by 1860, on which, with the aid of eight slaves, he raised cotton and corn. 1870 Census, La., Concordia, 4th Ward, Vidalia, 53; Ralph Wooster, "The Louisiana Secession Convention," *LHQ*, 34 (1951): 126; New Orleans directories (1870–71).

2. "An Act in Relation to the District Courts of the United States in the States of California and Louisiana," approved July 27, 1866. *Congressional Globe*, 39 Cong., 1 Sess., Appendix, p. 409.

3. These assertions are confirmed in Wooster, "Louisiana State Convention," 116, 117, 126.

4. See Appt. Files for Judicial Dists., La., Wade H. Hough, RG60, NA.

5. Despite Hough's "attachment to the Federal Union," he served in the Confederate forces as lieutenant colonel of the 12th La. Inf. *OR*, Ser. 4, Vol. 1: 750.

6. Hough did not get the job for, according to the act, the officials of the eastern district were to retain their positions. Thus, Edward H. Durrell remained judge. However, by 1870 Hough was the judge of a district court. *U.S. Off. Reg.* (1865–67); 1870 Census, La., Concordia, 4th Ward, Vidalia, 53.

7. Cotton factor John B. Bres (*fl*1901) was in partnership with Hough in 1869–70. New Orleans directories (1861–1901).

Message re *Resolution on Restoration of Tennessee*

WASHINGTON, D.C., *July* 24, 1866.

To the House of Representatives:

The following "joint resolution restoring Tennessee to her relations to the Union" was last evening presented for my approval:

"Whereas, in the year eighteen hundred and sixty-one, the government of the State of Tennessee was seized upon and taken possession of by persons in hostility to the United States, and the inhabitants of said State, in pursuance of an act of Congress, were declared to be in a state of insurrection against the United States; and whereas said State government can only be restored to its former political relations in the Union by the consent of the law-making power of the United States; and whereas the people of said State did, on the twenty-second day of February, eighteen hundred and sixty-five, by a large popular vote, adopt and ratify a constitution of government whereby slavery was abolished and all ordinances and laws of secession, and debts contracted under the same, were declared void; and whereas a State government has been organized under said constitution, which has ratified the amendment to the Constitution of the United States abolishing slavery, also the amendment proposed by the thirty-ninth Congress, and has done other acts proclaiming and denoting loyalty: Therefore,

"Be it resolved by the Senate and House of Representatives of the United States in Congress assembled, That the State of Tennessee is hereby restored to her former practical relations to the Union, and is again entitled to be represented by senators and representatives in Congress."

The preamble simply consists of statements, some of which are assumed, while the resolution is merely a declaration of opinion. It comprises no legislation, nor does it confer any power which is binding upon the respective houses, the Executive, or the States. It does not admit to their seats in Congress the senators and representatives from the State of Tennessee; for, notwithstanding the passage of the resolution, each house, in the exercise of the constitutional right to judge for itself of the elections, returns, and qualifications of its members, may, at its discretion, admit them, or continue to exclude them. If a joint resolution of this character were necessary and binding as a condition precedent to the admission of members of Congress, it would happen, in the event of a veto by the Executive, that senators and representatives could only be admitted to the halls of legislation by a two-thirds vote of each of the two houses.

Among other reasons recited in the preamble for the declarations contained in the resolution is the ratification, by the State government of Tennessee, of "the amendment to the Constitution of the United States abolishing slavery, and also the amendment proposed by the thirty-ninth Congress." If, as is also declared in the preamble, "said State government can only be restored to its former political relations in the Union by the consent of the law-making power of the United States," it would really seem to follow that the joint resolution which, at this late day, has received the sanction of Congress, should have been passed, approved, and placed on the statute books before any amendment to the Constitution was submitted to the legislature of Tennessee for ratification. Otherwise, the inference is plainly deducible that, while, in the opinion of Congress, the people of a State may be too strongly disloyal to be entitled to representation, they may, nevertheless, during the suspension of their "former proper practical relations to the Union," have an equally potent voice with other and loyal States in propositions to amend the Constitution, upon which so essentially depend the stability, prosperity, and very existence of the nation.

A brief reference to my annual message of the 4th of December last will show the steps taken by the Executive for the restoration to their constitutional relations to the Union of the States that had been affected by the rebellion.

Upon the cessation of active hostilities, provisional governors were appointed, conventions called, governors elected by the people, legislatures assembled and senators and representatives chosen to the Congress of the United States. At the same time the courts of the United States were reopened, the blockade removed, the custom-houses re-established, and postal operations resumed. The amendment to the Constitution abolishing slavery forever within the limits of the country was also submitted to the States, and they were thus invited to, and did participate in its ratification, thus exercising the highest functions pertaining to a State. In addition, nearly all of these States, through their conventions and legislatures, had adopted and ratified constitutions "of government, whereby slavery was abolished, and all ordinances and laws of secession, and debts contracted under the same, were declared void."

So far, then, the political existence of the States and their relations to the federal government had been fully and completely recognized and acknowledged by the executive department of the government; and the completion of the work of restoration, which had progressed so favorably, was submitted to Congress, upon which devolved all questions pertaining to the admission to their seats of the senators and representatives chosen from the States, whose people had engaged in the rebellion.

All these steps had been taken, when, on the 4th day of December, 1865, the 39th Congress assembled. Nearly eight months have elapsed since that time; and no other plan of restoration having been proposed by Congress for the measures instituted by the Executive, it is now declared in the joint resolution submitted for my approval, "that the State of Tennessee is hereby restored to her former proper practical relations to the Union, and is again entitled to be represented by senators and representatives in Congress." Thus, after the lapse of nearly eight months, Congress proposes to pave the way to the admission to representation of one of the eleven States whose people arrayed themselves in rebellion against the constitutional authority of the federal government.

Earnestly desiring to remove every cause of further delay, whether real or imaginary, on the part of Congress to the admission to seats of loyal senators and representatives from the State of Tennessee, I have, notwithstanding the anomalous character of this proceeding, affixed my signature to the resolution. My approval, however, is not to be construed as an acknowledgment of the right of Congress to pass laws preliminary to the admission of duly qualified representatives from any of the States. Neither is it to be considered as committing me to all the statements made in the preamble, some of which are, in my opinion, without foundation in fact, especially the assertion that the State of Tennessee has ratified the amendment to the Constitution of the United States proposed by the 39th Congress. No official notice of such ratification has been received by the Executive, or filed in the Department of State; on the contrary, unofficial information from most reliable sources induces the belief that the amendment has not yet been constitutionally sanctioned by the legislature of Tennessee. The right of each house, under the Constitution, to judge of the elections, returns, and qualifications of its own members is undoubted, and my approval or disapproval of the resolution could not in the slightest degree increase or diminish the authority in this respect conferred upon the two branches of Congress.

In conclusion, I cannot too earnestly repeat my recommendation for the admission of Tennessee, and all other States, to a fair and equal participation in national legislation, when they present themselves in the persons of loyal senators and representatives, who can comply with all the requirements of the Constitution and the laws. By this means harmony and reconciliation will be effected, the practical relations of all the States to the federal government re-established, and the work of restoration, inaugurated upon the termination of the war, successfully completed.

ANDREW JOHNSON.

House Ex. Docs., 39 Cong., 1 Sess., No. 151, pp. 1–3 (Ser. 1267).

From Thomas C. Ready[1]

Washington D.C.   July 24th 1866

Sir—

I had hoped to have had the pleasure of a personal interview with you, and to that end called this morning in Company with Hon Mr Noell of Mo.[2] but found you engaged. My stay being limited in your city, I, therefore address you this communication, and trust you may give the subject matter of it, due consideration.

I am here as the Representative of the staid sober, grey haired citizens of Jackson Co Mo to call your attention to their wrongs, and to ask your aid in redressing those wrongs. You are doubtless aware that Gov Fletcher[3] has organized armed equipped and stationed his Militia in Jackson co. The ostensible object, claimed by him is, that it is done for the preservation of Law and order, and that without bayonets, the laws, could not be enforced in that County.[4] This, I am deputed to deny in the strongest language, & to assert, that in all the elements, which go to constitute, a perfect peace & quiet we are excelled by no people in the union. It is true that Jackson co furnished a large number of soldiers to the Confederate Army, & that these soldiers, at the close of the War, returned to the County & resumed their citizenship. But it is still no less true, that, not one single individual since that time, has been in armed hostility to the Government, but on the Contrary, having accepted the issues of the war, have conformed their actions strictly to their obligations and have been quietly & industriously endeavoring to build up their wasted fortunes. No charge of riot, or dissension can be laid at their doors, and no sin can be found, with which to condemn them save, that most grave of all enormities, in the eyes of Gov Fletcher and the Radical Party, That they all with one accord, have heartily & freely approved of the Policy of your Excellency, in the restoration of the Government. This was the dread sin, that has determined Gov Fletcher to reestablish his Militia in our County. Since the organization of this Company, (the Captain of which is a citizen of Kansas) our County, so quiet & peaceful, before—has become the theatre of anarchy & confusion.

Every day brings its record of fresh outrages & indignities. No man lies his head upon his pillow at night, but dreads to hear the tread of soldiery, & the report of the death dealing musket ere morn. The scenes of

1861 are being daily enacted & no security is felt, in either life or property. On Tuesday the 17th inst the first act in the bloody drama was enacted. A squad of Militia under the command of a certain Mr Meador,[5] a Deputy Sheriff, went before daylight to the residence of one of our citizens, (a gentlemen of the highest respectability)[6] in search of his son,[7] who had been in the Confederate Army, but who for the last year had been at home, quietly engaged at work. Finding the son absent, engaged in harvesting at a neighbor's and knowing he would return home by sunrise, they secreted themselves in the brush, & behind fences & awaited his coming. Anon he came, dismounted from his horse, & whilst in the act of crossing the yard fence, this murderous representative of Civil Law, without demanding his surrender ordered his ruffians to fire upon him, & fire they did. Young Hultz fell, with four balls in his body. The gallant soldiers then rifled his pockets of $20 of hard earned money, took his pistols & horse & returned to Independence, to report to the Sheriff, that he had resisted an arrest & fired upon them, and they were compelled to kill him. Fortunately the wounds did not prove fatal, but the act so murderous in intent and cowardly in execution, has aroused a feeling among the people, even to the hoary headed veterans, which threatens to plunge the County again into war, the horrors of which will exceed four fold, that we have passed through. In this condition of affairs we have counselled forbearance, to those aggrieved, and have assured them that the strong arm of the Government, would be extended to protect them. And now sir I ask you, have we promised them too much. May we not rely upon you to carry into effect, those measures, outlined in your recent interview with the Hon Mr Noell[8] viz. That you would see that Missouri's citizens were protected, & were allowed to exercise the elective franchise in November next. We ask but peace, nothing more. Can you not aid us in gaining that? Our people have the most implicit confidence in your ability & determination to execute the laws, and are prepared to stand by you, in any means adopted by you to accomplish that end.

We now pray you to disband this murderous militia, and if necessary to quarter among us, Regular Soldiers, and we guarantee to aid them in the preservation of Law & order & the full & successful execution of all the laws.[9]

Hoping you may spare time from your onerous duties, to give this matter consideration. . . .

Thos. C. Ready

ALS, DLC-JP.

1. An Independence, Missouri, physician until 1852, Ready (1828–1883) spent the rest of his career as a merchant in St. Louis. Howard L. Conrad, ed., *Encyclopedia of the History of Missouri* (6 vols., St. Louis, 1901), 5: 306–8.

2. Rep. Thomas E. Noell.

4. During the war Jackson County had been an area of much guerrilla warfare, but not a scene of postwar problems until the advent of the militia. Parrish, *Radical Rule*, 89; Roger Jones to R. M. Sawyer, Aug. 15, 1866, Johnson Papers, LC.

5. There were at least seven Meador families in Jackson County in 1860. 1860 Census, Mo., Jackson, City of Independence, 16, 22,33; Blue Twp., Independence, 100, 101; Sniabar Twp., Pink Hill, 194, 198.

6. Perhaps either of the Jackson County farmers Samuel D. Hulse (1817–c1883) or Freeman Hulse (b. c1813). *A Memorial and Biographical Record of Kansas City and Jackson County, Mo.* (Chicago, 1896), 263–64; *Vital Statistics of Jackson County, Missouri, 1826–1876* (Kansas City, 1933–34), 342; 1860 Census, Mo., Jackson, Blue Twp., Independence, 122.

7. Maj. Roger Jones described several acts of violence in Jackson County and confirmed this account but did not give the first name of "Hultz" who had been with William Quantrill's Confederate raiders. Samuel D. Hulse had three sons: Melville (b.c1844), Greenville (b.c1846), and Arriste (b.c1848). Freeman Hulse had two sons of the proper age: Zadoch (b.c1840) and William (b.c1842). 1860 Census, Mo., Jackson, Sniabar Twp., Oak Grove, 184; Blue Twp., Independence, 122; Roger Jones to R.M. Sawyer, Aug. 15, 1866, Johnson Papers. LC.

8. The date of this visit has not been found.

9. In an endorsement on the letter Noell also requested the removal of the militia. Ready's letter, in part, caused Johnson to confer with Gen. William T. Sherman about the Missouri situation on August 1. Sherman, in turn, sent Major Jones to investigate the problems and met on August 9 with Governor Fletcher and two important conservatives, Thomas T. Gantt and Samuel T. Glover. As a result, Fletcher agreed to organize the militia on a less partisan basis and was promised the aid of federal troops, should the need arise. Parrish, *Radical Rule*, 91–95; Sherman to Johnson, Aug. 9, 1866; Gantt to John Hogan, Aug. 10. 1866; Roger Jones to R.M. Sawyer, Aug. 15, 1866, Johnson Papers, LC.

From James W. Throckmorton

Austin Texas   July 24th 1866—

I have just arrived, and am led to believe, that a Strong Effort based upon the most flagrant misrepresentation of Public Sentiment will be made to continue the Provisional Government here.[1]

Please telegraph me on the Subject at this point as there is a deep interest felt in the matter. The Legislature meets on the 6th day of August prox.

As Governor Elect I am here for the purpose of installation.

I deem it but proper to assure you that Should the State Government be turned over to those elected, it will pass from the hands opposed to, into that of those who are alike the friends of your policy and the lovers of the Union of the States.[2]

J W Throckmorton

ALS, DLC-JP.

1. There were indeed rumors to this effect, but nothing actually happened to prevent Throckmorton and the other officials from taking office. Ramsdell, *Reconstruction in Texas*, 112–13.

2. Throckmorton was inaugurated on August 9, 1866, but authorization from Washington was rather slow in arriving. Henry Stanbery, acting secretary of state, telegraphed Governor Hamilton on August 11, ordering him to turn over his office to Throckmorton. The new governor assumed his responsibilities on August 13. Ibid.; Stanbery to A. J. Hamilton, Aug. 11, 1866; Stanbery to Throckmorton, Aug. 11, 1866; Throckmorton to Stanbery, Aug. 14, 1866, *Louisville Courier*, Aug. 22, 1866. See also James H. Bell to Johnson, July 2, 1866.

From Washington Merchants and Property Holders[1]

Washington D.C.   July 24th, 1866

The undersigned Property Holders and Merchants doing business on Louisiana Avenue between Sixth and Seventh Streets respectfully represent that their consent to the erection of the Fair Building for the benefit of Orphans and Widows of Soldiers and Sailors was granted for that specific purpose for the space of Twenty-days and (none other.)[2] The Obstruction has now been standing for nearly Sixty days without a word of complaint from your Petioners. Said Building has been seriously detrimental to our business and we were to day much suprised to learn of the Joint Resolution's having passed both Houses of Congress granting to the Directors of the Fair the privilege of retaining the Building untill May 1867.[3] We beg leave to inform Your Excellency that Said Building is located in "C" Street North, thereby obstructing Said Street and is now being used for purposes other than of a Fair[4] and we are credibly informed that if the said Joint Resolution is approved by you the Building is to be let for Public Meetings, Concerts, Balls and other purposes for which it can be used and we have no evidence that the Orphans and Widows of Soldiers and Sailors are to be benefited thereby.[5] The parties now occupying said Building are now selling Tickets for a Gift enterprize and have promised $25,000 of the proceeds of said Sales to the Managers of the Fair. The sales several days ago had realized nearly $80,000 and we are credibly informed that not one Dollar has yet been paid over on account of the Fair.[6]

From all the facts before us we feel assured that the sole object of obtaining said grant is to benefit private parties and not for the purpose expressed in the Joint Resolution and further that said Building being constructed entirely of Wood seriously endangers valuable property in the neighborhood.[7]

Pet, DNA-RG48, Patents and Misc. Div., Lets. Recd.

1. There were 36 signatories, headed by John H. Semmes (c1822–fl1898), a wholesale grocer and proprietor of Seaton House, who drafted the petition. 1870 Census, D.C., Washington, 4th Ward, 458; Washington, D.C., directories (1855–98).

2. The joint resolution passed by the Washington city council in mid-May 1866 permitted the managers of the National Soldiers' and Sailors' Orphans' Home Association to erect a building at the corner of Seventh Street and Pennsylvania Avenue, provided that the building was removed in "about two weeks." Consent of the property holders in the neighborhood and approval by the secretary of the interior were both obtained. Meanwhile, Congress authorized the use of surplus government lumber for the "temporary" building. *Congressional Globe*, 39 Cong., 1 Sess., Appendix, p. 428; *National Intelligencer*, May 15, 21, 25, 1866.

3. For the joint resolution introduced by Nathaniel P. Banks on July 20 and passed by Congress a few days later, see *Congressional Globe*, 39 Cong., 1 Sess., pp. 3974, 4023, Appendix, p. 432.

4. A reference to a meeting which occurred at the Fair building on the evening of July 19, when Ohio Rep. Robert C. Schenck, Gen. John A. Logan of Illinois, and A. J. Hamil-

ton of Texas bitterly denounced the forthcoming Philadelphia Union Convention and made a "violent party assault" upon President Johnson. *National Intelligencer*, July 20, 23, 1866.

5. The National Soldiers' and Sailors' Orphans' Home was incorporated by act of Congress on July 25, 1866, and the institution continued to function in the nation's capital at least through 1877. *Congressional Globe*, 39 Cong., 2 Sess., p. 55; *Washington Evening Star*, Sept. 21, 1866; Washington, D.C., directories (1868–78).

6. Thrice postponed, the Grand National Gift Concert netted $8,575, over half of which was earmarked for the Soldiers' and Sailors' Orphans' Home fund. *National Intelligencer*, Oct. 15, 16, 1866.

7. Presented to Johnson on July 28, the joint resolution met with a pocket veto on July 28 when Congress adjourned. Yet the Fair building remained until it was finally torn down in January 1867. *House Docs.*, 70 Cong., 2 Sess., No. 493, pp. 13–14 (Ser. 9035); *National Intelligencer*, July 31, Nov. 6, 1866, Jan. 26, 1867.

From David W. Ballard[1]

Executive Office   Boise City I.T.
July 25th, 1866

Sir,

The exigencies of the case must serve as the apology for binging before you the greatly embarrassed condition of the affairs of our Territory.

On my arrival here on the 14th Ult. I found that my Predecessor Ex. gov. Lyon[2] & the Territorial secretary Horace C. Gilson, had both been absent from the Territory for some months. My only means of ascertaining the condition of Territorial affairs was through Mr. Howlett,[3] Acting Secretary under appointment of Ex. Gov. Lyon, whom I found to be a very competent gentleman, and well versed in the Financial affairs of the Territory, and whom I have recommended to the Department of State as a suitable person to be duly appointed Territorial Secretary. From the records in his office the present outstanding indebtedness of the Government is nearly sixty five thousand dollars ($65,000) not including the incidental printing of the last session of the Legislature & the Laws thereof.[4]

The annual expenses for office rent, court rooms & Legislative Halls will not fall below eight thousand five hundred dollars ($8,500).

Such is the depreciated condition of the government credit, that the Acting Secretary has for some time past been compelled to furnish at his own cost, all the necessaries required to supply both his own and the executive office, not being able to obtain any thing on the faith of a government voucher.

The Legislative Assembly is required to meet on the first monday in December next. Unless prompt action be taken at once to pay off the present indebtedness, and to place at the disposal of the Territorial Secretary, the funds requisite for the current year, it will be impossible to furnish the necessaries for the next session of the Legislature, and the probabilities are that it will be impossible for that body to hold a session next winter.[5]

In this country where money readily commands thirty per cent interest, Merchants and Tradesman have grown tired of investing their means in government vouchers, with the expectation of waiting for their pay from one to two years. Consequently if the government machinery is kept up it is essentially necessary that the requisite means should be forwarded.

You are aware that Ex Officio I am superintendent of Indian affairs.

The affairs of the Idaho Superintendency are in an equally embarrassed condition. I have transmitted to the Department of the Interior all the information in my possession on that subject.[6]

D. W. Ballard
Gov. & Ex offcio Superintendent of Ind. Affairs of Idaho.

ALS, DNA-RG59, Territorial Papers, Idaho (M445, Roll 1).

1. Ballard (1824–1883), an Indiana native, moved to Lebanon, Oregon, in the early 1850s, where he practiced medicine. Although he applied for the post of commissioner to Hawaii, he was appointed governor of Idaho instead. Despite a number of attempts by Democrats to unseat him, he managed to retain his position until 1870 when he returned to Oregon and the practice of medicine. McMullin and Walker, *Territorial Governors*, 129–30; Hubert H. Bancroft, *History of Washington, Idaho, and Montana, 1845–1889* (San Francisco, 1890), 470; Merle W. Wells, "David W. Ballard, Governor of Idaho, 1866–1870," *OHQ*, 54 (1953): 6–7.

2. Caleb Lyon.

3. Solomon R. Howlett, a native of New York and an "early settler" of the Idaho Territory, served as Governor Lyon's private secretary. When Lyon left the territory in April 1866, Howlett became both acting secretary and acting governor until Ballard arrived in June. Commissioned territorial secretary in July 1866, Howlett had several disputes with the legislature and was removed in 1869. *U.S. Off. Reg.* (1867); W. Turrentine Jackson, "Indian Affairs and Politics in Idaho Territory, 1863–1870," *PHR*, 14 (1945): 312–13; Pomeroy, *The Territories*, 135–36; Wells, "David W. Ballard," 9–15; Hailey, *Idaho*, 167.

4. Part of the territorial debt resulted from the activities of Secretary Gilson, who left Idaho on February 10, 1866, to arrange for a territorial printing contract in San Francisco and then fled to Hong Kong with over $30,000 in territorial funds. He embezzled so cleverly that it took nearly a year for Howlett to discover his theft. Merle W. Wells, "Clinton DeWitt Smith, Secretary, Idaho Territory, 1864–1865," *OHQ*, 52 (1951): 51–52.

5. The Democratic-controlled legislature did meet in December 1866 and caused numerous problems for the Radical Republicans Ballard and Howlett, including cutting their salaries in half by removing the supplement paid by the legislature, an action supposedly necessitated by economics. Howlett, in turn, withheld the federal funds sent to pay the legislators, because the latter refused to take the test oath mandated by Congress, and nearly caused a riot. Wells, "David W. Ballard," 7ff.

6. Ballard did not yet know that Lyon had absconded with over $46,000 intended for the Indians. Lyon first claimed that he had never received the money. Later he said that it had been stolen from under his pillow on a train. Despite the obvious contradiction of his statements, Lyon escaped conviction. Ibid., 5–6; McMullin and Walker, *Territorial Governors*, 128.

From Citizens of Virginia and North Carolina Counties[1]

[July 25, 1866][2]

We the undersigned, loyal citizens, of Stokes, and Forsyth Counties, of N.C., and Patrick County Va.; do sincerely pray, that some protection, or lenientcy, be shown us, from the U.S. Government. We who have been, inhumanly persecuted, for three or four years, of the most infamous, and cruel rebellion. We say cruel, because the most tyrannical, acts of atrocity, were perpetrated, on every advocate of loyalty: consequently, we or part of us, were compelled, to seek refuge, in holes, and dens in the woods; leaving our wives, and little ones, to the mercy of the most fiendish, traitors. Our homes have been visited, every few days, and locks broken, and plundered, of the contents. In many instances, our houses have been burnt, our provision taken, our horses, cattle, hogs, and in a word, every thing, on which to subsist, have been wrested from our hands, as punishment, of our disobedience, to the Rebel Government. Our wives have, been insulted, and maltreated, robbed of even their wearing apparel; their finger-rings, torn from their fingers, and bestowed upon the wives, and daughters, of rebel traitors. Some of our wives, have been torn from their suckling-babes, and thrown into camp, guarded by rebel ruffians, from two, to three weeks duration, and subjected to the most, insulting, and cruel tortures: to wit, their hands, have been put under, fence-rails, and hung up, by their thumbs, in order, to extort from them the hiding places, of their husbands, and sons. When ourselves, and sons were taken by them, we were tied with ropes, our shoes taken off, robbed of our money and clothing, compelled to walk, from 25 to 60 miles, barefooted through the snow, and cold thence carried, to Castle-Thunder, and punished beyon the power of pen to describe. They tried to perish us out, by taking our provision: some of us living in caves, and some over the lines, members of the U.S. army. A few of us obliged to keep from starving, were compelled to treat them likewise, to keep soul and body together. In this critical condition, did Gen. Stoneman's Raiders, find us, and some of them remained behind, and proffered to us their protection, collected up, some of these cruelly treated men, from their hiding places, went around, and made a few of the rebel traitors, give up a portion of their property, they had taken. It was then, that they appeared seemingly, penitent, and asked for letters of protection, which were granted. During the rebellion, they were the most influential, part of the community; now they are still in the ascendency. Our civil tribunals, seem to be governed, and ruled by them, and our destinies, as it were, are in the palms of their hands. In every instance where any property was taken, we have been indicted, and our property taken to pay this cost, while our cases are thrown out of court, with the plea, that they were authorized by the Rebel Government, to take our property, while we had no authority, under which to act. We who have fled our homes, crossed the lines, joined the U.S. army, and lent every assistance in the preservation, and extenuation, of our glorious old Union, are now oppressed, by these hated traitors. We assert that the great mass of the Secesh rebels, of this country are not loyal. It is an every day occurrence, that they speak hard things, of the U.S. Goverment, and say, that they would rather, be under the protection, of England, and France, than the U.S. And are we still to be persecuted? No; we appeal to the President, and Congress, for a redress of our grievences. With faith in God, we look to thee, with a certainty of success.

Mem, DLC-JP.
    1. The memorial was signed by several hundred citizens of Stokes and Forsyth counties in North Carolina and Patrick County, Virginia.
    2. This is the date of the cover letter from Benjamin S. Hedrick in which the memorial was enclosed.

From Martin R. Delany[1]

PORT ROYAL ISLAND, S.C., July 25, 1866.
Sir:
    I propose, simply as a black man,—one of the race most directly interested in the question of *enfranchisement* and the *exercise* of suffrage,—*a cursory view of the basis of security for perpetuating the Union.*

When the compact was formed, the British—a foreign nation—threatened the integrity and destruction of the American colonies. This outside pressure drove them together as independent states, and so long as they desired a Union,—appreciating the power of the enemy, and comprehending their own national strength,—it was sufficient security against any attempt at a dissolution or foreign subjugation.

So soon, however, as, mistaking their own strength, or designing an alliance with some other power, a portion of those states became dissatisfied with the Union, and recklessly sought its dissolution by a resort to the sword, so nearly equally divided were the two sections, that foreign intervention or an exhausting continuance of the struggle would most certainly have effected a dissolution of the Union.

But an element, heretofore latent and unthought of,—a power passive and unrecognized,—suddenly presented itself to the American mind, and its arm to the nation. This power was developed in the blacks, heretofore discarded as a national nonentity—a dreg or excrescence on the body politic. Free, without rights, or slaves, mainly,—therefore *things* constructively,—when called to the country's aid they developed a force which proved the balance precisely called for, and essentially necessary as an elementary part of the national strength. Without this force, or its equivalent, the rebellion could not have been subdued, and without it as an inseparable national element, the Union is insecure.

What becomes necessary, then, to secure and perpetuate the integrity of the Union, is simply the *enfranchisement* and recognition of the *political equality* of the power that saved the nation from destruction in a time of imminent peril—a recognition of the *political equality* of the blacks with the whites in all of their relations as American citizens. Therefore, with the elective franchise, and the exercise of suffrage in all of the Southern States recently holding slaves, there is no earthly power able to cope

with the United States as a military power; consequently nothing to en-
danger the national integrity. Nor can there ever arise from this element
the same contingency to threaten and disturb the quietude of the country
as that which has just been so happily disposed of. Because, believing
themselves sufficiently able, either with or without foreign aid, the rebels
drew the sword against their country, which developed a power in national means—military, financial, and statesmanship—that astonished
the world, and brought them to submission. Hence, whatever their disposition or dissatisfaction, the blacks, nor any other fractional part of the
country, with the historic knowledge before them of its prowess, will ever
be foolhardy enough to attempt rebellion or secession. And their own
political interest will ever keep them true and faithful to the Union,
thereby securing their own liberty, and proving a lasting safeguard as a
balance in the political scale of the country.

As the fear of the British, as an outside pressure, drove, and for a time
kept and held the Union together, so will the fear of the loss of liberty and
their political status, as an element in this great nation, serve as the outside pressure *necessary* to secure the fidelity of the blacks to the Union.
And this fidelity, unlike that of the rebels, need never be mistrusted; because, unlike them, the blacks have before them the *proofs* of the *power*
and *ability* of the Union to maintain unsullied the *prestige* of the national
integrity, even were they, like them, traitorously disposed to destroy their
country, or see it usurped by foreign nations.

This, sir, seems to me conclusive, and is the main point upon which I
base my argument against the contingency of a future dissolution of the
American Union, and in favor of its security.

M. R. DELANY,
Major 104th U.SC.T.

Frank A. Rollin, *Life and Public Services of Martin R. Delany* (Boston, 1868), 278–80.
    1. Delany (1812–1885) had had a career in medicine and in the abolitionist movement
prior to the outbreak of the Civil War. After the war Delany served with the Freedmen's
Bureau and then as customs house inspector at Charleston. *DAB.*

From Clifford N. Fyffe

Charlestown Mass   July 25th 1866

Sir,

About this time last summer I had the honor and pleasure to be presented to you by your friend—my Father—Rev. Granville Moody of
Ohio.

Emboldened by your kind courtesy, I ventured to present to you the
interest of Lieut. Fyffe[1] U.S. Navy who is since my Husband. You kindly
promised me then to do all you could for him, and we have to thank you
sincerely for the interest with which you have listened to my Father[2] &
others in regard to this matter and for your desire to aid us. As you will, I

hope remember—my Husband desires to be restored to the Active List of the Navy, and to his original position—which would be next below Mr. Pendergrast[3] in the list of Lieut Comdrs. to date from July 1863.[4] You will remember too that when in Nov. last you signified your desire that this "be done if no other preventing cause appeared than the charge of intemperance" (upon which Lieut. Fyffe was retired, and which my Father proved to your satisfaction on longer existed.) The Hon. Secy. of the Navy stated that action upon the case was the province of Congress and not the Executive and you signified to my Father in the letter before mentioned that as soon as the necessary action of Congress opened the way for it, you would give the desired nomination.

Accordingly application was made to Congress to pass an act to restore Lieut. Fyffe to the active list. This bill,[5] my friends in Congress believe would have passed last winter, but for Mr. Welles misconstruing an application of my Husband for sea service into a withdrawal of his claims to Congress and so informing the respective Chairmen of the committees. Out of respect to the Departt. Lieut Fyffe consented to postpone the final action till next winter, when we are assured that Messrs Grimes & Rice[6] will themselves introduce the bill. The Department offered my Husband a position upon the Frigate Chattanooga, if he would agree to postpone his application for three years—which proposition he declined to accept. Since then, four months ago, he was ordered to duty in the Boston Navy Yard—where he now is.

I can only trust to your own kindness to pardon all this detail, and to look favorably upon the request which I am about to make & which is the object of this letter. A Bill has been sent to you from Congress "to define the number & regulate the appointments of Officers of the Navy."[7] This provides for 20 additional Lieut. Comdrs. and also for promotion for bravery, high qualifications or distinguished conduct." I believe it is accorded to my Husband that during the last war he evinced great bravery. Admiral Lee[8] recommended the Departt. to promote him to his proper position in view of his fine ability and good behaviour in action under his own eye. After this, he fought and drove back the Rebel Rams, and did other valuable and important services. Mr. Welles himself in a letter to me certified that Lieut. Fyffe is a fine officer and his superior officers here will testify to his qualifications. I ask of your Excellency as a favor whose importance to us you can hardly estimate and as an act whose justice will I hope be apparent to you to nominate my Husband to his original position in the service—by virtue of the Authority vested in you by the said act of Congress. I believe my Husband will be restored next winter at all events, but the boon would come with tenfold value from the hands of my Father's friend and as a reward for services. I ask it in name of the nineteen yrs of the best of his life which my Husband has given to his country in view of the fact that in him centers the hopes of his Father,[9] prematurely old, maimed and diseased by the accidents and exposures of war and of my Father whose services you know and to whom my Husband stands in the place of the son who won a soldier's grave with honor ere he was twenty two.[10] If I am overbold will you attribute it to the importance of this matter to me and remember that your kind Courtesy to me last summer has merged my fear of the "President" in my gratitude and regard for the Gentleman. I write entirely on my own responsibility. Whether you grant my request or not will you have the goodness to make this letter a private and personal matter as regards the Secretary of the Navy who has throughout actively opposed every effort made on this matter, tho it does seem to me he ought to "rejoice more over this one sinner that repenteth" than over the one hundred and forty four Lieut Comdrs. who went not astray openly.[11]

I again earnestly request your favorable consideration and action, and pray that God in whose hands is the "*Kings* heart"—may turn you "as the rivers of water are turned," in such direction as will bring the speedy accomplishment of our hope and ambition.

I can only trust that your own kindness and the vital importance of the matter to us will make the apology that I am not bold enough to attempt for so far occupying your time.[12]

Clifford N. Fyffe

ALS, DLC-JP.

1. Joseph P. Fyffe.

2. See Granville Moody to Johnson, Jan. 26, 1866, *Johnson Papers*, 9: 644.

3. Austin Pendergrast (1829–1874) was promoted to the grade of commander on July 25, 1866, by virtue of the congressional act cited in footnote 7. *Appleton's Cyclopaedia*; Callahan, *List of Navy and Marine Corps*, 428.

4. 1862.

5. Rep. William Lawrence of Ohio had introduced the measure on January 15, 1866. *House Journal*, 39 Cong., 1 Sess., p. 150 (Ser. 1243).

6. James W. Grimes and Alexander H. Rice, chairmen of the Senate and House committees on naval affairs, respectively.

7. Introduced in April by Senator Grimes, the bill was approved by Johnson on July 25. *Senate Journal*, 39 Cong., 1 Sess., pp. 350, 731 (Ser. 1236). For the act itself, see *Congressional Globe*, 39 Cong., 1 Sess., Appendix, pp. 382–83.

8. Samuel Phillips Lee.

9. Edward P. Fyffe (1810–1867) attended West Point before earning his medical degree and commanding an Ohio infantry regiment during the war. Hunt and Brown, *Brigadier Generals*.

10. William H.H. Moody (1842–1864), first lieutenant, 74th Ohio Vol. Inf., had died of disease during the war. Sylvester Weeks, ed., *A Life's Retrospect: Autobiography of Rev. Granville Moody, D.D.* (Cincinnati, 1890), 178; *Off. Army Reg.: Vols.*, 5: 168.

11. Fyffe draws upon the parable of "The Lost Sheep," Luke 15: 3–7.

12. Fyffe's letter was endorsed by Representative Lawrence, who called the President's attention to the petition. In March 1867 Joseph Fyffe was commissioned lieutenant commander to date from July 16, 1862, and his promotion to the grade of commander was authorized by Johnson the following December. Ser. 6B, Vol. 2: 93, 96, Johnson Papers, LC.

From Ladies of Warren County[1]

White Sulphur Springs   Warren County N.C.
July 25th 1866

Sir:

The ladies of this county solicit your Excellency to grant Robert E. Lee an extension of his parole in order that he may be present with his family at religious services incident to erection of a monument 8th August next over remains his daughter Annie C. Lee who died these Springs October 1862.[2]

Tel, DNA-RG107, Tels. Recd., President, Vol. 5 (1866–67).
  1. The telegram was sent by a committee of seven ladies.
  2. Annie (1839–1862) was the second oldest of the general's four daughters. Her father did not attend the August 1866 ceremony but finally visited her grave in late March 1870. Lee, *Lee of Virginia*, 455, 456; Manly W. Wellman, *The County of Warren North Carolina, 1586–1917* (Chapel Hill, 1959), 163–64.

From Andrew C. Maxwell[1]

Bay City; July 25th, 1866.

Dear Sir,

Samuel N. Warren[2] of Flint is collector of the 6th Congressional District of Michigan and Townsend North[3] of Vassar is the Assessor. Both of these men are ridical abolitionists and are opposed to your administration. Warren is a noisy, talkative man, and makes no secret of his dislike for you or the course of your administration. North is a brother-in-law of Judge Edmunds,[4] late of the General Land office, equally positive in his views, but not so noisy. The Conservative people here who approve of the course of your administration desire their removal, and that other and better men may be appointed in their places. They have desired me to write you and to recommend Col. William B. McCreery[5] of Flint for Collector and Brevet Brig. Genl. Benjamin F. Partridge[6] of Bay city for assessor. Both of these men rose from the ranks to the office of Colonel—of their respective regiments, and each has a fair and honorable record as a soldier. Genl. Partridge was Colonel of the 16th Michigan Infantry and Col. McCreery was Colonel of the twenty first Regiment of Michigan Infantry.[7]

I am a member of the Legislature of this State—elected as a democrat, and heartily sustain your policy and the course of your administration, and in what is here stated I believe I express the views of all favorable to you in this District.

A. C. Maxwell

LS, DNA-RG56, Appts., Internal Revenue Service, Assessor, Mich, 6th Dist., Townsend North.

1. Maxwell (1831–1901), an attorney, teacher, and later circuit judge, had been elected to the Michigan legislature in 1864. Augustus H. Gansser, ed., *History of Bay County, Michigan and Representative Citizens* (Chicago, 1905), 384.

2. A native of Vermont, Warren (1813–1904) worked variously as a teacher, town justice and supervisor, postmaster, and school superintendent, in addition to his stint with the Treasury Department. *Early History of Michigan with Biographies of State Officers, Members of Congress Judges and Legislators* (Lansing, 1888), 673; Samuel W. Beakes, *Past and Present of Washtenaw County, Michigan* (Chicago, 1906), 521.

3. North (1814–*fl*1888), a lumber dealer, farmer, merchant, realtor, and register of deeds, had been appointed as assessor in 1862. He was later reappointed by Grant and served a number of years. *Early History of Michigan*, 494–95.

4. James M. Edmunds.

5. Currently serving as the mayor of Flint, McCreery (1836–1896), had seen a good bit of action during the Civil War. He was later elected as state treasurer and held a consular appointment under Benjamin Harrison. McCreery was highly recommended by a number of prominent leaders. Edwin O. Wood, *History of Genesee County, Michigan: Her People, Industries and Institutions* (2 vols., Indianapolis, 1916), 1: 531; Appts., Internal Revenue Service, Collector, Mich., 6th Dist., Wm. B. McCreery, RG56, NA.

6. Before the war Partridge (1822–1892) labored as a merchant, surveyor and civil engineer; during the war he participated in as many as fifty-two different engagements. His appointment as assessor was also urged by many of the same people who had endorsed McCreery's. Hunt and Brown, *Brigadier Generals*; *American Biographical History of Eminent and Self-Made Men: Michigan Volume* (Cincinnati, 1878), 8th Dist.: 41–42; Appts., Internal Revenue Service, Assessor, Mich., 6th Dist., B. F. Partridge, RG56, NA.

7. Johnson did exactly as Maxwell and his fellow conservatives prescribed. Both Warren and North were removed and soon replaced by McCreery and Partridge, but their nominations were rejected by the Senate in February 1867. Ser. 6B, Vol. 3: 539; Vol. 4: 275, Johnson Papers, LC.

From David S. Goodloe

Washington D.C. July 26th/66.

Sir.

In an interview had with you last evening concerning my removal from the office as Assessor of the 7th District of Kentucky—and the appointment of Benjamin Gratz Esq. thereto, you were kind enough to suggest that there was certainly some good reasons for the change, and if I would obtain the true state of facts from the Treasury Department, in relation thereto, you would favor me with another interview.

I have this morning visited the several offices, and being unwilling to farther intrude upon your patience I deemed this—a written communication —the most expeditious way of laying before you the result of my investigation, which will contain all the material facts relative to my case.

Commissioner Rollins certifies that my office is under the best of management, and that I have fulfilled my duties with credit alike to myself and advantage to the Government.

The special Agent of the Treasury Department[1] recently sent West, and who personally inspected my office, cordially testifies both to my fidelity and capacity.

Mr McCulloch plainly stated that he was guided in such matters by the representations of the member from the District, and that Mr

Shanklin had joined in the endorsement of Mr Gratz. I also learned at the same Department—that Mr Montgomery Blair had urged the change upon grounds of relationship to Mr Gratz, and referred the Secretary to the letter of Mr Shanklin upon the subject.[2]

It would have been folly in me Mr President to have expected any other course from Mr Shanklin, as his politics and mine have for the past few years been diametrically opposed. I—as Chairman of the Union Executive State Committee—earnestly advocated the election of Lincoln & Johnson. Mr Shanklin opposed them. In August last I supported the candidates who were in favor of the Constitutional Amendment abolishing slavery. Mr Shanklin was elected in opposition to that measure.

I have been Mr President an earnest advocate of your policy, both as President and as a Union man, and firm supporter of your Administration, which has brought upon me the censures of many friends who charge me with having deserted the party, and now I am removed at the instigation of a gentleman who did not support you, to make way for another who likewise voted against you.

I have no objections to urge against Mr Gratz personally, but on the contrary cordially endorse him as a gentleman: nor would I be here now, were it not at the solicitations of numerous friends in Kentucky—who now anxiously await your decision; they being unwilling to believe your policy was any other than the most patriotic and statesmanlike, and feeling convinced that if a true statement of my case could reach you, that injustice could not be done me. I leave the matter entirely in your hands,[3] as I depart this evening for Kentucky.

D. S. Goodloe.

ALS, DNA-RG56, Appts., Internal Revenue Service, Assessor, Ky., 7th Dist., D. S. Goodloe.

1. Unknown.
2. See George S. Shanklin to Johnson, Apr. 20, 1866.
3. Despite Goodloe's attempt to regain the office, Gratz retained the post and was renominated in January 1867. See Appts., Internal Revenue Service, Assessor, Ky., 7th Dist., D. S. Goodloe, RG56, NA; Ser. 6B, Vol. 4: 241–42, Johnson Papers, LC.

From Henry Stanbery

Washington, July 26th 1866

Sir,

I have the honor to acknowledge the receipt of a Resolution of the House of Representatives, passed July 23d 1866, (referred to me for report) asking information as to the application for pardon of G. E. Pickett who acted as a Major General of rebel forces in the late rebellion.[1]

I transmit you herewith, Sir, a copy of all the papers filed in support of the petition.[2] No action has been had by this Office upon these papers, nor has this Office information of any proceedings instituted against the said Pickett at any time for cruelty to prisoners, or any other offense against the laws of war.

Henry Stanbery   Attorney General

ALS, DLC-JP.

1. See *Congressional Globe*, 39 Cong., 1 Sess., p. 4047.

2. For papers related to Pickett's pardon, see Pickett to Johnson, June 1, 1866, Johnson Papers, LC; Amnesty Papers (M1003, Roll 67), Va., G. E. Pickett; *House Ex. Docs.*, 39 Cong., 2 Sess., No. 11, pp. 1–9 (Ser. 1288).

From James Harlan

Washington D.C.   July 27th 1866

Having heretofore informed you of my readiness to withdraw from the Cabinet whenever it might accord with your pleasure and convenience to name my successor, and in pursuance of an understanding arrived at in a recent interview,[1] I hereby tender my resignation of the office of Secretary of the Interior to take effect on the first day of September next.

In thus severing my official connection with your administration, I would do injustice to my own feelings were I not to present my sincere thanks, for the uniform courtesy and kindness shown me by you, during my term of Service.

Praying that the Supreme Ruler of Nations may bless you with health and vigor to endure the arduous labors incident to your high position, and wisdom to carry into effect such wise measures of policy as Congress may devise to secure domestic peace and National unity. . . .

Jas. Harlan

ALS, DLC-JP.

1. On the morning of July 27, Harlan met with Johnson, who informed him that he wanted to name the secretary's successor and to have it acted upon before Congress adjourned the next day. Johnson named Orville H. Browning to replace Harlan. Randall, *Browning Diary*, 2: 86.

From Cyrus W. Field[1]

Heart's Content [Newfoundland]   July 28th 1866—

Sir:—

The Atlantic cable was successfully Completed this morning. I hope that it will prove a blessing to England and the United States, and increase the intercourse between our own Country and the Eastern hemisphere.[2]

Cyrus W. Field

Tel, DLC-JP.

1. Field (1819–1892) was a successful merchant and promoter of the Atlantic cable. After incredible difficulties the first cable was completed in the summer of 1858; after a few weeks of operation, however, the cable failed. Undaunted, Field launched another cam-

paign to place a cable under the Atlantic Ocean and was eventually successful in 1866. *DAB*.

2. The President congratulated Field and expressed the hope that the new cable would "perpetuate peace and harmony." Johnson to Field, July 29, 1866, Tels. Sent, Sec. of War, RG 107, NA; *National Intelligencer*, July 30, 1866.

From Samuel T. Hulce[1]

Richmond Va   July 28th 1866.

Sir.

I am a private citizen perhaps scarcely known outside the city; formerly however of New-York State, but here for the last twenty five years.

I was before the war, during the war, and am since the war a Union Man, opposed to the *principle* of Slavery, but these questions of contention of former times are all now settled, & what I would write of is this. The Government at Washington is receiving from time to time representations from Gen Terry,[2] delegations of Negroes, and such unprincipled renegades as J. W. Hunnicutt,[3] B. Wardwell[4] Etc all *Exparte*. We are suffering from real injuries to which we are compelled to submit, and more from apprehensions, we fear to execute the laws lest Gen Terry proclaim "Marshal Law." Negroes hold nightly meetings where the most inflammatory & incindiary speeches are listened to delivered by Disunionists such as those above named, the Negroes authorized by the Gen. to drill armed & with Music in the streets a thing never allowed *white* Soldiers except on 4th of July & 22nd February. All this is countenanced by Gen Terry, and to day, on the Holy Sabbath, while the white citizens are not allowed Arms, the Negroes are in hundreds Marching through the streets, drums beating and the citizens submitting rather than give Gen Terry any excuse to interfere. All last night these Negro Soldiers in Squads were marching through the Streets;[5] their object is doubtless to incite some demonstration before the meeting of the Philadelphia convention. There is not one semblance of truth in the reports of injustice to negroes in our Courts. The Negroes are idle relying on the F Bureau, and stealing, and of course many are convicted in courts but have all the privileges of white citizens & most of their difficulties are with each other. We could easily manage them so as to secure our own safety, & satisfy them were it not for such officers & incendiaries as I have named. Cannot we hope you will secure us from imminent apprehended evil and yet continue to us the blessings of Civil law?

I would refer you to J. M. Botts Esq. as to the reliance to be placed on what I state.

S. T. Hulce

ALS, DLC-JP.

1. Hulce (*c*1813–*fl*1869) was a prewar teacher and overseer in Richmond. Afterwards, he served as a policeman for that city. 1850 Census, Va., Henrico, Western Dist., 1036; (1860), Richmond, 3rd Ward, 5; *Boyd's Directory of Richmond City* (1869).

2. Alfred H. Terry.

3. James W. Hunnicutt (1814–*fl*1870), Baptist minister and native of South Carolina, denounced both northern abolitionists and southern fire-eaters during the secession crisis and fled north in 1861. He later was a champion of black rights and was heralded as the Apostle of Radicalism in Virginia. Both before and after the war Hunnicutt edited a religious newspaper. Following his unsuccessful quest for governor in 1868, he became a moderate Republican and later left Virginia. 1870 Census, Va., Stafford, Aquia Twp., 8; Richard Lowe, *Republicans and Reconstruction in Virginia, 1856–70* (Charlottesville, 1991), 58, 148; Michael B. Chesson, *Richmond after the War, 1865–1890* (Richmond, 1981), 110; *Bristol News*, Dec. 6, 1867; *NUC*; *House Reports*, 39 Cong., 1 Sess., No. 30, pt. 2: 149 (Ser. 1273). See also *Louisville Courier*, Sept. 28, 1866.

4. Burnham Wardwell.

5. See *Richmond Dispatch*, July 28, 1866.

From William H. Johnson et al.[1]

Fernandina Fla.   July 28th 1866

Sir:

Early in the spring Mr Daniel Richards[2] came to Florida holding your commission as a Direct Tax Commissioner. Within a week after his arrival he wrote to General U. S. Grant a most calumnious letter[3] of that portion of our citizens who had reclaimed their land from the Direct Tax Sale, charging them with being rebels, while the fact is such persons to effect a redemption of their property from tax sale proved to the satisfaction of the Direct Tax Commissioner, not only that they had been loyal, but that they had given no aid or encouragement to the insurgents in rebellion against the Govement of the United States.

On the 4th of July last Mr Richards addressed an assembly of people in the following terms:

I cannot speak to you on this occasion without referring to other things. We have conquered these (Southern) people. The aristocracy of the South was the cause of the struggle. The spirit of the aristocrats has been put down by the force of our arms, but this spirit is cropping up again, and unless it is met in time by us and crushed again, we shall have another and bloodier conflict. It therefore becomes our duty to unite and to do all in our power to crush them and to keep this spirit down. To do this, it is necessary that we should get hold of the reigns of the State Government. It is our right and our privilege to legislate for these rebels, and to hold the offices, and we will not rest until we have them. We must have them. They are rebels, and as such, they have forfeited all right to make laws and to hold office. We are the only loyal people—we must govern them and rule them. We have achieved this right by the force of our arms, and we must have it. It is true, the war is closed, but only nominally. The conflict still exists, and ought to exist, and must be continued on till we put down the rebels, crush their spirit, and achieve our object. Only then will we be safe in the possession of our property and the enjoyment of our rights. Tell me we have laws in this State! There is no such thing as law existing here. The rebels have made what they call a Constitution, enacted laws and elected officers, but none are valid. Rebels cannot make a Constitution and execute laws for us loyal people. We must and will make a Constitution and laws for this State—one that will be valid and just, and under which all men can live and be protected.

The editorial comments of the Fernandina Courier which follow we vouch for as correct. It is no misrepresentation of this Union League to say that the leading object of its organization is to defeat your plan of reconstructing this Governmt & of restoring peace & tranquility to the country.

Mr Richards is an active persistent, and, as he has shown himself, an unscrupulous opponent of your administration & of its supporters.

We therefore respectfully ask that he be removed from the office of Direct Tax Commissioner of Florida.[4]

LS, DNA-RG58, Direct Tax Commission for Fla., Records Relating to Personnel Actions (1864–66).

1. Johnson (b. *c*1819), a farmer, and thirty-one others signed this letter. 1870 Census, Fla., Nassau, Fernandina, 23.

2. Richards (1821–1872) moved in 1855 from New York to Sterling, Illinois, where he was a hardware merchant. After a term (1862–63) as state senator he studied law in Chicago and on February 5, 1866, was confirmed as one of the Florida direct tax commissioners. For the next few years he was one of the most vocal leaders of the Radical Republicans in that state. He returned to Illinois shortly before his death. *The Biographical Record of Whiteside County, Illinois* (Chicago, 1900), 417–21; Ser. 6B, Vol. 4: 175, Johnson Papers, LC; Jerrell H. Shofner, *Nor Is It Over Yet: Florida in the Era of Reconstruction, 1863–1877* (Gainesville, 1974), 169–206 passim.

3. This letter to the general was dated April 12, 1866. Simon, *Grant Papers*, 15: 408n.

4. Johnson's August 13, 1866, decision was to "Issue an order for the dismissel of Daniel Richards at once," and the next day the papers were referred to Secretary of the Treasury McCulloch. Perplexing, however, is Johnson's undated endorsement, "Suspend action in this case for the present," on Richards's July 25, 1866, letter to Internal Revenue Commissioner E. A. Rollins, wherein Richards claimed his July 4th speech had been misrepresented. Although the failure to date this latter endorsement clouds any conclusion about the dismissal of Richards, one historian accepts as truth that Richards was removed. Shofner, *Nor Is It Over Yet*, 169; Direct Tax Commission for Fla., Records Relating to Personnel Actions (1864–66), RG58, NA.

From David Kilgore[1]

Muncie Ind   July 28 1866

President

Will you be so kind as to have the appointment of Henry C Marsh as Post Master at Muncie Ind made at once[2] The Senate having refused to act on his appointment. Your enemies are laboring to have some other person appointed[3]—who he is they keep a profound secret hence I am certain he is not your friend.[4]

David Kilgore

Tel, DLC-JP.

1. Kilgore (1804–1879), a former Republican congressman (1857–61) and member of the state legislature, was a delegate to the Philadelphia convention. *BDAC*.

2. Marsh (*c*1839–*fl*1875) had been nominated as Muncie's postmaster earlier, but his appointment was not secured until early August. 1860 Census, Ind., Delaware, Muncie, 122; Frank D. Haimbaugh, ed., *History of Delaware County Indiana* (2 vols., Indianapolis, 1924), 1: 456; *Senate Ex. Proceedings*, Vol. 14, pt. 2: 680, 690; *House Ex. Docs.*, 39 Cong., 2 Sess., No. 96, p. 36 (Ser. 1293).

3. On February 28, 1867, Johnson nominated William A. McClellan (1837–1891), formerly captain, 84th Ind. Inf., in place of Marsh, but he was not confirmed by the Senate. Perhaps McClellan was the person to whom Kilgore alludes. *Senate Ex. Proceedings*, Vol. 15, pt. 1: 296; pt. 2: 499; Pension Records, William A. McClellan, RG15, NA.

4. Following McClellan's rejection, Johnson renominated Marsh in March 1867, who was this time confirmed, and he continued serving as Muncie's postmaster through Johnson's and most of Grant's administration. Ibid., 1: 456; *Senate Ex. Proceedings*, Vol. 15, pt. 2: 571.

From A. Toomer Porter[1]

Warrenton Va   July 28" 1866

Sir

Since my interview with you when Gen O. O. Howard was with me,[2] I have been through the North endeavouring to raise the money for the purchase of the Marine Hospital in Charleston S C for a Freedmens School.

I have so far failed, but I have Succeeded in getting a friend[3] to purchase the building & I have just received a telegram from him Saying he has bought the building for Nine Thousand five hundred Dollars for which I am responsible. So anxious are we to get this in operation that I have run the risk, trusting to the *true* friends of the Negro to help me out, & hoping that the Government will be lenient with me till I can pay it all. Will it Suit Your Excellency to let me have the One Thousand Dollars you so generously subscribed to my object? Please address Rev. A Toomer Porter Charleston So Ca where I will be in a few days.[4] Assuring Your Excellency you have my humble but heartfelt prayers for Success in your administration & blessings temporal & Spiritual. . . .

A Toomer Porter

ALS, DLC-JP.
1. Porter (1828–1902), an Episcopal clergyman and educator, had been a Confederate chaplain (Hampton's Legion and the 25th S.C. Inf.). *Cyclopedia of Eminent and Representative Men of the Carolinas of the Nineteenth Century* (2 vols., Spartanburg, 1972 [1892]), 1: 493–95; Adams, *American Authors*, 543.
2. The exact date of the alleged interview has not been established.
3. Unidentified.
4. Although the press had already reported that Johnson had given "his check for $1,000, in aid of the [South Carolina] Theological Institute," not until August 9 did the President authorize a draft "payable to the order of the Agent of the Government to whom the whole amount of the price of the Marine Hospital in Charleston is to be paid." *Washington Evening Star*, July 13, 1866; Johnson to Porter, Aug. 9, 1866, Johnson-Bartlett Collection, Greeneville. See also Porter to Johnson, Oct. 26, 1866; Porter to William E. Chandler, Oct. 26, 1866; Chandler to Johnson, Oct. 31, Nov. 10, 1866, ibid.; Porter to Johnson, July 29, 1867, Johnson Papers, LC.

From Christian F. Sussdorff[1]

Garysburg North Hampton Co. North Carolina
July 28th 1866—

Excellency,

An unknown and obscure individual like myself may possible be considered presumptious in addressing the President of the U. States except on official business, but my motive in writing I trust your Excellency will, at the end perceive, and pardon the freedom.

Opposed as you must be to circumlocution I will therefore go strait to the subject and tell you in the beginning why I write these lines. I am in humble life and earn my bread by my own labour, have travelled for 30 years in N. Carolina S. Car. Georgia, Virginia and Tennessee, am by profession a tuner and repairer of Pianoes and in this capacity have come, for these long years and do now come in contact with the best and most educated part to say the least "the most influencial part" of the community every day. I hear their conversations and take part in it, and consequently form an idea of their feelings in reference to matters present, past or future. I am a German by birth, 59 years of age and came to South Car. in 1830 never held a slave, yet not by any means a radical.

In the position your Excellency occupies it is absolutely nessessary in order to act with wisdom to know the feelings and aims of the people over whom you preside and for whose benefit you are determined to risk all. In various documents emanating from your Excellency you have desired to have the support of the people every where, who love the Constitution and laws and to bring the government back to its original purity. For my own part, and I can say that for thousands, we are heart and hand with you in the plan of restoration and we bless you and pray for you that the "*Lord*" in his infinit goodness may take you in His special keeping in order to safe us and the Land from utter destruction. We owe you a great deal of gratitude for the stand you have taken in our behalf. We may have erred, still the people as a mass thought they had a right to cut loose from the old ship, but most of them have seen the folly and are perfectly willing to abide by the constitution henceforth.

Mr President, the feelings that pass through my mind when I think of the position you have taken and maintained against a fearful and unscrupulous opposition, I can not explain to you—suffice it to say, without flattery or ostentation, that I carry your likeness next my heart in a small case and it shall ever gratefully be cherished there.

In Congress and in the News Papers North we hear a great deal said about the disloyalty of the people south &c. because the people will not take northren men that come among us by the hand at once and make a big to do over them, or lick their boots. You may have been somewhat missled in the matter, even by southron men (pardon me) but I will tell your Excellency frankly, how it is. When some of these men or women come here, they conduct themselves in such a way as to disgust our folks. They boast what they can do, talk abusively about the sins of slavery and glorify the North. Well we have been punished severely enough, God knows and to be continually told that we are whipped and deserve destruction, is not calculated to put us in a very amiable mood towards them, is true. If disloyalty means to hate these noisy fellows and Radicals in Congress and out of it who mean to change the Constitution in a man-

ner that not a vestige is left of the original document, then are we truely
so; but on the contrary if loyalty means to be true to the Constitution as
set forth in the amnesty proclamation and oath—then are we truely loyal
to that instrument and the Government.

Presidents, Kings and Rulers as a general thing are surrounded by
flatterers, time servers and spies. Knowing these facts, and wishing to
hear truths told them, they generally employed wise men and gave them
the priviledge of saying any thing they pleased and to any body without
taking offence, and went under the name of "Court fools"!

Your Excellency will pardon me when I allude to one person whom
you appointed to office in this State I mean Ex Gov. Holden who tried
hard to be made Governor by the vote of the people imidiately before the
war but failed. This soured his temper considerable. Still he preached the
doctrine of Secession, took the state out of the Union and told us that it
was a just, holy and righteous cause. He further more encouraged volun-
teering and said the last dollar and the last cent must be spent. He had a
great share in impuing the people with the right of secession and had he
been elected in place of Ellis[2] at the second term would have made as
strong a Southron as ever drew a sowrd. He praised Vance[3] and recommended him to the people. For a year or so he worked in concert with
him; at last though he grew cold, turned square round and did all to de-
fead the movement he had sed in motion. He now calls himself loyal and
sitts in judgement over those he missled for recommindations for executive pardons. He speakes constantly about the disaffection in North Carolina and seems to make the Government believe that we can't be trusted,
says: look at the election of Worth, who was elected by Sesesh! You Mr
President appointed me and in rejecting me, they have rejected you and
your policy! Not so fast I say Mr. Holden—the President was not rejected, but Worth being a Union man from first to last, they simple voted
for him because they believed Gov. Worth was consistant and that it
would please you better, supposing in appointing Holden, you knew of
no other man, whom you could give the office on the spur of the moment
and before the smoke of the battle had cleared away.

I was at one time a sincere Holden man and believed as thousand did in
his integrity, but he missled us forsooke us and now sits in judgement
over us. I ask you in all honesty, is it not humiliating and can you blame
us, "the common people["] of having no more faith in him? Spare us this
humiliation in future Mr. President and in rejecting W. W. Holden—we
by no manner of means reflect upon you any disgrace. We love and honour you and you might come among us unattended and no harm would
befall you, but honour and respect would be heaped upon you, because
you stand as firm as a rock upon what is just and mercy. Let Holden say
what he pleases about Gov. Worth, he is nevertheless true to you and the
Constitution. Were your Excellency inclined to change your mind and
run a second time for President I am confident the whole South would

vote for you, with perhaps some few exceptions, and I don't know, judging folks by their passed conduct—W. W. Holden might be of that class at last.

In order to safe the Government from going to wreck we must be united and all past differences laid aside for it will take herculean strength [to] right the ship of State. We have to deal with a party that aims at a central Government and whip out the individuality of the States—they have been hammering at it for 7 or 8 ms. and still continue their aim, and would have played havoc, if it had not been for your firmness. Surely the Lord raised you up to be our shield and bucklar, and with you as our Josuah of old we will follow you in into the thickest of the field inscribing on our Banner the Constist. and the laws and Andrew Johnston our leader—and give the "Lord our God the Glory" His Holy name be praised!

With your Excellency permission I will now relate a few little insidents: That the people should be stunned by the great upheavings in the South, loss of property &c. is very natural, but that this leathargy should be heralded forth to their injury and oppression is cruel in the extreem. In my intercourse with the people I find that they are loath to take News Papers and I have to go sometimes for several weeks without seeing a sentence of what is going on in the outer world. I ask what's the reason you don't take a paper? Well if we take one, we hear nothing but abuse—the Radicals have it all their own way any how! Thats not true, is not the President a whole team in himself to hold their radical wagon back and has he not done it? Yes he has done wonders, but they will prove too many for him in the end. Exactly so, if all were actuated by the same spirit they might, but that's not going to happen if we show as much moral courage as we showed brute.

One gentleman in a high social position kept no Papers. When I asked the reason he said: he had kept at least ten before the war, but now he was done with politics &c. and if he had served his God as well as his political party would call himself a good Christian. I told him it was not worth while to jump from one extreem into another, and if you are afraid to hear of what the Radicals are concocting, you remind me very much of the Ostrich who when pursued and about being overtaken sticks his head into the Sand, believing that the enemy wont discover him and perishes foolishly. I told him I wanted to face the music under the President boldly—he said that was his doctrine too. I assure your Excellency that if we can make a tolerable good crop this year—the spirit will revive—we will be able to pay our taxes readier and all will wear a new face.

In all your Excellency's reply to depredations I perceive an intimate knowledge of the southren Character, impulsive but chivalric, brave to a falt, giving no insult and taking none, constitution loving and forgiving when honour is satisfyed. You said in one of your replys "the Southren People must be trusted!" Never did Solomon utter a truer sentence and had your counsel been followed up by Congress, the Union and good feeling would have been almost perfect as of old, for every one was disposed to prove how sincerely rependant he could be. I speak of the Southron people—how it would have been in the North is quit a different question.

I believe that in the providence of God it was so ordained that the Radicals should have an overwhelming majority in order that they had full swing to show to the world what the meant to do—if let alone. Their proceedings opened the eys of all conservative men and made them pause and reflect and see the real design of these mad revolutionists. Had they been compelled to work more covertly, they might have undermined the political fabric stealthily by degrees. All is plain now and there is no excuse for them and they will reap their reward yet. I hope the Philadelphia Convention will be properly attended by every Southren and Northren State so that thy people may once more come together and shake hands and may the Lord bless their doings! I want peace and harmony to reign over this land once more, and he who can produce that desirable object will live in history for ever, and I trust that Andrew Johnston Pres. of the U.S. will be that man.

Fearing that I have wearied you too long I must come to a close asking humble and reverently of your kind heart a favour and that is that you may be pleased in mercy to take into consideration the unpardoned condition of Ex Gov. William Graham, Ex Gov Vance and Brigadier Genl. Scals[4] all of this State. Allow me to say that more honourable men are no where to be found and if they pass to you their word that they will observe the Const. & the Laws they will surely do it. I know their character. You have pardoned many it is true but extend your mercy a little further. Recollect Mr. Pres: to *"Err is human—to forgive divine"* and North Carolinians will love you the more for it and bless you. Now Mr. Johnston my honoured Sir, if I have said too much accord it to my ignorance. I am but a mechanic and never had a collegiate education. To write an english letter correctly is a difficult thing to do, but take, please, the will for the deed.

You are constantly in my thoughts and at night when I appeal to the throne of Grace to forgive my many sins and failings I inclose you and yours as I have heard the same done in many private families, to pray that the Lord may graciously protect you and guide you in the proper way, and keep your mind sound and steadfast to His Glory and Renoun![5]

C. F. Sussdorff

ALS, DLC-JP.

1. Sussdorff (1807–1886), a German by birth, was also a landscape gardener and music teacher. Donald W. Stanley et al., eds., *Forsyth County, North Carolina Cemetery Records* (5 vols., Winston-Salem, 1976–78), 5: 1151; Gwynne S. Taylor, *From Frontier to Factory: An Architectural History of Forsyth County* (Winston-Salem, 1981), 228.

2. John W. Ellis (1820–1861), a lawyer at Salisbury, served as a legislator (1840s), superior court judge (1848–58), and governor (1858–61). Wakelyn, *BDC*, 179.

3. Zebulon B. Vance.

4. Alfred M. Scales (1827–1892), lawyer, legislator, and congressman (1857–59, 1875–84), during the war had been promoted brigadier general from captain and colonel of the 13th N.C. Inf. In the 1880s he was North Carolina's governor. Warner, *Gray*.

5. Sussdorff wrote a letter to Eliza Johnson on the same date as the one to the President. In it he explained that he was sending the latter to Mrs. Johnson so that she could read it and if she found it "worthy of his notice" she should "hand it to him at a leausur moment." Sussdorff to Mrs. Johnson, July 28, 1866, Johnson Papers, LC.

From Albert Voorhies and Andrew S. Herron[1]

New Orleans La.   July 28, 1866

Prest. Johnson.

Radical mass meeting composed mainly of large number of negroes last night Ending in a riot.[2] The committee of arrangements of said meeting assembling tonight. Violent and incendiary speeches made, negroes called to arm themselves,[3] You bitterly denounced. Speakers Field, Dostie, Hawkins, Henderson, Heirstand & others.[4] Gov. Wells arrived last night but sides with the Convention move. The whole matter before grand jury, but impossible to execute Civil process without certainty of riot. Contemplated to have the members of the Convention arrested under process from the Criminal Court of this District. Is the military to interfere to prevent process of Court?[5]

Albert Voohees   Lt. Governor of La. &
Andrew J.[S] Herron   Atty. Gen. of La.

Tel, DLC-JP.

1. Herron (c1824–fl1873), a lawyer from East Baton Rouge, had been Louisiana secretary of state (1852–60). During the war he rose to the rank of colonel in the Confederate army. Elected state attorney general in 1865, Herron was removed from office by Sheridan in 1867 as a result of Herron's refusal to prosecute those who attacked the Convention. In the 1870s Herron served in the state legislature. *New Orleans Picayune*, Jan. 6, 1873; Thomas R. Landry, "The Political Career of Robert Charles Wickliffe, Governor of Louisiana, 1856–1860," *LHQ*, 25 (1942): 680; Albert Leonce Dupont, "The Career of Paul Octave Hebert, Governor of Louisiana, 1853–1856," *LHQ*, 31 (1948): 501, 503; *House Reports*, 39 Cong., 2 Sess., No. 16, pp. 243–47 (Ser. 1304); Taylor, *La. Reconstructed*, 139.

2. The meeting of July 27 did not end in a riot. See, for example, *House Reports*, 39 Cong., 2 Sess., No. 16, pp. 1, 3 (Ser. 1304).

3. Ezra Hiestand characterized some of the remarks as "intemperate." Others who heard the speeches said that Dr. Anthony P. Dostie, the most radical speaker, so far from urging the blacks to come armed to the convention and incite a riot, had told them to go home peacefully but defend themselves if attacked. Ibid.; Donald E. Reynolds, "The New Orleans Riot of 1866, Reconsidered," *La. Hist.*, 5 (1964): 23–26.

4. Alexander P. Field (1800–c1876), after serving in the Illinois state legislature and as Illinois secretary of state, moved his law practice to New Orleans in 1849. He was elected to Congress from Louisiana in 1863 and 1864 but was not seated. Supporting the Radical Republicans and the so-called "Customhouse Faction," Field was elected state attorney general in 1872. The *Picayune* mentioned a "Judge Hawkins" speaking at the Mechanics' Institute meeting, but no other account of the meeting indicates his presence. The man could, perhaps, have been Jacob Hawkins (fl1876), lawyer and, in the 1870s, judge of the Superior District Court, or the reporter could have listed Hawkins mistakenly instead of the Rev. Mr. Horton, who did speak. John Henderson, Jr. (c1821–1866), a lawyer, died as a result of wounds received in the riot on July 30. Ezra Hiestand (c1816–fl1873) was a

The New Orleans riot
Harper's Weekly, September 8, 1866

lawyer who had been a member of the Louisiana state legislature, attorney of the city of New Orleans, justice of the peace, and judge. Conrad, *La. Biography*; *New Orleans Picayune*, July 28, 31, Aug. 1, Sept. 13, 1866; McCrary, *Lincoln and Reconstruction*, 250; New Orleans directories (1850–77); *Augusta Constitutionalist*, Aug. 7, 1866; 1860 Census, La., Orleans, New Orleans, 3rd Ward, 214; *House Reports*, 39 Cong., 2 Sess., No. 16, p. 1 (Ser. 1304).

5. Voorhies and Herron wanted to arrest the members of the Convention for unlawful assembly. Johnson replied that "The military will be expected to sustain and not to obstruct or interfere with the proceedings of the Courts." The actual riot took place on July 30. See Jacob Barker to Johnson, July 31, 1866; *House Reports*, 39 Cong., 2 Sess., No. 16, pp. 243–45 (Ser. 1304); Johnson to Voorhies, July 28, 1866, Johnson Papers, LC.

To J. Madison Wells

Washington City, July 28. 1866.

I have been advised that you have issued a proclamation convening the Convention Elected in 1864. Please inform me under and by what authority this has been done; and by what authority this Convention can assume to represent the whole people of the state of Louisiana.[1]

Andrew Johnson.

Tel, DLC-JP.

1. Wells replied that he had not issued a proclamation about the Convention. "This was done by the President of that body by virtue of resolution adjourning the Convention subject to his order, and in that case authorizing him to call upon the proper officer to issue writs of election in unrepresented parishes. My proclamation is in response to that call ordering an election on the 3d of Sept. As soon as vacancies can be ascertained an election will be held to fill them, when the entire State will be represented." Wells to Johnson, July 28, 1866, Johnson Papers, LC.

From William S. Cheatham

No 20 high Street   Nashville Tennessee
July 29th 1866

Dear Sir

The object of this letter is to ask you to issue an order for the release of Mr W B Shapards Sr[1] house on high Street between Church and union Streets So Mr Shapard Can get possession. I am informed that it is occupied by two men who are in the army. Mr Shapard is a very old man and his wife[2] is Sixty five years of age. The Government has had possession of his house for four or five years. Mr Shapard is an ardent Supporter of you and your restoration policy. Now as Congress has adjourned I hope you will remove every man who is opposed to you and your policy that holds a position under the Government. I would like for you to appoint me assessor of Eutaw Territory.[3]

A little over four hundred voters in this County have been registered and nearly all of those are Soldiers who are opposed to you and your policy. The Constitutional amendment that Governor Brownlow Telegraphed to Forney[4] had passed the Legislature did not passed as they had no

Quorum in the house. There was only fifty four members present. At the time the vote was taken they had two members under arrest who was not present when the vote was taken. They had to have fifty Six members to make a Quorum which they did not have. I never Saw Such oppression in my life as there is on the people of Tennessee at this time. The Radicals here abuse you for every thing they Can. Would to heaven that a Military Governor was appointed here and every thing this Legislature has done was declared null and void. Rember me to your family.

W S Cheatham

ALS, DLC-JP.

1. William B. Shapard (1797–1870) was a prominent banker in Nashville and served as the city's mayor in 1854. *Nashville Union and American*, Jan. 20, 1870; Jeanette T. Acklen, comp., *Tennessee Records: Tombstone Inscriptions and Manuscripts* (2 vols., Baltimore, 1967 [1933]), 1: 40.

2. Margery Childress Shapard (1801–1879) was a native of North Carolina. Ibid.

3. No evidence to indicate that Cheatham secured an appointment in Utah has been found. He was something of a habitual or persistent seeker after federal positions. See, for example, his letters to Johnson, Mar. 9, 1865, Johnson Papers, LC; and Mar. 22, 1865, *Johnson Papers*, 7: 530–31.

4. See John S. Brien and John C. Gaut to Johnson, July 19, 1866. The famous telegram from Brownlow to John W. Forney of July may be found in a number of different publications. Two of the more convenient ones are Patton, *Unionism and Reconstruction*, 223–24, and Coulter, *Brownlow*, 315.

From Sam Milligan

private

Greeneville Ten   July 29. 1866

Dear Sir:

It is imposible for me to shake off the fearful apprehension, that another great political crisis is rapidly pressing itself upon the American people. I have looked with silent interest upon the movements of the Radical party in Congress. They at once amaze and confound me. I have charity enough to hope, they do not seek the distruction of the Government; but I confess, I have not segacity to see that their policy tends to any other end. It is captious, and arogant—inconsistent, and without constitutional warrant. The grounds upon which the war was waged, and the principles upon which it was conducted, have all been abandoned; and a new theory inaugurated, wholly unknown to international law, or the principles of our own constitution. The idea, that under the usages of civilized nations, or the forms of our constitution, the Government of the United States, by the suppression of a rebellion, within its own Constitutional limits, and by its own people, can confer upon the Government, rights of sovereignty, which it did not previously possess, is at once anomolus and absurd. Such a doctrine, is an error—a grave and fundimental error. By conquest, the conquering power, gains complete sovereign rights where it had none before. This of necessity, is alone applicable to a foreign war. It can not apply to a rebellion; for how can a nation make conquest of its own territory? Sovereign rights are the highest rights, that can be exercised by any nation; and with what propriety can it be said, a nation by suppressing a rebellion within its own territory, over which before the rebellion it had sovereign power, thereby gained only what it had before? This is absurd nonsense! But what follows the suppression of hostilities in a nation? It is clear, that if a hostile power, either from within or without a nation, takes possession, and holds absolute dominion over any part of its territory, and such nation, by force of arms, expells or overthrows the enemy, & suppresses all hostilities, it acquires no new title,—no additional rights,—no sovereignty it did not enjoy before; but it merely suppresses hostilities within its own limits, and thereby regains exactly the same rights it enjoyed before, which had been temporarily suspended.

Now does it not follow as a corrolary, when the rebellion was suppressed, that the States remained with all there rights in the Union? If they held a constitutional organization in the Union, before the rebellion, and there can be no conquest, by the United States, of its own territory, they must of necessity occupy now their former position. If their governments were republican before the war, and as such recognized by the Federal Government, they certainly can not be less so now. They are, as to all their former rights & relations to the Metropolitan Government, precisely the same; and where is the necessity of changing the Constitution now, that they may be made republican. The fact that the negros are all free, does not alter the principle. Some of them were free before the war, and none of them, in any of the Southern States, were recognized as citizens, yet all the State governments were, by the acts of Congress admitting them as States, admitted to have republican constitutions and Governments. True, by constitutional amendment, slavery is abolished in every State, but how does that place the negro on any higher ground, than the freedman occupied before the emancipation of his race in the United States?

The relation of the States to the Federal Government being fixed the whole question is settled. Your policy, nor the policy of the Radicals, (if in deed they can be said to have any policy, which I was never able to see,)— does not propose to make rebels loyal. No policy can effect that, and yet that is the great difficulty. We must meet the difficulty, as all other enlightened christian nations, as modern times have met it—by judicious amnesties and pardons, and renewed trust and confidence. There is no other alternative. It is imperative. The radical policy, if they have any— no less than your own ends in this. The one postpones perhaps, what you more wisely propose to meet now. If the rebel element again betray, the confidence & magnanimity, the remedy is *the sword*. Try and hang some of the leaders now, for crimes already committed. Establish the power of the civil government to punish for treason, and then make, by judicious legislation, the civil arm of the Government, a strong, effectual, watchful, and ever present power, to punish crime, and trust all the rest—and all will be well. If not the sword—the sword!

We will have a delegation at Philadelphia. My position does not admit of my taking the stump, but I think, I have and am doing, in a quiet way, without boast, as much perhaps any one in the State to sustain your policy.

Sam Milligan

I will soon write you the state of things here.[1]

ALS, DLC-JP.
1. This sentence was written in the margin of the first page of Milligan's letter.

From Edmund Burke

Newport, N.H.   July 30th 1866.

Sir.

Some days since I enclosed a letter from Henry Hubbard Esq.[1] of Charlestown, in this State, recommending James C. Stebbins for the office of Postmaster of that town.[2]

Today, I have received a letter from Mr. Hubbard, which I enclose for your perusal,[3] in which he informs me that the Postmaster Genl. Mr. Randall, has promised the Hon Mr. Patterson,[4] Representative in Congress from this District, to appoint a man by the name of Kimball[5] to the office. Mr. Hubbard further writes that Mr. Stebbins has been grossly defamed in his character by his opponents and rivals for the appointment in question.

In view of recent appointments in this State I do not know that the recommendations of one belonging to the Democratic Party can avail in any case. But, notwithstanding, I deem it proper to say that Mr. Hubbard is a gentleman who stands as high, personally, as any other of any party in this State. He is incapable of falsehood or wilful misrepresentation. And what he says in relation to the character of Mr. Stebbins may be implicitly relied upon.

I will add my own testimony in favor of Mr. Stebbins. I have known him for twenty five years, during all which time he has occupied a respectable position in the town of his residence, and for many years he has filled the office of Sheriff. The attacks upon his character, if any have been made, are unfounded and false.

But it is not denied that he is a democrat, and if that fact is a bar to his appointment, his friends will not complain.

When I saw you in Washington a few weeks since, I inferred from your conversation that a new policy with regard to appointments would be instituted in this State—that the enemies of the policy of the Administration would *not* be appointed to office, and that its friends would be. The recent appointment of Senator Clark[6] to the office of District Judge, and that of Henry P. Rolfe[7] to the office of Postmaster at Concord, afford strong ground for inferring that the policy of appointing Radicals, the enemies of yourself and your policy, is to be continued.

Do not understand me as censuring this policy. I have no right, nor would it be respectful for me, to do so. The President will, of course, pursue that system of policy which he deems best. But, the policy which he does pursue is subject to the judgment of the People. My interview with you (had with the concurrence and approbation of the leaders of the Democratic Party of this State) led me to believe that you desired the alliance and co-operation of the Democracy of this State against an Radical Party supporting Congress and its policy. The appointments referred to, give ground for a contrary inference. Indeed, I may say that no appointment could more repel the Democratic Party from the support of the Administration than that of Mr. Clark especially. No man in New Hampshire is more offensive to the Democracy than he is. From those appointments the Democracy are like to infer that the Administration looks to the Radicals alone for support. And with this understanding, the Democratic Party, while it will support the measures of the Administration which are in principle Democratic, will be obliged to look only to its own organization for its future success.

I will again repeat what I assured you was the fact when I saw you in Washington, that the Administration has no support in this State outside the Democratic Party. The Democratic newspapers are the only papers in this State which support the Administration, or favor the Philadelphia Convention. With this I send you a copy of the "Independent Democrat,"[8] the leading organ of the Radicals in this State. One of its editors is Fogg,[9] late minister to Switzerland, and recently Commissioner to New Orleans, appointed by Mr. McCulloch. You will see that it ridicules your policy, and denounces the Philadelphia Convention. Yet, the honors and offices are given to this stripe of politician. Of course such a policy is suicidal.

Recurring again to the Post Office of Charlestown, if a democrat can in no event be appointed, a moderate Radical will be recommended instead of Mr. Stebbins. Mr. Hubbard assures me that there is no bitterer enemy of the Administration in Charlestown, than Mr. Kimball, who it is said, has the promise of it from the P.M. General. He is connected with a Shoemakers establishment which gives about 60 votes against the Administration, and controls the politics of the town as I am informed. If Kimball shall be appointed, it will be fatal to any movement in this country in view of getting up a party to support the Administration.

Edmund Burke

ALS, DLC-JP.
    1. Hubbard (b. c1818) was a well-to-do farmer. 1860 Census, N.H., Sullivan, Charlestown, 99.

2. Records indicated that Stebbins (c1806–fl1870) was appointed Charlestown postmaster in late August 1866 to replace Charles C. Kimball, who was removed for political reasons. Ibid., 98; (1870), 413; *House Ex. Docs.*, 39 Cong., 2 Sess., No. 96, p. 4 (Ser. 1293).

3. Hubbard to Burke, July 28, 1866, Johnson Papers, LC.

4. Alexander W. Randall and James W. Patterson, respectively.

5. Charles C. Kimball (c1830–fl1870) served both before and after the war in the state legislature and also as town clerk of Charlestown. Later he became postmaster of Charlestown. 1870 Census, N.H., Sullivan, Charlestown, 412; D. Hamilton Hurd, ed., *History of Cheshire and Sullivan Counties, New Hampshire* (Philadelphia, 1886), 38–39; *U.S. Off. Reg.* (1869–75).

6. Daniel Clark.

7. A Dartmouth graduate and former Democratic-turned-Republican legislator, Rolfe (1821–1898) was nominated postmaster at Concord on July 23, 1866, and confirmed by the Senate three days later. Removed from office by March 1867, he later served as a district attorney during most of Grant's administration. Stearns, *History of New Hampshire*, 1145; Ser. 6B, Vol. 4: 10, Johnson Papers, LC.

8. Not found.

9. George G. Fogg (1813–1881) was founding editor of the *Independent Democrat* of Concord before accepting Lincoln's appointment to a foreign mission in 1861. *DAB*.

From Kate Coyle[1]

32 Missouri Ave [Washington] July 30th [1866][2]

My dear Mr President

I wish to call your attention to the promise made me sometime since that you would think of Mr Coyle, when Congress would take the proposed action on the Paris Exposition. Now that it, has disposed of that object and leaves to you the disignation of the Commissioners; I am anxious that you should not overlook my request amidst the other importunities to which you will doubtless be subjected. What I particularly desire is, that Mr C__ may be *one* of *the ten* that are to be appointed for specific objects.[3]

The Press being a great power in our Country, in fact the Power since it moulds, as well as expresses, the opinions from which public action springs, it occurs to me that it deserves a special mission on an occasion of such importance; and as the Intelligencer is considered somewhat of a grand mother among our newspapers and enjoys a respect abroad unsurpassed by any, I think the old lady might be allowed to air her Cap ruffles at the Parisian Exposition. There is no doubt but that she would support abroad with a great deal of dignity the conservatism for which she is so distinguished at home. Let me commend this idea My dear President to your particular attention, and beg you to let it have due weight with you in the exercise of your discretionary power.

I am going to the Philadelphia Convention to do a great deal of talking and mightly little listening.

Kate Coyle

ALS, DLC-JP.

1. A resident of Washington, Kate Coyle (b. c1826) was a native of Maryland; she and

her husband were the parents of two children. 1860 Census, D.C., Washington, 4th Ward, 266.

2. Internal evidence *re* the Paris Exposition indicates that this is an 1866 document.

3. John F. Coyle did not get the appointment. *Washington Evening Star*, July 30, 1866.

From John B. Cresson[1]

Philada.   July 30th 1866

Mr President

Having noticed the passage by Congress of the long pending Bill for the Reorganization of the Regular Army,[2] making many vacancies to be filled by thy appointment, I would most respectfully beg permission to call thy attention to the case of my Son Colonel Charles C Cresson Jr,[3] who has for more than four years been an applicant & was promised it by Secy Cameron for a position in the Regular Service. He entered the Volunteer Service in July 61 as 2nd Lieut in the 66th Pa Vols, was transferred to the 73rd Penna. Vols, rose, by a *Wound* at *each promotion*, to be *Colonel* as per commission of Gov Curtin of the 73rd Penn Vet Vols.

The will find his Record in the War Office with strong & flattering Reccommendations from nearly all his commanding Officers Genls Hooker, Howard, Slocum[4] John W Geary, P. H Jones,[5] & numerous Civillians asking his appointment as Major: I know thee will do him Justice in this matter & in thy hands I rest it.

John B Cresson

Hon Thomas E Franklin[6] Lancaster

"   Green Adams   Kentucky

"   William D Kelley   Pa

"   Leonard Myers   do

"   Edgar Cowan   do

"   Joseph Bailley   do late Representative

"   Andrew G Curtin   Gov: Penna

"   John Covode   late Representative do

"   Morton McMichael Mayor Philada. & very many others are his strong Friends without distinction of Party in this matter & have their Reccommendations on File, most of them soliciting his promotion to Major in the Regular Army under the new Bill which was expected & *was* passed on Saturday last.

John B Cresson
No 1618 Mt Vernon St
or Powers & Weightmans[7] 9th & Parrish Sts Philada.

I have recd since writing above notification of Colonel Cressons appointment & confirmation as 2nd Lieutenant in the Regulars,[8] for which please accept my sincere thanks, but I still leave it with thee to see if he cannot be promoted to Major under the new Bill.[9]

ALS, DNA-RG94, ACP Branch, File C-5339-CB-1871, Charles C. Cresson.

1. Cresson (*fl*1876) was a merchant and druggist. He had written Johnson at least twice before regarding his son's appointment. Philadelphia directories (1865–78); John B. Cresson to Johnson, May 14, 28, 1866, ACP Branch, File C-5339-CB-1871, Charles C. Cresson, RG94, NA.

2. The measure passed by Congress on July 27 and approved by Johnson later in the day prescribed forty-five majors for the infantry branch. *Congressional Globe*, 39 Cong., 1 Sess., Appendix, p. 420; *Senate Journal*, 39 Cong., 1 Sess., pp. 781, 788 (Ser. 1236).

3. Cresson (1845–1906), mustered out of volunteer service in August 1865, had applied four months later for an appointment in the regular army. Pension Records, Adelia Cresson, RG15, NA; Charles C. Cresson, Jr., to Johnson, Dec. 6, 1865, Johnson Papers, LC.

4. Joseph Hooker, Oliver O. Howard, and Henry W. Slocum.

5. Patrick H. Jones (1830–1900) was at this time serving as clerk of the New York court of appeals. During the war he had commanded a New York regiment at Chancellorsville, where he was wounded and captured, and afterwards was engaged in the western theater. Grant appointed him postmaster of New York City in 1869. Warner, *Blue*.

6. Franklin (1810–1884) was a longtime lawyer in Lancaster who had served as a district attorney and subsequently as Pennsylvania's attorney general. He was also involved in banking and railroad interests. Franklin Ellis and Samuel Evans, *History of Lancaster County, Pennsylvania* (Philadelphia, 1883), 234–35; *Biographical Annals of Lancaster County Pennsylvania* (Chicago, 1903), 402.

7. A chemical firm operated by Thomas H. Powers (*c*1813–1878), William Weightman (1813–1904), and sometimes a third partner. Philadelphia directories (1865–70); 1870 Census, Pa., Philadelphia, Philadelphia, 23rd Dist., 8th Ward, 65; *DAB*.

8. Appointed on May 11, Cresson was commissioned on July 27, the date of the passage of the army reorganization act. Ser. 6B, Vol. 2: 41, Johnson Papers, LC.

9. Although the President later approved Cresson's transfer from the 17th to the 35th Inf. and his promotion to the rank of first lieutenant, he did not appoint him major. In 1879 Cresson retired from the army as a brevet lieutenant colonel, after having transferred to the cavalry and performed "gallant and meritorious service" in subduing the Modoc and the Nez Percé. Ibid., 48, 85; Powell, *Army List*, 263.

From Ulysses S. Grant

Washington, July 30th 1866.

Dear Sir:

A dispatch rec'd from Gen. Sherman in reply to mine[1] requesting him to come by Washington to receive directly from the hands of the President his commission of Lieut. General[2] announces that he will be here ready to call at the Executive Mansion at any time to-morrow that may suit the President.[3]

U. S. Grant   General

ALS, DLC-JP.

1. On July 28 Grant wired the following message to Sherman, who was in Buffalo, New York: "The President desires to present your commission of Lieutenant General to you in person, and you will come to Washington for this purpose immediately." Simon, *Grant Papers*, 16: 261–62n; *Washington Evening Star*, Aug. 2, 1866.

2. Grant's promotion to general allowed the way for Sherman's elevation to lieutenant general. Grant had recommended to both Johnson and Stanton that Sherman be promoted and had asked Johnson if he and Sherman could receive their commissions at the same time. Buckalew et al. to Johnson, ca. July, 1866; "Notes of Colonel W.G. Moore, Private Secretary to President Johnson, 1866–1868," *AHR*, 19 (1913): 102; Simon, *Grant Papers*, 16: 261.

3. Sherman arrived from Buffalo on July 31 and on the following day received his commission from the President at the White House. Grant attended the presentation. Ibid., 262n.

From Thomas A. Hendricks

Indianapolis, Ind   July 30, 1866

Sir

I have the honor to renew this recommendation made by myself and Justice Davis[1] of V. C. Hanna[2] for Paymaster in the Army. Maj Hanna servd. in this position throughout the war, and was an honest and efficient officer. He is a worthy gentleman, and I will be much gratified at his appointment, and I am sure it will be gratifying to a large portion of the people of this portion of the state.

T. A. Hendricks

P.S.   Of such of the paymasters that may be appointed from this state I earnestly request that Maj Hanna may be one.[3]

T. A H

ALS, DNA-RG94, ACP Branch, File H-4889-CB-1873, V. C. Hanna.
1. David Davis. Indiana's other senator, Henry S. Lane, was the third signatory. See Hendricks et al. to Johnson, Mar. 6, 1866, ACP Branch, File H-4889-CB-1873, V. C. Hanna, RG94, NA.
2. On the eve of the war, Valentine C. Hanna (d. 1884) had been a commission merchant in Indianapolis. He was mustered out of the volunteer army with the rank of brevet lieutenant colonel on July 20, 1866. Powell, *Army List*, 354; *Indianapolis Directory* (1861).
3. Also recommended by Indiana's delegation to the Philadelphia Convention (which included Hendricks) and Rep. James Wilson, Hanna was appointed as a major in the Pay Department in January 1867 and commissioned in March. He retired from the army ten years later. Ser. 6B, Vol. 2: 134, Johnson Papers, LC; Powell, *Army List*, 354; Solomon Meredith et al. to Johnson, July 19, 1866, ACP Branch, File H-4889-CB-1873, V. C. Hanna, RG94, NA.

To Andrew S. Herron

Washington, D.C.   July 30th 1866.

You will call on Genl. Sheridan, or whoever may be in command for sufficient force to sustain the civil authority in suppressing all illegal or unlawful assemblies who usurp or assume to exorcise any power or authority without first having obtained the consent of the people of the State. If there is to be a Convention, let it be composed of delegates chosen fresh from the people of the whole state. The people must be first consulted in reference to changing the organic law of the state. Usurpation will not be tolerated, the law and the constitution must be sustained and thereby peace & order.[1]

Andrew Johnson

Tel, DNA-RG107, Tels. Sent, President, Vol. 3 (1865–68).
1. Johnson is referring, of course, to stopping the proposed meeting of the reconvened

Convention of 1864. See also Albert Voorhies and Andrew S. Herron to Johnson, July 28, 1866; Herron to Johnson, July 31, 1866.

From A. Cameron Hunt[1]

Denver C.T.   July 30th 1866

I have the honor to herewith inform you that under the administration of the late President Lincoln I was appointed U.S. Marshal in and for the Territory of Colorado and held that position for the last four years; and my loyalty to the Government has never been doubted.

On the 24 inst. a Convention was held calling itself *Union* though ignoring the present administration. After its deliberations One G. M. Chilcott[2] was placed in nomination for delegate to Congress.

Said Chilcott now holds a prominent and lucretive position under the present administration and by your indulgence, and that your Excellency may be aware of the sentiments of the So Called *Union* Convention and its candidate I herewith submit for your perusal the enclosed Circular[3] to their secret society organized here by the radicals a short time since.[4]

A. Cameron Hunt

ALS, DLC-JP.

1. Alexander Cameron Hunt (1825–1894), an Illinoisian who had prospered in California, lost all his money in the panic of 1857, and moved to Colorado in 1859 where he served as judge and U.S. marshal (1862–66). *NCAB*, 6: 447–48.

2. George M. Chilcott's allegedly lucrative position was register of the U.S. Land Office (1863–67). Hunt was unhappy about Chilcott's nomination because he was also a candidate for delegate. *BDAC*; Lamar, *Far Southwest*, 260.

3. Not found.

4. Chilcott narrowly defeated Hunt in a closely contested election. Nevertheless, Gov. Alexander Cummings, a Hunt partisan, certified Hunt as the delegate, but Congress seated Chilcott. Hunt became governor instead. Lamar, *Far Southwest*, 260–63; Hall, *Colorado*, 1: 384–92.

To Queen Victoria

Washington D.C., July 30th 1866.

The President of the United States acknowledges with profound gratification the receipt of her Majestys despatch,[1] and cordially reciprocates the hope that the cable which now unites the Eastern and the Western hemispheres may serve to strengthen and to perpetuate peace and unity[2] between the government of England and the Republic of the United States.

Andrew Johnson

Tel, DNA-RG107, Tels. Sent, President, Vol. 3 (1865–68).

1. The Queen congratulated Johnson upon the completion of the Atlantic cable, declaring her hope that it might "serve as an additional bond of union between the United States & England." Queen Victoria to Johnson, July 27, 1866, Johnson Papers, LC. The wire

reached Johnson on July 30 because of a problem with the cable between Heart's Content, Newfoundland, and the mainland.

2. The original draft in the Johnson Papers reads "peace and amity."

From James M. Woolworth[1]

Omaha Nebraska, July, 30th, 1866.

Sir:—

The people of this Territory were surprised, saturday night, by telegraphic information that the two Houses of Congress have passed a resolution, for the admission of Nebraska as a state.[2] An extended statement cannot be made to your Excellency, of the reasons why this resolution should not be approved. The undersigned only proposes here to state a few facts bearing on the matter, to show that, while unscrupulous men, anxious only for office, have declared that the people have adopted the proposed constitution, the vote was clearly the otherway.

The official canvas made by Gov. Saunders Ch. Justice Kellogg[3] is enclosed; showing a majority of one hundred for the constitution. I propose to show that this is incorrect & fraudulent.

There is in Cass County a precinct known as Rock Bluffs. Its settlers are agriculturalists, who have lived there between ten & twelve years. Its farms are as well stocked, fenced & cultivated, as any in Nebraska. Its schools and churches as well attended, its people as intelligent. The Election was held there on the 2d of June. The usual vote of 158 was polled, of wh there a majority of 78 against the constitution. Under the law, the judges & clerks of Elections return the poll book, tally list, & abstract to the County Clerk. He selects two freeholders of the County, who, with him, canvas the returns from the precincts, and certify the result to the governor. The proper papers, that is, the poll book, tally sheet & abstract, were duly sent up from Rock Bluffs to the County Clerk. He and the two freeholders who composed the County board rejected the vote of that precinct, and sent up to the Governor the county vote without Rock Bluffs counted. The reason for this action was, as the Clerk alleged, because the poll book & tally sheet were not separately certified, although the three papers were bound together as a book, and all certified, together; and also because the Election board adjourned for dinner & supper. No fraud is pretended. The law does not make the Clerk & other members of the County board other than mere ministrial officers, to count the returns & return the result. Not only has this always been the custom, but two successive Chief Justices & two separate territorial boards have so construed the law. The arbitrary act of a County Clerk has disfranchised that precinct.

Again Poll Creek precinct in Merrick County where Eleven majority was given against the constitution, was thrown out, in the same way.

Col. Mathewson,[4] Agent of the Winebagos, although he had been here but four months, while the law requires six to constitute a qualified Elector, voted for the constitution; and also procured eighteen others— who were not qualified electors, because they were halfbreed Indians to vote for that measure.

At the soldiers polls at Fort Kearney, forty men voted for the constitution, who enlisted in Iowa, & who, throughout the war, have voted at Elections, held by Iowa Commissions, for Iowa officers; and in fact did so only so lately as last falls Elections.[5]

The case then stands thus:—

Rock Bluffs majority ag't state	— 78
Merrick County " " "	— 11.
Col. Mathewson & his Indians voting for state altho" not qualified	— 18.
Iowa soldiers voting —	40
Illegal votes for & legal votes against	— 147
Majority as claimed	100
Majority against state	— 47

It is impossible to lay before your Excellency the proofs of these allegations. On the Rock Bluffs matter, the Evidence is collected & of record in the Secretary's office, having been taken in a contest for seats in the Legislature. The same is true of Merrick County. Col. Mathewson's conduct has been Examined by the Grand Jury of the United States, and a large number of indictments found on account of it. Officers of undoubted veracity, have stated the above facts to the undersigned, relative to the soldiers.

This very imperfect statement is made on behalf of the large majority of the people, & particularly influencial conservatives, who support your Excellency's policy.

It may not be amiss to add, that the proposition to admit us as a state, made by Congress under the "Enabling act," was rejected by a vote of four to one; and that the constitution, now alleged to be adopted, was prepared by the Territorial Legislature, which was Elected, without any idea on the part of the people of this project.[6]

Jas. M. Woolworth.

ALS, DNA-RG59, Territorial Papers, Nebraska (M228, Roll 1).

1. Woolworth (1829–1906), a lawyer, moved to Nebraska from New York in 1856, and later became president of the American Bar Association (1896–97). *Who Was Who in America*, 1: 1381.

2. Sen. Benjamin Wade introduced a bill for the admission of Nebraska on July 23, 1866, and pushed it through Congress, receiving approval from both houses on July 27, just before they adjourned on the 28th. Johnson received the bill on the 28th and pocket vetoed it, since he disapproved of the admission of Nebraska. *Congressional Globe*, 39 Cong., 1 Sess., pp. 4044, 4072, 4116, 4205–13, 4219–22, 4237; Trefousse, *Johnson*, 273.

3. Alvin Saunders and William Kellogg. Ohio native Kellogg (1814–1872) practiced law in Illinois and served in the U.S. House of Representatives (1857–63). He was appointed Chief Justice by Johnson in December 1865. *BDAC*.

4. Charles Mathewson (*fl*1869), former colonel of the 12th Conn. Inf., was appointed agent in September 1865 and had arrived in Omaha by November 3, 1865. Thus he should have been eligible to vote in a June 1866 election. He remained as agent until early 1869. *Omaha Herald*, Oct. 27, Nov. 3, 1865; Hill, *Indian Affairs*, 208.

5. According to Judge Kellogg, no more than nineteen soldiers voted and these nineteen "said they had taken up their residence in the Territory of Nebraska and were going to continue to reside there and do reside there." *Congressional Globe*, 39 Cong., 1 Sess., p. 4220.

6. Congress passed the Enabling Act on April 19, 1864. Nebraskans did not vote down the proposition to become a state; rather, they elected men to the constitutional convention who opposed statehood and adjourned without drawing up a constitution, primarily because they feared additional taxes. The constitution submitted to Congress had been drawn up by the legislature under rather unusual secretive circumstances, and there were alleged irregularities at the election. Nebraska was not admitted as a state until March 1, 1867. *U.S. Statutes at Large*, 13: 47–50; Olson, *Nebraska*, 129–33.

From Jacob Barker

New Orleans, July 31st 1866.

Honored Sir:

As the chosen representative of this city to the Congress of the United States,[1] I feel it incumbent on me to inform you of the nature of the riot which unhappily pervaded our city yesterday.

Shortly before the restoration of peace there was an election ordered by Genl. Banks for members of a convention to assemble in this city. A few Parishes participated therein. Great frauds were committed at the polls by disregarding the laws of Louisiana regulating the registry of voters.

The persons thus elected assembled & prepared a new Constitution for the state which was submitted & adopted by the electors of the Union Parishes.[2]

When they adjourned they made an effort to perpetuate the power thus fraudulently obtained by authorizing the presiding officer[3] to reconvene them when occasion should require. This he refused to do on the repeated application of certain persons adverse to the peace & tranquillity of the State & subsequently left for the North, when some numbers of the members believed to be a minority, taking advantage of his absence, assembled & appointed a President pro tem,[4] and met again yesterday in opposition to the known will of this community & to the determination of the civil authorities not to permit such a revolutionary proceeding.

Certain misguided citizens induced a large number of the colored population to believe that the object of the Convention was to extend the right of suffrage, influencing the idle freedmen to come armed & protect the assemblage in their deliberations. They did so, when a conflict ensued between the Police force of the city and the leaders & abettors of the deluded colored men, resulting in their dispersion & the death & wounding of others. Those employed generally refused to take part therein. Several in my employ remained at their work throughout the day, seeming to be as much opposed to meddling with public affairs as were their employers. The Police dispersed the mob & quelled the riot. The military were called out & soon restored order. The citizens at large took no part in the disturbance—they are loyal to the United States to a man, excepting the agitators against the Constitution who are insignificant in character & in numbers, yet sufficient to keep the colored population at all times in a state of excitement.[5]

We acquiesced in the Constitution of 1864, the work of a small minority, impalatable as many of its provisions are, and shall give it a fair and honest support until we can get a better one, which we are prepared for whenever an election shall be authorized according to the laws of the State.

If military authority should be continued, General Fullerton[6] would be the most acceptable man to our citizens that could be appointed Military Governor of Louisiana.

Jacob Barker

ALS, DLC-JP.

1. Barker was elected but not seated. See Cuthbert Bullitt to Johnson, Nov. 7, 1865, *Johnson Papers*, 9: 353–54.

2. For a description of the election, convention, and constitution, see Taylor, *La. Reconstructed*, 42–52.

3. Judge Edward H. Durell.

4. Rufus K. Howell (*fl*1880) moved to New Orleans in 1850 where he directed a school until he was elected district judge in 1857, a position he held intermittently until 1877. Conrad, *La. Biography*; New Orleans directories (1870–80).

5. Other accounts of the riot by witnesses, generally laying the blame on the police, can be found in *House Reports*, 39 Cong., 2 Sess., No. 16, pp. 1–6, 46–49, 66–68 (Ser. 1304); Philip H. Sheridan to Johnson, Aug. 6, 1866, Johnson Papers, LC.

6. Joseph S. Fullerton. Fullerton was popular with conservative white Louisianans because, as temporary head of the Freedmen's Bureau in the state in 1865, he had catered to some of their desires. Gilles Vandal, *The New Orleans Riot of 1866: Anatomy of a Tragedy* (Lafayette, La., 1983), 91.

From John F. Coyle

Office National Intelligencer
Washington, July 31 [1866]

I called yesterday and to-day with Genl. Rousseau and Mr Blair Senr. to ask the appointment of C. Wendell Esq. to the office of Superintendent of Public Printing, declined by our mutual friend Genl. Steedman, who will on his arrival here—to-morrow—join in the recommendation.[1] This appointment or some other relief is *actual necessary* for our Continuance in such a manner as to be of use to the administration. No warmer or more active friend that Mr Wendell can be found. He is now absent on business of the National Union Executive Committee. If you have any objection to Mr Wendell *that is insuperable*, allow us to name some one else, but at the same time, I assure you he is the very best man, for the Government and your friends.[2]

John F. Coyle

ALS, DLC-JP.
1. Steedman had been nominated by Johnson on July 27 to be Superintendent of Public Printing. However, the following day, he declined the appointment. *Washington Evening Star*, July 28, 1866; Steedman to Johnson, July 28, 1866, Tels. Recd., President, Vol. 5 (1866–67), RG107, NA.
2. In late August Cornelius Wendell was appointed Superintendent of Public Printing and on September 1, 1866, "formally entered on his duties." *Washington Evening Star*, Aug. 28, Sept. 1, 1866.

From Andrew S. Herron

New Orleans La   July 31st 1866

Your dispatch received.[1] Genl Baird[2] has declared martial law in this City. The grand jury has indicted the members of the Convention, who met yesterday, as an unlawful assembly. Process for their arrest in hands of sheriff[3] suspended by Genl Baird until he receives direct instructions from Washington. I showed him your dispatch to me.

Andrew S. Herron   Atty Genl

Tel, DLC-JP.
1. See Johnson to Herron, July 30, 1866.
2. Gen. Absalom Baird was the military commander of Louisiana as well as superintendent of the Freedmen's Bureau for the state. Dawson, *Army Generals and Reconstruction*, 35.
3. Harry T. Hays.

From Kentucky Democratic Central Committee[1]

Frankfort, Ky., July 31, 1866.

Sir.

Without presuming or desiring, in any manner, officiously, to interfere with your affairs, or to dictate to you upon the Subject of the Executive patronage in the State of Kentucky, we have, after mature deliberation, determined to ask your attention to a brief statement of facts with regard thereto.

Our original purpose was to wait until after our election in August to address you; but in view of the fact, which we learn from the news papers, that changes are now being made in the Officials subject to Executive appointment in the state, and, evidently under the advice of parties, either not familiar with the condition of parties or the position of individuals in Ky, we feel called upon, now, to address you.

You will observe that we represent the Democratic party in the State; and we do avouch to you that ours is the only political organization in the State which indorses your administration, and from which you can hope for any support, in the contest with the Radicals, as represented by the majority of the present Congress.

Our opponents—Calling themselves the "*Union*" party—are, as a mass, in full sympathy with Sumner Stevens & Speed; and, though in some instances professing friendship for you—hoping for immediate profit—whenever the time comes & the issue is made, will array themselves upon the side of Congress. There are exceptions—Some men acting at present with the Union (?) party in the state are your friends, in good faith; but the great mass of them *are not*.

Further, we state to you, that all the while, since your accession to the Presidency the Executive appointees in Kentucky, have been men who are your real enemies, and the friends of the Ultra Radicals. And though some changes have been made by you recently, and we doubt not, with a view to correcting this state of fact; yet, Sir, it is true that, in most instances, no change has been made in the sentiments of the appointee; And today, the whole power of your patronage, in Kentucky, is being used against the real friends of your administration and in behalf of your enemies.

We make these statements to you, because we suppose you desire to strengthen your friends rather than weaken them by your patronage; and we therefore venture the suggestion that, for the present, you hold up the changes and appointments from Ky.

It is but a few days now till our election, when the real position of Kentucky will be defined, and the strength of your true friends developed.

Enclosed we hand you the platform and position of the party[2] we represent to which we beg to urge your attention.

We assure you that, upon these positions we will carry the state by a large majority, and that we are ranged upon the side of your administration in your noble efforts to restore the Union upon the basis of the Constitution; and will support you with earnestness and zeal.

We have forborne any attempts to set the matter in a correct light before you—notwithstanding we have been fully aware of the efforts which have been, and are being made to convey a false impression as to our purposes—for the reason that we did not wish to trouble you, or in any degree embarrass or complicate you in your delicate duties. But, in view of the facts, herein—before set forth, we feel that further silence upon our part would be inexcusable.

For the present we ask nothing, but that you hold up the matter of the Kentucky patronage until such time as it may take to make your self assured of the real state of parties here.

Some of the late appointees in this state, as we observe in the public prints, are really as obnoxious to your true friends in the state as those whose places they fill.

Disclaiming any other than those of a sincere wish to promote the success of your administration and assuring you of our highest personal esteem & regard. . . .

LS, DLC-JP.
1. The chairman of the committee was Robert W. Scott (1808–1886), who was admitted to the bar in 1829. While serving as president of the Southern Rights Convention in Frankfort in 1861 and as a member and subsequent chairman of the Democratic Central

Committee, Scott was best known for his leadership in Kentucky agriculture and his advances in livestock breeding. Carl E. Kramer, *Capital on the Kentucky* ([Frankfort], 1986), 149; *Biographical Encyclopaedia of Kentucky*, 222–27.

2. Although not found enclosed, the platform and position of the party to which the committee refers could be the resolutions adopted at the party's state convention in Louisville on May 1. See *Cincinnati Enquirer*, May 3, 1866.

From James W. Nesmith

Washington   July 31st 1866

On yesterday I had a conversation with the Secretary of the Treasury in which he manifested a desire to remove the present Collector of Customs at Astoria in Oregon,[1] and appoint some person as his successor who is not a resident of the state. I have filed with the Secretary a protest against such appointment and have asked him to defer any action in the matter until next Fall.[2] My reason for doing this is founded upon the fact that the disposition of that office will have its influence in the coming Senatorial elections in Oregon. If you desire my return to the Senate or that of a person friendly to your policy, I think that I should be permitted to controll the Federal patronage within the state. I therefore respectfully ask that none of the Federal Officers in Oregon be changed until after the Senatorial election in that State which will be early in September.[3] I put this request in writing because I believe that it will be more effective than an oral communication. I leave the city tomm—for College Hill Ohio which will be my post office address until the meeting of Congress.

J W Nesmith

ALS, DNA-RG56, Appts., Customs Service, Collector, Astoria, Orlando Humason.

1. William L. Adams (1821–1906), a native of Ohio, moved to Oregon from Illinois in 1848. He preached, taught school, and edited an ardently Republican paper, the *Argus*, at Oregon City. Lincoln rewarded him with the collectorship at Astoria. *DAB*; Hubert H. Bancroft, *History of Oregon, Vol. 2, 1848–1888* (San Francisco, 1888), 170, 458; George H. Williams, "Political History of Oregon from 1853 to 1865," *OHQ*, 2 (1901): 27, 31.

2. Johnson and McCulloch seem to have acceded to Nesmith's request. Nesmith recommended the appointment of Orlando Humason of Dalles City, Oregon, a brigadier general in the state militia during the war and a member of the state legislature. Although Humason was nominated, his appointment was rejected by the Senate on February 23, 1867. Nesmith to Johnson, Oct. 4, 1866, Appts., Customs Service, Collector, Astoria, Orlando Humason, RG56, NA; Ser. 6B, Vol. 4: 357, Johnson Papers, LC; Charles H. Carey, *History of Oregon* (Chicago, 1922), 676.

3. Nesmith was defeated by Henry W. Corbett, who served a single term in the Senate. *BDAC*.

From Dan Rice

Lockport New York, July 31st 1866.

Dear Sir

I promised in my last letter to discover how Daniel Livingston of the 19th District of Penn. regarded national affairs and his duties, as a public officer to those principles which every government official should uphold with all the power he possesses. But alas! he is unmindful of these sacred obligations and wantonly abuses his benefactor, and I fear he is so far commited to Judge Scofield[1] the present Representative of the 19th Dis't that he is beyond converting to the *Christian Cause*. Consequently I think the sooner he is removed the better,[2] for he is using not only his official influence but is constantly talking in favor of the re-nomination of Scofield for Congress. I do not know who to recommend in his place but if you think it advisable for me to look up a proper man I will do so. I think the more expeditious you are in removing such men particularly such sycophants as Douglass the Collector and Wheeler the assistant Assessor,[3] the sooner you will consumate what you have been and are so patrioticaly laboring for, a restored Union. You will recollect I sent you the names of parties for the positions of Collector of Revenue for the 19th District and assistant Assessor, both Soldiers. Major Swan is now very busy throughout Erie County in converting the people to the "Andy Johnson Policy" and one of the best hits you ever made in an appointment, you will make in this. Do not fail to appoint Swan Collector of Internal Revenue for the 19th District.[4]

I have spent several days in Buffalo N.Y. and have talked to over twenty thousand people in the six performances I gave, and thank God (notwithstanding I was hissed by several, each performance) I opened the eyes of the multitude and converted many to our side. I think an entire change in all the Government departments of the 30th District should take place as soon as proper men can be found to fill them, because *delay is dangerous* to the object you have in view. I have recommended two persons, one for Post Master in place of Clapp[5] the present incumbent, who is Editor of the Buffalo Express and the most vituperous black-guard I know of, with the exception of the "Dead Duck."[6] I inclose you the application of Cha's Stow Esq.[7] for Collector of Internal Revenue in place of Philip Dorsheimer[8] who by the way would not sign the call for an Andy Johnson Convention.

My attention has been specially directed to Erie County New York as a field of great political importance and to ascertaining the tendency of popular opinion and the value to be attached to the call for a Mass Convention on the 10th ins't, to appoint delegates, to the Philadelphia Convention, known to be sustainers of your Administration. Very careful investigation and conference with prominent and so to speak unpartisan citizens, thoroughly satisfied me that the Call is very generally sanctioned by men of worth and standing, irrespective of party. Many leading Republicans hitherto classed as Radicals, endorse it as an approval of a firm and yet conciliatory policy. I have no doubt that by judicious management the conservative strength of the County can be so managed as to materially further the best interests of the whole Union. In order to accomplish this desirable end however, I am of the opinion that a some what different course ought to be pursued, than that which appears to me to have heretofore guided Republican appointments in the County. The dash, vim, and hearty earnestness of Young America, particularly valuable in a crisis like the present, is borne down and discouraged by prominent Officials who either lack the ability to pursue an active and intelligent policy, are unfitted by Age, or through the acquirement of a competency have grown careless as to results. As a prominent instance of this I feel it my duty to cite the present Collector of Internal Revenue, Mr Philip Dorsheimer, who in my opinion falls under each of the above named objections. Being a German he was supposed to have great influence with the Germans. His power in this regard was always greatly over estimated, and there can be no doubt of his great unpopularity with the mass of German Republican voters, now. In fact I seriously question whether out side the limits of his Office he can control a dozen votes. Extremely radical, his influence such as it is, is detrimental. Many of his appointments are extremely unpopular, and injurious to your Excellency's Administration. The notorious fact that his son[9] rules him in all decisions, and pockets large fees at the expense of the public, gives very serious cause of complaint against the Government. In view of this condition of affairs I trust I may be pardoned for urging the early attention of your Excellency to the management of the Internal Revenue Office in Erie County. The Republican Party in Erie County has for several years been divided into two factions, known as the Express and the Commercial cliques. A bitter and irreconcilable feud exists between them, carried to such an extent that neither are to be fully relied upon, as either would sacrafice general results for the sake of defeating the other. The Call for the Convention heretofore refered to, promises not a compromise between them, but the inauguration of a new party, really independent of both and yet containing their best elements of strength. The movement consequent upon this Call will be an earnest and hearty one, encouraging you in the good work of reunion and reconciliation. The infusion of young enthusiastic spirit into it will greatly contribute to its success, and I would there fore most earnestly advocate the policy of enlisting active and competent young men, by recognizing, rewarding and encouraging their services, so far as you may deem compatible with public interests. I believe Erie County to be one of the battle fields upon which the fate of your policy is to be decided, and I am deeply desirous that your arm may be upheld in the approaching day of trial by those strong and willing hands to whose keeping I believe, and pray, you will be able to consign a glorious and restored Union.

                                                                    Dan Rice

ALS, DLC-JP.
    1. Glenni W. Scofield.
    2. Michael A. Frank was appointed on September 18 to replace Livingston as internal revenue assessor of the Nineteenth District of Pennsylvania. But neither Frank nor a subsequent Johnson appointee were confirmed by the Senate, and Livingston apparently re-

tained his position at least through September 1867. Ser. 6B, Vol. 3: 161; Vol. 4: 84, 87, Johnson Papers, LC; *U.S. Off. Reg.* (1867).

3. John W. Douglass and T. C. Wheeler.

4. A few months later Rice withdrew his nomination of Andrew F. Swan, indicating to Johnson that "his appointment would prove very unsatisfactory to the people," and recommended instead Calvin J. Hinds, an Erie County attorney. Rice to Johnson, ca. Sept. 11, 1866, Appts., Internal Revenue Service, Collector, Pa., 19th Dist., Calvin J. Hinds, RG56, NA.

5. Almon M. Clapp (1811–*fl*1899) served as editor of the *Buffalo Express* from 1846 until 1869, when he relocated to Washington to assume the superintendency of the U.S. Government Printing Office, and edited the *National Republican* before his retirement in 1881. Originally appointed by Lincoln as postmaster of Buffalo, Clapp was succeeded on October 1, 1866, by Joseph Candee. *NCAB*, 1: 359–60; Washington, D.C., directories (1892–99); *U.S. Off. Reg.* (1865–67); White, *Erie County*, 1: 453.

6. John W. Forney.

7. A Conservative Republican who had worked in the editorial department of the *Buffalo Express* during much of the war, Stow (c1838–1907) later gained renown as a publicity agent for Barnum and Bailey and other circuses and variety shows. Rice to Johnson, July 31, 1866, Appts., Internal Revenue Service, Collector, New York, 30th Dist., Charles Stone, RG56, NA; *New York Times*, Aug. 23, 1907; Brown, *Dan Rice*, 231.

8. Dorsheimer (c1800–c1867), hotel proprietor and a Republican party organizer who had served as state treasurer prior to being appointed by Lincoln as collector at Buffalo, was removed in mid-September 1866, despite the protests of Francis P. Blair, Sr., Gen. John A. Dix, and other prominent New York politicians. Dorsheimer's replacement was not Stow, however, but Nelson K. Hopkins, who failed to win Senate confirmation in February 1867. 1860 Census, N.Y., Erie, 1st Ward Buffalo City, 209; Buffalo directories (1849–68); White, *Erie County*, 456; G. W. Clinton to Johnson, Sept. 15, 1866; Blair to Hugh McCulloch, n.d.; Dix to Johnson, Oct. 5, 1866, Appts., Internal Revenue Service, Collector, N.Y., 30th Dist., Philip Dorsheimer, RG56, NA; *U.S. Off. Reg.* (1863–67); Ser. 6B, Vol. 4: 51, Johnson Papers, LC.

9. In 1867 Johnson appointed William Dorsheimer (1832–1888) as U.S. attorney for the northern district of New York. A Greeley supporter in 1872, Dorsheimer later served as Democratic lieutenant governor (1874–79) before his election to Congress in 1882 and appointment as U.S. attorney for the southern district in 1885. *DAB*.

From Henry H. Sibley
Confidential

St. Paul, Minn.   July 31, 1866

My dear Sir.

We served together four years in Congress, as you will doubtless recollect, and I recal my acquaintance with you during that long period, with great gratification.

I take the liberty to enclose herein, a programe and leading editorial (*both written by myself*) in the St. Paul Pioneer,[1] the oldest and most influential paper in the State, which has now passed into the hands of the Conservative democracy, and will henceforth sustain your policy of reconstruction, in opposition to that of the *destructives* in Congress.

We have good reason to believe that we shall carry this Congressional Dist. next fall.[2] I have been applied to by leading Conservative Republicans as well as Democrats, to permit my name to go before the Convention, as they state I can be elected without any doubt, but I have felt it my duty to decline, as my private affairs, after four years service as Brig. & Brevet Major Genl., in the Army, require all my attention.[3]

H. H. Sibley

ALS, DLC-JP.

1. The *St. Paul Pioneer* was a Republican paper until it changed owners at the end of July 1866. The first issue published by the new proprietors proclaimed that the *Pioneer* would now be a "live Democratic" paper, which "will support the administration of Andrew Johnson, so far as his acts shall continue to be in harmony with the sentiments of the real Union party of the country, which is the Democratic party." The paper supported the admission of the southern representatives to Congress. Sibley's articles were unsigned. *St. Paul Pioneer*, July 29, 31, 1866.

2. Contrary to Sibley's hopes Minnesota's two Republican representatives, Ignatius Donnelly and William Windom, were both reelected by substantial margins. Sibley did not run. Ben: Perley Poore, ed., *The Political Register and Congressional Directory* (Boston, 1878), 373, 706.

3. Sibley had commanded troops on the northern Indian frontier. Warner, *Blue*.

From Edwin M. Stanton

Washington City   July 31 1866

Mr. President

Enclosed you will find the *Orders* referred to this morning,[1] also a copy of a telegram just received from General Baird relating to the riot in New Orleans yesterday.[2] If it is later in date than the despatch you showed me from the Lieutenant Governor,[3] the affair seems to have been more serious than was supposed.

Edwin M Stanton   Sec of War

ALS, DLC-JP.

1. Not found.

2. This is probably Baird's telegram sent from New Orleans on the evening of July 30 and received in Washington at 1:00 p.m. on July 31. Baird reported that "A serious riot has occurred here today." It "commenced unexpectedly and before the troops could reach the scene of action a number of persons were killed and wounded. I have felt compelled to declare martial law, and have appointed a military Governor of the City. All is quiet now. Several prominent gentlemen connected with the Convention are killed or wounded." Later on July 31 Baird sent another telegram which expanded on his previous message. "Nearly all unite in attributing the chief blame to the police for the trouble yesterday. Thirty seven (37) persons are reported as killed. All belonging to the Convention or friendly to it." Absalom Baird to Stanton, July 30, July 31, 1866, Johnson Papers, LC.

3. Albert Voorhies had telegraphed Johnson on the afternoon of the riot: "Convention met. A riot broke out in the City. So far the police has the upperhand. Several white and colored persons killed. Called on Gen Baird for assistance which is cheerfully tendered. Intense excitement. Convention broken up." Voorhies to Johnson, July 30, 1866, ibid.

Appendix I

[Adapted from Robert Sobel, ed., *Biographical Directory of the United States Executive Branch, 1774–1971* (Westport, Conn., 1971).]

Office	Name
Secretary of State, 1865–69	William H. Seward
Secretary of the Treasury, 1865–69	Hugh McCulloch
Secretary of War, 1865–68	Edwin M. Stanton
Secretary of War ad interim, 1867–68	Ulysses S. Grant
Secretary of War, 1868–69	John M. Schofield
Attorney General, 1865–66	James Speed
Attorney General, 1866–68	Henry Stanbery
Attorney General ad interim, 1868*	Orville H. Browning
Attorney General, 1868–69	William M. Evarts
Postmaster General, 1865–66	William Dennison
Postmaster General, 1866–69	Alexander W. Randall
Secretary of the Navy, 1865–69	Gideon Welles
Secretary of the Interior, 1865	John P. Usher
Secretary of the Interior, 1865–66	James Harlan
Secretary of the Interior, 1866–69	Orville H. Browning

*from March 13, 1868, when Stanbery resigned, until July 20, 1868, when Evarts assumed office, Browning discharged the duties of attorney general in addition to his functions as head of the Interior Department.

Appendix II

VETO MESSAGES, PROCLAMATIONS, AND EXECUTIVE ORDERS
(FEBRUARY–JULY 1866)

[Asterisks indicate documents printed in Volume 10; all are printed in James D. Richardson, comp., *A Compilation of the Messages and Papers of the Presidents* (10 vols., Washington, D.C., 1896–99), Volume 6.]

Date	Veto Message	Richardson, *Messages*
Feb. 19	*Freedmen's Bureau Bill	398–405
Mar. 27	*Civil Rights Bill	405–13
May 15	*Colorado Statehood Bill	413–16
June 15	New York & Montana Iron Co. Land Purchase Bill	416–22
July 16	*Freedmen's Bureau Bill	422–26
July 28	Bill Creating Surveying District of the Territory of Montana	426–27

Proclamation

Feb. 12	Withdrawal of recognition of Rogers as Chile consul at New York	427–28
Mar. 26	Withdrawal of recognition of Habicht as Sweden and Norway consul at New York	428
Mar. 26	Withdrawal of recognition of Svenson as Sweden and Norway vice-consul at New Orleans	429
Apr. 2	*End of Insurrection	429–32
May 30	Restoration of rights of Habicht and Svenson	432
June 6	Warning against actions by U.S. citizens *re* colonies, districts, and peoples of British North America	433

Executive Order

Apr. 7	*Re* Appointments to Office	439–40
May 29	Closing of Executive Departments for funeral of Winfield Scott	442

Appendix III

MEMORANDUM *re* SAMUEL C. POMEROY'S VISIT
TO THE EXECUTIVE MANSION

Monday, March 19th, 1866.

The Hon. S. C Pomeroy called at the Executive Mansion this afternoon, in compliance with the request of the President, who informed the Senator that he desired to call his attention to a statement contained in a letter[1] addressed by the Reverend Henry Ward Beecher to Mr. J. D. Defrees,[2] Superintendent of Public Printing.

At the request of the President, Colonel Wm G. Moore then read from the letter referred to an extract, to the effect that Mr. Beecher had been told by Mr. Lincoln,[3] the Postmaster at Brooklyn, that during a visit to Washington he (Mr. Lincoln) had been informed by Mr. Pomeroy that he (the Senator) had, on occasions when he had visited the Executive Mansion, seen the President, and the President's son and son-in-law in an intoxicated condition.

Mr Pomeroy said that he had heard of the letter, and was glad of the opportunity to make an explanation. The facts were simply these: Mr. Lincoln had called on him, bringing with him a speech made by Mr. Beecher at the Cooper Institute, in the city of New York. Mr. Lincoln, during his visit, said to him, "The report is that President Johnson drinks too much. Do you know any thing about it?" I said, "I do not know any thing about it. All I know is, that his son and son-in-law drink, for I have seen them when I thought they were disguised in liquor; but as to the President, I know not a word of the kind. I never saw him drunk." Mr Lincoln then asked, "Shall I tell Beecher that? He always comes in my office and reads the papers? What shall I say to him?" I replied "Tell him whatever you are mind to?"

["]Our relations, Mr President, are friendly and kind, and I thought, when I saw you, I would make a clean breast of this matter. The whole truth is that I have seen your son and son-in-law when I thought they were disguised in liquor, but I never saw you drink a drop or smell a drop, nor have I ever smelt a drop about you. I have written a letter upon the subject to Mr. Beecher, stating what did occur, word for word, and I will write to Mr. Lincoln to-night. I assure you, if I can do any thing to contradict the statement contained in the letter of Mr. Beecher, I will do So any where and under oath."

D, DLC-JP.

1. Not found in the Johnson Papers, LC. On March 16 Hugh McCulloch had shown the letter to Gideon Welles, who advised that the President be informed of its contents. Later that evening the two cabinet officers had a meeting with Johnson at the White House. Beale, *Welles Diary*, 2: 453–54.

2. John D. Defrees (1810–1882) edited Indianapolis newspapers before being appointed by Lincoln in 1861 to manage the government printing office in Washington. By September 1, 1866, Defrees had been removed and replaced, but several months later was restored to office by special congressional legislation and continued serving until 1869. William W. Woolen, *Biographical and Historical Sketches of Early Indiana* (Indianapolis, 1883), 485–88; "John D. Defrees," *InMH*, 2 (1906): 147–50; Lanman, *Biographical Annals*, 511; *U.S. Statutes at Large*, 14: 398–99.

3. George B. Lincoln.

Index

Primary identification of a person is indicated by an italic *n* following the page reference. Identifications found in earlier volumes of the *Johnson Papers* are shown by providing volume and page numbers, within parentheses, immediately after the name of the individual. The only footnotes which have been indexed are those that constitute identification notes.